LEADING U.S. FIRMS

Federal Home Loan Mortgage,
  McLean, VA
Federated Department Stores,
  Cincinnati, OH
First Chicago NBD Corp., Chicago, IL
First Data, Hackensack, NJ
First Union Corp., Charlotte, NC
Firstenergy, Akron, OH
Fleet Financial Group, Boston, MA
Fleetwood Enterprises, Riverside, CA
Fleming, Oklahoma City, OK
Florida Progress, St. Petersburg, FL
Fluor, Irvine, CA
FMC, Chicago, IL
Food 4 Less, Compton, CA
Ford Motor, Dearborn, MI
Forster Wheeler, Clinton, NJ
Fort James, Richmond, VA
Fortune Brands,
  Old Greenwich, CT
Foundation Health Systems,
  Woodland Hill, CA
FPL Group, Juno Beach, FL
Fred Meyer, Portland, OR
Gannett, Arlington, VA
GAP, San Francisco, CA
Gateway 2000, North Sioux City, SD
Genamerica, St. Louis, MO
General Dynamics, Falls Church, VA
General Electric, Fairfield, CT
General Mills, Minneapolis, MN
General Motors, Detroit, MI
General Re, Stamford, CT
Genuine Parts, Atlanta, GA
Georgia-Pacific, Atlanta, GA
Giant Food, Landover, MD
Gillette, Boston, MA
Golden West Financial Corp.,
  Oakland, CA
Goodyear Tire & Rubber, Akron, OH
GPU, Morristown, NJ
Graybar Electric, St. Louis, MO
GTE, Stamford, CT
Guardian Life Ins. Co. of America,
  New York, NY
H.F. Ahmanson, Irwindale, CA
H.J. Heinz, Pittsburgh, PA
Halliburton, Dallas, TX
Hannaford Bros., Scarborough, ME
Harcourt General, Chestnut Hill, MA
Harnischfeger Industries,
  St. Francis, WI
Harris, Melbourne, FL
Hartford Financial Services,
  Hartford, CT
Hasbro, Pawtucket, RI
Healthsouth, Birmingham, AL
Hershey Foods, Hershey, PA
Hewlett-Packard, Palo Alto, CA
Hilton Hotels, Beverly Hills, CA
Home Depot, Atlanta, GA
Honeywell, Minneapolis, MN
Hormel Foods, Austin, MN
Household International,
  Prospect Heights, IL

Houston Industries, Houston, TX
Hum[...]
IBP, [...]
Ikor[...]
Illin[...]rks, Glenview, IL
IMC Global, Northbrook, IL
Inacom, Omaha, NE
Ingersoll-Rand, Woodcliff Lake, NJ
Ingram Micro, Santa Ana, CA
Inland Steel Industries, Chicago, IL
Intel, Santa Clara, CA
International Paper, Purchase, NY
Interpublic Group, New York, NY
Interstate Bakeries, Kansas City, MO
Intl. Business Machines, Armonk, NY
ITT, New York, NY
ITT Industries, White Plains, NY
J.C. Penney, Plano, TX
J.P. Morgan & Co., NY
Jefferson Smurfit, St. Louis, MO
John Hancock Mutual Life Ins.,
  Boston, MA
Johnson & Johnson,
  New Brunswick, NJ
Johnson Controls, Milwaukee, WI
Kellogg, Battle Creek, MI
Kelly Services, Troy, MI
Keycorp, Cleveland, OH
Kimberly-Clark, Irving, TX
Kmart, Troy, MI
Knight-Rider, Miami, FL
Kohl's, Menomonee Falls, WI
Kroger, Cincinnati, OH
Lear, Southfield, MI
Leggett & Platt, Carthage, MO
Lehman Brothers Holdings,
  New York, NY
LG&E Energy, Louisville, KY
Liberty Mutual Insurance Group,
  Boston, MA
Limited, Columbus, OH
Lincoln National, Fort Wayne, IN
Litton Industries,
  Woodland Hills, CA
Lockheed Martin, Bethesda, MD
Loews, New York, NY
Long Island Lighting, Hicksville, NY
Longs Drug Stores
  Walnut Creek, CA
Lowe's, North Wilkesboro, NC
LTV, Cleveland, OH
Lucent Technologies, Murray Hill, NJ
Lutheran Brotherhood,
  Minneapolis, MN
Lyondell Petrochemical,
  Houston, TX
Manpower, Milwaukee, WI
Mapco, Tulsa, OK
Marriott International, Bethesda, MD
Marsh & McLennan, New York, NY
Masco, Taylor, MI
Massachusetts Mutual Life Ins.,
  Springfield, MA
Mattel, El Segundo, CA
Maxxam, Houston, TX

May Department Stores,
  St. Louis, MO
Maytag, Newton, IA
MBNA, Wilmington, DE
McDonald's, Oak Brook, IL
McGraw-Hill, New York, NY
MCI Communications,
  Washington, D.C.
McKesson, San Francisco, CA
Mead, Dayton, OH
Medpartners, Birmingham, AL
Mellon Bank Corp., Pittsburgh, PA
Mercantile Stores, Fairfield, OH
Merck, Whitehouse Station, NJ
Merisel, El Segundo, CA
Merrill Lynch, New York, NY
Metropolitan Life Insurance,
  New York, NY
Microage, Tempe, AZ
Micron Technology, Boise, ID
Microsoft, Redmond, WA
Millennium Chemicals,
  Red Bank, NJ
Minnesota Mining & Mfg.,
  St. Paul, MN
Mobil, Fairfax, VA
Monsanto, St. Louis, MO
Morgan Stanley Dean Witter
  Discover, New York, NY
Morton International, Chicago, IL
Motorola, Schaumburg, IL
Mutual of Omaha Insurance,
  Omaha, NE
Nach Finch, Edina, MN
National City Corp., Cleveland, OH
NationsBank Corp., Charlotte, NC
Nationwide Ins. Enterprise,
  Columbus, OH
Navistar International, Chicago, IL
NCR, Dayton, OH
New Century Energies, Denver, CO
New York Life Insurance,
  New York, NY
New York Times, New York, NY
Newell, Freeport, IL
NGC, Houston, TX
Niagara Mohawk Power,
  Syracuse, NY
Nike, Beaverton, OR
Nordstrom, Seattle, WA
Norfolk Southern, Norfolk, VA
Northern States Power,
  Minneapolis, MN
Northop Grumman,
  Los Angeles, CA
Northwest Airlines, St. Paul, MN
Northwest Utilities, Berlin, CT
Northwestern Mutual Life Ins.,
  Milwaukee, WI
Norwest Corp., Minneapolis, MN
Nucor, Charlotte, NC
Occidental Petroleum,
  Los Angeles, CA
Office Depot, Delray Beach, FL
OfficeMax, Shaker Heights, OH

(Continued on next page)

LEADING U.S. FIRMS

Olsten, Melville, NY
Omnicom Group, New York, NY
Oracle, Redwood City, CA
Owens & Minor, Glen Allen, VA
Owens Corning, Toledo, OH
Owens-Illinois, Toledo, OH
Oxford Health Plans, Norwalk, CT
Paccar, Bellevue, WA
Pacific Enterprises, Los Angeles, CA
Pacific Life Insurance,
    Newport Beach, CA
Pacificare Health Systems,
    Santa Ana, CA
Pacificorp, Portland, OR
Paine Webber Group, New York, NY
Parker Hannifin, Cleveland, OH
Peco Energy, Philadelphia, PA
Penn Traffic, Syracuse, NY
PepsiCo, Purchase, NY
Peter Kiewit Sons', Omaha, NE
Pfizer, New York, NY
PG&E Corp., San Francisco, CA
Pharmacia & Upjohn,
    Bridgewater, NJ
Phelps Dodge, Phoenix, AZ
Philip Morris, New York, NY
Phillips Petroleum, Bartlesville, OK
Phoenix Home Life Mutual Ins.,
    Hartford, CT
Pitney Bowes, Stamford, CT
Pittson, Glen Allen, VA
PNC Bank Corp., Pittsburgh. PA
PP&L Resources, Allentown, PA
PPG Industries, Pittsburgh, PA
Praxair, Danbury, CN
Principal Financial, Des Moines, IA
Procter & Gamble, Cincinnati, OH
Proffitt's, Birmingham, AL
Progressive, Mayfield Village, OH
Prosource, Coral Cables, FL
Provident Cos., Chattanooga, TN
Prudential Ins. Group of America,
    Newark, NJ
Public Service Enterprise Group,
    Newark, NJ
Publix Super Markets, Lakeland, FL
Quaker Oats, Chicago, IL
Quantum, Milpitas, CA
R.R. Donnelley & Sons, Chicago, IL
Ralston Purina, St. Louis, MO
Raytheon, Lexington, MA
Reader's Digest Association,
    Pleasantville, NY
Reebok International,
    Stoughton, MA
Reliance Group Holdings,
    New York, NY
Republic Industries,
    Fort Lauderdale, FL
Republic New York Corp.,
    New York, NY
Reynolds Metals , Richmond, VA
Richfood Holdings,
    Mechanicsville, VA
Rite Aid, Camp Hill, PA

RJR Nabisco Holdings,
    New York, NY
Rockwell International,
    Costa Mesa, CA
Rohn & Haas, Philadelphia, PA
Ryder System, Miami, FL
Rykoff-Sexton, Wilkes-Barre, PA
Safeco, Seattle, WA
Safeway, Pleasanton, CA
Sara Lee, Chicago, IL
SBC Communications,
    San Antonio, TX
Schering-Plough, Madison, NJ
SCI Systems, Huntsville, AL
Seagate Technology,
    Scotts Valley, CA
Sears Roebuck, Hoffman Estates, IL
Service Merchandise,
    Brentwood, TN
ServiceMaster, Downers Grove, IL
Shaw Industries, Dalton, GA
Sherwin-Williams, Cleveland, OH
Silicon Graphics,
    Mountain View, CA
SLM Holdings, Reston, VA
Smithfield Foods, Norfolk, VA
Solectron, Milpitas, CA
Sonat, Birmingham, AL
Sonoco Products, Hartsville, SC
Southern, Atlanta, GA
Southwest Airlines, Dallas, TX
Sprint, Westwood, KS
St. Paul Cos., St. Paul, MN
Staples, Westborough, MA
State Farm Insurance Company,
    Bloomington, IL
State Street Corp., Boston, MA
Stone Container, Chicago, IL
Sun, Philadelphia, PA
Sun Microsystems, Palo Alto, CA
Suntrust Banks, Atlanta, GA
Supermarkets Genl. Holdings,
    Woodbridge, NJ
Supervalu, Eden Prairie, MN
Sysco, Houston, TX
Tandy, Fort Worth, TX
Tech Data, Clearwater, FL
Tele-Communications,
    Englewood, CO
Temple-Inland, Diboll, TX
Tenet Healthcare,
    Santa Barbara, CA
Tenneco, Greenwich, CT
Texaco, White Plains, NY
Texas Instruments, Dallas, TX
Texas Utilities, Dallas, TX
Textron, Providence, RI
Thermo Electron, Waltham, MA
3 Com, Santa Clara, CA
Tiaa-Cref, New York, NY
Time Warner, New York, NY
Times Mirror, Los Angeles, CA
TJX, Framingham, MA
Tosco, Stamford, CT
Toys "R" Us, Rochelle Park, NJ

Trans World Airlines, St. Louis, MO
TransAmerica, San Francisco, CA
Travelers Group, New York, NY
Truserv, Chicago, IL
TRW, Cleveland, OH
Turner Corp., New York, NY
Tyco International, Exeter, NH
Tyson Foods, Springdale, AR
U.S. Bancorp, Minneapolis, MN
U.S. Office Products, Washington, DC
UAL, Elk Grove Township, IL
Ultramar Diamond Shamrock,
    San Antonio, TX
Unicom, Chicago, IL
Union Camp, Wayne, NJ
Union Carbide, Danbury, CT
Union Pacific, Dallas, TX
Unisource, Berwyn, PA
Unisys, Blue Bell, PA
United Healthcare,
    Minnetonka, MN
United Parcel Service, Atlanta, GA
United Services Automobile Assn.,
    San Antonio, TX
United Technologies,
    Hartford, CT
Universal, Richmond, VA
Unocal, El Segundo, CA
Unum, Portland, ME
US Airways Group, Arlington, VA
US West, Englewood, CO
USF&G, Baltimore, MD
USG, Chicago, IL
USX, Pittsburgh, PA
Utilicorp United, Kansas City, MO
Vencor, Louisville, KY
VF, Wyomissing, PA.
Viacom, New York, NY
W.R. Grace, Boca Raton, FL
W.W. Grainger, Lincolnshire, IL
Wachovia Corp., Winston-Salem, NC
Wal-Mart Stores, Bentonville, AR
Walgreen, Deerfield, IL
Walt Disney, Burbank, CA
Warner-Lambert, Morris Plains, NJ
Washington Mutual, Seattle, WA
Waste Management, Oak Brook, IL
Wellpoint Health Networks,
    Woodland Hills, CA
Wells Fargo & Co.,
    San Francisco, CA
Western Atlas, Houston, TX
Western Digital, Irvine, CA
Westvaco, New York, NY
Weyerhaeuser, Federal Way, WA
Whirlpool, Benton Harbor, MI
Whitman, Rolling Meadows, IL
Williams, Tulsa, OK
Winn-Dixie Stores, Jacksonville, FL
Willamette Industries, Portland, OR
Woolworth, New York, NY
Worldcom, Jackson, MS
Xerox, Stamford, CT
Yellow, Overland Park, KS
York International, York, PA

The
Legal Environment
of Business
A Critical Thinking Approach
second edition

Nancy K. Kubasek
Bartley A. Brennan
M. Neil Browne

Bowling Green State University

Prentice Hall, Upper Saddle River, New Jersey 07458

Senior Editor: Don Hull
Editorial Assistant: Paula D'Introno
Editor-in-Chief: Natalie Anderson
Marketing Manager: Tamara Wederbrand
Senior Production Editor: Judy Leale
Managing Editor: Dee Josephson
Manufacturing Buyer: Ken Clinton
Manufacturing Supervisor: Arnold Vila
Manufacturing Manager: Vincent Scelta
Designer: Cheryl Asherman
Design Manager: Patricia Smythe
Interior Design: Jill Yutkowitz
Cover Design: Jill Yutkowitz
Cover Illustration: Salem Krieger
Composition: UG

Library of Congress Cataloging-in-Publication Data
Kubasek, Nancy.
    The legal environment of business : a critical-thinking approach /
Nancy K. Kubasek, Bartley A. Brennan, M. Neil Browne.—2nd ed.
        p.   cm.
    Includes bibliographical references and index.
    ISBN 0-13-922253-7 (hc.)
    1. Industrial laws and legislation—United States.   2. Trade
regulation—United States.   3. Critical thinking—United States.
I. Brennan, Bartley A.   II. Browne, M. Neil.   III. Title.
KF1600.K83   1998
346.7307—dc21   98-23947
                                                        CIP

Prentice-Hall International (UK) Limited, London
Prentice-Hall of Australia Pty. Limited, Sydney
Prentice-Hall Canada, Inc., Toronto
Prentice-Hall Hispanoamericana, S.A., Mexico
Prentice-Hall of India Private Limited, New Delhi
Prentice-Hall of Japan, Inc., Tokyo
Simon & Schuster Asia Pte. Ltd., Singapore
Editora Prentice-Hall do Brasil, Ltda., Rio de Janeiro

Printed in the United States of America

10 9 8 7 6 5 4 3

To the numerous students who appreciate the importance of developing their critical thinking skills for their personal growth and development.

Nancy K. Kubasek and M. Neil Browne

To my parents.

Bartley A. Brennan

BRIEF CONTENTS

C O N T E N T S

---

*Cases highlighted in magenta type indicate cases that are followed by Critical Thinking about the
Law material.

PREFACE

Writing a preface for a second edition is a great opportunity to thank the many readers who have assisted us in improving this new version of *The Legal Environment of Business: A Critical Thinking Approach*. We have listened to your advice and counsel, and the new edition represents the high level of your scholarship and your passion for teaching and learning. We have been graced by the insights of many readers and certainly urge all of you to pass along any ideas you have about how we can improve the book even more.

INTRODUCTION

Law can be conceptualized as either a set of rules or as a process whereby current rules have developed and new rules will evolve. This latter approach, which we will take in this book, sees law as an intricate, always incomplete tapestry, a piece of art with an identifiable, yet evolving, structure. It emerges and develops. This dynamic approach to the law as it relates to the business world is what our book hopes to encourage.

The readers of this book will typically be prospective managers of public and private enterprise. How can a text best prepare these future managers for functioning in the ever changing global legal environment of business? Critical thinking skills are the essential ingredient for understanding current legal rules and making future business decisions that both comply with and contribute to emergent law. The importance of these skills for contemporary organizations has been recognized not only by educators, but also by those in the business community.

The initial motivation for this book was the authors' perception that there was no legal environment book available that explicitly and adequately facilitated the development of students' critical thinking skills. Teaching students in a systematic manner that developed their critical thinking skills required the use of a supplemental critical thinking textbook, which was cumbersome, to say the least.

Some people may argue that merely using the traditional method of case analysis allows them to develop their students' critical thinking skills. The problem with such an approach, however, is that the case method focuses only on the students' analytical skills, ignoring the evaluative component that is really the essence of critical thinking. Another problem with the traditional method of case analysis is that it does not include an ethical component. To engage in critical thinking necessarily includes consideration of the impact of values on the outcome being considered.

The use of cases in the legal environment of business classroom, however, can provide an excellent opportunity for the development of students' critical thinking abilities when the traditional case method is modified to emphasize the development of critical thinking skills. So, the initial two authors of this text contacted M. Neil Browne, one of the authors of the best-selling critical thinking textbook, *Asking the Right Questions* (Prentice Hall, 5th Edition, 1998), and asked him whether he would be interested in collaborating on a legal environment of business textbook that incorporated the teaching of critical thinking skills. Because he has a law degree, and in fact, has written articles about the relationship between critical thinking and traditional case analysis, he was interested in the project.

The result of this collaboration is a textbook that explicitly lays out in the first chapter the critical thinking skills that the students are to acquire. It provides a modified approach to case analysis that gives students the opportunity to practice these skills throughout the semester, whenever they read either a case or an article containing legal analysis. Case questions that focus on various critical thinking skills appear after several cases throughout the book and are clearly identified by a "*CT*" critical thinking icon.

The feedback we received from the users of the first edition of this book told us that many faculty did in fact want to use a critical thinking approach, however, they did not want this approach limited to just the cases. Thus, an especially significant change to the second edition is the addition of critical thinking questions at the beginning of each chapter to get the students thinking critically about the material from the start.

DISTINCTIVE FEATURES OF THE TEXT

CONTAINS AN EXPLICIT CRITICAL THINKING MODEL

This is the first legal environment of business textbook that tells the students what critical thinking is and gives them the opportunity to explicitly work on developing those critical thinking skills. The critical thinking materials were developed by M. Neil Browne, a recognized authority in the field of critical thinking, who also has a law degree.

The model of critical thinking provided in the book is one that can also be easily adapted to essays, so that students can internalize the kinds of questions they ask when analyzing cases or an editorial in the newspaper.

The book was written in a manner that will give instructors maximum flexibility in terms of the degree to which they want to emphasize the development of the students' critical thinking skills. Those who want to maximize the development of students' critical thinking skills may find it helpful to spend a significant amount of time discussing the critical thinking material in chapter 1 and have the students apply this to every case, as well as answer the questions in the critical thinking boxes, which appear at the beginning of each chapter and follow some of the cases. Dr. Browne has also written a new student workbook for the text that will provide additional practice opportunities for anyone wishing to emphasize critical thinking skills. These instructors may also want to use the additional critical thinking questions and assignments in the instructor's manual.

Other instructors, who do not wish to emphasize critical thinking, may simply instruct the students to think about their responses to questions in the critical thinking boxes when they read the material, but then concentrate their class discussions on the substantive material in the text.

EMPHASIZES THE ROLE OF ETHICS

One of the issues professors continually grapple with is how to integrate ethics into the legal environment of business course. The critical thinking model introduced in chapter 1 incorporates ethics into the case analysis. Questioning how a person's ethics influences his or her decision making therefore becomes a routine part of a student's evaluative behavior. For those who prefer a more traditional approach to ethics, or who would like to spend additional time discussing ethics, we have included a new chapter on ethics and social responsibility in this edition.

CONTAINS CURRENT AND CLASSIC CASES

The textbook contains many of the most significant contemporary cases, including important United States Supreme Court decisions handed down as recently as 1998. The book includes many of the more recent controversial cases such as the case of Paula Jones against President Clinton, and the Cattle Ranchers' law suit against talk show host Oprah Winfrey. Yet it also retains many of those classic cases whose holdings have continued to have a significant impact on the legal environment of business for years after they were decided.

EMPHASIZES THE IMPORTANCE OF THE GLOBAL ENVIRONMENT

In recognition of the growing importance of the global environment, we have introduced the international environment of business to the students in the third chapter of the text. Of course, individual instructors may always choose to have the students read this chapter later, but its placement reflects the importance the authors place on international considerations, an importance stressed recently by the AACSB.

We have also incorporated into every chapter a section that focuses on the international dimensions of the subject matter of the chapter. In this way, international issues may be discussed throughout the semester.

STRESSES VOCABULARY DEVELOPMENT

We all recognize the importance of being able to use the "language of the law." Our text recognizes the importance of students' acquiring the necessary vocabulary to discuss legal issues by providing a running glossary in the margin.

CONTAINS NUMEROUS CHARTS, TABLES, AND EXHIBITS

Student learning is facilitated by the use of charts, tables, and exhibits. These matters convey the material to the students in a slightly different form, sometimes making concepts easier to comprehend. We have therefore incorporated them wherever possible. The publisher has carefully designed these elements in full color for effective comprehension by the student.

CONTAINS WEB SITES FOR EACH CHAPTER

We cannot ignore the fact that many of our students feel more comfortable on the Web than in the library. Therefore, at the end of each chapter, we have provided numerous Web sites to which they can go to learn more about the topics covered in the chapter.

COVERAGE

The AACSB mandates coverage of global and ethical issues; the influence of political, social, legal and regulatory, and environmental and technological issues; and the impact of demographic diversity on organizations. This book covers every one of the topics listed in the AACSB mandate and is especially strong in its emphasis on ethics and international issues. The critical thinking approach of the book makes the students recognize that ethics plays a significant role in every business decision they make.

ORGANIZATION

The book is conveniently organized into three parts. Part one introduces the student to the legal, social, political, global, international, and regulatory environment. Part two explores those areas of private law that have a significant impact on how businesses operate. Part three then focuses on the regulatory environment of business, familiarizing students with all of the areas of regulation they will be forced to respond to when they are managers.

CHANGES MADE TO THE SECOND EDITION

UPDATED CASES

Reviewers and users of the first edition have commented extensively on the interesting cases we have included in the text. As would be expected for a new edition, we have updated our cases to ensure inclusion of the most recent changes in the law. New cases are not only featured in the text, but have also been used to replace some of the older case problems. As with our initial case selection, we tried to find cases that not only illustrated important legal concepts, but contained fact patterns that would captivate the students' interest.

IMPROVED CRITICAL THINKING MATERIALS

We have made a number of changes in response to our users and reviewers suggestions. The first of these changes was to better incorporate the critical thinking materials into the text by beginning each chapter with a series of critical thinking questions. These questions will get the students thinking critically from the very start of the chapter.

WEB SITES FOR EACH CHAPTER

As noted earlier in the preface, we have now included the addresses for numerous relevant Web sites at the end of each chapter.

EXPANDED CONTRACTS AND SALES MATERIALS

A number of users wanted a little more material on contracts and sales, and so this edition features two chapters on contracts and sales, including additional Uniform Commercial Code materials.

NEW COVERAGE OF EMPLOYEE BENEFITS

The material on labor law has been reorganized, and we have added an additional chapter that covers issues fundamental to employee security, including such topics as unemployment compensation, workers compensation, and employee privacy rights.

SUPPLEMENTS

A wide range of supplements are available to make this course administratively easier for the instructor, and to enable the instructor to provide the students access to a broader range of educational experiences than would be available with the textbook alone.

INSTRUCTOR'S RESOURCE MANUAL

Once again, our instructor's resource manual has been expertly prepared by Andrea Giampetro-Meyer, of Loyola College, a recipient of teaching awards from the ALSB, her college, and Beta Gamma Sigma. Because she uses the textbook, the authors asked her to incorporate ideas into the manual that have actually been tested in the class. The author is also someone who has expertise in the area of critical thinking, having written numerous articles on the topic. The manual includes the following features:
- discussion outlines for each chapter, with references to other supplements when appropriate
- answers to questions in Critical Thinking Boxes
- answers to end of the chapter questions
- additional critical thinking questions and assignments

STUDENT STUDY GUIDE/CRITICAL THINKING SUPPLEMENT

M. Neil Browne, who authored the critical thinking materials in the text, has written a new *Student Study Guide* for the second edition. This study guide provides significant opportunities for students to practice and improve their critical thinking skills, in addition to providing them with exercises to test their knowledge of the substantive materials provided in the text. The idea for this supplement grew out of users' requests that we provide more opportunities for students to focus on developing their critical thinking skills.

PowerPoint Slides

Developed by Howard Ellis of Millersville University, Millersville, PA. Students today are visually oriented, and perhaps one of the best methods for keeping their attention in class is to have color graphics available. Each chapter of the text is supported by a substantial number of content-oriented graphics that will enhance the student's classroom experience.

Prentice Hall Custom Video Series

Fifteen core topics in business law and legal environment of business are expertly illustrated in this new, custom video series just for legal studies in business. The videos sharply illustrate the important connection between business and management issues and the law. Available in fall 1998. Contact your local Prentice Hall sales representative for details.

The Prentice Hall/*New York Times* Contemporary View Program

The *New York Times* and Prentice Hall are sponsoring "Themes of the Times," a program designed to enhance student access to current information of relevance in the classroom. Through this program, the core subject matter provided in the text is supplemented by a collection of time-sensitive articles from one of the world's most distinguished newspapers, the *New York Times*. These articles demonstrate the vital, ongoing connection between what is learned in the classroom and what is happening in the world around us.

Prentice Hall and the *New York Times* are proud to co-sponsor "Themes of the Times." We hope it will make the reading of both textbooks and newspapers a more dynamic, involving process.

Prentice Hall Custom Test

Based on the number one best-selling, state-of-the-art test generation software program developed by Engineering Software Associates (ESA), Prentice Hall Custom Test is not only suitable for your course, but can be customized to your personal needs. With Prentice Hall Custom Test's user-friendly test creation and powerful algorithmic generation, you can create tailor-made tests quickly, easily and error-free. Whether you are on Macintosh, Windows, or DOS, you can create an exam, administer it traditionally or on-line, evaluate and track student's results, and analyze the success of the exam—all with a simple click of the mouse.

Web Site Support

Prentice Hall has been a leader in on-line support of both professors and students. The legal studies Web site is part of the number one Web site for business faculty and students— PHLIP (Prentice Hall Learning on the Internet Partnership). PHLIP generates about 500,000 "hits" per month. Both faculty and students add to their in- and out-of-class experience by making PHLIP part of their course. PHLIP supports several Prentice Hall legal studies texts with current events links, cases, discussion questions, student study hall, "ask the tutor," faculty supplements and much more. Visit PHLIP at ⟨http://www.phlip.marist.edu⟩.

Case Updates

Adopters of the book may subscribe to a list service that will provide regular case updates via e-mail, consisting of edited versions of newly decided cases and accompanying critical thinking questions that may be used to stimulate discussions about these cases.

TotaLaw CD-ROM for Legal Studies in Business

TotaLaw is packaged **free** with every copy of the text and is a comprehensive resource. It contains thirty important acts and statutes that have a direct impact on business in the United States and in international arenas every day. Students can search by key word and will never find an undergraduate textbook with the comprehensiveness of *TotaLaw*.

ACKNOWLEDGMENTS

Numerous people have contributed to the success of this project, without which this book would not have become a reality. We would therefore like to acknowledge their contributions. Our sincere thanks for all of their work go to the professionals at Prentice Hall: Don Hull, our editor; Paula D'Introno, his assistant; Judy Leale, our production editor; and Margo Quinto, our copy editor. Tamara Wederbrand, marketing manager, has worked with us to design the right strategy and marketing communications.

We wish to thank the following reviewers whose numerous comments, suggestions, and criticisms significantly improved the content of this textbook: Louis Aranda, Arizona State; Roy J. Girasa, Pace University; Jane A. Malloy, Delaware Valley CC; Ernest W. King, University of Southern Mississippi; James Marshall, Michigan State University; John McGee, Southwest Texas State University; Royce Barondes, Louisiana State University; and Debra Burke, Western Carolina University. Andrea Giampetro-Meyer, the author of the Instructor's Manual, also provided numerous helpful suggestions to both the first and second editions.

We wish to acknowledge our colleague Robert Holmes, who generously agreed to share his expertise in the labor and employment fields by reviewing those chapters for the first edition with painstaking care. His comments and suggestions were invaluable. His subsequent comments based on his use of the book provided additional assistance to us in our revisions.

We thank Don Boren, the Chair of our Legal Studies Department, whose careful reading of the text when he used it for his classes stimulated a number of conversations about issues raised in the text. As a result of these conversations, many complex issues have been clarified in the second edition.

We thank Wesley J. Hiers, a Ph.D. student in industrial relations at Cornell University, who provided unusually dedicated and creative assistance for this project and also our research assistants, Carrie Williamson, who drafted a number of the graphics for the new edition and Michael Meuti, who provided substantial assistance to us in the final stages of the book's production. We also thank the word processing staff at Bowling Green State University who retyped numerous versions of this manuscript without complaint: Joyce Hyslop, Karen Masters, and Tami Thomas.

And finally, we thank the numerous students who used the book and made suggestions.

The authors hope that this book will help fulfill its purpose of providing a useful tool for students who wish to develop their critical thinking skills while gaining a better understanding of the legal environment of business. Toward that end, the authors would be happy to correspond with any readers via e-mail. So if you have any questions while reading the text, please feel free to contact Nancy Kubasek at nkubase@cba.bgsu.edu or Neil Browne at nbrown2 @cba.bgsu.edu.

ABOUT THE AUTHORS

Nancy Kubasek is a Professor of Legal Studies at Bowling Green State University, where she teaches the Legal Environment of Business, Environmental Law, and Women and the Law. For eight years she team-taught a freshman honors seminar on critical thinking and values analysis. She has published an undergraduate textbook entitled *Environmental Law*, second edition (Prentice Hall, 1996) and more than 40 articles. Her articles have appeared in such journals as the *American Business Law Journal*, the *Journal of Legal Studies Education,* the *Harvard Women's Law Journal*, the *Georgetown Journal of Legal Ethics,* and the *Harvard Journal on Legislation*. She received her J.D. from the University of Toledo College of Law and her B.A. from Bowling Green State University.

"The most important thing that a teacher can do is to help his or her students develop the skills and attitudes necessary to become lifelong learners. Professors should help their students learn the types of questions to ask to analyze complex legal issues, and to develop a set of criteria to apply when evaluating reasons. If we are successful, students will leave our legal environment of business classroom with a basic understanding of important legal concepts, a set of evaluative criteria to apply when evaluating arguments that includes an ethical component, and a desire to continue learning.

To attain these goals, the classroom must be an interactive one, where students learn to ask important questions, define contexts, generate sound reasons, point out the flaws in erroneous reasoning, recognize alternative perspectives, and consider the impacts that their decisions (both now and in the future) have on the broader community beyond themselves."

Bartley A. Brennan is a Professor of Legal Studies at Bowling Green State University. He is a graduate of the School of Foreign Service, Georgetown University (B.S. International Economics); the College of Law, State University of New York at Buffalo (J.D.); and Memphis State University (M.A. Economics). He was a volunteer in the United States Peace Corps, was employed by the Office of Opinions and Review of the Federal Communications Commission, and worked in the general counsel's office of a private international corporation. He has received appointments as a visiting associate professor, the Wharton School, University of Pennsylvania, and as a Research Fellow, Ethics Resource Center, Washington, D.C. He is the author of articles dealing with the Foreign Corrupt Practices Act of 1977, as Amended; the business judgment rule; law and economics; and business ethics. He has published numerous articles in such journals as the *American Business Law Journal, University of North Carolina Journal of International Law*, and the *Notre Dame University Journal of Legislation*. He is a co-author of *Modern Business Law* (third edition). He has testified on amending the Foreign Corrupt Practices Act before the Sub-Committee on International Economics and Finance of the House Commerce, Energy, and Telecommunications Committee.

His teaching goals include the following:

1. to assist students in developing an understanding of the role of law in managerial decision making

2. to help develop students' critical thinking skills that can assist them for their total lives, inclusive of careers

3. to help develop communication skills that can assist students throughout their careers

4. to help students develop an understanding of the international dimensions of law and ethics in making management and personal decisions.

M. Neil Browne is a Distinguished Teaching Professor of Economics at Bowling Green State University. He received a J.D. from the University of Toledo and a Ph.D. from the University of Texas. He is the co-author of seven books and more than one hundred research articles in professional journals. One of his books, *Asking the Right Questions: A Guide to Critical Thinking,* fifth edition, is a leading text in the field of critical thinking. His most recent book, *Striving for Excellence in College: Tips for Active Learning,* provides learners with practical ideas for expanding the power and effectiveness of their thinking. Professor Browne has been asked by dozens of colleges and universities to aid their faculty in developing critical thinking skills on their respective campuses. He also serves on the editorial board of the *Korean Journal of Critical Thinking.* In 1989, he was a silver medalist in the Council for the Advancement and Support of Education's National Professor of the Year award. Also in 1989, he was named the Ohio Professor of the Year. He has won numerous teaching awards on both a local and national level.

"When students come into contact with conflicting claims, they can react in several fashions; my task is to enable them to evaluate these persuasive attempts. I try to provide them with a broad range of criteria and attitudes that reasonable people tend to use as they think their way through a conversation. In addition, I urge them to use productive questions as a stimulus to deep discussion, a looking below the surface of an argument for the assumptions underlying the visible component of the reasoning. The eventual objectives are to enable them to be highly selective in their choice of beliefs and to provide them with the greater sense of meaning that stems from knowing that they have used their own minds to separate sense from relative nonsense."

AN INTRODUCTION TO THE
LAW AND THE LEGAL
ENVIRONMENT OF BUSINESS

PART ONE

$\mathcal{P}$art One introduces the concept of critical thinking that provides the framework for our study of the legal environment of business. It also gives an overview of this legal environment through our exploration of alternative philosophies of law, alternative philosophies of ethics, how the constitutional foundations of our legal system works to resolve both criminal and civil disputes, how the American system works, and alternative methods of resolving disputes. It concludes with a discussion of that corrosion of the legal environment of business known as white collar crime.

1

CRITICAL THINKING AND LEGAL REASONING

- **THE IMPORTANCE OF CRITICAL THINKING**

- **A CRITICAL THINKING MODEL**

- **THE CRITICAL THINKING STEPS**

- **USING CRITICAL THINKING TO MAKE LEGAL REASONING COME ALIVE**

- **APPLYING THE CRITICAL THINKING APPROACH**

4

Part One

*An Introduction to the Law
and the Legal Environment
of Business*

critical thinking skills The
ability to understand the
structure of an argument and
apply a set of evaluative criteria
to assess its merits.

THE IMPORTANCE OF CRITICAL THINKING

Success in the modern business firm requires the development of **critical thinking skills**: the ability to understand what someone is saying and then to apply evaluative criteria to assess the quality of the reasoning offered to support the conclusion. Because they are under increasing competitive pressure, business and industry need managers with advanced thinking skills.[1] Highlighting this need, a recent report by the Secretary of Education states that because "one of the major goals of business education is preparing students for the workforce, students and their professors must respond to this need for enhancing critical thinking skills."[2]

Calls for improvements in critical thinking skills also come from persons concerned about business ethics: "Managers stand in need of sharp critical thinking skills that will serve them well [in tackling] ethical issues," according to an editorial in *Management Accounting*.[3] As a future business manager, you will experience many ethical dilemmas. Where should our facilities be located? Whom should we hire? What are the boundaries of fair competition? What responsibilities do firms owe various stakeholders? All such questions require legal analysis and ethical understanding, *guided by critical thinking*.

The message is clear: success in business today requires critical thinking skills, and there is no better context in which to develop them than in the study of the laws that affect business. Critical thinking skills learned in the legal environment of business course will be easily transferred to your eventual role as a manager, entrepreneur, or other business professional.

Remember, as you learn about our legal system and how its evolution affects the legal environment of business, you will also be developing your critical thinking skills. You will find that, as your critical thinking skills develop, your understanding of the law will be enhanced. The skills are mutually beneficial.

Legal reasoning is like other reasoning in some ways and different in others. When people, including lawyers and judges, reason, they do so for a purpose. Some problem or dilemma bothers them. The stimulus that gets them thinking is the issue. It is stated as a question because it is a call for action. It requires them to *do* something, to think about answers.

For instance, in our legal environment of business course we will be interested in such issues as the following:

1. When are union organizers permitted under the National Labor Relations Act to trespass on an employer's property?
2. Do tobacco manufacturers have liability for the deaths of smokers?
3. Must a business fulfill a contract when the contract is made with an unlicensed contractor in a state requiring that all contractors be licensed?

These questions have several different answers. Which one should you choose as your answer? Here is where critical thinking is essential to your business success. Some of your answers could get you into trouble; others could advance your purpose. Each answer is called a **conclusion**. The conclusion is a position or stance on an issue.

conclusion A position or stance on an issue; the goal toward which reasoning moves.

Business firms encounter legal conclusions in the form of laws or court decisions. Business managers are therefore both consumers of and contributors to legal conclusions. As businesses learn about and react to decisions or conclusions made by courts, they have two primary methods of response: They can

1. Memorize the conclusions or rules of law as a guide for future business decisions, or they can
2. Make judgments about the quality of the conclusions.

---

[1]C. Sormunen and M. Chalupa, *Critical Thinking Skills Research: Developing Evaluation Techniques*, 69 J. Educ. Bus. 172 (1994).
[2]*Id.*
[3]P. Madsen, *Moral Mazes in Management*, Mgmt. Acct., July 1990, at 56.

This book encourages you to do both. What is unique about this text is its practical approach to evaluating legal reasoning. This approach is based on using critical thinking skills to understand and evaluate the law as it affects business.

There are many forms of critical thinking, but they all share one characteristic: They focus on the quality of someone's reasoning. Critical thinking is active; it challenges each of us to form judgments about the quality of the link between someone's reasons and conclusions. In particular, we will be focusing on the link between a court's reasons and conclusions.

You will be interested in the legal environment of business not just to understand the current rules governing your business decisions but also to help you evaluate the rules you will encounter as a business manager.

A CRITICAL THINKING MODEL

You will learn critical thinking by practicing it. The text will tutor you. But your efforts are the key to your skill as a critical thinker. Because people often learn best by example, we will introduce you to critical thinking by demonstrating it in a model that you can easily follow.

We now turn to a sample of critical thinking in practice. The eight critical thinking questions listed in Exhibit 1–1 and applied in the sample case that follows it illustrate the approach you should follow when reading cases to develop your critical thinking abilities.

COOK V. RHODE ISLAND DEPARTMENT OF MENTAL HEALTH, RETARDATION AND HOSPITALS
UNITED STATES FIRST CIRCUIT COURT OF APPEALS 10F.2D 17 (1993)

Plaintiff Cook, a woman who stood 5 feet 2 inches tall and weighed over 320 pounds, applied for a vacant position as an institutional attendant. She had previously held this same position. The State of Rhode Island, the defendant, refused to hire her because of her obesity. She sued on the grounds that their discriminatory refusal to rehire her violated the 1973 Rehabilitation Act. The trial court found in her favor and the defendant appealed.

JUDGE SELYA

Section 504 of the 1973 Rehabilitation Act provides that "[n]o otherwise qualified individual . . . shall, solely by reason of her or his disability, . . . be subjected to discrimination under any program or activity receiving Federal financial assistance." Section 504 embraces not only those persons who are in fact disabled, but also those who bear the brunt of discrimination because prospective employers view them as disabled.

Section 504's perceived disability model can be satisfied whether or not a person actually has a physical or mental impairment. Also, regulations define the term "physical or mental impairment" broadly to include any physiological disorder or condition significantly affecting a major bodily system, e.g., musculoskeletal, respiratory, or cardiovascular.

The state asserts that "mutable" [changeable] conditions are not the sort of impairments that can find safe harbor in the lee of Section 504. It claims that morbid obesity is a mutable condition and that, therefore, one who suffers from it is not handicapped within the meaning of the federal law because she can simply lose weight and rid herself of any concomitant disability.

The jury had before it credible evidence that metabolic dysfunction, which leads to weight gain in the morbidly obese, lingers even after weight loss. Given this evidence, the jury reasonably could have found that, though people afflicted with morbid obesity can treat the manifestations of metabolic dysfunction by fasting or perennial undereating, the physical impairment itself—a dysfunctional metabolism—is permanent.

The state also asserts that, because morbid obesity is caused, or at least exacerbated, by voluntary conduct, it cannot constitute an impairment falling within the ambit of Section 504. But the statute contains no language suggesting that its protection is linked to how an individual became impaired, or whether an individual contributed to his or her impairment. On the contrary, the statute indisputably applies to numerous conditions that may be caused or exacerbated by voluntary conduct, such as alcoholism, AIDS, diabetes, cancer resulting from cigarette smoking, and heart disease resulting from excesses of various types.

The regulations define "major life activities" to include walking, breathing, working, and other manual tasks. In this case, the state refused to hire the applicant because it believed that her morbid obesity interfered with her ability to undertake physical activities, including walking, lifting, bending, stooping, and kneeling, to such an extent that she would be incapable of working as an attendant. On this basis alone, the jury plausibly could have found that the state viewed the applicant's suspected impairment as interfering with major life activities.

We think that detached jurors reasonably could have found that the state's pessimistic assessment of the applicant's capabilities demonstrated that it regarded her condition as substantially limiting a major life activity—being able to work.

We next consider whether there was sufficient evidence for the jury to conclude that the applicant was "otherwise qualified" to work as an attendant. An otherwise qualified person is one who is able to meet all of a program's requirements in spite of her handicap. Although an employer is not required to be unfailingly correct in assessing a person's qualifications for a job, an employer cannot act solely on the basis of subjective beliefs. An unfounded assumption that an applicant is unqualified for a particular job, even if arrived at in good faith, is not sufficient to forestall liability under Section 504.

The state's position is that the applicant's morbid obesity presented such a risk to herself and the facility's residents that she was not otherwise qualified, or, in the alternative, that it was reasonable for the state to believe that she was not otherwise qualified.

The state has not offered a hint of any non-weight-related reason for rejecting the plaintiff's application. On this record, there was considerable room for a jury to find that the state declined to hire the applicant "due solely to" her perceived handicap. In a society that all too often confuses "slim" with "beautiful" or "good," morbid obesity can present formidable barriers to employment. Where, as here, the barriers transgress federal law, those who erect and seek to preserve them must suffer the consequences.

Affirmed in favor of Plaintiff, Cook.

As a citizen, entrepreneur, or manager, you will encounter cases like the one above. How would you have responded? What do you think about the quality of Judge Selya's reasoning? Let's apply some critical thinking to this case. First, review the eight steps of a critical thinking approach to legal reasoning in Exhibit 1–1. We will call these the critical thinking questions throughout the book.

Notice the primary importance of the first four steps; their purpose is to discover the vital elements in the case and the reasoning behind the decision. Failure to consider these four foundational steps might result in our reacting too quickly to what a court or legislature has said.

The answers to these four questions enable us to understand how the court's argument fits together and to make intelligent use of legal decisions. These answers are the necessary first step in a critical thinking approach to legal analysis. The final four questions are the critical thinking component of legal reasoning. We ask them to form our reaction to what the court decided.

Our reactions to legal arguments shape our efforts to either support the status quo in the legal environment of business or support the institution of particular changes. Without the last four questions, legal reasoning would be sterile. Why are we even curious about the legal environment? The answer is we want it to be the best we can create. But improvement requires our very best critical thinking.

EXHIBIT 1–1

The Eight Steps to Legal Reasoning

8. Is there relevant missing information?

7. How appropriate are the legal analogies?

6. What ethical norms are fundamental to the court's reasoning?

5. Does the legal argument contain significant ambiguity?

4. What are the relevant rules of law?

3. What are the reasons and conclusion?

2. What is the issue?

1. What are the facts?

You will develop your own workable strategies for legal reasoning, but we urge you to start by following our structure. Every time you read a case, ask yourself these eight questions. Then improve upon this set of questions as you become comfortable with them.

The remainder of this section will demonstrate the use of each of the eight steps in order. Notice that the order makes sense. The first four follow the path that best allows you to discover the basis of a particular legal decision; the next four assist you in deciding what you think about the worth of that decision.

THE CRITICAL THINKING STEPS

FACTS

First we look for the most basic building blocks in a legal decision or argument. These building blocks, or facts, provide the environment or context in which the legal issue is to be resolved. Certain events occurred; certain actions were or were not taken; particular persons behaved or failed to behave in specific ways. All of these and many more possibilities together make up the intricate setting for the playing out of the issue in question. We always wonder: What happened in this case? Let's now turn our attention to the *Cook* case:

1. A woman applied for and was denied a job she had previously held in a state-operated facility for retarded persons.
2. At the time of denial she was 5 feet 2 inches tall and weighed over 320 pounds.
3. A federal law against discrimination based on disability in any organization or activity receiving federal funds exists.

ISSUE

In almost any legal conflict, finding and expressing the issue is an important step in forming our reaction. The issue is the question that caused the lawyers and their clients to enter the legal system. Usually there are several reasonable perspectives concerning the correct way to word the issue in dispute.

1. To what extent does metabolic dysfunction explain morbid obesity?
2. Does obesity interfere with major life activities and thus place it under the 1973 Rehabilitation Act? (1 and 2 are versions of the same issue.)
3. Do the regulations associated with Section 504 imply a broad interpretation of its scope, permitting obesity to fall under its jurisdiction?

Do not let the possibility of *multiple* useful ways to word the issue cause you any confusion. The issue is certainly not just anything that we say it is. If we claim something is an issue, our suggestion must fulfill the definition of an issue *in this particular factual situation*.

REASONS AND CONCLUSION

Judge Selya found it reasonable for a jury to believe that the state unlawfully declined to hire the plaintiff solely because she was obese. This finding by Judge Selya is his conclusion; it serves as his answer to the legal issue. Why did he answer this way? Here we are calling for the **reasons**, explanations or justifications provided as support for a conclusion.

reason An explanation or justification provided as support for a conclusion.

1. Medical evidence exists that even when a person works hard to lose weight, metabolic dysfunction (which is out of the person's control) continues.
2. The Rehabilitation Act applies even to conditions that the individual may have caused.
3. The state failed to check adequately to see whether the woman could do the attendant's job.
4. Most fundamentally, the Rehabilitation Act forbids discrimination in such facilities.

8

Part One

*An Introduction to the Law
and the Legal Environment
of Business*

Let's not pass too quickly over this very important critical thinking step. When we ask Why? of any opinion, we are showing our respect for reasons as the proper basis for any assertion. We want a world rich with opinions so we can have a broad field of choice. But we should agree with only those legal opinions that have convincing reasons supporting the conclusion. So to ask Why? is our way of saying, "I want to believe you, but you have an obligation to help me by sharing the reasons for your conclusion."

RULES OF LAW

Judges cannot offer just any reasoning that they please. They must always look back over their shoulders at the laws and previous court decisions that together provide an anchor for current and future decisions.

This particular case is an attempt to match the words of the 1973 Rehabilitation Act and its regulations with the facts in this instance. Because no case law is cited, the rule is the statute itself. What makes legal reasoning so complex is that statutes and findings are never *crystal* clear. They may be clear, but judges and businesspeople have room for interpretive flexibility in their reasoning.

AMBIGUITY

ambiguous Susceptible to two or more possible interpretations.

The court's reasoning leans on its implied assumptions about the meaning of several ambiguous words. (An **ambiguous** word is one capable of having more than one meaning in the context of these facts.) For instance, Judge Selya stated that metabolic dysfunction "lingers" after weight loss. Does it linger in the sense of forcing or stimulating probable weight gain? Or does it linger only in that it is always lurking as a remotely possible future problem? Answering these questions would be relevant to the appropriateness of using AIDS as an analogy to argue that the act includes protection for conditions made worse by voluntary conduct. Conduct is not just voluntary or involuntary. The degree of involuntary disability is relevant to the amount of compassion we feel for the person allegedly harmed in a legal conflict.

Another illustration of important ambiguity in the decision is the court's use of the term *subjective* to describe the state's belief that the plaintiff could not in her current condition fulfill job requirements. Does *subjective* here mean "there was no scientific investigation of her capabilities"? If so, is this standard realistic?

Or does *subjective* mean that "the state's refusal to hire the person arose solely from past experience with people of the plaintiff's size"? The next questions then would be how vast was this experience and how frequently do people in her condition surprise us by their ability to perform jobs our experience might suggest they could not do. Any decision by an employer has heavy subjective components. Hence, until we know what *subjective* means, we cannot fairly decide that the employer treated the employee inappropriately.

ETHICAL NORMS

The primary ethical norms that influence judges' decisions are justice, security, freedom, and efficiency. Judge Selya expresses himself as a defender of *justice*. (Here is a good place to turn ahead to Exhibit 1–2 to check alternative definitions of justice.) He is obviously bothered by the potential abuse of stereotypes by those who have heard or have a hunch that many work outcomes of a person who possesses a particular characteristic are predictable. He asks us to consider whether the fact of obesity should automatically prevent someone from being considered for a job.

Although the court does not explicitly address its feelings about *efficiency*, that ethical norm is assigned low priority by the reasoning. The costs to the firm of hiring suspect employees or paying for less "subjective" methods of evaluating employees play no apparent role in shaping the court's argument.

We certainly cannot say as a result that Judge Selya does not value efficiency. Surely he does! But for this fact pattern, efficiency has a lower ethical pull on the reasoning than is provided by the ethical norm of justice.

Is obesity enough like AIDS, diabetes, and cancer that we can take the accepted jurisdiction of the Rehabilitation Act over those diseases and use it to announce comparable jurisdiction over obesity? Ordinarily, our examination of legal analogies will require us to compare legal precedents cited by the parties with the facts of the case we are examining. Those precedents are the analogies on which legal decision making depends.

However, in this case, no precedent is directly cited. Instead, we are reminded by the court that AIDS, diabetes, and cancer are all linked to the voluntary behavior of persons who have those diseases *and* that persons who suffer those diseases are covered by the statute in question. So, the court asks, what is different about obesity?

The worth of this analogy depends on a greater understanding of obesity than most of us have. As stated earlier, even when we label an action as "voluntary," we know that certain accidental factors pushed and pulled on the choice. Are you voluntarily reading this chapter? Isn't "yes and no" the correct answer? Did your parents and their teaching (an event external to you, over which you lacked control) have any impact on the probability that you would read the chapter?

To feel comfortable with the analogy, we would need to be persuaded that, like cancer, obesity has a largely involuntary cause, despite its link to voluntary activities.

MISSING INFORMATION

In the search for relevant missing information, it is important not to say just anything that comes to mind. For example, where did the plaintiff last eat Thanksgiving dinner? Anyone hearing that question would understandably wonder why it was asked. Ask only questions that would be helpful in understanding the reasoning in this particular case.

To focus on only *relevant* missing information, we should include with a request for additional information an explanation for why we want it. We have listed a few examples below for the *Cook* case. You can probably identify others.

1. How large was the plaintiff when she first held the job that she was later denied? If her size in the first instance was similar to her current size and she performed her job adequately, her position is greatly strengthened.

2. Congress, as it does with any legislation, discussed the Rehabilitation Act before passing it. Does that discussion contain any clues as to Congress' intent with respect to the extent of involuntary causation that is required for a plaintiff to fall under the protection of this law? The answer would conceivably clarify the appropriateness of this extension of the statute's coverage.

3. How much evidence did the employer consider before rejecting the plaintiff? The reason for being curious about this evidence is that the answer would address Judge Selya's appropriate concern about justice in this case. Was the plaintiff treated fairly or arbitrarily? Did the employer make a hasty or a thoughtful determination of her capabilities?

Many other critical thinking skills could be applied to this and other cases. In this book we are focusing on the ones especially valuable for legal reasoning. Consistently applying this critical thinking approach will enable you to understand the reasoning in the cases and to increase your awareness of alternative approaches our laws could take to many problems you will encounter in the legal environment of business. The remaining portion of this chapter examines each of the critical thinking questions in greater depth to help you better understand the function of each.

You will have plenty of practice opportunities in this text to apply this set of critical thinking questions to the cases you read. You should also answer the questions contained in the "Critical Thinking about the Law" boxes that follow many of the cases.

10

Part One

*An Introduction to the Law
and the Legal Environment
of Business*

*"I still don't have all the answers, but I'm
beginning to ask the right questions."*

USING CRITICAL THINKING TO MAKE LEGAL REASONING COME ALIVE

Our response to an issue is a conclusion. It is what we want others to believe about the issue. For example, a court might conclude that an employee, allegedly fired for her political views, was actually a victim of employment discrimination and is entitled to a damage award. Conclusions are reached by following a path that is produced by reasoning. Hence, examining reasoning is especially important when we are trying to understand and evaluate a conclusion.

There are many paths by which we may reach conclusions. For instance, I might settle all issues in my life by listening to voices in the night, asking my uncle, studying astrological signs, or just playing hunches. Each method could produce conclusions. Each could yield results.

But our intellectual and legal tradition demands a different type of support for conclusions. In this tradition, the basis for our conclusions is supposed to consist of reasons. When someone has no apparent reasons or the reasons don't match the conclusion, we feel entitled to say, "But that makes no sense." We aren't impressed by claims that we should accept someone's conclusion "just because."

This requirement that we all provide reasons for conclusions is what we mean in large part when we say we are going to think. We will ponder what the reasons and conclusion are and whether they mesh. This intense study of how a certain conclusion follows from a particular set of reasons occupies much of the time involved in careful decision making.

Persons trained to reason about court cases have a great appreciation for the unique facts that provoked a legal action. Those facts and no others provide the context for our reasoning. If an issue arises because environmentalists want to prevent an interstate highway from extending through a wilderness area, we want to know right away—What are the facts?

Doesn't everyone want to know about the context for an event? Unfortunately, the answer is no. Many people rush to judgment once they know the issue. One valuable lesson you can take with you as you practice legal analysis is the fundamental importance of the unique set of facts that provide the setting for the legal dispute.

Legal reasoning encourages unusual and necessary respect for the particular factual situation that stimulated disagreement between parties. These *fact patterns*, as we call them, bring the issue to our attention and limit the extent to which the court's conclusion can be applied to other situations. Small wonder that the first step in legal reasoning is to ask and answer the question: What are the facts?

LEGAL REASONING

STEP 1:   What Are the Facts?

The call for the facts is not a request for all facts but only those that have a bearing on the dispute at hand. That dispute tells us whether a certain fact is pertinent. In some cases the plaintiff's age may be a key point; in another it may be irrelevant noise.

Only after we have familiarized ourselves with the relevant legal facts do we begin the familiar pattern of reasoning that thoughtful people use. We then ask and answer the following question: What is the issue?

STEP 2:   What Is the Issue?

The issue is the question that the court is being asked to answer. For example, courts face groups of facts relevant to issues such as the following:

1.   Does Title VII apply to sexual harassment situations when the accused and the alleged victim are members of the same sex?
2.   Does a particular merger between two companies violate the Sherman Act?
3.   When does a governmental regulation require compensation to the property owner affected by the regulation?

As we pointed out earlier, the way we express the issue guides the legal reasoning in the case. Hence, forming an issue in a very broad or a highly narrow manner has implications for the scope of the effect stemming from the eventual decision. You can appreciate now why parties to a dispute work very hard to get the court to see the issue in a particular way.

You will read many legal decisions in this book. No element of your analysis of those cases is more important than careful consideration of the issue at hand. The key to issue spotting is asking yourself what question do the parties want to be answered by the court. The next logical step in legal analysis is to ask: What are the reasons and conclusion?

STEP 3:   What Are the Reasons and Conclusion?

The issue is the stimulus for thought. The facts and the issue in a particular case get us started thinking critically about legal reasoning. But the conclusion and the reasons for that conclusion provide flesh to the court's reaction to the legal issue. They tell us how the court has responded to the issue.

To find the conclusion, use the issue as a helper. Ask yourself: How did the court react to the issue? The answer is the conclusion. The reasons for that conclusion provide the answer to the question: Why did the court prefer this response to the issue, rather than any alternative? One part of the answer to that question is the answer to another question: What are the relevant rules of law?

12

Part One

*An Introduction to the Law
and the Legal Environment
of Business*

STEP 4: What Are the Relevant Rules of Law?

The fourth step in legal reasoning reveals another difference from general, non-legal reasoning. The issue arises in a context of existing legal rules. We do not treat each legal dispute as if it were the first such dispute in human history. On the contrary, society has already addressed similar disputes in its laws and court findings. It has already responded to situations much like the ones now before the court.

The historical record of pertinent judicial decisions provides a rich source of reasons on which to base the conclusion of courts. These prior decisions, or legal precedents, provide legal rules that those in a legal dispute must defer to. Thus, the fourth step in legal reasoning requires a focus on those rules. These legal rules are what the parties to a dispute must use as the framework for their legal claims. How those rules and the reasoning and conclusions built on them are expressed, however, is not always crystal clear. So another question—one that starts the critical thinking evaluation of the conclusion—is: Does the legal argument contain significant ambiguity?

STEP 5: Does the Legal Argument Contain Significant Ambiguity?

Legal arguments are expressed in words, and words rarely have the clarity we presume. Whenever we are tempted to think that our words speak for themselves, we should remind ourselves of Emerson's observation that "to be understood is a rare luxury." Hence, legal reasoning possesses elasticity. It can be stretched and reduced to fit the purpose of the attorney or judge.

As an illustration, a rule of law may contain the phrase "public safety." At first glance, as with any term, some interpretation arises in our mind. But as we continue to consider the extent and limits of "public safety," we realize it is not so clear. To be more certain about the meaning we must study the intent of the person making the legal argument. Just how safe must the public be before an action provides sufficient threat to public safety to justify public intervention?

As a strategy for critical thinking, the request for clarification is a form of evaluation. The point of the question is that we cannot make the reasoning our own until we have determined what we are being asked to embrace.

What we are being asked to embrace and the reasoning behind it usually involve some ethical component. So an important question to ask is: What ethical norms are fundamental to the courts reasoning?

STEP 6: What Ethical Norms Are Fundamental to the Court's Reasoning?

norm A standard of conduct.

The legal environment of business is established and modified according to ethical norms. A **norm** is a standard of conduct, a set of expectations that we bring to social encounters. For example, one norm we collectively understand and obey is that our departures are ordinarily punctuated by "good bye." We may presume rudeness or preoccupation on the part of someone who leaves our presence without bidding us some form of farewell.

ethical norms Standards of conduct that we consider good or virtuous.

Ethical norms are special because they are steps toward achieving what we consider good or virtuous. Goodness and virtue are universally preferred to their opposites, but the preference has little meaning until we look more deeply into the meaning of these noble aims. As you are well aware, there are dozens of alternative visions about what it means to be good or to have a good society.

Conversations about ethics explore these alternative visions. They do so by comparing the relative merit of human behavior that is guided by one ethical norm or another. Ethical norms represent the abstractions we hold out to others as the most fundamental standards defining our self-worth and value to others.

For example, any of us would be proud to know that others see us as meeting the ethical norms we know as honesty, dependability, and compassion. Ethical norms are the standards of conduct we most want to see observed by our children and our neighbors.

The legal environment of business has received ethical guidance from many norms. Certain norms, however, play a particularly large role in legal reasoning.

A judge's claiming or implying allegiance to a particular ethical norm focuses our attention on a specific category of desired conduct. We have or think we have an understanding of what is meant by freedom and other ethical norms.

But do we? Ethical norms are, without exception, complex and subject to multiple interpretations. Consequently, to identify the importance of one of the ethical norms in a piece of legal reasoning, we must look at the context to figure out *which form* of the ethical norm is being used. The types of conduct called for by the term *freedom* not only differ depending on the form of freedom being assumed, but at times they can contradict each other.

As a future business manager, your task is to be aware that there are alternative forms of each ethical norm. Then a natural next step is to search for the form used by the legal reasoning so you can understand and later evaluate that reasoning.

The following alternative forms of the four primary ethical norms can aid you in that search.

ETHICAL NORM	FORMS
1. Freedom	To act without restriction from rules imposed by others.
	To possess the capacity or resources to act as one wishes.
2. Security	To possess a large enough supply of goods and services that basic needs are met.
	To be safe from those wishing to interfere with your property rights.
	To achieve the psychological condition of self-confidence such that risks are welcomed.
3. Justice	To receive the product of your labor.
	To treat all humans identically, regardless of class, race, gender, age, and so on.
	To provide resources in proportion to need.
	To possess anything that someone else was willing to grant you.
4. Efficiency	To maximize the amount of wealth in our society.
	To get the most from a particular input.
	To minimize costs.

Consequently, we highlight what we will refer to as the four **primary ethical norms**: freedom, security, justice, and efficiency. (See Exhibit 1–2 for clarification of these norms.) The interplay among these four provides the major ethical direction for the laws governing business behavior. As you examine the cases in this text, you may identify other ethical norms that influence judicial opinions.

As critical thinkers we will want to always search for the relevant ethical norms. To do so requires us to infer their identity from the court's reasoning. Courts often do not announce their preferred pattern of ethical norms, but the norms are there anyway, having their way with the legal reasoning. As critical thinkers, we want to use the ethical norms, once we find them, as a basis for evaluating the reasoning.

Another element used in arriving at legal conclusions is the device of reasoning by analogy. Part of the critical thinking process in the evaluation of a legal conclusion is another question: How appropriate are the legal analogies?

primary ethical norms The four norms that provide the major ethical direction for the laws governing business behavior: freedom, security, justice, and efficiency.

STEP 7: How Appropriate Are the Legal Analogies?

A major difference between legal reasoning and other forms of analysis is the heavy reliance on analogies. Our legal system places great emphasis on the law as it has evolved in previous decisions. This evolutionary process is our heritage, the collective judgments of our historical mothers and fathers. We give them and their intellects our respect by using legal precedents as the major support structure for judicial decisions. By doing so, we do not have to approach each fact pattern with new eyes; instead, we are guided by similar experiences that our predecessors have already studied.

14

Part One

*An Introduction to the Law
and the Legal Environment
of Business*

analogy A comparison based on the assumption that if two things are alike in some respect, they must be alike in other respects.

The use of precedent to reach legal conclusions is so common that legal reasoning can be characterized as little but analogical reasoning. An **analogy** is a verbal device for transferring meaning from something we understand quite well to something we have just discovered and have, as yet, not understood satisfactorily. What we already understand in the case of legal reasoning is the precedent; what we hope to understand better is the current legal dispute. We call on the precedent for enlightenment.

To visualize the choice of legal analogy, imagine that we are trying to decide whether a waitress or waiter can be required to smile for hours as a condition of employment. (What is artificial about such an illustration, as we hope you already recognize, is the absence of a more complete factual picture to provide context.) The employer in question asks the legal staff to find appropriate legal precedents. They discover the following list of prior decisions:

1. Professional cheerleaders can be required to smile within reason, if that activity is clearly specified at the time of employment.
2. Employees who interact regularly with customers can be required as a condition of employment to wear clothing consistent with practice in the trade.
3. Employers may not require employees to lift boxes over 120 pounds without the aid of a mechanical device under the guidelines of the Employee Health Act.

Notice that each precedent has similarities to, but each has major differences from, the situation of the waiter or waitress. To mention only a few:

- Is a smile more natural to what we can expect from a cheerleader than from a waiter or waitress?
- Were the restaurant employees told in advance that smiling is an integral part of the job?
- Is a smile more personal than clothing? Are smiles private, as opposed to clothing, which is more external to who we are?
- Is a plastered-on smile, held in place for hours, a serious risk to mental health?
- Is a potential risk from smiling as real a danger as the one resulting from physically hoisting huge objects?

The actual selection of precedent, and consequently the search for appropriate analogies, is channeled by the theory of logic we find most revealing *in this case*. For example, if you see the requirement to smile as an invasion of privacy, you will likely see the second precedent as especially appropriate. Both the precedent and the case in question have employment situations with close customer contact.

However, the differences could be significant enough to reject that analogy. Do you see your clothing as part of your essence in the same fashion as you surely see the facial form you decide to show us at any given moment? Furthermore, the second precedent contains the phrase "consistent with practice in the trade." Would not a simple field trip to restaurants demonstrate that a broad smile is a pleasant exception?

As you practice looking for similarities and differences in legal precedents and the legal problem you are studying, you will experience some of the fun and frustration of legal reasoning within a business context. The excitement comes when you stumble upon just the perfect, matching fact pattern; then, after taking a closer look, you are brought back to earth by those annoying analogical differences that your experience warns you are always present.

Ambiguity, ethical norms, and legal analogies are all areas in which legal arguments may be deficient. But even if you are satisfied that all those considerations meet your standards, there is a final question that must not be overlooked in your critical analysis of a conclusion: Is there relevant missing information?

When we ask about the facts of a case, we mean the information presented in the legal proceedings. However, we are all quite aware that the stated facts are just a subset of the complete factual picture responsible for the dispute. How could any of us expect to ever have all the facts about a situation? We know we could use more facts than we have, but at some point we have to stop gathering information and settle the dispute.

You might not be convinced that the facts we know about a situation are inevitably incomplete. But consider how we acquire facts. If we gather them ourselves, we know the limits on our own experience and perceptions. We often see what we want to see, and we consequently select certain facts to file in our consciousness. Other facts may be highly relevant, but we ignore them. We can neither see nor process all the facts.

Our other major source of information is other people. We implicitly trust their intentions, abilities, and perspective when we take the facts they give us and make them our own. But no one gives us a complete version of the facts. For several reasons, we can be sure that the facts shared with us are only partial.

Armed with your awareness of the incompleteness of facts, what can you do as a future businessperson or employee to effectively resolve disagreements and apply legal precedents?

You can seek a more complete portrayal of the facts. Keep asking for detail and context to aid your thinking. For example, once you learn that a statute requires a firm to use the standard of conduct in the industry, you should not be satisfied with the following fact:

> *On 14 occasions, our firm attempted to contact other firms to determine the industry standards. We have bent over backwards to comply with the ethical norms of our direct competitors.*

Instead, you will persist in asking probing questions designed to generate a more revealing pattern of facts. Among the missing information you might ask for would be the extent and content of actual conversations about industry standards, as well as some convincing evidence that "direct" competitors are an adequate voice, representing "the industry."

APPLYING THE CRITICAL THINKING APPROACH

Now that you have an understanding of the critical thinking approach, you are ready to begin your study of the legal environment of business. Remember to apply each of the questions to the cases as you read them.

After you become proficient at asking these questions of every case you read, you may find that you start asking these evaluative questions in other contexts. For example, you might find that, when you read an editorial in the *Wall Street Journal*, you start asking whether the writer has used ambiguous terms that affect the quality of the reasoning or you start noticing when important relevant information is missing. Once you reach this point, you are well on your way to becoming a critical thinker whose thinking skills will be extremely helpful for functioning in the legal environment of business.

- -

 On the Internet

http://www2.andrews.edu/~mattingl/courses/phys253/think.html   This page lists the distinguishing features of a critical thinker.

http://www.sonoma.edu/CThink/University/univlibrary/Pseudo/outline.nclk   Sponsored by the Center for Critical Thinking at Sonoma State University, this site contains extensive information about critical thinking, including articles and a glossary.

http://www.bucks.edu/library/resources/criteval.htm   Here is a site that illustrates how to apply critical thinking skills to Web resources.

- -

2

INTRODUCTION TO LAW AND THE LEGAL
ENVIRONMENT OF BUSINESS

- **DEFINITION OF THE LEGAL ENVIRONMENT OF BUSINESS**

- **DEFINITION OF LAW AND JURISPRUDENCE**

- **SOURCES OF LAW**

- **CLASSIFICATIONS OF LAW**

- **INTERNATIONAL DIMENSIONS OF THE LEGAL ENVIRONMENT**

  OF BUSINESS

This book is about the legal environment in which the business community operates today. Although we concentrate on law and the legal variables that help shape business decisions, we have not overlooked the ethical questions that often arise in business decision making. In this chapter, we are especially concerned with legal variables in the context of critical thinking, as outlined in chapter 1. In addition, we examine the international dimensions of several areas of law. In an age of sophisticated telecommunication systems and computers, it would be naive for readers to believe that, as citizens of a prosperous, powerful nation situated between two oceans, they can afford to ignore the rest of the world. Just as foreign multinational companies must interact with U.S. companies and government agencies, so must U.S. entities interact with them.

The United States, Canada, and Mexico created the North American Free Trade Agreement (NAFTA) to lower trade barriers among themselves. In the Asian-Pacific Economic Cooperation (APEC) forum, the United States and 17 Pacific Rim nations are discussing easing barriers to trade and investments among themselves and creating a Pacific free trade zone extending from Chile to China.[1] The General Agreement on Trade and Tariffs and Trade/World Trade Organization continues to lower trade barriers among the 124 nations that have joined it. No nation is an island today, and economic globalization is sure to continue—even accelerate—as we move into the twenty-first century. (See chapter 3 for discussion of the international legal environment of business.)

Critical Thinking about the Law

THIS CHAPTER SERVES AS AN INTRODUCTION to the legal and ethical components in the environment of business. You will learn about different schools of jurisprudence and about sources and classifications of law. In addition, this chapter offers the opportunity to practice the critical thinking skills you just learned in chapter 1. The following critical thinking questions will help you better understand the introductory topics discussed in this chapter.

1. Why should we be concerned with the ethical components of the legal environment of business? Why shouldn't we just learn the relevant laws regarding businesses?

   CLUE Which critical thinking questions address the ethical components of the legal environment of business?

2. As you will soon discover, judges and lawyers often subscribe to a particular school of legal thought. However, judges and lawyers will probably not explicitly tell us which school of thought they prefer. Why do you think this knowledge might be beneficial when critically evaluating a judge's reasoning?

   CLUE Think about why we look for missing information. Furthermore, why do we want to identify the ethical norms fundamental to a court's reasoning?

3. You tell your landlord that your front door look is broken, but he doesn't repair the lock. A week later, you are robbed. You decide to sue the landlord, and you begin to search for an attorney. As a legal studies student, you ask the potential lawyers what school of jurisprudence they prefer. Although you find a lawyer who prefers the same school of jurisprudence you prefer, your decision is not complete. What else might you want to ask the lawyer?

   CLUE Think about the other factors that might affect a lawyer's performance.

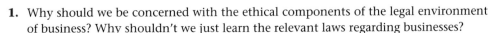

---

[1]*See* N.Y. Times, November 11, 1994, at A6.

18

Part One

An Introduction to the Law
and the Legal Environment
of Business

DEFINITION OF THE LEGAL ENVIRONMENT OF BUSINESS

Scholars define the "legal environment of business" in various ways, according to the purposes of their studies. For our purposes, the study of the legal environment of business shall include:

- The study of legal reasoning, critical thinking skills, ethical norms, and schools of ethical thought that interact with the law.
- The study of the legal process and our present legal system, as well as alternative dispute resolution systems, such as private courts, mediation, arbitration, and negotiations.
- The study of the administrative law process and the role of businesspeople in that process.
- The study of selected areas of public and private law, such as securities regulation, antitrust, labor, product liability, contracts, and consumer and environmental law. In each of these areas, we emphasize the processes by which business managers relate to individuals and government regulators.
- The examination of the international dimensions of the legal environment of law.

Our study of the legal environment of business is characterized by five features:

1. *It develops critical thinking skills.*
2. *It helps to establish legal literacy.* A survey by the Hearst Corporation found that 50 percent of Americans believe that it is up to the criminally accused to prove their innocence, despite our common law heritage that a person is presumed innocent until proven guilty. Only 41 percent were able to identify the then chief justice (Warren Burger) and the first woman Supreme Court justice (Sandra Day O'Connor). Of those responding to the survey, 49.9 percent had served on a jury, and 31 percent were college graduates.
3. *It develops an understanding that the law is dynamic not static.* The chapters on discrimination law, securities regulation, antitrust law, and labor law, especially, have had to be constantly updated during the writing of this book because federal regulatory agencies issue new regulations, rules, and guidelines almost daily.
4. *It deals with real-world problems.* You will be confronted with real, not theoretical, legal and ethical problems. As the great American jurist Oliver Wendell Holmes once pointed out, the law is grounded in "experience." In reading the cases excerpted in this book, you will see how business leaders and others either were ignorant of the legal and ethical variables they faced or failed to consider them in making important decisions.

EXHIBIT 2-1 *Top Ten Reasons for Studying the Legal Environment of Business*

1. Becoming aware of the rules of doing business.
2. Familiarizing yourself with the legal limits on business freedom.
3. Forming an alertness to potential misconduct of competitors.
4. Appreciating the limits of entrepreneurship.
5. Being able to communicate with your lawyer.
6. Making you a more fully informed citizen.
7. Developing an employment-related skill.
8. Exploring the fascinating complexity of business decisions.
9. Providing a heightened awareness of business ethics.
10. Opening your eyes to the excitement of the law and business.

5. *It is interdisciplinary.* We interweave into our discussions of the legal environment of business materials from other disciplines that you either are studying now or have studied in the past, especially economics, management, finance, marketing, and ethics. You may be surprised to learn how often officers of the court (judges and attorneys) are obliged to consider material from several disciplines in making decisions. Your own knowledge of these other disciplines will be extremely helpful to understanding the court decisions set out in this book.

As you will learn throughout the semester, there are a number of benefits to be gained by studying the legal environment of business. Exhibit 2-1 highlights the top ten reasons for studying the legal environment of business.

DEFINITION OF LAW AND JURISPRUDENCE

Jurisprudence is the science or philosophy of law, or law in its most generalized form. Law has been defined in different ways by scholarly thinkers. Some idea of the range of definitions can be gained from the following quote from a distinguished legal philosopher:

> *We have been told by Plato that law is a form of social control; by Aristotle that it is a rule of conduct, a contract, an ideal of reason; by Cicero that it is the agreement of reason and nature, the distinction between the just and the unjust; by Aquinas that it is an ordinance of reason for the common good; by Bacon that certainty is the prime necessity of law; by Hobbes that law is the command of the sovereign; by Hegel that it is an unfolding or realizing of the idea of right.[2]*

jurisprudence The science or philosophy of law; law in its most generalized form.

The various ideas of law expressed in that passage represent different schools of jurisprudence. To give you some sense of the diversity of meaning the term *law* has, we will examine seven accepted schools of legal thought: (1) natural law, (2) positivist, (3) sociological, (4) American realist, (5) critical legal theory, (6) feminist, and (7) law and economics. Table 2-1 summarizes the outstanding characteristics of each of these schools of jurisprudence.

NATURAL LAW SCHOOL

For adherents of the natural law school, which has existed since 300 B.C., law consists of the following concepts: (1) There exist certain legal values or value judgments (e.g., a presumption of innocence until guilt is proved); (2) these values or value judgments are unchanging because their source is absolute (e.g., Nature, God, or Reason); (3) these values or value judgments can be determined

TABLE 2-1   *Schools of Jurisprudence*

SCHOOL	SOME CHARACTERISTICS
Natural Law School	Source of law is absolute (Nature, God, or Reason).
Positivist School	Source of law is the sovereign.
Sociological School	Source of law is contemporary community opinion and customs.
American Realist School	Source of law is actors in the legal system and scientific analysis of their actions.
Critical Legal Theory School	Source of law is a cluster of legal and nonlegal beliefs that must be critiqued to bring about social and political change.
Feminist School	Jurisprudence reflects a male-dominated executive, legislative, and judicial system in which women's perspectives are ignored and women are victimized.
Law and Economics School	Applies classical economic theory and empirical methods to all areas of law in order to arrive at decisions.

[2]*See* H. Cairns, *Legal Philosophy from Plato to Hegel* (Baltimore: Johns Hopkins University Press, 1949).

20

Part One

*An Introduction to the Law
and the Legal Environment
of Business*

by human reason; and (4) once determined, they supersede any form of human law. Perhaps the most memorable statement of the natural law school of thought in this century was made by Martin Luther King Jr. in his famous letter from a Birmingham, Alabama, city jail. Here is how he explained to a group of ministers why he had violated human laws that discriminated against his people:

> *There are just laws and there are unjust laws. I would be the first to advocate obeying just laws. One has not only a legal but moral responsibility to obey just laws. Conversely, one has a moral responsibility to disobey unjust laws. I would agree with Saint Augustine that "An unjust law is no law at all."*
>
> *Now what is the difference between the two? How does one determine when a law is just or unjust? A just law is a man-made code that squares with the moral law or the law of God. An unjust law is a code that is out of harmony with the moral law. To put it in the terms of Saint Thomas Aquinas, an unjust law is a human law that is not rooted in eternal and natural law. Any law that uplifts human personality is just. Any law that degrades human personality is unjust. All segregation statutes are unjust because segregation distorts the soul and damages the personality. . . .*
>
> *Let us turn to a more concrete example of just and unjust law. An unjust law is a code that a majority inflicts on a minority that is not binding on itself. This is difference made legal. On the other hand, a just law is a code that a majority compels a minority to follow that it is willing to follow itself. This is sameness made legal.*
>
> *Let me give another explanation. An unjust law is a code inflicted upon a minority which that minority had no part in enacting or creating because they did not have the unhampered right to vote.[3]*

Adherents of other schools of legal thought view King's general definition of law as overly subjective. For example, they ask, "Who is to determine whether a man-made law is unjust because it is 'out of harmony with the moral law'?" Or: "Whose moral precepts or values are to be included in the 'moral law'?" The United States is a country of differing cultures, races, ethnic groups, and religions, each of which may reflect unique moral values.

POSITIVIST SCHOOL

Early in the 1800s, followers of positivism developed a school of thought in opposition to the natural law school. Its chief tenets are: (1) Law is the expression of the will of the legislator or sovereign, which must be followed; (2) morals are separate from law and should not be considered in making legal decisions (thus judges should not take into consideration extralegal factors such as contemporary community values in determining what constitutes a violation of law); and (3) law is a "closed logical system" in which correct legal decisions are reached solely by logic and the use of precedents (previous cases decided by the courts).

Disciples of the positivist school would argue that when the Congress of the United States has not acted on a matter, the United States Supreme Court has no power to act on that matter. They would argue, for example, that morality has no part in determining whether discrimination exists when a business pays workers differently on the basis of their sex, race, religion, or ethnic origin. Only civil rights legislation passed by Congress, and previous cases interpreting that legislation, should be considered.

Positivism has been criticized by adherents of other schools of thought as too narrow and literal-minded. Critics argue that the refusal to consider social, ethical, and other factors makes for a static jurisprudence that ill serves society.

---

[3]*See* M.L. King "Letters from a Birmingham Jail" (April 16, 1963) *reprinted in* M. McGuaigan, *Jurisprudence* (New York: Free Press, 1979), p. 63.

SOCIOLOGICAL SCHOOL

Followers of the sociological school propose three steps in determining law: (1) A legislator or a judge should make an inventory of community interests; (2) judges and legislators should use this inventory to familiarize themselves with the community's standards and mores; and (3) they should rule or legislate in conformity with those standards and mores. For those associated with this school of legal thought, human behavior or contemporary community values are the most important factors in determining the direction the law should take. This philosophy is in sharp contrast to that of the positivist school, which relies on case precedents and statutory law. Adherents of the sociological school seek to change the law by surveying human behavior and determining present community standards. For example, after a famous U.S. Supreme Court decision stating that material could be judged "obscene" on the basis of "contemporary community standards,"[4] one mayor of a large city immediately went out and polled his community on what books and movies they thought were obscene. (He failed to get a consensus.)

Critics of the sociological school argue that this school would make the law too unpredictable for both individuals and businesses. They note that contemporary community standards change over time, and, thus, the law itself would be changing all the time and the effects could harm the community. For example, if a state or local legislature offered a corporation certain tax breaks as an incentive to move to a community, and then revoked those tax breaks a few years later because community opinion on such matters had changed, other corporations would be reluctant to locate in that community.

AMERICAN REALIST SCHOOL

The American realist school, though close to the sociological school in its emphasis on people, focuses on the actors in the judicial system instead of on the larger community to determine the meaning of law. This school sees law as a part of society and a means of enforcing political and social values. In a book entitled *The Bramble Bush*, Karl Llewellyn wrote: "This doing of something about disputes, this doing it reasonably, is the business of the law. And the people who have the doing of it are in charge, whether they be judges, or clerks, or jailers, or lawyers, they are officials of the law. What these officials do about disputes is, to my mind, the law itself."[5] For Llewellyn and other American realists, anyone who wants to know about law should study the judicial process and the actors in that process. This means regular attendance at courthouses and jails, as well as scientific study of the problems associated with the legal process (e.g., plea bargaining in the courtroom).

Positivists argue that if the American realist definition of law were accepted, there would be a dangerous unpredictability to the law.

CRITICAL LEGAL STUDIES SCHOOL

A contemporary extension of American legal realism, critical legal studies seeks to connect what happens in the legal system to the political-economic context within which it operates. Adherents of critical legal jurisprudence believe that law reflects a cluster of beliefs that convinces human beings that the hierarchal relations that they live and work under are natural and must be accommodated. According to this school, this cluster of beliefs has been constructed by elitists to rationalize their dominant power. Using economics, mass communications, religion, and, most of all, law, society's elite have constructed an interlocking system of beliefs that reinforces established wealth and privilege. Only by critiquing these belief structures, critical legal theorists believe, will people be able to break out of a hierarchical system and bring about democratic social and political change.

---

[4]Roth v. United States, 354 U.S. 476, 479 (1957).
[5]K. Llewellyn, *The Bramble Bush* (Dobbs Ferry, N.Y.: Oceana Publications, 1950), p. 12.

Traditional critics argue that the critical legal theorists have not developed concrete strategies to bring about the social and political changes they desire but have constructed an essentially negative position.

FEMINIST SCHOOL

There is a range of views as to what constitutes feminist jurisprudence. Most adherents of this school, believing that significant rights have been denied to women, advocate lobbying legislatures and litigating in courts for changes in laws to accommodate women's views. They argue that our traditional common law reflects a male emphasis on individual rights, which at times is at odds with women's views that the law should be more reflective of a "culture of caring." To other adherents of this school of jurisprudence, the law is a means of male oppression. For example, some feminists have argued that the First Amendment forbidding Congress from making any laws abridging the freedom of speech was authored by men and is presently interpreted by male-dominated U.S. courts to allow pornographers to make large profits by exploiting and degrading women.

Traditional critics of feminist jurisprudence argue that it is too narrow in scope and that it fails to account for changes taking place in U.S. society such as the increasing number of women students in professional and graduate schools and their movement into higher-ranking positions in both the public and private sectors.

LAW AND ECONOMICS SCHOOL

The law and economics school of jurisprudence started to evolve in the 1950s, but it has been applied with some rigor for the last 20 years. It advocates using classical economic theory and empirical methods of economics to explain and predict judges' decisions in such areas as torts, contracts, property, criminal administrative law, and law enforcement. The proponents of the law and economics school argue that most court decisions, and the legal doctrines they depend on, are best understood as efforts to promote an efficient allocation of resources in society.

Critics of the school of law and economics argue that there are many schools of economic thought, and thus no single body of principles governs economics. For example, neo-Keynesians and classical market theorists have very different views of the proper role of the state in the allocation of resources. A related criticism is that this school takes a politically conservative approach to the legal solution of economic or political problems. Liberals and others argue that it is a captive of conservative thinkers.

SOURCES OF LAW

The founders of this country created in the United States Constitution three direct sources of law and one indirect source. The legislative branch (Article I) is the maker or creator of laws; the executive branch (Article II), the enforcer of laws; and the judicial branch (Article III), the interpreter of laws. Each branch represents a separate source of law while performing its functions (Table 2-2). The fourth (indirect) source of law is administrative agencies, which will be briefly discussed in this chapter and examined in detail in chapter 16.

THE LEGISLATURE AS A SOURCE OF STATUTORY LAW

Article I, Section 1, of the U.S. Constitution states, "All legislative Powers herein granted shall be vested in a Congress of the United States which shall consist of a House and Senate." It is important to understand the process by which a law (called a *statute*) is made by the Congress because this process and its results have an impact on such diverse groups as consumers, businesspeople, taxpayers, and unions. It should be emphasized that at every stage of the process, each of the groups potentially affected seeks to influence the proposed piece of legislation through lobbying. The federal legislative process described here (Exhibit 2-2) is

TABLE 2-2 *Where to Find the Law*

LEVEL OF GOVERNMENT	LEGISLATIVE LAW	EXECUTIVE ORDERS	COMMON LAW/ JUDICIAL INTERPRETATIONS	ADMINISTRATIVE REGULATIONS
Federal	• United States Code (U.S.C.) • United States Code Annotated (U.S.C.A.) • United States Statutes at Large (Stat.)	• Title 3 of the Code of Federal Regulations • Codification of Presidential Proclamations and Executive Orders	• United States Reports (U.S.) • Supreme Court Reporter (S. Ct.) • Federal Reporter (F., F.2d) • Federal Supplement (F. Supp.) • Federal agency reports (titled by agency; e.g., F.C.C. Reports) • Regional reporters • State reporters	• Code of Federal Regulations (C.F.R.) • Federal Register (Fed. Reg.)
State	• State code or state statutes (e.g., Ohio Revised Code Annotated, Baldwin's)		• Regional reporters • State reporters	• State administrative code or state administrative regulations
Local	• Municipal ordinances		• Varies; often difficult to find. Many municipalities do not publish case decisions but do preserve them on microfilm. Interested parties usually must contact the clerk's office at the local courthouse.	• Municipality administrative regulations

similar in most respects to the processes used by state legislatures, though state constitutions may prescribe some differences.

STEPS IN THE LEGISLATIVE PROCESS

Step 1. A *bill* is introduced into the U.S. House of Representatives or Senate by a single member or by several members. It is generally referred to the committee of the House or Senate that has jurisdiction over the subject matter of the bill. (In most cases, a bill is simultaneously introduced into the Senate and House. Within each body, committees may vie with each other for jurisdictional priority.)

Let's briefly follow through the House of Representatives a bill proposing to deregulate the trucking industry by doing away with the rate-making power of the Interstate Commerce Commission (ICC). This bill would be referred to the House Committee on Energy and Commerce, which, in turn, would refer it to the appropriate subcommittee.

Step 2. The House subcommittee holds hearings on the bill, listening to testimony from all concerned parties and establishing a hearing record.

Step 3. After hearings, the bill is "marked up" (drafted in precise form) and then referred to the subcommittee for a vote.

Step 4. If the vote is affirmative, the subcommittee forwards the bill to the full House Energy and Commerce Committee, which either accepts the subcommittee's recommendation, puts a hold on the bill, or rejects it. If the House committee votes to accept the bill, it reports it to the full House of Representatives for a vote by all members.

Step 5. If the bill is passed by the House of Representatives and a similar bill is passed by the Senate, the bills go to a Senate-House Conference Committee to reconcile any differences in content. After compromise and reconciliation of the two bills, a single bill is reported to the full House and Senate for a vote.

Step 6. If there is a final affirmative vote by both houses of Congress, the bill is forwarded to the president, who may sign it into law or veto it. When the president signs the bill into law, it becomes known as a *statute*, meaning it is

24

Part One

*An Introduction to the Law
and the Legal Environment
of Business*

EXHIBIT 2-2 *How a Bill becomes a Law*

This graphic shows the typical way in which proposed legislation is enacted into law. There are more complicated, as well as simpler, routes, and most bills fall by the way-side and never become law. The process is illustrated with two hypothetical separate bills: House bill No. 1 (HR 1) and Senate bill No. 2 (S 2). In practice, most legislation begins as similar proposals in both houses.) Each bill must be passed by both houses of Congress in identical form before it can become law. The path of HR 1 is traced by a blue line, that of S 2 by a red line.

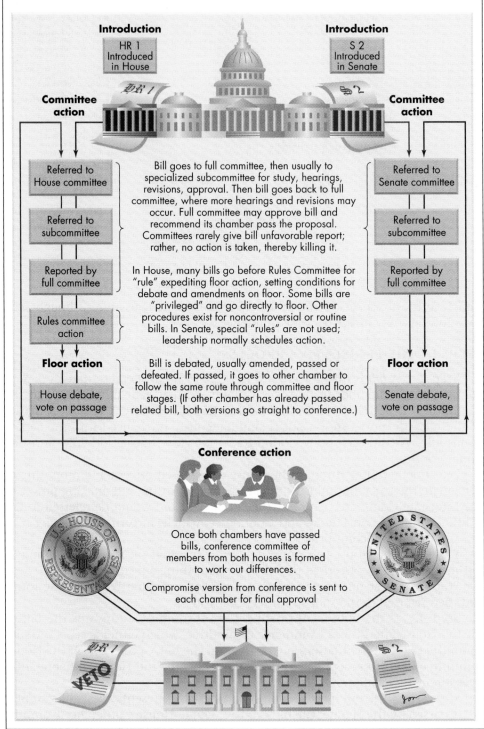

Reprinted with the permission of Congressional Quarterly, Inc.

written down and codified in the *United States Code Annotated*. In the event of a presidential veto, a two-thirds vote of the Senate and House membership is required to override the veto. If the president takes no action within ten days of receiving the bill from Congress, it automatically becomes law without the president's signature.

The single exception to this procedure occurs when Congress adjourns before the ten-day period has elapsed: In that case, the bill would not become law. It is said to have been "pocket-vetoed" by the president: The president "stuck the bill in a pocket" and vetoed it by doing nothing. With either type of veto, the bill is dead and can be revived only by being reintroduced in the next session of Congress, in which case the procedure begins all over again.

THE JUDICIAL BRANCH AS A SOURCE OF CASE LAW

The federal courts and most state courts make up the judicial branch of government. They are charged by their respective constitutions with interpreting the *constitution* and *statutory law* on a case-by-case basis. Most *case* interpretations are reported in large volumes called *reporters*. These constitute a compilation of our federal and state *case law*.

When two parties disagree about the meaning of a statute, they bring their case to court for the court to interpret. For example, when the bill to deregulate the trucking industry and take away the rate-making function of the ICC (Interstate Commerce Commission) was signed by the president and became law, two parties could have disagreed about its meaning and asked the federal courts to interpret it. If the law had been challenged, the court would have first looked at the law's legislative history in order to determine the *intent* of the legislature. This history was found in the hearings held by the subcommittees and committees previously referred to, as well as any debates on the Senate and House floors. Hearings are published in the *U.S. Congressional News and Administrative Reports*, which may be ordered from the Government Printing Office or found in most university libraries in the government documents section. Debates on a bill are published in the daily *Congressional Record*, which may also be found in most university libraries.

The U.S. Supreme Court and most state supreme courts have the power of judicial review—that is, the power to determine whether a statute is constitutional. Although this power was not expressly provided for in the U.S. Constitution, the Supreme Court established it for the judiciary in the landmark case *Marbury v. Madison*[6] (see chapter 5 for a discussion of this case). As was seen in the case of *United States v. Nixon*,[7] the right of judicial review gives the U.S. Supreme Court the ultimate power to check the excesses of either the legislative or the executive branch.

Further, these decisions establish *case law precedents*, which are followed by all federal and state courts. Thus, through its case-by-case interpretation of the Constitution and statutes, the U.S. Supreme Court establishes a line of authoritative cases on a particular subject that have to be followed by the lower courts, both federal and state. Similarly, state supreme courts establish precedents that must be followed by lower courts in their particular state systems.

THE EXECUTIVE BRANCH AS A SOURCE OF LAW

The executive branch is composed of the president, the president's staff, and the cabinet, which is made up of the heads of each of the executive departments (e.g., the Secretary of State, the Secretary of Labor, the Secretary of Defense, and the Secretary of the Treasury) and the counselor to the president. The Executive Office is composed of various offices, such as the Office of Management and Budget (OMB) and the Office of Personnel Management (OPM). The executive branch is a source of law in two ways.

---

[6]5 U.S. (1 Branch) 137 (1803).
[7]418 U.S. 683 (1974).

26

Part One

*An Introduction to the Law
and the Legal Environment
of Business*

TREATY MAKING   The president has the power, subject to the advice and consent of the Senate, to make treaties. These treaties become the law of the land, on the basis of the Supremacy Clause of the United States Constitution (Article VI), and supersede any state law. When President Carter entered into a treaty returning the Panama Canal Zone to the nation of Panama under certain conditions, it became the law of the land, and the treaty provisions superseded any federal or state laws inconsistent with the treaty.

EXECUTIVE ORDERS   Throughout history, the president has made laws by issuing executive orders. For example, as we shall see in chapter 16, President Reagan, by virtue of an executive order, ruled that all executive federal agencies must do a cost-benefit analysis before setting forth a proposed regulation for comment by interested parties. President Truman, by executive order, directed the secretary of commerce to seize all the nation's steel mills to prevent a strike in this essential industry during the Korean War. President Johnson issued Executive Order No. 11246 requiring government contractors to set out an affirmative action plan for hiring and promoting minorities and women. (This executive order is discussed in chapter 19.)

The executive order as a source of law is also used by state governors to deal with emergencies and with budget functions. Often a governor will call out the national guard or, in some states, implement particular aspects of the budget by executive order. For example, a governor may order a freeze on the hiring of employees in the state university system or order an across-the-board cut in budgets in all state departments.

ADMINISTRATIVE AGENCIES AS A SOURCE OF LAW

Less well known as a source of law are the federal regulatory agencies, among which are the Securities and Exchange Commission (SEC), the Federal Trade Commission (FTC), the Equal Employment Opportunity Commission (EEOC), and the Occupational Safety and Health Administration (OSHA). As will be discussed in chapter 14, Congress has delegated to these agencies the authority to make rules governing the conduct of business and labor in certain areas. This authority was delegated because it was thought to be in the public interest, convenience, and necessity. Because each of the agencies must notify the public of proposed rule making and set out a cost-benefit analysis, all proposed and final rules can be found in the *Federal Register*. Administrative agencies constitute what many have called a "fourth branch of government." They exist at the state and local levels as well.

CLASSIFICATIONS OF LAW

statutory law Law made by the legislative branch of government.

Besides **statutory law** made by the legislative branch and **case law** resulting from judicial interpretation of constitutions and statutes, there are several other classifications of law that are necessary to know about in order to understand the legal environment of business.

case law Law resulting from judicial interpretations of constitutions and statutes.

CRIMINAL LAW AND CIVIL LAW

criminal law Composed of federal and state statutes prohibiting wrongful conduct ranging from murder to fraud.

Criminal law comprises those federal and state statutes that prohibit wrongful conduct such as arson, rape, murder, extortion, forgery, and fraud. The purpose of criminal law is to punish offenders by imprisonment or fines. The plaintiff in a criminal case is the United States, State X, County X, or City X, representing society and the victim against the defendant, who is most likely to be an individual but may also be a corporation, a partnership, or a single proprietorship. The plaintiff must prove *beyond a reasonable doubt* that the defendant committed a crime.

Crimes are generally divided into felonies and misdemeanors. In most states, *felonies* are serious crimes (e.g., rape, arson, and criminal fraud) that are punishable by incarceration in a state penitentiary. *Misdemeanors* are less serious crimes (e.g., driving while intoxicated) that are usually punishable by shorter periods of imprisonment in a county or city jail or by fines. An act that is a misdemeanor in one state could be a felony in another, and vice versa. White collar crime felonies and misdemeanors are discussed in chapter 7.

    Civil law comprises federal and state statutes governing litigation between two private parties. Neither the state nor the federal government is represented in most civil cases (exceptions will be pointed out in future chapters). Rather than prosecutors, there are plaintiffs, who are usually individuals or businesses suing other individuals or businesses (the defendants) to obtain compensation for an alleged breach of a private duty. For example, *A*, a retailer, enters into a contract with *B*, a manufacturer who agrees to supply *A* with all the bicycles of a certain brand that the retailer can sell. *A* advertises, and sales exceed all expectations. *B* refuses to ship any more bicycles, and *A*'s customers sue him for reneging on the raincheck he gave them. In turn, *A* sues *B* for breach of contract. *A* must show by a *preponderance of evidence* (a lower standard of proof than the "beyond a reasonable doubt" standard that prevails in criminal cases) that *B* is liable (legally obligated) to fulfill the contract. Note that *A* is not seeking to put *B* in prison or to fine *B*. *A* is seeking only to be compensated for his advertising costs, his lost sales, and what it may cost him in lawyers' fees, court costs, and damages to settle with his customers.

> **civil law** Law governing litigation between two private parties.

PUBLIC AND PRIVATE LAW

Public law deals with the relationship of government to individual citizens. Constitutional law, criminal law, and administrative law fit this classification. *Constitutional law* (discussed in chapter 4) comprises the basic principles and laws of the nation as set forth in the U.S. Constitution. It determines the powers and obligations of the government and guarantees certain rights to citizens. Examples of questions that fall under constitutional law are: Does an individual citizen have a Sixth Amendment right to counsel when stopped by a police officer, taken into custody, and interrogated? Is it cruel and unusual punishment under the Eighth Amendment to electrocute a person when that person has been found guilty of certain crimes, such as first-degree murder or killing a police officer in the line of duty? We have already touched upon criminal law (which is discussed more fully in chapter 7). *Administrative law* (examined in chapter 16) covers the process by which individuals or businesses can redress grievances against regulatory agencies such as the Federal Trade Commission (FTC) and the Securities and Exchange Commission (SEC). It prevents the agencies from acting in an arbitrary or capricious manner and from extending their power beyond the scope that Congress has given them. For example, when the Federal Communications Commission (FCC) ruled that cable television corporations had to set aside so many channels for access by *any* public group that requested time, the court reversed this FCC rule, deciding that it was beyond the agency's authority and in violation of a provision of the Federal Communications Act. Administrative law also covers the process whereby government agencies represent individuals or classes of individuals against business entities—for example, when the Equal Employment Opportunity Commission (EEOC) represents individuals alleging discrimination in pay under the provisions of the Civil Rights Act of 1964.

> **public law** Law dealing with the relationship of government to individual citizens.

    Private law is generally concerned with the enforcement of private duties between individuals, between an individual and a business, and between two businesses. Contracts, torts, and property law fall under this classification. Note that the government is not a concerned party in most private law cases.

> **private law** Law dealing with the enforcement of private duties.

INTERNATIONAL DIMENSIONS OF THE LEGAL ENVIRONMENT OF BUSINESS

At the beginning of this chapter, we stated that managers need to be aware of the impact of international variables on their business. As of the mid-1990s, approximately 30 percent of all jobs in the United States are dependent on ex-

28

Part One

*An Introduction to the Law
and the Legal Environment
of Business*

ports, and, in the view of many experts, that percentage will rise to 50 percent early in the next century. Trade treaties will make the international dimensions of the legal environment of business increasingly important to U.S. firms. Throughout this book, therefore, we discuss the international dimensions of product liability, tort, contracts, labor, securities and antitrust law, as well as ethics whenever appropriate. For example, current U.S. securities laws include the Foreign Corrupt Practices Act of 1977 (FCPA), as amended in 1988. If the laws of Country X do not forbid bribery in order to obtain a $10 million contract to build an oil pipeline, should U.S. companies be constrained by the FCPA prohibitions against such bribery? Ethical and cultural relativists would say no; "When in Rome do as the Romans do." Normative ethical theorists, such as rule utilitarians, would say yes, arguing that rules agreed upon by the world community, or a preponderance of it, cannot be compromised by a particular situation. They would point out that both the United Nations' Multinational Code and the laws of most of the UN's member states prohibit bribery.

SUMMARY

The study of the legal environment of business includes the study of legal reasoning, critical thinking skills, and ethical norms; the legal and administrative law processes; selected areas of public and private law; and relevant international law. Jurisprudence is the science or philosophy of law, or law in its most generalized form. The major schools of jurisprudence are natural law, positivism, sociological, American realism, critical legal theory, feminism, and law and economics.

The three direct sources of law are the legislative (statutory), judicial (case law), and executive (executive orders) branches of government. Administrative agencies, which promulgate regulations and rules, constitute the fourth (indirect) source of law.

The international dimensions of law include legal, financial, economic, and ethical variables that have an impact on business decision making.

REVIEW QUESTIONS

2-1. Contrast the natural law school's definition of law with that of the positivist school.

2-2. Explain how the critical legal theory and the feminist school of jurisprudence are similar.

2-3. Describe how the executive branch of government is a source of law.

2-4. What is the difference between statutory law and case law? Explain.

2-5. If the president vetoes a bill passed by Congress, is there any way that the bill can become law? Explain.

2-6. Distinguish between the pairs of terms in each of these three classifications of law:

a. public law, private law

b. civil law, criminal law

c. felonies, misdemeanors

REVIEW PROBLEMS

2-7. Three men are trapped in a cave with no hope of rescue and no food. They roll dice to determine who will be killed and eaten by the others in order to survive. The two survivors are rescued ten days later and tried for murder. Judge A finds them guilty, saying that the unjustifiable killing of another is against the homicide laws of State X. He bases his decision solely on statutory law and case precedents interpreting the law. To which school of legal thought does Judge A belong? Explain.

2-8. Basing his decision on the same set of facts as given in Problem 2-7, Judge B rules that the survivors are not guilty because they were cut off from all civilized life and, in such a situation, the laws of nature apply, not man-made laws. To which school of legal thought does Judge B belong? Explain.

2-9. Basing her decision on the same set of facts as given in Problem 2-7, Judge C rules that the two survivors are not guilty because, according to a scientific survey of the community by a professional polling organization, the public believes that the survivors' actions were defensible. To which school of legal thought does Judge C belong? Explain.

2-10. Imagine that you were a judge in the case set forth in Problem 2-7. How would you decide the case? On the basis of your reasons for your decision, explain which legal philosophy you think you hold.

2-11. Madison and his adult son lived in a house owned by Madison. At the request of the son, Marshall painted the house. Madison did not authorize the work, but he knew that it was being done and raised no objection. Madison refused to pay Marshall, arguing that he had not contracted to have the house painted.

   Marshall asked his attorney if Madison was legally liable to pay him. The attorney told Marshall that in their state several appellate court opinions had established that when a homeowner allows work to be done on his home by a person who would ordinarily expect to be paid, a duty to pay exists. The attorney stated that, on the basis of these precedents, it was advisable for Marshall to bring a suit to collect the reasonable value of the work he had done. Explain what the attorney meant by *precedent* and why the fact that precedent existed was significant.

2-12. Smith was involved in litigation in California. She lost her case in the trial court. She appealed to the California appellate court, arguing that the trial court judge had incorrectly excluded certain evidence. To support her argument, she cited rulings by the Supreme Court of North Dakota and the Supreme Court of Ohio. Both the North Dakota and Ohio cases involved facts that were similar to those in Smith's case. Does the California court have to follow the decisions from North Dakota and Ohio? Support your answer.

CASE PROBLEMS

2-13. Howard was charged with violating the Federal Black Bass Act. The act made it unlawful to transport black bass if such transportation is contrary to the law of the state from which fish are transported. The Florida Fish and Game Commission had a rule prohibiting the transportation of black bass out of the state. The commission was authorized by the state constitution. Howard's attorney argued that the federal act did not apply because the commission's rule was not a "law of the state." Discuss the validity of this defense. What types of law, on the basis of the classifications set out in the chapter, are present in this problem? Explain. *United States v. Howard*, 352 U.S. 212 (1956)

2-14. Butler and others organized a corporation ostensibly to help small business firms secure loans. They were to be compensated by a finder's fee. The firms were solicited by mail. If a firm indicated an interest, it was visited by a salesperson. The entire scheme was a fraud. The corporation retained the membership fees and did nothing to secure loans.

   The corporation, Butler, and 29 others were prosecuted in a single action for mail fraud. Several of the defendants asked to have their cases severed and tried separately, arguing that combining this number of defendants in a single case was unfair. Discuss the validity of a government argument based on stare decisis and citing a number of cases in which

30

Part One

*An Introduction to the Law
and the Legal Environment
of Business*

larger numbers of defendants had been tried in a single case. Is the trial court bound by these cases? If so, which schools of jurisprudence discussed in this chapter apply to this problem. Explain. *Butler v. United States*, 317 F.2d 249 (1963)

2-15. When the Republican National Convention was taking place in 1984, Gregory Lee Johnson and other demonstrators marched through the Dallas streets, protesting the policies of the Reagan administration. During the march, Johnson unfurled an American flag, doused it with kerosene, and set it on fire. While the flag burned, the protestors chanted, "America, the red, white, and blue, we spit on you." Johnson was convicted under Texas law of the crime of desecrating a venerated object. He was sentenced to one year in prison and fined $2,000. Johnson appealed his conviction to the U.S. Supreme Court, claiming that the law violated his First Amendment right to free expression. Was this law he allegedly violated a public law or a private law? *Texas v. Johnson*, 109 S. Ct. 2535 (1990)

2-16. Section 301(a) of the Federal Food, Drug, and Cosmetics Act prohibits the introduction into interstate commerce of any drug that is misbranded. According to Section 502(a), a product is misbranded if its "labeling is false or misleading" and if the labeling does not bear "adequate directions for use." The term *labeling* is defined to mean "all labels and other written, printed, or graphic matter (1) upon any article or any of its containers or (2) accompanying such article." Violation of the act is a crime.

Kordel sells health-food products that are compounds of vitamins, minerals, and herbs. These items are sold to stores. In addition to supplying the product, Kordel separately furnishes pamphlets describing the products. Much of the literature is shipped separately from the products and at different times—both before and after shipments. Kordel is charged with violating the Food and Drug Act. On the basis of the above facts, outline a defense available to him. Explain how the prosecution might overcome this defense.

2-17. The federal Equal Employment Opportunity Commission (EEOC) brought suit against the Commonwealth of Massachusetts, challenging a statute mandating that state police must retire at 50 as a violation of the Age Discrimination Act. In an earlier suit brought by a state policeman named Mahoney, who held a desk job, the federal courts upheld the Massachusetts law on the grounds that being under 50 was a bona fide occupational requirement. The district court rejected the EEOC's challenge to the law on the basis of the ruling in Mahoney's case. The EEOC appealed, arguing that Mahoney's case should not be considered binding precedent for all members of the state police force. How did the EEOC appeal this case? Did it represent the agency or individuals or both? Who won? *EEOC v. Trabucco*, 791 F.2d 283 (1986)

2-18. Laurence Powell, Stacey Koon, and other Los Angeles police officers apprehended and arrested Rodney King after a high-speed chase. King was severely beaten during the arrest. The beating was videotaped by a nearby resident and was played prominently on TV. The police officers were charged with assault. They petitioned to have their criminal trial moved from the County of Los Angeles to another county in California, claiming that they could not receive a fair trial in Los Angeles. The trial court rejected their request, and they appealed to the California Court of Appeal, an intermediate appellate court.

The court issued an unsigned "by the court" opinion delivered jointly by all four judges who heard the case. Who won? Why was the criminal case sought to be moved? *Powell v. California*, 232 Cal. App. 3d 785 (1991)

On the Internet

http://www.lawlib.uh.edu/guides/a_encycl.html   Going to this site is the equivalent to looking at an encyclopedia of jurisprudence.

http://www.seanet.com/~rod/marbury.html   Learn about the jurisprudence of access to justice from this page.

http://lark.cc.ukans.edu/~akdclass/femlit/femjur.html   Here is a starting point for finding resources on the Web related to feminist jurisprudence.

http://www.lectlaw.com//def/j025   This site contains an alternative definition of jurisprudence.

3

THE INTERNATIONAL LEGAL ENVIRONMENT
OF BUSINESS

- **DIMENSIONS OF THE INTERNATIONAL ENVIRONMENT OF BUSINESS**

- **METHODS OF ENGAGING IN INTERNATIONAL BUSINESS**

- **RISKS OF ENGAGING IN INTERNATIONAL BUSINESS**

- **LEGAL AND ECONOMIC INTEGRATION AS A MEANS**

  OF ENCOURAGING INTERNATIONAL BUSINESS ACTIVITY

- **INTERNATIONAL DISPUTE RESOLUTION**

At the outset of chapter 2, we noted that U.S. managers can no longer afford to view their firms as doing business on a huge island between the Pacific and Atlantic oceans. Existing and pending multilateral trade agreements will open vast opportunities to do business in Europe and Asia, throughout the Americas, and indeed throughout the world. If present and future U.S. managers do not become aware of these opportunities, as well as the attendant risks, they and their firms will be at a competitive disadvantage vis-à-vis foreign competitors from all over the world.

This chapter (1) introduces the international environment of business; (2) sets forth the methods by which companies may engage in international business; (3) indicates the risks involved in such engagement; (4) describes organizations that work to bring down tariff barriers and thus encourage companies of all nations to engage in international business; and (5) indicates the means by which disputes between companies doing business in the international arena are settled. Please note carefully that when we use the word *companies* in an international context, we are referring not only to private-sector firms but also to nation-state subsidized entities and government agencies that act like private-sector companies.

Critical Thinking about the Law

BECAUSE OF THE WIDESPREAD INTERNATIONAL OPPORTUNITIES and advances in communication, business managers must be aware of the global legal environment of business. As you will soon learn, the political, economic, cultural, and legal dimensions are all important international business considerations. The following questions will help sharpen your critical thinking about the international legal environment of business.

1. Consider the number of countries that might participate in an international business agreement. Why might ambiguity be a particularly important concern in international business?

   CLUE Consider the variety of cultures as well as the differences in languages. How might these factors affect business agreements?

2. Why might the critical thinking questions about ethical norms and missing information be important for international businesses?

   CLUE Again, consider the variety of cultures involved in international business. Why might identifying the primary ethical norms of a culture be helpful?

3. What ethical norm might influence the willingness to enter into agreements with foreign companies?

   CLUE How might international agreements differ from agreements between two U.S. companies? (See chapter 1.)

DIMENSIONS OF THE INTERNATIONAL ENVIRONMENT OF BUSINESS

Doing international business has political, economic, cultural, and legal dimensions. Although this chapter emphasizes the legal dimensions of international business transactions, business managers need to be aware of those other important dimensions as well. (Ethical dimensions will be examined in chapter 8.)

POLITICAL DIMENSIONS

Managers of firms doing international business must deal with different types of governments, ranging from democracies to totalitarian states (Table 3-1). They are concerned with the stability of these governments and with whether

TABLE 3-1 *Categorization of Countries by Degree of Freedom,* 1992

FREE

1.0
Andorra
Australia
Austria
Barbados
Belgium
Belize
Canada
Cyprus
Denmark
Finland
Iceland
Kiribati
Liechtenstein
Luxembourg
Malta
Marshall Islands
Micronesia
Netherlands
New Zealand
Norway
Portugal
San Marino
Sweden
Switzerland
Tuvalu
United States

1.5
Bahamas
Cape Verde
Costa Verde
Costa Rica
Czech Republic
Dominica
France

Germany
Grenada
Hungary
Ireland
Italy
Mauritius
Monaco
Palau
St. Lucia
St. Vincent and the
    Grenadines
Sao Tome and Principe
Slovenia
Solomon Islands
Spain
Trinidad and Tobago
United Kingdom

2.0
Bulgaria
Chile
Greece
Guyana
Israel
Japan
Korea, South
Lithuania
Nauru
Poland
St. Kitts-Nevis
Uruguay
Vanuatu
Western Samoa

2.5
Argentina

Benin
Bolivia
Botswana
Ecuador
Estonia
Jamaica
Latvia
Malawi
Mongolia
Namibia
Panama
Slovakia
South Africa

Related Territories
1.0
Aland Islands (Finland)
American Samoa (U.S.)
Azores (Port.)
Bermuda (U.K.)
British Virgin Islands (U.K.)
Canary Islands (Spain)
Cayman Islands (U.K.)
Cocos (Keeling Islands) (Austral.)
Faeroe Islands (Den.)
Gilbraltar (U.K.)
Greenland (Den.)
Guam (U.S.)
Isle of Man (U.K.)
Madeira (Port.)
Montserrat (U.K.)
Pitcairn Islands (U.K.)
St. Pierre-Miquelon (France)
Turks and Caicos (U.K.)
U.S. Virgin Islands (U.S.)

1.5
Anguilla (U.K.)
Aruba (Neth.)
Ceuta (Spain)
Channel Islands (U.K.)
Cook Islands (N.Z.)
Falkland Islands (U.K.)
French Guiana (France)
French Polynesia (France)
Guadeloupe (France)
Martinique (France)
Mayotte (Mahore) (France)
Melilla (Spain)
Netherlands Antilles (Neth.)
Niue (N.Z.)
Norfolk Island (Austral.)
Northern Marianas (U.S.)
Puerto Rico (U.S.)
St. Helena and Dependencies
    (U.K.)

2.0
New Caledonia (France)
Rapanui (Easter Island)
    (Chile)
Reunion (France)
Svalbard (Norway)
Tokelau (N.Z.)
Wallis and Futuna Islands
    (France)

2.5
Christmas Island (Austral.)

PARTLY FREE

3.0
Bangladesh
Brazil
El Salvador
Honduras
Madagascar
Mali
Papua New Guinea
Suriname
Taiwan
Venezuela

3.5
Albania
Antigua and Barbuda
Armenia
Central African
    Republic
Colombia
Dominican Republic
Fiji
Guinea-Bissua
Kyrgystan
Macedonia

Nepal
Paraguay
Philippines
Romania
Russia
Seychelles
Ukraine
Zambia

4.0
Belarus
Comoros

Congo
Croatia
India
Jordan
Lesotho
Mexico
Moldova
Mozambique
Niger
Pakistan
Thailand
Tonga

TABLE 3-1 *(cont.)*

PARTLY FREE

4.5	5.0	5.5	4.0
Burkina Faso	Georgia	Lebanon	Kurdistan (Iraq)
Cambodia	Haiti		
Gabon	Kuwait	**Related Territories**	**5.0**
Ghana	Morocco	**3.0**	Macao (Port.)
Guatemala	Singapore	Cyprus (Turkey)	
Malaysia	Turkey		
Nicaragua	Uganda	**3.5**	
Peru	Zimbabwe	Hong Kong (U.K.)	
Senegal		Northern Ireland (U.K.)	
Sri Lanka			

NOT FREE

5.5		7.0	**Related Territories**
Cameroon	Maldives	Afghanistan	**5.5**
Chad	Oman	Algeria	Occupied Territories
Eritrea	Tanzania	Angola	and Palestinian
Ethiopia	Yugoslavia (Serbia and	Bhutan	Autonomous Areas
Guinea	Montenegro)	Burma	(Israel)
Ivory Coast (Cote		China	
D'Ivoire)	**6.5**	Cuba	**6.0**
Kazakhstan	Brunei	Equatorial Guinea	Vojvodina (Yugoslavia)
Swaziland	Burundi	Iraq	
Togo	The Gambia	Korea, North	**6.5**
Tunisia	Indonesia	Libya	Western Sahara (Morocco)
United Arab	Iran	Mauritania	
Emirates	Laos	Rwanda	**7.0**
Yemen	Liberia	Saudi Arabia	East Timor (Indonesia)
	Nigeria	Somalia	Irian Jaya (West Papua)
6.0	Qatar	Sudan	(Indonesia)
Azerbaijan	Sierra Leone	Syria	Kashmir (India)
Bahrain	Zaire	Tajikistan	Kosovo (Yugoslavia)
Bosnia-Herzegovina		Turkmenistan	Nagorno-Karabakh
Djibouti		Uzbekistan	(Armenia/Azerbaijan)
Egypt		Vietnam	Tibet (China)
Kenya			

*1 represents the highest degree of freedom, 7 the least degree of freedom.

Source: This list is based on data developed by Freedom House's Comparative Survey of Freedom. The Survey analyzes factors such as the degree to which fair and competitive elections occur, individual and group freedoms are guaranteed in practice, and press freedom exists. In some countries, the category reflects active citizen opposition rather than political rights granted by a government. More detailed and up-to-date Survey information may be obtained from Freedom House. Freedom House Survey Team, *Freedom in the World: The Annual Survey of Political Rights and Civil Liberties, 1994–1995.* (New York: Freedom House, 1995).

economic decisions are centralized or decentralized. In the Marxist form of government, such as existed in the former Soviet Union and in Eastern Europe until recent years, economic decisions were centralized and there was political stability. This would seem to be an ideal environment in which to do business from a multinational business manager's perspective. But it was not ideal, because a centralized economy limits the supply of goods coming from outside a country, the price that can be charged for goods inside the country, and the amount of currency that can be taken out of the country by multinational businesses.

Despite the collapse of communism and the development of new political systems professing support of free enterprise in Eastern Europe and throughout the former Soviet Union, companies in the industrialized nations have delayed investing in most of these areas because they are uncertain of their political sta-

36

Part One

*An Introduction to the Law
and the Legal Environment
of Business*

bility and willingness to adhere to economic agreements. The situation is similar in China, where an early rush to invest has been slowed by foreign companies' experiences with a seemingly capricious government. For example, McDonald's leased a prime location in Beijing from the centralized government but found itself ousted a few years later when the government revoked the lease in order to allow a department store to be built on that site. Moreover, doubts about the Chinese government's intention to honor its agreement with the British government that Hong Kong will retain its separate political and economic status for 50 years after the 99-year British lease expired in 1997 has led one long-time Hong Kong trading company, Jardine, to move its headquarters to the Bahamas. Others are expected to follow.

ECONOMIC DIMENSIONS

Every business manager should do a *country analysis* (Table 3-2) before doing business in another nation-state. Such an analysis not only examines political variables but also dissects a nation's economic performance as demonstrated in its rate of economic growth, inflation, budget, and trade balance. There are four economic factors that especially affect business investment:

1. *Differences in size and economic growth rate of various nation-states.* For example, when McDonald's decided to engage in international business, the company initially sited its restaurants only in countries that already had high growth rates. As more and more developing nations moved toward a market economy, McDonald's expanded into Russia, China, Brazil, Mexico, and other countries deemed to have potentially high growth rates.

2. *The impact of central planning versus a market economy on the availability of supplies.* When McDonald's went into Russia, it had to build its own food-processing center to be certain it would get the quality of beef it needed. Further, because of distribution problems, it used its own trucks to move supplies.

3. *The availability of disposable income.* This is a tricky issue. Despite the fact that the price of a Big Mac, french fries, and a soft drink equals the average Russian worker's pay for four hours of work, McDonald's is serving an estimated 540,000 customers a day at its Moscow restaurant.

4. *The existence of an appropriate transportation infrastructure.* Decent roads, railroads, and ports are needed to bring in supplies and then to transport them within the host country. McDonald's experience in Russia is commonplace. Multinational businesses face transportation problems in many developing countries.

CULTURAL DIMENSIONS

culture The learned norms of a society that are based on values, beliefs, and attitudes.

Culture may be defined as learned norms of a society that are based on values, beliefs, and attitudes. For example, if people of the same area speak the same *language* (e.g., Spanish in most of Latin America, with the exception of Brazil and a few small nations), the area is often said to be culturally homogeneous. *Religion* is a strong builder of common values. In 1995, the Iranian government outlawed the selling and use of satellite communications in Iran on the grounds that they presented "decadent" Western values that were undermining Muslim religious values.

A failure to understand that some cultures are based on *ascribed group membership* (gender, family, age, or ethnic affiliation) rather than on *acquired group membership* (religious, political, professional, or other associations), as in the West, can lead to business mistakes. For example, gender- and family-based affiliations are very important in Saudi Arabia, where a strict interpretation of Islam prevents women from playing a major role in business. Most Saudi women who work hold jobs that demand little or no contact with men, such as teaching or acting as doctors only for women.

Another important cultural factor is the *attitude toward work.* Mediterranean and Latin American cultures base their group affiliation on *family* and place more emphasis on *leisure* than on work. We often say that the Protestant ethic,

TABLE 3-2 *World Bank Categories for Economies*

HIGH-INCOME ECONOMIES (42 COUNTRIES WITH 1994 PER CAPITA GNP OF U.S. $8,956 OR MORE)	UPPER-MIDDLE-INCOME ECONOMIES (35 COUNTRIES WITH 1994 PER CAPITA GNP BETWEEN U.S. $2,896 AND $8,955)	LOWER-MIDDLE-INCOME ECONOMIES (53 COUNTRIES WITH 1994 PER CAPITA INCOME BETWEEN U.S. $726 AND $2,895)	LOW-INCOME ECONOMIES (53 COUNTRIES WITH 1994 PER CAPITA INCOME OF U.S. $725 OR LESS)
Andorra	American Samoa	Algeria	Afghanistan
Aruba	Antigua and Barbuda	Angola	Albania
Australia	Argentina	Belarus	Armenia
Austria	Bahrain	Belize	Azerbaijan
Bahamas	Barbados	Bolivia	Bangladesh
Belgium	Brazil	Botswana	Benin
Bermuda	Chile	Bulgaria	Bhutan
Brunei	Czech Republic	Colombia	Bosnia and Herzegovina
Canada	French Guiana	Costa Rica	Burkina Faso
Cayman Islands	Gabon	Croatia	Burundi
Channel Islands	Greece	Cuba	Cambodia
Cyprus	Guadeloupe	Djibouti	Cameroon
Denmark	Guam	Dominica	Cape Verde
Faeroe Islands	Hungary	Dominican Republic	Central African Rep.
Finland	Isle of Man	Ecuador	Chad
France	Korea, Rep.	El Salvador	China
French Polynesia	Libya	Estonia	Comoros
Germany	Malaysia	Fiji	Congo
Greenland	Malta	Grenada	Côte d'Ivoire
Hong Kong	Martinique	Guatemala	Egypt, Arab Rep.
Iceland	Mauritius	Indonesia	Equatorial Guinea
Ireland	Mayotte	Iran, Islamic Rep.	Eritrea
Israel	Mexico	Iraq	Ethiopia
Italy	New Caledonia	Jamaica	Gambia
Japan	Oman	Jordan	Georgia
Kuwait	Puerto Rico	Kazakhstan	Chana
Luxembourg	Reunion	Kiribati	Guinea
Macao	Saudi Arabia	Korea, Dem. Rep.	Guinea-Bissau
Netherlands	Seychelles	Latvia	Guyana
Netherlands Antilles	Slovenia	Lebanon	Haiti
New Zealand	South Africa	Lithuania	Honduras
Norway	St. Kitts and Nevis	Macedonia, FYR	India
Portugal	St. Lucia	Maldives	Kenya
Qatar	Trinidad and Tobago	Marshall Islands	Kyguz Republic
Singapore	Uruguay	Micronesia, Fed. Sts.	Laos
Spain		Moldova	Lesotho
Sweden		Morocco	Liberia
Switzerland		Namibia	Madagascar
United Arab Emirates		Northern Mariana Is.	Malawi
United Kingdom		Panama	Mali
United States		Papua New Guinea	Mauritania
Virgin Islands		Paraguay	Mongolia
		Peru	Mozambique
		Philippines	Myanmar
		Poland	Nepal
		Romania	Nicaragua
		Russian Federation	Niger
		Slovak Republic	Nigeria
		Solomon Islands	Pakistan
		St. Vincent	Rwanda
		Suriname	Sao Tome and Principe
		Swaziland	Senegal
		Syrian Arab Republic	Sierra Leone

Source: From *World Development Report 1996* by the International Bank for Reconstruction and Development/The World Bank. Used by permission of Oxford University Press.

38

Part One

*An Introduction to the Law
and the Legal Environment
of Business*

stressing the virtues of hard work and thrift, is prevalent in Western and other industrialized nations. Yet the Germans refuse to work more than 35 hours a week and take 28 days of paid vacation every year. The average hourly wage is higher in Germany than in the United States, and German workers' benefits far outpace those of U.S. workers.

Business managers must carefully consider language, religion, attitudes toward work and leisure, family versus individual reliance, and numerous other cultural values when planning to do business in another nation-state. They also need to find a method of reconciling cultural differences between people and companies from their own nation-state and those from the country they intend to do business in.

LEGAL DIMENSIONS

Business managers have to be guided both by the national legal systems of their own country and the host country and by international law when they venture into foreign territory.

NATIONAL LEGAL SYSTEMS When deciding whether to do business in a certain country, business managers are advised to learn about the legal system of that country and its potential impact in such areas as contracts, investment, and corporate law. The five major families of law are: (1) common law, (2) civil law, (3) Islamic law, (4) socialist law, and (5) Hindu law (Table 3-3).

The *common law* family is most familiar to companies doing business in the United States, England, and 26 former British colonies. The source of law is primarily case law, and decisions rely heavily on case precedents. As statutory law has become more prominent in common law countries, the courts' interpretation of laws made by legislative bodies and of regulations set forth by administrative agencies has substantially increased the body of common law.

Countries that follow the *Romano-Germanic civil law* (e.g., France, Germany, and Sweden) organize their legal systems around legal codes rather than around cases, regulations, and precedents, as do common law countries. Thus judges in civil law countries of Europe, Latin America, and Asia resolve disputes primarily by reference to general provisions of codes and secondarily by reference to statutes passed by legislative bodies. However, as the body of written opinions in civil law countries grows, and as they adopt computer-based case and statutory systems such as Westlaw and Lexus, the highest courts in these countries

TABLE 3-3 *Families of National Law and How They Affect International Business*

FAMILY	CHARACTERISTICS
Common law	Primary reliance is on case law and precedent instead of statutory law. Courts can declare statutory law unconstitutional.
Romano-Germanic civil law	Primary reliance is on codes and statutory law rather than case law. In general, the high court cannot declare laws of parliament unconstitutional (an exception is the German Constitutional Court).
Islamic law	Is derived from the *Shari'a*, a code of rules designed to govern the daily lives of all Muslims.
Socialist law	Is based upon the teaching of Karl Marx. No private property is recognized. Law encourages the collectivization of property and the means of production and seeks to guarantee national security. According to classical Marxist theory, both the law and the state will fade away as people are better educated to socialism and advance toward the ultimate stage of pure communism.
Hindu law	Is derived from the *Sastras*. Hindu law governing the behavior of people in each caste (hereditary categories that restrict members' occupations and social associations). Primarily concerned with family matters and succession. Has been codified into India's national legal system.

are taking greater note of case law in their decisions. Civil law systems tend to put great emphasis on private law: that is, law that governs relationships between individuals and corporations or between individuals. Examples are the *law of obligations*, which includes common law contracts, torts, and creditor-debtor relationships. In contrast to common law systems, civil law systems have an inferior *public law*: this is law that governs the relationships between individuals and the state. In fact, their jurists are not extensively trained in such areas as criminal, administrative, and labor law.[1]

More than 600 million Muslims in approximately 30 countries that are predominantly Muslim, as well as many more Muslims living in countries where Islam is a minority religion, are governed by Islamic law.[2] In many countries, Islamic law, as encoded in the *Shari'a*, exists alongside the secular law. In nations that have adopted Islamic law as their dominant legal system (e.g., Saudi Arabia), citizens must obey the *Shari'a*, and anyone who transgresses its rules is punished by a court. International business transactions are affected in many ways by Islamic law. For example, earning interest on money is forbidden, though a way around this stricture can be found by setting up Islamic banks, that, in lieu of paying interest on accounts, pay each depositor a share of the profits made by the bank.

Socialist law systems are based upon the teaching of Karl Marx and Vladimir Lenin (who was, incidentally, a lawyer). Right after the Bolshevik Revolution of 1917 in Russia, the Czarist legal system, which was based on the Romano-Germanic civil law, was replaced by a legal system consisting of People's Courts staffed by members of the Communist Party and peasant workers. By the early 1930s, this system had been replaced by a formal legal system with civil and criminal codes that has lasted to this day. The major goals of the Russian legal system, which are quite different from those of other legal systems, are (1) to encourage collectivization of the economy; (2) to educate the masses as to the wisdom of socialist law; and (3) to maintain national security.[3] Most property belongs to the state, particularly industrial and agricultural property. Personal (not private) property exists, but it may be used only for the satisfaction and needs of the individual, not for profit—which is referred to as "speculation" and is in violation of socialist law. Personal ownership ends either with the death of the individual or with revocation of the legal use and enjoyment of the property. Socialist law is designed to preserve the authority of the state over agricultural land and all means of production. It is still enforced in North Korea, Cuba, and to some degree, Libya, but the countries that made up the old Soviet Union and the East European bloc have been moving toward Romano-Germanic civil law systems and private-market economies in the last decade.

Hindu law, called *Sharmasastra*, is linked to the revelations of the Vedas, a collection of Indian religious songs and prayers believed to have been written between 100 B.C. and A.D. 300 or 400.[4] It is both personal and religious. Hindus are divided into social categories called *castes*, and the rules governing their behavior are set out in texts known as *Sastras*. The primary concerns of Hindu law are family matters and property succession. Four-fifths of all Hindus live in India; most of the other fifth are spread throughout Southeast Asia and Africa, with smaller numbers living in Europe and the Americas. After gaining independence from England in 1950, India codified Hindu law. Today it plays a prominent role in Indian law alongside secular statutory law, which, especially in the areas of business and trade, uses legal terminology and concepts derived from common law. Both the Indian criminal and civil codes strongly reflect the British common law tradition.[5]

---

[1]*See* R. Davids and J. Brierly, *Major Legal Systems in the World Today* (New York: Free Press, 1978), pp. 76–77.
[2]*Id.* at 437–438.
[3]*Id.* at 176–179.
[4]*Id.* at 449.
[5]*Id.* at 468–471.

40

Part One

*An Introduction to the Law
and the Legal Environment
of Business*

public international law Law
that governs the relationships
between nation-states.

private international law
Law that governs the
relationships between private
parties involved in international
transactions. Includes
international business law.

INTERNATIONAL LAW The law that governs the relationships between
nation-states is known as **public international law. Private international law** governs the relationships between private parties involved in transactions across national borders. In most cases, the parties negotiate between
themselves and set out their agreements in a written document. In some cases,
however, nation-states subsidize the private parties or are signators to the agreements negotiated by those parties. In such instances, the distinction between
private and public international law is blurred.

The sources of international law can be found in (1) custom; (2) treaties between nations, particularly treaties of friendship and commerce; (3) judicial decisions of international courts such as the International Court of Justice; (4) decisions of national and regional courts such as the U.S. Supreme Court, the
London Commercial Court, and the European Court of Justice; (5) scholarly
writings; and (6) international organizations. These sources will be discussed
throughout the text.

International business law includes laws governing (1) exit visas and work
permits; (2) tax and antitrust matters and contracts; (3) patents, trademarks,
and copyrights; (4) bilateral treaties of commerce and friendship between nations and multilateral treaties of commerce such as the North American Free
Trade Agreement (NAFTA), the European Union (EU), and the World Trade Organization (WTO). All will be explored later in this chapter.

METHODS OF ENGAGING IN INTERNATIONAL BUSINESS

For purposes of this chapter, methods of engaging in international business are
classified as (1) trade, (2) international licensing and franchising, and (3) foreign direct investment.

TRADE

international trade The
export of goods and services from
a country and the import of
goods and services into a
country.

We define **international trade** as exporting goods and services from a country and importing goods and services into a country. There are two traditional
theories of trade relationships. The theory of *absolute advantage*, which is the
older theory, states that an individual nation should concentrate on exporting
the goods that it can produce most efficiently. For example, Sir Lanka (formerly
Ceylon) produces tea more efficiently than most countries can, and thus any
surplus in Sri Lanka's tea production should be exported to countries that produce tea less efficiently. The theory of *comparative advantage* arose out of the re-
alization that a country did not have to have an absolute advantage in producing a good in order to export it efficiently; rather, it would contribute to global
efficiency if it produced specialized products simply *more* efficiently than others
did. To illustrate this concept, let's assume that the best attorney in a small
town is also the best legal secretary. Because this person can make more money
as an attorney, it would be most efficient for her to devote her energy to working as a lawyer and to hire a legal secretary. Similarly, let's assume that the
United States can produce both wheat and tea more efficiently than Sri Lanka
can. Thus, the United States has an absolute advantage in its trade with Sri
Lanka. Let us further assume that U.S. wheat production is comparatively
greater than U.S. tea production vis-à-vis Sri Lanka. That is, by using the same
amount of resources, the United States can produce two and a half times as
much wheat but only twice as much tea as Sri Lanka. The United States then
has a comparative advantage in wheat over tea.[6]

In this simplified example, we made several assumptions: that there were
only two countries and two commodities involved; that transport costs in the
two countries were about the same; that efficiency was the sole objective; and
that political factors were not significant. In international trade, things are far
more complex. There are many nations and innumerable products involved,
and political factors are often more potent than economic considerations.

---

[6]J. Daniels and L. Radebaugh, *International Business*, 7th ed. (Reading, Mass.: Addison-Wesley,
1995), pp. 174, 175.

Trade is generally considered to be the least risky means of doing international business because it demands little involvement with a foreign buyer or seller. For small and middle-sized firms, the first step toward involvement in international business is generally to hire an *export management company*, which is a company licensed to operate as the representative of many manufacturers with exportable products. These management companies are privately owned by citizens of various nation-states and have long-standing links to importers in many countries. They provide exporting firms with market research, identify potential buyers, and assist the firms in negotiating contracts.

Export trading companies, which are governed by the Export Trading Act in the United States, comprise those manufacturers and banks that either buy the products of a small business and resell them in another country or sell products of several companies on a commission basis. Small and medium-sized exporting companies may also choose to retain *foreign distributors*, which purchase imported goods at a discount and resell them in the foreign or host country. Once a company has had some experience selling in other countries, it may decide to retain a *foreign sales representative*. Sales representatives differ from foreign distributors in that they do not take title to the goods being exported. Rather, they usually maintain a principal-agency relationship with the exporter.

INTERNATIONAL LICENSING AND FRANCHISING

International licensing is a contractual agreement by which a company (licensor) makes its trade secrets, trademarks, patents, or copyrights (intellectual property) available to a foreign individual or company (licensee) in return either for royalties or for other compensation based on the volume of goods sold or a lump sum. All licensing agreements are subject to restrictions of the host country, which may include demands that its nationals be trained for management positions in the licensee company, that the host government receive a percentage of the gross profits, and that licensor technology be made available to all host country nationals. Licensing agreements can differ vastly from country to country.

international licensing A contractual agreement by which a company (licensor) makes its intellectual property available to a foreign individual or company (licensee) for payment.

International franchising permits a licensee of a trademark to market the licensor's goods or services in a particular nation (e.g., Kentucky Fried Chicken franchises in China). Often, companies franchise their trademark to avoid a nation-state's restrictions on foreign direct investment. Also, political instability is less likely to be a threat to investment when a local franchisee is running the business. Companies considering entering into an international franchise agreement should investigate bilateral treaties of friendship and commerce between the franchisor's nation and the franchisee's nation, as well as the business laws of the franchisee country.

international franchising A contractual agreement whereby a company (licensor) permits another company (licensee) to market its trader marked goods or services in a particular nation.

In some instances, licensing and franchising negotiations are tense and drawn out because businesses in many industrialized nations are intent on protecting their intellectual property against "piracy" or are adamant about getting assurances that franchising agreements will be honored. These are major, legitimate concerns. For example, in 1994, 1995, and 1996, the United States threatened to impose sanctions against China because of that nation's sale of pirated U.S. goods as well as its failure to comply with international franchising requirements. A series of last-minute agreements encouraged by Chinese and U.S. businesses averted the sanctions, which would have proved expensive for private and public parties in both countries.

FOREIGN DIRECT INVESTMENT

Direct investment in foreign nations is usually undertaken only by established multinational corporations. Foreign direct investment may take one of two forms: The multinational either creates a wholly or partially owned and controlled foreign subsidiary in the host country or enters into a joint venture with an individual, corporation, or government agency of the host country. In both cases, the risk for the investing company is greater than is the risk in interna-

42

Part One

*An Introduction to the Law
and the Legal Environment
of Business*

foreign subsidiary A company
that is wholly or partially owned
and controlled by a company
based in another country.

tional trade and international franchising and licensing because serious amounts of capital are flowing to the host country that are subject to its government's restrictions and its domestic law.

Large multinationals choose to create **foreign subsidiaries** for several reasons: (1) to expand their foreign markets, (2) to acquire foreign resources, including raw materials, (3) to improve their production efficiency, (4) to acquire knowledge, and (5) to be closer to their customers and competitors. Rarely do all these reasons pertain in a single instance. For example, U.S. companies have set up foreign subsidiaries in Mexico, Western Europe, Brazil, and India for quite different reasons. Mexico provided cheap labor and a location close to customers and suppliers for U.S. automobile manufacturers. In the case of Western Europe, the impetus was both a threat and an opportunity. The member nations of the European Union (EU) have been moving to eliminate all trade barriers among themselves, while at the same time imposing stiffer tariffs on goods and services imported from non-EU countries. United States companies have been rushing to establish foreign subsidiaries in EU countries not only to avoid being shut out of this huge lucrative market but also to expand sales among its approximate 380 million people. Brazil is not only the largest potential market in Latin America; it also offers low labor and transportation costs, which makes it ideal for U.S. automakers desiring to export to neighboring Latin American countries. Union Carbide, Inc., a producer of chemicals and plastics, decided to establish a subsidiary in India, where cheap labor (including highly skilled chemists and engineers) and low-cost transportation enabled the parent company to produce various materials cheaply, and thus boost its bottom line. The Indian subsidiary turned out to be a very expensive investment for Union Carbide after the Bhopal disaster. The civil suit that resulted illustrates an issue that is often overlooked by managers of multinationals when setting up subsidiaries in foreign nation-states: Should a parent corporation be held liable for the activities of its foreign subsidiary? Although the case presented here is framed in a jurisdictional context (whether a U.S. court or an Indian court should hear the suit), you should bear in mind the issue of corporate parent liability as you read it.

IN RE UNION CARBIDE CORPORATION GAS PLANT DISASTER AT BHOPAL, INDIA IN DECEMBER, 1984 V. UNION CARBIDE CORPORATION

UNITED STATES COURT OF APPEALS 809 F.2D 195 (2D CIR. 1987)

The government of India (UOI) and several private class action plaintiffs (Indian citizens) sued Union Carbide India Limited (UCIL) and the parent corporation, Union Carbide Corporation (UCC), for over $1 billion after a disaster at a chemical plant operated by UCIL in 1984. There was a leak of the lethal gas methylisocyanate from the plant on the night of December 2, 1984. The deadly chemicals were blown by wind over the adjacent city of Bhopal, resulting in the deaths of more than 2,000 persons and the injury of more than another 200,000. UCIL is incorporated under the laws of India; 50.9 percent of the stock is owned by UCC, 22 percent is owned or controlled by the government of India, and the balance is owned by 23,500 Indian citizens. The federal district court (Judge Keenan) granted UCC's motion to dismiss the plaintiffs' action on the grounds that Indian courts, not U.S. courts, were the appropriate forum for the suit. The plaintiffs appealed this decision.

JUDGE MANSFIELD

As the district court found, the record shows that the private interests of the respective parties weigh heavily in favor of dismissal on grounds of *forum non conveniens*. The many witnesses and sources of proof are almost entirely located in India, where the accident occurred, and could not be compelled to appear for trial in the United States. The Bhopal plant at the time of the accident was operated by some 193 Indian nationals, including the managers of seven operating units employed by the Agricultural Products Division of UCIL, who reported to Indian Works Managers in Bhopal. The plant was maintained by seven functional departments employing over 200 more Indian nationals. UCIL kept daily, weekly and monthly records of plant operations and records of maintenance, as well as records of the plant's Quality Control, Purchasing, and Stores branches, all operated by Indian employees. The great majority of documents bearing on the design, safety, start-up and operation of the plant, as well as the safety training of the plant's employees, is located in India. Proof to be offered at trial would be derived from interviews of these witnesses in India and study of the records located there to determine whether the accident was caused by negligence on the part of the management or employees in the operation of the plant, by fault in its design, or by sabotage. In short, India has greater ease of access to the proof than does the United States.

The Plaintiffs seek to prove that the accident was caused by negligence on the part of UCC in originally contributing to the design of the plant and its provision for storage of excessive amounts of the gas at the plant. As Judge Keenan found, however, UCC's participation was limited and its involvement in plant operations terminated long before the accident. Under 1973 agreements negotiated at arm's-length with UCIL, UCC did provide a summary "process design package" for construction of the plant and the services of some of its technicians to monitor the progress of UCIL in detailing the design and erecting the plant. However, the UOI controlled the terms of the agreements and precluded UCC from exercising any authority to "detail design, erect and commission the plant," which was done independently over the period from 1972 to 1980 by UCIL process design engineers who supervised, among many others, some 55 to 60 Indian engineers employed by the Bombay engineering firm of Humphreys and Glasgow. The preliminary process design information furnished by UCC could not have been used to construct the plant. Construction required the detailed process design and engineering data prepared by hundreds of Indian engineers, process designers and sub-contractors. During the ten years spent constructing the plant, the design and configuration underwent many changes.

In short, the plant has been constructed and managed by Indians in India. No Americans were employed at the plant at the time of the accident. In the five years from 1980 to 1984, although more than 1,000 Indians were employed at the plant, only one American was employed there and he left in 1982. No Americans visited the plant for more than one year prior to the accident, and during the five-year period before the accident the communications between the plant and the United States were almost non-existent.

The vast majority of material witnesses and documentary proof bearing on causation of and liability for the accident is located in India, not the United States, and would be more accessible to an Indian court than to a United States court. The records are almost entirely in Hindi or other Indian languages, understandable to an Indian court without translation. The witnesses for the most part do not speak English but Indian languages understood by an Indian court but not by an American court. These witnesses could be required to appear in an Indian court but not in a court of the United States.

India's interest is increased by the fact that it has for years treated UCIL as an Indian national, subjecting it to intensive regulations and governmental supervision of the construction, development and operation of the Bhopal plant, its emissions, water and air pollution, and safety precautions. Numerous Indian government officials have regularly conducted on-site inspections of the plant and approved its machinery and equipment, including its facilities for storage of the lethal methylisocyanate gas that escaped and caused the disaster giving rise to the claims. Thus India has considered the plant to be an Indian one and the disaster to be an Indian problem. It therefore has a deep interest in ensuring compliance with its safety standards.

Affirmed in favor of Defendant, Union Carbide.

Critical Thinking about the Law

1. Highlight the importance of the facts in shaping a judicial opinion by writing an imaginary letter that, had it been introduced as evidence, would have greatly distressed Union Carbide Corporation.

   CLUE Review the first part of the decision, in which Judge Mansfield discusses the extent of UCC's involvement in the plant where the accident occurred. What facts would counter his statement that the parent company had only "limited" involvement?

2. Suppose a U.S. plant exploded, resulting in extensive deaths in the United States. Further suppose that all the engineers who built the plant wrote and spoke German only. Could Judge Mansfield's decision be used as an analogy to seek dismissal of a negligence suit against the owners of the plant?

   CLUE Review the discussion of the use of legal analogies in chapter 1 and apply what you read to this question.

3. What additional information, were it to surface, would strengthen Union Carbide's request for a dismissal of the case described?

   CLUE Notice the wide assortment of facts that Judge Mansfield organized to support his decision.

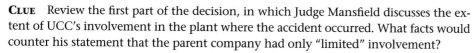

44

Part One

*An Introduction to the Law
and the Legal Environment
of Business*

COMMENT: The Bhopal victims filed their claims in U.S. courts against UCC because the parent company had more money than the subsidiary (UCIL). Also, suing the parent made it more likely that the case would be heard in U.S. courts, which are considered to be far better forums for winning damages in personal injury actions than Indian courts are. After the lawsuits were removed to an Indian court, UCC agreed to pay $470 million to the Bhopal disaster victims. Union Carbide's stock substantially decreased in value, and UCC was threatened by a takeover (the attempt was thwarted in 1985). More than half of UCC was subsequently sold or spun off, including the Indian subsidiary (UCIL). About 12,000 people worked for UCC in 1995, in contrast to the 110,000 employed by the company a decade earlier. Still, UCC recovered quite well from the disaster; it has been a Dow Industrial (top 30) stock since 1992.

Joint ventures, which involve a relationship between two or more corporations or between a foreign multinational and an agency of a host country government or a host country national, are usually set up for a specific undertaking over a limited period of time. Many developing countries (such as China) allow foreign investment only in the form of a joint venture between host country nationals and the multinationals. Recently, there have been three-way joint ventures among United States–based multinationals (e.g., automobile companies such as Chrysler and General Motors), Japanese multinationals (e.g., Mitsubishi and Honda), and Chinese government agencies and Chinese nationals. Joint ventures are also used in host countries with fewer restrictions on foreign investment, often to spread the risk or to amass required investment sums that are too large for one corporation to raise by itself. Some of these joint ventures are private associations, with no host government involvement.

joint venture Relationship between two or more persons or corporations; or an association between a foreign multinational and an agency of the host government or a host country national; set up for a specific business undertaking or a limited time period.

RISKS OF ENGAGING IN INTERNATIONAL BUSINESS

Unlike doing business in one's own country, the "rules of the game" are not always clear when engaging in business in a foreign country, particularly in what we have classified as middle- and low-income economies (see Table 3-2). Here we set out the four primary risks that managers engaged in international business may face: (1) expropriation of private property by the host foreign nation; (2) the application of the sovereign immunity doctrine and the act-of-state doctrine to disputes between foreign states and U.S. firms; (3) export and import controls; and (4) currency controls and fluctuations in currency values.

EXPROPRIATION OF PRIVATE PROPERTY

expropriation The taking of private property by a host country government for political or economic reasons.

Expropriation—the taking of private property by a host country government either for political or for economic reasons—is one of the greatest risks companies take when they engage in international business. Thus, it is essential for business managers to investigate the recent behavior of host country government officials, particularly in countries that are moving from a centrally planned economy toward one that is market-oriented (e.g., Russia and Eastern European nations). One method of limiting risk in politically unstable countries is to concentrate on exports and imports (trade) and licensing and franchising. Another is to take advantage of the low-cost insurance against expropriation offered by the Overseas Private Investment Corporation (OPIC). If a U.S. plant or other project is insured by OPIC and is expropriated, the U.S. firm receives compensation in return for assigning to OPIC the firm's claim against the host country government.

bilateral investment treaty Treaty between two parties to outline conditions for investment in either country.

Bilateral investment treaties (BITs), which are negotiated between two governments, obligate the host government to show fair and nondiscriminatory treatment to investors from the other country. The BIT also includes a promise of prompt, adequate, and effective compensation in the event of expropriation or nationalization.

SOVEREIGN IMMUNITY DOCTRINE

sovereign immunity doctrine States that a government expropriating foreign-owned private property is immune from the jurisdiction of courts in the owner's country.

Another risk for companies engaged in international business is the **sovereign immunity doctrine**, which allows a government expropriating foreign-owned private property to claim that it is immune from the jurisdiction of courts in the owner's country because it is a government not a private-sector entity. In these cases, the company whose property was expropriated often receives nothing because it cannot press its claims in its own country's courts, and courts in the host country are seldom amenable to such claims.

The sovereign immunity doctrine has been a highly controversial issue between the United States and certain foreign governments in developing nations. To give some protection to foreign businesses without impinging on the legitimate rights of other governments, the U.S. Congress in 1976 enacted the Foreign Sovereign Immunities Act (FSIA), which shields foreign governments from U.S. judicial review of their public, but not their private, acts. The FSIA grants foreign nations immunity from judicial review by U.S. courts unless they meet one of the FSIA's private exceptions. One such exception is the foreign government's involvement in *commercial* activity. The case detailed below clarifies the U.S. Supreme Court's definition of commercial activity under the FSIA. Note how the Court emphasizes the *nature* of the Argentine government's action by asking whether it is the type of action a private party would engage in.

REPUBLIC OF ARGENTINA V. WELTOVER, INC. ET AL.

UNITED STATES SUPREME COURT 112 S. CT. 2160 (1992)

As part of a plan to stabilize defendant-petitioner Argentina's currency, that country and petitioner bank (collectively "Argentina") issued bonds, called "Bonods," which provided for repayment in U.S. dollars through transfer on the market in one of several locations, including New York City. Concluding that it lacked sufficient foreign exchange to retire the Bonods when they began to mature, Argentina unilaterally extended the time for payment and offered bondholders substitute instruments as a means of rescheduling the debts. Plaintiff-respondent bondholders, two Panamanian corporations and a Swiss bank, declined to accept the rescheduling and insisted on repayment in New York. When Argentina refused, plaintiffs brought a breach-of-contract action in the District Court, which denied Argentina's motion to dismiss. The Court of Appeals affirmed, ruling that the District Court had jurisdiction under the Foreign Sovereign Immunities Act of 1976 (FSIA), which subjects foreign states to suit in American court for, *inter alia*, acts taken "in connection with a commercial activity" that have "a direct effect in the United States." The Supreme Court of the United States granted Argentina's petition for review.

JUSTICE SCALIA

This case requires us to decide whether the Republic of Argentina's default on certain bonds issued as part of a plan to stabilize its currency was an act taken "in connection with a commercial activity" that had a "direct effect on the United States" so as to subject Argentina to suit in an American court under the Foreign Sovereign Immunities Act of 1976.

The Foreign Sovereign Immunities Act of 1976 (FSIA), establishes a comprehensive framework for determining whether a court in this country, state or federal, may exercise jurisdiction over a foreign state. Under the Act, a "foreign state shall be immune from the jurisdiction of the courts of the United States and of the States" unless one of several statutorily defined exceptions applies. The FSIA thus provides the "sole basis" for obtaining jurisdiction over a foreign sovereign in the United States. The most significant of the FSIA's exceptions—and the one at issue in this case—is the "commercial" exception, which provides that a foreign state is not immune from suit in any case

> in which the action is based upon a commercial activity carried on in the United States by the foreign state; or upon an act performed in the United States in connection with a commercial activity of the foreign state elsewhere; or upon an act outside the territory of the United States in connection with a commercial activity of the foreign state elsewhere and that act causes a direct effect in the United States.

The key question is whether the activity is "commercial" under the FSIA. The FSIA defines "commercial activity" to mean:

> [E]ither a regular course of commercial conduct or a particular commercial transaction or act. The commercial character of an activity shall be determined by reference to the nature of the course of conduct or particular transaction or act, rather than by reference to its purpose.

This definition, however, leaves the critical term "commercial" largely undefined: The first sentence simply establishes that the commercial nature of an activity does not depend upon whether it is a single act or a regular course of conduct, and the second sentence merely specifies what element of the conduct determines commerciality (i.e., nature rather than purpose), but still without saying what "commercial" means. We conclude that when a foreign government acts, not as regulator of a market, but in the manner of a private player within it, the foreign sovereign's actions are "commercial" within the meaning of the FSIA. Moreover, because the Act provides that the commercial character of an act is to be determined by reference to its "nature" rather than its "purpose," the question is not whether the foreign government is acting with a profit motive or instead with the aim of fulfilling uniquely sovereign objectives. Rather, the issue is whether the particular actions that the foreign state performs (whatever the motive behind them) are the *type* of actions by which a private party engages in "trade and traffic or commerce." Thus, a foreign government's issuance of regulations limiting foreign currency exchange is a sovereign activity, because such authoritative control of commerce cannot be exercised by a private party; whereas a contract to buy army boots or even bullets is a "commercial" activity, because private companies can similarly use sales contracts to acquire goods.

The commercial character of the Bonods is confirmed by the fact that they are in almost all respects garden-variety debt instruments: they may be held by private parties; they are negotiable and may be traded on the international market (except in Argentina); and they promise a future stream of cash income.

We agree with the Court of Appeals that it is irrelevant why Argentina participated in the bond market in the manner of a private actor; it matters only that it did so. We conclude that Argentina's insurance of Bonods was a "commercial activity" under the FSIA.

Affirmed in favor of Plaintiff-Respondents, Bondholders.

ACT-OF-STATE DOCTRINE

act-of-state doctrine States that each sovereign nation is bound to respect the independence of every other sovereign nation and that the courts of one nation will not sit in judgment on the acts of the courts of another nation.

The **act-of-state doctrine** holds that each sovereign nation is bound to respect the independence of every other sovereign state and that the courts of one nation will not sit in judgment on the acts of the courts of another nation done within that nation's own sovereign territory. This doctrine, together with the sovereign immunity doctrine, substantially increases the risk of doing business in a foreign country. Like the sovereign immunity doctrine, the act-of-state doctrine includes some court-ordered exceptions, such as when the foreign government is acting in a *commercial* capacity or when it seeks to repudiate a commercial obligation.

Congress made it clear in 1964 that the act-of-state doctrine shall not be applied in cases in which *property is confiscated* in violation of international law unless the president of the United States decides that the federal courts should apply it. As the case below demonstrates, the plaintiff has the burden of proving that the doctrine should *not* apply—that is, that the courts *should* sit in judgment of public acts of a foreign government, in this case, a former government.

REPUBLIC OF THE PHILIPPINES V. FERDINAND E. MARCOS
UNITED STATES CIRCUIT COURT OF APPEALS 862 F.2D 1355 (9TH CIR. 1988)

The Republic of the Philippines (plaintiff) brought a civil suit against its former president, Ferdinand Marcos, and his wife, Imelda (defendants), asserting claims under the Racketeer Influenced Corrupt Organizations Act (RICO) and other applicable U.S. law. The Republic alleges that the Marcoses (and other defendants) arranged for investments in real estate in Beverly Hills, California, of $4 million fraudulently obtained by the Marcoses; that the Marcoses arranged for the creation of two bank accounts in the name of Imelda Marcos at Lloyds Bank of California totaling over $800,000, also fraudulently obtained by the Marcoses; and that the Marcoses transported into Hawaii money, jewels, and other property worth over $7 million, also fraudulently obtained by them. The key to the Republic's entire case is the allegation that the Marcoses stole public money. The federal district court entered a preliminary injunction enjoining the Marcoses from disposing of any of their assets except to pay attorneys and their living expenses. The Marcoses appealed.

JUDGE NOONAN

Before determining whether issuance of an injunction was appropriate we must consider two defenses which, if accepted, would block trial of the case the Marcoses maintain. First, that their acts are insulated because they were acts of state not reviewable by our courts, and second, that any adjudication of these acts would involve the investigation of political questions beyond our court's competence.

The classification of certain acts as "acts of state," with the consequence that their validity will be treated as beyond judicial review, is a pragmatic device, not required by the nature of sovereign authority and inconsistently applied in international law. The purpose of the device is to keep the judiciary from embroiling the courts and the country in the affairs of the foreign nation whose acts are challenged. Minimally viewed, the classification keeps a court from making pronouncements on matters over which it has no power: maximally interpreted, the classification prevents the embarrassment of a court defending a foreign government that is "extant at the time of suit."

The "continuing vitality" of the doctrine depends on its capacity to reflect the proper distribution of functions between the judicial and political branches of the government on matters bearing upon foreign relations.

As a practical tool for keeping the judicial branch out of the conduct of foreign affairs, the classification of "act of state" is not a promise to the ruler of any foreign country that his conduct, if challenged by his own country after his fall, may not become the subject of scrutiny in our courts. No estoppel exists insulating a deposed dictator from accounting. No guarantee has been granted that immunity may be acquired by an ex-chief magistrate invoking the magic words "act of state" to cover his or her past performance.

In the instant case the Marcoses offered no evidence whatsoever to support the classification of their acts as acts of state. The burden of proving acts of state rested upon them. They did not undertake the proof.

Bribetaking, theft, embezzlement, extortion, fraud, and conspiracy to do these things are all acts susceptible of concrete proof that need not involve political questions. The court, it is true, may have to determine questions of Philippine law in determining whether a given act was legal or illegal. But questions of foreign law are not beyond the capacity of our courts. The court will be examining the acts of the president of a country whose immediate political heritage is from our own. Although sometimes criticized as a ruler and at times invested with extraordinary power, Ferdinand Marcos does not appear to have had the authority of an absolute autocrat. He was not the state, but the head of the state, bound by the laws that applied to him. Our courts have had no difficulty in distinguishing the legal acts of a deposed ruler from his acts for personal profit that lack a basis in law.

Affirmed for Plaintiff, Republic of the Philippines.

Critical Thinking about the Law

1. At the outset of the case, Judge Noonan acknowledges a key ambiguity in this case that will require clarification before announcing his decision. How does that ambiguity affect the reasoning?

   CLUE Notice the key concept in the first of the two defenses used by the Marcoses.

2. What behavior of the Marcoses made it highly unlikely that the first defense would be effective?

   CLUE Review Judge Noonan's rationale for not honoring the defense.

3. What ethical norm is implicit in the Marcoses' struggle against the preliminary injunction?

   CLUE Look back at the discussion of the ethical norms and eliminate those that seem inconsistent with the Marcoses' behavior and interests.

EXPORT AND IMPORT CONTROLS

EXPORT CONTROLS Export controls are usually applied by governments to militarily sensitive goods (e.g., computer hardware and software) to prevent unfriendly nations from obtaining these goods. In the United States, the Department of State, the Department of Commerce, and the Defense Department bear responsibility, under the Export Administration Act and the Arms Export Control Act, for authorizing the export of sensitive technology. Both criminal and administrative sanctions may be imposed on corporations and individuals who violate these laws. In the aftermath of the Persian Gulf War of 1989, several companies were convicted of supplying Iraq with parts and weapons before the war. In pleas settling the cases, each defendant corporation indicated that it was encouraged to make such sales by U.S. government agencies (e.g., the Central Intelligence Agency) in order to further the U.S. policy of preventing Iran from triumphing over Iraq in the lengthy war between those two countries during the 1980s.

Export controls often prevent U.S. companies from living up to negotiated contracts. Thus they can damage the ability of U.S. firms to do business abroad.

48

Part One

*An Introduction to the Law
and the Legal Environment
of Business*

IMPORT CONTROLS   Nations often set up import barriers to prevent foreign companies from destroying home industries. Two such controls are *tariffs* and *quotas*. For example, the United States has sought historically to protect its domestic automobile and textile industries, agriculture, and intellectual property (copyrights, patents, trademarks, and trade secrets). Intellectual property has become an extremely important U.S. export in recent years, and Washington has grown more determined than ever to prevent its being pirated. After several years of frustrating negotiations with the People's Republic of China, the U.S. government decided to threaten imposition of 100 percent tariffs on approximately $1 billion of Chinese imports in 1995, and again in 1996 and 1997. In retaliation, the Chinese government has threatened several times to impose import controls on many U.S. goods. Washington took action only after documenting that hundreds of millions of dollars' worth of "pirated" computerized software (including videodiscs, law books, and movies) was being produced for sale within China and for export to Southeast Asian nations in violation of the intellectual property laws of both China and the United States, as well as international law. The documentation showed that 29 factories owned by the state or Communist Party officials were producing pirated goods. A last-minute settlement in which the Chinese government pledged to honor intellectual property rights prevented a trade war that would have had bad implications for workers in import-export industries in both countries. American consumers also would have suffered because Chinese imports would have been twice as expensive had the 100 percent tariff taken effect—though the effect on consumers would have been offset by an increase in imports of the affected goods from other foreign countries (e.g., English and Japanese bikes would have replaced Chinese bikes in demand).

This, one of the largest import trade retaliation cases in U.S. history, would also have had far-reaching political and economic implications for China. The United States had been blocking China's entrance into the World Trade Organization (WTO) because of its pirating practices, as well as its failure to conform to WTO tariff standardizations, and its human rights record. A trade war between the two nations would have sealed China's exclusion for some time to come. As of this writing, the economic reforms begun by the former Chinese premier Deng Ziaoping—including changes in laws governing trade, licensing, and direct investment by foreigners—seem to be continuing as the government works toward a form of private- and public-sector development in several industries.

By permission of Chip Box and Creators Syndicate.

CURRENCY CONTROLS Currency controls are usually found in lower-income and lower-middle-income countries where regulations may restrict the conversion of domestic currency into foreign currency (e.g., the U.S. dollar) and the *repatriation* of foreign currency (e.g., taking U.S. dollars out of India). The latter type of restriction limits foreign multinationals from repatriating more than a certain percentage of the funds they have invested in the host country. Some countries impose an income (withholding) tax on repatriated earnings. Businesspeople need to be aware that currency controls are common in developing nations and that doing business in countries that impose them requires investment for the long term.

CURRENCY FLUCTUATIONS Doing international business involves the exchange of foreign currencies in the buying and selling of goods and services. Significant fluctuations in currency values, especially if they are unanticipated, and therefore unprepared for, can present painful problems for businesses. For example, in July through September of 1997 the world saw currencies of some Asian countries vis-à-vis the U.S. dollar fall dramatically (Exhibit 3-1). For many years, these countries had linked their currencies to the dollar. When their currencies were delinked, high growth rates, inflation, and easy bank loans led to financial crises. Some Asian political leaders blamed the crises on monetary speculators, who in turn placed the blame on more fundamental economic indicators. With the resulting devaluation of currencies, such countries as Malaysia, Thailand, Indonesia, the Philippines, and South Korea saw their exports to developed nations plunge and investors flee. If it took many more ringgits (Malaysia), bahts (Thai), rupiahs (Indonesia), pesos (Philippines), and wons (Korea) per U.S. dollar to recover their return on investments, investors looked for other locations (e.g., United States, Europe, Latin America) to move their money. In economies that were highly dependent on foreign investment this strategy led to cutbacks on major projects that would have provided local growth and employment. Most important, in October and November 1997, stock markets fell worldwide for several days, showing the interdependency of national and international institutions. The International Monetary Fund, the U.S. government, and private U.S. commercial banks "pumped" more than $100 million into the five nations mentioned here in January of 1998.

In such a financial crises, U.S. and other exporters *hedge* against exchange risks by contracting with a bank. In return for a fee (based on risk), the bank assumes the risk of currency fluctuation by guaranteeing the exporter a fixed

---

EXHIBIT 3-1 *Tracking the Asian Currency Crisis*

Daily closing values of selected currencies per U.S. dollar (scales are inverted)

Source: The Wall Street Journal, September 9, 1997. Reprinted by permission of The Wall Street Journal, © 1997 Dow Jones & Company, Inc. All Rights Reserved Worldwide.

hedging Exporting companies contract with a bank that guarantees the exporter a fixed number of U.S. dollars in exchange for payment of the goods it receives in a foreign currency. The exporting company pays a fee to the bank. The fee is based upon the risk the bank is taking that the foreign currency will fluctuate.

number of dollars in exchange for the foreign currency it receives. **Hedging** is a practice managers doing international business should be thoroughly informed of, especially if they are dealing with developing nations, where currency fluctuations can be quite erratic.

LEGAL AND ECONOMIC INTEGRATION AS A MEANS OF ENCOURAGING INTERNATIONAL BUSINESS ACTIVITY

Table 3-4 summarizes a number of groups that have been formed to assist businesspeople in carrying out international transactions. These groups range from the World Trade Organization (formerly the General Agreement on Tariffs and Trade), which is attempting to reduce tariff barriers worldwide, to the proposed South American Common Market, which would form a duty-free zone for all the nations of South America. The most ambitious organization is the European Union (EU), which is in the process of forming a West European political and economic community with a single currency and a common external tariff barrier toward nonmembers.

Multinational corporations are learning that doing international business is much easier when they are aware of the worldwide and regional groups listed in Table 3-4. We will describe three of these groups: the WTO, the EU, and the North America Free Trade Agreement (NAFTA). We chose to examine these three because they represent three different philosophies and structures of legal and economic integration, not because we do not appreciate the major efforts of other integrative groups outlined in Table 3-4.

THE WORLD TRADE ORGANIZATION

PURPOSE AND TERMS   On January 1, 1995, the 47-year-old General Agreement on Tariffs and Trade (GATT) organization was replaced by a new umbrella group, the World Trade Organization (WTO). The WTO has the power to enforce the new trade accord that evolved out of seven rounds of GATT negotiations, with more than 140 nations participating. All 124 signators to this accord have agreed to reduce their tariffs and subsidies by an average of one-third on most goods over the next decade, agricultural tariffs and subsidies included. Economists estimate that this trade pact will result in tariff reductions totaling $744 billion over the next ten years.

Moreover, the accord, which the WTO will supervise, prohibits member countries from placing limits on the quantity of imports (quotas). For example, Japan will have to end its ban on rice imports, and the United States will have to end its import quotas on peanuts, dairy products, and textiles. Furthermore, the agreement bans the practice of requiring high *local content* of materials for manufactured products such as cars. It also requires all signatory countries to protect *patents, trademarks, copyrights*, and *trade secrets*. (See chapter 13 for discussion of these topics, which fall under the umbrella of intellectual property.)

GENERAL IMPACT   The accord created the World Trade Organization, which consists of all nations whose governments approved and met the GATT–Uruguay Round Accord.[7] Each member state has one vote in the *Ministerial Conference*, with no single nation having a veto. The Conference meets at least biannually, and a *General Council* meets as needed. The Conference may amend the charter created by the pact—in some cases, by a two-thirds vote; in others, by a three-fourths vote. Changes will apply to all members, even those that voted no.

The WTO has been given the power to set up a powerful dispute-resolution system with three-person arbitration panels. Each panel follows a strict schedule for dispute-resolution decisions, and WTO members may veto its findings. This is a matter of great concern to the United States, and it figured promi-

---

[7]Uruguay Round Amendments Act, Pub. L. 103–465 was approved by Congress on December 8, 1994. One hundred and eight states signed the final act embodying the results of the Heruguay round of multilateral trade negotiations. Bureau of National Affairs, *International Reporter*, vol. 11, p. 11 (April 20, 1994). Sixteen more states have joined since 1944.

TABLE 3-4 *Legally and Economically Integrated Institutions*

NAME	MEMBERS AND PURPOSE
World Trade Organization (WTO)	Replaced General Agreement on Tariffs and Trade (GATT) in 1995. 124 member nations. Goal is to get the nations of the world to commit to the trade principles of nondiscrimination and reciprocity so that, when a trade treaty is negotiated between two members, the provisions of that bilateral treaty will be extended to all WTO members (i.e., all will have MFN—"most favored nation"—status). All members are obligated to harmonize their trade laws or face sanctions. The WTO, through its arbitration tribunals, is to mediate disputes and recommend sanctions.
European Union	Composed of 15 West European member states. Established as the European Economic Community (later called the European Community) by the Treaty of Rome in 1957. Goal is to establish an economic "common market" by eliminating custom duties and other quantitative restrictions on the import and export of goods and services between member states. In 1986 the treaty was amended by the Single European Act (SEA), providing for the abolition of all customs and technical barriers between nations by December 31, 1992. In 1991, the Maastricht Summit Treaty proposed monetary union, political union, and a "social dimension" (harmonizing labor and social security regulations) among EU members, but the treaty has not yet been ratified by all member states.
North American Free Trade Agreement (NAFTA)	The United States, Canada, and Mexico are members at present; Chile has been invited to join. NAFTA seeks to eliminate barriers to the flow of goods, services, and investments among member nations over a 15-year period, starting in 1994, the year of its ratification. Unlike the European Union, NAFTA is not intended to create a common market. Whereas European Union states have a common tariff barrier against non-EU states, members of NAFTA maintain their own individual tariff rates for goods and services coming from non-NAFTA countries.
Organization for Economic Cooperation and Development (OECD)	Established in 1961. Western European nations with Australia, New Zealand, United States, Canada, Japan, Russia, and some Eastern European nations as associate members. The OECD's original purpose was to promote economic growth after World War II. Today it recommends and evaluates options on environmental issues for its members and establishes guidelines for multinational corporations when operating in developed and developing countries.
European Free Trade Association (EFTA)	Founded in 1960 and originally composed of Finland, Sweden, Norway, Iceland, Lichtenstein, Switzerland, and Austria. EFTA has an intergovernment council that negotiates treaties with the EU. Finland, Sweden, and Austria left the EFTA in 1995 and joined the EU. EFTA in the future will have only minor significance.
Andean Common Market (ANCOM)	Composed of Bolivia, Venezuela, Columbia, Ecuador, and Peru, ANCOM seeks to integrate these nations politically and economically through a commission, the Juanta Andean Development Bank, and a Reserve Fund and a Court of Justice. Founded in 1969, its goals have been set back by national interests.
Mercado Commun del Ser Mercosul (Mercosul)	Composed of Argentina, Brazil, Paraguay, and Uruguay. Mercosul's purposes are to reduce tariffs and eliminate nontariff barriers among members and to establish a common external tariff. The organization was founded in 1991, and these goals were to be met by December 31, 1994. For political reasons they have not been fully met.
South American Common Market	A duty-free common market comprised of countries in the ANCOM and Mercosul groups came about on January 1, 1995. On that date, tariffs were ended on 95 percent of goods traded between Brazil, Argentina, Paraguay, and Uruguay. All these nations adopted common external tariffs.
Asia-Pacific Economic Cooperation Group (APEC)	Formed in 1989. A loosely organized group of 15 developed and developing Pacific nations, including Japan, China, United States, Canada, and New Zealand. APEC is not a trading bloc and has no structure except for a secretariat.
Association of Southeast Asian Nations (ASEAN)	Formed in 1967. Composed of Indonesia, Malaysia, Vietnam, Philippines, Singapore, Thailand, and Brunei. ASEAN's purpose is to encourage economic growth of member nations by promoting trade and industry. There have been tariff reductions between members, and ASEAN's secretariat has represented nations vis-à-vis other regional groups such as the EU.
African Economic Community (AEC)	Founded in 1991 for the purpose of implementing a common market among its 51 members over a 20-year period.
Gulf Cooperation Council (GCC)	Founded in 1982. Composed of Saudi Arabia, Kuwait, Bahrain, Qatar, the United Arab Emirates, and Oman. The GCC's purposes are to standardize industrial subsidies, eliminate trade barriers among members, and negotiate with other regional groups to obtain favorable treatment for GCC goods, services, and investments.

52

Part One

*An Introduction to the Law
and the Legal Environment
of Business*

nently in the House and the Senate debates preceding approval of the WTO. United States farmers (and other groups), who had previously won decisions before GATT panels, saw these decisions vetoed by the European Union countries that subsidize the production of soybeans and other agricultural products; they enthusiastically supported the new WTO process. Environmentalists and consumer groups, on the other hand, feared that the WTO would overrule U.S. environmental laws and in other ways infringe on the sovereignty of the nation. To assuage these fears, the framers of the accord added a provision that allows any nation to withdraw upon six months' notice. Congress also attached a condition to its approval that calls for the setting up of a panel of U.S. federal judges to review the WTO panels' decisions.

IMPACT ON CORPORATE INVESTMENT DECISION MAKING The WTO pact makes it less risky for multinationals to source parts—that is, to have them built in cheap-labor countries and then brought back to the multinational's home country for use in making a product (e.g., brakes for automobiles). Industries that are expected to shift quickly to buying parts from all over the world for their products include computers, telecommunications, and other high-tech manufacturing. It is anticipated that with a freer flow of goods across borders, business will gain increased economies of scale by building parts-manufacturing plants at a location that serves a wide market area.

Because the tariff cuts are to be introduced gradually over a six-year period and are to be finalized only after ten years, the impact on trade will not be immediate. However, once the major nations ratify the WTO pact, companies will begin to make investment and employment decisions predicated on dramatic reductions in tariffs, subsidies, and other government-established deterrents to free trade.

EXHIBIT 3-2 *The European Union Member States and Applicants*

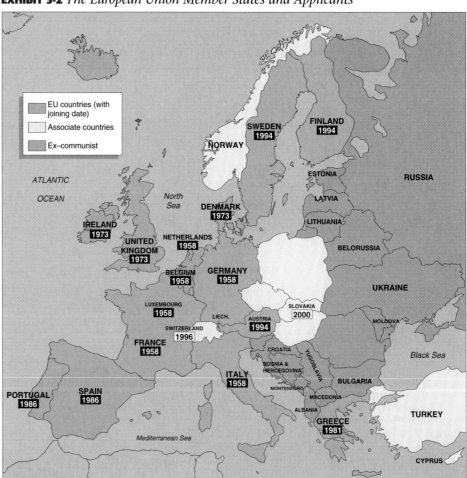

From The Economist, July 11, 1992. © 1992 The Economist Newspaper Group, Inc. Reprinted with permission. Further reproduction prohibited.

PURPOSE Today's 15-member European Union (EU) grew out of the European Economic Community (later called the European Community) established by six West European nations through the Rome Treaty of 1957. Its goals were, and are, to create a "customs union" that would do away with internal tariffs among the member states and to create a uniform external tariff to be applied to all nonmembers. The EU is thoroughly committed to achieving the free movement of goods, services, capital, and people across borders (Exhibit 3-2).

The EU's ambitious plan to create an immense West European "Common Market" of 380 million people and $4 trillion worth of goods was greatly strengthened by the 1986 signing of the Single European Act (SEA), which set a deadline for economic integration of December 31, 1992, and instituted new voting requirements to make passage of EU legislation easier. A treaty that was proposed at the Maastricht Summit in 1991 was ratified in 1993. It provided for (1) monetary union through the creation of a single currency for the entire EU, (2) political union, and (3) a "social dimension" through the establishment of uniform labor and social security regulations. The leaders of the then 12 nations agreed to the creation of a European Monetary Institute by 1994, a European Central Bank by 1998, and a uniform European currency unit (ECU) (Table 3-5) by 1999. Three new members (Finland, Austria, and Sweden) joined the EU in 1994, bringing the total to 15 nations. Former Eastern bloc nations and Turkey have applied for membership.

TABLE 3-5 *Key Elements of the Treaty of Maastricht*

AGREEMENT	GOALS AND STUMBLING BLOCKS
Monetary Union	• European Monetary Institute to be created on January 1, 1994, and to start operating on January 1, 1999, at the earliest.
	• A single currency issued any day after January 1, 1999, is the goal of 11 nations who presently meet three standards: (1) annual budget deficit cannot exceed the ceiling of 3 percent of gross domestic product; (2) the public debt limit for each country must not exceed 60 percent of gross domestic product; and (3) a country's inflation rate must be lower than 2.9 percent, based upon a complex formula set out in 1997.
	• Great Britain was allowed to stay out of the EC currency union until an unspecified date. It opposes monetary union for ideological reasons. It appears that all 15 members except Italy, Spain and Greece will meet the criteria for entry.
	• Denmark was also allowed to opt out pending a referendum on the issue, a constitutional requirement. The Danish government backs monetary union.
Political Union	• EC jurisdiction in areas including industrial affairs, health, education, trade, environment, energy, culture, tourism, and consumer and civil protection. Member states vote to implement decisions.
	• Increased political cooperation under a new name—European Union. Permanent diplomatic network of senior political officials created in the EC capitals.
	• Great Britain rejected EC-imposed labor legislation, forcing the removal of the so-called social chapter from the treaty. It will be implemented separately by the other 14 members, officials said.
Federalism	• EC leaders dropped reference to an EC "with a federal goal." Instead, the political union accord describes the community as "an ever-closer union in which political decisions have to be taken as near to the people as possible."
	• Great Britain rejected the "federalism" as the embodiment of what it feels would be an encroaching EC superstate.
Foreign Affairs	• EC states move toward a joint foreign policy, with most decisions requiring unanimity
	• Great Britain wanted the ability to opt out of any joint decision. How this provision will be interpreted by the various sides is yet to be seen.
Defense	• The Western European Union, a long-dormant group of nine EC states, will be revived to act as the EC's defense body but linked to the NATO alliance.
	• France and Germany had supported a greater military role for the union, but Great Britain, Italy, and others did not want to see NATO's influence diluted.
European Parliament	• The 518-member EC assembly gets a modest say in shaping some EC legislation. Its new powers fall short of what the assembly had sought (i.e., an equitable sharing of the right to make EC laws with the EC governments).
	• Great Britain and Denmark refused to grant the assembly broader powers.
Rich-Poor Gap	• Spain got a formal commitment from its richer partners for more money for itself, Ireland, Greece, and Portugal. The EC will review its bookkeeping methods and take more account of the relative wealth of EC members.

54

Part One

*An Introduction to the Law
and the Legal Environment
of Business*

STRUCTURE   The European Union consists of a Council of Ministers, a Commission, a Parliament (Assembly), and the European Court of Justice (with the addition of the Court of First Instance).

Council of Ministers.   The Council of Ministers is composed of one representative from each of the member nations. Its purposes are to coordinate the economic policies of member states and, more recently, to negotiate the economic policies of member states and to negotiate with nonmember states. In the past, the Council generally rubber-stamped legislation proposed by the Commission, but this docility is less assured as the Council begins to flex some of the authority granted it by the SEA and the Maastricht Treaty.

Commission.   The Commission consists of 20 members who represent the EU, not national concerns. It is responsible for the EU's relations with international organizations such as the United Nations and GATT (WTO). Member states are apportioned voting power in the Commission on the basis of their population and economic power. The Commission elects a president from among its members. Each Commission member supervises a functional area (e.g., agriculture or competition) that may be affected by several directorates. There are 22 directorates (Exhibit 3-3), which are actually run by "supranational" civil servants called director generals. In theory, the directorates serve the Commission, but, in fact, the director generals often heavily influence legislation as it moves through the Commission.

Parliament.   The Parliament (Assembly) is made up of representatives elected from each nation-state for a term set by the nation-state. The representatives come from most of the major European political factions (Socialists, Christian Democrats, Communists, Liberals, and so on), and each of the parties in the Parliament also exists in the member states. The Parliament elects a president to preside over its deliberations. The Parliament's general powers are to (1) serve as a consultative body to the Council, (2) refer matters affecting EU interests to the Commission or Council, (3) censure the Commission when neces-

---

EXHIBIT 3-3 *Directorates of the European Union*

- External Relations
- Economic and Financial Affairs
- Internal Market and Industrial Affairs
- Competition
- Employment, Social Affairs, and Education
- Agriculture
- Transportation
- Development
- Personnel and Administration
- Information, Communication, and Culture
- Environment, Nuclear Safety, and Civil Protection, Science, Research and Development
- Telecommunication, Information Industry, and Innovation
- Fisheries
- Financial Institutions and Company Law
- Regional Policy
- Energy
- Credit and Investment
- Budgets
- Financial Control
- Customs Union and Indirect Taxation
- Coordination of Structural Instruments
- Enterprise Policy, Distributive Trades, Tourism, and Cooperatives

sary, (4) assent to trade agreements with countries outside the EU, (5) amend the EU budget, and (6) participate with the Commission in the legislative procedure.

European Court of Justice. The European Court of Justice performs the functions of arbiter and final decision maker in conflicts between EU law and individual member states. The national courts of member states are obligated to follow EU law and Court of Justice decisions. The *Court of First Instance* was established in 1989 to reduce the workload of the Court of Justice. It has jurisdiction over appeals of the Commission's decisions on mergers and acquisitions. It also sets the penalties for price fixing when non-EU companies are involved.

IMPACT

Unity of Law. Agricultural, environmental, and labor legislation is being made uniform throughout the 15 member nations, with allowances and subsidies for the poorer members. The national courts of member states are now following decisions of the European Court of Justice.

Economic Integration. The SEA and the Maastricht Treaty have pushed the EU members to eliminate tariff and nontariff barriers among themselves. British and French differences over the creation of a single currency have forced the suspension of this goal.

Political Union. The political union envisioned by the Maastricht Treaty has been an elusive goal for the EU because member states (and their citizens) have proved more reluctant to make the necessary compromises on national sovereignty than the treaty's architects anticipated. Nonetheless, the EU is the only regional organization that has in place the sophisticated structure required to make political union a realistic possibility.

NORTH AMERICAN FREE TRADE AGREEMENT

PURPOSE The North American Free Trade Agreement, ratified in 1994, seeks to eliminate barriers to the flow of goods, services, and investments among Canada, the United States, and Mexico over a 15-year period (see pre-NAFTA comparison, Table 3-6). NAFTA envisions a gradual phasing out of these barriers, with the length of the phaseout varying from industry to industry. The ultimate goal is a totally free trade zone among the three member states, with eventual inclusion of the Central and Latin American countries. So far, the only country invited to join the founding members is Chile.

STRUCTURE NAFTA is administered by a three-member Trade Commission, which overseas a Secretariat and Arbitral Panels.

Trade Commission. Staffed by trade ministers from each of the three nations, the Trade Commission meets once a year and makes its decisions by consensus. It supervises the implementation of the treaty and resolves disputes over interpretation. The daily operations of NAFTA are conducted by ad hoc working groups appointed by the three governments.

Secretariat. The permanent Secretariat is composed of national sections (departments) representing each member country. Its purposes are to provide technical support for the Trade Commission and to put together arbitral panels to resolve disputes between members.

Arbitral Panels. The treaty has detailed arbitration provisions for settling disputes, particularly those involving dumping of goods (selling a good in a member country at a lower price than at home) and interpretations of the treaty. Though the arbitration proceedings are designed especially to resolve disputes between member nations, the treaty encourages private parties to use them as well. If they do, they must agree to abide by the arbitral panel's decision.

Each arbitral panel has five members, chosen from a roster of 30 legal experts from NAFTA and non-NAFTA countries. Within 90 days, the panel will give the disputant countries a confidential report. Over the next 14 days, the disputants may present their comments on the report to the panel. Within 30 days of the issuance of the initial report, the arbitral panel must present its final

56

Part One

*An Introduction to the Law
and the Legal Environment
of Business*

TABLE 3-6   *Comparison of pre-NAFTA Partners*

	CANADA	MEXICO	UNITED STATES
Population	27 million	88 million	253 million
Gross domestic product per person	$21,960	$3,220	$22,420
Hourly pay and benefits (automobile industry)	$19.20	$2.75	$21.90
Hourly pay and benefits (textiles)	$11.90	$1.95	$10.30
Total exports	$128 billion	$27 billion	$417 billion
Total imports	$120 billion	$38 billion	$490 billion
Exports to Canada		$2.1 billion	$85.1 billion
Exports to Mexico	$.390 billion		$33.3 billion
Exports to United States	$93.7 billion	$31.9 billion	

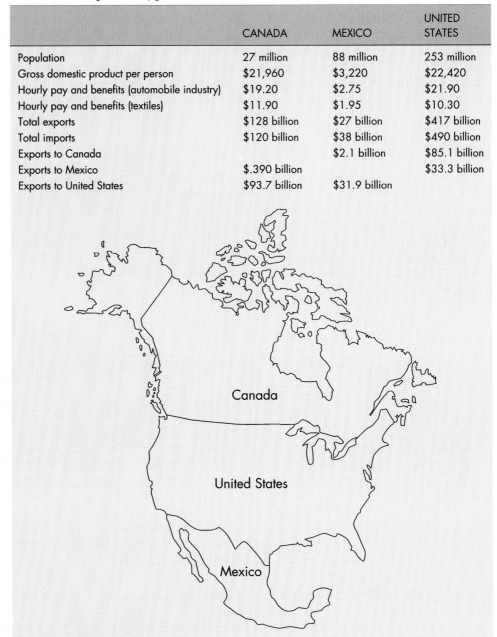

Source: International Monetary Fund (1991).

report to the parties and to the Trade Commission, which publishes it. The countries then have 30 days to resolve their dispute, or if the panel has found one party wrong, the other may legally retaliate.

IMPACT   NAFTA has not only brought together three North American neighbors of different historical and cultural background; it has also provided a model of economic integration for other countries in Central and Latin America (see Table 3-4).

It has had an impact on each country's exports and imports. It has served as an institution to arbitrate disputes. In 1995, the U.S. government filed a complaint on behalf of United Parcel Service (UPS), and one of the first arbitration panels was set up. UPS believed it was being hampered by NAFTA government regulations in Mexico, which limit the size of delivery trucks to be used in delivering packages. The arbitration panel ruled in favor of UPS.

INTERNATIONAL DISPUTE RESOLUTION

Many times, when private or public parties enter into an international business agreement, they incorporate means for resolving future disputes (e.g., arbitration clauses) into the agreement. Another form of protection for firms doing business internationally is the insurance some nation-states offer domestic companies to encourage them to export (e.g., United States Overseas Private Investment Corporation). Still, the two methods used most frequently to resolve irreconcilable differences between parties involved in international transactions are arbitration and litigation.

ARBITRATION

Arbitration is a dispute-resolution process whereby parties submit their disagreements to a private individual decision maker they agree on or to a panel of decision makers whose selection has been provided for in the contract the parties signed. *Arbitration clauses* in contracts involving international business transactions should meticulously stipulate what law will govern the arbitration, where and when the arbitration will take place, what language will be used, and how the expenses of arbitration will be shared. They also stipulate to a waiver of judicial (court) review by both parties to the dispute. All these matters should be carefully negotiated when the contract is being drafted.

arbitration A dispute-resolution method whereby the disputant parties submit their disagreement to a mutually agreed upon neutral decision maker or one provided for by statute.

Arbitration of disputes may also come about through *treaties*. For instance, the United Nations Convention on the Recognition of Foreign Arbitral Awards encourages use of arbitration agreements and awards. The World Bank's International Center for the Settlement of Investment Disputes (ICSID), created in 1965 by treaty (the Washington Convention), provides to disputants, arbitration rules as well as experienced arbitrators, and the International Chamber of Commerce offers a permanent arbitration tribunal. Finally, individual countries have arbitration associations that provide experienced arbitrators to parties desiring assistance in settling their disputes.

We present a detailed explanation of the arbitration process in chapter 6. Here we provide a case that demonstrates how important it is for businesses to understand the nature of international arbitration and the meaning of any documents they sign.

REPUBLIC OF NICARAGUA V. STANDARD FRUIT COMPANY AND STEAMSHIP COMPANY
UNITED STATES COURT OF APPEALS 937 F.2D 469 (9TH CIR. 1991)

Plaintiff-appellant Nicaragua sued Standard Fruit and its parent companies, the defendants. Standard Fruit, a wholly owned subsidiary of Standard Fruit Company (SFC) and Steamship Company (Steamship), was involved in the production and purchase of bananas in Nicaragua. Steamship purchased the bananas from SFC. In 1979, a Nicaraguan rebel group known as the Sandinistas overthrew the government of Nicaragua and attempted to negotiate with Standard Fruit for more control over the banana industry in their country. When the negotiations proved unsuccessful, the Sandinistas took over the industry by decree and nullified all leases of plantations and purchase contracts. Standard Fruit stopped doing business in Nicaragua. After three days of negotiations, Steamship signed a Memorandum, termed "an agreement in principal" that provided for the renegotiation of existing contracts and included an arbitration clause that stated:

> *Any and all disputes arising under the arrangements contemplated hereunder . . . will be referred to mutually agreed mechanisms or procedures of international arbitration, such as the rules of the London Arbitration Association.*

The implementing contracts provided for in the Memorandum were never renegotiated, but Standard Fruit resumed business in Nicaragua for two years and then left the country for good in 1982. Nicaragua then sued in a United States District Court, requesting the court to compel Steamship to arbitrate Nicaragua's breach-of-contract suit. Steamship argued that the arbitration clause in the Memorandum was too vague and broad to be enforceable and that it merely referred to the creation of a formal clause that would be included in the renegotiated contracts. The district court agreed and ruled in favor of the defendants, granting their request for a summary judgment. Nicaragua appealed.

We hold that although it was the court's responsibility to determine the threshold question of arbitrability, the district court improperly looked to the validity of the contract as a whole and erroneously determined that the parties had not agreed to arbitrate this dispute. Instead, it should have considered only the validity and scope of the arbitration clause itself. In addition, the district court ignored strong evidence in the record that both parties intended to be bound by the arbitration clause. As all doubts over the scope of an arbitration clause must be resolved in favor of arbitration, and in light of the strong federal policy favoring arbitration in international commercial disputes, Nicaragua's motion to compel arbitration should have been granted. Whether the Memorandum was binding, whether it covered banana purchases, and whether Standard Fruit Company was bound by it are all questions properly left to the arbitrators. Finally, genuine disputes of fact exist as to the intent of the parties and the validity and scope of the Memorandum.

Reversed in favor of Plaintiff-Appellant, Nicaragua.

LITIGATION

litigation A dispute-resolution process that involves going through the judicial system; a lawsuit.

When contracts do not contain arbitration clauses and there is no other alternative (such as mediation or conciliation) available, **litigation** may be the only way to resolve a dispute between parties. In some private international business contracts, a *choice-of-forum* clause is included so that the parties know which family of law is to be applied in case of a dispute and what nation's courts will be used. When negotiating contracts in the international arena, managers should make sure that choice-of-forum clauses are specific on both these questions, for what family of law governs and which nation's courts are used can make a major difference in the outcome. Because there is no single international court or legal system capable of resolving all commercial disputes between private parties, a choice-of-forum clause should be negotiated in all agreements involving major transactions. London's Commercial Court, established in 1895, is the most popular neutral forum for resolving commercial litigation owing to its 100 years of experience.

Most of the international and regional organizations discussed in this chapter emphatically encourage the arbitration of private contractual disputes because the arbitration process is a quicker and less public means of resolving disputes than litigation. In certain areas of the world (particularly the Far East), companies and governments seek to avoid litigation.

SUMMARY

The political, economic, cultural, and legal dimensions of the international environment of business need to be considered by managers undertaking international business ventures, although the emphasis in this book is on legal and ethical issues.

The major families of law are common law, which relies primarily on case law and precedent; civil law, which relies primarily on codes and statutory law; Islamic law, which relies on the *Shari'a*, a religious code of rules; socialist law, which is based on Marxism-Leninism and does not recognize private property; and Hindu law, which relies primarily on the *Sastras*, a religious code.

International law is divided into public international law, governing the relationships between nation-states, and private international law, governing the relationships between private parties involved in international transactions.

The major methods of engaging in international business are trade, international licensing and franchising, and foreign direct investment. The principal risks of engaging in international business are expropriation, the sovereign immunity doctrine and the act-of-state doctrine, export and import controls, and currency controls and fluctuations (particularly in developing nations).

World and regional integrative organizations, especially the World Trade Organization, the European Union, and NAFTA are making a strong impact on international business. Arbitration and litigation are the major methods of international dispute resolution.

REVIEW QUESTIONS

3-1. Contrast the common law family with the socialist law family.

3-2. Which of the methods of engaging in international business discussed in this chapter is least risky for a foreign multinational company? Explain.

3-3. Define the following.

    a. expropriation

    b. doctrine of sovereign immunity

    c. act-of-state doctrine

    d. arbitration clause

    e. choice-of-forum clause

3-4. Explain how currency fluctuations affect companies doing international business.

3-5. Why was the GATT Pact, creating the World Trade Organization, so important to doing international business? Explain.

3-6. Why is arbitration preferred to litigation as a means of resolving international business disputes? Explain.

REVIEW PROBLEMS

3-7. Royal Bed and Spring Co., a U.S. distributor of furniture products, entered into an exclusive distributorship agreement with a Brazilian manufacturer of furniture products. Under the terms of the contract, Royal Bed was to distribute in Puerto Rico the furniture products manufactured by Famossul in Brazil. The contract contained forum-selection and choice-of-law clauses, which designated the juridical district of Curitiba, State of Parana, Brazil, as the judicial forum and the Brazilian Civil Code as the law to be applied in the event of any dispute. Famossul terminated the exclusive distributorship and suspended the shipment of goods without just cause. Puerto Rican law refuses to enforce forum-selection clauses providing for foreign venues as a matter of public policy. In what jurisdiction should Royal Bed bring suit? Explain.

3-8. A, a U.S. company, entered into a contract with C, a Swiss subsidiary of General Motors, to sell Chevrolet automobiles in Aruba. An arbitration clause in the parties' agreement provided that all disputes would be settled by arbitration in accordance with Aruban law. Aruba follows Dutch civil laws. A argues that only U.S. law can apply because the contact was made in the United States. Is A correct? Explain.

3-9. Zapata entered into a contract with a German corporation to use one of Zapata's oil-drilling rigs off the coasts of Italy. The contract stated: "Any dispute arising must be treated before the London Court of Justice." A severe storm damaged the oil rig as it was being towed through the Gulf of Mexico. Zapata filed suit in federal district court. Does the U.S. court have jurisdiction to decide the dispute? What is the purpose behind a choice-of-forum clause, and should the clause be enforced?

3-10. The members of the International Association of Machinists (IAM) were disturbed by the high price of oil and petroleum-derived products in the United States. They believed that the actions of the Organization of Petroleum Exporting Countries (OPEC) were the cause of the high prices. Therefore, the IAM sued OPEC's member countries in a federal district court, alleging that these countries' price-setting activities violated U.S. antitrust law. OPEC argued the act-of-state doctrine as a defense. Who do you think won? Explain why.

3-11. Dr. Will Pirkey, a U.S. otolaryngologist, signed an employment contract in which he agreed to work for two years at the King Faisal Hospital in Saudi Arabia. Before his departure, Pirkey received his employment contract,

60

Part One

*An Introduction to the Law
and the Legal Environment
of Business*

which contained a clause providing that his agreement with the hospital would be construed in accordance with Saudi Arabian law. Because of the assassination of King Faisal and for other reasons, Pirkey did not go to Saudi Arabia as agreed and is now contesting the choice-of-law provision of his employment contract as unconscionable. He asks that his home state's laws (New York) should apply. Who will win this case? Explain why.

3-12. U.S. Company owned a subsidiary in France that had a contract to deliver compressors for use in the Soviet natural gas pipeline then under construction. The U.S. government banned the export of goods to the Soviet Union by U.S. companies or U.S.-controlled foreign companies, and U.S. Company complied with the ban by ordering its French subsidiary to stop delivery of the compressors. The French government, however, ordered delivery. U.S. Company delivered the compressors. The U.S. government thereupon instituted a criminal action against U.S. Company. What is U.S. Company's defense? Explain.

CASE PROBLEMS

3-13. Mitsubishi entered into a joint venture with Chrysler to distribute automobiles in Puerto Rico. When they entered into the agreement they specified that "all disputes shall be finally settled by arbitration in Japan in accordance with the rules and regulations of the Japan Commercial Arbitration Association." Mitsubishi brought an action in the U.S. District Court to compel arbitration when a dispute arose regarding the contract. Can such a contract clause be enforced? On what basis will a court compel arbitration on such a claim? *Mitsubishi Motors v. Soler Chrysler-Plymouth*, 105 S. Ct. 3346 (1985)

3-14. Two Liberian corporations with significant U.S. connections executed a contract in New York City that chartered a tanker, the *Hercules*, belonging to the Amerada Hess Corporation. After leaving oil at the Hess refinery in the Virgin Islands, the *Hercules* began a return voyage to Valdez, Alaska. The United States notified both Argentina and Britain that the *Hercules* was outside the war zone and 500 miles from both Argentina and the Falkland Islands when it was bombed twice by Argentine aircraft. This bombing occurred despite messages from the ship's captain and the hoisting of a white flag. The extensively damaged ship contained an undetonated bomb and was scuttled. The Liberian corporations first tried to sue in Argentina but could find no one to take their case. They then filed suit in U.S. district court. The case went to the Supreme Court, where in 1989 the Court concluded that there was no basis for jurisdiction over Argentina. What other options disclosed in this chapter are available to the Liberian corporations? *Argentine Republic v. Amerada Hess Shipping Corp.*, 109 S. Ct. 683 (1989)

3-15. The plaintiff, a Swiss corporation, entered into contracts to purchase chicken from the defendant, B.N.S. International Sales Corporation, a New York corporation. The English-language contracts called for the delivery of "chicken" of various weights. When the birds were shipped to Switzerland, the two-pound sizes were not young broiling chickens as the plaintiff had expected but mature stewing chickens or fowl. The plaintiff protested, claiming that in German the term *chicken* referred to young broiling chicken. The question for the court was what kind of chicken did the plaintiff order. Was it "broiling chicken," as the plaintiff argued, or any chicken weighing 2 pounds, as the defendant argued? See *Frigaliment Importing C., Ltd. v. B.N.S. International Sales Corp.*, 190 F. Supp. 116 (S.D.N.Y. 1960). What could the parties have done to avoid this misunderstanding? What alternative besides going to court could have been used by the parties to settle this dispute? Explain.

On the Internet

http://lawlib.wvcc.edu/washlaw/forint/forintmain.html   This page
provides links to primary foreign and international legal resources, research
aids, and sites useful for international business.

http://www.noord.bart.n1/~bethleham/law.htm   This page provides
A to Z information about international law.

http://www.law.osaka-u.ac.ip/legal-info/worldlist/world/st.htm
A resource list for more than 70 countries can be found at this site.

http://www.icj-cij.org/   This page contains information about and rulings
of the International Court of Justice.

4

CONSTITUTIONAL PRINCIPLES

- **THE CONSTITUTION**

- **FEDERALISM**

- **SEPARATION OF POWERS**

- **THE IMPACT OF THE COMMERCE CLAUSE ON BUSINESS**

- **THE IMPACT OF THE AMENDMENTS ON BUSINESS**

Fiercely independent, highly individualistic, and very proud of their country would be a good characterization of Americans. Many say there is no place they would rather live than the United States. Much of their pride stems from a belief that we have a strong Constitution, which secures for all individuals their most fundamental rights. Most people, however, are not aware of precisely what their constitutional rights are or of how to go about enforcing those rights. This chapter provides the future business manager with basic knowledge of the constitutional framework of our country as well as an overview of how some of the constitutional provisions have a significant impact on the legal environment of business.

THE CONSTITUTION

The Constitution provides the legal framework for our nation. The articles of the Constitution set out the basic structure of our government and the respective roles of the state and federal governments. The Amendments to the Constitution, especially the first ten, were primarily designed to establish and protect individual rights.

Critical Thinking about the Law

THE CONSTITUTION SECURES NUMEROUS RIGHTS FOR U.S. citizens. If we did not have these rights, our lives would be very different. Furthermore, businesses would be forced to alter their practices because they would not enjoy the various constitutional protections. As you will soon learn, various components of the Constitution, such as the Commerce Clause and the Bill of Rights, offer guidance and protection for businesses. The following questions will help sharpen your critical thinking about the protection and guidance for businesses offered by the Constitution.

1. One of the basic elements in the Constitution is the separation of powers in the government. What ethical norm would guide the framers' thinking in creating a system with a separation of powers and a system of checks and balances?

   CLUE   Consider what might happen if one branch of government became too strong.

2. If the framers of the Constitution wanted to offer the protection of unrestricted speech for citizens and businesses, what ethical norm would they view as most important?

   CLUE   Return to the list of ethical norms in chapter 1. Which ethical norm might the framers view as least important in protecting unrestricted speech?

3. Why should you, as a future business manager, be knowledgeable about the basic protections offered by the Constitution?

   CLUE   If you were ignorant of the constitutional protections, how might your business suffer?

FEDERALISM

Underlying the system of government established by the Constitution is the principle of **federalism**, which means that the authority to govern is divided between two sovereigns, or supreme lawmakers. In the United States, these two sovereigns are the state and federal governments. Federalism allocates the power to control local matters to local governments. This allocation is embodied in the U.S. Constitution. Under the Constitution, all powers that are neither given exclusively to the federal government nor taken from the states are reserved to the states. The federal government has only those powers granted to it in the Constitution. Therefore, whenever federal legislation that affects business is passed, the question of the source of authority for that regulation always arises. The Commerce Clause is the predominant source of authority for the federal regulation of business, as we will see later.

federalism A system of government in which power is divided between a central authority and constituent political units.

EXHIBIT 4-1 *Application of the Supremacy Clause to State Regulation*

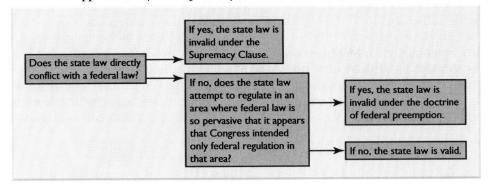

In some areas, the state and federal governments have *concurrent* authority; that is, both governments have the power to regulate the matter in question. This situation arises when authority to regulate in an area has been expressly given to the federal government by the Constitution. In such cases, a state may regulate in the area as long as its regulation does not conflict with any federal regulation of the same subject matter. A conflict arises when a regulated party cannot comply with both the state and the federal law at the same time. When the state law is more restrictive, such that compliance with the state law is automatically compliance with the federal law, the state law will usually be valid. For example, as discussed in chapter 20, in many areas of environmental regulation, states may impose much more stringent pollution-control standards than those imposed by federal law.

SUPREMACY CLAUSE

Supremacy Clause Provides that the U.S. Constitution and all laws and treaties of the United States constitute the supreme law of the land; found in Article V.

The outcome of conflicts between state and federal laws is dictated by the **Supremacy Clause**. This clause, found in Article V of the Constitution, provides that the Constitution, laws, and treaties of the United States constitute the supreme law of the land, "any Thing in the Constitution or Laws of any State to the Contrary notwithstanding." This principle is known as the principle of **federal supremacy**: Any state or local law that directly conflicts with the federal Constitution, laws, or treaties is void. Federal laws include rules promulgated by federal administrative agencies. Exhibit 4-1 illustrates the application of the Supremacy Clause to state regulation.

federal supremacy Principle that states that any state or local law that directly conflicts with the federal Constitution, laws, or treaties is void.

FEDERAL PREEMPTION

federal preemption In an area in which federal regulation is pervasive, state legislation cannot stand.

The Supremacy Clause is also the basis for the doctrine of **federal preemption**. This doctrine is used to strike down a state law that, although it does not directly conflict with a federal law, attempts to regulate an area in which federal legislation is so pervasive that it is evident that the U.S. Congress wanted only federal regulation in that general area. It is often said in these cases that federal law "preempts the field." Cases of federal preemption are especially likely to arise in matters pertaining to interstate commerce, in which a local regulation imposes a substantial burden on the flow of interstate commerce through a particular state. This situation is discussed in some detail in the section on the Commerce Clause.

SEPARATION OF POWERS

The U.S. Constitution, in its first three articles, establishes three independent branches of the federal government, each with its own predominant and independent power. These three are the legislative, executive, and judicial branches. Each branch was made independent of the others and was given a separate sphere of power to prevent any one source from obtaining too much power and consequently dominating the government.

separation of powers Constitutional doctrine whereby the legislative branch enacts laws and appropriates funds, the executive branch sees that the laws are faithfully executed, and the judicial branch interprets the laws.

The doctrine of **separation of powers** calls for Congress, the legislative branch, to enact legislation and appropriate funds. The president is comman-

EXHIBIT 4-2 *System of Checks and Balances*

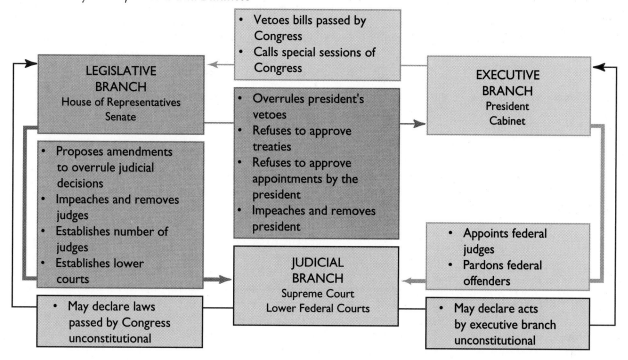

der-in-chief of the armed forces and is also charged with ensuring that the laws are faithfully executed. The judicial branch is charged with interpreting the laws in the course of applying them to particular disputes. No member of one branch owes his or her tenure in that position to a member of any other branch; no branch can encroach on the power of another. This system is often referred to as being a system of checks and balances; that is, the powers given to each branch operate to keep the other branches from being able to seize enough power to dominate the government. Exhibit 4-2 provides a portrait of this system.

Despite this delicate system of checks and balances, there have been numerous occasions when a question arose as to whether one branch was attempting to encroach on the domain of another. This situation most recently arose in an unusual context: a sexual harassment charge against President Bill Clinton.

WILLIAM JEFFERSON CLINTON V. PAULA CORBIN JONES
SUPREME COURT OF THE UNITED STATES 117 S.CT. 1636 (1997)

Plaintiff Paula Jones filed a civil action against defendant President Bill Clinton, alleging that he made "abhorrent" sexual advances. She sought $75,000 in actual damages and $100,000 in punitive damages.

Defendant Clinton sought to dismiss the claim on the grounds of presidential immunity, or, alternatively, to delay the proceedings until his term of office had expired.

The district court denied the motion to dismiss and ordered discovery to proceed, but it also ordered that the trial be stayed until the end of the president's term. The Court of Appeals affirmed the denial of the motion to dismiss and reversed the stay of the trial. President Clinton appealed to the U.S. Supreme Court.

JUSTICE STEVENS

Petitioner's principal submission—that "in all but the most exceptional cases," the Constitution affords the President temporary immunity from civil damages litigation arising out of events that occurred before he took office—cannot be sustained on the basis of precedent.

Only three sitting presidents have been defendants in civil litigation involving their actions prior to taking office. Complaints against Theodore Roosevelt and Harry Truman had been dismissed before they took office; the dismissals were affirmed after their respective inaugurations. Two companion cases arising out of an automobile accident were filed against John F. Kennedy in 1960 during the Presidential campaign. After taking office, he unsuccessfully argued that his status as Commander in Chief gave him a right to a stay. The motion for a stay was denied by the District Court, and the matter was settled out of court. Thus, none of those cases sheds any light on the constitutional issue before us.

The principal rationale for affording certain public servants immunity from suits for money damages arising out of their official acts is inapplicable to unofficial conduct. In cases involving prosecutors, legislators, and judges we have repeatedly explained that the immunity serves the public interest in enabling such officials to perform their designated functions effectively without fear that a particular decision may give rise to personal liability.

That rationale provided the principal basis for our holding that a former president of the United States was "entitled to absolute immunity from damages liability predicated on his official acts." Our central concern was to avoid rendering the President "unduly cautious in the discharge of this official duties."

This reasoning provides no support for an immunity for *unofficial* conduct. . . . "[T]he sphere of protected action must be related closely to the immunity's justifying purposes." But we have never suggested that the President, or any other official, has an immunity that extends beyond the scope of any action taken in an official capacity.

Moreover, when defining the scope of an immunity for acts clearly taken *within* an official capacity, we have applied a functional approach. "Frequently our decisions have held that an official's absolute immunity should extend only to acts in performance of particular functions of his office."

Petitioner's strongest argument supporting his immunity claim is based on the text and structure of the Constitution. The President argues for a postponement of the judicial proceedings that will determine whether he violated any law. His argument is grounded in the character of the office that was created by Article II of the Constitution, and relies on separation-of-powers principles.

As a starting premise, petitioner contends that he occupies a unique office with powers and responsibilities so vast and important that the public interest demands that he devote his undivided time and attention to his public duties. He submits that—given the nature of the office—the doctrine of separation of powers places limits on the authority of the Federal Judiciary to interfere with the Executive Branch that would be transgressed by allowing this action to proceed.

We have no dispute with the initial premise of the argument. We have long recognized the "unique position in the constitutional scheme" that this office occupies.

It does not follow, however, that separation of powers principles would be violated by allowing this action to proceed. The doctrine of separation of powers is concerned with the allocation of official power among the three co-equal branches of our Government. The Framers

"built into the tripartite Federal Government . . . a self-executing safeguard against the encroachment or aggrandizement of one branch at the expense of the other." Thus, for example, the Congress may not exercise the judicial power to revise final judgments, or the executive power to manage an airport.

. . . [I]n this case there is no suggestion that the Federal Judiciary is being asked to perform any function that might in some way be described as "executive." Respondent is merely asking the courts to exercise their core Article III jurisdiction to decide cases and controversies. Whatever the outcome of this case, there is no possibility that the decision will curtail the scope of the official powers of the Executive Branch. The litigation of questions that relate entirely to the unofficial conduct of the individual who happens to be the President poses no perceptible risk of misallocation of either judicial power or executive power.

Rather than arguing that the decision of the case will produce either an aggrandizement of judicial power or a narrowing of executive power, petitioner contends that—as a by-product of an otherwise traditional exercise of judicial power—burdens will be placed on the President that will hamper the performance of his official duties. We have recognized that "[e]ven when a branch does not arrogate power to itself . . . the separation-of-powers doctrine requires that a branch not impair another in the performance of its constitutional duties." As a factual matter, petitioner contends that this particular case—as well as the potential additional litigation that an affirmance of the Court of Appeals judgment might spawn—may impose an unacceptable burden on the President's time and energy, and thereby impair the effective performance of his office.

Petitioner's predictive judgment finds little support in either history or the relatively narrow compass of the issues raised in this particular case. If the past is any indicator, it seems unlikely that a deluge of such litigation will ever engulf the presidency. As for the case at hand, if properly managed by the District Court, it appears to us highly unlikely to occupy any substantial amount of petitioner's time.

Of greater significance, petitioner errs by presuming that interactions between the Judicial Branch and the Executive, even quite burdensome interactions, necessarily rise to the level of constitutionally forbidden impairment of the Executive's ability to perform its constitutionally mandated functions. Separation of powers does not mean that the branches "ought to have no *partial agency* in, or no *control* over the acts of each other." The fact that a federal court's exercise of its traditional Article III jurisdiction may significantly burden the time and attention of the Chief Executive is not sufficient to establish a violation of the Constitution. Two long-settled propositions . . . support that conclusion.

First, we have long held that when the President takes official action, the Court has the authority to determine whether he has acted within the law. Perhaps the most dramatic example of such a case is our holding that President Truman exceeded his constitutional authority when he issued an order directing the Secretary of Commerce to take possession of and operate most of the Nation's steel mills, in order to avert a national catastrophe. *Youngstown Sheet & Tube Co. v. Sawyer*, 343 U.S. 579 (1952).

Second, it is also settled that the President is subject to judicial process in appropriate circumstances. We . . . held that President Nixon was obligated to comply with a subpoena commanding him to produce certain tape recordings of his conversations with his aides. As we explained, "neither the doctrine of separation of powers, nor the need for confidentiality of high-level communications, without more, can sustain an absolute, unqualified presidential privilege of immunity from judicial process under all circumstances."

Sitting Presidents have responded to court orders to provide testimony and other information with sufficient frequency that such interactions between the Judicial and Executive Branches can scarcely be thought a novelty. President Ford complied with an order to give a deposition in a criminal trial, and President Clinton has twice given videotaped testimony in criminal proceedings.

In sum, "[i]t is settled law that the separation-of-powers doctrine does not bar every exercise of jurisdiction over the President of the United States." If the Judiciary may severely burden the Executive Branch by reviewing the legality of the president's official conduct, and if it may direct appropriate process to the president himself, it must follow that the federal courts have power to determine the legality of his unofficial conduct. The burden on the president's time and energy that is a mere by-product of such review surely cannot be considered as onerous as the direct burden imposed by judicial review and the occasional invalidation of his official actions. We therefore hold that the doctrine of separation of powers does not require federal courts to stay all private actions against the President until he leaves office.

In all events, the question whether a specific case should receive exceptional treatment is more appropriately the subject of the exercise of judicial discretion than an interpretation of the Constitution.

Reversed in part. *Affirmed* in part
in favor of Respondent, Jones.

COMMENT: After this case was sent back for trial on the merits, the case was ultimately dismissed on April 1, 1998, on a motion for summary judgment on grounds that the plaintiffs' allegations, even if true, failed to state a claim of criminal sexual assault or sexual harassment. It is ironic that despite the high courts' claim that the case would be "highly unlikely to occupy any substantial amount of the petitioners time," matters arising out of this case managed to not only occupy so much of the President's time and become such a focus of a media frenzy that many people were calling for the media to reduce coverage of the issues so the President could do his job.[1]

Cases like *Clinton v. Jones* are not common. The reason is not that each branch generally operates carefully within its own sphere of power. Rather, the explanation lies in the fact that because it is difficult to determine where one branch's authority ends and another's begins, each branch rarely challenges the power of its competing branches. The powers of each branch were established so that, although the branches are separate, each branch still influences the actions of the others. And, although the branches are independent and have their own separate functions, there is still a substantial amount of interaction among the three.

THE IMPACT OF THE COMMERCE CLAUSE ON BUSINESS

THE COMMERCE CLAUSE AS A SOURCE OF FEDERAL AUTHORITY

The primary powers of Congress are listed in Article I of the Constitution. It is important to remember that Congress has only *limited* legislative power. Congress possesses only that legislative power granted to it by the Constitution. Thus, all acts of Congress not specifically authorized by the Constitution or necessary to accomplish an authorized end are invalid.

The **Commerce Clause** provides the basis for most of the federal regulation of business today. This clause empowers the legislature to "regulate Commerce with foreign Nations, and among the several States, and with the Indian Tribes." Early in our history, the Supreme Court was committed to a laissez-faire ideology, an ideology that was grounded in individualism. A narrow interpretation of the Commerce Clause means that only a limited amount of trade or exchange can be regulated by Congress.

Under the Court's initial narrow interpretation, the Commerce Clause was interpreted to apply to only the transportation of goods. Manufacturing of

Commerce Clause Empowers Congress to regulate commerce with foreign nations, with Indian tribes, and among the states; found in Article I.

---

[1]Paula Corbin Jones v. William Jefferson Clinton and Danny Ferguson, 1998 WL 148370 (E.D. Ark.)

68

Part One

*An Introduction to the Law
and the Legal Environment
of Business*

goods, even of goods that were going to be sold in another state, did not have a direct effect on interstate commerce and thus was not subject to federal regulation. Businesses conducted solely in one state were similarly excluded from the authority of Congress. Under this restrictive interpretation, numerous federal regulations, such as laws attempting to regulate the use of child labor in manufacturing plants,[2] were struck down.

In the early 1930s, the Supreme Court's interpretation of the Commerce Clause was broadened to allow a greater scope for federal regulations. In *NLRB v. Jones & Laughlin Steel Corp.,*[3] for example, the Court said that "[a]lthough activities may be intrastate in character when separately considered, if they have such a close and substantial relationship to interstate commerce that their control is essential or appropriate to protect that commerce from burdens or obstructions, Congress cannot be denied the power to exercise that control." The following case illustrates just how broad the reach of Congress is under the current interpretation of the Commerce Clause.

JAMES JEFFERSON MCLAIN ET AL. V. REAL ESTATE BOARD OF NEW ORLEANS, INC.
UNITED STATES SUPREME COURT 444 U.S. 232 (1980)

A federal antitrust law, the Sherman Act, prohibits businesspersons from entering into price-fixing agreements that would have a harmful effect on interstate commerce. The plaintiffs in this case alleged that the defendant real estate brokers engaged in a conspiracy to control, fix, and uniformly raise prices for the purchase and sale of realty in Greater New Orleans through the use of a number of noncompetitive practices such as using fixed commission rates, splitting fees, and suppressing of market information in violation of the Sherman Act. The complaint alleged that, because of the defendant's actions, residential property prices were artificially raised, thereby injuring plaintiffs when they employed defendants in real estate transactions. The plaintiffs sought damages and injunctive relief (a court order requiring the defendants to stop engaging in the allegedly unlawful acts).

The defendants filed a motion to dismiss the case on the grounds that the transactions were purely intrastate and therefore federal law could not regulate the activities. The District Court agreed and dismissed the case, finding that brokerage activities "neither occur in nor substantially affect interstate commerce." The Court of Appeals affirmed the dismissal. Plaintiffs appealed to the U.S. Supreme Court.

CHIEF JUSTICE BURGER

The broad authority of Congress under the Commerce Clause has, of course, long been interpreted to extend beyond activities actually in interstate commerce to reach other activities, while wholly local in nature, nevertheless substantially affecting interstate commerce.

The conceptual distinction between activities "in" interstate commerce and those which "affect" interstate commerce has been preserved in the cases. . . . It can no longer be doubted, however, that the jurisdictional requirement of the Sherman Act may be satisfied by either the "in commerce" or the "effect on commerce" theory.

[J]urisdiction may not be invoked under that statute unless the relevant aspect of interstate commerce is identified; it is not sufficient to merely rely on identification of a relevant local activity and to presume an interrelationship with some unspecified aspect of interstate commerce. [A] plaintiff must allege . . . either that the defendants' activity is itself in interstate commerce or, if it is local in nature, that it has an effect on some other appreciable activity demonstrably in interstate commerce. [I]t would be sufficient for petitioners to demonstrate a substantial effect on interstate commerce generated by respondents' brokerage activity.

[In this case] [i]t is clear that an appreciable amount of commerce is involved in the financing of residential property . . . and in the insuring of titles to such property. [L]ending institutions in the area committed hundreds of millions of dollars to residential financing. Funds were raised from out-of-state investors and from interbank loans obtained from interstate financial institutions. Multistate lending institutions took mortgages insured under federal programs which entailed interstate transfers of premiums and settlements. Before making a mortgage loan . . . lending institutions usually . . . required title insurance, which was furnished by interstate corporations.

Brokerage activities necessarily affect both the frequency and the terms of residential sales transactions. Ultimately,

---

[2]Hammer v. Dagenhart, 247 U.S. 251 (1918).
[3]301 U.S. 1 (1937).

whatever stimulates or retards the volume of residential sales, or has an impact on the purchase price, affects the demand for financing and title insurance, those two commercial activities that on this record are shown to have occurred in interstate commerce. Where, as here, the services of respondent real estate brokers are often employed in transactions in the relevant market . . . respondents' activities have a not insubstantial effect on interstate commerce.

Reversed in favor of Plaintiffs, McLain et al.

As the foregoing case illustrates, any activity, even if purely intrastate, can be regulated by the federal government if it substantially affects interstate commerce. The effect may be direct or indirect, as the U.S. Supreme Court demonstrated in the 1942 case of *Wickard v. Filburn*,[4] when they upheld federal regulation of the production of wheat on a farm in Ohio that produced only 239 bushels of wheat solely for consumption on the farm. The Court's rationale was that even though one wheat farmer's activities might not matter, the combination of a lot of small farmers' activities could have a substantial impact on the national wheat market. This broad interpretation of the Commerce Clause has made possible much of the legislation covered in other sections of this book.

Most economic regulation by the federal government is now presumed to be constitutional. In determining whether Congress has the authority to enact legislation under the Commerce Clause, the Supreme Court asks whether there is any rational basis for Congress to find that the activity to be regulated affects interstate commerce. If there is, the Court asks whether there is any reasonable connection between the ends asserted and the regulatory scheme selected to achieve those ends. If there is, the legislation stands. Exhibit 4-3 illustrates some additional cases in which purely local activities were found to affect interstate commerce sufficiently to justify federal regulation.

THE COMMERCE CLAUSE AS A RESTRICTION ON STATE AUTHORITY

Because the Commerce Clause grants authority to regulate commerce to the federal government, a conflict arises over the extent to which granting such authority to the federal government restricts the states' authority to regulate commerce. The courts have attempted to resolve the conflict over the impact of the Commerce Clause on state regulation by distinguishing between regulations of commerce and regulations under the state police power. **Police power** means the residual powers retained by the state to enact legislation to safeguard the health and welfare of its citizenry. When the courts perceived state laws to be attempts to regulate interstate commerce, these laws would be struck down. But when the courts found state laws to be based on the exercise of the state police power, the laws were upheld.

police power The state's retained authority to pass laws to protect the health, safety, and welfare of the community.

EXHIBIT 4-3 *Intrastate Activities That Affected Interstate Commerce*

CASE	FEDERAL STATUTE	ACTIVITY AND RATIONALE FOR DECISION
United States v. Lake, 985 F.2d 265 (1995)	Federal Mine Safety and Health Act	Defendant operated a mine whose coal was sold locally, and he purchased mining supplies from local dealers and consumed commercially produced electricity. "Even if coal production at the mine was small and sales of coal were entirely local . . . such small-scale efforts, when combined with others, could influence interstate coal pricing and demand."
International House of Pancakes v. Theodore Pinnock, 844 F. Supp. 574 (1993)	Americans with Disabilities Act	Although defendant's restaurant was located in a single state, it was located within two miles of two interstate highways and there were three hotels within walking distance. The restaurant was also a franchise of a large, international, publicly held corporation that had 547 franchises in 35 states, Japan, and Canada. These facts were sufficient evidence that the restaurant's activities affected interstate commerce.
Perez, Petitioner v. United States, 402 U.S. 146 (1971)	Consumer Credit Protection Act	Loansharking activities, whereby criminals use extortion to collect loan payments, is a local activity, "but in its national setting it is one way that organized interstate crime holds its guns to the heads of the poor . . . and syphons funds from numerous locations to finance its national operations" and thereby affects interstate commerce.

[4]317 U.S. 111 (1942).

70

Part One
_____

*An Introduction to the Law
and the Legal Environment
of Business*

Since the mid-1930s, whenever states have enacted legislation that affects interstate commerce, the courts have applied a two-pronged test. First, they ask: Is the regulation rationally related to a legitimate state end? If it is, then they ask: Is the regulatory burden imposed on interstate commerce outweighed by the state interest in enforcing the legislation? If it is, the state's regulation is upheld.

OREGON WASTE SYSTEMS, INC. V. DEPARTMENT OF ENVIRONMENTAL QUALITY OF THE STATE OF OREGON
SUPREME COURT OF THE UNITED STATES U.S.L.W. 511 U.S. 93 (1994)

The state of Oregon passed legislation imposing an $0.85 per ton fee on in-state disposal of solid wastes generated within Oregon and a $2.25 per ton disposal charge on wastes generated outside the state. Plaintiffs brought an action alleging that the surcharge violated the Commerce Clause by favoring in-state economic interests over those out-of-state parties who would have to pay the higher surcharge. The State Court of Appeals upheld the Oregon legislation, and the Oregon Supreme Court affirmed. The case was appealed to the U.S. Supreme Court.

JUSTICE THOMAS

Though phrased as a grant of regulatory power to Congress, the Commerce Clause has long been understood to have a "negative" aspect that denies the States the power unjustifiably to discriminate against or burden the interstate flow of articles of commerce. . . .

[W]e have held that the first step in analyzing any law subject to judicial scrutiny under the negative Commerce Clause is to determine whether it "regulates evenhandedly with only 'incidental' effect on interstate commerce, or discriminates against interstate commerce." . . . As we use the term here, "discrimination" simply means differential treatment of in-state and out-of-state economic interests that benefits the former and burdens the later.

In *Chemical Waste Management, Inc. v. Hunt*, we easily found Alabama's surcharge on hazardous waste from other States to be facially discriminatory because it imposed a higher fee on the disposal of out-of-state waste than on the disposal of identical in-state waste. We deem it equally obvious here that Oregon's $2.25 per ton surcharge is discriminatory on its face. The surcharge subjects waste from other States to a fee almost three times greater than the $.85 per ton charge imposed on solid in-state waste. It is well-established that a law is discriminatory if it "tax[es] a transaction or incident more heavily when it crosses state lines than when it occurs entirely within the state."

Respondents argue, and the Oregon Supreme Court held, that the statutory nexus between the surcharge and "the [otherwise uncompensated] costs to the State of Oregon and its political subdivisions of disposing of solid waste generated out-of-state," necessarily precludes a finding that the surcharge is discriminatory. We find respondents' narrow focus on Oregon's compensatory aim to be foreclosed by our precedents. Even if the surcharge merely recoups the costs of disposing of out-of-state waste in Oregon, the fact remains that the differential charge favors shippers of Oregon waste over their counterparts handling waste generated in other States. In making that geographic distinction, the surcharge patently discriminates against interstate commerce.

Because the Oregon surcharge is discriminatory, the surcharge must be invalidated unless respondents can "sho[w] that it advances a legitimate local purpose that cannot be adequately served by reasonable nondiscriminatory alternatives." Our cases require that justifications for discriminatory restrictions on commerce pass the "strictest scrutiny."

No claim has been made that the disposal of waste from other States imposes higher costs on Oregon and its political subdivisions than the disposal of in-state waste. Also, respondents have not offered any safety or health reason unique to nonhazardous waste from other States for discouraging the flow of such waste into Oregon.

Respondents' principal defense of the higher surcharge on out-of-state waste is that it is a "compensatory tax" necessary to make shippers of such waste pay their "fair share" of the costs imposed on Oregon by the disposal of their waste in the State. In *Chemical Waste* we noted the possibility that such an argument might justify a discriminatory surcharge or tax on out-of-state waste. In making that observation, we implicitly recognized the settled principle that interstate commerce may be made to "'pay its way.'"

Although it is often no mean feat to determine whether a challenged tax is a compensatory tax, we have little difficulty concluding that the Oregon surcharge is not such a tax. Oregon does not impose a specific charge of at least $2.25 per ton on shippers of waste generated in Oregon, for which the out-of-state surcharge might be considered compensatory. Respondents' failure to identify a specific charge on intrastate commerce equal to or exceeding the surcharge is fatal to their claim.

Respondents argue that, despite the absence of a specific $2.25 per ton charge on in-state waste, intrastate commerce does pay its share of the costs underlying the surcharge through general taxation. Whether or not that is true is difficult to determine, as "[general] tax payments are received for the general purposes of the [government], and are, upon proper receipt, lost in the general revenues." Even assuming, however, that various other means of general taxation, such as income taxes, could serve as an identifiable intrastate burden roughly equivalent to the out-of-state surcharge, respondents' compensatory tax argument fails because the in-state and out-of-state levies are not imposed on substantially equivalent events.

We conclude that, far from being substantially equivalent, taxes on earning income and utilizing Oregon landfills are "entirely different kind[s] of tax[es]."

Respondents' final argument is that Oregon has an interest in spreading the costs of the in-state disposal of Oregon waste to all Oregonians. That is, because all citizens of Oregon benefit from the proper in-state disposal of waste from Oregon, respondents claim it is only proper for Oregon to require them to bear more of the costs of disposing of such waste in the State through a higher general tax burden. At the same time, however, Oregon citizens should not be required to bear the costs of disposing of out-of-state waste, respondents claim. The necessary result of that limited cost-shifting is to require shippers of out-of-state waste to bear the full costs of in-state disposal, but to permit shippers of Oregon waste to bear less than the full cost.

We fail to perceive any distinction between respondents' contention and a claim that the State has an interest in reducing the costs of handling in-state waste. Our cases condemn as illegitimate, however, any governmental interest that is not "unrelated to economic protectionism," and regulating interstate commerce in such a way as to give those who handle domestic articles of commerce a cost advantage over their competitors handling similar items produced elsewhere constitutes such protectionism.

Because respondents have offered no legitimate reason to subject waste generated in other States to a discriminatory surcharge approximately three times as high as that imposed on waste generated in Oregon, the surcharge is facially invalid under the negative Commerce Clause.

Reversed in favor of Plaintiff, Oregon Waste Systems.

DISSENT

CHIEF JUSTICE REHNQUIST, WITH WHOM JUSTICE BLACKMUN JOINS, DISSENTING

Landfill space evaporates as solid waste accumulates. State and local governments expend financial and political capital to develop trash control systems that are efficient, lawful, and protective of the environment. The State of Oregon responsibly attempted to address its solid waste disposal problem through enactment of a comprehensive regulatory scheme for the management, disposal, reduction, and recycling of solid waste. For this Oregon should be applauded. The regulatory scheme included a fee charged on out-of-state solid waste. The Oregon Legislature directed the Commission to determine the appropriate surcharge "based on the costs . . . of disposing of solid waste generated out-of-state." The Commission arrived at a surcharge of $2.25 per ton, compared to the $.85 per ton charged on in-state solid waste. The surcharge works out to an increase of about $.14 per week for the typical out-of-state solid waste producer. This seems a small price to pay for the right to deposit your "garbage, rubbish, refuse . . . ; sewage sludge, septic tank and cesspool pumpings or other sludge; . . . manure, . . . dead animals, [and] infectious waste" on your neighbors.

We confirmed in *Sporhase v. Nebraska ex rel. Douglas*, that a State may enact a comprehensive regulatory system to address an environmental problem or a threat to natural resources within the confines of the Commerce Clause. [W]here a State imposes restrictions on the ability of its own citizens to dispose of solid waste in an effort to promote a "clean and safe environment," it is not discriminating against interstate commerce by preventing the uncontrolled transfer of out-of-state solid waste into the State.

The availability of safe landfill disposal sites in Oregon did not occur by chance. Through its regulatory scheme, the State of Oregon inspects landfill sites, monitors waste streams, promotes recycling, and imposes an $.85 per ton disposal fee on in-state waste, all in an effort to curb the threat that its residents will harm the environment and create health and safety problems through excessive and unmonitored solid waste disposal. Depletion of a clean and safe environment will follow if Oregon must accept out-of-state waste at its landfills without a sharing of the disposal costs. The Commerce Clause does not require a State to abide this outcome where the "natural resource has some indicia of a good publicly produced and owned, in which a State may favor its own citizens in times of shortage."

Far from neutralizing the economic situation for Oregon producers and out-of-state producers, the Court's analysis turns the Commerce Clause on its head. Oregon's neighbors will operate under a competitive advantage against their Oregon counterparts as they can now produce solid waste with reckless abandon and avoid paying concomitant state taxes to develop new landfills and clean up retired landfill sites. While we once recognized that "'the collection and disposal of solid wastes should continue to be primarily the function of State, regional, and local agencies,'" the Court today leaves States with only two options: become a dumper and ship as much waste as possible to a less populated State, or become a dumpee, and stoically accept waste from more densely populated States.

The Court asserts that the State has not offered "any safety or health reasons" for discouraging the flow of solid waste into Oregon. I disagree. The availability of environmentally sound landfill space and the proper disposal of solid waste strike me as justifiable "safety or health" rationales for the fee.

I think that the $2.25 per ton fee that Oregon imposes on out-of-state waste works out to a similar "fair approximation" of the privilege to use its landfills.

The Court begrudgingly concedes that interstate commerce may be made to "pay its way," yet finds Oregon's nominal surcharge to exact more than a "just share" from interstate commerce. It escapes me how an additional $.14 per week cost for the average solid waste producer constitutes anything but the type of "incidental effects on interstate commerce" endorsed by the majority. Even-handed regulations imposing such incidental effects on interstate commerce must be upheld unless "the burden imposed on such commerce is clearly excessive in relation to the putative local benefits."

Critical Thinking about the Law

WITH BOTH THE MAJORITY AND DISSENTING opinions included, this case provides you with an excellent opportunity to test your critical thinking skills.

As you recall, legal disagreements often reflect disputes about the meaning of ambiguous language or about appropriate legal precedents. The interpretive conflict between Justices Thomas and Rehnquist is no different.

1. Justices Thomas and Rehnquist argue their cases on the basis of different legal precedents. In doing so, each Justice is arguing that Oregon Waste Systems is analogous to the cited precedent and thus calls for similar treatment. Evaluate the quality of the analogy made by Justice Thomas.

   CLUE A necessary step in determining your answer will be listing the reasons the justice gives for selecting his precedent and then evaluating these reasons.

2. Besides legal precedents, ambiguities are also a major point of contention in the disagreement between Justices Thomas and Rehnquist. Make an argument for what you believe to be the most important ambiguity.

   CLUE Refer to each Justice's thoughts on the extent to which Oregon charges out-of-state dumpers.

THE IMPACT OF THE AMENDMENTS ON BUSINESS

The first ten amendments to the U.S. Constitution, known as the Bill of Rights, have a substantial impact on governmental regulation of the legal environment of business. These amendments prohibit the federal government from infringing on certain freedoms that are guaranteed to individuals living in our society. The Fourteenth Amendment extends most of the provisions in the Bill of Rights to the behavior of states, prohibiting their interference in the exercise of those rights. Many of the first ten amendments have also been held to apply to corporations because corporations are treated, in most cases, as "artificial persons." The activities protected by the Bill of Rights and the Fourteenth Amendment are not only those that occur in one's private life but also those that take place in a commercial setting. Several of these amendments have a significant impact on the regulatory environment of business, and they are discussed in the remainder of this chapter.

THE FIRST AMENDMENT

First Amendment Guarantees freedom of speech, press, and religion and the right to peacefully assemble and to petition the government for redress of grievances.

The **First Amendment** guarantees freedom of speech and of the press. It also prohibits the abridgment of the right to assemble peacefully and to petition for redress of grievances. Finally, it prohibits the government from aiding the establishment of a religion and from interfering with the free exercise of religion (Exhibit 4-4).

Although we say these rights are guaranteed, they obviously cannot be absolute. Most people would agree that a person does not have the right to yell "Fire!" in a crowded theater. Nor does one's right of free speech extend to making false statements about another that would be injurious to that person's reputation. Because of the difficulty of determining the boundaries of individual rights, a large number of First Amendment cases have been decided by the courts. Attempts to regulate new technologies also raise first amendment issues. For example, Congress passed the Communications Decency Act of 1996 (CDC) to protect minors from harmful material on the Internet. But the United States Supreme Court found that provisions of the CDC that criminalized and prohibited the "knowing" transmission of "obscene or indecent" messages to any recipient under the age of 18 by means of telecommunications devices or through the use of interactive computer services were content-based blanket restrictions on freedom of speech. Because these provisions of the statute were too vague

EXHIBIT 4-4

73

Chapter 4

Constitutional Principles

The first amendment protects a broad range of activities.

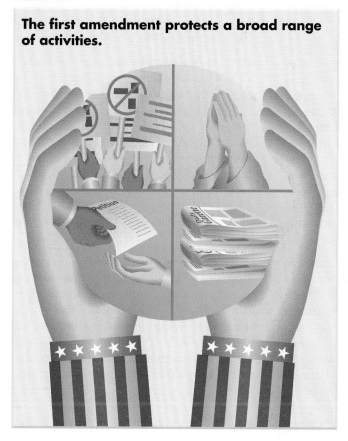

and overly broad, repressing speech that adults have the right to make, these provisions were found to be unconstitutional.[5]

CORPORATE SPEECH Numerous cases have arisen over the extent to which First Amendment guarantees are applicable to corporate commercial speech. The doctrine currently used to analyze commercial speech is discussed in the following case.

CENTRAL HUDSON GAS & ELECTRIC CORPORATION V. PUBLIC SERVICE COMMISSION OF NEW YORK
UNITED STATES SUPREME COURT 100 S. CT. 2343 (1980)

Plaintiff Central Hudson Gas and Electric Corporation filed an action against Public Service Commission of New York to challenge the constitutionality of a regulation that completely banned promotional advertising by the utility but permitted "informational" ads—those designed to encourage shifting consumption from peak to nonpeak times. The regulation was upheld by the trial court. On appeal by the utility, the New York Court of Appeals sustained the regulation, concluding that governmental interests outweighed the limited constitutional value of the commercial speech at issue. The utility appealed.

JUSTICE POWELL

The Commission's order [enforcing the regulation's advertising ban] restricts only commercial speech, that is, expression related solely to the economic interests of the speaker and its audience. The First Amendment, as applied to the States through the Fourteenth Amendment, protects commercial speech from unwarranted governmental regulation. Commercial expression not only serves the economic interest of the speaker, but also assists consumers and furthers the societal interest in the fullest possible dissemination of information. In applying the First Amendment to this area, we have rejected the "highly paternalistic" view that government has complete power to suppress or regulate commercial speech. Even when advertising communicates only an incomplete version of the relevant facts, the First Amendment presumes that some accurate information is better than no information at all. Nevertheless, our decisions have recognized "the 'common sense'

---

[5]Janet Reno v. American Civil Liberties Union, 117 S.Ct. 2329 (1997).

distinction between speech proposing a commercial transaction, which occurs in an area traditionally subject to government regulation, and other varieties of speech."

The Constitution therefore accords a lesser protection to commercial speech than to other constitutionally guaranteed expression. The protection available for particular commercial expression turns on the nature both of the expression and of the governmental interests served by its regulation. Two features of commercial speech permit regulation of its content. First, commercial speakers have extensive knowledge of both the market and their products. Thus, they are well situated to evaluate the accuracy of their messages and the lawfulness of the underlying activity. In addition, commercial speech, the offspring of economic self-interest, is a hardy breed of expression that is not "particularly susceptible to being crushed by overboard regulation."

If the communication is neither misleading nor related to unlawful activity, the government's power is more circumscribed. The State must assert a substantial interest to be achieved by restrictions on commercial speech. Moreover, the regulatory technique must be in proportion to that interest. The limitation on expression must be designed carefully to achieve the State's goal. Compliance with this requirement may be measured by two criteria. First, the restriction must directly advance the state interest involved; the regulation may not be sustained if it provides only ineffective or remote support for the government's purpose. Second, if the governmental interest could be served as well by a more limited restriction on commercial speech, the excessive restrictions cannot survive.

The second criterion recognizes that the First Amendment mandates that speech restrictions be "narrowly drawn." The regulatory technique may extend only as far as the interest it serves. The State cannot regulate speech that poses no danger to the asserted state interest, nor can it completely suppress information when narrower restrictions on expression would serve its interest as well.

In commercial speech cases, then, a four-part analysis has developed. At the outset, we must determine whether the expression is protected by the First Amendment. For commercial speech to come within that provision, it at least must concern lawful activity and not be misleading. Next, we ask whether the asserted governmental interest is substantial. If both inquiries yield positive answers, we must determine whether the regulation directly advances the governmental interest asserted, and whether it is not more extensive than is necessary to serve that interest.

The Commission does not claim that the expression at issue is inaccurate or relates to unlawful activity. Yet the New York Court of Appeals questioned whether Central Hudson's advertising is protected commercial speech. Because appellant holds a monopoly over the sale of electricity in its service area, the state court suggested that the Commission's order restricts no commercial speech of any worth.

In the absence of factors that would distort the decision to advertise, we may assume that the willingness of a business to promote its products justifies belief that consumers are interested in the advertising. Since no such extraordinary conditions have been identified in this case, appellant's monopoly position does not alter the First Amendment's protection for its commercial speech.

The Commission offers two state interests as justifications for the ban on promotional advertising. The first concerns energy conservation. Any increase in demand for electricity—during peak or off-peak periods—means greater consumption of energy. The Commission argues that the State's interest in conserving energy is sufficient to support suppression of advertising designed to increase consumption of electricity. In view of our country's dependence on energy resources beyond our control, no one can doubt the importance of energy conservation. Plainly, therefore, the state interest asserted is substantial.

We come finally to the critical inquiry in this case: whether the Commission's complete suppression of speech ordinarily protected by the First Amendment is no more extensive than necessary to further the State's interest in energy conservation. The Commission's order reaches all promotional advertising, regardless of the impact of the touted service on overall energy use. But the energy conservation rationale, as important as it is, cannot justify suppressing information about electric devices or services that would cause no net increase in total energy use. In addition, no showing has been made that a more limited restriction on the content of promotional advertising would not serve adequately the State's interests.

Appellant insists that but for the ban, it would advertise products and services that use energy efficiently. These include the "heat pump," which both parties acknowledge to be a major improvement in electric heating, and the use of electric heat as a "backup" to solar and other heat sources. Although the Commission has questioned the efficiency of electric heating before this Court, neither the Commission's Policy Statement nor its order denying rehearing made findings on this issue.

The Commission's order prevents appellant from promoting electric services that would reduce energy use by diverting demand from less efficient sources, or that would consume roughly the same amount of energy as do alternative sources. In neither situation would the utility's advertising endanger conservation or mislead the public. To the extent that the Commission's order suppresses speech that in no way impairs the State's interest in energy conservation, the Commission's order violates the First and Fourteenth Amendments and must be invalidated.

The Commission also has not demonstrated that its interest in conservation cannot be protected adequately by more limited regulation of appellant's commercial expression. To further its policy of conservation, the Commission could attempt to restrict the format and content of Central Hudson's advertising. It might, for example, require that the advertisements include information about the relative efficiency and expense of the offered service, both under current conditions and for the foreseeable future.

Reversed in favor of Plaintiff, Central Hudson.

Critical Thinking about the Law

IN THIS CASE, THE COURT HAD to balance government interests in energy efficiency as well as fair and efficient pricing with the conflicting constitutional value of Central Hudson's right to free commercial speech. Having affirmed the validity of government's substantial interests in regulating the utility company, the Court sought to determine if these interests could have been sufficiently served with more limited restrictions. Because this determination is of central importance to the Court's reversal of the earlier court's judgment, it will be the focus of the questions that follow.

1. What primary ethical norm is implicit in the legal requirement that regulations on commercial speech *must be of the most limited nature possible* in carrying out the desired end of advancing the state's substantial interest?

   CLUE Review the four primary ethical norms. You want to focus not on the government regulation but on the rationale for limits on that regulation.

2. What information missing from the Court's opinion must you, as a critical thinker, know before being satisfied entirely with the decision?

   CLUE You want to focus on the issue about which the Public Service Commission and Central Hudson have conflicting viewpoints. What information would you want to know before accepting the soundness of the Court's judgment in resolving this conflict?

COMMENT: The test set forth in Central Hudson was reaffirmed by the U.S. Supreme Court in two decisions handed down in the summer of 1995, when it applied the test in *Rubin v. Coors Brewing Co.*[6] and *Florida Bar v. Went for It and John T. Blakely.*[7] In the first case, Coors challenged a regulation of the Federal Alcohol Administration Act that prohibited beer labels from disclosing the beer's alcohol content. The court found that the government's interest in suppressing "strength wars" among beer producers was "substantial" under the Central Hudson test, but the ban failed to meet the asserted government interest and is no more extensive than necessary to serve that interest.

A restriction that passed the Central Hudson test was the Florida ethics rule upheld in the latter case. The rule requires lawyers to wait 30 days before sending targeted direct mail solicitation letters to victims of accidents or disasters. The high court found a substantial interest both in protecting the privacy and tranquility of victims and their loved ones against invasive and unsolicited contact by lawyers and in preventing the erosion of confidence in the profession that such repeated invasions have caused. The bar association had established, by unrebutted survey data, that Floridians considered immediate postaccident direct-mail solicitation to be an invasion of victims' privacy that reflects poorly on lawyers. The Court also found that the ban's scope is reasonably well tailored to meet the stated objectives. It is limited in duration, and there are other ways for injured Floridians to learn about the availability of legal services during the ban. Thus the ban was upheld as directly advancing the asserted legitimate interest in a manner no more extensive than necessary to serve that interest.

CORPORATE POLITICAL SPEECH Not all corporate speech is considered commercial speech. Sometimes, for example, corporations might spend funds to support political candidates or referenda. At one time, states restricted the amount of advertising firms could engage in because of a fear that, with their huge assets, corporations' speech on behalf of a particular candidate or issue would drown out other voices. But in the 1978 case of *First National Bank of*

---

[6]115 S. Ct. 1585 (1995).
[7]115 S. Ct. 2371 (1995).

76

Part One

An Introduction to the Law
and the Legal Environment
of Business

Boston v. Bellotti,[8] the U.S. Supreme Court struck down a state law that prohibited certain corporations from making contributions or expenditures influencing voters on any issues that would not materially affect the corporate assets or business. Stating that "the concept that the government may restrict speech of some elements of our society in order to enhance the relative voice of others is wholly foreign to the First Amendment," the high court ruled that corporate political speech should be protected to the same extent as the ordinary citizen's political speech.

THE FOURTH AMENDMENT

Fourth Amendment Protects the right of individuals to be secure in their persons, homes, and personal property by prohibiting the government from conducting unreasonable searches of individuals and seizing their property.

The **Fourth Amendment** protects the right of individuals to be secure in their persons, their homes, and their personal property. It prohibits the government from conducting unreasonable searches of individuals and seizing their property to use as evidence against them. If such an unreasonable search and seizure occurs, the evidence obtained from it cannot be used in a trial.

An unreasonable search and seizure is basically one conducted without the government official's having first obtained a warrant from the court. The warrant must specify the items sought. Government officials are able to obtain such a warrant only when they can show probable cause to believe that the search will turn up the specified evidence of criminal activity. Supreme Court decisions, however, have recently narrowed the protection of the Fourth Amendment by providing for circumstances in which no search warrant is needed. Improvements in technology have also caused problems in the application of the Fourth Amendment because it is now simpler to eavesdrop on people and to engage in other covert activities.

The Fourth Amendment protects corporations as well as individuals. This protection is generally applicable, as noted above, in criminal cases. However, Fourth Amendment issues also arise when government regulations authorize, or even require, warrantless searches by administrative agencies.

Although administrative searches are presumed to require a search warrant, an exception has been carved out. If an industry is one that has been subject to pervasive regulation, a warrantless search would not be unreasonable. In such industries, warrantless searches are required in order to make sure that regulations are being upheld.

The standard as it now stands is difficult to interpret. A warrantless search authorized by the Gun Control Act or the Federal Mine Safety and Health Act would be legal. A warrantless search under the Occupational Safety and Health Act, however, would violate the Fourth Amendment because there is no history of pervasive legislation on working conditions before the act's passage.

THE FIFTH AMENDMENT

Fifth Amendment Protects individuals against self-incrimination and double jeopardy and guarantees them the right to trial by jury; protects both individuals and businesses through the Due Process Clause and the Takings Clause.

The **Fifth Amendment** provides many significant protections to individuals. For instance, it protects against self-incrimination and double jeopardy, that is, being tried twice for the same crime. Of more importance to businesspersons, however, is the **Due Process Clause** of the Fifth Amendment. This provision provides that one cannot be deprived of life, liberty, or property without *due process* of law.

Due Process Clause Provides that no one can be deprived of life, liberty, or property without "due process of law"; found in Fifth Amendment.

There are two types of due process: *procedural* and *substantive*. Originally, due process was interpreted only procedurally. **Procedural due process** requires that a criminal whose life, liberty, or property would be taken by a conviction be given a fair trial: that is, that he or she is entitled to notice of the alleged criminal action and the opportunity to confront his or her accusers before an impartial tribunal. The application of procedural due process soon spread beyond criminal matters, especially after passage of the Fourteenth Amendment, discussed in the next section, which made the requirement of due process applicable to state governments.

procedural due process Procedural steps to which individuals are entitled before losing their life, liberty, or property.

---

[8]435 U.S. 765 (1978).

Today, the Due Process Clause has been applied to such diverse situations as the termination of welfare benefits,[9] the discharge of a public employee from his or her job, and the suspension of a student from school. It should be noted, however, that the types of takings to which the due process clause applies are not being continually increased. In fact, after a broad expansion of the takings to which this clause applied, the courts began restricting the application of this clause during the 1970s and have continued to do so since then. The courts restrict the clause's application by narrowing the interpretation of property and liberty. This narrowing is especially common in interpreting the due process clause as it applies to state governments under the Fourteenth Amendment.

What procedural safeguards does procedural due process require? The question is not easily answered. The procedures that the government must follow when there may be a taking of an individual's life, liberty, or property vary according to the nature of the taking. In general, as the magnitude of the potential deprivation increases, the extent of the procedures required also increases.

The second type of due process is substantive due process. The concept of **substantive due process** refers to the basic fairness of laws that may deprive an individual of his or her liberty or property. In other words, when a law is passed that will restrict individuals' liberty or their use of their property, the government must have a proper purpose for the restriction or it violates substantive due process.

substantive due process
Requirement that laws depriving individuals of liberty or property be fair.

During the late nineteenth and early twentieth centuries, this concept was referred to as *economic substantive due process* and was used to strike down a number of pieces of social legislation, including laws that established minimum wages and hours. Business managers successfully argued that such laws interfered with the liberty of employer and employee to enter into whatever type of employment contract they might choose. Analogous arguments were used to defeat many laws that would have allegedly helped the less fortunate at the expense of business interests. Economic substantive due process flourished only until the late 1930s. Today, many pieces of social legislation are in force that would have been held unconstitutional under the old concept of economic substantive due process.

The concept of substantive due process is not dead. However, its use today protects not economic interests, but personal rights, such as the still-evolving right to privacy. The right to privacy is a liberty now deemed to be protected under the Constitution. In order for a law restricting one's right to privacy to conform to substantive due process, the restriction in question must bear a *substantial* relationship to a *compelling* governmental purpose.

The Fifth Amendment further provides that if the government takes private property for public use, it must pay the owner just compensation. This provision is referred to as the **Takings Clause**. Unlike the protection against self-incrimination, which does not apply to corporations, both the Due Process Clause and the provision for just compensation are applicable to corporations. This provision for just compensation has caused considerable litigation recently. One significant issue that has arisen is the question of what constitutes a "public use," for which the government can take property. This issue is discussed in greater detail in chapter 13.

Takings Clause Provides that if the government takes private property for public use, it must pay the owner just compensation; found in Fifth Amendment.

A second issue under this takings provision is the question of when a government regulation can become so onerous as to constitute a taking for which just compensation is required. Environmental regulations, because they often have an impact on the way landowners may use their property, have been increasingly challenged as unconstitutionally violative of the takings provision. In the following case, the Supreme Court examined a state regulation challenged as violating the Fifth Amendment, as applied to the state by the Fourteenth Amendment.

---

[9]Goldberg v. Kelly, 90 U.S. 101 (1970). In this case, the U.S. Supreme Court stated that the termination of a welfare recipient's welfare benefits by a state agency without affording him or her the opportunity for an evidentiary hearing before termination violates the recipient's procedural due process rights.

DAVID LUCAS V. SOUTH CAROLINA COASTAL COMMISSION
SUPREME COURT OF THE UNITED STATES 112 U.S. 2886 (1992)

In 1986, plaintiff David Lucas paid $975,000 for two beachfront lots on the Isle of Palms along the South Carolina coast, planning to eventually build one home for himself and another for a wealthy buyer. Nineteen months later the state passed a Beachfront Management Act, which banned construction close to the shore in order to prevent flying debris and other environmental damage from Atlantic storms. Because the new regulation prevented his constructing either house, which he believed rendered his land "valueless," he sued the state, seeking "just compensation" under the Takings Clause of the Fifth Amendment. The trial court found in favor of Lucas and awarded him $1.2 million. On appeal, the state argued successfully that a landowner had no right to harm his land, which Lucas would be doing by constructing the homes, and the trial court verdict was reversed. Lucas then appealed the case to the U.S. Supreme Court.

JUSTICE SCALIA

Prior to Justice Holmes' exposition in *Pennsylvania Coal Co.* v. *Mahon*, it was generally thought that the Takings Clause reached only a "direct appropriation" of property, or the functional equivalent of a "practical ouster of [the owner's] possession."

Nevertheless, our decision in *Mahon* offered little insight into when, and under what circumstances, a given regulation would be seen as going "too far" for purposes of the Fifth Amendment. In 70-odd years of succeeding "regulatory takings" jurisprudence, we have generally eschewed any "'set formula'" for determining how far is too far. We have, however, described at least two discrete categories of regulatory action as compensable without case-specific inquiry into the public interest advanced in support of the restraint. The first encompasses regulations that compel the property owner to suffer a physical "invasion" of his property. In general (at least with regard to permanent invasions), no matter how minute the intrusion, and no matter how weighty the public purpose behind it, we have required compensation.

The second situation in which we have found categorical treatment appropriate is where regulation denies all economically beneficial or productive use of land. As we have said on numerous occasions, the Fifth Amendment is violated when land-use regulation "does not substantially advance legitimate state interests or *denies an owner economically viable use of his land.*"

Affirmatively supporting a compensation requirement is the fact that regulations that leave the owner of land without economically beneficial or productive options for its use—typically, as here, by requiring land to be left substantially in its natural state—carry with them a heightened risk that private property is being pressed into some form of public service under the guise of mitigating serious public harm.

The trial court found Lucas's two beachfront lots to have been rendered valueless by respondent's enforcement of the coastal-zone construction ban. Under Lucas's theory of the case, which rested upon our "no economically viable use" statements, that finding entitled him to compensation.

By neglecting to dispute the findings enumerated in the Act or otherwise to challenge the legislature's purposes, petitioner "concede[d] that the beach/dune area of South Carolina's shores is an extremely valuable public resource; that the erection of new construction contributes to the erosion and destruction of this public resource; and that discouraging new construction in close proximity to the beach/dune area is necessary to prevent a great public harm." In the court's view, these concessions brought petitioner's challenge within a long line of this Court's cases sustaining against Due Process and Takings Clause challenges against the State's use of its "police powers" to enjoin a property owner from activities akin to public nuisances [e.g., order to destroy diseased cedar trees to prevent infection of nearby orchards].

It is correct that many of our proper opinions have suggested that "harmful or noxious uses" of property may be proscribed by government regulation without the requirement of compensation. For a number of reasons, however, we think the South Carolina Supreme Court was too quick to conclude that that principle decides the present case. The "harmful or noxious uses" principle was the Court's early attempt to describe in theoretical terms why government may, consistent with the Takings Clause, affect property values by regulation without incurring an obligation to compensate—a reality we nowadays acknowledge explicitly with respect to the full scope of the State's police power.

The legislature's recitation of a noxious-use justification cannot be the basis for departing from our categorical rule that total regulatory takings must be compensated. If it were, departure would virtually always be allowed.

Where the State seeks to sustain regulation that deprives land of all economically beneficial use, we think it may resist compensation only if the logically antecedent inquiry into the nature of the owner's estate shows that the proscribed use interests were not part of his title to begin with.

Where "permanent physical occupation" of land is concerned, we have refused to allow the government to decree it anew (without compensation), no matter how weighty the asserted "public interests" involved, though we assuredly *would* permit the government to assert a permanent easement that was a preexisting limitation upon the landowner's title. We believe similar treatments must be accorded confiscatory regulations, i.e., regulations that prohibit all economically beneficial use of land.

On this analysis, the owner of a lake bed, for example, would not be entitled to compensation when he is denied the requisite permit to engage in a landfilling operation that would have the effect of flooding others' land. Such regulatory action may well have the effect of eliminating the land's only economically productive use, but it does not proscribe a productive use that was previously permissible under relevant property and nuisance principles. The use of these properties for what are now expressly prohibited purposes was *always* unlawful, and it was open to the State at any point to make the implication of those background principles of nuisance and property law explicit.

The "total taking" inquiry we require today will ordinarily entail analysis of, among other things, the degree of harm to public lands and resources, or adjacent private property, posed by the claimant's proposed activities, the social value of the claimant's activities and their suitability to the locality in question, and the relative ease with which the alleged harm can be avoided through measures taken by the claimant and the government (or adjacent private landowners) alike. The fact that a particular use has long been engaged in by similarly situated owners ordinarily imports a lack of any common-law prohibition (though changed circumstances or new knowledge may make what was previously permissible no longer so). So also does the fact that other landowners, similarly situated, are permitted to continue the use denied to the claimant.

It seems unlikely that common-law principles would have prevented the erection of any habitable or productive improvements on petitioner's land. We emphasize that to win its case . . . South Carolina must identify background principles of nuisance and property law that prohibit the uses he now intends in the circumstances in which the property is presently found. Only on this showing can the State fairly claim that, in proscribing all such beneficial uses, the Beachfront Management Act is taking nothing.

Reversed and *remanded* in favor of Appellant, Lucas.

Critical Thinking about the Law

A S DO OTHER CASES WE HAVE studied, *Lucas* represents a conflict between two sets of interests. Society in the form of government has many legitimate concerns—safety, environmental protection, maintenance of a transportation network, and so on—that interfere with the interests of individual property owners. On the other hand, imagine the outrage felt by individual property owners when they see an outside body in the form of the state seizing their property.

Critical thinking about the legal reasoning used by Judge Scalia can help improve your response to this conflict of legitimate interests.

1. Justice Scalia dismisses the "noxious use" principle as an inappropriate tool for determining compensation under the Takings Clause on the grounds that this principle is ambiguous. Yet, while dismissing this principle, Scalia himself offers in its place another ambiguous basis for justifying a taking. Try to identify the ambiguity in Scalia's own principle for a legitimate state "taking."

   CLUE Locate the section in the decision where Scalia spells out what is required for a legal "taking."

2. Environmentalists were very distressed by this decision. Yet, one thing we have stressed in our approach to critical thinking about the law is the importance of the specifics in the fact pattern. How do the facts in this case make the decision much less a threat to environmental regulation than it might appear to be at first?

   CLUE Imagine that you could *create* facts related to *Lucas*. Which facts would you change that would have moved Scalia in the direction of affirming the decision of the South Carolina Supreme Court?

Many advocates of private property rights now believe that the Takings Clause has taken on a new importance because of recent cases such as *Lucas* and *Whitney v. United States*,[10] wherein a federal court found that the federal *Surface Mining and Reclamation Act* constituted a taking with respect to one mining company whose land became completely useless as a result of the act. Whether the "Property Firsters," as they call themselves, will be successful in the future

---

[10]926 F.2d 1169 (1991).

80

Part One

*An Introduction to the Law
and the Legal Environment
of Business*

remains to be seen, but they have clearly brought back attention to an argument against regulation that had been fairly dormant for the past 50 years. And they are using their arguments primarily to challenge a broad range of environmental laws involving matters from forcing cleanups of hazardous waste sites to restricting grazing and rationing water.

Regardless of the success of the property rights movement, one impact that can already be seen is that states are being a little more cautious in the regulations they are passing. In May of 1992, for example, Arizona passed a law requiring state agencies to assess whether regulations they are considering might result in their having to compensate property owners.

A final problem that often causes confusion among businesspersons is the question of the extent of Fifth Amendment protections for corporations. The Fifth Amendment protection against self-incrimination has not been held to apply to corporations. However, some decisions have raised questions about this longstanding interpretation. In *United States v. Doe*,[11] the U.S. Supreme Court determined that even though the contents of a document may not be protected under the Fifth Amendment, a sole proprietor should have the right to show that the act of producing the documents would entail testimonial self-incrimination as to admissions that the records existed. Therefore, the sole proprietor could not be compelled to produce the sole proprietorship's records.

In the subsequent case of *Braswell v. United States*,[12] however, the Court clearly distinguished between the role of a custodian of corporate records and a sole proprietor. In *Braswell*, the defendant operated his business as a corporation, with himself as the sole shareholder. When a grand jury issued a subpoena requiring him to produce corporate books and records, Braswell argued that to do so would violate his Fifth Amendment privilege against self-incrimination. The U.S. Supreme Court denied Braswell's claim and said that, clearly, subpoenaed business records are not privileged, and, because Braswell was a custodian for the records, his act of producing the records would be in a representative capacity, not a personal one, so the records must be produced. The Court stated that, had the business been a sole proprietorship, Braswell would have had the opportunity to show that the act of production would have been self-incriminating. Because his business was a corporation, he was acting as a representative of a corporation, and regardless of how small the corporation, he could not claim a privilege.

FOURTEENTH AMENDMENT

Fourteenth Amendment
Applies the entire Bill of Rights, excepting parts of the Fifth Amendment, to the states.

The **Fourteenth Amendment** is important because it applies the Due Process Clause to the state governments. It has been interpreted to apply almost the entire Bill of Rights to the states, with the exceptions of the Fifth Amendment right to indictment by a grand jury for certain types of crimes and the right to trial by jury.

The Fourteenth Amendment is also important because it contains the Equal Protection Clause, which prevents the states from denying "the equal protection of the laws" to any citizen. This clause has been a useful tool for people attempting to reduce discrimination in this country. Its significance in this area is examined in chapter 19.

SUMMARY

The framework of our nation is embodied in the U.S. Constitution, which established a system of government based on the concept of federalism. Under this system, the power to regulate local matters is given to the states; the federal government is granted limited powers to regulate activities that substantially affect interstate commerce. All powers not specifically given to the federal government are reserved to the states.

---

[11]465 U.S. 605 (1984).
[12]487 U.S. 99 (1988).

The Commerce Clause is the primary source of the federal government's authority to regulate business. The same clause restricts states from passing regulations that would interfere with interstate commerce.

The state and federal governments are limited in their regulations by the amendments to the Constitution, especially the Bill of Rights. The First Amendment, for example, protects our individual right to free expression; commercial speech is also entitled to a significant amount of protection in this area.

Other important amendments for the businessperson are the Fourth Amendment, which protects one's right to be free from unwarranted searches and seizures, and the Fifth Amendment, which establishes our right to due process. A final amendment that has a significant impact on the legal environment is the Fourteenth Amendment, which applies most of the Bill of Rights to the states and also contains the Equal Protection Clause.

REVIEW QUESTIONS

4-1. Explain the relationship between the Supremacy Clause and the doctrine of federal preemption.

4-2. How does the Commerce Clause affect federal regulation of business activities?

4-3. What is police power?

4-4. How does the Commerce Clause affect state regulation of business?

4-5. Explain why you believe the courts have found each of the following to either constitute or not constitute a regulatory taking: a. a city ordinance reduced the size limit for freestanding signs within the city limits, forcing plaintiff to replace his sign. b. a city ordinance prohibiting billboards along roads in residential areas of the city. c. the refusal of the Army Corps of Engineers to grant Florida Rock Company a permit to allow them to mine limestone that lay beneath a track of wetlands.

4-6. How does the First Amendment Protection of private speech differ from the protection of commercial speech?

REVIEW PROBLEMS

4-7. Voters in the state of California decide that the tobacco industry is having too great an impact on the outcome of local referenda limiting smoking in public places. To curb the influence of that powerful lobby, so that the fate of the legislation is more clearly reflective of the will of "the people," they pass a law prohibiting firms in the tobacco industry and tobacco industry associations from (1) purchasing any advertising related to any smoking-related referenda and (2) making any cash contributions to any organizations involved in campaigns related to antismoking legislation. Several tobacco firms challenge the law. What is the constitutional basis for their challenge? Why will they be likely to either succeed or fail?

4-8. Ms. Crabtree is given a one-year, nontenured contract to teach English at Haddock State University, a public institution. After her contract year ends, she is not offered a contract for the next year and is not given any explanation as to why she is not being rehired. She sues the school, arguing that her right to procedural due process has been violated. Is she correct?

4-9. The State of Ohio decides that Ohio's landfills are becoming too full at too rapid a pace, so they pass a law banning the import of waste generated out of state. Several landfill operators have contracts with out-of-state generators, so they sue the state to have the statute declared void. What arguments will each side make in this case? What is the most likely decision? Why?

4-10. Chen opens a small business. As business thrives, he decides to incorporate. He becomes the corporation's president and also its sole shareholder. Chen comes under investigation for tax fraud and is subpoenaed to pro-

82

Part One

*An Introduction to the Law
and the Legal Environment
of Business*

duce the corporate tax records for the prior three years. He challenges the subpoena on the grounds that it violates his Fifth Amendment right not to incriminate himself. Must he comply with the subpoena?

4-11. Congress passed the Americans with Disabilities Act requiring, among other provisions, that places of public accommodation remove architectural barriers to access where such removal is "readily achievable." If such removal is not "readily achievable," the firm must make its goods or services available through alternative methods if such methods are readily achievable. To comply with the law, Ricardo's Restaurant will have to construct a ramp at the entrance to the restaurant and two ramps within the dining area, rearrange some of the tables and chairs, and remodel the restrooms so that they will accommodate wheelchairs. Because of the expenditures Ricardo will have to make to comply with the law, he challenges the law as being a taking of private property without just compensation in violation of the Fifth Amendment. Does the law violate the Fifth Amendment?

4-12. Plaintiffs owned a piece of lakeside property. The land was subsequently rezoned to prohibit high-density apartment complexes and restrict the use of the property to single family dwellings. On what basis would the plaintiffs claim their constitutional rights had been violated by the zoning change? Would they be correct?

CASE PROBLEMS

4-13. Petitioner, a Maine non-profit corporation, operated a camp for primarily out-of-state residents. Petitioner paid over $20,000 per year in real estate and personal property tax from 1989–1991. A Maine statute provided an exemption from most of those taxes for any charity incorporated in Maine and serving primarily Maine residents. Those serving primarily nonresidents, however, qualified for a much more limited benefit, and only if they charged less than $30 per week per person for their services. Because petitioners charged $400 per week per camper, and was therefore ineligible for any tax benefit. Petitioner challenged the constitutionality of the statute. Initially, petitioner was granted summary judgment. This decision was reversed, and petitioner appealed to the United States Supreme Court. On what grounds would petitioner argue the statute was unconstitutional? Why do you believe the petitioner won or lost? *Camps Newfound/Owatona v. Town of Harrison, Maine,* 117 S. Ct. 1590 (1997)

4-14. Congress passed the Gun-Free School Zones Act, making it a federal offense for any individual knowingly to possess a firearm in any place the individual knows or has reasonable cause to believe is a school zone. The law was challenged on the grounds that Congress had exceeded its Commerce Clause authority in passing this legislation. Provide the arguments that you believe opponents and proponents of the law would have made. How do you believe the U.S. Supreme Court decided this case? Why? *United States v. Lopez,* 115 S. Ct. 1624 (1995)

4-15. Lawn Builders' president, Mr. Shadoian, was summoned to appear before the IRS and produce corporate records for examination in conjunction with an IRS investigation into Lawn Builders' tax liability for the years 1984, 1985, and 1986. Shadoian refused to produce any records or to appear on the grounds that he and the corporation had a Fifth Amendment privilege against self-incrimination that prevented them from having to appear and produce the records at issue. Was Shadoian correct in asserting the privilege on behalf of himself and the corporation? *Lawn Builders of New England, Inc. and James T. Shadoian v. United States of America,* 856 F.2d 388 (1988)

4-16. A federal law prohibited the broadcast of lottery advertising by licensees located in nonlottery states. Edge Broadcasting Co., a licensee located in a nonlottery state close to the border of a lottery state challenged the ban as violative of the First Amendment. Do you think the Court found this law to be constitutional? Why or why not? United States and Federal Communications *Commission v. Edge Broadcasting Co.*, 113 S. Ct. 2696 (1993)

4-17. A woman distributed leaflets concerning a school tax that were signed "Concerned Parents and Taxpayers." She was convicted of violating a state law mandating that political campaign literature must include the name and address of the sender. She appealed on the grounds that the law under which she was convicted was unconstitutional. Make the constitutional argument that would have been made on her behalf. Do you think the U.S. Supreme Court decided in her favor? Why or why not? *McIntyre v. Ohio Elections Commission*, 115 S. Ct. 1511 (1995)

4-18. The Port Authority of New Jersey and New York banned "the continuous or repetitive . . . distribution of printed or written material" and the solicitation for funds within their airport terminals. The Court of Appeals upheld the ban on solicitation but struck down the ban on leafletting. How do you think the U.S. Supreme Court decided the case on appeal? Why? *International Society for Krishna Consciousness, Inc. v. Walter Lee, Superintendent of Port Authority Police*, 112 S. Ct. 2711 (1992)

 On the Internet

http://www.constitution.org   This site, constructed by a constitutional society, is dedicated to research and public education about the principles of constitutional republican government.

http://asa.oglilib.umich.edu/chdocs/rights/citizen.html   This site is a guide to resources that explain the rights of Americans under federal law.

http://www.law.cornell.edu:80/constitution/constitution overview.html   Go to this site if you wish to download the United States Constitution.

http://www.freedomforum.org/   This site, The Freedom Forum, is a place to go if you are interested in first amendment issues.

http://www.aclu.org/issues/freespeech/info.html   The ACLU, one of the largest organizations devoted to protecting free speech, maintains this site.

5

THE AMERICAN LEGAL SYSTEM

- **JURISDICTION**

- **VENUE**

- **THE STRUCTURE OF THE COURT SYSTEM**

- **THE ACTORS IN THE LEGAL SYSTEM AND THEIR RELATIONSHIP**

  TO THE BUSINESS COMMUNITY

- **THE ADVERSARY PROCESS**

- **STEPS IN CIVIL LITIGATION AND THE ROLE OF BUSINESSPERSONS**

- **INTERNATIONAL DIMENSIONS OF THE AMERICAN LEGAL SYSTEM**

We are all subject to both state and federal laws. Under our dual court system, all lawsuits must be brought in either the federal or the state court system. In some cases, an action may be brought in either. It is thus important that persons in the business community understand how the decisions are made as to which court system can resolve their grievances. This chapter first considers the principles that determine which court system has the power to hear various types of cases and then examines in greater detail the structure of the two basic divisions of our dual court system. Next, it focuses on the actors who play major roles in our litigation process. Finally, it examines the philosophy behind our American legal system and traces the procedures that must be followed when using one of our courts.

Critical Thinking about the Law

OUR AMERICAN LEGAL SYSTEM CAN SEEM confusing at first. Using your critical thinking skills to answer the following questions as you read this chapter will help you understand how our legal system operates.

1. Critical thinkers recognize that ambiguous words—words that have multiple possible meanings—can cause confusion. Sam boldly asserts that the court of common pleas has jurisdiction over *Jones v. Smith*, while Clara asserts equally strongly that the court of common pleas does not have jurisdiction over the case. Explain the ambiguity that allows these two apparently contradictory statements to both be true.

   CLUE Is it possible for a court to have one type of jurisdiction and not another?

2. Our legal system contains numerous procedural requirements. Which of the ethical norms is furthered by these requirements?

   CLUE Review the four ethical norms described in chapter 1.

3. Many legal scholars say that the adversary system is consistent with the U.S. culture. What value that is furthered by our adversary system is important to our culture?

   CLUE Can you go beyond the four ethical norms described in chapter 1 and think of any other important values?

JURISDICTION

The concept of jurisdiction is at once exceedingly simple and, at the same time, exceedingly complex. At its simplest level, **jurisdiction** is the power of the courts to hear a case and to render a decision that is binding on the parties. Jurisdiction is complex, however, because there are several types of jurisdiction that a court must have in order to hear a case.

jurisdiction The power of a court to hear a case and render a binding decision.

ORIGINAL VERSUS APPELLATE JURISDICTION

Perhaps the simplest type of jurisdiction to understand is the distinction between original and appellate jurisdiction, which refers to the role the court plays in the judicial hierarchy. A court of **original jurisdiction**, usually referred to as a trial court, has the power to initially hear and decide a case. It is in the court of original jurisdiction that a case originates; hence its name. A court with **appellate jurisdiction** has the power to review a previously made decision to determine whether the trial court erred in its decision.

original jurisdiction The power to initially hear and decide (try) a case.

appellate jurisdiction The power to review a previously made decision by the trial court.

JURISDICTION OVER PERSONS AND PROPERTY

IN PERSONAM JURISDICTION Before the court can render a decision affecting a person, the court must have **in personam jurisdiction**, or **jurisdiction over the person**. In personam jurisdiction is the power to render a decision affecting the specific persons before the court. When a person files a lawsuit,

in personam jurisdiction (jurisdiction over the person) The power of a court to render a decision that affects the legal rights of a specific person.

plaintiff Party on whose behalf the complaint is filed.

defendant Party against whom an action is being brought.

complaint The initial pleading in a case that states the names of the parties to the action, the basis for the court's subject matter jurisdiction, the facts on which the party's claim is based, and the relief that the party is seeking.

summons Order by a court to appear before it at a certain time and place.

service Providing the defendant with a summons and a copy of the complaint.

long-arm statute A statute authorizing a court to obtain jurisdiction over an out-of-state defendant when that party has sufficient minimum contacts with a state.

that person, called the **plaintiff**, gives the court in personam jurisdiction over him or her. By filing a case, the plaintiff is asking the court to make a ruling affecting his or her rights. The court must acquire jurisdiction over the party being sued, the **defendant**, by *serving* him or her with a copy of the plaintiff's **complaint** and a **summons**. The complaint, discussed in more detail later in this chapter, is a detailed statement of the basis for the plaintiff's lawsuit and the relief being sought. The summons is an order of the court notifying the defendant of the pending case and telling him or her how and when to respond to the complaint.

Personal **service**, whereby a sheriff or other person appointed by the court hands the summons and complaint to the defendant, has been the traditional method of service. Today, other types of service are more common. *Residential service* may be used, whereby the summons and complaint are left by the representative of the court with a responsible adult at the home of the defendant. Certified mail or, in some cases, ordinary mail is also used to serve defendants. Once the defendant has been properly served, the court has in personam jurisdiction over him or her and may render a decision affecting his or her legal rights, regardless of whether the defendant responds to the complaint.

When one thinks about how the rules of service would apply to a suit against a corporation, the question arises: How do you serve a corporation? The legal system has solved that question. Most states require that corporations appoint an *agent for service* when they are incorporated. This agent is a person who has been given the legal authority to receive service for the corporation. Once the agent has been served, the corporation is served. In most states, service on the president of the corporation also constitutes service on the corporation.

A court's power is generally limited to the borders of the state in which it is located. So, traditionally, a defendant had to be served within the state in which the court was located in order for the court to acquire jurisdiction over the person of the defendant. This restriction imposed severe hardships when a defendant who lived in one state entered another state and injured the plaintiff. If the defendant never again entered the plaintiff's state, the plaintiff could bring an action against the defendant only in the state in which the defendant lived. Obviously, this restriction would prevent many legitimate actions from being filed.

To alleviate this problem, most states enacted **long-arm statutes**. These statutes enable the court to serve the defendant outside the state as long as the defendant has engaged in certain acts within the state. Those acts vary from state to state, but most statutes include such acts as committing a tort within the state or doing business within the state. The following case demonstrates the application of a long-arm statute.

WORLD-WIDE VOLKSWAGEN CORPORATION V. WOODSON, DISTRICT JUDGE OF CREEK COUNTY
UNITED STATES SUPREME COURT 444 U.S. 286 (1980)

Mr. and Mrs. Robinson, the plaintiffs, filed a product liability action against defendant World-Wide Volkswagen in a state court in Oklahoma to collect compensation for damages they incurred as a result of an accident involving an Audi they had purchased in New York. The defendants, the retailer (Seaway) and the wholesaler of the car (World-Wide Volkswagen), were both New York corporations.

Defendants claimed that the Oklahoma court could not exercise jurisdiction over them because they were nonresidents and they lacked sufficient "minimum contacts" with the state to be subject to its in personam jurisdiction.

The trial court rejected defendant-petitioner's claims. The Oklahoma Supreme Court likewise rejected their claims, so they petitioned the U.S. Supreme Court. (Justice Woodson

is the state supreme court justice whose ruling in this case is being challenged.)

JUSTICE WHITE

The issue before us is whether, consistently with the Due Process Clause of the Fourteenth Amendment, an Oklahoma court may exercise *in personam* jurisdiction over a nonresident automobile retailer and its wholesale distributor in a products-liability action, when the defendants' only connection with Oklahoma is the fact that an automobile sold in New York to New York residents became involved in an accident in Oklahoma.

As has long been settled, and as we reaffirm today, a state court may exercise personal jurisdiction over a nonresident defendant only so long as there exist "minimum contacts" between the defendant and the forum State. The concept of minimum contacts, in turn, can be seen to perform two related, but distinguishable, functions. It protects the defendant against the burdens of litigating in a distant or inconvenient forum. And it acts to ensure that the States, through their courts, do not reach out beyond the limits imposed on them by their status as coequal sovereigns in a federal system.

The protection against inconvenient litigation is typically described in terms of "reasonableness" or "fairness." We have said that the defendant's contacts with the forum State must be such that maintenance of the suit "does not offend 'traditional notions of fair play and substantial justice.'"

The limits imposed on state jurisdiction by the Due Process Clause, in its role as a guarantor against inconvenient litigation, have been substantially relaxed over the years. This trend is largely attributable to a fundamental transformation in the American economy:

> Today many commercial transactions touch two or more States and may involve parties separated by the full continent. With this increasing nationalization of commerce has come a great increase in the amount of business conducted by mail across state lines. At the same time modern transportation and communication have made it much less burdensome for a party sued to defend himself in a State where he engages in economic activity.

Nevertheless, we have never accepted the proposition that state lines are irrelevant for jurisdictional purposes, nor could we, and remain faithful to the principles of interstate federalism embodied in the Constitution.

Applying these principles to the case at hand, we find in the record before us a total absence of those affiliating circumstances that are a necessary predicate to any exercise of state-court jurisdiction. Petitioners carry on no activity whatsoever in Oklahoma. They close no sales and perform no services there. They avail themselves of none of the privileges and benefits of Oklahoma law. They solicit no business there either through salespersons or through advertising reasonably calculated to reach the State. Nor does the record show that they regularly sell cars at wholesale or retail to Oklahoma customers or residents or that they indirectly, through others, serve or seek to serve the Oklahoma market. In short, respondents seek to base jurisdiction on one, isolated occurrence and whatever inferences can be drawn therefrom: the fortuitous circumstance that a single Audi automobile sold in New York to New York residents, happened to suffer an accident while passing through Oklahoma.

It is argued, however, that because an automobile is mobile by its very design and purpose it was "foreseeable" that the Robinsons' Audi would cause injury in Oklahoma. Yet "foreseeability" alone has never been a sufficient benchmark for personal jurisdiction under the Due Process Clause.

If foreseeability were the criterion, a local California tire retailer could be forced to defend in Pennsylvania when a blowout occurs there, a Wisconsin seller of a defective automobile jack could be hauled before a distant court for damage caused in New Jersey, or a Florida soft-drink concessionaire could be summoned to Alaska to account for injuries happening there.

This is not to say, of course, that foreseeability is wholly irrelevant. But the foreseeability that is critical to due process analysis is not the mere likelihood that a product will find its way into the forum State. Rather, it is that the defendant's conduct and connection with the forum State are such that he should reasonably anticipate being hauled into court there.

When a corporation "purposefully avails itself of the privilege of conducting activities within the forum State," it has clear notice that it is subject to suit there, and can act to alleviate the risk of burdensome litigation by procuring insurance, passing the expected costs on to customers, or, if the risks are too great, severing its connection with the State. Hence if the sale of a product of a manufacturer or distributor such as Audi or Volkswagen is not simply an isolated occurrence, but arises from the efforts of the manufacturer or distributor to serve, directly or indirectly, the market for its product in other States, it is not unreasonable to subject it to suit in one of those States if its allegedly defective merchandise has there been the source of injury to its owner or to others.

But there is no such or similar basis for Oklahoma jurisdiction over World-Wide or Seaway in this case. Seaway's sales are made in Massena, N.Y. World-Wide's market, although substantially larger, is limited to dealers in New York, New Jersey, and Connecticut. There is no evidence of record that any automobiles distributed by World-Wide are sold to retail customers outside this tristate area. It is foreseeable that the purchasers of automobiles sold by World-Wide and Seaway may take them to Oklahoma. But the mere "unilateral activity of those who claim some relationship with a nonresident defendant cannot satisfy the requirement of contact with the forum State."

Reversed in favor of Petitioner, World-Wide Volkswagen Corp.

IN REM JURISDICTION If a defendant has property within a state, the plaintiff may seek to bring the action directly against the property rather than against the owner. For example, if a Michigan defendant owned land in Idaho on which taxes had not been paid for ten years, the state could bring an action to recover those taxes. The Idaho court would have **in rem jurisdiction** over the property, and, in an in rem proceeding, could order the property sold to pay the taxes. Such proceedings are often used when the owner of the property cannot be located for personal service.

in rem jurisdiction The power of a court to render a decision that affects property directly rather than the owner of the property.

88

Part One

*An Introduction to the Law
and the Legal Environment
of Business*

subject matter jurisdiction
The power of a court to render a
decision in a particular type of
case.

state court jurisdiction
Applies to cases that may be
heard only in the state court
system.

SUBJECT MATTER JURISDICTION

One of the most important types of jurisdiction is **subject matter jurisdiction**, the power of the court to hear certain kinds of cases. Subject matter jurisdiction is extremely important because if a judge renders a decision in a case over which the court does not have subject matter jurisdiction, the decision is void, or meaningless. The parties cannot give the court subject matter jurisdiction. It is granted by law as described in the subsequent sections.

At the beginning of the chapter, you learned that we have a dual court system, comprising of both a state and a federal system. The choice of which system to file a case in is not purely a matter of deciding which forum is most convenient or which judge would be most sympathetic. Subject matter jurisdiction determines what court may hear the case. When you think about the concept of subject matter jurisdiction, it is easiest to think of it in two steps. First, in which court system does the case fall, or, in other words, under what jurisdiction does the case fall? There are three possible answers: state jurisdiction, exclusive federal jurisdiction, or concurrent jurisdiction. Exhibit 5-1 illustrates the relationship among these three. Once you know which court system has jurisdiction over the case, you then need to ask whether there is a special court within that system that hears that specific type of case.

STATE JURISDICTION The **state court** system has subject matter jurisdiction over all cases not within the exclusive jurisdiction of the federal court system. Only a very limited number of cases fall within the exclusive jurisdiction of the federal courts. Consequently, almost all cases fall within the state courts' jurisdiction. Suits for breach of contract, product liability actions, and divorces are just a few of the types of cases that fall within the state court system's jurisdiction.

EXHIBIT 5-1

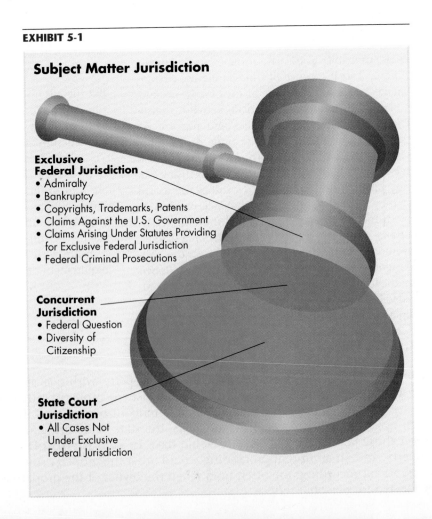

Subject Matter Jurisdiction

Exclusive Federal Jurisdiction
• Admiralty
• Bankruptcy
• Copyrights, Trademarks, Patents
• Claims Against the U.S. Government
• Claims Arising Under Statutes Providing for Exclusive Federal Jurisdiction
• Federal Criminal Prosecutions

Concurrent Jurisdiction
• Federal Question
• Diversity of Citizenship

State Court Jurisdiction
• All Cases Not Under Exclusive Federal Jurisdiction

EXCLUSIVE FEDERAL JURISDICTION   A few types of cases may be heard only in the federal courts. Such cases are within the **exclusive jurisdiction** of the federal court system. If these cases were tried in a state court, any decision rendered by the judge would be void. Cases that fall within the exclusive jurisdiction of the federal courts include such matters as admiralty, bankruptcy, federal criminal prosecutions, claims against the U.S. government, and claims arising under those federal statues that include a provision for exclusive federal jurisdiction. Many of these last cases are of particular concern to persons in business. For example, one statute that gives exclusive jurisdiction to the federal court system is the National Environmental Policy Act, discussed in chapter 20. Cases brought under this act must be filed in a federal district court.

exclusive federal jurisdiction Applies to cases that may be heard only in the federal court system.

CONCURRENT FEDERAL JURISDICTION   Many cases may be heard in either a federal or a state court. These cases are said to fall within the federal court's **concurrent jurisdiction**, meaning that *both* court systems have jurisdiction, so the plaintiff may file in the trial court of either system. There are two types of such cases. The first are *federal question* cases. If a case requires an interpretation of the U.S. Constitution, a federal statute, or a federal treaty, it is said to involve a federal question and may be heard in either the state or the federal court system. Many people make the mistake of thinking that when a person believes that his or her rights under the federal Constitution have been violated, the case *must* go to the federal courts. They are wrong. Such a case involves a federal question and is therefore within the concurrent jurisdiction of both court systems and can be heard in either.

concurrent jurisdiction Applies to cases that may be heard in either the federal or the state court system.

The second means by which a case may fall within the federal court's concurrent jurisdiction is through *diversity of citizenship*. If the opponents in a case are from different states, there is said to be diversity of citizenship. The diversity must be complete. If any two parties on opposing sides reside in the same state, diversity is lost. For example, if the plaintiff is an Ohio resident and one of the defendants lives in Michigan and the other in Indiana, diversity exists. However, if an Ohio plaintiff is bringing an action against a Michigan defendant and an Ohio defendant, there is not complete diversity and therefore no concurrent federal jurisdiction. When the basis for federal jurisdiction is diversity of citizenship, there must be an amount in excess of $75,000 in controversy (increased from $50,000 in 1996).

When a case falls within the federal court's concurrent jurisdiction because of either a federal question or diversity of citizenship, the suit may be filed in either state or federal court. If the case is filed in state court, the defendant has a *right of removal*, which means that he or she may have the case transferred to federal court. All the defendant has to do is file a motion with the court asking to exercise his or her right of removal and the case must be transferred to federal court; the judge has no discretion but must comply with the request.

The right of removal arises *only* when the case is filed in state court; there is no right of removal from a federal to a state court. As a result, whenever there is a case under concurrent jurisdiction, if either party wants the case to be heard in federal court, that is where it will be heard.

Why should both parties have the right to have such a case heard in federal court? In certain cases, a party may fear local prejudice in a state court. Juries for a state court are generally drawn from the county in which the court is located. The juries for federal district courts are drawn from the entire district, which encompasses many counties. Juries in state court are therefore usually more homogeneous than are those in a district court. One problem that this homogeneity may present to the out-of-state corporate defendant occurs when the county in which the court is located is predominantly rural. If the case involves an injury to a member of this rural community, the defendant may feel that the rural jurors would be more sympathetic to the local injured party, whereas jurors drawn from a broader area, including cities, may be more likely to view the victim less sympathetically. City residents are also more likely to work for a corporation and thus may not regard corporations as unfavorably as might rural residents.

90

Part One

*An Introduction to the Law
and the Legal Environment
of Business*

When a case involves a federal question, some people believe that federal judges are better qualified to hear such cases because they have more experience in resolving questions that require an interpretation of federal statutes. Finally, if a party anticipates that it may be necessary to appeal the case to the U.S. Supreme Court, bringing the case first in a federal district court may save one step in the appeals process.

When one party wishes to have the case tried in federal court and the other prefers state court, the issue of whether the case is within the concurrent jurisdiction of the federal courts sometimes arises. The following case provides an illustration of such a situation.

GAFFORD V. GENERAL ELECTRIC COMPANY
UNITED STATES COURT OF APPEALS 997 F.2D 150 (1993)

Plaintiff Carol Gafford filed an action against defendant General Electric Co. for violating the Kentucky Civil Rights Statute by discriminating against her on grounds of gender. She filed the case in the state court. The defendant filed a motion to exercise its right of removal, and the case was accordingly transferred to the federal district court over the plaintiff's objection. The trial was held, and the plaintiff lost. She appealed on the grounds that the case should never have been tried in federal court because there was not sufficient evidence of (1) $50,000 in controversy or (2) that the defendants' principle place of business was New York. Therefore, the diversity requirement had not been met.

JUDGE JONES

"The appropriate test for determining threshold jurisdictional amount when the complaining papers seek no specific award is still unclear." A survey of the case law reveals at least three different burdens of proof to be placed upon the defendant in such a circumstance.

We conclude that the "preponderance of the evidence" ("more likely than not") test is the best alternative. We believe that this test best balances the competing interests of protecting a defendant's right to remove (the case from state court) and limiting diversity jurisdiction.

The principal policy behind a defendant's statutorily created right to remove is protection from local bias. We believe that the "preponderance of the evidence" test comports with the balance struck. It does not place upon the defendant the daunting burden of proving, to a legal certainty, that the plaintiff's damages are not less than the amount-in-controversy requirement. Such a burden might well require the defendant to research, state and prove the plaintiff's claim for damages. On the other end of the spectrum, requiring the defendant to prove that the amount in controversy "may" meet the federal requirement would effectively force the plaintiff seeking remand to prove in rebuttal that only a relatively small amount of damages is legally possible.

We believe that the mean between the extremes unsettles to the least extent the balance struck between the defen-

dant's right to remove and the federal interest in limiting diversity jurisdiction.

Gafford contends that GE never met its burden of proving that the amount in controversy exceeded $50,000 once she set that issue in controversy. GE responds that Senior Counsel, [of] GE's Appliance Park facility in Louisville, Kentucky, testified at the pretrial hearing on jurisdiction that, should Gafford prevail on her claims, she would be entitled to a sum greater than $50,000 for backpay, as well as additional amounts for attorney fees and other damages.

Gafford did not offer any rebuttal witnesses at the jurisdiction hearing. Nor were any affidavits filed to contradict Jones' [agent for GE] testimony. Given GE's burden of proof settled upon above, we find that the district court did not err in finding that the amount in controversy exceeded $50,000.

Gafford also takes issue with the district court's determination that diversity of citizenship among the parties was complete. Gafford is a citizen of Kentucky. For purposes of determining diversity jurisdiction, a corporation can be a citizen of two states: (1) its state of incorporation; and (2) the state of its principal place of business. GE is incorporated in New York.

What is disputed is whether GE's principal place of business is in Kentucky. Gafford basically argues that, given the size of the GE facility in Kentucky, which encompasses over 9,000 employees, "[i]t would be reasonable to conclude that Jefferson County, Kentucky is a principal place of business for General Electric."

Gafford maintains that GE did not make a sufficient showing of workforce distribution and the like in order to meet its burden of proof, which we take to be a preponderance of the evidence.

By common sense and by law, a corporation can have only one principal place of business for purposes of establishing its state of citizenship. GE submitted evidence to the court that Schenectady, New York is its principal place of business, where basic corporate and personnel records are maintained. At the hearing, Earl F. Jones produced a copy of the 10-K form GE had filed with the United States Securities and Exchange Commission for the fiscal year ended December 31, 1990.

The following testimony was then introduced:

[MR. JONES]. . . . [O]n page two of this document, indicates that General Electric's address is 1 River Road, Schenectady, New York and that is in fact the principal place of business of the corporation.

[COUNSEL FOR GE]. Okay. Has the principal place of business been New York at all times material to this case?

[MR. JONES]. Yes.

In the affidavit submitted by GE, Jones also noted:

> *There are many states in the United States in which General Electric has extensive manufacturing operations. Several of those states contain General Electric business operations that generate more revenue for General Electric than Appliance Park in Kentucky.*

Gafford presented no evidence to rebut the affidavit or the testimony put forth by Jones at the jurisdiction hearing.

"The question of a corporation's principal place of business is essentially one of fact, to be determined on a case-by-case basis, taking into account such factors as the character of the corporation, its purposes, the kind of business in which it is engaged, and the situs of its operations."

In making this determination, courts have followed various approaches, or "tests." The "nerve center" test emphasizes the situs of corporate decision-making authority and overall control. The "corporate activities"/"place of activity" test emphasizes the location of production activities or service activities. These tests are not mutually exclusive.

Where a corporation carries on its business in a number of states and no one state is clearly the state in which its business is principally conducted, the state in which the substantial part of its business is transacted and from which centralized general supervision of its business is exercised is the state in which it has its principal place of business.

Since General Electric is neither incorporated nor has its principle [sic] place of business in Kentucky, it is not a citizen of the state for the purposes of diversity.

Given GE's basic corporate structure, it was not clearly erroneous to conclude that the significant administrative activity in New York justified finding New York to be GE's principal place of business.

Affirmed in favor of Defendant, General Electric Co.

Critical Thinking about the Law

LEGAL REASONING HAS TWO BASIC ELEMENTS: a conclusion and some reasons. The reasons provide a basis whereby we are urged to have confidence in the conclusion. For reasons to do their job, they must provide support, something reliable that moves our understanding in the direction of the conclusion.

Some courts provide reasons that restate in different words the conclusion they have chosen. These so-called reasons are disappointing because they do not do the job we expect from reasons.

1. This case has an unusually large amount of these pseudo-, or false, reasons. Locate an instance in which the Court writes as if it is providing a reason but is actually simply rewording its conclusion.

   CLUE Words such as *because* often signal us that the writer believes she or he is about to provide a reason.

VENUE

Subject matter jurisdiction should not be confused with venue. Once it is determined which court system has the power to hear the case, **venue** determines which of the many trial courts in that system is appropriate (Exhibit 5-2). Venue, clearly prescribed by statue in each state, is a matter of geographic location. It is usually based on the residence of the defendant, the residence of the plaintiff, the location of the property in dispute, or the location in which the incident out of which the dispute arose occurred. When there are multiple defendants who reside in various geographic locations, the party filing the lawsuit may usually choose from among the various locales. If the location of the court in which the case is filed presents a hardship or inconvenience to one of the parties, that person may request that the case be moved under the doctrine of *forum non conveniens*, which simply means that the location of the trial court is inconvenient. The judge in the

venue County of the trial court; prescribed by state statute.

92

Part One

*An Introduction to the Law
and the Legal Environment
of Business*

EXHIBIT 5-2 *Venue*

> *Venue is appropriate*
> - in the county of plaintiff's residence.
> - in the county of defendant's residence.
> - in the county where the dispute in issue arose.

case will consider the party's request and decide whether to grant it. Unlike the right of removal, the request for change of venue is granted at the judge's discretion. There will usually be a hearing on the issue of whether the judge should grant the motion because the plaintiff generally filed the case in a particular court for a reason and will therefore be opposed to the defendant's motion.

THE STRUCTURE OF THE COURT SYSTEM

As noted previously, our system has two parallel court structures, one federal and one state system. Because of subject matter jurisdiction limitations, one often does not have a choice as to which system to file the case in. Once a case is filed in a system, it will stay within that system, except for appeals to the U.S. Supreme Court. The following sections set forth the structure of the two systems. As you will see, they are indeed very similar. Their relationship is illustrated in Exhibit 5-3.

THE FEDERAL COURT SYSTEM

FEDERAL TRIAL COURTS   As you already know, trial courts are the courts of original jurisdiction. In the federal court system, the trial courts are the *United States district courts.* The United States is divided into 96 districts, and each district has at least one trial court of *general jurisdiction. General jurisdiction* means that the court has the power to hear cases involving a wide variety of subject matter and that it is not limited in the types of remedies that it can grant. All cases to be heard in the federal system are filed in these courts, except those cases for which Congress has established special trial courts of *limited jurisdiction.*

Trial courts of *limited jurisdiction* in the federal system are limited in the type of cases they have the power to hear. Special federal trial courts of limited jurisdiction have been established for bankruptcy cases, claims against the U.S. government, and copyright, patent, and trademark cases. In an extremely limited number of cases, the U.S. Supreme Court also functions as a trial court of limited jurisdiction. Such cases include controversies between two or more states and suits against foreign ambassadors. During 1995, a total of 283,200 cases were filed in federal district courts. This figure is up slightly over the 1990 figure of 264,400, but down from the 312,200 cases filed during 1985.

INTERMEDIATE COURTS OF APPEAL   The second level of courts in the federal system is made up of the *United States circuit courts of appeal.* The United States is divided into 11 geographic areas, and the District of Columbia, each of which has a circuit court of appeals. Exhibit 5-4 illustrates this division. There is also a federal circuit court of appeals and a recently established United States Veterans' Court of Appeals. Each circuit court of appeals hears appeals from all of the district courts located within its geographic area. These courts also hear appeals from administrative agencies located within their respective circuits. In some cases, appeals from administrative agencies are heard by the Federal Circuit Court of Appeals. The Veterans Appeals Court hears appeals of benefits decisions made by the Veteran's Administration. U.S. Circuit Courts of Appeals heard a total of 47,269 cases during 1995.

EXHIBIT 5-3 *The Structure of the Court System*

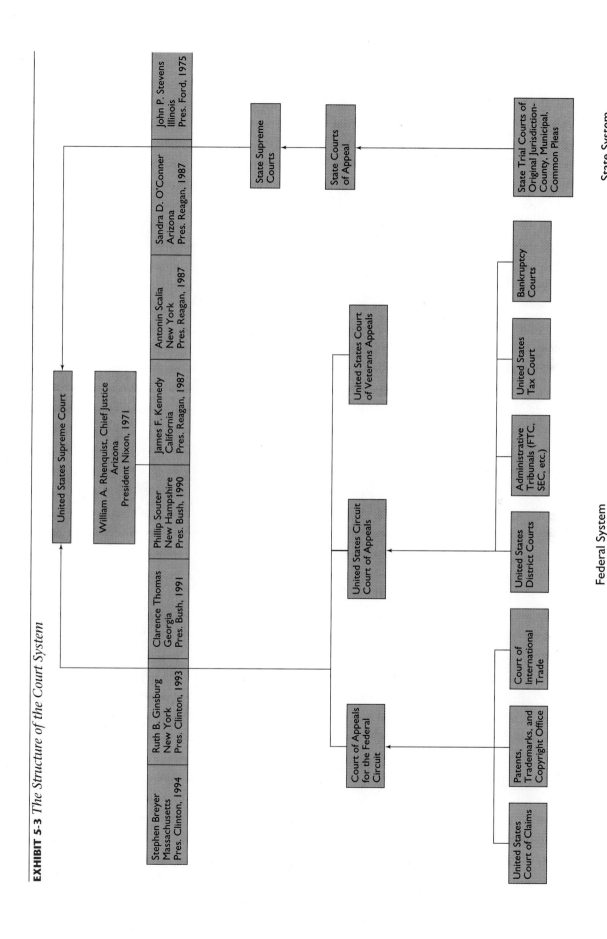

EXHIBIT 5-4

Geographic Boundaries of
United States Courts of Appeals and United States District Courts

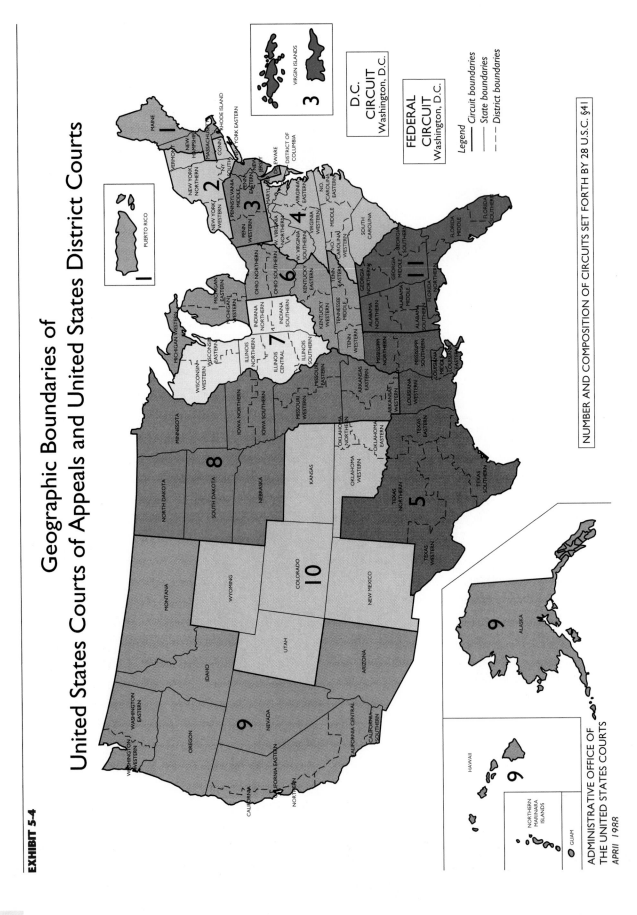

Legend
— Circuit boundaries
—— State boundaries
--- District boundaries

NUMBER AND COMPOSITION OF CIRCUITS SET FORTH BY 28 U.S.C. §41

ADMINISTRATIVE OFFICE OF
THE UNITED STATES COURTS
APRIL 1988

COURT OF LAST RESORT   The United States Supreme Court is the final appellate court in the federal system. In a limited number of instances, discussed later in this chapter, the U.S. Supreme Court also hears cases from the court of last resort in a state system. As previously noted, the U.S. Supreme Court also functions as a trial court in a limited number of cases.

STATE COURT SYSTEMS

There is no uniform state court structure because each state has devised its own court system. Most states, however, follow a general structure similar to that of the federal court system.

STATE TRIAL COURTS   In state court systems, most cases are originally filed in the *trial court of general jurisdiction*. As in the federal system, state trial courts of general jurisdiction are those that have the power to hear all the cases that would be tried in the state court system, except those cases for which special trial courts of limited jurisdiction have been established. These trial courts of general jurisdiction are distributed throughout each state, usually by county. The names of these courts vary from state to state but are usually called *courts of common pleas* or *county courts*. New York uniquely calls it trial courts of general jurisdiction *supreme courts*. In some states, these courts may have specialized divisions, such as domestic relations or probate.

Most states also have trial courts of limited jurisdiction. These courts are usually limited in the remedies that they may grant. Some may not issue injunctions or orders for specific performance. A common court of limited jurisdiction in most states is the small claims court, which may not grant damage awards in excess of specified amounts. Some courts of limited jurisdiction are limited to certain types of cases, such as traffic cases. Some criminal courts of limited jurisdiction may be limited to hearing misdemeanors. It is difficult to generalize about these courts because they vary so much from state to state. The main distinction between trial courts of general and limited jurisdiction, however, is that the former hear almost all types of cases that are filed in the state system and are unlimited in the remedies they can provide, whereas the latter hear only a particular type of case or may award only limited remedies.

INTERMEDIATE COURTS OF APPEAL   Intermediate courts of appeal, analogous to the federal circuit courts of appeal, exist in approximately half the states. These courts usually have broad jurisdiction, hearing appeals from courts of general and limited jurisdictions as well as from state administrative agencies. The names of these courts also vary by state. They may be called *courts of appeal* or *superior courts*.

COURTS OF LAST RESORT   In almost all cases filed in the state court system, the last appeal is to the state court of last resort. This court is frequently called the *supreme court*. In some states, it is known as the *court of appeals*. In approximately half of the states, it is the second court to which an appeal can be made; in the remaining states, it is the only appellate court.

THE ACTORS IN THE LEGAL SYSTEM AND THEIR RELATIONSHIP TO THE BUSINESS COMMUNITY

THE ATTORNEY

An understanding of the structure of the legal system would be incomplete without an awareness of the primary actors within the system. The party with whom businesspersons usually have the most frequent contact is the attorney. Although the exact qualifications for being an attorney vary from state to state, most states require that an attorney have a law degree, have passed the state's bar examination, and be of high moral character. Attorneys are the legal representatives of the parties before the court. Some corporations have full-time at-

96

Part One

*An Introduction to the Law
and the Legal Environment
of Business*

attorney-client privilege
Provides that information furnished by a client to an attorney in confidence, in conjunction with a legal matter, may not be revealed by the attorney without the client's permission.

work-product doctrine
Provides that formal and informal documents prepared by an attorney in conjunction with a client's case are privileged and may not be revealed by the attorney without the client's permission.

torneys, referred to as *in-house counsel*. Other corporations send all their legal work to an outside law firm. Many large businesses have in-house counsel and also use outside counsel when a problem arises that requires a specialist.

ATTORNEY-CLIENT PRIVILEGE The attorney can provide effective representation only when he or she knows all the pertinent facts of the case. The businessperson who withholds information from his or her attorney may cause irreparable harm if the hidden facts are revealed by the opposing side in court. The **attorney-client privilege** was established to encourage client honesty. This privilege provides that information furnished in confidence to an attorney, in conjunction with a legal matter, may not be revealed by that attorney without permission from the client. There is, however, an important exception to this rule. If the lawyer knows that the client is about to commit a crime, the lawyer *may* reveal confidential information in order to prevent the commission of that crime. Revealing such information, however, is not *required* of the attorney, it is simply allowed. This protection also extends to the attorney's work product under what is known as the **work-product doctrine**. The work product includes those formal and informal documents prepared by the attorney in conjunction with a client's case.

One of the problems arising out of the use of the attorney-client privilege in the corporate setting is the definition of the client. The client is the corporation, but the communication sought to be protected is that between the attorney and upper-, middle-, or lower-level employees of the corporation. In such cases, the corporate attorney usually tries to rely on the work-product doctrine to protect the information that he or she has gathered from employees, especially when such information is in the form of written communications. Such an approach has generally been successful, but the courts have not yet precisely defined the parameters of the attorney-client privilege and the work-product doctrine as they apply to the corporate setting.

ADDITIONAL FUNCTIONS OF THE ATTORNEY Attorneys are probably best known for representing clients in litigation, but they also provide other services for business clients. Attorneys represent their clients not only in courtroom litigation but also before administrative boards. Attorneys may be called on to represent their corporate clients in negotiations with labor unions or with other firms.

Corporate attorneys also serve as advisers or counselors, reviewing proposed corporate activities and advising management of legal problems that may arise as a result of such activities. In-house counsel familiar with the various activities of the firm are often in the best position to fulfill this role. Thus, businesspersons should attempt to establish a good working relationship with in-house counsel, using them as a resource whenever legal issues arise. Managers should not assume that they know all the legal ramifications of all the business activities in which they engage. Most in-house counsel would prefer to be consulted *before* an activity is undertaken rather than *after* it results in a legal problem.

Finally, the attorney may serve as a draftsperson, drawing up contracts, deeds, the corporate charter, securities registration statements, and all other legal documents needed by the corporation. Thus, is it clear that the attorney is one actor in the U.S. legal system who is of special importance to the business manager.

THE JUDGE

The role of the judge is especially important in our legal system. The judge's function changes, depending on whether he or she is a trial or an appellate court judge. A trial court judge presides over the trial, making sure that the case is heard with reasonable speed, ruling on all motions made in the case, and deciding all *questions of the law*. One of the most crucial functions of the trial court judge is ruling on whether certain pieces of evidence are admissible. Failure of the judge to admit certain items into evidence may be determinative of the outcome of a case, and a judge's ruling on any piece of evidence may subsequently become the basis for the appeal of an unfavorable decision. If the parties waive their rights to a jury trial, or if they are not entitled to a jury, the judge also decides the facts in the case and renders a decision accordingly. A single judge presides over each case.

Appellate judges serve on panels. They review lower-court cases to determine whether errors of law were committed by the lower courts. Their review consists primarily of reading the transcript of the trial, reading written arguments by counsel for both parties, and sometimes hearing oral arguments from both parties' attorneys.

State court judges are usually elected, although some are appointed, whereas federal court judges are appointed by the president with the advice and consent of the Senate. This appointment process is a good example of how the legislative and executive branches serve as checks on each other. The president has the greatest role because he makes the nomination, but he cannot choose just anyone. The president will usually select a list of potential nominees that will then be rated by a committee of the American Bar Association. The Bar Association will look at the nominees' legal experience and read their written opinions and published articles in an attempt to ensure that only the best-qualified candidates will be named to the federal bench. The Senate will also scrutinize the list and give the president an idea in advance of whether the various potential nominees will have a high likelihood of being confirmed. Once the president makes a nomination, the Senate Judiciary Subcommittee will hold formal hearings on the nominees' fitness for office. After the hearings, the full Senate will vote on the nomination. The President will generally try to nominate someone with an ideological background similar to his, but if the Senate is dominated by the opposite political party, a nominee who has too strong an ideology is not likely to be confirmed. In recent years, the appointment process has become familiar to most Americans as the hearings on Supreme Court nominees have been televised. Federal court judges serve for life, whereas state court judges generally serve a definite term, the length of which varies from state to state.

There is a lot of debate over whether federal judges should be appointed for life or elected for specific terms. The rationale behind appointment for life is that it takes the politics out of the judicial process. A judge will be selected on the basis of his or her credentials as opposed to the quality of his or her campaign skills. Once in office, the judge is free to make honest decisions without having to worry about the impact of any decision on reelection.

Of course, that independence is just what makes some people prefer elected judges. They argue that the members of every other branch of government are elected and are, therefore, forced to represent the will of the people, and judges should represent the people no less than members of the other branches.

THE POWER OF JUDICIAL REVIEW   One very important power that the judges have is the power of judicial review, that is, the power to determine whether a law passed by the legislature violates the Constitution. Any law that violates the Constitution must be struck down as null and void. The justices of the Supreme Court are the final arbiters of the constitutionality of our statutory laws.

This power of judicial review was not explicitly stated in the Constitution. It was established in the classic 1803 case of *Marbury v. Madison*,[1] wherein the Supreme Court stated, "It is emphatically the province and duty of the judicial department to say what the law is. Those who apply the rule to particular cases must of necessity expound and interpret that rule. If two laws conflict with each other, the courts must decide which of these conflicting rules governs the case. This is the very essence of judicial duty."

When individual justices exercise the power of judicial review, they do so with different philosophies and attitudes. Their philosophies can have a power-

---
[1] 5 U.S. (1 Branch) 137 (1803).

Part One

An Introduction to the Law
and the Legal Environment
of Business

judicial restraint A judicial philosophy that says courts should refrain from determining the constitutionality of a legislative act unless absolutely necessary and that social, political, and economic change should come out of the political process.

judicial activism A judicial philosophy that says the courts need to take an active role in encouraging political, economic, and social change.

ful effect on how they make decisions. One distinction that is frequently made with respect to judicial philosophies is the difference between judicial activism and judicial restraint. A judge who believes in **judicial restraint** believes that the three branches are co-equal and that the judiciary should refrain from determining the constitutionality of an act of Congress unless doing so is absolutely necessary. The intent behind the philosophy of judicial restraint is to keep the judiciary from interfering in the congressional sphere of power. These justices tend to believe that social, economic, and political change should result from the political process, not from judicial action. They consequently give great deference to actions of the state and federal legislatures.

Those who believe in judicial restraint will be much less likely than judicial activists to overturn an existing precedent. They tend to focus much more on the facts than on questioning whether the law needs to be changed. They tend to uphold lower-court decisions unless the decisions are clearly wrong on the facts.

Judicial activists tend to see a need for the court to take an active role in encouraging political, economic, and social change because the political process is often too slow to bring about necessary changes. They believe that constitutional issues must be decided within the context of today's society and that the framers meant for the Constitution to be an evolving document. Judicial activists are much less wedded to precedent than are adherents of judicial restraint. Adherents to a philosophy of judicial activism are result-oriented, and therefore much more likely to listen to arguments about what result is good for society. Activist judges are responsible for many social changes, especially in the civil rights area.

THE JURY

The jury is the means by which citizens participate in our judicial system. It had its roots in ancient Greek civilization, and it is often seen as the hallmark of democracy. A jury is a group of individuals, selected randomly from the geographic area in which the court is located, who will determine questions of fact. There are two types of juries: petit and grand.

petit jury A jury of 12 citizens impaneled to decide on the facts at issue in a criminal case and to pronounce the defendant guilty or not guilty.

PETIT JURIES Businesspersons are primarily concerned with **petit juries**, which serve as the finders of fact for trial courts. Originally composed of 12 members, most juries in civil cases are now allowed to have fewer members in many jurisdictions. Traditionally, jury decisions had to be unanimous. Today, however, more than half the jurisdictions no longer require unanimity in civil cases. This change in the jury system has been made primarily to speed up trial procedures.

An important decision to be made by any corporate client and her or his attorney is whether to have a jury. In any civil action in which the plaintiff is seeking a remedy at law (money damages), a jury may hear the case. If both parties to the case agree, however, the jury may be waived and a judge will decide the facts of the case. There is no rule about when a jury should be chosen, but a few factors should be considered. One is the technical nature of the case. A case that is highly technical may be one that can be more fairly decided by a judge, especially one who has expertise in the area in dispute. Another factor is the emotional appeal of the case. If the case is one for which the opponent's arguments may have strong emotional appeal, a judge may render a fairer decision than a jury would.

indictment A formal written accusation in a felony case.

grand jury A group of 12 to 23 citizens convened in private to decide whether enough evidence exists to try the defendant for a felony.

GRAND JURIES Grand juries are used only in criminal matters. The Fifth Amendment requires that all federal prosecutions for "infamous" crimes (including all federal offenses that carry a term of imprisonment in excess of one year) be commenced with an **indictment** (a formal accusation of the commission of a crime, which must be made before a defendant can be tried for the crime) by a **grand jury**. This jury hears evidence presented by the prosecutor and determines whether there is enough evidence to justify charging a defendant. The prudent business manager who carefully heeds the advice of an attorney should not be faced with a potential indictment by a grand jury. Increasingly, however, corporate managers *are* facing criminal charges for actions taken to benefit their corporate employers. Such cases are discussed in chapter 7.

THE ADVERSARY PROCESS

Our system of litigation is accurately described as an adversarial system. In an **adversarial system**, a neutral fact finder, a jury (or judge in a bench trial), hears evidence and arguments presented by both sides and then makes an objective decision based on the facts as presented by the proponents of each side and the law. Strict rules govern the types of evidence that the fact finder may consider. Theoretically, the adversarial system is the best way to bring out the truth, for each side will aggressively seek all the evidence that supports its position and will attempt to make the strongest possible argument for its position.

adversarial system System of litigation in which the judge hears evidence and arguments presented by both sides in a case and then makes an objective decision based on the facts and the law as presented by each side.

CRITICISMS OF THE ADVERSARY SYSTEM

Many people criticize this system. They argue that because each side is searching for only that evidence which supports its position, a proponent who discovers evidence helpful to the other side will not bring such evidence to the attention of the court. This tendency to ignore contrary evidence prevents a fair decision, one based on *all* the available evidence, from being rendered.

Another argument of the critics is that the adversarial process is extremely time-consuming and costly. Two groups of "investigators" are seeking the same evidence. Thus, there is a duplication of effort that lengthens the process and increases the cost unnecessarily.

Others argue that the adversarial system, as it functions in this country, is unfair. Each party in the adversarial process is represented by an attorney. Having the most skillful attorney is a tremendous advantage. Because the wealthier a party is, the better the attorney she or he can afford to hire, the system unjustifiably favors the wealthy.

Law professor Marc Galanter has written an interesting critique of our adversarial system that has generated a lot of discussion.[2] He argues that, given the structure of our system, certain parties tend to have a distinct advantage. Galanter divides litigants into two groups: the repeat players (RPs), those who are engaged in similar litigations over time, and the one-shotters (OSs), those who have only occasional recourse to the courts. Repeat players would typically be large corporations, financial institutions, landlords, developers, government agencies, and prosecutors. Typical one-shotters would be debtors, employees with grievances against their employers, tenants, and victims of accidents.

According to Galanter, the RPs have a distinct advantage over the OSs in litigation. Because of their experience, RPs are better prepared for trial; they know what kinds of records to keep and how to structure transactions so that they will have an advantage in court. Repeat players will have developed expertise in the area and will have access to specialists. They will have low "start-up costs" for a case because they have been through the same type of case before. Repeat players will have developed helpful informal relationships with persons at the courthouse. Knowing the odds of success better than the OS does, the RP can use experience and knowledge to calculate whether to settle. Finally, RPs can litigate for rules or for an immediate outcome.

Thus, in a typical case involving an RP and an OS, the RP has a distinct advantage. Some people believe that this advantage is significant enough to prevent our current system from dispensing justice in these cases.

---

[2]M. Galanter, *Why the Haves Come Out Ahead: Speculation on the Limits of Legal Change*, 9 J.L. & Soc. Rev. 96 (1974).

Part One

---

*An Introduction to the Law
and the Legal Environment
of Business*

STEPS IN CIVIL LITIGATION AND THE ROLE OF BUSINESSPERSONS

THE PRETRIAL STAGE

Every lawsuit is the result of a dispute. Business disputes may result from a breach of contract, the protested firing of an employee, or the injury of a consumer who uses the corporation's product. This section focuses on dispute resolution in this country under the adversary system. It examines the procedure used in a civil case, the stages of which are outlined in Exhibit 5-5. The rules that govern such proceedings are called the **rules of civil procedure**. There are federal rules of civil procedure, which apply in all federal courts, as well as state rules, which apply in the state courts. Most of the state rules are based on the federal rules.

rules of civil procedure The rules governing proceedings in a civil case; federal rules of procedure apply in all federal courts, and state rules apply in state courts.

INFORMAL NEGOTIATIONS   For the businessperson involved in a dispute, the first step is probably going to be to discuss the dispute directly with the other disputing party. When it appears that the parties are not going to be able to resolve the problem themselves, the businessperson will then discuss the dispute with an attorney. It is important that the attorney be given all relevant information, even if it does not make the businessperson look good. The more relevant facts the attorney has, the better the attorney's advice will be. Together, the attorney and the client may be able to resolve the dispute informally with the other party.

INITIATION OF A LEGAL ACTION   Once a party decides that an informal resolution is not possible, the parties enter what is often called the *pleading stage* of the lawsuit. **Pleadings** are papers filed by a party in court and then served on the opponent. The basic pleadings are the *complaint*, the *answer*, the *counterclaim*, and the *motion to dismiss*. Exhibit 5-6 provides an illustration of a typical complaint. The attorney of the businessperson who feels that he or she has been wronged initiates a lawsuit by filing a complaint in the appropriate court. A complaint is a document that states the names of the parties to the action, the basis for the court's subject matter jurisdiction, the facts on which the party's claim is based, and the relief that the party is seeking. Remember that the party on whose behalf the complaint is filed is the *plaintiff*, and the *defendant* is the party against whom the action is being brought.

pleadings Papers filed by a party in court and then served on the opponent in a civil lawsuit.

In determining the appropriate court in which to file the complaint, the attorney must determine which court has *subject matter jurisdiction* over the case. Once that determination has been made, the attorney must ascertain the proper *venue* for the case. The means used by the attorney to determine the subject matter jurisdiction and venue were discussed earlier in this chapter.

SERVICE OF PROCESS   Once the complaint has been filed, the court *serves* a copy of the complaint and a summons on the defendant. The reader should remember that service is the procedure used by the court to ensure that the defendant actually receives a copy of the summons and the complaint. Service of process gives the court in personam jurisdiction over the defendant and provides his or her due process right of notice of the charges filed against him or her.

DEFENDANT'S RESPONSE   Once the defendant has been properly served, he or she files an answer and possibly a counterclaim. The **answer** is a response to the allegations in the plaintiff's complaint. The answer must admit, deny, or state that the defendant has no knowledge about the truth of each of the plaintiff's allegations. The answer may also contain *affirmative defenses*, which consist of facts that were not stated in the complaint that would provide justification for the defendant's actions *and* a legally sound reason to deny relief to the plaintiff. These defenses must be stated in the answer. If they are not raised in

answer Defendant's response to the allegations in the plaintiff's complaint.

Plaintiff files *complaint*, which is
served on defendant along with *summons*.

↓

Defendant files *answer, counterclaim,*
and/or *motion to dismiss.*

↓

Plaintiff may file a *reply*
to defendant's counterclaim.

↓

Plaintiff or defendant may file a
motion for judgment on the pleadings
or *motions for preliminary relief.*

↓

Discovery occurs, including
interrogatories, requests for production
of documents, and depositions.

↓

Plaintiff or defendant may file a
motion for summary judgment.

↓

Pretrial conference is held.

↓

The *trial* occurs. The plaintiff's case is presented,
followed by the defendant's case.

↓

In a trial by jury, the judge *instructs the jury*, they recess to
make their findings, and then return their *verdict.*

↓

After a jury trial, the losing party may file a
posttrial motion, such as *motion for a new trial* or a
motion for a judgment notwithstanding the verdict.

↓

The judge hands down the *judgment.*

↓

Losing party may *appeal* judgment
of the trial court.

EXHIBIT 5-6 *Complaint*

THE COURT OF COMMON PLEAS
OF LUCAS COUNTY, OHIO

Pam Streets, Plaintiff v. Daniel Lane, Defendant
COMPLAINT FOR NEGLIGENCE
Case No. _____

Now comes the plaintiff, Pam Streets, and, for her complaint, alleges as follows:

1. Plaintiff, Pam Streets, is a citizen of Lucas County, in the state of Ohio, and Defendant, Daniel Lane, is a citizen of Lucas County in the state of Ohio.

2. On December 1, 1987, the Plaintiff was lawfully driving her automobile south on Main Street in Toledo, Ohio.

3. At approximately 4:00 p.m., on December 1, 1987, the Defendant negligently ran a red light on Star Avenue, and as a result crashed into Plaintiff's car.

4. As a result of the collision, the Plaintiff suffered lacerations to the face and a broken leg, incurring $10,000 in medical expenses.

5. As a result of the above described collision, her car was damaged in the amount of $12,000.

6. As a result of the foregoing injuries, the Plaintiff was required to miss eight weeks of work, resulting in a loss of wages of $2,400.

WHEREFORE, Plaintiff demands judgment in the amount of $24,000, plus costs of this action.

Sam Snead
Attorney for Plaintiff
124 East Broadway
Toledo, OH 43605

JURY DEMAND
Plaintiff demands a trial by jury in this matter.

Sam Snead
Attorney for Plaintiff

the answer, the court might not allow these defenses to be raised later. The defendant is required to plead his or her affirmative defenses in the answer in order to give the plaintiff notice of all the issues that will be raised at the trial.

As an illustration, two affirmative defenses to a breach of contract action might be that the plaintiff procured the defendant's signature on the contract through fraud and that the contract was illegal because its enforcement would result in a violation of the antitrust laws. Another example could arise, if a manufacturer were being sued because the plaintiff was injured by the manufacturer's negligently produced defective product. The defendant might raise the affirmative defense of contributory negligence, arguing that the plaintiff's injury would not have occurred if the plaintiff had not also been negligent. Notice the use of an affirmative defense in the sample answer in Exhibit 5-7. It is important that the businessperson who is being sued try immediately to think of any potential affirmative defenses that might excuse his or her actions.

When a defendant, upon receiving the complaint, believes that even if all of the plaintiff's factual allegations were true the plaintiff would not be entitled to a favorable judgment, the defendant may file a **motion to dismiss**. There are no factual issues being debated, so the judge accepts the facts as stated by the plaintiff and makes a ruling on the legal questions in the case. Judges are generally not receptive to such motions, granting them only when it appears

motion to dismiss Defendant's application to the court to put the case out of judicial consideration because even if the plaintiff's factual allegations are true, the plaintiff is not entitled to relief.

THE COURT OF COMMON PLEAS
OF LUCAS COUNTY, OHIO

_____

Pam Streets, Plaintiff v. Daniel Lane, Defendant
ANSWER AND COUNTERCLAIM
Case No. _____

Now comes the defendant, Daniel Lane, and answers the complaint of plaintiff herein as follows:

FIRST DEFENSE

1. Admits the allegations in paragraphs 1 and 2.

2. Denies the allegation in paragraph 3.

3. Is without knowledge as to the truth or falsity of the allegations contained in paragraphs 4, 5, and 6.

SECOND DEFENSE

4. If the court believes the allegations contained in paragraph 3, which the defendant expressly denies, plaintiff should still be denied recovery because she was negligently driving in excess of the speed limit and without her glasses, both of which contributed to the cause of the accident.

COUNTERCLAIM

5. Defendant lawfully drove his automobile in an eastbound direction on Starr Avenue on December 1, 1987.

6. At approximately 4:00 p.m., on December 1, 1987, plaintiff negligently drove her automobile at an excessive speed through a red light on Main Street where Said Street crosses Starr Avenue, colliding into defendant's automobile.

7. As a result of the collision, defendant suffered bruises and a concussion, resulting in $5,000 in medical bills.

8. Defendant further suffered $6,000 in property damage to his automobile.

WHEREFORE, defendant prays for a judgment dismissing the plaintiff's complaint, granting the defendant a judgment against plaintiff in the amount of $11,000 plus costs of this action.

Shelly Shaker
Attorney for Defendant
216 Nevada
Toledo, OH 43605

beyond doubt that the plaintiff can prove no set of facts in support of his claim that would entitle him to relief.

A defendant who believes that he or she has a cause of action against the plaintiff will include a **counterclaim**. The form of a counterclaim is just like that of a complaint. The defendant states the facts supporting his or her claim and asks for the relief to which he or she feels entitled. Exhibit 5-7 also contains a counterclaim.

If the defendant files a counterclaim, the plaintiff generally files a *reply*. A reply is simply an answer to a counterclaim. In the reply, the plaintiff admits, denies, or states that he or she is without knowledge of the truth of the facts asserted by the defendant in the counterclaim. Any affirmative defenses that are appropriate must be raised in the reply.

PRETRIAL MOTIONS   The early pleadings just described serve to establish the legal and factual issues of the case. Once those issues have been established, either the plaintiff or the defendant may file a motion designed to bring the case to an early conclusion or to gain some advantage for the party filing the

counterclaim Defendant's statement of facts showing cause for action against the plaintiff and a request for appropriate relief.

104

Part One

*An Introduction to the Law
and the Legal Environment
of Business*

motion. A *motion* is simply a request by a party for the court to do something. A party may request, or move, that the court do almost anything pertaining to the case. For example, a party might make a motion for some form of temporary relief until a decision has been rendered; in a suit brought over the right to a piece of property, the court may grant a motion prohibiting the current possessor of that property from selling it.

When a party files any motion with the court, a copy is always sent to the opposing attorney. That attorney may respond to the motion, usually requesting that the judge deny the motion. In many cases, the judge will simply rule on the motion, either granting or denying it. In some cases, the judge will hold a hearing at which the two sides orally present their arguments.

DISCOVERY   Once the initial pleadings and motions have been filed, the parties gather information from each other through **discovery**. At this stage, the businessperson is frequently asked by her or his attorney to respond to the opponent's discovery requests. There are a number of tools of discovery. One of the most common is *interrogatories*, which are a series of written questions that are sent to the opposing party, who must truthfully answer them under oath. The interrogatories are frequently accompanied by a *request to admit certain facts*. The attorney and the client work together to answer these interrogatories and requests for admission of facts.

discovery The pretrial gathering of information from each other by the parties.

A *request to produce documents* or other items is another tool of discovery. Unless the information requested is privileged or is irrelevant to the case, it must be produced. Photographs, contracts, written estimates, and forms that must be filed with government agencies are among the items that might be requested. One party might also request that the other party submit to a mental or a physical examination. This motion will be approved only when the party's mental or physical health is at issue in the case.

deposition Pretrial testimony by witnesses who are examined under oath.

Finally, testimony before trial might be obtained by the taking of a **deposition**. At a deposition, a witness is examined under oath by attorneys. A court reporter (stenographer) records every word spoken by the attorneys and witnesses. The testimony is usually transcribed so that both parties have a written copy. If a businessperson is to be deposed in a case, it is very important that he or she and the attorney talk extensively about what kinds of questions could come up at the deposition and how such questions are to be answered. The party who requested the deposition is not only seeking information but is also laying the groundwork for identifying any inconsistencies that might arise between a person's testimony at the deposition and in court. If such inconsistencies exist, they will be brought to the attention of the fact finder and may result in a loss of credibility for the person giving testimony in the courtroom. Depositions may also be used when a potential witness is old or ill and might die before the trial. They are useful if witnesses might be moving or for some other reason might not be available at the time of the trial.

As a result of discovery, each party should have knowledge of most of the facts surrounding the case. This process is supposed to prevent surprises from occurring in the courtroom. Parties must comply with requests for discovery, or the court could order that the facts sought to be discovered be deemed to be admitted. Thus, it is important that the businessperson involved in litigation produce for the attorney all requested discovery material. An attorney who feels that certain material should not be discovered makes arguments about its lack of relevance to the case, but if the court disagrees, the information must be supplied.

PRETRIAL CONFERENCE   If the judge finds that questions of fact do exist, he or she usually holds a pretrial conference. This is an informal meeting of the judge with the lawyers representing the parties. At this meeting, they try to narrow the legal and factual issues and to work out a settlement if possible. When the lawsuit begins, there are many conflicting assertions as to what events actually led up to the lawsuit. Questions about what actually happened are referred to as *questions of fact*. Many times, as a result of discovery, parties come to agree on most of the facts. Remaining factual disputes can often be resolved at the conference. Then the only questions left are how to apply the law to the facts and what damages, if any, to award. By the time of the pretrial conference, the businessperson should have determined the limits on any settlement to which he or she is willing to agree and should have communicated those limits to his or her attorney, who may be able to reach a settlement at the conference. Judges frequently try very hard to help the parties reach agreement before trial. If no settlement can be reached, the attorneys and the judge discuss the administrative details of the trial, its length, the witnesses, and any pretrial stipulations of fact or law to which the parties can agree.

THE TRIAL

Once the pretrial stage has concluded, the next step is the trial. As stated previously, if the plaintiff is seeking a legal remedy (money damages), he or she is usually entitled to a jury trial. The judge is the fact finder only when an equitable remedy (an injunction or other court order) is being sought or the parties have waived their right to a jury. For example, a plaintiff in a product liability action requesting a judgment for $10,000 in medical expenses would be seeking a legal remedy and would be entitled to a jury trial. But a plaintiff seeking an injunction, under the antitrust laws, to prohibit two defendant corporations from merging would be requesting an equitable remedy and would not be entitled to a jury. It is important for the business manager to determine at the outset whether a jury is desirable because a jury must be demanded in the complaint.

The stages of the trial are (1) jury selection, (2) the opening statements, (3) the plaintiff's case, (4) the defendant's case, (5) the conference on jury instructions, (6) closing arguments, and (7) post-trial motions.

JURY SELECTION An important part of a jury trial is the selection of the jury. A panel of potential jurors is selected randomly from a list of citizens. In the federal court system, voter lists are used. In a process known as **voir dire,** the judge or the attorneys, or both, question potential jurors to determine whether they could render an unbiased opinion in the case.

When a juror's response to a question causes an attorney to believe that this potential juror cannot be unbiased, the attorney will ask that the potential juror be removed "for cause." For example, in an accident case, a potential juror might reveal that he had been in a similar accident. Or the potential juror may have filed a similar lawsuit against one of the defendant's competitors five years ago. Attorneys are given an unlimited number of challenges for cause. In most states, each attorney is allowed to reject a minimal number of potential jurors without giving a reason. These rejections are called *peremptory challenges*.

Although the legitimate rationale for peremptories is that they recognize a lawyer's "gut reaction" to a potential juror who does not say anything that technically reveals a bias, there has been some abuse of preemptories in the past. One potential source of abuse was to use peremptories to discriminate against certain classes, such as race or gender.

In 1989, in the case of *Batson v. Kentucky*[3] the U.S. Supreme Court ruled that prosecutors could not use race-based peremptory challenges in criminal cases. Subsequently, the Supreme Court extended the ban to the use of race-based challenges by either party in civil cases. Several unsuccessful attempts were made to extend the prohibition to challenges based on gender. Finally, in 1992, the court in the following case extended the equal protection guarantee to cover gender.

voir dire Process whereby the judge and/or the attorneys question potential jurors to determine whether they will be able to render an unbiased opinion in the case.

---

[3]476 U.S. 79 (1986).

J.E.B. V. ALABAMA *EX REL.* T.B.

UNITED STATES SUPREME COURT 114 S. CT. 1419 (1994)

On behalf of T.B., the unwed mother of a minor child, the State of Alabama filed a complaint for paternity and child support against J.E.B. Twelve males and 24 females were called by the court as potential jurors. After the court had removed three individuals for cause, only ten males remained. The state used its peremptory challenges to remove nine male jurors, J.E.B. removed the tenth, resulting in an all-female jury. The court rejected J.E.B.'s objection to the gender-based challenges, and the jury found J.E.B. to be the father.

J.E.B. appealed to the court of appeals, who affirmed the trial court's decision that the Equal Protection Clause does not prohibit gender-based challenges. The Alabama Supreme Court denied certiorari (discussed later), and J.E.B. then appealed to the U.S. Supreme Court.

JUSTICE BLACKMUN

Today we reaffirm what should be axiomatic: Intentional discrimination on the basis of gender by state actors violates the Equal Protection Clause, particularly where, as here, the discrimination serves to ratify and perpetuate invidious, archaic, and overbroad stereotypes about the relative abilities of men and women.

Discrimination on the basis of gender in the exercise of peremptory challenges is a relatively recent phenomenon. Gender-based peremptory strikes were hardly practicable for most of our country's existence, since, until the 19th century, women were completely excluded from jury service.

Many States continued to exclude women from jury service well into the present century, despite the fact that women attained suffrage upon ratification of the Nineteenth Amendment in 1920.

Despite the heightened scrutiny afforded distinctions based on gender, respondent argues that gender discrimination in the selection of the petit jury should be permitted, though discrimination on the basis of race is not. Respondent suggests that "gender discrimination in this country . . . has never reached the level of discrimination" against African-Americans, and therefore gender discrimination, unlike racial discrimination, is tolerable in the courtroom.

While the prejudicial attitudes toward women in this country have not been identical to those held toward racial minorities, the similarities between the experiences of racial minorities and women, in some contexts, "overpower those differences." Certainly, with respect to jury service, African-Americans and women share a history of total exclusion.

Discrimination in jury selection, whether based on race or on gender, causes harm to the litigants, the community, and the individual jurors who are wrongfully excluded from participation in the judicial process. The litigants are harmed by the risk that the prejudice which motivated the discriminatory selection of the jury will infect the entire proceedings. The community is harmed by the State's participation in the perpetuation of invidious group stereotypes and the inevitable loss of confidence in our judicial system that state-sanctioned discrimination in the courtroom engenders.

When state actors exercise peremptory challenges in reliance on gender stereotypes, they ratify and reinforce prejudicial views of the relative abilities of men and women. Because these stereotypes have wreaked injustice in so many other spheres of our country's public life, active discrimination by litigants on the basis of gender during jury selection "invites cynicism respecting the jury's neutrality and its obligation to adhere to the law."

In recent cases we have emphasized that individual jurors themselves have a right to nondiscriminatory jury selection procedures.

As with race-based *Batson* claims, a party alleging gender discrimination must make a prima facie showing of intentional discrimination before the party exercising the challenge is required to explain the basis for the strike. When an explanation is required, it need not rise to the level of a "for cause" challenge; rather, it merely must be based on a juror characteristic other than gender and the proffered explanation may not be pretextual.

Equal opportunity to participate in the fair administration of justice is fundamental to our democratic system. It reaffirms the promise of equality under the law—that all citizens, regardless of race, ethnicity, or gender, have the chance to take part directly in our democracy. When persons are excluded from participation in our democratic processes solely because of race or gender, this promise of equality dims, and the integrity of our judicial system is jeopardized.

In view of these concerns, the Equal Protection Clause prohibits discrimination in jury selection on the basis of gender, or on the assumption that an individual will be biased in a particular case for no reason other than the fact that the person happens to be a woman or happens to be a man. As with race, the "core guarantee of equal protection, ensuring citizens that their State will not discriminate . . . , would be meaningless were we to approve the exclusion of jurors on the basis of such assumptions, which arise solely from the jurors' [gender]."

Reversed and remanded in favor of Defendant, J.E.B.

JUSTICE SCALIA, DISSENTING

Today's opinion is an inspiring demonstration of how thoroughly up-to-date and right-thinking we Justices are in matters pertaining to the sexes, and how sternly we disapprove the male chauvinist attitudes of our predecessors. The price to be paid for this display—a modest price, surely—is that most of the opinion is quite irrelevant to the case at hand. The hasty reader will be surprised to learn, for example, that this lawsuit involves a complaint about the use of peremptory challenges to exclude *men* from a petit jury. To be sure, petitioner, a man, used all but one of *his* peremptory strikes to remove *women* from the jury (he used his last challenge to strike the sole remaining male from the pool), but the validity of *his* strikes is not before us. Nonetheless, the Court treats itself to an extended discussion of the historic exclusion of women not only from jury service, but also from service at the bar (which is rather like jury service, in that it involves going to the courthouse a lot). All this, as I say, is irrelevant since the case involves state action that allegedly discriminates against men.

The Court also spends time establishing that the use of sex as a proxy for particular views or sympathies is unwise and perhaps irrational. The opinion stresses the lack of statistical evidence to support the widely held belief that, at least in certain types of cases, a juror's sex has some statistically significant predictive value as to how the juror will behave. This assertion seems to place the Court in opposition to its earlier Sixth Amendment "fair cross-section" cases. ("Controlled studies . . . have concluded that women bring to juries their own perspectives and values that influence both jury deliberation and result".)

Of course the relationship of sex to partiality *would have been* relevant if the Court had demanded in this case what it ordinarily demands: that the complaining party have suffered some injury. Leaving aside for the moment the reality that the defendant himself had the opportunity to strike women from the jury, the defendant would have some cause to complain about the prosecutor's striking male jurors if male jurors tend to be more favorable towards defendants in paternity suits. But if men and women jurors are (as the Court thinks) fungible, then the only arguable injury from the prosecutor's "impermissible" use of male sex as the basis for his peremptories is injury to the stricken juror, not to the defendant. Indeed, far from having suffered harm, petitioner, a state actor under precedents, has himself actually *inflicted* harm on female jurors. The Court today presumably supplies petitioner with a cause of action by applying the uniquely expansive third-party standing analysis of according petitioner a remedy because of the wrong done to male jurors. Insofar as petitioner is concerned, this is a case of harmless error if there ever was one; a retrial will do nothing but divert the State's judicial and prosecutorial resources, allowing either petitioner or some other malefactor to go free.

The core of the Court's reasoning is that peremptory challenges on the basis of any group characteristic subject to heightened scrutiny are inconsistent with the guarantee of the Equal Protection Clause. That conclusion can be reached only by focusing unrealistically upon individual exercises of the peremptory challenge, and ignoring the totality of the practice. Since all groups are subject to the peremptory challenge (and will be made the object of it, depending upon the nature of the particular case) it is hard to see how any group is denied equal protection.

Even if the line of our later cases guaranteed by today's decision limits the theoretically boundless *Batson* principle to race, sex, and perhaps other classifications subject to heightened scrutiny, much damage has been done. It has been done, first and foremost, to the peremptory challenge system, which loses its whole character when (in order to defend against "impermissible stereotyping" claims) "reasons" for strikes must be given. The right of peremptory challenge " 'is', as Blackstone says, 'an arbitrary and capricious right; and it must be exercised with full freedom, or it fails of its full purpose.' "

And damage has been done, secondarily, to the entire justice system, which will bear the burden of the expanded quest for "reasoned peremptories" that the Court demands. The extension of *Batson* to sex, and almost certainly beyond, will provide the basis for extensive collateral litigation, . . . Another consequence, as I have mentioned, is a lengthening of the voir dire process that already burdens trial courts.

The irrationality of today's strike-by-strike approach to equal protection is evident from the consequences of extending it to its logical conclusion. If a fair and impartial trial is a prosecutor's only legitimate goal; if adversarial trial stratagems must be tested against that goal in abstraction from their role within the system as a whole; and if, so tested, sex-based stratagems do not survive heightened scrutiny—then the prosecutor presumably violates the Constitution when he selects a male or female police officer to testify because he believes one or the other sex might be more convincing in the context of the particular case, or because he believes one or the other might be more appealing to a predominantly male or female jury. A decision to stress one line of argument or present certain witnesses before a mostly female jury—for example, to stress that the defendant victimized women—becomes, under the Court's reasoning, intentional discrimination by a state actor on the basis of gender.

I dissent.

Critical Thinking about the Law

THE REASONING IN THIS CASE IS played out with *Batson v. Kentucky* standing tall and visible in the background. The legal system reinforces our ethical preference for order. The resulting dependability of our legal rules serves as a guide for business decisions, facilitating the many transactions required by modern business.

Yet the courts recognize that rules must evolve as our social needs and understandings change. Hence the courts must struggle with achieving a balance between order and flexibility. *J.E.B.* provides an opportunity to use our critical thinking to see this tension in action.

1. Justice Blackmun disagrees with the respondent concerning the comparative "level of discrimination" experienced by nonwhites and women. Our reasoning frequently contains phrases such as "level of discrimination" that require some numerical determination. Recognize that *clear* numbers measuring such a level are hard to come by. As critical thinkers you can often see soft spots in reasoning by asking: Now how are they measuring that concept? Could you help Justice Blackmun measure "level of discrimination" by suggesting what data might be useful for this determination?

   CLUE Start with the number of people affected, the probability that they would be affected, and the extent of the harm.

2. Justice Scalia does not categorically disagree with extension of *Batson*. What facts would have had to be different for Scalia to have concurred with the majority?

   CLUE Find the section in his dissent where he explains the inadequacies in the majority's reasoning.

The voir dire process has changed significantly over the years, and many lawyers see a successful voir dire as being the essential element in winning a case. Jury selection today has become a "science," and in most cases involving large potential judgments at least one side, and often both, use a professional jury selection service. These companies provide a wide array of services to the customers. Some of these services include identifying demographic data to help lawyers build a profile of the ideal juror, helping design questions for the lawyers to ask during voir dire, and providing such post–voir dire services as mock juries and shadow juries. A **mock jury** is a group of individuals whose demographic makeup matches that of the actual jury. The lawyers practice their case before the mock jury to find out how receptive the "jurors" are to the arguments and how the mock jurors relate to the witnesses. Lawyers can gain valuable information about what they need to change before presenting the case. Depending on how much money a client has, lawyers may go through multiple "trials" in front of a mock jury. A **shadow jury** again matches the demographics of the real jury, but the shadow jury actually sits in the courtroom during the trial. They "deliberate" at the end of each day so that the lawyer will have an ongoing idea of how the case is going. The shadow jury's deliberations may let a lawyer know when damage has been done to the case that needs to be repaired. After the trial is finished, the shadow jury deliberates for a predetermined, brief period of time. Their "verdict" then helps the lawyer decide whether to try to settle the case before the jury comes back with a verdict. (Remember, the parties can agree to settle at any time until the jury hands down the final decision in the case.)

You can see from this brief discussion how valuable a jury selection service can be. You can also see why many critics argue that such services should not be allowed. After all, they give a tremendous advantage to the client who has more money to spend on the trial.

OPENING STATEMENTS Once a jury has been impaneled, or selected, the case begins with the opening statements. Each party's attorney explains to the judge and the jury what facts he or she intends to prove, the legal conclusions to which those facts will lead, and how the case should be decided.

mock jury Group of individuals, demographically matched to the actual jurors in a case, in front of whom lawyers practice their arguments before presenting their case to the actual jury.

shadow jury Group of individuals, demographically matched to the actual jurors in a case, that sits in the courtroom during a trial and then "deliberates" at the end of each day so that lawyers have continuous feedback of how their case is going.

PLAINTIFF'S CASE   The plaintiff then presents his or her case, which consists of examining witnesses and presenting evidence. The procedure for each witness is the same. First, the plaintiff's attorney questions the witness in what is called *direct examination*. The plaintiff's lawyer asks questions designed to elicit from the witnesses facts that support the plaintiff's case. Then the opposing counsel may *cross-examine* the witness; only questions pertaining to the witness's direct examination may be asked. The purpose of cross-examination is often to "poke holes" in the witness's testimony or to reduce the credibility of the witness. The plaintiff's attorney then has the opportunity for redirect examination, to repair any damage done by the cross-examination. The opposing counsel then has a last opportunity to cross-examine the witness to address facts brought out in redirect examination. This procedure is followed for each of the plaintiff's witnesses.

Immediately after the plaintiff's case, the defendant may make a *motion for a directed verdict*. In making such a motion, the defendant is stating to the court that even if all the plaintiff's factual allegations are true, the plaintiff has not proved his or her case. For example, as will be discussed in chapter 11, to prove a case of negligence, the plaintiff must prove that the defendant breached his duty to the plaintiff and, in so doing, caused compensable injury. If the plaintiff offers no evidence of any compensable injury, then there can be no judgment for the plaintiff even if the defendant did breach his duty. In such a case, a motion for a directed verdict would be granted, and the case would be dismissed. Such motions are rarely granted because the plaintiff will usually introduce some evidence of every element necessary to establish the existence of his or her case.

A motion for a directed verdict also may be made by either party after the presentation of the defendant's case. The party filing the motion (the moving party) is saying that even if the judge looks at all the evidence in the light most favorable to the other party, it is overwhelmingly clear that the only decision the jury could come to is that the moving party is entitled to judgment in his or her favor.

DEFENDANT'S CASE   If the defendant's motion for a directed verdict is denied, the trial proceeds with the defendant's case in chief. The defendant's witnesses are questioned in the same manner as were the plaintiff's, except that it is the defendant's attorney who does the direct and redirect examination and the plaintiff's attorney is entitled to cross-examine the witnesses.

CONFERENCE ON JURY INSTRUCTIONS   If the case is being heard by a jury, the attorneys and the judge then retire for a conference on jury instructions. Jury instructions are the court's explanation to the jury of what legal decision they must make if they find certain facts to be true. Each attorney presents to the judge the set of jury instructions he or she feels will enable the jury to accurately apply the law to the facts. Obviously, each attorney tries to state the law in the manner most favorable to his or her client. The judge confers with the attorneys regarding their proposed instructions and then draws up the instructions for the jury.

CLOSING ARGUMENTS   The attorneys' last contact with the jury then follows. The attorneys present their closing arguments. The party who has the burden of proof, the plaintiff, presents the first closing argument; the defendant's closing argument follows. Finally, the plaintiff is entitled to a rebuttal. The judge then reads the instructions to the jury, and the jurors retire to the jury room to deliberate. When they reach a decision, the jurors return to the courtroom, where their verdict is read.

POST-TRIAL MOTIONS   The party who loses has a number of options. *A motion for a judgment notwithstanding the verdict* may be made. This motion is a request for the judge to enter a judgment contrary to that handed down by the jury on the ground that, as a matter of law, the decision could only have been different from that reached by the jury. For example, if a plaintiff requests dam-

110

Part One

*An Introduction to the Law
and the Legal Environment
of Business*

ages of $500 but introduces evidence of only $100 in damages, the jury cannot award the plaintiff the $400 for unsubstantiated damages. If they do so, the defendant will file a motion for a judgment notwithstanding the verdict. Alternatively, the dissatisfied party may file a *motion for a new trial* on the ground that the verdict is clearly against the weight of the evidence. If neither motion is granted and the judge enters a judgment in accordance with the verdict, the losing party may appeal the decision.

APPELLATE PROCEDURE

As explained earlier, the court to which the case is appealed depends on the court in which the case was originally heard. If a case was heard in a federal district court, it is appealed to the U.S. circuit court of appeals for the geographic region in which the district court is located. If heard in a state trial court, the case is appealed to that state's intermediate appellate court or, if none exists, to the state's final appellate court.

To appeal a case, the losing party must allege that a *prejudicial error of law* occurred during the trial. A prejudicial error is one that is so substantial that it could have affected the outcome of the case. For example, the judge may have ruled as admissible in court certain evidence that had a major impact on the decision, when that evidence was legally inadmissible. Or the party may argue that the instructions that the judge read to the jury were inaccurate and resulted in a misapplication of the law to the facts.

When a case is appealed, there is not a new trial. The attorney for the appealing party (the appellant) and the attorney for the party who won in the lower court (the appellee) file briefs, or written arguments, with the court of appeals. They also generally present oral arguments before the appeals court. The court considers these arguments, reviews the record of the case, and renders a decision. The decisions of the appellate court can take a number of forms. The court may accept the decision of the lower court and **affirm** that decision. Alternatively, the appellate court may conclude that the lower court was correct in its decision, except for granting an inappropriate remedy, and so it will **modify** the remedy. If the appellate court decides that the lower court was incorrect in its decision, that decision will be **reversed**. Finally, the appeals court may feel that an error was committed, but it does not know how that error would have affected the outcome of the case, so it will **remand** the case to the lower court for a new trial.

Although the appeals procedure may sound relatively simple compared with the initial trial procedure, appeals require a great deal of work on the part of the attorneys. They are consequently expensive. Thus, when deciding whether to appeal, the businessperson must consider how much money he or she wishes to spend. If a judgment is rendered against a businessperson, it may be less expensive to pay the judgment than to appeal.

Another factor to be considered when one is deciding whether to appeal is the precedential value of the case. The case may involve an important issue of law that a party hopes will be decided in her or his favor by an appeals court. If she or he anticipates similar suits arising in the future, it may be important to get a favorable ruling, and if the case appears to be strong, an appeal may be desirable.

Appellate courts, unlike trial courts, are usually composed of a bench of at least three judges. There are no juries. The decision of the court is determined by the majority of the judges. One of the judges who votes with the majority records the court's decision and their reasons in what is called the *majority opinion*. These have precedential value and are used by judges to make future decisions and by attorneys in advising their clients as to the appropriate course of behavior in similar situations. If any of the judges in a case agrees with the ultimate decision of the majority but for different reasons, he or she may write a *concurring opinion*, stating how this conclusion was reached. Finally, the judge or judges disagreeing with the majority may write their *dissenting opinion*, giving their reasons for reaching a contrary conclusion. Dissenting opinions may be cited in briefs by attorneys arguing that the law should be changed. Dissents may also be cited by an appellate judge who decides to change the law.

affirm Term used for an appellate court's decision to uphold the decision of a lower court in a case that has been appealed.

modify Term used for an appellate court's decision that, although the lower court's decision was correct, it granted an inappropriate remedy that needs to be changed.

reverse Term used for an appellate court's decision that the lower court's decision was incorrect and cannot be allowed to stand.

remand Term used for an appellate court's decision that an error was committed that may have affected the outcome of the case and that therefore the case must be returned to the lower court.

For most cases, only one appeal is possible. In some states, where there is both an intermediate and a superior court of appeals, a losing party may appeal from the intermediate appellate court to the state court of last resort. In a limited number of cases, a losing party may be able to appeal from a state court of last resort or a federal circuit court of appeals to the U.S. Supreme Court.

APPEAL TO THE UNITED STATES SUPREME COURT   Every year, thousands of individuals attempt to have their appeals heard by the U.S. Supreme Court. But the Court hears, on average, only about 150 to 200 cases every year. When a party wishes to have his or her case heard by the highest court in the nation, he or she files a petition with the Court, asking them to issue a *writ of certiorari*, which is an order to a lower court to send the record of the case to a higher court, in this case the Supreme Court.

As you may guess from the number of cases heard by the Supreme Court, it issues very few such writs. The justices review the petitions they receive and will issue a writ only when at least four justices vote to hear the case. The Court is most likely to issue a writ when: (1) the case presents a *substantial federal question* that has not yet been addressed by the Supreme Court; (2) the case involves a matter that has produced conflicting decisions from the various circuit courts of appeal and is therefore in need of resolution; (3) a state court of last resort holds that a federal law is invalid or upholds a state law that has been challenged as violating federal law; or (4) a federal court has ruled that an act of Congress is unconstitutional.

It is often difficult to predict whether the Court will hear a case. In the first instance described above, for example, a federal question is simply an issue arising under the federal Constitution, treaties, or statutes. Substantiality is a more difficult issue to define. If the decision would affect a large number of people or is likely to arise again if not decided, it may be considered substantial. But sometimes a case may in fact involve a very important federal question of statutory interpretation, yet the Supreme Court may believe that the problem was unclear drafting by Congress, and so they may choose to not hear the case in anticipation of an amendment of the federal statute whose interpretation is at issue. The Supreme Court's refusal to hear a case has no precedential effect.

INTERNATIONAL DIMENSIONS OF THE AMERICAN LEGAL SYSTEM

This chapter has focused on the American legal system. With the growth of multinationals and increasing trade among nations, U.S. businesses will increasingly become involved in disputes in foreign nations, and foreigners will increasingly become involved in disputes with U.S. citizens and corporations.

When parties make international agreements, they can incorporate as a term of the agreement their choice of which nation's court will hear any disputes arising under the agreement. Because of differences between our litigation system and others, it is important to compare the procedures in the two countries before choosing a forum. For example, in Japan, there is no procedure comparable to discovery, so parties go to trial not knowing what evidence the other side has.

With the increase in trade, many foreigners now purchase U.S. goods. Because of some differences between court systems, many citizens of foreign countries injured by U.S. corporations will prefer to sue in the United States. In Japan, for example, there are no contingency fees, and an injured plaintiff must pay his or her lawyer's fees up front, at a cost of 8 percent of the proposed recovery plus nonrefundable court costs. Also, in Japan, there are no class actions.

SUMMARY

Our American legal system is really two systems: a federal system and a state system. When one has a legal dispute, subject matter jurisdiction determines which court system will hear the case. Almost all cases fall within the state court's jurisdiction. Only the limited number of cases within the exclusive juris-

112

Part One

*An Introduction to the Law
and the Legal Environment
of Business*

diction of the federal courts do not. A case may be heard in either court when there is concurrent jurisdiction. Concurrent jurisdiction exists when (1) the case involves a federal question or (2) there is diversity of citizenship between the plaintiff and the defendant. Besides having subject matter jurisdiction, a court must also have inpersonam jurisdiction and proper venue to hear a case.

Cases are filed in courts of original jurisdiction. In the state system, these courts are usually called the courts of common pleas, or county courts. In the federal system, the courts of original jurisdiction are called the district courts. In the state system, state courts of appeals and state supreme courts have appellate jurisdiction. Depending on the state, there may be either one or two levels of appeal. In the federal system, cases are appealed to the circuit court of appeals and then to the U.S. Supreme Court.

Cases are guided through the courts by attorneys. Juries act as finders of fact in trials. Judges resolve questions of law and, in bench trials, also serve as finders of fact.

There are four basic stages in a lawsuit. In the pretrial stage, there are (1) informal negotiations, (2) pleadings, (3) pretrial motions, (4) discovery, and (5) a pretrial conference. Next comes the trial, with (1) jury selection, (2) opening statements, (3) the plaintiff's case, (4) the defendant's case, (5) jury instructions, and (6) closing arguments. Third comes the post-trial motions, which may include a motion for a judgment notwithstanding the verdict or a motion for a new trial. The final stage is the appellate stage, during which the party who lost at the trial appeals his or her case.

REVIEW QUESTIONS

5-1. Identify the different types of jurisdiction and explain why each is important.

5-2. Explain the two situations that cause the state and federal courts to have concurrent jurisdiction.

5-3. What is venue?

5-4. What is the relationship between federal district courts and courts of common pleas?

5-5. What is the attorney-client privilege, and what is the rationale for its existence?

5-6. Explain the importance of the work-product doctrine.

REVIEW PROBLEMS

5-7. Jacobson, a Michigan resident, sued Hasbro Corporation for negligence after one of Hasbro's truck drivers fell asleep and ran his semi off the road and into Jacobson's house, causing structural damage of approximately $80,000. Hasbro has a small plant in Michigan, one in Ohio, and a third in Indiana. The company is incorporated in Illinois and has its central offices there. Jacobson files his case in the state court in Michigan. Hasbro files a motion for removal, which Jacobson contests, arguing that the case does not fall within the concurrent jurisdiction of the federal courts. Should the case be transferred? Why or why not?

5-8. Bill, a white male, is charged with spousal abuse. His attorney uses his peremptory challenges to remove all the white females from the jury. The prosecution objects. Was there any impropriety in the jury selection process?

5-9. Marx Corporation is incorporated in the state of Delaware, but all of the firm's business is conducted within the state of New York. Sanders, a Delaware resident, is injured by one of Marx Corporation's products and subsequently files suit against Marx Corporation in Delaware State Court. Marx files a motion to dismiss the case on grounds that Delaware cannot assert jurisdiction over the corporation because they do not conduct business in Delaware and only incorporated there because they gained certain legal advantages from incorporating in that state. Explain why the Delaware state court system does or does not have jurisdiction over this case.

5-10. Carson is a resident of Clark County, Nevada. He sued Stevens, a resident of Washoe County, Nevada, for injuries he received in an accident that took place in Washoe County. Carson filed the case in Clark County. Can Stevens get the case moved to Washoe County? How would he try to do so?

5-11. Attorney Fox represented Davis in a number of drunk driving cases. Davis shows up at Fox's office to discuss having the attorney draw up a will for him. The attorney recognizes that Davis is clearly intoxicated. The attorney offers to pay for a cab to take Davis home, but he refuses the offer. Fox's secretary suggests that he call the state highway patrol. If Fox calls the highway patrol, is he violating the attorney-client privilege? Why or why not?

5-12. Watson brought a negligence case against the Ferndale Drug Store to recover damages for injuries he received from falling on the wet floor of the store. He thought the store was negligent for marking the floor with only a small sign that said "Slippery When Wet." The trial court refused to let Watson introduce evidence that, after his fall, the store started marking wet floors with cones and a large sign saying "Caution—Floor Is Wet and Slippery." Watson lost in the trial court and lost his appeals to the state appeals court and state supreme court. Will he be able to appeal to the U.S. Supreme Court? Why or why not?

CASE PROBLEMS

5-13. International Shoe Corporation, which had its principal place of business in Missouri, employed in the state of Washington 11 to 13 salespersons, who exhibited samples and solicited orders for shoes from prospective buyers within that state. International Shoe Company was assessed by the state of Washington for contributions to a state unemployment fund. The assessment was personnally served on one of the defendant's sales representatives within the state and a copy was sent by registered mail to the company's headquarters in Missouri. International Shoe's representative showed up at court to challenge the assessment on numerous grounds, including the ground that the corporation had not been properly served. Is the corporation's defense valid? Why or why not? *International Shoe Co. v. Washington*, 326 U.S. 310 (1945)

5-14. Rudzewicz, a Michigan resident, entered into a franchise agreement with Burger King, a Florida Corporation whose principal offices are in Miami, to operate a Burger King in Michigan. The governing contracts provide that the franchise relationship is established in Miami and governed by Florida law. All payments and notices go to Miami. When Rudzewicz began falling behind in his franchise payments and the parties could not resolve their dispute, Burger King filed a breach of contract action in the District Court in Miami, alleging diversity jurisdiction. Burger King won, but the Court of Appeals reversed, holding that the District Court could not exercise jurisdiction over Rudzewicz under the Florida long-arm statute. How do you think the U.S. Supreme Court ruled on appeal? Explain. *Burger King Corporation v. Rudzewicz*, 471 U.S. 462 (1985)

5-15. George Rush, a New York City resident who worked as a columnist for the New York *Daily News*, wrote a column in which he criticized Berry Gordy, president of Motown Records. Gordy, a California resident, filed an action in a California state court against Rush and the *News* for libel (making a false statement that hurts the reputation of another). The newspaper is distributed primarily in New York but it does have 13 California subscribers who receive the newspaper in the mail. The newspaper also regularly sends reporters to California to cover entertainment news. Explain

114

Part One

*An Introduction to the Law
and the Legal Environment
of Business*

why the state court in California can or cannot exercise personal jurisdiction over the defendants. *Gordy v. Daily News, L.P.,* 93 F.3d 829 (1996)

5-16. Edmonson, a black construction worker, was injured at a job site. He sued Leesville Concrete Co. for negligence, arguing that the company allowed one of its trucks to roll backward and pin him against some construction equipment. During the voir dire, Leesville used two of its three peremptory challenges to remove potential black jurors from the jury pool. Edmonson requested that the judge require Leesville to provide a race-neutral explanation for the peremptories. The judge refused because the case involved a civil, not a criminal, action. The jury found for Edmonson but, under a comparative negligence standard, found that Edmonson himself was 80 percent responsible for his own injuries and reduced the amount of the award accordingly. On appeal, Edmonson challenged the judge's failure to require a race-neutral justification for the peremptories. Do you think that the U.S. Supreme Court found the trial court judge's ruling on the peremptories to be in accordance with the law? Why or why not? *Edmonson v. Leesville Concrete Company,* 500 U.S. 614 (1991)

5-17. Luis Santiago was convicted on felony drug charges. During the voir dire for the case, the prosecutor had used peremptory strikes to remove three obese members of the jury pool. On appeal, Santiago challenged the prosecutor's use of the peremptory challenges as being discriminatory in violation of the Fourteenth Amendment. Did the court of appeals overturn Santiago's conviction? Why or why not? *United States v. Santiago,* 58 F.3d 422 (1995)

5-18. Command Transportation sued Y.S. Line Corporation for libel and tortious interference with contract. The basis for the lawsuit was an allegedly libelous letter written by Joyce, a former employee of Y.S. Line. The plaintiff sought to discover communications between Joyce and the corporate counsel regarding information contained in the letter. Y.S. Line argued that such communications were privileged. How do you think the court should have ruled on this issue? Why? *Command Corporation Inc. v. Y.S. Line Corporation,* 116 F.R.D. 94 (1987)

 On the Internet

http://www.courtinfo.ca.gov/onlinereference/soj091397.htm From this site, you can learn about one state's court system which is illustrious of how most state court systems are set up.

http://users.anet-stl.com/~hvmlr/hm_pg9.html This site contains some thought-provoking ideas for reforming our legal system.

http://www.uexpress.com/ups/opinion/column/wb/archive/wb970408.html This page contains a not-too-optimistic perspective on the potential for reform of the jury system.

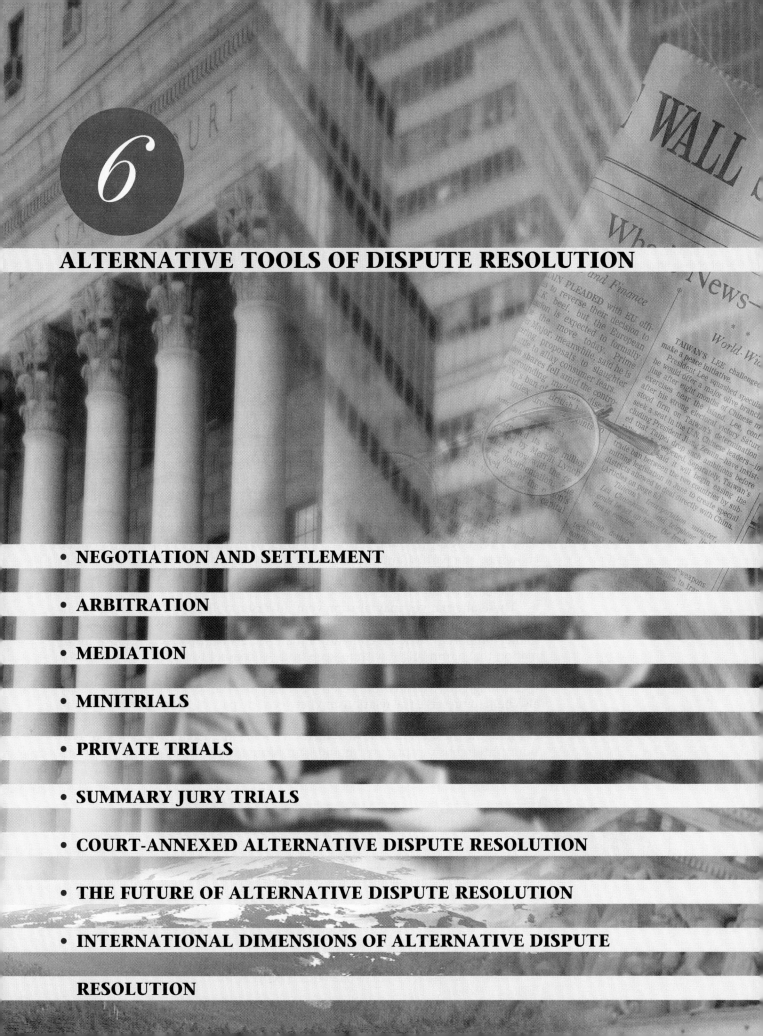

6

ALTERNATIVE TOOLS OF DISPUTE RESOLUTION

- **NEGOTIATION AND SETTLEMENT**

- **ARBITRATION**

- **MEDIATION**

- **MINITRIALS**

- **PRIVATE TRIALS**

- **SUMMARY JURY TRIALS**

- **COURT-ANNEXED ALTERNATIVE DISPUTE RESOLUTION**

- **THE FUTURE OF ALTERNATIVE DISPUTE RESOLUTION**

- **INTERNATIONAL DIMENSIONS OF ALTERNATIVE DISPUTE**

  RESOLUTION

116

Part One

*An Introduction to the Law
and the Legal Environment
of Business*

**alternative dispute
resolution (ADR)** Resolving
legal disputes through methods
other than litigation, such as
negotiation and settlement,
arbitration, mediation, private
trials, minitrials, and summary
jury trial.

Recently, Pacific Gas and Electric Company (PG & E) was faced with six disputes stemming from the crash of a helicopter that hit one of their electrical lines. Officials at PG & E knew that they were facing the expensive and time-consuming litigation process described in chapter 5. They were aware that a trial would take about two years to wind its way through the court system, with litigation costs of $300,000 if the matter were settled before the trial and double that amount if the case were tried through to a verdict. Instead, the case was resolved within 10 months, and legal fees and administrative costs were kept to around $20,000.[1] How?

Like a growing number of would-be litigants who see the trial process as unwieldy, time-consuming, and expensive, PG & E decided to consider resolving their dispute outside the court, through what is often referred to as **alternative dispute resolution**, or **ADR**. Many judges now encourage the increased use of these alternatives to litigation, which include (1) negotiation and settlement, (2) arbitration, (3) mediation, (4) minitrials, (5) private trials, and (6) summary jury trials. The ADR method that PG & E successfully opted for was mediation.

These options are becoming so common that many law and some business schools now offer courses covering alternative dispute-resolution methods. In the business world itself, 600 of the nation's largest corporations have signed a pledge to not sue another corporation before first trying to resolve the conflict out of court.[2] Nearly every state court has some ADR program in place.

Almost all of these alternative methods share certain advantages over litigation. First, they are generally less expensive. For example, PG & E shifted toward an aggressive litigation alternative approach in 1988, and, by 1993, their legal department's operation costs, including legal fees, had fallen by 9 percent. The amount they paid out in judgments and settlements during that time fell by 25 percent.[3] Second, most ADR methods are more convenient for the participants: They are less time-consuming, and the formal hearing times and places can be set to accommodate the parties. Admittedly, it is difficult to estimate the time required by a given ADR case. However, studies of private commercial arbitration cases have shown that the average time lag from filing date to the decision date is 145 days. Third, the persons presiding over the resolution process can be chosen by the parties, and, in many cases, they are chosen because they would be more familiar with the subject matter of the dispute than a randomly assigned judge would be.

These alternatives may also prevent adverse publicity, which could be ruinous to a business. Similarly, they preserve confidentiality, which may be extremely important when a company's trade secrets are involved. A lot of information that a firm might wish to keep from its competitors could come out in a lawsuit but would not be subject to public disclosure when the matter was settled through an ADR method. Finally, the less adversarial of these methods may also help to preserve the relationship between the parties, many of whom desire to continue doing business with one another. In the following sections, we will examine the most important ADR methods in greater detail. From these discussions, future businesspersons should gain some awareness of typical situations in which each of these alternatives may be preferable to litigation.

Critical Thinking about the Law

WHY WOULD ONE WANT TO USE an alternative method for dispute resolution? Alternative dispute resolution seems to be advantageous compared with the traditional method of litigation for several reasons. For example, ADR methods are less time-consuming than litigation. The following questions will help you learn to think critically about alternative dispute resolution.

---

[1]E. J. Pollock, *Mediation Firms Alter the Legal Landscape*, Wall St. J., March 22, 1993, at 1.
[2]M. Chambers, *Sua Sponte*, Nat'l L.J., September 27, 1993, at 21, col. 1.
[3]Pollock, *supra* note 1.

1. What are the reasons offered to suggest that ADR is advantageous compared with litigation?

   CLUE   Reread the introductory section.

2. What primary ethical norms are behind the reasons given to suggest that ADR is advantageous?

   CLUE   Examine the reasons given in response to Question 1. Consider the list of ethical norms given in chapter 1. For example, ADR methods are less time-consuming. Which ethical norm is being upheld in this reason?

NEGOTIATION AND SETTLEMENT

The oldest, and perhaps the simplest, alternative to litigation is negotiation and settlement. **Negotiation and settlement** is the process by which the parties to a dispute come together informally, either with or without their lawyers, and attempt to resolve their dispute. No independent or neutral third party is involved.

To successfully negotiate a settlement, each party must, in most cases, give up something in exchange for getting something from the other side. Almost all lawyers will attempt to negotiate a settlement before taking a case to trial or going to some other more formal type of dispute-resolution method. Attempts at negotiation and settlement are so common that we often do not even consider negotiation as an alternative to litigation.

negotiation and settlement
An alternative dispute-resolution method in which the disputant parties come together informally to try to resolve their differences.

ARBITRATION

One of the most well known alternatives to litigation, *arbitration*, is the resolution of a dispute by a neutral third party outside the judicial setting. The arbitration hearing is similar to a trial, but there is no prehearing discovery process. In addition, the stringent rules of evidence applicable in a trial are generally relaxed. Each side presents its witnesses and evidence and has the opportunity to cross-examine its opponent's witnesses. The arbitrator frequently takes a much more active role in questioning the witness than would a judge. If the arbitrator needs to know more information, he or she generally does not hesitate to ask for that information from witnesses.

As a general rule, no official record of the arbitration hearing is made. Rather, the arbitrator and each of the parties usually take their own notes of what happens. However, the parties and the arbitrator may agree to have a stenographer record the proceedings at the expense of the parties. Although attorneys may represent parties in arbitration, legal counsel is not required. Individuals may represent themselves or have nonlawyers represent them. For example, in a labor dispute, as discussed in chapter 18, the union may be represented by one of its officers. In addition to the oral presentation, in some cases, the arbitrator may request written arguments from the parties. These documents are called *arbitration briefs*.

The arbitrator usually provides a decision for the parties within 30 days of the hearing. In many states, this deadline is mandated by statute. The arbitrators' decision is called the **award**, even if no monetary compensation is ordered. The award does not have to state any findings of fact or conclusions of law. Nor must the arbitrator cite any precedent for the decision or give any reasons. He or she must only resolve the dispute. If the arbitrator, however, hopes to continue to be selected by parties, he or she should provide reasons for the decision.

award The arbitrator's decision.

For a number of reasons, the arbitrator's decision is much more likely to be a compromise decision than a decision handed down by a court. First, the arbitrator is not as constrained by precedent as are judges. An arbitrator is interested in resolving a factual dispute, not in establishing or strictly applying a rule

118

Part One

*An Introduction to the Law
and the Legal Environment
of Business*

of law. Second, the arbitrator may be more interested than a judge in preserving an ongoing relationship with the parties. A compromise is much more likely to achieve this result than is a clear win-or-lose decision. Finally, because an arbitrator frequently decides cases in a particular area, he or she wants to maintain a reputation of being fair to both sides. For example, a person who focuses on labor arbitrations would not want to gain a reputation as being pro-labor or pro-management.

The decision rendered by the arbitrator is legally binding. In some cases, such as labor cases, a decision may be appealed to the district court, but there are few such appeals. Of the more than 25,000 labor cases decided by arbitrators each year, fewer than 200 are challenged. The following U.S. Supreme Court case demonstrates the deference the courts give to arbitrator's decisions.

UNITED STEELWORKERS OF AMERICA V. ENTERPRISE WHEEL & CAR CORPORATION
UNITED STATES SUPREME COURT 363 U.S. 593 (1960)

Employees represented by the plaintiff union were fired during the term of a collective bargaining agreement. That agreement provided for arbitration of differences as to the meaning and application of the agreement and for reinstatement and back pay for persons fired in violation of the agreement. A grievance was filed, and when respondent finally refused to arbitrate, this suit was brought for specific enforcement of the arbitration provisions of the agreement. The district court ordered arbitration. After the employees' discharge and before the arbitration award the collective bargaining agreement expired.

The question of whether the employees should have been fired was then taken to arbitration, in accordance with the district court's order. The arbitrator found that the discharge of the men was not justified, though their conduct, he said, was improper. In his view, the facts warranted at most a suspension of the men for ten days each. The arbitrator awarded reinstatement with back pay minus (1) wages obtained through other work and (2) pay for a ten-day suspension period. The defendant, Enterprise Wheel & Car Corp., refused to comply with the award. The district court directed the defendant to comply. The court of appeals reversed in favor of the defendant, and the plaintiff appealed to the U.S. Supreme Court.

JUSTICE DOUGLAS

The refusal of courts to review the merits of an arbitration award is the proper approach to arbitration under collective bargaining agreements. The federal policy of settling labor disputes by arbitration would be undermined if courts had the final say on the merits of the awards. The arbitrators under these collective agreements are indispensable agencies in a continuous collective bargaining process. They sit to settle disputes at the plant level—disputes that require for their solution knowledge of the custom and practices of a particular factor or of a particular industry as reflected in particular agreements.

When an arbitrator is commissioned to interpret and apply the collective bargaining agreement, he is to bring his informed judgement to bear in order to reach a fair solution of a problem. This is especially true when it comes to formulating remedies. There the need is for flexibility in meeting a wide variety of situations. The draftsmen may never have thought of what specific remedy should be awarded to meet a particular contingency. Nevertheless, an arbitrator is confined to interpretation and application of the collective bargaining agreement; he does not sit to dispense his own brand of industrial justice. He may of course look for guidance from many sources, yet his award is legitimate only so long as it draws its essence from the collective bargaining agreement. When the arbitrator's words manifest an infidelity to this obligation, courts have no choice but to refuse enforcement of the award.

The opinion of the arbitrator in this case, as it bears upon the award of back pay beyond the date of the agreement's expiration and reinstatement, is ambiguous. It may be read as based solely upon the arbitrator's view of the requirements of enacted legislation, which would mean that he exceeded the scope of the submission. Or it may be read as embodying a construction of the agreement itself, perhaps with the arbitrator looking to "the law" for help in determining the sense of the agreement. A mere ambiguity in the opinion accompanying an award, which permits the inference that the arbitrator may have exceeded his authority, is not a reason for refusing to enforce the award. Arbitrators have no obligation to the court to give their reasons for an award. To require opinions free of ambiguity may lead arbitrators to play it safe by writing no supporting opinions. This would be undesirable, for a well-reasoned opinion tends to engender confidence in the integrity of the process and aids in clarifying the underlying agreement. Moreover, we see no reason to assume that this arbitrator has abused the trust the parties confided in him and has not stayed within the areas marked out for his consideration. It is not apparent that he went beyond the submission. The Court of Appeals' opinion refusing to enforce the reinstatement and partial back pay portions of the award was not based upon any finding that the arbitrator did not premise his award on his construction of the contract. It merely disagreed with the arbitrator's construction of it.

The collective bargaining agreement could have provided that if any of the employees was wrongfully discharged, the remedy would be reinstatement and back pay up to the date they were returned to work. Respondent's major argument seems to be that by applying correct principles of law to the interpretation of the collective bargaining agreement it can be determined that the agreement did not so provide, and that therefore the arbitrator's decision was not based upon the contract. The acceptance of this view would require courts, even under the standard arbitration clause, to review the merits of every construction of the contract. This plenary review by a court of the mer-

its would make meaningless the provisions that the arbitrator's decision is final, for in reality it would almost never be final. . . . [T]he question of interpretation of the collective bargaining agreement is a question for the arbitrator. It is the arbitrator's construction which was bargained for; and so far as the arbitrator's decision concerns construction of the contract, the courts have no business overruling him because their interpretation of the contract is different from his.

Reversed and remanded in favor of Plaintiff, United Steelworkers of America.

Critical Thinking about the Law

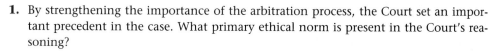

LEGAL REASONING IS NOT ALWAYS BASED on tangible evidence. On some occasions, the legal reasoning that determines judicial decisions is based on what potentially could happen given factor X, Y, or Z.

In this particular case, the Court in large part argues its position on such a basis. Keep this consideration in mind while answering the following questions, especially Question 2.

1. By strengthening the importance of the arbitration process, the Court set an important precedent in the case. What primary ethical norm is present in the Court's reasoning?

   CLUE Think about what it means to support delegated authority. What end does the means of delegating authority serve?

2. In its decision, the Court was particularly attentive to the implications of its decision for the future. What key concern compelled the Court to rule as it did?

   CLUE Reexamine the Court's reasoning. What did the Court believe would result from excessive regulation of arbitrators' decisions?

The policy of deferring to the arbitrator laid down in *United Steelworkers* v. *Enterprise Wheel* has since been extended to arbitration in areas other than labor contracts. Unless there is a clear showing that the arbitrator's decision is contrary to law or there was some defect in the arbitration process, the decision will be upheld. Section 10 of the Federal Arbitration Act, the federal law enacted to encourage the use of arbitration, sets forth the four grounds on which the arbitrator's award may be set aside:

1. The award was the result of corruption, fraud, or other "undue means."
2. The arbitrator exhibited bias or corruption.
3. The arbitrator refused to postpone the hearing despite sufficient cause, refused to hear evidence pertinent and material to the dispute, or otherwise acted to substantially prejudice the rights of one of the parties.
4. The arbitrator exceeded his or her authority or failed to use such authority to make a mutual, final, and definite award.

METHODS OF SECURING ARBITRATION

Arbitration may be secured voluntarily, or it may be imposed upon the parties. The first voluntary means of securing arbitration is by including a **binding arbitration clause** in a contract. Such a clause provides that all or certain disputes arising under the contract are to be settled by arbitration. The clause should also include the means by which the arbitrator is to be selected. More

binding arbitration clause
A provision in a contract mandating that all disputes arising under the contract be settled by arbitration.

119

Part One

*An Introduction to the Law
and the Legal Environment
of Business*

EXHIBIT 6-1 *Sample Binding Arbitration Clause*

> *Any controversy, dispute, or claim of whatever nature arising out of, in connection with, or in relation to the interpretation, performance or breach of this agreement, including any claim based on contract, tort, or statute, shall be resolved, at the request of any party to this agreement, by final and binding arbitration conducted at a location determined by the arbitrator in (City,), (State) administered by and in accordance with the then existing Rules of Practice and Procedure of Judicial Arbitration & Mediation Services, Inc. (J.A.M.S.), and judgment upon any award rendered by the arbitrator may be entered by any state or federal court having jurisdiction thereof.*

than 95 percent of the collective bargaining agreements in force today have some provision for arbitration.[4] Exhibit 6-1 contains a sample binding arbitration clause that could be included in almost any business contract.

If their contract contains no binding arbitration clause, the parties may secure arbitration by entering into a **submission agreement**, an example of which is provided in Exhibit 6-2 on page 122. This contract can be entered into at any time. It is a written contract that states that the parties wish to settle their dispute by arbitration. Usually, it specifies the following conditions:

submission agreement
Separate agreement providing that a specific dispute be resolved through arbitration.

- How the arbitrator will be selected
- The nature of the dispute
- Any constraints on the arbitrator's authority to remedy the dispute
- The place where the arbitration will take place
- A time by which the arbitration must be scheduled

Usually, both parties will declare their intent to be bound by the arbitrator's award.

If the parties have entered into a submission agreement or have included a binding arbitration clause in their contract, they will be required to resolve their disputes through arbitration. Both federal and state courts must defer to arbitration if the contract in dispute contains a binding arbitration clause. This constraint was mandated by the U.S. Supreme Court in the following case.

SOUTHLAND CORPORATION V. KEATING
SUPREME COURT OF THE UNITED STATES 52 U.S.L.W. 4131 (1984)

Plaintiffs, a group of individuals who ran 7-Eleven stores franchised by the Southland Corporation, sued the defendant corporation for breach of contract, fraud, and violation of the California Franchise Investment Law. The defendant responded by filing a motion to compel arbitration because their contract included a clause stating that any claim or controversy related to the agreement would be settled by arbitration in accordance with the rules of the American Arbitration Association. The trial court held that the fraud and breach of contract claims should be arbitrated but that the cause of action (or claim) filed under the state franchise law should be litigated. The California Court of Appeals held that all claims should be subject to arbitration. The court stated that to allow the state fran-

chise law claim to be litigated would be to contravene the Federal Arbitration Act, which withdraws from the courts claims covered by an arbitration clause. The California Supreme Court reversed the decision of the court of appeals and reinstated the trial court's decision. The defendant corporation appealed to the U.S. Supreme Court.

CHIEF JUSTICE BURGER

The California Franchise Investment Law provides:

> *Any condition, stipulation or provision purporting to bind any person acquiring any franchise to waive compliance with any provision of the law or any rule or order hereunder is void.*

---

[4]M. Jacobs, *Required Job Arbitration Stirs Critics*, Wall St. J., June 22, 1993, at B3, col. 1.

The California Supreme Court interpreted this statute to require judicial consideration of claims brought under the State statute and accordingly refused to enforce the parties' contract to arbitrate such claims. So interpreted, the California Franchise Investment Law directly conflicts with Section 2 of the Federal Arbitration Act and violates the Supremacy Clause.

In enacting Section 2 of the Federal Act, Congress declared a national policy favoring arbitration and withdrew the power of the states to require a judicial forum for the resolution of claims which the contracting parties agreed to resolve by arbitration. The Federal Arbitration Act provides:

> *A written provision in any maritime transaction or a contract evidencing a transaction involving commerce to settle by arbitration a controversy thereafter arising out of such contract or transaction, or the refusal to perform the whole or any part thereof, or an agreement in writing to submit to arbitration an existing controversy arising out of such a contract, transaction, or refusal, shall be valid, irrevocable, and enforceable, save upon such grounds as exist at law or in equity for the revocation of any contract.*

Congress has thus mandated the enforcement of arbitration agreements.

We discern only two limitations on the enforceability of arbitration provisions governed by the Federal Arbitration Act: they must be part of a written maritime contract or a contract "evidencing a transaction involving commerce" and such clauses may be revoked upon "grounds as exist at law or in equity for the revocation of any contract." We see nothing in the Act indicating that the broad principle of enforceability is subject to any additional limitations under State law.

The Federal Arbitration Act rests on the authority of Congress to enact substantive rules under the Commerce Clause. The Court examined the legislative history of the Act and concluded that the statue "is based upon . . . the incontestable federal foundations of 'control over interstate commerce and over admiralty.' "

We reaffirmed our view that the Arbitration Act "creates a body of federal substantive law" and expressly stated what was implicit, the substantive law the Act created was applicable in state and federal court.

Although the legislative history is not without ambiguities, there are strong indications that Congress had in mind something more than making arbitration agreements enforceable only in the federal courts. The House Report plainly suggests the more comprehensive objectives:

> *The purpose of this bill is to make valid and enforceable agreements for arbitration contained* in contracts involving interstate commerce *or within the jurisdiction or admiralty, or which may be the subject of litigation in the Federal courts.*

The broader purpose can also be inferred from the reality that Congress would be less likely to address a problem whose impact was confined to federal courts than a problem of large significance in the field of commerce. The Arbitration Act sought to "overcome the rule of equity, that equity will not specifically enforce any arbitration agreement."

And since the overwhelming proportion of all civil litigation in this country is in the state courts, we cannot believe Congress intended to limit the Arbitration Act to disputes subject only to *federal* court jurisdiction. Such an interpretation would frustrate Congressional intent to place "an arbitration agreement . . . upon the same footing as other contracts, where it belongs."

In creating a substantive rule applicable in state as well as federal courts, Congress intended to foreclose state legislative attempts to undercut the enforceability of arbitration agreements. We hold that Section 31512 of the California Franchise Investment Law violates the Supremacy Clause.

Reversed in favor of Defendant, Southland Corp.

Critical Thinking about the Law

B Y NOW, YOU REALIZE THAT LEGAL reasons have degrees of quality, reliability, and acceptability. A claim is not valid simply because reasons are given for its truth or merit.

The following questions will refresh your appreciation of this point.

1. Crucial to the Court's reasoning is its claim that the Congress intended the Federal Arbitration Act's authority to extend to the state courts. What evidence does the Court provide for this claim?

   CLUE Reread the section that begins with this claim.

2. Having answered Question 1, you now know that the Court relies to some extent on the legislative history of the act to support its position. What are the dangers with this type of evidence?

   CLUE Think about your own personal history. Have your intentions always been expressed in a form that everyone who knew you could interpret accurately?

122

Part One

*An Introduction to the Law
and the Legal Environment
of Business*

EXHIBIT 6-2 *Sample Submission Agreement*

American Arbitration Association

SUBMISSION TO DISPUTE RESOLUTION

Date: _____

The named parties hereby submit the following dispute for resolution under the _____

_____ Rules* of the American Arbitration Association:

Procedure Selected: ❑ Binding Arbitration   ❑ Mediation Settlement

                        ❑ Other _____
                                        (Describe)

FOR INSURANCE CASES ONLY:

_____ _____ to _____   _____
Policy Number   Effective Dates   Applicable Policy Limits

_____   _____
Date of Incident   Location

Insured: _____   Claim Number: _____

Name(s) of Claimant(s)	**Check if a Minor**	**Amount Claimed**
_____	❑	_____
_____	❑	_____

Nature of Dispute and/or Injuries Alleged (attach additional sheets if necessary):

Place of Hearing: _____

We agree that, if binding arbitration is selected, we will abide by and perform any award rendered hereunder and that a judgement may be entered on the award.

To Be Completed by the Parties

Name of Party	Name of Party
Address	Address
City, State, and ZIP Code	City, State, and ZIP Code
( ) _____ Telephone Fax	( ) _____ Telephone Fax
Signature†	Signature†
Name of Party's Attorney or Representative	Name of Party's Attorney or Representative
Address	Address
City, State, and ZIP Code	City, State, and ZIP Code
( ) _____ Telephone Fax	( ) _____ Telephone Fax
Signature†	Signature†

Please file three copies with the AAA.

* *If you have a question as to which rules apply, please contact the AAA.*
† *Signatures of all parties are required for arbitration.*

Form G1 - 6/91

Source: Reproduced with permission of the American Arbitration Association, 140 West 51st Street, New York, NY 10020.

The U.S. Supreme Court had the opportunity to reexamine its holding in *Southerland v. Keating* in 1985 when it agreed to hear the case of *Allied-Bruce-Termix Cos. v. Dobson.*[5] In that case, a Mr. Gibbs and a termite exterminator had entered into a termite control contract that included a clause providing that all disputes under the contract would be settled exclusively by arbitration. Dobson had purchased Gibbs's house and took over the contract. When Allied-Bruce-Termix was unable to fulfill the terms of the contract, Dobson filed suit in court, asking the state to uphold a state law invalidating predispute arbitration clauses. The state's highest court upheld the state law, saying that the Federal Arbitration Act did not apply to this case because the parties did not contemplate any interstate transaction under the contract. On the

[5]63 U.S.L.W. 4079 (1995).

appeal before the U.S. Supreme Court, 20 state attorneys general signed an *amicus curiae* (friend of the court) brief arguing in favor of overruling *Southerland* and upholding the Alabama court's decision. The Court, however, overruled the Alabama court, and upheld *Southerland* saying that the contract clearly involved interstate commerce because Termix was a multistate operation and further, the materials used by the company were purchased in another state. The Court thereby reinforced its intent to interpret the statute broadly.

The drafters of either a submission agreement or a binding arbitration clause must be precise because courts will enforce the agreements as written. And parties who decide to specify that a certain state's laws govern an agreement should be familiar with all of the laws that might be applicable, including the state laws governing the arbitration procedures themselves.

In addition to the two voluntary means, arbitration may also be mandated by state law for certain types of conflicts. For instance, in some states, public employees must submit collective bargaining disputes to binding arbitration. In other states, disputes involving less than a certain amount of money automatically go to arbitration.

SELECTION OF AN ARBITRATOR

Once the decision to arbitrate has been made, an arbitrator must be selected. Arbitrators are generally lawyers, professors, or other professionals. They are frequently selected on the basis of their special expertise in some area. If the parties have not agreed on an arbitrator before a dispute, they generally use one of two sources for selecting one: the Federal Mediation and Conciliation Services (FMCS), a government agency discussed further in chapter 14, or the American Arbitration Association (AAA), a private, nonprofit organization founded in 1926, whose stated purpose is "to foster the study of arbitration in all of its aspects, to perfect its techniques under arbitration law, and to advance generally the science of arbitration for the prompt and economical settlement of disputes." Its slogan is "Speed, Economy, and Justice." The AAA now resolves more

EXHIBIT 6-3 *The Arbitrator's Code of Ethics*

Canon 1
- An arbitrator will uphold the integrity and fairness of the arbitration process.

Canon 2
- If the arbitrator has an interest or relationship that is likely to affect his or her impartiality or that might create an appearance of partiality or bias, it must be disclosed.

Canon 3
- An arbitrator, in communicating with the parties, should avoid impropriety or the appearance of it.

Canon 4
- The arbitrator should conduct the proceedings fairly and diligently.

Canon 5
- The arbitrator should make decisions in a just, independent, and deliberate manner.

Canon 6
- The arbitrator should be faithful to the relationship of trust and confidentiality inherent in that office.

Canon 7
- In a case where there is a board of arbitrators, each party may select an arbitrator. That arbitrator must ensure that he or she follows all the ethical considerations in this type of situation.

124

Part One

*An Introduction to the Law
and the Legal Environment
of Business*

than 50,000 disputes each year. The parties may also turn to one of the private arbitration services.

When the disputants contact one of these agencies, they receive a list of potential arbitrators along with a biographical sketch of each. The parties will jointly select an arbitrator from the list. Once the arbitrator has been selected, the parties and the arbitrator agree on the time, the date, and the location of the arbitration. They also agree on the substantive and procedural rules to be followed in the arbitration.

Regardless of whether the arbitrator is selected through the AAA, the FMCS, or some private association, he or she will be subject to the Arbitrator's Code of Ethics. Organized by canons of ethics, the code is designed to ensure that arbitrators perform their duties diligently and in good faith, thereby maintaining public confidence in the arbitration process. Exhibit 6-3 contains the seven canons of the Arbitrator's Code of Ethics.

COMMON USES OF ARBITRATION

As noted earlier, arbitration is frequently used to resolve grievances under collective bargaining agreements. It is so frequently used in these cases that it is sometimes identified primarily as a means for resolving labor disputes, but it is also used to resolve a much broader range of issues, as Exhibit 6-4 illustrates. For example, many consumer complaints are now being handled by arbitration sponsored by Better Business Bureaus (BBBs) in more than 100 cities. Under the BBBs' National Consumer Arbitration Program, which has been in effect since 1972, the consumer first files a complaint with the BBB, whose representative attempts to negotiate a solution between the consumer and the business. If negotiation fails, the consumer and the business representative sign a submission agreement specifying the disputed issues. Then they select an arbitrator from a panel of five trained volunteers from the local community. After the hearing (at which the parties are usually not represented by counsel), the arbitrator has ten days to render a decision.

EXHIBIT 6-4 *American Arbitration Association Statistics on Use of Arbitration*

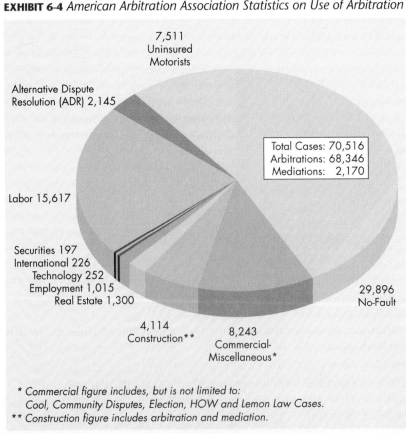

Total Cases: 70,516
Arbitrations: 68,346
Mediations: 2,170

** Commercial figure includes, but is not limited to:
Cool, Community Disputes, Election, HOW and Lemon Law Cases.*
** Construction figure includes arbitration and mediation.

The National Consumer Arbitration Program is limited in that arbitrators cannot award damages beyond the value of the product in question. They cannot, for example, award punitive damages or damages for personal injuries suffered as a result of a defective product. Despite these limitations, this program provides an excellent forum for disputes that often would not be resolved in court because the cost of litigation would probably exceed or come close to the amount of the damage award. The use of arbitration in consumer cases is further discussed in chapter 23.

An area in which arbitration is increasingly being used is in employment disputes. Before the following case, there was some uncertainty as to whether employees could be required to resolve all of their employment disputes through arbitration; that issue was initially resolved as follows.

GILMER V. INTERSTATE/JOHNSON LANE CORPORATION
UNITED STATES SUPREME COURT 111 S. CT. 1647 (1991)

Plaintiff Robert Gilmer filed a charge with the Equal Employment Opportunity Commission (EEOC) and sued his employer, defendant Interstate/Johnson Lane Corporation. Gilmer alleged that his employer violated the Age Discrimination in Employment Act (ADEA). When he was hired by the defendant as a registered securities dealer, Gilmer had signed an agreement to settle by arbitration any disputes arising out of that employment. The employer therefore filed a motion to compel arbitration. The trial court denied the defendant's motion and defendant appealed to the circuit court. The circuit court reversed in favor of the defendant and the plaintiff appealed to the U.S. Supreme Court.

JUSTICE WHITE

The question presented in this case is whether a claim under the Age Discrimination in Employment Act of 1967 (ADEA) can be subjected to compulsory arbitration pursuant to an arbitration agreement in a securities registration application. As required by his employment, Gilmer registered as a securities representative with several stock exchanges, including the New York Stock Exchange (NYSE).

His registration application provided, among other things, that Gilmer "agree[d] to arbitrate any dispute, claim or controversy" arising between him and Interstate "that is required to be arbitrated under the rules, constitutions or bylaws of the organizations with which I register."

It is by now clear that statutory claims may be the subject of an arbitration agreement, enforceable pursuant to the FAA. Indeed, in recent years we have held enforceable arbitration agreements relating to claims arising under the Sherman Act, Sec. 10(b) of the Securities Exchange Act of 1934; the civil provisions of the Racketeer Influenced Corrupt Organizations Act (RICO); and Sec. 12(2) of the Securities Act of 1933.

In these cases we recognized that "by agreeing to arbitrate a statutory claim, a party does not forgo the substantive rights afforded by the statute; it only submits to their resolution in an arbitral, rather than a judicial, forum."

Although all statutory claims may not be appropriate for arbitration, "[h]aving made the bargain to arbitrate, the party should be held to it unless Congress itself has evinced an intention to preclude a waiver of judicial remedies for the statutory rights at issue." The burden is on Gilmer to show that Congress intended to preclude a waiver of a judicial forum for ADEA claims. If such an intention exists, it will be discoverable in the text of the ADEA, its legislative history, or an "inherent conflict" between arbitration and the ADEA's underlying purposes. Throughout such an inquiry, it should be kept in mind that "questions of arbitrability must be addressed with a healthy regard for the federal policy favoring arbitration."

Gilmer concedes that nothing in the text of the ADEA or its legislative history explicitly precludes arbitration. He argues, however, that compulsory arbitration of ADEA claims pursuant to arbitration agreements would be inconsistent with the statutory framework and purposes of the ADEA. Like the Court of Appeals, we disagree.

Congress enacted the ADEA in 1967 "to promote employment of older persons based on their ability rather than age; to prohibit arbitrary age discrimination in employment; [and] to help employers and workers find ways of meeting problems arising from the impact of age on employment." To achieve those goals, the ADEA, among other things, makes it unlawful for an employer "to fail or refuse to hire or to discharge any individual or otherwise discriminate against any individual with respect to his compensation, terms, conditions, or privileges of employment, because of such individual's age." This proscription is enforced both by private suits and by the EEOC.

We also are unpersuaded by the argument that arbitration will undermine the role of the EEOC in enforcing the ADEA. An individual ADEA claimant subject to an arbitration agreement will still be free to file a charge with the EEOC, even though the claimant is not able to institute a private judicial action. Indeed, Gilmer filed a charge with the EEOC in this case. In any event, the EEOC's role in combating age discrimination is not dependent on the filing of a charge; the agency may receive information concerning alleged violations of the ADEA "from any source," and it has independent authority to investigate age discrimination. Moreover, nothing in the ADEA indicates that Congress intended that the EEOC be involved in all employment disputes. Such disputes can be settled, for example, without any EEOC involvement. Finally, the mere involvement of an administrative agency in the enforcement of a statute is not sufficient to preclude arbitration. For example, the Securities Exchange Commission is heavily involved in the enforcement of the Securities Exchange Act of 1934 and the Securities Act of 1933, but we have held that claims under both of those statutes may be subject to compulsory arbitration.

Gilmer also argues that compulsory arbitration is improper because it deprives claimants of the judicial forum provided for by the ADEA. Congress, however, did not explicitly preclude arbitration or other nonjudicial resolution of claims, even in its recent amendments to the ADEA. Moreover, Gilmer's argument ignores the ADEA's flexible approach to resolution of claims. The EEOC, for example, is directed to pursue "informal methods of conciliation, conference, and persuasion," which suggests that out-of-court dispute resolution, such as arbitration, is consistent with the statutory scheme established by Congress.

In arguing that arbitration is inconsistent with the ADEA, Gilmer also raises a host of challenges to the adequacy of arbitration procedures. Such generalized attacks on arbitration "res[t] on suspicion of arbitration as a method of weakening the protections afforded in the substantive law to would-be complainants," and as such, they are "far out of step with our current strong endorsement of the federal statutes favoring this method of resolving disputes."

Gilmer also complains that the discovery allowed in arbitration is more limited than in the federal courts, which he contends will make it difficult to prove discrimination. It is unlikely, however, that age discrimination claims require more extensive discovery than other claims that we have found to be arbitrable, such as RICO and antitrust claims. Although those procedures might not be as extensive as in the federal courts, by agreeing to arbitrate, a party "trades the procedures and opportunity for review of the courtroom for the simplicity, informality, and expedition of arbitration."

It is also argued that arbitration procedures cannot adequately further the purposes of the ADEA because they do not provide for broad equitable relief and class actions. As the court below noted, however, arbitrators do have the power to fashion equitable relief. Indeed, the NYSE rules applicable here do not restrict the types of relief an arbitrator may award, but merely refer to "damages and/or other relief."

Affirmed in favor of Defendant, Johnson/Lane Interstate Corp.

Gilmer essentially upheld the validity of the National Association of Securities Dealers' policy of requiring all employees who execute, buy, or sell orders at brokerages or investment banks to agree to arbitrate all employment grievances as a condition of their employment. The initial impact of this ruling was to increase the use of mandatory arbitration agreements in employment contracts in all industries. In fact, about 100 large companies soon moved to follow the securities industry's policy.

However, some courts and the EEOC became increasingly concerned about whether arbitration agreements that had to be accepted as a condition of employment were really voluntary. On July 10, 1997, the EEOC issued a policy statement saying that the mandatory "arbitration of discrimination claims as a condition of employment are [sic] contrary to the fundamental principles of employment discrimination laws." The EEOC chairman stated that the agency strongly supported agreements to arbitrate once a dispute had arisen but did not believe that a prospective employee could make a voluntary agreement to arbitrate future disputes as part of a "take it or leave it" contract of employment.

In response to the EEOC's policy statement, on August 7, 1997, the National Association of Securities Dealers announced a new policy that would allow employees to choose between entering into private arbitration agreements with their employers and reserving the right to file a case in federal or state court for statutory discrimination claims.

Other areas in which arbitration is prevalent include malpractice cases, environmental disputes, community disputes and elections, and commercial contract conflicts. It is also being increasingly used to handle insurance liability claims arising from accidents.

PROBLEMS WITH ARBITRATION

Despite the growing use of arbitration, the process is not free of criticism, especially in the securities industry. From 1991, when the U.S. Supreme Court affirmed the authority of the securities industry to do so, until 1997 securities firms required that employees who execute, buy, or sell orders at brokerages or investment banks take all their employment disputes—including allegations of race, sex, and age discrimination—to arbitration instead of to court.

According to a study by the General Accounting Office (GAO), those disputes are most likely to be filed by women and minorities. They are also the cases most likely to be heard by white males over 60. Only 11 percent of the arbitrators are female, and fewer than 1 percent are Asian or black. Arbitrators in the securities industry come from the New York Stock Exchange and the National Association of Securities Dealers. Most are retired or semiretired executives or professionals, so they frequently lack subject matter expertise in the discrimination matters.

Although not criticizing the fairness of the outcomes in any particular cases, the GAO did recommend that the industry appoint as arbitrators in discrimination cases people who had some knowledge about discrimination. They also recommended that the industry track the outcome of discrimination cases and establish criteria to keep individuals with records of regulatory violations or other disciplinary actions from becoming arbitrators. Finally, the report expressed concern over the lack of regularized SEC oversight of the arbitration process in general, including the thousands of broker-customer disputes arbitrated each year. The GAO asked the SEC to establish a regular cycle of reasonably frequent reviews of all securities arbitrations, which the SEC has agreed to do.

The trend toward greater use of compulsory arbitration in employment and termination cases concerns some lawyers and legal scholars. They are concerned that such a requirement erodes workers' rights. Thus, an employee who is subject to mandatory arbitration gives up the right to a public trial, the ability to get an injunction to stop unlawful practices, and the right to bring a class action suit.

Another potential problem is the arbitrator's background. For example, although about half of the AAA's arbitrators are lawyers, often an arbitrator is merely someone with expertise in the area in which the dispute arose. He or she may be solving a legal dispute without any real understanding of the applicable law.

A related problem that some fear is that if more employers (and other institutions) turn to mandatory arbitration, arbitration may start to become more and more like litigation. Those forced to give up their day in court may start pressing for their "due process" rights in arbitration. They may also argue that arbitrators should be allowed to grant the same remedies as courts. Ultimately, arbitration proceedings could be burdened with the same kinds of formalities that plague litigation—that is, the same disadvantages that have given rise to ADR in the first place.

Some also question the absence of written opinions. Without such opinions, legal precedents cannot develop to reflect changing circumstances. Finally, there is a question of whether the public interest is harmed by allowing an industry to use arbitration to "hide" its disputes from the public. If, for example, a bank required all billing disputes to be handled by arbitration, the public would never know if that bank was continually making overbilling errors. If such cases went to court, the public would be informed about the bank practices and inefficiencies. In addition, of course, firms that are secure in the knowledge that their operations will not be publicized are more likely to be lax than are firms that know they are subject to public scrutiny.

MEDIATION

Another method of dispute resolution is mediation. **Mediation** primarily differs from arbitration and litigation in that the mediator makes no final decision. She or he is simply a facilitator of communication between disputing parties.

mediation An alternative dispute-resolution method in which the disputant parties select a neutral party to help them reconcile their differences by facilitating communication and suggesting ways to solve their problems.

128

Part One

*An Introduction to the Law
and the Legal Environment
of Business*

*Parties conclude their successful mediation with a handshake while
the mediator looks at them approvingly.*

Mediation is an informal process in which the two disputants select a party, usually one with expertise in the disputed area, to help them reconcile their differences. It is sometimes characterized as a creative and collaborative process involving joint efforts of the mediator and the disputants.

Even though different mediators use different techniques, their overall goals are the same. They try to get the disputants to listen to each other's concerns and understand each other's arguments with the hope of eventually getting the two parties communicating. Once the parties are talking, the mediator attempts to help them decide how to solve their problem. The agreed upon resolution should be "fair, equitable," and "based upon sufficient information."

Although there is no guarantee that a decision will be reached through mediation, once a decision is reached the parties generally enter into a contract that embodies the terms of their settlement. Skilled mediators will attempt to help the parties to draft agreements that reflect the principles that underlie mediation; that is, the agreement should not attempt to assess blame either implicitly or explicitly but should reflect mutual problem solving and consensual agreement. If one party does not live up to the terms of the settlement, he or she can then be sued for breach of contract. Often, however, the parties are more likely to live up to the terms of the agreement than they are to obey a court order because they were the ones who reached the agreement. The agreement is their idea of how to solve the dispute, not some outsider's solution.

If the mediation is not successful and the parties subsequently take their dispute to arbitration or litigation, nothing that was said during mediation can be used by either party at a later proceeding. Whatever transpires during the mediation is confidential.

SELECTION OF A MEDIATOR

Mediators are available from several sources. In addition to the nonprofit AAA described earlier, private companies providing mediators are thriving. Two of the biggest, Judicial Arbitration and Mediation Services (JAMS) and Endispute, merged in 1996, and their new company, JAMS/Endispute, generated an estimated $45 million in revenues during 1997.

One factor to consider when selecting a mediator is what type of background he or she has. Some companies use only former judges, whereas others use judges, lawyers, and nonlawyers as mediators. There is, not surprisingly, a lot of contention over who makes the best mediator. Many people prefer judges because of their legal knowledge, but others say that judges are too ready to make a decision because they spend most of their careers making decisions.

COMMON USES OF MEDIATION

Perhaps the best-known use of mediation is in collective bargaining disputes. Under the National Labor Relations Act, before engaging in an economic strike to achieve better wages, hours, or working conditions under a new collective bargaining agreement, a union must first contact the Federal Mediation and Conciliation Services and attempt to mediate contract demands.

Mediation is also used increasingly to resolve insurance claim disputes and commercial contract problems. More and more frequently a mediation clause is being included in commercial contracts in conjunction with a standard arbitration clause. Under such clauses, if mediation is unsuccessful the parties would then submit the dispute to arbitration. Going through *both* of these processes is still generally less time-consuming and expensive than litigation, especially when one considers the drawn-out discovery process.

Some argue that mediation should play a greater role in employment disputes. Often such disputes arise out of miscommunication, and mediation helps to open the lines of communication. There are a wide variety of creative remedies that might be applicable to the employment situation. In fact, Endispute offers three basic employment dispute options: standard mediation, streamlined mediation, and a mediation-arbitration combination.

A growing area for mediation is in the resolution of environmental disputes. Many advocate the use of mediation for environmental matters because the traditional dispute-resolution methods are designed to handle a problem between two parties, whereas environmental disputes often involve multiple parties. Mediation can easily accommodate multiple parties. Environmental matters are often likely to involve parties who will have to deal with one another in the future, so preservation of their relationship is of utmost importance. For example, you might have a dispute over a new development in which a local citizen group, a developer, the municipality, and an environmental interest group might all have concerns. Mediation could theoretically resolve their problems in a way that would prevent greater problems in the future. Mediation also offers the potential for creative solutions, which are often needed for environmental disputes.

ADVANTAGES OF MEDIATION

The primary advantage of mediation is that because of its nonadversarial nature, it tends to preserve the relationship between the parties to a greater extent than would a trial or any of the other alternatives to litigation. Because the parties are talking to each other, not talking about each other and trying to make the other look bad, there is less of the bitterness that often results from a trial. Parties will almost always come away from a trial with increased hostility toward the other side, whereas even if the parties cannot resolve their differences completely, they almost always leave mediation with a little better understanding of each other's position. Thus, it is used more and more frequently in cases in which the parties will have an ongoing relationship once the immediate dispute is settled.

Another important advantage to mediation is its ability to result in creative solutions. Because the parties are not searching for a decision in their favor or an award of money damages, they are more open to finding some sort of creative solution that may allow both parties to receive some benefit from the situation. Finally, as with other ADR methods, mediation is usually less expensive and less time-consuming than litigation. It's difficult to measure precisely how successful mediation is, however, because settlements are not made public.

130

Part One

*An Introduction to the Law
and the Legal Environment
of Business*

CRITICISMS OF MEDIATION

The process of mediation has its critics. They argue that the informal nature of the process represses and denies certain irreconcilable structural conflicts, such as the inherent strife between labor and management. They also argue that this informal process tends to create the impression of equality between the disputants when no such equality exists. The resultant compromise between unequals is an unequal compromise, but it is clothed in the appearance of equal influence.

The mediation process can also arguably be abused. A party who believes that he or she will ultimately lose a dispute may enter the mediation process in bad faith, dragging the process out as long as possible.

MINITRIALS

minitrial An alternative dispute-resolution method in which lawyers for each side present the case for their side at a proceeding referred by a neutral adviser, but settlement authority usually resides with senior executives of the disputing corporations.

A relatively new means of resolving commercial disputes, probably first used in the United States in 1977 to resolve a dispute between TRW and Telecredit, is the minitrial. A **minitrial** is presided over by a neutral adviser, but the settlement authority resides with senior executives of the disputing corporations. Lawyers for each side make a presentation of the strengths and weaknesses of their respective positions. The adviser may be asked to give his or her opinion as to what the result would be if the case went to trial. Then the corporate executives meet, without their attorneys, to discuss settlement options. Once they reach a settlement, they can make it binding by entering into a contract that encompasses the terms of the settlement.

The use of a minitrial before resorting to arbitration or litigation may be provided for in a clause in the contract. One modification of the minitrial is to give the neutral adviser the authority to settle the case if the corporate executives cannot agree on a means of resolving the dispute within a given period of time.

The minitrial is seen by some as more desirable than arbitration because the disputes involve complex matters that may be better understood by parties directly involved in the contract than by an outside arbitrator. The process also requires intensive, direct communication between the disputants, which may help them better understand the other party's position and may ultimately help their relationship. Minitrials, in some cases, also have the advantage of being less costly than arbitration.

PRIVATE TRIALS

private trial An alternative dispute-resolution method in which cases are tried, usually in private, by a referee who is selected by the disputants and empowered by statute to enter a binding judgment.

In several states, legislation now permits **private trials**. Cases are tried by a referee selected and paid by the disputants. These referees are empowered by statute to enter legally binding judgments. Referees usually need not have any special training, but they are frequently retired judges, hence the disparaging reference to this ADR method as "rent-a-judge." The time and place of the trial are set by the parties at their convenience. Cases may be tried in private, a provision that ensures confidentiality.

On hearing the case, the referee states findings of facts and conclusions of law in a report with the trial court. The referee's final judgment is entered with the clerk when the report is filed. Any party who is dissatisfied with the decision can move for a new trial before the trial court judge. If this motion is denied, the party can appeal the final judgment.

Until recently, private trials did not involve juries. But private jury trials are now offered by a small number of private firms, most notably JAMS/Endispute. Jurors in these cases tend to be slightly better educated than the typical jury, and many will have served on several previous private juries. Whether having "semiprofessional" jurors serving on many cases perverts the idea of a "jury of one's peers" is currently being debated.

Like other forms of ADR, private trials are subject to criticisms. Many people, for example, are concerned that the use of private trials may lead to the development of a two-tier system of justice. Disputants with sufficient resources will be able to channel their disputes through an efficient, private system; everyone else will have to resolve their complaints through a slower, less efficient public system. Similarly, critics suggest that as wealthier individuals and corporations opt for the private courts, they will be less willing to channel their tax dollars into the public system. With less funding, the public system would then become even less effective. Finally, there is the same question that was raised with respect to arbitration of whether the public interest is harmed by allowing an industry to use private trials to "hide" its disputes from the public.

SUMMARY JURY TRIALS

Originating in a federal district court in Cleveland, Ohio, in 1983 as a way to clean up an overcrowded docket, **summary jury trials** are today used in many state and federal courts across the nation for that purpose. The primary advantage of a summary jury trial is that it lasts one day. The judge first instructs a jury on the law. Each side then has a limited amount of time to make an opening statement and to present a summary of the evidence it would have presented at a regular trial.

> **summary jury trial** An alternative dispute-resolution method that consists of an abbreviated trial, a nonbinding jury verdict, and a settlement conference.

The jury, which is usually composed of no more than six people, then retires to reach a verdict. The verdict, however, is only advisory, although jurors are usually not aware that their decision does not have a binding effect.

Immediately after receiving the verdict, the parties retire to a settlement conference. Roughly 95 percent of all cases settle at this point. If the parties do not settle, the case is then set for trial. If a case goes to trial, nothing from the summary trial is admissible as evidence.

COURT-ANNEXED ALTERNATIVE DISPUTE RESOLUTION

USE OF COURT-ANNEXED ADR IN THE STATE AND FEDERAL SYSTEMS

In an attempt to relieve the overburdened court systems, and in partial recognition of the success of voluntary ADR, many state and federal jurisdictions are mandating that disputants go through some formal ADR process before certain types of cases may be brought to trial. It is difficult to generalize about the use of ADR in the court system, however, because practices vary from jurisdiction to jurisdiction, and even from court to court, as courts experiment with a broad range of programs and approaches. Some courts mandate ADR; others make it voluntary. Some refer almost all civil cases to ADR; others target certain cases by subject matter or by amount in controversy.

In the federal system, for example, since 1984, ten federal districts have adopted programs for mandatory, nonbinding arbitration of disputes involving amounts of less than $100,000. Ten other districts have programs involving nonmandatory arbitration. These programs have been highly successful, with less than 10 percent of the cases referred to arbitration going to trial. Experimentation in the federal courts with these types of programs is therefore likely to continue and spread to other districts.

Experimentation with the use of ADR is also going on at the appellate level in the federal system. Today, nearly 50 percent of the federal appellate courts have adopted rules governing the use of ADR in certain federal appeals.

More than half of the states have enacted legislation authorizing ADR in the courts or have established statewide task forces to develop ADR programs. And probably every state has at least one court that has experimented with some form of ADR. Mediation appears to be the most common form of ADR used, perhaps because of its informality compared with other types of ADR or perhaps because it allows the lawyers and parties to retain greater control over their cases.

The aggressiveness with which a state encourages the use of ADR methods varies a great deal. In some states, such as Missouri, a completely voluntary approach is used. Courts are simply required to provide all parties with a notice of the availability of ADR services and names and addresses of persons or agencies

132

Part One

*An Introduction to the Law
and the Legal Environment
of Business*

who can provide such services. Although such a casual approach is criticized on grounds that few people will voluntarily use such services, defenders point out that if people choose ADR, their commitment to the process will be stronger than if they are forced into it, and therefore it is more likely to work. Many states have adopted programs that require parties to take certain types of cases either to mandatory nonbinding arbitration or to mediation. It is only when the parties cannot reach an agreement through mediation or when one party disagrees with the arbitrator's decision that the court will hear the case.

In Minnesota, parties must consult with each other and decide within 45 days of filing a case which form of ADR they would like to use. Their decision is reported to the court. If the parties cannot agree, or the judge disagrees with their selection, a conference with the judge is held and the judge then orders participants to use a particular ADR method.

Similarly, in the Western District of Missouri, approximately one-third of litigants must select a form of ADR to use. If the litigants cannot decide, an administrator of the court will meet with the parties and their lawyers and make a decision for them.

Some state systems also use ADR at the appellate level. South Carolina was the first state to do so. Under their system, arbitration at the appellate level is optional, but once arbitration has been selected, the decision of the arbitrator is binding.

DIFFERENCES BETWEEN COURT-ANNEXED AND VOLUNTARY ADR

ARBITRATION   Probably the major difference between court-annexed arbitration and voluntary arbitration is that, in most cases, the court-mandated arbitration is not binding on the parties. If either party objects to the outcome, the case will go to court for a full trial. As you remember from earlier sections of this chapter, the outcome of voluntary arbitration is binding. The right of a dissatisfied party to reject a court-mandated arbitration decision is really necessary, however, in order to preserve the disputants' due process rights. In the interests of streamlining the justice system, the government cannot take away a person's right to her day in court.

Of course, a person who chooses to go forward with a trial after rejecting an arbitrator's decision may still be penalized to some extent in a number of states. In some systems, a party who rejects an arbitrator's decision and does not receive a more favorable decision from the trial court may be forced to pay the opposing counsel's court fees. In other systems, that party may be required to pay the costs of the arbitration or other court fees.

Another difference between court-mandated and voluntary arbitration lies in the rules of evidence, which are generally more relaxed in arbitration than in litigation. A few states do treat evidence in court-mandated arbitration in this same relaxed fashion, either allowing almost any evidence to be admitted regardless of whether it would be admissible in court or allowing the arbitrator to decide what evidence is admissible. However, in most states, the same rules of evidence apply to court-annexed arbitration that apply to trials.

MEDIATION   The primary difference between court-mandated mediation and voluntary mediation is in the attitudes of the parties toward the process. In voluntary mediation, the parties are likely to enter the mediation process with a desire to work out an agreement; in court-ordered mediation, they are much more likely to view mediation as simply a hurdle to go through before the trial.

THE FUTURE OF ALTERNATIVE DISPUTE RESOLUTION

You are already familiar with some of the problems associated with each of the ADR methods. You should also be aware of some of the concerns raised about the overall increase in the use of ADR.

First, some legal scholars are concerned about whether a dispute resolution firm can be truly unbiased when one of the parties to the dispute is a major client of the dispute-resolution provider. For example, if a major insurance company includes a binding arbitration clause in all its contracts and specifies that JAMS/Endispute will provide the arbitrator, it may be tempting for JAMS/Endispute to favor the insurance company to try to ensure that they will continue to benefit from the firm's business in the future. The more intense the competition among ADR providers, the more tempted the providers may be to favor large firms. Another issue raised by some critics is whether it is fair for consumers to be coerced into an ADR forum and thereby forced to give up their right to a trial, especially when (1) they may be much more likely to get a higher award from a jury than from an arbitrator and (2) they may find themselves having "agreed" to arbitration not really voluntarily, but because of a clause stuck in a purchase agreement that they failed to read. Despite these concerns, however, interest in ADR continues to grow, and there is no reason to think this growth will end in the near future. JAMS/Endispute reported that during the first three months of 1998, it was showing a 13 percent increase in monthly caseload over 1997.

INTERNATIONAL DIMENSIONS OF ALTERNATIVE DISPUTE RESOLUTION

Internationally, alternative dispute-resolution methods are highly favored. Seventy-three countries currently belong to the United Nations Convention on the Recognition and Enforcement of Foreign Arbitral Awards, commonly referred to as the New York Convention. The primary function of this treaty is to ensure that an arbitration award made in any of the signatory countries is enforceable in the losing party's country. Defenses to enforcement that are allowed under the treaty include: one of the parties to the contract lacked the legal capacity to enter into a contract; the losing party did not receive proper notice of the arbitration; the arbitrator was acting outside the scope of his authority when making the awards.

Organizations exist to provide alternative dispute-resolution services for firms of different nations. The most commonly known to U.S. businesspersons is probably the American Arbitration Association. Others include the United Nations Commission of International Trade Law, the London Court of International Arbitration, the Euro-Arab Chamber of Commerce, and the International Chamber of Commerce.

The United States' policy favors arbitration of international disputes. The following case demonstrates this policy.

MITSUBISHI MOTORS CORPORATION V. SOLER CHRYSLER-PLYMOUTH
UNITED STATES SUPREME COURT 473 U.S. 614 (1985)

Plaintiff Mitsubishi, a Japanese corporation, and Chrysler International, a Swiss corporation, formed a joint venture company, Mitsubishi Motors, to distribute worldwide motor vehicles manufactured in the United States and bearing Mitsubishi and Chrysler trademarks. Defendant Soler Chrysler-Plymouth, a dealership incorporated in Puerto Rico, entered into a distributorship agreement with Mitsubishi that included a binding arbitration clause. When Soler began having difficulty selling the requisite number of cars, it first asked Mitsubishi to delay shipment of several orders and then subsequently refused to accept liability for its failure to sell vehicles under the contract.

Plaintiff Mitsubishi filed an action to compel arbitration. The district court ordered arbitration of all claims, including defendants' allegations of antitrust violations. The

court of appeals reversed in favor of the defendant. The plaintiff, Mitsubishi, appealed to the U.S. Supreme Court.

JUSTICE BLACKMUN

We granted certiorari primarily to consider whether an American court could enforce an agreement to resolve antitrust claims by arbitration when that agreement arises from an international transaction. Soler reasons that because it falls within a class of whose benefit the federal and local antitrust laws were passed, the clause cannot be read to contemplate arbitration of these statutory claims.

We do not agree, for we find no warrant in the Arbitration Act for implying in every contract a presumption against arbitration of statutory claims. The "liberal federal policy favoring arbitration agreements," manifested by the Act as a whole, is at bottom a policy guaranteeing the enforcement of private contractual arrangements: the Act simply "creates a body of federal substantive law establishing and regulating the duty to honor an agreement to arbitrate."

There is no reason to depart from these guidelines where a party bound by an arbitration agreement raises claims founded on statutory rights. Of course, courts should remain attuned to well-supported claims that the agreement to arbitrate resulted from the sort of fraud or overwhelming economic power that would provide grounds "for the revocation of any contract." But, absent such compelling considerations, the Act itself provides no basis for disfavoring agreements to arbitrate statutory claims.

By agreeing to arbitrate a statutory claim, a party does not forgo the substantive rights afforded by the statute, it only submits to their resolution in an arbitral, rather than a judicial, forum. It trades the procedures and opportunity for review of the courtroom for the simplicity, informality, and expedition of arbitration.

We now turn to consider whether Soler's antitrust claims are nonarbitrable even though it agreed to arbitrate them. . . . [W]e conclude that concerns of international comity, respect for the capacities of foreign and transnational tribunals, and sensitivity to the need of the international commercial system for predictability in the resolution of disputes require that we enforce the parties' agreement, even assuming that a contrary result would be forthcoming in a domestic context.

There is no reason to assume at the outset of the dispute that international arbitration will not provide an adequate mechanism. To be sure, the international arbitral tribunal owes no prior allegiance to the legal norms of particular states; hence, it has no direct obligation to vindicate their statutory dictates. The tribunal, however, is bound to effectuate the intentions of the parties. Where the parties have agreed that the arbitral body is to decide a defined set of claims that includes, as in these cases, those arising from the application of American antitrust law, the tribunal therefore should be bound to decide that dispute in accord with the national law giving rise to the claim.

As international trade has expanded in recent decades, so too has the use of international arbitration to resolve disputes arising in the course of that trade. The controversies that international arbitral institutions are called upon to resolve have increased in diversity as well as in complexity. Yet the potential of these tribunals for efficient disposition of legal disagreements arising from commercial relations has not yet been tested. If they are to take a central place in the international legal order, national courts will need to "shake off the old judicial hostility to arbitration," and also their customary and understandable unwillingness to cede jurisdiction of a claim arising under domestic law to a foreign or transnational tribunal. To this extent, at least, it will be necessary for national courts to subordinate domestic notions of arbitrability to the international policy favoring commercial arbitration.

Accordingly, we "require this representative of the American business community to honor its bargain," . . . by holding this agreement to arbitrate "enforce[able] in accord with the explicit provisions of the Arbitration Act."

[As to the issue of arbitrability] *Reversed and remanded*, in favor of the Plaintiff, Mitsubishi.

SUMMARY

As the burden on our court system increases, many disputants are turning to alternative ways of resolving disputes. These alternatives include (1) negotiation and settlement, (2) arbitration, (3) mediation, (4) minitrials, (5) private trials, and (6) summary jury trials.

Which, if any, alternative is best for an individual depends on the situation. The primary benefits that come from these alternatives, in varying degrees include (1) less publicity, (2) less time, (3) less expense, (4) more convenient proceedings, and (5) a better chance to have a reasonable relationship with the other disputant in the future.

Alternative dispute resolution (ADR) also has its critics. Some of their concerns are that compulsory ADR may force parties to give up their "day in court," that a party who consistently procures ADR services from one firm will end up with a "neutral" that is biased toward that party, and that we will end up with a two-tier system of justice—an efficient private system and an overburdened public one.

REVIEW QUESTIONS

6-1. Explain why the use of ADR is increasing.

6-2. When will a judge overturn an arbitrator's decision?

6-3. Explain how one secures arbitration as a means of resolving a dispute.

6-4. Why are some people opposed to the growing use of arbitration?

6-5. What are the basic obligations of an arbitrator according to the Arbitrator's Code of Ethics?

6-6. Identify the factors that would lead a disputant to favor mediation as a dispute-resolution method.

REVIEW PROBLEMS

6-7. McGraw and Duffy have a contract that includes a binding arbitration clause. The clause provides for arbitration of any dispute arising out of the contract. The clause also provides that the arbitrator is authorized to award damages of up to $100,000 in any dispute arising out of the contract. McGraw allegedly breaches the contract. Duffy seeks arbitration, and the arbitrator, given the willfulness of the breach and the magnitude of its consequences, awards Duffy $150,000 in damages. Would a court uphold the award? Why or why not?

6-8. Sam and Mary enter into a contract that does not include a provision for arbitration. Mary wants to arbitrate the dispute, but Sam believes that arbitration is not possible because there is no binding arbitration clause in the contract. How can the parties secure arbitration?

6-9. Howard and Hannah decide to resolve a contract dispute through arbitration. They select their arbitrator through a private service. The arbitrator returns a significant award for Howard. The weekend after receiving a notice of the award, Hannah finds out from one of Howard's co-workers that, although the arbitrator and Howard acted as if they did not know each other, they actually had been college roommates. Does Hannah have any basis for getting the award set aside?

6-10. Eloise is hired as a pharmacist and signs an employment agreement that includes a provision that she will submit any employment disputes to arbitration. After being on the job for three years, she is denied a promotion that she feels she deserved. She files a sex discrimination charge with the EEOC and a lawsuit in the federal district court. The employer files a motion to compel arbitration. Will she be forced to arbitrate her claims? Why or why not?

6-11. Boxley Corporation and Eberly Corporation have a contract dispute before an arbitrator. Eberly wants to present evidence of prior contract disputes the two have had, but the arbitrator refuses to receive that evidence, saying it is not relevant to the alleged breach of contract at issue before him. When Boxley receives an award from the arbitrator that entitles it to significant damages from Eberly, the latter appeals the arbitrator's decision on the grounds that the excluded evidence would have changed the outcome. Why is Eberly likely or unlikely to have the award overturned?

6-12. Marshall files a complaint against S.A. & E., a brokerage firm registered with the Securities and Exchange Commission. The complaint alleges a violation of the Securities Exchange Act by engaging in fraudulent excessive trading. S.A. & E. files a motion to dismiss the case because Marshall had signed a customer agreement that included in its terms a promise to submit all disputes arising under their accounts to arbitration. Marshall argues that, owing to the egregious nature of S.A. & E.'s conduct, Marshall should be entitled to his "day in court" and the binding arbitration clause should be nullified. Why will the court grant or deny S.A. & E's motion?

CASE PROBLEMS

6-13. Saturn adopted a "Mission and Philosophy" of manufacturing and selling cars. As part of this mission, all of their dealer agreements contained a binding alternative dispute-resolution clause. This clause provides for a

136

Part One

*An Introduction to the Law
and the Legal Environment
of Business*

mandatory two-step process that includes mediation and binding arbitration, which provides for document discovery and a hearing. The decision of the arbitration panel is final and unappealable, except as provided by the Federal Arbitration Act. Saturn refuses to contract with anyone who refuses to agree to this provision.

Virginia passed a law that prohibited automobile manufacturers and dealers from entering into agreements that contain mandatory alternative dispute-resolution provisions, such as Saturn's contracts include. Saturn challenged the law as being preempted by the Federal Arbitration Act. Was Saturn's challenge successful? Why or why not? *Saturn Distributing Corp. v. Williams*, 905 F.2d 259 (1990)

6-14. Simmons was in an automobile accident with an uninsured motorist, from which he sustained personal injuries. He notified his insurance company that he was making a claim under his uninsured motorist coverage. His policy provided that if the insured and the insurer could not agree on the amount due under the claim, the dispute would be resolved by arbitration. Eventually, a claim for arbitration was made by Simmons. His insurance company refused to appoint arbitrators until a court order was obtained compelling their appointment. The arbitration resulted in an award of $8,900 in Simmons's favor, including a claim of the United States for $2,835. The insurance company refused to pay the award, and an action was finally brought to confirm and enforce the award.

The insurance company claimed that the arbitrator had exceeded his authority to enter any award relating to the claim of the United States because they were not represented at the arbitration by any government attorney. Simmons's lawyer had an affidavit from an Air Force captain giving him the authority to represent the government's claims in the matter. Explain why the arbitrator either did or did not exceed his authority. *Transnational Insurance Co. v. Larry Simmons*, 507 P.2d 693

6-15. AMF and Brunswick compete in the manufacture of bowling equipment. In earlier litigation over allegedly false and deceptive advertising, they entered into a settlement agreement that any future dispute involving an advertised claim of "data-based comparative superiority" of any bowling product would be submitted to a named advisory panel to determine whether there was experimental support for the claims. The party accused of making the false representation would be required to provide the panel the evidence upon which the claims were based in order for the panelists to make a fair decision.

Subsequently, Brunswick advertised that one of its products, Armor Plate 3000, a bowling lane material, was superior in durability to wood lanes. When AMF requested that the claim be submitted to the advisory party, Brunswick refused, arguing that the advertisement did not fall within the terms of the agreement, so AMF brought an action to compel nonbinding arbitration of the issue in accordance with the terms of agreement.

Did the court order this dispute to be submitted to the panel? Why or why not? *AMF Inc. v. Brunswick Corp.*, 621 F. Supp. 456 (1985)

6-16. Misco, Inc. had a collective bargaining agreement with the United Paperworkers International Union that authorized the submission to arbitration of any grievance that arose from interpretation or application of the agreement's terms. One of the employer's work rules provided that the employer had the right to discharge an employee for the possession or use of a controlled substance on company property. Cooper, a union member covered by the agreement who operated a hazardous piece of equipment was caught by the police in the backseat of someone else's car in the employer's parking lot. There was marijuana smoke in the air and a lighted marijuana cigarette in the front ashtray. A police search of Cooper's car revealed marijuana gleanings. After learning of this incident, the employer discharged Cooper for violating the disciplinary rule.

Cooper filed a grievance, arguing that his discharge was not justified under the rule. The arbitrator found in Cooper's favor and ordered him to be reinstated. The employer appealed to the district court, where the judge vacated the arbitration award, holding that to uphold the arbitrator's remedy would violate the public policy "against the operation of dangerous machinery by persons under the influence of drugs." The judge also disagreed with the arbitrator's findings that there was not sufficient cause for terminating the employee under the rule.

The union appealed the district court decision on behalf of the employee. The court of appeals affirmed. How do you think the U.S. Supreme Court decided this case? Why? *United Paperworkers International Union v. Misco, Inc.* 108 S. Ct. 364 (1987)

6-17. Alphonse Fletcher, an African American male, worked for Kidder, Peabody, & Company as a trader analyst. He believed that the firm breached his employment agreement with him by withholding 50 percent of his bonus compensation, deferring payment for up to 18 months, and requiring him to pay for trading losses on a dollar-for-dollar basis. No white traders were subject to similar treatment. Further, he was allegedly told by one of the firm's officers that he should not complain because he was "one of the highest paid black males" in the country.

A little more than a year later, Fletcher resigned and sued the firm for race discrimination in violation of state law. The firm filed a motion to compel arbitration on the grounds that the employment contract contained a binding arbitration clause, and therefore this claim should be subject to arbitration. The trial court denied the motion and was reversed on appeal. How do you believe this case was ultimately decided by New York's highest court? What factual issue do you think would be most important in this case? *Fletcher v. Kidder, Peabody, & Co.*, 619 N.E.2d 998 (1993)

6-18. McGhee Communications, Inc. (McGhee) filed an action against Firelock Incorporated (Firelock) for damages of less than $50,000 for Firelock's failure to provide advertising services for which McGhee had paid. McGhee sought to have the case arbitrated under the state's mandatory arbitration law. In his answer, Firelock sought to have the state's mandatory arbitration struck down as violative of his rights under the Colorado Constitution to access to the courts and a trial by jury and to his rights under the United States Constitution to equal protection and due process.

Under the law, a framework of mandatory arbitration for civil disputes in which $50,000 or less is at issue was established for eight of Colorado's judicial districts. All such cases must go to arbitration before a "qualified" arbitrator selected in accordance with statutory procedures, but if either party does not agree with the arbitrator's decision, he or she may file a motion for a new trial within 30 days of having received the unsatisfactory decision. The party will be entitled to the trial. However, if the trial award does not result in an improvement of the position of the demanding party by more than 10 percent, the demanding party must pay the costs of the arbitration proceeding including arbitrator's fees, in an amount not to exceed $1,000.

Thoroughly explain why Colorado's law either will or will not withstand this constitutional challenge. *Firelock Inc. v. The District Court in and of the 20th Judicial District of Colorado*, 776 P.2d 1090 (1989)

138

Part One

*An Introduction to the Law
and the Legal Environment
of Business*

 On the Internet

http://adrr.com/   This ADR site contains substantial on-line materials for ADR and particulary for mediation.

http://www.law.harvard.edu/Programs/pon   This Harvard Law School page is dedicated to improving the theory and practice of negotiation and dispute resolution.

http://www.com.ljextra.com/practice/arbitration/incex.html   This page contains recent cases resolved through ADR methods, as well as numerous detailed hotlinks.

http://www.adr.org   This site is the home page of the American Arbitration Association.

7

WHITE COLLAR CRIME AND
THE BUSINESS COMMUNITY

- **CRIME AND CRIMINAL PROCEDURE**

- **DISTINGUISHING FEATURES OF WHITE COLLAR CRIME**

- **COMMON WHITE COLLAR CRIMES**

- **PREVENTION OF WHITE COLLAR CRIME**

- **FEDERAL LAWS USED IN THE FIGHT AGAINST WHITE COLLAR CRIME**

- **STATE LAWS USED IN THE FIGHT AGAINST WHITE COLLAR CRIME**

- **INTERNATIONAL DIMENSIONS OF WHITE COLLAR CRIME**

140

Part One

*An Introduction to the Law
and the Legal Environment
of Business*

In 1998, a Georgetown lawyer pleaded guilty to wire fraud and money laundering and admitted to stealing more than $300,000 while managing real estate money for a title company. His crimes were not all that unusual; he just happened to get caught. During the previous year, telemarketing fraud resulted in losses in the United States and Canada of close to $40 billion, while health care fraud in the United States alone was estimated to be as high as $100 billion. It is estimated that billions of dollars will be lost this year by Americans who will fall victim to one of the fastest growing white collar crimes: *identity theft*, a crime whereby a thief obtains credit in someone else's name and charges thousands of dollars in that person's name.

White collar crimes—crimes committed in a commercial context—occur every day. Collectively, these crimes often result in millions of dollars of damages. In recent years, as corporate crimes like the ones detailed in Table 7-1 are becoming more publicized, people's attitudes toward corporations and white collar crime are being affected.

Critical Thinking about the Law

WHY SHOULD WE BE CONCERNED ABOUT white collar crime? You can use the following critical thinking questions to help guide your thinking about white collar crime as you study this chapter.

1. If a judge strongly valued justice, do you think she would give an easier sentence to a business manager who embezzled $50,000 than she would give to a person who robbed a bank of $50,000? Why?

   CLUE Think about the definitions of justice offered in chapter 1.

2. As a future business manager, you may be forced to make tough decisions regarding white collar crime. Imagine that you discover that one of your employees planned to offer a bribe to an agent from the Environmental Protection Agency to prevent your company from being fined. Although the result of the potential bribe could greatly benefit your company, you know that the bribe is illegal. What conflicting ethical norms are involved in your decision?

   CLUE Review the list of ethical norms offered in chapter 1.

3. White collar crime is typically not violent crime. Therefore, many people assume that street crime is more serious and should receive harsher punishments. Can you generate some reasons why that assumption is false? Why might white collar crime deserve a more severe sentence?

   CLUE Reread the introductory paragraphs that provide information about white collar crime. Why might a business manager deserve a more severe sentence than a young woman committing a robbery? What are the consequences of both actions?

The future manager must be prepared to respond to a growing lack of public confidence and to avoid becoming a corporate criminal. This chapter will help the reader prepare to face the challenges posed by corporate crime. The first section defines crime and briefly explains criminal procedure. Next, the factors that distinguish corporate crime from street crime are discussed. The third section explains in detail some of the more common white collar crimes. The fourth section introduces some ideas for how we can reduce the incidence of white collar crime. The fifth and sixth sections discuss respectively the federal and state responses to white collar crime. An overview of the international dimensions of white collar crime is then provided.

TABLE 7-1 *Recent White Collar Crimes*

Martin Bramson, Businessman. Sentence: 30 Years

Bramson, 52, directed the largest malpractice insurance scam in U.S. history. His decade-long insurance scam swindled doctors across the country out of more than $10 million and siphoned millions of dollars through a maze of phony companies and nearly 600 bank accounts worldwide. Bramson ran the scam with the help of his brother and father, setting up 53 foreign-licensed insurance companies and selling cut-rate malpractice insurance over the phone to physicians nationwide. The Bramsons collected premiums but refused to pay large claims from doctors and their patients, prosecutors said.

Bramson pleaded guilty in 1997 to conspiracy, mail fraud, and money laundering. He was sentenced to 30 years in prison and was fined in excess of $1 million. As part of his plea bargain, Bramson agreed to cooperate with efforts to locate millions in assets still believed to be hidden in banks around the world. In exchange, the government dropped seven counts and agreed not to call him to testify against another brother, Carl, still under investigation. Eight other people, including lawyers and insurance underwriters, also have pleaded guilty in the case.

Eddie Antar, Corporate Founder. Sentence: $12\frac{1}{2}$ Years

Antar, 45, head of the Crazy Eddie discount electronics chain that promoted itself with television commercials pitching "insaaaaane" prices, organized an $80 million stock fraud by inflating his companies' inventory and sales figures before the company went public in 1984. Antar sold out for a huge profit by 1987, and in 1989 the company filed for bankruptcy and went out of business. He was tried and convicted of conspiracy, racketeering, and securities and mail fraud.

In April 1994, in addition to a sentence of twelve and one half years in prison, Antar was ordered to pay $121 million in restitution to former stockholders. As of June, 1997, authorities had recovered $135 million, including $77 million Antar had stashed in foreign bank accounts.

Tom Billman, Banker. Sentence: 40 Years

Billman, 54, as president and chief executive of the now defunct Community Savings and Loan Association of Bethesda, Maryland, embezzled $29.5 million from depositors. Billman fled in 1988 after wiring $22 million to Swiss bank accounts. He lived lavishly on two yachts in the Mediterranean before he was arrested in 1993 in Paris, where he was posing as a champagne entrepreneur. He was tried and convicted of federal mail fraud.

In June 1994, Billman was sentenced to 40 years in prison and was ordered to pay $25 million in restitution. Billman claimed to be "hopelessly insolvent," but by October 1994 police had discovered $9 million hidden in Europe.

Herbert Steindler, International Sales Manager. Sentence: 7 Years

Steindler, 55, a General Electric Company executive in charge of military jet-engine sales to Israel, conspired to divert $11 million from defense contracts between GE and the Israeli government. The contracts were financed under a U.S. foreign military aid program. Most of the money was transferred to Swiss bank accounts for the benefit of Steindler and Rami Dotan, a former Israeli Air Force general. Steindler plead guilty to money laundering.

Steindler was sentenced in November 1994 to seven years in prison and two years of supervised release. GE previously plead guilty and in 1992 paid $69 million in fines and penalties to settle charges of conspiracy, money laundering, and failure to make and keep accurate books and records.

John Morberg, Government Official. Sentence: $6\frac{1}{2}$ Years

Morberg, 44, former Michigan House Fiscal Agency Director, masterminded a conspiracy to bilk taxpayers of up to $1.8 million. Morberg embezzled money for purposes of arranging the sale of military weapons to Croatia, buying a landfill in Michigan's Upper Peninsula, underwriting vacation trips and home improvements, and paying pals and business associates as no-work employees and consultants. He plead guilty to racketeering, tax evasion, and embezzlement.

Morberg was sentenced in September 1994 to six and one half years in prison and must repay $834,000 to the state and $10,477 to the IRS. Morberg will forfeit his $1,977 monthly state pension while in prison, and after release $1,727 of the pension will go to the state, with the rest earmarked for private debts of more than $100,000.

Part One

*An Introduction to the Law
and the Legal Environment
of Business*

CRIME AND CRIMINAL PROCEDURE

CRIME

Criminal law is designed to punish an offender for causing harm to the public health, safety, or morals. Criminal laws prohibit certain actions and specify the range of punishments for such conduct. The proscribed conduct generally includes a description of both a wrongful behavior (an act or failure to act where one has a duty to do so) and a wrongful intent or state of mind. The legal term for wrongful intent is *mens rea* (guilty mind). An extremely limited number of crimes do not require *mens rea*. These crimes are the "strict liability," or regulatory, crimes. They occur most commonly in heavily regulated industries and arise when a regulation has been violated. Regulatory crimes are created when the legislature decides that the need to protect the public outweighs the traditional requirement of *mens rea*. Because of the absence of the *mens rea* requirement for regulatory crimes, punishment for their violation is generally less severe than it is for wrongful behavior. In some states, punishment is limited to fines.

Crimes are generally classified as treason, felony, misdemeanor, or petty crime, on the basis of the seriousness of the offense. Treason is engaging in war against the United States or giving aid or comfort to its enemies. **Felonies** include serious crimes such as murder or rape, punishable by death or imprisonment in a penitentiary. **Misdemeanors** are considered less serious crimes and are punishable by a fine or by imprisonment in a local jail. An assault (a threat to injure someone) would be an example of a misdemeanor. A **petty crime** is a minor federal crime punishable by a fine or by incarceration for six months or less. The statute defining the crime generally states whether it is a felony, misdemeanor, or petty crime. The more serious the offense, the greater the stigma that attaches to the criminal.

CRIMINAL PROCEDURE

Criminal proceedings are initiated somewhat differently from civil proceedings. The procedures may vary slightly from state to state. In general, however, the case begins with an **arrest** of the defendant. The police must, in almost all cases, obtain an arrest warrant before arresting the defendant and taking him or her into custody. The arrest warrant will be issued by a magistrate when there is **probable cause** to believe that the suspect committed the crime. A magistrate is a public official who has the power to issue warrants; he or she is the lowest ranking judicial official. Probable cause exists if it appears, from the available facts and circumstances, likely that the defendant committed the crime. An arrest may be made by a police officer without a warrant, but only if probable cause exists and there is not time to secure a warrant. An arrest without a warrant would most commonly be made when police are called to the scene of a crime and catch the suspect committing the crime or fleeing from the scene.

At the time of the arrest, the suspect must be informed of her or his legal rights. These rights are referred to as the **Miranda rights**, and if the defendant is not informed of these rights, any statements the defendant makes at the time of the arrest will be inadmissible at the defendant's trial. These rights are listed in Table 7-2.

After the defendant has been arrested, he or she will be taken to the police station for *booking*, the filing of criminal charges against the defendant. The arresting officer will then file a *criminal complaint* against the defendant. Shortly after the complaint is filed, the defendant will make his or her **first appearance** before the magistrate. At this time, the magistrate will determine whether there was probable cause for the arrest. If there was not, the suspect will be set free and the case will be dismissed.

If the offense is a minor one, and the defendant pleads guilty, the magistrate may accept the guilty plea and sentence the defendant. Most defendants however, maintain they are innocent. The magistrate will make sure the defen-

felony A serious crime that is punishable by death or imprisonment in a penitentiary.

misdemeanor A less serious crime than a felony that is punishable by fine or imprisonment in a local jail.

petty crime A minor crime punishable, under federal statutes, by fine or incarceration of no more than six months.

arrest To seize and hold under the authority of the law.

probable cause The reasonable inference from the available facts and circumstances that the suspect committed the crime.

Miranda rights Certain legal rights—such as the right to remain silent to avoid self-incrimination and the right to an attorney—that a suspect must be immediately informed of upon arrest.

first appearance Appearance of the defendant before a magistrate, who determines whether there was probable cause for the arrest.

Before any questioning by authorities, the following statements must be made to the defendant:

1. "You have the right to remain silent and refuse to answer any questions."
2. "Anything you say may be used against you in a court of law."
3. "You have the right to consult an attorney before speaking to the police and have an attorney present during any questioning now or in the future."
4. "If you cannot afford an attorney, one will be appointed for you before the questioning begins."
5. "If you do not have an attorney available, you have the right to remain silent until you have had an opportunity to consult with one."
6. "Now that I have advised you of your rights, are you willing to answer any questions without an attorney present?"

dant has a lawyer and, if the defendant is indigent, will appoint a lawyer for him or her. The magistrate will also set bail at this time. **Bail** is an amount of money that is paid to the court to ensure that the defendant will return for trial. In some cases, especially in white collar crimes, if the magistrate believes that the defendant has such "ties to the community" that he or she will not try to flee the area to avoid prosecution the defendant may be released without posting bail. In such cases, the defendant is said to be released "on his own recognizance."

If the crime is a misdemeanor, the next step is the prosecutor's issuance of an **information**, a formal written accusation or charge. The information is usually issued only after the prosecutor has presented the facts to a magistrate who believes that the prosecution has sufficient grounds to bring the case.

In felony cases, the process begins with a presentation by the *prosecutor* (the prosecuting officer representing the United States or the state) of the facts surrounding the crime to a *grand jury*, a group of individuals under oath who are presented with evidence of a crime. The grand jury has the power to subpoena witnesses and require them to produce documents and tangible evidence. If the grand jury is convinced by a preponderance of the evidence that there is reason to believe that the defendant may have committed the crime, an *indictment* (a formal, written accusation) is issued against the defendant. A grand jury does *not* make a finding of guilt; it simply decides whether there is enough evidence that the defendant committed the crime to justify bringing the defendant to trial. Government resources are limited, and the prosecution may not always believe they have sufficient evidence to get an indictment, let alone prove beyond a reasonable doubt that the defendant committed the crime, so not every crime is prosecuted. The prosecutor's office must make the decision in each case. Usually their decision as to whether to seek an indictment depends upon whether they believe they can get a conviction and whether the interests of justice would be served by prosecuting the crime.

At the federal level, almost all criminal prosecutions are initiated by the indictment process, and the decision whether to prosecute is generally guided by the *Principles of Federal Prosecution*, published by the Justice Department in 1980. These *Principles* state that the primary consideration in the indictment decision is whether the existing admissible evidence is sufficient to obtain a conviction for a federal crime. Even if sufficient evidence does exist, the prosecutor's office might choose not to prosecute a crime if no substantial federal interest would be served by doing so, if the defendant could be efficiently prosecuted in another jurisdiction, or if an adequate noncriminal alternative to criminal prosecution exists. The factors that influence whether a substantial federal interest exists are listed in Table 7-3.

The *Principles* clearly recognize that, at least when a federal crime is at issue, other noncriminal actions may offer fairer or more efficient ways to respond to the criminal conduct. Some alternatives might be to institute civil proceedings against the defendant or to refer the complaint to a licensing board or the professional organization to which the criminal belongs.

bail An amount of money the defendant pays to the court upon release from custody as security that he or she will return for trial.

information A formal written accusation in a misdemeanor case.

TABLE 7-3 *Factors for Determining a Substantial Federal Interest and the Principles for Federal Prosecution*

1. Federal law enforcement priorities: established by the Department of Justice
2. Deterrent effect
3. The subject's culpability
4. The subject's willingness to cooperate
5. The subject's personal circumstances
6. The probable sentence
7. The possibility of prosecution in another jurisdiction
8. Noncriminal alternatives to prosecution

Another alternative to indictment is *pretrial diversion*, often referred to as PTD. Pretrial diversion attempts to divert certain criminal offenders from the traditional criminal justice system into a program of supervision and services. A PTD participant signs an agreement with the government acknowledging responsibility for the act at issue, but not admitting guilt. The participant agrees to be supervised by the U.S. Probation Office and to comply with the terms established for the agreed upon period of the agreement, up to 18 months. Special conditions, which vary according to the alleged circumstances and the criminal activity, might include participating in community programs or paying restitution. If the participant complies with the agreement, the matter is closed. If not, he or she will then be prosecuted.

arraignment Formal appearance of the defendant in court to answer the indictment by entering a plea of guilty or not guilty.

Once there has been an indictment, the next step is the **arraignment**. The defendant appears in court and enters a plea of guilty or not guilty. A defendant who enters a plea of not guilty is entitled to a trial before a *petit jury*. If the defendant declines a jury trial, the case is heard by a judge. This procedure is called a *bench trial*.

nolo contendere A plea of no contest that subjects the defendant to punishment but is not an admission of guilt.

A defendant may also enter a plea of **nolo contendere**. This plea is one by which the defendant does not admit guilt but agrees to not contest the charges. The advantage of a nolo contendere plea over a plea of guilty is that the former cannot be used against the defendant in a civil suit.

plea bargaining The negotiation of an agreement between the defendant's attorney and the prosecutor whereby the defendant pleads guilty to a certain charge or charges in exchange for the dropping the reduction of the charges by the prosecution.

PLEA BARGAINING   At any time during the proceedings, the parties may engage in **plea bargaining**, which is a process of negotiation between the defense attorney and the public prosecutor or district attorney. The result of this process is that the defendant pleads guilty to a lesser offense, in exchange for which the prosecutor drops or reduces some of the charges. Plea bargaining benefits the criminal by eliminating the risk of a greater penalty. It benefits the prosecutor by giving her or him a sure conviction and by reducing what is generally an overwhelming caseload. It saves both parties the time and expense of a trial.

Plea bargaining is used extensively for white collar crimes, generally at a much earlier stage than for street crimes. In white collar cases, plea bargaining often occurs even before the indictment. This process, as well as other modifications of criminal procedures in white collar crime cases, helps to make the white collar criminal seem "less a criminal" and thus reduces the likelihood of severe punishment.

BURDEN OF PROOF   If the case goes to trial, the burden of proof is usually on the prosecutor. The burden of proof has two aspects: the *burden of production of evidence* and the *burden of persuasion*. The burden of production of evidence of all of the elements of the crime is placed on the prosecution. Thus, the prosecution must present physical evidence and testimony that prove all elements of the crime. The burden of producing evidence of any affirmative defenses (defenses in which the defendant admits to doing the act but claims some reason for not being held responsible, such as insanity, self-defense, intoxication, or coercion) lies with the defendant.

The prosecution also bears the burden of persuasion. This means that the prosecutor must convince the jury *beyond a reasonable doubt* that the defendant committed the crime. In some states, a defendant who presents evidence of an affirmative defense must persuade the jury of the existence of the defense by a preponderance of the evidence. This means that the defense must prove that it is more likely than not that the defense exists. In other states, the burden of persuasion lies with the prosecutor to show beyond a reasonable doubt that the defense does not exist.

The actual trial itself is similar to a civil trial, and the role of the prosecutor or district attorney is similar to that of the plaintiff's attorney. One major difference, however, is that the defendant in a criminal case cannot be compelled to testify, and the finder of fact is not to hold the exercise of this right against the defendant. This right to not testify is guaranteed by the constitutional provision in the Fifth Amendment that no person "shall be compelled in any criminal case to be a witness against himself."

DEFENSES   Obviously, one of the most common defenses is that the defendant did not do the act in question. But even if the defendant did commit the act, there are a number of affirmative defenses that might be raised to preclude the defendant from being convicted of the crime. Affirmative defenses may be thought of as excuses for otherwise unlawful conduct. Four of the most common are entrapment, insanity, duress, and mistake.

Entrapment occurs when the idea for the crime was not the defendant's but was, instead, put into the defendant's mind by a police officer or other government official. An extreme example might be a case in which a government official first suggests to an employee that he or she could make good money by altering certain corporate records. Then the official shows up at the employee's home at night with a key to the office where the records are kept and reminds the employee that the record keeper is on vacation that week. The official also reminds the employee that most of the other workers rarely stay late on Friday nights, so Friday after work might be an ideal time to get the books. If prosecuted for fraud, the employee could raise the defense of entrapment.

Entrapment is not always easy to prove, however. Police are allowed to set up legitimate "sting" operations to catch persons engaged in criminal activity. The key to a legitimate sting is that the defendant was "predisposed" to commit the crime; the officer did not put the idea in the defendant's head. If an officer dresses up like a prostitute and parades around in an area where prostitution is rampant, a potential customer who solicits sex could not raise the charge of entrapment against a charge of soliciting a prostitute. Most cases, however, fall between our two examples, and it is often difficult to predict whether the entrapment defense will be successful.

Insanity is one of the best-known criminal defenses, although it is not used nearly as frequently as its notoriety might imply. Insanity is a defense when a person's mental condition prevents him or her from understanding the wrongful nature of the act he or she committed or from distinguishing wrong from right.

Duress occurs when a person is forced to commit a wrongful act by a threat of immediate bodily harm or loss of life, and the affirmative **duress defense** can be used by a person who claims he or she was forced to commit a crime. For example, if Sam holds a gun to Jim's head and tells him to forge his employer's signature on a company check or he will be shot, Jim can raise the defense of duress to a charge of forgery. This defense is generally not available to a charge of murder.

A **mistake of fact** may sometimes be raised when that mistake vitiates the criminal intent. For example, if Mary takes Karen's umbrella from a public umbrella rack, thinking it is hers, she can raise mistake as a defense to a charge of theft.

A mistake of law, however, is generally not a defense. A person could not, for example, fail to include payment received for a small job on his or her income tax return because of a mistaken belief that income for part-time work of under $100 did not have to be reported.

entrapment An affirmative defense claiming that the idea for the crime did not originate with the defendant but was put into the defendant's mind by a police officer or other government official.

insanity defense An affirmative defense claiming that the defendant's mental condition precluded understanding the wrongful nature of the act he or she committed or distinguishing wrong from right in general.

duress defense An affirmative defense claiming that the defendant was forced to commit the wrongful act by threat of immediate bodily harm or loss of life.

mistake-of-fact-defense An affirmative defense claiming that a mistake made by the defendant vitiates criminal intent.

146

Part One

*An Introduction to the Law
and the Legal Environment
of Business*

EXHIBIT 7-1 *Steps of a Criminal Prosecution*

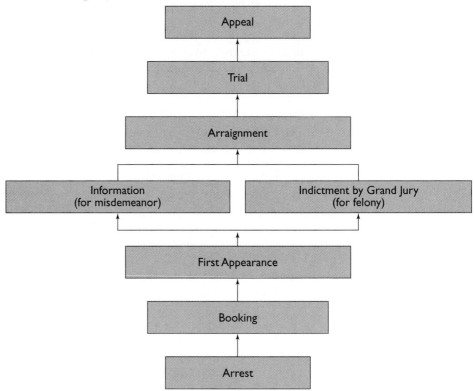

Any defendant who does not prevail at the trial court can appeal the decision, just as in a civil case. The steps of a criminal action are set out in Exhibit 7-1.

DISTINGUISHING FEATURES OF WHITE COLLAR CRIME

An initial problem with any discussion of white collar crime is its definition. The term **white collar crime** does not have a precise meaning. The term was first made popular in 1939 by sociologist Edwin Sutherland, who defined white collar crime as "crime committed by a person of respectability and high social status in the course of his occupation." Traditionally, it has been the classification of those crimes committed in a commercial context by members of the professional and managerial classes. It includes such diverse acts as bribery of corporate or government officials and violations of federal regulations such as the Occupational Safety and Health Act and the Internal Revenue Service Code. In this book, we will be using the traditional definition.

white collar crime A crime committed in a commercial context by a member of the professional-managerial class.

THE CORPORATION AS A CRIMINAL

One of the distinguishing features of white collar crime is that sometimes the "criminal" may be difficult to identify. In a street crime, the identity of the criminal is fairly clear: It is the person who committed the act. If a person hires another to commit a crime, the person doing the hiring is likewise guilty of a crime. In the case of white collar crime, the crime is often committed on behalf of a corporation, which is defined as an artificial legal entity or an artificial person. An important question, then, is whether liability can be imposed on the corporation for the criminal acts committed by employees of the corporation on behalf of the corporation.

Initially, the courts said no. Because a corporation had no mind, it could not have the mental state necessary to commit a crime. This rule was first eroded by the imposition of liability on corporations for so-called **strict liability offenses**, those for which no state of mind is required. These generally

strict liability offense One for which no state of mind is required.

were cases in which corporate employees failed to take some action required by a regulation. For example, under most *blue sky laws* (state regulations of securities), it is a violation to file a false statement of a company's financial condition with a state's secretary of state. Filing a false statement is a crime, even if the corporate officer filing the statement believed it was true, as no state of mind is required to commit the crime.

The courts then began to impose liability on corporations for criminal acts of the employees by imputing the state of mind of the employee to the corporation. Today, as a general rule, the only crimes for which a corporation is not held liable are those that are punishable only by incarceration. Obviously, the rationale for this rule is that the punishment could not be carried out. Some states have even eliminated this problem by passing a statute that provides for specific fines for corporations that commit offenses otherwise punishable by incarceration only.

Many corporate executives may not realize the extent to which a corporation today can be held liable for the acts of its employees. That liability can extend down to acts of even the lowest-level employees and even to acts in violation of corporate directives, as long as two conditions are met. First, the conduct must be within the scope of the employee agent's authority. Second, the action must have been undertaken, at least in part, to benefit the corporation. Some examples of employee actions for which corporations have been held liable include a mid-level manager's rigging a bid in violation of the Sherman Act,[1] clerical employees of a retail eye-wear chain conspiring to falsify Medicare claims,[2] and a car salesman's obtaining automobile loans for the dealership's customers by misrepresenting financial data to the lending bank.[3]

Many states have passed statutes imposing criminal liability on partnerships under the same circumstances as those under which liability is imposed on a corporation. In the absence of such a statute, liability is not imposed on the partnership because a partnership is not a legal person.

ARGUMENTS IN SUPPORT OF CORPORATE LIABILITY

Needless to say, there is no consensus about whether, as a matter of policy, corporations *should* be held criminally liable. Some of the arguments in favor of such liability include the following:

1. Imposing financial sanctions against the corporation will result in lower dividends for the shareholders, which, in turn, will prompt the shareholders to take a more active role in trying to make sure that the corporation behaves legally. They will carefully select directors who will scrupuously monitor corporate behavior and will express concern when anything appears to be unethical or illegal.

2. In situations in which the crime is an omission and the responsibility for performing the omitted duty is not clearly delegated to any specific party, the duty rests with no particular individual. Therefore there is no one to blame, and the corporation cannot be held responsible. If no one, not even the corporation, is held liable, there is no incentive to obey the laws.

3. Closely related to reason 2 is the fact that there are a tremendous number of suspects in a corporation. Most enforcement agencies do not have the resources to investigate the large number of employees involved and to build cases against each. It is much easier and less expensive for the government to investigate and bring a case against the corporation as an entity.

4. The fact that many decisions are committee decisions—or else decisions made by an initial person or group and then approved by several tiers of management—again makes it hard to point the finger at one individual. Sometimes, one individual is responsible for making an initial decision, and then someone else is responsible for implementing that decision.

---

[1]United States v. Koppers, 652 F.2d 290 (2d Cir. 1981).
[2]United States v. Gold, 743 F.2d 800 (11th Cir. 1984).
[3]Commonwealth v. Duddie Ford, Inc. 551 N.E.2d 1211 (1990).

148

Part One

*An Introduction to the Law
and the Legal Environment
of Business*

5. A further reason is that corporate personnel are expendable. To lose a manager because of a conviction does not really harm the enterprise that profited from the wrongdoing. In fact, it allows the firm to externalize the costs of the criminal behavior, that is, to absolve themselves of guilt in the eyes of the public. The manager takes the blame, and the corporation, which profited from the manager's illegal act, continues to thrive.

6. Even if one could impose liability on one or two individuals, it is unfair to single them out for punishment when the behavior in question probably resulted from a pattern of behavior common to the entire corporation.

7. Some people assume that the beneficiaries of crime committed on behalf of the corporation are the shareholders, because they may get higher dividends if corporate crime keeps costs lower. To fail to impose sanctions on the corporation would be to allow the shareholders to benefit from the illegal activity.

8. If an action is taken against the corporation, the criminal act will be linked to the corporation in the public's mind. In a market-oriented society such as ours, disclosure of full information about businesses is essential for consumers to make informed decisions about the types of firms with which they want to transact business.

ARGUMENTS IN OPPOSITION TO CORPORATE LIABILITY

The following are arguments against imposing liability on corporations.

1. Imposing fines on corporations is a waste of time and effort because the fines are never going to be severe enough to act as a deterrent. Even if more substantial fines were imposed the firms would simply pass on the losses to consumers in the form of increased product prices. Thus, it would really be the consumers of the corporation's products who would be punished.

"Honesty is the best policy, Fernbaugh, but it's not company policy."

2. Some people believe that the shareholders' dividends may be reduced if fines are imposed on the corporation because the cost of the fines will reduce the profits available for dividend payments. Reducing dividends, it is argued, is unfair because in most corporations, the shareholders really do not have any power to control corporate behavior.

3. Because criminal prosecutions of corporations are not well publicized, they do not harm the corporation's public image. The corporations have enough money and public relations personnel to easily overcome any negative publicity with a well-run advertising campaign designed to polish their public image. For example, the prosecution of Revco of Ohio for defrauding Medicaid of hundreds of thousand of dollars resulted in only a temporary decline of the value of Revco's stock.[4]

IMPOSITION OF LIABILITY ON CORPORATE EXECUTIVES

Another potential candidate for liability in the case of white collar crime is the corporate executive. Top-level corporate executives, as a group, have tremendous power through their control over national corporations. When these corporations earn record-setting profits, top-level executives rush forward to take credit for their corporations' successes. However, these same executives do not rush forward to take responsibility for their corporations' criminal violations.

In their study of corporate crime, sociologists Marshall Clinard and Peter Yeager found that in only 1.5 percent of all enforcement actions (actions requiring compliance with federal regulations) was a corporate official penalized for failure to carry out a legal responsibility to the company.[5] Primarily because of the delegation of responsibility to lower tiers of management and reliance on unwritten orders, top-level management is often able to protect itself from liability for the results of its policy decisions.

Traditionally, imposing liability on executives has been difficult because the criminal law usually requires an unlawful act to be accompanied by an unlawful intent (*mens rea*). In cases of violations of federal regulations, corporate executives often argue that they are not the ones directly responsible for filing the documents or conducting the studies. They certainly never explicitly ordered that such regulations be disregarded. As the following case shows, however, the courts are now recognizing that corporate executives who have the power and authority to secure compliance with the law have an affirmative duty to do so. Failure to uphold that duty can lead to criminal sanctions.

UNITED STATES V. PARK
UNITED STATES SUPREME COURT 421 U.S. 658 (1975)

Defendant Park, the president of a national food-chain corporation, was charged, along with the corporation, with violating the federal Food, Drug, and Cosmetic Act by allowing food in the warehouse to be exposed to rodent contamination. Park had conceded that he was responsible for the sanitary conditions as part of his responsibility for the "entire operation" but claimed that he had turned the responsibility for sanitation over to dependable subordinates. He admitted at the trial that he had received a warning letter from the Food and Drug Administration regarding the unsanitary conditions at one of the company's warehouses.

The trial court found the defendant guilty. The court of appeals reversed. The case was appealed to the U.S. Supreme Court.

CHIEF JUSTICE BURGER

The question presented was whether "the manager of a corporation, as well as the corporation itself, may be pros-

---

[4]D. Vaughan, *Controlling Unlawful Organizational Behavior* (Chicago: University of Chicago Press, 1983).

[5]M. Clinard and P. Yeager, *Corporate Crime* (New York: Free Press, 1980), p. 272.

ecuted under the Federal Food, Drug, and Cosmetic Act of 1938 for the introduction of misbranded and adulterated articles into interstate commerce. In *Dotterweich*, a jury had disagreed as to the corporation, a jobber purchasing drugs from manufacturers and shipping them in interstate commerce under its own label, but had convicted Dotterweich, the corporation's president and general manager.

In reversing the judgment of the Court of Appeals and reinstating Dotterweich's conviction, this Court looked to the purposes of the Act and noted that they "touch phases of the lives and health of people which, in the circumstances of modern industrialism, are largely beyond self-protection." It observed that the Act is of "a now familiar type" which "dispenses with the conventional requirement for criminal conduct—awareness of some wrongdoing. In the interest of the larger good it puts the burden of acting at hazard upon a person otherwise innocent but standing in responsible relation to a public danger."

Central to the Court's conclusion that individuals other than proprietors are subject to the criminal provisions of the Act was the reality that "the only way in which a corporation can act is through the individuals who act on in its behalf." The Court also noted that corporate officers had been subject to criminal liability under the Federal Food and Drugs Act of 1906, and it observed that a contrary result under the 1938 legislation would be incompatible with the expressed intent of Congress to "enlarge and stiffen the penal net" and to discourage a view of the Act's criminal penalties as a " 'license fee for the conduct of an illegitimate business.' "

At the same time, however, the Court was aware of the concern which was the motivating factor in the Court of Appeals' decision, that literal enforcement "might operate too harshly by sweeping within its condemnation any person however remotely entangled in the proscribed shipment." A limiting principle, in the form of "settled doctrines of criminal law" defining those who "are responsible for the commission of a misdemeanor," was available. In this context, the Court concluded, those doctrines dictated that the offense was committed "by all who . . . have . . . a responsible share in the furtherance of the transaction which the statute outlaws."

The rule that corporate employees who have "a responsible share in the furtherance of the transaction which the statute outlaws" are subject to the criminal provisions of the Act was not formulated in a vacuum. Cases under the Federal Food and Drugs Act of 1906 reflected the view both that knowledge or intent were not required to be proved in prosecutions under its criminal provisions, and that responsible corporate agents could be subjected to the liability thereby imposed. Moreover, the principle had been recognized that a corporate agent, through whose act, default, or omission the corporation committed a crime, was himself guilty individually of that crime.

The rationale of the interpretation given the Act in *Dotterweich*, as holding criminally accountable the persons whose failure to exercise the authority and supervisory responsibility reposed in them by the business organization, resulted in the violation complained of, has been confirmed in our subsequent cases. Thus, the Court has reaffirmed the proposition that "the public interest in the purity of its food is so great as to warrant the imposition of the highest standard of care on distributors." In order to make "distributors of food the strictest censors of their merchandise," the Act punishes "neglect where the law requires care, and inaction where it imposes a duty." "The accused, if he does not will the violation, usually is in a position to prevent it with no more care than society might reasonably expect and no more exertion than it might reasonably extract from one who assumed his responsibilities."

Thus, *Dotterweich* and the cases which have followed reveal that in providing sanctions which reach and touch the individuals who execute the corporate mission—and this is by no means necessarily confined to a single corporate agent or employee—the Act imposes not only a positive duty to seek out and remedy violations when they occur but also, and primarily, a duty to implement measures that will insure that violations will not occur. The requirements of foresight and vigilance imposed on responsible corporate agents are beyond question demanding, and perhaps onerous, but they are not more stringent than the public has a right to expect of those who voluntarily assume positions of authority in business enterprises whose services and products affect the healthy and well-being of the public that supports them.

The Act does not, as we observed in *Dotterweich*, make criminal liability turn on "awareness of some wrongdoing" or "conscious fraud." The duty imposed by Congress on responsible corporate agents is, we emphasize, one that requires the highest standard of foresight and vigilance, but the Act, in its criminal aspect, does not require that which is objectively impossible. The theory upon which responsible corporate agents are held criminally accountable for "causing" violations of the Act permits a claim that a defendant was "powerless" to prevent or correct the violation to "be raised defensively at a trial on the merits."

. . . [I]t is equally clear that the Government established a prima facie case when it introduced evidence sufficient to warrant a finding by the trier of the facts that the defendant had, by reason of his position in the corporation, responsibility and authority either to prevent in the first instance, or promptly to correct, the violation complained of, and that he failed to do so. The failure thus to fulfill the duty imposed by the interaction of the corporate agent's authority and that statute furnishes a sufficient causal link. The considerations which prompted the imposition of this duty, and the scope of the duty, provide the measure of culpability.

Reversed in favor of the Government.

Critical Thinking about the Law

ALTHOUGH IT NEVER EXPLICITLY STATED IT as such, the Court in this case was guided by a fundamental principle: To the extent that one has authority, she or he also has responsibility and can be liable for criminal action. This guiding principle played a significant role in the Court's justification (i.e., reasoning) for its decision.

Context was very important in the formulation of this principle as well as in its application to this case. Key facts, primary ethical norms, and judicial precedent were important elements of this context. Consequently, the questions that follow will focus on those aspects of the case.

1. What key fact was very important to the Court in its determination of Park's guilt?

CLUE Think again about the Court's guiding principle in this case. You want to identify the key fact that allowed the Court to apply the principle to this particular case.

2. Precedent plays a crucial role in the Court's reasoning and, thus, in its decision. What key precedent in criminal law did the *Dotterweich* decision dispense with, thereby clearing the way for the guiding principle discussed above to have greater significance and making conviction in the present case possible?

CLUE Reread the section in which Justice Burger discusses the *Dotterweich* decision.

Although the *Park* case demonstrates that corporate executives *may* be found guilty of committing a corporate crime, few actually *are* convicted. Even when they are convicted, harsh penalties are not likely to be imposed.

A primary reason for the limited number of convictions is the diffusion of responsibility. It is often difficult to establish who was responsible for the criminal act. Another problem related to corporate structure is that everyone usually has a specific job, and putting all of the pieces of the crime together is difficult. The reader should remember that the burden of proof is on the prosecution. Corporate executives also tend to have high-caliber counsel who specialize in defending white collar criminals. These skilled attorneys, often paid for by the corporation or, when not unlawful, by an insurance carrier, usually get involved during the initial investigation of the case and perceive one of their key functions as keeping evidence out of the hands of the prosecutor. They often regard themselves as having lost the case if they do not prevent their client from being indicted or if they do not at least get the charge reduced to the lowest possible misdemeanor.[6] Another alleged reason for the limited number of convictions of corporate executives is that they are generally persons with a great deal of knowledge, including knowledge of inefficiencies and improprieties on the part of the government officials who are regulating them. It is argued that regulators are unlikely to press for prosecution when their own ineptness may be revealed in the process.

IMPOSITION OF LIABILITY ON LOWER-LEVEL CORPORATE CRIMINALS

Although much debate has been generated over the extent to which the corporation and its top executives should be held liable for crimes committed on behalf of the corporation, it is important to remember that lower- and mid-level corporate employees can also be held liable for their individual criminal actions, and imposition of liability on the corporation does not in any way preclude the imposition of liability on the individual actor. It is likewise no excuse

---

[6]K. Mann, *Defending White Collar Crime* (New Haven: Yale University Press, 1985), p. 10.

152

Part One

*An Introduction to the Law
and the Legal Environment
of Business*

on the part of an employee that he was committing the wrongful act only because his employer instructed him to do so.

FACTORS ENCOURAGING THE COMMISSION OF WHITE COLLAR CRIME

White collar crime can be distinguished from street crime by some of the factors that facilitate its commission (Table 7-4). Recognition of these factors is not meant to excuse this behavior; instead, it may be used to help devise ways to control corporate crime. As an informed corporate manager, your knowledge of these factors may help you to avoid the temptation to engage in criminal activities and to discourage others from doing so.

Initially, we must recognize that many people in our society value material success above all else. When the focus of our energies is on material success, we are much more willing to engage in illegal means to achieve our goal than we would be if our focus were on, for instance, ethical conduct. With the stress on success, the line between illegality and a shrewd business deal becomes blurred.

The culture of some corporations creates an atmosphere in which corporate crime may thrive. For instance, if rewards such as salary and promotion are tied to meeting short-term goals, employees may use whatever means available to help them achieve those goals.

Once illegal behavior is initiated, it tends to become institutionalized because of a phenomenon referred to by social psychologist Irving Janis as *groupthink*.[7] In groupthink, there is an implicit agreement not to bring up upsetting facts. In the corporation, where junior managers' success depends to some degree on the approval of senior managers, a junior manager would be extremely reluctant to criticize a senior manager's actions. One dramatic instance of this dynamic is the E. F. Hutton case, in which the practice of writing illegal checks spread throughout the company. Nobody wanted to bring up the upsetting fact that perhaps the practice was illegal. Instead, managers just went along.[8]

Another factor making white collar crime easy to commit is the fact that decision making is often distributed among various individuals. Because responsibility is diffuse, individuals may feel only very limited personal responsibility for the results of their actions. This spreading of responsibility also results in an awareness that the likelihood of getting caught is small. Another factor related to the complex organizational structure of a corporation is that once a decision has been made, it is implemented by many. Thus, even if a manager has second thoughts about a decision, it is often too late to stop the process. Also, once a decision has been made, when it is implemented by others the decision maker feels limited responsibility.

The businesspersons who are unlucky enough to get caught do not automatically lose their status among their peers. Some, in fact, may be admired. Violations of the law are not necessarily violations of businesspersons' ethical codes. It is important to note that, unlike street criminals, who usually recognize that they are committing crimes, white collar criminals are frequently regarded by themselves and their peers as respectable, law-abiding citizens.

TABLE 7-4 *Factors Facilitating the Commission of White Collar Crime*

1. Societal stress on material success, without equal emphasis on means of achieving success.
2. Linkage of corporate rewards of salary and promotion to accomplishing short-term goals.
3. Groupthink.
4. Ease of rationalizing illegal behavior.
5. Dispersion of decision making.
6. Retention of status by persons convicted of white collar crime.
7. The lack of an adversarial relationship between the corporation and government regulators.

---

[7]D. Goleman, *Following the Leader*, Science '85, October 1985, at 18.
[8]*Id.*

In some instances, corporate crime is facilitated because the supposed adversarial relationship between the corporation and the government agency "watchdog" does not exist. Top corporate executives and high-level government officials may share similar values and lifestyles. Business managers often make career moves directly to a government agency regulating that business, and then back to business. These factors may make some government officials reluctant to crack down on businesspersons, and businesspersons' awareness of this reluctance contributes to an environment in which white collar crime can be tolerated.

Sentencing of White Collar Criminals

A public perception that judges were not giving long enough sentences to white collar criminals and were not imposing large enough fines led to the adoption of the 1991 Sentencing Guidelines for use by federal judges. These guidelines are said to provide "just punishment, adequate deterrence, and incentives for organizations to maintain internal mechanisms for preventing, detecting, and reporting criminal conduct in all aspects of their activity."[9]

Under these sentencing guidelines, a fine is a product of a "base fine" and a "culpability score." The base fine is the greatest of either the company's gain, the victim's loss, or a dollar amount corresponding to an offense level. The culpability score provides a multiplier that is applied to the base fine. The culpability score is determined by looking at a chart of potential mitigating and aggravating factors. An example of an aggravating factor might be that high levels of management were aware of the criminal activity but did nothing to stop it. Mitigating factors would be having a meaningful compliance program in effect at the time of the offense and upper management's taking steps to remedy the harm, discipline the offender, and prevent a recurrence. Because of the difference that these aggravating and mitigating factors can have on the amount of the fine—a crime with a base fine of $5 million, for example, could be as low as $2 million or as high as $20 million, depending on the culpability score—supporters hope that the guidelines will not only result in fairer penalties but will actually have a major impact on the way firms operate. Exhibit 7-2 provides an

---

EXHIBIT 7-2 *Components of an Effective Program under
the Uniform Sentencing Guidelines*

- Compliance programs that could reasonably be expected to reduce the prospect of criminal conduct have been established.
- Specific high-level individuals have been assigned responsibility to oversee compliance with the standards and procedures.
- The organization has taken reasonable steps to achieve compliance with its standards by installing monitoring and auditing systems designed to detect criminal conduct.
- Evidence confirms that substantial discretionary authority has not been delegated to individuals who the organization knows or should have known have a propensity to engage in illegal activities.
- Standards and procedures have been communicated to all employees and agents through training programs and printed materials.
- Standards are consistently reinforced through appropriate disciplinary mechanisms.
- Appropriate responses are made to reported offenses, with action taken to prevent recurrence.

Source: S. Albert, "Federal Sentencing Guidelines," *Internal Auditor*, October 1992, pp. 46, 47.

---

[9]C. C. Dow and R. J. Muehl, *Are Policies Keyed to New Sentencing Guidelines?* 36 Sec. Mgmt. 98 (November 1992).

154

Part One

*An Introduction to the Law
and the Legal Environment
of Business*

illustration of the characteristics of an effective antifraud program under the federal sentencing guidelines that would operate as a mitigating factor.

When the sentencing guidelines were established, there was a concern about the lack of prison time served by most white collar criminals and the general judicial leniency for white collar crimes. Consequently, some confinement was mandated for almost all white collar offenses. Sentences are determined similarly to the way fines are, with a base sentence and culpability factor. However, judges were given discretion, under extraordinary circumstances, to modify the sentence and depart from the guidelines and may impose alternative penalties as described later in this section. Some of the factors that allow departure include "substantial cooperation" of the defendant; extraordinary effects of a prison sentence on third parties, including the defendant's family; an overstatement of loss from the crime; and diminished capacity.

Some critics of the guidelines argue that although prison sentences are required for a broad range of white collar crimes, the sentences for these crimes are still much less than for street crimes. For example, the base sentence for an antitrust violation is as low as two to eight months.[10] During 1997, the average sentence in the 5,983 cases of fraud was 18.7 months.

As noted above, extraordinary circumstances do allow the judge to depart from the sentencing guidelines, and nothing prohibits the use of alternative sentencing. One alternative to prison judges favor for white collar offenders is community service. Offenders have been assigned to perform such services as giving speeches about their wrongful acts to business and civic groups and working among the poor in drug rehabilitation clinics. A corporate criminal who dumped industrial waste into San Diego's sewers, claiming it was domestic sewage, received a $250 fine and three years' probation, with an unusual twist: For violating waste disposal laws, he was required to complete a hazardous materials course, perform 120 hours of volunteer work for the Veterans of Foreign Wars, and spend 40 hours at the city's pump station where waste is discharged by trucks into the city's sewage treatment system. The man was also ordered to inform the waste haulers who came into the pump station that he had falsified a report describing the type of waste he was discharging.[11]

Another popular alternative to prison is occupational disqualification. The white collar criminal is prohibited for a specific period from engaging in an occupation in which she or he would be able to commit the same crime again. Policing such a prohibition is difficult, so if a corporation really wants the convicted employee's services, it can easily adjust the employee's job title to make it appear the job is one the employee can legally hold.

Finally an alternative touted as saving money for the taxpayers is house arrest or home confinement. The criminal is not allowed to leave home for the period of incarceration and is compelled to wear an unremovable sensor that allows government officials to detect his or her location at all times. Finally, the defendant may be able to serve his or her term on weekends.

COMMON WHITE COLLAR CRIMES

Thus far, we have focused on the white collar criminal, but any study of white collar crime must include consideration of who the victims are and what some of the precise crimes are. The victims of white collar crime are widespread, and they vary according to the precise crime committed. White collar crimes may be committed against the public in general, as when environmental regulations are violated; against consumers, as when they are forced to pay higher prices because of violations of the antitrust laws or when they die because the products they purchased were made without undergoing the tests required by the Pure Food, Drug, and Cosmetic Act; against the taxpayers, as when income taxes are not paid; and against the corporation itself, as when employees steal

---

[10]Gregory N. Racz, *Exploring Collateral Consequences: Koon v. United States, Third Party Departures from Federal Sentencing Guidelines,* 72 N.Y.U.L. Rev. 1462 (1997).
[11]Kathryn Balint, *Falsifier on Waste,* San Diego Union-Tribune, Aug. 21, 1993.

from their employer. When the victims are the corporation the criminal works for, we sometimes refer to the crime as an intrabusiness crime. Estimates of the annual costs of intrabusiness crime range from $4 billion to $44 billion. In this section, we examine some of the more common white collar crimes, noting their elements and their victims.

BRIBERY

Bribery is the offering, giving, soliciting, or receiving of money or any object of value for the purpose of influencing a person's action, especially a government official. The law against bribery is necessary to protect the integrity of the government and to ensure that the government functions fairly and efficiently. Bribery would include paying a judge to rule in favor of a party and giving a senator free use of your condominium if he or she votes for a particular piece of legislation. A recent example of bribery involved a Denver zone manager for American Honda Company. On July 1, 1994, he pleaded guilty to charges of taking bribes from an auto dealer in return for giving him larger car allocations. The bribes included cash, gifts, and hidden ownership in a New Jersey car dealership, all worth a total of about $100,000.

Some states broaden their definition of bribery to include certain payoffs in a commercial context. It is often considered bribery to offer to confer a benefit upon an employee or agent of another in an attempt to influence that agent's behavior on behalf of his employer or principle without that employer or principle's knowledge. Thus, Sam's offer to pay a contracting officer $5,000 in exchange for that officer's promise to purchase all the widgets his employer needs the next year would be considered a bribe in many states.

VIOLATIONS OF FEDERAL REGULATIONS

During the past few decades, regulatory agencies have been created and federal regulations enacted to control business. Analogous state regulations have also been enacted. Some are primarily regulations of economic matters; others are designed to protect the health, safety, and welfare of employees, consumers, and the public in general. You will study many of the regulations in the public law part of this book, chapters 16 through 23.

Violation of any of these regulations constitutes a white collar crime. The victims of these crimes vary according to the regulation that has been violated. For example, Occupational Safety and Health Act standards are established to protect the health and safety of workers. When these standards are violated, the violation is a criminal act that victimizes the employee, who is working under less-safe or less-healthful conditions than those required by law. When examining these different regulations in later chapters of this book, the reader should consider who would be victimized by violations of each of the regulations. The reader who has a clear understanding of who might be hurt by such violations may be careful not to violate those regulations when he or she is a manager.

Violations of these regulations are often not perceived as criminal because they are frequently remedied outside the traditional courtroom setting. These regulations are often enforced by the appropriate regulatory agency through the issuance of a warning, a recall of defective products, or a *consent agreement* (a contract in which the violator agrees to cease engaging in the illegal activity). A *cease-and-desist order* may also be issued, ordering the corporation to cease violating the law and imposing a fine on the corporation for each day it violates the order. *Warning letters* are often the first approach of the regulatory agency, and the prudent businessperson should heed them. In cases of substantial violations, regulatory agencies may, of course, seek to impose fines on the corporation or manager responsible for the violation or may ask the court to impose a prison sentence on an offender.

The maximum monetary penalty that can be issued for violating federal regulations enacted to control business varies according to the regulation in question. For example, the maximum corporate penalty for violating the antitrust law is $1 million, a rarely awarded sum, which is not very large compared with the billions of dollars of assets and sales of some violators. For other acts, maximums are much lower. For example, $1,000 is the maximum for a first offense under the Pure Food, Drug, and Cosmetics Act, and $10,000 is the maximum for Occupational Health and Safety Act violations.

The maximum fines for individuals vary; $10,000 under acts such as the Pure Food, Drug, and Cosmetics Act and the Securities Exchange Act are typical. Maximum prison sentences usually range from six months to one year, with a few acts allowing up to five-year sentences. The imposition of maximum sentences is rare.

CRIMINAL FRAUD

criminal fraud Intentional use of some sort of misrepresentation to gain an advantage over another party.

Criminal fraud is a generic term that embraces a wide variety of means by which an individual intentionally uses some sort of misrepresentation to gain an advantage over another person. State fraud statutes vary, but most require proof of three elements: (1) an intent to defraud, (2) the commission of a fraudulent act, and (3) the accomplished fraud. It is very difficult to prove fraud, especially the first element: the intent to defraud. Some common fraudulent acts that occur in the corporate setting are:

1. *Defalcation*, the misappropriation of trust funds or money held in a fiduciary capacity.
2. *False entries*, the making of an entry into the books of a bank or corporation that is designed to represent the existence of funds that do not exist.
3. *False token*, a false document or sign of existence used to perpetrate a fraud, such as making counterfeit money.
4. *False pretenses*, a designed misrepresentation of existing facts or conditions by which a person obtains another's money or goods, such as the writing of a worthless check.
5. *Forgery*, the material altering of anything in writing that, if genuine, might be the foundation of a legal liability.
6. *Fraudulent concealment*, the suppression of a material fact that the person is legally bound to disclose.

This list is by no means all-inclusive, but it demonstrates the broad variety of actions captured by the term *fraud*.

A person or corporation that uses the mail to execute a scheme or artifice to defraud the public out of money or property may be prosecuted under the federal law that prohibits mail fraud. Likewise, a person or corporation that uses the telephone, telegraph, television, radio, or other device to transmit a fraudulent message may be prosecuted for the federal crime of wire fraud. Mail fraud claims can be brought in a wide range of situations. As the following case indicates, the mailings do not even have to be a central element to the fraud as long as they are related to a central element.

SCHMUCK V. UNITED STATES
UNITED STATES SUPREME COURT 109 S. CT. 1443 (1989)

Defendant-petitioner Schmuck was a used car dealer who had purchased cars, rolled back their odometers, and then resold them to Wisconsin retail dealers for prices artificially inflated because of the incorrect mileage readings. The final step in the resale was that the dealer who purchased the car would mail a title application form to the Wisconsin Department of Transportation on behalf of the customer. The jury found Schmuck guilty of 12 counts of mail fraud, with the mailing of the title being the requisite

use of the mail. The court of appeals affirmed the conviction. Schmuck appealed to the U.S. Supreme Court.

JUSTICE BLACKMUN

The federal mail fraud statute does not purport to reach all frauds, but only those limited instances in which the use of the mails is a part of the execution of the fraud, leaving all other cases to be dealt with by appropriate state law. To be part of the execution of the fraud, however, the use of the mails need not be an essential element of the scheme. It is sufficient for the mailing to be "incident to an essential part of the scheme," or "a step in [the] plot."

Schmuck, relying principally on this Court's decisions in *Kann*, argues that mail fraud can be predicated only on a mailing that affirmatively assists the perpetrator in carrying out his fraudulent scheme. The mailing element of the offense, he contends, cannot be satisfied by a mailing, such as those at issue here, that is routine and innocent in and of itself, and that, far from furthering the execution of the fraud, occurs after the fraud has come to fruition, is merely tangentially related to the fraud, and is counterproductive in that it creates a "paper trail" from which the fraud may be discovered. We disagree both with this characterization of the mailing in the present case and with this description of the applicable law.

We begin by considering the scope of Schmuck's fraudulent scheme. Schmuck was charged with devising and executing a scheme to defraud Wisconsin retail automobile customers who based their decisions to purchase certain automobiles at least in part on the low-mileage readings provided by the tampered odometers. This was a fairly large-scale operation. Thus, Schmuck's was not a "one-shot" operation in which he sold a single car to an isolated dealer. His was an ongoing fraudulent venture. A rational jury could have concluded that the success of Schmuck's venture depended upon his continued harmonious relations with, and good reputation among, retail dealers, which in turn required the smooth flow of cars from the dealers to their Wisconsin customers.

Under these circumstances, we believe that a rational jury could have found that the title-registration mailings were part of the execution of the fraudulent scheme, a scheme which did not reach fruition until the retail dealers resold the cars and effected transfers of title. Schmuck's scheme would have come to an abrupt halt if the dealers either had lost faith in Schmuck or had not been able to resell the cars obtained from him. These resales and Schmuck's relationships with the retail dealers naturally depended on the successful passage of title among the various parties. Thus, although the registration-form mailings may not have contributed directly to the duping of either the retail dealers or the customers, they were necessary to the passage of title, which in turn was essential to the perpetuation of Schmuck's scheme. As noted earlier, a mailing that is "incident to an essential part of the scheme," satisfies the mailing element of the mail fraud offense. The mailings here fit this description.

Here a jury rationally could have found that Schmuck by no means was indifferent to the fact of who bore the loss. The mailing of the title-registration forms was an essential step in the successful passage of title to the retail purchasers. Moreover, a failure of this passage of title would have jeopardized Schmuck's relationship of trust and goodwill with the retail dealers upon whose unwitting cooperation his scheme depended. Schmuck's reliance on our prior cases limiting the reach of the mail fraud statute is simply misplaced.

Affirmed in favor of the Prosecution.

Fraud can range from a single act that victimizes one individual to a long-term scheme that victimizes thousands. In the corporate setting, fraud is sometimes committed by managers to make themselves look better so that they can secure promotions at the expense of others who perhaps deserve the promotions. Fraudulent entries in corporate records may result in artificially inflating the purchase price of stock at the expense of its purchasers. Fraud may also be committed against the corporation, and thus against the shareholders, as when an employee on a bonus system fraudulently reports sales before they have been completed to collect an early bonus or "pads" his or her expense account. The more autonomy employees have, and the fewer people overseeing their actions, the greater the likelihood of their committing fraud.

Consumers may also be victims of corporate fraud, as when businesspersons make false representations in advertising and labeling. Consumers may also be victimized by the fraudulent substitution of inferior goods for higher-quality ones.

LARCENY

Another frequently occurring type of white collar crime is larceny. **Larceny** is a matter of state criminal law, so the definition may vary slightly by state, but it can generally be defined as the secretive and wrongful taking and carrying away of the personal property of another with the intent to permanently deprive the rightful owner of its use or possession. The means of carrying out this crime is *stealth*: Larceny is not carried out by means of fear or force, which is the means of committing a robbery, and it is not carried out by means of false representa-

larceny The secretive and wrongful taking and carrying away of the personal property of another with the intent to permanently deprive the rightful owner of its use or possession.

tion, which is one means of committing fraud. Larceny is commonly called *theft* by persons without legal training.

Most states distinguish petty larceny from grand larceny, with the distinction based on the value of the item. *Grand larceny* involves items of higher value than those involved in *petty larceny*. It is usually considered a felony and thus is punishable by either a more severe fine or a longer term of imprisonment, or both.

In the corporate context, larceny generally involves employees' taking the employer's property. Common instances of larceny include employee's taking home stationery or supplies from the office.

EMBEZZLEMENT

embezzlement The wrongful conversion of the property of another by one who is lawfully in possession of that property.

Another white collar offense is **embezzlement**. This crime is commonly defined as the wrongful conversion of the property of another by one who is lawfully in possession of that property. In some states, by statute, the crime may be committed only by certain classes of people, such as fiduciaries, attorneys, and public officials. As the reader might guess, larceny and embezzlement sometimes overlap.

Like larceny, embezzlement is usually divided into degrees based on the value of the property embezzled. Some states also treat different kinds of embezzlers differently; that is, those embezzling from different types of institutions or those holding different types of positions may be distinguished.

COMPUTER CRIMES

As technology evolves, so do ways of committing corporate crime. With the arrival of the computer and the increasing automation of many facets of business, an area of crime has developed that society has not yet found an effective means of handling. No one knows the exact cost of computer crime each year, but estimates range from $300 million to $40 billion.

For the most part, computer crime, rather than being a new type of crime, is a means of making traditional crimes easier to commit. See Exhibit 7-3 for examples of some typical computer crime techniques. Think about how many employees have access to a computer at work. When the number of individuals with home computers is added, there are myriad opportunities available for computer crime. Computer systems must now be protected from management, lower-level employees, and outsiders, sometimes known as *hackers*. With all these individuals having access to computers, a continuing increase in the amount of computer crime seems highly likely. Not only do computers make

---

EXHIBIT 7-3 *Common Computer Crime Techniques*

PIGGYBACKING–A nonauthorized person gains access to a terminal when an authorized person failed to sign off or an unauthorized person discovers an authorized user's password and signs on using that password.

IMPOSTER TERMINAL–Using a home computer with a telephone modem to gain access to a mainframe computer by cracking the password code and then using the computer free of charge.

TROJAN HORSE–Covertly placing instructions in a computer program that will generate unauthorized functions.

SALAMI SLICING–Stealing tiny amounts of money off large numbers of inputs (such as taking a penny off each entry) and transferring them into one's personal account.

crime easier, but it appears that computers also make crime more profitable. According to federal officials, the average loss in a bank robbery is $3,200 and the average loss in a nonelectronic embezzlement is $23,500. But in a computer fraud, the average loss is $500,000.

Computer crimes are also not frequently prosecuted; some analysts estimate that fewer than 1 percent of those who engage in computer fraud are actually prosecuted. One reason these criminals are so successful is that many computer crimes are extremely difficult to detect. Even if the crime is detected, if the victim is a business, they will often not prosecute because they do not want their competitors to know that their system was vulnerable. A final problem with convicting people of computer crimes is that the crimes sometimes do not fit precisely with the statutory definition of traditional crimes.

Partially in response to this lack of adequate statutes under which to prosecute computer crime, Congress passed the Counterfeit Access Device and Computer Fraud and Abuse Act of 1984. This act prohibits the unauthorized, knowing use of or access to computers in six broad categories. Crimes falling within the first category listed below are felonies; the remainder are misdemeanors.

1. The unauthorized use of or access to a computer to obtain classified military or foreign policy information with the intent to harm the United States or to benefit a foreign country.

2. The unauthorized use of a computer to collect financial or credit information protected under federal privacy law.

3. The unauthorized access to a federal computer and the use, modification, destruction, or disclosure of data it contains or the prevention of authorized persons' use of such data.

4. The alteration or modification of data in financial computers causing a loss of $1,000 or more.

5. The modification of data that impedes medical treatment to individuals.

6. The fraudulent transfer of computer passwords or other similar data that could aid unauthorized access that either (a) affects interstate commerce or (b) permits access to a government computer.

Even though these categories of wrongful acts may seem fairly comprehensive, there are still a number of computer crimes that do not fall into any of them. Those crimes must be prosecuted, if at all, under one of the state computer crime statutes or under one of the traditional crime statutes.

As society attempts to find ways to respond to computer crimes, we have initially attempted to categorize the crimes. Following is just one way to categorize and think about these crimes.

DESTRUCTION OF DATA   Destruction of data is one of the biggest problems facing business today. A person with expertise in programming can create what is commonly referred to as a **virus**, a program designed to rearrange, replace, or destroy data. Once a virus is planted in a computer's instructions, it can spread to other systems or programs by rapidly copying itself. Hence, if a computer virus is not caught early, it can be extremely destructive.

A number of software programs have been developed to detect and destroy viruses. These programs however, are reactive, not proactive. Every time a new type of virus is discovered, a new antiviral program must be developed.

Destruction of data may also be more limited. For example, a disgruntled employee who is fired might program his computer to destroy a section of data every time a file is saved. Before anyone realizes what has occurred, valuable data may be lost.

UNLAWFUL APPROPRIATION OF DATA OR SERVICES   Employees at work are often provided expensive computer systems and software. They have access to vast amounts of data. When employees use their work computers or

virus A computer program that destroys, damages, rearranges, or replaces computer data.

160

Part One

*An Introduction to the Law
and the Legal Environment
of Business*

data accessed through these computers in a manner not authorized by their employer, they have engaged in theft of computer services or data.

An early question was whether a theft could arise when there was no physical carrying away of the misappropriated matter. Remember, the traditional definition of larceny requires a physical removal of the property from the possession of its lawful owner. The following case demonstrates how many states today are getting around this problem.

STATE V. MCGRAW
COURT OF APPEALS OF INDIANA 459 N.E.2D 61 (1984)

Defendant McGraw was charged and convicted by a jury of two counts of theft of computer services for using his employer's computer in his personal business. He had used the computer to keep customer lists and inventory control, among other uses, despite having no authority to use the computer for personal matters. Defendant filed a motion to dismiss on the grounds that the indictment failed to state an offense. The trial court granted the defendant's motion, and the state appealed.

JUDGE NEAL

We deem that the sole issue under the motion to dismiss and the court's ruling thereon is whether the unauthorized use of another person's computer for private business is theft under the statute as a matter of law.

Theft is defined as follows: "A person who knowingly and intentionally exerts unauthorized control over property of another person with intent to deprive the other person of any part of its value or use, commits theft."

" 'Property' means anything of value and includes a gain or advantage or anything that might reasonably be regarded as such by the beneficiary: real property, personal property, money, labor, and services; intangibles; commercial instruments; written instruments concerning labor, services, or property; written instruments otherwise of value to the owner, such as a public record, deed, will, credit card, or letter of credit; a signature to a written instrument; extension of credit; trade secrets; contract rights, choices-in-action, and other interests in or claims to wealth; electricity, gas, oil, and water; captured or domestic animals, birds, and fish; food and drug; and human remains."

McGraw asserts that to be guilty of the offense, a specific prohibition of his conduct must exist. He contends that he could not deprive the city of the "use" of the computer unless his data caused an overload on the computer memory banks, or that he used the computer for his private business at a time which interfered with city use. He argues that the value of the services was de minimus. He finally claims that his activities were no more than

personal use of an office phone, calculator, or copy machine.

Inasmuch as the evidence clearly supports the fact that McGraw knowingly and intentionally used the city leased computer for his own monetary benefit, the only real question is whether "use" of a computer is a property subject to theft.

We deem McGraw's interpretation of the statutes overly restrictive. In short, he is arguing old common law precepts pertaining to larceny. In our view his contentions are inapposite to the plain meaning of the statutory sections involved herein.

Computer services, leased or owned, are a part of our market economy in huge dollar amounts. Like cable television, computer services are ". . . anything of value." Computer time is "services" for which money is paid. Such services may reasonably be regarded as valuable assets to the beneficiary. Thus, computer services are property within the meaning of the definition of property subject to theft. When a person "obtains" or "takes" those services, he has exerted control under the Code. Taking without the other person's consent is unauthorized taking. Depriving the other person of any part of the services' use completes the offense.

Property must be shown to have a value, however slight, but the monetary value of property is of no concern, and the jury may under proper instructions infer some value. The theft statue comprehends a broad field of conduct, and does not limit the means or methods by which unauthorized control of property may be obtained. We disagree that specific prohibition to exerting control is necessary to support the conviction theft. Further, we disagree that it is a defense to exerting unauthorized control that the owner was not using the property at the time.

We are of the opinion that Counts VIII and IX of the information state an offense.

Reversed, and the conviction reinstated.

Critical Thinking about the Law

AT ISSUE IN THIS CASE WAS whether a theft can occur without the removal of the misappropriated matter. The court responded to this issue affirmatively. Important to the court's response was a key fact in the case.

Consequently, the questions that follow will focus on that key fact's role in the court's decision. You will recall that a given fact is "key" to the extent that its presence is crucial in determining the outcome of the case and if its absence potentially could cause an alternative outcome.

1. What is the key fact in this case?

   CLUE Reread the discussion of the defense's arguments. An analogy offered by the defense suggests the implication of this key fact's alteration.

2. The court suggests that computers and cable television bear a substantial likeness for the sake of this case's decision. Evaluate this analogy.

   CLUE Important to any evaluation of an analogy is identifying similarities and differences between the two entities being compared.

ENTERING OF FRAUDULENT RECORDS OR DATA INTO A COMPUTER SYSTEM Entering fraudulent records includes altering a person's credit rating electronically and breaking into a university's computer system and changing someone's course grades.

FINANCIAL CRIMES Fraud, embezzlement, and larceny are now easier to accomplish by computer. An employee could electronically transfer ownership of funds from a corporate account to a personal account. Any object subject to lawful transfer electronically can also be stolen electronically.

PREVENTION OF WHITE COLLAR CRIME

We should all be interested in the prevention of white collar crime because we are all its victims in more than one aspect of our lives. We are victims as consumers, shareholders, responsible employees, taxpayers, and citizens in general. The suggested ways for reducing white collar crime are numerous and varied. Some ideas are utopian, but others can be put into practice immediately.

First, we will examine some of the ways in which corporate crime committed on behalf of the corporation may be prevented. One suggestion is to replace state chartering of corporations with federal chartering. Proponents argue that such chartering would prevent competition among states, which may lead to bribery and state officials' routinely overlooking corporate violations of the laws. As a part of federal chartering (or until then, by state law), corporations could be required to have outside directors (directors who are not also officers or managers). A counterargument to that suggestion is that outside directors do not have a significant impact on the behavior of management. They have neither the knowledge nor the interest to provide effective supervision.

An even more innovative suggestion, put forward by Christopher Stone,[12] is that each corporation doing over a certain amount of business be required to have a general public director (GPD). The GPD would have an office at the corporation with a small staff, would be given access to corporate books and records, and would represent the public interest in the ongoing functions of the

---

[12]C. Stone, *Where Law Ends: The Social Control of Corporations* (New York: Harper & Row, 1976), pp. 122–183.

162

Part One

*An Introduction to the Law
and the Legal Environment
of Business*

corporation. General public directors would sit on corporate committees and advise corporate officials about the legality of their activities. These public-interest watchdogs would be full-time workers paid from tax money. Stone further suggested that special public directors (SPDs), who would function like GPDs except that they would work in a special area such as workplace safety or antitrust, be assigned to corporations that have committed a series of violations in any specific area. Special public directors would attempt to prevent further violations of a similar nature.

Two other proposals are to link the amounts of fines to the benefits obtained by the violations or to increase the amount of both corporate and individual fines. Over 90 percent of the fines paid by corporations between 1975 and 1976 were less than $5,000. When imposed on a relatively small corporation, one with annual sales of $300 million, such fines are analogous to giving a person who earns $15,000 a year a two-and-a-half cent fine.[13] Hence, fines as they currently exist do not really serve any deterrent function. Likewise, requiring greater and mandatory prison sentences for corporate executives found to have violated federal and state regulations might cause them to take these laws more seriously. Some also suggest elimination of the nolo contendere plea.

Because it is believed that the courts are unlikely to impose stiff fines on either corporations or convicted executives, the imposition of *equity fines* has been proposed. If a company is convicted of a white collar crime, it would be forced to turn over a substantial block of its stock to a victims' compensation fund. This relinquishing of the company's stock would make its executives' holdings worth less. It would also provoke the ire of shareholders, whose holdings would be diluted, and might prompt them to call for the ouster of the responsible executives. Finally, it might put pressure on managers, who realize that the existence of a block of stock in one place would make a takeover attempt easier.

It is also believed that regulations are often broken because of ineffective monitoring by agencies. One remedy, it is argued, would be to increase the operating budgets of the regulatory agencies to allow them to hire more people to monitor corporations and to improve the training of regulatory agency employees. A related argument is that the regulations themselves are often vague and complex. Simplification of these laws would make them more understandable and easier to follow. It would also make violations of these laws easier to recognize and prosecute.

FEDERAL LAWS USED IN THE FIGHT AGAINST WHITE COLLAR CRIME

THE RACKETEER INFLUENCED CORRUPT ORGANIZATIONS ACT (RICO)

Racketeer Influenced Corrupt Organizations Act (RICO) Prohibits persons employed by or associated with an enterprise from engaging in a pattern of racketeering activity, which is broadly defined to include almost all white collar crimes as well as acts of violence.

In the eyes of many plaintiffs' attorneys and prosecutors, a major weapon in the fight against white collar crime can be found in Title IX of the Organized Crime Control Act of 1970,[14] the **Racketeer Influenced Corrupt Organizations Act**, or **RICO**, as it is commonly called. This statute was originally enacted to help fight organized crime, but its application in the commercial context soon became apparent. In fact, a study by the Task Force on Civil RICO of the American Bar Association revealed that only about 9 percent of the RICO cases involved what is commonly considered organized crime; 37 percent were cases involving common law fraud in a commercial setting, and 40 percent involved securities fraud allegations.[15]

---

[13]G. Stricharchuk and A. Pasztor, *New Muscle in False Claims Act May Help in Combating Fraud against the Government*, Wall St. J., December 19, 1986, at 19, col. 4.

[14]18 U.S.C.A. §§ 1961 et. seq. (West Pub. Co. 1998).

[15]Stricharchuk and Pasztor, *supra* note 13.

RICO is such a powerful statute because it allows any person whose business or property is injured by a violation of the statute to recover treble damages plus attorney's fees in a civil action. So this is a case in which a civil lawsuit may help prevent criminal action.

How does one violate RICO? RICO prohibits persons employed by or associated with an enterprise from engaging in a pattern of racketeering activity. Judicial interpretations have interpreted *pattern* to mean more than one act. Thus, RICO cannot be used against the one-time violator. What constitutes racketeering activity, however, has been very broadly defined to include almost all criminal actions, including acts of violence, the provision of illegal goods and services, bribery, antitrust violations, securities violations, and fraud.

RICO has been used so successfully in many of these areas that many corporate and brokerage firm attorneys are making appeals to the legislature through the press to limit the application of RICO. They argue that the statute is unfair because it does not require that a defendant be convicted of the alleged criminal activity before a civil RICO suit can be brought. They argue that this lack of a requirement of a prior conviction leads to spurious lawsuits and encourages out-of-court settlements by intimidated legitimate businesspersons. Opponents also argue that the courts are or will be "flooded" with such lawsuits and thus valuable resources will be wasted. They also argue that the law was designed to attack "organized crime" not employees of "legitimate businesses," against whom it is now being successfully used.

Proponents of RICO argue that the law should continue in force as it is. They point out that fraud is a national problem, costing the nation more than $200 billion each year.[16] Proponents further believe that given our lack of success in prosecuting criminal fraud cases in the past, we should retain this tool, which may allow us to punish persons who have been able to escape criminal prosecution. Criminal activity in "legitimate" businesses is a major problem facing the country today, and curing it can only enhance the reputations of those in the business world. If a corporation and its officers are not engaging in illegal or quasi-legal activities, they have nothing to fear from RICO.

FALSE CLAIMS ACT

A largely ignored 123-year-old federal law has come back to life since 1986, and is now being used vigorously in the fight against white collar crime. Under the False Claims Act, private citizens may sue employers on behalf of the government for fraud against the government. A successful party may receive 25 percent of the amount recovered if the government chooses to intervene in the action or 30 percent if the government does not participate in the suit.

The act also offers protection to persons using the law to sue their employer. An employer may be held liable to the employee for twice the amount of back pay plus special damages if found guilty of retaliation. During 1997, the Justice Department recovered $625 million dollars from 530 suits filed under this act. The record verdict in a single case was the 1998 verdict under which FMC corporation was ordered to pay $300 million when the plaintiff, an FMC engineer, convinced a jury that FMC lied about safety flaws in its armored infantry vehicle. Seventy percent of that judgment goes to the government.[17]

The False Claims Act has been used in a wide variety of circumstances. It has been used by an employee claiming that his employer, a school, helped its students fraudulently obtain millions of dollars in federal financial aid; by an employee who claimed that his employer, a defense contractor, knowingly manufactured defective parts for use in a guided missile system; and more recently by employees of hospitals, doctors and nursing homes that are over-

---

[16]Mann, *supra* note 6, at 86.
[17]Laurel Campbell, Health Care-Whistleblower 'Valuable Tool' Officials Use to Uncover Fraud, The Commercial Appeal, Memphis, Tennessee, 1998 WL 3667967.

164

Part One

*An Introduction to the Law
and the Legal Environment
of Business*

billing Medicare claims. Overcharging the government is another claim providing the basis for an action under this act.

Because of Justice Department estimates that fraud costs the taxpayers as much as $100 billion a year,[18] there are many propenents of the use of this act. Its use is encouraged because it motivates persons in the best position to be aware of fraud to report the occurrence thereof. Employers who know that their employees may bring an action if asked to engage in fraud may be deterred from engaging in such acts.

Opponents of the use of the False Claims Act cite a variety of reasons. Some fear that frivolous or politically motivated lawsuits may be brought. Others say that the 60-day time period during which the Justice Department has to decide whether to join in the action is too brief and places an undue burden on the Department. During that limited time period they must decide whether to join in a complex suit that may take years to resolve.

For now, at least, use of the False Claims Act is increasing, but the continuing viability of this act was called into question in October 1997. A federal district court struck down a case filed under this law, ruling that the federal law was unconstitutional because it did not present a "case or controversy" as required by Article III of the Constitution. The court said that because the plaintiff employee had not suffered any injury, he had no case. Four other district courts had previously ruled that the law did not violate the Constitution, so until the U.S. Supreme Court rules on the issue, there will be uncertainty about the use of this law by whistleblowers. The controversial district court decision has been appealed, but the circuit court has not yet ruled on the case.

STATE LAWS USED IN THE FIGHT AGAINST WHITE COLLAR CRIME

Some states have whistleblower statutes that protect employees who testify against their employers. Some state acts also allow government whistleblowers to bring actions against the state government, and a few—namely Texas, California, and Alaska—even allow government-employee whistleblowers to seek punitive damages.

Although a whistleblower statute with unlimited potential for recovery may sound like a good idea, not everyone supports such laws. Sometimes cases under these statutes have surprising outcomes. The following case demonstrates the application of Texas's Whistleblower Act.

TEXAS DEPARTMENT OF HUMAN SERVICES V. GEORGE GREEN
COURT OF APPEALS OF TEXAS 855 S.W. 2D 136 (1993)

Plaintiff-appellant George Green brought an action for retaliatory discharge against his former employer, the Texas Department of Human Services (DHS), alleging that he had been fired because he kept informing his supervisors of what he believed was a pattern of fraud and corruption among DHS procurement officers. He had reported a series of corrupt activities to his superiors, and, when they failed to take corrective actions, he had threatened to go outside the agency. He was then thoroughly investigated and ultimately terminated for a 13 cent unauthorized phone call and a missed physical therapy session while on sick leave. The trial court, in a jury trial, awarded him $3,459,831.87 in compensatory damages, $10 million in punitive damages, and $160,000 in attorney fees, plus interest. DHS appealed, and the court of appeals affirmed. DHS then filed a motion for rehearing with the court of appeals.

---

[18]Harvey Berleman, *A Few Big Penalties Make for a Record Year,* Nat'l. L.J., Oct. 24, 1994.

JUSTICE SMITH

In its first point of error, DHS argues that the trial court erred in rendering judgment on the verdict because governmental immunity bars both the suit and the liability for an award of damages against DHS, a state agency.

DHS argues that the legislature must not have intended to waive governmental immunity because the Whistleblower Act permits a public employee to recover actual and unlimited exemplary damages, "as the surreal verdict in this suit demonstrates." DHS maintains that the Act only creates a cause of action against individual state or local officials and not against the governmental entity itself as employer.

The relevant portions of the Act prohibiting retaliation and creating certain remedies for public employees state:

> *Sec. 2. A state or local governmental body may not suspend or terminate the employment of, or otherwise discriminate against, a public employee who reports a violation of law to an appropriate law enforcement authority if the employee report is made in good faith.*
>
> *Sec. 3. (a) A public employee whose employment is suspended or terminated in violation of this Act is entitled to:*
>
> *(1) reinstatement in his former position; (2) compensation for wages lost during the period of suspension or termination; and (3) reinstatement of any fringe benefits or seniority rights lost because of the suspension or termination.*

In determining whether the legislature unambiguously waived the State's governmental immunity with these words, we are guided by this Court's previous examination of the Act's text.... [W]e determined that the statute as a whole evidences two legislative purposes: (1) to protect public employees from retaliation by their employer when, in good faith, employees report a violation of law, and (2) in consequence, to secure lawful conduct on the part of those who direct and conduct the affairs of public bodies.

In effecting the first goal, the legislature directed its proscription of retaliatory firing against a "state or local governmental body," and not against the individual supervisors through whom that body might act. From the legislature's focus on the governmental body as the fountainhead of the prohibited conduct, we perceive an unambiguous intent to direct the Act's penalties at the same entity. This understanding is wholly consistent with the Act's second goal, securing lawful conduct from those who manage the affairs of the governmental body. In its wisdom, the legislature obviously determined that subjecting the governmental body, and not the individual agent, to the Act's highest penalties would enhance the Act's deterrent effect. Because it thus bears the primary risk for violations of the Act, the governmental body has the principal incentive to oversee the conduct of its agents to the greater protection of public employees.

In light of the legislature's purposes, we decline to read the Act as limiting a public employee's cause of action for retaliation to a suit against an individual supervisor. Indeed, such an interpretation cannot be reconciled with section 5(a) of the Act, which provides for a civil penalty not to exceed $1,000 to be imposed against individual supervisors for violations of the Act. The attorney general or appropriate prosecuting attorney sues to collect this penalty, and because any funds collected must be deposited in the state treasury's general revenue fund, an injured public employee derives no benefit from a penalty levied under section 5.

Nowhere else does the Act expressly refer to individual supervisors, much less target them for liability. Thus, the express mention of individual supervisors in section 5(a) and nowhere else constrains us to interpret the Act's other sections as excluding additional liability of individual supervisors. Because governmental bodies (including state agencies) are, therefore, the manifest object of the Act's other liability provisions, we must decline DHS's invitation to extend the liability of individual supervisors when the legislature itself has not done so.

Suit against a governmental body that retaliates for whistleblowing activities plainly falls within the terms, as well as the spirit and purpose, of the Whistleblower Act.

The Texas Supreme Court has noted the importance of the legislative safeguards afforded by a whistleblower cause of action:

> *In a democratic, free enterprise system, a commitment to whistleblowing represents a fundamental confidence in the ability of individuals to make a difference. Society can never eradicate wrongdoing, but it can shield from retaliation those citizens who, urged on by their integrity and social responsibility, speak out to protect its well-being.*

We conclude that the Act unambiguously waives the governmental immunity from suit. Complaints about "surreal verdicts" resulting from the Act's failure to limit liability for actual or exemplary damages should be addressed to the legislature, not the judiciary.

The jury's finding must be upheld unless it is so against the great weight and preponderance of the evidence as to be manifestly unjust or erroneous. We are not free to substitute our judgment for the jury's simply because we may disagree with the verdict.

We conclude that this is more than the scintilla of evidence required to defeat the no-evidence challenge to the jury's finding that Green's whistleblowing activities resulted in DHS's retaliatory firing; we also hold that the finding is factually sufficient.

Affirmed in favor of Plaintiff, Green.

Critical Thinking about the Law

THE PRIMARY OBJECTIVE OF THE COURT in this case was to examine whether a governmental body is subject to suit and liability for damages under the Whistleblower Act. In determining that governmental bodies indeed are subject to such legal remedies, the court offered rather elaborate reasoning, some of it based on precedent.

The purpose of these critical questions is to improve your skills in identifying a court's reasoning, for only after that has been done can you begin to evaluate.

1. One type of justification for its decision is the court's explanation of why a governmental body may be subject to suit and liability under the Whistleblower Act. Reproduce the court's support for this justification.

   CLUE The bulk of the support can be found within the court's discussion of the act's first goal.

2. Implicit beliefs (assumptions) often slip into legal reasoning. Their presence is normal and necessary. However, the accuracy of these beliefs needs to be questioned when they are both debatable and extremely important for the court's reasoning. Otherwise, unquestioned assumptions end up moving us toward a conclusion that a critical thinker might reject.

   For example, in this case the court claims that placing maximum penalties on the governmental body itself results in maximizing the deterrent effect intended by the act. Can you think of any reason why the result of this logic might *not* create the heightened supervision assumed by the court?

   CLUE Would you be more attentive to your behavior if a penalty could fall on you directly or if the penalty could fall only on the organization to which you belong?

INTERNATIONAL DIMENSIONS OF WHITE COLLAR CRIME

White collar crime is not a problem just in the United States. It is a worldwide problem. Ironically, improvements in technology have increased the amount of white collar crime on a worldwide scale by creating more opportunities for skilled employees to commit such crimes. For example, the availability of credit cards that can be used worldwide has increased the opportunities for credit card fraud.

When companies operate multinationally, they may be able to avoid regulation and escape the jurisdiction of any nation by not really basing their operations in any country. One example of a company that was able to successfully engage in criminal behavior for years without detection was Investor's Overseas Services (IOS). This company was much admired until its collapse in 1970. Using sales representatives recruited worldwide, IOS was able to get investors to invest $2.5 billion in a variety of mutual fund companies. Sales kept growing until the company finally went broke and the investors lost their money.

To some extent, IOS had been able to operate in a fraudulent manner because the company was not domiciled in any country or group of countries, and, thus, it was subject to no particular country's regulation. Managers registered and domiciled their funds wherever they could in order to avoid taxation and regulation. Consequently, they were able to do things that no company domiciled in one country could do. The prudent manager should make sure that any multinational firm with which he or she does business is domiciled in some country.

Another factor leading to the commission of white collar crime on an international scale is the unfortunate lack of cooperation among the police of different countries. Countries simply do not have the resources available to coordinate strong international links to try to apprehend white collar criminals.

SUMMARY

Criminal law is that body of laws designed to punish persons who engage in activities that are harmful to the public health, safety, or welfare. A crime generally requires a wrongful act and a criminal intent.

Criminal procedure is similar to civil procedure, but there are some significant differences. A criminal prosecution begins with the issuance of an information by a magistrate or an indictment by a grand jury. The next step is the arraignment, which is followed by the trial, and then, in some cases, an appeal.

White collar crime, crimes committed in a commercial context, may be as costly to society as street crime, but they are more difficult to prosecute and often carry relatively light sentences.

Some of the more common white collar crimes are larceny, the secretive and wrongful taking of another's property; embezzlement, the wrongful conversion of property that one has lawful possession of; and violations of federal regulations. Increasingly, computers are being used to commit white collar crime, making the detection of these crimes even more difficult.

Attempts are being made to fight white collar crime on the federal level through such statutes as RICO and the False Claims Act. Some states have now passed whistleblower statutes to help fight against white collar crime.

When thinking about white collar crime, it is important to remember that one of the drawbacks increasing globalization is that it has led to increasing amounts of white collar crime carried out across borders. Criminals have taken advantage of the lack of international cooperation among law enforcement officials.

REVIEW QUESTIONS

7-1. What is the purpose of criminal law?

7-2. Explain how crimes are classified.

7-3. Explain the basic procedural stages in a criminal prosecution.

7-4. State two alternative definitions of *white collar crime* and give an example of one crime that fits under both definitions and another crime that would fit only one of the definitions.

7-5. Explain the rationale for imposing criminal liability on corporations.

7-6. Explain two sentencing alternatives to prison for white collar criminals.

REVIEW PROBLEMS

7-7. Rawlsworth is an employer of General Sam Corporation. One of Rawlsworth's jobs is to monitor the amount of particular pollutants and to record the results on a form that is submitted to the Environmental Protection Agency. This self-monitoring is required by law to ensure that firms limit the amount of particular pollutants they discharge. One day the firm's equipment is malfunctioning, and so Rawlsworth records that the firm's discharge is in excess of the lawful amount. When Matheson, Rawlsworth's supervisor, sees what he has done, Matheson tells him to change the records to state that the firm *is* in compliance and in the future, never to record such violations. When Rawlston calls the vice president to report this violation, he is told that the vice president does not take care of such matters and does not want to know about them. Rawlsworth then falsifies the records as instructed. When the falsification is discovered, who can be held criminally liable? Why?

7-8. Several corporations were convicted of violating the Sherman Act as a result of an unlawful agreement among their agents that the suppliers who supported an association to attract tourists would be given preferential treatment over those who did not contribute financially to the association. The corporations appealed on the grounds that the corporate agents involved were acting contrary to general corporate policy. Was the defense valid?

168

Part One

*An Introduction to the Law
and the Legal Environment
of Business*

7-9. Defendant Laffal was the president of a corporation that operated a restaurant. It was alleged that prostitutes frequented the restaurant, picking up men there and returning them after a short time, thus making the restaurant an illegal "bawdy house" in violation of the state criminal law. Laffal argued that he could not be charged with operating a bawdy house because he was never present when any of the illegal acts took place and he did not even know they were going on. Was Laffal correct?

7-10. Evans was a loan officer for a bank and in this capacity had approved several loans to Docherty, all of which were legitimate and were repaid on time. Evans asked Docherty to apply for a loan from the bank for $2,000 and then to give the money to Evans, who would repay the loan. Evans explained that he could not obtain the loan himself because bank policy did not allow borrowing from the bank. Docherty agreed. Was Evans's or Docherty's behavior illegal?

7-11. Defendant managed a corporation charted for the purpose of "introducing people." He obtained a loan from a Mrs. Russ by telling her that he wanted the loan to build a theater on company property and that the loan would be secured by a mortgage on the property. The loan was not repaid; the mortgage was not given to the lender because the corporation owned no property. The defendant, in fact, simply deposited the money in the corporate account and used it to pay corporate debts. What crime, if any, had the defendant committed?

7-12. Jones worked for a small community college teaching business students how to set up inventories on various computer programs. The college had purchased the software and was licensed to use several copies of it for educational purposes. Jones started his own small business on the side and used the software for his own firm's inventory control. He saw his own use as "testing" the product to make sure he was teaching students to use a process that really worked. Is his behavior lawful or unlawful? Why?

CASE PROBLEMS

7-13. Becker was the target of a police sting operation. The police had stopped Valencea at a narcotics stop point, seized 5 ounces of cocaine from him, and asked him for the names of those with whom he was dealing. One of the names was Becker's. Police had Valencea offer to sell Becker some cocaine. When Valencea called Becker, he said he had some cocaine to sell and he also asked Becker about the money Becker owed him. Becker told him that he could repay the debt if Valencea would "bring him something decent." The next day Valencea called Becker and told him he had some weed and cocaine, and he would meet him at a motel to make the exchange. Police conducted surveillance of the meeting, at which Valencea tried to sell Becker all 5 ounces for $2,000. Becker negotiated the price and said that he had to go sell "quarters." Becker did not buy the marijuana, which was offered by an undercover policeman who was also in the room. Becker was arrested immediately.

Becker raised the defense of entrapment at trial, but the defense was rejected by the trial court. On appeal, was Becker successful in demonstrating that the entrapment defense should have been accepted by the trial court? Why or why not? *State of Minnesota v. Becker*, 1995 WL 265067 (unpublished opinion)

7-14. Kao, owner of the China Wok, was having trouble getting a sufficient rating from the county health inspector, Radcliff, stating that the restaurant met the regulations of the state and county. After several inspections, Radcliff went to the restaurant at Kao's insistence and was given an envelope containing "dollar bills" of an undetermined denomination and was told by Kao that he should "buy himself lunch" with it. Realizing what was in the envelope, Radcliff refused it and told his supervisor.

An undercover agent, Bond, was then sent to inspect the restaurant. On the third visit, Bond told Kao he needed money to fix his truck, which Kao gave to him with a warning not to tell anyone. The next day, Kao received a letter saying the health inspection had been postponed for eight days. Bond asked Kao whether he had done a good job and Kao said yes. Kao later admitted that he had given the money to Bond to get the inspection postponed.

Kao was charged with bribery for allegedly bribing Bond and was subsequently convicted. He appealed the conviction on the grounds that all of the elements of bribery had not been proved because Bond, because he was not really a health department inspector, could not in fact influence the inspection process. Does Kao have a legitimate reason for having his conviction overturned? Why or why not? *State of Nebraska v. Hang-Nan Kao*, 531 N.W.2d 555 (1995)

7-15. Orr was a deputy treasurer and bookkeeper for the treasurer's office of Washington County, Virginia. She received and recorded the county's daily revenue and deposited those funds into the county's account. Over the course of her employment, she kept several thousand dollars for herself instead of depositing it into the county's account. What crime was she prosecuted for committing? Was the prosecution successful? *Orr v. Commonwealth of Virginia*, 344 S.E.2d 627 (1986)

7-16. Dotterweich was the general manager of a pharmaceutical company. He and the company were charged with violating the federal Food, Drug, and Cosmetics Act by shipping misbranded drugs to a physician. Dotterweich had no personal connection with the shipments, but he was in general charge of all the company's business and had instructed employees to fill orders received from physicians. Could he be held criminally responsible for violating the act? *United States v. Dotterweich* 320 U.S. 277 (1943)

7-17. In September 1988, Neidorf and Riggs devised and began to implement a scheme to defraud Bell South Telephone Company. The objective of the fraud scheme was to steal Bell South's computer text file that contained information regarding Bell South's enhanced 911 system for handling emergency calls. In December of 1988, Riggs began executing the fraud by using his home computer in Decatur, Georgia, to gain unlawful access to South's computer system. Having retrieved it, he transferred the stolen computer text file to Neidorf, at the University of Missouri, via an interstate computer data network, and Neidorf cleaned up the file so no one would be able to detect that it had been stolen from Bell South. In February, Neidorf published the file in his PHRACK newsletter. What crimes could Riggs and Neidorf be charged with? Discuss the likelihood of successful prosecution for these crimes. *United States v. Riggs*, 730 F. Supp. 414 (1990)

7-18. Defendant Morris, a graduate student in computer science at Cornell University, designed and released into the Internet a computer program known as a "worm." It spread and multiplied and eventually caused computers at various educational and military institutions to cease functioning. His reason for taking this action was to demonstrate to fellow graduate students the lack of security protecting computer networks. With what crime was he most likely charged? Was this prosecution successful? *United States v. Robert Tappen Morris*, 928 F.2d 504 (1991)

 On the Internet

http://www.3.5k.sympatico.ca/rcmpccs/wcc.html   This site provides general overview of white collar crimes and detailed definitions.

170

Part One

*An Introduction to the Law
and the Legal Environment
of Business*

http://www.wwcatalog.com/nylp/pages/overmaier-white.html   This page covers in-depth perspectives of white collar crimes and regulatory offenses.

http://www.nwmissouri.edu/nwcourses/martin/deviance/whitcorp/index. htm   A slide show is given here outlining white collar crime and corporate deviance.

http://www.iir.com/nwcc/nwcc.htm   This site is the location of the National White Collar Crime Center, which provides investigative support services to fight against white collar crimes.

http://www.ffhsj.com/firmpage/publicist/wcc.htm   A bibliography of articles on white collar crime.

http://www.neptune.net/~dougk/crimol.htm   White collar crime links provide articles and additional hotlinks to valuable information regarding white collar crime.

8

ETHICS, SOCIAL RESPONSIBILITY, AND THE BUSINESS MANAGER

- **DEFINITION OF BUSINESS ETHICS AND SOCIAL RESPONSIBILITY**

- **THEORIES OF ETHICAL THOUGHT**

- **CODES OF ETHICS**

- **THEORIES OF SOCIAL RESPONSIBILITY**

172

Part One

*An Introduction to the Law
and the Legal Environment
of Business*

On December 2, 1984, in Bhopal, India, lethal methylisocyanate gas (MIC) leaked from a chemical plant owned by Union Carbide India Limited, killing approximately 2,000 people and injuring thousands more, many of whom are still receiving treatment. Union Carbide's chairman, Warren Anderson, a lawyer, flew to India with a pledge of interim assistance totaling $7 million and medical support. He was arrested and deported from the country. Lawsuits on behalf of the deceased and injured were brought by U.S. law firms as well as by the government of India.

The price of Union Carbide stock dropped from $48 to $33. In August of 1984 GAF Corporation attempted to take over Union Carbide. Union Carbide successfully fought off the takeover attempt. On May 13, 1986, a federal court judge dismissed the personal injury and wrongful death actions, stating that the complaints should be more properly heard in a court in India. The judge attached certain conditions to the dismissal, one of which was that Union Carbide would have to agree to pay any damages rendered by an Indian court. The trial began in August 1988 in a New Delhi court amidst rumors that a former disgruntled employee had sabotaged Union Carbide's Bhopal plant, causing the gas leakage. In January 1988, Union Carbide shares traded on the New York Stock Exchange for $49, and the much leaner company was one of 30 corporations making up the composite Dow Jones Industrial Average.

The Bhopal incident in 1984 and a stream of insider trading cases in 1986 and 1987 continuing into the 1990s have brought a heightened awareness to the business community of the need for continued debate on whether business has a responsibility solely to shareholders or to other stakeholders as well.

Such issues force us to ask ourselves: What should be the rules that businesses obey in their daily operations? These are ethical questions, in that they force us to consider how we should behave if we are to live in a better world. Business ethics is the study of the moral practices of the firms who play such an important role in shaping that better world.

We have already begun thinking about business ethics. Recall from chapter 1 that an important aspect of critical thinking is consideration of alternative ethical norms shaping particular legal arguments. The primary ethical norms—freedom, security, justice, and efficiency—are the meat and potatoes of creating a better world.

Whenever you wonder whether a business decision requires us to think about ethics, simply ask yourself: Will this decision affect the quality of life of other people? If the answer is yes, the decision involves ethics. We think you will agree that business ethics is an extremely important aspect of our legal environment because almost all business decisions influence the quality of our lives.

This chapter presents material on business ethics in a neutral way. Readers are left to make their own choices about what part ethics should play in business decision making and about whether the business community, the trade groups that represent it, and individual managers should act in a "socially responsible" manner. The chapter includes (1) a broad definition of ethics and social responsibility; (2) some recognized schools of ethical thought and their application to business problems; (3) a discussion of individual, corporate, trade association, and professional ethical codes; and (4) theories of social responsibility as applied to business problems. The chapter ends with a brief discussion of some current trends in the area of ethics and social responsibility as well as some proposals now being debated, which, if implemented, would change the structure of corporate governance.

Critical Thinking about the Law

BUSINESS ETHICS IS PERHAPS ONE OF the most personal and emotional areas in law. Business ethics can be confusing and complex because a right or wrong answer often does not exist. Because this area is so emotional and controversial, it is extremely important to use your critical thinking skills when thinking about business ethics. It would be very easy to make arguments based on your "gut" reaction to cases such as the

Bhopal gas incident. However, you should carefully use your critical thinking skills to draw an informed conclusion. The following questions can help you begin to understand the complexity surrounding business ethics.

1. As critical thinkers, you have learned that ambiguous words—words that have multiple possible meanings—can cause confusion in the legal environment. Perhaps the best example of ambiguity in the legal environment is the phrase *social responsibility*. What definitions of *responsibility* can you generate?

   CLUE Consider the Bhopal incident. Do you think Union Carbide would have the same definition of *social responsibility* as the families of the victims of the accident in India?

2. It is quite common for individuals, business, judges, and juries to each have different meanings of the phrase *social responsibility*. Preferences for certain ethical norms might account for these different meanings. If executives of a company thought that security was extremely important, how might their definition of *social responsibility* be affected?

   CLUE Remember the definitions of security in chapter 1. If Union Carbide valued security, how might the company treat the victims of the Bhopal incident?

3. Your friend discovers that you are taking a legal environment of business class. He says, "I'm extremely angry at the cigarette companies. They knew that cigarettes cause cancer. Don't those companies have a responsibility to protect us?" Because you are trained in critical thinking, you know that his question does not have a simple answer. Keeping your critical thinking skills in mind, how would you intelligently respond to his question?

   CLUE Consider the critical thinking questions about ambiguity, ethical norms, and missing information.

DEFINITION OF BUSINESS ETHICS AND SOCIAL RESPONSIBILITY

BUSINESS ETHICS

Ethics is the study of good and bad behavior. **Business ethics** is a subset of the study of ethics and is defined as the study of what makes up good and bad business conduct. This conduct occurs when the firm acts as an organization, as well as when individual managers make decisions inside the organization. For example, there may be differences between the way Warren Anderson, personally, looked at the Bhopal tragedy (a failure of the plant to implement company operating standards) and the way the corporation's board of directors and the chemical industry did (the Indian government allowed people to live too close to the plant). It is important to look at "business" ethics not as a single monolithic system but from the perspective of individual managers, corporations, and industry-wide ethical concerns. Each may judge a particular happening in a different way.

How these groups think depends on their ethical norms and on their philosophy or theory of ethics. To help you understand their thinking, we include a discussion of three schools of ethical thought. Individual managers, corporations, or industries may belong to any one of the schools, as each school has its advocates and refinements. In addition, each school attempts to explain why an action is right or wrong and how one knows it to be right or wrong.

THE SOCIAL RESPONSIBILITY OF BUSINESS

The **social responsibility** of business is defined as a concern by business about both its profit-seeking and its non-profit-seeking activities and their intended and unintended impact on groups and individuals other than manage-

ethics The study of what makes up good and bad conduct inclusive of related actions and values.

business ethics The study of what makes up good and bad conduct as related to business activities and values.

social responsibility Concern of business entities about profit and non-profit activities and their unintended impact upon others directly or indirectly involved.

174

Part One

*An Introduction to the Law
and the Legal Environment
of Business*

ment or the owners of a corporation (e.g., consumers, environmentalists, and political groups). Since the late 1960s, an outcry has arisen for business to be more socially responsible. This outcry of public concern has resulted from three factors.

1. *The complexity and interdependence of a postindustrial society.* No individual or business is an island unto itself. If a company builds a chemical plant in Bhopal, India, and its primary purpose is to make profits for its shareholders, can it be held responsible to the public that lives around the plant when there is a gas leak? The public are dependent on the firm's good conduct, and the firm is dependent on the public and its political representatives to supply labor, an adequate water supply, tax forgiveness, roads, and so on.

2. *Political influence* that has translated public outcry for socially responsible conduct into government regulation. Whether a malfunction occurs at a nuclear plant at Three Mile Island or a human disaster is caused by a gas leak in Bhopal, India, the political arm of government at all levels sees the solution in the form of more regulation. This attitude pleases the government's constituents and makes its officials more electable.

3. *Philosophical differences* about what should be the obligations of business. Neoclassical economic theory would argue that the sole purpose of business is to make a profit for its investing shareholders, who, in turn, reinvest, creating expanded or new businesses that employ more people, thus creating a higher standard of living.

   Others hold different theories of social responsibility. Some would argue for a managerial or coping approach; that is, "throw money" at the problem when it occurs, such as the Bhopal disaster, and it will go away. Others would argue a more encompassing theory of social responsibility that purports that business, like any other institution in our society (e.g., unions, churches), has a social responsibility not only to shareholders (or members or congregations) but also to diverse groups, such as consumers and political, ethnic, racial group, and gender-oriented organizations. These and other theories of social responsibility are discussed later in this chapter.

THEORIES OF ETHICAL THOUGHT

CONSEQUENTIAL THEORIES

Ethicists, businesspeople, and workers who adhere to a consequential theory of ethics judge acts ethically good or bad based on whether the acts have achieved their desired results. The actions of a business or any other societal unit are looked at as right or wrong only in terms of whether the results can be rationalized.

This theory is best exemplified by the *utilitarian school of thought*, which is divided into two subschools: act utilitarianism and rule utilitarianism. In general, adherents of this school judge all conduct of individuals or businesses on whether it brings net happiness or pleasure to a society. They judge an act ethically correct after adding up the risks (unhappiness) and the benefits (happiness) to society and obtaining a net outcome. For example, if it is necessary for a company to pay a bribe to a foreign official in order to get several billion dollars in airplane contracts, utilitarians would argue, in general, that the payment is ethically correct because it will provide net happiness to society; that is, it will bring jobs and spending to the community where the airplane company is located. If the bribe is not paid, the contracts, jobs, and spending will go to a company somewhere else.

Act utilitarians determine if an action is right or wrong on the basis of whether that individual act (the payment of a bribe) alone brings net happiness to the society as opposed to whether other alternatives (e.g., not paying the bribe or allowing others to pay the bribe) would bring more or less net happiness. *Rule utilitarians* argue that an act (the payment of the bribe) is ethically right if the performance of similar acts by all similar agents (other contractors) would produce the best results in society or has done so in the past. Rule utilitarians hold the position that whatever applicable rule has been established by political representatives must be followed and should serve as a standard in the evaluation of similar acts. If payment of bribes has been determined by the society to bring net happiness, and a rule allowing bribes exists, then rule utilitarians would allow the bribe. On the other hand, the Foreign Corrupt Practices Act of 1977, as amended in 1988, which forbids paying bribes to foreign government officials to get business that would not have been obtained without such a payment, is an example of a standard that rule utilitarians would argue must be followed but that would set a different result. So the act utilitarians might get the airplane plant, but the rule utilitarians, if they were following the Foreign Corrupt Practices Act, would not.

We must note that both act and rule utilitarians focus on the *consequences* of an act and not on the question of verifying whether an act is ethically good or bad.[1] Either one of these theories can be used by individuals or businesses to justify their actions.[2] Act utilitarians use the principle of utility (adding up the costs and benefits of an act to arrive at net happiness) to focus on an individual action at one point in time. Rule utilitarians believe that one should not consider the consequences of a single act in determining net happiness but, instead, should focus on a *general rule* that exemplifies net happiness for the whole society.

DEONTOLOGICAL THEORIES

Deontology is derived from a Greek word meaning "duty." For advocates of deontology, rules and principles determine whether actions are ethically good or bad. The consequences of individual actions are not considered. The Golden Rule, "Do unto others as you would have them do unto you," is the hallmark of the theory.

Absolute deontology claims that actions can be judged ethically good or bad on the basis of absolute moral principles arrived at by human reason regardless of the consequences of an action: that is, regardless of whether there is net happiness.[3] Immanual Kant (1724–1804) provided an example of an absolute moral principle in his widely studied "categorical imperative." He stated that a person ought to engage only in acts that he or she could see becoming a universal standard. For example, if a U.S. company bribes a foreign official in order to obtain a contract to build airplanes, then U.S. society and business should be willing to accept the principle that foreign multinationals will be free morally to bribe U.S. government officials in order to obtain defense contracts. Of course, the reverse will be true if nonbribery statutes are adopted worldwide. Kant, as part of his statement of the categorical imperative, assumed that everyone is a rational being having free will, and he warned that one ought to "treat others as having intrinsic values in themselves, and not merely as a means to achieve one's end."[4] For deontologists such as Kant, ethical reasoning means adopting universal principles that are applied to all equally. Segregation of one ethnic or racial group is unethical because it denies the intrinsic value of each human being and thus violates a general universal principle.

HUMANIST THEORIES

A third school of thought, the *humanist school*, evaluates actions as ethically good or bad depending on what they contribute to improving inherent human capacities such as intelligence, wisdom, and self-restraint. Many natural law theorists (examined in chapter 2) believe that humans would arrive by reason alone at standards of conduct that ultimately derive from a divine being or an-

---

[1]*See* W. La Croix, *Principles for Ethics in Business* (rev. ed., Washington, D.C.: University Press, 1979), p. 12.

[2]*See* B. Brennan, *Amending the Foreign Corrupt Practices Act of 1977: Clarifying or Gutting a Law*, 2 J. Legis. 78–81 (1984), for an examination of the rule and act utilitarian schools of thought within the context of the proposed amending process of the 1977 Foreign Corrupt Practices Act.

[3]La Croix, *supra* note 2, at 13.

[4]*Foundations of the Metaphysics of Moral Thought and Critical Essays* (R. Wolff ed., New York: Bobbs-Merrill, 1964), p. 44.

176

Part One

*An Introduction to the Law
and the Legal Environment
of Business*

other ultimate source such as nature. For example, if a U.S. business participates in bribing a foreign official, it is not doing an act that improves inherent human capacities such as intelligence and wisdom, and thus, the act is not ethical. In a situation that demanded choice, as well as the use of the intelligence and restraint that would prevent a violation of law (the Foreign Corrupt Practices Act of 1977), the particular business would have failed ethically as well as legally. In the case excerpted here ethical questions are raised that can be addressed by the use of each of the three ethical theories reviewed.

SINDELL V. ABBOTT LABORATORIES
SUPREME COURT OF CALIFORNIA 697 P.2D 924 (1980)

The plaintiff, Sindell, brought a class action against the defendant and ten other manufacturers of diethylstilbestrol (DES) for a malignant bladder tumor caused by her mother's use of DES during pregnancy some 20 years before. The plaintiff sought compensatory damages of $1 million and punitive damages of $10 million. Between 1941 and 1971, the defendant companies manufactured and marketed the drug for the purpose of preventing miscarriages. In 1947, the Food and Drug Administration (FDA) authorized the marketing of DES on an experimental basis, requiring a label that said it was only "experimental." In 1971, the FDA ordered defendants to cease marketing and promoting DES and to warn physicians and the general public that the drug should not be used by pregnant women because of the danger to the unborn child. As a result of scientific research, it is clear that DES can cause vaginal and bladder cancer in daughters exposed to it before birth. The cancer (adenocarcinoma) manifests itself after a minimal latency period of 12 years, is fast-spreading, and requires radical surgery, as in the case of the plaintiff. According to a Fordham Law Review article, 1.5 million to 3 million mothers had taken DES between 1947 and 1971. Thousands of daughters of these women have suffered from adenocarcinoma, and the incidence of cancerous vaginal growth among them is 30–90 percent. The lower courts in this case ruled in favor of the defendants. The plaintiff appealed.

JUSTICE MOSK

We begin with the proposition that, as a general rule, the imposition of liability depends upon a showing by the plaintiff that his or her injuries were caused by the act of the defendant or by an instrumentality under the defendant's control.

In our contemporary, complex, industrialized society advances in science and technology create fungible goods which may harm consumers and which cannot be traced to any specific producer ... [W]e acknowledge that some adaptation of the rules of causation and liability may be appropriate in these recurring circumstances.

From a broader policy standpoint, defendants are better able to bear the cost of injury resulting from the manufacture of a defective product. The manufacturer is in the best position to discover and guard against defects in its products and to warn of harmful effects; thus, holding it liable for defects and failure to warn of harmful effects will provide an incentive to product safety.

We hold it to be reasonable in the present context to measure the likelihood that any of the defendants supplied with the product which allegedly injured plaintiff by the percentage of the DES sold by each of them for the purpose of preventing miscarriage bears to the entire production of the drug sold by all for that purpose. Plaintiff asserts in her briefs that Eli Lilly and Company and five or six other companies produced 90 percent of the DES marketed.

If plaintiff joins in the action the manufacturers of a substantial share of the DES which her mother might have taken, the injustice of shifting the burden of proof to defendants to demonstrate that they could not have made the substance which injured plaintiff is significantly diminished.... [W]e hold only that a substantial percentage is required.

The presence in the action of a substantial share of the appropriate market also provides a ready means to apportion damages among the defendants. Each defendant will be held liable for the proportion of the judgment represented by its share of that market unless it demonstrates that it could not have made the product which caused plaintiff's injuries. In the present case, as we have seen, one DES manufacturer was dismissed from the action upon filing a declaration that it had not manufactured DES until after plaintiff was born. Once plaintiff has met her burden of joining the required defendants, they in turn may cross-complaint against other DES manufacturers, not jointed in the action, which they can allege might have supplied the injury-causing product.

Under this approach, each manufacturer's liability would approximate its responsibility for the injuries caused by its own products. Some minor discrepancy in the correlation between market share and liability is inevitable; therefore, a defendant may be held liable for a somewhat different percentage of the damage than its share of the appropriate market would justify. It is probably impossible, with the passage of time, to determine market share with mathematical exactitude.

Under the rule we adopt, each manufacturer's liability for an injury would be approximately equivalent to the damages caused by the DES it manufactured.

Reversed in favor of Plaintiff, Sindell.

CODES OF ETHICS

INDIVIDUAL CODES OF ETHICS

When examining business ethics, one must recognize that the corporations, partnerships, and other entities that make up the business community are a composite of individuals. If the readers of this book are asked where they obtained their ethical values, they might respond, from parents, church, peers, teachers, brothers and sisters, or the environment. In any event, corporations, and the culture of a corporation, are greatly influenced by what ethical values individuals bring to it. Often, business managers are faced with a conflict between their individual ethical values and those of the corporation. For example, a father of three young children, divorced, and their sole support, is asked by his supervisor to "slightly change" figures that will make the tests on rats of a new drug look more favorable when reported to the Food and Drug Administration. His supervisor hints that if he fails to do so he may be looking for another job. The individual is faced with a conflict in ethical values: individual values of honesty and humaneness toward potential users of the drug versus business values of profits, efficiency, loyalty to the corporation, and the need for a job. Which values should he adopt?

CORPORATE CODES OF ETHICS

The sum total of individual employees' ethical values influences corporate conduct, especially in a corporation's early years. The activities during these years, in turn, form the basis of what constitutes a "corporate culture," or an environment for doing business. In a free-market society, values of productivity, efficiency, and profits become part of the culture of all companies. Some companies seek to generate productivity by cooperation between workers and management; others motivate through intense production goals that may bring about high labor turnover. Some companies have marketed their product through emphasis on quality and service; others, by beating the competition through lower prices.[5] Over time, these production and marketing emphases have evolved into what is called a *corporate culture*, often set forth in corporate codes.

Approximately 90 percent of all major corporations have adopted codes of conduct since the mid-1960s. In general, the codes apply to upper- and middle-level managers. They are usually implemented by a chief executive officer or a designated agent. They tend to provide sanctions ranging from personal reprimands in one's files to dismissal. Some formal codes allow for due process hearings within the corporation in which an employee accused of a violation is given a chance to defend himself or herself. With many employees bringing wrongful dismissal actions in courts of law, more formal internal procedures are developing to implement due process requirements. A study of corporate codes reveals that the actions most typically forbidden are:[6]

1. Paying bribes to foreign government officials
2. Fixing prices
3. Giving gifts to customers or accepting gifts from suppliers
4. Using insider information
5. Revealing trade secrets

INDUSTRY CODES OF ETHICS

In addition to corporate ethical codes, industry codes exist, such as those of the National Association of Broadcasters or the National Association of Used Car Dealers. In most cases, these codes are rather general and contain either affirma-

---

[5]C. Power and D. Vogel, *Ethics in the Education of Business Managers* (Hastings-on-Hudson, N.Y.: Hastings Center, 1980), p. 6.
[6]*See* K. Chatov, *What Corporate Ethics Statements Say*, 22 Cal. Mgmt. Rev. 20 (1980).

178

Part One

*An Introduction to the Law
and the Legal Environment
of Business*

tive inspirational guidelines or a list of "shall-nots." A "hybrid model" including "dos and don'ts" generally addresses itself to subjects such as:[7]

1. Honest and fair dealings with customers

2. Acceptable levels of safety, efficacy, or cleanliness

3. Nondeceptive advertising

4. Maintenance of experienced and trained personnel, competent performance of services, and furnishing of quality products

Most trade associations were formed for the purpose of lobbying Congress, the executive branch, and the regulatory agencies, in addition to influencing elections through their political action committees (PACs). They have not generally been effective in monitoring violations of their own ethical codes. In light of the reasons for their existence and the fact that membership dues support their work, it is not likely that they will be very effective disciplinarians.

However, some effective *self-regulating mechanisms* do exist in industries. In chapter 22, the reader will see that self-regulating organizations (SROs) such as the National Association of Securities Dealers and the New York Stock Exchange have carried out authority delegated to them by the Securities and Exchange Commission in an extremely efficient manner. In addition, the Council of Better Business Bureaus, through its National Advertising Division (NAD), has provided empirical evidence that self-regulation can be effective. The NAD seeks to monitor and expose false advertising through its local bureaus and has done an effective job, receiving commendations from a leading consumer advocate, Ralph Nader.[8]

PROFESSIONAL CODES OF ETHICS

Within a corporation, managers often interact with individual employees who have "professional" codes of conduct that may supersede corporate or industry-wide codes in terms of what activities they can participate in and still remain licensed professionals. For example, under the Model Code of Professional Responsibility, a lawyer must reveal the intention of his or her client to commit a crime and the information necessary to prevent the crime.[9] When a lawyer, a member of the law department of Airplane Corporation X, learns that his company deliberately intends to bribe a high-level foreign official in order to obtain an airplane contract, he may be forced, under the Model Code, to disclose this intention because the planned bribe is a violation of the Foreign Corrupt Practices Act of 1977, an act that has criminal penalties. Failure to disclose could lead to suspension or disbarment by the lawyer's state bar. Management must be sensitive to this and to the several professional codes that are to be discussed.

Professionals is an often-overused term, referring to everything from masons to hair stylists to engineers, lawyers, and doctors. When discussing professions or professionals here, we mean a group that has the following characteristics:

1. Prelicensing mandatory university educational training, as well as continuing education requirements

2. Licensing-exam requirements

3. A set of written ethical standards that are recognized and continually enforced by the group

4. A formal association or group that meets regularly

5. An independent commitment to the public interest

6. Formal recognition by the public as a professional group

---

[7]*See* R. Jacobs, *Vehicles for Self-Regulation: Codes of Conduct, Credentialing and Standards, in* Self-Regulation, Conference Proceedings (Washington, D.C.: Ethics Resource Center, 1982), p. 83.

[8]*See* R. Tankersley, *Advertising: Regulation, Deregulation and Self-Regulation, in* Self-Regulation, Conference Proceedings, *supra* note 8, at 45.

[9]*See* Model Code of Professional Responsibility DR 4-401(C) and Formal Op. 314 (1965).

Management must often interact with the professions outlined in the following paragraphs. Each of them has a separate code of conduct. An awareness of this factor may lead to a greater understanding of why each acts as it does.

ACCOUNTING The American Institute of Certified Public Accountants (AICPA) has promulgated a Code of Professional Ethics and Interpretive Rules. The Institute of Internal Auditors has set out a Code of Ethics, as well as a Statement of Responsibilities of Internal Auditors. In addition, the Association of Government Accountants has promulgated a Code of Ethics.

Disciplinary procedures are set forth for individuals as well as for firms in the Code of Professional Ethics for Certified Public Accountants (CPAs). Membership in the AICPA is suspended without a hearing if a judgment of conviction is filed with the secretary of the institute as related to the following:

1. A felony as defined under any state law
2. The willful failure to file an income tax return, which the CPA as an individual is required to file
3. The filing of a fraudulent return on the part of the CPA for his or her own return or that of a client
4. The aiding in the preparation of a fraudulent income tax return of a client.[10]

The AICPA Division for CPA Firms is responsible for disciplining firms as opposed to individuals. Through its SEC Practice and its Private Company sections this division requires member firms to (1) adhere to quality-control standards, (2) submit to peer review of their accounting and audit practices every three years, (3) ensure that all professionals participate in continuing education programs, and (4) maintain minimum amounts of liability insurance.

INSURANCE AND FINANCE The American Society of Chartered Life Underwriters (ASCLU) has adopted a Code of Ethics consisting of eight Guides to Professional Conduct and six Rules of Professional Conduct. The Guides are broad in nature, whereas the Rules are specific. Enforcement of the Code of Ethics is left primarily to local chapters. Discipline includes reprimand, censure, and dismissal. A local chapter can additionally recommend suspension or revocation to a national board. Very few disciplinary actions have been forthcoming.[11]

In addition, the Society of Chartered Property and Casualty Underwriters (CPCC) has a Code of Ethics consisting of seven Specified Unethical Practices, as well as three Unspecified Unethical Practices of a more general nature. On receipt of a written and signed complaint, the president of the society appoints a three-member conference panel to hear the case. If a panel finds a member guilty of an "unspecified unethical practice," the president directs the member to cease such action. If a member is found guilty of a "specified unethical practice," the society's board of directors may reprimand or censure the violator or suspend or expel her or him from membership in the society.

LAW The American Bar Association's Model Rules of Professional Responsibility were submitted to the highest state courts and the District of Columbia for adoption, after the association's House of Delegates approved them in August 1983 (before then, the states had adopted the Model Code of Professional Responsibility). There are nine canons of professional responsibility. From these are derived Ethical Considerations and Disciplinary Rules. The Model Rules set out a minimal level of conduct that is expected of an attorney. Violation of any of these rules may lead to warnings, reprimands, public censure, suspension, or

---

[10]*See* AICPA Professional Standards, vol. 2, Disciplinary Suspension and Termination of Membership Hearing, BL 730.01.
[11]*See* R. Horn, *On Professions, Professionals, and Professional Ethics* (Malvern, Penn.: American Institute for Property and Liability Underwriters, 1978), p. 74.

180

Part One

*An Introduction to the Law
and the Legal Environment
of Business*

disbarment by the enforcement agency of the highest state court in which the attorney is admitted to practice. Most state bar disciplinary actions are published in state bar journals and local newspapers, so lawyers and the public in general are aware of attorneys who have been subject to disciplinary action.

The case excerpted here illustrates some legal problems surrounding professional ethical codes when they result in price fixing.

BATES V. STATE BAR OF ARIZONA
United States Supreme Court 433 U.S. 350 (1977)

Plaintiff-appellants Bates and O'Steen, licensed to practice law in the state of Arizona, opened a "legal clinic" in 1974. The clinic provided legal services to people with modest incomes for approximately two years, after which the clinic placed an advertisement in the *Arizona Republic*, a daily newspaper circulated in the Phoenix area, stating prices charged for legal services. The plaintiffs conceded that this advertisement was a violation of Disciplinary Rule 2-l0l(B) incorporated in Rule 29(a) of the Arizona Supreme Court rules, which stated in part:

> *A lawyer shall not publicize himself or his partner or associate, or any other lawyer affiliated with him or his firm, as a lawyer through newspapers, or magazine advertisements, radio, television announcements, display advertisements in the city telephone directories or other means of commercial publicity, nor shall he authorize others to do so in his behalf.*

A complaint was initiated by the president of the State Bar of Arizona, and a hearing was held before a three-member special local administrative committee. The committee recommended to the Arizona Supreme Court that each of the plaintiffs be suspended from practice for not less than six months. The court agreed and ordered the plaintiffs suspended. The plaintiffs appealed to the U.S. Supreme Court.

JUSTICE BLACKMUN

The heart of the dispute before us today is whether lawyers may constitutionally advertise the prices at which certain routine services will be performed. Numerous justifications are proffered for the restriction of such price advertising. We consider each in turn:

1. The Adverse Effect on Professionalism. Appellee places particular emphasis on the adverse effects that it feels price advertising will have on the legal profession. The key to professionalism, it is argued, is the sense of pride that involvement in the discipline generates. It is claimed that price advertising will bring about commercialization, which will undermine the attorney's sense of dignity and self-worth. The hustle of the marketplace will adversely affect the profession's service orientation, and irreparably damage the delicate balance between the lawyer's need to earn and his obligation selflessly to serve. Advertising is also said to erode the client's trust in his attorney. Once

the client perceives that the lawyer is motivated by profit, his confidence that the attorney is acting out of a commitment to the client's welfare is jeopardized. And advertising is said to tarnish the dignified public image of the profession.

We recognize, of course, and commend the spirit of public service with which the profession of law is practiced and to which it is dedicated. The present Members of this Court, licensed attorneys all, could not feel otherwise. And we would have reason to pause if we felt that our decision today would undercut that spirit. But we find the postulated connection between advertising and the erosion of true professionalism to be severely strained. At its core, the argument presumes that attorneys must conceal from themselves and from their clients the real-life fact that lawyers earn their livelihood at the bar. We suspect that few attorneys engage in such self-deception. And rare is the client, moreover, even one of modest means, who enlists the aid of an attorney with the expectation that his services will be rendered free of charge.

Moreover, the assertion that advertising will diminish the attorney's reputation in the community is open to question. Bankers and engineers advertise, and yet these professionals are not regarded as undignified. In fact, it has been suggested that the failure of lawyers to advertise creates public disillusionment with the profession. The absence of advertising may be seen to reflect the profession's failure to reach out and serve the community. Studies reveal that many persons do not obtain counsel even when they perceive a need because of the feared price of services or because of an inability to locate a competent attorney. Indeed, cynicism with regard to the profession may be created by the fact that it long has publicly eschewed advertising, while condoning the actions or the attorney who structures his social or civic associations so as to provide contacts with potential clients.

2. Inherently Misleading Nature of Attorney Advertising. It is argued that advertising of legal services inevitably will be misleading. The argument that legal services are so unique that fixed rates cannot meaningfully be established is refuted by the record in this case. The appellee State Bar itself sponsors a Legal Services Program in which the participating attorneys agree to perform services like those advertised by the appellants at standardized rates.

3. The Adverse Effect on the Administration of Justice. Advertising is said to have the undesirable effect of stirring up litigation. But advertising by attorneys is not an unmitigated source of harm to the administration of justice. It may offer great benefits. Although advertising might increase the use of the judicial machinery, we cannot accept the notion that it is always better for a person to suffer a wrong silently than to redress it by legal action.

4. The Undesirable Economic Effects of Advertising. It is claimed that advertising will increase the overhead costs of the profession, and that these costs then will be passed along to consumers in the form of increased fees. Moreover, it is claimed that the additional cost of practice will create a substantial entry barrier, deterring or preventing young attorneys from penetrating the market and entrenching the position of the bar's established members.

These two arguments seem dubious at best. Neither distinguishes lawyers from others and neither appears relevant to the First Amendment. The ban on advertising serves to increase the difficulty of discovering the lowest cost seller of acceptable ability. As a result, to this extent attorneys are isolated from competition, and the incentive to price competitively is reduced. Although it is true that the effect of advertising on the price of services has not been demonstrated, there is revealing evidence with regard to products; where consumers have the benefit of price advertising, retail prices often are dramatically lower than they would be without advertising. It is entirely possible that advertising will serve to reduce, not advance, the cost of legal services to the consumer.

The entry-barrier argument is equally unpersuasive. In the absence of advertising, an attorney must rely on his contacts with the community to generate a flow of business. In view of the time necessary to develop such contacts, the ban in fact serves to perpetuate the market position of established attorneys. Consideration of entry-barrier problems would urge that advertising be allowed so as to aid the new competitor in penetrating the market.

5. The Adverse Effect of Advertising on the Quality of Service. It is argued that the attorney may advertise a given "package" of service at a set price, and will be inclined to provide, by indiscriminate use, the standard package regardless of whether it fits the client's needs. . . . Even if advertising leads to the creation of "legal clinics" like that of appellants—clinics that emphasize standardized procedures for routine problems—it is possible that such clinics will improve service by reducing the likelihood of error.

6. The Difficulties of Enforcement. Finally, it is argued that the wholesale restriction is justified by the problems of enforcement if any other course is taken. Because the public lacks sophistication in legal matters, it may be particularly susceptible to misleading or deceptive advertising by lawyers.

It is at least somewhat incongruous for the opponents of advertising to extol the virtues and altruism of the legal profession at one point, and, at another, to assert that its members will seize the opportunity to mislead and distort. We suspect that, with advertising, most lawyers will behave as they always have: They will abide by their solemn oaths to uphold the integrity and honor of their profession and of the legal system.

In sum, we are not persuaded that any of the proffered justifications rise to the level of an acceptable reason for the suppression of all advertising by attorneys. As with other varieties of speech, it follows as well that there may be reasonable restrictions on the time, place, and manner of advertising.

The constitutional issue in this case is only whether the State may prevent the publication in a newspaper of appellants' truthful advertisement concerning the availability and terms of routine legal services. We rule simply that the flow of such information may not be restrained, and we therefore hold the present application of the disciplinary rule against appellants to be violative of the First Amendment.

Reversed in favor of Plaintiffs, Bates.

Critical Thinking about the Law

As YOU KNOW, A JUDGE'S REASONING is not always clear. In the course of writing an opinion, a judge may discuss an assortment of topics. Your task, as a reader, is to organize those topics into a meaningful pattern and then locate the reasoning in the decision. Only then are you ready to think critically about the case. The following questions should help you better understand the reasoning in the *Bates* case.

1. The Court clearly listed the reasons the State Bar of Arizona offered for restricting price advertising. Justice Blackmun evaluated those reasons. As critical thinkers, you realize that identifying the link between the conclusion and reasons is imperative. What reasons did the Court offer for allowing attorneys to advertise their prices?

    CLUE Remember that the Court concluded that, under the First Amendment, the state may not suppress advertising by attorneys. What reasons did Justice Blackmun use to reach this conclusion?

2. What primary ethical norm dominated the Court's consideration of the advertisement of prices for attorney services?

CLUE Go back to the court's examination of the reasons offered by the State Bar of Arizona. Look closely at Justice Blackmun's response to reason 3. Furthermore, consider the last two paragraphs of the opinion.

3. Suppose the State Bar of Arizona had introduced evidence that advertising causes the price of attorney's services to increase. Do you think Justice Blackmun would have come to a different conclusion? Why or why not?

CLUE Look at the discussion of undesirable economic effects on advertising. Consider the primary ethical norm you identified in Question 2. Do you think Justice Blackmun would consider this piece of evidence to be extremely persuasive?

THEORIES OF SOCIAL RESPONSIBILITY

Early in this chapter, the *social responsibility* of business was defined as concern by business about both its profit and its nonprofit activities and their intended and unintended impact on others. As you will see, theories of ethics and theories of social responsibility are not necessarily mutually exclusive. For example, the primary purpose of a steel company is to make a profit for its individual and institutional shareholders. The unintended effects of this company's actions might be that the surrounding community has polluted waters and homes are affected by ash that falls from the company's smokestack. Similarly, in the Union Carbide incident set out at the beginning of this chapter, the purpose of Union Carbide India Ltd. was to make a profit for its shareholders. By doing so, it was able to employ people. The unintended effect of this activity was a gas leak that killed approximately 2,000 people and injured many more. The question in both of these cases is, What responsibility, if any, do firms have for the unintended effects of their profit-seeking activity? This section of the chapter discusses five views of social responsibility that seek to answer that question: profit-oriented theory, managerial theory, institutional theory, professional obligation theory, and regulation theory. Each of these theories reflects, or is an implementation of, the ethical values or culture of a corporation. The reader should analyze each, realizing, as in the case of ethical theories, that each has its strong advocates but that the "answer" may not lie in any one.

PROFIT-ORIENTED THEORY

The *profit-oriented theory of social responsibility* begins with a market-oriented concept of the firm that most readers were exposed to in their first or second course in economics. Holders of this theory argue that business entities are distinct organizations in our society and that their sole purpose is to increase profits for shareholders. Businesses are to be judged solely on criteria of economic efficiency and how well they contribute to growth in productivity and technology. Corporate social responsibility is shown by managers who maximize profits for their shareholders, who, in turn, are able to reinvest such profits, providing for increased productivity, new employment opportunities, and increased consumption of goods. Classical economists, who advocate this position, recognize that there will be unintended effects of such profit-seeking activities (externalities) that affect society and cannot be incorporated into or passed on in the price of output. They would argue that this is the "social cost" of doing business. Such social costs are a collective responsibility of the government. Individual businesses should not be expected to voluntarily incorporate in their product's price the cost of cleaning up water or air, because this incorporation will distort the market mechanism and the efficient use of resources. Profit-seeking advocates argue that, when government needs to act in a collective manner, it should act in a way that involves the least interference with the efficiency of the market system, preferably through direct taxation.

In summary, efforts at pollution control, upgrading minority workers, and bringing equality of payment to the workforce are all tasks of government, not of the private sector, which is incapable of making such choices and is not elected in a democratic society to do so. Its sole responsibility is to seek profits for its shareholders.

MANAGERIAL THEORY

Advocates of the *managerial theory of social responsibility* argue that businesses, particularly large institutions, have a number of interest groups or constituents both internally and externally that they must deal with regularly, not just stockholders and a board of directors. A business has employees, customers, suppliers, consumers, activist groups, government regulators, and others that influence decision making and the ability of the entity to make profits. In effect, modern managers must balance conflicting claims on their time and the company's resources. Employees want better wages, working conditions, and pensions; suppliers want prompt payment for their goods; and consumers want higher-quality goods at lower prices. These often-conflicting demands lead advocates of a managerial theory of social responsibility to argue that the firm must have the trust of all groups, both internal and external. Thus, it must have clear ethical standards and a sense of social responsibility for its unintended acts in order to maximize profits and to survive in the short and long run. A firm that seeks to maximize short-run profits and ignores the claims of groups, whether they be unions, consumer activists, or government regulators, will not be able to survive in the complex environment that business operates in.

If one reviews the Union Carbide India Ltd. incident described earlier, it is clear that the explosion in Bhopal, India, had at least three consequences: It (1) precipitated to an attempt by GAF to take over the company; (2) Union Carbide made a successful but costly attempt to fight off this takeover; (3) the value of the stock decreased, and thus, the investors suffered large losses. Advocates of managerial theory would point to the investors' trust in management's ability to deal with this disaster as being important to how the market evaluated Union Carbide's stock. They also would argue that the management of Johnson & Johnson took decisive action in dealing with the poison in its Tylenol product and was thus perceived by investors and customers as being trustworthy.[12] As a result its stock value recovered relatively quickly.

INSTITUTIONAL THEORY

Advocates of an *institutional theory of social responsibility* for business argue that business entities have a responsibility to act in a manner that benefits all of society just as churches, unions, courts, universities, and governments have. Whether a single proprietorship, a partnership, or a corporation, a business is a legal entity in our society that must be held responsible for its activities. Proponents of this theory argue that the same civil and criminal sanctions should be applied to business activities that injure the social fabric of a society (e.g. the pollution of water and air) as are applied to acts of individuals and of other institutions. When managers fail to deal adequately with "externalities," they should be held accountable not only to their board of directors but also to government enforcement authorities and individual citizens as well.

PROFESSIONAL OBLIGATION THEORY

Advocates of a *professional obligation theory of social responsibility* state that business managers and members of boards of directors should be certified as "professionals" before they can assume managerial responsibility. In our discussion of professional ethical codes, we defined professionals as persons having (1) educational entrance requirements and continuing-education standards,

---

[12]*See* M. Krikorian, Ethical Conduct: An Aid to Management, Address at Albion College, Albion, Mich., (April 16, 1985).

184

Part One

*An Introduction to the Law
and the Legal Environment
of Business*

(2) licensing-exam requirements, (3) codes of conduct that are enforced, (4) a formal association that meets regularly, and (5) an independent commitment to the public interest. Advocates of a professional obligation theory argue that business directors and managers, like doctors and lawyers, have a responsibility to the public beyond merely making profits and that the public must be able to be sure that they are qualified to hold their positions. They should be licensed by meeting university requirements and passing a state or national test. They should be subject to a disciplinary code that could involve revocation or suspension of their license to "practice the management of a business" if they are found by state or national boards to have failed to meet their codified responsibilities. Such responsibilities would include accountability for the unintended effects of their profit-making activities (externalities).

REGULATION THEORY

A *regulation theory of social responsibility* sees all business units as accountable to elected public officials. Proponents of this theory argue that, because business managers are responsible only to a board of directors that represents shareholders, the corporation cannot be trusted to act in a socially responsible manner. If society is to be protected from the unintended effects of profit-making business activities (e.g., pollution, sex discrimination in the workplace, and injuries to workers), it is necessary for government to be involved. The degree of government involvement is much debated by advocates of this theory. Some would argue in the extreme for a socialist state. Others argue for government representatives on boards of directors, and still others argue that government should set up standards of socially responsible conduct for each industry. The last group advocates an annual process of reporting conduct, both socially responsible and not, similar to the independent financial audits required now by the SEC of all publicly registered firms.

SUMMARY

We have sought to define ethics and social responsibility within the context of business associations. We examined consequential theories of ethics based on the consequences of the company's actions. In contrast, deontology schools of ethics are based on duties. Humanist theories of ethics evaluates actions as good or bad on how the actions improved inherent human capacities. Codes of ethics emanating from businesses and professions were also examined. Finally, five theories of social responsibility based on the unintended effects of corporate and human conduct were examined.

REVIEW QUESTIONS

8-1. Define the humanist theory of ethics. On the basis of this theory and a reading of the Union Carbide case synopsis, do you think that Union Carbide acted ethically after the Bhopal, India, incident? Explain.

8-2. List the differing views of whether corporations should act in a socially responsible manner? Explain.

8-3. How are professional codes of ethics different from individual codes? Explain.

8-4. What actions are typically forbidden by corporate codes? Explain.

8-5. Why are industry ethical codes not generally effective? Explain.

REVIEW PROBLEMS

8-6. A, a middle-level manager of Drug Company X, has been told by her boss, B, to change some figures on the percentage of rats that died as a result of injections of a new drug that will need Food and Drug Administration approval. The percentage of animals that died in the testing will need to be reported as lower, she is told. A is the single mother of two children and makes $65,000 a year. Choose one ethical theory outlined in the chapter, and, on the basis of that theory, advise A what to do.

8-7. B knows that 200 percent cost overruns exist because of the negligence of the management of Company Y in carrying out a federal government contract to build an airplane. He works in the comptroller's office and has been told by his boss to "keep his mouth shut" when the auditors from the General Accounting Office (a government agency) come. He is told that there will be "severe consequences" if he does not keep quiet. He earns $65,000 annually and is the father of three children attending private colleges. His wife works at home but is not compensated. Select a single ethical theory and advise B what he should do.

8-8. C, a student at University Z, learns a method of bypassing the telephone system to make free telephone calls. C tells his roommate, D. How would you advise D to act on the basis of one of the ethical theories discussed in this chapter?

8-9. You are hiring a new manager for your department. You have several good applicants. Assume that the one who is best suited for the job in training and experience has also been found to have done one of the things listed below. How would knowing what the person has done affect your decision? Would your answer be the same regardless of which theory of ethical thought you applied?

a. The individual listed on his resume that he had an MBA from Rutgers. He does not have an MBA.

b. The individual listed that his prior salary was $40,000. The prior salary was $32,000.

8-10. You are a purchasing manager for Alphs Corporation. You are responsible for buying two $1 million generators. Your company has a written policy prohibiting any company buyer from receiving a gratuity in excess of $50 and requiring that all gratuities be reported. The company has no policy regarding whistleblowing. A salesperson for a generator manufacturer offers to arrange it so that you can buy a $20,000 car for $7,000. The car would be bought from a third party. You decline the offer. Do you now report it to your superior? To the salesperson's superior? How would the various schools of ethical thought influence your decision?

8-11. You are a lab technician for the Standard Ethical Drug Company. You run tests on animals and prepare a summary that is then doctored by your superior to make a drug appear safe when in fact it is not. Your supervisor determines your salary and has a significant influence on whether your retain the job. You are the sole source of support of your two children, have no close relative to help you, and are just making it financially. Jobs equivalent to yours are difficult to find. You are convinced that if the company markets the drug, the risk of cancer to the drug users will increase significantly. The drug provides significant relief for hemorrhoids. What will you do? How would the ethical schools of thought influence your decision?

CASE PROBLEMS

8-12. The Warner-Lambert Company has manufactured and distributed Listerine antiseptic mouthwash since 1897. Its formula has never changed. The company has represented it as being beneficial in preventing and curing colds and sore throats. In 1972, the Federal Trade Commission filed a complaint against Warner-Lambert alleging that the company engaged in false advertising in violation of federal law. In 1975, after examining the evidence, the FTC issued an opinion that held that the company's representations that Listerine prevented and cured colds and sore throats were false and that the company should spend a percentage of their advertising budget on corrective advertising indicating that Listerine is not a cure

186

Part One

*An Introduction to the Law
and the Legal Environment
of Business*

for the common cold. The court of appeals affirmed. To which school of ethical thought did Warner-Lambert company adhere? *Warner-Lambert v. Federal Trade Commission*, 562 F.2d 49 (1972)

8-13. Carolyn Hamaker sued Kenwel-Jackson Machine, Inc., for injuries allegedly resulting from an unreasonably dangerous notching machine. Kenwel Machine Company was a manufacturer of notching machines that were used to make notches in lumber stackers. The company secured a patent for model 3072, which they made for a number of years and then developed improvements, resulting in later models 3072A, 3072B, and 3072C, also patented. Kenwel sold its assets to the Jacksons for $140,000 on December 31, 1975. The agreement placed the responsibility for all liabilities on the seller. Sometime afterward, the Kenwel Machine Company was disbanded. The Jacksons formed a new company, Kenwel-Jackson Machine, Inc., which manufactured and sold notching machines. In March 1981, Carolyn Hamaker severed four fingers while using a 3072 notching machine. She sued Kenwel-Jackson, claiming that it was strictly liable for her injuries. The trial court granted summary judgment for the defendant. What school of social responsibility could the appellate court find the company had failed to adhere to? Explain. *Hamaker v. Kenwel-Jackson Machine, Inc.*, 387 N.W.2d 516 (1986)

- -

 On the Internet

http://ethics.acusd.edu/index.html   Ethics Updates is designed primarily to be used by ethics instructors and their students. It is intended to provide updates on current literature.

http://www.legalethics.com/   This comprehensive ethics page provides numerous hotlinks to other valuable Web sites.

http://webusers.anct-stl.com/~humir/hm_pg.html   This page looks at our legal system from an ethics perspective and suggests some possible alternatives for reform.

- -

PRIVATE LAW AND THE
LEGAL ENVIRONMENT
OF BUSINESS

*P*art Two explores areas of private law that impact on the legal environment of business. It opens with a discussion of contract law, then proceeds to examine the law of torts, product liability law, property law, agency law, and finally, the law of business associations.

9

THE LAW OF CONTRACTS AND SALES—I

- **DEFINITION, SOURCES, AND CLASSIFICATIONS OF CONTRACT LAW**

- **ELEMENTS OF A LEGAL CONTRACT**

- **CONTRACTS THAT MUST BE IN WRITING**

- **PAROL EVIDENCE RULE**

- **THIRD-PARTY BENEFICIARY CONTRACTS AND ASSIGNMENT**

  OF RIGHTS

It is a fundamental requirement of a free enterprise economy that entities in the private sector and at all levels of government be able to enter into agreements that are *enforceable* by courts of law. Without the assurance that business agreements are legally enforceable, everyday commercial dealings would be difficult to carry out. Contract law has evolved to provide enterprises with the sense of predictability and security they need to flourish and to produce quality products.

Contract law affects several other areas of law discussed in this book. When we take up the law of torts and product liability (chapters 11 and 12), for instance, much of our discussion will concern breaches of warranty of merchantability, fitness, or usefulness. In our review of the law of business associations (chapter 15), we will examine contracts between principal and agents, employer and employees, and partners in partnership agreements. You will see when we analyze antitrust law (chapter 22) that contracts that unreasonably restrain trade are prohibited. The basis for our discussion of labor law (chapter 18) is collective bargaining agreements and what practices incorporated into those agreements government regulation will tolerate. Finally, when we discuss the relationship between management and consumers (chapter 23), the law of contracts will be our starting point. So contract law is immensely significant in the legal environment of business.

This chapter begins with a definition and classification of contract law. It analyzes the six elements of a contract, then explains which contracts must be in writing in order to be enforceable, the parol evidence rule, and the nature of third-party beneficiary contracts and assignment of rights.

Critical Thinking about the Law

THE NEED FOR PREDICTABILITY IN BUSINESS dealings had a great deal to do with the rise of contract law. In addition, several ethical norms have shaped the evolution of that law. Preliminary to our discussion of the law of contracts, you can sharpen your thinking about contract principles by considering the relevant ethical norms that cause people to consider and pursue contract disputes.

This critical thinking activity is meant to heighten your sensitivity to the pervasiveness of ethical norms in discussions about contract law and to enrich your appreciation of the moral issues at stake in this area of the legal environment of business.

1. What ethical norms are especially important to someone who wants all agreements between people to be legally enforceable?

    CLUE Ask yourself, "What would society gain by holding people to all the agreements they make?" Review the ethical norms discussed in chapter 1 if you need help in answering this question.

2. What ethical norms are held in the highest regard by a business manager who wants the law to enforce only certain agreements made under certain conditions?

    CLUE Remember that firms often buy parts and services. What ethical norms is a business seeking to uphold when it urges the courts to be more flexible in enforcing agreements?

3. Now translate your answer to each of the first two questions into one of the four primary ethical norms: freedom, security, justice, and efficiency.

    CLUE Consider the variety of definitions given in chapter 1 for each of the primary ethical norms. Is there a rough match between any of those definitions and your answers to each of the first two questions? For example, predictability provides greater security in the sense of removing fear of disorder.

DEFINITION, SOURCES, AND CLASSIFICATIONS OF CONTRACT LAW

contract A legally enforceable exchange of promises or an exchange of a promise for an act.

DEFINITION

A **contract** is generally defined as a legally enforceable exchange of promises or an exchange of a promise for an act that assures parties to an agreement that their promises will be enforceable. Contract law brings predictability to the exchange. For example, if a corporation manufacturing video recorders enters into an agreement with a retailer to provide a fixed number of video recorders each month, the retailer knows that it can rely on the corporation's promise and advertise the availability of those video recorders to its customers because if the manufacturer reneges on the agreement, it is enforceable in a court of law. Contracts are essential to the workings of a private enterprise economy. They assist parties in the buying and selling of goods, and they make it possible to shift risks to parties more willing to bear them.

SOURCES OF CONTRACT LAW

Contract law is grounded in the case law of the state and federal courts as well as in state and federal statutory law. Case law, or what is often known as the common law because it originates with the law of English courts, governs contracts dealing with real property, personal property, services, and employment contracts. Statutory law, particularly the Uniform Commercial Code (UCC), generally governs contracts for the sale of goods. The UCC has been adopted in whole or in part by all 50 states and the District of Columbia. This chapter emphasizes case law because that is the source of most of the principles of contract law.

CASE LAW   The law of contracts originated in judicial decisions in England and the United States. Later, states and the federal courts modified their case law through the use of statutory law. Nonetheless, the formation of contract

"No, Mr. Foster, I'm afraid that keeping your fingers crossed during the signing of the contract did not render it unenforceable."

law and its understanding are based on fundamental principles set out by the courts and, more recently, in the *Restatement of the Law of Contracts*. The restatement summarizes contract principles as set out by legal scholars. Case law (or common law) applies to contracts that cover real property (land and anything attached permanently therein), personal property, services, and employment contracts.

UNIFORM COMMERCIAL CODE In order to obtain uniformity among state laws, particularly as applicable to sales contracts, the National Conference of Commissioners on Uniform State Laws and the American Law Institute drafted a set of commercial laws applicable to all states. This effort was called the *Uniform Commercial Code (UCC)*. (Article II of the Uniform Commercial Code: http://law.cornell.edu/ucc/2/overview.html) Gradually, the states adopted the document in whole or in part. Businesses now had uniform requirements that expedite interstate contracts. In general, Article II of the UCC allows more liberal requirements to form and perform contracts than are allowed in contracts based on common law principles. Particular differences are noted in sections of this and the next chapter. Article II is being revised to provide coverage of contracts dealing with electronic data processing, licenses, leases, and matters dealing with computer software.

CLASSIFICATIONS OF CONTRACTS

Terms that refer to types of contracts are sprinkled throughout this text. So that you will clearly understand what we are talking about, we define several classifications of contracts here.

express contract An exchange of oral or written promises between parties that are enforceable in a court of law.

EXPRESS AND IMPLIED CONTRACTS An **express contract** is an exchange of oral or written promises between parties that are enforceable in a court of law. Note that oral and written promises are equally enforceable. An **implied contract** is one that is established by the conduct of a party rather than by the party's written or spoken words. For example, if you go to the dentist in an emergency and have a tooth extracted, you and the dentist have an implied agreement contract: He will extract your throbbing tooth in a professional manner and you will pay him for his service. The existence and content of an implied contract are determined by the reasonable-person test: Would a reasonable person expect the conduct of the parties to constitute an enforceable contract?

implied contract One that is established by the conduct of a party rather than by the party's written or spoken words.

unilateral contract An exchange of a promise for an act.

UNILATERAL AND BILATERAL CONTRACTS A **unilateral contract** is defined as an exchange of a promise for an act. For example, if City A promises to pay a reward of $5,000 to anyone who provides information leading to the arrest and conviction of the individual who robbed a local bank, the promise is accepted by the act of the person who provides the information. A **bilateral contract** involves the exchange of one promise for another promise. For example, Jones promises to pay Smith $5,000 for a piece of land in exchange for Smith's promise to deliver clear title and a deed at a later date.

bilateral contract The exchange of one promise for another promise.

void contract One that at its formation has an illegal object of serious defects.

VOID, VOIDABLE, AND VALID CONTRACTS A contract is **void** if at its formation its object is illegal or it has serious defects in its formation (e.g., fraud). If Jones promises to pay Smith $5,000 to kill Clark, the contract is void at its formation because killing another person without court sanction is illegal. A contract is **voidable** if one of the parties has the option of either withdrawing from the contract or enforcing it. If Jones, a 17-year-old in a state where the legal age for entering an enforceable contract is 18, executes an agreement with Smith, an adult, to buy a car, Jones can rescind (cancel) the contract before he or she is 18 or shortly thereafter. A **valid contract** is one that is *not* void, is enforceable, and meets the six requirements discussed later in this chapter.

voidable contract One that gives one of the parties the option of withdrawing.

valid contract One that meets all legal requirements for a fully enforceable contract.

EXECUTED AND EXECUTORY CONTRACTS   An **executed contract** is one for which all the terms have been performed. In our earlier example, if Jones agrees to buy Smith's land for $5,000, and Smith, delivers clear title and a deed and Jones gives Smith $5,000, the necessary terms (assuming no fraud) have been carried out or performed. In contrast, an **executory contract** is one for which all the terms have not been completed or performed. If Jones agrees to paint Smith's house for $2,500 and Smith promises to pay the $2,500 upon completion of the paint job, the contract remains executory until the house is completely painted. The importance of complete performance will be shown when discharge and remedies for a breach of contract are examined in chapter 10.

QUASI-CONTRACT   A **quasi-contract** is a court-imposed agreement to prevent unjust enrichment of one party when the parties had not really agreed to an enforceable contract. For example, while visiting his neighbor, Johnson, Jones sees a truck pull up at his own residence. Two people emerge and begin cutting his lawn and doing other landscaping work. Jones knows that neither he nor his wife contracted to have this work performed; nevertheless, he likes the job that's being done, so he says nothing. When the landscapers finish, they put a bill in Jones's mailbox and drive off. It turns out that the landscapers made an honest mistake: They landscaped Jones's property when they were supposed to landscape Smith's. Jones refuses to pay the bill, arguing that he did not contract for this work. He even calls the landscapers unflattering names. The court orders Jones to pay, finding that he was unjustly enriched. (Jones would not have had to pay if he had not been in a position to correct the mistake before it took place. That is, Jones would not have had to pay had this mistaken landscaping occurred while he and his wife were vacationing in Paris.) Quasi-contracts are rare.

ELEMENTS OF A LEGAL CONTRACT

A valid contract has six elements: (1) legal offer, (2) legal acceptance, (3) consideration, (4) genuine assent, (5) competent parties, and (6) a legal object. When these six elements are present, a legally enforceable contract usually exists.

LEGAL OFFER

The contractual process begins with a **legal offer**. "I will pay you $2,000 for your 1978 Cutlass," Smith says to Jones. Smith has initiated a possible contract and is known as the *offeror*. Jones is the *offeree*. In order for Smith's offer to be valid, by common law principles, it must meet three requirements:

1. The offer must show *objective intent* to enter into the contract. The court will look at the words, conduct, writing, and, in some cases, deliberate omissions of the offer. The court will not concern itself with subjective measurements, such as what was in the person's mind at the time of entering the contract. It will simply ask whether a reasonable person who listened to Smith's statements would conclude that there was a serious intent to make an offer.

2. The offer must be *definite*; that is, there must be some reference to subject matter, quantity of items being offered, and price of the items. In Smith's offer, all three references are present. (Article II of the UCC, because it is intended to govern daily transactions in goods is less stringent. It allows the price and other terms—but not subject matter or quantity—to remain open or to be based on an industry standard of "reasonableness." X offers to sell "20 widgets that are needed" to Y at a "reasonable price with specific terms to be negotiated" is an example of the more open-ended approach to legal offers taken by the UCC.)

3. The offer must be *communicated* to the party (offeree) intended by the offeror. Smith's offer was communicated directly to Jones, but what of an

executed contract One for which all the terms have been performed.

executory contract One for which all the terms have not been performed.

quasi-contract A court-imposed agreement to present the unjust enrichment of one party when the parties had not really agreed to an enforceable contract.

legal offer An offer that shows objective intent to enter into the contract, is definite, and is communicated to the offeree.

offer by Bank X to pay for information leading to the arrest and conviction of Y, a robber? Z does not know of the reward, but several days after it is offered, she sees Y running out of a store with something in his hand. Z apprehends Y. Should she get the reward from Bank X? The bank's offer of a reward was not communicated to her, so the technical requirements of contract law have not been met. Most state courts, however, and many state statutes, provide that Z will be able to collect, for it is public policy to encourage citizens to assist in apprehending criminals.

In the following case, the court examined an advertisement's intent, its definiteness, and to whom it was communicated in determining whether a legal offer existed.

CHANG V. FIRST COLONIAL SAVINGS BANK
SUPREME COURT OF VIRGINIA 410 S.E.2D 928 (1991)

First Colonial Savings Bank ran an advertisement in a Richmond, Virginia, newspaper that read, in part:

> ### *You Win 2 ways*
> *WITH FIRST COLONIAL'S*
> ### *Savings Certificates*
> *1. Great Gifts & 2. High Interest*
>
> . . .
>
> *Saving at First Colonial is a very rewarding experience. In appreciation for your business we have Great Gifts for you to enjoy NOW—and when your investment matures you get your entire principal back PLUS GREAT INTEREST.*
>
> *Plan B: 3 $\frac{1}{2}$ Year Investment*
>
> . . .
>
> *Deposit $14,000 and receive two gifts: a Remington Shotgun and GE CB Radio, OR an RCA 20" Color-Trac TV and $20,136.12 upon maturity in 3 $\frac{1}{2}$ years.*
>
> *Substantial penalty for early withdrawal. Allow 4–6 weeks for delivery. Wholesale cost of gifts must be reported on IRS Form 1099. Rates shown are . . . 8 $\frac{3}{4}$ % for Plan B. All gifts are fully warranted by manufacturer. DEPOSITS INSURED TO $100,000 by FSLIC. Interest can be received monthly by check.*

Relying on this advertisement, the Changs deposited $14,000 in First Colonial and received a certificate of deposit and a color television. But when they returned three and one half years later to collect their interest, the bank informed them that the advertisement had contained a typographical error: They actually needed to have deposited $15,000 in order to receive $20,136.12 upon the maturing of the certificate of deposit. The bank did not inform the Changs of the typo until after the certificate had matured, but it did display pamphlets in its lobby containing the correct figures at the time the Changs made the deposit. The Changs argued that members of the public should be able to reasonably rely upon an advertisement that is so specific about the dollar amount to be received in interest upon maturity in return for a certain deposited sum; that is, the advertisement constituted a legal offer that could be accepted. The bank argued that the advertisement did not constitute a legal offer but only an invitation to the public to make an offer. The state district court ruled in favor of the Changs. The appeals court reversed in favor of the bank. The Changs appealed to the Supreme Court of Virginia.

JUDGE HASSELL

The general rule followed in most states, and which we adopt, is that newspaper advertisements are not offers, but merely invitations to bargain. However, there is a very narrow and limited exception to this rule. "[W]here the offer is clear, definite, and explicit, and leaves nothing open for negotiation, it constitutes an offer, acceptance of which will complete the contract."

Applying these principles to the facts before us, we hold that the advertisement constituted an offer which was accepted when the Changs deposited their $14,000 with the bank for a period of three and one-half years. A plain reading of the advertisement demonstrates that First Colonial's offer of the television and $20,136.12 upon maturity in three and one-half years was clear, definite, and explicit and left nothing open for negotiation.

Even though the bank's advertisement upon which the Changs relied may have contained a mistake caused by a typographical error, under the unique facts and circumstances of this case, the error does not invalidate the offer. First Colonial did not inform the Changs of this typographical error until after it had the use of the Changs' $14,000 for three and one-half years. Additionally, applying the general rule to which there are certain exceptions not applicable here, a unilateral mistake does not void an otherwise legally binding contract.

Reversed in favor of Appellants, Changs.

Critical Thinking about the Law

WHEN A COURT MAKES A DECISION it focuses on a particular group of facts. One aspect of legal reasoning that is distinct from reasoning in most other fields is its focus on the unique setting and circumstances of the individual case. Therefore, thinking critically about legal reasoning requires us to focus on that group of facts that the court has before it. The court is not making a general ruling that applies to any and all fact patterns; it is saying, rather, in this situation, here is how existing rules of law apply.

Consequently, the two questions here encourage you once again to find the key facts of the case and to consider their importance in shaping the finding of the court.

1. If you had to pick out one fact that is crucial to the court's reversal of the appeal court's finding for the defendant, what would it be?

   CLUE Reread the court's reasoning. What fact does the judge seem to rely on most to support his argument?

2. To demonstrate your appreciation of the importance of the specific context in determining the court's decision, construct a different advertisement that would have protected First Colonial from an adverse decision like this one.

   CLUE Use your answer to Question 1 to redesign the advertisement. Try to stick as closely as you can to the intent First Colonial had in its own advertisement. In other words, accomplish the bank's purpose, but avoid legal liability.

METHODS OF TERMINATION OF AN OFFER There are generally five methods of termination of an offer under the common law.

   1. *Lapse of time.* The failure of the offeree to respond within a reasonable time (e.g., 30 days) will cause an offer to lapse.
   2. *Death of either party.* However, the death of the agent of a corporation will not terminate the contract because the company will continue in most cases.
   3. *Destruction of the subject matter.* If the item contracted for cannot be replaced because of an accident not the fault of the offeror, the offer may be terminated.
   4. *Rejection by the offeree.* If the offeree does not accept the offer, it is terminated.
   5. *Revocation by the offeror.* If the offeror withdraws the offer before the offeree accepts it, the offer is terminated. The UCC differs somewhat from the common law in methods of termination of an offer. Here are some examples.

Rejection by the Offeree At *common law* a counteroffer by the offeree constitutes *rejection* (method 4 above) and brings about a termination of the offer. For example, suppose Jones offers to sell his house for $200,000 and no more or less. If Smith offers Jones $185,000, Smith has terminated the original offer and now has set forth a counteroffer ($185,000), which Jones can either accept or reject.

The *Uniform Commercial Code*, Section 2-207, allows for modification by offerees when dealing with the sale of goods. For example, in the case of *nonmerchants*, such as Smith and Jones above, a counteroffer by the offeree (Smith) does not constitute a rejection because there is still a clear intent to contract, but the additional term added by the offeree will not become part of the contract. For example, suppose Smith offers to sell his bicycle to Jones for $300. If Jones tells Smith that he will buy his bicycle for the amount of $300 if he (Smith) paints it black, a contract exists even if the painting of the bicycle was not part of the original offer by Smith.

If both parties to a contract for goods are *merchants*, under Section 2-207, added terms to a contract by an offeree will become additional terms and part of an enforceable contract unless one of the following conditions exists: (1) the added terms are material to the contract; or (2) the offeror limited the term of the original offer to the offeree by placing it in writing; or (3) one of the parties objects to any added term within a reasonable period of time.

Revocation by the Offeror   At *common law* the offer is terminated if the offeror notifies the offeree that the offer is no longer good before the offeree accepts it (revocation; method 5 above). An offeree can forestall that type of termination by paying an offeror an amount of money to keep the offer open for a time. This tactic is called an *option*, and usually it will exist for 30 days. During this time the offeror can neither sell the property to another nor revoke the offer. Under the *UCC* a firm offer made by a merchant in writing, and signed by the merchant with another, must be held open for a definite period (three months). The firm offer cannot be revoked, and no consideration is required (the offeree need not buy an option).

LEGAL ACCEPTANCE

legal acceptance An acceptance that shows objective intent to enter into the contract, that is communicated by proper means to the offeror, and that mirrors the terms of the offer.

Legal acceptance involves three requirements that must be met. In order for an acceptance to be valid:

1. An *intent* to accept must be shown by the offeree.
2. The intent must be *communicated* by proper means.
3. The intent must satisfy, or "mirror," the terms of the offer.

INTENT TO ACCEPT   There must be objective intent (words, conduct, writing) similar to that required of a legal offer. If Jones offers to sell Smith his 1978 Cutlass for $2,000 and Smith responds by stating, "I'll think it over," there is no objective intent to accept because there exists no present commitment on the part of Smith. In general, silence does not constitute acceptance unless prior conduct of the parties indicates that they assume that it does.

COMMUNICATION OF ACCEPTANCE   In general, any "reasonable means of communication" may be used in accepting an offer, and acceptances are generally binding upon the offeror when dispatched. Both industry custom and the subject matter will determine "reasonableness" in the eyes of a court. However, if the offeror requires that acceptance be communicated only in a certain form (e.g., letter) any other form that is used by the offeree (e.g., telegram) will delay the effectiveness of the acceptance until it reaches the offeror. If the offer states that "acceptance must be by mail" and the mails are used, the acceptance is effective upon deposit at the post office. If a telegram is used instead of mail, the acceptance will not be effective until it reaches the offeror.

Knowing whether there has been a valid acceptance is not always easy, as the following case against Pamela Lee Anderson, of *Baywatch* fame, illustrates.

THE PRIVATE MOVIE COMPANY, INC. V. PAMELA LEE ANDERSON ET AL.
SUPERIOR COURT OF CALIFORNIA, COUNTY OF LOS ANGELES (1997)

The plaintiff, Private Movie Company (Efraim), sued the defendant, Pamela Lee Anderson (Lee), for $4.6 million, alleging that she breached both an oral and a written contract so that she could work on a different project. The plaintiff claimed that an oral contract existed on November 18, 1994, when the parties agreed on all of the principal terms of a "deal," at the conclusion of a "business meeting" at the offices of defendant's personal manager. The plaintiff claimed that a written contract was entered into on December 21, 1994, when the plaintiff's lawyer sent the defendant copies of a "long-form" contract [Exhibit 10]. The plaintiff claimed that Exhibit 10 was a written embodiment of the oral agreement reached on November 18, 1994.

The somewhat confusing facts that were testified to, and disputed, at trial made it difficult for the judge to determine whether a contract existed. The events began in October of 1994, when plaintiff's attorney, Blaha, sent plaintiff's script to defendant's agent. After several conversations, an offer was sent to her agent. At trial, Efraim testified that Lee had said she loved the script and the character, but she testified that she was concerned about the nudity and sexual content of the script. Efraim said that he told Lee that the script would be rewritten and he would do whatever she wished regarding the nudity.

On November 18, a business meeting was held by Efraim, his attorney, the defendant's agents (Joel and Stevens) and manager (Brody), and the director, to negotiate a contract. Those present at the meeting testified that agreement was reached on: specific makeup person, security, trailer to be provided for Lee, start date, expenses and per diem. The issue of limiting the amount of nudity used in the trailer or any of the advertising material was raised. The issue of nudity in the film was apparently resolved by an understanding that Brody (defendant's manager) would provide a list of dos and don'ts and that Private Movie would abide by them. The structure of the agreement was also discussed with an understanding that there would be two contracts—i.e., an acting contract and a consulting contract—thereby allowing Private Movie to save money relating to payment of benefits. The issue of the sexual content or simulated sex in the movie script was not raised at the meeting. Nor was the issue of the rewrite of the script raised at the meeting. At the end of the meeting, Efraim asked Defendant's agent whether the deal was closed if Anderson's compensation was increased to $200,000. He said yes.

A few days later Efraim had his attorney draft the agreement with the increased compensation. Several drafts were exchanged between the attorney and defendant's agent, all containing the following nudity clause:

> NUDITY. The parties hereto acknowledge that the Picture will include "nude and/or simulated sex scenes." Player has read the screenplay of the Picture prior to receipt of the Agreement and hereby consents to being photographed in such scenes, provided that such "nude and simulated sex scenes" will not be hanged nor photographed in a manner different from what has been agreed to unless mutually approved by Artist and producer.

The rewritten script was sent to defendant on December 27, 1994. Plaintiff's attorney testified that he called defendant on December 29, 1994, and she said the script was great, but she wanted a different makeup artist and would split the difference in cost. Defendant testified that she recalled no such phone call. She said that she reviewed the script on January 1, 1995, saw that the simulated sex scenes remained, and called her manager to tell him she would not do the film.

Plaintiff found a less well known actress to make the film and brought his action against the defendant.

JUDGE HOROWITZ

When the parties orally or in writing agree that the terms of a proposed contract are to be reduced to writing and signed by them before it is to be effective, there is no binding agreement until a written contract is signed. If the parties have orally agreed on the terms and conditions of a contract with the mutual intention that it shall thereupon become binding, but also agree that a formal written agreement to the same effect shall be prepared and signed, the oral agreement is binding regardless of whether it is subsequently reduced to writing.

Whether it is the intention of the parties that the agreement should be binding at once, or when later reduced to writing, or to a more formal writing, is an issue to be determined by reference to the words the parties used, as well as [based on] all of the surrounding facts and circumstances.

One of the essential elements to the existence of a contract is the consent of the parties. This consent must be freely given, mutual, and communicated by each party to the other.

Consent is not mutual unless the parties all agree upon the same thing in the same sense. Ordinarily, it is the outward expression of consent that is controlling. Mutual consent arises out of the reasonable meaning of the words and acts of the parties, and not from any secret or unexpressed intention or understanding. In determining if there was mutual consent, the Court considers not only the words and conduct of the parties, but also the circumstances under which the words are used and the conduct occurs.

Parties may engage in preliminary negotiations, oral or written, before reaching an agreement. These negotiations only result in a binding contract when all of the essential terms are definitely understood and agreed upon even though the parties intend that formal writing including all of these terms shall be signed later.

An acceptance of an offer must be absolute and unconditional. All of the terms of the offer must be accepted without change or condition. A change in the terms set forth in the offer, or a conditional acceptance, is a rejection of the offer.

Plaintiff has presented no testimony that Lee, on 11/18/94, the date which Plaintiff alleged that an oral contract was created, personally agreed to perform in the movie Hello, She Lied; Plaintiff, therefore, has the burden of proving that Joel and/or Stevens, her "agent" and "manager," had the authority to bind her to an oral written contract.

The parties do not and did not agree on the definition of "simulated sex." Clearly the performance of simulated sexual scenes in the film was important and material to both Lee and Efraim. Efraim stated that he would abide by whatever Lee wanted in this regard.

Nudity and sexual content are material deal points that must be resolved before there can be a binding contract. An agreement concerning sexual content or simulated sex was not reached in this instance. Lee did not agree to the terms relating to simulated sex or to the script offered by the Plaintiff.

Plaintiff's letter of 1/13/95 to Lee claims she "agreed to perform simulated sex scenes, and the exact type of nudity had been agreed upon in detail." Efraim claimed in deposition that Lee agreed to perform simulated sex scenes and agreed to the draft contract to confirm that fact. Blaha testified that Paragraph 9 was a correct statement of the agreement. In deposition he stated it was a mistake. The rewritten script has three or four scenes that depict simulated sex. It is obvious that the "offer" made by Plaintiff concerning this issue was not complete and unqualified, nor was there any acceptance of this issue that was complete and unqualified.

Brody and Joel testified to their opinion that they thought they had "closed the deal" on 11/18/94 or shortly thereafter. Such perceptions have very little legal relevance. Brody testified that he had authority to negotiate this contract. Joel never spoke with Lee concerning the transaction and did not negotiate points such as script rewrite or sexual content.

Plaintiff has failed to prove by a preponderance of the evidence that Lee entered into an oral or written contract to perform in the movie *Hello, She Lied*.

Judgment in favor of Defendant, Lee.

SATISFYING, OR "MIRRORING," THE TERMS OF THE OFFER   Under the common law, to be valid, the acceptance must satisfy, or "mirror," the terms of the offer. For example, if Jones offers to sell Smith his Cutlass for $2,000, and Smith responds by saying, "I'll give you $1,800," this is not a legal acceptance but a counteroffer by Jones, which then must be accepted by Smith in order for the terms of the counteroffer to be satisfied and a contract to take place. Under the UCC, acceptance does not have to be a mirror image of the offer. Terms can be added to the contract without constituting a counteroffer if they meet one of the three conditions listed in the section on methods of termination of an offer.

CONSIDERATION

consideration A bargained-for exchange of promises in which a legal detriment is suffered by the promisee.

Consideration is defined as a bargained-for exchange of promises in which a legal detriment is suffered by the promisee. For example, Smith promises Jones that if she gives up her job with Stone Corporation, he will employ her at Brick Corporation. The two requirements of consideration are met: (1) Smith (promisor) has bargained for a return promise from Jones (promisee) that she will give up her job; (2) when Jones gives up her job, she has lost a legal right, the contractual right to her present job with Stone Corporation. The reader should note that *legal* detriment (giving up a *legal* right or refraining from exercising a legal right) must take place. *Economic* detriment is not necessary. For example, a student agrees to not go to any bars during fall semester in exchange for his mother's promise to give him $500. The student's giving up his right to go to the bars is a legal detriment because he now cannot do something he previously could legally do.

ADEQUACY OF CONSIDERATION   In general the courts have not been concerned with the amount of consideration involved in a contract, especially in a business context. If one party makes a bad deal with another party—that is, if the consideration is inadequate—the courts will usually refuse to interfere. Unless a party can show fraud, duress, undue influence, or mistake, the court will not intervene on behalf of a plaintiff. Sufficiency of consideration as opposed to adequacy will be examined by the court. Sufficiency of consideration requires both a bargained-for exchange of promises and legal detriment to the promisee.

PREEXISTING DUTY RULE   In defining consideration, we said that a legal detriment to a promisee requires the giving up of a legal right or the refraining from exercising a right. Logically, the courts have then declared that if a party merely agrees to do what he or she is required to do, there exists no detriment to the promisee. For example, Smith contracted with Jones for Jones to build him a house by April 1, 1988, for $150,000. On February 1, 1988, Jones came to

Smith and said that, because of the number of jobs he has, he wouldn't be able to finish by April unless Smith agreed to a bonus of $10,000. Smith agreed to the bonus, and the house was completed by April 1. Smith refused to pay, claiming that there was a *preexisting duty* on the part of Jones because he had a contractual duty to finish by April 1. Jones took him to court but lost the suit because no consideration existed for the bonus agreement. There is an important exception to the preexisting duty rule: the UCC, which applies to the sale of goods, states that an agreement modifying the original contract needs no consideration to be binding.

PROMISES ENFORCEABLE WITHOUT CONSIDERATION The courts have enforced certain contracts when the requirements of consideration were not met, using the doctrine of *promissory estoppel* to do so. This doctrine requires (1) a promise justifiably relied on by the promissee, (2) substantial economic detriment to the promissee, and (3) an injustice that cannot be avoided except by enforcing the contract. Consider this hypothetical example. An elderly couple pledged in writing to leave $1 million to their family church for a building fund if the church raised another $1 million. The church accepted the offer, raised the matching funds, and contracted with an architect and builder. The couple died and, in their will, left the money to another church. When the family church sued the deceased's estate on the basis of the promissory estoppel doctrine, the court awarded it the full amount pledged, even though a *bargained for exchange of promises* did not exist. There was a justifiable reliance by the family church upon the couple's promise, causing substantial economic injury to the church, and injustice could not be avoided in any other way.

LIQUIDATED AND UNLIQUIDATED DEBTS A *liquidated debt* exists when there is *no dispute* about the amount or other terms of the debt. If A owes B and C $500,000, and B and C agree to accept $100,000 as settlement for the debt, they are not precluded from suing A later on for the balance. The courts reason that the first agreement by A to pay a particular amount ($500,000) to B and C was supported by consideration. The second agreement to pay $100,000 was not because A had a preexisting duty to pay $500,000, and there was therefore no legal detriment on A's part to support B and C's promise to accept the lesser amount.

An *unliquidated debt* exists when there is a *dispute* between the parties as to the amount owed by the debtor. If an agreement similar to the one above, except that the amount A originally owed B, and C is in dispute, the general rule is that there exists consideration for the *second* agreement, and the creditors cannot come back and sue for the balance of what they thought they were owed. B and C would have no claim for the full $500,000, but would be limited to $100,000. The rationale is that new consideration was given for the second agreement. There exists a legal detriment because B and C are giving up a legal right to sue for an *unspecified* debt. The debtor is also giving up a legal right because there is *uncertainty* as to what he or she owes in an unliquidated debt situation.

GENUINE ASSENT

When two parties enter into a legally enforceable contract, it is presumed that they have entered of their own free will and that the two parties understand the content of the contract in the same way. If *fraud*, *duress*, *undue influence*, or *mutual mistake* exists, **genuine assent**, or a "meeting of the minds," has not taken place, and grounds for rescission (cancellation) of the contract exist. Table 9-1 lists the factors that prevent genuine assent.

FRAUD **Fraud** consists of (1) a misrepresentation of a *material* (significant) fact, (2) made with *intent to deceive* the other party, (3) who reasonably *relies* upon the misrepresentation, (4) and as a result is *injured*. For example, Smith enters into a contract to sell a house to Jones. The house is 12 years old, and Smith

genuine assent Assent to a contract that is free of fraud, duress, undue influence, and mutual mistake.

fraud Misrepresentation of a material fact made with intent to deceive the other party, who reasonably relied upon the misrepresentation and was injured as a result. See also criminal fraud.

TABLE 9-1 *Factors Preventing Genuine Assent*

- Fraud
- Duress
- Undue influence
- Mistake
    Bilateral
    Unilateral

notices that the basement is sinking. He fails to tell Jones. After Jones moves in, he finds that the house is sinking about two feet a year. In this case, there existed a misrepresentation of a material fact because there existed a duty on the part of Smith to disclose the fact that the house was sinking. Further, there existed knowledge of the fact with *intent to deceive.* The law does not require that an evil motive exist, but only that the selling party (Smith) knew and recklessly disregarded the fact that the house was sinking. *Reliance* existed on the part of Jones, who thought the house was habitable, and of course *injury* to Jones took place because the house was not worth what he paid for it. The cost of preventing further sinking of the house would be part of the damages involved. The case here illustrates fraud based upon a unique set of facts.

STAMBOVSKY V. ACKLEY AND ELLIS REALTY

SUPREME COURT, APPELLATE DIVISION STATE OF NEW YORK
169 A.D.2D 254 (1991)

Plaintiff Stambovsky purchased a home from Ackley, who was represented by Ellis Realty. After entering the contract but before closing, Stambovsky learned that the house was said to be possessed by poltergeists, reportedly seen by Ackley and her family on numerous occasions over the previous nine years. As a resident of New York City, Stambovsky was unaware that apparitions seen by the Ackleys were reported in the *Reader's Digest* and the local press of Nyack, New York. The house was also included in 1989 on a five-home walking tour, in which the house was described as "a riverfront Victorian (with ghost)." Stambovsky brought an action for rescission of the contract, arguing that the reputation of the house impaired the present value of the property and its resale value. He argued that the failure of the Ackleys and Ellis Realty Company to disclose the nature of the house as haunted was fraudulent in nature. The defendants argued that the principle of *caveat emptor* (buyer beware) applied in the state of New York and they had no affirmative duty to disclose nonmaterial matters. They moved for dismissal. The lower court granted the dismissal. The plaintiff appealed.

JUDGE RUBIN

While I agree with [the] Supreme Court [New York's trial court] that the real estate broker, as agent for the seller, is under no duty to disclose to a potential buyer the phantasmal reputation of the premises and that, in his pursuit of a legal remedy for fraudulent misrepresentation against

the seller, plaintiff hasn't a ghost of a chance, I am nevertheless moved by the spirit of equity to allow the buyer to seek rescission of the contract of sale and recovery of his down payment. New York law fails to recognize any remedy for damages incurred as a result of the seller's mere silence, applying instead the strict rule of caveat emptor. Therefore, the theoretical basis for granting relief, even under the extraordinary facts of this case, is elusive if not ephemeral.

"Pity me not but lend they serious hearing to what I shall unfold" (William Shakespeare, *Hamlet*, Act I, Scene V [Ghost]).

From the perspective of a person in the position of plaintiff herein, a very practical problem arises with respect to the discovery of a paranormal phenomenon: "Who you gonna' call?" as the title song to the movie *Ghostbusters* asks. Applying the strict rule of caveat emptor to a contract involving a house possessed by poltergeists conjures up visions of a psychic or medium routinely accompanying the structural engineer and Terminix man on an inspection of every home subject to a contract of sale. It portends that the prudent attorney will establish an escrow account lest the subject of the transaction come back to haunt him and his client—or pray that his malpractice insurance coverage extends to supernatural disasters. In the interest of avoiding such untenable consequences, the notion that a haunting is a condition which can and should be ascertained upon reasonable inspection of the premises is a hobgoblin which should be exorcised from the body of legal precedent and laid quietly to rest.

The doctrine of caveat emptor requires that a buyer act prudently to assess the fitness and value of his purchase and operates to bar the purchaser who fails to exercise due care from seeking the equitable remedy of rescission. For the purposes of the instant motion to dismiss the action, the plaintiff is entitled to every favorable inference which may reasonably be drawn from the pleadings; specifically, in this instance, that he met his obligation to conduct an inspection of the premises and a search of available public records with most meticulous inspection and the search would not reveal the presence of poltergeists at the premises or unearth the property's ghoulish reputation in the community. Therefore, there is no sound policy reason to deny plaintiff relief for failing to discover a state of affairs which the most prudent purchaser would not be expected to even contemplate.

The case law in this jurisdiction dealing with the duty of a vendor of real property to disclose information to the buyer is distinguishable from the matter under review. The most salient distinction is that existing cases invariably deal with the physical condition of the premises and other factors affecting its operation. No case has been brought to this court's attention in which the property value was impaired as the result of the reputation created by information disseminated to the public by the seller (or, for that matter, as a result of possession by poltergeists). Where a condition which has been created by the seller materially impairs the value of the contract and is peculiarly within the knowledge of the seller or unlikely to be discovered by a prudent purchaser exercising due care with respect to the subject transaction, nondisclosure constitutes a basis for rescission as a matter of equity. Any other outcome places upon the buyer not merely the obligation to exercise care in his purchase but rather to be omniscient with respect to any fact which may affect the bargain. No practical purpose is served by imposing such a burden upon a purchaser. To the contrary, it encourages predatory business practice and offends the principle that equity will suffer no wrong to be without a remedy.

In the case at bar, defendant seller deliberately fostered the public belief that her home was possessed. Having undertaken to inform the public at large, to whom she has no legal relationship, about the supernatural occurrences on her property, she may be said to owe no less a duty to her contract vendee. It has been remarked that the occasional modern cases which permit a seller to take unfair advantage of a buyer's ignorance but has created and perpetuated a condition about which he is unlikely to even inquire, enforcement of the contract (in whole or in part) is offensive to the court's sense of equity. Application of the remedy of rescission, within the bounds of the narrow exception to the doctrine of caveat emptor set forth herein, is entirely appropriate to relieve the unwitting purchaser from the consequences of a most unnatural bargain.

Reversed in favor of Plaintiff, Stambovsky.

DISSENTING OPINION

The parties herein were represented by counsel and dealt at arm's length. This is evidenced by the contract of sale which contained various riders and a specific provision that all prior understandings and agreements between the parties were merged into the contract, that the contract completely expressed their full agreement and that neither had relied upon any statement by anyone else not set forth in the contract. There is no allegation that defendants, by some specific act, other than the failure to speak, deceived the plaintiff. Nevertheless, a cause of action may be sufficiently stated where there is a confidential or fiduciary relationship creating a duty to disclose and there was a failure to disclose a material fact, calculated to induce a false belief. However, plaintiff herein has not alleged and there is no basis for concluding that a confidential or fiduciary relationship existed between these parties to an arm's length transaction such as to give rise to a duty to disclose. In addition, there is no allegation that defendants thwarted plaintiff's efforts to fulfill his responsibilities fixed by the doctrine of caveat emptor.

DURESS   Another factor that prevents genuine assent of the parties is **duress**, defined as any wrongful act or threat that prevents a party from exercising free will when executing a contract. The state of mind of the party at the time of entering into the contract is important. If Smith, when executing a contract with Jones to sell a house, holds a gun on Jones and threatens to shoot Jones if he refuses to sign the contract, grounds exist for rescission of the contract. Duress is not limited to physical threats, however. Threats of economic ruin or public embarrassment also constitute duress.

UNDUE INFLUENCE   If one party exerts mental coercion over the other party, there is **undue influence** and therefore no genuine assent. There are two court-established requirements for undue influence: (1) There must be a dominant-subservient relationship between the contrasting parties (e.g., a doctor-patient, lawyer-client, or any trusting relationship); (2) this dominant-subservient

duress Any wrongful act or threat that prevents a party from exercising free will when executing a contract.

undue influence Mental coercion exerted by one party over the other party to the contract.

relationship must allow one party to influence the other in a mentally coercive way. An example of coercion that meets these requirements is a dying patient's contracting with a family doctor to sell the doctor his family land at an unreasonably low price in order to pay his doctor bills. The case set out here illustrates the court's approach to fraud, duress, and (particularly) undue influence.

ODORIZZI V. BLOOMFIELD SCHOOL DISTRICT
CALIFORNIA COURT OF APPEALS 54 CAL. RPTR. 533 (1966)

Plaintiff-appellant Odorizzi was employed as a teacher in the Bloomfield School District (defendant-respondent) in 1964 and had signed a contract for the following year. He was arrested on June 11 and submitted his resignation on June 13 to the principal and superintendent. They accepted it. In July of 1964 criminal charges were dismissed, and he sought to be reinstated. When the district refused, he sued, claiming his resignation was invalid owing to fraud, duress, and undue influence. He asserted that on the day after his arrest, after he had been up all night, the superintendent of his district and the principal of the school came to his apartment and demanded his resignation, claiming that they would publicize his arrest and cause him great embarrassment if he did not resign. He claimed that they also stated that they would see that he never got another job. The trial court ruled in favor of the school district. Odorozzi appealed.

JUDGE FLEMING

Duress consists in unlawful confinement of another's person, or relatives, or property, which causes him to consent to a transaction through fear. Duress is often used interchangeably with menace, but in California menace is technically a threat of duress or a threat of injury to the person, property, or character of another. We agree with respondent's contention that neither duress nor menace was involved in this case, because the action is not unlawful unless the party making the threat knows the falsity of his claim. The amended complaint shows in substance that the school representatives announced their intention to initiate suspension and dismissal proceedings at a time when the filing of such proceedings was not only their legal right but their positive duty as school officials. Although the filing of such proceedings might be extremely damaging to plaintiff's reputation, the injury would remain incidental so long as the school officials acted in good faith in the performance of their duties. Neither duress nor menace was present as a ground for rescission.

Nor do we find a cause for fraud, either actual or constructive. Actual fraud involves conscious misrepresentation, or concealment, or non-disclosure of a material fact which induces the innocent party to enter the contract. A complaint for fraud must plea misrepresentation, knowledge of falsity, intent to induce reliance, justifiable reliance, and resulting damage. While the amended complaint charged misrepresentation, it failed to assert the elements of knowledge of falsity, intent to induce reliance, justifiable reliance, and resulting damage. A cause of action for actual fraud was therefore not stated.

Constructive fraud arises on a breach of duty by one in a confidential or fiduciary relationship to another which induces justifiable reliance by the latter to his prejudice. Plaintiff has attempted to bring himself within this category. Plaintiff, however, sets forth no facts to support his conclusion of a confidential relationship between the representatives of the school district and himself, other than that the parties bore the relationship of employer and employee to each other. Under prevailing judicial opinion no presumption of a confidential relationship arises from the bare fact that parties to a contract are employer and employee; rather, additional ties must be brought out in order to create the presumption of a confidential relationship between the two. The absence of a confidential relationship between employer and employee is especially apparent where, as here, the parties were negotiating to bring about a termination of their relationship. In such a situation each party is expected to look after his own interests, and a lack of confidentiality is implicit in the subject matter of their dealings. We think the allegations of constructive fraud were inadequate.

However, the pleading does set out a claim that plaintiff's consent to the transaction had been obtained through the use of undue influence.

Undue influence, in the sense we are concerned with here, is a shorthand legal phrase used to describe persuasion which tends to be coercive in nature, persuasion which overcomes the will without convincing the judgment. The hallmark of such persuasion is high pressure, a pressure which works on mental, moral, or emotional weakness to such an extent that it approaches the boundaries of coercion. In this sense, undue influence has been called overpersuasion.

Misrepresentations of law or fact are not essential to the charge, for a person's will may be overborne without misrepresentation. In essence, undue influence involves the use of excessive pressure to persuade one vulnerable to such pressure, pressure applied by a dominant subject to a servient object. In combination, the elements of undue susceptibility in the servient person and excessive pressure by the dominating person makes the latter's influence undue, for it results in the apparent will of the servient person being in fact the will of the dominant person.

In the present case plaintiff has pleaded that such weakness at the time he signed his resignation prevented him from freely and competently applying his judgment to the problem before him. Plaintiff declares he was under severe mental and emotional strain at the time because he had just completed the process of arrest, questioning, booking, and release on bail and had been without sleep for forty hours. It is possible that exhaustion and emotional turmoil may wholly incapacitate a person from exercising his judgment.

Undue influence in its second aspect involves an application of excessive strength by a dominant subject against a servient object. Judicial consideration of this second element in undue influence has been relatively rare, for there are few cases denying persons who persuade but do not misrepresent the benefit of their bargain. Yet logically, the same legal consequences should apply to the results of excessive strength as to the results of undue weakness. Whether from weakness on one side, or strength on the other, or a combination of the two, undue influence occurs whenever there results that kind of influence or supremacy of one mind over another by which that other is prevented from acting according to his own wish or judgment, and whereby the will of the person is overborne and he is induced to do or forbear to do an act which he would not do, or would do, if left to act freely. Undue influence involves a type of mismatch which our statute calls unfair advantage. Whether a person of subnormal capacities has been subjected to ordinary force or a person of normal capacities subjected to extraordinary force, the match is equally out of balance. If will has been overcome against judgment, consent may be rescinded.

Overpersuasion is generally accompanied by certain characteristics which tend to create a pattern. The pattern usually involves several of the following elements: (1) discussion of the transaction at an unusual or inappropriate time, (2) consummation of the transaction in an unusual place, (3) insistent demand that the business be finished at once, (4) extreme emphasis on untoward consequences of delay, (5) the use of multiple persuaders by the dominant side against a single servient party, (6) absence of third-party advisers to the servient party, (7) statements that there is no time to consult financial advisers or attorneys. If a number of these elements are simultaneously present, the persuasion may be characterized as excessive.

The difference between legitimate persuasion and excessive pressure, like the difference between seduction and rape, rests to a considerable extent in the manner in which the parties go about their business. For example, if a day or two after Odorizzi's release on bail the superintendent of the school district had called him into his office during business hours and directed his attention to those provisions of the Education Code compelling his leave of absence and authorizing his suspension on the filing of written charges, had told him that the District contemplated filing written charges against him, had pointed out the alternative of resignation available to him, had informed him he was free to consult counsel or any adviser he wished and to consider the matter overnight and return with his decision the next day, it is extremely unlikely that any complaint about the use of excessive pressure could ever have been made against the school district.

But, according to the allegations of the complaint, this is not the way it happened, and if it had happened that way, plaintiff would never have resigned. Rather, the representatives of the school board undertook to achieve their objective by overpersuasion and imposition to secure plaintiff's signature but not his consent to his resignation through a high-pressure carrot-and-stick technique—under which they assured plaintiff they were trying to assist him, he should rely on their advice, there wasn't time to consult an attorney, if he didn't resign at once the school district would suspend and dismiss him from his position and publicize the proceedings, but if he did resign the incident wouldn't jeopardize his chances of securing a teaching post elsewhere.

Plaintiff has thus pleaded both subjective and objective elements entering the undue influence equation and stated sufficient facts to put in issue the question whether his free will had been overborne by defendant's agents at a time when he was unable to function in a normal manner.

We express no opinion on the merits of plaintiff's case, or the propriety of his continuing to teach school, or the timeliness of his rescission. We do hold that his pleading, liberally construed, states a cause of action for rescission of a transaction to which his apparent consent had been obtained through the use of undue influence.

Reversed in favor of Plaintiff, Odorizzi.

MISTAKE   A **mistake** also prevents a meeting of the minds, or genuine assent. If both parties made an error as to a material fact a *mutual*, or *bilateral*, mistake has occurred, and as a general rule the courts will rescind such contracts. But if an error is made by only one party to the contract a *unilateral* mistake has occurred, and the courts will generally not grant the mistaken party a rescission of the contract. An exception to this rule is made if the nonmistaken party knew or should have known of the mistake. For example, if five contractors bid on a $10 million hospital project and Smith's bid is $2 million below all other bids because of an accountant's error, the hospital should have known of the error before accepting the bid, especially if Smith had immediately notified the hospital of the mathematical error and the contract was executory in nature.

mistake Error as to material fact. A *bilateral mistake* is one made by both parties; a *unilateral mistake* is one made by only one party to the contract.

competency A party's ability to understand the nature of the transaction and the consequences of entering into it at the time the contract was entered into.

The fifth essential element of a legally enforceable contract is **competency** of the parties. A person is presumed to be competent at the time of entering into a contract, so most people who raise the defense of a lack of capacity must prove that at the *time the contract was entered into* the individual did not have the ability to understand the nature of the transaction and the consequences of entering into it. This defense often arises when contracts involve minors or insane or intoxicated persons.

MINORS   A minor is a person under the legal age of majority. The states differ as to age of majority for entering into enforceable contracts. The age of majority for contractual capacity should not be confused with the age at which one can drink or can vote in state and federal elections. Contracts made by minors are voidable and can be *disaffirmed* by the minor at any time before the minor becomes of a majority age or shortly thereafter. If the minor fails to disaffirm a contract, he or she will be considered to have *ratified* (approved) it and is thus legally bound. For example Smith at age 17 years, three months, entered into a contract with Jones to buy the latter's automobile for $2,000. The state in which the contract was executed had a majority age of 18. After using the automobile for two years and a month, Smith returned the auto and asked for his $2,000 back, minus depreciation on the car, because he was only 17 when he entered the contract and he claimed that therefore the contract was voidable. Smith was not allowed to disaffirm his contract because he had ratified the agreement by failing to disaffirm it before age 18 or shortly thereafter.

A minor is generally liable for the reasonable value (not the contract or the market value) of *necessaries* (food, clothing, shelter) which enable the minor to live in a manner he or she is accustomed to. To avoid the issues of what constitutes a necessary, prudent businesspeople check purchasers' ages very carefully and require a parent or guardian to co-sign a loan when the borrower is a minor. For example, a student who is a minor for contractual purposes is not able to obtain a loan at a bank without a parent's signature, and merchants generally will check to see if a charge card in the possession of a minor is issued in a parent's name.

The following case illustrates the principle of disaffirmance and ratification by a minor. The court ruled in favor of the minor, allowing her to disaffirm the release and to sue the gymnastics club. Her mother, as an adult, was not allowed to disaffirm the release and thus could not sue.

TARA SIMMONS V. PARKETTE GYMNASTICS TRAINING CENTER
UNITED STATES DISTRICT COURT 670 F. SUPP. 140 (E.D. PA. 1987)

Tara Simmons, a minor, and her mother sued the defendant, a gymnastics organization, claiming injury as a result of the negligent acts or omissions of the defendant's employee. The defendant asserted that it was not responsible for Tara's injury because both she and her mother had signed a release absolving the gym from all liability for injuries suffered by the plaintiffs.

JUDGE TROUTMAN

The release asserted by the defendant provides as follows:

In consideration of my participation in Parkettes, I, intending to be legally bound, do hereby, for myself, my heirs, executors, and administrators, waive and release any and all right and claims for damages which I may hereafter accrue to me

against the United States Gymnastic Federation, the Parkette National Gymnastic Team, their officers, representatives, successors, and/or assigns for any and all damages which may be sustained and suffered by me in connection with my association with the above gymnastic program, or which may arise out of my traveling to or participating in and returning from any activity associated with the program.

Gymnast's Signature _____
/s/Tara Simmons

Signature of Parent _____
or Guardian   *(Father)*

_____
/s/Sharon Grenell   *(Mother)*

As can be seen, the release is prospective in nature, i.e., it purports to exculpate the defendant from future liability, as opposed to a release compromising and settling an already existing claim for damages. . . .

It is axiomatic under Pennsylvania law that a valid release is an absolute bar to recovery for everything included in the release, and it can only be set aside as *any contract* . . . in the presence of clear, precise and indubitable evidence of fraud, accidental means or *incompetence of the party who is alleged to have signed it.*

A. The Adult Plaintiff.

[1] As to the minor plaintiff's mother's claim, i.e., Count II of the complaint, we conclude that her cause of action is indeed barred by the exculpatory agreement she signed.

B. The Minor Plaintiff.

[2] The effect of the exculpatory agreement upon the minor plaintiff's claim for damages, i.e., Count I of the complaint, presents a somewhat more difficult question. It is hornbook contract law that a minor, with certain exceptions, is not competent to enter into a "valid" contract. . . . Where a minor executes a contract, however, the agreement is not "void," but rather "voidable." . . . After reaching the age of majority, the minor may disaffirm the contract, thereby rendering it a nullity. . . . An exculpatory agreement such as that involved herein is simply a specific type of contract. Syllogistically, therefore, one would assume that the minor plaintiff may nullify the release by disaffirming it and, apparently in response to the defendants' motion, this is what she has purported to do. . . .

Finally, it is this Court's experience that agreements such as that involved herein have become commonplace in our society with regard to organizations such as little league, scouting, midget football and so on. Thus, we believe our decision represents an important one because of the impact it may have upon such organizations.

Judgement in favor of Minor Plaintiff (child), and against Adult Plaintiff (mother).

INSANITY   If a person is adjudicated by a court of law to be insane, or is *de facto* (in fact) insane at the time of entering into a contract, the individual will be allowed to disaffirm a contract. Court-appointed guardians may also disaffirm such agreements.

INTOXICATION   A person who is intoxicated to the degree that understanding the nature of the contract and its consequences is impossible will be able to disaffirm a contract in all cases but those involving necessaries. It is the degree of intoxication that the court will look at. In order to disaffirm, the intoxicated individual will have to return the item bought. In the case of necessaries, the intoxicated individual is not allowed to disaffirm but is held liable for the reasonable value of such items.

LEGAL OBJECT

The sixth necessary element of a contract is a **legal object**. This means that the subject matter of the agreement must be lawful. If it is not, the contract is void at its inception. Contracts that are in violation of state or federal statutes, as well as those in violation of case law, are void as a matter of public policy.

legal object Contract subject matter that is lawful under statutory and case law.

STATUTORY LAW   State statutes that forbid wagering agreements (betting), usurious (defined as exorbitant) finance charges or interest rates on loans, as well as those aimed at licensing and regulation have been the source of much adjudication. If Smith practices law in a state without being admitted to practice before its highest state court, the courts will generally not enforce any contracts Smith made with clients for services rendered. Smith may also be subject to criminal charges. State statutes require licensing of nurses, doctors, accountants, real estate agents, electricians, and many other groups (the list varies from state to state) in order to protect the public from incompetents. Some opponents of these statutes argue that they were enacted at the behest of interest groups to decrease the supply of individuals in a particular profession or trade and hence prevent competition. Whatever their origin, however, courts will not enforce contracts made by unlicensed providers of these services.

CASE LAW   Often, when there is a question as to whether a contract has a lawful object, statutory law does not indicate clearly whether the contract is void or unenforceable. For example, agreements not to compete are found to be contrary to the public policy of fostering competition, and there are federal and state antitrust laws (statutes) making price fixing between competitors illegal and void. However, when an otherwise lawful contract of employment contains a no-competition clause whereby an employee agrees not to be employed by a competitor of his or her employer, the courts will look at whether the restriction on the employee is for a *reasonable* time and area. In addition, it will look at the relative bargaining power of the employer and employee and the hardship on the employee contractually forbidden to work for another employer in the same industry. As the following case shows, each factual situation is carefully examined, and the standard of reasonableness is used to determine whether the contract is enforceable.

NALCO CHEMICAL COMPANY V. HYDRO TECHNOLOGIES, INCORPORATED
UNITED STATES COURT OF APPEALS 984 F.2D 801 (7TH CIR. 1993)

Nalco Chemical Company ("Nalco") produces water treatment chemicals and services, offering to its customers more than 3,100 products and programs. It is a big company, employing more than 6,000 people in 12 operating groups. Two of those employees were Daniel Girmscheid and Thomas Broge. When Girmscheid and Broge began working for Nalco, they signed employment agreements containing clauses stating that they would not compete with Nalco if they left the company. The agreements are a form that Nalco uses for all employees.

> *Employee will not, directly or indirectly, during his employment and for the period of two (2) years immediately after its termination, engage or assist in the same or any similar line of business, competing with the line of business now or hereafter conducted or operated by Nalco during the term of Employee's employment by Nalco, whether as consultant, employee, officer, director, or representative of such competing business within the United States of America, provided, however, that in the event that the Employee's position with Nalco immediately prior to termination is that of field representative, then the geographic area of the non-competition covenant shall be limited to the geographic area within the United States of America for which Employee was responsible at any time during the two year period immediately preceding termination.*

Girmscheid and Broge were employed in the "Watergy" group, part of the Water and Waste Treatment Division. The Watergy group geographically divides the American market into districts. Girmscheid and Broge were assigned to district G-14, eastern Wisconsin and northern Illinois. Girmscheid was an account manager, and Broge was a district sales representative. Girmscheid and Broge left Nalco to work for a competitor, Hydro Technologies, Inc. (Hydro). Hydro conducts the same business as Nalco's Watergy division, and more than 20 Nalco customers switched to Hydro when Broge and Girmscheid joined the company.

Nalco sued Hydro for immediate enforcement of the employment agreements to bar Broge and Girmscheid from having contact with any more Nalco customers. The dis-

trict court construed paragraph five as prohibiting Girmscheid and Broge from contacting former or potential customers for two years in their district and issued a preliminary injunction. Hydro appealed.

JUDGE BAUER

Paragraph five is indisputably a covenant not to compete. It bars Broge and Girmscheid from competing for two years in the same or any similar business to Nalco's in the geographic area for which they were responsible immediately preceding their termination. Girmscheid's and Broge's attack on the clause is two-fold. First, that "the same or any similar business conducted or operated by Nalco" encompasses virtually all aspects of water treatment, not merely that conducted by the Watergy division. Second, that the geographic area for which they were responsible is not a reasonable restraint; the district is large, and the men serviced customers in only a few of the areas within the district.

Covenants not to compete are disfavored. Nonetheless, some covenants are enforceable. To determine if paragraph five is enforceable, we consider whether it (1) is necessary to protect Nalco's legitimate interests; (2) provides a reasonable time restriction; (3) provides a reasonable territorial restriction; (4) is harsh or oppressive to Girmscheid and Broge; and (5) is contrary to public policy.

Paragraph five states specifically that Broge and Girmscheid cannot "engage or assist in the same or any similar line of business, competing with the line of business now or hereafter conducted or operated by Nalco during the term of Employee's employment by Nalco. . . . " Nalco is a very large company, engaged in many facets of water treatment. It has a diverse organization of groups and divisions. The Waste and Water Treatment division is but one of twelve. The Watergy group is one of four within that division. Other divisions provide chemical products and services to many types of industries. The parties do not dispute that Girmscheid and Broge did not deal with any of these various enterprises. Therefore, the Nalco restraint exceeds the bounds of reason.

The business activity restraint is overbroad and violates three of the five factors under which noncompetition clauses are analyzed. First, it is much greater than that necessary to protect Nalco's legitimate interests; second, it is both harsh and oppressive to Girmscheid and Broge; and finally, such a broad restraint violates a public policy against barriers to competition.

Reversed in favor of Defendants, Hydro and Girmscheid and Broge.

Critical Thinking about the Law

*N*ALCO V. HYDRO IS A TYPICAL incident in the legal environment of business. Nalco has legitimate interests. After all, it trained and nurtured Girmscheid and Broge. Is it fair for the return on Nalco's investment to be received by Hydro?

Yet Hydro and its new employees have appropriate interests as well. Ordinarily an employer should be legally encouraged to hire the best possible employees. Girmscheid and Broge are not slaves. Isn't employee mobility a lubricant toward increased business efficiency?

Still another set of interests demands our allegiance. Notice that the court defends the need to promote competition. We, the consuming public, gain from the tension of multiple competitors, each striving to please us with high quality and low prices. Should Nalco's future profits be protected by reducing this productive tension?

1. As with any case, the *Nalco* decision was made on the basis of an incomplete set of facts. Study the three sets of interests outlined above. What missing information would you find useful to help you decide whether you believe the court reached a proper decision?

   CLUE View the situation from Nalco's perspective. What facts (not before the court, but yet quite possibly accurate) would have moved the court more toward upholding the agreement Nalco had with its two former employees?

2. Evaluate the implied analogy in the following analysis of *Nalco.*

   From the *Nalco* decision, I am convinced that a restrictive clause preventing an employee from working for a competitor cannot be enforced. Just as an agreement between an infant and an adult is invalid, an employee will not be held liable for agreements with large, complex employers like Nalco.

   CLUE Review the court's reasoning. Focus on *why* the agreement between Nalco and its former employees was not upheld. Now consider the elements in the attempted analogy.

CONTRACTS THAT MUST BE IN WRITING

Most contracts need not be in writing. They are enforceable as long as the six elements of a contract exist. However, the Statute of Frauds, which originated in England in 1677, requires certain business contracts to be in writing. Originally, those contracts listed in this section, and some other nonbusiness contracts, were required to be in writing because they were thought to be the most likely situations in which perjury would occur. Today, each state requires by statute that various contracts be written in order to be enforceable.

In most states, the requirements for a written contract include some evidence of writing and the signature of the party being sued. The writing should reasonably outline the terms and state who are the parties to the agreement. Contracts governed by the UCC do not have these requirements. The party suing may have the only evidence of writing with his or her signature on it. Often, between merchants, confirmation memoranda summarize oral agreements and are satisfied by only one party. The nonsigning party must simply review the memorandum. The Statute of Frauds is satisfied if the nonsigning party agrees to its content.

The business-related contracts in this section are those that most frequently fall *within* the Statute of Frauds. They therefore must be in writing to be enforceable.

CONTRACTS FOR THE SALE OF AN INTEREST IN LAND

An "interest in land" includes mortgages, easements (an easement is a contract that allows a party to cross your land, for example, with electrical wires), and of course the land itself and the buildings on it. Leases for longer than one year usually have to be in writing.

A notable exception to the requirement that contracts for sale of an interest in land must be written is part performance. For example, if substantial improvements have been made on a piece of property by a lessee in reliance on an oral commitment by the lessor to sell, the oral contract will be enforced.

CONTRACTS TO PAY THE DEBTS OF ANOTHER

If Smith promises to pay Jones's debt to the bank should Jones be unable to pay it, this contract must be in writing under the statute of frauds. In this case, Smith has *secondary liability to the bank*. If, however, Smith tells the bank that he will act as a surety for Jones's debt, Smith has a *primary liability to the bank*. This agreement is not within the Statue of Frauds, and therefore may be enforced even if oral.

In the first situation, Smith's promise was *conditional* in nature. That is, on condition that Jones does not pay, the bank may look to Smith, but first it must look to Jones. In the second situation, the bank may first look to Smith. It does not have to go to Jones at all because it has a guarantor or surety agreement with Smith.

CONTRACTS NOT PERFORMABLE IN ONE YEAR

A contract must be in writing if it specifies that it will last longer than one year. For example, in most states, a baseball player who agrees to play for a team for three years at $2 million a year must sign a written contract in order for it to be enforceable. If, however, no date is set in the contract for the completion of performance, the contract need not be in writing. For example, an agreement to provide help for a person until that person dies does not fall within the Statute of Frauds and thus does not have to be in writing to be enforceable.

SALE OF GOODS OF $500 OR MORE

Under the Uniform Commercial Code, contracts for the sale of goods of $500 or more fall within the Statute of Frauds and must be in writing to be enforced. There are three exceptions to this rule: (1) One of the parties to a suit admits in writing or in court to the existence of an oral contract; (2) a buyer accepts and uses the goods; (3) the contract is between merchants, and the merchant who is sued received a written confirmation of the oral agreement and did not object within ten days. In all of these instances, the oral contract will be enforced even if for goods worth $500 or more.

In the following case, the plaintiff claimed that an oral contract existed under the "merchants" and "partial performance" exceptions to the Statute of Frauds.

THOMSON PRINTING MACHINERY COMPANY V. B.F. GOODRICH COMPANY
UNITED STATES COURT OF APPEAL 714 F.2D 744 (7TH CIR. 1983)

Thomson Printing buys and sells used printing machinery. On Tuesday, April 10, 1979, the president of Thomson Printing, James Thomson, went to Goodrich's surplus machinery department in Akron, Ohio, to look at some used printing machinery that was for sale. James Thomson dis-

cussed the sale terms, including a price of $9,000, with Goodrich's surplus equipment manager, Ingram Meyers. Four days later, on Saturday, April 14, 1979, James Thomson sent to Goodrich in Akron a purchase order for the equipment and a check for $1,000 in part payment. Thomson Printing sued Goodrich when Goodrich refused to perform. Goodrich asserted by way of defense that no contract had been formed and that in any event the alleged oral contract was unenforceable due to the Statute of Frauds. Thomson Printing argued that a contract had been made and that the "merchants" and "partial performance" exceptions to the Statute of Frauds were applicable and satisfied. The jury found for Thomson Printing, but the district court entered a judgment for Goodrich on the grounds that the Statute of Frauds barred enforcement of the contract in Thomson's favor. Plaintiff, Thomson appealed.

JUDGE CUDAHY

A modern exception to the usual writing requirement is the "merchants" exception of the U.C.C. § 2-201(2), which provides:

> Between merchants if within a reasonable time a writing in confirmation of the contract and sufficient against the sender is received and the party receiving it has reason to know its contents, it satisfies the [writing requirement] against such party unless written notice of objection to its contents is given within 10 days after it is received.

We must emphasize that the only effect of this exception is to take away from a merchant who receives a writing in confirmation of a contract the Statute of Frauds defense if the merchant does not object. The sender must still persuade the trier of fact that a contract was in fact made orally, to which the written confirmation applies.

In the instant case, James Thomson sent a "writing in confirmation" to Goodrich four days after his meeting with Ingram Meyers, a Goodrich employee and agent. The purchase order contained Thomson Printing's name, address, telephone number and certain information about the machinery purchase. The check James Thomson sent to Goodrich with the purchase order also had Thomson's name and address on it. Goodrich argues, however, that Thomson's writing in confirmation cannot qualify for the 2-201(2) exception because it was not received by anyone at Goodrich who had reason to know its contents. Goodrich claims that Thomson erred in not specifically designating on the envelope, check or purchase order that the items were intended for Ingram Meyers or the surplus equipment. Consequently, Goodrich contends, it was unable to "find a home" for the check and purchase order despite attempts to do so, in accordance with its regular procedures, by sending copies of the documents to several of its various divisions. Ingram Meyers testified that he never learned of the purchase order until weeks later when James Thomson called to arrange for removal of the machines. By then, however, the machines had long been sold to someone else.

We think Goodrich misreads the requirements of 2-201(2). First, the literal requirements of 2-201(2), as they apply are that a writing "is received" and that Goodrich "has reason to know its contents." There is not dispute that the purchase order and check were received by Goodrich, and there is at least no specific or express requirement that the "receipt" referred to in 2-201(2) be by any Goodrich agent in particular.

These issues are not resolved by [2-201(2)], but it is probably a reasonable projection that a delivery at either the recipient's principal place of business, a place of business from which negotiations were conducted, or to which the sender may have transmitted previous communications, will be an adequate receipt.

As for the "reason to know its contents" requirement, this element "is best understood to mean that the confirmation was an instrument which should have been anticipated and therefore should have received the attention of appropriate parties."

Thus, the question comes down to whether Goodrich's mailroom, given the information it had, should have notified the surplus equipment manager, Ingram Meyers, of Thomson's confirmatory writing. At whatever point Meyers should have been so notified, then at that point Thomson's writing was effective even though Meyers did not see it.

We note that the jury verdict for Thomson Printing indicates that the jury found as a fact that the contract had in fact been made and that the Statute of Frauds had been satisfied. Also, Goodrich acknowledges those facts about the handling of the purchase order which we regard as determinative of the "merchants" exception question. We think that there is ample evidence to support the jury findings both of the existence of the contract and of the satisfaction of the Statute.

Reversed in favor of Plaintiff, Thomson.

NONBUSINESS CONTRACTS

Non-business-related contracts that must be in writing to be enforceable are (1) contracts in consideration of marriage and (2) contracts of an executor or administrator to answer for the debts of a deceased person.

PAROL EVIDENCE RULE

The **parol** (oral) **evidence rule** states that when parties have executed a *written* agreement, which is complete on its face, *oral* agreements made *prior to* or at the *same time as* the written agreement that *vary*, *alter*, or *contradict* it are in-

parol evidence rule When parties have executed a written agreement that is complete on its face, oral agreements made prior to, or at the same time as, the written agreement that vary, alter, or contradict it are invalid.

209

TABLE 9-2   *Exceptions to the Parol Evidence Rule*

1. Oral agreements used to prove a subsequent modification of the written agreements are admissible.
2. Oral agreements to clear up ambiguity in the written agreement are admissible.
3. Oral agreements to prove fraud, mistake, illegality, duress, undue influence, or lack of capacity are admissible.
4. Oral agreements concerning collateral matters not germane to the written agreement are admissible.

valid. Such oral agreements will not be allowed to be introduced in evidence by most state courts. For example, suppose that Smith enters into a written contract with Jones to sell him a two-year-old Chevy Citation for $5,000 and "all warranties are excluded" under the terms of the contract. At the time of signing, Smith orally tells Jones, "Don't worry, we'll warranty all parts and labor." This oral agreement made at the time of execution will not be allowed into evidence because it varies from the written agreement. Exceptions to the parol evidence rule are set out in Table 9-2.

Under the UCC, written memoranda that are intended to be a final expression of the parties' agreement cannot be contradicted by prior or contemporaneous oral agreement but may be explained or supplemented orally by course of dealing or usage of trade, by course of performance, or by evidence of consistent additional terms. This UCC rule allows the courts to admit into evidence oral testimony with regard to written agreements that would ordinarily be inadmissible under case law.

THIRD-PARTY BENEFICIARY CONTRACTS AND ASSIGNMENT OF RIGHTS

TYPES OF THIRD-PARTY BENEFICIARY CONTRACTS

So far, our discussion has focused on contracts between two parties (usually Smith and Jones). However, two parties may enter into a contract with the clear *intent* to benefit a third party; in these cases, there is a *third-party beneficiary contract*. There are two kinds of third-person beneficiary contracts: donee and creditor.

donee-beneficiary contract One in which the promisee obtains a promise from the promisor to make a gift to a third party.

A **donee-beneficiary contract** exists when the purpose of the promisee in obtaining a promise from the promisor is to make a gift to a third person. For example, Liberty Insurance Company (promisor) promises to pay Smith (third party) a sum of $100,000 upon the death of Jones (promisee) in exchange for Jones's payment of a yearly premium. Under this third-party donee-beneficiary contract, Smith may sue Liberty Insurance Company if it fails to pay the $100,000 upon the death of Jones.

creditor-beneficiary contract One in which the promisee obtains a promise from the promisor to fulfill a legal obligation of the promisee to a third party.

A third-party **creditor-beneficiary contract** exists when the purpose of the promisee in requiring a promisor's performance to be made to a third person is to fulfill a legal obligation of the promisee to the third person. For example, Smith (promisee) works for Jones (promisor) in exchange for Jones's promise to pay Taylor $6,000 that Smith owes. Under this third-party creditor-beneficiary contract, if Smith does the work and Jones refuses to pay, Taylor may sue both Jones and Smith.

Note that insurance contracts and all forms of creditor collection agreements are third-party beneficiary contracts. These types of agreements are obviously very important in our economy.

ASSIGNMENT OF RIGHTS

assignment The present transfer of an existing right.

An **assignment** is the *present* transfer of an existing right. Contracts between two parties may be assigned to a third party under certain conditions. Suppose that B, a manufacturing company, sells A, a retail company, 600 bicycles at

A (Obligor-Promisor) ‑ ‑ ‑ ‑ ‑ ‑ → **B** (Obligee-Promisee-Assignor)

C (Assignee)

$100 apiece on credit. A, known as the obligor-promisor, agrees to pay B, the obligee-promisee-assignor, $60,000. A does not pay, and therefore B has the right to sue A. But B has another choice: to assign this right to C, a collection agency, and receive immediate cash from C. In effect, B is assigning to C, known as the assignee, A's promise to pay in the future in exchange for receiving cash from C now (Exhibit 9-1). C has the right to sue both A and B. That is, if the collection agency is unable to collect the money from the retailer, it may sue not only the retailer but also the manufacturer to recover the cash it advanced in anticipation of collecting the debt.

The conditions attached to most assignments are that unless the obligor (A) receives notice of assignment by the obligee-assignor (B), the obligor has no duty to the assignee (C). Once that notice is received, however, the assignee "stands in the shoes" of the obligee.

Certain classes of assignments are not recognized by law:

1. Assignments that materially change the duty of the obligor.
2. Assignments forbidden by state statute.
3. Any assignment forbidden by the original contract between the obligor-promisor and the obligee-promisee.

SUMMARY

A contract is defined as a legally enforceable exchange of promises. The sources of contract law are case law from state and federal courts and statutory law from the federal and state legislatures, particularly from the Uniform Commercial Code. Contracts may be classified as express or implied, unilateral or bilateral, void or voidable or valid; executed, executory; and quasi.

The six necessary elements of a legal contract are: (1) a legal offer, (2) a legal acceptance, (3) a consideration, (4) genuine assent, (5) competent parties, and (6) a legal object. The Uniform Commercial code differs somewhat from the common law in its requirements for contracts. Table 9-3 outlines some of the differences.

TABLE 9-3 *Comparison between Common Law and the Uniform Commercial Code (UCC)*

AREA OF COMPARISON	COMMON LAW	UCC
Contract application	Real property, services, and employment contracts	Sale of goods contracts
Requirements for offer	Includes subject matter, price, and quantity	Includes subject matter and quantity while leaving price and other terms open
Option agreements	Needs consideration for all option agreements	No consideration needed
Requirements for acceptance	Terms of acceptance are mirror image of offer	Mirror image not necessary; additional terms allowed if one of three requirements is met
Requirements for consideration	Consideration required for contract to be enforceable except under doctrine of promissory estoppel	Consideration not needed for modifications
Statute of Frauds (contracts that must be in writing)	Real estate contracts, contracts not performable in one year; paying the debt of another	Sale of goods of $500 or more with three exceptions

Some types of contracts fall within the Statute of Frauds and therefore must be in writing to be enforceable. The parol evidence rule invalidates most oral agreements made before or at the same time as a written contract that alter or contradict the terms of the contract.

Third-party beneficiary contracts may be of either the donor-beneficiary or the creditor-beneficiary type. A contract made between two parties may be assigned to a third party under certain conditions.

REVIEW QUESTIONS

9-1. How is a contract generally defined?

9-2. Explain the distinction between a void and a voidable contract; between an executed and an executory contract; between a unilateral and a bilateral contract.

9-3. Describe the three requirements for a valid acceptance.

9-4. Describe the three requirements for a valid offer.

9-5. Explain how an offer can be terminated.

9-6. Explain the difference between liquidated and unliquidated debts.

REVIEW PROBLEMS

9-7. Fisher, an employment agency, sued Catani, a minor, for breach of contract for the balance due the agency of $101.25 as a commission for finding Catani employment. The defendant disaffirmed his contract with the agency while still a minor two months after obtaining the job and one month after he quit. Can he disaffirm? Explain.

9-8. Robinson was employed as an assistant manager in Gallagher Drug Company Store. He was accused of theft and embezzlement, which he admitted to, and was fired. The following day, at company headquarters, he signed a contract promising to repay the company $2,000. Robinson made payments totaling $741, and then stopped. Gallagher sued for the balance. Robinson's defense was that he had signed the agreement under duress. What logical problem would there be in Robinson's arguing that he became aware of the duress after he attended a support group for unemployed managers?

9-9. Osborne, a former chairman of the board of Locke Steel Company, entered into an agreement with Locke that, on retirement, he would hold himself available for consultation and would not work for any direct or indirect competitors of the company. In exchange for these promises, the company agreed to pay Osborne $15,000 a year for the rest of his life. After paying for two years, the company stopped payments when Osborne refused to consent to a modification of the agreement. The defendant argued that there was no consideration because the contract was based on past services, and thus there was no detriment to the promisee (Osborne). Who won? Explain.

9-10. Fisher, an inexperienced businessman, bought equipment and chinchillas from Division West Chinchilla in order to start a chinchilla ranch. Fisher got into the business because Division West had told him that chinchilla ranching was an "easy undertaking.... and no special skills were required." Fisher lost money operating the ranch. He sued, claiming that he had relied on Division West's fraudulent representations. Who won? Explain.

9-11. William Story promised his nephew that he would pay him $5,000 if he gave up "using tobacco, swearing, and playing cards and billiards until he was 21." The nephew did so and asked his uncle for the money. His uncle agreed to pay, but died before he did so. The uncle's estate refused to pay, arguing that there was no consideration for the uncle's promise. Should the court uphold the agreement in this case? Why or why not?

9-12. Mellen showed an interest in buying Johnson's cottage. Johnson wrote to Mellen that the cottage was for sale and that she was also writing to several other people who had expressed interest in buying the cottage. Mellen interpreted the letter as an offer and accepted. Johnson sold the property to someone else. Mellen sued Johnson in a Massachusetts state court. Who won? Explain. *Mellen v. Johnson,* 76 N.E.2d 658 (1948)

9-13. Soheil Sadri, a California resident, owed Caesar's Tahoe Casino $22,000 after a two-day gambling spree. On January 13 and 14, he wrote the casino two personal checks for $2,000 and $10,000. On January 14, he executed two memoranda of indebtedness for $5,000 each. Sadri subsequently stopped payment on the checks and memoranda, which were drawn on his account at a California bank. Caesar's Tahoe transferred its rights in the checks and memoranda to Metropolitan Creditors Service (MCS) of Sacramento for collection. MCS sued Sadri in California. Who won? Explain. *Metropolitan Creditors Service of Sacramento v. Sadri,* 19 Cal. Rptr. 2d 646 (1993)

9-14. Charles and Judy Orr were divorced in 1970. Their divorce agreement included a provision that Charles would pay for the college or professional school education of their two children, then minors. In 1990, Jennifer Orr, the Orrs' daughter, filed a petition to compel Charles to pay for college expenses based on a third-party beneficiary theory. The trial court dismissed the action on the ground that Jennifer, as an adult child of the involved parties, did not have standing because she was not a party to the original divorce agreement. Jennifer appealed. Who won? Explain. *Orr v. Orr,* 592 N.E.2d 343 (1992)

9-15. Time Warner and Fox, two powerful, experienced, and skilled electronic-media giants, negotiated for, but failed to reach agreement on, the carriage of the Fox News Channel by Time Warner. Fox filed an action against Time Warner for fraud and promissory estoppel, relying on Time Warner's oral assurances during the negotiations to the effect of: "We are in agreement," "We will certainly reach agreement," "Signing an agreement with you is our top priority after we arrange an important merger," and "All the details are set," when in fact, the gritty details had not been agreed upon. Simultaneously, Time Warner was considering alternate arrangements with others which they ultimately embraced—to Fox's disappointment—partly, it can be assumed, because some of Time Warner's management was hostile to, and never wanted an agreement with, Fox. The parties did participate in intensive and complex negotiations, but they never reached—or even approached—agreement on the essentials to a contractual relationship. Time Warner filed a motion for summary judgement. Why do you believe the court did or did not grant Time Warner's motion? *Fox News Network, L.L.C. v. Time Warner, Inc.,* 1997 WL 271720 (E.D.N.Y., May 16, 1997)

9-16. Southwest Engineering Company was preparing to submit a bid to the U.S. Army Corps of Engineers for construction of runway lighting facilities. On April 28, Southwest met with Martin Tractor Company to negotiate the price of a standby generator and accessory equipment to be used for the project. At this meeting, the agent for Martin Tractor noted each required item and its price on a memorandum, which he then gave to Southwest's agent. Martin's agent did not sign the memorandum but had printed his name and that of his company in the upper left corner. On May 24, Martin Tractor wrote to Southwest refusing to supply the generator and equipment. Southwest repeatedly tried to convince Martin Tractor to supply the equipment, until September 6, when it got the required items from another supplier at a cost of $6,041 more than the figures listed by Martin Tractor on the memorandum. Southwest filed suit for breach of contract claiming that the memorandum fell within the Statute of Frauds. Who won? Explain. *Southwest Engineering Co. v. Martin Tractor Co.,* 473 P.2d 186 (1970)

On the Internet

http://www.uchasting.edu/plri/fall94/whipple.html   This page contains a discussion of issues related to the Statute of Frauds.

http://www.loc.gov   From this site you can find links to a wealth of information about contracts.

http://law.cornell.edu.topics/contracts.html   This site will provide more links to information about contract law.

http://qsilver.queensu.ca/~law120/   A model for contract development and implementation is provided at this site.

http://www.lectlaw.com/formb.htm   Multiple contract examples and forms are provided on this Web site.

http://www.legalinformation.net.infonet/consumer/contracts.html   This site provides consumer legal information about making contracts, breaking contracts, form contracts, and reading the fine print.

10

THE LAW OF CONTRACTS AND SALES—II

- **METHODS OF DISCHARGING A CONTRACT**

- **REMEDIES FOR A BREACH OF CONTRACT**

- **INTERNATIONAL DIMENSIONS OF CONTRACT AND SALES LAW**

At the outset of the law of contracts in chapter 9 we were concerned that agreements be *enforceable*. We noted that without enforceability of contract law by a court there would be no *predictability* for enterprises who produce and sell goods. Without this there would be no *security* for a firm and financial stability. We would see the risk of loss increase and entrepreneurship decline if contracts were not enforceable at all levels of the manufacturing, marketing and distribution of services and goods.

In this chapter we will carefully examine the methods by which a contract can be discharged (particularly through performance), as well as the remedies that are to be had for firms and individuals who are injured by a breacher of contracts both for the sale of goods (Article 2) and for leases (Article 2A of the UCC). This chapter also addresses the international dimensions of the discharge and enforcement of contracts.

Critical Thinking about the Law

IN THE PREVIOUS CHAPTER, WE EMPHASIZED the importance of predictability and stability for those who enter into contracts. Yet, we do not want parties to jump immediately to the belief that they have a contract every time they talk about an exchange. Instead, we want to make it possible for people to talk about an exchange without having actually made a commitment to the exchange. Why?

To aid your critical thinking about issues surrounding contract formation and performance, let's look at a fact pattern involving concert tickets.

Jennifer and Juan were recently involved in a breach of contract case. Juan had two extra tickets to a Garth Brooks concert, and he agreed to sell these tickets to Jennifer. After they had agreed about the price, Juan promised to give the tickets to Jennifer the next day. But the next day, Jennifer did not want the tickets. Jennifer had discovered that it was an outdoor, afternoon concert. Jennifer argued that she should not have to buy the tickets because she is allergic to sunlight and unable to spend any extended period of time outside. The judge ruled in favor of Jennifer.

1. What ethical norms seem to dominate the judge's thinking?

   CLUE We have said that security is one reason for enforcing contracts. Review your list of ethical norms. Which norms seem to conflict with security in this case?

2. What missing information might be helpful in this case?

   CLUE To help you think about missing information, ask yourself the following question. Would the fact that Juan knew that Jennifer was allergic to sunlight affect your thinking about this case?

3. What ambiguous words might be troublesome in this case?

   CLUE Examine the reasoning that Jennifer uses to argue that she should be released from the contract.

METHODS OF DISCHARGING A CONTRACT

When a contract is terminated, it is said to be *discharged*. A contract may be discharged by performance (complete of substantial), mutual agreement, conditions precedent and subsequent, impossibility of performance, or commercial impracticality.

DISCHARGE BY PERFORMANCE

In most cases, parties to an agreement discharge their contractual obligation by doing what was required by the terms of the agreement. Many times, however, performance is substantial rather than complete. Traditional common law allowed suits for breach of contract if there was not **complete performance** of every detail of the contract. Today, however the standard is **substantial performance**. This standard requires (1) completion of nearly all the terms of the agreement, (2) an honest effort to complete all the terms, (3) no *willful* departure from the terms of the agreement. Courts usually find substantial performance when there is only a *minor* breach of contract. For example, A, a contractor, agreed to build a house with five bedrooms for B. By the terms of the agreement each of the rooms was to be painted blue. By mistake, one was painted pink, and B refused to pay A the $10,000 balance due on the house. The court awarded A $10,000 minus the cost of painting the wrongly painted room, finding that the departure from the contract terms was slight and unintentional and therefore insufficient for B to refuse to perform (pay) as agreed to in the contract.

If the breach is *material*, the injured party may terminate the contract and sue to recover damages. A material breach is one that is substantial and, usually, intentional. Today, courts allow a party to "cure" a material breach if the time period within which a contract is supposed to be performed has not lapsed.

The following classic case concerns a dispute over whether there was a minor or a material breach of contract by a home builder and which of two rules the court should use to measure damages.

complete performance
Completion of all the terms of the contract.

substantial performance
Completion of nearly all the terms of the contract plus an honest effort to complete the rest of the terms coupled with no willful departure from any of the terms.

PLANTE V. JACOBS
SUPREME COURT OF WISCONSIN 103 N.W.2D 296 (1960)

Plaintiff-appellee Plante sued defendants-appellants the Jacobs to obtain a lien on their property to recover $26,765 owed Plante by the Jacobs. Plante had agreed to build a house on a lot owned by the Jacobs according to specifications. A dispute arose when the misplacement of a wall caused the living room to be smaller than specified. The amount unpaid was approximately 25 percent of the contracting price. The wall would cost $4,000 to tear down and rebuild. Real estate experts claimed that the value of the house was not affected by the smaller width of the living room. The plaintiff conceded that he had failed to provide gutters and downspouts, a sidewalk, closed clothes poles, and other small items amounting to $1,601.95. However, he claimed that he had substantially performed the contract. Defendants argued that Plante had not substantially performed, and therefore there was a material breach of the contract. The lower court ruled in favor of Plante for $4,152.90. The Jacobs appealed.

JUSTICE HALLOWS

Substantial performance as applied to construction of a house does not mean that every detail must be in strict compliance with the specifications and the plans. Something less than perfection is the test of specific performance unless all details are made the essence of the contract. This was not done here. There may be situations in which features or details of construction of special or of great personal importance, which if not performed, would prevent a finding of substantial performance of the contract. In this case the plan was a stock floor plan. No detailed construction of the house was shown on the plan.

There were no blueprints. The specifications were standard printed forms with some modifications and additions written in by the parties. Many of the problems that arose during the construction had to be solved on the basis of practical experience. No mathematical rule relating to the percentage of the price, of cost of completion or of completeness can be laid down to determine substantial performance of a building contract. Although the defendants received a house with which they are dissatisfied in many respects, the trial court was not in error in finding the contract was substantially performed.

The next question is what is the amount of recovery when the plaintiff has substantially, but incompletely, performed. For substantial performance the plaintiff should recover the contract price less the damages caused the defendant by the incomplete performance. Both parties agree the correct rule for damages due to faulty construction amounting to such incomplete performance is the difference between the value of the house if it had been constructed in strict accordance with the plans and specifications. This is the diminished-value rule. The cost of replacement or repair is not the measure of such damage, but is an element to take into consideration in arriving at value under some circumstances. The cost of replacement or the cost to make whole the omissions may equal or be less than the difference in value in some cases and, likewise, the cost to rectify a defect may greatly exceed the added value to the structure as corrected. The defendants argue that under this rule their damages are $10,000. The plaintiff on review argues the defendants' damages are only $650. Both parties agree the trial court applied the wrong rule to the facts.

The trial court applied the cost-of-repair or replacement rule as to several items, stating when there are a number of small items of defect or omission which can be remedied without the reconstruction of a substantial part of the building or a great sacrifice of work or material already wrought in the building, the reasonable cost of correcting the defect should be allowed.

The trial court disallowed certain claimed defects because they were not proven. This finding was not against the great weight and clear preponderance of the evidence and will not be disturbed on appeal. Of the remaining defects claimed by the defendants, the court allowed the cost of replacement or repair except as to the misplacement of the living-room wall. Whether a defect should fall under the cost-of-replacement rule or be considered under the diminished-value rule depends upon the nature and magnitude of the defect. This court has not allowed items of such magnitude under the cost-of-repair rule as the trial court did. Viewing the construction of the house as a whole and its cost we cannot say, however, that the trial court was in error in allowing the cost of repairing the plaster cracks in the ceilings, the cost of mud jacking and repairing the patio floor, and the cost of reconstructing the non-weight-bearing and nonstructural patio wall. Such reconstruction did not involve an unreasonable economic waste.

The item of misplacing the living room wall under the facts of this case was clearly under the diminished-value rule. There is no evidence that defendants requested or demanded the replacement of the wall in the place called for by the specifications during the course of construction. To tear down the wall now and rebuild it in its proper place would involve a substantial destruction of the work, if not all of it, which was put into the wall and would cause additional damage to other parts of the house and require replastering and redecorating the walls and ceilings of at least two rooms. Such economic waste is unreasonable and unjustified. The rule of diminished value contemplates the wall is not going to be moved. Expert witnesses for both parties, testifying as to the value of the house, agreed that the misplacement of the wall had no effect on the market price. The trial court properly found that the defendants suffered no legal damage, although the defendants' particular desire for specified room size was not satisfied.

It would unduly prolong this opinion to detail and discuss all the disputed items of defects of workmanship or omissions. We have reviewed the entire record and considered the points of law raised and believe the findings are supported by the great weight and clear preponderance of the evidence and the law properly applied to the facts.

Affirmed in favor of Plaintiff, Plante.

UNIFORM COMMERCIAL CODE AND PERFORMANCE   The substantial performance doctrine does not apply to the sale of goods. The performance of a sale or lease contract requires the seller or lessor to transfer and deliver what is known as *conforming goods* (perfect tender rule). The buyer or lessee must accept and pay for the conforming goods. The UCC states an exception to the perfect tender rule. If the goods or tender of delivery fail to conform to the contract in any respect, the buyer has the following options: (1) to reject all the goods, (2) to accept all that are tendered, or (3) to accept any number of units the buyer chooses to and reject the rest. The buyer must generally give notice to the seller of any defect in the goods or tender of delivery and then allow the seller a reasonable time to "cure" the defect.

DISCHARGE BY MUTUAL AGREEMENT

Subsequent to the making of a contract, the parties may agree that they should *rescind* (cancel) the contract because some unforeseen event took place that makes its fulfillment financially impracticable. For example, if A agrees to build B a house for $150,000, and then, when building the basement, runs into an unforeseen and incorrectable erosion factor, both parties may want to cancel the agreement, with restitution to A for expenditures on the basement construction. The contract is then said to be discharged by mutual agreement.

Sometimes the parties wish to rescind an original agreement and substitute a new one for it. This type of discharge by mutual agreement is called *accord and satisfaction*. If the parties wish to substitute new parties for the original parties to the agreement, this is called *novation*. Note that novation does not change contractual *duties*; it merely changes the parties that will perform those duties. Suppose a rock star (original party) is unable to perform at a concert because of illness and a star of the same stature (substitute party) agrees to appear instead. If all parties, including the concert impresario, agree to the substitution, there is discharge by mutual agreement. See the following case.

ELLENBOGEN & GOLDSTEIN, P.C. V. BRANDES

SUPREME COURT APPELLATE DIVISION, FIRST DEPARTMENT 641 N.Y.S.2D 28 (1995)

Ellenbogen & Goldstein, P.C., represented Iris Brandes in her divorce action. The law firm sent monthly bills to Brandes, most of which she did not pay. Brandes and the firm agreed to an accord, under which the firm would accept as payment the first $25,000 that she and her husband realized from the sale of their house. The firm sent Brandes a final bill, which went unpaid for four and a half months. Finally, the firm filed a suit in a New York state court against Brandes, seeking $112,281.07. Brandes asserted that the firm had orally agreed to render legal services without charge and orally advised her to ignore its bills. The firm filed a motion for summary judgment, which the court granted. Brandes appealed.

MEMORANDUM DECISION

... Defendant's [Brandes's] assertions ... are ... contradicted by the ... unsatisfied accord between the parties. ... While there was clearly an accord that plaintiff would accept defendant's payment of the first $25,000 defendant and her former husband ... realized from the sale of the marital residence, it is equally clear that there was no satisfaction, and that plaintiff therefore remains free to sue on its original claim.

Affirmed in favor of Plaintiff, Ellenbogen & Goldstein.

DISCHARGE BY CONDITIONS PRECEDENT AND SUBSEQUENT

CONDITION PRECEDENT   A **condition precedent** is a particular event that must take place in order to give rise to a duty of performance. If the event does not take place, the contract may be discharged. For example, when Smith enters into a contract with Jones to sell a piece of real estate, a clause in the agreement requires that title must be approved by Jones's attorney *before* closing and execution of the contract for sale. If Jones's attorney does not give this approval before the closing, then Jones is discharged from the contract.

condition precedent A particular event that must take place to give rise to a duty of performance of a contract.

CONDITION SUBSEQUENT   A **condition subsequent** is a particular future event that, when following the execution of a contract, terminates the contract. For example, a homeowner's insurance contract may discharge the insurer from responsibility for coverage in the event of an "act of war" (condition subsequent).

condition subsequent A particular event that when following the execution of a contract terminates it.

DISCHARGE BY IMPOSSIBILITY OF PERFORMANCE

In early common law, when disruptive unanticipated events (e.g., war) occurred after parties entered into a contract, the contract was considered enforceable anyway. Thus, if a shipping line could not transport goods it had agreed to transport because of a wartime blockade, or if it could transport the goods but had to take a more expensive route to do so, it (or its insurance carrier) was required to pay damages or absorb the costs of a longer route. Courts today take the view that if an unforeseeable event makes a promisor's performance *objectively* impossible, the contract is discharged by **impossibility of performance**. "Objectively impossible" is defined as meaning that no person or company could legally or physically perform the contract.

impossibility of performance Situation in which the party cannot legally or physically perform the contract.

This defense for nonperformance is used most frequently in three circumstances. First is the *death or illness of a promisor* whose personal performance is required to fulfill the contract when no substitute is possible. Say a world-renowned artist is commissioned to paint an individual's portrait. If the artist dies, the contract is discharged because there is no substitute for the artist. Second is a *change of law* making the promised performance illegal. For example, if A enters into a contract with B to sell B her home to be used for residential purposes, and subsequent to their agreement the property is zoned commercial, the contract will be discharged. The final circumstance is the *destruction of the subject matter*. If A enters into a contract with B to buy all the hay in B's barn and the barn burns down with the hay in it before shipment takes place, the contract is discharged because performance is impossible.

commercial impracticability
Situation that makes
performance of a contract
unreasonably expensive,
injurious, or costly to a party.

DISCHARGE BY COMMERCIAL IMPRACTICABILITY The courts have sought to enlarge the grounds for discharge of a contract by adding the concept of **commercial impracticability**, defined as a situation in which performance is impracticable because of unreasonable expense, injury, or loss to one party. In effect, a situation that was not foreseeable, or whose nonoccurrence was assumed at the time the contract was executed, occurs, making performance of the contract unreasonably expensive or injurious to a party. For example, a plastics manufacturer becomes extremely short of raw materials because of a war and an embargo on oil coming from the Middle East. The manufacturer's contracts with his retailers for plastic goods will be discharged in most cases if the court finds that the manufacturer could not have anticipated the war and had no alternative source of materials costing about the same price. See the following case.

SYROVY TRUST V. ALPINE RESOURCES, INCORPORATED
COURT OF APPEALS OF WASHINGTON 841 P.2D 1270 (1992)

The George Syrovy Trust (Syrovy) agreed to sell Alpine Resources, Inc., all of the timber from Syrovy's property that Alpine could harvest over a two-year period for $140,000. Over the next two years, Alpine harvested some timber and paid Syrovy $50,000. When Syrovy sued for the contract balance of $90,000, Alpine claimed that it should be released from its obligation to pay the remainder of the contract price on the ground of commercial impracticability. Alpine claimed that bad weather conditions during both winters and the fact that Alpine could not engage in logging operations during the hunting season made it impossible to harvest the quantity of timber it had planned to harvest when the contract was formed. The trial court granted Syrovy's motion for summary judgment, and Alpine appealed.

JUDGE SWEENEY

. . . [Under the defense of impracticability] performance is excused if events occur that are not foreseen or antici-

pated—a "wholly unexpected contingency." Difficulties that are assumed by a party, at the time of contracting, cannot form the basis of an impracticability defense.

Alpine argues that the winters of 1988 and 1989 were so severe that harvesting became impossible. However, Mr. Reoh [who negotiated the contract for Alpine] is a logger with considerable experience in purchasing timber. It would be unreasonable to suggest that weather conditions were an unforeseeable event. Also, there is no evidence to support the assertion that the weather was so remarkable that contract performance was impossible.

Alpine also argues that it did not have access to the property during hunting season. . . . Access problems were foreseeable and the risk was allocated in the contract. The problems cannot be asserted as a basis for an impracticability defense.

Affirmed in favor of Plaintiff, Syrovy.

REMEDIES FOR A BREACH OF CONTRACT

The fact that a court will enforce a contract does not mean that one party will automatically sue if the other breaches. Businesspeople need to consider several factors before they rush to file a lawsuit: (1) the likelihood of the suit's succeeding, (2) whether they wish to maintain a business relationship with the breaching party, (3) the possibility of arbitrating the dispute through a third party, thus avoiding litigation, and (4) the cost of arbitration or litigation as opposed to the revenues to be gained from enforcing the contract.

Remedies for a breach of contract are generally classified according to whether the plaintiff requests monetary damages ("legal" remedies) or nonmonetary damages (equitable remedies).

monetary damages Dollar
sums awarded for a breach of
contract; "legal" remedies.

compensatory damages
Monetary damages awarded for a
breach of contract that results in
higher costs or lost profits for the
injured party.

MONETARY DAMAGES ("LEGAL" REMEDIES)

Monetary damages include compensatory, punitive, nominal, and *liquidated* damages.

COMPENSATORY DAMAGES The purpose of **compensatory damages** is to place the injured (nonbreaching) party to a contract in the position that that party would have been in had the terms of the contract been performed. For example, if a firm contracted to buy 8,000 widgets at $10 apiece to be delivered by August 15, the buyer has a right to go out and buy the widgets from another source if they are not delivered by the contract date. Suppose the widgets bought from the other source cost $10.50 apiece. In that case, the buyer can sue for the fifty cent difference in price per unit plus court costs. If the buyer cannot obtain widgets anywhere else, it can sue for lost profits.

The courts have set out three standards that the plaintiff-buyer must meet in order to recoup lost profits:

1. The plaintiff-buyer must show that it was *reasonably foreseen* by the defendant-seller that if she did not deliver the promised goods, the buyer would have no alternative source and thus would lose profits.

2. The plaintiff-buyer must show the amount of the damages with *reasonable certainty*; the buyer cannot just speculate about what this amount is.

3. The plaintiff-buyer must show that she did everything possible to *mitigate damage*—that is, that she looked for other possible sources of the goods.

In the landmark case that follows, a famous actor and dancer (whose brother is well known in the movie business) is involved in the litigation of a contract that involves the mitigation of damages.

SHIRLEY PARKER V. TWENTIETH CENTURY-FOX FILM CORPORATION
SUPREME COURT OF CALIFORNIA 474 P.2D 689 (1970)

Shirley Parker was a well-known actress (Shirley MacLaine) who contracted with Twentieth Century-Fox Film Corporation to play the female lead in a picture entitled *Bloomer Girl*, a musical. The film corporation decided against making the film, and so notified Parker, but offered to employ her in another film, *Big Country*. The compensation was the same but the picture was a western to be shot in Australia as opposed to a musical. Parker was given one week to accept. She didn't and sued Twentieth-Century Fox, seeking recovery of $750,000 plus interest. The defendants argued against the awarding for damages to Parker because, they claimed, she failed to mitigate damages by accepting the part in *Big Country*. The trial court awarded summary judgment to Parker. Twentieth Century-Fox appealed.

JUSTICE BURKE

The complaint sets forth two causes of action. The first is for money due under the contract; the second, based upon the same allegations as the first, is for damages resulting from defendant's breach of contract. Defendant, in its answer, admits the existence and validity of the contract, that plaintiff complied with all the conditions, covenants and promises and stood ready to complete the performance, and that defendant breached and "anticipatorily repudiated" the contract. It denies, however, that any money is due to plaintiff either under the contract or as a result of its breach, and pleads as an affirmative defense to both causes of action plaintiff's allegedly deliberate failure to mitigate damages, asserting that she unreasonably refused to accept its offer of the leading role in *Big Country*.

Plaintiff moved for summary judgment under Code of Civil Procedure section 437c, the motion was granted, and summary judgment for $750,000 plus interest was entered in plaintiff's favor. This appeal by defendant followed.

As stated, defendant's sole defense to this action which resulted from its deliberate breach of contract is that in rejecting defendant's substitute offer of employment plaintiff unreasonably refused to mitigate damages.

The general rule is that the measure of recovery by a wrongfully discharged employee is the amount of salary agreed upon for the period of service, less the amount which the employer affirmatively proves the employee has earned or with reasonable effort might have earned from other employment. However, before projected earnings from other employment opportunities not sought or accepted by the discharged employee can be applied in mitigation, the employer must show that the other employment was comparable, or substantially similar, to that of which the employee has been deprived; the employee's rejection of or failure to seek other available employment of a different or inferior kind may not be resorted to in order to mitigate damages.

In the present case defendant has raised no issue of reasonableness of efforts by plaintiff to obtain other employment; the sole issue is whether plaintiff's refusal of defendant's substitute offer of *Big Country* may be used in mitigation. Nor, if the *Big Country* offer was of employment different or inferior when compared with the original *Bloomer Girl* employment, is there an issue as to whether or not plaintiff acted reasonably in refusing the substitute offer. Despite defendant's arguments to the contrary, no case cited or which our research has discovered holds or suggests that reasonableness is an element of a wrongfully discharged employee's option to reject, or fail to seek, different or inferior employment lest the possible earnings therefrom be charged against him in mitigation of damages.

Applying the foregoing rules to the record in the present case, with all intendment in favor of the party opposing the summary judgment motion—here, defendant—it is clear that the trial court correctly ruled that plaintiff's failure to accept defendant's tendered substitute employment could not be applied in mitigation of damages because the offer of the *Big Country* lead was of employment both different and inferior, and that no factual dispute was presented on that issue. The mere circumstances that *Bloomer Girl* was to be a musical review calling upon plaintiff's talents as a dancer as well as an actress, and was to be produced in the City of Los Angeles, whereas *Big Country* was a straight dramatic role in a "Western Type" story taking place in an opal mine in Australia, demonstrates the difference in kind between the two employments; the female lead as a dramatic actress in a western style motion picture can by no stretch of imagination be considered the equivalent of or substantially similar to the lead in a song-and-dance production.

Additionally, the substitute *Big Country* offer proposed to eliminate or impair the director and screenplay approvals accorded to plaintiff under the original *Bloomer Girl* contract, and thus constituted an offer of inferior employment. No expertise or judicial notice is required in order to hold that the deprivation or infringement of an employee's rights held under an original employment contract converts the available "other employment" relied upon by the employer to mitigate damages, into inferior employment which the employee need not seek or accept.

In view of the determination that defendant failed to present any facts showing the existence of a factual issue with respect to its sole defense—plaintiff's rejection of its substitute employment offer in mitigation of damages—we need not consider plaintiff's further contention that for various reasons, plaintiff was excused from attempting to mitigate damages.

Affirmed in favor of Plaintiff, Parker.

Critical Thinking about the Law

REMEDIES ARE AMONG THE MORE VISIBLE actions by which judges express their views about ethical norms. Notice that in the *Parker* decision the California Supreme Court could conceivably have affirmed the trial court's judgment for Parker and then decided to reduce the damages. However, the court was disturbed enough by the harm caused by Twentieth Century-Fox that it affirmed what was at the time a substantial damage award.

1. Decide what damage award each of the four primary ethical norms outlined in chapter 1 compels in this case and present a rationale for why that norm compels that particular damage award. You are not looking so much for a specific number here. Instead, you are asking the question: "Which of these norms propel the damage award higher and which argue for minimal damages?"

   CLUE Remember that one form of ethical reasoning focuses on the consequences of following an ethical norm in a particular situation. For instance, what would be the impact on efficiency if the damage award were even higher than that affirmed by the court?

2. If you were the judge in this case, what argument would you make in defending the size of the damages awarded by the trial court?

   CLUE Use ethical reasoning to support your desired remedy.

---

punitive damages Monetary damages awarded in excess of compensatory damages for the sole purpose of deterring similar conduct in the future.

nominal damages Monetary damages of a very small amount (e.g., $1) awarded to a party that is injured by a breach of contract but cannot show real damages.

liquidated damages Monetary damages for nonperformance that are stipulated in a clause in the contract.

PUNITIVE DAMAGES Damages in excess of compensatory damages that the court awards for the sole purpose of *deterring* the defendant and others from doing the same act again are known as **punitive damages**. They are infrequently awarded in contract cases.

NOMINAL DAMAGES Sometimes the court awards a very small sum (usually $1) in **nominal damages** to a party that is injured by a breach of contract but cannot show real damages. Generally in these cases, the court also enables the injured party to recover court costs, though not attorney's fees.

LIQUIDATED DAMAGES **Liquidated damages** are usually set in a separate clause in the contract. The clause generally stipulates that the parties agree to pay so much a day for every day beyond a certain date that the contract is not completely performed. Liquidated damage clauses are frequently found in general contractors' agreements with individuals, corporations, and state or local agencies in situations in which it is essential that a building project be completed on time. Such clauses help the contracting parties avoid going to court and seeking a judicial determination of damages—with all the attendant delays and expenses.

EQUITABLE REMEDIES

When dollar damages are inadequate or impracticable as a remedy, the injured party may turn to nondollar, or **equitable remedies**. Equitable remedies include rescission, reformation, specific performance, and injunction.

RESCISSION **Rescission** is defined as the canceling of a contract. Plaintiffs who wish to be put back in the position they were in before entering into the contract often seek rescission. In cases of fraud, duress, mistake, or undue influence (discussed in chapter 9) the courts will generally award rescission.

REFORMATION The correction of terms in an agreement so that they reflect the true understanding of the parties is known as **reformation**. For example, if A enters into an agreement to sell B 10,000 widgets at $.50 a unit when the figure should have been $5.50 a unit, A will petition the court for reformation of the contract.

SPECIFIC PERFORMANCE A court order compelling a party to perform in such a way as to meet the terms of the contract is called **specific performance**. Courts are reluctant to order specific performance unless (1) a unique object is the subject matter of the contract (e.g., an antique or artwork) or (2) real estate is involved. To obtain a specific performance order, the plaintiff must generally show that dollar damages (damages "at law") are inadequate to compensate for the defendant's breach of contract. Even then, a court will often refuse to grant the order if it is incapable of or unwilling to supervise it. For these reasons, specific performance in contract cases is infrequently granted.

INJUNCTIONS **Injunctions** are *temporary* (30 days) or *permanent* orders of the court preventing a party to a contract from doing something. The plaintiff must show the court that dollar damages are inadequate and that irreparable harm will be done if the injunction is not granted. For instance, if an opera singer contracts with an opera company to sing exclusively for the company and then later decides to sing for other opera companies, the court may grant an injunction to prevent her from singing for the other companies. Injunctions, like specific performance, are seldom granted in contract law cases.

equitable remedies Nonmonetary damages awarded for breach of contract when monetary damages would be inadequate or impracticable.

rescission Cancellation of a contract.

reformation Correction of terms in an agreement so that they reflect the true understanding of the parties.

specific performance A court order compelling a party to perform in such a way as to meet the terms of the contract.

injunction Temporary or permanent court order preventing a party to a contract from doing something.

POTTER V. OSTER
SUPREME COURT OF IOWA 426 N.W.2D 148 (1988)

The parties, though sharing a common interest in agribusiness, present a study in contrasts. Plaintiff Charles Potter is a farm laborer, and his wife, Sue, is a homemaker and substitute teacher. They have lived all their lives within a few miles of the real estate in question. Defendant Merrill Oster is an agricultural journalist and recognized specialist in land investment strategies. He owns Oster Communications, a multimillion dollar publishing concern devoted to furnishing farmers the latest in commodity market analysis and advice on an array of farm issues.

In May 1978, Oster contracted with Florence Stark to purchase her 160-acre farm in Howard County, Iowa, for $260,000 on a ten-year contract at 7 percent interest. Oster then sold the homestead and nine acres to Charles and Sue Potter for $70,000. The Potters paid $18,850 down and executed a ten-year installment contract for the balance at 8.5 percent interest. Oster then executed a contract with Robert Bishop for the sale of the remaining 151 acres as part of a package deal that included the sale of 17 farms for a sum exceeding $5.9 million.

These back-to-back contracts collapsed like dominoes in March 1985 when Bishop failed to pay Oster and Oster failed to pay Stark the installments due on their respective contracts. Stark commenced forfeiture proceedings (proceedings to retake the property because Oster failed to perform a legal obligation—payment under the contract—and thus forfeited his right to the land). The Potters had paid every installment when due under their contract with Oster and had included Stark as a joint payee with Oster on their March 1, 1985, payment. But they were financially unable to exercise their right to advance the sums due on the entire 160 acres in order to preserve their interest in the nine acres and homestead. As a result, their interest in the real estate was forfeited along with Oster's and Bishop's and they were forced to move from their home in August 1985.

The Potters then sued Oster to rescind their contract with him, claiming restitution damages for all consideration paid. Trial testimony revealed that the market value of the property had decreased markedly since its purchase. Expert appraisers valued the homestead and nine acres between $27,500 and $35,000. Oster himself placed a $28,000 value on the property; Potter $39,000. Evidence was also received placing the reasonable rental value of the property at $150 per month, or a total of $10,800 for the six-year Potter occupancy.

The district court concluded that the Potters were entitled to rescission of the contract and return of the consideration paid including principal and interest, cost of improvements, closing expenses, and taxes for a total of $65,169.37. From this amount the court deducted $10,800 for six years' rental, bringing the final judgment to $54,369.37.

On appeal, Oster challenged the judgment. He claimed that Potter had an adequate remedy at law for damages which should have been measured by the actual economic loss sustained.

JUDGE NEUMAN

This is a suit in equity brought by the plaintiffs to rescind an installment land contract based on the seller's inability to convey title. The question on appeal is whether, in an era of declining land values, returning the parties to the status quo works an inequitable result. We think not. Accordingly, we affirm the district court judgment for rescission and restitution.

The facts are largely undisputed. Because the case was tried in equity, our review is de novo. We give weight to the findings of the trial court, particularly where the credibility of witnesses is concerned, but we are not bound thereby.

Rescission is a restitutionary remedy which attempts to restore the parties to their positions at the time the contract was executed. The remedy calls for a return of the land to the seller, with the buyer given judgment for payments made under the contract plus the value of improvements, less reasonable rental value for the period during which the buyer was in possession. The remedy has long been available in Iowa to buyers under land contracts when the seller has no title to convey.

Rescission is considered an extraordinary remedy, however, and is ordinarily not available to a litigant as a matter of right but only when, in the discretion of the court, it is necessary to obtain equity. Our cases have established three requirements that must be met before rescission will be granted. First, the injured party must not be in default. Second, the breach must be substantial and go to the heart of the contract. Third, remedies at law must be inadequate.

The first two tests are easily met in the present case. Potters are entirely without fault in this transaction. They tendered their 1985 installment payment to Oster before the forfeiture, and no additional payments were due until 1986. On the question of materiality, Oster's loss of equitable title [ownership rights protected in equity] to the homestead by forfeiture caused not only substantial, but total breach of his obligation to insure peaceful possession [an implied promise made by a landowner, when selling or renting land, that the buyer or tenant will not be evicted or disturbed by the landowner or a person having a lien or superior title] and convey marketable title under the Oster-Potter contract.

Only the third test—the inadequacy of damages at law—is contested by Oster on appeal. . . . Restoring the status quo is the goal of the restitutionary remedy of rescission. Here, the district court accomplished the goal by awarding Potters a sum representing all they had paid under the contract rendered worthless by Oster's default. Oster contends that in an era of declining land values, such a remedy goes beyond achieving the status quo and results in a windfall to the Potters. Unwilling to disgorge the benefits he has received under the unfulfilled contract, Oster would have the court shift the "entrepreneurial risk" [the risk assumed by one who initiates, and provides or controls the management of, a business enterprise] of market loss to the Potters by limiting their recovery to the difference between the property's market value at breach ($35,000) and the contract balance ($27,900). In other words, Oster claims the court should have awarded . . . damages. . . .

. . . [L]egal remedies are considered inadequate when the damages cannot be measured with sufficient certainty. Contrary to Oster's assertion that Potters' compensation should be limited to the difference between the property's fair market value and contract balance at time of breach, . . . damages are correctly calculated as the difference between contract price and market value at the time of performance. Since the time of performance in this case would have been March 1990, the market value of the homestead and acreage cannot be predicted with any certainty, thus rendering such a formulation inadequate.

Most importantly, the fair market value of the homestead at the time of forfeiture is an incorrect measure of the benefit Potters lost. It fails to account for the special value Potters placed on the property's location and residential features that uniquely suited their family. For precisely this reason, remedies at law are presumed inadequate for breach of a real estate contract. Oster has failed to overcome that presumption here. His characterization of the transaction as a mere market loss for Potters, compensable by a sum which would enable them to make a nominal down payment on an equivalent homestead, has no legal or factual support in this record. . . .

. . . In summary, we find no error in the trial court's conclusion that Potters were entitled to rescission of the contract and return of all benefits allowed thereunder, less the value of reasonable rental for the period of occupancy. . . .

Affirmed in favor of Plaintiff, Potter.

INTERNATIONAL DIMENSIONS OF CONTRACT AND SALES LAW

As more nations in Europe, Latin America, and Asia have shifted toward market-oriented economies, international trade has increased, and, along with it, contracts implementing transactions between foreign entities (either governments or private companies) and U.S. companies have increased. International and regional treaties lowering or eliminating tariffs have hastened the trend to free trade. (See chapter 3 for a detailed description of recent trade pacts.)

Given this accelerating trend toward free trade, the United Nations Commission on International Trade Law drafted the *Convention on Contracts for the International Sale of Goods* (CISG) to provide uniformity to international transactions. The CISG covers all contracts for the sale of goods in countries that have ratified it (Table 10-1). Parties to a contract can choose to adhere to all or part of the CISG, or they may select other laws to govern their transactions.

On January 1, 1988, CISG was approved as a treaty and incorporated into U.S. federal law. As a treaty, it overrides conflicting state laws dealing with contracts. Each of the 50 states is now examining conflicts between the Uniform Commercial Code (as adopted in the state) and the CISG, which supersedes it.

Some of these differences between the CISG and the UCC are highly significant. For example, under the CISG, a contract is formed when the seller (offeror) receives the acceptance from the offeree, whereas under the UCC, a contract is formed when the acceptance is mailed or otherwise transmitted. To take another example, under the CISG, a sales contract of any amount is enforceable if it is oral, whereas the UCC requires a written contract for a sale of goods of $500 or more.

TABLE 10-1 *Countries That Ratified or Acceded to the CISG by 1994*

Argentina	Lesotho
Australia	Mexico
Austria	Netherlands
Bulgaria	Norway
Belarus	People's Republic of China
Chile	Poland
The Czech and	Romania
Slovak Republics	Singapore
Denmark	Spain
Ecuador	Sweden
Egypt	Switzerland
Finland	Syrian Arab Republic
France	Uganda
Germany	Ukrainian Republic
Ghana	United States
Guinea	Venezuela
Hungary	Yugoslavia
Iraq	Zambia
Italy	

Present and future business managers must become knowledgeable about these and other differences between the UCC and the CISG to avoid costly and time-consuming litigation as international transactions in goods increase. You might want to review chapter 3 at this point to refresh your memory of the methods and details of international transactions.

SUMMARY

Contracts are discharged by performance, mutual agreement, conditions precedent and subsequent, and sometimes through impossibility of performance. Remedies for breach of contract include dollar remedies such as lost profits, punitive, nominal, and liquidated damages. Often, when dollar damages are insufficient, the court will rely upon equitable remedies (nondollar damages) such as rescission, restitution, specific performance, and reformation.

Contract laws became more uniform with the ratification by many nations of the Convention on Contracts for the International Sale of Goods. This has wide implications for the conduct of international transactions.

REVIEW QUESTIONS

10-1. Describe the criteria used by the courts in determining lost profits.

10-2. What is the CISG? Why is it important to present and future businesspeople?

10-3. What is meant by "impossibility of performance"?

10-4. What is the standard a court uses to award dollar damages when lost profits are involved?

10-5. Why should a party who has not breached a contract be required to mitigate the damages of the breaching party?

10-6. What equitable remedies are available when a contract is breached?

REVIEW PROBLEMS

10-7. Silver was a journeyman electrician who was occasionally employed by A.O.C. Corporation, an apartment management company. He did some electrical work for A.O.C. over a four-month period and submitted a bill for $893. The defendant refused to pay, claiming the contract lacked a legal object because the plaintiff was not licensed as an electrical contractor in Detroit or the state of Michigan. The state licensing statute exempted "minor work," and the plaintiff claimed that his work rewiring a hallway in an apartment building managed by A.O.C. was "minor." What critical thinking skills would you use to speculate on who might win this case?

10-8. Ace contracted with Jones to do certain remodeling work on the building owned by Jones. Jones supplied the specifications for the work. The contract price was $70,000. After the work was completed, Jones was dissatisfied and had Clay, an expert, compare the work done with the specifications provided. Clay testified that the work had been done improperly by Ace and that it would cost about $6,000 to correct the mistakes of Ace. If Jones refuses to pay any amount to Ace, what recourse, if any, does Ace have against Jones? Explain.

10-9. On January 4, General Contractors, Inc. entered into a contract with Julius and Penelope Jones to construct a house fit for occupancy by June 1. What is the legal consequence if General Contractors fails to complete the house by June 1, but does finish it by June 20? What would be the consequence if the contract stated that with regard to the June 1 deadline, "time is of the essence"? Suppose further that by May 10 no work has yet been started by General Contractors. When contacted by Julius, General Contractors' president states that due to other projects still pending, he is unable to build the house until late November. What legal recourse, if any, do Julius and Penelope have against General Contractors?

10-10. A contractor agreed to build a skating rink for the plaintiff at a price of $180,000. The rink was to be completed by December 1 and was designed to replace a similar but older rink that the plaintiff rented for $800 a month. A clause in the contract awarded the plaintiff "$100 per day in liquidated damages" for each day after December 1 that the rink was not completed. Was this a valid liquidated damages clause? Explain.

10-11. On April 15, Don Construction contracted to build a house for Jessup. The contract price was $55,000. The agreement contained a provision stating that the builder would deduct $1,000 a day from the contract price for each day the house was not completed after August 15. It was not completed until September 15. Don Construction refused to deduct $30,000 from the contract price. Jessup refused to sue. Don Construction sued, claiming the $1,000 a day was a penalty clause, not a liquidated damages clause. What was the result? Explain.

10-12. Julius W. Erving ("Dr. J") entered into a four-year contract to play exclusively for the Virginia Squires of the American Basketball Association. After one year, he left the Squires to play for the Atlanta Hawks of the National Basketball Association. The contract signed with the Squires provided that the team have his contract set aside for fraud. The Squires counterclaimed and asked for arbitration. Who won? Explain.

10-13. TWA had a sale/leaseback agreement with Connecticut National Bank. Because of the Gulf War, air travel was decreased and they were having trouble making their payments. Discuss the extent to which TWA could use commercial impracticability or impossibility as a defense for nonpayment.

CASE PROBLEMS

10-14. McLanahan's Lamborghini was stolen and had been extensively damaged. A provision in the insurance policy stated that the coverage for theft damages was subject to certain terms and conditions, including the condition that any person claiming coverage under the policy must allow Farmers (the insurance company) "to inspect and appraise the damaged vehicle before its repair or disposal." McLanahan, without notifying Farmers and without giving Farmers an opportunity to inspect the vehicle, sold the car to a wholesale car dealer. Farmers then denied coverage, and McLanahan brought suit to recover for the damages caused to his car by the theft. Did McLanahan have a valid claim against the insurance company? Explain. *McLanahan v. Farmers Insurance Co. of Washington*, 831 P.2d 160 (1992)

10-15. Mishara Construction Company was the general contractor for a construction project. It contracted with the Transit Mixed Concrete Company to supply all the ready-mixed concrete needed for the project. Under the contract, Mishara was to specify the dates and amounts of deliveries. In April 1967, a labor dispute stopped work on the project. Work resumed in June, but the workers maintained their picket line for two more years. Transit Mixed Concrete made few deliveries during the two-year period, and Mishara had to get concrete from other sources. Mishara sued for damages as a result of Transit's delays and the higher cost of purchasing concrete elsewhere. Transit defended on the basis of impossibility of performance. Who won? Explain. *Mishara Construction Co. v. Transit Mixed Concrete Co.*, 310 N.E.2d 363 (1974)

10-16. Lininger operates the Lodge on the Desert restaurant in Tucson. He contracted with Dine Out Corporation to participate in their two-for-one dining program, whereby participants have coupons in a booklet that entitles them to buy one dinner and get another free. During the first year, Lininger served 3,901 coupon customers. During the second year, however, Dine Out did not advertise the program the way they had promised, and Lininger had only six coupon customers. How do you think the court should calculate Lininger's damages? *Lininger v. Dine Out Corp.*, 639 P.2d 350 (1981)

10-17. Erik Madsen was trying to develop a pool table that, like a pinball machine, would produce light and sound effects. Madsen contracted with Murrey & Sons, a pool table manufacturer, to purchase 100 pool tables specially designed to accommodate electronic lighting and sound effects to be designed and installed by Madsen. The total contract price was $55,000, of which $42,500 was paid by Madsen in advance. Madsen was unable to develop a proper design for the electronic components and advised Murrey & Sons that he would be unable to take delivery of the 100 custom-designed tables. Murrey & Sons, which had already completed the tables, dismantled them and sold them for salvage and firewood. Madsen sued to recover his advance payment. Who won? Explain. *Madsen v. Murrey* 743 P.2d 1112 (1987)

10-18. Bill's Coal and Cherokee Coal (the sellers) were under contract with the Board of Public Utilities of Springfield, Missouri (the purchaser) to supply the purchaser with all the coal that it required until the expiration date of the contract. The contract enabled the purchaser to terminate the contract early if it could find another supplier that could provide the coal at a price of 15 to 20 percent lower than the contract price. Citing this provision, the purchaser tried to terminate the contract. The sellers disputed purchaser's right to terminate and sued. The purchaser was eventually judged to have breached the contract, and the sellers were awarded the difference between the contract price and the market price. Despite this victory, the sellers appealed, claiming they were lost-volume sellers and hence entitled to recover their lost profits. Who won? Explain. *Bill's Coal v. Board of Public Utilities*, 9 U.C.C. Rep. Serv. 1238 (1989)

- -

 On the Internet

http://cisgw3.law.pace.edu/cisg/text/database.html   The CISG can be found at this page, set up by the Institute of Commercial Law.

- -

11

THE LAW OF TORTS

- **THE GOALS OF TORT LAW**

- **DAMAGES AVAILABLE IN TORT CASES**

- **CLASSIFICATIONS OF TORTS**

- **INTERNATIONAL DIMENSIONS OF TORT LAW**

tort An injury to another's
person or property ; a civil
wrong.

We said in chapter 2 that the law is divided into criminal law and civil law. The division, however, is not airtight. Although a given set of actions may constitute a crime or a wrong against the state, and thus may give rise to a criminal prosecution, the same set of actions may also constitute a tort, a civil wrong that gives the injured party the right to bring a lawsuit against the wrongdoer to recover compensation for the injuries. We define a **tort** as an injury to another's person or property.

This chapter discusses torts as if they were the same across the country—and, in general, they are—but you should keep in mind that tort law is *state law* and so may vary somewhat from state to state. The total amount of tort litigation has been declining since 1990.[1] Even so, tort law is, and will continue to be, an important area of law and an essential subject for the student of the legal environment of business.

Critical Thinking about the Law

TORT LAW ALLOWS COMPENSATION FOR INDIVIDUALS whose person or property has been injured. Applying some critical thinking questions to tort law can help you better understand this chapter.

1. As discussed in chapter 1, courts have preferences for certain ethical norms. Using critical thinking skills will help us understand how those norms have shaped legal reasoning about tort law. It is quite possible for two judges hearing a tort case to disagree on a verdict. One reason for the different verdicts is their disagreement over which ethical norms are most important. When conflicting ethical norms are inherent in tort law?

   CLUE Think of the definitions of the primary ethical norms in chapter 1. If a judge strongly values freedom, what ethical norm might conflict with the judge's loyalty to freedom? Why?

2. Loyalty to certain ethical norms will influence one's attitude toward compensating injured individuals. Remember that the majority of civil jury trials involve torts. If you value efficiency, how might the large number of tort cases in the court system affect your thinking about tort law?

   CLUE Why would this large number of tort cases not trouble a person who values justice over efficiency?

3. One of the critical thinking skills you have learned to use is identifying ambiguous words. Words with multiple possible meanings can result in different interpretations of a law. In tort law, this issue is especially important. Look at the definition of a tort. How does the definition of the word *injury* influence thinking about tort cases?

   CLUE Again, consider the number of tort cases in the courts. How would the number of court cases change if we loosely defined the word *injury*? What ethical norms would influence our definition of injury?

THE GOALS OF TORT LAW

Tort cases are commonly referred to as *personal injury cases*, although a tort case may involve harm solely to property. The primary goal of tort law is to compensate innocent persons who are injured—or whose property is injured—as a result of another's conduct, but tort law also fulfills other important societal goals. It discourages private retaliation by injured persons and their friends. It

---

[1]B. Ostron and N. Kauder, Examining the Work of State Courts, 1994: A National Perspective from the Court Statistics Project 26 (National Center for State Courts 1996).

also promotes citizens' sense of a just society by forcing responsible parties to pay for the injuries they have caused. Finally, it deters future wrongs because potential wrongdoers are aware that they will have to pay for the consequences of their harmful acts.

For example, if Sam takes Judy's car without her permission and wrecks it, he has committed a tort. If there were no tort law, she would get no compensation from Sam and would have to use her own money to have the car repaired or to buy a new one. She would feel that she lived in an unjust world. She might even be tempted to seek revenge against Sam by breaking his car window. Others, seeing what Sam has gotten away with, would be less likely to be careful with other people's property in the future. However, because we have tort law, Judy can sue Sam and receive compensation from him for the damage he did to her car. She will then feel that she has received justice and will not be inclined to take any private retaliatory actions against Sam. Others, knowing that Sam had to pay for the harm he caused, may be deterred from committing torts themselves.

DAMAGES AVAILABLE IN TORT CASES

The victim of a tort may sue the wrongdoer, or *tortfeasor*, and has the potential to recover from among three types of damages: *compensatory, nominal*, and *punitive* (Table 11-1). All three types of damages were defined and discussed in chapter 10 in relation to breaches of contract. Here we describe their specific application to tort cases.

COMPENSATORY DAMAGES

The most common type of damages sought in tort cases are compensatory damages. Compensatory damages are designed to make the victim whole again—that is, to put the victim in the position he or she would have been in had the tort never taken place. They include compensation for all of the injuries to the victim and his or her property that were caused by the tortfeasor. Typical items covered by this class of damages are medical bills, lost wages, property repair bills, and compensation for pain and suffering. Note that attorneys' fees are *not* considered an item of compensatory damages, even though it would be virtually impossible for a victim to bring suit without the services of an attorney. Because the plaintiffs in personal injury cases must usually pay their attorneys by giving them a portion of the compensatory damages they are awarded, some people argue that compensatory damages do not fully compensate tort victims.

NOMINAL DAMAGES

Sometimes the plaintiff is unable to prove damages that would necessitate compensation. In such a case, the court may award the victim nominal damages (damages in name only). The sum of such awards is minuscule, usually $1, but recovery of nominal damages may be important because it allows the plaintiff to seek punitive damages. Punitive damages cannot be awarded alone but must accompany an award of compensatory or nominal damages.

TABLE 11-1 *Types of Tort Damages*

TYPE	PURPOSE	AMOUNT
Compensatory	To put the plaintiff in the position he or she would have been in had the tort never occurred	Sufficient to cover all losses caused by the tort, including compensation for pain and suffering
Nominal	To recognize that the plaintiff has been wronged	A nominal amount—usually $1–5
Punitive	To punish the defendant	Determined by the severity of the wrongful conduct and the wealth of the defendant

When the act of the tortfeasor is flagrant, unconscionable, or egregious, the court may award the victim punitive damages. These damages are designed to not only punish the tortfeasor for willfully engaging in extremely harmful conduct but also to deter others from engaging in similar conduct. Punitive damages are considered by some legal scholars to be especially useful in deterring manufacturers from making unsafe products. If there were no possibility of incurring punitive damages, manufacturers might calculate how much money they would have to spend fighting and settling lawsuits resulting from the sale of a defective product and then calculate the cost of making a safer product. If it turned out to be cheaper to produce the defective product and compensate injured victims than to make a safer product, rational manufacturers would be likely to produce the defective product. The risk of incurring punitive damages, however, is often sufficient to convince manufacturers to produce the safe product.

Some people disagree with this reasoning. They claim that the costs of compensatory damages alone are a sufficient incentive to produce only safe products. They further argue that the almost unrestricted ability to award punitive damages gives juries too much power.

In recent years, there have been many attempts by insurance companies and "tort reform" groups to limit the amount of punitive damages that can be assessed. These advocates of tort reform have tried repeatedly to get the courts to strike down punitive damages as unconstitutional on the grounds that such damages violate defendants' due process rights. This argument was unsuccessful until 1994. That year, in the case of *Honda Motor Company v. Oberg*,[2] the Supreme Court handed business firms their first victory in their campaign against punitive damages. This case, in which the High Court struck down a punitive damages award as being violation of due process, was unusual in two respects. First, the punitive damages were over five times the amount of the compensatory damages. Second, the state law had no provision for judicial review of the amount of the punitive damage award, whereas every other state allows such a review. It was Oregon's denial of judicial review of the amount of punitive damages that the U. S. Supreme Court said violated the Due Process Clause. Because of its unusual facts, *Honda v. Oberg* was not very instructive as to when punitive damages would be so excessive as to violate due process. In the following case, the Supreme Court finally set forth a workable test.

BMW OF NORTH AMERICA, INCORPORATED V. IRA GORE, JR.
UNITED STATES SUPREME COURT 116 S. CT. 1589 (1995)

Plaintiff Ira Gore, Jr. brought an action against BMW's American distributor and the dealer who had sold him a car, alleging that the dealer's failure to disclose that the car had been repainted after being damaged before delivery constituted suppression of a material fact. The failure to notify the plaintiff was consistent with the company policy not to advise its dealers, and hence their customers, of predelivery damage to new cars when the cost of repair amounted to less than 3 percent of the car's suggested retail price. The jury returned a verdict finding BMW liable for compensatory damages of $4,000. In addition, the jury assessed $4 million in punitive damages, based on a determination that the nondisclosure policy constituted "gross, oppressive or malicious" fraud. The Alabama Circuit Court affirmed. The distributor and manufacturer appealed. The Alabama Supreme Court conditionally affirmed the punitive damage award after reducing the award to $2 million.

JUSTICE STEVENS

The Due Process Clause of the Fourteenth Amendment prohibits a State from imposing a "grossly excessive" punishment on a tortfeasor. The question presented is whether a $2 million punitive damages award . . . exceeds the constitutional limit.

Punitive damages may properly be imposed to further a State's legitimate interests in punishing unlawful conduct and deterring its repetition. In our federal system, States necessarily have considerable flexibility in determining the level of punitive damages that they will allow in different

---

[2]114 S. Ct. 2331 (1994).

classes of cases and in any particular case. Most States that authorize exemplary damages afford the jury similar latitude, requiring only that the damages awarded be reasonably necessary to vindicate the State's legitimate interests in punishment and deterrence. Only when an award can fairly be categorized as "grossly excessive" in relation to these interests does it enter the zone of arbitrariness that violates the Due Process Clause of the Fourteenth Amendment.

For that reason, the federal excessiveness inquiry appropriately begins with an identification of the state interests that a punitive award is designed to serve. We therefore focus our attention first on the scope of Alabama's legitimate interests in punishing BMW and deterring it from future misconduct.

No one doubts that a State may protect its citizens by prohibiting deceptive trade practices and by requiring automobile distributors to disclose presale repairs that affect the value of a new car. But the States need not, and in fact do not, provide such protection in a uniform manner. That diversity demonstrates that reasonable people may disagree about the value of a full disclosure requirement.

We may assume, arguendo, that it would be wise for every State to adopt Dr. Gore's preferred rule, requiring full disclosure of every presale repair to a car, no matter how trivial and regardless of its actual impact on the value of the car. But while we do not doubt that Congress has ample authority to enact such a policy for the entire Nation, it is clear that no single State could do so, or even impose its own policy choice on neighboring States. Similarly, one State's power to impose burdens on the interstate market for automobiles is not only subordinate to the federal power over interstate commerce, but is also constrained by the need to respect the interests of other States. We think it follows from these principles of state sovereignty and comity that a State may not impose economic sanctions on violators of its laws with the intent of changing the tortfeasors' lawful conduct in other States.

The award must be analyzed in the light of the same conduct, with consideration given only to the interests of Alabama consumers, rather than those of the entire Nation. When the scope of the interest in punishment and deterrence that an Alabama court may appropriately consider is properly limited, it is apparent—for reasons that we shall now address—that this award is grossly excessive.

Elementary notions of fairness enshrined in our constitutional jurisprudence dictate that a person receive fair notice not only of the conduct that will subject him to punishment but also of the severity of the penalty that a State may impose. Three guideposts, each of which indicates that BMW did not receive adequate notice of the magnitude of the sanction that Alabama might impose for adhering to the nondisclosure policy lead us to the conclusion that the $2 million award against BMW is grossly excessive: the degree of reprehensibility of the nondisclosure; the disparity between the harm or potential harm suffered by Dr. Gore and his punitive damages award; and the difference between this remedy and the civil penalties authorized or imposed in comparable cases.

Perhaps the most important indicium of the reasonableness of a punitive damages award is the degree of reprehensibility of the defendant's conduct. As the Court stated nearly 150 years ago, exemplary damages imposed on a defendant should reflect "the enormity of his offense." Thus, we have said that "nonviolent crimes are less serious than crimes marked by violence or the threat of violence." Similarly, "trickery and deceit" are more reprehensible than negligence.

In this case, none of the aggravating factors associated with particularly reprehensible conduct is present. The harm BMW inflicted on Dr. Gore was purely economic in nature. The presale refinishing of the car had no effect on its performance or safety features, or even its appearance for at least nine months after his purchase. BMW's conduct evinced no indifference to or reckless disregard for the health and safety of others. To be sure, infliction of economic injury, especially when done intentionally through affirmative acts of misconduct, or when the target is financially vulnerable, can warrant a substantial penalty. But this observation does not convert all acts that cause economic harm into torts that are sufficiently reprehensible to justify a significant sanction in addition to compensatory damages.

Dr. Gore contends that BMW's conduct was particularly reprehensible because nondisclosure of the repairs to his car formed part of a nationwide pattern of tortious conduct. Certainly, evidence that a defendant has repeatedly engaged in prohibited conduct while knowing or suspecting that it was unlawful would provide relevant support for an argument that strong medicine is required to cure the defendant's disrespect for the law.

Dr. Gore's second argument for treating BMW as a recidivist is that the company should have anticipated that its actions would be considered fraudulent in some, if not all, jurisdictions. This contention overlooks the fact that actionable fraud requires a material misrepresentation or omission. This qualifier invites line drawing of just the sort engaged in by States with disclosure statutes and by BMW. We do not think it can be disputed that there may exist minor imperfections in the finish of a new car that can be repaired (or indeed, left unrepaired) without materially affecting the car's value. There is no evidence that BMW acted in bad faith when it sought to establish the appropriate line between presumptively minor damage and damage requiring disclosure to purchasers. For this purpose, BMW could reasonably rely on state disclosure statutes for guidance. In this regard, it is also significant that there is no evidence that BMW persisted in a course of conduct after it had been adjudged unlawful on even one occasion, let alone repeated occasions.

Finally, the record in this case discloses no deliberate false statements, acts of affirmative misconduct, or concealment of evidence of improper motive.

We accept, of course, the jury's finding that BMW suppressed a material fact which Alabama law obligated it to communicate to prospective purchasers of repainted cars in that State. But the omission of a material fact may be less reprehensible than a deliberate false statement, particularly when there is a good faith basis for believing that no duty to disclose exists. That conduct is sufficiently reprehensible to give rise to tort liability, and even a modest award of exemplary damages, does not establish the high degree of culpability that warrants a substantial punitive damages award. Because this case exhibits none of the circumstances ordinarily associated with egregiously improper conduct, we are persuaded that BMW's conduct was not sufficiently reprehensible to warrant imposition of a $2 million exemplary damages award.

The second and perhaps most commonly cited indicium of an unreasonable or excessive punitive damages award is its ratio to the actual harm inflicted on the plaintiff. The principle that exemplary damages must bear a "reasonable relationship" to compensatory damages has a long pedigree. Our decisions in both *Haslip* and *TXO* endorsed the proposition that a comparison between the compensatory award and the punitive award is significant.

In *Haslip* we concluded that even though a punitive damages award of "more than four times the amount of compensatory damages," might be "close to the line," it did not "cross the line into the area of constitutional impropriety." *TXO* refined this analysis by confirming that the proper inquiry is "'whether there is a reasonable relationship between the punitive damages award and the harm likely to result from the defendant's conduct as well as the harm that actually has occurred.'" Thus, in upholding the $10 million award in *TXO*, we relied on the difference between that figure and the harm to the victim that would have ensued if the tortious plan had succeeded. That difference suggested that the relevant ratio was not more than 10 to 1.

The $2 million in punitive damages awarded to Dr. Gore by the Alabama Supreme Court is 500 times the amount of his actual harm as determined by the jury. Moreover, there is no suggestion that Dr. Gore or any other BMW purchaser was threatened with any additional potential harm by BMW's nondisclosure policy. The disparity in this case is thus dramatically greater than those considered in *Haslip* and *TXO*.

Of course, we have consistently rejected the notion that the constitutional line is marked by a simple mathematical formula, even one that compares actual and potential damages to the punitive award. Indeed, low awards of compensatory damages may properly support a higher ratio than high compensatory awards, if, for example, a particularly egregious act has resulted in only a small amount of economic damages. A higher ratio may also be justified in cases in which the injury is hard to detect or the monetary value of noneconomic harm might have been difficult to determine.

Comparing the punitive damages award and the civil or criminal penalties that could be imposed for comparable misconduct provides a third indicium of excessiveness. [A] reviewing court should "accord 'substantial deference' to legislative judgments concerning appropriate sanctions for the conduct at issue." In this case the $2 million economic sanction imposed on BMW is substantially greater than the statutory fines available in Alabama and elsewhere for similar malfeasance.

We cannot accept the conclusion of the Alabama Supreme Court that BMW's conduct was sufficiently egregious to justify a punitive sanction that is tantamount to a severe criminal penalty.

The fact that BMW is a large corporation rather than an impecunious individual does not diminish its entitlement to fair notice of the demands that the several States impose on the conduct of its business. Indeed, its status as an active participant in the national economy implicates the federal interest in preventing individual States from imposing undue burdens on interstate commerce. While each State has ample power to protect its own consumers, none may use the punitive damages deterrent as a means of imposing its regulatory policies on the entire Nation.

As in *Haslip*, we are not prepared to draw a bright line marking the limits of a constitutionally acceptable punitive damages award. Unlike that case, however, we are fully convinced that the grossly excessive award imposed in this case transcends the constitutional limit.

Reversed and remanded in favor of Appellant, BMW.

COMMENT: The impact of the *BMW* case has spread beyond tort cases. The *BMW* test handed down for determining whether a punitive award is excessive—by looking at (1) the reprehensibility of the conduct, (2) the ratio of punitive damages to compensatory damages, and (3) comparable civil and criminal penalties for the same crime—was used to hold as unreasonable a punitive damages award in a recent discrimination case.

Major punitive damages awards by juries have made headlines and fueled the debate over limiting punitive damages, but most people fail to recognize that the huge jury awards they read about in the headlines are rarely paid. In September of 1995, for example, a federal jury in Alaska slapped Exxon Corporation with the largest punitive damage award ever imposed on a corporation—$5 billion, awarded to 14,000 people who were injured by the *Exxon Valdez* oil spill in March 1989. Before the time for filing post-trial material had closed, Exxon had filed a total of 22 motions. See Table 11-2 for some examples of appeals courts' reductions of extravagant punitive damages awarded by juries.

TABLE 11-2 *Some Major Punitive Damages Awards in Recent Years*

CASE	JURY AWARD	ULTIMATE RESOLUTION
Conroy v. Owens-Corning Fiberglass	A jury awarded $3.37 million in compensatory damages and $54 million in punitive damages to the families of three men who contracted mesothelioma from long-term workplace exposure to asbestos.	On appeal, punitive damages were reduced from $18.2 million per plaintiff to $1 million and one cent per plaintiff. Plaintiffs then settled for an undisclosed amount.
In re FPI/Agretech Securities Litigation	A jury ordered Ernst & Young to pay $8.9 million in compensatory damages and $10 million in punitive damages for the firm's failure to discover accounting irregularities that caused plaintiff-investors to lose about $100 million.	On appeal, circuit court judge threw out all of the punitive damages and reduced the total judgment to $8 million plus interest. A new trial on punitive damages was set, but defendants paid $17 million to settle the case.
Liebeck v. McDonald's	A jury awarded Stella Liebeck $2.9 million in damages, including $2.7 million in punitive damages for extensive burns she received when she spilled hot coffee (170°F) on her legs. Jurors were influenced by McDonald's having known that prior customers had received severe burns from the coffee.	The trial court reduced the award by 77 percent to $640,000. The parties subsequently settled the case for an undisclosed amount.
Proctor v. Davis	In 1991, a jury ordered the defendant to pay plaintiff Proctor and his wife $127.78 million in damages, including $124.57 million in punitive damages. Mr. Proctor's left eye had shriveled when an ophthalmologist accidentally injected an Upjohn product called Depo-Medrol into the plaintiff's eye.	In 1992, the trial judge cut nearly $90 million from the punitive award, reducing the judgment to $38.2 million. In 1994, the appellate judge reduced the punitive damages to the amount of the compensatory damages, leaving a judgment of $6.2 million.

The recent trend is for state courts to take a more active role in limiting punitive damages. For example, on February 2, 1994, the Texas Supreme Court handed down a decision in the case of *Transportation v. Morill*[3] that is expected to make it more difficult for plaintiffs in that state to recover punitive damages, and many commentators believe that the ruling will influence decision makers in other states. Morill suffered a broken pelvis and became impotent as a result of having a stack of countertops fall on him while he was working. He sued the insurance company when it delayed payment on some of his medical bills. The jury awarded Morill $101,000 in compensatory damages, with $100,000 of that total being for mental anguish, and $1 million in punitive damages. The state court of appeals affirmed the verdict. The Texas Supreme Court struck down the punitive damages award, holding that an insurance company's refusal to pay a

---

[3]879 S.W. 2d 194 (1994).

claim does not justify punitive damages unless the failure to pay was in bad faith *and* the insurer knew that its action would probably bring about extraordinary harm such as "death, grievous physical injury or genuine likelihood of financial catastrophe."

Many pieces of legislation designed to reform tort law have been unsuccessfully proposed at both the state and federal levels during the past several years. The majority of these proposals contained provisions limiting punitive damages. For example, in 1995, the Common Sense Legal Reform Act proposed in the U. S. Congress contained a provision limiting punitive damages in certain types of tort cases—namely, torts involving defective products (so-called product liability cases, which are discussed in chapter 12). This legislation would allow punitive damages in such cases only when the plaintiff could prove by clear and convincing evidence that the harm suffered was caused by "actual malice." Such damages would also be limited to $250,000 or three times the actual economic harm incurred by the plaintiff, whichever was greater. Part of this legislation, including the cap on punitive damages, was passed in 1996, but was vetoed by President Clinton. Reformers at the federal level have had no success since then.

State legislatures are also working on so-called tort reform. Between 1986 and 1988, a number of states passed some sort of tort reform legislation. In 1995, 19 states enacted tort reform measures[4]; 11 did so in 1996[5] and 10 in 1997.[6] By February of 1997, supreme courts in half the states had invalidated all or part of many of the tort reform acts that attempted to limit damages or place other hurdles to discourage tort suits.[7]

CLASSIFICATIONS OF TORTS

There are three classifications of torts: intentional, negligent, and strict liability. The primary distinguishing feature among them is the degree of willfulness of the wrongful conduct. **Intentional torts** are those wherein the defendant took some purposeful action that he or she knew, or should have known, would harm the plaintiff. **Negligent torts** involve carelessness on the part of the defendant. Finally, **strict liability torts** involve inherently dangerous actions and impose liability on the defendant regardless of how careful he or she was. Defenses for the various categories of torts differ, as do the types of damages generally awarded (Table 11-3).

INTENTIONAL TORTS

Intentional torts, the most "willful" torts, include a substantial number of carefully defined wrongful acts. What each of these acts has in common is the element of intent. *Intent* here does not mean a specific determination to cause harm to the plaintiff; rather, it means the determination to do a specific physical act that may lead to harming the plaintiff's person, property, or economic interests.

Intentional torts can be divided into three categories based on the interest being harmed: torts against persons, torts against property, and torts against economic interests. The following sections discuss a number of specific torts that fall into each category, along with the defenses to each.

intentional tort A civil wrong that involves taking some purposeful action that the defendant knew, or should have known, would harm the person, property, or economic interests of the plaintiff.

negligent tort A civil wrong that involves a failure to meet the standard of care a reasonable person would meet, and because of that failure, harm to another resulted.

strict liability tort A civil wrong that involves taking action that is so inherently dangerous under the circumstances of its performance that no amount of due care can make it safe.

---

[4]American Tort Reform Association, Issue by Issue Look at the Number of States enacting Tort Reform Legislation (April 28, 1998, http://www.aaabiz.com/atra/atri2.htm).
[5]*Id.*
[6]American Tort Reform Association, 1997 Tort Reform Enact. as of August 31, 1997 (April 28, 1998, http://www.aaabiz.com/atra/atri2.htm).
[7]Bruce Finzen, Barbara Haley, Kevin Shaw, *Illinois High Court Latest to Nix Tort Reform Law*, Nat'l. L.J., Feb. 16, 1998, B9 col. 2.

TABLE 11-3 *Categories of Torts*

TYPE	DESCRIPTION AND EXAMPLES	COMMON DEFENSES	TYPE OF DAMAGES USUALLY AWARDED
Intentional Torts	Purposeful action that results in harm	Specific to subtype	
Against persons	Assault and battery	• Self-defense • Defense of another • Defense of property	Compensatory damages for medical bills, lost wages, and pain and suffering

	Defamation	• Truth
		• Privilege
		   Absolute (congressional and courtroom speech)
		   Conditional (speech concerning public figures or in employment context)
			Compensatory damages for measurable financial losses

	Invasion of privacy	• Waiver by plaintiff of right to privacy • Posted warnings of observation	Compensatory damages for any resultant economic loss and pain and suffering
	False imprisonment	• Shopkeepers' privilege	Compensatory damages for treatment of physical injuries and lost time at work
	Intentional infliction of emotional distress		Compensatory damages for treatment of physical illness resulting from the emotional distress
Against property	Trespass to realty		Compensatory damages for harm caused to property and losses suffered by rightful owner
	Trespass to personalty		Compensatory damages for harm to the property
	Conversion		Compensatory damages for full value of converted item
Against economic interests	Disparagement	• Truth	Compensatory damages for actual economic loss
	Intentional interference with a contract	• No knowledge of contract	Compensatory damages for loss of expected benefits from the contract
	Unfair competition		Compensatory damages for lost profits
	Misappropriation	• Independent origination • Denial of discussion of idea	Compensatory damages for economic losses
Negligent Torts	Careless action that results in harm	• No duty • No breach of duty • No causation (actual or proximate) • No damages suffered by the plaintiff • Contributory negligence by plaintiff • Pure comparative negligence • Modified comparative negligence	Compensatory damages for injuries, including medical bills, lost time from work, harm to property, and pain and suffering
Strict Liability Torts	Action that is so inherently dangerous that no amount of due care can make it safe	• Assumption of the risk	Compensatory damages for personal injury and harm to property

assault Intentional placing of a person in fear or apprehension of an immediate, offensive bodily contact.

INTENTIONAL TORTS AGAINST PERSONS There are a number of torts against persons. We will discuss five of the most common ones: assault and battery, defamation, privacy torts, false imprisonment, and intentional infliction of emotional distress.

Assault and Battery. Torts against persons consist of harms to another's physical or mental integrity. One of the most common torts against the person is assault. An **assault** is the intentional placing of another in fear or apprehension of an immediate, offensive bodily contact. All of those elements must be present for an assault to exist. Thus, if the defendant pointed a gun at the plaintiff and threatened to shoot, and the plaintiff believed the defendant would shoot, an assault would have taken place. However, if the plaintiff thought the defendant was joking when making the threat, there was no assault because there was no *apprehension* on the part of the plaintiff. Likewise, a threat to commit harm in a week is not an assault because there is no question of *immediate* bodily harm. But a threat made with an unloaded gun, as long as the plaintiff does not know the defendant is incapable of carrying out the threat, *is* an assault.

battery Intentional unwanted and offensive bodily contact.

An assault is frequently, but not always, followed by a **battery**, which is an intentional, unwanted, offensive bodily contact. Punching someone in the nose is a battery. However, accidentally bumping into someone on a crowded street is not. The term *bodily contact* has been broadly interpreted to include such diverse situations as the defendant's using a projectile, such as a gun, to make physical contact with the plaintiff, and a defendant's pulling a chair out from under the plaintiff.

Defenses to Assault and Battery. The most common defense to a battery is *self-defense*. If one is attacked, one may repel the attacker—but with only that degree of force reasonably necessary to protect oneself. In most states, if a third person is in trouble, one may defend that person with the same degree of force that one would reasonably use to defend oneself, so long as the third party is unable to act in his or her own defense and there is a socially recognized duty to defend that person. This defense is often referred to as *defense of another*.

A third defense that may be raised against a charge of battery is *defense of property*. A person can use reasonable force to defend home and property from an intruder. However, deadly force in defense of property is rarely, if ever, considered justified.

defamation Intentional publication (communication to a third party) of a false statement that is harmful to the plaintiff's reputation.

libel Publication of a defamatory statement in permanent form.

slander Spoken defamatory statement.

Defamation. Another tort that most people have heard of is defamation. **Defamation** is the intentional publication (communication to a third party) of a false statement that is harmful to the plaintiff's reputation. To recover damages in a defamation case, the plaintiff must have suffered harm that resulted in measurable financial loss. If the defamation is published in a permanent form—for example, in a piece of writing or on television—the tort is called **libel**; if it is spoken, it is called **slander**.

Two questions have arisen since people began to communicate over the Internet. First, when does a false statement made over this information network constitute defamation? Second, who can be held liable if defamation does exist? The following case illustrates one court's approach to these issues.

CUBBY V. COMPUSERVE

SOUTH DISTRICT COURT OF NEW YORK 776 F. SUPP 135 (1991)

Plaintiff Cubby developed Skuttlebut, a computer database designed to electronically publish and distribute news and gossip. Rumorville, a competitor of Skuttlebut, allegedly published defamatory statements about Skuttlebut through CompuServe. CompuServe is an online informa-

tion service that, for a fee, provides subscribers with access to thousands of information sources, among them Rumorville—a publication available through the Journalism Forum, one of 150 special-interest forums accessible through CompuServe's Information Service (CIS). Plaintiff sued defendant CompuServe for libel, whereupon defendant filed this motion for a summary judgment.

JUDGE LEISURE

CompuServe has no opportunity to review Rumorville's contents before DFA [the publisher of Rumorville] uploads it into CompuServe's computer banks, from which it is immediately available to approved CIS [subscribers]. CompuServe receives no part of any fees that DFA charges for access to Rumorville, nor does CompuServe compensate DFA for providing Rumorville to the Journalism Forum; the compensation CompuServe receives for making Rumorville available to its subscribers is the standard online time usage and membership fees charged to all CIS subscribers, regardless of the information services they use. CompuServe maintains that, before this action was filed, it had no notice of any complaints about the contents of the Rumorville publication or about DFA.

Plaintiffs base their libel claim on the allegedly defamatory statements contained in the Rumorville publication that CompuServe carried as part of the Journalism Forum. CompuServe argues that, based on the undisputed facts, it was a distributor of Rumorville, as opposed to a publisher of the Rumorville statements. CompuServe further contends that, as a distributor of Rumorville, it cannot be held liable on the libel claim because it neither knew nor had reason to know of the allegedly defamatory statements. Plaintiffs, on the other hand, argue that the Court should conclude that CompuServe is a publisher of the statements and hold it to a higher standard of liability.

Ordinarily, "one who repeats or otherwise republishes defamatory matter is subject to liability as if he had originally published it." The requirement that a distributor must have knowledge of the contents of a publication before liability can be imposed for distributing that publication is deeply rooted in the First Amendment, made applicable to the states through the Fourteenth Amendment. "[T]he constitutional guarantees of the freedom of speech and of the press stand in the way of imposing" strict liability on distributors for the contents of the reading materials they carry. In *Smith*, the Court struck down an ordinance that imposed liability on a bookseller for possession of an obscene book, regardless of whether the bookseller had knowledge of the book's contents. The Court reasoned that "Every bookseller would be placed under an obligation to make himself aware of the contents of every book in his shop. It would be altogether unreasonable to demand so near an approach to omniscience." And the bookseller's burden would become the public's burden, for by restricting him the public's access to reading matter would be restricted. If the contents of bookshops and periodical stands were restricted to material of which their proprietors had made an inspection, they might be depleted indeed.

Although *Smith* involved criminal liability, the First Amendment's guarantees are no less relevant to the instant action: "What a State may not constitutionally bring about by means of a criminal statute is likewise beyond the reach of its civil law of libel."

CompuServe's CIS product is in essence an electronic, for-profit library that carries a vast number of publications and collects usage and membership fees from its subscribers in return for access to the publications. CompuServe and companies like it are at the forefront of the information industry revolution. High technology has markedly increased the speed with which information is gathered and processed; it is now possible for an individual with a personal computer, modem, and telephone line to have instantaneous access to thousands of news publications from across the United States and around the world. While CompuServe may decline to carry a given publication altogether, in reality, once it does decide to carry a publication, it will have little or no editorial control over that publication's contents. This is especially so when CompuServe carries the publication as part of a forum that is managed by a company unrelated to CompuServe.

With respect to the Rumorville publication, the undisputed facts are that DFA uploads the text of Rumorville into CompuServe's data banks and makes it available to approved CIS subscribers instantaneously. CompuServe has no more editorial control over such a publication than does a public library, book store, or newsstand, and it would be no more feasible for CompuServe to examine every publication it carries for potentially defamatory statements than it would be for any other distributor to do so. "First Amendment guarantees have long been recognized as protecting distributors of publications. . . . Obviously, the national distributor of hundreds of periodicals has no duty to monitor each issue of every periodical it distributes. Such a rule would be an impermissible burden on the First Amendment." Plaintiffs have not set forth anything other than conclusory allegations as to whether CompuServe knew or had reason to know of the Rumorville statements, and have failed to meet their burden on this issue.

Plaintiffs have not set forth any specific facts showing that there is a genuine issue as to whether CompuServe knew or had reason to know of Rumorville's contents. Because CompuServe, as a news distributor, may not be held liable if it neither knew nor had reason to know of the allegedly defamatory Rumorville statements, summary judgment in favor of CompuServe on the libel claim is granted.

Judgment in favor of Defendant, CompuServe.

Critical Thinking about the Law

TENSION BETWEEN THE FIRST AMENDMENT RIGHT to free speech and libel law is inevitable. Courts often have a problem distinguishing between lawful free speech and libel because the boundary between them is hazy. In this case, the court uses a legal analogy to make the distinction. The worth of the distinction is only as good as the worth of the analogy used in making it.

Consequently, one objective of the following questions is for you to evaluate the appropriateness of the legal analogy found in the court's reasoning.

1. Is the legal analogy used by the court relevant?

CLUE Besides evaluating the court's reasons for the analogy's relevance, consider whether technological changes merit new interpretations of First Amendment rights and responsibilities with respect to speech.

2. To demonstrate the significance of primary ethical norms in court decisions such as this one, identify the ethical norm that would have reversed the *Cubby* decision.

CLUE This norm is related to prioritizing the plaintiff's rights over those of the defendant in cases like this one.

COMMENT: The holding in this case has been reaffirmed in several cases since then, including *Stratton Oakmont, Inc. v. Prodigy Services Company,*[8] filed in late 1994. In the *Prodigy* case, the alleged defamatory statement was made on MoneyTalk, an electronic bulletinboard transmitted by the computer network Prodigy, and remained posted on that bulletinboard for 19 days. In its defense, Prodigy relied on the analogy to booksellers used by the court in deciding *Cubby*, arguing that with 75,000 postings submitted every day for their 1,000 bulletinboards, it is impossible to scan every posting for libel. But the judge in the trial court in New York found a significant difference between the two cases. Prodigy marketed itself as a "family-oriented" computer network and used a computer program to screen out obscene messages and offensive language. Prodigy also published guidelines that requested that users refrain from posting "insulting" notes, and warned that notes offensive to community standards would be removed when brought to Prodigy's attention. The trial court, denying the defendant's motion for summary judgment, found that by actively using technology and personnel to delete notes from its bulletinboard for "offensiveness" and "bad taste," Prodigy was clearly making content decisions, which constitute editorial control. This editorial control made them a publisher, not a distributor. The court was very careful to point that they were in full agreement with the *Cubby* decision, but in Prodigy's case, the network's conscious choice to gain the benefits of editorial control altered the scenario and mandated the finding that Prodigy was a publisher.

The parties to the case, however, subsequently reached an agreement that Prodigy would publicly apologize and the case would be dropped.

This affirmative defense was used in the 1997 on-line libel case filed by White House adviser Sidney Blumenthal against Matt Drudge and America On Line (AOL). The $30 million libel action was based on a statement Drudge had published on-line on his AOL forum, in which he claimed that Mr. Blumenthal "has a spousal abuse problem that has been effectively covered up." The court granted A.O.L.'s motion for summary judgment, dismissing the Internet service provider from the case on the grounds that telecommunications carriers, with no practical way of keeping track of the communications they submit, cannot be held liable.

---

[8]63 U.S.L.W. 2765 (1995).

The 1996 Communications Decency Act basically affirmed the reasoning in *Cubby* and created an affirmative defense for online service providers. The Act States: "No provider or user of an interactive computer service shall be treated as the publisher or speaker of any information provided by another information content provider."[9] A number of parts of this law were declared unconstitutional by the U.S. Supreme Court in the case of *Reno v. ACLU*,[10] but this provision limiting the Internet service provider's liability was not struck down.

Defenses to Defamation.   There are two primary types of defenses to a defamation action: truth and privilege. It is often stated that *truth* is an absolute defense. In other words, if I make an honest statement that harms the reputation of the defendant, there has been no defamation. However, for the ordinary plaintiff, a defendant cannot use the excuse that he or she *thought* the statement was true. It is only when a possible privilege exists that the defendant's incorrect belief about the truth of the statement is important.

Privilege is the second type of defense in a defamation action. Most privileges arise under certain circumstances in which our society has decided that encouraging people to speak is more important than protecting people's reputations.

There are two types of privilege: absolute and qualified, or conditional. When an **absolute privilege** exists, one can make any statement, true or false, and cannot be sued for defamation. There are very few situations in which such a privilege exists. The Speech and Debate Clause of the U.S. Constitution gives an absolute privilege to individuals speaking on the House and Senate floors during congressional debate. This privilege will encourage the most robust debate possible over potential legislation. Another absolute privilege arises in the courtroom during a trial.

> **absolute privilege** The right to make any statement, true or false, about someone and not be held liable for defamation.

The other type of privilege is a qualified or **conditional privilege**. A conditional privilege provides that one will not be held liable for defamation unless the false statement was made with *malice*. Malice has a special meaning in a defamation case. Malice means knowledge of the falsity of the statement or reckless disregard for the truth. In other words, the defendant either knew the statement was false or could have easily discovered whether it was false.

> **conditional privilege** The right to make a false statement about someone and not be held liable for defamation provided the statement was made without malice.

The most often used conditional privilege is the *public figure privilege*. People in the public eye, such as politicians, often find themselves the victims of false rumors. When a defendant has made a false statement about a public figure, a person who has thrust herself or himself into the public eye and who generally has access to the media, the defendant will raise the public figure privilege as a defense for defamation. If the defendant proves that the plaintiff is a public figure, the plaintiff will have to additionally prove that the defamation was made with *malice* (defined as knowledge of the falsity or reckless disregard for the truth) in order to recover for defamation.

The reason for this privilege to comment freely about public figures as long as statements are made without malice is to encourage open discussion about persons who have a significant impact on our lives. Also, because these people generally have access to the media, they are in a position to defend themselves and therefore need less protection than an ordinary private citizen.

A libel or slander case brought by a public figure sometimes appears quite complex. First, the public figure plaintiff proves that the defendant made a false statement that harmed the plaintiff's reputation. Then the defendant must prove that the plaintiff is in fact a public figure. Then the burden of proof shifts back to the plaintiff, who must prove that the statements were made with malice (Exhibit 11-1).

There are two kinds of public figures: *public figures for all purposes* and *public figures for a limited purpose*. The public figure for all purposes was defined in the foregoing paragraph. Movie stars, musicians, and politicians fall into that category. The public figure for a limited purpose is a private figure who achieves

---

[9]47 U.S.C. §230(c)1.
[10]117 S. Ct. 2329 (1997).

EXHIBIT 11-1 *The Shifting Burden of Proof in a Defamation Case*

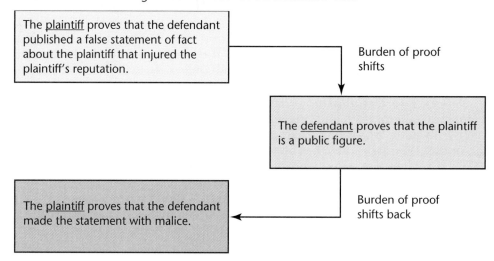

substantial media attention for a specific activity. That person is then considered a public figure for matters related to that activity. For example, the leader of an anti-abortion group would be considered a public figure for matters related to abortion. Thus, if the activist brought a defamation suit against a defendant who falsely stated that the activist had undergone three abortions as a teenager, the activist would have to prove that the defendant knew the statement was false, or acted recklessly, without even trying to check the veracity of the claim. On the other hand, had the defendant claimed that the activist had stolen money from at least three former employers, no public figure privilege would arise and it would not be necessary for the activist to prove that the claim had been made with malice.

Some people are trying to argue that the public figure privilege should apply in another context: when the defamatory statement is published over the Internet. The rationale for this privilege is twofold. First, remember that part of the reason for the public figure privilege is that the public figure who has been defamed has access to the media and therefore has the ability to defend himself or herself. Likewise, when a person is defamed over the Internet, with a few keystrokes, the defamed party can respond. Thus, there is less need for the stronger legal protection we ordinarily give to the private party. A second reason is that we want to encourage free expression and the exchange of ideas on the Internet. Requiring a plaintiff to prove malice would encourage such free discussion because people would not have to be worried about making errors when they speak about others.

Another use of the conditional privilege arises with respect to job recommendations. To encourage employers to give honest assessments of their former employees, an employer who makes a false statement about a former worker can be held liable only if the statement is made with malice. The following case demonstrates how defamation cases may arise in the employment context.

IDA WALKER V. GRAND CENTRAL SANITATION AND NOLAN PERIN

SUPERIOR COURT OF PENNSYLVANIA 634 A.2D 236 (1993)

Plaintiff Ida Walker applied for a position on a team that was being put together to bid for a recycling job. Mr. Tolbert, the organizer of the team spoke with defendant Nolan Perin, president of Grand Central Sanitation, Walker's former employer, for a reference. Tolbert informed Walker that because of the response of her former

employer, Tolbert could not put her on the team. Tolbert's recycling business, however, never materialized.

Plaintiff sued the defendant for defamation. A jury awarded her $23,500. Defendant appealed on the grounds that he should have been granted a motion notwithstanding the verdict because Walker had offered no evidence of damages.

JUSTICE OLSZEWSKI

Perin's (defendant's agent) words in a letter to Walker [from Tolbert]:

> Dear Ida,
>
> . . . Mr. Perin said that he "didn't know if she can to it." "[Pocono] didn't have a lot of success with her. Maybe she could do it for someone else. Perhaps the Pocono position was beyond her capabilities."
>
> I asked Mr. Perin what your problem was as he saw it. He told me that you "had a problem meeting goals," that you were "too liberal with personnel," and that you "wouldn't come into work Monday after working a hard week. I [Perin] just couldn't make money operating like that . . . maybe you can, but I can't. I just got tired of it and let her go."
>
> With this kind of reference, I believe that it would be difficult to successfully respond to a Request for Qualifications from the City if you were a key member of the applicants' group.
>
> Very Truly Yours,
> Rudolph V. Tolbert

Perin claims first that his statements are incapable of defamatory meaning. Any defamation action begins with the court's legal determination of whether the spoken words are capable of impugning the reputation of the person who alleges the defamation. A publication is defamatory if it is intended to harass the reputation of another so as to lower him or her in the estimation of the community or if it tends to deter third persons from associating or dealing with him or her. When considering defamatory meaning, the court must determine what effect the statement is fairly calculated to produce and the impression it would naturally engender in the minds of average persons among whom it is intended. . . . A statement which ascribes to another conduct, character, or a condition which would adversely affect her fitness for the proper conduct of her lawful business, trade or profession is defamatory. It is well established, however, that a statement which is a mere expression of opinion is not. Viewing Perin's statements in the context in which they were made, it is clear that many of his statements were opinions. Perin's assertion that he "did not have a lot of success" with Walker was nothing more than an assessment of her performance in light of his expectations. Likewise, his feeling that "I don't know if she can do it," the statement that Walker was "too liberal with personnel" and his conclusion that "I just can't make money like that" cannot be interpreted as reflecting on Walker's reputation within the business community because they express Perin's subjective viewpoint. Whether Perin is "picky" or "unfair," as Walker testified, is not subject to scrutiny. Perin is entitled to value Walker's addition to his business in any way he wishes, so long as these are his personal judgments. We find that these particular statements are not actionable as slander.

We cannot say the same for the remaining statements, however, for even if they could be viewed as part of Perin's overall assessment of his business judgment regarding Walker's performance, they "imply the existence of undisclosed defamatory facts justifying the opinion," and thus are capable of defamatory meaning. For example, Perin's statement that Walker's position at Pocono might have been "beyond her capabilities" implies that Walker's background or ability is somehow deficient for a position in the recycling/marketing field. This implication could tend to undermine the community's confidence in her ability for potentially fallacious reasons. Moreover, Perin's accusation that Walker did not show up for work on Mondays after working a hard week is not an opinion at all—it is a statement of fact which, if proven to be untrue, could have a devastating effect on Walker's reputation. Since we must view the evidence in a light most favorable to Walker, we conclude that these comments, even though laden with opinions, were capable of defamatory meaning.

Perin claims next that judgement notwithstanding the verdict should have been granted because Walker suffered no damage; Tolbert's venture never transpired and he was unaffected by the utterance of the words. Contrarily, Walker argues that since Perin's statements impugned her business reputation, she was a victim of slander per se. She therefore contends that damages are presumed and further inquiry into damages flowing from the statements is unnecessary. We cannot agree with Walker's contention.

[A] defendant who publishes a statement which can be considered slander per se is liable for the proven, actual harm the publication causes. Moreover, our holding is consistent with our state's policy of compensating, in full, a plaintiff who has proven her right to redress, while ensuring that we do so in a manner that is not unfair to the liable party:

[D]amages are to be compensatory to the full extent of the injury sustained, but the award should be limited to compensation and compensation alone.

Requiring the plaintiff to prove general damages in cases of slander per se accommodates the plaintiff's interest in recovering for damage to reputation without specifically identifying a pecuniary loss as well as the court's interest in maintaining some type of control over the amount a jury should be entitled to compensate an injured person.

Here, it becomes clear upon reviewing the record that the jury was not presented with evidence upon which it could base an award of damages, even if it could have found that Perin was not privileged to make the statements he did. The defamatory statement was spoken to one person, Tolbert, so that he could evaluate Walker and develop a marketing team for a venture that never transpired. Tolbert testified that he thought no less of Walker personally and that his opinion of her capabilities was unaffected by the defamation. There was no evidence that the words were repeated to anyone other than Tolbert or that they had any adverse effect on her job search. Walker did not testify that she suffered any adverse emotional reaction or that they impeded her ability to gain employment. These circumstances cannot permit recovery for a slander per se.

Judgment notwithstanding the verdict should have been granted in favor of Perin and Grand Central.

Reversed in favor of Defendants, Grand Central Sanitation and Perin.

Critical Thinking about the Law

THIS DEFAMATION CASE ILLUSTRATES AGAIN THE **significance of context for legal reasoning.** Not only is the context in which an action is committed important to the outcome of a case, so, too, is the unique perspective of the court ruling on the case. For instance, in a murder case, we have all heard of "hanging judges"; yet, at the same time, we recognize that not all judges are eager to hang defendants.

Because of the importance of an offense's context as well as the perspective of the court, the following questions emphasize these two considerations.

1. What primary ethical norm (i.e., what particular perspective) dominates the court's consideration of the circumstances under which a plaintiff should receive compensation in a defamation suit?

CLUE Refer to the court's extensive discussion of damages and compensation.

2. Being able to identify the connection (or lack thereof) between the reasons and the conclusion of an argument is necessary to being a good critical thinker. Identify the court's reasons for not awarding the plaintiff compensation.

CLUE Pay particular attention to the extent to which the court found the plaintiff to be damaged by the defamation.

---

public disclosure of private facts A privacy tort that consists of unwarranted disclosure of a private fact about a person.

false light A privacy tort that consists of intentionally taking actions that would lead observers to make false assumptions about the person.

appropriation A privacy tort that consists of using a person's name or likeness for commercial gain without the person's permission.

invasion of privacy A privacy tort that consists of encroaching upon the solitude, seclusion, or personal affairs of someone who has the right to expect privacy.

Privacy Torts. Although truth may be an absolute defense to defamation, one is not necessarily allowed to reveal everything one knows about another person. The recently developed tort of *invasion of privacy* is used to allow a person to keep private matters confidential. Just as defamation has two forms, libel and slander, the tort of invasion of privacy is really four distinct torts: (1) public disclosure of private facts, (2) false light, (3) appropriation, and (4) invasion of privacy.

Public disclosure of private facts occurs when the defendant makes public a fact about the plaintiff that the plaintiff is entitled to keep private. The disclosure must be unwarranted and the plaintiff must have not waived his or her right to privacy. For example, if the defendant worked in a clinic and revealed the names of women who had obtained abortions at the clinic, the defendant would be liable for public disclosure of private facts.

False light occurs when you do not actually make a defamatory statement about someone, but by your actions you place the person in a false light. For example, a neighborhood newsletter publishes a story captioned "Gang Warfare Growing in Our Community," and between the caption and the article is an untitled photo of four girls sitting on the hood of a car. The photo is clear enough that the girls' identities are obvious. If these girls are not gang members, they have been placed in a false light and may sue the publisher.

Appropriation of a person's name for commercial gain occurs when a defendant uses another's name or likeness without that person's permission for commercial gain. This tort, for example, prohibits a cereal company from putting an athlete's picture on their cereal box without obtaining the athlete's permission.

The final privacy tort is **invasion of privacy**, which occurs when someone invades another's solitude, seclusion, or personal affairs when that person has the right to expect privacy. Some examples of invasion of privacy would include wiretapping and using someone's password to gain access to the person's electronic mail messages. Or, an owner of an ice skating rink who installed two-way mirrors in the women's dressing room would have committed an invasion of privacy because the skaters should be able to expect a certain degree of privacy in a dressing room. Of course, the degree of privacy one should reasonably expect varies greatly. For example, if one is trying on clothes in a department store fitting room where signs are posted saying that "area is under observation to deter shoplifting," it would not be unreasonable for the store to have authorized security guards of the same sex as the dressing room occupants observing the dressing rooms.

False Imprisonment.   **False imprisonment** is the intentional restraint or confinement of a person against that person's will and without justification. The tort protects our freedom of movement. The confinement cannot be by moral force alone or by threats of future harm. There must be either physical restraint, such as locking a door; physical force, such as holding someone down; or threats of physical force.

Most cases of false imprisonment are brought against security guards and retailers. In fact, this tort is brought so frequently against retailers who have detained a person suspected of shoplifting that it has become known as the "shopkeeper's tort." In most states, retailers who detain suspected shoplifters for questioning are entitled to raise the "shopkeepers' privilege." Under this privilege a merchant who has reason to believe a person has shoplifted may detain the person for questioning about the incident. The detention must be conducted in a reasonable manner, and the suspect can be held for only a reasonable time. The following case illustrates this privilege.

false imprisonment The intentional restraint or confinement, by force or threat of force, of a person against that person's will and without justification.

GORTAREZ V. SMITTY'S SUPER VALU
ARIZONA SUPREME COURT 1400 P.2D 807 (1984)

Plaintiff Earnest Gortarez Jr. accompanied his cousin Hernandez to Smitty's Bit Town #10, where Hernandez purchased a $22 power booster in the auto supply department. Gortarez picked up a $.59 vaporizer and asked whether he could pay for it up front when he finished shopping. The clerk said yes. The boys wandered around looking at other merchandise and left the store through an unattended checkout aisle. As the boys walked into the parking lot, a clerk, assistant manager, and security guard ran after them, pushed Hernandez against the car and started searching him. Gortarez tried to help his cousin, and the security guard used a chokehold on him. They were finally released when a checkout boy said the vaporizer was in a basket at the unattended checkout aisle. Gortarez required medical treatment for injuries from the chokehold.

Plaintiff Gortarez brought this action for false imprisonment, as well as assault. The defendant made a motion for a directed verdict on the false imprisonment claim, which was granted. Plaintiff appealed.

JUDGE FELDMAN

As Prosser noted, shoplifting is a major problem, causing losses that range into millions of dollars each year. There have been a number of decisions which permit a business person for reasonable cause, to detain a customer for investigation. [P]rivilege, however, is narrow; it is confined to what is reasonably necessary for its limited purpose, of enabling the defendant to do what is possible on the spot to discover the facts. There will be liability if the detention is for a length of time beyond that which is reasonably necessary for such a short investigation, or if the plaintiff is assaulted, insulted or bullied, or public accusation is made against him, or the privilege is exercised in an unreasonable manner.

To invoke the privilege, therefore, "reasonable cause" is only the threshold requirement. Once reasonable cause is established, there are two further questions regarding the application of the privilege. We must ask whether the purpose of the shopkeeper's action was proper (i.e., detention for questioning or summoning a law enforcement officer). The last question is whether the detention was carried out in a reasonable manner and for a reasonable length of time. If the answer to any of the three questions is negative, then the privilege granted by statute is inapplicable, the seizure is tortious.

Under statutes permitting the detention of suspected shoplifters, "reasonable cause" generally has the same meaning as "probable cause."

In the case at bench, the facts supporting reasonable cause are as follows: the clerk saw Gortarez with the item when he asked if he could pay for it at the front. The clerk followed the two young men through the store, and did not see them either deposit the item or pay for it as they left.

The nature and extent of investigation is part of the determination of reasonable cause. Actual verification by seeing the customer leave the store with merchandise without paying for it is not a necessary element to establish reasonable cause under this statutory privilege.

The statute provides this privilege for the express and limited purpose of detention for investigation by questioning or summoning a law enforcement officer. There was no evidence of either questioning or summoning of officers. Although there was no questioning, it is possible that the intent of the employee was to question or call officers.

Assuming there was reasonable cause for the detention, and that the detention was for a proper purpose, the privilege still may not attach if the merchant does not detain in a reasonable manner and for a reasonable time.

Restatement (Second) of Torts states that the use of force is never privileged unless the resistance of the suspected thief makes the use of such force necessary for the actor's self-defense.

Reasonable force may be used to detain the person; but . . . the use of force intended or likely to cause serious bodily harm is never privileged for the sole purpose of detention to investigate, and it becomes privileged only where the resistance of the other makes it necessary for the actor to use such force in self-defense. In the ordinary case, the use of any force at all will not be privileged until the other has been requested to remain; and it is only where there is not time for such a request, or it would obviously be futile, that force is justified.

We hold that the principle quoted is applicable to our statutory requirement that the detention be carried out in a "reasonable manner." Under the restrictions given above, there was a question whether the use of force in the restraint of Gortarez was reasonable. There was no request that the two young men remain. No inquiry was made with regard to whether Hernandez had the vaporizer. Gibson testified that Hernandez gave no indication of resistance and made no attempt to escape. The possible theft of a $.59 item hardly warrants apprehension that the two were armed or dangerous. There was, arguably, time to make a request to remain before Gibson seized Hernandez and began searching him. Also, there is no indication that such a request would obviously have been futile. The evidence adduced probably would have supported a finding that the manner of detention was unreasonable as a matter of law. At best, there was a question of fact; there was no support for the court's presumptive finding that as a matter of law the detention was performed reasonably.

The court directed a verdict for defendants on the false arrest and imprisonment counts. In so doing, it necessarily found as a matter of law that there was reasonable cause, and the seizure and detention were undertaken for a proper purpose and in a reasonable manner. We hold that the court erred in the findings with respect to both the purpose and manner of detention. This requires reversal and retrial. At the new trial evidence on the three issues should be measured against the principles set forth in this opinion.

Reversed and remanded in favor of Plaintiff, Gortarez.

Even if one is successful in bringing an action for false imprisonment, damages are often not easy to prove. Obviously, a person who is physically restrained might have medical bills for treatment of physical injuries, but most cases do not involve physical harm. Usually plaintiffs ask for a monetary award to compensate them for lost time off work, pain and suffering from the mental distress, and humiliation.

Intentional Infliction of Emotional Distress. One of the newest torts against the person is **intentional infliction of emotional distress**. This tort arises when the defendant engages in outrageous, intentional conduct that is likely to cause extreme emotional distress to the party toward whom such conduct is directed. For example, if a debt collector called a debtor and told him that he was a police officer and he was sorry to inform him that his wife had just been killed in an auto accident, and her last words to the medic at the scene of the crash had been, "God must be punishing me for our not paying our debts," such conduct would most likely be interpreted as the intentional infliction of emotional distress.

In most states, to recover damages for intentional infliction of emotional distress, the plaintiff must demonstrate some physical symptoms caused by his or her emotional distress. For example, in the above example, if the plaintiff had high blood pressure, and after hearing the message he had a heart attack, the heart attack would provide the basis for his injury. Other physical symptoms commonly arising from emotional distress include headaches, a sudden onset of high blood pressure, hives, chills, inability to sleep, or inability to get out of bed.

The following case provides an illustration of this tort.

intentional infliction of emotional distress
Intentionally engaging in outrageous conduct that is likely to cause extreme emotional pain to the person toward whom the conduct is directed.

M.B.M. COMPANY, INC., PETITIONER V. SHIRLEY ANN COUNCE, RESPONDENT
SUPREME COURT OF ARKANSAS 596 S.W.2D 681 (1980)

Plaintiff Shirley Counce sued defendant M.B.M. Company for intentional infliction of emotional distress. She was laid off by M.B.M. initially because she "was not needed." Subsequently, she was accused of stealing money; on her last day of work she was told she would not get her last check unless she took a polygraph test. She passed the test, but when she received her last check, $36 was deducted, with the deduction explained to her as being her share of the missing money. She applied for unemployment compensation, but her claim was denied because the employer reported that the plaintiff had been fired because of numerous customer complaints, a bad attitude, and violating company rules. Ms. Counce then filed this lawsuit. The trial court judge granted the defendant's motion for summary judgment. The court of appeals reversed and defendant appealed.

CHIEF JUSTICE FOGELMAN

The evolutionary process demonstrated by our own decisions caused Prof. William T. Prosser to say, in 1939, that it was time that the courts recognize that they had created a new tort. According to him, the new tort consisted of intentional, outrageous infliction of mental suffering in the extreme form and that it resembled assault. He pointed out that, in spite of the fact that mental anguish had been recognized in early assault cases, the law had been reluctant to accept interest in peace of mind as entitled to independent legal protection. He described the matter dealt with in this new tort as outrageous conduct of a kind especially calculated to cause serious mental and emotional disturbance. Prof. Prosser pointed out that in many cases in which recovery for mental suffering was permitted as parasitic damage, that element was the only substantial damage actually sustained.

We can and do now recognize that one who by extreme and outrageous conduct wilfully or wantonly causes severe emotional distress to another is subject to liability for such emotional distress and for bodily harm resulting from the distress.

It is of little consequence that different terms are used in describing the element of compensable damages involved as mental suffering, mental anguish, emotional distress, etc. Prosser sees the term mental anguish comprehensive enough to cover everything from nervous shock to emotional upset, and agrees that the words emotional distress may well be used. In his view they include all highly unpleasant mental reactions, such as fright, horror, grief, shame, humiliation, anger, embarrassment, chagrin, disappointment, worry and nausea. The emotional distress for which damages may be sought must be so severe that no reasonable person could be expected to endure it. It must be reasonable and justified under the circumstances. Liability arises only when the distress is extreme.

By extreme and outrageous conduct, we mean conduct that is so outrageous in character, and so extreme in degree, as to go beyond all possible bounds of decency, and to be regraded as atrocious, and utterly intolerable in a civilized society.

Since we recognize the tort of intentional infliction of emotional distress, we conclude that granting a summary judgment was error. Ms. Counce has no cause of action for intentional infliction of emotional distress because of petitioner's action in discharging, because petitioner is not liable for doing that which it had the legal right to do.

M.B.M.'s conduct subsequent to her discharge is a different matter. Prosser states that there are cases in which the extreme and outrageous nature of the conduct arises not so much from what is done as from the abuse by the defendant of a relationship with the plaintiff which gives him power to damage the plaintiff's interests. Certainly there was such a relationship so long as Ms. Counce was not paid for her work until the time of her discharge. Such a relationship also existed with reference to her entitlement to unemployment compensation benefits. The facts disclose that, in order to receive her pay, Ms. Counce was forced to submit to a polygraph test after her employment had been terminated and to cause a labor department investigation to collect $36 of the $36.81 due her. There is, at this point, no satisfactory explanation of the basis for withholding this money after she had passed the polygraph test. The different reasons given for her discharge are a significant circumstance, particularly when Coleman Moss' unsatisfactory explanation of the basis for the statement made by M.B.M. to the Employment Security Division is taken into account. We have no hesitation in saying that there was a material issue of fact as to whether M.B.M.'s conduct was extreme and outrageous.

We cannot say, with the degree of certainty that we should where summary judgment is involved, that there is no material issue of fact as to her unpleasant mental reactions such as anguish, shock, anger, embarrassment, chagrin, disappointment or worry.

Affirmed in favor of Plaintiff, Counce.

trespass to realty (trespass to real property) Intentionally entering the land of another or causing an object to be placed on the land of another without the landowner's permission.

trespass to personalty Intentionally exercising dominion and control over another's personal property.

conversion Intentional permanent removal of property from the rightful owner's possession and control.

disparagement Intentionally defaming a business product or service.

INTENTIONAL TORTS AGAINST PROPERTY   The foregoing torts arise when persons are harmed. The second category of intentional torts involve damage to property. **Trespass to realty**, also called **trespass to real property**, occurs when a person intentionally enters the land of another or causes an object to be placed on the land of another without the landowner's permission. Trespass to realty also occurs when one originally enters another's land with permission, is told to leave, and yet remains on the land. It is no defense to argue that one did not know that the land belonged to another; the intent refers to intentionally being on that particular piece of land.

   Trespass to personalty occurs when one intentionally exercises dominion and control over another's personal property. It is usually of short duration, and the trespasser is liable for any harm caused to the property or any loss suffered by the true owner as a result of the trespasser's having the property.

   Conversion is a more extreme wrong. It requires the defendant's permanent removal of the property from the owner's possession and control. With conversion, the item cannot be recovered or restored to its original condition. The plaintiff usually recovers damages for the full value of the converted item.

   If I take my neighbor's car for a drive without permission, but I return it unharmed before the owner knows I have it, I have committed trespass to personalty, but the true owner has no damages. If I take the car and hit a tree, damaging the bumper before I return the car, I have again committed trespass to personalty and will be liable for the cost of repairing the car. If I take the car and sell it to a salvage firm that tears the car apart and sells its parts, I have committed conversion and will be liable for replacing the car.

INTENTIONAL TORTS AGAINST ECONOMIC INTERESTS   Torts against economic interests are the torts that most commonly arise within the business context. One such tort, the tort of **disparagement**, is a form of a tort you previously read about: defamation. Disparagement can be thought of as defamation of a business product or service.

   To win a disparagement case, a plaintiff must prove four elements. First, the defendant made a false statement of a material fact about the plaintiff's business product or service. In general, the type of statements that are actionable are statements about the quality, honesty, or reputation of the business, as well as statements about the ownership of the business property. The second element is publication. Remember, publication in the context of any kind of defamation action means communication to a third party. So if the defendant makes disparaging comments about the plaintiff's business in a public address to a consumer group or in an advertisement, the defendant has published the statement.

   Third, there must be harm to the reputation of the business, product, or service. Finally, there must be actual economic loss as a result of the false statements. Proving the economic loss that provides a basis for compensatory damages is not always easy. Usually damages will be based on a decrease in profits that can be linked to the publication of the false statement. An alternative, although a less common way to prove damages would be to demonstrate that the plaintiff had been negotiating a contract with a third party, but the third party lost interest shortly after the publication of the false statement. The profits the plaintiff would have made on the contract would be the damages. Table 11-4 lists the elements of disparagement.

TABLE 11-4   *Elements of Disparagement*

1. A false statement of a material fact about the plaintiff's product or service
2. Publication
3. Damage to the reputation of the product or service
4. Economic loss

In 13 states, a closely related tort has recently been created: *food disparagement*. Dubbed "veggie libel" and "banana bills" by their critics, these laws provide ranchers and farmers a cause of action when someone spreads false information about the safety of a food product.

The first major test of one of these laws came in a $6.7 million case filed by a rancher in a federal district court against talk show host Oprah Winfrey and one of her guests. They were discussing the potential for U.S. cattle to contract mad cow disease, and, at one point, Oprah said that was it; the conversation had stopped her from ever eating a burger again. After the broadcast, which the show's producers said tried to show both sides of the issue, the price of cattle futures fell.

The Texas law at issue provides that anyone who says that a perishable food product is unsafe, and knows the statement is false, may be required to pay damages to the producer of the product. The defendants originally asked that the case be dismissed on the grounds that the law unconstitutionally interferes with free speech. The judge dismissed the food disparagement claims on the grounds that the cattlemen did not prove that "knowingly false" statements were made and that a perishable food was involved. The jury then decided there was no case under traditional business disparagement law, either. But the plaintiffs were not deterred; a week later they filed a second "veggie" libel case against Winfrey in a Texas state court. At publication time, the fate of this second lawsuit had not been decided.

Another tort against economic interests is the tort of **intentional interference with a contract**, a complex and difficult tort to prove. In order to prove the tort of intentional interference with a contract, the plaintiff must demonstrate that:

> **intentional interference with a contract** Knowingly and successfully taking action for the purpose of enticing a third party to breach a valid contract with the plaintiff.

1. The plaintiff had a valid contract with a third party.
2. The defendant knew of the contract and its terms.
3. The defendant took action knowing that it was highly likely to cause the third party to breach the contract with the plaintiff.
4. The defendant undertook the action for the purpose of causing the third party to breach the contract.
5. The third party did in fact breach the contract.
6. As a result of the breach, the plaintiff was injured.

Some of the most common intentional interference with contract cases in the business setting involve employers' taking employees from another firm when they know the employee has a contract for a set period of time. Luring an employee from a successful competitor is often a delicate situation. There is no problem if the employee does not have a contract for a fixed period of time, but if the employee is indeed bound by a contract of employment for a fixed term or by a contractual agreement to not work for a competitor for a set period of time, then pursuit of the employee makes a second employer with knowledge of the contract open to liability.

A third tort against economic interest is **unfair competition**. Our legal system assumes that individuals go into business for the purpose of making a profit. Competition is supposed to drive inefficient firms out of business because the more efficient firms will be able to provide less expensive goods and services. For this system to work, however, firms must be in business to make a profit. Therefore, it is unlawful for a person to go into business for the purpose of causing a loss of business to another without regard for his or her own profit.

> **unfair competition** Entering into business for the sole purpose of causing a loss of business to another firm.

For example, assume that Mark wants to open a painting business, but his father wants him to go to college. When Mark opens his business, his father starts a competing firm, and is able to underbid every job his son bids because he, the father, is willing to lose money. He just wants to force his son out of business. The father, in this case, is engaging in unfair competition.

Misappropriation is another tort against economic interest that is difficult to prove. Misappropriation occurs when a person presents an unsolicited

> **misappropriation** Use of an unsolicited idea for a product, service, or marketing method without compensating the originator of the idea.

idea for a product, service, or even method of marketing to a business with the expectation of compensation if the idea is used by the firm and the firm subsequently uses the idea without compensating the individual. The individual may have the basis for an action for misappropriation.

The firm may always defend on the grounds that they had already independently come up with the idea that the plaintiff had proposed. They may also deny that the idea was even discussed. It is therefore extremely important that anyone offering an unsolicited idea to a firm have that idea and the offer to the firm documented.

NEGLIGENT TORTS

ELEMENTS OF NEGLIGENCE   The second classification of torts is negligent torts. **Negligence** results not from the willful wrongdoing of a party but from carelessness. A person is said to be negligent when her or his behavior falls below the standard of care necessary to protect others from an unreasonable risk of harm. To prove negligence, a plaintiff must establish four elements: (1) duty, (2) breach of duty, (3) causation, and (4) damages. Failure to establish any one of those elements precludes recovery by the plaintiff.

The first element to be proved is *duty*. The duty is the standard of care that the defendant owes the plaintiff. Under certain circumstances, a law establishes the duty of care for a particular party, but the courts generally use a "reasonable person" standard. Under this standard, the defendant must have exercised the degree of care and skill that a reasonable person would have exercised in similar circumstances to protect the plaintiff from an unreasonable risk of injury.

The next element is a *breach of duty*. Once the plaintiff establishes the duty required of the defendant under the circumstances, the plaintiff must show that the defendant's conduct was not consistent with that duty. For example, a reasonable person does not leave a campfire burning unattended in the woods. A defendant who builds a campfire and then goes home without putting out the campfire has breached her or his duty of care to the owner of the campground and to other campers whose safety is endangered by the unguarded campfire.

The third element is *causation*. This is really two elements, actual cause and proximate cause. *Actual cause* is a factual matter of whether the defendant's conduct resulted in the plaintiff's injury. The breach of the duty must have resulted directly in the plaintiff's harm. To ascertain whether the breach of duty was the actual cause of the plaintiff's harm, one asks oneself, "If the defendant had obeyed his or her duty, would the plaintiff still have been injured?" If the answer is no, then the defendant's breach was the actual cause of the plaintiff's harm.

Proximate cause is a question of how far the society wishes to extend liability. In the majority of states, proximate cause is defined as foreseeability. Proximate cause exists if both the plaintiff and the type of injury incurred by the plaintiff are foreseeable. For example, it is foreseeable that if a tire falls off a car, the car may run off the road and hit a pedestrian. It is not foreseeable that the pedestrian will be carrying dynamite, which he will throw when he sees the car moving toward him, causing the dynamite to explode, causing vibrations that shatter a window six blocks away, causing glass to fly and cut a secretary. Neither the secretary nor the secretary's injury would be foreseeable, so the secretary would not succeed in a suit for negligence against the manufacturer of the car in most states because of the lack of proximate cause. Proximate cause, however, would not prevent the pedestrian from suing in this example because a pedestrian is a foreseeable victim when a car goes out of control.

In a minority of states, the courts do not differentiate between actual and proximate cause; once actual cause is proved, proximate cause is said to exist. Thus, in the minority of states, both the pedestrian and the secretary would be able to recover in the foregoing example.

Damages, or compensable injury, are the final element. The defendant's action must have resulted in some harm to the plaintiff for which the plaintiff can be compensated. A party cannot bring an action in negligence seeking only nominal damages.

negligence Failure to live up to the standard of care that a reasonable person would meet to protect others from an unreasonable risk of harm.

Thus, in any negligence case, the plaintiff must show that the defendant owed a duty of care to the plaintiff and breached that duty, causing foreseeable harm to the plaintiff for which the plaintiff is seeking compensation. Place yourself in the plaintiff's position to see that proving negligence would often be difficult. Frequently, direct proof of the defendant's negligent conduct does not exist because it was destroyed and there were no witnesses to the negligent act. To make it easier for plaintiffs to recover in negligence cases, most courts have adopted two doctrines: *res ipsa loquitur* and *negligence per se.*

Res ipsa loquitur literally means "the thing speaks for itself." The plaintiff uses this doctrine to allow the judge or jury to *infer* that the defendant's negligence was the cause of the plaintiff's harm when there is no direct evidence of the defendant's lack of due care. To establish res ipsa loquitur in most states, the plaintiff must demonstrate that:

1. The event was of a kind that ordinarily does not occur in the absence of negligence.
2. Other responsible causes, including the conduct of third parties and the plaintiff, have been sufficiently eliminated.
3. The indicated negligence is within the scope of the defendant's duty to the plaintiff.

> **res ipsa loquitur** Legal doctrine that allows a judge or a jury to infer negligence on the basis of the fact that accidents of the type that happened to the plaintiff generally do not occur in the absence of negligence on the part of someone in the defendant's position.

Proof of these elements does not *require* a finding of negligence; it merely permits it.

One of the earliest uses of res ipsa loquitur was the case of *Escola v. Coca Cola.*[11] In that case, the plaintiff, a waitress, was injured when a bottle of Coca Cola that she was removing from a case exploded in her hand. From the facts that (1) bottled soft drinks ordinarily do not spontaneously explode, and (2) the bottles had been sitting in a case, undisturbed, in the restaurant for approximately 36 hours before the plaintiff simply removed the bottle from the case, the jury reasonably inferred that the defendant's negligence in the filling of the bottle resulted in its explosion. The plaintiff therefore could recover without direct proof of the defendant's negligence. The doctrine has subsequently been used in numerous accident cases in which there has been no direct evidence of negligence. Note that the jury does not have to infer negligence, but they may. The defendant's best response to the use of this doctrine is to try to demonstrate other possible causes of the accident.

Another doctrine that may aid the plaintiff is **negligence per se**. If a statute is enacted to prevent a certain type of harm and a defendant violates that statute, causing that type of harm to befall the plaintiff, the plaintiff may use proof of the violation of the statute as proof as negligence. For example, it is unlawful to sell certain types of glue to minors because they may inhale it to obtain a euphoric feeling. Such a use of the glue may lead to severe health problems or death. If a retailer sold such glue to a minor who died from sniffing the glue, proof of the sale in violation of the statute establishes negligence per se by the retailer.

> **negligence per se** Legal doctrine that says when a statute has been enacted to prevent a certain type of harm and the defendant violates that statute, causing that type of harm to befall the plaintiff, the plaintiff may use proof of the violation as proof of negligence.

DEFENSES TO NEGLIGENCE   While the courts have created the two foregoing doctrines to help the plaintiff establish his or her case, the courts also accept certain defenses that will relieve a defendant from liability, even if the plaintiff has successfully established the elements of negligence.

Initially, all states made available a strong defense to negligence: **contributory negligence**. Under this defense, the defendant must prove that (1) the plaintiff did not exercise the degree of care that one would ordinarily exercise to protect oneself from an unreasonable risk of harm, and (2) this failure contributed to causing the plaintiff's own harm. Proof of such contributory negligence is an absolute bar to recovery. In other words, once the defendant proves that the plaintiff was contributorily negligent, the defendant wins the lawsuit

> **contributory negligence** A defense to negligence that consists of proving the plaintiff did not exercise the ordinary degree of care to protect against an unreasonable risk of harm and that this failure contributed to causing the plaintiff's harm.

---

[11]150 P.2d 436 (1944).

EXHIBIT 11-2 *Application of the Last-Clear-Chance Doctrine*

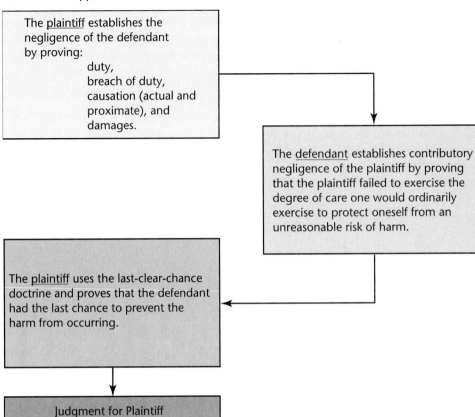

The plaintiff establishes the
negligence of the defendant
by proving:
    duty,
    breach of duty,
    causation (actual and
    proximate), and
    damages.

The defendant establishes contributory
negligence of the plaintiff by proving
that the plaintiff failed to exercise the
degree of care one would ordinarily
exercise to protect oneself from an
unreasonable risk of harm.

The plaintiff uses the last-clear-chance
doctrine and proves that the defendant
had the last chance to prevent the
harm from occurring.

Judgment for Plaintiff

comparative negligence A
defense that allocates recovery
based on percentage of fault
allocated to plaintiff and
defendant; available in either
pure or modified form.

and will not have to pay any damages to the plaintiff. Because of the harshness
of this defense, many states adopted the *last-clear-chance doctrine* (Exhibit 11-2).
Under this doctrine, once the defendant establishes contributory negligence on
the part of the plaintiff, the plaintiff may still recover by showing that the defendant had the last clear opportunity to avoid the accident that resulted in the
plaintiff's loss.

The adoption of this doctrine, however, still left a lot of situations in which
an extremely careless defendant caused a great deal of harm to a plaintiff who
was barred from recovery because of minimal contributory negligence. Thus,
today, most states have replaced the contributory negligence defense with either pure or modified **comparative negligence**. Under a *pure comparative negligence* defense, the court determines the percentage of fault of the defendant,
and that is the percentage of damages for which the defendant is liable. Damages under *modified comparative negligence* are calculated in the same manner,
except that the defendant must be more than 50 percent at fault before the
plaintiff can recover. Twenty-eight states have modified comparative negligence, thirteen have pure comparative negligence, and nine have contributory
negligence. Remember, every state adopts one of these three defenses. The parties do not get to pick from among them. However, if a party resides in a state
that uses a defense that is not favorable to that party, he or she can always
argue that the state should change its law to accept a different defense. For example, a plaintiff residing in a state that still allows the contributory negligence
defense might try to argue that the state should follow the trend and modernize
its law by moving to modified comparative negligence and abolishing the contributory negligence defense.

assumption of the risk A
defense to negligence based on
showing that the plaintiff
voluntarily and unreasonably
encountered a known risk and
that the harm that the plaintiff
suffered was the harm that was
risked.

Another defense that may be used in a negligence case is **assumption of
the risk**. The defendant must show that the plaintiff voluntarily and unreasonably encountered a known risk. To successfully use this defense, the defen-

dant must establish that the harm suffered was indeed the risk assumed. For example, in a 1976 case, a plaintiff was using a grinding wheel wearing only his eyeglasses and not the safety goggles provided by his employer to keep the pieces of stone chips and dust from flying into his eyes. The defective grinding wheel exploded into three pieces, and one piece flew into the plaintiff's eye, blinding him. When the plaintiff sued the defendant manufacturer, the defendant raised the defense of assumption of the risk. The court struck down that attempted use of the defense, noting that the wearing of safety goggles was not intended to prevent harm from exploding grinding wheels, and that if any risks were assumed, it was the risk of getting a small stone chip in his eye. As the plaintiff could not have known that the wheel would explode, he could not have assumed the risk.

STRICT LIABILITY TORTS

A third type of tort is a strict liability tort. Under this theory, the defendant is engaged in an activity that is so inherently dangerous under the circumstances of its performance that no amount of due care can make it safe. The activity does have some social utility, however, so we do not want to prohibit it entirely. Consequently, we allow people to engage in such activities but hold them strictly liable for any damages caused by engaging in these activities. Inherently dangerous activities include blasting in a populated area and keeping nondomesticated animals. As the reader will see in the next chapter, in today's society, strict liability has had perhaps its greatest impact on cases involving products that are considered unreasonably dangerous.

INTERNATIONAL DIMENSIONS OF TORT LAW

With the increasing globalization of business, it is becoming more common for citizens of foreign countries to temporarily reside in the United States, as well as for U.S. citizens to reside abroad for long periods of time. There are also a number of people with dual citizenship. It is therefore a realistic possibility that one might get a tort judgment in the United States and need to enforce that judgment in a foreign nation.

Although many European nations are signatories to treaties regarding enforcement of foreign judgments, the United States has not signed any such treaties. Therefore, the extent to which a U.S. judgment will be enforced in a foreign nation depends on that nation's laws. For example, some nations will review the judgment to ensure that it does not offend their country's notion of due process.

One area in which at least two nations have been unwilling to fully enforce U.S. judgments is with respect to punitive damage awards. Both a German federal court and English court have ruled that punitive damage awards violate their nation's public policy interest in maintaining a purely compensatory tort system. They have therefore refused to enforce U.S. punitive damages awards. As international business, and thus international litigation, continue to grow, the U.S. business manager will have to become increasingly familiar with the policies of foreign courts.

SUMMARY

Tort law provides a means for an injured party to obtain compensation from the party whose actions caused the injury. Tort law provides three types of damages. Compensatory damages, which are the most common, are designed to put the plaintiff in the position he or she would have been in had the tort not occurred. Nominal damages, available only in intentional tort cases, are a minimal amount, such as $1, and signify that the defendant's behavior was wrongful but caused no harm. Punitive damages are assessed in addition to compensatory damages when the defendant's conduct is egregious. Punitive damages are designed primarily to punish the defendant and deter such conduct in the future.

Torts are classified as intentional, negligent, or strict liability, depending on the degree of willfulness required for the tort. The most willful are the intentional torts, which are further categorized by the interest that is injured. Intentional torts against the person include assault, battery, defamation, intentional infliction of emotional distress, false imprisonment, and the privacy torts. Intentional torts against property include trespass to realty, trespass to personalty, and conversion. Intentional torts against economic interests include disparagement, intentional interference with contractual relations, misappropriation and unfair competition.

Negligence can be thought of as the tort of carelessness. To prove negligence, one must prove four elements: (1) duty of care, (2) breach of duty, (3) causation, and (4) damages. Negligence per se and res ipsa loquitur are two doctrines that may help the plaintiff prove negligence. Defenses to negligence include contributory negligence, modified and pure comparative negligence, and assumption of the risk.

Strict liability occurs when one causes injury to another by engaging in an unreasonably dangerous activity.

As more citizens of foreign nations reside in the U.S., and more residents of foreign countries reside in the U.S., it becomes increasingly likely that one might get a tort judgment in the United States and need to enforce it in a foreign country. The enforceability of such a judgment depends upon that foreign nation's laws. And if one is attempting to enforce that judgment in either Germany or England, any punitive damages award will not be enforced.

REVIEW QUESTIONS

11-1. Evaluate the arguments for and against restricting the availability of punitive damages. Explain why you would tend to agree more with one position than the other.

11-2. Distinguish intentional torts from negligent torts.

11-3. Define an assault and a battery, and explain how the two are related.

11-4. Explain why it is harder to win a defamation action if you are a public figure.

11-5. Explain the relationship between trespass to personalty and conversion.

11-6. Your state is proposing to pass a food disparagement law. Construct the strongest arguments in support of and in opposition to such a law. Explain how emphasizing the importance of different ethical norms could lead to a different attitude toward the proposed law.

REVIEW PROBLEMS

11-7. Karen writes Bob a long letter in which she falsely accuses him of stealing her bike. Bob is outraged because no one has ever questioned his character in that way before. He is so incensed that he shows the letter to several colleagues, as well as to his boss.

A few weeks later, he applies for a promotion and is turned down. When he asks his boss why he lost the promotion, his boss, very reluctantly, says he believed that a number of people were concerned about his integrity in light of the recent accusations about his involvement in a bicycle theft. Bob sues Karen for defamation and intentional infliction of emotional distress. Why will he probably succeed or fail on each claim?

11-8. Madeline enters into a contract with Canyon Canoes to go on a week-long canoe trip down a river. The contract states that, although the firm provides experienced guides and high-quality equipment, they are not insurers of the adventurers' safety. The firm cannot be responsible for harm resulting from ordinary dangers of outdoor activities. Madeline is injured when the Coleman stove she was provided with explodes. The explosion was caused by an inadequate repair that had been made by Canyon Canoes. The company raises the defense of assumption of the risk when she sues them for negligence. Why is or is this not a valid defense?

11-9. Action Advertising hired Alice Jones as an account executive. She signed an employment contract under which she agreed to work for the agency for a one-year term for an annual salary of $45,000. After the manager of Creative Ads had seen an exceptional set of ads Jones had created, he called Jones, asking her whether she would be interested in changing jobs. When Jones explained that she was bound by contract for six more months, the manager said that the contract was unenforceable, and further offered to double her salary if she came to work for him because he did not believe she was being paid what she was worth. If Jones quits and goes to work for Creative, is there a tort? If so, what would the remedy be? If not, why not?

11-10. Sam was driving in excess of the speed limit and ran a red light at 11 P.M. He hit Suzanne's car, which was crossing the intersection when he ran the red light. Sam had not seen Suzanne's car because of his excess speed and also because she was driving a black car and had not turned on her headlights. Suzanne suffered extensive injuries, and sued Sam for negligence. Detail the manner in which she tried to prove her case and describe how Sam attempted to defend himself. How do you think the court would resolve this dispute? How would the state in which the case arose affect the outcome?

11-11. Bill is having marital difficulties and has an affair with Sara, from whom he contracts herpes. Hoping to work out his marital problems, he does not inform his wife of his infection. Four years later, Bill and his wife, Eva, divorce. A month later, before she has had any relationships with other men, Eva discovers she has herpes. Knowing she could have contracted the disease from only one person, she sues her husband for negligence, battery, and intentional infliction of emotional distress. What arguments would she make to support each of these causes of action? Explain how you believe the court would respond to each argument.

11-12. Devo Dynamite is imploding a building. Despite taking every known safety precaution and imploding the building at a time when the least traffic is likely to be in the area, the implosion is not perfect, and Ron, a passerby, is injured by a piece of flying debris. What tort may Devo be accused of committing? Explain why Ron is either likely or unlikely to be successful in his legal action.

CASE PROBLEMS

11-13. Briney owned an unoccupied farmhouse. Frustrated by vandals entering the house, he set up a spring gun to discharge in the event that anyone entered a bedroom of the old building. Katko and his companion had broken into the house to find and steal old bottles and dated fruit jars. When they opened the bedroom door, the gun automatically discharged, shooting Katko in the leg. He sued Briney for battery. The jury entered an award for Katko for $20,000 in actual damages and $10,000 in punitive damages. Briney filed a motion for a new trial, which the trial court judge denied. He appealed the denial of the motion to the state supreme court. How do you think the court ruled? Why? *Katko v. Briney*, 183 N.W.3d 657 (1971)

11-14. Hank Fishel was shopping at a supermarket when he was stopped by a security guard, who accused him of stealing a bottle of aspirin that he had in his sweater pocket. When the guard called the manager, Fishel explained that he had just previously bought the aspirin at a drugstore and was comparing prices. He said that if they would accompany him to the drugstore, they would find the package in the trash bin in front of the drugstore. Fishel said also that if they would count all the aspirins in the bottle, they would find two missing: the two he had taken outside the store. The manager refused both requests, and they took Fishel to the stockroom, where they searched him and handcuffed him to a large metal container, where he waited until the police arrived. The manager filed a complaint against him. Charges were dropped when the security guard failed to appear to testify. Fishel then sued the store. On what grounds was his suit based? Was he successful? *Colonial Stores v. Fishel*, 288 S.E. 21 (1981)

11-15. On October 2, 1990, a tabloid published by Globe International Publishing Inc., the *Sun*, ran a front-page story entitled "Pregnancy Forces Granny to Quit Work at Age 101." Accompanying the headline was a photograph of Nellie Mitchell, a 96-year-old woman from Arkansas, although the story purported to be about a woman from Australia named Audrey Wiles. Mrs. Mitchell was severely humiliated and embarrassed by the publication of her picture in the *Sun* and subsequently sued Globe International. For what tort did she sue the publisher? Was her action successful? *Mitchell v. Globe International Publishing, Inc.*, 978 F.2d 1065 (1992)

11-16. Plaintiff Mark Goldfarb, a former state prisoner, was enrolled in the defendant's class. During one class meeting, an unidentified person came in, threw a pie that struck the professor, and then left. The professor immediately accused Goldfarb of the assault. The next day, when Goldfarb attempted to take his seat for class, the professor had him ejected from the building. In front of the class, the professor accused Goldfarb of attempting to blackmail him. Goldfarb sued the professor for intentional infliction of emotional distress, claiming that the professor's actions had caused him extreme mental anguish, humiliation, and emotional distress. Does Goldfarb have a valid cause of action against the professor? Why or why not? *Goldfarb v. Baker*, 547 S.W.2d 567 (1977)

11-17. Apple growers of Washington filed an action for defamation and disparagement against CBS's *60 minutes* and local affiliates that broadcast the segment featuring an investigative report of an allegedly cancer-causing chemical used in the production of apples. The local affiliates, who exercised no editorial control over the content of the broadcast, could have preempted the show. However, they did not know in advance that the show would be controversial; all they knew was that the show was going to be about the inability of federal regulators to prevent known carcinogens from being sprayed on produce. The affiliates filed a motion to have the case against them dismissed. On what grounds would they make this motion? Was it successful? *Grady Auvil v. CBS "60 Minutes" et al.*, 800 F. Supp. 928 (1992)

11-18. Pyrodyne Corporation was hired to put on a fireworks display for the Fourth of July. During the display, one of their mortars was knocked into a horizontal position, from which position it ignited and sent the rocket inside shooting forward 500 feet, right into the crowd, where it exploded, injuring Danny and Marion Klein. They brought an action against the company, basing their case on a theory of strict liability. The company moved for summary judgment, arguing that the case, if brought at all, should be decided on the basis of negligence principles. The trial court denied the motion and found Pyrodyne strictly liable. What was the result on appeal? Why? *Klein v. Pyrodyne Corp.*, 810 P.2d 917 (1991)

On the Internet

http://www.law.cornell.edu/clr/80-4.htm   What happens when a tort affects a large number of people in the same way? This site discusses issues related to such situations.

http://www.pstweb.com/schmidt/tort.html   This site provides numerous links to resources related to tort reform.

http://www.public-policy.org/~ncpa/pd/law/lawb.html   Reading and evaluating this justification for tort reform provides an opportunity to test your critical thinking skills while considering an important issue.

http://www.cspinet.org/foodspeak   If you were bothered by the idea of "veggie libel laws," you will want to check out this site maintained by the Foodspeak Coalition.

12

PRODUCT AND SERVICE LIABILITY LAW

- **THEORIES OF RECOVERY IN PRODUCT LIABILITY CASES**

- **ENTERPRISE LIABILITY**

- **SERVICE LIABILITY**

- **INTERNATIONAL DIMENSIONS OF PRODUCT LIABILITY LAW**

When consumers enter a store to purchase a product, they assume that the product that will do the job the manufacturer claims it will do without injuring the consumer or anyone else. The consumer may not be aware that each year, more than 20 million injuries result from the use of products purchased in the U.S. marketplace. The National Commission on Product Safety estimates that among those injured, 30,000 persons die and another 100,000 are permanently disabled. Such injuries have resulted in the filing of numerous lawsuits, with estimates of the number of product liability cases ranging as high as 1 million a year.[1] Given the substantial number of product-related injuries and the amount of ensuing litigation, the businessperson in today's society will probably become involved in some aspect of product liability litigation, either as a plaintiff or as an employee of a defendant. This chapter discusses the most significant aspects of this area of law, known as *product liability*, in order to help the student function as a prudent consumer and businessperson.

Product liability law developed out of *tort law*, discussed in the previous chapter. This chapter begins by introducing the three primary theories of recovery in product liability cases and the defenses raised in such cases. When examining these theories, the reader should recognize how they rely on the traditional tort theories discussed in chapter 11. These sections are followed by an introduction to the concept of enterprise liability, a concept that has slightly broadened the potential reach of product liability cases. Closely related to the concept of product liability is service liability, which is discussed in the next section. Although they are not obvious at first, product liability law does have international implications, and these are discussed in the final section of this chapter.

Critical Thinking about the Law

Manufacturers owe a certain responsibility to consumers. Consumers should be able to reasonably use a product without its causing harm to them or others. After you read the following case, answer the critical thinking questions that will enhance your thinking about product liability law.

Katherine purchased a can of hair spray from her local drugstore. When she removed the cap from the hair spray can, the can exploded in her hands. She suffered third-degree burns on her hands and face and was unable to work for three months. Katherine sued the hair spray manufacturer after she discovered that another woman had suffered an identical accident when using the same brand of hair spray. The jury awarded Katherine $750,000 in compensatory damages.

1. Katherine's lawyer described a previous case in which an individual was injured because a product exploded. Two years earlier, a woman walking down a row of hair care products in a supermarket had been injured when three cans of hair spray spontaneously exploded. She lost her sight because of the explosion, and a jury awarded her $2.2 million in damages. Katherine's lawyer argued that because the previous woman had been compensated, Katherine should be awarded $2 million in damages for her injuries. Do you think the earlier case is similar enough to Katherine's case for Katherine to recover damages? Why?

   Clue How are the cases similar and different? How does the fact that Katherine purchased the product affect your thinking about the earlier case?

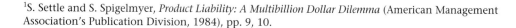

[1]S. Settle and S. Spigelmyer, *Product Liability: A Multibillion Dollar Dilemma* (American Management Association's Publication Division, 1984), pp. 9, 10.

2. The manufacturer argued that, because they place a warning on the hair spray cans, they are free from responsibility for injury. The can states, "Warning: Flammable. Contents under pressure." However, the jury ruled in favor of Katherine. What ethical norm seems to have shaped the jury's thought?

CLUE Study the list of ethical norms in chapter 1. The manufacturer argued that they should not have to assume responsibility because the can has a warning. What ethical norm is consistent with offering greater protection for the consumer?

3. What additional information about this case would make you more willing to state your own opinion about the situation?

CLUE What information about the product would change your thinking about the responsibility of the manufacturer? For example, suppose that Katherine discovered that an identical accident occurred with the same brand of hair spray. How might knowing the date that the similar accident occurred influence your thinking about Katherine's case?

THEORIES OF RECOVERY IN PRODUCT LIABILITY CASES

Product liability law developed out of tort law. A glance at the three primary theories of recovery in product liability cases reveals a relationship between product liability and tort law. The three theories of recovery used in product liability cases are *negligence, breach of warranty,* and *strict product liability.* A plaintiff usually brings an action alleging as many of these three grounds as possible, although usually a suit based on strict product liability is the easiest to prove.

NEGLIGENCE

Negligence has been one of the theories traditionally used by plaintiffs in product liability cases. To successfully recover using a negligence theory, the plaintiff must prove the elements of negligence explained in chapter 11. The plaintiff must establish that the defendant manufacturer owed a duty of care to the plaintiff, that the defendant breached that duty of care, that this breach of duty caused the plaintiff's injury, and that the plaintiff suffered actual, compensable injury.

THE PRIVITY LIMITATION   An early problem using negligence as a theory of recovery for an injury caused by a defective product was the problem of establishing duty. Originally, the courts said that a plaintiff who was not the purchaser of the defective product could not establish a duty of care and thus could not recover. This limitation was based on the concept of *privity.* Privity means that one is a party to a contract. In the earliest known product liability case, *Winterbottom v. Wright,*[2] the British court in 1842 laid the basis for the long-standing rule that to recover for an injury caused by a defective product, the plaintiff must establish privity. In other words, before a manufacturer or seller of a defective good could owe a duty to the plaintiff, the plaintiff must have purchased that good directly from the defendant who manufactured it. Because plaintiffs rarely purchase goods from the manufacturer, few such suits were initially brought.

The years of the privity limitation tended to be a grim period for injured consumers. Gradually, especially in cases of defective food, the courts began to do away with the requirement of privity, and it was essentially abolished in the landmark 1916 case of *MacPherson v. Buick Motor Co.*[3]

In *MacPherson v. Buick,* the court held the remote manufacturer of an automobile with a defective wheel liable to the plaintiff when the wheel broke and

---

[2]152 Eng. Rep. 402 (1842).
[3]111 N.E. 1050 (1916).

the plaintiff was injured. Judge Cardozo stated in that case that the presence of a sale does not control the duty; if the elements of a product are such that it is harmful to individuals if negligently made, and if the manufacturer knows that the product will be used by other than the purchaser without new tests, then "irrespective of contract, the manufacturer of this thing is under a duty to make it carefully." By the holding in this New York case, which was quickly followed by similar holdings in other states, the court did away with the requirement of privity, thereby allowing a negligent manufacturer to be held responsible for a defective product's causing injuries to someone with whom the defendant manufacturer had no contract.

Eradication of the privity requirement and the subsequent increase in the liability of producers and sellers reflected a shift in social policy toward placing responsibility for injuries on those who market a product that could foreseeably cause harm if proper care were not taken in its design, manufacture, and labeling. Increasingly, the courts indicated that defendants should be responsible for their affirmative acts when they knew that such actions could cause harm to others. Also, because the manufacturer and seller derive economic benefits from the sale and use of the product, it seemed fair to impose liability on them if they earned profits from a defectively made product.

Thus, the abolition of the privity limitation opened the door for negligence as a theory of liability to be used in cases in which people were injured because of the lack of care of a product manufacturer or seller. There are now a number of negligent acts or omissions that typically give rise to negligence-based product liability actions, which are listed in Table 12-1 below.

NEGLIGENT FAILURE TO WARN Most of the product liability actions grounded in negligence involve allegations of failure to warn or inadequate warning. To bring a successful negligence case for failure to warn, the plaintiff must demonstrate that the defendant knew or should have known that, without a warning, the product would be dangerous in its ordinary use or in any *reasonably foreseeable* use. There is generally no duty to warn of dangers arising from unforeseeable misuses of a product or from obvious dangers. A producer, for example, need not give a warning that a sharp knife could cut someone. In determining whether a reasonable manufacturer would have given a warning in a particular situation, the courts frequently consider the likelihood of the injury, the seriousness of the injury, and the ease of warning (Exhibit 12-1).

Often, a defendant gives a warning but does so in a manner not clearly calculated to reach those whom the defendant should expect to use the product. If the product is to be used by someone other than the original purchaser, the manufacturer is generally required to put some sort of warning on the product itself, not just in a manual that comes with the product. If children or those who are illiterate are likely to come into contact with the product and risk harm from its use, picture warnings may be required.

Products designed for intimate bodily use, especially drugs and cosmetics, often give rise to actions based on negligent failure to warn because the use of these products frequently causes adverse reactions. When a toxic or allergic reaction causes harm to the user of a cosmetic or an over-the-counter drug, many courts find that there is no duty to warn unless the plaintiff proves (1) that the product contained an ingredient to which an appreciable number of people would have an adverse reaction, (2) that the defendant knew or should have known, in the exercise of ordinary care, that this was

TABLE 12-1 *Common Negligent Actions Leading to Product Liability Cases*

- Negligent failure to warn
- Negligent provision of an inadequate warning
- Negligent manufacture
- Negligent testing or failure to test
- Negligent advertising

EXHIBIT 12-1

It is not always easy for a company to know whether a warning is necessary—and, if it is, where to place that warning. After a jury awarded Stella Liebeck $2.9 million (later reduced by the judge to $640,000 and settled for an undisclosed amount), some fast-food restaurants began warning their drive-through customers that their coffee was *very* hot by placing warnings on the packaging and also on their drive-through windows.

so, and (3) that the plaintiff's reaction was due to his or her membership in this abnormal group.[4]

Other courts, however, determine negligence in such cases by looking at the particular circumstances of the case and weighing the amount of danger to be avoided with the ease of warning. For example, in a 1995 case against McNeil Consumer Products Co., a jury awarded over $8.8 million to a man who suffered permanent liver damage as a result of drinking a glass of wine with a Tylenol capsule. The corporation knew in 1977 that combining a normal dose of Tylenol with a small amount of wine may cause massive liver damage in some people, but the company failed to put a warning to that effect on the label. The company attempted to justify the lack of warning by pointing out how rare such a reaction was, but the jury did not accept that defense.[5]

The marketing of prescription drugs is unique because the manufacturer almost never has any communication with the user, only with the physician who prescribes the drug for the user. In these cases, the courts have generally held that drug manufacturers have a duty to provide adequate warnings to physicians to enable them to decide whether to prescribe the drug or to disclose the risk to the patient. The manufacturer must warn the physician of any chance of a serious adverse reaction, no matter how small the risk may be.

---

[4]W. Page et al., *Prosser and Keeton on Torts* (5th ed. St. Paul: West 1984), p. 687.
[5]Benedi v. McNeil Consumer Products Co., 1994 W.L. 729052 (L.R.P. Jury).

Initially, almost all successful product liability actions based on negligence were for breach of the duty to warn. The range of successful actions was so limited because a number of influential people believed the idea that competition and the open marketplace provided the best means for ensuring that products will contain optimal safety. Those who believe in the sanctity of the market feel that the manufacturer's job is to see that the purchaser is an *informed* purchaser and is not deceived about the safety of a product.[6]

NEGLIGENT DESIGN   The foregoing attitude generally prevailed until approximately 1960, when the courts began, in a limited number of cases, to impose liability based on negligence in the sale of *defectively designed products*. Such liability is imposed only when a reasonable person would conclude that despite any warnings given with the product, the risk of harm outweighed the utility of the product as designed. In bringing an action for negligence in design, a plaintiff must generally prove that the product design (1) is inherently dangerous, (2) contains insufficient safety devices, or (3) consists of materials that do not satisfy standards acceptable in the trade.

In general, an action for product liability based on negligence is accompanied by a claim grounded in strict liability (discussed later). The strict liability claims are usually easier to prove. With the growing acceptance of strict liability, negligence has become less important as a theory of liability. Another reason for the lack of favor for negligence as a theory of recovery is the broad range of defenses available for such actions.

NEGLIGENCE PER SE   In the previous chapter, the concept of negligence per se was introduced. As you know from that discussion, violation of a statutory duty is considered negligence per se. That concept is also used in negligence-based product liability cases.

When a statute establishes product standards, the manufacturer has a duty to meet those standards imposed by the statute. If a manufacturer does not meet those standards, the manufacturer has breached his duty of reasonable care and as long as the plaintiff can establish that the breach of the statutory duty caused injury, the plaintiff can recover under negligence per se.

Statutes that might be violated and lead to negligence per se actions include the Flammable Fabrics Act of 1953, the Food, Drug, and Cosmetics Act of 1938, and the Hazardous Substances Labeling Act of 1960.

DEFENSES TO A NEGLIGENCE-BASED PRODUCT LIABILITY ACTION
All of the defenses to negligence discussed in the negligence section of the torts chapter are available in product liability cases based on negligence. Remember that the plaintiff's own failure to act reasonably can provide a defense. Depending on the state in which the action is brought, the plaintiff's negligence will allow the defendant to raise the defense of *contributory, modified comparative*, or *pure comparative negligence*. If contributory negligence is proved, the plaintiff is barred from recovery. In a state where the defense of pure comparative negligence is allowed, the plaintiff can recover for only that portion of the harm attributable to the defendant's negligence. In a modified contributory negligence state, the plaintiff can recover the percentage of harm caused by the defendant as long as the jury finds the plaintiff's negligence responsible for less than 50 percent of the harm. So, if a jury finds the defendant to be responsible for 60 percent of the plaintiffs' harm, the plaintiff could recover nothing in a contributory negligence state and recover damages for 60 percent of his or her injuries in a modified or pure comparative negligence state. If the defendant were only 40 percent responsible, however, the plaintiff would be able to recover for 40 percent of his or her injuries only in the pure comparative negligence state and nothing in the other two.

---

[6]*See* R. Coase, *The Problem of Social Cost*, 3 L. & Econ. 1 (1960).

Another defense available in product liability cases based on negligence is *assumption of the risk*. A plaintiff is said to assume the risk when he or she voluntarily and unreasonably encounters a known danger. If the consumer knows that a defect exists but still proceeds unreasonably to make use of the product, he or she is said to have voluntarily assumed the risk of injury from the defect and cannot recover.

In deciding whether the plaintiff did indeed assume the risk, the trier of fact may consider such factors as the plaintiff's age, experience, knowledge, and understanding. The obviousness of the defect and the danger it poses are also relevant factors. If a plaintiff knows of a danger but does not fully appreciate the magnitude of the risk, the applicability of the defense is a question for the jury to determine. In most cases, when an employee uses an unsafe machine at work, she or he is not presumed to assume the risk because most courts recognize that the concept of voluntariness is an illusion in the workplace. Earlier, however, employees attempting to sue manufacturers of defective machines for injuries at work were defeated by this defense.

In many states, *misuse* of the product is raised as a defense in negligence-based product liability cases. It is generally accepted that such a misuse must be unreasonable or unforeseeable to constitute a defense. When a defendant raises the defense of product misuse, what he or she is really arguing is that the harm was caused not by the defendant's negligence but by the plaintiff's failure to use the product in the manner in which it was designed to be used.

Statutory defenses are also available to defendants. To ensure that there will be sufficient evidence from which a trier of fact can make a decision, states have **statutes of limitations** that limit the time within which all types of civil actions may be brought. In most states, the statute of limitations for tort actions, and thus for negligence-based product liability cases, is from one to four years from the date of injury.

statute of limitations A statute that bars actions arising more than a specified number of years after the cause of the action arises.

States also have **statutes of repose**, which provide an additional limitation in product liability cases by barring actions arising more than a specified number of years after the product was purchased. Statues of repose are usually much longer than statutes of limitations; they are often at least 10 years, and frequently are 25 or 50 years. Statutes of repose may seem unduly harsh on consumers who may be injured as a result of a latent defect in a product. On the other hand, to make the manufacturer liable in perpetuity is felt by some to be unduly harsh on manufacturers and sellers because of the resulting uncertainty about possible liability. Those who worry about the seller's liability, however, should remember that the older the product is, the more difficult it will be for the plaintiff to prove negligence on the part of the defendant.

statute of repose A statute that bars actions arising more than a specified number of years after the product was purchased.

The **state-of-the-art defense** is used by the defendant to demonstrate that his or her alleged negligent behavior was reasonable, given the available scientific knowledge existing at the time the product was sold or produced. If a case is based on the defendant's negligent defective design of a product, the state-of-the-art defense refers to the technological feasibility of producing a safer product at the time the product was manufactured. In cases of negligent failure to warn, the state-of-the-art refers to the scientific knowability of a risk associated with a product at the time of its production. This is a valid defense in a negligence case because the focus is on the reasonableness of the defendant's conduct. Demonstrating that, given the state of scientific knowledge, there was no feasible way to make a safer product does not always preclude liability. The court may find that the defendant's conduct was still unreasonable because even in the product's technologically safest form, the risks posed by the defect in the design so outweighed the benefits of the product that the reasonable person would not have produced a product of that design.

state-of-the-art defense A product liability defense based on adherence to existing technologically feasible standards at the time the product was manufactured.

An earlier section revealed that failure to comply with a safety standard may lead to the imposition of liability. An interesting question is whether the converse is true. Does *compliance with safety regulations* constitute a defense? There is no clear answer to that question. Sometimes, however, compliance with federal laws may lead to the defense that use of state tort law is preempted by a federal statute designed to ensure the safety of a particular class of products.

The following case illustrates one situation in which the court accepted the pre-emption argument and found that compliance with a federal statute designed to regulate medical devices relieved a manufacturer from potential tort liability.

IRENE M. GREEN AND MARTIN GREEN, APPELLANTS V. RICHARD L. DOLSKY, M.D. AND COLLAGEN CORPORATION
SUPERIOR COURT OF PENNSYLVANIA 641 A.2D 600 (1994)

Plaintiff Irene Green developed an autoimmune disease after she was treated with Zyderm collagen implant. Zyderm is injected under the skin to fill in wrinkles and is regulated as a Class III medical device under the Medical Device Amendments Act of 1976 (MDA). When Plaintiff Green sued Defendants Collagen Corporation and the doctor who treated her on the basis of theories of negligence, strict liability, and breach of warranty, the defendants filed a motion for summary judgment on the grounds that the MDA preempted the Green's state tort claims. The trial court agreed and granted the motion. Plaintiffs appealed to the Pennsylvania Superior Court.

JUDGE JOHNSON

Under the supremacy clause of the United States Constitution, federal law is "the supreme Law of the Land; and the Judges in every State shall be bound thereby, any Thing in the Constitution or Laws of any State to the Contrary notwithstanding." As a result, all conflicts between federal and state laws must be resolved in favor of federal law. In determining whether a conflict between state and federal law exists, a court looks to congressional intent.

Generally, preemption may be express or implied, and it is compelled whether Congress' command is explicitly stated in the statute's language or implicitly contained in its structure and purpose. When Congress is silent on the matter, state law will be preempted by federal law "when (a) compliance with both state and federal law is impossible or (b) when state law stands as an impediment to a federal purpose."

Pursuant to the MDA, the FDA classifies all medical devices into one of three categories. Class III devices, such as Zyderm, are subject to the most extensive controls "to provide reasonable assurance of . . . safety and effectiveness." Class III devices must obtain pre-market approval from the FDA because they "present a potential unreasonable risk of illness or injury."

Thus, the extensive pre-market approval process requires a manufacturer to submit a detailed application to the FDA, including information pertaining to product specifications, intended use, manufacturing methods, and proposed labeling. An appointed panel of experts conducts a comprehensive review of the application and prepares a report and recommendation. Within six months of receipt of the application, the FDA must either approve the device for sale, or reject it for additional information or testing. The MDA also imposes extensive post-approval regula-

tions to keep the FDA apprised of any new information or safety findings relating to Class III devices. The FDA may withdraw approval of the product permanently, or suspend its approval temporarily if it determines that the device has become unsafe or its labeling inadequate.

In enacting the MDA, Congress was not only interested in protecting the individual use, but it was also interested in encouraging research and development and allowing new and improved medical devices to be marketed without delay. In the MDA, Congress included an express preemption provision.

State requirements which, in effect, establish new substantive requirements for a medical device in a regulated area, such as labeling, are preempted. Since Congress has provided an express preemption provision in the MDA, we must determine whether the Green's state law tort claims fall within the scope of that provision by imposing requirements in addition to or different from those mandated by the FDA.

In *King v. Collagen Corp.* [a similar case], the plaintiff, Jane King, contracted an auto-immune disease after receiving a test dose of Zyderm. King filed suit against Collagen, the manufacturer, alleging strict liability, breach of warranty of merchantability, negligence. . . . Collagen filed a motion for summary judgment on the basis that the MDA preempted King's claims. The United States District Court for the District of Massachusetts agreed.

The First Circuit Court of Appeals affirmed after finding that (1) the extensive pre-market approval process and the similarly extensive post-approval regulations were indications that the FDA had established specific "requirements" within the meaning of §360k of the MDA and (2) King's state law tort claims would impose additional or different requirements than those mandated by the FDA, in contravention of §360k.

In *Stamps v. Collagen Corp* [another similar case], guided by the express language of §360k(a), the Fifth Circuit Court of Appeals determined that Stamps' claims were preempted by federal law because first, the state tort law claims would constitute requirements in addition to or different from the MDA, and, second, these requirements would relate to either the safety or effectiveness of Zyderm and Zyplast. "State tort causes of action—to the extent they relate to safety, effectiveness, or other MDA requirements—constitute requirements 'different from, or in addition to' the Class III process; they are, therefore, preempted."

In the present case, the Greens claim that the district court erred in granting summary judgment on the basis that the MDA preempted their state tort law claims. Here, we are constrained to agree with the rationale in *King*, and *Stamps*, and we conclude that a finding in favor of the Greens on any of their alleged state tort law claims would impose additional or different requirements on Collagen, whose product, Zyderm, has already received FDA approval. Such requirements are in conflict with the MDA and thus, the Greens' state law claims are therefore preempted.

Affirmed in favor of Defendants, Dolsky and Collagen Corp.

The court's decision in the *Green* case turned to a great extent on the intent of Congress in passing the legislation that set the standards. Each preemption case requires careful scrutiny of the purpose of the statute, and the opposite result often occurs. For example, in *Tebbetts v. Ford Motor Co.*,[7] the plaintiff alleged that the 1988 Ford Escort was defectively designed because it did not have a driver's side air bag. Ford raised the preemption defense, arguing that it had complied with federal safety regulations under the National Traffic and Motor Vehicle Safety Act (NTMVS), and that such compliance preempted recovery under state product liability laws. The court analyzed the legislative history of the act, as well as the language of the law itself. Finding a clause in the law that stated that "[c]ompliance with any Federal motor vehicle safety standard issued under this act does not exempt any person from any liability under common law," the court found that the Tebbetts were not preempted from bringing their product liability action.

From the foregoing discussion of negligence, it is apparent that negligence is a valid theory on which to base a product liability case. However, from a plaintiff's perspective, it offers too many defenses to the manufacturer and the seller. An alternative theory of liability is breach of warranty.

STRICT LIABILITY IN CONTRACT FOR BREACH OF WARRANTY

warranty A guarantee or binding promise that goods (products) meet certain standards of performance.

express warranty A warranty that is clearly stated by the seller or manufacturer.

implied warranty A warranty that automatically arises out of a transaction.

implied warranty of merchantability A warranty that a good is reasonably fit for ordinary use.

The Uniform Commercial Code (UCC) provides the basis for recovery against a manufacturer or seller on the basis of breach of warranty. A **warranty** is a guarantee or a binding promise. Warranties may be either **express** (clearly stated by the seller or manufacturer) or **implied** (automatically arising out of a transaction). Either may give rise to liability (Table 12-2). Two types of implied warranties may provide the basis for a product liability action: warranty of merchantability and warranty of fitness for a particular purpose.

IMPLIED WARRANTY OF MERCHANTABILITY The **implied warranty of merchantability** is a warranty or guarantee that the goods are reasonably fit for ordinary use. This warranty arises out of every sale, unless it is expressly and clearly excluded. According to the UCC, to meet the standard of merchantability, the goods:

1. Must pass without objection in the trade under the contract description.
2. Must be of fair or average quality within the description.
3. Must be fit for the ordinary purpose for which the goods are used.

TABLE 12-2 *Warranties That May Give Rise to Liability*

EXPRESS WARRANTIES	IMPLIED WARRANTIES
• Written or oral description of good • Promise or affirmation of fact about the good • Sample or model of the good	• Of merchantability • Of fitness for a particular purpose

[7]665 A.2d 345 (N.H. 1995).

4. Must run, with variations permitted by agreement, of even kind, quality, and quantity within each unit and among all units involved.

5. Must be adequately contained, packaged, and labeled as the agreement may require.

6. Must conform to any affirmations or promises made on the label or the container.[8]

If the product does not conform to those standards and, as a result of this nonconformity, the purchaser or his or her property is injured, the purchaser may recover for breach of implied warranty of merchantability. The UCC expressly provides that an injury to a person or property proximately caused by a breach of warranty is a recoverable type of consequential damage. The use of this warranty is limited, however, in two respects: (1) It is made only by one regularly engaged in the sale of that type of good, and (2) the seller may sometimes avoid liability by expressly disclaiming liability, or by limited liability to replacement of the defective goods. The UCC, however, has restricted the applicability of the latter limitation by a provision declaring that a limitation of consequential damages for injury to a person in the case of consumer goods is prima facie "unconscionable." *Unconscionability* is a concept meaning gross unfairness. Under the UCC, unconscionable contract clauses are unenforceable. Thus, if a disclaimer is unconscionable, it will not be enforced.

Privity is not a problem in an action based on breach of warranty because of UCC Section 2-318. This section allows states to adopt one of three alternatives to allow nonpurchasers to recover for breach of warranty. The most liberal alternative allows any person injured by the defective product to sue.

One issue that frequently arises in product liability cases involving breach of the warranty of merchantability is whether there is a breach of this warranty when the alleged breach arises from a naturally occurring characteristic of the product. This problem typically arises in cases involving food. Is it a breach of the warranty of merchantability when there is a bone in a fish fillet or a pit in an olive jar labeled "pitted olives"? The following case sets forth the two tests that are used in various jurisdictions.

WILLIAMS V. BRAUM ICE CREAM STORES, INCORPORATED
OKLAHOMA COURT OF APPEALS 534 P.2D 700 (1974)

Plaintiff Williams purchased a cherry-pecan ice cream cone from the defendant's shop. While eating the ice cream, she broke her tooth on a cherry pit that was in the ice cream. She sued defendant Braum Ice Cream Stores, Inc., for breach of implied warranty of merchantability. The trial court ruled in favor of the defendant, and the plaintiff appealed.

JUDGE REYNOLDS

There is a division of authority as to the test to be applied where injury is suffered from an object in food or drink sold to be consumed on or off the premises. Some courts hold there is no breach of implied warranty on the part of a restaurant if the object in the food was "natural" to the food served. These jurisdictions recognize that the vendor is held to impliedly warrant the fitness of food, or that he may be liable in negligence in failing to use ordinary care

in its preparation, but deny recovery as a matter of law when the substance found in the food is natural to the ingredients of the type of food served. This rule, labeled the "foreign-natural test" by many jurists, is predicated on the view that the practical difficulties of separation of ingredients in the course of food preparation (bones from meat or fish, seeds from fruit, and nutshell from the nut meat) is a matter of common knowledge. Under this natural theory, there may be a recovery only if the object is "foreign" to the food served. How far can the "foreign-natural test" be expanded? How many bones from meat or fish, seeds from fruit, nut shells from the nut meat or other natural indigestible substances are unacceptable under the "foreign-natural test"?

The other line of authorities hold that the test to be applied is what should "reasonably be expected" by a customer in the food sold to him.

---

[8]U.C.C. § 2-314.

[State law] provides in pertinent part as follows:

(1) . . . a warranty that the goods shall be merchantable is implied in a contract for their sale if the seller is a merchant with respect to goods of that kind. Under this section the serving for value of food or drink to be consumed either on the premises or elsewhere is a sale.

(2) Goods to be merchantable must be at least such as . . . (c) are fit for the ordinary purposes for which such goods are used; . . .

In *Zabner v. Howard Johnson's Inc. . . .* the Court held:

The "Foreign-natural" test as applied as a matter of law by the trial court does not recommend itself to us as being logical or desirable. The reasoning applied in this test is fallacious because it assumes that all substances which are natural to the food in one stage or another of preparation are, in fact, anticipated by the average consumer in the final product served. . . .

Categorizing a substance as foreign or natural may have some importance in determining the degree of negligence of the processor of food, but it is not determinative of what is unfit or harmful in fact for human consumption. A nutshell natural to nut meat can cause as much harm as a foreign substance, such as a pebble, piece of wire or glass. All are in-

digestible and likely to cause injury. Naturalness of the substance to any ingredients in the food served is important only in determining whether the consumer may reasonably expect to find such substance in the particular type of dish or style of food served.

The "reasonable expectation" test as applied to an action for breach of implied warranty is keyed to what is "reasonably" fit. If it is found that the pit of a cherry should be anticipated in cherry pecan ice cream and guarded against by the consumer, then the ice cream was reasonably fit under the implied warranty.

In some instances, objects which are "natural" to the type of food but which are generally not found in the style of the food as prepared, are held to be the equivalent of a foreign substance.

We hold that the better legal theory to be applied in such cases is the "reasonable expectation" theory, rather than the "naturalness" theory as applied by the trial court. What should be reasonably expected by the consumer is a jury question, and the question of whether plaintiff acted in a reasonable manner in eating the ice cream cone is also a fact question to be decided by the jury.

Reversed and remanded in favor of Plaintiff, Williams.

Critical Thinking about the Law

THE CRITERIA SELECTED ARE IMPORTANT IN determining the outcome of a case. Simply put, depending upon the court's selection from many possible criteria, it can reach multiple conclusions. Judging a case according to criteria X, Y, and Z can yield a vastly different decision than if the same case were judged according to criteria A, B, and C.

This particular case illustrates the above assertion. The trial court had made a legal decision based on criterion X, namely the "foreign-natural" test. However, the appeals court held that the trial court must redecide the case, this time on the basis of criterion Y, or the "reasonable expectation" test.

The critical thinking questions enable you to examine carefully the key differences between the two tests, including the possible implications. The larger project of the questions is to increase your awareness of the extent to which a legal decision is dependent upon the criteria chosen to reach that decision.

1. What is the fundamental difference between the nature of the two tests discussed by the court?

CLUE Reread the discussion of the two tests to formulate your answer.

2. Which of the two tests is more likely to yield ambiguous reasoning when applied?

CLUE Refer to your answer to Question 1.

IMPLIED WARRANTY OF FITNESS FOR A PARTICULAR PURPOSE A second implied warranty that may be the basis for a product liability case in the **implied warranty of fitness for a particular purpose.** This warranty arises when a seller knows that the purchaser wants to purchase a good for a particular use. The seller tells the consumer that the good can be used for that purpose, and the buyer reasonably relies on the seller's expertise and purchases the product. If the good cannot be used for that purpose, and, as a result of the

implied warranty of fitness for a particular purpose A warranty that arises when the seller tells the consumer a good is fit for a specific use.

purchaser's attempt to use the good for that purpose, the consumer is injured, a product liability action for breach of warranty of fitness for a particular purpose is justified. For example, if a farmer needed oil for his irrigation engine, and he went to a store and told the seller exactly what model irrigation engine he needed oil for, the seller would be creating an implied warranty of fitness for a particular purpose by picking up a can of oil, handing it to the farmer, and saying, "This is the product you need." If the farmer purchases the recommended oil, uses it in the engine, and the engine explodes because the oil was not heavy enough, the seller would have breached the warranty of fitness for a particular purpose. If the farmer were injured by the explosion, he would be able to recover on the basis of breach of warranty.

EXPRESS WARRANTIES   The seller or the manufacturer may also be held liable for breach of an express warranty. An express warranty is created by a seller in one of three ways: by describing the goods, by making a promise or affirmation of fact about the goods, or by providing a model or sample of the good. If the goods fail to meet the description, fail to do what the seller claimed they would do, or fail to be the same as the model or sample, the seller has breached an express warranty. For example, if a 200-pound man asks a seller whether a ladder will hold a 200-pound man without breaking, the seller who says that it will is affirming a fact and is thus expressly warranting that the ladder will hold a 200-pound man without breaking. If the purchaser takes the ladder home and climbs up on it, and if it breaks under his weight, causing him to fall to the ground, he may bring a product liability action against the seller on the basis of breach of an express warranty.

DEFENSES TO BREACH-OF-WARRANTY ACTIONS   Two common defenses used in cases based on breach of warranty arise from the UCC and make sense in a commercial setting when a transaction is between two businesspeople, but they make little sense in the context of a consumer injury. Therefore, the courts have found ways to limit the use of these defenses in product liability cases in most states.

The first such defense is that the purchaser failed to give the seller notice within a reasonable time after he or she knew or should have known of the breach of warranty, as required by the UCC. Obviously, most consumers would not be aware of this rule, and as a result, many early breach-of-warranty cases were lost. Most courts today avoid this requirement by holding (1) that a long delay is reasonable under the particular circumstances, (2) that the section imposing the notice requirement was not intended to apply to personal injury situations, or (3) that the requirement is inapplicable between parties who have not dealt with each other, as when a consumer is suing a manufacturer.

The second defense is the existence of a **disclaimer**. A seller or manufacturer may relieve himself or herself of liability for breach of warranty in advance through the use of disclaimers. The disclaimer may say (1) that no warranties are made ("as is"), (2) that the manufacturer or seller warrants only against certain consequences or defects, or (3) that liability is limited to repair, replacement, or return of the product price.

Again, these disclaimers make sense in a commercial context but seem somewhat harsh in the case of consumer transactions. Thus, the courts do not look with favor on disclaimers. First, the disclaimer must be clear; in many cases, courts have rejected the defendant's use of a disclaimer as a defense on the grounds that the retail purchaser either did not see the disclaimer or did not understand it. Thus, any businessperson using disclaimers to limit liability must be sure that the disclaimers are very plainly stated on an integral part of the product or package that will not be removed before retail purchase by the consumer. In some cases, however, despite clear disclaimers, courts have held disclaimers to consumers invalid, stating either that these disclaimers are unenforceable *adhesion contracts* resulting from gross inequities of bargaining power and are therefore unenforceable, or that they are *unconscionable* and contrary to the policy of the law. The UCC, in fact, now contains a provision stating that a

disclaimer Disavowal of liability for breach of warranty by the manufacturer or seller of a good in advance of the sale of the good.

limitation of consequential damages for injury to a person in the case of consumer goods is prima facie unconscionable.

The *statute of limitations* may also be used defensively in a case based on strict liability for breach of warranty. Under the UCC, the statute of limitations runs four years from the date on which the cause of action arises. In an action based on breach of warranty, the cause of action, according to the UCC, arises at the time of the sale. This rule would severely limit actions for breach of warranty, as defects often do not cause harm immediately. Section 2-725(2) of the UCC, however, changes the time that the cause of action arises to the date when the breach of warranty is or should have been discovered when a warranty "explicitly extends to the future performance of the goods, and the discovery of the breach must await the time of performance." This section, when applicable, makes the statue of limitations less of a potential problem for the plaintiff. In a few states, courts have simply decided to apply the tort statute of limitations as running from the date of injury or the date when the defect was or should have been discovered to all product liability cases grounded in breach of warranty.

STRICT LIABILITY IN TORT

The third and most prevalent theory of product liability used during the past three decades is strict liability in tort, established in the 1963 case of *Greenman v. Yuba Power Products Co.*[9] and incorporated in Section 402A of the *Restatement (Second) of Torts.*[10] This section reads as follows:

> (1) One who sells any product in a defective condition, unreasonably dangerous to the user or consumer or his family is subject to liability for physical harm thereby caused to the ultimate user or consumer, or to this property, if
>   (a) the seller is engaged in the business of selling such a product, and
>   (b) it is expected to and does reach the consumer or user without substantial change in the condition in which it was sold.
> (2) The rule stated in Subsection (1) applies although
>   (a) the seller has exercised all possible care in the preparation and sale of his product, and
>   (b) the user or consumer has not bought the product from or entered into any contractual relation with the seller.

Under this theory, the manufacturer, distributor, or retailer may be held liable to any reasonably foreseeable injured party. Unlike causes of action based on negligence or, to a lesser degree, breach of warranty, product liability actions based on strict liability in tort focus on the *product*, not on the producer or seller. The degree of care exercised by the defendant is not an issue in these cases. The issue in such cases is whether the product was in a "defective condition, unreasonably dangerous" when sold. To succeed in a strict liability action, the plaintiff must prove that:

1. The product was defective when sold,
2. The defective condition rendered the product unreasonably dangerous, and
3. The product was the cause of the plaintiff's injury.

The defect is usually the most difficult part of the case for the plaintiff to establish. A product may be defective because of (1) some flaw or abnormality in its construction or marketing that led to its being more dangerous than it otherwise would have been, (2) a failure by the manufacturer or seller to adequately warn of a risk or hazard associated with the product, or (3) a design that is defective.

---

[9]59 Cal. 2d 57 (1962).
[10]Restatement (Second) of Torts § 402A.

A defect in manufacture or marketing generally involves a specific product's not meeting the manufacturer's specifications. Proof of such a defect is generally provided in one or both of two ways: (1) Experts testify as to the type of flaw that could have caused the accident that led to the plaintiff's injury; (2) evidence of the circumstances surrounding the accident lead the jury to infer that the accident must have been caused by a defect in the product.

When a plaintiff is seeking recovery based on a design defect, he or she is not impugning just one item, but an entire product line. If a product is held to be defectively designed in one case, a manufacturer or seller may recognize that this particular case may stimulate a huge number of additional lawsuits. Thus, defendants are very concerned about the outcome of these cases. Therefore, the availability of this type of action has a greater impact on encouraging manufacturers to produce safe products than does the availability of any other type of product liability action.

Although all the states agree that manufacturers may not market defectively designed products, there is no uniform definition of a defective design. Two tests have evolved to determine whether a product is so defective as to be unreasonably dangerous. The first test, set out in the *Restatement (Second) of Torts*, is the **consumer expectations test**. This test asks the question: Did the product meet the standards that would be expected by a reasonable consumer? Such a test relies on the experiences and expectations of the ordinary consumer and thus is not answered by the use of expert testimony about the merits of the design.

The second is the **feasible alternatives test**, sometimes referred to as the risk-utility test. In applying this test, the court generally looks at seven factors:

1. The usefulness and desirability of the product—its utility to the user and to the public as a whole.
2. The safety aspects of the product—the likelihood that it will cause injury, and the probable seriousness of the injury.
3. The availability of a substitute product that would meet the same need and not be as unsafe.
4. The manufacturer's ability to eliminate the unsafe character of the product without impairing its usefulness or making it too expensive to maintain its utility.
5. The user's ability to avoid danger by the exercise of care in the use of the product.
6. The user's anticipated awareness of the dangers inherent in the product and their avoidability, because of general public knowledge of the obvious condition of the product or of the existence of suitable warnings or instructions.
7. The feasibility, on the part of the manufacturer, of spreading the loss by adjusting the price of the product or carrying liability insurance.[11]

The following case illustrates the difference between these two tests.

consumer expectations test A test used by courts to determine whether a product is so defective as to be unreasonably dangerous that asks whether the product performed as would be expected by a reasonable consumer.

feasible alternatives test A test used by courts to determine whether a product is so defective as to be unreasonably dangerous that focuses on whether, given available alternatives, the product's design was reasonable; the risk utility test.

SPERRY-NEW HOLLAND, A DIVISION OF SPERRY CORPORATION V. JOHN PAUL PRESTAGE AND PAM PRESTAGE
SUPREME COURT OF MISSISSIPPI 617 So. 2D 248 (1993)

Plaintiff-appellees John and Pam Prestage sued defendant for damages arising out of an accident in which Mr. Prestage's foot and lower leg were caught in a combine manufactured by defendant-appellant Sperry-New Holland. Plaintiffs' first cause of action was based on the theory of strict product liability. A jury awarded John $1,425,000 for his injuries and Pam $218,750 for loss of consortium (the ability to engage in sexual relations with one's spouse). Defendant appealed.

---

[11]J. Wade, *On the Nature of Strict Tort Liability for Products*, 44 Miss. L.J. 825 (1994).

JUDGE PRATHER

Sperry raises several issues . . .

Issue A: The court erred in applying a "risk-utility" analysis instead of a "consumer expectation" analysis.

This case requires a re-examination of Mississippi products liability law. Two competing theories of strict liability in tort can be extrapolated from our case law. While our older decisions applied a "consumer expectations" analysis in products cases, recent decisions have turned on an analysis under "risk-utility." In this case, Sperry claims that the trial court erred in applying a "risk-utility" theory of recovery, and not a "consumer expectations" theory. Prestage argues that while "consumer expectations" was the law at one time, recent cases have embraced "risk-utility." We today apply a "risk-utility" analysis and write to clarify our reasons for the adoption for that test.

The purpose of [strict] liability is to insure that the costs of injuries resulting from defective products are borne by the manufacturers that put such products on the market rather than by the injured persons who are powerless to protect themselves.

State Stove explicitly holds that the extent of strict liability of a manufacturer for harm caused by its product is not that of an insurer. However, strict liability does relieve the plaintiff of the onerous burden of proving negligence (i.e., fault). Fault is supplied as a matter of law.

Section 402A is still the law in Mississippi. How this Court defines the phrases "defective conditions" and "unreasonably dangerous" used in 402A dictates whether a "consumer expectations" analysis or a "risk-utility" analysis will prevail. Problems have arisen because our past decisions have been unclear and have been misinterpreted in some instances.

"Consumer Expectations" Analysis

The term "consumer expectations" comes from comment i to Section 402A. It states:

> The rule stated in this section applies only where the defective condition of the product makes it unreasonably dangerous to the user or consumer. . . . The article sold must be dangerous to an extent beyond that which would be contemplated by the ordinary consumer who purchases it, with the ordinary knowledge common to the community as to its characteristics.

In a "consumer expectations" analysis, "ordinarily the phrase 'defective condition' means that the article has something wrong with it, that it did not function as expected." Comment g of Section 402A defines "defective condition" as "a condition not contemplated by the ultimate consumer, which will be unreasonably dangerous to him." Thus, in a "consumer expectations" analysis, for a plaintiff to recover, the defect in a product which causes his injuries must not be one which the plaintiff, as an ordinary consumer, would know to be unreasonably dangerous to him. In other words, if the plaintiff, applying the knowledge of an ordinary consumer, sees a danger and can appreciate that danger, then he cannot recover for any injury resulting from that appreciated danger.

"Risk-Utility" Analysis

In a "risk-utility" analysis, a product is "unreasonably dangerous" if a reasonable person would conclude that the danger-in-fact, whether foreseeable or not, outweighs the utility of the product. Thus, even if a plaintiff appreciates the danger of a product, he can still recover for any injury resulting from the danger provided that the utility of the product is outweighed by the danger that the product creates. Under the "risk-utility" test, either the judge or the jury can balance the utility and danger-in-fact, or risk, of the product.

Around the country, the test generally employed to determine liability for products defects is the "risk-utility" test. In recent years, the "risk-utility" test has replaced the "consumer expectations" test in defective design cases. "Risk-utility" has become the trend in most federal and state jurisdictions.

This Court has clearly moved away from a "consumer expectations" analysis and has moved towards "risk-utility." Consistent with the national trend, the two most recent decisions of this Court applied a "risk-utility" analysis to strict products liability.

A "risk-utility" analysis best protects both the manufacturer and the consumer. It does not create a duty on the manufacturer to create a completely safe product. Creating such a product is often impossible or prohibitively expensive. Instead, a manufacturer is charged with the duty to make its product reasonably safe, regardless of whether the plaintiff is aware of the product's dangerousness. This is not to say that a plaintiff is not responsible for his own actions. In balancing the utility of the product against the risk it creates, an ordinary person's ability to avoid the danger by exercising care is also weighed.

Having here reiterated this Court's adoption of a "risk-utility" analysis for products liability cases, we hold, necessarily, that the "patent danger" bar is no longer applicable in Mississippi. Under a "risk-utility" analysis, the "patent danger" rule does not apply. In "risk-utility," the openness and obviousness of a product's design is simply a factor to consider in determining whether a product is unreasonably dangerous.

There is sufficient evidence to show that Prestage tried his case under a "risk-utility" analysis. It is also clear from the record that the trial court understood "risk-utility" to be the law in Mississippi and applied that test correctly.

Affirmed in favor of Plaintiff, Prestage.

Critical Thinking about the Law

THIS CASE PROVIDES ANOTHER ILLUSTRATION OF the importance of criteria selection in determining the outcome of a case. When Sperry-New Holland appealed the case, it did not focus on the facts or on the court's conclusion. Instead, the appeal focused on the test used by the court to decide the case. There was the presumption in the defendant's appeal that if the "consumer expectations" test had been used instead of the "risk-utility" analysis, the decision likely would have been different.

The questions that follow will help you to think more critically about the court's decision to use "risk-utility" analysis.

1. To demonstrate your awareness of the guiding power of ethical norms, identify the primary ethical norm that would lead to the use of risk-utility analysis.

   CLUE To answer this question, you want to reread the court's discussion of each test.

2. In this case, the court selects "risk-utility" analysis as the test to apply in making its decision. What are its reasons for making this selection?

   CLUE You know the court's holding. Every group of sentences that answers the question. "*Why* is that the holding?" provides a reason.

IMPACT OF THE RESTATEMENT (THIRD) OF TORTS Even though elements of Section 402A of the *Restatement (Second) of Torts* have come to be adopted in all states, and it is generally considered to be the foundation of modern product liability law, there has been a lot of dissatisfaction over the law. That dissatisfaction resulted in what may be the biggest change in product liability law since the passage of Section 402A: the adoption on May 20, 1997, of the American Law Institute's *Restatement (Third) of Torts: Product Liability*, which is intended to replace Section 402A.

Under the Restatement (Third), "[O]ne engaged in the business of selling or otherwise distributing products who sells or distributes a defective product is subject to liability for harm to persons or property caused by the defect." The seller's liability, however, is determined by a different standard, depending on which type of defect is involved: (1) a manufacturing defect, (2) a design defect, or (3) a defective warning.

When the defect is one in the manufacture, liability is strict. A manufacturing defect is said to exist when "the product departs from its intended design." The new rule imposes liability in such a case regardless of the care taken by the manufacturer.

The Restatement (Third) adopts a reasonableness standard for design defects. It states that "a product is defective in design when the foreseeable risks of the harm posed by the product could have been reduced or avoided by the adoption of a reasonable alternative design by the seller . . . and the omission of the alternative design renders the product not reasonably safe." In the comments, the Restatement lists a number of factors the court can use to determine whether a reasonable alternative design renders the product not reasonably safe. These factors include: "the magnitude and probability of the foreseeable risks of harm, the instructions and warnings accompanying the product, and the nature and strength of consumer expectations regarding the product, including expectations arising from product portrayal and marketing . . . the relative advantages and disadvantages of the product as designed and as it alternatively could have been designed . . . the likely effects of the alternative design on product longevity maintenance, repair and esthetics, and the range of consumer choice among products." Thus, the Restatement (Third) has in effect shifted to a risk-utility test.

Regarding the third category, warning defects, the Restatement (Third) has likewise adopted a reasonableness standard. "A product is defective because of inadequate instructions or warnings when the foreseeable risks of harm posed by the product could have been reduced or avoided by the provision of reasonable instructions or warnings by the seller . . . and the omission of the warnings renders the product not reasonably safe."

Many lawyers think that the changes brought about by the newest Restatement will have a deep impact on product liability law well into the twenty-first century.

BYSTANDER LIABILITY Sometimes the person injured by the defective product is not a purchaser, nor even an owner of the product. The question arises as to whether strict product liability can be used by someone other than the owner or user of the product. The following case provides the rationale of one court that chose to allow recovery by a bystander.

JAMES A. PETERSON, ADMINISTRATOR OF THE ESTATE OF MARADEAN PETERSON ET AL. V. LOU BACKRODT CHEVROLET COMPANY

APPELLATE COURT OF ILLINOIS 307 N.E.2D 729 (1974)

An automobile sold by the defendant, Lou Backrodt Chevrolet, had a defective brake system at the time it was sold. The defective brakes failed, causing the driver to strike two minors, killing one and injuring the other. The deceased minor's estate brought this product liability action against the seller of the defective automobile. The trial court dismissed the action against the defendant on the grounds that bystanders did not have a cause of action. The plaintiff appealed.

JUSTICE GUILD

The question of whether a bystander can employ the doctrine of strict liability in a lawsuit has been thoroughly considered by reviewing courts and legal commentators. These authorities indicate that permitting the bystander to maintain an action based on strict tort liability is the more enlightened approach. This has been the result when this issue has been considered in light of Illinois law.

The rationale behind this result is best expressed by this statement of the California Supreme Court in *Elmore v. American Motors Corp.*

If anything, bystanders should be entitled to greater protection than the consumer or user where injury to bystanders from the defect is reasonably foreseeable. Consumers and users, at least, have the opportunity to inspect for defects and to limit their purchases to articles manufactured by reputable manufacturers and sold by reputable retailers, whereas the bystander ordinarily has no such opportunities. In short, the bystander is in greater need of protection from defective products which are dangerous, and if any distinction should be made between bystanders and users, it should be made . . . to extend greater liability in favor of the bystanders.

. . . the doctrine of strict liability in tort is available in an action for personal injuries by a bystander against the manufacturer and the retailer.

We agree with the California Supreme Court's cogent reasoning and hold that it is equally applicable when directed to those in the business of selling used cars.

Reversed and remanded in favor of Plaintiff, Peterson.

Critical Thinking about the Law

SOME OF THE MOST IMPORTANT DECISIONS made by the courts concern the scope of a given law. With their decisions, courts determine what classes, groups, and so on will or will not be protected by certain laws. Inevitably, courts must grapple with questions related to the four primary ethical norms in making these decisions.

In this case, the court supported the applicability of strict tort liability to third parties, or "bystanders." The primary objective of the questions that follow is to enable you to recognize the role ethical norms played in the court's liberal interpretation of strict tort liability.

1. What primary ethical norm dominates the court's reasoning?

   CLUE To answer this question, you want to reread the excerpted paragraph from the California Supreme Court decision.

2. To demonstrate your ability to recognize the importance of judicial decision in shaping law, identify the term used by the court that is potentially ambiguous and most likely will require further interpretation in future cases.

   CLUE This ambiguous term is not an adjective as is the general rule. Its interpretation will decide who will or will not be protected.

DEFENSES TO A STRICT PRODUCT LIABILITY ACTION *Product misuse*, discussed as a defense to a negligence-based action, is also available in a strict product liability case. *Assumption of the risk* is likewise raised as a defense in a strict liability action.

However, controversy has arisen over whether the *state-of-the-art defense* should be allowed in cases in which the cause of action is based on strict liability. In most strict liability cases, courts have rejected the use of this defense, stating that the issue is not what the producers knew at the time the product was produced, but whether the product was defectively dangerous. In the 1984 case of *Elmore v. Owens Illinois, Inc.*[12] a claim arose from the plaintiff's contracting asbestosis. The plaintiff's job required him to handle a product manufactured by the defendant that contained 15 percent asbestos. The Supreme Court of Missouri ruled that the state of the art of a product has no bearing on the outcome of a strict liability claim because the issue is the defective condition of the product, not the manufacturer's knowledge, negligence, or fault.

The refusal of most courts to allow the state-of-the-art defense in strict liability cases makes sense if we consider the social policy reasons for imposing strict liability. One of the reasons for imposing strict liability is that the manufacturers or producers are best able to spread the cost of the risk; this risk-spreading function does not change with the availability of scientific knowledge.

The argument against this position, however, is equally compelling to some. If the manufacturer has indeed done everything as safely and carefully as available technology allows, it seems unfair to impose liability on the defendant. After all, how else could he or she have manufactured the product?

ENTERPRISE LIABILITY

In recent years, a new problem has developed in products liability law. Injuries resulting from defects in a number of products began showing up 10 or 20 years after exposure to the product. By this time, even though injury could be traced to the defective product, the plaintiffs could not trace the product to any particular manufacturer. Often, there were a number of manufacturers producing the same product, and the plaintiff would have no idea whose product had been used. Often, a plaintiff had used more than one manufacturer's product. The courts had to balance the interests of the plaintiffs in recovering for injuries caused by defective products against the manufacturers' interests in not being held liable for injuries caused by a product they did not produce. The primary means used to resolve this dilemma today is termed **enterprise liability**, or the **market share theory**. It was created in 1982 by the California Supreme Court in the case of *Sindell v. Abbott Laboratories*[13], excerpted in chapter 2.

In the *Sindell* case, the plaintiffs' mothers had all taken a drug known as diethylstilbestrol (DES) during pregnancies that had occurred before the drug was banned in 1971. Because the drug had been produced 20 years before the plain-

enterprise liability (market share theory) A theory of recovery in liability cases according to which damages are apportioned among all the manufacturers of a product, based on their market share at the time the plaintiffs' cause of action arose.

---

[12]673 S.W.2d 434 (Mo. 1984).
[13]607 P.2d 924 (1980).

tiffs suffered any effects from the drug their mothers had taken, it was impossible to trace the defective drug back to each manufacturer who had produced the drug that had caused each individual's problems. In order to balance the competing interests of the victims, who had suffered injury from the drug, and the defendants, who did not want to be held liable for a drug they did not produce, the court allowed the plaintiffs to sue all of the manufacturers who had produced the drug at the time that the plaintiffs' mothers had used the drug. Then the judge apportioned liability among the defendant-manufacturers on the basis of the share of the market they had held at the time that the drug had been produced.

Since *Sindell*, a number of other courts have applied and refined the market share theory, primarily in drug cases. One trial court judge in a Pennsylvania DES case laid out the four factors that are generally necessary for applying market share liability: (1) All defendants are tortfeasors; (2) the allegedly harmful products are identical and share the same defective qualities; (3) plaintiff is unable through no fault of her own to identify which defendant caused her injury; and (4) the manufacturers of substantially all of the defective products in the relevant area and during the relevant time are named as defendants.[14]

Other courts have modified the market share approach of *Sindell*. For example, in *Collins v. Eli Lilly Co.*,[15] a 1984 DES case, the court rejected the market share theory applied in *Sindell* and instead held that the plaintiff need sue only one maker of the allegedly defective drug. If the plaintiff can prove that the defendant manufactured a drug of the type taken by the plaintiff's mother at the time of the mother's pregnancy, that defendant can be held liable for all damages. However, the defendant may join other defendants and the jury may apportion liability among all defendants. The court stated that this approach could also be applied to cases that were factually similar to the DES cases.

Not all states have adopted the enterprise liability or market share theory. At least one case has questioned whether the theory could be applied to cases based on fraud or breach of warranty. In *Brown v. Abbott Laboratories*,[16] the court refused to extend the theories to such cases because they focused not on the *product*, but on the behavior of the manufacturer. Likewise, at least one California court has refused to allow the market share theory to be used to award punitive damages.[17]

SERVICE LIABILITY

Along with the growth in lawsuits for defective products, there has also been an increase in the number of lawsuits brought for defective services. These actions are generally brought when someone or someones' property is harmed as a result of an inadequately performed service.

Unlike in the product liability area, strict liability has rarely been applied to services. The few cases in which a strict liability standard has been applied involved cases in which the defendant provided both a good and a service, such as a restaurant owner's serving spoiled food.

Most service liability cases involve services provided by professionals, such as doctors, lawyers, engineers, real estate appraisers, and accountants. Actions against these professionals are generally referred to as **malpractice** cases and are usually based on a theory of negligence, breach of contract, or fraud. Malpractice actions against professionals are rising at an extremely rapid rate. For example, by the early 1970s, there had been only about 700 legal malpractice decisions reported; today that many legal malpractice cases occur each year.

The businessperson, however, is most likely to become involved in a malpractice action involving accountant malpractice. The next section, therefore, explores the liability of accountants.

malpractice suits Service liability suits brought against professionals, usually based on a theory of negligence, breach of contract, or fraud.

---

[14]*Erlich v. Abbott Lab.*, 5 Phila. 249 (1981).
[15]342 N.W.2d 37 (Sic. 1984).
[16]751 P.2d 470 (1995).
[17]*Magallanes v. E.R. Squibb & Sons*, 167 Cal. App. 878 (1985).

One group that has seen increasing liability is accountants. Much of their potential liability has come from the securities laws. Accountants' liability under these laws is discussed in chapter 21.

Accountant's liability for malpractice generally arises under actions for negligence, fraud, or breach of contract. Under a malpractice action based on negligence, the plaintiff must prove the same elements discussed in previous sections on negligence: duty, breach of duty, causation, and damages.

The accountant's duty is said to be that of using the degree of care, skill, judgment, and knowledge that can reasonably be expected of a member of the accounting profession. Two sets of standards have been developed by the American Institute of Certified Public Accountants, the professional accountants' association, that help determine reasonable care. A reasonable accountant should at minimum, follow the Generally Accepted Accounting Principles (GAAPs) and the Generally Accepted Auditing Standards (GAASs). These two codes provide standards against which to measure an accountant's practices.

A major issue in accounting malpractice is the question of to whom the accountant's duty is owed. States are not in agreement about to whom an accountant can be held liable. Of course, the accountant is always liable to his or her clients. Third parties who have relied on the accountants' work present a problem, however.

There are three alternative rules used by states to define the parameters of the accountants' liability to third parties. The first, and oldest, rule is often referred to as the **Ultramares Doctrine**. Under this rule, the accountant is liable to only those in a privity of contract relationship. In other words, only the party who contracted for the accountant's work may sue. For example, if a client contacted an accountant to prepare a statement that the accountant knew was going to be used to secure a loan from the First Founding Bank, First Founding could not sue the accountant for malpractice in a state that followed the Ultramares Doctrine because there was no contractual relationship between First Founding and the accountant.

A somewhat more liberal rule is found in Section 552 of the *Restatement (Second) of Torts*. This rule holds that accountants will be liable to a limited class of intended users of the information. Thus, the accountant owes a duty to the client and any class of persons the accountant knows is going to be receiving a copy of his or her work. Under this rule, First Founding *could* recover in the above example.

Ultramares Doctrine Rule making accountants liable only to those in a privity of contract relationship with the accountant.

EXHIBIT 12-2 *Liability of Accountants to Third Parties*

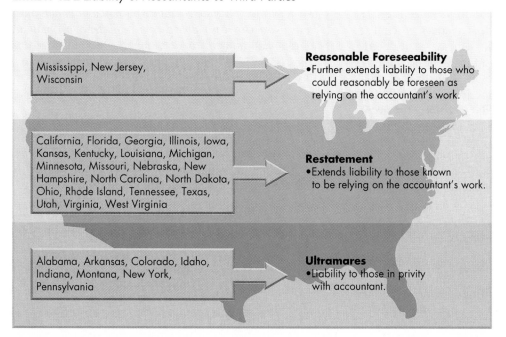

Mississippi, New Jersey, Wisconsin

Reasonable Foreseeability
• Further extends liability to those who could reasonably be foreseen as relying on the accountant's work.

California, Florida, Georgia, Illinois, Iowa, Kansas, Kentucky, Louisiana, Michigan, Minnesota, Missouri, Nebraska, New Hampshire, North Carolina, North Dakota, Ohio, Rhode Island, Tennessee, Texas, Utah, Virginia, West Virginia

Restatement
• Extends liability to those known to be relying on the accountant's work.

Alabama, Arkansas, Colorado, Idaho, Indiana, Montana, New York, Pennsylvania

Ultramares
• Liability to those in privity with accountant.

The broadest rule applies in an extremely limited number of states. The smallest minority of states holds the accountant liable to any reasonably foreseeable user of the statement the accountant prepares (Exhibit 12-2).

In the following case, the Supreme Court of Florida in 1990 decided to increase the extent of liability of accountants. In explaining their rationale for the extension, the court provided a good discussion of the alternative rules of liability.

FIRST FLORIDA BANK V. MAX MITCHELL AND COMPANY
SUPREME COURT OF FLORIDA 558 SO. 2D 9 (1990)

Plaintiff First Florida Bank sued defendant accounting firm Max Mitchell for preparing inaccurate financial statements that plaintiff had relied upon when it decided to make a loan to Max Mitchell's client. The statements were prepared by Max Mitchell and Company with knowledge that they were to be used by the plaintiff in its loan decision, and were in fact delivered to the plaintiff bank by the defendant. The trial court decided in favor of the plaintiff bank, and defendant accounting firm appealed.

JUSTICE GRIMES

When an accountant fails to exercise reasonable and ordinary care in preparing the financial statements of his clients and where that accountant personally delivers and presents the statements to a third party to induce that third party to loan to or invest in the clients, knowing that the statements will be relied upon by the third party in loaning to or investing in the client, is the accountant liable to the third party in negligence for the damages the third party suffers as a result of the accountant's failure to use reasonable and ordinary care in preparing the financial statements, despite a lack of privity between the accountant and the third party?

The seminal case on this subject is *Ultramares Corp. v. Touche*. In that case the court held that a lender which had relied upon inaccurate financial statements to its detriment had no cause of action against the public accounting firm which had prepared them because of the lack of privity between the parties. In declining to relax the requirement of privity, the court observed: "If liability for negligence exists, a thoughtless slip or blunder, the failure to detect a theft or forgery beneath the cover of deceptive entries, may expose accountants to a liability in an indeterminate (sic) amount for an indeterminate (sic) time to an indeterminate (sic) class. The hazards of a business conducted on these terms are so extreme as to kindle doubt whether a flaw may not exist in the implication of a duty that exposes one to these consequences."

The doctrine of privity has undergone substantial erosion in Florida. Indeed, in cases involving injuries caused by negligently manufactured products the requirement that there be privity between the plaintiff

and the manufacturer has been abolished. Further, this Court held that a general contractor could sue an architect or engineer for damages proximately caused by their negligence on a building project despite the absence of privity of contract between the parties.

In the more than fifty years which have elapsed since *Ultramares*, the question of an accountant's liability for negligence where no privity exists has been addressed by many courts. There are now essentially four lines of authority with respect to this issue.

1. Except in cases of fraud, an accountant is only liable to one with whom he is in privity or near privity.

2. An accountant is liable to third parties in the absence of privity under the circumstances described in section 552, Restatement (Second) of Torts (1976), which reads in pertinent part:

"§552. Information Negligently Supplied for the Guidance of Others (1) One who, in the course of his business, profession or employment, or in any other transaction in which he has a pecuniary interest, supplies false information for the guidance of others in their business transactions, is subject to liability for pecuniary loss caused to them by their justifiable reliance on the information, if he fails to exercise reasonable care or competence in obtaining or communicating the information. (2) Except as stated in Subsection (3), the liability stated in Subsection (1) is limited to loss suffered

(a) by the person or one of a limited group of persons for whose benefit and guidance he intends to supply the information or know that the recipient intends to supply it: and

(b) through reliance upon it in a transaction that he intends the information to influence or knows that the recipient so intends or in a substantially similar transaction."

3. An accountant is liable to all persons who might reasonably be foreseen as relying upon his work product.

4. An accountant's liability to third persons shall be determined by the balancing of various factors, among which are the extent to which the transaction was intended to affect the plaintiff, the fore-

seeability of harm to him, the degree of certainty that the plaintiff suffered injury, the closeness of the connection between the defendant's conduct and the injury suffered, the moral blame attached to the defendant's conduct, and the policy of preventing future harm.

We are persuaded by the wisdom of the rule which limits liability to those persons or classes of persons whom an accountant "knows" will rely on his opinion rather than those he "should have known" would do so because it takes into account the fact that an accountant controls neither his client's accounting records nor the distribution of his reports.

We conclude that the standard set forth in the Restatement (Second) of Torts § 552 (1976) represents the soundest approach to accountants' liability for negligent misrepresentation. It constitutes a middle ground between the restrictive *Ultramares* approach advocated by defendants and the expansive "reasonably foreseeable" approach advanced by plaintiffs. It recognizes that liability should extend not only to those with whom the accountant is in privity or near privity, but also to those persons, or classes of persons, whom he knows and intends will rely on this opinion, or whom he knows his client intends will so rely. On the other hand, as the commentary makes clear, it prevents extension of liability in situations where the accountant "merely knows of

the ever-present possibility of repetition to anyone, and the possibility of action in reliance upon (the audited financial statements), on the part of anyone to whom it may be repeated." As such it balances, more so than the other standards, the need to hold accountants to a standard that accounts for their contemporary role in the financial world with the need to protect them from liability that unreasonably exceeds the bounds of their real undertaking.

There remains the need to apply this rule to the facts at hand. At the time Mitchell prepared the audits for C. M. Systems, it was unknown that they would be used to induce the reliance of First Florida Bank to approve a line of credit for C. M. Systems. Therefore, except for the unusual facts of this case, Mitchell could not be held liable to the bank for any negligence in preparing the audit. However, Mitchell actually negotiated the loan on behalf of his client. He personally delivered the financial statements to the bank with the knowledge that it would rely upon them in considering whether or not to make the loan. Under this unique set of facts, we believe that Mitchell vouched for the integrity of the audits and that his conduct in dealing with the bank sufficed to meet the requirements of the rule which we have adopted in this opinion.

Reversed and remanded in favor of Plaintiff, First Florida Bank.

Critical Thinking about the Law

THIS CASE PROVIDES ANOTHER ILLUSTRATION OF the extent to which the criteria selected by the court shapes their judgment about the case. Because of our esteem for the court and the judicial system in general, we tend to believe that any set of criteria used to judge the facts and circumstances of a case are *the* criteria for judging that case. We presume that judging the case by those criteria yields the "right" judgment. Justice Grimes himself explicitly stated that there existed four different sets of criteria that have been used to judge such cases. He chose one.

Consequently, one project of the questions that follow is to prod you to think more deeply about the extent to which the standards (i.e., criteria) we use to judge the world influence that judgment, with the courtroom being no exception.

1. Understanding the issue at hand is a necessary condition for critically thinking about legal reasoning. What key fact makes the issue of the case an issue at all?

   CLUE Under certain circumstances there would have been no question of the accountant's liability. Why is there a question of his liability in this case?

2. To ensure that you understand the importance of criteria selection for legal decisions, explain the likely outcome of the case had the court adopted the criteria used in the *Ultramares* case.

   CLUE Read again the court's review of *Ultramares*.

The rule in this case has been used to extend liability to third parties adversely affected by the performance of other professionals. For example, in 1991, the case was cited to justify allowing a condominium association to sue an engineer who had been retained to inspect buildings and to make structural reports before an apartment building was converted into a condominium.[18] The case was also cited to allow a real estate appraiser to be sued by a bank who relied on an inaccurate appraisal of property.[19]

The potential of accountants' being sued is not only being expanded by the slow demise of the Ultramares Doctrine, which extends the number of persons who can sue the accountant, but the activities for which they can be held liable is also expanding. In 1994, a jury in California handed down the first massive verdict against an accounting firm for its work as a litigation consultant in *Mattco Forge, Inc. v. Arthur Young*.[20] In 1986, Mattco filed suit against General Electric Co. and hired Ernst & Young as litigation consultants to provide a damage analysis. The firm made numerous errors, including recreating documents that existed before the lawsuit. When the recreations were discovered, the case against G.E. was dismissed. Mattco then sued Ernst & Young for malpractice and fraud. The case was initially dismissed, but on appeal the Supreme Court of California held that accountants were "not immune for malpractice arising out of litigation support services." The case was then tried and resulted in the award of $14.2 million compensatory damages and $27.8 million in punitive damages. On appeal, the plaintiff's damages were reduced to out-of-pocket expenses because the plaintiffs had failed to prove an essential element of a malpractice claim: that had it not been for the malpractice of the defendants, the plaintiff would have won the case. It is only by proving this "case within a case" that the plaintiff in such a malpractice case can show damages. Thus the appellate court clarified the standard for malpractice cases arising out of litigation support services.

INTERNATIONAL DIMENSIONS OF PRODUCT LIABILITY LAW

Businesspersons are concerned with the transnational aspects of products liability law primarily in two situations: (1) when they sell an imported product that causes injury to a consumer in the United States and (2) when they manufacture and export a product that causes harm to a consumer in a foreign country. In both instances, the U.S. corporation may be subject to liability for the injury.

Liability for a defective product that injures a consumer may be imposed on everyone in the chain of distribution of the product from the retailer to the manufacturer. In about 80 percent of the cases, it is the manufacturer on whom plaintiffs tend to concentrate[21] because the manufacturer is usually responsible for the defect and has the greatest assets. If the manufacturer of a defective product is a company located in another country, a U.S. importer, wholesaler, distributor, or retailer may find herself or himself liable for the injuries caused by a defective imported product. When a manufacturer is located in a foreign country, the plaintiff often simply sues only the retailer and the wholesaler. Because they do business in the state where the consumer lives, the court can easily assert personal jurisdiction over them. The foreign corporation may sometimes argue successfully that the corporation does not have enough minimum contracts with the state to allow the assertion of jurisdiction over the foreign manufacturer under the state's long-arm statute.

Even if the long-arm statute is satisfied, a potential problem arises in conjunction with service. Although the means of service acceptable in the United States are acceptable for serving corporations in most countries, the Hague Con-

---

[18]Bay Garden Manor Condominium Association v. James Marks, 576 So.2d 744 (1991).
[19]First State Bank v. Albright and Associates of Ocala, Inc. 561 So.2d 1326 (1990).
[20]5 Cal. App. 4th 39 (1992).
[21]J. Siegmund, *Current Developments in Product Liability Affecting International Commerce,* 4 J. Prod. Liab. 109, 111 (1981).

vention on the Service of Judicial and Extrajudicial Documents in Civil and Commercial Matters (adhered to by 28 countries, including most of the major trading partners of the United States) requires that the foreign defendant receive actual notice of the suit. This requirement is sometimes difficult to satisfy.

Still another consideration for the plaintiff is the collectability of the judgment. If the foreign defendant has no assets in the United States and refuses to pay, the plaintiff will be forced to ask the courts in the country where the manufacturer is located to execute a judgment against the defendant's assets there. With all of these potential problems resulting from an action against a foreign manufacturer, a plaintiff is very likely to simply sue those U.S. businesses in the chain of distribution. The prudent businessperson who sells foreign goods should be aware of this potential liability problem.

In the case of U.S. products sold abroad, U.S. manufacturers may be brought before the foreign courts. Since the late 1970s, European and other foreign countries have been adopting increasingly strict product liability rules, holding manufacturers, distributors, and retailers liable for injuries caused by defective products on theories similar to those used in the United States, such as breach of warranty, negligence, and strict liability.

Each country has its own set of rules, so the prudent businessperson will become familiar with the rules of the country to which he or she is exporting a product. New Zealand, for example, took a unique approach in its 1972 Accident Compensation Act. This law provides for almost automatic payment of compensation for pecuniary damages, such as medical expenses and lost wages, while excluding most claims for pain and suffering.[22] Another example of how foreign laws may vary is found in France, where the courts systematically refuse to enforce contract clauses that attempt to limit a manufacturer's liability to repairing or replacing defective products in cases of both personal and commercial loss.

Foreign importers, retailers, and wholesalers of goods manufactured in the United States are not at all reluctant to join U.S. manufacturers in lawsuits in order to distribute the cost of the judgment. Obtaining jurisdiction over U.S. manufacturers presents some difficulties for some foreign courts, but most countries are more permissive than the U.S. courts in their grounds for jurisdiction, so it is much easier for a foreign court to obtain jurisdiction over a U.S. manufacturer than it is for a U.S. court to obtain jurisdiction over a foreign manufacturer. United States courts generally enforce judgments rendered by foreign courts as long as the principles used to obtain jurisdiction over the person are reasonably similar to those accepted in the United States and the substantive law reasonably conforms to our sense of justice.[23] Thus, it is extremely important that businesspersons remember that selling a product overseas does not mean freedom from product liability considerations. Product standards for goods sold overseas should be just as high as for goods sold domestically. In fact, extra precautions may need to be taken. For example, warning labels and instructions should always be printed in the languages spoken in the countries where the goods will be sold.

SUMMARY

Product liability law grew out of tort law and relies on basic tort theories. A product liability action can be based on negligence, breach of warranty, or strict product liability. The easiest of these to prove is strict product liability.

A product liability action may be brought by any party who is injured by a defective product, even if he or she did not purchase the product. An action based on strict product liability may even be brought by a bystander.

The defendant may be a retailer, distributor, or manufacturer. Sometimes, when the producer of the product cannot be clearly identified, as in the case of

---

[22]G. Palmer, *Compensation for Personal Injury: A Requiem for the Common Law in New Zealand,* 21 J. Comp. L. 1 (1973).
[23]*Id.* at 132.

a drug, the theory of enterprise liability (market share theory) may be used to bring an action against all manufacturers of a product.

Service liability is analogous to product liability, but is for defective services. Another difference between the two is that negligence is generally the only theory of liability available in a service liability case. Most service liability cases involve professional malpractice, such as accountant or medical malpractice.

Just because a U.S. corporation manufactures goods for sale overseas, the goods should not be less safe than those produced for American consumption. The manufacturer of a shoddy exported product may find himself or herself defending an action brought in a foreign court. Conversely, an importer in the United States should be especially careful inspecting the imported goods because a U.S. plaintiff may not want to sue the foreign producer, leaving the U.S. importer as the primary defendant.

REVIEW QUESTIONS

12-1. Explain what privity is and what impact it had on the development of product liability law.

12-2. Explain the elements one would have to prove to bring a successful product liability case based on negligence.

12-3. Explain the defenses one can raise in a product liability case based on negligence.

12-4. Explain the various types of warranties that provide the basis for product liability cases based on breach of warranty.

12-5. Explain the difference between the "foreign-natural" and consumer expectations tests.

12-6. Explain the defenses available in a breach of warranty case.

REVIEW PROBLEMS

12-7. Jack Clark was eating a chicken enchilada at Mexacoli Rose restaurant when he swallowed a chicken bone. The bone lodged in his throat and had to be removed in the emergency room of a local hospital. What is the primary factor that will determine whether Mr. Clark's product liability lawsuit is successful?

12-8. Five people died of carbon monoxide poisoning from a gas heater that had been improperly installed in a cabin by the owner, who had not extended the vent pipe far enough above the roof line. The instruction manual had stated that the pipe needed to be vented outside but did not specify how far outside the vent pipe needed to extend, other than having a drawing that showed it extending beyond the roof line. The manual also said, "Warning: to ensure compliance with local codes, have installed by a gas or utility inspector." Do the decedents' estates have a product liability action for failure to warn? Why or why not?

12-9. The plaintiff was injured when a fire extinguisher failed to work when it was needed to put out a fire. Could the defendant manufacturer of the fire extinguisher raise the defense of contributory negligence against the plaintiff if the plaintiff's negligence started the fire? Why or why not?

12-10. Mattie was injured when she lost control of the car she was driving because of a tire blowout. The tire was guaranteed by the manufacturer "against failure from blowouts." The guarantee also limited the manufacturer's liability to repair or replacement of any defective tire. Can Mattie sue under strict liability breach of warranty and recover damages for her injury? Why or why not?

12-11. Bob was waiting at the crosswalk for the light to turn green. As he stood there, a car that was stopped in the road next to him suddenly exploded. There had been a defect in the engine that had caused the explosion.

Will Bob be able to bring a strict product liability action against the manufacturer of the engine?

12-12. National Bank was deciding whether to loan money to Pateo Corporation. They asked Pateo to provide them with a copy of the company's most recent audit. When doing the audit, the auditors, Hamble & Humphries, failed to follow up on evidence indicating that one of the firm's managing partners might be siphoning money out of the corporation's funds. Relying on the audit, the bank made the loan. Six months later Pateo went into bankruptcy, primarily because one partner had stolen funds from the corporation and then had fled the country. Can the bank bring an action against Hamble & Humphries? Why is your answer dependent on the state in which the case arose?

CASE PROBLEMS

12-13. Mello purchased a hydraulic jack at K-Mart. The jack's packaging stated that the jack was manufactured in Hong Kong for the K-Mart Corporation and bore a K-Mart label. Mello was injured when the jack malfunctioned, so he brought an action against K-Mart for negligent design and manufacture of the jack. K-Mart moved for summary judgment on the grounds that it did not design or manufacture the jack and that it was not designed specifically for K-Mart. Discuss why K-Mart's motion either was or was not denied. *Mello v. K-Mart Corp.*, 604 F. Supp. 769 (1985)

12-14. Yong Cha Hong bought some take-out fried chicken from Roy Rogers Restaurant, owned by the Marriott Corporation. When she was eating one of the chicken wings she had purchased, she bit into something that she thought was a worm. The experience caused her extreme physical and emotional distress, and she sued the Marriott Corporation for breach of implied warranty of merchantability, seeking damages of $500,000. Marriott provided evidence of expert analysis that showed that the object at issue was not a worm or other parasite, but was probably either a chicken aorta or trachea, and argued for summary judgment on the grounds that there could be no recovery as a matter of law because the offending item was a part of the chicken, and therefore not a foreign object. Discuss the outcome of Marriott's motion for summary judgment. *Yong Cha Hong v. Marriott Corp.*, 3 UCC Rep. Serv. 2d 83 (1987)

12-15. Mrs. Maybank went to New York City to visit her grandson. She borrowed her daughter's camera to take with her so she could photograph her grandson. At a K-Mart store (owned by S. S. Kresge Company), she purchased a box of flash cubes manufactured by G.T.E. Sylvania. The box that the bulbs came in said that each bulb was safety-coated. When Mrs. Maybank attempted to take a photograph of her grandson, the flash cube exploded, knocking off Mrs. Maybank's glasses and cutting her eye, resulting in her being hospitalized for eight days. Mrs. Maybank sued S. S. Kresge. Discuss the outcome of this case. *Maybank v. S. S. Kresge Co.*, 266 S.E.2d 409 (1980)

12-16. Connie Daniell felt "overburdened" and attempted to commit suicide by climbing into the trunk of her Ford LTD and closing it behind her. While inside, she changed her mind, but she could not get out. She was locked inside for nine days before she was discovered and rescued. She then brought a strict liability action against Ford for a defective design because the trunk did not have an internal release mechanism. She also alleged that Ford should be held liable for its failure to warn of the absence of an internal trunk release mechanism. She sought to recover for physical and psychological injuries sustained during her period of being trapped in the car. Discuss the defense Ford was most likely to raise and the likelihood of their success in raising this defense. *Daniell v. Ford Motor Co., Inc.*, 581 F. Supp. 728 (1984)

12-17. Anthony Sipari leased a golf cart from the Villa Olivia Country Club. When he leased the cart, a woman presented him with a card, approximately three by four inches in size, and said, "Will you sign this for your deposit?" He signed the card and received the key to the three-wheeled golf cart. While he was driving the cart along the fairway, the back of the cart elevated, forward motion stopped immediately, and he flew out of the cart. He landed on the ground, and the cart rolled on top of him, injuring him. Sipari sued the country club and the manufacturer of the allegedly defectively designed cart. The country club raised the defenses of assumption of the risk, misuse, and that an exculpatory clause on the rental ticket relieved them of any liability in the matter. A jury found in favor of the plaintiff, but the country club filed a motion for, and was granted, a directed verdict. What was the outcome on appeal? *Sipari v. Villa Olivia Country Club & Club Car, Inc.*, 380 N.E.2d 819 (1978)

12-18. Smith was a hemophiliac who received injections of a blood protein antihemophiliac factor (AFH) concentrate. Subsequently, Smith was diagnosed with human immunodeficiency virus. It was not known which of the drug companies manufactured the AFH that Smith injected. How did Smith's inability to identify the manufacturer of the AFH affect the case? *Smith v. Cutter Biological, Inc.*, 823 P.2d 717 (1991)

- -

 On the Internet

http://www.public-policy.org/~ncpa/pd/law/lawb.html For an international perspective, find out about Japan's product liability law from this site.

http://www.eurunion.org/news/press/1997-4/pr63-97.htm Another perspective can be found by reading this proposal for reforming product liability law in the European Union.

- -

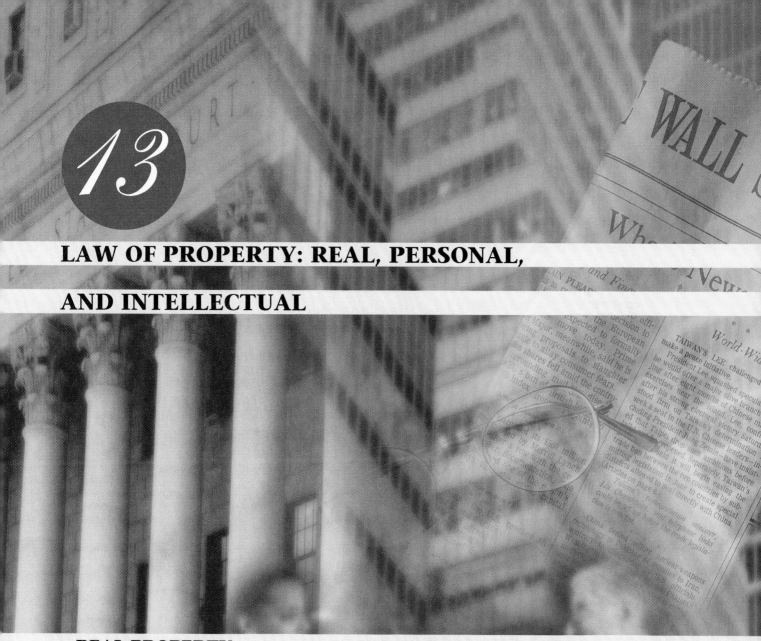

13

LAW OF PROPERTY: REAL, PERSONAL, AND INTELLECTUAL

- **REAL PROPERTY**

- **INTERESTS IN REAL PROPERTY**

- **VOLUNTARY TRANSFER OF REAL PROPERTY**

- **INVOLUNTARY TRANSFER OF REAL PROPERTY**

- **RESTRICTIONS ON LAND USE**

- **PERSONAL PROPERTY**

- **INTELLECTUAL PROPERTY**

- **INTERNATIONAL DIMENSIONS OF PROPERTY LAW**

When people hear the word *property*, they generally think of physical objects: land, houses, cars. However, this pattern of thought reflects an incomplete understanding of the concept of property. **Property** is a bundle of rights and interests in relation to other persons with reference to a tangible or intangible object (Exhibit 13-1). The essence of the concept of property is that the state provides the mechanism to allow the owner to exclude other people.

By virtue of this right, persons with great amounts of property have an especially significant amount of power. Because possessing property facilitates the acquisition of even more property, the identification of those who possess a disproportionate amount of property rights provides insight into the dynamics of influence and authority in our society.

Critical Thinking about the Law

PROPERTY IS DIRECTLY RELATED TO THE power that one has in society. Some individuals argue that the government should offer more protection for property owners. Others argue that in a fair country citizens would have similar amounts of property because property provides a basis for so many other decisions. Property rights actually exist as a matter of degree. A property owner has some rights, but he or she must tolerate some restrictions on those rights. The following questions will help you think critically about the link between property rights and power.

1. If a group of politicians passed a law to increase protection of property rights, what ethical norm probably led to this legislation?

   CLUE Review the list of ethical norms in chapter 1. Which ethical norm seems most likely to cause increased protection of property?

2. If a group of radical politicians proposed a law that reduced personal property protection and redistributed some property rights to the poor, what ethical norm was probably behind this action?

   CLUE Again, review the list of ethical norms.

3. According to the Bill Gates's Web site, Bill Gates has a net worth that makes him richer than all but 48 countries. His development of intellectual property has created his considerable wealth. How do you think he would react to Questions 1 and 2?

   CLUE Which law do you think he would be most willing to support? Why?

Property rights are not the same in every society, nor are they static. In reading this chapter, think about how property rights could be different and what impact that difference would have both on the legal environment of business and on society as a whole.

Because different types of property give their owners different rights, and because different bodies of law govern different types of property, we will discuss the three primary types of property in separate sections. Initially, this chapter focuses on *real property*, that is, land and anything permanently attached to it. The next section discusses *personal property*, both tangible (capable of being detected by the senses) and intangible (incapable of being detected by the senses). The third section shifts to *intellectual property*, that is, things created primarily by mental rather than physical processes.

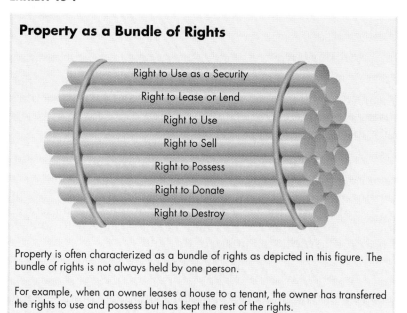

Property as a Bundle of Rights

Right to Use as a Security

Right to Lease or Lend

Right to Use

Right to Sell

Right to Possess

Right to Donate

Right to Destroy

Property is often characterized as a bundle of rights as depicted in this figure. The bundle of rights is not always held by one person.

For example, when an owner leases a house to a tenant, the owner has transferred the rights to use and possess but has kept the rest of the rights.

REAL PROPERTY

Real property is land and everything permanently attached to it. One's rights to a property depend on the type of interest that one has in that property. These types of interests are described in detail in the next section. Once one has an interest, the law provides the means to convey or transfer that interest. Although most conveyances are voluntary, the government may require involuntary conveyances to benefit the public and may place restrictions on the use of property to protect the public health, safety, and welfare.

real property Land and everything permanently attached to it.

DEFINITION OF REAL PROPERTY

Although the definition of *real property* in the previous paragraph may have sounded straightforward, many disputes have arisen over whether certain items are real or personal property. The law says that an item that is *attached* to the land is a part of the realty. What does *attached* mean? Usually, an item is considered attached if its removal would cause damage to the property. Thus, built-in appliances are generally a part of the real property, whereas free-standing ones are not. Sometimes, however, an item is not really permanently affixed to the land, but its functioning is said to be essential to the functioning of the structure. In such cases, the courts usually find the item to be part of the real property.

FIXTURES   An item that is initially a piece of personal property, but is later attached permanently to the realty, is known as a **fixture** and is treated as part of the realty. Thus, if a person rents another's property and installs a built-in microwave oven, the oven is a fixture and becomes part of the realty. The tenant may not remove the oven when he or she leaves. There are two exceptions to this rule.

fixture An item that is initially a piece of personal property but is later attached permanently to the realty and is treated as part of the realty.

First, the parties may agree that specific fixtures will be treated as personal property. To be enforceable, such an agreement must be in writing.

The second exception is for *trade fixtures*. A trade fixture is a piece of personal property that is affixed to realty in conjunction with the lease of a property for a business. When an entrepreneur opens an ice cream parlor in a leased building, the freezers he installs are trade fixtures. These are treated as personal property because of a presumption that neither party intends such

water rights The legal ability to use water flowing across or underneath one's property.

mineral rights The legal ability to dig or mine the minerals from the earth below the surface of one's land.

fee simple absolute The right to own and possess the land against all others, without conditions.

fixtures to become a permanent part of the realty. The businessperson will need the items at any new location, and new business tenants will have different needs.

Extent of Ownership

Any concept of land obviously includes the surface of the land, but legally, more is included. The landowner is entitled to the air space above the land, extending to the atmosphere. Ownership of land also includes **water rights,** the legal ability to use water flowing across or underneath one's property. Water rights, however, are somewhat restricted, in that one cannot divert water flowing across the property in such a manner as to deprive landowners downstream of the use of water from the stream.

Ownership of land usually also encompasses the land below the surface, including **mineral rights,** the legal ability to dig or mine the minerals from the earth. However, these mineral rights may be sold or given to someone other than the person who owns the surface of the land.

INTERESTS IN REAL PROPERTY

Not all interests in land are permanent. The duration of one's ownership depends on the type of *estate* one is said to hold. The estate that one has also determines what powers one has in regard to using the land. Exhibit 13-2 briefly summarizes these interests, which are described in detail in the following sections.

Fee Simple Absolute

The most complete estate is the **fee simple absolute**. When most people talk about owning property, they usually have in mind a fee simple absolute. If one has a fee simple absolute, one has all rights to own and possess that land. When the owner of a fee simple absolute interest dies, the interest passes to the owner's heirs.

EXHIBIT 13-2 *Estates in Land*

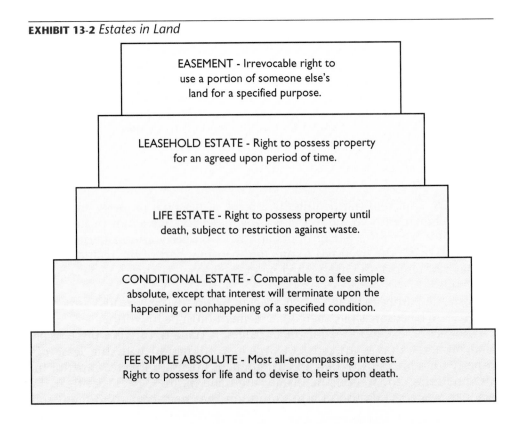

CONDITIONAL ESTATE

The interest of a **conditional estate** is the same as that of a fee simple absolute, except that it is subject to a *condition*, the happening or nonhappening of which will terminate the interest. For example, Rose may own a farm subject to the condition that Rose never grow cotton. Once Rose grows cotton, the condition has occurred, and the land either reverts to the former owner or is transferred in accordance with the terms of the deed (the instrument that is used to convey real property). Conversely, a conditional estate could be set up so that the holder would own the farm as long as the primary crop planted every year was corn. Failure to meet the condition would terminate the estate.

conditional estate The right to own and possess the land, subject to a condition whose happening (or nonhappening) will terminate the estate.

LIFE ESTATE

A **life estate** is the right to own and possess property until one dies. The use of a life estate may be more restricted than that of a fee simple absolute. The party who will take possession of the property upon the death of the holder of the life estate has an interest in making sure that the value of the property does not substantially decline as a result of neglect or abuse by the holder of the life estate. Thus, the holder is not allowed to *waste* the property. The holder cannot use the property in such a way as to destroy its value to future holders. Nor can the life tenant neglect to make necessary repairs to the property to prevent its destruction.

life estate The right to own and possess the land until one dies.

The following case provides an illustration of the type of behavior that the courts have found to constitute waste.

SAULS V. CROSBY
DISTRICT COURT OF APPEALS OF FLORIDA 258 SO. 2D 326 (1972)

Appellant and defendant Annie Sauls conveyed a future interest in certain property to plaintiff-appellees Dan and Bertha Crosby, reserving for herself a life estate in the property. When she attempted to cut timber on the property to sell, the holders of the future interest sought to enjoin her from doing so. The district court held that defendant Sauls was not entitled to cut timber and keep the proceeds for herself. Defendant Sauls appealed.

JUDGE RAWLS

On the 9th day of October 1968, appellant conveyed to appellees certain lands situated in Hamilton County, Florida, with the following reservation set forth in said conveyance: "The Grantor herein, reserves a life estate in said property." By this appeal appellant now contends that the trial court erred in denying her, as a life tenant, the right to cut merchantable timber and enjoy the proceeds.

The English common law, which was transplanted on this continent, holds that it is waste for an ordinary life tenant to cut timber upon his estate when the sole purpose is to clear the woodlands. American courts today as a general rule recognize that an ordinary life tenant may cut timber and not be liable for waste if he uses the timber for fuel; for repairing fences and buildings on the estate; for fitting the land for cultivation; or for use as pasture if the inheritance is not damaged and the acts are conformable to good husbandry; and for thinning or other purposes which are necessary for the enjoyment of the estate and are in conformity with good husbandry.

In this jurisdiction a tenant for life or a person vested with an ordinary life estate is entitled to the use and enjoyment of his estate during its existence. The only restriction on the life tenant's use and enjoyment is that he not permanently diminish or change the value of the future estate of the remainderman. This limitation places on the "ordinary life tenant" the responsibility for all waste of whatever character.

An instrument creating a life tenancy may absolve the tenant of responsibility for waste by stating that the life tenant has the power to consume or that the life tenant is without impeachment for waste. Thus, there is a sharp distinction in the rights of an ordinary life tenant or life tenant without impeachment for waste or life tenant who has the power to consume. An ordinary life tenant has no right to cut the timber from an estate for purely commercial reasons and so to do is tortious conduct for which the remainderman may sue immediately.

In the case before us, the trial court was concerned with the rights of an ordinary life tenant and correctly concluded that appellant "does not have the right to cut merchantable timber from the land involved in this suit unless the proceeds of such cutting and sale are held in trust for the use and benefit of the remaindermen. . . ."

Affirmed in favor of Plaintiff, Crosby.

Critical Thinking about the Law

A JUDGE'S REASONING EXPLAINS THE CONDITIONS under which certain actions are either legal or illegal. These conditions reveal the extent to which a court's decision depends on not only the existence of a certain set of facts but also the court's earlier determinations about the appropriate structure of those conditions.

Though brief, the court's decision in this particular case is loaded with contingencies or limits to the boundaries of the decision. The following questions will help you both to identify and to evaluate those contingencies.

1. To ensure that you are aware of the contingent nature of the court's decision, identify all of the conditions listed by the court that would have made the defendant's actions legally acceptable.

   CLUE Go back through the court's reasoning and pinpoint when it is acceptable for an ordinary life tenant to cut timber.

2. As you now know from performing the task assigned in Question 1, the court provides a condition under which Sauls could have cut timber for commercial purposes. What ethical norm is implicit in this condition?

   CLUE Think about what a person who objects to the plaintiff's being allowed to keep the money would say. Would such a person say that this allowance is unjust, inefficient, a detriment to security, or a violation of liberty?

---

future interest The present right to possess and own the land in the future.

FUTURE INTEREST   A person's present right to possession and ownership of land in the future is a **future interest** and usually exists in conjunction with a life estate or a conditional estate. For example, Sam owns a life estate in Blueberry Farm, and, on Sam's death, fee simple absolute ownership of the land will pass to Jane. Jane has a future interest in Blueberry Farm. As a result of her interest, she may sue Sam to enjoin him from engaging in waste of the property.

LEASEHOLD ESTATES

leasehold The right to possess property for an agreed-upon period of time stated in a lease.

lease The contract that transfers possessory interest in a property from the owner (lessor) to the tenant (lessee).

A **leasehold** is not an ownership interest. It is a *possessory* interest. One who has a leasehold is entitled to exclude all others, including the property owner under most circumstances, for the period of the lease and is entitled to use the property for any legal purpose that is not destructive of other occupiers' rights or prohibited by the terms of the lease. The **lease** is the contract that transfers the possessory interest. It generally specifies the property to be leased, the amount of the rent payments and when they are due, the duration of the leasehold, and any special duties or rights of either party. It is signed by both parties. The owner of the property is the lessor, or landlord. The holder of the lease is the lessee, or tenant.

Although the rights and obligations of the landlord and the tenant may be altered by the lease, some states have statutes requiring landlords to keep the premises in good repair and allowing tenants to withhold their rent if the landlord fails to do so. The landlord may enter the property only in an emergency, with permission of the tenant to make repairs, or with notice to the tenant near the end of the leasehold to show the property to a potential tenant. If the tenant fails to make the agreed-upon rental payments, the landlord may bring an action to evict the tenant.

Unless prohibited by the lease, a tenant may move out of the property and sublease it to another party. The initial tenant, however, still remains liable to the landlord for payment of rent due for the entire term of the lease.

EASEMENTS

An **easement** is an irrevocable right to use some portion of another's land for a specific purpose. The party holding the easement does not own the land in question but has only the right to use it. Easements generally arise in one of three ways: express agreement, prescription, or necessity.

An easement by *express agreement* arises when the landowner expressly agrees to allow the holder of the easement to use the land in question for the agreed-upon purpose. For example, a utility company may have an easement to run power lines across one's property. The easement should be described on the deed to the property or recorded in the county office that keeps property records to protect the holder of the easement when the property is sold.

An *easement by prescription* arises under state law. When one openly uses a portion of another's property for a statutory period of time, an easement arises. In many states, the time period is 25 years.

An *easement by necessity* arises when a piece of property is divided and, as a result, one portion is landlocked. The owner of the landlocked portion has an easement to cross the other parcel for purposes of entrance to and exit from the land.

easement An irrevocable right to use some portion of another's land for a specific purpose.

CO-OWNERSHIP

We have been referring to the holders of interest in land in the singular. Ownership of land may also be held by multiple persons, as well as by business organizations. Whenever there is ownership by multiple parties, it is important to know what type of ownership exists because different forms give different rights to the owners.

The three types of **co-ownership** are tenancy in common, joint tenancy, and tenancy by the entirety. Regardless of which type of tenancy exists, all tenants have the equal right to occupy all the property. Their other interests are described below and are summarized in Table 13-1.

Tenancy in common occurs most frequently. Owners may own unequal shares of the property, may sell their interest without consent of the other owners, and may have their interest attached by a creditor. Upon the death of the tenant in common, his or her heirs receive the property interest.

Under **joint tenancy**, all are co-owners of equal shares and may sell their shares without the consent of other owners. Their interest can be attached by creditors. Upon the death of a joint tenant, his or her interest is divided equally among the remaining joint owners.

Tenancy by the entirety exists only when co-owners are a married couple. One cannot sell his or her interest without the consent of the other, and creditors of only one cannot attach the property. Upon the death of one, full ownership of the property passes to the other. Upon divorce, tenancy by the entirety automatically becomes tenancy in common.

co-ownership Ownership of land by multiple persons or business organizations; all tenants have an equal right to occupy all of the property.

tenancy in common Form of co-ownership of real property in which owners may have equal or unequal shares of the property, may sell their shares without the consent of the other owners, and may have their interest attached by creditors.

joint tenancy Form of co-ownership of real property in which all owners have equal shares in the property, may sell their shares without the consent of the other owners, and may have their interest attached by creditors.

tenancy by the entirety Form of co-ownership of real property, allowed only to married couples, in which one owner cannot sell without the consent of the other and the creditors of only one owner cannot attach the property.

TABLE 13-1 *Joint Ownership*

TYPE	DIVISION OF OWNERSHIP	RIGHTS OF OWNERS' CREDITORS	OWNERSHIP OF PROPERTY UPON DEATH
Tenancy in common	Equal or unequal shares	Can attach interest	Transferred to heirs
Joint tenancy	Equal shares	Can attach interest	Divided among other joint tenants
Tenancy by the entirety	Equal shares	Cannot attach interest	Goes to surviving spouse

LICENSES

A license is a temporary, revokable right to be on someone else's property. When one opens a business, the public is given a license to enter the property to purchase the good or services provided by the business.

VOLUNTARY TRANSFER OF REAL PROPERTY

The value of property is heightened by the owner's ability to transfer that property. In general, the owner may transfer the property to anyone for any amount of consideration or for no consideration. He or she may transfer all or any portion of the property.

In order to transfer property, however, the owner must follow the proper procedures. These are *execution, delivery, acceptance,* and, to protect the recipient of the property, *recording* (Exhibit 13-3). Unless something to the contrary is stated, it is presumed that a conveyance of ownership is the conveyance of a fee simple absolute.

EXECUTION

deed Instrument of conveyance of property.

The first step in a voluntary transfer is the *execution* of the deed. The **deed**, as shown in Exhibit 13-4, is the instrument of conveyance. A properly drafted deed:

1. Identifies the grantor (the person conveying the property) and the grantee (the person receiving the property).
2. Contains words that express the grantor's intent to convey the property.
3. Identifies the type and percentage of ownership.
4. States the price paid for the property, if any.
5. Contains a legal description of the physical boundaries of the property (not the street address).
6. Specifies any easements or restrictions on use of the land.
7. Identifies any warranties or promises made by the grantor in conjunction with the conveyance.

EXHIBIT 13-3 *Steps in a Conveyance*

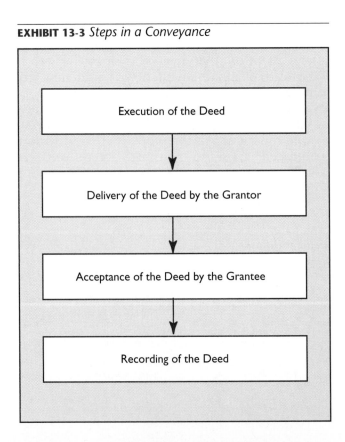

Execution of the Deed

↓

Delivery of the Deed by the Grantor

↓

Acceptance of the Deed by the Grantee

↓

Recording of the Deed

Form 1-A   8   Legal News, Toledo, Ohio

WARRANTY DEED

Received and Recorded at _____M.	TRANSFERRED _____
RECORDER	AUDITOR
	PER_____

Know All Men By These Presents:

That   Sam Seller

in consideration of $88,000   *the grantor* ,

    to be   *paid by*   Betty Buyer

                                         the grantee

whose present mail address is   2028 North Main, Bowling Green, Ohio

the receipt whereof is hereby acknowledged, do es   *hereby BARGAIN, SELL and CONVEY to said Grantee*

and her   *heirs, successors and assigns forever, the following described real estate, situate in the County of*
         Wood   *, State of Ohio: viz:*

                          Lot 57, plat 32 in
                          Green Hills Subdivision

and all the estate, right, title and interest said grantor   ha s   *or ought to have in and to said described premises, together with the privileges and appurtenances to the same belonging, but subject to zoning ordinances, restrictions of record and public utility or other easements of record.*

    Grantor   *acquired title to the above described premises by instrument recorded in Vol.* LXVI *, Page* 12 *.*

    To Have and To Hold the same to the said Grantee   *, and to* his   *heirs, successors and assigns forever;*
Grantor is   *hereby covenanting that he is*   *the true and lawful owner*   *of said premises and he*
is   *well seized of the same in fee simple, and ha s*   *good right and full power to bargain, sell and convey the same in the manner aforesaid, and that the premises so conveyed are clear, free and unencumbered and that* he   will *warrant and defend the same against all claims whatsoever, except taxes and assessments due and payable -*

    IN WITNESS WHEREOF, The said   Sam Seller *has*

hereunto set his   *hand this* 17   *day of* May   *in the year of our Lord*
One Thousand Nine Hundred and eighty-eight

        Signed, acknowledged and
        Delivered in the presence of

The State of Ohio,_____ Wood _____County, ss.

    BE IT REMEMBERED, That on the 17th   *day of* May   *in the year of our Lord*
One Thousand Nine Hundred and eighty eight   *, before me, the subscriber, a Notary Public within and for said county, personally came* Sam Seller

the grantor   *in the above conveyance, and acknowledged the signing thereof to be* his   *voluntary act and deed, for the purpose therein mentioned.*

    IN WITNESS WHEREOF, I have hereunto subscribed my name and affixed my official seal on the day and year aforesaid.

                         Notary Public, _____ Lucas _____ County, Ohio.

This Instrument Prepared By: **Andrea Attorney**   My Commission Expires 9-28-95

GENERAL WARRANTY DEED

Two basic types of deeds are generally used to transfer ownership of property. The first, a **general warranty deed**, is preferred by grantees because it contains certain warranties or promises by the grantor. Although such covenants may vary slightly from state to state, they generally include the following.

1. The covenant of *seisen*, a promise that the grantor owns the interest that he or she is conveying.

2. The covenant of the *right to convey*, a promise that the grantor has the right to convey the property.

general warranty deed A deed that promises that the grantor owns the land and has the right to convey it and that the land has no encumbrances other than those stated in the deed.

3. The covenant against *encumbrances*, a promise that there are no mortgages or liens against the property that are not stated in the deed.

4. The covenant for *quiet enjoyment*, a promise that the grantee will not be disturbed by anyone who has a better claim to title of the property and a promise to defend the grantee's title against such claims or to reimburse the grantee for any money spent in the defense or settlement of such claims.

5. The covenant of *further assurances*, the promise that the grantor will provide the grantee with any additional documents that the grantee needs to perfect his or her title to the property.

quitclaim deed A deed that simply transfers to the grantee the interest that the grantor owns in the property.

QUITCLAIM DEED The other type of deed, which is more desirable from the grantor's perspective, is the **quitclaim deed**. With such a deed, the grantor simply transfers to the grantee the interest that the grantor owns in the property being conveyed. The grantor makes no additional covenants. Obviously, most grantees would be very reluctant to accept a quitclaim deed.

Once the properly drafted deed has been signed by the grantor and the grantee, it is said to have been *executed*. Many states require the signing of the deed to be witnessed or notarized (witnessed by an official of the state who certifies that she or he saw the parties sign the deed and was provided evidence that the signatories were who they purported to be).

DELIVERY

Once executed, the deed must be *delivered*, or transferred, to the grantee with the intent of transferring ownership to the grantee. The delivery may be made directly to the grantee or to a third party who has been instructed to transfer the deed to the grantee.

ACCEPTANCE

The final essential step is *acceptance* by the grantee. This is the grantee's expression of intent to possess the property. Acceptance is presumed when the grantee retains possession of the deed.

RECORDING

Recording is not essential for the transfer of ownership, but it is so important to securing the grantee's rights to the property that is should always be a part of the process of conveyance. Recording is the filing of the deed (as well as any other documents related to realty, such as mortgages) with the appropriate county office. This office varies by state and may be the county clerk's office or the county recorder's office. Recording gives the world notice of the transfer. It is significant because in many states, if there are two deeds allegedly conveying the same piece of property, the owner of the property is the one whose deed was recorded first.

INVOLUNTARY TRANSFER OF REAL PROPERTY

Transfer of ownership interests in property may also occur without the owner's knowledge, or even against his or her will, by either adverse possession or condemnation.

ADVERSE POSSESSION

adverse possession Acquiring ownership of realty by openly treating it as one's own, with neither protest nor permission from the real owner, for a statutorily established period of time.

Most states provide that when a person openly treats realty as his or her own, without protest or permission from the real owner, for a statutorily established period of time, ownership is automatically vested in that person. Each state has its own exact requirements for **adverse possession**, but the necessary possession is often described as having to be *actual* (the party resides on or uses the land as would an owner), *open* (not secretive), and *notorious* (without the owner's permission). Some state laws require specific acts such as the payment of real estate taxes. Others require that the adverse possessor took possession of the land "under color of title," that is, thinking that he or she was the lawful possessor of the land.

CONDEMNATION

Condemnation is a process by which the government acquires the ownership of private property for a public use over the protest of the owner of the property. The property owner may have been contesting either the taking itself or the price that the government was willing to pay for the taking. Condemnation proceedings occur as a result of the government's exercise of its right of **eminent domain**, which was briefly discussed in chapter 4. Remember from the discussion of the Takings Clause that the right of eminent domain is the constitutional right of the government to take private property, on payment of just compensation, for a purpose that will benefit the general welfare. This taking may be by any level of government or, in limited cases, by private companies fulfilling a public or governmental function.

Under the right of eminent domain, the government first approaches the property owner with an offer of payment. If the owner objects to the transfer or the parties cannot agree on a price, the government institutes condemnation proceedings. The court then determines whether the governmental purpose is legitimate. If it determines that it is, the court then determines the fair market value of the property. Once this price has been paid, ownership is transferred to the governmental body that brought the action.

Sometimes the government wishes to use its eminent domain power to take property and the owner questions whether the taking is really for a public purpose. That question may be especially difficult when the property to be acquired will be subsequently conveyed to another private individual. The following case involves such an issue.

condemnation The process whereby the government acquires the ownership of private property for a public use over the protest of the owner.

eminent domain The constitutional right of the government to take privately owned real property for a public purpose in exchange for a just compensation to the owner.

POLETOWN NEIGHBORHOOD COUNCIL V. CITY OF DETROIT AND THE DETROIT ECONOMIC DEVELOPMENT CORPORATION
SUPREME COURT OF MICHIGAN 304 N.W.2D 455 (1981)

Defendant Detroit Economic Development Corporation sought to acquire a large parcel of land on which members of the plaintiff organization, Poletown Neighborhood Council, resided and had small businesses. Once they had acquired the land, through the use of the city's eminent domain power, the land would be conveyed to General Motors to expand their plant. Plaintiffs, who did not want their community destroyed, sued the city and the development council on the grounds that they were attempting to abuse their power of eminent domain to take private property for a private use.

The trial court found in favor of the defendants, allowing the condemnation of the property. The court of appeals affirmed. Plaintiffs appealed to the state supreme court.

PER CURIAM

This case raises a question of paramount importance to the future welfare of this state and its residents: Can a municipality use the power of eminent domain granted to it by the Economic Development Corporations Act, to condemn property for transfer to a private corporation to build a plant to promote industry and commerce, thereby adding jobs and taxes to the economic base of the municipality and state?

Plaintiffs-appellants do not challenge the declaration of the legislature that programs to alleviate and prevent conditions of unemployment and to preserve and develop industry and commerce are essential public purposes. Nor do they challenge the proposition that legislation to accomplish this purpose falls within the Constitutional grant of general legislative power to the legislature.

What plaintiffs-appellants do challenge is the constitutionality of using the power of eminent domain to condemn one person's property to convey it to another private person in order to bolster the economy. They argue that whatever incidental benefit may accrue to the public, assembling land to General Motors' specifications for conveyance to General Motors for its uncontrolled use in profit making is really a taking for private use and not a public use because General Motors is the primary beneficiary of the condemnation.

The defendants-appellees contend, on the other hand, that the controlling public purpose in taking this land is to create an industrial site which will be used to alleviate and prevent conditions of unemployment and fiscal distress. The fact that it will be conveyed to and ultimately used by a private manufacturer does not defeat this predominant public purpose.

There is no dispute about the law. All agree that condemnation for a public use or purpose is permitted. All agree that condemnation for a private use or purpose is forbidden. Similarly, condemnation for a private use cannot be authorized whatever its incidental public benefit and condemnation for a public purpose cannot be forbidden whatever the incidental private gain. The heart of this dispute is whether the proposed condemnation is for the primary benefit of the public or the private user.

The Legislature has determined that governmental action of the type contemplated here meets a public need and serves an essential public purpose. The Court's role after such a determination is made is limited.

The determination of what constitutes a public purpose is primarily a legislative function, subject to review by the courts when abused, and the determination of the legislative body of that matter should not be reversed except in instances where such determination is palpable and manifestly arbitrary and incorrect.

In the court below, the plaintiffs-appellants challenged the necessity for the taking of the land for the proposed project. In this regard the city presented substantial evidence of the severe economic conditions facing the residents of the city and state, the need for new industrial development to revitalize local industries, the economic boost the proposed project would provide, and the lack of other adequate available sites to implement the project.

As Justice Cooley stated over a hundred years ago "the most important consideration in the case of eminent domain is the necessity of accomplishing some public good which is otherwise impracticable, and the law does not so much regard the means as the need." When there is such public need, "(t)he abstract right (of an individual) to make use of his own property in his own way is compelled to yield to the general comfort and protection of community, and to a proper regard to relative rights in others."

In the instant case the benefit to be received by the municipality invoking the power of eminent domain is a clear and significant one and is sufficient to satisfy this Court that such a project was an intended and a legitimate object of the Legislature when it allowed municipalities to exercise condemnation power even though a private party will also, ultimately, receive benefit as an incident thereto.

The power of eminent domain is to be used in this instance primarily to accomplish the essential public purposes of alleviating unemployment and revitalizing the economic base of the community. The benefit to a private interest is merely incidental.

Our determination that this project falls within the public purpose, as stated by the Legislature, does not mean that every condemnation proposed by an economic development corporation will meet with similar acceptance simply because it may provide some jobs or add to the industrial or commercial base. If the public benefit was not so clear and significant, we would hesitate to sanction approval of such a project. Where, as here, the condemnation power is exercised in a way that benefits specific and identifiable private interests, a court inspects with heightened scrutiny the claim that the public interest is the predominant interest being advanced. Such public benefit cannot be speculative or marginal but must be clear and significant if it is to be within the legitimate purpose as stated by the Legislature. We hold this project is warranted on the basis that its significance for the people of Detroit and the state has been demonstrated.

Affirmed in favor of Defendant, Detroit Economic Development Corporation.

DISSENTING

JUSTICE FITZGERALD

. . . Because I believe the proposed condemnation clearly exceeds the government's authority to take private property through the power of eminent domain, I dissent.

Our approval of the use of eminent domain power in this case takes this state into a new realm of takings of private property; there is simply no precedent for this decision in previous Michigan cases.

The city places great reliance on a number of slum clearance cases here and elsewhere in which it has been held that the fact that the property taken is eventually transferred to private parties does not defeat a claim that the taking is for a public use. Despite the superficial similarity of these cases to the instant one based on the ultimate disposition of the property, these decisions do not justify the condemnation proposed by the city. The public purpose that has been found to support the slum clearance cases is the benefit to the public health and welfare that arises from the elimination of existing blight, even though the ultimate disposition of the property will benefit private interests. As we said in *In re* Slum Clearance, supra:

"It seems to us that the public purpose of slum clearance is in any event the one controlling purpose of the condemnation. The jury were not asked to decide any necessity to condemn the parcels involved for any purpose of resale, but only for slum clearance.

"(T)he resale (abating part of the cost of clearance) is not a primary purpose and is incidental and ancillary to the primary and real purpose of clearance."

However, in the present case the transfer of the property to General Motors after the condemnation cannot be considered incidental to the taking. It is only through the acquisition and use of the property by General Motors that the "public purpose" of promoting employment can be achieved. Thus, it is the economic benefits of the project that are incidental to the private use of the property.

The city also points to decisions that have found the objective of economic development to be a sufficient "public purpose" to support the expenditure of public funds in aid of industry. What constitutes a public purpose in a context of governmental taxing and spending power cannot be equated with the use of that term in connection with eminent domain powers. The potential risk of abuse in the use of eminent domain power is clear. Condemnation places the burden of aiding industry on the few, who are likely to have limited power to protect themselves from the excesses of legislative enthusiasm for the promotion of industry.

Second, it is worth noting that the Maryland and Minnesota cases cited above are distinguishable in that in each it was the governmental unit that selected the site in question for commercial or industrial development. By contrast, the project before us was initiated by General Motors Corporation's solicitation of the city for its aid in locating a factory site.

The condemnation contemplated in the present action goes beyond the scope of the power of eminent domain in that it takes private property for private use. I would reverse the judgment of the circuit court.

Critical Thinking about the Law

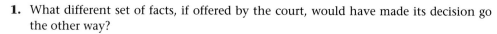

UPON READING THE OPINIONS OF BOTH the majority and the dissent, we learn that the former's reasoning primarily consists of both a set of facts and a legal analogy. This type of reasoning, as you know by now, is very common.

Whenever any entity, including a court, makes a conclusion based on a set of facts supported by an analogy, it is important that we as critical thinkers examine those foundations. Question 1 will prod you to think about the significance of the facts selected by the majority in its opinion. Question 2 will do the same concerning the legal analogy.

1. What different set of facts, if offered by the court, would have made its decision go the other way?

   CLUE The judge states explicitly that the main issue is whether the condemnation primarily advances the public purpose. What facts allowed the court to say that the condemnation provided such an advancement?

2. The dissenting judge attacks the majority's use of slum clearance as a legal analogy. On what grounds is such an attack made?

   CLUE Pay attention to the ways in which the dissent differentiates the present case from those pertaining to slum clearances.

RESTRICTIONS ON LAND USE

No one is allowed to use the land in a *completely* unrestricted manner. As previously indicated, the doctrine of waste prohibits some uses and abuses of land. There are other such restrictions, both voluntary and involuntary.

RESTRICTIVE COVENANTS

Parties may voluntarily enter into **restrictive covenants**, that is, promises to use or not to use their land in particular ways. These covenants are generally included in the deeds and are binding on the owners as long as the covenants are for lawful acts. For example, a restrictive covenant not to construct buildings higher than three stories would be lawful and enforceable, whereas a covenant never to convey property to minorities would be unlawful and thus unenforceable.

restrictive covenants
Promises by the owner, generally included in the deed, to use or not to use the land in particular ways.

ZONING

Zoning is the restriction of the use of property to allow for the orderly growth and development of a community and to protect the health, safety, and welfare of its citizens. Zoning may restrict the type of use to which land may be put, such as residential, commercial, industrial, or agricultural. Zoning laws may also regulate land use in geographic areas on the basis of such factors as the intensity (single or multifamily dwellings), the size, or the placement of buildings.

zoning Government restrictions on the use of private property in order to ensure the orderly growth and development of a community and to protect the health, safety, and welfare of citizens.

variance Permission given to a
landowner to use a piece of his or
her land in a manner prohibited
by the zoning laws; generally
granted to prevent undue
hardship.

When new zoning ordinances are enacted by a community, there is generally a public hearing on the proposed change in zoning. Often, the community allows a *nonconforming use* of a particular property when the zoning of an area changes. This exception to the zoning law occurs when the property in question was being used for a purpose not allowed under the new zoning statutes, but because of the prior use, the owner is allowed to continue using the property in the nonconforming manner.

A landowner who wished to use her or his land in a manner prohibited by zoning laws may seek a *variance* from the appropriate governmental unit, usually a zoning board or a planning commission. A **variance** is permission to use a piece of land in a manner prohibited by the zoning laws. Variances are generally granted to prevent undue hardship.

Sometimes, persons negatively affected by a zoning law challenge that ordinance. Zoning is allowed under the police power, the power of the state to regulate to protect the health, safety, and welfare of the public. To be a valid exercise of such power, the zoning ordinance must not be arbitrary or unreasonable. An ordinance is unreasonable if (1) it encroaches on the private property rights of landowners without a substantial relationship to a legitimate government purpose, or (2) there is no reasonable relationship between the ends sought to be obtained and the means used to attain those ends.

Zoning is also unreasonable if it is totally destructive of the economic value of a property holder's land. In such cases, the zoning is really a constructive taking of the property, and the party whose land is so affected is entitled to just compensation. This type of challenge is frequently made, but it is rarely successful.

OTHER STATUTORY RESTRICTIONS ON LAND USE

In addition to zoning ordinances, states often use their police power to pass laws affecting individuals' use of their property. For example, some states have passed historic preservation statutes whereby certain buildings with historical importance are subject to certain restrictions. Owners of such structures may be required to keep the buildings in good repair or might be required to have any alternations to the buildings' facade approved prior to modification.

Like zoning laws, any laws restricting peoples' use of their property may be subject to constitutional challenge. The following case illustrates the type of land use regulations that are increasingly being challenged. In this case, the Court clarified and toughened its requirement that government planners produce specific justifications when they condition building permits on a party's rendering a portion of the property for public use.

DOLAN V. CITY TIGARD
UNITED STATES SUPREME COURT 114 S. CT. 2309 (1994)

Plaintiff Dolan sought a permit from defendant City of Tigard to expand her store and pave her parking lot. The city conditioned granting her permit on her dedication of a portion of her property for (1) a public greenway to minimize flooding that would otherwise be likely to result from her construction and (2) a pedestrian/bicycle pathway to decrease congestion in the business district.

Plaintiff Dolan appealed the decision of the planning commission to the Land Use Board of Appeals, which found that the land dedication requirements were reasonably related to her proposed construction, and therefore did not constitute a taking. The state court of appeals and state supreme court both affirmed the decision in favor of

the city. Plaintiff Dolan appealed to the U.S. Supreme Court.

JUSTICE REHNQUIST

One of the principal purposes of the Takings Clause is "to bar Government from forcing some people alone to bear public burdens which, in all fairness and justice, should be borne by the public as a whole." Without question, had the city simply required petitioner to dedicate a strip of land along Fanno Creek for public use, rather than conditioning the grant of her permit to redevelop her property on such a dedication, a taking would have occurred. Such public access would deprive petitioner of the right to exclude others, "one of the most essential sticks in the bundle of rights that are commonly characterized as property."

On the other side of the ledger, the authority of state and local governments to engage in land use planning has been sustained against constitutional challenge. . . . A land use regulation does not effect a taking if it "substantially advance[s] legitimate state interests" and does not "den[y] an owner economically viable use of his land."

Petitioner contends that the city has forced her to choose between the building permit and her right under the Fifth Amendment to just compensation for the public easements. Petitioner does not quarrel with the city's authority to exact some forms of dedication as a condition for the grant of a building permit, but challenges the showing made by the city to justify these exactions. She argues that the city has identified "no special benefits" conferred on her, and has not identified any "special quantifiable burdens" created by her new store that would justify the particular dedications required from her which are not required from the public at large.

In evaluating petitioner's claim, we must first determine whether the "essential nexus" exists between the "legitimate state interest" and the permit condition exacted by the city. If we find that a nexus exists, we must then decide the required degree of connection between the exactions and the projected impact of the proposed development.

Undoubtedly, the prevention of flooding along Fanno Creek and the reduction of traffic congestion in the Central Business District qualify as the type of legitimate public purposes we have upheld. It seems equally obvious that a nexus exists between preventing flooding along Fanno Creek and limiting development within the creek's 100-year floodplain. Petitioner proposes to double the size of her retail store and to pave her now-gravel parking lot, thereby expanding the impervious surface on the property and increasing the amount of stormwater run-off into Fanno Creek.

The same may be said for the city's attempt to reduce traffic congestion by providing for alternative means of transportation. In theory, a pedestrian/bicycle pathway provides a useful alternative means of transportation for workers and shoppers: "Pedestrians and bicyclists occupying dedicated spaces for walking and/or bicycling . . . remove potential vehicles from streets, resulting in an overall improvement in total transportation system flow."

The second part of our analysis requires us to determine whether the degree of the exactions demanded by the city's permit conditions bear the required relationship to the projected impact of petitioner's proposed development.

"The distinction, therefore, which must be made between an appropriate exercise of the police power and an improper exercise of eminent domain is whether the requirement has some reasonable relationship or nexus to the use

to which the property is being made or is merely being used as an excuse for taking property simply because at that particular moment the landowner is asking the city for some license or permit."

We think a term such as "rough proportionality" best encapsulates what we hold to be the requirement of the Fifth Amendment. No precise mathematical calculation is required, but the city must make some sort of individualized determination that the required dedication is related both in nature and extent to the impact of the proposed development.

We turn now to analysis of whether the findings relied upon by the city here, first with respect to the floodplain easement and second with respect to the pedestrian/bicycle path, satisfied these requirements.

It is axiomatic that increasing the amount of impervious surface will increase the quantity and rate of stormwater flow from petitioner's property. The city has never said why a public greenway, as opposed to a private one, was required in the interest of flood control. We conclude that the findings upon which the city relies do not show the required reasonable relationship between the floodplain easement and the petitioner's proposed new building.

With respect to the pedestrian/bicycle pathway, we have no doubt that the city was correct in finding that the larger retail sales facility proposed by petitioner will increase traffic on the streets of the Central Business District. Dedications for streets, sidewalks, and other public ways are generally reasonable exactions to avoid excessive congestion from a proposed property use. But on the records before us, the city has not met its burden of demonstrating that the additional number of vehicle and bicycle trips generated by the petitioner's development reasonably relate to the city's requirement for a dedication of the pedestrian/bicycle pathway easement.

As Justice Peterson of the Supreme Court of Oregon explained in his dissenting opinion, however, "[t]he findings of fact that the bicycle pathway system 'could offset some of the traffic demand' is a far cry from a finding that the bicycle pathway system will, or is likely to, offset some of the traffic demand." No precise mathematical calculation is required, but the city must make some effort to quantify its findings in support of the dedication for the pedestrian/bicycle pathway beyond the conclusory statement that it could offset some of the traffic demand generated.

Cities have long engaged in the commendable task of land use planning, made necessary by increasing urbanization particularly in metropolitan areas such as Portland. The city's goals of reducing flooding hazards and traffic congestion, and providing for public greenways, are laudable, but there are outer limits to how this may be done. "A strong public desire to improve the public condition [will not] warrant achieving the desire by a shorter cut than the constitutional way of paying for the change."

Reversed and remanded in favor of Plaintiff, Dolan.

PERSONAL PROPERTY

personal property All property that is not real property; may be tangible or intangible.

tangible property Personal property that is material and movable (e.g., furniture).

intangible property Personal property that does not have a physical form and is usually evidenced in writings (e.g., an insurance policy).

All property that is not real property is **personal property**. As previously explained, personal property may be either tangible or intangible. **Tangible property** includes movable items, such as furniture, cars, and other goods. **Intangibles** include such items as bank accounts, stocks, and insurance policies. Because most intangibles (with the exception of some of those classified as intellectual property and discussed later) are evidenced by writings, most of the following discussion applies to both tangible and intangible property. The primary concerns that arise in conjunction with personal property involve (1) the means of acquiring ownership of the property and (2) the rights and duties arising out of a *bailment*. Both are discussed here in detail.

VOLUNTARY TRANSFER OF PERSONAL PROPERTY

title Ownership of property.

The most common means by which personal property is acquired is by its voluntary transfer, as a result of either a purchase or a gift. Ownership of property is referred to as **title**, and title to property passes when the parties so intend. When there is a purchase, the acquiring party gives some consideration to the seller in exchange for title to the property. In most cases, this transfer of ownership requires no formalities, but in a few cases, changes of ownership must be registered with a government agency. The primary transfers requiring such formalities include sales of motor vehicles, watercraft, and airplanes. Transfer of such property requires that a certificate of title be signed by the seller, taken to the appropriate governmental agency, and then reissued in the name of the new owner.

Gifts are distinguished from purchases in that there is no consideration given for a gift. As the reader knows, a promise to make a gift is therefore unenforceable. Once properly made, however, a gift is an irrevocable transfer.

donative intent Intent to transfer ownership to another at the time the donor makes actual or constructive delivery of the gift to the donee.

For a valid gift to occur, three elements must be present (Exhibit 13-5). First, there must be a *delivery* of the gift. This delivery may be actual, that is, the physical presentation of the gift itself. Or it may be constructive, that is, the delivery of an item that gives access to the gift or represents it, such as the handing over of the keys to a car. Second, the delivery must be made with **donative intent** to make a present, as opposed to future, gift. The donor makes the delivery with the purpose of turning over ownership at the time of delivery. The final element is *acceptance*, a willingness of the donee to take the gift from the donor. Usually, acceptance is not a problem, although a donee may not want to accept a gift because he or she does not want to feel obligated to the donor or because he or she believes that ownership of the gift may impose some unwanted legal liability.

INVOLUNTARY TRANSFERS OF PERSONAL PROPERTY

Involuntary transfers involve the transfer of ownership of property that has been abandoned, lost, or mislaid. The finder of such property *may* acquire ownership rights to such property through possession.

Abandoned property is property that the original owner has discarded. Anyone who finds that property becomes its owner by possessing it.

Lost property is property that the true owner has unknowingly or accidentally dropped or left somewhere. He or she has no way of knowing how to retrieve it. In most states, the finder of lost property has title to the lost good against all except the true owner.

EXHIBIT 13-5 *Elements of a Gift*

- Delivery
- Donative intent
- Acceptance

Mislaid property differs from lost property in that the owner has intentionally placed the property somewhere but has forgotten its location. The person who owns the realty on which the mislaid property was placed has the right to hold the mislaid property. The reason is that it is likely that the true owner will return to the realty looking for the mislaid property.

In some states, the law requires that before becoming the owner of lost or mislaid property, a finder must place an ad in the paper that will give the true owner notice that the property has been found or must leave the property with the police for a statutorily established reasonable period of time. Some state laws require both.

BAILMENTS

A **bailment** of personal property is a special relationship in which one party, the *bailor*, transfers possession of personal property to another, the *bailee*, to be used by the bailee in an agreed-on manner for an agreed-on time period.

One example of a bailment is when a person leaves his or her coat in a coat-check room. The person hands his or her coat to the clerk and is given a ticket identifying the object of the bailment so that it can be reclaimed. The bailment may be gratuitous or for consideration. It may be to benefit the bailor, the bailee, or both. If the bailment is intended to benefit only the bailor, the bailee is liable for damage to the property caused by the bailee's gross negligence. If the bailment is solely for the bailee's benefit, then the bailee is responsible for harm to the property caused by even the slightest lack of due care on the part of the bailee. If the bailment is for the mutual benefit of both bailee and bailor, the bailee is liable for harm to the bailed property arising out of the bailee's ordinary or gross negligence. If the property is harmed by an unpreventable "act of God," there is not liability on the part of the bailee under any circumstances. These general rules notwithstanding, the parties to a bailment contract can limit or expand the liability of the bailee by contract. In general, conspicuous signs (e.g., "We are not responsible for lost items") have been held sufficient to limit liability.

If the bailee is to receive compensation for the bailment, the bailee may retain possession of the bailed property until payment is made. In most states, when the bailor refuses to provide the agreed-upon compensation to the bailee, the property may ultimately be sold by the bailee after proper notice and a hearing. The proceeds are first used to pay the bailee and to cover the costs of the sale. The remaining proceeds then go to the bailor.

In addition to their duty to pay bailees their agreed-on compensation, a bailor must also warn the bailee of any hidden defects in the bailed goods. If such a warning is not given and the defect injures the bailee, the bailor is liable to the bailee for the injuries.

bailment A relationship in which one person (the bailor) transfers possession of personal property to another (the bailee) to be used in an agreed-upon manner for an agreed-upon period of time.

INTELLECTUAL PROPERTY

Intellectual property consists of the fruits of one's mind. The laws of intellectual property protect property that is primarily the result of mental creativity rather than physical effort. This category includes trademarks, trade secrets, patents, and copyrights, all of which are discussed in the following paragraphs.

TRADEMARKS

A **trademark** is a distinctive mark, word, design, picture, or arrangement used by a seller in conjunction with a product and tending to cause the consumer to identify the product with the producer. Even the shape of a product or package may be a trademark if it is nonfunctional.

Even though the description of a trademark is very broad, there has still been substantial litigation over precisely what features can and cannot serve as trademark. In the following case, the U.S. Supreme Court grappled with the issue of whether a color can be a trademark.

trademark A distinctive mark, word, design, picture, or arrangement used by the producer of a product that tends to cause consumers to identify the product with the producer.

For years, Plaintiff, Qualitex Co., colored the dry-cleaning press pads it manufactured a special shade of green-gold. When Jacobson products, a competitor, started coloring its pads the same shade of green-gold, Qualitex sued Jacobson Products for trademark infringement. The defendant challenged the legitimacy of the trademark, arguing that color alone should not qualify for registration as a trademark.

The district court found in favor of the plaintiff, but the ninth circuit reversed, holding that color alone could not be registered as a trademark. The plaintiff appealed to the U.S. Supreme Court.

JUSTICE BREYER

The Lanham Act gives a seller or producer the exclusive right to "register" a trademark, to prevent his or her competitors from using that trademark. Both the language of the Act and the basic underlying principles of trademark law would seem to include color within the universe of things that can qualify as a trademark. The language of the Lanham Act describes that universe in the broadest of terms. It says that trademarks "includ[e] any word, name, symbol, or device, or any combination thereof." Since human beings might use as a "symbol" or "device" almost anything at all that is capable of carrying meaning, this language, read literally, is not restrictive. The courts and the Patent and Trademark Office has [sic] authorized for use as a mark a particular shape (of a Coca-Cola bottle), a particular sound (of NBC's three chimes) and even a particular scent (of plumeria blossoms on sewing thread). If a shape, a sound, and a fragrance can act as symbols why, one might ask, can a color not do the same?

A color is also capable of satisfying the more important part of the statutory definition of a trademark, which requires that a person "us[e]" or "inten[d] to use" the mark

> To identify and distinguish his or her goods, including a unique product, from those manufactured or sold by others and to indicate the source of the goods, even if that source is unknown.

True, a product's color is unlike "fanciful," "arbitrary," or "suggestive" words or designs, which almost automatically tell a customer that they refer to a brand. The imaginary word "Suntost," or the words "Suntost Marmalade," on a jar of orange jam immediately would signal a brand or a product "source"; the jam's orange color does not do so. But, over time, customers may come to treat a particular color on a product or its packaging (say, a color that in context seems unusual such as pink on a firm's insulating material or red on the head of a large industrial bolt) as signifying a brand. And, if so, that color would have come to identify and distinguish the goods—i.e. "to indicate" their "source"—much in the way that descriptive words

on a product (say, "Trim" on nail clippers or "Car-Freshener" on deodorizer) can come to indicate a product's origin. In this circumstance, trademark law says that the word (e.g., "Trim"), although not inherently distinctive, has developed "secondary meaning." ("Secondary meaning" is acquired when "in the minds of the public, the primary significance of a product feature . . . is to identify the source of the product rather than the product itself"). Again, one might ask, if trademark law permits a descriptive word with secondary meaning to act as a mark, why would it not permit a color, under similar circumstances, to do the same?

It would seem, then, that color alone, at least sometimes, can meet the basic legal requirements for use as a trademark. It can act as a symbol that distinguishes a firm's goods and identifies their source, without serving any other significant function. The green-gold color acts as a symbol. Having developed secondary meaning (for customers identified the green-gold color as Qualitex's), it identifies the press pads' source. And, the green-gold color serves no other function. Accordingly, unless there is some special reason that convincingly militates against the use of color alone as a trademark, trademark law would protect Qualitex's use of the green-gold color on its press pads.

Respondent Jacobson Products says that there are four special reasons why the law should forbid the use of color alone as a trademark. We shall explain why we find them unpersuasive.

Jacobson says that, if the law permits the use of color as a trademark, it will produce uncertainty and unresolvable court disputes about what shades of a color a competitor may lawfully use. Because lighting will affect perceptions of protected color, competitors and courts will suffer from "shade confusion" as they try to decide whether use of a similar color on a similar product does, or does not, confuse customers and thereby infringe a trademark.

We do not believe that color, in this respect, is special. Courts traditionally decide quite difficult questions about whether two words or phrases or symbols are sufficiently similar, in context, to confuse buyers. They have had to compare, for example, such words as "Bonamine" and "Dramamine" (motion-sickness remedies); "Huggies" and "Dougies" (diapers); "Cheracol" and "Syrocol" (cough syrup): "Cyclone" and "Tornado" (wire fences): and "mattres" and "1-800-Mattres" (mattress franchisor telephone numbers). Legal standards exist to guide courts in making such comparisons. We do not see why courts could not apply those standards to a color, replicating, if necessary, lighting conditions under which a colored product is normally sold. Indeed, courts already have done so in cases where a trademark consists of a color plus a design, i.e., a colored symbol such as a gold stripe (around a sewer pipe), a yellow strand of wire rope, or a "brilliant yellow" band (on ampules).

Jacobson argues that colors are in limited supply. If one of many competitors can appropriate a particular color for use as a trademark, and each competitor then tries to do the same, the supply of colors will soon be depleted.

This argument is unpersuasive, however, largely because it relies on an occasional problem to justify a blanket prohibition. When a color serves as a mark, normally alternative colors will likely be available for similar use by others. Moreover, if that is not so—if a "color depletion" or "color scarcity" problem does arise—the trademark doctrine of "functionality" normally would seem available to prevent the anticompetitive consequences that Jacobson's argument posits.

The functionality doctrine forbids the use of a product's feature as a trademark where doing so will put a competitor at a significant disadvantage because the feature is "essential to the use or purpose of the article" or "affects [its] cost or quality." For example, this Court has written that competitors might be free to copy the color of a medical pill where that color serves to identify the kind of medication (e.g., a type of blood medicine) in addition to its source. And, the federal courts have demonstrated that they can apply this doctrine in a careful and reasoned manner, with sensitivity to the effect on competition. Lower courts have permitted competitors to copy the green color of farm machinery (because customers wanted their farm equipment to match) and have barred the use of black as a trademark on outboard boat motors (because black has the special functional attributes of decreasing the apparent size of the motor and ensuring compatibility with many different boat colors).

Where a color serves a significant nontrademark function courts will examine whether its use as a mark would permit one competitor (or a group) to interfere with legiti-mate (nontrademark-related) competition through actual or potential exclusive use of an important product ingredient. That examination should not discourage firms from creating aesthetically pleasing mark designs, for it is open to their competitors to do the same. But, ordinarily, it should prevent the anticompetitive consequences of Jacobson's hypothetical "color depletion" argument, when, and if, the circumstances of a particular case threaten "color depletion."

Jacobson points to many older cases—including Supreme Court cases—in support of its position. These Supreme Court cases, however, interpreted trademark law as it existed before 1946, when Congress enacted the Lanham Act. The Lanham Act significantly changed and liberalized the common law to "dispense with more technical prohibitions," most notably, by permitting trademark registration of descriptive words (say, "U-Build-It" model airplanes) where they had acquired "secondary meaning." The Lanham Act extended protection to descriptive marks by making clear that (with certain explicit exceptions not relevant here), "Nothing . . . shall prevent the registration of a mark used by the applicant which has become distinctive of the applicant's goods in commerce." This language permits an ordinary word, normally used for a nontrademark purpose (e.g., description), to act as a trademark where it has gained "secondary meaning." Its logic would appear to apply to color as well.

Jacobson argues that there is no need to permit color alone to function as a trademark because a firm already may use color as part of a trademark, say, as a colored circle or colored letter or colored word. This argument begs the question. One can understand why a firm might find it difficult to place a usable symbol or word on a product and, in such instances, a firm might want to use color, pure and simple, instead of color as part of a design.

Reversed in favor of Plaintiff, Qualitex Company.

A trademark used *intrastate* is protected under state common law. To be protected in *interstate* use, the trademark must be registered with the U.S. Patent Office under the Lanham Act of 1947. Several types of marks, listed in Table 13-2, are protected under this act.

If a mark is registered, the holder of the mark may recover damages from an infringer who uses it to pass off goods as those of the mark owner. The owner may also obtain an injunction prohibiting the infringer from using the mark. Only the latter remedy is available for an unregistered mark.

TABLE 13-2   *Types of Marks Protected under the Lanham Act*

1. *Product trademarks:* Marks affixed to a good, its packaging, or its labeling.
2. *Service marks:* Marks used in conjunction with a service.
3. *Collective marks:* Marks identifying the producers as belonging to a larger group, such as a trade union.
4. *Certification marks:* Marks licensed by a group that has established certain criteria for use of the mark, such as "U.L. Tested" or "Good Housekeeping Seal of Approval."

To register a mark with the Patent Office, one must submit a drawing of the mark and indicate when it was first used in interstate commerce and how it is used. The Patent Office conducts an investigation to verify those facts and will register a trademark as long as it is not generic, descriptive, immoral, deceptive, the name of the person whose permission has not been obtained, or substantially similar to another's trademark.

It is sometimes difficult to determine whether a trademark will be protected. And once the trademark is issued, it is not always easy to predict when a similar mark will be found to infringe upon the registered trademark. The following case demonstrates a typical analysis used in a trademark infringement suit.

TOYS "R" US, INC. V. CANARSIE KIDDIE SHOP, INC.
DISTRICT COURT OF THE EASTERN DISTRICT OF NEW YORK 559 F. SUPP. 1189 (1983)

Beginning in 1960, plaintiff Toys "R" Us, Inc., sold children's clothes in stores across the country. The firm obtained a registered trademark and service mark for Toys "R" Us in 1961 and aggressively advertised and promoted their products using these marks. In the late 1970s, defendant Canarsie Kiddie Shop, Inc., opened two kids' clothing stores within two miles of a Toys "R" Us Shop, and contemplated opening a third. The owner of Canarsie Kiddie Shop, Inc., called the stores Kids "r" Us. He never attempted to register the name. Toys "R" Us sued for trademark infringement in the federal district court.

JUDGE GLASSER

In assessing the likelihood of confusion and in balancing the equities, this Court must consider the now classic factors. . . .

1. Strength of the Senior User's Mark

. . . "[T]he term 'strength' as applied to trademarks refers to the distinctiveness of the mark, or more precisely, its tendency to identify goods sold under the mark as emanating from the particular, although possibly anonymous, source." A mark can fall into one of four general categories which, in order of ascending strength, are: (1) generic; (2) descriptive; (3) suggestive; and (4) arbitrary or fanciful. The strength of a mark is generally dependent both on its place upon the scale and on whether it has acquired secondary meaning.

A generic term "refers, or has come to be understood as referring to the genus of which the particular product is a species." A generic term is entitled to no trademark protection whatsoever, since any manufacturer or seller has the right to call a product by its name.

A descriptive mark identifies a significant characteristic of the product, but is not the common name of the product. A mark is descriptive if it "informs the purchasing public of the characteristics, quality, functions, uses, ingredients, components, or other properties of a product, or conveys comparable information about a service." To achieve trademark protection a descriptive term must have attained secondary meaning, that is, it must have "become distinctive of the applicant's goods in commerce."

A suggestive mark is one that "requires imagination, thought and perception to reach a conclusion as to the nature of the goods." These marks fall short of directly describing the qualities or functions of a particular product or service, but merely suggest such qualities. If a term is suggestive, it is entitled to protection without proof of secondary meaning.

Arbitrary or fanciful marks require no extended definition. They are marks which in no way describe or suggest the qualities of the product.

The Toys "R" Us mark is difficult to categorize.

The strength of the plaintiff's mark must be evaluated by examining the mark in its entirety. . . . I agree that the Toys "R" Us mark serves to describe the business of the plaintiff, and in this sense is merely descriptive. This descriptive quality, however, does require some "imagination, thought, and perception" on the part of the consumer since the plaintiff's mark, read quite literally, conveys the message, "we are toys," rather than "we sell toys."

Whether the "leap of imagination" required here is sufficient to render the mark suggestive rather than descriptive is a question with no clear-cut answer. Such an absolute categorization is not essential, however, since the defendants concede that through the plaintiff's marketing and advertising efforts the Toys "R" Us mark has acquired secondary meaning in the minds of the public, at least in relation to its sale of toys. Such secondary meaning assures that the plaintiff's mark is entitled to protection even if it is viewed as merely descriptive. Because I find that through the plaintiff's advertising and marketing efforts the plaintiff's mark has developed strong secondary meaning as a source of children's products, it is sufficient for purposes of this decision to note merely that the plaintiff's mark is one of medium strength, clearly entitled to protection, but falling short of the protection afforded an arbitrary or fanciful mark.

2. Degree of Similarity between the Two Marks

... [T]he key inquiry is ... whether a similarity exists which is likely to cause confusion. This test must be applied from the perspective of prospective purchasers. Thus, it must be determined whether "the *impression* which the infringing [mark] makes upon the consumer is such that he is likely to believe the product is from the same source as the one he knows under the trademark." In making this determination, it is the overall impression of the mark as a whole that must be considered.

Turning to the two marks involved here, various similarities and differences are readily apparent. The patent similarity between the marks is that they both employ the phrase, "R Us." Further, both marks employee the letter "R" in place of the word "are," although the plaintiff's mark uses an inverted capitalized "R," while the defendants generally use a non-inverted lower case "r" for their mark.

The most glaring difference between the marks is that in one the phrase "R Us" is preceded by the word "Toys," while in the other it is preceded by the word "Kids." Other differences include the following: plaintiff's mark ends with an exclamation point, plaintiff frequently utilizes the image of a giraffe alongside its mark, plaintiff's mark is set forth in stylized lettering, usually multi-colored, and plaintiff frequently utilizes the words, "a children's bargain basement" under the logo in its advertising.

I attach no great significance to the minor lettering differences between the marks, or to the images or slogans usually accompanying the plaintiff's mark.... While the marks are clearly distinguishable when placed side by side, there are sufficiently strong similarities to create the possibility that some consumers might believe that the two marks emanated from the same source. The similarities in sound and association also create the possibility that some consumers might mistake one mark for the other when seeing or hearing the mark alone. The extent to which these possibilities are "likely" must be determined in the context of all the factors present here.

3. Proximity of the Products

Where the products in question are competitive, the likelihood of consumer confusion increases.

... [B]oth plaintiff and defendants sell children's clothing; ... the plaintiff and defendants currently are direct product competitors.

4. The Likelihood That Plaintiff Will "Bridge the Gap"

... "[B]ridging the gap" refers to two distinct possibilities; first, that the senior user presently intends to expand his sales efforts to compete directly with the junior user, thus creating the likelihood that the two products will be directly competitive; second, that while there is no present intention to bridge the gap, consumers will assume otherwise and conclude, in this era of corporate diversification,

that the parties are related companies. . . . I find both possibilities present here.

5. Evidence of Actual Confusion

Evidence of actual confusion is a strong indication that there is a likelihood of confusion. It is not, however, a prerequisite for the plaintiff to recover.

6. Junior User's Good Faith

The state of mind of the junior user is an important factor in striking the balance of the equities. In the instant case, Mr. Pomeranc asserted at trial that he did not recall whether he was aware of the plaintiff's mark when he chose to name his store Kids "r" Us in 1977.

I do not find this testimony to be credible. In view of the proximity of the stores, the overlapping of their products, and the strong advertising and marketing effort conducted by the plaintiff for a considerable amount of time prior to the defendants' adoption of the name Kids "r" Us, it is difficult to believe that the defendants were unaware of the plaintiff's use of the Toys "R" Us mark.

The defendants adopted the Kids "r" Us mark with knowledge of plaintiff's mark. A lack of good faith is relevant not only in balancing the equities, but also is a factor supporting a finding of a likelihood of confusion.

7. Quality of the Junior User's Product

If the junior user's product is of a low quality, the senior user's interest in avoiding any confusion is heightened. In the instant case, there is no suggestion that the defendants' products are inferior, and this factor therefore is not relevant.

8. Sophistication of the Purchasers

The level of sophistication of the average purchaser also bears on the likelihood of confusion. Every product, because of the type of buyer that it attracts, has its own distinct threshold for confusion of the source or origin.

The goods sold by both plaintiff and defendants are moderately priced clothing articles, which are not major expenditures for most purchasers. Consumers of such goods, therefore, do not exercise the same degree of care in buying as when purchasing more expensive items. Further, it may be that the consumers purchasing from the plaintiff and defendants are influenced in part by the desires of their children, for whom the products offered by plaintiff and defendants are meant.

9. Junior User's Goodwill

[A] powerful equitable argument against finding infringement is created when the junior user, through concurrent use of an identical trademark, develops goodwill in their mark. Defendants have not expended large sums advertising their store or promoting its name. Further, it appears that most of the defendants' customers are local "repeat shoppers," who come to the Kids "r" Us store primarily because of their own past experiences with it. In light of this lack of development of goodwill, I find that the defendants do not have a strong equitable interest in retaining the Kids "r" Us mark.

Conclusion on Likelihood of Confusion

[T]he defendants use of the Kids "r" Us mark does create a likelihood of confusion for an appreciable number of consumers.

In reaching this determination, I place primary importance on the strong secondary meaning that the plaintiff has developed in its mark, the directly competitive nature of the products offered by the plaintiff and defendants, the plaintiff's substantially developed plans to open stores similar in format to those of the defendants', the lack of sophistication of the purchasers, the similarities between the marks, the defendants' lack of good faith in adopting the mark, and the limited goodwill the defendants have developed in their mark.

Judgement for the Plaintiff, Toys "R" Us.

Critical Thinking about the Law

LEGAL REASONING AND DECISION MAKING ALMOST always entail a reliance on tradition. Yet, in this particular case, the court's deference to tradition is especially strong. In applying the "classic factors" to the case, the court judges the present case on the basis of the way in which an allegedly similar earlier case was judged.

The implications of relying on tradition in legal reasoning are quite significant. The questions that follow will help you to consider this significance more deeply.

1. To demonstrate your ability to recognize analogous reasoning, identify the implicit analogy that pervades the court's reasoning.

   CLUE Consider the source of the "classic factors."

2. What important piece of missing information hinders your ability to make a sound critical judgement about the appropriateness of the court's reasoning?

   CLUE Refer to your answer to Question 1; it is directly related to this question.

TRADE SECRETS

trade secret A process, product, method of operation, or compilation of information used in a business that is not known to the public and that may bestow a competitive advantage on the business.

A **trade secret** is a process, product, method of operation, or compilation of information that gives a businessperson an advantage over his or her competitors. Inventions and designs may also be considered trade secrets. A trade secret is protected by the common law from unlawful appropriation by competitors as long as it is kept secret and comprises elements not generally known in the trade.

Competitors may discover the "secret" by any lawful means, such as reverse engineering or by going on public tours of plants and observing the use of trade secrets. Discovery of the secret means there is no longer a trade secret to be protected.

In order to enjoin a competitor from continuing the use of a trade secret or to recover damages caused by the use of the secret, a plaintiff must prove that:

1. A trade secret actually existed.
2. The defendant acquired it through unlawful means such as breaking into the plaintiff's business and stealing it or securing it through misuse of a confidential relationship with the plaintiff or one of the plaintiff's present or former employees.
3. The defendant used the trade secret without the plaintiff's permission.

PATENTS

patent Grants the holder the exclusive right to produce, sell, and use a product, process, invention, machine, or asexually reproduced plant for 17 years.

A **patent** protects a product, process, invention, machine, or plant produced by asexual reproduction. For this protection to be granted, certain criteria must be satisfied (Exhibit 13-6). First, the object of the patent must be *novel*, or new. No

- Novel
- Useful
- Nonobvious

one else must have previously made or published the plans for this object. The second criterion is that it be *useful*, unless it is a design patent. It must provide some utility to society. The final criterion is that it be *nonobvious*. The invention must not be one that the person of ordinary skill in the trade could have easily discovered. When a patent is issued for an object, it gives its holder the exclusive right to produce, sell, and use the object of the patent for 17 years. The holder of the patent may *license*, or allow others to manufacture and sell, the patented object. In most cases, patents are licensed in exchange for the payment of *royalties*, a sum of money paid for each use of the patented process.

The only restrictions on the patent holder are that he or she may not use the patent for an illegal purpose. The two most common illegal purposes would by *tying arrangements* and *cross-licensing*. A **tying arrangement** occurs when the patent holder issues a license to use the patented object only if the licensee agrees also to buy some nonpatented product from the holder. **Cross-licensing** occurs when two patent holders license each other to use their patents *only* on the condition that neither licenses anyone else to use his or her patent without the other's consent. Both of these activities are unlawful because they tend to reduce competition.

To obtain a patent, one generally contacts an attorney licensed to practice before the U.S. Patent Office. The attorney does a *patent search* to make sure that no other similar patent exists. If it does not, the attorney fills out a patent application and files it with the Patent Office. The Patent Office evaluates the application, and, if the object meets the criteria already described, a patent is issued.

Once the patent is issued, the holder may bring a patent infringement suit in a federal court against anyone who uses, sells, or manufacturers the patented invention without the permission of the patent holder. A successful action may result in an injunction prohibiting further use of the patented item by the infringer and also an award of damages. Sometimes, however, the result of the case is that the holder loses the patent. This loss would occur when the infringer is able to prove that the Patent Office should not have issued the patent in the first place.

A common dilemma facing an inventor is whether to protect an invention through patent or trade secret law. If the inventor successfully patents and defends the patent, the patent holder has a guarantee of an exclusive monopoly on the use of the invention for 17 years, a substantial period of time. The problem is that, once this period is over, the patented good goes into the public domain and everyone has access to it. There is also the risk that the patent may be successfully challenged and the protection lost prematurely.

Trade secret law, on the other hand, could protect the invention in perpetuity. The problem is that once someone discovers the secret lawfully, the protection is lost.

tying arrangement A restraint of trade wherein the seller permits a buyer to purchase one product or service only if the buyer agrees to purchase a second product or service. For example, a patent holder issues a license to use a patented object on condition that the licensee agree to also buy nonpatented products from the patent holder.

cross-licensing An illegal practice in which two patent holders license each other to use their patented objects only on condition that neither will license anyone else to use those patented objects without the other's consent.

COPYRIGHTS

Copyrights protect the *expression* of creative ideas. They do not protect the ideas themselves but only their fixed form of expression. Copyrights protect a diverse range of creative works, such as books, periodicals, musical compositions, plays, motion pictures, sound recordings, lectures, works of art, and computer programs. Titles and short phrases may not be copyrighted.

There are three criteria for a work to be copyrightable (Exhibit 13-7). First, it must be *fixed*, which means set out in a tangible medium of expression. Next, it must also be *original*. Finally, it must be *creative*.

copyright The exclusive legal right to reproduce, publish, and sell the fixed form of expression of an original creative idea.

EXHIBIT 13-7 *Criteria for a Copyright*

- Fixed Form
- Original
- Creative

A copyright automatically arises under common law when the idea is expressed in tangible form and carries appropriate notice. However, if the work is freely distributed without notice of copyright, the work falls into the public domain. A copyrighted work that is reproduced with the appropriate notice affixed is protected for the life of its creator plus 50 years.

Under the common law of copyright, any infringer may be enjoined from reproducing a copyrighted work. For the creator to be able to sue the infringer to recover damages arising from the infringement, however, the copyrighted work must be registered. One may register a work by filing a form with the Register of Copyright and providing two copies of the copyrighted materials to the Library of Congress. Whenever the work is reproduced, it must be accompanied by the appropriate notice of copyright. Printed works, for example, must be published with the word *copyright* and the symbol © or the abbreviation *copr.*, followed by the first date of publication and the name of the copyright owner. Once the work is registered, as long as it is always accompanied by the notice of copyright when reproduced, the holder of the copyright has the additional right to sue any infringer for damages caused by the infringer's use of the copyrighted materials and to recover any profits made by the infringer on the copyrighted material.

fair use doctrine A legal doctrine providing that a copyrighted work may be reproduced for purposes of "criticism, comment, news reporting, teaching (including multiple copies for classroom use), scholarship, and research."

A source of controversy involving copyrighted works is the application of the **fair use doctrine**. This doctrine provides that a copyrighted work may be reproduced for purposes of "criticism, comment, news reporting, teaching (including multiple copies for classroom use), scholarships, and research." In the following decision, the judge discusses some of the factors used to determine whether the fair use doctrine is applicable as a defense to an allegation of copyright infringement when the alleged infringer is engaged in a parody.

LUTHER CAMPBELL, A.K.A. LUKE SKYWALKER V. ACUFF-ROSE MUSIC, INC.

UNITED STATES SUPREME COURT 510 US 569 (1994)

Defendant-petitioner Luther Campbell's band recorded a bawdy version of the romantic 1964 rock song, "Oh, Pretty Woman." The band copied the original song's opening bass rift and the first line of lyrics. The new song then turned into a play on words, substituting shocking new lyrics that derisively demonstrated how bland and banal the original was. The plaintiff filed a copyright infringement action against the petitioners. The district court granted summary judgment for the defendants, saying that the song was a parody that made fair use of the original. The court of appeals reversed, holding that the commercial nature of the parody rendered it presumptively unfair. The defendant appealed to the U.S. Supreme Court.

JUSTICE SOUTER

The first factor in a fair use enquiry is "the purpose and character of the use, including whether such use is of a commercial nature or is for nonprofit educational pur-

poses." The central purpose of this investigation is to see whether the new work merely "supersede[s] the objects" of the original creation, or instead adds something new, with a further purpose or different character, altering the first with new expression, meaning, or message; it asks, in other words, whether and to what extent the new work is "transformative." Although such transformative use is not absolutely necessary for a finding of fair use, the goal of copyright, to promote science and the arts, is generally furthered by the creation of transformative works. [T]he more transformative the new work, the less will be the significance of other factors, like commercialism, that may weigh against a finding of fair use.

Suffice it to say now that parody has an obvious claim to transformative value. Like less ostensibly humorous forms of criticism, it can provide social benefit, by shedding light on an earlier work, and, in the process, creating a new one. We thus line up with the courts that have held that parody, like other comment or criticism, may claim fair use under § 107.

Modern dictionaries accordingly describe a parody as a "literary or artistic work that imitates the characteristic style of an author or a work for comic effect or ridicule," or as a "composition in prose or verse in which the characteristic turns of thought and phrase in an author or class of authors are imitated in such a way as to make them appear ridiculous." For the purposes of copyright law, the nub of the definitions, and the heart of any parodist's claim to quote from existing material, is the use of some elements of a prior author's composition to create a new one that, at least in part, comments on that author's works. Parody needs to mimic an original to make its point, and so has some claim to use the creation of its victim's imagination.

[P]arody, like any other use, has to work its way through the relevant factors, and be judged case by case, in light of the ends of the copyright law.

Here, the District Court held, and the Court of Appeals assumed, that 2 Live Crew's "Pretty Woman" contains parody, commenting on and criticizing the original work, whatever it may have to say about society at large.

The threshold question when fair use is raised in defense of parody is whether a parodic character may reasonably be perceived. Whether, going beyond that, parody is in good taste or bad does not and should not matter to fair use.

While we might not assign a high rank to the parodic element here, we think it fair to say that 2 Live Crew's song reasonably could be perceived as commenting on the original or criticizing it, to some degree. 2 Live Crew juxtaposes the romantic musings of a man whose fantasy comes true, with degrading taunts, a bawdy demand for sex, and a sigh of relief from paternal responsibility. The later words can be taken as a comment on the naivete of the original of an earlier day, as a rejection of its sentiment that ignores the ugliness of street life and the debasement that it signifies. It is this joinder of reference and ridicule that marks off the author's choice of parody from the other types of comment and criticism that traditionally have had a claim to fair use protection as transformative works.

The Court of Appeals, however, immediately cut short the enquiry into 2 Live Crew's fair use claim by confining its treatment of the first factor essentially to one relevant fact, the commercial nature of the use.

The second statutory factor, "the nature of the copyrighted work," draws on the "value of the materials used." This factor calls for recognition that some works are closer to the core of intended copyright protection than others, with the consequence that fair use is more difficult to establish when the former works are copied. We agree that the Orbison original's creative expression for public dissemination falls within the core of the copyright's protective purposes. This fact, however, is not much help in this case, or ever likely to help much in separating the fair use sheep from the infringing goats in a parody case, since parodies almost invariably copy publicly known, expressive works.

The third factor asks whether "the amount and substantiality of the portion used in relation to the copyrighted work as a whole," "the quantity and value of the materials used," are reasonable in relation to the purpose of the copying. We recognize that the extent of permissible copying varies with the purpose and character of the use.

We think the Court of Appeals was insufficiently appreciative of parody's need for the recognizable sight or sound when it ruled 2 Live Crew's use unreasonable as a matter of law. It is true, of course, that 2 Live Crew copied the characteristic opening bass riff (or musical phrase) of the original, and true that the words of the first line copy the Orbison lyrics. But if quotation of the opening riff and the first line may be said to go to the "heart" of the original, the heart is also what most readily conjures up the song for parody, and it is the heart at which parody takes aim. Copying does not become excessive in relation to parodic purpose merely because the portion taken was the original's heart. If 2 Live Crew had copied a significantly less memorable part of the original, it is difficult to see how its parodic character would have come through.

In parody, as in news reporting, context is everything, and the question of fairness asks what else the parodist did besides go to the heart of the original. It is significant that 2 Live Crew not only copied the first line of the original, but thereafter departed markedly from the Orbison lyrics for its own ends. 2 Live Crew not only copied the bass riff and repeated it, but also produced otherwise distinctive sounds, interposing "scraper" noise, overlaying the music with solos in different keys, and altering the drum beat. This is not a case, then, where "a substantial portion" of the parody itself is composed of a "verbatim" copying of the original. It is not, that is, a case where the parody is so insubstantial, as compared to the copying, that the third factor must be resolved as a matter of law against the parodists.

The fourth fair use factor is "the effect of the use upon the potential market for or value of the copyrighted work." It requires courts to consider not only the extent of market harm caused by the particular actions of the alleged infringer, but also whether unrestricted and widespread conduct of the sort engaged in by the defendant . . . "would result in a substantially adverse impact on the potential market" for the original.

Since fair use is an affirmative defense, its proponent would have difficulty carrying the burden of demonstrating fair use without favorable evidence about relevant markets. In moving for summary judgment, 2 Live Crew left themselves at just such a disadvantage when they failed to address the effect on the market for rap derivatives, and confined themselves to uncontroverted submissions that there was no likely effect on the market for the original. They did not, however, thereby subject themselves to the evidentiary presumption applied by the Court of Appeals.

No "presumption" or inference of market harm that might find support in *Sony* is applicable to a case involving something beyond mere duplication for commercial purposes. Indeed, as to parody pure and simple, it is more likely that the new work will not affect the market for the original in a way cognizable under this factor, that is, by acting as a substitute for it. This is so because the parody and the original usually serve different market functions.

We do not, of course, suggest that a parody may not harm the market at all, but when a lethal parody, like a scathing theater review, kills demand for the original, it does not produce a harm cognizable under the Copyright Act. Because "parody may quite legitimately aim at garroting the original, destroying it commercially as well as artistically," the role of the courts is to distinguish between "[b]iting criticism [that merely] suppresses demand [and] copyright infringement[, which] usurps it."

It was error for the Court of Appeals to conclude that the commercial nature of 2 Live Crew's parody of "Oh, Pretty Woman" rendered it presumptively unfair. No such evidentiary presumption is available to address either the first factor, the character and purpose of the use, or the fourth, market harm, in determining whether a transformative use, such as parody, is a fair one. The court also erred in holding that 2 Live Crew had necessarily copied excessively from the Orbison original, considering the parodic purpose of the use.

Reversed in favor of Petitioner, Campbell, and *remanded*.

INTERNATIONAL DIMENSIONS OF PROPERTY LAW

The primary international protection for intellectual property is offered through multilateral conventions. These treaties are generally administered by the World Intellectual Property Organization, a specialized agency of the United Nations.

THE BERNE CONVENTION OF 1886

The Berne Convention of 1886, to which 81 countries are now signatories, is the oldest treaty designed to protect artistic rights. Four basic principles underlie obligations of signatories to the treaty:

1. The *national treatment principle* requires each member nation to protect artists of all signatory nations equally.

2. The *nonconditional protection principle* requires that protection not be conditioned on the use of formalities although the country of origin may require registration or a similar formality.

3. The *protection independent of protection in the country of origin principle* allows nationals of nonsignatory countries to protect works if they are created in a member country.

4. The *common rules principle* establishes minimum standards for granting copyrights that all nations must meet.

UNIVERSAL COPYRIGHT CONVENTION

Although the United States, China, and Russia are now signatories to the Berne Convention, they and other nations had not signed the treaty in the 1950s because they disagreed with some of its provisions. Consequently, they decided to enter into another convention that would not contravene the rights of anyone under the Berne convention and would be loose enough for all nations to sign. This new document was the Universal Copyright Convention. The document went into effect in 1950 and was revised, along with the Berne Convention, in 1971. Today, 93 nations have signed either the 1952 or the 1971 version.

The Universal Copyright Convention differs from the Berne Convention primarily by allowing members to establish formalities for protection and making exceptions to common rules as long as the exceptions are not inconsistent with the essence of the treaty. It also does not require signatory countries to protect authors' rights.

THE PARIS CONVENTION OF 1883

The Paris Convention now has 101 members who have agreed to protect so-called industrial rights, such as inventions and trademarks. Unfair competition is also restricted under the Paris Convention.

The treaty has been revised several times, and not all members have signed all versions. Although the treaty is highly complex, it has three basic principles: (1) *national treatment*, as defined under the Berne Convention; (2) *the right of priority*, which allows a national of a member state 12 months after filing in his home nation to file an application in any other member state and have the date of application be considered the date of the filing in the home nation; and (3) *common rules*, which set out minimum standards of protection in all states. These common rules include such items as outlawing false labeling and protecting trade names of companies from member states even without registration.

PATENT COOPERATION TREATY

The Patent Cooperation Treaty contains a provision for making application for a patent in any member state an international application that would be as effective as filing individually in all member states. When the application is filed in any member state, the application is then forwarded to an international search authority.

Despite the existence of such agreements, enforcement in foreign countries is often very lax. In 1994, problems with blatant trademark infringement in China was so severe that President Clinton threatened to impose trade sanctions if enforcement were not improved.

SUMMARY

Property is a bundle of rights in relation to a tangible object, the most significant of which is probably the right to exclude others. Property can be divided into three categories: real property, land and anything permanently attached to it; personal property, tangible movable objects and intangible objects; and intellectual property, property that is primarily the result of one's mental rather than physical efforts.

Real property can be transferred voluntarily or involuntarily. Voluntary transfers include transfer by gift or sale. Adverse possession and condemnation are the two involuntary means. Personal property likewise can be transferred voluntarily through a gift or sale. It may also be transferred involuntarily if it is lost or mislaid.

The primary forms of intellectual property we protect are trademarks, copyrights, patents, and trade secrets. Unlike most property, which is protected by state law, the first three forms of intellectual property are protected by federal statutes. Intellectual property is protected internationally primarily by the use of treaties. Such treaties include the Universal Copyright Convention, the Berne Convention, and the Paris Convention of 1883.

REVIEW QUESTIONS

13-1. Explain why each of the following is or is not real property.
   a. A fence
   b. A tree
   c. A house trailer
   d. A built-in oven
   e. A refrigerator

13-2. Define the primary estates in land.

13-3. Explain the circumstances under which each of the following types of ownership would be most desirable. Give reasons for your responses.
   a. Joint tenancy
   b. Tenancy in common
   c. Tenancy by the entirety

13-4. Explain how the ownership of land may be transferred.

13-5. Explain how a general warranty deed differs from a quitclaim deed.

13-6. What are the similarities and differences between condemnation and adverse possession?

REVIEW PROBLEMS

13-7. The plaintiff owned land in an area zoned for buildable private parks. The city rezoned the land to allow only parks open to the public. This rezoning effectively prohibited the plaintiff from generating any sort of income from the land. Was the plaintiff correct in his contention that this constituted a deprivation of property without due process of law?

13-8. Judy worked the morning shift at Wild Oats. She bought a Pepsi but got too busy to drink it, so she left it on a shelf behind the counter to drink the next day. Sindy was working that afternoon. She got thirsty and asked her coworkers if the Pepsi belonged to any of them. When no one claimed it, she opened the bottle, saw some fine print on the underside of the cap, and read, "You have won a million dollars." When Judy found out what happened, she confronted Sindy and claimed the prize as hers. Explain who should receive the prize money and why.

13-9. Hallman spent the night at the New Colonial Hotel. On inquiry, he was told that the bellboy would take care of his car. The bellboy took the car to a nearby parking lot and left the car and keys with the lot attendant. He gave Hallman a claim check bearing the name of the lot and stamped "New Colonial." When Hallman went to pick up his car, the side window was broken and over $500 worth of personal property was missing. Who was liable for the missing personalty and the damage to the car? Why?

13-10. Thrifty Inn decides to open a motel along an interstate that will provide cheap lodging. It calls the motel Sleep McCheap. McDonald's seeks to enjoin Thrifty Inns from using the name, claiming that it violates the McDonald's trademark as well as the McStop trademark that the firm has for its one-stop business that provides cheap food, cheap lodging, and cheap gas. Will the injunction be granted? Why or why not?

13-11. Amerec Corporation had developed a secret, unpatented process for producing methanol and had built a special plant where they were going to use this process. The Christophers were hired by a competitor of Amerec to take aerial photographs of the construction. Amerec sued the photographers for misappropriation of trade secrets. What defenses might the Christophers raise? Would these be successful?

13-12. Professor Kendall wants students to read three articles from a recently published journal. The professor, who is concerned about the students' expenditures for books, photocopies the articles and places them on reserve. The publisher of the journal sues the professor for copyright infringement. What defense will the professor raise? Would this defense be successful?

CASE PROBLEMS

13-13. Everyone who purchased property in the Mains Farm subdivision received a copy of the restrictive covenants, which stated that property within the subdivision would be used only for single-family dwellings. Worthington read the restrictive covenant when she purchased her home. Yet, shortly after moving there, she began running a for-profit, supervised adult home, where she provided 24-hour supervision and care for four unrelated adults. The Mains Farm Homeowners Association brought an action against her, seeking to enforce the restrictive covenant. Is it enforceable? *Mains Farm Homeowners Ass'n v. Worthington*, 854 P.2d 1072 (1993)

13-14. First Chicago Bank sold a number of used storage cabinets to a second-hand furniture dealer. He sold some of these cabinets to Strayer, who gave one of them, a locked one without a key, to his friend Michael. Six weeks later, Michael was moving the cabinet and it fell over, causing the lock to break. Inside the cabinet were several certificates of deposit, many made payable to bearer, worth $666,687,948.85. Michael called the FBI, who took possession of the certificates. Michael filed an action to have the court determine ownership of the certificates. In whose favor did the court rule, Michael's or First Chicago Bank's? Why? *Michael v. First Chicago Corp.*, 487 N.E.2d 403 (1986)

13-15. Amerson asked to borrow Howell's drill. Howell knew that the drill had shocked the last three people who had used it, injuring none of them. He informed Amerson of this fact, and before giving the drill to Amerson, replaced the plug and tested it, receiving no shock. Amerson used the drill and received a fatal shock. Amerson's estate sued Howell. Was Howell liable? Why or why not? *Howell v. Amerson*, 156 S.E.2d 371 (1967)

13-16. Miller Brewing produced a reduced-calorie beer called "Miller Lite," which it began selling in the 1970s and spent millions of dollars advertising. In 1980, Falstaff Brewing Corp. started marketing a reduced-calorie beer, "Falstaff Lite." Miller filed an action seeking an injunction against Falstaff to prevent them from using the term *Lite*. What was the outcome of the case? *Miller Brewing Co. v. Falstaff Brewing Corp.*, 655 F.2d 5 (1987)

13-17. The Coca-Cola Company filed an action suit against the Koke Company of America, seeking an injunction preventing them from using the word *Koke* on their beverages because the use of that term was an infringement of the Coca Cola trademark. The Koke Company raised the defense that the trademark should have never been issued because the term Coca Cola fraudulently implies that cocaine is an ingredient of the beverage. The district court found in favor of Coca Cola and granted the injunction. The appellate court reversed. How do you think the U.S. Supreme Court ultimately decided the case? Why? *Coca Cola Co. v. Koke Co. of America*, 254 U.S. 143 (1920)

13-18. Nike, Inc., has trademarks for its name, a "woosh" design, and a phrase, "just do it." These marks appear on Nike clothing, hats, shoes, and other athletic products. Mike and his daughter started, for a summer project, Just Did It Enterprises, to manufacture and sell through mail order, t-shirts and sweatshirts that had the name Mike and a swoosh emblazoned on them. The project lost money, and Nike sued them for trademark infringement. Discuss the likely outcome of Nike's suit. *Nike, Inc. v. Just Did It Enterprises*, 6 F.3d 1225 (1993)

- -

 On the Internet

http://www.benedict.com   Find out more about copyrights from "The Copyright Website."

http://www.uspto.gov   This is the Web site of the United States Patent and Trademark Office.

http://www.unicc.org/wipo/   This is the home page of the World Intellectual Property Organization.

http://www.fpk.edu/tfield/ipbasics.htm   This site is a source of basic trademark and copyright information.

http://www.cornell.edu/topics/patent.html   Here is a place for information about patents and to get an official form for filing a patent application.

- -

14

AGENCY LAW

- **DEFINITION AND TYPES OF AGENCY RELATIONSHIPS**

- **CREATION OF AN AGENCY RELATIONSHIP**

- **DUTIES OF AGENTS AND PRINCIPALS**

- **PRINCIPAL'S AND AGENT'S LIABILITY TO THIRD PARTIES**

- **TERMINATION OF THE PRINCIPAL-AGENT RELATIONSHIP**

- **INTERNATIONAL DIMENSIONS OF AGENCY LAW**

Agency law has become more prominent in our complex postindustrial society. In an earlier period, when business owners (principals) did most or all of their business on a one-to-one basis with their customers (third parties), agents played a very small role in the business environment. As business entities became larger and conducted farflung transactions within the United States and worldwide, businesspeople felt a need to hire domestic and foreign agents to represent their interests to potential customers.

This chapter examines the following matters: (1) the definition and creation of an agency relationship, as well as the employment relationships formed; (2) the rights and duties of agents and principals toward each other and toward third parties; (3) the law of contracts and torts as they affect agency relationships; and (4) the international dimensions of agency law.

Critical Thinking about the Law

AGENCY LAW IS BASED ON A trusting relationship between two parties or individuals. Critical thinking skills, such as identifying ethical norms and missing information, are especially important when thinking about agency relationships.

1. Agency relationships are frequently used in modern society. Businesses increasingly rely on agents to conduct their business with customers. What ethical norms would businesses expect their agents to hold in carrying out their responsibilities?

   CLUE Look at the list of ethical norms and ask yourself: Which would be most important to a business?

2. As you will soon learn, agency relationships can be formed by informal oral agreements or by formal written contracts. Judges are often faced with the task of determining whether an agency relationship exists in informal oral agreements or formal written contracts or whether an agency relationship exists after an agent has performed a task. What kinds of information would be especially important to a judge in deciding whether an agency relationship had been established?

   CLUE What would tend to happen if a business formed a relationship with an employee to carry out a task?

3. Consider the definitions of justice in chapter 1. How might the fact that the agent has already performed the task affect the judge's decision?

   CLUE Do any of the definitions of justice give special guidance here?

DEFINITION AND TYPES OF AGENCY RELATIONSHIPS

DEFINITION OF AGENCY

Agency is defined as a fiduciary relationship (one of trust and confidence) between two persons in which they mutually agree that one person (the agent) will act on the behalf of the other (the principal) and be subject to the latter's control and consent.[1] For example, a corporate officer who enters into contracts that legally bind the corporation is representing the corporation as an agent.

Provided they are able to understand the instructions of a principal, most people have the capacity to act as agents. For example, a minor can be employed by a principal to act as an agent in making an offer of employment to a third person. The minor's lack of capacity to enter a contract is immaterial here because the contract is between the principal and the third party. (However, the

agency A fiduciary relationship between two persons in which one (the agent) acts on behalf of, and is subject to the control of, the other (the principal).

---

[1]Restatement (Second) of Agency, §1(1) "Agency": "the fiduciary relation which results from the manifestation of consent by one person to another that the other shall act on his behalf and subject to his control, and consent by the other . . ." 1933, 1958.

minor's lack of contractual capacity means that any agreement between the minor and the principal may be voided by the minor before he or she reaches majority age or shortly thereafter.)

TYPES OF AGENCY RELATIONSHIPS

Agency law is concerned with three types of relationships: principal-agent, employer-employee, and employer-independent contractor. These relationships are summarized in Table 14-1.

principal-agent relationship One in which the principal gives the agent expressed or actual authority to act on the former's behalf.

PRINCIPAL-AGENT   The **principal-agent relationship** is one in which the principal (usually an employer) hires an agent (employee) and gives the agent either expressed or actual authority to act on the principal's behalf. **Expressed authority** arises from specific statements made by the principal to the agent. **Actual authority** includes expressed authority and implied authority—that authority customarily given to an agent in an industry, trade, or profession. The principal-agent relationship is the most basic type of agency relationship. It is, in fact, the foundation of the next two types of agency relationships we discuss: that between employer and employee and that between principal and independent contractor.

expressed authority Authority that arises from specific statements made by the principal (employer) to the agent (employee).

actual authority Includes expressed authority as well as implied authority, or that authority customarily given to an agent in an industry, trade, or profession.

EMPLOYER-EMPLOYEE   The employer-employee relationship evolved out of the traditional master-servant relationship, in which a master employed a servant to perform services and the servant's conduct was subject to the master's physical control. Under the doctrine of **respondant superior**, the master was responsible for the acts of servants that were within the scope of their employment. In the postindustrialized version of this arrangement, the **employer-employee relationship**, the employee is subject to the control of the employer and, in accordance with expressed or implied authority, may enter into contractual relationships on behalf of the employer. In general, any agent who works for pay is considered an employee, and any employee, unless specifically limited, who deals with a third party is given agent's status. The employer-employee relationship is the only agency relationship that encompasses workers' compensation, Social Security, and unemployment compensation laws (as well as numerous other state and federal laws), thus its importance. It is also important to distinguish the *employer-employee* relationship from a **principal-(employer)—independent contractor** relationship, which normally does not fall under these statutes, and that is an important distinction in the legal environment of business.

respondant superior Legal doctrine imposing liability on a principal for torts committed by an agent who is employed by the principal and subject to the principal's control.

employer-employee relationship One in which an agent (employee) who works for pay and is subject to the control of the principal (employer) may enter into contractual relationships on the latter's behalf.

employer-independent contractor relationship One in which the agent (independent contractor) is hired by the principal (employer) to do a specific job but is not controlled with respect to physical conduct or details of work performance.

EMPLOYER-INDEPENDENT CONTRACTOR   Independent contractors are hired by the employer to do a specific job but are not controlled with respect to their physical conduct or the details of their work performance. In this type of agency relationship, the employer is normally not subject to payments into workers' compensation pools and Social Security or to liability for the torts of the independent contractor. (Torts, you will recall, are wrongful acts, other than breaches of contract, for which damages may be obtained.) For example, the employer of a taxi driver who is an independent contractor and owns his or

TABLE 14-1   *Types of Agency Relationships*

Principal-agent	Agent is hired by principal to act on his or her behalf subject to the latter's control and consent.
Employer-employee	Employer controls the physcial conduct and determines the details of performance of employee.
Employer-independent contractor	Employer does not control the details of performance and conduct of independent contractor.

her own cab is not liable in most cases for damages when the driver injures another person in an accident.

When courts are called upon to distinguish between an *employee* and an *independent contractor*, it is the *degree of control* the employer has over the agent that they scrutinize. Courts also consider such factors as: (1) whether the hired persons had a distinct occupation or profession, (2) whether they supplied their own tools and equipment, (3) whether they were employed only for a specific time period, (4) whether they are paid hourly or on completion of a job, and (5) what degree of skill is required to do the job.

In order to escape paying unemployment insurance taxes, as well as medical benefits, many employers in recent years have classified their workers as independent contractors or part-time workers. A common strategy in the highly competitive business environment of the 1990s is to "downsize" by cutting back on the number of employees in a corporation through early retirement plans and layoffs and then to "restructure" by rehiring them as "consultants" (independent contractors) to accomplish the same work they did as employees. This is essentially a cost-cutting measure. The "consultants" draw a per diem or lump sum instead of a salary for the job they are hired to perform, and the company saves on health care, unemployment compensation, and Social Security benefits. In turn, the independent contractors are free to work for others besides their old employer, perhaps while receiving a pension from the employer. The case that follows indicates the scrutiny courts are presently giving to employers' classification of workers as independent contractors.

DAWS CRITICAL CARE REGISTRY, INCORPORATED V. DEPARTMENT OF LABOR, EMPLOYMENT SECURITY DIVISION
CONNECTICUT SUPERIOR COURT 622 A.2D 222 (1992)

Daws Critical Care Registry (plaintiff), a professional nurse agency, is appealing a decision by the administrator of the Connecticut Unemployment Compensation Act of the Connecticut Department of Labor (defendant) that Daws should pay unemployment taxes to the department. Daws argues that the nurses it supplies to medical facilities are independent contractors and therefore it is not liable for this tax. Daws supplies nurses to medical facilities upon request from a list of nurses it maintains, then bills the medical facilities and pays the nurses a set wage depending on their qualifications. Nurses may work for other agencies as well as Daws.

JUSTICE HEALY

Under the Unemployment Compensation Act the term "employment" means: "Service performed by an individual shall be deemed to be employment subject to this chapter irrespective of whether the common law relationship of master and servant exists, unless and until it is shown to the satisfaction of the administrator that (A) such individual has been and will continue to be free from control and direction in connection with the performance of such service; and (B) such service is performed either outside the usual course of the business for which the service is performed or is performed outside of all the places of business of the enterprise for which the service is performed; and (C) such individual is customarily engaged in an independently established trade, occupation, profes-

sion or business of the same nature as that involved in the service performed. . . ." This is the act's ABC test.

This statute not only codifies common law rules used to determine the existence of an employer-employee relationship, but also incorporates what is known "in Connecticut and throughout the country in similar legislation as the 'ABC test' [which is used] to ascertain whether an employer-employee relationship exists under the act." For the plaintiff to prove that it is not an employer and, thus, has no liability under the act for unemployment taxes, it must show that it has satisfied all three prongs of the ABC test.

In taking up the ABC test in the present case, part A will be examined first. Under that part Daws bore the burden of proving under the statute that its nurses have "been and will continue to be free from any control or direction" in connection with the performance of such service, "both under (their) contract (for the performance of service) and in fact." Part A of the test invokes essentially the same criteria as the independent contractor test at common law: The fundamental distinction between an employee and an independent contractor depends upon the existence or nonexistence of the right to control the means and methods of work. The test of the relationship is the right to control. It is not the fact of actual interference with the control, but the right to interfere, that makes the difference between an independent contractor and a servant or agent.

The court is aware that the test of the relationship does not depend upon the actual exercise of the right to control by Daws but that the existence of the right to control is sufficient. But it is submitted that Daws did not have the general right to control their nurses. It had no such control or even the right to control over the means and methods of the nurses' services rendered at the medical facilities where their assignments took them. Daws' function, after satisfying itself that a nurse was "competent" was fairly limited to arranging times mutually convenient for the nurse and the particular medical facility where the nurse's services were to be rendered and examining a nurse's pay invoices when submitted to it for payment and in making payment. It did not have "the right to general control of the activities." Once the assignment to a particular medical facility was offered by Daws and undertaken by a Daws nurse, the nurse went there and, subject to the protocol of that facility, rendered her professional services under that facility's direction. The lack of a right to control is further indicated by the proof that no representative of Daws ever visited a medical facility to check on the performance of any of their nurses. The court also notes that Daws did not conduct any orientations for its nurses nor did it have any manual of instructions that it issued to them . . . There is no question but that Daws processed the invoices submitted to it by its nurses for payment for their nursing services at whatever medical facility they might work. These invoices were on forms provided by Daws and the times indicated thereon as having been worked had to be certified to by a supervisor at that particular facility before being processed by Daws. Payment was at an hourly rate. The defendant, in arguing that the Daws nurses are employees, maintains that "the hourly rate of pay criterion is not merely satisfied; instead a comprehensive pay scheme on an hourly and continuing basis during a nurse's performance of service is established." This apparently is to suggest that the "hourly rate criterion" he contends for is to be distinguished, as the defendant claims, from payment of an independent contractor at the end of an entire project without taking account of the number of hours worked on the project. This court believes otherwise. "The manner of remuneration, whether in wages, salary commission, by piece or job, is not decisive or controlling in determining whether one is an employee or an independent contractor exercising control over the manner of his own work." In other words, the methods used to determine the payment to be made for the work done is not of controlling significance. The reality is that the payor (Daws), in effect, served in the nature of conduit for payment.

Under all the evidence, the court concludes that the facts demonstrate . . . that Daws did satisfy part A of the ABC test.

Part B of the ABC test in our statute says: "such service is performed either outside the usual course of the business for which the service is performed or is performed outside of all the places of business of the enterprise for which the service is performed."

Daws argues that it, in effect, brokers nursing personnel. A "broker" has been said generally to be one whose business it is to bring buyer and seller together. A "broker" has also been said to be a "middleman or negotiator between parties." There can be little question but that Daws is in the business of providing, indeed brokering, nurses to its clients: medical facilities. There also can be little question but that the nurses so provided furnished their professional services at the particular medical facility. Once, however, they went on an assignment, Daws had no control over them, certainly, as to how they performed their services. Daws was not in the business of providing health care at any client's medical facility. The simple and overriding fact is that Daws does not perform patient care but it brokers nurses. In so doing it is Daws' nurses who perform nursing services when at medical facilities, which is a function beyond the usual course of Daws' business and beyond what, in fact, it holds itself out to do. Part B has been satisfied by the plaintiff and the defendant's conclusion to the contrary cannot stand.

Part C of the ABC test provides that "such individual is customarily engaged in an independently established trade, occupation, profession or business of the same nature as that involved in the service performed." Here the court notes that part C in our statute refers to "an independently established trade, occupation, profession or business . . ." The Daws nurses were in a "profession." The term "profession" implies "knowledge of an advanced type in a given field of science or learning gained by a prolonged course of specialized instruction and study." The Daws nurses were in an independently established profession as the result of having been licensed by the state after completing a long course of instruction and study. They were also "customarily" so engaged in that profession as defined. This called is "independently established." [W]ell over a majority of Daws nurses worked for other agencies at other medical facilities performing similar services while also working on assignments through Daws. The performance of such "like services" was independent of "whatever connection" they had with Daws and the continued performance of such "like services" was "not subject to their relationship with the principal (Daws)." The independently established nature of their nursing profession permits them to continue therein even after their relationship with Daws terminates.

Reversed in favor of Plaintiff, Daws.

CREATION OF AN AGENCY RELATIONSHIP

Agency relationships can be informal oral agreements or they can be formal written contracts. Under the Statute of Frauds (see chapter 9), some states require that all agency contracts be in writing.

Most such relationships grow out of the consent of two parties, the principal indicating in some way that the agent should act on its behalf and the agent agreeing to do so. An agency relationship may be formed through: (1) expressed agency, (2) implied authority, (3) ratification of the agent's previous acts by the principal, or (4) apparent agency (Table 14-2).

EXPRESSED AGENCY OR AGENCY BY AGREEMENT

An agency relationship formed through oral or written agreement between the principal and agent is known as an **expressed agency**, or **agency by agreement**. Under the Statute of Frauds (discussed in chapter 9), agency agreements that will last longer than one year must be in writing. An *exclusive agency contract* is a type of agreement whereby the principal agrees that it will not employ any other agent for a period of time or until a particular job is completed. If the principal fails to live up to this agreement, the agent may file a breach-of-contract suit to recover monetary damages plus court costs and attorney's fees.

A legal document used to establish an agency relationship is called a **power of attorney**. It gives the agent the authority to sign legal documents on behalf of the principal. Many states allow powers of attorney for both business and health care purposes. In the latter kind of power of attorney, the principal designates in writing an individual (agent) who will act for the principal in the event of a serious illness that renders the principal mentally incompetent to make decisions concerning his or her own medical care. The agent is usually given the authority to make such decisions in consultation with physicians. The power of attorney for business purposes may be a general document that gives the agent broad powers to act on the principal's behalf (Exhibit 14-1), or it may be a more limited document that authorizes the agent to act only in matters enumerated in the agreement. Many people now incorporate by reference powers of attorney for both health and business purposes into their wills or trusts.

AGENCY BY IMPLIED AUTHORITY

When a principal and agent create an agency, they often do not set out every detail of the agent's authority in the written or oral agreement. In **agency by implied authority**, customs, circumstances, and the facts of a situation determine the authority of the agent to do business on behalf of the principal.

expressed agency (agency by agreement) Agency relationship formed through oral or written agreement.

power of attorney An agency agreement used to give an agent authority to sign legal documents on behalf of the principal.

agency by implied authority Agency relationship in which customs and circumstances, rather than a detailed formal agreement, determine the agent's authority.

TABLE 14-2   *How Agency Relationships Are Created*

AGENCY RELATIONSHIP	METHOD OF CREATION
Expressed agency, or agency by agreement	Formed by detailed written or oral agreement. A power-of-attorney document is often used to establish this relationship.
Agency by implied authority	Formed in situations in which custom and circumstances determine the agent's authority to do business for the principal.
Agency through ratification	Formed when an unauthorized act of an agent is accepted by the principal.
Agency by estoppel or apparent authority	Formed when a principal leads a third party to believe that a certain person is acting as agent for the principal. The principal is estopped from denying the agency relationship.

EXHIBIT 14-1 *Power of Attorney*

Power of Attorney

Know All Men by These Presents: That _____

_____

the undersigned (jointly and severally, if more than one) hereby make, consitute and
appoint _____

_____

My true and lawful Attorney for me and in my name, place and stead and for my use and benefit:

    (a) To ask, demand, sue for, recover, collect and receive each and every sum of money, debt, account, legacy, bequest, interest, dividend, annuity and demand (which now is or hereafter shall become due, owing or payable) belonging to or claimed by me, and to use and take any lawful means for the recovery thereof by legal process or otherwise, and to execute and deliver a satisfaction or release therefor, together with the right and power to compromise or compound any claim, or demand;

    (b) To exercise any or all of the following powers as to real property, any interest therein and/or any building thereon; To contract for, purchase, receive and take possession thereof and of evidence of title thereto; to lease the same for any term or purpose, including leases for business residence, and oil and/or mineral development; to sell exchange, grant or convey the same with or without warranty; and to mortgage, transfer in trust, or otherwise encumber or hypothecate the same to secure payment of a negotiable or non-negotiable note or performance of any obligation or agreement;

    (c) To exercise any or all of the following powers as to all kinds of personal property and goods, wares and merchandise, chosen in action and other property in possession or in action; To contract for, buy sell, exchange, transfer and in any legal manner deal in and with the same and to mortgage, transfer in trust, or otherwise encumber of hypothecate the same to secure payment of a negotiable or non-negotiable note or performance of any obligation or agreement.

    (d) To borrow money and to execute and deliver negotiable or non-negotiable notes therefore with or without security; and to loan money and receive negotiable or non-negotiable notes therefor with such security as said Attorney shall deem proper;

    (e) To create, amend, supplement and terminate any trust and to instruct and advise the trustee of any trust wherein I am or may be trustor or beneficiary, to present and vote stock, exercise stock rights, accept and deal with any dividend, distribution or bonus, join in any corporate financing, reorganization, merger, liquidation, consolidation or other action and the extension, compromise, conversion, adjustment, enforcement or foreclosure, singly or in conjunction with others of any corporate stock, bond, note, debenture or other security; to compound, compromise, adjust, settle and satisfy any obligation secured or unsecured, owing by or to me and to give or accept any property and/or money whether or not equal to or less in value than the amount owing in payment settlement or satisfaction thereof;

    (f) To transact business of any kind or class and as my act and deed to sign, execute, acknowledge and deliver any deed, lease, assignment or lease, covenant, indenture indemnity, agreement, mortgage, deed of trust, assignment of mortgage or of the beneficial interest under deed of trust, extension or renewal of any obligation, subordination or waiver or priority, hypothecation, bottomry, charter-party, bill of lading, bill of sale, bill, bond, note, whether negotiable, receipt, evidence of debt, full or partial release or satisfaction of mortgage judgment and other debt, request for partial or full reconveyance of deed or trust and such other instruments in writing of any kind or class as may be necessary or proper in the premises. **Giving and Granting** unto my said Attorney full power and authority to do and perform all and every act and thing whatsoever, requisite, necessary or appropriate to be done in and about the premises as fully to all intents and purposes as I might or could do if personally present, hereby ratifying all that my said Attorney shall lawfully do or cause to be done by virtue of these presents. The powers and authority hereby conferred upon my said Attorney shall be applicable to all real and personal property or interests therein now owned or hereafter required by me and wherever situate.

    My said Attorney is empowered hereby to determine in said Attorney s sale discretion the time when, purpose for and manner in which any power herein conferred upon said Attorney shall be exercised, and the conditions, provisions and covenants of any instrument or document which may be executed by said Attorney pursuant hereto and in the acquisition or disposition of real or personal property, my said Attorney shall have exclusive power to fix the terms thereof for cash, credit, and/or property, and if on credit with or without security.

    The undersigned, if a married person, hereby further authorizes and empowers my said Attorney, as my duly authorized agent, to join in my behalf, in the execution of any instrument by which any community real property or any interest therein, now owned or hereafter acquired by my spouse and myself, or either of us, is sold, leased, encumbered, or conveyed.

    When the contest to requires, the masculine gender includes the feminine and/or neuter, and the singular number includes the plural.

Witness my hand this _____ day of _____ , 19 _____.
STATE OF OHIO
COUNT OF WOOD   } SS

On _____ before me, the undersigned,
a Notary Public in and for said State personally
appeared _____

_____

_____

_____ personally known
to me (or proved to me on the basis of satisfactory
evidence) to be the person _____ whose name
_____ subscribed to the within instrument and
acknowledged that _____ executed the same.
WITNESS my hand and official seal.
Signature _____

_____
    Name (Typed or Printed)   (This area for official seal)

Unless the agency contract says otherwise, courts have generally allowed agents to:

1. Receive payments of money due principal.
2. Enter into contracts for incidentals.
3. Employ or discharge employees.
4. Buy equipment and supplies.

In the following case, the court indicates the extent to which implied authority will be granted to an agent.

PENTHOUSE INTERNATIONAL V. BARNES

UNITED STATES COURT OF APPEALS 792 F.2D 943 (9TH CIR. 1986)

Priscilla Barnes was a hostess at a club in Hollywood, California when she was approached by a freelance photographer (Dunas) who sold nude photographs to *Penthouse* magazine. Dunas was an independent contractor. He asked Barnes to pose nude. She agreed but did not want her actual name used. Dunas agreed to her terms, and Barnes signed a "Release, Authorization and Agreement Form" that gave *Penthouse* the right to "republish photographic pictures or portraits." Dunas added the term "AKA" ("also known as") on the contract to indicate that the photographs would not be published under her actual name but under a pseudonym. *Penthouse* did so in 1976. Later Barnes became a well-known television broadcaster for a station in Los Angeles. When Penthouse informed her, in 1983, that they wished to republish her nude photograph she threatened to sue, claiming Dunas had implied agency to write the term "AKA" and thus *Penthouse* was bound. *Penthouse* requested a declaratory judgment from the federal district court allowing it to republish a nude photo of the defendant. The district court found for Barnes and issued an injunction against *Penthouse*. *Penthouse* appealed.

JUDGE BOOCHEVER

Under California law, questions regarding the existence of agency are questions of fact that we review for clear error. California Civil Code Section 2316 defines actual authority as "such as a principal intentionally confers upon the agent, or intentionally, or by want of ordinary care, allows the agent to believe himself to possess." At issue is whether Dunas contracted to act on behalf of Penthouse.

Penthouse instructed photographers "to get a signed model release and not to alter the release in any way, without our permission." However, Penthouse carried Dunas's name on its masthead, gave him blank Penthouse contracts, may have given him business cards, and had him present contracts to models. Thus, although the record conflicts as to whether Dunas was an actual agent of Penthouse, on review, we cannot find that the district court clearly erred in finding Dunas to be a Penthouse agent.

Having found that the district court did not err in characterizing Dunas as an agent, we next turn to whether Dunas was acting within the scope of his authority by modifying the contract. Barnes does not contend nor is there evidence that Dunas possessed express actual authority to modify the contract. Dunas, however, had implied actual authority. Implied actual authority requires that (1) Dunas believe he was authorized to modify the contract based on Penthouse conduct known to him or (2) such a belief was reasonable.

Circumstantial evidence exists that Dunas placed "AKA" on other contracts with no objection from Penthouse. In June 1974, a year and a half before Barnes posed, contracts prepared by Dunas had "AKA" on them. Further, Penthouse internal memoranda reflect an understanding among Penthouse employees that "AKA" added to a contract meant that Penthouse was to associate a fictitious name with a woman's photograph. The evidence thus indicates that Dunas reasonably believed he was authorized to add "AKA" and modify the contract to require that only a fictitious name be used.

Affirmed in favor of Defendant, Barnes.

AGENCY THROUGH RATIFICATION BY PRINCIPAL

Agency by ratification occurs when a person misrepresents him- or herself as an agent and the principal accepts (ratifies) the unauthorized act. If the principal accepts the results of the agent's act, then the principal is bound, just as if he or she had authorized the individual to act as an agent. Two conditions are necessary for the ratification to be effective: (1) The principal must have full knowledge of the agent's action, and (2) the existence of the principal must be clear to the third party at the time of the agent's unauthorized act. For example, Max Black tells his friend Mary Ann Jones, a realtor, that if she ever finds anyone who is ready, willing, and able to sell a certain kind of computer franchised store, he will buy it. Jones finds such a store, cannot reach Brown, and has never been his agent, but she enters into the agreement with the franchisor anyway and signs the contract "Mary Ann Jones, agent for Max Black." Jones is not Black's agent. However, if Black decides to honor the contract, he will have ratified an agency relationship, and Jones will most likely get a commission.

agency by ratification Agency relationship in which an unauthorized agent commits the principal to an agreement and the principal later accepts the unauthorized agreement, thus ratifying the agency relationship.

AGENCY BY ESTOPPEL, OR APPARENT AUTHORITY

If a third person is led to believe by a principal that a certain individual is the principal's agent, then there appears to be authority for the agent to act and the principal is *estopped* from denying that the individual is an agent. It is the writing, words, or acts, or some combination thereof, of the principal that create the **agency by estoppel**, or **apparent authority** for the agent to act; the third party relies on the principal's conduct. In reading the case that follows, note carefully the court's focus on the principal's actions in the negative application of the legal doctrine of **estoppel**.

HAMILTON HAULING, INCORPORATED V. GAF CORPORATION
MISSOURI COURT OF APPEALS 719 S.W.2D 841 (MO. APP. 1986)

Hamilton Hauling (plaintiff) sued GAF (defendant) for a breach of contract. Bajt, a purchasing agent for GAF, entered into a long-term contract with Hamilton Hauling for the purchase of $6 million worth of wood chips, and GAF refused to acknowledge the contract. Company policy required approval of such contracts at corporate headquarters, which Bajt had never sought. Bajt had never before entered into a long-time agreement for GAF. GAF notified Hamilton that it would not go through with the contract since Bajt had had no expressed or apparent authority to enter into it. The trial court found for GAF. Hamilton appealed.

JUSTICE DIXON

It is generally held that when a principal "holds out" another as possessing certain authority, thereby inducing others reasonably to believe that authority exists, the agent has apparent authority to act even though as between himself and the principal, such authority has not been granted. Apparent authority differs from actual authority in that the principal communicates directly with a third person to create apparent authority; to create actual authority, the principal communicates directly with the agent.

When a principal has by his voluntary act placed an agent in such a situation that a person of ordinary prudence, conversant with business usages and the nature of the particular business, is justified in presuming that such agent has authority to perform a particular act on behalf of his principal, the principal is estopped from denying the agent's authority to perform the act.

It must be emphasized that the third party must reasonably rely on the authority held out by the principal.... Apparent authority is that which a reasonably prudent man, using diligence and discretion, in view of the principal's conduct would suppose the agent to possess.

Establishment of apparent authority by direct, express statements is obvious. The other methods of creating apparent authority by "position" and by "prior acts" have both been recognized.... Apparent authority may result from a prior relation of agent and principal. The principal by allowing an agent to carry out prior similar transactions may create an appearance of authority of the agent to carry out such acts.

There was no evidence to show that GAF knowingly permitted Bajt to enter into the contract in question. Bajt had never entered into a long-term contract before. Bajt admitted he did not send a copy of the contract to corporate headquarters and no one at GAF seemed to know about the contract. Clearly, the Contract was made in violation of internal corporate policy and nothing was presented to show that GAF generally "ignored" its policy in making long-term multi-million dollar contracts.

Hamilton Hauling claims Bajt's authority came from his position [.] [H]owever, there was no evidence of any sort in this case as to the usual authority of purchasing agents generally. There was nothing to support an inference that a vendor dealing with a purchasing agent expects that agent to have the power to make a contract like the long-term agreement in evidence.... There was no evidence that Bajt had ever entered into a long-term contract on behalf of GAF; in fact, Bajt admitted that in all his years at GAF, he had not made any other such contract. Bajt was not clothed with apparent authority by virtue of his position. Moreover, there was no evidence to support Hamilton's claim that he reasonably relied on Bajt's authority. Hamilton admitted that the contracts he had entered into with other corporations were signed at corporate headquarters, not locally.

Affirmed in favor of Defendant, GAF.

Critical Thinking about the Law

A S A FUTURE BUSINESS MANAGER, YOU need to recognize the complexity of both the lines of authority in a company and the legal rights of that company. This case illustrates the kind of confusion and conflict that can arise when employees undertake a business transaction without their employer's consent. The general issue here is: Under what conditions is an employee an agent of a company? The following questions will help you understand how the court resolved this issue and, consequently, how to deal with related dilemmas you may face in your career.

1. The court recognizes the ambiguity of the word *authority* and confronts it. What is the result?

   CLUE You are looking for a distinction.

2. In attempting to establish that Bajt had "apparent" authority, the court says that one of three conditions must be met. What are they?

   CLUE Look for the paragraph in which the court states this explicitly.

DUTIES OF AGENTS AND PRINCIPALS

PRINCIPAL'S DUTIES TO AGENT

Through an evolution of case law and scholarly writing, it is now generally recognized that a principal (employer) owes four duties to an agent (employees): (1) a duty of *compensation*, (2) a duty of *reimbursement* and *indemnification*, (3) a duty of *cooperation*, and (4) a duty to provide *safe working conditions*. These duties are either part of a written contract or implied by law.

DUTY OF COMPENSATION   In the absence of a written agreement, it is implied that a principal will compensate the agent for services rendered, either when services are contracted for or when they are completed. If the parties cannot agree on the amount, courts will usually indicate that the compensation should be calculated on the basis of what is reasonable or customary. For example, lawyers and real estate brokers are sometimes paid on a **contingency fee** (commission) basis.

> **contingency fee** Agent's compensation that consists of a percentage of the amount the agent secured for the principal in a business transaction.

DUTY OF REIMBURSEMENT AND INDEMNIFICATION   An **indemnity** is an obligation on the part of an individual (principal) to make good (or reimburse) another person (agent) against any losses incurred when the latter is acting on the former's behalf. All *necessary* expenses can be recouped by the agent, but the agent is not entitled to expenses arising out of tortious conduct (e.g., negligence) or unlawful activities (e.g., bribes paid to suppliers).

> **indemnity** Obligation of the principal to reimburse the agent for any losses the agent incurs while acting on the principal's behalf.

DUTY OF COOPERATION   The principal must do nothing to interfere with the reasonable conduct of an agent as agreed upon in an express or implied contract. For example, if a franchisor (principal) agrees with a franchisee (agent) that the latter has an exclusive right to sell a specific item within a geographic territory, the franchisor cannot legally compete with the franchisee by setting up another franchisee within that territory. If the franchisor does establish a competitive franchisee, the first franchisee can sue for breach of contract, asking either for lost profit, court costs, and attorney's fees or for specific performance.

DUTY TO PROVIDE SAFE WORKING CONDITIONS   The principal has a duty to its agent to provide safe working conditions. Federal legislation such as the Occupational Safety and Health Act (discussed in chapter 17) set standards designed to create a safe working environment for employees. Employers who repeatedly violate those standards may be fined or imprisoned or both.

AGENT'S DUTIES TO PRINCIPAL

Just as a principal has legal duties to an agent, the agent has legal obligations toward the principal. They are loyalty, obedience, accounting, and performance.

DUTY OF LOYALTY   Courts have often indicated that the agent's most important obligation is *fiduciary*. The fiduciary obligation includes loyalty to the principal—that is, acting on behalf of *one* principal only to avoid conflicts of interest, communicating all material information to the principal, and refraining from acting in a manner that is adverse to the principal's interest.

DUTY OF OBEDIENCE   The agent has the duty to follow all *reasonable* and *lawful* instructions of the principal. If the manufacturer of a drug to alleviate the symptoms of the common cold tells his advertising department, salespeople, and distributors to tout the product as a *cure* for the common cold, these agents have no duty to follow the instructions because they are in violation of Section 5 of the Federal Trade Commission Act (see chapter 23).

DUTY OF ACCOUNTING   Whenever the principal requests an accounting of money or property, it is the duty of the agent to hand over the requested material. When courts have been asked to determine how the duty of accounting is met, their answers have varied from case to case, but the keeping of accurate books that can be viewed by the principal is the minimum activity expected.

DUTY OF PERFORMANCE   In all agency relationships, courts have indicated that agents must use reasonable care and skill in performing their work. This is generally taken to mean that agents must live up to the standards of performance expected of people in their occupation. Note in the following case the court's concern about whether an insurance company (agent) failed to meet the duty of performance to the deceased (principal) because it did not buy a life insurance contract.

BIAS V. ADVANTAGE INTERNATIONAL, INCORPORATED
UNITED STATES COURT OF APPEALS 905 F.2D 1558 (D.C. CIR. 1990)

Leonard Bias's estate (plaintiff) sued Advantage International Inc. (defendant), claiming that Advantage had failed to obtain a $1 million insurance policy on Leonard Bias as directed to. Bias was an outstanding basketball player at the University of Maryland. On June 17, 1986, he was drafted in the first round by the Boston Celtics of the National Basketball Association. On June 19, 1986, he died in his dormitory room of an overdose of cocaine. Advantage obtained a summary judgment from the trial court, in which the court noted that even if Advantage had attempted to obtain an insurance policy, it would have been denied because of Bias's cocaine use. The estate appealed to the U.S. Court of Appeals, arguing that there was a genuine issue of fact as to whether Bias was a cocaine user and that that fact should have been presented to the jury.

JUSTICE SENTELLE

The testimony of Long and Gregg (former teammates of Bias) clearly tends to show that Bias was a cocaine user.

The testimony of Bias's parents to the effect that they knew Bias well and did not know him to be a drug user does not rebut the Long and Gregg testimony about Bias's drug use on particular occasions. The drug test results offered by the Estate may show that Bias had no cocaine in his system on the dates when the tests were administered, but, as the District Court correctly notes, these tests speak only to Bias's abstention during the periods preceding the tests. The tests do not rebut the Long and Gregg testimony that on a number of occasions Bias ingested cocaine in their presence.

The Estate could have deposed Long and Gregg, or otherwise attempted to impeach their testimony. The Estate also could have offered the testimony of other friends or teammates of Bias who were present at some of the gatherings described by Long and Gregg, who went out with Bias frequently, or who were otherwise familiar with his social habits. The Estate did none of these things. The Estate is not entitled to reach the jury merely on the supposition that the jury might not believe the defendants' witnesses. We thus agree with the District Court that there was no genuine issue of fact concerning Bias's status as a cocaine user.

The defendants offered evidence that every insurance company inquires about the prior drug use of an applicant for a jumbo policy at some point in the application process. The Estate failed to name a single particular company or provide other evidence that a single company ex- isted which would have issued a jumbo policy in 1986 without inquiring about the applicant's drug use. Because the Estate has failed to do more than show that there is "some metaphysical doubt as to the material facts," the District Court properly concluded that there was no gen- uine issue of material fact as to the insurability of a drug user.

Affirmed in favor of Defendant, Advantage.

Critical Thinking about the Law

YOU SHOULD BE ALERT TO THE human element that figures into all legal reasoning. Be- cause a human being and not a computer is weighing the evidence in a case and rendering decisions, there is always the possibility that reasonable people will dis- agree about legal judgments. Judges, as humans, are not infallible.

Therefore we need to focus on *how* a decision is reached as opposed to blindly ac- cepting the decision itself. Indeed, as we emphasized in chapter 1, the *process* of legal de- cision making is central to critical thinking about the law. The questions that follow will aid you in the process-centered task of thinking critically about the judge's treatment of the evidence presented in this case.

1. What evidence concerning Bias's alleged drug use is in conflict?

CLUE Examine the judge's discussion of whether Bias was a regular cocaine user.

2. The judge resolves this conflicting evidence by ruling that the testimony affirming Bias's drug use is not disproved by evidence to the contrary. You might have reached a different conclusion. Even if you did not, how and why might someone else have made a different judgment?

CLUE You want to think about not only the quality of the evidence that suggests that Bias was *not* a drug user but also the quality of the evidence that suggests that he was.

PRINCIPAL'S AND AGENT'S LIABILITY TO THIRD PARTIES

Principals are normally responsible for the acts of their agents if those acts come within the scope of the agents' employment. Principals, then, can be held liable when agents enter contracts, commit torts within the scope of their em- ployment, and commit crimes while acting on behalf of the principal.

CONTRACTUAL LIABILITY

The purpose of a principal-agency relationship is to enable the principal to ex- pand business through the use of agents who can negotiate agreements with third parties that the principal would find it difficult or impossible to contact. To do their job, therefore, agents must be authorized to enter into contracts. A principal's liability for an agent's contracts depends in large part on whether the principal is disclosed or undisclosed to the third party at the time of the ex- ecution of the agreement.

LIABILITY OF DISCLOSED AND PARTIALLY DISCLOSED PRINCIPALS

A **disclosed principal** is one whose identity is known by the third party at the time he or she enters into the agreement; the third party is aware that the agent is acting on behalf of *this* principal. A **partially disclosed principal** is one whose identity is not known to the third party at the time of the agree- ment; the third party does know, however, that the agent represents *a* princi-

disclosed principal One whose identity is known by the third party when the latter enters into an agreement negotiated by the agent.

partially disclosed principal One whose identity is not known to the third party at the time of the agreement, though the third party does know the agent represents a principal. **325**

pal. In both these cases, the agent has *actual authority*, and therefore the principal is liable. For example, if Jones (agent) enters into an agreement with Thomas (third party) to buy a new car on behalf of Smith, Inc. (principal), Smith will be liable for the contract. Disclosure of a principal is usually shown in the agent's signature on the contract (e.g., "Smith, Inc. by Jones, Agent").

LIABILITY OF UNDISCLOSED PRINCIPAL

undisclosed principal One whose identity and existence are both unknown to the third party.

When the third party is aware of neither the identity of the principal nor the agency relationship, the agent may be liable to the third party if the principal does not perform the terms of the contract. **Undisclosed principal**-agent relationships are lawful and are often used by wealthy people to conceal their involvement in a negotiation. For example, Jones, a famous tycoon, hires Smith to go to an auction to bid on a castle. Jones wishes to remain undisclosed because he fears the other bidders will "bid up" the price if they know he is bidding. In this case, both Jones and Smith are liable to the seller whose castle is being auctioned.

TORT LIABILITY

Under the doctrine of respondant superior, a principal (employer) may be liable for the intentional or negligent torts of his or her agent (employee) if such acts are committed *within the scope of the agent's employment.* If the unauthorized acts are committed outside the scope of employment, liability shifts to the agent. So the crucial issue for the courts is whether the employee was acting within the scope of employment when the tort took place.

Two criteria used by the courts to decide this issue are: (1) Was the agent or employee acting in the principal's interest? (2) Was the agent or employee authorized to be in the particular place that he or she was in at the time of the commission of the tort? For example, Smith, an employee of Brennan Pizza Company, is authorized to deliver pizza in a vehicle owned by the company but not to make any stops in between delivering the pizza and returning the company vehicle to Brennan Pizza. Smith stops off at a local tavern after delivering her last pizza. She comes out of the tavern and hits a third party, Jones, who is walking across the street in a legal manner. If Jones sues the company and Smith, the court must decide these questions: Should the company be held liable? Should the agent, Smith, be held liable? Or should they be held liable jointly and severally? In most states, the agent would be liable given this factual situation because she was not authorized to be where she was at the time of the accident. Where company rules against the tortious activity are in place, courts generally rule against the agent. Were the company and Smith found to be **jointly/severally liable**, the agent would have had to indemnify the principal for what the company has to pay. Practically speaking, though, an agent like Smith usually does not have the money to pay either damages or indemnities. Under the "deep pocket" concept, Brennan Pizza Company alone would pay damages because it has the money to do so. Whether an employee was acting within the scope of his or her employment at the time of an accident is often not clear-cut, as the following case illustrates.

joint/several liability The legal principle that makes two or more people liable for a judgment, either as individuals or in any proportional combination. Under this principle, a person who is partially responsible for a tort can end up being completely liable for damages.

LAZAR V. THERMAL EQUIPMENT CORPORATION

COURT OF APPEALS OF CALIFORNIA 195 CAL. RPTR. 890 (1983)

Lazar (plaintiff) sued Thermal Equipment (defendant) for injuries suffered when one of Thermal's employees (Lanno) hit him, causing bodily injury and injury to his car. Lanno was allowed by the company to take his truck home daily, and he was provided with gasoline and au-

thorized to use the truck for personal purposes. While on his way home from work, he stopped at a store that was in the opposite direction both from work and from his home and hit Lazar. The trial court jury found for Lazar. Thermal appealed.

JUDGE SCHAVER

Under the doctrine of respondant superior, an employer is responsible for the torts of his employee if these torts are committed within the scope of employment. The "going and coming" rule acts to limit an employer's liability under respondant superior. This rule deems an employee's actions to be outside the scope of employment when these actions occur while the employee is going to or returning from work. The "going and coming" rule, in turn, has been limited in recent years. Under the modern rule, if the employee's trip to or from work "involves an incidental benefit to the employer not common to commute trips made by ordinary members of the work force," the "going and coming" rule will not apply.

In the [present] case, the trial court was presented with uncontroverted evidence that Thermal derived a special benefit from Lanno's commute. This commute was made in the company vehicle, and an object of the commute was to transport the vehicle to Lanno's home where it would be ready for business use in case Lanno received emergency after-hours calls for repair from the employer's customers. In traveling to and from work, Lanno was thus acting in the scope of his employment, conferring a tangible benefit on his employer; the "going and coming" rule is thus inapplicable.

A further issue, however, is presented in this case. Lanno decided that, before going home, he would stop at a shop and buy a certain, now forgotten, item. To further complicate the question, this shop and item were located in the opposite direction from the Lanno home.

One traditional means of defining this foreseeability is seen in the distinction between minor "deviations" and substantial "departures" from the employer's business. The former are deemed foreseeable and remain within the scope of employment; the latter are unforeseeable and take the employee outside the scope of his employment.

Witkin [an authority on the law of agency] describes the traditional distinction as follows: "The question is often one of fact, and the rule now established is that only a substantial deviation or departure takes the employee outside the scope of his employment. If the main purpose of his activity is still the employer's business, it does not cease to be within the scope of the employment by reason of incidental personal acts, slight delays, or deflections from the most direct route . . ."

In the [present] case, we are asked to decide whether Lanno's personal errand was a foreseeable deviation from the scope of his employment, or whether evidence or inferences therefrom have been presented which would lead a jury to believe that this errand was an unforeseeable, substantial departure from his duties.

The evidence presented to the trial court was not controverted. Lanno testified that on the day of the accident he left work and headed away from his home, planning to buy an item and then return directly home. The evidence thus clearly showed that Lanno planned a minor errand to be carried out, broadly speaking, on the way home. Lanno further testified that this type of errand occurred with his employer's permission. No evidence was presented, nor could any inference be drawn from the evidence, showing that Lanno had any other object in mind that day than a brief stop at a store before going home.

The evidence, then, leads ineluctably to the conclusion that Lanno's errand was a minor deviation from his employer's business. Here, it would have been unreasonable and inconvenient for Lanno to drive his truck home, stop there, then return to purchase the needed item, passing work on the way. The decision to stop to buy the item on the way home was one reasonably necessary to Lanno's comfort and convenience. For this reason the detour must be considered a minor deviation.

Affirmed for Plaintiff, Lazar.

CRIMINAL LIABILITY

Principals are generally not liable for criminal acts (e.g., murder, rape, price fixing, extortion) of their agents because it is difficult to show the intent of the principal that is required for liability for such crimes. However, this general rule has two major exceptions: (1) when a principal participates directly in the agent's crime and (2) when the principal has reason to know there is a violation of law taking place by employees or agents. (see *United States v. Park* in chapter 7). For an example of the first exception assume that a refinery threatens to terminate Jones (employee) unless he agrees to set the prices of gasoline in a certain location and communicate those prices to all company-owned and independent dealers using the refinery's gasoline. If Jones does what he is told and is caught, both the refinery and Jones will be prosecuted under the Sherman Act for price fixing (see chapter 23). The defense of Jones that he was just an employee following his employer's orders when he fixed prices will not be acceptable. On the other hand, if Jones refuses to do what his employer is demanding and is discharged, he can sue the refinery on the basis of the tort of wrongful discharge (see chapter 19).

TERMINATION OF THE PRINCIPAL-AGENT RELATIONSHIP

The principal-agent relationship may be terminated by agreement or by operation of law.

TERMINATION BY AGREEMENT

Either of the parties may decide to terminate the principal-agent relationship. When such a relationship is terminated, all third parties who dealt with the agent should be given *actual notice* by the principal. *Constructive notice* may be given to others through advertisement in newspapers published in areas where the agent operated on behalf of the principal.

Some agency relationships are terminated by a *lapse of time*. For example, Jones agrees with Smith that Smith will serve as his agent for business purposes until May 20, 1996. On that day, Smith's actual or apparent authority lapses. Once again, the principal should notify all relevant third parties at the termination.

TERMINATION BY LAW

When the principal-agent relationship is terminated by law, there is no requirement to give notification to relevant third parties. The five most common methods of termination by operation of law are (1) *death of one of the parties*, even if the other party is unaware of that death, (2) *insanity of one of the parties*, (3) *bankruptcy of the principal*, (4) *impossibility of performance*, which may come about through the destruction or loss of subject matter or a change in the law, (5) an *outbreak of war*, particularly when the agent's country is at war with the principal's country.

INTERNATIONAL DIMENSIONS OF AGENCY LAW

As global business by multinationals, midsize, and even small corporations has expanded, many U.S. businesses have hired foreign agents to represent them abroad. With the lowering of tariff barriers through such treaties as the North American Free Trade Agreement and the World Trade Organization, foreign agents will become ever more essential to the movement of goods and services across national boundaries. So it behooves managers in businesses of all sizes to become knowledgeable about the exporting companies, distributors, and sales agents they contract with and the rules that govern those agents in their own countries. We covered the general aspects of these treaties and the international legal environment of business in chapter 3. Here we encapsulate some of the major differences between agency law and practice in the United States and in two importing trading partners of U.S. business: Japan and the European Union.

JAPAN

In Japan, agents must disclose whom they are representing, and third parties often require proof that agents are acting on behalf of a particular principal. Unlike in the United States, an agent in Japan must have expressed authority to act, and principals are held liable for acts of agents within their limited range.

EUROPEAN UNION (EU)

European Union principals are bound to act in good faith toward their agents. If there is no written contract, compensation is based on customary practice in the location where the agent is acting. Agents are also expected to act in good faith. All items in negotiations must be communicated to the principal, and the agent is bound to follow the principal's instructions quite literally. Most agency agreements are assumed to be for an indefinite time; thus notice of one, two, and three months, respectively, is required to terminate a relationship of one, two, and three years' duration.

From just these two examples you can see how agency law elsewhere can differ significantly from agency law in the United States. Managers should carefully review a host country's laws on agency before carrying on business in that country.

There are special complications for managers when the law of the host country conflicts with the Foreign Corrupt Practices Act (FCPA) of 1977, as amended in 1988. Although that act allows remuneration to lower-level foreign agents and officials to expedite the handling of goods U.S. businesses are seeking to sell in another country, it strictly forbids payments to political officials of a certain level. Because companies are liable for both civil and criminal sanctions for violating the FCPA, managers must keep a close watch over the actions of hired foreign agents as well as over the actions of their own employees abroad.

SUMMARY

An agency relationship is a fiduciary relationship in which the agent acts on behalf of, and is subject to the control of, the principal. There are three types: principal-agent, employer-employee, and employer-independent contractor. The four methods of creating an agency relationship are (1) through expressed agency (agency by agreement), (2) by implied authority, (3) through ratification by the principal, and (4) by estoppel, or apparent authority. The duties of the principal to the agent are compensation for services rendered, reimbursement for expenses and indemnification for losses, cooperation, and provision of providing safe working conditions. Those of the agent toward the principal are loyalty, obedience to reasonable and lawful instructions, an accurate accounting, and skillful and careful performance.

Principals are liable to third parties for contracts made by their agents on their behalf, torts committed by the agent within the scope of the agent's employment, and crimes committed by the agent at the principal's direction.

Agency relationships may be terminated by mutual consent or by operation of law.

Managers doing international business need to be aware of the sometimes significant differences between agency law in the United States and agency law in other countries.

REVIEW QUESTIONS

14-1. Explain the doctrine of respondant superior.

14-2. Define apparent and actual authority.

14-3. Describe the agent's duties to the principal.

14-4. Distinguish an agent from an independent contractor.

14-5. Is a principal responsible for all contracts entered into by an agent? Explain.

14-6. Why must a principal notify a third party of the termination of an agency relationship? Explain.

REVIEW PROBLEMS

14-7. Profit Corporation authorized Anderson, an employee, to find a buyer for used equipment that Profit intended to sell. Anderson believed that he had authority to contract for the sale of the equipment, but in fact he did not. Anderson found a prospective buyer, Caveat Corporation, and contracted with Caveat on behalf of Profit for the sale of the equipment to Caveat. In this contract, Anderson warranted that the equipment was fit for Caveat's particular needs. A responsible officer of Profit read the contract and directed that the equipment be shipped to Caveat. The equipment did not meet the special needs of Caveat, and Caveat refused to pay for it. Profit sued Caveat for the contract price. Who will win this case and why?

14-8. Mrs. Terry sees a cashmere sweater she likes in Peters Department Store but notices that it is slightly soiled. Alice, the salesclerk, agrees to mark it down from $55 to $40, which she has no authority to do. Mrs. Terry consents, asks that the sweater be delivered, and promises to pay COD. The manager of Peters sees the item being wrapped, corrects the bill, and sends it out to Mrs. Terry. On seeing her sweater accompanied by a bill for $55, Mrs. Terry calls and is told by Peters that Alice had no authority to knock down the price and that she should either pay the bill or return the sweater. Is Mrs. Terry entitled to the bargain? Why or why not?

14-9. Owner orally authorized Agent to sell his house. Agent completed a sale of the house to Buyer. When Buyer attempted to enforce the contract against Owner, Buyer was told that the contract was not enforceable because Owner's agency relation with Agent was not in writing. Must Owner have given Agent written authorization?

14-10. Owner listed his house with Penelope, a real estate broker, granting Penelope an exclusive right to sell Owner's house. Penelope entered negotiations with Buyer, who seemed interested in purchasing the property. Buyer found the price agreeable but he insisted on including in the sales contract a clause giving him the right to cancel the contract if he could not get a loan to finance his purchase. At the closing, Buyer exercised his right to cancel, giving as his reason inability to procure a loan. Penelope turned to Owner and claimed that she was entitled to her commission even though the sale did not go through. Must Owner pay Penelope a commission?

14-11. Julius and Olga Sylvester owned an unimproved piece of land near King of Prussia, Pennsylvania. They were approached by Beck, a real estate broker, who asked if they were willing to sell their land, stating that an oil company was interested in buying, renting, or leasing the property. The Sylvesters said that they were only interested in selling, and they authorized Beck to sell the property for $15,000. Several weeks later, Beck phoned the Sylvesters and offered to buy the property for himself for $14,000. Olga asked, "What happened to the oil company?" and Beck responded, "They are not interested. You want too much money for it." The Sylvesters sold the property to Beck. A month later, Beck sold the property to Epstein for $25,000. When the Sylvesters learned that Beck had realized a huge profit in a quick resale of the property, they sued Beck, claiming that he owed them the $9,000 profit. Does Beck owe the Sylvesters the money?

14-12. Peter authorized Arnon, a grain broker, to buy at the market 20,000 bushels of wheat for Peter. At the time, Arnon had in storage 5,000 bushels belonging to Johnson, who had authorized Arnon to sell for him. Arnon also had 15,000 bushels that she owned. Arnon transferred these 20,000 bushels to Peter's name and charged Peter the current market price. Shortly thereafter, and before Peters had used or sold the wheat, the market price declined sharply. Peters refused to pay for the wheat and tried to cancel the contract. Can he cancel? Explain.

CASE PROBLEMS

14-13. The National Biscuit Company is a corporation that produces and distributes cookies and other food products to grocery stores and other outlets across the nation. Nabisco hired Ronnell Lynch as a cookie salesman-trainee. Lynch was assigned his own sales territory. Lynch's duties involved making sales calls, taking orders, and making sure that shelves of stores in his territory were stocked with Nabisco products.

On May 1, 1969, Lynch visited a grocery store that was managed by Jerome Lange. An argument developed between Lynch and Lange. Lynch became very angry and started swearing. Lange, the store manager, told Lynch to stop swearing or leave the store. Lynch became angry and went behind the counter and dared Lange to a fight. When Lange refused to fight, Lynch proceeded to assault and batter Lange, causing severe injuries. Lange sued Nabisco. The jury returned a verdict in favor of Nabisco. The court refused to grant plaintiff Lange's motion for judgment notwithstanding the verdict. Lange appealed. Who won? Explain. *Lange v. National Biscuit Co.*, 211 N.W.2d 783 (1983)

14-14. Arlen Gatzke was a district manager for Walgreen Company. Gatzke was sent to Duluth, Minnesota, to supervise the opening of a new Walgreen restaurant. While in Duluth, Gatzke stayed at the Edgewater Motel. While there, Gatzke was "on call" 24 hours a day to other Walgreen stores located in his territory. Gatzke, after working 17 hours, went with several other Walgreen employees to the Bellows Restaurant to drink. Within an hour, Gatzke had consumed three "double" and one single brandy Manhattans. A fire broke out in Gatzke's room about 2 A.M. at the Edgewater Motel. Gatzke escaped from his burning room, but the fire spread and caused extensive damage to the motel.

Evidence showed that Gatzke smoked two packs of cigarettes a day. An expert fire witness testified that the fire started in or next to the wastepaper basket in Gatzke's room. Edgewater Motels, Inc., sued Gatzke, Walgreen, and the Bellows Restaurant. The parties stipulated that the damage to the Edgewater Motel was $330,360. The jury returned a verdict against defendant Gatzke and Walgreen. The court granted Walgreen's motion for a judgment notwithstanding the verdict of the jury in favor of the defendants. The defendants appealed. Who won? Explain. *Edgewater Hotels v. Walgreen Co.*, 277 N.W.2d 11 (1979)

14-15. Venezio, a real estate broker, conducted his business under the name "King Realty." On May 19, 1984, King Realty entered into a contract to purchase property located in the Town of Rotterdam, Schenectady County, from Bianchi. Venezio signed the end of the contract "King Realty for Customer." On May 23, 1984, King Realty entered into a contract to sell the property to Attanasio. However, Bianchi refused to sell the property to King Realty, alleging that because the original contract failed to adequately identify the purchaser, there was not a binding contract. Venezio, King Realty, brought this action for specific performance against Bianchi. The trial court granted Venezio's motion for summary judgment. Bianchi appealed. Who won? Explain. *Venezio v. Bianchi*, 508 N.Y.2d 549 (1986)

14-16. In February 1980 Richard Seib, president of Aztec Petroleum Corporation engaged Donnie Douglas to buy a 4,900-acre block of oil and gas leases for Aztec. For his services, Douglas was to receive $5,000, together with an assignment of royalty interest in the leases obtained.

On February 23, 1980, Aztec sent Douglas a $5,000 payment in advance for buying the leases and two other checks totaling $124,180 to pay for leases. By the end of March all but a few tracts had been leased by Douglas.

During the acquisition period Aztec sent Douglas $343,557.36. Forty-two thousand dollars was kept as cash by Douglas and never deposited. When he made the final account to Aztec in June 1980, Douglas sent bogus receipts to show that the cash went to lessors. He later admitted at trial that he did not really obtain receipts for cash payments but that his wife had forged all of those sent to Aztec by transposing signatures of lessors from other documents.

Once most of the leases were obtained, Douglas wished to receive his override royalty. However, Seib kept badgering Douglas for an accounting. Douglas concocted a false account by using forged receipts and altering the amount and payee of the checks to plug in whatever figure was necessary to come to $343,557.36, the amount committed to his charge. He then forwarded the forged receipts to Aztec's Dallas headquarters.

Upon receipt of the account, Seib contacted some of the lessors and discovered several who were not paid the amounts reported. With this knowledge he refused to convey the override royalty to Douglas.

Douglas sued Aztec for the override royalty. Aztec denied liability and counterclaimed for actual and exemplary damages. A jury resulted in a judgment denying Douglas the override royalty and awarding Aztec $107,834.57 in actual damages and $100,000 in exemplary damages. Douglas appealed to the Texas Court of Appeals. Who won? Explain. *Douglas v. Aztec Petroleum*, 6695 S.W.2d 312 (1985)

14-17. McKeehan, looking for investment opportunities, dealt directly with Malcolm and Jacob Wittels of Wittels Investment Company. McKeehan entrusted $28,813 to them. The Wittelses invested this money in a deed of trust in property. After the investments matured, McKeehan repeatedly demanded that her funds be returned. The Wittelses, disregarded the instructions and renewed the investments without her consent. Tax liens existed on all properties in the investments, and there was evidence that the Wittelses were aware of these tax liens. McKeehan sued the Wittelses for damages, alleging that they had breached their fiduciary duties to her. The trial court entered judgment in favor of McKeehan in the amount of $29,942.65 actual damages and $25,000 punitive damages. The Wittelses appealed to the Missouri Court of Appeals. Who won? Explain. *McKeehan v. Wittelses*, 508 S.W.2d 277 (1977)

14-18. From May 17, 1973, Bob Harvey was employed by the Magnolia Health Center as a laboratory technician. While at Magnolia, Harvey ordered laboratory testing services from Bio-Chem Medical laboratories over his signature. Harvey left Magnolia on June 13, 1973, to assume an administrative position with another clinic. Later that month he received a bill from Bio-Chem for the testing services he ordered while at Magnolia. Harvey claimed that he had contracted for these services in a representative capacity for his employer and therefore was not obligated to pay the bill.

Bio-Chem sued Harvey to recover the amount owed for the lab testing services, and the trial court entered judgment against Harvey. Harvey appealed to the Louisiana Court of Appeals. Who won? Explain. *Bio-Chem v. Harvey*, 310 S.W. 173 (1973)

 On the Internet

http://www.indiana.edu/~swp/9601.htm   On this page you can find a discussion of important issues related to agency law.

15

LAW AND BUSINESS ASSOCIATIONS

- **THE THREE MAJOR FORMS OF BUSINESS ORGANIZATION**

  IN THE UNITED STATES

- **FACTORS INFLUENCING A BUSINESS MANAGER'S CHOICE**

  OF ORGANIZATIONAL FORM

- **SPECIALIZED FORMS OF BUSINESS ASSOCIATIONS**

- **INTERNATIONAL DIMENSIONS OF BUSINESS ASSOCIATIONS**

The world of business is much more complex than is ordinarily supposed. Businesses vary greatly in size, of course, but they also differ dramatically in form, and organizational form has a tremendous impact on the amount of regulation to which a business is subject, as well as on the rights and responsibilities of its owners.

The first section of this chapter introduces the three major types of business associations found in this country—the sole proprietorship, the partnership, and the corporation. It describes how these organizational forms are created and terminated and identifies some of the important players in each. The second section presents a detailed look at the factors that cause businesspeople to choose one of these three organizational forms initially and the reasons they sometimes change from one form to another.

There are other types of business associations that are less well known than the principal three, and the third section discusses several of those specialized forms. The final section raises some of the questions business managers need to ask before they decide on the form their involvement in international markets will take.

Critical Thinking about the Law

WE HAVE POINTED OUT THAT THE organizational form of the business will determine the amount of regulation that a firm experiences. Furthermore, owners will have different rights and responsibilities according to the organizational form. Although you will learn about the three major organizational forms later in this chapter, you can prepare to use your critical thinking skills while you consider business associations by asking yourself the following questions.

1. (This question is not a formal critical thinking question, but it lays the groundwork for critical thinking about forms of business organization.) Think about the businesses that you interact with everyday. For example, where do you buy groceries? Who cuts your hair? Where did you buy this book? Why should the community even care whether these businesses are owned by a single person or by hundreds of shareholders?

   CLUE Ask yourself what the community expects from businesses and how these different forms of ownership would affect the extent to which those expectations are fulfilled.

2. Joan wants to open a business that specializes in selling fine wines. She believes that, as long as she follows the law of selling alcohol only to individuals 21 years of age or older, the government should not impose any other regulation on her business activity. What ethical norm seems to dominate Joan's thinking?

   CLUE Think about the list of ethical norms in chapter 1. Which norm seems most consistent with little or no governmental regulation? Which ethical norm seems to conflict with the idea of little governmental regulation?

3. One of the factors that might influence business owners to choose one organizational form over another is the liability associated with that organizational form. For example, in a sole proprietorship, the owner is liable for all losses, whereas owners in a corporation have limited liability. Vanessa has a chance to be either a sole proprietor or a shareholder in a corporation. She chooses to become a sole proprietor, even though she considers this option to be riskier. Which ethical norms might be guiding her decision to become a sole proprietor?

   CLUE Look closely at the list of ethical norms. Which norms seem consistent with Vanessa's choice? Can you generate any other ethical norms that seem to influence her decision?

THE THREE MAJOR FORMS OF BUSINESS ORGANIZATION IN THE UNITED STATES

The most common forms of business organization in the United States are the sole proprietorship, the partnership, and the corporation (Table 15-1). We examine each of these organizational forms in turn, beginning with the oldest and simplest: the sole proprietorship.

THE SOLE PROPRIETORSHIP

Someone who decides to go into business alone is creating a **sole proprietorship**. Forming a sole proprietorship requires few legal formalities, and the enterprise is subject to minimal governmental regulation. The proprietor has total control of management and retains all profits of the business, which are taxed as personal income to the proprietor. The proprietor is also personally liable for all losses incurred by the proprietorship.

sole proprietorship A business owned by one person, who has sole control over management and profits.

THE PARTNERSHIP

TYPES OF PARTNERSHIP When two or more people wish to be involved in the ownership of a business, either a *limited* or a general partnership may be formed. Under the Uniform Partnership Act (UPA), the law that governs partnerships in most states, a **partnership** is defined as a voluntary association of two or more persons formed to carry on a business as co-owners for profit. As in a sole proprietorship, the profits of a partnership are taxed only as income to the partners. More recently the Revised Uniform Partnership Act has been adopted in 18 states as of 1998. This Act (RUPA) when adopted no longer dissolves a partnership just because a partner leaves; clarifies the fiduciary duties of partners; and establishes a formula for valuing a partnership interest during a buyout. It also provides greater protection for the limited liability partner (to be discussed later in this chapter).

partnership A voluntary association of two or more persons formed to carry on a business as co-owners for profit.

In a **general partnership**, all profits are divided among the partners, and all partners are personally liable for partnership debts. For example, if James and Carol decide to operate a florist shop as co-owners in a general partnership, each of them makes an initial contribution in the form of cash, realty, business supplies, or services. They take an equal role in the management of the business, with each expected to contribute services. They split the profits equally (assuming that no other proportion has been specified in a written partnership agreement). At the end of the first year, they file a partnership return with the Internal Revenue Service that shows the partnership's profit or loss. If the partnership makes a profit, James and Carol each pay income tax on half the profits; if the partnership incurs a loss, each deducts one-half of that loss from his or her ordinary income. The partnership itself pays no taxes. If the business

general partnership A partnership in which management responsibilities and profits are divided (usually equally) among the partners, and all partners have unlimited personal liability for the partnership's debts.

TABLE 15-1   *Alternative Forms of Business Organization*

Sole proprietorship	Person going into business on his or her own, responsible for all profits and losses.
Partnership (general)	Voluntary association of two or more persons to carry on a business as co-owners for profit. A *limited liability* partnership is a voluntary association, as is a general partnership, but one or more partners contribute capital *only*, and those partners play no role in management. Their liability is limited to the amount of capital they contribute.
Corporation	A legal entity created by state law that raises capital by issuing stocks and bonds to investors, who become shareholders and owners of the corporation. Corporations can be classified as *public* or *private* and are further distinguished as *multinational, professional, closely held, subchapter S,* and *limited liability corporations.*

limited partnership A partnership that has one general partner, who is responsible for managing the business, and one or more limited partners, who invest in the partnership but do not participate in its management and whose liability is limited to the amount of capital they contribute.

fails, both James and Carol can be sued by creditors and forced to pay the partnership's debts out of their personal resources.

Now suppose that Shelly wishes to invest in James and Carol's partnership but has no desire to take part in its management because she does not want to incur unlimited liability. In most states, she could join the business as a limited partner, and the partnership would then become a limited partnership. **Limited partnerships** have at least one general partner and one limited partner and are easily identifiable because they must include the word *limited* (or an abbreviation of it) in their names. Except for the special status accorded to limited partners and the necessity of strictly following the statutory scheme for the formation of a limited partnership (described later in this section), general and limited partnerships function similarly. The primary law governing limited partnerships is the Revised Uniform Limited Partnership Act (RULPA), which has been adopted by 48 states. The question of how much management activity a limited partner can engage in before losing the special status granted by statute is still unsettled. The following case concerns a limited partner who acted to secure credit for the partnership.

PITMAN V. FLANAGAN LUMBER CO.

SUPREME COURT OF ALABAMA 567 SO. 2D 1335 (1990)

Plaintiff Flanagan sued defendant Pitman, claiming that, although Pitman was a limited partner in Ramsey Homebuilders, he was responsible for that company's debt under the Revised Uniform Limited Partnership Act. Ramsey, the general partner in the business had a poor credit history, so Pitman secured an account with the Flanagan Lumber Company in the partnership's name. After the partnership failed to pay its debts, Flanagan sued. Pitman's defense was that he was a limited partner who did not participate in management or control, and hence was not liable. The trial court ruled in favor of Flanagan. Pitman appealed.

JUSTICE HOUSTON

Pitman argues that the evidence does not support the trial court's finding that he participated in the control of the partnership's business. He also contends that he had no written agreement with Flanagan to pay the partnership's account and, therefore, he cannot be held responsible for the debt.

"Control" is defined in Black's Law Dictionary as "the [p]ower or authority to manage, direct, superintend, restrict, regulate, govern, administer, or oversee." In the

present case, the evidence showed that Pitman interceded on behalf of the partnership in order to secure an account with Flanagan. The trial court could have found from this evidence that Pitman participated in the "control" of the partnership's business by securing one of the things that the partnership needed to survive—a source of building materials that would be provided on credit. Furthermore, the evidence supports the trial court's finding that Flanagan reasonably relied on Pitman's participation in the partnership's business by extending credit to the partnership. The trial court's judgment was not plainly and palpably wrong.

With regard to Pitman's second contention (i.e., that [the Statute of Frauds] protects him from liability because he had no written agreement with Flanagan to pay the partnership's debt), the trial court did not adjudge Pitman liable on the ground that he had an agreement with Flanagan to pay the account, but on the ground that he had lost his limited partner status under [the Revised Uniform Limited Partnership Act, Section 303(a)], and, therefore [,] became liable as a general partner for the partnership's debt.

Affirmed in favor of Plaintiff, Flanagan.

Limited Liability Limited Partnership (LLLP). The liability of a general partner is the same as that of the limited partners. The liability is to the amount of investment made in the firm by each partner.

Limited Liability Partnership (LLP). This form is for professionals who do business as partners. The major advantage allows a partnership to continue even if there exists liability for one of the partners for tort liability. If a client sues one of the partners for malpractice and wins a large judgment, and the firm's insurance does not cover it all, all the partners are not jointly and separately liable.

CREATING A PARTNERSHIP Initially in many partnerships, there is no written partnership agreement; the partners informally split the capital contribution and work between them. In the absence of a written agreement, the Uniform Partnership Act (UPA) controls. For example, the UPA requires partners to share profits equally. Now James and Carol may not have intended an equal distribution of profits when they went into business, and such a distribution may be unfair because Carol does 90 percent of the work and the less energetic James does a mere 10 percent. But if they have no written agreement, James can legally claim 50 percent of the profits. To avoid conflicts over management responsibilities, borrowing power, profit sharing, and other common bones of contention in a partnership, the partners should set out the rights and responsibilities of each partner in a written partnership agreement at the outset. Exhibit 15-1 lists some of the items that should be included in such an agreement.

Under the RUPA, which is noted at the beginning of this chapter, most of the Act consists of rules that will apply unless the partnership agreement states differently. This will force all partnerships to be carefully created. All parties engaged in an existing partnership or creating a new one should be careful to see if the RUPA has been adopted in the state where the partnership agreement is formed.

RELATIONSHIP BETWEEN PARTNERS The Uniform Partnership Act requires that each partner have a fiduciary relationship to the partnership and act in good faith for the benefit of the partnership. In most general partnerships, each partner has one vote in decisions pertaining to the management of the business, though in some instances—such as a decision to merge with another partnership—a unanimous vote may be required.

Read Exhibit 15-1 carefully, for it will give you a good idea of the issues that should be resolved before people enter into a business partnership. The relationship between partners will go much more smoothly if the parties agree beforehand on how much each will invest, the management duties each will undertake, methods of dispute resolution, banking arrangements and borrowing policies for the business, and how the books will be kept. Then look at Exhibit 15-2, which is a model form for a general partnership agreement. It does not contain variables it might be wise to include for specific kinds of partnerships, but it is a useful starting point for drafting such an agreement.

EXHIBIT 15-1 *Items to Be Included in Partnership Agreements*

Name and address of partnership.

Name and address of partners.

Purpose of partnership.

Duration of partnership.

Amount and type of investment of each partner (e.g., cash, realty, services).

Loans to partnership.

How profits and losses are to be shared.

Management and voting power of each partner.

Method of settling disputes that should arise.

Cross-insurance of partners.

Duties of each partner.

How books are to be set up and maintained.

Banking arrangements—who has authority to deposit and withdraw.

Who has authority to borrow money in the name of partnership.

Who does the hiring and firing of employees.

EXHIBIT 15-2 *Model General Partnership Agreement Form*

Kubasek-Brennan-Browne
PARTNERSHIP AGREEMENT

This agreement, made and entered into as of the [Date], by and among Kubasek-Brennan-Browne (referred to as "Partners").

WITNESSETH:

Whereas, the Parties hereto desire to form a General Partnership (hereinafter referred to as the "Partnership"), for the term and upon the conditions hereinafter set forth;

Now, therefore, in consideration of the mutual covenants hereinafter contained, it is agreed by and among the Parties hereto as follows:

Article I
BASIC STRUCTURE

Form. The Parties hereby form a General Partnership pursuant to the Laws of the State of Newgarth.

Name. The business of the Partnership shall be conducted under the name of Kubasek-Brennan-Browne.

Place of Business. The principal office and place of business of the Partnership shall be located at 2130 Foot Street, Justin, Newgarth, or such other place as the Partners may from time to time designate.

Term. The Partnership shall commence on [Date], and shall continue for [Number] years, unless earlier terminated in the following manner;

    (a) By the completion of the purpose intended, or

    (b) Pursuant to this Agreement, or

    (c) By applicable Newgarth law, or

    (d) By death, insanity, bankruptcy, retirement, withdrawal, resignation, expulsion, or disability of all of the then Partners.

Article II
MANAGEMENT

Managing Partners. The Managing Partner(s) shall be all partners.

Voting. All Managing Partner(s) shall have the right to vote as to the management and conduct of the business of the Partnership according to their then Percentage Share of [Capital/Income]. Except otherwise herein set forth a majority of such [Capital/Income] shall control.

Percentage Share of Profits. Distribution of the Partners of net operating profits of the Partnership shall be made quarterly in the percentage agreed upon (40%, 40%, 20%).

TERMINATING A PARTNERSHIP A partnership, unlike a corporation, does not have perpetual existence. It can "die" when partners leave the partnership, the partnership is merged with another business or goes bankrupt, or the partnership agreement expires.

On its "deathbed," a partnership goes through a process called "dissolution and winding-up." *Dissolution* prevents any new business from taking place, whereas **winding-up** involves completing all unfinished transactions, paying off the debts, dividing any remaining profits, and distributing assets.

winding-up The process of completing all unfinished transactions, paying off outstanding debts, distributing assets, and dividing remaining profits after a partnership has been terminated, or dissolved.

EXHIBIT 15-2 *(continued)*

339

Chapter 15

Law and Business Associations

Article III
DISSOLUTION

Dissolutions. In the event that the Partnership shall hereafter be dissolved for any reason whatsoever, a full and general account of its assets, liabilities and transactions shall at once be taken. Such assets may be sold and turned into cash as soon as possible and all debts and other amounts due the Partnership collected. The proceeds thereof shall thereupon be applied as follows:

(a) To discharge the debts and liabilities of the Partnership and the expenses of liquidation.

(b) To pay each Partner or his legal representative any unpaid salary, drawing account, interest or profits to which he shall then be entitled and in addition, to repay to any Partner his capital contributions in excess of his original capital contribution.

(c) To divide the surplus, if any, among the Partners or their representatives as follows: (1) First (to the extent of each Partner's then capital account) in proportion to their then capital accounts.

Then according to each Partner's then Percentage Share of Capital/Income.

Right To Demand Property. To partner shall have the right to demand and receive property in kind for his distribution.

Article IV
MISCELLANEOUS

Accounting Year, Books, Statements. The Partnership's fiscal year shall commence on January 1st of each year and shall end on December 31st of each year. Full and accurate books of account shall be kept at such place as the Managing Partner(s) may from time to time designate, showing the condition of the business and finances of the Partnership; and each Partner shall have access to such books of account and shall be entitled to examine them at any time during ordinary business hours.

Arbitration. Any controversy or claim arising out of or relating to this Agreement shall only be settled by arbitration in accordance with the rules of the American Arbitration, one Arbitrator, and shall be enforceable in any court having competent jurisdiction.

Witnesses	**Partners**
J. Foster	Kubasek-Brennan-Browne

THE CORPORATION

The partnership is the most common form of business organization in the United States. However, the dominant business organization form is the **corporation**, a legal entity created by state law that raises capital by issuing stock to investors, who own the corporation. Although the corporation may have many owners, it is legally treated as a single person. Before we go into the laws governing the creation, financing, and operation of corporations, we need to explain how corporations are classified.

corporation An entity formed and authorized by state law to act as a single person and to raise capital by issuing stock to investors who are the owners of the corporation.

closely held corporation One whose stock is not traded on the national securities exchanges but is privately held by a small group of people.

publicly held corporation One whose stock is traded on at least one national securities exchange.

multinational (transnational) corporation One whose production, distribution, ownership, and management span several nations.

Subchapter S corporation A business that is organized like a corporation but, under Internal Revenue Code Subchapter S, is treated like a partnership for tax purposes so long as it abides by certain restrictions pertaining to stock, shareholders, and affiliations.

professional corporation One organized by doctors, dentists, lawyers, accountants, and other professionals specified in state statutes.

limited liability corporation (LLC) A hybrid corporation-partnership like the Subchapter S corporation, but with far fewer restrictions.

CLASSIFICATION OF CORPORATIONS All corporations are broadly classified as either public or private. They are further differentiated as closely held, publicly held, multinational, Subchapter S, professional, or limited liability corporations.

Closely Held Corporation. The greatest number of corporations in this country are private, or **closely held corporations**. The stock of these corporations is not traded on any of the national securities exchanges. Instead, it is usually held by a small group of people, often members of the same family or close friends, who serve as directors as well as officers and active managers of the corporation. When the corporation is formed, these original owners frequently enter into an agreement to restrict the sale of stock to the initial shareholders. By limiting ownership in this way, they retain control of the corporation.

Publicly Held Corporation. Those corporations whose stock is traded on the national exchanges are known as **publicly held corporations**. Although technically governed by the same rules as closely held corporations (except for securities law, which are discussed in chapter 21), their operations are much different from those of closely held corporations. Publicly held corporations have numerous shareholders who are simply investors. Real control rests in the hands of the officers and managers, who may own some stock, though generally not a majority or controlling amount.

When the term *corporation* is used in this book, a publicly held corporation is meant unless otherwise specified. Although some regulations apply only to publicly held corporations, in most instances the same laws apply to both public and private corporations. The impact of such laws differs, though, depending on whether the affected corporation is public or private. The reason for our focus on public rather than private corporations is the same as our reason for emphasizing corporations rather than partnerships: impact on society. Public corporations are wealthier than any other form of business organization, and therefore the impact of regulation on these corporations has the greatest effect on society.

Multinational or Transnational Corporation. This relatively new type of publicly held corporation now dominates the world economy. It is called a **multinational,** or **transnational, corporation** because it does not restrict its production to a single nation and generally maintains worldwide distribution sites. Its stock is usually traded on the securities exchanges of several nations, and its managers are often citizens of different countries. Through their tremendous wealth, power, and reach, multinationals have a strong impact on societies all over the world.

Subchapter S Corporation. This type of closely held corporation is best described as a hybrid of the corporation and the partnership. The **Subchapter S corporation** is organized and operates as a regular business corporation, but for tax purposes is treated like a partnership. To qualify for Subchapter S treatment under the Internal Revenue Code, a domestic corporation must (1) have no more than 35 shareholders, all of whom are individuals, estates, or certain types of trusts, and none of whom is a nonresident alien; (2) have only one class of stock outstanding; and (3) not be a member of an affiliated group of corporations. All shareholders must consent to the election of Subchapter S status.

Professional Corporation. The **professional corporation** is a fairly new form of business organization intended for doctors, lawyers, dentists, accountants, and other professionals who were once unable to incorporate legally. Most states now have passed statutes permitting specified professionals to incorporate so that they can take the tax advantages of deductions for health and pension plans that are allowable under the corporate form. In most states, the professional corporation differs from other corporations in that the owners are not accorded limited liability for professional acts (it is generally considered contrary to public policy to grant professionals limited liability for their negligence).

Limited-Liability Corporation (LLC). Like the Subchapter S corporation, the **limited liability corporation (LLC)** is a hybrid form of business organization. It allows entrepreneurs and small businesspeople to enjoy the same limited personal liability that shareholders in a corporation have while retaining the status of partners in a partnership. The LLC is federally taxed, not as a corporation, but as a partnership, so taxes are paid personally by members of the LLC. Limited liability corporation members share in the profits from the business and exercise management control without these actions affecting their profit share or limited liability status. The LLC differs from the Subchapter S corporation in that other corporations, partnerships, and foreign investors can be LLC members, and there is no limit on the number of members.

Before the publication of an Internal Revenue Service Review Procedure on January 17, 1995, an LLC possessing more than two of the following four characteristics would be liable for income taxes:

1. Limited liability
2. Continuity of life
3. Free transferability of interest
4. Centralization of management

Because every LLC, by definition, has limited liability, LLCs could not have more than one of the other three characteristics. Under the new Review Procedure, it is clear that the IRS will interpret the other three characteristics liberally and in a pro-LLC fashion.[1]

Limited liability corporations have been proliferating, especially in the mobile and wireless telecommunications area, ever since the IRS ruling. Approximately 47 states now have LLC statutes,[2] and LLCs are subject to supervision by state courts, although little case law exists on this new form of business enterprise. At present, the Securities and Exchange Commission (SEC) is investigating whether LLC ownership interests should be considered securities that must be registered under federal and state securities laws. Already, some states have placed restrictions on the transfer of members' interests.

CREATING A CORPORATION   Corporations are creatures of state, *not* federal, law. Each of the 50 states, as well as the District of Columbia, Puerto Rico, and Guam has a general incorporation statute that stipulates the articles of incorporation to be used in that state. These articles, generally standardized forms, identify the name of the corporation, its registered address and resident agent, the general purpose of the business, the classes of stock to be issued by the corporation and their face value, and the names and mailing addresses of the incorporators (Exhibit 15-3). The articles, accompanied by the required fees, are filed with the secretary of state of the state of incorporation, who then issues a certificate of incorporation. Upon issuance of the certificate, the corporation holds its first board meeting, at which a board of directors is elected, bylaws are enacted, and corporate stock is issued. The bylaws are the governing regulations of the corporation and often are the basis for litigation when directors act on behalf of the shareholders of the corporation. The Delaware Supreme Court is considered the most influential of all courts in the nation with regard to corporate governance and the chief arbiter of conflicts between corporations and between shareholders and a single corporation. More than 50 percent of Fortune 100 companies are registered in Delaware. Anyone who merges, sues, or manages a Delaware corporation is subject to Delaware law as interpreted by its courts. More recently there has been significant controversy surrounding the appointment and reappointment of new and state supreme court justices and the politicizing of appointments made by the commission that recommends candidates to the governor.

Two primary foci of state corporate laws are the financing of the corporation and its operation. These two areas are necessarily entwined, but they are separated here for discussion purposes. Laws governing these two areas of corporate activity are primarily state regulations, though most states are guided by

---

[1]*See* J. Dan *LLC's Get Big Boost*, Law. Wkly. USA, January 16, 1995, at 1.
[2]*Id.* at 11.

EXHIBIT 15-3 *Articles of Incorporation of Brennan-Kubasek Corporation*

ARTICLE I

Name

The name of this corporation is Brennan-Kubasek Corporation.

ARTICLE II

Registered Office and Resident Agent

The registered office of the corporation is 15650, Id Rd., Newgarth, Ohio.

The resident agent at that address is M. Neil Browne.

ARTICLE III

Nature of Business

The nature and purpose of the business to be conducted or promoted are:

To engage in any lawful conduct or activity for which corporations may be organized in the State of Ohio.

ARTICLE IV

Capital Stock

This corporation is authorized to issue forty thousand (40,000) shares of common stock without par value.

ARTICLE V

Incorporators

The name and mailing addresses of the incorporators are as follows:

B. A. Brennan—600 Jelly Street, Newgarth, Ohio

N. Kubasek—800 Minor Street, Newgarth, Ohio

ARTICLE VI

Initial directors

The powers of the incorporators are to terminate upon the filing of these Articles of Incorporation, and the name and mailing address of the persons who are to serve as directors until the first annual meeting of stockholders or until their successors are elected and qualified are:

B. A. Brennan—600 Jelly Street, Newgarth, Ohio

N. Kubasek—800 Minor Street, Newgarth, Ohio

ARTICLE VII

Bylaws

The power to adopt, repeal and amend the bylaws of this corporation shall reside in the Board of Directors of this corporation.

IN TESTIMONY WHEREOF, we have hereunto set our names this _____ day of _____.

---

a modified version of the federal Revised Model Business Corporations Act (RMBCA).

FINANCING A CORPORATION *Financing* is the acquiring of funds or capital for the operation or expansion of a corporation. Corporations generally engage in two types of financing: debt and equity. *Debt financing* may be described as the taking out of loans; *equity financing* is accomplished by the sale of ownership interest in the corporation.

Debt Financing. A corporation can issue three primary types of debt instruments: notes, bonds, and debentures. **Notes** are short-term loans. **Bonds**

notes Short-term loans.

bonds Long-term loans secured by a lien or mortgage on corporate assets.

are usually long-term loans secured by a lien or mortgage on corporate assets. **Debentures** are usually unsecured long-term corporate loans.

In all forms of debt financing, corporations incur a liability to the holder of the debt security. Periodic interest payments are generally required. Interest payments on debt securities are tax deductible, whereas dividend payments made to owners under equity financing are not. This difference in the tax treatment of the two types of financing is one reason for the heavy reliance on debt financing by corporations. Even though debt financing offers distinct tax advantages to both the corporation and investors, there is always the risk that a corporation that relies too much on debt financing will be deemed too thinly capitalized by the Internal Revenue Service (IRS), which will then treat any loans made by shareholders as capital contributions.

Equity Financing. All business corporations must raise operating capital through the sale of **stock**, or *equity securities*. Exhibit 15-4 reproduces a stock certificate, which evidences one's ownership of stock. *Shareholders*—persons who purchase shares of stock—generally acquire rights to control the corporation through voting, to receive income through dividends, and, upon dissolution of the corporation, to share in the net assets in direct proportion to the number of shares they own.

The number of shares of stock must be authorized in the corporation's articles of incorporation. All shares authorized by the articles need not be issued or sold to shareholders immediately, but no shares may be issued that are not authorized. Under the Revised Model Business Corporations Act, the articles of incorporation must authorize (1) one or more classes of stock that entitle their owners to unlimited voting rights and (2) one or more classes of stock (these may be the same classes as those with voting rights) that entitle their owners to receive the net assets of the corporation upon dissolution. This provision of the RMBCA ensures that there will be a class of shareholders with the power to elect directors and make other important decisions and a class of shareholders who will share in the residuary (remaining assets) of the corporation on its termination.

Classes of Stock. Most states allow corporations to authorize and issue different classes of stock, with different rights attaching to the different classes. The limitations and preferences of each class must be stated in the articles of incorporation. The two primary classes of stock are common and preferred.

Traditionally, **common stock** has carried with it the right to vote, the right to participate in income through dividends, and the right to participate in the net assets on liquidation. Common stock has no preferential rights (described in the next paragraphs), and therefore common stockholders bear the greatest risk of loss. If a corporation has only one class of stock, it is ordinarily assumed to be common stock.

Preferred stock is given special preferences relating to either the payment of dividends or the distribution of assets. Most preferred stock is preferred as to dividends, meaning that in every year in which the corporation pays a dividend, the preferred shareholders are paid before the common shareholders at a rate stipulated in the articles of incorporation.

If the stock is *cumulative preferred*, the preferred shareholders do not lose their rights to a dividend during a year in which no dividends are paid. Rather, their rights to each year's unpaid dividends accumulate. Thus, during the next year in which dividends are paid, the preferred shareholders receive all past dividends that have accumulated plus the present year's dividend before any dividends are paid to the common shareholders.

If the stock is *participating preferred*, the preferred shareholders first receive their dividends at the preferred rate. The common shareholders receive dividends at the same rate. The remaining income is shared, on a pro rata basis, by the common and preferred stockholders.

If the stock is *liquidation preferred*, upon liquidation of the corporation, preferred shareholders receive either the par value of their stock or a specified monetary amount before the common shareholders share pro rata in the remainder of the assets. Liquidation preferences may also be participating.

debentures Unsecured long-term corporate loans.

stock The capital that a corporation raises through the sale of shares that entitle their holders to certain rights of ownership.

common stock A class of stock that entitles its owner to vote for the corporation's board of directors, to receive dividends, and to participate in the net assets upon liquidation of the corporation.

preferred stock A class of stock that entitles its owner to special preferences relating to either dividends or the distribution of assets.

EXHIBIT 15-4 *Stock Certificate*

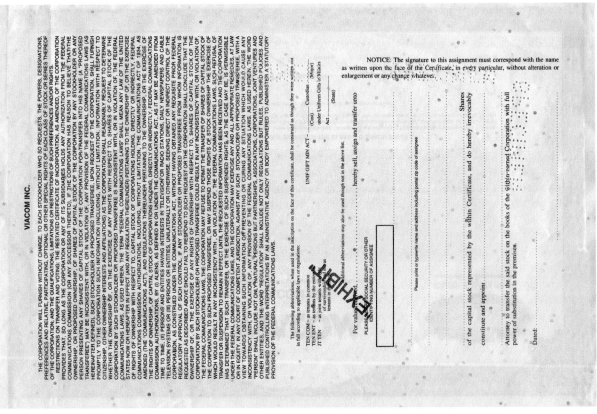

Authorized use by Viacom International Inc.

Finally, preferred stock may be *convertible.* At the holder's request, such stock may be exchanged for common stock at a stated ratio.

Preferred stock frequently has limited voting rights. It is also generally redeemable, meaning that the corporation has the right to exchange each preferred share for a prespecified monetary amount.

All these distinctions may become irrelevant as more states adopt the Revised Model Business Corporations Act. The RMBCA stipulates that the various classes of stock and the number of shares in each class that may be issued must be stated in the articles of incorporation, but it omits references to such classes of stock as "preferred" and "common." If only one class of stock is designated in the articles of incorporation, it is presumed that the shares carry both the right to vote and the right to participate in corporate assets. If more than one class of stock is authorized, either the distinguishing designation and preferences, limitations, and rights of those classes must be listed or the board of directors must be authorized to designate such features at a later date.

This broad flexibility given to the directors to affect the **capital structure** of the corporation may be desirable from management's perspective. However, it does not benefit the shareholders, because it may dilute their interests. It is also contrary to present trends in securities regulations (discussed in chapter 21).

Under the RMBCA, corporations can also issue rights to purchase a stated number of shares at a stated price, usually for a stated period of time. Legal documents, called **stock warrants**, that certify these rights may be freely traded. Employees may receive such rights as compensation in the form of **stock options.** However, when employees are granted the rights to purchase shares at a stated price, these rights cannot be traded.

Consideration. Stocks and warrants are issued in return for consideration—that is, something of value. That consideration cannot be less than the *stated value* of the shares. If a corporation issues shares for less than the stated value, the shareholder remains liable to the corporation for the difference between the stated value and the amount of consideration actually paid.

Traditionally, the minimum amount for which a share could be issued was called the **par value.** In general, this amount was so low (often $1) that the likelihood of a buyer not paying at least that much for the stock was slim. The total par value of all stock initially issued by a corporation was known as *stated capital.* Some states allowed the issuance of *no-par stock,* which is stock that does not have a stated par value, but when a corporation issued no-par stock, the board of directors still had to designate a stated value for the stock. The sum of the stated values was the stated capital of the corporation.

The RMBCA has done away with the terms *par, no par,* and *stated capital.* Now, before issuing any shares, the board of directors must determine that the amount of consideration received or about to be received is adequate. When the corporation receives the consideration for which the board of directors authorized the issuance of the shares, the shares are deemed *fully paid.*

Under the RMBCA and most current state laws, the consideration paid for the stock may be in the form of money, property, or past services. The RMBCA also allows for payment by promissory notes and agreements to provide future services.

In some states, problems can arise over the valuation of a nonmonetary consideration. Most states use the *good faith rule,* which presumes that the valuation of the property or services given as consideration for the stock was fair as long as it was honestly made—in other words, there was no fraud or bad faith on the part of the directors in making their valuation, and they exercised the degree of care that ordinarily prudent persons in their position would exercise.

OPERATION OF THE CORPORATION The question of how the corporation is financed can be answered relatively easily. As the previous section explained, the corporation is financed by debt and equity security holders. The answer to the question of who manages the corporation is not quite so simple. Even legal experts disagree to some extent over who actually manages the corporation, as well as over who *should* manage it.

capital structure The percentage of each type of capital—debt, preferred stock, and common equity—used by the corporation.

stock warrant A document authorizing its holder to purchase a stated number of shares of stock at a stated price, usually for a stated period of time; may be freely traded.

stock option A stock warrant issued to employees; cannot be traded.

par value The nominal or face value of a stock or bond.

Three groups theoretically have a voice in the management of the corporation: the shareholders, the board of directors, and the corporate officers and managers. Formal responsibility for management of the corporation is vested in its board of directors, who are elected by the shareholders. These directors determine policy matters and appoint the officers who carry out those policies and manage the everyday affairs of the corporation. Exhibit 15-5 illustrates the division of responsibility in this corporate hierarchy of shareholders, board of directors, and officers and managers.

The Role of the Shareholders. The shareholders are the owners of the corporation, yet they have no direct control over its operation. They are not agents of the corporation and cannot act on its behalf. Their control of the corporation is limited to exercising their right to vote at shareholders' meetings and, through that voting, to select the board of directors who will set corporate policy.

Most corporations are obliged to hold an annual shareholders' meeting at a time specified in the corporate bylaws. In addition, special shareholders' meetings may be called by the board of directors, the holders of more than 5 percent of the shares entitled to cast a vote at such meetings, or anyone else authorized to do so under the corporate bylaws.

Shareholders vote at the shareholders' meetings either in person or by a **proxy**, which is a written delegation of authority to cast one's votes. Most shareholders vote by proxy, and it is this process of proxy election that has led many people to question whether shareholders really have any say in operating the corporation.

The proxy election is usually run by a proxy committee of corporate executives, who, under the Security and Exchange Commission's Proxy Rules, must use a ballot form to solicit proxies. The form must state that the shares held by the shareholder will be voted in accordance with the way the shareholder marks the ballot. The shareholder has the option to indicate on the ballot that

proxy A document by which a shareholder or a publicly held company can transfer his or her right to vote at a shareholders meeting to a second party.

EXHIBIT 15-5 *The Corporate Hierarchy*

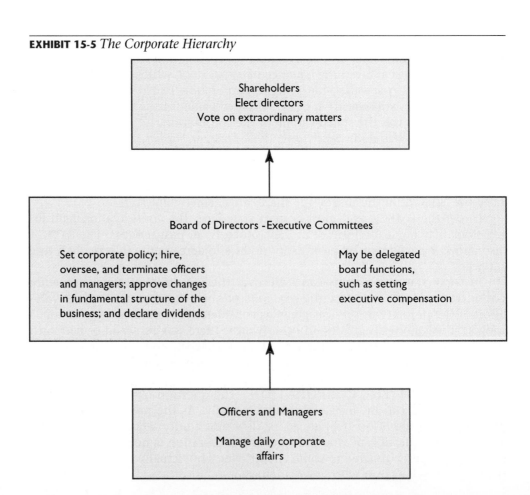

he or she wishes to allow the proxy committee to vote the shares in any way they see fit. The proxy committee also sends all shareholders a statement of resolutions on which the shareholders are to vote, as well as a biographical sketch of each of the candidates for the board of directors.

This process sounds efficient, even benign. However, because shareholders of major corporations are scattered across the country and could not realistically attend a shareholders' meeting, the proxy process gives management effective control over the election. By placing on the ballot only the names of those candidates management wishes to see elected to the board of directors, management, in essence, selects the board. Although a shareholder can write in the name of another candidate, the cost of communicating with other shareholders makes the prospects for a write-in candidate quite slim.

Any shareholder may also engage in proxy solicitation. However, the costs of doing so are almost prohibitive. In a fight between a shareholder and the corporate proxy committee for proxies, the corporate committee has access to corporate funds, corporate office materials such as paper and duplicating machinery, corporate clerical personnel, and also the corporate legal staff. The shareholders have only their personal funds.

In recent years, the proxy forms sent out by proxy committees of major corporations have sometimes contained resolutions submitted by politically active shareholders who understand how the corporate machinery operates. Most of these resolutions have sought to change the corporation's social policies; for example, resolutions seeking to prohibit the corporation from investing in countries that practice apartheid and from withholding information from shareholders regarding the environmental impact of the corporation's activities have been popular in the last decade or so. The public-interest proxy resolution shown in Exhibit 15-6 was proposed by a shareholder of General Motors in the proxy statement for the 1985 annual meeting. Its objective was to force GM to be politically neutral.

When these types of resolutions appear on proxy forms, the management of the corporation usually suggests that shareholders vote against them. Management also generally includes a strong argument against such resolutions on the proxy statement on which the proposal appears. Thus even if a shareholder does get a resolution on the ballot, the chances of its passing are slim, though there are more frequent and more vigorous fights over policy resolutions than over the election of directors.

Recognizing that shareholder voting occurs primarily by proxy, and thus that the shareholders' meeting really serves no purpose but to fulfill the demands of the law, Delaware decided to abolish the requirement that corpora-

---

EXHIBIT 15-6 *Shareholder Resolution*

Resolved: That the stockholders of General Motors, assembled in annual meeting in person and by proxy, hereby recommended that the Corporation affirm the political nonpartisanship of the Corporation. To this end the following practices are to be avoided.

(a) The handing of contribution cards of a single political party to an employee by a supervisor.

(b) Requesting an employee to send a political contribution to an individual in the corporation for subsequent delivery as part of a group of contributions to a political party or fund-raising committee.

(c) Requesting an employee to issue personal checks blank as to payee for subsequent forwarding to a political party, committee, or candidate.

(d) Using supervisory meetings to announce that contribution cards of one party are available and that anyone desiring cards of a different party will be supplied one on request to his supervisor.

(e) Placing a preponderance of contribution cards of one party at mail station locations

tions hold an annual shareholders' meeting. Other states may soon follow Delaware's example.

The Role of the Board of Directors. Most incorporation laws state that the corporation shall be managed by the board of directors. Although such a rule may reflect the behavior of the directors of a closely held corporation who are also its officers, it does not describe the behavior of the directors of publicly held corporations. Nor does it describe the behavior that most people expect from directors of publicly held corporations.

Recognizing that most directors are not going to become involved in corporate affairs, the RMBCA in its statement of the role of the board of directors says merely that the corporation shall be managed "under the direction of" the board. This provision does seem to make it clear, however, that the directors are expected to function at least as overseers and policymakers. In this role, the board of directors generally must authorize or approve (1) the payment of dividends, changes in financing, and other capital changes; (2) the selection, supervision, and removal of officers and other executive personnel; (3) the determination of executive compensation and pension plans; (4) the adoption, amendment, or repeal of the corporate bylaws; and (5) the establishment of policy regarding products, services, and labor relations. Unfortunately, most corporate boards abdicate their policymaking function and merely rubber-stamp decisions already made by the officers and managers of the corporation. Rarely does a board challenge an action taken by its corporate officers.

The board, like the shareholders, must function as a group. Unlike shareholders, however directors are not allowed to vote by proxy. Instead, they are supposed to vote in person at a formal directors' meeting. The rationale for this traditional restriction is that corporations derive benefits from the consultation, discussion, and collective judgment of their boards. Today, however, the laws in most states have been relaxed enough so that board members may act informally, without a meeting, when all the directors consent to such action in writing.

The Role of the Officers and Managers. The officers and managers are responsible for the actual management of corporate affairs. Unlike directors and shareholders, officers are agents of the corporation. Technically, they are appointed and supervised by the board of directors, but, since the officers of the company control the proxy election, it is usually the directors who serve at the pleasure of the corporate officers.

Traditional statutes provided that a corporation must have certain officers, such as a president, a vice president, and a treasurer. The RMBCA, however, makes no such stipulations.

Fiduciary Obligation of Directors, Officers, and Managers. As previously noted, the shareholders do not have any direct control over the corporation's operations. Whenever the property of one party is placed in the control of another, however, a fiduciary relationship exists between the two. Thus certain obligations, called *fiduciary duties*, are placed on property holders to ensure that they will treat the property as carefully as if it were their own. Because the shareholders own the corporation (property) but its care is entrusted to the directors, officers, and managers, a fiduciary relationship exists between the shareholders and the officers, managers, and directors. The standards of conduct—and thus the fiduciary duties—imposed by the RMBCA on officers and directors of corporations are almost identical. Both are required to exercise their duties:

> *(1) in good faith; (2) with the care an ordinarily prudent person in a like position would exercise under similar circumstances; and (3) in a manner he reasonably believes to be in the best interests of the corporation. (Sections 8.30 and 8.42 of the RMBCA)*

corporate opportunity doctrine A doctrine, established by case law, that says corporate officers, directors, and agents cannot take personal advantage of an opportunity that in all fairness should have belonged to the corporation.

There is a potential breach of this duty to act in the best interests of the corporation when a corporate officer or director takes personal advantage of an opportunity that, in all fairness, should have belonged to the corporation. The following case illustrates this **corporate opportunity doctrine**.

IRVING TRUST COMPANY V. DEUTSCH
UNITED STATES COURT OF APPEALS 73 F.2D 121 (2D CIR. 1934)

The plaintiff, Irving Trust, was the trustee in bankruptcy proceedings for Sonora Products Corporation of America (formerly Acoustic Products Company). The defendants were directors of Acoustic Products. Before it went bankrupt, Acoustic had tried to secure certain patent rights held by De Forest Radio Company. An agent of Acoustic, named Bell, made an offer on the company's behalf for a third of the stock in De Forest, which would have increased Acoustic's chances of getting the patent rights. Acoustic's president, Deutsch, was authorized to obtain financing for the stock purchase but was unable to do so. He and two other directors and Bell then purchased the stock themselves and later sold it for a substantial profit. When Irving Trust sought to hold the defendants liable to the corporation for the amount of the profits, the district court dismissed the trustee's petition for relief. Irving Trust appealed.

JUSTICE SWAN

The theory of the suit is that a fiduciary may make no profit for himself out of a violation of duty to his cestui [the beneficiary or person for whom the trust was established] even though he risks his own funds in the venture, and that anyone who assists in the fiduciary's dereliction is likewise liable to account for the profit so made. Concretely, the argument is that members of the Biddle syndicate, three of whom, Messrs. Biddle, Deutsch, and Hammond, were directors and one, Mr. Bell, its agent in procuring the contract, appropriated to themselves Acoustic's rights under its contract with Reynolds & Co., for 200,000 shares of De Forest stock, when as fiduciaries they were obligated to preserve those rights for Acoustic and were forbidden to take a position where personal interest would conflict with the interest of their principal. The other defendants are claimed to have assisted in their dereliction. In answer to this argument, the defendants do not deny the principle, but dispute its applicability to the facts.

The main defense asserted is that Acoustic by reason of its financial straits had neither the funds nor the credit to make the purchase and that the directors honestly believed that by buying the stock for themselves they could give Acoustic the advantage of access to the De Forest patents, while at the same time taking a stock speculation for their own benefit. In support of the proposition that the prohibition against corporate officers acting on their own behalf is removed if the corporation is itself financially unable to enter into the transaction, the appellees cite *Hannerty v. Standard Theater*

Co., 109 Mo. 297, 19 S.W. 82. While these facts raise some question whether Acoustic actually lacked the funds or credit necessary for carrying out its contract, we do not feel justified in reversing the District Court's finding that it did. Nevertheless, they tend to show the wisdom of a rigid rule forbidding directors of a solvent corporation to take over for their own profit a corporate contract on the plea of the corporation's financial inability to perform. If the directors are uncertain whether the corporation can make the necessary outlays, they need not embark upon the venture; if they do, they may not substitute themselves for the corporation any place along the line and divert possible benefits into their own pockets. "Uncompromising rigidity has been the attitude of courts of equity when petitioned to undermine the rule of undivided loyalty by the 'disintegrating erosion' of particular exceptions."

The defendant Bell was Acoustic's agent in the original negotiations with Reynolds, and it is urged by the plaintiff that as such agent he was a fiduciary precluded from making profits out of the subject-matter of his agency. On his behalf it is contended that his agency was ended when he delivered to Acoustic the written offer of Reynolds & Co. and that his participation in the Biddle syndicate was not by virtue of his former agency relationship nor because of any information he had obtained as Acoustic's agent; that he stands like any stranger to whom the syndicate might have offered a participation. But, even if the fact of his agency be disregarded, we think there is an applicable principle which requires him to account, namely, that one who knowingly joins a fiduciary in an enterprise where the personal interest of the latter is or may be antagonistic to his trust becomes jointly and severally liable with him for the profits of the enterprise. Although Bell testified that "My knowledge of what Acoustic did or intended to do with respect to Reynolds' offer of March 31st was limited to what Deutsch told me around the 9th of April," and although precisely what he was told does not appear, nevertheless Bell says that on April 7th or 9th he agreed with Mr. Deutsch that, if the latter was not successful in raising the purchase money for the stock from his own associates, he would join him to the extent of $25,000. This agreement, made at a time when the offer was still open for acceptance by the corporation, brings Bell within the principle above enunciated.

Reversed as against Bell, Biddle, Deutsch, and Hammond.
Affirmed as to the other defendants.

Critical Thinking about the Law

THIS CASE FOLLOWS A LONG LINE of precedents in which corporations have been protected from any disloyalty on the part of their agents. Presumably, there is a significant temptation to reap personal gain from what one has learned as an agent of a corporation—personal gain that replaces what could have been the corporation's gain. The fiduciary relationship between a director and the corporation forbids reaping personal gain in such a manner. The logic of the courts is that, without this case law to restrain them, agents of a corporation would often act in their own immediate self-interest rather than in the interest of the corporation that is employing them.

There is a primary ethical norm implicit in this law, termed the *corporate opportunity doctrine*. There are certain circumstances in which this doctrine is and is not applicable to the case at hand. Both the norm and the circumstances under which it is applicable are explored in the questions that follow.

1. In delivering the opinion of the court, Justice Swan identified the wisdom of a "rigid rule" that prevents directors from taking personal profit that could have been the corporation's. To the extent that this "rigid rule" is both enduring and unchanging, what primary ethical norm is implicit in its application?

   CLUE The rule's primary function is the preservation of the corporation's interest. You want to answer this question by considering what primary ethical norm would be violated or weakened if such a rule did not exist.

2. What key fact implicates Bell, the former agent of the corporation, in the violation of the law?

   CLUE Reread the end of the court's opinion and identify the fact that, had it been slightly different, might have exempted Bell from the unfavorable judgment. Keep in mind that it was the corporate *opportunity* doctrine that Bell violated.

Although a *corporate opportunity* must be offered to the corporation, it will not necessarily be accepted by the corporation. Once an opportunity is rejected by a vote of the disinterested members of the board of directors, that opportunity no longer belongs to the corporation.

When the corporation cannot take advantage of an opportunity because of financial constraints, a director or officer must do his or her best to secure financing of the opportunity by the corporation, although neither need go so far as to lend the corporation money. In general, taking personal advantage of the opportunity when financing is clearly unavailable is allowed. However, as *Irving Trust v. Deutsch* demonstrates, some courts have strictly applied the duty of undivided loyalty and held that such action usurps a corporate opportunity.

Another potentially troublesome situation occurs when an officer or a director, or a corporation in which the officer or director has an interest, enters into a transaction with the corporation. This problem, known as a **conflict of interest**, is specifically addressed by the RMBCA. The act provides that a transaction will not be voided because of a conflict of interest when any one of the following is true: (1) The material facts of the transaction and the director's interest were disclosed or known to the board of directors or a committee thereof, and they authorized, approved, or ratified the transaction; (2) the material facts of the transaction and the director's interest were known or disclosed to the shareholders entitled to vote, and they approved, authorized, or ratified the transaction; or (3) the transaction was fair to the corporation. Use of the broad language, "the transaction was fair," seems to give the utmost flexibility to directors. In many states that have not adopted the RMBCA, directors can protect themselves from conflict-of-interest charges through full disclosure and ratification by the board of directors.

conflict of interest A conflict that occurs when a corporate officer or director enters into a transaction with the corporation in which he or she has a personal interest.

We have said that officers and directors are required to exercise their duties in a manner they reasonably believe to be in the best interests of the corporation. Under the **business judgment rule**, the courts generally avoid second-guessing corporate executives and let stand any business decisions made in good faith that are uninfluenced by personal considerations.

In determining whether a *director's* conduct fulfills the duty of care, the courts are aided by RMBCA, which states that a director is entitled to rely on information and reports provided or prepared by (1) officers or employees of the corporation whom the director reasonably believes are reliable and competent, (2) legal counsel or accountants in regard to matters that the director believes are within that professional's competence, or (3) a committee of directors of which the director is not a part, if he or she reasonably believes they merit confidence. The use courts make of the business judgment rule is illustrated by the following case.

business judgment rule A rule that says corporate officers and directors are not liable for honest mistakes of business judgment.

SMITH V. VAN GORKOM
DELAWARE SUPREME COURT 488 A.2D 858 (1985)

In order to take advantage of a favorable tax situation, defendant Van Gorkom, chief executive of Trans Union Corporation ("Trans Union" or "the Company"), solicited a merger offer from Pritzker, an outside investor. Van Gorkom acted on his own and arbitrarily arrived at a buyout price of $55 per share. Without any investigation, the full Trans Union board accepted the offer informally. The offer was proposed two more times before its formal acceptance by the board. Plaintiff Smith and other shareholders brought suit, claiming that the board had failed to give due consideration to the offer. The trial court held that the shareholder vote approving the merger should not be set aside because the stockholders had been "fairly informed" by the board of directors before they voted on it.

It also found that, because the board had considered the offer three times before formally accepting it, it had acted in an informed manner and was therefore entitled to the protection of the business judgment rule. Plaintiffs appealed.

JUSTICE HORSEY

On Friday, September 19, Van Gorkom called a special meeting of the Trans Union Board for noon the following day. . . .

Van Gorkom began the Special Meeting of the Board with a twenty-minute oral presentation. Copies of the proposed Merger Agreement were delivered too late for study before or during the meeting. He reviewed the Company's ITC and depreciation problems and the efforts theretofore made to solve them. He discussed his initial meeting with Pritzker and his motivation in arranging that meeting. Van Gorkom did not disclose to the Board, however, the methodology by which he alone had arrived at the $55 figure, or the fact that he first proposed the $55 price in his negotiations with Pritzker.

Van Gorkom outlines the terms of the Pritzker offer as follows: Pritzker would pay $55 in cash for all outstanding shares of Trans Union stock upon completion of which Trans Union would be merged into New T Company, a subsidiary wholly-owned by Pritzker and formed to implement the merger; for a period of 90 days, Trans Union could receive, but could not actively solicit, competing offers; the offer had to be acted on by the next evening, Sunday, September 21; Trans Union could only furnish to competing bidders published information, and not proprietary information; the offer was subject to Pritzker obtaining the necessary financing by October 10, 1980; if the financing contingency were met or waived by Pritzker, Trans Union was required to sell to Pritzker one million newly-issued shares of Trans Union at $38 per share.

The Board meeting of September 20 lasted about two hours. . . . The directors approved the proposed Merger Agreement. . . .

On February 10, the stockholders of Trans Union approved the Pritzker merger proposal. Of the outstanding shares, 69.9% were voted in favor of the merger, 7.25% were voted against the merger; and 22.85% were not voted.

The determination of whether a business judgment is an informed one turns on whether the directors have informed themselves "prior to making a business decision of all material information reasonably available to them."

In the specific context of a proposed merger of domestic corporations, a director has a duty under 8 Del. C. 251(b), along with his fellow directors, to act in an informed and deliberate manner in determining whether to approve an agreement of merger before submitting the proposal to the stockholders. Certainly in the merger context, a director may not abdicate that duty by leaving to the shareholders alone the decision to approve or disapprove the agreement.

On the record before us, we must conclude that the Board of Directors did not reach an informed business judgment on September 20, 1980 in voting to "sell" the Company for $55 per share pursuant to the Pritzker cash-out merger proposal. Our reasons, in summary, are as follows:

The directors (1) did not adequately inform themselves as to Van Gorkom's role in forcing the "sale" of the Company and in establishing the per share purchase price; (2) were uninformed as to the intrinsic value of the Company; and (3) given these circumstances, at a minimum, were grossly negligent in approving the "sale" of the Company upon two hours' consideration, without prior notice, and without the exigency of a crisis or emergency.

Without any documents before them concerning the proposed transaction, the members of the Board were required to rely entirely upon Van Gorkom's 20-minute oral presentation of the proposal. No written summary of the terms of the merger was presented; the directors were given no documentation to support the adequacy of $55 price per share for sale of the Company; and the Board had before it nothing more than Van Gorkom's statement of his understanding of the substance of an agreement which he admittedly had never read, nor which any member of the Board had ever seen.

There was no call by the Board, either on September 20 or thereafter, for any valuation study or documentation of the $55 price per share as a measure of the fair value of the Company in a cash-out context. It is undisputed that the major asset of Trans Union was its cash flow. Yet, at no time did the Board call for a valuation study taking into account that highly significant element of the Company's assets.

The record also establishes that the Board accepted without scrutiny Van Gorkom's representation as to the fairness of the $55 price per share for sale of the Company—a subject that the Board had never previously considered. The Board thereby failed to discover that Van Gorkom had suggested the $55 price to Pritzker and, most crucially, that Van Gorkom had arrived at the $55 figure based on calculations designed solely to determine the feasibility of a leveraged buy-out. No questions were raised either as to the tax implications of a cash-out merger or how the price for the one million share option granted Pritzker was calculated.

We do not say that the Board of Directors was not entitled to give some credence to Van Gorkom's representation that $55 was an adequate or fair price.... The issue is whether the directors informed themselves as to all information that was reasonably available to them. Had they done so, they would have learned of the source and derivation of the $55 price and could not reasonably have relied thereupon in good faith.

The defendants ultimately rely on the stockholder vote of February 10 for exoneration. The defendants contend that the stockholders' "overwhelming" vote approving the Pritzker Merger Agreement had the legal effect of curing any failure of the Board to reach an informed business judgment in its approval of the merger.

The burden must fall on defendants who claim ratification based on shareholder vote to establish that the shareholder approval resulted from a fully informed electorate. On the record before us, it is clear that the Board failed to meet that burden.

To summarize: we hold that the directors of Trans Union breached their fiduciary duty to their stockholders (1) by their failure to inform themselves of all information reasonably available to them and relevant to their decision to recommend the Pritzker merger; and (2) by their failure to disclose all material information such as a reasonable stockholder would consider important in deciding whether to approve the Pritzker offer.

We hold, therefore, that the Trial Court committed reversible error in applying the business judgment rule in favor of the director defendants in this case.

Reversed in favor of Plaintiff, Smith.

Critical Thinking about the Law

THE STANDARDS WE USE TO MAKE judgments are often ambiguous. For example, in judging someone's character we might consider whether that person is fair, honest, and reasonable. To the extent that standards such as "fair" and "honest" and "reasonable" do not have universal meanings, they are ambiguous.

As you are well aware by this time, courts are not exempt from this tendency to use ambiguous standards in judging. The facts of a case are important in determining how ambiguous standards will be applied.

An important critical thinking skill is the ability to recognize ambiguous language in a court's opinion, for without this recognition, you are not prepared to make an informed decision about whether the court's application of standards was merited by the facts of the case. The questions that follow are intended to help you improve this critical thinking skill.

1. To demonstrate your ability to recognize ambiguous language, identify at least two examples of such language in the court's opinion.

CLUE Remember that adjectives are often ambiguous.

2. The court applies this ambiguous language in a manner unfavorable to the defendant. What reasons does the court provide for doing so?

CLUE If the defendant had met the standards by which he was being judged, the decision would have been favorable to him. Another way of phrasing this question is: Why didn't the court find that he met these standards?

COMMENT: In *Cinerama Inc. v. Technicolor Inc.*, 663 A.2d 1156 (1995) the Supreme Court of Delaware distinguished the *Van Gorkom* case and held that the defendant (Technicolor) board of directors did not violate their duty of loyalty when as *interested* directors they participated in a unanimous vote to repeal the company's supermajority provisions. The court stated that an "entire fairness analysis is required" when considering how a board of directors discharges its fiduciary duties. The Delaware Supreme Court affirmed the chancery court's decision in favor of the defendants despite the fact that the *interested* directors had played a major part in negotiating the merger of their company without disclosing their material conflicts of interest to shareholders such as the plaintiff, Cinerama.

FACTORS INFLUENCING A BUSINESS MANAGER'S CHOICE OF ORGANIZATIONAL FORM

There is no ideal form for a business venture. Each of the forms we discussed in the first section of this chapter has advantages and disadvantages. The entrepreneur, with the counsel of an attorney and an accountant or tax expert, should carefully weigh the advantages and disadvantages of different organizational forms for the type of business the entrepreneur wishes to open. The principal factors influencing the choice of organizational form are (1) tax ramifications, (2) control considerations, (3) potential liability of the owners, (4) ease and expense of formation and operation, (5) transferability of ownership interests, and (6) the projected life of the organization. Table 15-2 gives an overview of how these six factors differ for each organizational form.

SPECIALIZED FORMS OF BUSINESS ASSOCIATIONS

In addition to the three major forms of business association emphasized in this chapter, there are several specialized forms of doing business. These forms, summarized in Table 15-3, have become increasingly significant for raising capital, producing goods and services, and marketing them—in many cases, across national borders. You will note in our discussion of these specialized forms that they arise out of private contractual relationships and often are not regulated by state or federal governments.

COOPERATIVE

A **cooperative** is a not-for-profit organization formed by individuals to market products. For example, farmers often agree to pool their crops in order to sell them in larger quantities so they can get the best price from distributors. Any profits made by the cooperative are shared by members. The dividends of a cooperative are paid to members in direct proportion to the amount of business they conduct with the organization yearly.

cooperative A not-for-profit organization formed by individuals to market products.

JOINT STOCK COMPANY

A **joint stock company** is a partnership agreement in which members agree to stock ownership in exchange for partnership liability. Although members own shares that are transferable (as in a corporation), the joint

joint stock company A partnership agreement in which members of the company own shares that are transferable, but all goods are held in the name of the members, who assume partnership liability.

TABLE 15-2 *Comparison of Alternative Forms of Business Organization*

ORGANIZATIONAL FORM	TAX RAMIFICATIONS	CONTROL CONSIDERATIONS
Sole proprietorship	Profits taxed directly to proprietor as ordinary income and losses deducted by proprietor	Sole proprietor has total control.
General partnership	A federal income tax return must be filed for information only. Profits taxed to partners as ordinary income, and losses deducted by partners. Profits and losses shared equally unless changed by partnership agreement.	Each partner is entitled to equal control. Can be changed by partnership agreement.
Limited partnership (Limited liability partnership)	Same as general partnership.	Same as for general partners. Limited partners cannot take part in management.
Public corporation	Profits taxed as income to corporation and . again as income to owners when distributed as dividends.	Separation of ownership and . control. No control over daily management decisions.
Subchapter S corporation	Taxed as a partnership.	Separation of ownership and control. No control over daily management decisions.
Limited liability corporation	Taxed as a partnership.	Control over daily management decisions.

LIABILITY	EASE AND EXPENSE OF FORMATION	TRANSFERABILITY OF OWNERSHIP INTERESTS	LIFETIME
Sole proprietor has unlimited personal liability.	No formalities or expenses required other than those specific to the business to be operated.	Nontransferable.	Limited to life of proprietor.
Each partner has unlimited personal liability for debts of the partnership.	No formalities or expenses required other than those specific to the business to be operated. Written agreement advisable.	Nontransferable.	Limited to life of partners.
Same as for general partners. Liability of limited partner is limited to his or her capital contribution.	Added expense and time required to draw up and file written partnership agreement. Failure to comply with formalities will result in loss of limited partnership.	Nontransferable.	Limited to life of general partners.
Liability limited to loss of capital contribution.	Expense and time required to comply with statutory formality. Must receive charter from state; usually required to register and pay fees to operate in states other than state of incorporation.	Generally unlimited, except by shareholder agreements.	Unlimited.
Liability limited to loss of capital contribution.	Same as for public corporation; must follow IRS rules carefully or lose Subchapter S status.	Ownership interests limited to no more than 35 shareholders; all must be individuals, estates, or certain types of trusts, and no shareholder may be a nonresident alien. Shares may not be issued or transferred to more than 35 shareholders.	Unlimited.
Liability limited to loss of capital contribution. carefully or lose limited liability status.	Same as for public corporation; must follow IRS rules	No limitation on number of shareholders.	Unlimited.

TABLE 15-3 *Specialized Forms of Business Association*

FORM	DESCRIPTION
Cooperative	A not-for-profit business created by individuals to market products.
Joint stock company	A partnership agreement in which individuals agree to take stock ownership while retaining partnership liability.
Syndicate	An investment group created primarily for the purpose of financing a purchase, usually a single transaction.
Joint venture	A partnership, individual, or corporation that pools labor and capital for a limited period of time.
Franchising	A method of marketing goods through a private agreement whereby the franchisor allows use of its trade name, trademark, or copyright in exchange for a percentage of the gross profits made by the franchisee.

stock company is treated as a partnership because all goods are held in the name of the partners, who are held personally liable when sued successfully by a third party.

SYNDICATE

syndicate An investment group that privately agrees to come together for the purpose of financing a large commercial project that none of the syndicate members could finance alone.

A **syndicate** is an investment group that makes a private agreement to come together for the purpose of financing a large commercial project (e.g., a hotel or a sports team) that the individual members (partnerships or corporations) could not finance alone. The advantage of a syndicate is that it can raise large amounts of capital quickly. The disadvantage is if the project fails, the syndicate members may be held liable for a breach of the agreement by a third party.

JOINT VENTURE

joint venture Relationship between two or more persons or corporations; or an association between a foreign multinational and an agency of the host government or a host country national; set up for a specific business undertaking or a limited time period.

When individuals, partnerships, or corporations make a private agreement to finance, produce, and sell goods, securities, or commodities for a limited purpose and/or a limited time, they have formed a **joint venture**. Joint ventures are a popular way for developing nations (e.g., China) to attract foreign capital. Typically, two companies (say, Chrysler and Bank of America) join with foreign companies (say, Chinese State Auto Companies) to finance, produce, and market goods. In the United States, General Motors and Toyota Corporation entered into a joint venture to produce the highly successful Saturn line of cars.

FRANCHISING

franchising A commercial agreement between a party that owns a trade name or trademark (the franchisor) and a party that sells or distributes goods or services using that trade name or trademark (the franchisee).

A **franchising** relationship is based on a private commercial agreement between the franchisor, who owns a trade name or trademark, and the franchisee, who sells or distributes goods using the trade name or trademark. It is a method of marketing goods or services.

The franchisee usually pays a percentage of the gross sales to the franchisor in exchange for use of the trademark name, construction of the building, and numerous other services. Usually the franchisee is a local entrepreneur whom the franchisor supplies with goods to be sold under conditions set out under the agreement. Failure to meet such conditions (e.g., not keeping a fast-food restaurant clean) may lead to termination of the franchise agreement. The following case revolves around the need to balance both parties' interests when terminating a franchise.

BECK OIL COMPANY ET AL. V. TEXACO REFINING & MARKETING COMPANY, INC.

UNITED STATES DISTRICT COURT 822 F. SUPP. 1326 (1993)

Franchisees (plaintiffs) sued franchisor TRMI (defendant) for terminating their franchise agreement. TRMI was a subsidiary of Texaco, Inc., which refined and marketed motor fuels. It was formed by Texaco after Texaco acquired Getty Oil Company. When TRMI withdrew from the area of Illinois where the plaintiffs (franchisees) were located, it terminated the franchise agreement. Both parties moved for summary judgment.

JUDGE MILLS

Defendant states that the decision to terminate was based on three factors: (1) the closing of Defendant's Lawrenceville, Illinois, refinery; (2) the inability of Defendant to economically supply the withdrawal area; and (3) the unreasonable and uneconomical Getty supply system in the withdrawal area. The Lawrenceville refinery was technologically outdated and by late 1984, the cost of finished gasoline produced there resulted in a $2.00 per barrel loss for each barrel of oil refined. In addition, Defendant did not have another refinery in the location with an efficient means of transporting Defendant's products to the withdrawal area.

The Petroleum Marketing Practices Act (PMPA) governs the termination of motor fuel product franchises. Under the PMPA, the following are grounds for termination of any franchise: a determination made by the franchisor in good faith and in the normal course of business to withdraw from the marketing of motor fuel through retail outlets in the relevant geographic market area in which the marketing premises are located, if (i) such determination (I) was made after the date such franchise was entered into or renewed, and (II) was based upon the occurrence of changes in relevant facts and circumstances after such date; (ii) the termination or nonrenewal is not for the purpose of converting the premises, which are the subject of the franchise, to operation by employees or agents of the franchisor for such franchisor's own account.

In this case, after the Getty acquisition, Texaco reorganized and reevaluated its operations to determine their efficiency and profitability. The affidavits submitted by TRMI demonstrate concerns about uneconomical distribution methods in the area served by the Lawrenceville refinery. Accordingly, the Court must conclude that TRMI's decision to withdraw was made in good faith and was part of the normal decision making process once TRMI began examining its operations after the Getty acquisition.

Summary judgment in favor of Defendant, TRMI.

INTERNATIONAL DIMENSIONS OF BUSINESS ASSOCIATIONS

It is inevitable that the worldwide trend to market-oriented economies will raise the demand for the investment capital and manufactured goods and services of the industrialized world. This certainty, together with the forging of international and regional agreements to lower or eliminate tariffs and other barriers to trade in recent years (see chapter 3), is spurring many corporations, partnerships, and proprietorships that were once strictly domestic businesses to become transnational, multinational, or international buyers and sellers of goods and services.

In deciding whether to take the plunge into international waters, managers of small, mid-size, and large businesses need to ask the following questions:

- Is there a demand for the product in the targeted country or countries?
- Are there legal obstacles in the targeted country that need to be carefully considered?
- Is managing an international business at a distance a realistic possibility for the firm?
- Will management be able to deal successfully with currency fluctuations?
- Is the risk of political interference by the target country's government too great to make doing business in that country worthwhile?
- Is there a serious risk of nonperformance, nonpayment, or loss of property or freight in the country or region the firm is considering entering?

If the responses to those questions indicate that the firm should go ahead, managers need to determine the optimal level of international involvement by answering these questions:

- Should the firm *directly export* to another firm in the target country, or should it hire an export trading company to market its products?

- Should the firm license the use of its products under an international *licensing agreement*? For example, international franchising is a form of licensing in which franchisees in the targeted countries are allowed to use the franchisor's name in exchange for a percentage of the gross profits. This specialized business form is the preferred way to go international among fast-food retailers such as McDonald's, Wendy's, and Pizza Hut. If the firm holds a patent, trademark, or copyright on its product, however, it must always be concerned about possible efforts by businesses or individuals in the target country to circumvent multilateral and bilateral international agreements.

- Should the firm go international by *joint ventures, mergers*, or *acquisitions*? These alternatives, which involve investment of large sums of capital, seem most appropriate for large multinational companies.

In summary, managers must carefully weigh the risks and rewards before committing the business to an international market.

SUMMARY

The sole proprietorship, the partnership, and the corporation are the three major forms of business organization in the United States.

Factors influencing the choice of one of these three types of business associations include tax ramifications, control considerations, liability of owners, and, less significantly, ease and expense of ownership, transferability of properties, and the projected life of the business. The sole proprietorship allows the owner to have total control of management, assets, and profits; the owner also has unlimited personal liability. General partners usually exercise equal control over management and profits; they, too, incur unlimited personal liability. Limited partners forgo management control in return for limited liability. In both sole proprietorships and partnerships, profits are taxed as personal income to the owners. All corporations offer limited liability to owners. Owners of private corporations often exercise managerial control. In Subchapter S and limited liability corporations, profits are taxed as in a partnership. Owners (shareholders) of public corporations exert no managerial control; profits of these corporations are subject to double taxation.

Specialized forms of business associations are the cooperative, the joint stock company, the syndicate, the joint venture, and franchising.

Business organizations should ask some basic questions before they enter global markets. Once they have decided to go ahead, they need to decide the optimal level of involvement and marketing methods.

REVIEW QUESTIONS

15-1. Identify the primary differences between a limited partnership and a general partnership.

15-2. Describe the various types of corporations discussed in this chapter.

15-3. Identify the factors that an entrepreneur should consider in selecting an organizational form for a business.

15-4. Describe the circumstances under which a partnership would offer greater tax advantages than a corporation.

15-5. Explain why is it somewhat misleading to assert that the corporate form provides limited liability for its owners, whereas the partnership form saddles its owners with unlimited liability.

15-6. What is the difference between a joint venture and a cooperative?

REVIEW PROBLEMS

15-7. A truck owned by Thoni Trucking Company was involved in an accident that caused severe injuries to the Fosters (plaintiffs). After learning of the accident, the owner (defendant) of all but two shares of the stock in

Thoni Trucking and the rest of the board of directors, which consisted of the majority owner's wife and his father, transferred substantial corporate assets to themselves as salary and dividends. The remaining assets and business operations were transferred to another company that the defendant owned. In the midst of these activities, the defendant kept sending misleading information to the plaintiffs, first telling them to seek recovery from the defendant corporation, then advising them that the corporation had no assets. Would the defendant's actions allow him to reduce his liability?

15-8. Jumping Jills, Inc., was a corporation that provided trampolines for the use of the public. Defendant Jones owned 80 percent of the stock of Jumping Jills, Inc.; his wife owned 10 percent; and his stepson owned the remaining 10 percent. Jones also owned a drive-in theater located next to the trampoline business. The finances of the two businesses were kept completely separate; the family finances were kept separate from both businesses. The public had no notice that the ownership of the two businesses was similar. Jumping Jills employed two persons. It had been in business for only three months when young Banks was injured on one of its trampolines. Jumping Jill's insurance company went bankrupt, and thus could not compensate Banks for his injuries. The corporation itself had no assets, so Banks sought to recover from the major shareholder, Jones. Would Banks be successful?

15-9. Alder, Svingos, and Shaw owned an equal number of shares in a corporation that was organized to run a restaurant. They entered into a shareholders' agreement that provided, among other things, that all corporate changes, including changes in the corporate structure, would have to be approved by a unanimous vote of the shareholders. When Alder and Shaw tried to sell the business, Svingos alleged that this sale would violate the shareholders' agreement. Shaw and Alder argued that the pertinent provision was void because it should have been contained in the articles of incorporation not in the shareholders' agreement. Was the shareholders' agreement enforceable in this case?

15-10. Dunn and Welch both appeared to operate Ruidoso Downs Feed Concession. Dunn sought to obtain credit for Ruidoso Downs from Anderson Hay and Grain Co. Relying on Dunn's financial position, Anderson extended the credit. Dunn was the person who was responsible for making sure that the payments were made. When Ruidoso Downs could not pay Anderson, Anderson brought an action against Dunn, alleging that, as a partner, Dunn was personally liable for the debts the partnership could not repay. Dunn defended on the grounds that he was not a partner because there was no formal partnership agreement between him and Welch. Was Dunn liable?

15-11. Kline was both president and one of two directors of Fayes, Inc. The business, the ladies' ready-to-wear department of a department store, was supervised by a general manager and operated under a five-year written lease. In March, the renewal lease was sent to Kline, as president. He held the lease for eight months and then had it redrawn as a personal lease in his name. The new lease became effective July 1, but the corporation continued to operate until July 31, when Kline seized all of the assets, including the inventory and fixtures. Did the corporation have any legal recourse?

15-12. Hugo and Charles were brothers who did business as partners for several years. When Hugo died, Charles was appointed administrator of his estate. Tax returns disclosed that the partnership business continued to operate just as it had before Hugo's death and that Hugo's estate received the profits and was charged with the losses of the business. Did Charles have the authority to continue the partnership business after the dissolution of the partnership brought about by Hugo's death, and are the assets of Hugo's estate chargeable with the liabilities of the partnership incurred after Hugo's death?

CASE PROBLEMS

15-13. Gilbert, the owner of record of 17 shares of Transamerica Corporation, wrote the management of the company and submitted four proposals that he wanted to be presented for action by shareholders at the next annual stockholders' meeting. The Securities and Exchange Commission (SEC) demanded that Transamerica comply with Gilbert's request, but the company refused. The SEC brought an action to forbid Transamerica from making use of any proxy solicited by it for use at the annual meeting, from making use of the mails or any instrumentality of interstate commerce to solicit proxies, or from making use of any soliciting material without complying with the SEC's demands. Transamerica claimed that the shareholder may interest himself only in a subject in respect to which he is entitled to vote at a stockholders' meeting when every requirement of state law and of the provisions of the charter and bylaws has been fulfilled. State law states that a certificate of incorporation may set forth provisions that limit, regulate, and define the powers and functions of the directors and stockholders.

A bylaw of Transamerica vested in the board of directors the power to decide whether any proposal should be voted on at an annual meeting of stockholders. Three of Gilbert's proposals were: (1) to have independent public auditors of the books of Transamerica elected by the stockholders, (2) to eliminate from a bylaw the requirement that notice of any proposed alteration or amendment of the bylaws be contained in the notice of meetings, (3) to require an account or a report of the proceedings at the annual meetings to be sent to all stockholders. Is Gilbert entitled to make such demands? What are the reasons for and against the proposals made by Gilbert? Will the power of shareholders go to an extreme if small shareholders like Gilbert can exert so much pressure? *Securities and Exchange Comm'n v. Transamerica Corp.*, 163 F.2d 511 (3d Cir. 1947), *cert. denied*, 332 U.S. 847 (1948)

15-14. Emerson Electric Company acquired 13.2 percent of the outstanding common stock of Dodge Manufacturing Company through a tender offer made in an unsuccessful attempt to take over Dodge. Shortly thereafter, the shareholders of Dodge approved a merger with Reliance Electric Company. Emerson decided to dispose of enough of its shares to bring its holdings below 10 percent in order to immunize the disposal of the remainder of its shares from liability under Section 16(b) of the Securities Exchange Act of 1934. Section 16(b) provides that a corporation may recover for itself the profits realized by an owner of more than 10 percent of its shares from a purchase and sale of its stock within any six-month period, provided the owner held more than 10 percent at the time of both purchase and sale. Emerson sold some shares of Dodge, reducing its holdings in Dodge to 9.96 percent of the outstanding shares. Several weeks later, Emerson sold the remainder of the Dodge shares to Dodge. Reliance demanded the profits realized on both sales, since the purchase and two sales all occurred within a three-month period. Emerson does not dispute the fact that the profits from the first sale should now be turned over. It contends that after the first sale it no longer held more than 10 percent and should not be treated as an "insider" but like any other investor, and consequently, should be able to keep its profit. Who should prevail? If Emerson should lose, is there any time it can keep its profit, or will it always be penalized since it once held more than 10 percent of Dodge's stock? *Reliance Electric Co. v. Emerson Electric Co.*, 404 U.S. 418 (1972)

15-15. Pillsbury had long opposed the Vietnam War. He learned that Honeywell, Inc. had a substantial part of its business in the production of munitions used in the war and also that Honeywell had a large government contract to produce antipersonnel fragmentation bombs. Pillsbury was determined to stop this production. He bought one share of Honeywell in his name in order to get himself a voice in Honeywell's affairs so he could persuade the company to cease producing munitions. Pillsbury submitted demands to Honeywell requesting that it produce its original shareholder ledger, current shareholder ledger, and all corporate records dealing with weapons and munitions manufacture. Honeywell refused. Pillsbury brought suit to compel Honeywell to let him inspect the requested records. Pillsbury claimed that he wished to inspect the records in order to correspond with other shareholders with the hope of electing to the board one or more directors who represented his particular viewpoint. Should the court let Pillsbury inspect the records? Does Pillsbury have a proper purpose germane to his interest as a shareholder? Should a shareholder be allowed to persuade a company to adopt his social and political views? *State ex rel. Pillsbury v. Honeywell, Inc.*, 291 Minn. 322, 191 N.W.2d 406 (1971)

15-16. Cole Real Estate Corporation was a closely held corporation that owned, managed, and rented residential apartment properties. Mrs. Helen Cole was the majority stockholder, owning all but 86 of the 4,120 outstanding shares of common stock. Peoples Bank & Trust Company of Indianapolis held the remaining 86 shares in a trustee capacity. Mrs. Cole had been a director, the president, and treasurer of the corporation since its organization in 1935. Cole corporation was a "one-woman corporation," and little evidence of corporate identity was maintained.

The most recent board of directors meeting was held in 1954, when the corporation was reorganized. At that meeting, the last stock dividend was declared on previously outstanding preferred shares. Mrs. Cole testified that a shareholder meeting had not been held owing to lack of interest, even though she knew Indiana law required annual shareholder meetings. As the corporation's sole employee, Mrs. Cole lived in a home owned and operated by the corporation. The home also was the corporate office, and she paid no rent or utilities. Two automobiles—owned, operated, and maintained by the corporation—provided Mrs. Cole with her only means of transportation. She set her own salary during the years 1964–1970 without consulting the board of directors.

Peoples Bank & Trust, as minority shareholder, brought a lawsuit for an accounting, recovery of corporate assets, and a declaration of dividends. Mrs. Cole argued that a closed corporation should be justifiably distinguished from a public corporation when questions of corporate formality and internal operations are at issue. Peoples Bank contended that corporate law prevents an officer and a director of a corporation from using the assets of a corporate entity for personal gain. Who won? Was there excessive compensation and/or converted corporate assets? Should a dividend have been declared? *Cole Real Estate Corp. v. Peoples Bank & Trust Co.*, 310 N.E.2d 275 (1974)

15-17. Wiberg, a director of Gulf Coast Land and Development Company, and another director contracted with the corporation to devote their full time to selling a new line of its stock, for which they were to receive a commission on sales. The corporate resolution creating this contract was passed by the votes of these two directors and by a third director. The resolution was later ratified by holders of a majority of the shares at a special meeting in which the three directors, who were the majority shareholders, voted to ratify their action as directors. After two years the corporation terminated the contract and refused to pay Wiberg his commission. Wiberg sued to recover his commission.

The defendant contended that the contract was void as against public policy because two of the three directors who had voted for it had a personal interest in the transaction and because it had not been ratified by 100 percent of the shareholders. Wiberg argued that the contract is enforceable even when the corporation makes a contract with a director; that the director's vote is necessary to authorize the contract if the contract appears to be fair, just, and beneficial to the corporation; and that the director personally made a full disclosure and the contract was then ratified by a majority of the stockholders. Assuming that the contract was what Wiberg contended it was—that is, fair, just, and beneficial to the corporation—did Wiberg prevail? Even though Wiberg had a personal interest in the contract, do you think he acted fairly and honestly in the corporation's interests? *Wiberg v. Gulf Coast Land and Development Co.*, 360 S.W.2d 563 (1962)

15-18. Tigrett suffered an on-the-job injury. She sued the Heritage Building Company to recover workmen's compensation benefits at a time when the company's liabilities exceeded its debts. Shortly after she sued, all the company's assets were transferred to Pointer, the president and sole stockholder, in consideration of the company's indebtedness to him. He, in turn, on the same day transferred these assets to another of his corporations, Heritage Corporation. Tigrett won a judgment against Heritage Building Company, but the company had no assets from which to satisfy a judgment. Tigrett then filed a suit against Pointer and the Heritage Corporation. What was the result? Was Pointer held personally liable? *Tigrett v. Pointer*, 580 S.W.2d 375 (1979)

 On the Internet

http://www.ib.be/invest-belgium/legal.html   For another perspective on the creation of a business, use this site to find out how a corporation is established in Belgium.

http://www.hia.com/llcweb/ll-home.html   This site provides information about limited liability corporations.

http://www.farr.law.com/sb-main.htm   This site briefly provides advantages and disadvantages for sole proprietorships, corporations, etc.

PUBLIC LAW
AND THE LEGAL
ENVIRONMENT OF BUSINESS

*P*art Three focuses on the public laws that regulate the legal environment of business. Because most public laws governing the legal environment are administered and created by administrative agencies, this part opens with a chapter introducing administrative agencies. After this foundational chapter, this part focuses on those laws affecting the employee in the workplace: laws governing employee benefits, labor-management relationships, and employment discrimination. The focus then shifts to laws governing the physical environment, followed by laws governing securities, antitrust, and consumer protection.

16

THE LAW OF ADMINISTRATIVE AGENCIES

The first two federal administrative agencies—the Interstate Commerce Commission (ICC) (now extinct) and the Federal Trade Commission (FTC)—were created by Congress in the late nineteenth century and early twentieth century, an era of reform. Congress felt that the anticompetitive conduct of railroads and other corporations could best be controlled by separate administrative agencies with defined statutory mandates. In another era of reform following the stock market crash of 1929 and the beginning of the Great Depression, Congress saw a need for additional agencies to assist a free market economy and to act in the public interest—hence the creation of such agencies as the Securities and Exchange Commission (SEC), the National Labor Relations Board (NLRB), and the Federal Communications Commission (FCC). From time to time since then, new administrative agencies have been established, until today there are some 76 federal administrative agencies affecting nearly every aspect of life in the United States.[1] For example, the clothes we wear are subject to regulation by the Consumer Product Safety Commission (CPSC); the cars we drive are subject to regulation by the National Highway Safety Transportation Board (NHSTB) and the Environmental Protection Agency (EPA); and the television we watch and the out-of-state telephone calls we make are subject to regulation by the Federal Communications Commission (FCC). (See Exhibit 16-1 on page 368 for a broad picture of the federal government's reach through its departments, agencies, and corporations.)

Because government agencies have such a powerful effect on business, businesspeople need to understand the *law* (regulations) these agencies are empowered to create and the rules of *procedure* they use to make such laws. The impact of administrative agency regulations on business and society is a primary focus of this text. Although we emphasize the role of federal administrative agencies, each of the 50 states, the District of Columbia, and Puerto Rico, as well as counties, cities, and some towns, have administrative agencies that also regulate business and societal conduct. In this chapter, we define administrative law and administrative agencies and discuss the reasons for their growth, how they were created, and their functions. We also explore the federal administrative agencies' relationship to the executive, legislative, and judicial branches of government, as well as the institutions and laws that limit the power of administrative agencies. We end the chapter with a brief consideration of the international dimensions of administrative agencies.

Critical Thinking about the Law

AS A FUTURE BUSINESS LEADER, YOU will certainly encounter many governmental regulations. Congress created administrative agencies, in part, because they could not hope to address the enormous variety and number of concerns that are now covered by administrative agencies. Although you will not learn about every administrative agency in this chapter, you can jumpstart your thinking about administrative agencies by answering these critical thinking questions.

1. Your roommate states that people do not have to follow the regulations passed by administrative agencies because these regulations are not laws. She argues that only Congress can make laws. Which critical thinking question needs to be applied to settle this disagreement?

    CLUE Do they agree on the meaning of the words your roommate is using?

---

[1]Office of the Register, *General Index: Code of Federal Regulations* (rev. ed., Washington, D.C.: National Archives, General Services Administration, January 1, 1994).

2. Some individuals may argue that the creation of regulations by administrative agencies promotes unfair restrictions on business. What ethical norm seems to be behind this thought?

   CLUE If you want fewer restrictions from the government, what ethical norm is influencing your thought? What ethical norm seem to conflict with the wish for fewer governmental regulations?

3. Congress assumes that the administrative agencies will effectively address problems in their respective areas. For example, the EPA ensures compliance with environmental laws. If Matt makes the assumption that environmental problems are so complex and widespread that the EPA could not hope to make a difference, what conclusion do you think Matt would draw regarding administrative agencies?

   CLUE Think about a contrary assumption. If Matt assumed that the administrative agencies were effective, would he be more likely to support the regulations passed by the various agencies?

INTRODUCTION TO ADMINISTRATIVE LAW AND ADMINISTRATIVE AGENCIES

ADMINISTRATIVE LAW

For the purposes of this text, **administrative law** is defined broadly as any rule (statute or regulation) that affects, directly or indirectly, an administrative agency. These rules may be procedural or substantive, and they may come from the legislative, executive, or judicial branch of government or from the agencies themselves. A **procedural rule** generally has an impact on the internal processes by which the agencies function or prescribes methods of enforcing rights. For example, under the Administrative Procedure Act, an administrative agency must give adequate notice to all parties involved in an agency hearing. A **substantive rule** defines rights of parties. An example is an act of Congress that forbids the Federal Trade Commission (FTC) from applying the antitrust laws to all the Coca-Cola bottlers in the United States. In this instance, the rights and regulations of both the FTC and the Coca-Cola bottlers were defined by Congress.

> **administrative law** Any rule (statue or regulation) that directly or indirectly affects an administrative agency.
>
> **procedural rule** A rule that governs the internal processes of an administrative agency.
>
> **substantive rule** A rule that creates, defines, or regulates the legal rights of administrative agencies and the parties they regulate.

ADMINISTRATIVE AGENCIES

An **administrative agency** is any body that is created by the legislative branch (e.g., Congress, a state legislature, or a city council) to carry out specific duties. Some agencies are not situated wholly in the legislative, executive, or judicial branch of government. Instead, they may have legislative power to make rules for an entire industry, judicial power to adjudicate (decide) individual cases, and executive power to investigate corporate misconduct. Examples of such independent federal administrative agencies are the Environmental Protection Agency, the Federal Communications Commission, and the Interstate Commerce Commission; at the state level, examples are public utilities commissions and building authorities; at the city level, examples are city planning commissions and tax appeals boards.

> **administrative agency** Any body that is created by the legislative branch to carry out specific duties.

TYPES Administrative agencies are generally classified as independent or executive. **Independent administrative agencies**, such as the FTC and the SEC, are usually headed by a board of commissioners, who are appointed for a specific term of years by the president with the advice and consent of the Senate. A commissioner can be removed before serving out a full term only for causes defined by Congress, not at the whim of the president—which is why these agencies are called independent.

Executive administrative agencies are generally located within departments of the executive branch of government. For example, the Occupational

> **independent administrative agency** An agency whose appointed heads and members serve for fixed terms and cannot be removed by the president except for reasons defined by Congress.
>
> **executive administrative agency** An agency located within a department of the executive branch of government; heads and appointed members serve at the pleasure of the president.

THE CONSTITUTION

LEGISLATIVE BRANCH
THE CONGRESS

Senate   House

Architect of the Capital
General Accounting Office
Government Printing Office
Library of Congress
United States Botanic Garden
Office of Technology Assessment
Congressional Budget Office
Copyright Royalty Tribunal

EXECUTIVE BRANCH

The President

Executive Office of the President

White House Office
Office of Management and Budget
Council of Economic Advisers
National Security Council
Office of Policy Development
Office of the U.S. Trade
    Representative
Council on Environmental Quality
Office of Science and Technology
    Policy
Office of Administration

JUDICIAL BRANCH

The Supreme Court of the
    United States

Circuit Courts of Appeals of the
    United States
District Courts of the United States
United States Court of Claims
United States Court of
    International Trade
United States Tax Court
United States Court of Military
    Appeals
Territorial Courts
Federal Judicial Center
Administrative Office of the
    United States Courts

Department of State	Department of the Treasury	Department of Defense	Department of Justice	Department of the Interior
Department of Agriculture	Department of Commerce	Department of Labor	Department of Transportation	Department of Energy

Dept. of Health and Human Serv.	Dept. of Housing and Urban Dev.	Dept. of Education

---

INDEPENDENT ESTABLISHMENTS AND GOVERNMENTAL CORPORATIONS

ACTION
Administrative Conference of
    the United States
African Development Foundation
American Battle Monuments
    Commission
Appalachian Regional
    Commission
Board for International
    Broadcasting
Central Intelligence Agency
Civil Aeronautics Board
Commission on Civil Rights
Commission of Fine Arts
Commodity Futures
    Trading Commission
Consumer Product Safety
    Commission
Environmental Protection
    Agency
Equal Employment
    Opportunity Commission
Export-Import Bank of the
    United States

Farm Credit Administration
Federal Communications
    Commission
Federal Deposit Insurance
    Corporation
Federal Election Commission
Federal Emergency
    Management Agency
Federal Home Loan Bank
    Board
Federal Labor Relations
    Board
Federal Maritime Commission
Federal Mediation and
    Conciliation Service
Federal Reserve System
Federal Trade Commission
General Services
    Administration
Inter-American Foundation

Interstate Commerce
    Commission
Merit Systems Protection
    Board
National Aeronautics and
    Space Administration
National Capital Planning
    Commission
National Credit Union
    Administration
National Foundation on
    the Arts and Humanities
National Labor Relations
    Board
National Mediation Board
National Science
    Foundation
National Transportation
    Safety Board
National Regulatory
    Commission
Occupational Safety and
    Health Review Commission
Office of Personnel
    Management

Panama Canal Commission
Peace Corps
Pennsylvania Avenue
    Development Corporation
Pension Benefit Guaranty
    Corporation
Postal Rate Commission
Railroad Retirement Board
Securities and Exchange
    Commission
Selective Service System
Small Business
    Administration
Tennessee Valley Authority
U.S. Arms Control and
    Disarmament Agency
U.S. Information Agency
U.S. International
    Development Corporation
    Agency
U.S. International Trade
    Commission
U.S. Postal Service
Veterans Administration

Source: Adapted from D.V. Edwards, *The American Political Experience: An Introduction to Government* 4th ed., (Prentice Hall, 1988). Data from *United States Government Manual, 1987/1988* (Government Printing Office). Reprinted in *The Legal Environment of Business* G. Spriro, (Prentice Hall, 1993).

Safety and Health Administration (OSHA) is located in the Department of Labor, the National Transportation Safety Board (NTSB) in the Department of Transportation. Heads and members of these boards have no fixed term of office. They serve at the pleasure of the president, meaning they can be removed from their positions by the chief executive at any time.

Table 16-1 lists the major independent and executive agencies of the federal government.

INDEPENDENT AGENCIES	EXECUTIVE AGENCIES
Commodity Futures Trading Commission (CFTC)	Federal Deposit Insurance Corporation (FDIC)
Consumer Product Safety Commission (CPSC)	General Services Administration (GSA)
Equal Employment Opportunity Commission (EEOC)	International Development Corporation Agency (IDCA)
Federal Communications Commission (FCC)	National Aeronautics and Space Administration (NASA)
Federal Trade Commission (FTC)	National Science Foundation (NSF)
Interstate Commerce Commission (ICC)	Occupational Safety and Health Administration (OSHA)
National Labor Relations Board (NLRB)	
National Transportation Safety Board (NTSB)	Office of Personnel Management (OPM)
Nuclear Regulatory Commission (NRC)	Small Business Administration (SBA)
Securities and Exchange Commission (SEC)	Veterans Administration (VA)

REASONS FOR GROWTH Administrative agencies have proliferated rapidly since the late 1890s for the following reasons:

1. *Flexibility.* Unlike the court proceedings studied in chapter 5, administrative agency hearings are not governed by strict rules of evidence. For example, hearsay rules are waived in most cases.

2. *Need for expertise.* The staff of each of the agencies has technical expertise in a relatively narrow area, gained from concentrating on that area over the years. It would be impossible, for example, for 435 House of Representatives members and 100 Senators to regulate the television, radio, and satellite communication systems of the United States on a daily basis. Only the FCC staff has that expertise.

3. *Prevention of overcrowding in courts.* If all the administrative agencies in Exhibit 16-1 did not exist, our highly complex, often litigious, society would have to seek redress of grievances through the federal and state court systems. As was explained in chapter 6, both corporations and individuals are already seeking alternatives to the overburdened court system.

4. *Expeditious solutions to national problems.* After the 1929 Crash and the ensuing Depression, Congress sought to give investors confidence in the securities markets by creating the Securities and Exchange Commission in 1934. The SEC was intended to be a "watchdog" agency that would ensure full disclosure of material information to the investing public and prevent a repetition of the fraudulent practices that marked the freewheeling 1920s. When the public became concerned about the deterioration of the nation's water, land, and air, Congress created the Environmental Protection Agency to implement clean air, water, and waste regulations.

All those reasons for the existence of administrative agencies are now being challenged by proponents of *deregulation*—or no regulation—of industry. The debate between advocates of returning to a period in our history when market forces were the sole regulators of business conduct and champions of administrative agency regulation is highlighted throughout the public law section of this text.

CREATION OF ADMINISTRATIVE AGENCIES

Exhibit 16-2 gives an idea of the proliferation of administrative agencies at the federal level from 1900 to 1990. Because all these agencies affect individuals, the business community, and society as a whole, it is important for you to know how and why they were created.

Congress creates these agencies through statutes called **enabling legislation**. In general, an enabling statute delegates to the agency congressional **legislative power** for the purpose of serving the "public interest, convenience, and necessity." Armed with this mandate, the administrative agency

enabling legislation
Legislation that grants lawful power to an administrative agency to issue rules, investigate potential violations of rules or statutes, and adjudicate disputes.

legislative power The power delegated by Congress to an administrative agency to make rules that must be adhered to by individuals and businesses regulated by the agency; these rules have the force of law.

EXHIBIT 16-2 *Growth of Federal Regulatory Agencies*

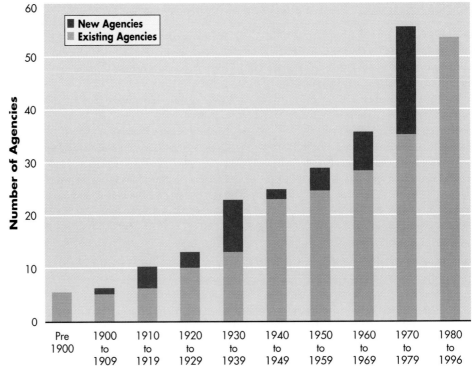

Source: From *Business and Government in the Global Marketplace*, 6/e, by Weidenbaum, Murray L., © 1999. Reprinted by permission of Prentice Hall, Inc., Upper Saddle River, NJ, and the Center for the Study of American Business.

executive power The power delegated by Congress to an administrative agency to investigate whether the rules enacted by the agency have been properly followed by businesses and individuals.

judicial power The power delegated by Congress to an administrative agency to adjudicate cases through an administrative proceeding; includes the power to issue a complaint, hold a hearing by an administrative law judge, and issue either an initial decision or a recommended decision to a head(s) of an agency.

can issue rules that control individual and business behavior. In many instances, such rules carry criminal as well as civil penalties. In chapter 22, you will see how the SEC, using its mandate under the 1933 and 1934 Securities Acts, can both fine and criminally prosecute individuals involved in insider trading. The enabling statute also delegates **executive power** to the agency to investigate potential violations of rules or statutes. Chapter 22 sets out the wide-ranging investigative powers of the SEC staff. Finally, the enabling statutes delegate **judicial power** to the agency to settle or adjudicate any disputes it may have with businesses or individuals. For example, the SEC, using its congressional mandate under the 1933 and 1934 Securities Acts, has prescribed rules governing the issuance of, and trading in, securities by businesses as well as by brokers and underwriters. The SEC staff adjudicates individual cases in which individuals or corporations may have violated the rules.

Because the framers of the U.S. Constitution carefully separated the legislative, executive, and judicial powers of government into three distinct branches, some people complain that allowing administrative agencies to exercise all three powers violates the spirit of the Constitution. Critics go so far as to state that these agencies constitute a "fourth branch of government." In 1995 the House of Representatives and the Senate overwhelmingly passed a bill that would require all administrative agencies (both executive and independent) to do a cost-benefit analysis of any proposed regulation that would cost the economy more than $25 million. All agencies would also have to identify possible alternatives to the proposed regulation that would require no government action, as well as varying actions customized for different regions of the country, and "the use of market-based mechanisms." The Office of Management and Budget (OMB) reviews all proposed rules judged to be "major."

FUNCTIONS OF ADMINISTRATIVE AGENCIES

Administrative agencies perform the following functions: (1) *rule making*; (2) *adjudication* of individual cases brought before administrative law judges by agency staff; and (3) *administrative activities*, which include (a) informal advising of individual businesses and consumers, (b) preparing reports and doing studies of industries and of consumer activities, and (c) issuing guidelines for the business community and others as to what activities are legal in the eyes of the agency staff.

RULE MAKING

We said that administrative agencies are authorized to perform the legislative function of making rules or regulations by virtue of the enabling statutes. For example, the enabling statute of the Occupational Safety and Health Administration (OSHA) gave the secretary of labor authority to set "mandatory safety and health standards applicable to businesses affecting interstate commerce." The secretary was also given the power to "prescribe such rules and regulations that he may deem necessary to carry out the responsibilities under this act." In some cases, the procedures for implementing the rule-making function are

EXHIBIT 16-3 *Steps in the Informal Rule-Making Process*

Step 1.
Agency drafts
rules in consultation
with interested parties.

Step 2.
Proposed rules are
published in *Federal Register.*

Step 3.
Interested parties can file
written comments on the
written draft usually within
a 30-day period from
publication in the
Federal Register.

Step 4.
Final draft of a rule is published
in *Federal Register* 30 days
before it takes effect. A
statement of its purpose and cost
benefit analysis must accompany
its publication.

Step 5.
Agency receives feedback from
interested parties during 30-day
period and makes decision on
whether final draft should be
rewritten. If not it becomes
law.

Administrative Procedure Act (APA) Establishes the standards and procedures federal administrative agencies must follow in their rule-making and adjudicative functions.

spelled out in the enabling act. If they are not, agencies follow the three major rule-making models—formal, informal, and hybrid—outlined in the **Administrative Procedure Act (APA).**

FORMAL RULE MAKING   Section 553(c) of the APA requires formal rule making when an enabling statute or other legislation states that all regulations or rules must be enacted by an agency as part of a formal hearing process that includes a complete transcript. This procedure provides for (1) an agency notice of proposed rule making to the public in the *Federal Register*; (2) a public hearing at which witnesses give testimony on the pros and cons of the proposed rule, each witness is cross-examined, and the rules of evidence are applied; and (3) the making and publication of formal findings by the agency. On the basis of these findings, an agency may or may not promulgate a regulation. Because of the expense and time involved in creating a formal transcript and record, most enabling statutes do not require agencies to go through a formal rule-making procedure when promulgating regulations.

INFORMAL RULE MAKING   As provided by Section 553 of the APA, informal rule making applies in all situations in which the agency's enabling legislation or other congressional directives do not require another form. The APA requires that the agency (1) give prior notice of the proposed rule by publishing it in the *Federal Register*; (2) provide an opportunity for all interested parties to submit written comments; and (3) publish the final rule, with a statement of its basis and purpose, in the *Federal Register*. Exhibit 16-3 on page 371 lays out the five-step process for promulgating a rule according to the informal rule-making model. Executive and independent agencies are required to set out a cost benefit analysis in Step 1 of the process.

Informal rule making is the model most often used by administrative agencies because it is efficient in terms of time and cost. No formal public hearing is required, and no formal record need be established, as in formal rule making. However, parties opposed to a particular rule arrived at through informal rule making often seek to persuade the appellate courts that the agency in question did not take important factors into account when the rule was being made.

AMERICAN DENTAL ASSOCIATION V. MARTIN
UNITED STATES COURT OF APPEALS 984 F.2D 823 (7TH CIR. 1993)

In 1991, the Occupational Safety and Health Administration (OSHA) promulgated a rule to protect health care workers from viruses that can be transmitted in the blood of patients. The rule requires employers in the health care industry to take certain precautions relating to the handling of contaminated instruments (such as needles), the disposal of contaminated waste, and the use of protective clothing (such as gloves, masks, and gowns). The rule also requires employers to provide vaccinations for hepatitis B for their employees and confidential blood testing of workers following accidental exposures (such as being stuck with a contaminated needle). The American Dental Association (ADA) and two other groups asked a federal court to review the rule. The ADA argued, among other things, that OSHA had failed to establish that dental workers were sufficiently at risk to benefit from the rule. Furthermore, the rule would unnecessarily burden consumers with increased medical costs and, hence, diminished care.

JUDGE POSNER

In deciding to impose this extensive array of restrictions on the practice of medicine, nursing, and dentistry, OSHA did not (indeed is not authorized to) compare the benefits with the costs and impose the restrictions on finding that the former exceeded the latter. Instead it asked whether the restrictions would materially reduce a significant workplace risk to human health without imperiling the existence of, or threatening massive dislocation to, the health care industry.

OSHA cannot impose onerous requirements on an industry that does not pose substantial hazards to the safety or health of its workers. But neither is the agency required to proceed workplace by workplace, which would require it to promulgate hundreds of thousands of separate rules. It is not our business to pick the happy medium between these extremes. It is OSHA's business. If it provides a rational explanation for its choice, we are bound. It explained that while the cost of compliance with the precautions that the CDC has recommended (and OSHA has required) against bloodborne pathogens varies in a readily determinable fashion from industry to industry, the risk of infection does not. The risk goes with practices (so protective clothing is required only where being splashed with blood or other infective liquid can reasonably be anticipated, whether it is a dentist's office or a hospital operating room) rather than with industries, and the rule is therefore based on practices rather than on industries. The HIV or HBV carrier bears menace with him as he makes the rounds from health care provider to health care provider. The risk of blood splatters and needlesticks is greater in some medical procedures than in others, but a dental hygienist is as likely to be splattered by blood contained in saliva as is many a worker in a hospital or a doctor's office. The idea behind requiring universal precautions for health care workers is to protect those workers in any situation in which there is a nontrivial risk of physical contact with a patient's blood, and these situations arise in dentists' offices as well as in doctors' offices and hospitals. OSHA was required neither to quantify the risk to workers' health nor to establish the existence of significant risk to a scientific certainty. It is true that because fewer people have dental than medical insurance, and therefore more people pay for dental care out of their own pockets, the higher price of dentistry that is a likely consequence of the rule will have a greater impact on demand; and inadequate dental care is a source of pain and suffering. But again the dental association made no effort to quantify this impact, though techniques for doing so exist in economics.

The dental association complains that the rule goes too far in requiring dentists to "ensure" that their employees comply with the requirements of the rule. They say this imposes strict liability, which OSHA acknowledges it cannot do. It is reasonably plain, however, that OSHA did not by using the word "ensure" seek to impose strict liability. It explained that the employer's responsibility doesn't end with furnishing his employees with protective gear, for example; he must do everything he can reasonably be expected to do to see that they use it. Like an employer made liable for his employee's conduct not by the principle of respondeat superior (a form of strict liability) but by the negligence principle, the employer subject to OSHA's rule on bloodborne pathogens must take all reasonable measures to prevent his employees from violating the rule, but if despite these measures the employee violates the rule, the employer is off the hook.

The costs of compliance with OSHA's rule, once the issue of strict liability for unforeseeable misconduct by employees is laid to one side, can hardly be thought so great as to imperil dentistry. Annualized, these costs are estimated to be equal to less than one-third of one percent of the industry's annual revenue. This may overstate the actual cost, not to society as a whole but to the industry.

[T]he dental association's argument [is] that OSHA's rule is likely to cause a deterioration in dental care as dental patients flee the higher prices resulting from the industry's efforts to shift some of the costs of compliance with the rule to its customers. There are some omitted costs, as we have noted, but not enough to make a decisive difference; nor does the association emphasize them.

Plaintiff ADA's petition to review the rule *denied*.

HYBRID RULE MAKING   Interested parties often complained that informal rule making gave them little opportunity to be heard other than in writing. Both Congress and the executive branch wanted administrative agencies to do a cost-benefit analysis of proposed regulations. Out of this input from the public and two branches of government came hybrid rule making, which combines some of the aspects of formal and informal rule making. This model requires the agency to give notice of a proposed regulation, set a period for public comments, hold a public hearing, and have a cost-benefit analysis done by an independent executive agency.

EXEMPTED RULE MAKING   Section 553 of the APA allows the agencies to decide whether there will be public participation in rule-making proceedings relating to "military or foreign affairs" and "agency management or personnel," as well as in proceedings relating to "public property, loans, grants, benefits or contracts" of an agency. Public notice and comment are also not required when the agency is making interpretive rules or general statements of policy.

It is generally conceded that proceedings dealing with military and foreign affairs often require speed and secrecy, both of which are incompatible with public notice and hearings. The other exemptions, however, are becoming more difficult to justify in the eyes of the courts, as the case of *Public Citizens v. National Economic Commission* shows (see the next section of this chapter).

JUDICIAL REVIEW OF RULE MAKING   After a regulation is promulgated by an administrative agency and is published in the Federal *Register*, it generally becomes law. Appellate courts have accepted agency-promulgated regulations as law unless a business or other affected groups or individuals can show that:

1.   The congressional delegation of legislative authority in the enabling act was unconstitutional because it was *too vague* and not limited.

2.   An agency action *violated a constitutional standard*, such as the right to be free from unreasonable searches and seizures under the Fourth Amendment. For example, if an agency such as OSHA promulgated a rule that allowed its inspectors to search a business property at any time without its owners' permission and without an administrative search warrant, that rule would be in violation of the Fourth Amendment.

3.   The act of an agency was *beyond the scope of power* granted to it by Congress in its enabling legislation.

Judicial review of administrative agency action provides a check against agency excesses that can prove very costly to the business community. Excerpted here is a case that exemplifies that kind of judicial review when constitutional standards are important.

RUBIN V. COORS BREWING COMPANY
UNITED STATES SUPREME COURT 115 S. CT. 1585 (1995)

Coors Brewing Company (respondent) brews beer. In 1987, it applied to the Bureau of Alcohol, Tobacco, and Firearms (BATF) for approval of proposed labels and advertisements that disclosed the alcohol content of its beer. BATF refused to approve the disclosure under section 205(e)(2) of the Federal Alcohol Administration Act (FAAA), which prohibits the selling, shipping, or delivery of malt beverages, distilled spirits, or wines in bottles:

> *unless such products are bottled, packaged, and labeled in conformity with such regulations, to be prescribed by the Secretary of the Treasury, with respect to packaging, marking, branding, and labeling and size and fill of container . . . as will provide the consumer with adequate information as to identify the quality of the products, the alcohol content thereof, the net contents of the package, and the manufacturer or bottler or importer of the product.*

Regulations related to this statutory restriction (27 C.F.R. § 7.26(a)) prohibit the disclosure of alcohol content on beer labels.

In addition to prohibiting numerical indications of alcohol content, the labeling regulations proscribe descriptive terms that suggest high content, such as "strong," "full strength," "extra strength," "high test," "high proof," "pre-war strength," and "full oldtime alcoholic strength." (27 C.F.R. § 7.29(f)). The prohibitions do not preclude labels from identifying a beer as "low alcohol," "reduced alcohol," "non-alcoholic," or "alcohol-free."

When BATF refused to approve the labels, Coors filed suit in federal district court challenging the regulation as violative of the First Amendment. BATF (the government) argued that the ban on alcohol content in labels was needed to prevent "strength wars" among brewers who would then compete in the marketplace on the potency of their beers.

The district court found for Coors, but the U.S. Court of Appeals for the Tenth Circuit reversed. It remanded the case to the trial court for determining whether the ban was an appropriate means of avoiding strength wars. The lower court found there was no evidence of any relationship between the disclosure on labels of alcohol content and competition on the basis of content. The court of appeals (on the second appeal) concluded that BATF's regulation violated the First Amendment.

JUSTICE THOMAS

Both the lower courts and the parties agree that respondent seeks to disclose only truthful, verifiable, and nonmisleading factual information about alcohol content on its beer labels. Thus, our analysis focuses on the substantiality of the interest behind § 205(e)(2) and on whether the labeling ban bears an acceptable fit with the Government's goal. A careful consideration of these factors indicates that § 205(e)(2) violates the First Amendment's protection of commercial speech.

According to the Government, the FAAA's restriction prevents a particular type of beer drinker—one who selects a beverage because of its high potency—from choosing beers solely for their alcohol content. In the Government's view, restricting disclosure of information regarding a particular product characteristic will decrease the extent to which consumers will select the product on the basis of that characteristic.

Respondent counters that Congress actually intended the FAAA to achieve the far different purpose of preventing brewers from making inaccurate claims concerning alcohol content.

Rather than suppressing the free flow of factual information in the wine and spirits markets, the Government seeks to control competition on the basis of strength by monitoring distillers' promotions and marketing. The respondent quite correctly notes that the general thrust of federal alcohol policy appears to favor greater disclosure of information, rather than less.

The Government carries the burden of showing that the challenged regulation advances the Government's interest "in a direct and material way." That burden "is not satisfied by mere speculation and conjecture; rather, a governmental body seeking to sustain a restriction on commercial speech must demonstrate that the harms it recites are real and that its restriction will in fact alleviate them to a material degree."

The Government attempts to meet its burden by pointing to current developments in the consumer market. It claims that beer producers are already competing and advertising on the basis of alcohol strength in the "malt liquor" segment of the beer market. The Government attempts to show that this competition threatens to spread to the rest of the market by directing our attention to respondent's motives in bringing this litigation. Respondent allegedly suffers from consumer misperceptions that its beers contain less alcohol than other brands. According to the Government, once respondent gains relief from § 205(e)(2), it will use its labels to overcome this handicap.

Under the Government's theory, § 205(e)(2) suppresses the threat of such competition by preventing consumers from choosing beers on the basis of alcohol content. It is assuredly a matter of "common sense," that a restriction on the advertising of a product characteristic will decrease the extent to which consumers select a product on the basis of that trait. In addition to common sense, the Government urges us to turn to history as a guide. According to the Government, at the time Congress enacted the FAAA, the use of labels displaying alcohol content had helped produce a strength war. Section 205(e)(2) allegedly relieved competitive pressures to market beer on the basis of alcohol content, resulting over the long term in beers with lower alcohol levels.

We conclude that § 205(e)(2) cannot directly and materially advance its asserted interest because of the overall irrationality of the Government's regulatory scheme. While the laws governing labeling prohibit the disclosure of alcohol content unless required by state law, federal regulations apply a contrary policy to beer advertising. The failure to prohibit the disclosure of alcohol content in advertising, which would seem to constitute a more influential weapon in any strength war than labels, makes no rational sense if the government's true aim is to suppress strength wars.

While we are mindful that respondent only appealed the constitutionality of § 205(e)(2), these exemptions and inconsistencies bring into question the purpose of the labeling ban. To be sure, the Government's interest in combating strength wars remains a valid goal. But the irrationality of this unique and puzzling regulatory framework ensures that the labeling ban will fail to achieve that end. There is little chance that § 205(e)(2) can directly and materially advance its aim, while other provisions of the same act directly undermine and counteract its effects.

The Government argues that a sufficient "fit" exists here because the labeling ban applies to only one product characteristic and because the ban does not prohibit all disclosures of alcohol content—it applies only to those involving labeling and advertising. In response, respondent suggests several alternatives, such as directly limiting the alcohol content of beers, prohibiting marketing efforts emphasizing high alcohol strength (which is apparently the policy in some other Western nations), or limiting the labeling ban only to malt liquors, which is the segment of the market that allegedly is threatened with a strength war. We agree that the availability of these options, all of which could advance the Government's asserted interest in a manner less intrusive to respondent's First Amendment rights, indicates that § 205(e)(2) is more extensive than necessary.

Affirmed in favor of Respondent, Coors.

ADJUDICATION

In carrying out its adjudicative function in individual cases as opposed to rule making for whole industries, the administrative agency usually pursues a four-step process. After receiving a complaint alleging violation of an administrative law, the agency notifies the party against whom the complaint is made and conducts an investigation into the merits of the complaint. If the agency staff finds the complaint has merit, it next negotiates with the party to see if it can get the party to voluntarily stop the violation. If negotiation is unsuccessful, the third step is to file a complaint with an administrative law judge (ALJ). Step 4 consists of a hearing and decision by the ALJ. The party may appeal the ALJ's decision to the full commission or agency head, and ultimately to a federal court of appeals and the U.S. Supreme Court.

All these steps are guided by the APA, which sets out minimum procedural standards for administrative agency adjudication. Enabling statutes that create agencies often add other procedural requirements. Finally, case law arising out of appeals of agency decisions to the U.S. circuit courts of appeal and the U.S. Supreme Court provides further guidelines for agencies in carrying out their adjudicative function. In the following detailed description of the four-step adjudicative process for federal administrative agencies, we use the Federal Trade Commission (FTC) as a representative agency. You will find it easier to follow our discussion if you look first at the organizational outline of the FTC provided in Exhibit 16-4 and the summary of adjudication and judicial review of agency decision making given in Exhibit 16-5.

Federal Trade Commission (FTC) An independent regulatory agency entrusted by Congress with promoting a competitive business environment.

INVESTIGATION AND COMPLAINT The **Federal Trade Commission (FTC)**, which includes the Bureau of Competition and the Bureau of Consumer Protection, is obliged to conduct an investigation whenever it receives a complaint from other government agencies, competitors, or consumers. For example, upon receiving a complaint about a mouthwash product that is advertised as killing germs and protecting people from sore throat, the commission examines the product to see if the statement has any scientific validity. Should the commission's staff find that the advertising is "deceptive" or "unfair" within the meaning of Section 5 of the Federal Trade Commission Act, it will seek to stop the advertising campaign in one of two ways:

1. *Voluntary compliance.* The staff will ask the corporation to voluntarily stop the advertising campaign. Usually, no penalty is assessed if the company agrees to do this.

2. *Consent order.* If voluntary compliance is not obtained, the staff notifies the mouthwash company that it has ten days to enter into a *consent order*, or the staff will issue a formal complaint.

EXHIBIT 16-4 *Federal Trade Commission*

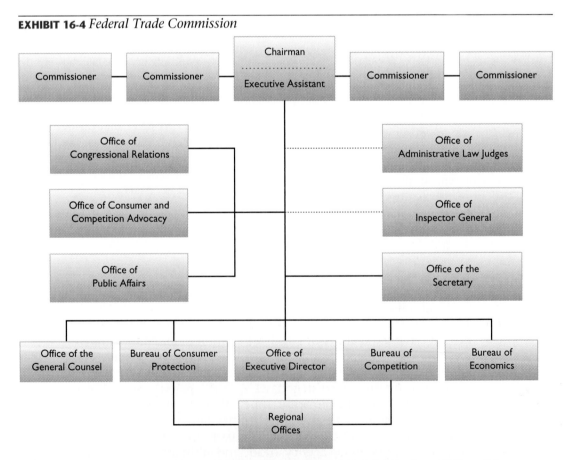

Source: U.S. Government Manual 1992–93 (Washington, D.C.: Office of the *Federal Register*, 1992), p. 615.

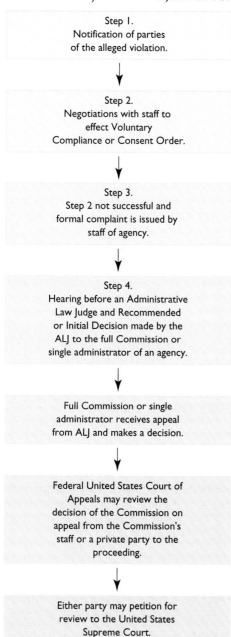

Step 1.
Notification of parties
of the alleged violation.

Step 2.
Negotiations with staff to
effect Voluntary
Compliance or Consent Order.

Step 3.
Step 2 not successful and
formal complaint is issued by
staff of agency.

Step 4.
Hearing before an Administrative
Law Judge and Recommended
or Initial Decision made by the
ALJ to the full Commission or
single administrator of an agency.

Full Commission or single
administrator receives appeal
from ALJ and makes a decision.

Federal United States Court of
Appeals may review the
decision of the Commission on
appeal from the Commission's
staff or a private party to the
proceeding.

Either party may petition for
review to the United States
Supreme Court.

Most cases are closed at this stage because, under a **consent order**, the company does not have to admit that it was deceptive or unfair in its advertising; it only has to promise that it will not do such unlawful advertising again and agree to the remedy that the commission imposes. The latter may be some form of corrective advertising that tells the public that the mouthwash does not kill germs. A consent order helps the commission staff to obtain a binding cease-and-desist order with limited effort and time. It also benefits the company, because by agreeing to a consent order, the company avoids both an admission of guilt and the cost of litigation and shareholder and consumer lawsuits that might ensue if the next steps in the adjudication process—a formal complaint and a hearing by an administrative law judge—resulted in a adverse decision for the company.

consent order An agreement by a business to stop an activity an administrative agency alleges to be unlawful and to accept the remedy the agency imposes; no admission of guilt is necessary.

FORMAL COMPLAINT AND HEARING   If the case is not settled by voluntary compliance or a consent order, the commission's staff, usually through the FCC's Office of the General Counsel (see Exhibit 16-4), will issue a formal complaint listing the charges against the mouthwash company and will request that certain penalties be assessed by the **administrative law judge (ALJ)**. Administrative law judges, who number approximately 1,150, are selected on the basis of a merit exam and are assigned to specific administrative agencies. They usually come from within the federal administrative bureaucracy and are given life tenure. Administrative law judges are noted for their independence, even though they may be assigned to a particular independent or executive agency for a number of years.[2]

A hearing before an ALJ may take several months or years. It resembles a judicial proceeding in that it includes notice to the parties, discovery, and the presentation of evidence by both the staff of the commission and the accused party (the respondent), direct examination and cross-examination of the witnesses, and presentation of motions and arguments to the ALJ. However, there is no jury at these hearings, and they are more informal than court proceedings. For instance, an ALJ will often intervene to ask questions and to take note of evidence that neither of the parties has introduced. At times, in fact, the ALJ becomes a severe questioner of both parties, especially in hearings involving disability and welfare claims. Thus adjudicative proceedings are less adversarial and more investigative, or inquisitorial, than court proceedings.

INITIAL OR RECOMMENDED DECISION   After the hearing is completed, both the commission staff and the respondent submit proposed findings of facts and conclusions of law. Under the APA, the ALJ must then prepare an initial or recommended decision. An *initial decision* becomes the final agency action unless an appeal is taken to the full commission by either the staff or the respondent. In contrast, a *recommended decision* is not final; it has to be acted on by the full commission or by the head of the agency. Agency heads and commissions are not required to defer to the ALJ's factual findings. It should be remembered that commissioners and agency heads are political appointees of the president and may have political or policy reasons for overruling an ALJ's decision. Should either the staff or the respondent appeal a full commission's decision to a federal circuit court of appeals, the court is likely to give deference to the ALJ's factual findings because the ALJ is the person who actually heard the witnesses testify and read the submitted exhibits.

APPEAL TO THE FULL COMMISSION   If the losing party (the agency staff or the respondent) does not agree with the ALJ's decision, it may appeal to the full commission, in the case of the FTC, or to the head of an executive department (or agency), in the case of an executive agency. In the mouthwash case we are using as an example, a majority of the commission members must rule in favor of one of the parties on the basis of a **preponderance of evidence** (51 percent or more) standard. The APA requires that the commission state factual, legal, and policy bases for its decision. This requirement makes the agency responsible for its decision both to the public and to the courts that may later review it.

JUDICIAL REVIEW OF ADJUDICATIVE PROCEEDINGS   If the party that loses at the full-commission or agency-head level in an adjudicative proceeding wishes to appeal, it must file a motion for appeal with the federal circuit court of appeals that has jurisdiction in the case. Briefs are filed by both parties, and the court hears oral argument. The court also reviews the whole record, including the ALJ's findings, in the case. It does not review the commission's *factual* findings as long as they are supported by *substantial evidence* in the record. (The *substantial evidence rule* requires that the court find that a reasonable person, after reviewing the record, would make the same findings the agency did.)

---

[2]*See Administrative Law Judges Are Washington's Potent Hybrids*, N.Y. Times, December 3, 1980; and *Symposium: Administrative Law Judges*, 6 W. New Eng. L. Rev. 1 (1984).

Rather, it reviews the commission's *legal* findings to ensure that (1) it acted in a constitutionally approved way; (2) it acted within the scope of its jurisdiction as outlined by the enabling statute; and (3) it followed proper statutory procedures and did not act in an arbitrary or capricious manner. In the following case, you will note the court's application of some of these standards.

WARNER LAMBERT V. FEDERAL TRADE COMMISSION
UNITED STATES COURT OF APPEALS 562 F.2D 49 (D.C. CIR. 1977)

The product Listerine was advertised by the Warner Lambert Company (petitioner) as a preventive or cure for the common cold. Listerine had been on the market since 1879 and had been advertised as described since 1921. The FTC ordered Warner Lambert to cease and desist its advertising and to allocate $10 million to corrective advertising that included a statement "Contrary to prior advertising." The ALJ ruled in favor of the FTC staff. The petitioner appealed to the full commission, which affirmed most of the ALJ's findings. Warner Lambert appealed to the court of appeals.

JUDGE WRIGHT

The first issue on appeal is whether the Commission's conclusion that Listerine is not beneficial for colds or sore throats is supported by the evidence. The Commission's findings must be sustained if they are supported by substantial evidence on the record viewed as a whole. We conclude that they are.

Both the ALJ and the Commission carefully analyzed the evidence. They gave full consideration to the studies submitted by petitioner. The ultimate conclusion that Listerine is not an effective cold remedy was based on six specific findings of fact.

First, the Commission found that the ingredients of Listerine are not present in sufficient quantities to have any therapeutic effect. This was the testimony of two leading pharmacologists called by Commission counsel. The Commission was justified in concluding that the testimony of Listerine's experts was not sufficiently persuasive to counter this testimony.

Second, the Commission found that in the process of gargling it is impossible for Listerine to reach the critical areas of the body in medically significant concentration. The liquid is confined to the mouth chamber. Such vapors as might reach the nasal passage would not be in therapeutic concentration. Petitioner did not offer any evidence that vapors reached the affected areas in significant concentration.

Third, the Commission found that even if significant quantities of the active ingredients of Listerine were to reach the critical sites where cold viruses enter and infect the body, they could not interfere with the activities of the virus because they could not penetrate the tissue cells.

Fourth, the Commission discounted the results of a clinical study conducted by petitioner that contends that in a four-year study school children who gargled with Listerine had fewer colds and cold symptoms than those who did not gargle with Listerine. The Commission found that the design and execution of the "St. Barnabas Study" made its results unreliable. For the first two years of the four-year test no placebo was given to the control group. For the last two years the placebo was inadequate: the control group was given colored water which did not resemble Listerine in smell or taste. There was also evidence that the physician who examined the test subjects was not blinded from knowing which children were using Listerine and which were not, that his evaluation of the cold symptoms of each child each day may have been imprecise, and that he necessarily relied on the non-blinded child's subjective reporting. Both the ALJ and the Commission analyzed the St. Barnabas Study and the expert testimony about it in depth and were justified in concluding that its results are unreliable.

Fifth, the Commission found that the ability of Listerine to kill germs by millions on contact is of no medical significance in the treatment of colds or sore throats. Expert testimony showed that bacteria in the oral cavity, the "germs" which Listerine purports to kill, do not cause colds and play no role in cold symptoms. Colds are caused by viruses. Further, "while Listerine kills millions of bacteria in the mouth, it also leaves millions. It is impossible to sterilize any area of the mouth, let alone the entire mouth."

Sixth, the Commission found that Listerine has no significant beneficial effect on the symptoms of sore throat. The Commission recognized that gargling with Listerine could provide temporary relief from a sore throat by removing accumulated debris irritating the throat. But this type of relief can also be obtained by gargling with salt water or even warm water. The Commission found that this is not the significant relief promised by petitioner's advertisements. It was reasonable to conclude that "such temporary relief does not 'lessen the severity' of a sore throat any more than expectorating or blowing one's nose 'lessens the severity' of a cold."

Petitioner contends that even if its advertising claims in the past were false, the portion of the Commission's order requiring "corrective advertising" exceeds the Commission's statutory power. The argument is based upon a literal reading of Section 5 of the Federal Trade Commission Act, which authorizes the Commission to issue "cease and desist" orders against violators and does not expressly mention any other remedies. The Commission's position, on the other hand, is that the affirmative disclosure that Listerine will not prevent colds or lessen their severity is absolutely necessary to give effect to the prospective cease and desist order; a hundred years of false claims could have built up a large reservoir of erroneous consumer belief which would persist, unless corrected, long after petitioner ceased making the claims.

The need for the corrective advertising remedy and its appropriateness in this case are important issues. But the threshold question is whether the Commission has the authority to issue such an order. We hold that it does based on the legislative history of the Federal Trade Commission Act of 1914, the Wheeler-Lea Act Amendments of 1938, and the 1975 amendments, along with case precedents interpreting the act.

Having established that the Commission does have the power to order corrective advertising in appropriate cases, it remains to consider whether use of the remedy against Listerine is warranted and equitable. We have concluded that part 3 of the order should be modified to delete the phrase "Contrary to prior advertising." With that modification, we approve the order.

Our role in reviewing the remedy is limited. The Supreme Court has set forth the standard:

> *The Commission is the expert body to determine what remedy is necessary to eliminate the unfair or deceptive trade practices which have been disclosed. It has wide latitude for judgment and the courts will not interfere except where the remedy selected has no reasonable relation to the unlawful practices found to exist.*

The Commission has adopted the following standard for the imposition of corrective advertising:

> *If a deceptive advertisement has played a substantial role in creating or reinforcing in the public's mind a false and material belief which lives on after the false advertising ceases, there is clear and continuing injury to competition and to the consuming public as consumers continue to make purchasing decisions based on the false belief. Since this injury cannot be averted by merely requiring respondent to cease disseminating the advertisement, we may appropriately order respondent to take affirmative action designed to terminate the otherwise continuing ill effects of the advertisement.*

We think this standard is entirely reasonable. It dictates two factual inquiries: (1) Did Listerine's advertisements play a substantial role in creating or reinforcing in the public's mind a false belief about the product? and Would this belief linger on after the false advertising ceases? It strikes us that if the answer to both questions is not yes, then Listerine may be wasting their massive advertising budgets. Indeed, it is more than a little peculiar to hear petitioner assert that its commercials really have no effect on consumer belief.

Affirmed with modifications in favor of Respondent, Commission.

Critical Thinking about the Law

AS A FUTURE BUSINESS MANAGER YOU likely will have consultants who will attempt to persuade you of the quality and appropriateness of their proposals. Important to you will be not only *what* the proposal is, but *why* you should accept it. Whenever we ask the question Why? we are looking for reasons.

Learning to ask Why? is a relatively simple but crucial skill to develop. Unless you ask a consultant why you should accept a proposal, you might approve a bad proposal or reject a good one for no good reason.

The case presents you with an opportunity to develop the skill of asking why.

1. The court gives a rationale for its finding that the FTC has the authority to order corrective advertising. What missing information do you need before you can evaluate the quality of this rationale?

   CLUE Find the paragraph in which the court provides its rationale. Ask yourself why the court believes the rationale is sound. Next ask yourself what more you would like to know before being confident about the quality of the court's rationale.

2. The court ordered that "contrary to prior advertising" be deleted from the corrective advertising. What reasons did the court give for this deletion?

   CLUE Imagine that the court is asked to explain why the deletion is desirable.

3. When trying to stop false advertising and seeking a remedy for it, the FTC is faced with a clash between two primary ethical norms. Identify those norms.

   CLUE Tackle this question one part at a time. What primary ethical norm is promoted by eliminating false advertising? What primary ethical norm is promoted by permitting the advertising?

In addition to rule making and adjudication, executive and independent agencies perform a variety of tasks that are less well known but equally important to the average individual or business. The most significant of these are:

1. *Advising* businesses and individuals concerning what an agency considers legal or not legal. The antitrust merger guidelines we discuss in chapter 22 are an example of an attempt by the Justice Department and the FTC to advise all interested parties about what conduct will be considered violations of Section 7 of the Clayton Act. More generally, lawyers representing interested parties meet daily with agency officials to receive informal comments or advice.

2. *Conducting studies* of industry and markets. Agencies such as the FTC, the OSHA, and the FDA (Food and Drug Administration) carry out studies to determine the level of economic concentration in an industry, dangerous products in the workplace, and the harmful effects of legal drugs.

3. *Providing information* to the general public on myriad matters through answering phone calls, distributing pamphlets, and holding seminars.

4. *Licensing* of businesses in certain areas, such as radio and television stations (FCC).

5. *Managing property*. The General Services Administration (GSA) is the largest landlord in the country. It buys, sells, and leases all property used by the U.S. government.

LIMITATIONS ON ADMINISTRATIVE AGENCIES' POWERS

STATUTORY LIMITATIONS

Certain federal statutes, summarized in Table 16-2 on page 383, limit the power of administrative agencies and their officials. We have already discussed the Administrative Procedure Act. You should carefully review the brief descriptions of the other statutes listed in the table. It is important that you know, both as a future business manager and as an individual citizen, their major provisions. For instance, under the Federal Register Act of 1933, the Federal Privacy Act of 1974, and the Freedom of Information Act of 1966 as amended in 1974 and 1976, the decision-making processes of administrative agencies are open to the public. This legislation prevents secret, arbitrary, or capricious activity by the "fourth branch of government." And, as you have seen, judicial review of administrative agencies' rule-making and adjudication functions serves a similar purpose. Note also that private citizens have a means of relief against improper acts by employees of federal administrative agencies through the Federal Tort Claims Act of 1946, which forces agencies to waive sovereign immunity for their tortious actions and those of their employees. Tortious actions under this act include assault, battery, abuse of prosecution, false arrest, and trespass. For example, if an inspector from the EPA illegally enters a business property after being told to leave, the inspector, as well as the agency, may be held liable.

We said earlier that agencies were exempted from holding open hearings in certain circumstances, chiefly when proceedings concern military matters of foreign affairs. Some agencies, such as the National Economic Commission in the following case, have tried to stretch the exemption to cover proceedings in other "sensitive" matters.

PUBLIC CITIZENS V. NATIONAL ECONOMIC COMMISSION
UNITED STATES DISTRICT COURT 703 F. SUPP. 113 (D.D.C. 1989)

Plaintiff Public Citizens sought to enjoin the National Economic Commission (NEC) from holding closed hearings. During the late fall of 1989, the NEC and the administrator of the General Services Administration sought to close upcoming January meetings of the NEC. At those meetings, the NEC was to hear expert testimony and discuss economic issues confronting the nation, including "economic assumptions" regarding growth, inflation, interest rates, and unemployment, as well as "budget options," such as revenue sources and budget cuts. The NEC sought closure of all meetings at which these issues would be discussed, alleging that participants and witnesses would be inhibited from speaking candidly if the meetings were open to the public. The NEC also asserted that information obtained at open meetings would lead to unwarranted speculation over future economic policy, which in turn might disrupt national markets. Public Citizen, a public-interest group, and others, including the *Washington Post* and the *Wall Street Journal*, sought to prevent the closure of the meetings.

JUDGE GREEN

In previous cases, the Nuclear Regulatory Commission sought to close a series of meetings to discuss preparation of the agency's annual budget request for fiscal year 1982, invoking exemption 9(B) of the Sunshine Act. The Court concluded that there "is no blanket exemption for agency meetings at any stage of the budget preparation process. The availability of exemptions for specific portions of budgetary discussions must be determined upon the facts of each case." The Court recognized that "specific items discussed at Commission budget meetings might be exempt from the open-meeting requirement of the Act, and might justify closing portions of the Commission meeting." However, [the Court] made it clear beyond any doubt that this could only be done "on an individual and particularized basis." Furthermore, the burden is on the party seeking to close the meeting to establish that the invoked exemption properly applies.

Defendants in the instant case are not seeking to close specific portions of the scheduled meetings on an "individual and particularized" basis. On the contrary, defendants wish to shield the internal debate from the public by closing, in their entirety, all working sessions of the [NEC]. They have not carried their burden of establishing that exemption 9(B) applies to all of the scheduled meetings of the [NEC].

Rather than singling out discrete portions of some meetings on an individual and particularized basis with justification for such limited closure, defendants assert a sweeping and broad deliberative process privilege, shielding their internal debate and operation from the public. The legislative history of the Sunshine Act as well as the relevant case law prohibits this.

The district court permanently enjoins the NEC from closing its meetings.

INSTITUTIONAL LIMITATIONS

EXECUTIVE BRANCH The power of administrative agencies is limited by the executive branch through (1) the power of the president to appoint the heads of the agencies, (2) the power of the Office of Management and Budget (OMB) to recommend a fiscal year budget for each agency, and (3) presidential executive orders.

The president not only appoints the head of each administrative agency but also designates some lower-level heads of departments and divisions that do not come under the federal civil service system. Naturally, presidential appointees tend to have the same philosophical bent as the chief executive and are often of the same party. In this way, the president gains some influence over both independent and executive agencies.

Presidents exercise even greater influence over executive agencies through the budget process and executive orders. In 1981, for instance, President Reagan signed Executive Order 12291, which requires executive agencies to perform a cost-benefit analysis before promulgating a *major* federal regulation. A major federal regulation is one that will cost business $100 million or more to comply with. To take another example, this one concerning the budget process, Executive Order 12498, signed in 1985 (also by President Reagan), extended the OMB's powers so that it now has authority over "pre-rule-making action" by executive agencies. This executive order requires civilian government agencies to submit a Draft Regulatory Program listing all pre-rule-making and other significant actions they intend to take in a fiscal year. These Draft Regulatory Programs become part of the Administration's Regulatory Program. Once that program is published by the OMB, no agency may deviate from the plan without approval from the OMB unless forced to do so by the courts. Note that these executive orders affect *executive* administrative agencies. *Independent* administrative agencies have been requested to comply voluntarily with these orders and some have done so. A bill passed by the House of Representatives and the Senate in 1995, and discussed in this chapter under "Cre-

TABLE 16-2 *Federal Statutes Limiting Administrative Agencies' Authority*

STATUTE	SUMMARY OF PROVISIONS
Federal Register of Act of 1933	Created the Federal Register system, which mandates the publication of all notices of federal agency meetings, proposed regulations, and final regulations in the *Federal Register*. The Federal Register system includes the *Government Manual*, which lists information, updated yearly, about each administrative agency, and the *Code of Federal Regulations* (CFR), which codifies regulations promulgated by agencies of the federal government.
Freedom of Information Act of 1966 (FOIA)	Requires each agency to publish in the *Federal Register* places where the public can get information from the agency, procedural and substantive rules and regulations, and policy statements. Also, the FOIA requires each agency to make available for copying on request such items as satff manuals, staff instruction orders, and adjudicated opinions, as well as interpretations of policy statements. Nine exceptions exist that enable an agency to deny an FOIA request by the public, a business, or other groups.
Government in Sunshine Act of 1976 (Sunshine Act)	Requires each agency headed by a collegiate body to hold every portion of a business meeting open to public attendance. A collegiate body exists if the agency is headed by two or more individuals, the majority of whom are appointed by the president and confirmed by the Senate.
Federal Privacy Act of 1974 (FPA)	Prevents an agency from disclosing any record in a system of records, by any means of communication, to any person or agency without the written authority of the individual. Eleven exceptions to the statute allow information to be released by the agency without the consent of individuals. Some exceptions are (1) to meet an FOIA request; (2) for use by the Selective Service System; (3) for use by another federal agency in civil or criminal law enforcement; (4) for use by a committee of the Congress; or (5) to meet a court order. Also, under the FPA, an individual may obtain information and correct errors in his or her record.
Administrative Procedure Act (APA)	The APA requires that certain uniform procedures be followed by all federal administrative agencies when performing their rule-making and adjudicative functions.
Federal Tort Claims Act of 1946 (FTCA)	Requires the federal government to waive sovereign immunity and to assume liability for the tortious act of its employees if nondiscretionary functions are being carried out by the employee.

ation of Administrative Agencies" applies to both executive and independent administrative agencies.

LEGISLATIVE BRANCH Congress limits the authority of administrative agencies through its (1) oversight power, (2) investigative power, (3) power to terminate an agency, and (4) power to advise and consent on presidential nominations for heads of administrative agencies.

When Congress creates an agency, it delegates to that agency its own legislative power over a narrow area of commerce, say, human rights. Each year, through one of its oversight committees, it determines whether the agency has been carrying out its mandated function. Suppose, for example, that the House Energy and Commerce Committee's Subcommittee on Consumer, Finance, and Telecommunications finds that the SEC is not enforcing laws against insider trading and fraud. The full committee will investigate and, if it finds dereliction, will order the SEC to enforce the laws as it is charged to do.

The greatest legislative limitation on agency power, however, lies in Congress's right to approve or disapprove an agency budget submitted by the executive branch (the OMB). If Congress disagrees with the agency's actions, it can slash the budget or refuse to budget the agency at all. The latter action, of course, will shut down the agency. On the other hand, if Congress believes that the executive branch is shortchanging an agency for some reason, it can raise that agency's budget above the amount proposed by the OMB.

JUDICIAL BRANCH The courts can curb administrative agencies' rule-making and adjudicative excesses by reversing or modifying such actions, as we explained earlier in this chapter. You might want to go back to that portion of the chapter at this point and reread the standards used by the courts in reviewing these agency functions.

INTERNATIONAL DIMENSIONS OF ADMINISTRATIVE AGENCIES

Like the United States, other nations have created administrative agencies to carry out important government functions. In some cases, they have more unfettered authority than their U.S. counterparts. Japan's Ministry of International Trade and Industry, Ministry of Finance, and Ministry of Foreign Affairs, for example, are often thought to be more powerful than elected Japanese politicians. Educated Japanese compete to work for these powerful agencies, which deeply influence trade, foreign affairs, and domestic issues.

The U.S. Trade Representative's Office, the Commerce Department's International Division, and the State Department share power over trade matters and regularly meet with and influence their administrative agency counterparts in Japan and Europe, particularly in the European Union. Recently, the Securities and Exchange Commission (SEC) entered into memoranda of agreement with Switzerland and other European countries, as well as with several Caribbean nations, to obtain disclosure of numbered bank accounts suspected of being used to harbor illegal profits from insider trading and other fraudulent activities in the United States (this topic is discussed in chapter 22).

SUMMARY

Administrative law is defined broadly as any rule (statute or regulation) that directly or indirectly affects an administrative agency. The Administrative Procedure Act (APA) provides procedural guidelines for federal agencies; these guidelines are often copied, in whole or in part, by state and local administrative agencies.

The major functions of administrative agencies are rule making, adjudication, and the carrying out of numerous administrative activities. The executive, judicial, and legislative branches of government limit the power of federal agencies in numerous ways. In addition, several federal statutes limit the authority of administrative agencies.

Federal administrative agencies meet with their counterparts in other nations and enter into international agreements that aid the enforcement powers of U.S. agencies.

REVIEW QUESTIONS

16-1. Why did Congress create administrative agencies?

16-2. What are the two major functions of administrative agencies?

16-3. Explain the distinction between executive administrative agencies and independent administrative agencies.

16-4. Describe how the courts check the power of administrative agencies.

16-5. Describe how the executive branch of government checks the power of administrative agencies.

16-6. Describe how the legislative branch of government checks the power of administrative agencies.

16-7. The Occupational Safety and Health Administration (OSHA) promulgated a rule limiting employees' exposure to cotton dust during the manufacture of cotton products because serious diseases were traced to exposure to such dust. The cotton industry argued that the standard was beyond the scope of OSHA's authority in that it failed to reflect a reasonable relationship between the costs of compliance for the industry and the benefits to people working in the cotton industry. OSHA and the Secretary of Labor argued that they did not need to perform a cost-benefit analysis to justify the standard but needed only to show that the standard reduced the risk of illness to an extent that was technologically and economically feasible. Who won this case, and why?

16-8. Under the Clean Air Act, the EPA can regulate gasoline additions if they "endanger the public welfare." Scientific evidence showed that lead emissions from gasoline constituted 90 percent of all the lead in the air and that this lead could be absorbed into the body. The EPA promulgated regulations requiring a step-by-step reduction of the lead content of gasoline. Gasoline manufacturers challenged EPA's rule-making procedure, claiming that it was arbitrary and capricious because the evidence supporting the agency's decision was unsound. They claimed that air was only one of several sources of the lead absorbed by the body. The EPA argued that the evidence it had marshaled was sufficient to justify the regulations. Who won this case, and why?

16-9. The Federal Communications Commission (FCC) promulgated rules prohibiting cable television from broadcasting feature films more than three years old but less than ten years old in addition to certain other programs. Home Box Office (HBO) argued that these rules were arbitrary and capricious and that they discriminated against cable companies. The FCC countered that the regulations were necessary to prevent siphoning off of movies by cable companies from (free) network television. Who won this case, and why?

16-10. In 1969, the Secretary of Transportation approved a plan to extend an interstate highway through Overton Park in Memphis, Tennessee. A group of environmentalists petitioned the courts, seeking to enjoin the Department of Transportation (DOT) from financing the project. They argued that under the Federal Aid Highway Act, federal funds could not be used for highway construction through a public park if a "feasible and prudent alternative" existed. DOT personnel produced affidavits indicating that the secretary had considered other alternatives and argued that, unless there was substantial evidence to the contrary, the secretary's decision should be upheld by the reviewing court. Who won this case, and why?

16-11. The Federal Trade Commission (FTC) instituted proceedings against The Soft Drink Bottling Co., alleging violations of laws prohibiting unfair methods of competition. The complaint against Soft Drink Bottling challenged the validity of exclusive bottling agreements between the company and franchised bottlers, who have agreed not to sell the company's products outside a designated territory. Soft Drink Bottling asked the FTC to include the 513 bottlers in the case. The FTC refused to do so on the ground that inclusion of so many bottlers would make the case unmanageable—although it said that any bottlers who wished to could intervene in the case. Soft Drink Bottling decided to appeal the decision to a federal court. Did the court entertain the action?

16-12. One of the hottest business issues today is the outrageousness lavish pay of many chief executive officers (CEOs) vis-à-vis corporate profits. In 1990, for example, United Airlines' CEO got $18.3 million—1,200 times what a new flight attendant makes—even though United's profits had fallen by

71 percent that year! The Interstate Commerce Commission would like to regulate CEO pay. Does it have the authority to do so? Explain.

CASE PROBLEMS

16-13. George Carlin, a satiric humorist, recorded a 12-minute monologue "Filthy Words." He began by referring to "the words you couldn't say on the public airwaves" and then listed those words, repeating them over and over again. A New York radio station owned by Pacifica Foundation (Pacifica) broadcast Carlin's "Filthy Words" monologue. A father who heard the broadcast while driving with his young son filed a complaint with the Federal Communications Commission (FCC). The Federal Communications Act forbids the use of "any obscene, indecent, or profane language by means of radio communications." Therefore, FCC issued an order granting the complaint and informing Pacifica that the order would be considered in future licensing decisions involving Pacifica. Is the FCC regulation legal? *Federal Communications Commission v. Pacifica Foundation*, 438 U.S. 726 (1978)

16-14. The Food and Drug Administration (FDA) is charged with enforcing the Food, Drug, and Cosmetics Act. This statute mandates that FDA limit the amount of "poisonous or deleterious substances" in food. The FDA established certain "action levels" of unavoidable contaminants. Food producers that sell products that are contaminated above the set action level are subject to enforcement proceedings initiated by FDA. FDA argues that the "action levels" are merely interpretive rules or statements of policy that do not require notice and comment. The Community Nutrition Institute, groups, sued to require FDA to follow the notice and comment procedure. Who wins? *Community Nutrition Institute v. Young*, 818 F.2d 943 (D.C. Cir. 1987)

16-15. In 1970, Congress concluded that work-related deaths and injuries had become a national problem, it enacted the Occupational Safety and Health Act of 1970 (OSHA). The act creates a new statutory duty for employers to avoid maintaining unsafe and unhealthy working conditions and empowers the secretary of labor (Secretary) to promulgate health and safety standards.

A government inspector cited Atlas Roofing Company, Inc. (Atlas), for violating an OSHA rule that required roof-opening covers to be installed to prevent accidents. An employee's death had resulted from the violation. The Secretary issued an order of abatement and proposed a $600 civil penalty. Atlas contested the citation and was afforded a hearing before an Administrative Law Judge (ALF). The ALF and Secretary affirmed the findings of a violation and issued the order of abatement and civil penalty. Atlas sought judicial review. The court of appeals affirmed. Atlas appealed. Who won? Explain. *Atlas Roofing v. Occupational Safety and Health Review Commission*, 430 U.S. 442 (1977)

16-16. On August 2, 1967, The New York Landmark Preservation Commission designated the Grand Central Terminal (Terminal) as a landmark building and the city block it occupies as a landmark site. Terminal, which is owned by the Penn Central Transportation Company (Penn Central), is one of New York City's most famous buildings.

In January 1968, Penn Central filed an application with Commission to construct a 55-story office building in the airspace above the existing façade of Terminal. The Commission denied Penn Central's application. Commission stated:

We have no fixed rule against making additions to designated buildings–it all depends on how they are done. But to balance a 55-story office tower above a flamboyant Beaux Arts façade seems nothing more than an esthetic joke. Quite simply, the tower would overwhelm the Terminal by its sheer mass.

Penn Central filed suit in New York Supreme Court. The trial court held in favor of Penn Central and granted an injunction and declaratory relief. The appellate division reversed. The court of appeals affirmed. Penn Central appealed. Who won? Explain. *Penn Central v. City of New York*, 438 U.S. 104 (1978)

 On the Internet

http://plague.law.umkc.edu/Xfiles/x30.htm   A brief overview of the role of administrative agencies can be found on this page.

http://rs7.loc.gov/loc/guides/govt.html   This site provides a guide to government information about administrative agencies on the Internet.

http://www.itpolicy.gsa.gov/mka/itdirect/faindex.htm   This site provides the names and telephone numbers for most administrative agencies.

http://www.cei.org/ebb/delegate.html   Find an interesting discussion about accountability of administrative agencies on this page.

http://www.abanet.org/adminlaw/process.html   Here is the site to go to if you have ideas about how to improve the way administrative agencies operate.

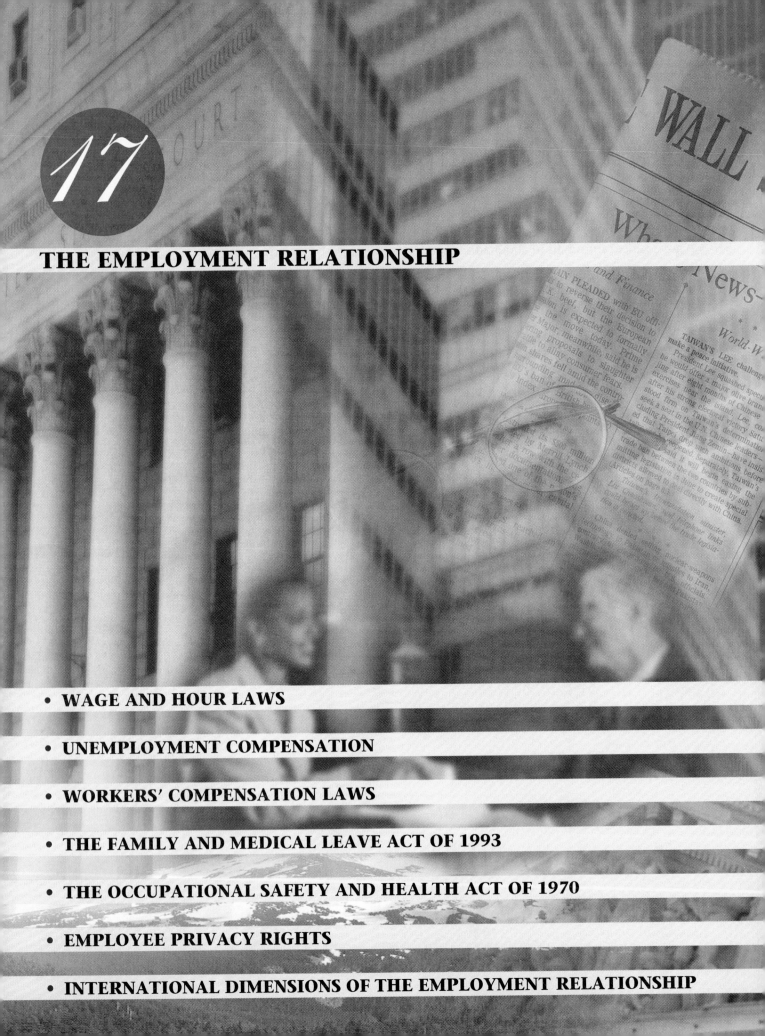

17

THE EMPLOYMENT RELATIONSHIP

- **WAGE AND HOUR LAWS**

- **UNEMPLOYMENT COMPENSATION**

- **WORKERS' COMPENSATION LAWS**

- **THE FAMILY AND MEDICAL LEAVE ACT OF 1993**

- **THE OCCUPATIONAL SAFETY AND HEALTH ACT OF 1970**

- **EMPLOYEE PRIVACY RIGHTS**

- **INTERNATIONAL DIMENSIONS OF THE EMPLOYMENT RELATIONSHIP**

One way to think about the employment relationship is that it is a contractual relationship between the employer and employee: The employer agrees to pay the employee a certain amount of money in exchange for the employee's agreement to render specific services. Early in our history, the employer and employee were free to determine all the conditions of their employment relationship. Today, however, both the federal and state governments specify many of the conditions under which that relationship exists.

This chapter will explain many of the conditions that the government imposes. The first four sections will focus on the laws that affect employee wages and benefits: wage and hour laws; unemployment compensation legislation; state workers' compensation laws; and the Family and Medical Leave Act. The fifth and sixth sections shift to protecting worker safety and health and privacy rights. The final section focuses on the international dimensions of the employment relationship.

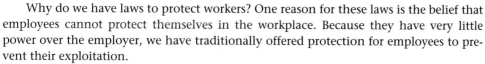

Critical Thinking about the Law

EMPLOYERS ARE REQUIRED BY LAW TO provide specific employment conditions for their employees. For example, minimum wage and hours laws help to ensure that the worker will be not be required to work an extraordinary number of hours for little pay.

Why do we have laws to protect workers? One reason for these laws is the belief that employees cannot protect themselves in the workplace. Because they have very little power over the employer, we have traditionally offered protection for employees to prevent their exploitation.

After you read the following case, answer the critical thinking questions that will sharpen your thinking about employee benefits.

Mike works full-time at a large factory. As he is preparing to go home after his shift, he sees his boss yelling angrily at the television in his office. The news station had just reported a new law passed by Congress that requires employers to provide paid leave for the birth of a child. Both mothers and fathers will receive the paid leave. Mike's boss thinks the new law is an outrageous restriction on employers. Mike, however, is happy about the new law because his wife is pregnant. He will be happy to stay home with his wife when she has the baby.

1. Mike's opinion and his employer's opinion about the new law obviously conflict. Their respective ethical preferences are one important cause of their disagreement. What ethical norm seems to be dominating the employer's thought?

   CLUE Why is the employer upset? Review your list of ethical norms; try to match one of the norms to the reason why the employer is angry.

2. Mike's boss makes the following argument: "It is ridiculous that the government would make me pay my employees to sit at home! They are my employees. I should get to decide if employees should be allowed to leave for the birth of a child." Do you see any problems with this argument?

   CLUE How does the employer's argument conflict with the reason for offering employee benefits?

3. Before you make a judgment about the worth of the new law, is there any additional information that would help your thinking?

   CLUE What information seems to be missing? Several crucial pieces of information about the paid leave are not offered in the news report.

WAGE AND HOUR LAWS

Employers do not have the complete freedom any more to pay workers any wages they choose or to require them to work any number of hours. Several federal laws impose minimum wage and hour requirements. For example, the Davis-Bacon Act[1] requires that contractors and subcontractors working on government projects pay the "prevailing wage." The most pervasive law regulating wages and hours, however, is the Fair Labor Standards Act[2] (FLSA), a law that covers all employers engaged in interstate commerce or the production of goods for interstate commerce.

One of the most significant aspects of the FLSA is its requirement that a minimum wage of a specified amount be paid to all employees in covered industries. This specified amount is periodically raised by Congress to compensate for increases in the cost of living caused by inflation. The most recent increase took effect on September 1, 1997, when the minimum wage rose to $5.15 per hour.

The FLSA also requires that employees who work more than 40 hours in a week be paid no less than one and one half times their regular wage for all the hours beyond the standard 40-hour work week. Four categories of employees, however, are excluded from this provision of the law: executives, administrative employees, professional employees, and outside salespersons. To prevent employers from taking advantage of these exemptions, however, the act generally requires that these employees earn at least a minimum amount of income and spend a certain amount of time engaged in specified activities before they can fall into each of those exempted categories.

UNEMPLOYMENT COMPENSATION

Having a minimum wage provides a great deal of security for employees when they are working, but what happens to those who lose their jobs? In 1935, Congress passed the Federal Unemployment Tax Act[3], which created a state system that provides unemployment compensation to qualified employees who lose their jobs. Under this act, employers pay taxes to the states. These tax dollars are deposited into the federal government's Unemployment Insurance Fund.

Each state then has an account from which it has access to the money in the fund. States then set up their own system of allocating these funds, determining such matters as how the amount of compensation is determined and how long it can be collected. Eligibility requirements must also be set, with most states requiring, at minimum, that an applicant was not fired for just cause or did not voluntarily quit.

WORKERS' COMPENSATION LAWS

Unlike many other laws affecting the employment relationship, workers' compensation legislation is purely state law. Our coverage of this topic must therefore be rather generalized. Prudent businesspeople will familiarize themselves with the workers' compensation statutes of the states within which their companies operate.

COVERAGE

workers' compensation laws
State laws that provide financial compensation to covered employees, or their dependents, when employees are injured on the job.

Workers' compensation laws provide financial compensation to employees or their dependents when the covered employee of a covered employer is injured on the job. For administrative convenience, most states exclude certain types of businesses and small firms from coverage. A few states also allow employers to "opt out" of the system. These states may likewise give the employee the opportunity to reject coverage.

---

[1] 40 U.S.C. § 276a–276a-5 (1998).
[2] 29 U.S.C. §§ 201–260 (1998).
[3] 26 U.S.C. §§ 3301–3310.

Workers' compensation is said to be "no fault" because recovery does not depend on showing that the injury was caused by an error of the employer. Think of workers' compensation as analogous to insurance: The employer pays premiums based on the frequency of accidents in the employer's business, and the employees receive insurance-like benefits if injured.

To recover workers' compensation benefits, the injured party must demonstrate that she or he is an *employee*, as opposed to being an independent contractor. This distinction, which was discussed in chapter 14, is based on the degree of control the employer can exert over the worker: The greater the degree of control, the more likely the party will be considered an employee. Factors showing employer control include the employer's dictating how the job is to be done, providing the tools to do the job, and setting the worker's schedule. In contrast, in employer-independent contractor relationships, the employer generally specifies the task to be accomplished but has no control over how the task is done. A broker hired by a firm to sell a piece of property is an example of an independent contractor.

The employee must also establish that the *injury occurred on the job*. This means it must have taken place during the time and within the scope of the claimant's employment. Once an employee is on company property, the courts generally find that the employee was on the job. This finding is based on the application of what is commonly called the *premises rule*.

More difficult, however, is the situation of the employee who is injured on the way to or from work. If the employee works fixed hours at a fixed location, injuries on the way to or from work are generally noncompensable. But some states provide for exceptions to this rule. One exception, known as the *special-hazards exception*, applies when a necessary means of access to the employer's premises presents a special risk, even if the hazardous area is beyond the control of the employer. For example, if an employee must make a left-hand turn across a busy thoroughfare to enter the company parking lot, this situation has been held to be risk of employment; therefore employees involved in accidents while making a left-hand turn into their employer's parking lots have been allowed compensation under this exception.

Another exception occurs when an employee is requested to *run an errand* for the employer on the way to or from work. In general, compensation is allowed for injuries sustained during the course of running the errand.

Sometimes, as a consequence of the job, an employee is forced to *temporarily stay away from home*. What if the employee is injured while away from home? In some states, reasonable injuries suffered while away from work are covered. In a New York case, a typist was required to travel to Canada to transcribe depositions. While showering in her hotel, she fell and injured herself. She filed a successful workers' compensation claim.

The elements necessary for recovery under workers' compensation laws are summarized in Exhibit 17-1.

RECOVERABLE BENEFITS

The amounts and types of benefits recoverable under workers' compensation are specified by each state's relevant statute. Most statutes cover medical, hospital, and rehabilitation expenses. In some cases, expenses for unusual items have been allowed as necessary. For example, a New York court ruled that a claimant

---

EXHIBIT 17-1 *Elements Required for a Successful Workers' Compensation Claim*

1. Claimant is an employee, as opposed to an independent contractor.
2. Both claimant and employer are covered by the state workers' compensation statute.
3. The injury occurred while the claimant was on the job and acting within the scope of the claimant's employment.

who had become a quadriplegic as a result of a work-related accident was entitled to recover the cost of building a self-contained apartment attached to his parents' home. The claimant, who had formerly been highly independent, had been placed in a nursing home after the accident, but the depression caused by his injury was so compounded by being surrounded by infirm, elderly people that he had tried to commit suicide three times. Thus the court felt that, in this case, the apartment qualified under the statute as "other treatment" or "appliances" necessary to treat the worker for his work-connected injury.

Compensation under state statutes also generally includes payment for lost wages. When employees become disabled as a result of their injury, most states have a schedule that determines the amount of compensation for the disability, as well as compensation schedules for loss of body parts. Thus, an employee who lost a toe in an industrial accident, even though not disabled as a result, would be entitled to some compensation for the loss.

THE CLAIMS PROCESS

Most workers' compensation claims are handled by a state agency responsible for administering the compensation fund and adjudicating claims. In general, an employee who is injured fills out a claim form and files it with the responsible administrative agency. A representative of the agency then verifies the claim with the employer. If the employer does not contest the claim—and most do not—an employee of the bureau (usually called a "claims examiner") investigates the claim and determines the proper payment.

If either the amount or the validity of the claim is contested, there is an informal hearing before a regional office of the agency. Most states provide for an appeals process within the agency. A dissatisfied party who has exhausted the administrative appeals process may appeal to the state trial court of general jurisdiction.

BENEFITS OF THE WORKERS' COMPENSATION SYSTEM

Workers' compensation systems are often touted as benefitting workers. In many ways, they do. Before we had workers' compensation statutes, an employee who was injured on the job could successfully gain compensation from his employer only if able to prove that the injury was caused by the employer's negligence. Such proof was often difficult to produce.

Recovery was further restricted by the availability of powerful defenses. If the employee's own negligence contributed to the injury, the employee could not recover because of the _defense of contributory negligence._ Under the _fellow servant rule_, an employee could not recover if the act of another employee caused or contributed to the injury. And in some cases, the courts would say that if the claimant employee engaged in work knowing that it presented a particular safety risk, that employee had _assumed the risk_ of injury, and therefore the employer was not liable.

Overall, then, workers' compensation helps employees because it has removed from them the burden of having to prove employer negligence and has made all the defenses just mentioned irrelevant to compensation claims. Today, employees can obtain compensation in situations in which, formerly, they could not have recovered. The system also helps employees because they do not need to hire an attorney to recover. Many injured workers have never used attorneys and would not know how to seek legal help. They might also fear retaliation from their employers for bringing suit.

Certain aspects of workers' compensation, however, work to the detriment of employees and to the benefit of employers. In most states, employees who are covered by workers' compensation statutes do not have the right to bring personal injury lawsuits against their employers. Because the payment schedule adopted under any state law is a political compromise heavily influenced by business lobbies, the amount of compensation given is minimal—generally far less than the amount a party could recover through a successful lawsuit brought against the employer.

ADVANTAGES	DISADVANTAGES
Guaranteed recovery for on-the-job injury.	Employees give up the right to bring a negligence action, which might have yielded a much larger recovery.
No need to hire a lawyer to recover.	
Employees' own negligence does not bar recovery.	Because employers do not have to fear large damage awards to workers who suffer substantial injuries, they may be less concerned about safe working conditions.
Negligence of other workers does not bar recovery.	

Some people argue that claimants are not completely compensated under most payment schedules and that workers' compensation laws compel employees to give up the chance of a large (or full) recovery in exchange for certain, but minimal, recovery. Because employers simply make regular payments to the workers' compensation fund, the costs of occupational injuries are a routine part of their operating expenses. Companies do not have to worry about incurring substantial unanticipated losses; at most, they may find their premiums increased if the number of claims filed against them goes up. Some people argue that, by reducing potential costs for workplace injuries in this manner, workers' compensation has made employers more careless about employee safety than they would be if they had to fear huge damage awards.

Table 17-1 provides a quick comparison of the advantages and disadvantages of workers' compensation from the employee's point of view.

THE FAMILY AND MEDICAL LEAVE ACT OF 1993

On August 5, 1993, the **Family and Medical Leave Act (FMLA)** went into effect. This law was designed to guarantee that workers facing an unexpected medical catastrophe or the birth or adoption of a child would be able to take needed time off from work. The act was hailed by its supporters as a "breakthrough" in U.S. law, and it was feared by its opponents as an unwieldy encumbrance upon business. So far, the jury is still out on the act's effectiveness.

Family and Medical Leave Act (FMLA) A law designed to guarantee that workers facing a medical catastrophe or certain specified family responsibilities will be able to take needed time off from work without pay, but without losing medical benefits or their job.

MAJOR PROVISIONS

The Family and Medical Leave Act is a highly complex piece of legislation, containing six titles divided into 26 sections. The regulations, designed to guide the implementation of the act, are eight times longer than the statute itself! No wonder many employers were still not in full compliance with the act a year after it became effective.

The act covers all public employers and private employers of 50 or more employees. Covered employers must formulate a family leave policy and revise employee handbooks accordingly. The policy must provide all eligible employees with up to 12 weeks of leave during any 12-month period for any of the following family-related occurrences:

- The birth of a child.
- The adoption of a child.
- The placement of a foster child in the employee's care.
- The care of a seriously ill spouse, parent, or child.
- A serious health condition that renders the employee unable to perform any of the essential functions of his or her job.

To exercise one's rights under the FMLA, an employee whose need for a leave is foreseeable must advise the employer of that need at least 30 days prior to the anticipated date on which the leave needs to begin, or as soon as practicable. A typical foreseeable leave would be one for the birth of a child.

If the leave is unforeseeable, notice must be given as soon as practicable. "As soon as practicable" is defined as within one or two business days from when the need for the leave becomes known.

The act does not provide a clear definition of exactly what type of notice is necessary. At minimum, the employee must inform the employer of why the employee needs the leave, and, if possible, the length of time needed. The FMLA does not have to be specifically mentioned in the request.

Courts look at the facts of each case individually to determine whether notice was sufficient. The following case illustrates how confusing the issue of adequacy of notice can be.

REICH, SECRETARY OF LABOR V. MIDWEST PLASTIC ENGINEERING
UNITED STATES DISTRICT COURT 934 F. SUPP. 266 (W.D. MICH 1995)

Ms. Van Dosen worked for Defendant Midwest Plastic Engineering, Inc. from July, 1988 through November 29, 1993. On November 15, 1993, she telephoned her employer to say that she had been to the emergency room the previous night because she thought she had chickenpox and she would not be at work that day because she was going to see her doctor. On November 16, she called again to say she had chickenpox. She did not return to work until November 29, because she had ultimately been hospitalized for the chickenpox. Her only communication with the employer between November 16 and 29 was when a friend picked up her paycheck and said that Van Dosen had a doctor's appointment. When she returned to work, Ms. Van Dosen was fired for excessive absenteeism. She then filed a charge claiming that her termination constituted a violation of the FMLA.

DISTRICT JUDGE HOLMES BELL

The Act is silent regarding the notice which an employee must provide to her employer when the need for leave is not foreseeable. The regulations, however, provide: . . . "An employee shall provide at least verbal notice sufficient to make the employer aware that the employee needs FMLA-qualifying leave, and the anticipated timing and duration of the leave. The employee need not expressly assert rights under the FMLA, but may only state that leave is needed for [a cover reason]. The employer should inquire further of the employee if it is necessary to have more information about whether FMLA leave is being sought by the employee, and obtain the necessary details of the leave to be taken. In the case of medical conditions, the employer may find it necessary to inquire further to determine if the leave is because of a serious health condition and may request medical certification to support the need for such leave.

[T]he Court must now determine whether Ms. Van Dosen informed Midwest of her condition with sufficient detail to make it evident that the requested leave was protected as FMLA-qualifying leave. The Court can illustrate . . . with a hypothetical involving two eligible employees. Both employees were involved in separate car accidents on Sunday.

The first employee incurred substantial injuries as a result of his accident which necessitated his being hospitalized for several weeks. The second employee sustained no injuries in his accident.

Neither employee came to work on Monday, the first because he was in the hospital and the second because he decided to go fishing. Each employee called the employer on Monday morning and reported that he would not be at work that day and that he had been involved in a car accident on Sunday. Under the Act and the regulations, the first employee clearly had a "serious health condition," and the second clearly did not. But neither employee provided the employer with adequate notice of his need for FMLA-leave. While each employee told the employer that he had been involved in a car accident on Sunday, neither employee informed the employer of his condition with sufficient detail to make it evident to the employer that the absence was protected as FMLA-qualifying leave—a person who is involved in a car accident does not necessarily incur a serious health condition.

To provide adequate notice to the employer of his need for FMLA leave, the first employee should have stated that he had been hospitalized as the result of the accident. Such a statement by the employee would have informed his employer of his condition with sufficient detail to make it evident that the requested leave was protected as FMLA-qualifying leave. An employer should not have to speculate as to the nature of an employee's condition.

Turning to the present case, Ms. Van Dosen communicated with Midwest regarding her condition and need for leave on only three occasions prior to the termination of her employment on November 29—her November 15 telephone message, her November 16 conversation with Mr. Adams, and [her friend's] conversation with Mr. Long on November 19. In the course of these communications, Ms. Van Dosen failed to communicate sufficient information to inform Midwest of her condition with sufficient detail to make it evident to Midwest that her leave was as the result of a "serious health condition" and was, therefore, protected as FMLA-qualifying leave.

Specifically, the Court finds that she did not communicate that she was under the continuing treatment of a health care provider for her condition of chicken pox, nor did she communicate that she had received inpatient care at Vencor Hospital as the result of her having chicken pox.

Furthermore, even if Midwest had not already terminated Ms. Van Dosen's employment prior to her November 29 conversation with Mr. Long, and even if she had communicated these facts to Mr. Long during that conversation, the Court nevertheless concludes that the defendants still did not violate the Act. As previously indicated, [the act] required that Ms. Van Dosen provide notice to Midwest "as soon as practicable." Surely, if Ms. Van Dosen was able to go to the bank on the afternoon of November 19, she was "practicably" able to notify Midwest of her condition at least by that date.

Finally, Midwest was permitted to require Ms. Van Dosen to report periodically on her status and intent to return to work. Mr. Long specifically told [her friend] to have Ms. Van Dosen bring in a doctor's slip verifying her condition on Monday, November 22. Ms. Van Dosen failed to do this. Moreover, she failed even to call in on that day to explain either her absence or her failure to bring in the slip and did not call in on November 23, 24, or 29.

Thus, even if she had adequately notified Midwest of her need for FMLA leave—which she did not do—she failed to update Midwest as to her status and intent to return to work as Mr. Long had demanded and Midwest's policies required. This alone gave Midwest a ground to terminate Ms. Van Dosen's employment.

Judgment in favor of Defendant, Midwest Plastic Engineering.

Upon termination of their leaves, employees must be restored to the same position or one that involves substantially equivalent skills, effort, responsibility, and authority. And, although the leave can be unpaid, the employer must continue health insurance benefits during the leave period. The employer may also require an employee to substitute paid time off for unpaid leave. For example, an employee who has four weeks of accrued sick leave and two weeks of vacation and wishes to take a 12-week leave for the birth of a new baby may be required to take the paid vacation and sick leave plus six weeks of unpaid leave.

SERIOUS MEDICAL CONDITION

One of the most contentious issues under the FMLA is what constitutes a medical condition that is serious enough to invoke the protections of the act. That issue is discussed in the following case.

BAUER V. DAYTON-WALTHER CORPORATION
UNITED STATES DISTRICT COURT 910 F. SUPP. 306 (E.D. KY. 1996)

Plaintiff Bauer had worked for Defendant since 1992, under a labor agreement that incorporated a "no-fault" attendance policy whereby employees incur certain numbers of points for absenteeism. Upon the accumulation of six absenteeism points in a six-month period, the employee could be automatically terminated. Bauer acquired six points in the following manner. He earned one point for leaving work two hours early to visit a sick relative; a second point for just taking off some "personal time"; a third point for taking off a day for rectal bleeding and a cold; a fourth point for leaving early because of illness, which he later said was rectal bleeding; a fifth point for leaving work early for a doctor's appointment to check out the rectal bleeding; and then a sixth and seventh point for taking off work without notice for no reason. He was then terminated pursuant to the attendance policy.

Bauer sued his former employer for violation of the Family and Medical Leave Act (FMLA) because he believed that several of his absences were due to his "serious health condition." Defendant employer moved for summary judgment.

DISTRICT JUDGE HOOD

Central to the resolution of this motion is a determination of whether Bauer's condition constituted a "serious health condition" under the FMLA.

[Bauer] does admit that he could have performed the essential functions of his job despite his condition. [He] claims that during the period of time up to [his doctor's] appointment, his rectal bleeding continued. Nevertheless, he missed no work from June 21 to July 11 and apparently had no difficulties performing his job duties. Specifically,

Bauer maintains that he was assessed certain points without regard for his "serious medical condition" and thus in violation of the FMLA.

Dayton-Walther argues that it is entitled to summary judgment because Bauer's situation is not protected by the FMLA. Dayton-Walther contends that Bauer's illness does not constitute a "serious health condition." Bauer, on the other hand, takes issue with the "no-fault" attendance policy claiming that it takes no account of the protections afforded by the FMLA. Bauer maintains that an individual might be faced with a Catch-22: foregoing an examination to discover a potentially serious medical condition or incurring an absentee point under a "no-fault" attendance policy.

[O]nly three different days of absenteeism could possibly implicate the protections of the FMLA. First, one point was incurred on June 18. Various explanations have been presented for this absence. Dayton-Walther points out that Bauer claims he had a common illness such as a cold. Bauer, on the other hand, suggests that his rectal bleeding prevented him from working that day. Second, on June 21 Bauer again incurred one point when he left work early. He claims that he left due to heavy bleeding and reported his situation to his supervisor. Third, on July 11, Bauer left work early for his appointment with Dr. Eckert.

The FMLA guarantees eligible employees the right to take up to twelve weeks unpaid leave per year in certain specified situations . . . [including] where the employee has "a serious health condition that makes the employee unable to perform the essential functions of the position of such employee."

Bauer's claim rests on him [sic] having a "serious health condition" as understood through this final provision. The FMLA and the regulations thereunder prohibit an employer from discriminating against an employee who has used FMLA leave or otherwise interfering with the exercise or attempted exercise of FMLA rights.

The regulations specifically provide that FMLA leave time cannot be counted under a "no-fault" attendance policy. The relevant issue, therefore, is whether Bauer's condition, viewed as he alleges it to be, qualifies for protection under the FMLA. The relevant statutory definition of serious health condition includes ". . . an illness, injury, impairment, or physical or mental condition that involves . . . continuing treatment by a health care provider."

The regulations, intended to illuminate the contours of the scope of the statutory definition, set out six different definitions of serious health condition involving continuing treatment. Only three of those definitions are relevant here: first, "a period of incapacity (i.e., inability to work . . .) of more than three consecutive calendar days. . . ."; second, a "period of incapacity or treatment for such incapacity due to a chronic health condition" (that is, one which requires periodic visits for treatment, continues

over an extended period of time, and may cause an episodic rather than continuing period of incapacity); third, a "period of absences to receive multiple treatments . . . for a condition that would likely result in a period of incapacity of more than three consecutive calendar days in the absence of medical intervention or treatment. . . ."

A review of the record reveals that Bauer's claims of health related absences could never qualify under the first regulatory definition because, even assuming incapacity, it never lasted more than three days. The June 18 absence, whatever the exact cause, lasted only one day. The day after the June 21 absence, Bauer came to work and worked an entire shift. Likewise with the July 11 absence.

Nor did Bauer suffer from a "chronic serious health condition" as defined in the regulations. Bauer sought medical attention on only one occasion due to his condition. Apparently, no treatment of this condition was ever administered. Bauer's condition falls far short of the sort of chronic serious health problems such as diabetes and epilepsy within the purview of the FMLA.

Finally, there is absolutely no support in the record for the contention that Bauer received multiple treatments for a condition which, if left untreated, would have resulted in incapacity for more than three consecutive calendar days. Further, it is not clear that without treatment his condition was such that he would have missed work for the requisite period. [I]t becomes clear that the term "serious health condition" was not intended to include Bauer's condition.

In *Seidle*, the federal district court entertained the question of whether a potentially "serious health condition" could fall within the purview of the FMLA. This Court agrees with the approach taken in Seidle with respect to the potentiality of a condition to become worse. The condition must be taken for what it was during the relevant time period, and not for what it could have conceivably become. Bauer's condition of rectal bleeding, whatever medical label we might attribute to it, is simply not the sort of serious medical condition which Congress contemplated to be covered by the FMLA. Rectal bleeding is nowhere listed in the nonexclusive list of examples of "serious health conditions" which includes afflictions such as heart attacks, most cancers, and pneumonia.

Finally, the Court notes that if Bauer was in a Catch-22 then it was only by his own device. Bauer was not faced with only two options: to forego medical assistance or to incur an absentee point. Nothing prevented Bauer from attempting to set up another appointment time when he was not working. Apparently, Bauer made no effort to accommodate his work schedule. Reconciling appointments with a work schedule is commonplace.

Summary judgment granted in favor of Defendant, Dayton-Walther.

Critical Thinking about the Law

As A CONCERNED CITIZEN, YOU SHOULD pay attention to the reasoning offered by politicians, business people, and other citizens. Furthermore, as a future business manager, you will probably be asked to explain why you make certain decisions. Therefore, you should make it a habit to pay attention to reasoning.

The *Bauer* case addressed the issue of determining when a medical condition is serious enough to provide protection under the FMLA. The following questions can help you understand the reasoning the court used to respond to this issue.

1. Judge Hood clearly identified the issue of the case and concluded that Bauer's condition did not qualify for protection under the FMLA. What reasons did Judge Hood offer for the conclusion that Bauer's condition was not covered?

   CLUE Pay close attention to the judge's response to the definitions of "serious condition."

2. Judge Hood was influenced by the decision in *Seidle*. What was the decision in *Seidle*, and why was Judge Hood persuaded by that decision?

   CLUE Remember that judges are not always necessarily clear in their reasoning.

REMEDIES FOR VIOLATIONS OF FMLA

If an employer fails to comply with the FMLA, the penalties can be substantial. The plaintiff may recover damages for unpaid wages or salary, lost benefits, denied compensation, and actual monetary losses up to an amount equivalent to the employee's wages for 12 weeks, as well as attorney fees and court costs. If the plaintiff can prove bad faith on the part of the employer, double damages may be awarded. An employee may also be entitled to reinstatement or promotion.

Although most awards under FMLA have not been extremely large, the size of the awards is beginning to grow. Two of the large awards were made in 1996. The largest award, for $313,000, was awarded in California to a worker who was demoted, and then fired, for taking time off from work for surgery for a brain tumor.[4] An Illinois court handed down the second largest award of $58,000 to a woman who was fired for taking off three weeks of work to care for her sick children.[5] Many employment law specialists are now seeing the FLMA as an act that employers must carefully follow.

THE OCCUPATIONAL SAFETY AND HEALTH ACT OF 1970

Employees worry about more than compensation. They also want to work in a safe environment. And working can be hazardous to one's health and safety. But not all jobs are equally hazardous. The most dangerous industry is mining, followed by construction, agriculture, and transportation. The safest industries are the service industries. Fortunately for workers, their workplaces are getting safer. Exhibit 17-2 illustrates the declining rates of occupational injuries in the U.S. workplace.

The primary regulatory measure designed to provide a safer workplace is the **Occupational Safety and Health Act** of 1970 **(OSH Act)**. The OSH Act requires every employer to "furnish to each of his employees . . . employment . . . free from recognized hazards that are likely to cause death or serious physical harm . . ." To ensure that this objective will be met, Congress, under the OSH Act, authorized the creation of three agencies: the Occupational Safety and

Occupational Safety and Health Act (OSH Act) A regulatory act designed to provide a workplace free from recognized hazards that are likely to case death or serious harm to employees.

---

[4]*Kline v. Walmart Stores, Inc.*, No. CA-95-0056-H (post-trial motions *denied*, October, 1996).
[5]96 *Lawyer's Weekly* 973 (1996).

EXHIBIT 17-2 *Occupational Injury and Illness Incidence Rates (per 100 full-time workers, selected years)*

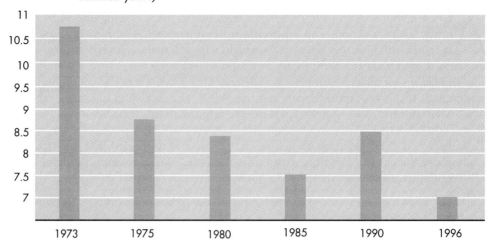

Source: Adapted from ⟨http://stats.bls.gov/news.release/osh.t06.htm⟩.

Health Administration (OSHA), the National Institute for Occupational Safety and Health (NIOSH), and the Occupational Safety and Health Review Commission (OSHRC).

OCCUPATIONAL SAFETY AND HEALTH ADMINISTRATION (OSHA)

Occupational Safety and Health Administration (OSHA) The agency responsible, under the OSH Act, for setting and enforcing standards for occupational health and safety.

The most important of these agencies is the **Occupational Safety and Health Administration (OSHA)**. It has both a standard-setting and an enforcement role. In addition, it undertakes educational programs among employers and employees.

STANDARD SETTING OSHA sets the standards for occupational health and safety in the United States. These standards are frequently opposed by labor and management, but for different reasons. In general, labor organizations criticize them for insufficiently protecting employees' health and safety, whereas employer groups claim they are unnecessarily stringent and too costly.

In establishing health standards, OSHA has used the following four-step process since 1981:

1. The agency asks whether the hazard presents a "significant risk" that warrants intervention.
2. If it does, OSHA decides whether regulatory action can reduce the risk.
3. If it can, the agency establishes a standard to reduce the risk "to the extent feasible," taking into account both technological and economic feasibility.
4. OSHA then analyzes the cost effectiveness of various implementation options to determine which will achieve its goals most efficiently.[6]

ENFORCEMENT OSHA is charged with enforcing the OSH Act through unannounced inspections and the levying of fines against violators. The goals of OSHA inspections are to find and correct existing hazards and to encourage employers to eliminate hazards *before* inspection.

OSHA conducts several different types of inspections. In order of priority, these are: *imminent danger inspections*, when OSHA learns of a hazard that can be expected to cause physical harm or death; *catastrophe and fatality investigations*, whenever an accident hospitalizes five or more workers or causes a death; *em-*

[6]*Preventing Illness and Injury in the Workplace* (Washington, D.C.: Office of Technology Assessment, 1985), p. 4.

ployee complaints, when an employee alleges a violation and requests an inspection; *special inspection programs*, including those aimed at certain hazards or industries; and finally, *programmed or random inspections*. *Follow-up inspections* may also be conducted at any time.

However, there are only 2,451 federal and state inspectors to regulate 96.7 million workers. It would take each inspector 167 years for every workplace in the U.S. to be inspected.[7] Total OSHA inspections in the U.S. have fallen from 42,377 in 1994 to 24,024 in 1996.[8]

Inspection Procedure The safety and health compliance officer conducting the inspection arrives at the plant, usually unannounced, presents his or her credentials, and asks to meet with the person in charge and a union representative to explain the purpose of the visit. The inspector then asks to see any relevant records. Since 1981, the policy of OSHA has been for the inspector in a safety inspection to calculate from these employer records the average lost-workday rate of injury. If it is lower than the average for the industry, the inspection is ended. If it is higher, the inspector walks through the workplace, taking notes, pictures, and exposure samples when relevant. An employer or an employee representative, or both, may accompany the inspector on this tour. After the inspection, the inspector discusses any apparent violations with the employer. Any citations are usually mailed to the employer at a later date.

As we noted in chapter 4, an employer has the constitutional right to refuse to allow an inspection if the inspector does not have a warrant. If the employer does refuse to allow an inspection, however, the OSHA representative generally just goes to court and obtains a warrant. In 1997, OSHA launched a cooperative compliance program under which about 500 companies with the highest accident and illness rates or the greatest number of OSHA citations would get full inspections, whereas about 12,250 firms with more modest records were asked to create health and safety programs to avoid tough inspections.

Penalties When violations are found, compliance inspectors may issue citations for violations. These violations fall into three categories: willful or repeat, serious, and nonserious. The maximum fines for serious or nonserious violations is $7,000 per day of noncompliance, whereas the maximum for a willful or repeat violation is up to $70,000 per violation. If a willful violation results in the death of a worker, criminal penalties may be imposed. For a first conviction, a fine of up to $10,000 and six months in jail is possible. For subsequent convictions, the penalty may be up to $20,000 and one year in jail. During 1996, a total of 55,100 citations were issued, down 62% from 145,900 in 1994.[9] Unfortunately, the greatest number of these citations are for paperwork violations.[10]

PUBLIC EDUCATION OSHA provides on-site consultations with employers seeking to bring their business up to OSHA standards. In 1994, OSHA conducted 23,728[11] of these on-site consultations. OSHA also sponsors a Targeted Training Program, which provides short-term grants to employers, employees, and nonprofit organizations to address health and safety issues about which OSHA has particular concern.

STATE PLANS Under the present OSH Act, a state may regulate its own workplaces if it establishes a program providing for the establishment and enforcement of standards that will be at least as effective as the federal standards. As of April 1995, 25 states had established such programs.

---

[7]Sandy Cain, "Safety First: OSHA Reforms in The Works," 20. *Orange County Business Journal* 22, November 24, 1997.

[8]*Id.*

[9]*Id.*

[10]*Id.*

[11]Telephone conversation with Arlene Perkins, OSHA, April 26, 1995.

OCCUPATIONAL SAFETY AND HEALTH REVIEW COMMISSION (OSHRC)

The **Occupational Safety and Health Review Commission (OSHRC)** is an independent review body before which an employer can contest the issuance of a citation by OSHA, the amount of the penalty, or the time within which abatement is expected. A hearing is conducted before an administrative law judge, whose ruling becomes OSHRC's final order 30 days after it is issued, provided it is not contested. Within the 30-day period, any party may request a review of the decision by OSHRC, which is automatically granted. A final order is issued after the review is completed. The final order may be appealed to a circuit court of appeals.

NATIONAL INSTITUTE FOR OCCUPATIONAL SAFETY AND HEALTH (NIOSH)

The **National Institute for Occupational Safety and Health (NIOSH)** was established under the OSH Act to identify occupational health and safety problems, to develop controls to prevent occupational accidents and diseases, and to disseminate its findings. This body functions primarily as a research facility that attempts to make its findings on hazards available to those who can use them. Although independent of OSHA, NIOSH provides OSHA with information on which the agency bases many of its "criteria documents," recommendations for health and safety standards that contain supporting evidence and bibliographical references.[12]

OSHA, NIOSH, and OSHRC work together to implement the OSH Act. By taking advantage of the assistance offered by these agencies and by meeting the standards that OSHA has established, businesspeople can make their workplaces safer and more healthful. It may even be in their interests to do so, for often the increased costs of providing a safer workplace are more than offset by the benefits employers derive from reduced absenteeism, fewer workers' compensation claims, and less work time lost because of accident investigations.

EMPLOYEE PRIVACY RIGHTS

Safety is an important concern of employees, but they are increasingly concerned about privacy on the job. Privacy issues arise in a broad array of contexts including the hiring process, monitoring of employee performance on the job, and the use of new technology.

ELECTRONIC MONITORING AND COMMUNICATION

Increasing use of technology in the workplace has raised a number of new privacy issues. When, for example, can employers monitor employees' telephone conversations, read their e-mail, or listen to their voice mail? The legal issues related to workplace privacy involve the common law tort of invasion of privacy (discussed in chapter 11), and the Omnibus Crime Control and Safe Streets Act of 1968,[13] as amended by the Electronic Communications Privacy Act (ECPA) of 1986.[14]

The Omnibus Crime Control Act prohibits employers from listening to the private telephone conversations of employees or disclosing the contents of those conversations. Employers are allowed to ban personal calls and monitor calls for compliance, but once they determine that a call is personal, they are not allowed to continue listening to the conversation. Violators may be subject to fines of up to $10,000.

The Electronic Communications Act extended employee's privacy rights to electronic forms of communication including e-mail and cellular phones. The act prohibits the intentional interception of electronic communications or the intentional disclosure or use of the information obtained through such inter-

---

[12]*Id.*
[13]18 U.S.C. § 2210 et seq.
[14]18 U.S.C. §§ 2510–2521.

ception. The act, however, includes a "business-extension exemption" that allows employers to monitor employee telephone conversations in the ordinary course of their employment, as long as the employer does not continue to listen to conversations once he recognizes that they are of a personal nature. Such monitoring is often needed by employers to improve job performance and to offer some protection to employees from harassing calls from the public. A second exception arises when the employees consent to the monitoring of their conversations. The following case illustrates the application of this law.

LA PRIEL B. JAMES V. NEWSPAPER AGENCY CORPORATION
UNITED STATES COURT OF APPEALS 591 F.2D 579 (10TH CIR. 1979)

Plaintiff James sued her former employer, Defendant Newspaper Agency Corporation, for willfully and unlawfully intercepting wire and oral communications by monitoring telephone calls she made on her work telephone. The District Court found in favor of the defendant. Plaintiff appealed.

CIRCUIT JUDGE MCWILLIAMS

James alleged that her erstwhile employer had been guilty of willful and unlawful interception of wire and oral communications in violation of 18 U.S.C. § 2510, et seq.

On January 5, the defendant decided to install a telephone monitoring device on the telephones in certain departments, particularly those departments dealing with the general public. All affected personnel were notified, in writing, of this decision. James' telephone was one of several telephones that was thus monitored.

The monitoring system was installed by the Bell system. The purpose was to allow supervisory personnel to monitor business calls to the end that employees could be given training and instruction as to how to better deal with the general public, and also to serve as some protection for employees from abusive calls. One of James' main assignments was to collect unpaid bills from transient advertisers by use of the telephone.

[The law] provides that it is unlawful for any person to use "any electronic, mechanical, or other device to intercept any oral communication . . ." [It] defines "electronic, me-

chanical, or other device" as follows: "any device or apparatus which can be used to intercept a wire or oral communication other than (a) any telephone or telegraph instrument, equipment or facility, or any component thereof, (i) furnished to the subscriber or user by a communications common carrier in the ordinary course of its business and being used by the subscriber or user in the ordinary course of its business; or (ii) being used by a communications common carrier in the ordinary course of its business."

[T]he defendant had requested the telephone company to install a monitoring device which would permit the defendant to listen in on telephone conversations between its employees and its advertisers, and others. This was a part of the service rendered by the phone company on request. [T]he reason for the installation was the concern by management over abusive language used by irate customers when called upon to pay their bills, coupled with the possible need to give further training and supervision to employees dealing with the public. The installation was not done surreptitiously. Rather, all employees were advised in advance, in writing, of the proposed installation, and there was no protest. In our view, the present case comes squarely within the exception provided in 18 U.S.C. § 2510(5)(a), and it is on this basis that we affirm the summary judgment granted the defendant on the second claim. Here the installation was not surreptitious, but with advance knowledge on the part of both management and its employees, and was for a legitimate business purpose.

Affirmed in favor of Defendant, Newspaper Agency.

The key question in cases involving employer monitoring and interception of employee communications via e-mail, telephone, or voice mail is whether the employee had a reasonable expectation of privacy with respect to the communication in question. Therefore, many employment law specialists recommend that, to minimize the likelihood of being sued by employees for invasion of privacy and to keep good morale in the workplace, employers should have written employee privacy policies that are explained to employees and printed in employee handbooks. The Society of Human Resource Management, in a 1997 survey, found that nearly 80 percent of participants had e-mail, yet only 36 percent had policies defining proper e-mail use and only 34 percent had written privacy policies.

Privacy policies should cover matters from employer surveillance policies, to control of and access to medical and personnel records, to drug testing, and to all issues unique to the electronic workplace. Exhibit 17-3 provides a sample of a good electronic mail policy.

A related privacy concern in the workplace is the use of surveillance cameras. Again, the courts fall back on the reasonable expectation of privacy. Closed-circuit cameras are increasingly being used to combat employee theft, to monitor employee performance, and to safeguard employees. Clearly visible cameras are generally not challenged. As one arbitrator said, "Since one of the supervisor's jobs is to observe employees at work, such supervision cannot be said to interfere with an employee's right to privacy, even if it is done by a camera."

Hidden cameras may generally be placed in areas where employees do not have reasonable expectation of privacy, such as hallways. Installation of video

---

EXHIBIT 17-3 *Electronic Mail Policy and Employee Acknowledgment*

ELECTRONIC MAIL POLICY

* E-mail is the property of the company and should be used solely for work-related purposes.

* Employees are prohibited from sending messages that are harassing, intimidating, offensive or discriminatory.

* Each employee will be given a password to access e-mail. Your password is personal and should not be shared with anyone else. However, the company retains a copy of all passwords and has a right to access E-mail at any time for any reason without notice to the employee. The Employee has NO expectation of privacy or confidentiality in the E-mail System.

* The employee must sign and return an Acknowledgment & Consent form indicating receipt and acceptance of our company's policy.

ACKNOWLEDGMENT

I understand that the company's electronic mail and voice mail systems (herein together referred to as "the company's systems") are company property and are to be used for company business. I understand that [excessive] use of the company's systems for the conduct of personal business is strictly prohibited.

I understand that the company reserves the right to access, review, and disclose information obtained through the company's systems at any time, with or without advance notice to me and with or without my consent. I also understand that I am required to notify my supervisor and the company's Security Department if I become aware of any misuse of the company's systems.

I confirm that I have read this employee acknowledgment and have had an opportunity to ask questions about it. I also agree to abide by the terms of the company's policy in this regard a copy of which has been provided to me.

AGREED TO THIS_____ DAY OF_____ ,19 _____.

_____

Witness _____ Employee Signature _____

Source: Copyright 1997, Robert B. Fitzpatrick, Fitzpatrick & Associates, reprinted from "Technology Advances in the Information Age: Effects on Workplace Privacy Issues," SB ALI-ABA 261(1997).

cameras in bathrooms, however, may prompt claims of invasion of privacy. In cases in which a plant is unionized, the courts may consider the installation of a closed-circuit television monitoring system to be an issue that the firm must bargain over with the union because it changes working conditions.

DRUG TESTING

In the interests of safety, and also to have a more productive workforce, employers have been increasingly interested in using drug testing for employees. Employer interest in drug testing was also encouraged by Congress in 1988, when it passed the Drug-Free Workplace Act, which required employers that receive federal aid or do business of $25,000 or more with the federal government to develop an antidrug policy for employees, provide drug-free awareness programs for them, make them aware of assistance programs for those with drug problems, and warn them of penalties for violating the company's drug-free policies.

Employers, however, must be careful when establishing drug-testing policies because employees may challenge such policies on grounds that they violate their state or federal constitutional rights, their common law privacy rights, or state or local drug-testing laws. Because of the variation among states regarding drug testing, employers must examine both the statutory and case law in their state very closely before implementing a drug-testing policy. With that caution in mind, however, some broad generalizations can be made.

Drug testing generally arises in four different contexts, and standards may be different for each. The most commonly occurring drug testing is preemployment testing. Most states allow preemployment drug testing. Most states also recognize the legitimacy of drug testing as a part of a periodic physical, assuming that proper standards for drug testing are followed. The third context in which drug testing may be used is one in which the employer has a reasonable suspicion that an employee may be under the influence of drugs in the workplace. "Reasonable suspicion" generally requires the employer to have some evidence, such as an unexplainable drop in performance, to justify the tests. If the employer does have such sound evidence, the test is generally upheld. The most controversial area is that of random drug testing, on which the courts are split. Random drug testing is most likely to be upheld when an employee may pose a safety risk to others by doing a job while under the influence of drugs and when employees have been informed in advance in writing of the random drug-testing policy.

Private-sector employers have much greater freedom to require drug testing than do employers in the public sector. Whereas private employers may be restricted only by state constitutions and state and local laws, federal entities are also restricted by the Constitution. The following case provides the Supreme Court's most recent response to a challenge to drug testing as a violation of individuals' Fourth Amendment right to be free from unreasonable searches.

CHANDLER V. MILLER, ET AL
UNITED STATES SUPREME COURT 117 S. CT. 1295 (1997)

A Georgia statute requires candidates for designated state offices to certify that they have taken a urinalysis drug test within 30 days prior to qualifying for nomination or election and that the test result was negative. Plaintiffs, Libertarian Party nominees for state offices including Chandler, filed an action one month before the deadline for submission of the certificates, naming the governor (Miller) and state administrative officials as defendents. They asserted that the drug tests required by the law violated their rights under the First, Fourth, and Fourteenth Amendments to the United States Constitution.

JUSTICE GINSBURG

The Fourth Amendment requires the government to respect "[t]he right of the people to be secure in their persons . . . against unreasonable searches and seizures." This restraint on government conduct generally bars officials from undertaking a search or seizure absent individualized suspicion. Searches conducted without grounds for suspicion of particular individuals have been upheld, however, in "certain limited circumstances."

We confront in this case the question of whether [Georgia's] requirement ranks among the limited circumstances in which suspicionless searches are warranted. Relying on this Court's precedents sustaining drug-testing programs for student athletes, customs employees, and railway employees, the United States Court of Appeals for the Eleventh Circuit judged Georgia's law constitutional.

Georgia was the first, and apparently remains the only, State to condition candidacy for state office on a drug test.

It is settled law, the court accepted, that the drug tests required by the statute rank as searches. But, as was true of the drug-testing programs at issue in *Skinner* and *Von Raab*, the [Circuit] court reasoned, § 21–2–140 serves "special needs," interests other than the ordinary needs of law enforcement. The court therefore endeavored to "'balance the individual's privacy expectations against the Government's interests to determine whether it [was] impractical to require a warrant or some level of individualized suspicion in the particular context.'" Examining the state interests involved, the court acknowledged the absence of any record of drug abuse by elected officials in Georgia. Nonetheless, the court observed, "[t]he people of Georgia place in the trust of their elected officials . . . their liberty, their safety, their economic well-being, [and] ultimate responsibility for law enforcement." Consequently, "those vested with the highest executive authority to make public policy in general and frequently to supervise Georgia's drug interdiction efforts in particular must be persons appreciative of the perils of drug use." The court further noted that "[t]he nature of high public office in itself demands the highest levels of honesty, clear-sightedness, and clear-thinking."

Turning to petitioners' privacy interests, the Eleventh Circuit emphasized that the tests could be conducted in the office of the candidate's private physician, making the "intrusion here . . . even less than that approved in *Von Raab*." Furthermore, the candidate would control release of the test results: Should the candidate test positive, he or she could forfeit the opportunity to run for office, and in that event, nothing would be divulged to law enforcement officials.

Another consideration, the court said, is the reality that "candidates for high office must expect the voters to demand some disclosures about their physical, emotional, and mental fitness for the position." Concluding that the State's interests outweighed the privacy intrusion caused by the required certification, the court held the statute, as applied to petitioners, not inconsistent with the Fourth and Fourteenth Amendments.

[W]e note, first, that the testing method the Georgia statute describes is relatively noninvasive; therefore, if the "special need" showing had been made, the State could not be faulted for excessive intrusion. The State permits a candidate to provide the urine specimen in the office of his or her private physician; and the results of the test are given first to the candidate, who controls further dissemination of the report.

Because the State has effectively limited the invasiveness of the testing procedure, we concentrate on the core issue: Is the certification requirement warranted by a special need? Our precedents establish that the proffered special need for drug testing must be substantial—important enough to override the individual's acknowledged privacy interest, sufficiently vital to suppress the Fourth Amendment's normal requirement of individualized suspicion. Georgia has failed to show a special need of that kind. Respondents' defense of the statute rests primarily on the incompatibility of unlawful drug use with holding high state office. The statute is justified, respondents contend, because the use of illegal drugs draws into question an official's judgment and integrity; jeopardizes the discharge of public functions, including antidrug law enforcement efforts; and undermines public confidence and trust in elected officials. The statute, according to respondents, serves to deter unlawful drug users from becoming candidates and thus stops them from attaining high state office. Notably lacking in respondents' presentation is any indication of a concrete danger demanding departure from the Fourth Amendment's main rule. Nothing in the record hints that the hazards respondents broadly describe are real and not simply hypothetical for Georgia's polity.

In contrast to the effective testing regimes upheld in [precedents, omitted] Georgia's certification requirement is not well designed to identify candidates who violate antidrug laws. Nor is the scheme a credible means to deter illicit drug users from seeking election to state office. The test date—to be scheduled by the candidate any time within 30 days prior to qualifying for a place on the ballot—is no secret. As counsel for respondents acknowledged at oral argument, users of illegal drugs, save for those prohibitively addicted, could abstain for a pretest period sufficient to avoid detection. Moreover, respondents have offered no reason why ordinary law enforcement methods would not suffice to apprehend such addicted individuals, should they appear in the limelight of a public stage.

What is left, after close review of Georgia's scheme, is the image the State seeks to project. By requiring candidates for public office to submit to drug testing, Georgia displays its commitment to the struggle against drug abuse. The suspicionless tests, according to respondents, signify that candidates, if elected, will be fit to serve their constituents free from the influence of illegal drugs. But Georgia asserts no evidence of a drug problem among the State's elected officials, those officials typically do not perform high-risk, safety-sensitive tasks, and the required certification immediately aids no interdiction effort. The need revealed, in short, is symbolic, not "special," as that term draws meaning from our case law.

The greatest dangers to liberty lurk in insidious encroachment by men of zeal, well-meaning but without understanding. However well-meant, the candidate drug test Georgia has devised diminishes personal privacy for a symbol's sake. The Fourth Amendment shields society against that state action.

Reversed in favor of Plaintiff, Chandler.

Critical Thinking about the Law

THE PRIMARY OBJECTIVE IN THIS CASE was to determine whether the state of Georgia could require candidates for state offices to be tested for drugs before qualifying for election. However, a more abstract version of the same issue is the following: When may a public employer impinge on the privacy rights of a potential employee? The court provides an answer to the question, and your task as a critical thinker is to find the answer and evaluate its worth. The following critical thinking questions will help you complete that task.

1. If the state of Georgia could have demonstrated one element, they would have won their case. What is that element, and why would Georgia have won?

CLUE This question requires you to identify the conclusion and reasons. If one element had been demonstrated by the state, the court would have come to a different conclusion.

2. The court uses a certain definition of "special need." Do you think this definition is adequate?

CLUE Go back to the definition of "special need" in the reasoning. Then reread the ambiguity section in the first chapter of this book. On the basis of what you know about ambiguity, make a judgment about the clarity of the definition.

OTHER TESTING

Employers have also used other forms of testing, some of which have been restricted by state and federal laws. For example, in 1988, Congress passed the Employee Polygraph Protection Act. This law prevents employers from using lie detector tests while screening job applicants. It also prohibits administering lie detector tests randomly, but it does allow their use in specific instances in which there has been an economic injury to the employer's business. The act also provides an exception to allow private security companies and those selling controlled substances to use lie detector testing of applicants and current employees. The Labor Department may seek fines of up to $10,000 against firms that violate the act.

INTERNATIONAL DIMENSIONS OF THE EMPLOYMENT RELATIONSHIP

Although some of the benefits described in this chapter may seem significant, laws in some other nations ensure much greater benefits for workers. One area in which other nations provide significantly greater benefits is parental leave. Workers in this country are guaranteed up to 12 weeks of *unpaid* leave; most European countries require a guaranteed *paid* leave. For example, in France, Austria, and Finland, paid parental leave begins six weeks before childbirth and extends to ten weeks after birth in France, eight weeks in Austria, and almost one year in Finland. French working mothers are then entitled to an additional unpaid job-protected leave until their children reach the age of three. Altogether, over 120 nations require paid maternity leave, with the Czech Republic providing 24 weeks of paid leave. One of the reasons why such extensive benefits can be offered in those nations, however, is that the tax-funded social insurance/social security systems provide most of the money for these benefits.

To try to ensure that workers around the world receive the rights and benefits described in this chapter, the United Nations Commission on Human Rights developed the International Covenant on Economic, Social, and Cultural Rights. This covenant does not really bind any employers, but it gathers its strength by documenting and publicizing where its terms are not followed.

SUMMARY

The employment relationship today is still a contract between the employer and employee, but the national and state governments specify certain parameters of this relationship. Laws that affect wages and hours include the Davis-Bacon Act, the Fair Labor Standards Act, and the Federal Unemployment Tax Act.

The Family and Medical Leave Act ensures that workers will be able to take necessary time off from work when they or members of their family suffer from a serious medical condition. The Occupational Safety and Health Act tries to secure safe working conditions for employees, but if they are injured on the job, workers' compensation laws provide benefits for them to compensate them for the injury or disability they receive.

A final concern of workers and employers is the extent of worker privacy rights. Federal employees have more rights in this area than private employees, because the public employer has to comply with the Fourth Amendment, but private employers must still be sure they do not violate state and federal laws designed to protect worker privacy. The prudent employer today will have a written privacy policy that clearly sets out when employees should have a reasonable expectation of privacy and when they should not. When comparing other countries' employee benefits with those in the United States, one area where the United States offers less protection to employees is with respect to family leave benefits.

REVIEW QUESTIONS

17-1. What benefits do employees receive under the Fair Labor Standards Act?

17-2. Explain how workers' compensation laws benefit both employers and employees, but in different ways.

17-3. What requirements are imposed on an employer by the Family and Medical Leave Act?

17-4. What remedies can an employee seek if an employer violates the Family and Medical Leave Act?

17-5. Explain the relationship between OSHA and NIOSH.

17-6. Explain the principles you would want to keep in mind when drafting an employee privacy policy for a firm.

REVIEW PROBLEMS

17-7. In early December, Decco Manufacturing Corporation underwent a major downsizing and laid off 40 percent of its employees. Robert Banks was not laid off, but he thought that he probably would be laid off in the near future unless business got dramatically better. In fact, his supervisor told him that he would probably be laid off in early January. Robert decided that if he were going to get laid off anyway, he would rather have the time between jobs over the holidays, so he quit and filed for unemployment compensation. Should he be able to collect workers' compensation?

17-8. Karen Jenner was a teacher at Northwood Junior High. Every year, to raise money for charity, the school sponsored a faculty-student basketball game. Teachers were required to participate in the event in some manner, either by playing on the team, selling tickets, or working at the concession stand. Karen chose to play on the team and was injured when she collided with another player during the game. She filed a claim for workers' compensation, which her employer contested. Explain why you believe her claim is either valid or invalid.

17-9. Nellie Mandle worked as a machine operator. She had been told on numerous occasions that if her press ever jammed up, she was not to stick her hand in to unjam it, but rather, was to use a special safety fork with a long handle that would allow her to unjam the machine without inserting any part of her hand into the press. Her machine jammed, and she looked around for the safety fork. Realizing that the worker on the previous shift must have removed the fork, she reached her hand inside the machine to unjam it. Before she could remove her hand, the machine cycled, catching her hand and injuring it severely. She filed a workers' compensation claim, which her employer contested because she caused the injury by her disobedience of the safety rules. Evaluate the employer's argument.

17-10. Caroline Williams works for a firm that has a written policy that prohibits the use of company telephones for personal use. Employees have been told that the company randomly monitors telephone conversations to enforce this policy. Caroline uses a company telephone to call her doctor to find out the results of a blood test she had taken to determine whether she had contracted a sexually transmitted disease. Her employer intercepted the phone call and, once he heard her question, he stayed on the line to find out the results of her test. Discuss why you believe the employer's behavior is lawful or unlawful. If unlawful, what penalty should he receive?

17-11. Michael Meuter was an employee in a hospital emergency room. He used an extension phone to call one of the workers in the pharmacy to order some drugs for the emergency room. After placing his request, he started to complain to the pharmacy worker about his supervisor, calling him a number of offensive names. Unknown to Michael, his supervisor was listening to the conversation. Was the supervisor's listening to the conversation lawful?

17-12. Ginny Morris applied for a job as an executive assistant to the president of a software firm. She received high evaluations from those on the hiring committee and was told that she looked like an excellent candidate for the job, but before a final decision could be made, she would have to take a drug test so that the firm could be confident that she did not use any illegal drugs and a lie detector test to ensure that she would be someone who could be entrusted with trade secrets. Discuss whether you believe there are any problems with the firm's requests.

CASE PROBLEMS

17-13. Mark Moeller, a 32-year-old meat cutter, had been employed by Ralph's for 10 years. He died of a heart attack while at home Sunday evening, June 1. Moeller had not worked at Ralph's since the previous October, when he had been on disability leave owing to an industrial injury to his finger. Because of declining sales, Moeller had been laid off in November, a month after he had gone on disability leave. On the day before Moeller was scheduled to return to work from the layoff, Ralph's telephoned Moeller at home and told him to report back to work the next day. Ralph's said that the best the firm could offer Moeller was a part-time meat cutter's position without benefits. This offer was less than what Moeller, who was in financial difficulty, had hoped to receive.

When Moeller received the back-to-work phone call, the news that he would be working only part-time without benefits was so stressful to him that it triggered a sudden heart arrhythmia which, because of Moeller's congenital heart muscle disease, caused a fatal heart attack. Moeller's widow, Anna Moeller, filed a claim for workers' compensation death benefits and petitioned to be appointed guardian ad litem and trustee for the minors. Ralph's denied the claim.

The worker's compensation judge (WCJ) found, accepting Mrs. Moeller's expert medical witness' opinion and rejecting Ralph's conflicting medical evidence, that the back-to-work phone call was so stressful it triggered a sudden arrhythmia and fatal heart attack. The WCJ further found the phone call arose out of and occurred during the course of employment, despite the undisputed evidence that Moeller had not worked at Ralph's since October, had been laid off since November 1991, and had died the day before he was to return to work. After the board rejected Ralph's petition for reconsideration, Ralph's appealed. Who do you think won the case on appeal? Why? *Workers' Compensation Appeals Board and Casey Renee Moeller*, 58 Cal. App. 4th 647 (1997)

17-14. Ronald Smith's contract as a high school math instructor, girl's baseball coach, and girl's basketball coach also contained a clause stating that he "may be required to devote a reasonable amount of time to other duties" in addition to his instructional obligations. Such duties often included supervising and sponsoring out-of-the-classroom student activities. The high school's math club invited Mr. Smith to their annual end-of-the-year outing, which was held at a reservoir. Mr. Smith attended with his family. One of the students brought a windsurfer, which several students used. Mr. Smith tried using the windsurfer, fell, and was seriously injured. He subsequently died. His wife filed a claim for workers' compensation benefits, to which the employer objected. What was the basis for their objection? Explain why the court ultimately did or did not agree with the employer. *Smith v. Workers' Compensation Appeals Board*, 2326 Cal. Rptr. 248 (1987)

17-15. Audrey worked for Provident Mutual Life Insurance Company. Her son was running a fever on October 12, so she took him to the doctor, who found his temperature to be 99.8 degrees. The doctor diagnosed an infection in the boy's right ear and prescribed an oral antibiotic, which the child was to take for ten days. No eardrops were prescribed, nor did the doctor recommend that Audrey take her son to a hospital. He did suggest, however, that she keep him home from day care for at least 48 hours, or until he felt better. By late that evening, the boy's fever was gone, but he did not eat supper and had only juice for breakfast the next morning. He stayed home that day and mostly watched television, and though he did not complain about his ear hurting, he did not have much of an appetite. On the 16th, he went to the supermarket with his mother and started talking and playing a little more, as well as hearing a little better. On the 18th, Audrey finally took him back to day care and returned to work. When she was terminated for her four-day absence, she argued that she was entitled to the time off under the Family and Medical Leave Act. She therefore sued her employer. Both plaintiff and defendant filed motions for summary judgment, with the issue being whether the child's ear infection constituted a serious health condition, as required under the act. How do you think the court resolved this case? Why? *Audrey M. Seidle v. Provident Mutual Life Insurance Co.*, 871 F. Supp. 238 (1994)

17-16. Marsden was employed by CIS Enterprise from July 12, 1993, through July 28, 1994. On April 23, 1994, her daughter was injured in a car accident. In June 1994, Marsden asked to be given reduced hours so she could accompany her daughter to therapy. Her supervisor agreed, and for two weeks Marsden worked the reduced schedule. She then told her supervisor that her daughter's therapy time had been changed, so she needed a four-week leave of absence under the Family and Medical Leave Act. The supervisor told Marsden that she needed the approval of the personnel manager for an extended leave. Marsden did not obtain the required approval.

Marsden did not show after July 1, 1994. On July 19, 1994, CIS sent her a registered letter telling her to contact CIS within 48 hours. On July 28,1994, CIS sent Marsden a letter of termination. When Marsden's application for unemployment benefits was denied because she had been terminated for "just cause," she appealed, arguing that her termination was not for just cause because (1) she had not been warned that she could be terminated for excessive absences and (2) that her termination was in violation of the FMLA. Explain why you believe she was or was not successful in her appeal. *Marsden v. Review Board of Indiana Employment Security Division*, 654 N.E.2d 907 (1995)

17-17. Pillsbury Company provided an e-mail system for its employees so they could communicate with one another. Employees were told that their e-mail was confidential and would not be used against them. Smyth, a Pillsbury employee, wrote an e-mail message to his supervisor in which he criticized sales management at the firm and threatnd to "kill the backstabbing bastards." When other members of the management team intercepted his e-mail message, Smyth was fired for transmitting inappropriate and unprofessional comments. Smyth believed that his termination violated his privacy rights. Do you think the court agreed with Smyth? Why or why not? *Smyth v. Pillsbury Co.*, 914 F. Supp. 97 (1996)

17-18. The Customs Service instituted a drug-testing program that analyzed urine specimens of employees who applied for promotion to positions involving interdiction of illegal drugs, requiring them to carry firearms or handle classified materials. The employee union challenged the program as unconstitutional because there was no history of drug abuse problems among Customs Service employees. The U.S. district court upheld the drug-testing program. Explain how you believe the U.S. Supreme Court ruled on appeal and why they reached that conclusion. *Service Employees, National Treasury Employees Union, et al., Petitioners v. William Von Raab, Commissioner, United States Customs Service*, 489 U.S. 660 (1989)

 On the Internet

http://www.benefitslink.com/index.html   BenefitsLink is a site that provides information about employee benefits, including articles about employee benefits, the full texts of new regulations, and links to other related sites.

http://www.osha-slc.gov   The Web page of the Occupational Safety and Health Administration provides information about worker health and safety, including how to file a complaint. It also provides the text of the Occupational Safety and Health Act of 1970, as well as OSHA standards, regulations, and directives.

http://hr.ucdavis.edu/elr/fmla97b.htm   This site contains a document entitled "Family and Medical Leave . . . What Every Supervisor Should Know," which provides a good overview of the FMLA and illustrates its implementation by a public employer.

http://www.umn.edu.edu/humanrts/instree/b2esc.htm   At this page, you can find the International Covenant on Economic, Social, and Cultural Rights.

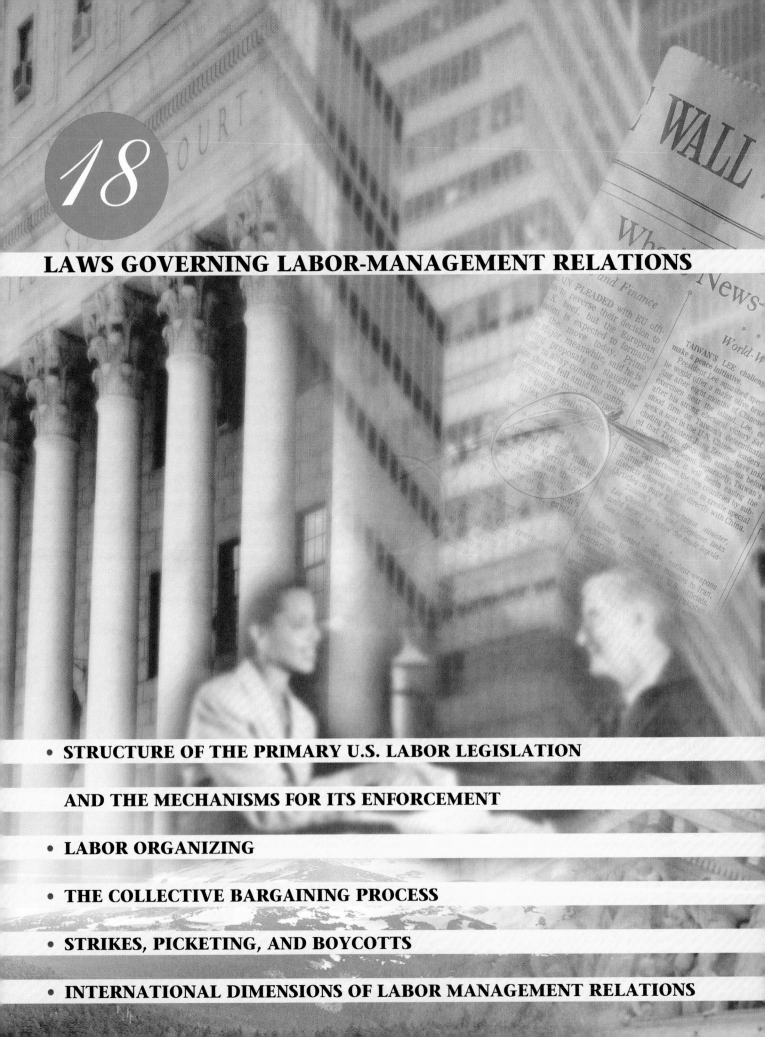

18

LAWS GOVERNING LABOR-MANAGEMENT RELATIONS

- **STRUCTURE OF THE PRIMARY U.S. LABOR LEGISLATION**

  AND THE MECHANISMS FOR ITS ENFORCEMENT

- **LABOR ORGANIZING**

- **THE COLLECTIVE BARGAINING PROCESS**

- **STRIKES, PICKETING, AND BOYCOTTS**

- **INTERNATIONAL DIMENSIONS OF LABOR MANAGEMENT RELATIONS**

In the early 1800s, labor unions were very rare. Despite the mistreatment of workers by management during the Industrial Revolution, most attempts to organize employees throughout the nineteenth and early twentieth centuries were treated by the courts as criminal conspiracies. Finally, in the midst of the economic chaos of the Great Depression, Congress enacted laws giving employees the right to organize and to bargain collectively over wages and terms and conditions of employment.

Union strength has fluctuated in the years since unions were legalized. Over a third of U.S. workers were organized in the post–World War II period. By 1983, however, only 20.1 percent of workers were unionized, and, by 1997, the percentage had fallen to 14.1 percent. Not all occupations are equally organized. Exhibit 18-1 shows the percentages of workers organized by occupational group in 1996.

Although organized workers are still not in as powerful a position as their employers, they are distinctly better off than they were during most of our nation's existence. The primary basis for their improved status is the National Labor Relations Act (NLRA), which was passed in 1935. The NLRA is the focus of this chapter.

The first section briefly outlines the structure and enforcement of the NLRA and the Landrum-Griffin Act, the primary pieces of operative labor legislation. The next three sections discuss specific areas of labor-management relations governed by the NLRA: organizing, collective bargaining, and the collective activities of striking, picketing, and boycotting. The chapter concludes with a consideration of the international dimensions of labor law.

Before you start to read about our system of labor laws, take a few minutes to examine Table 18-1, which summarizes the two conflicting views of the role of unions in economics and society. Whether one thinks labor laws should strengthen or restrain labor organizations depends largely on which of the two "faces" of unions one thinks is "prettiest."

Critical Thinking about the Law

Many people hold strong feelings about unions. Workers who belong to unions often view unions as positive forces that work to their benefit. On the other hand, employers are often suspicious of the activity of unions. As you consider the aspects of labor law in this chapter, be aware of the role of biases in complex legal issues. The following critical thinking questions will help you consider the role of biases and ethical norms in labor legislation.

1. In the language of ethical norms, what function do unions serve for workers?

   Clue Remember the list of ethical norms, and reread the beginning paragraphs of this chapter. How do labor unions help workers? Can you match this answer to an ethical norm?

2. What role do you think personal ethical norms should play in thinking about labor legislation?

   Clue Could paying attention to these ethical norms benefit the workers or employers in any manner?

3. Your co-workers have been excitedly talking for days about plans to unionize. You are unsure if you will join the union. One of your co-workers argues that joining the union will help you get a raise. What questions do you have for your co-worker about missing information?

   Clue Think about any possible costs associated with getting a raise.

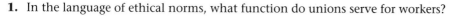

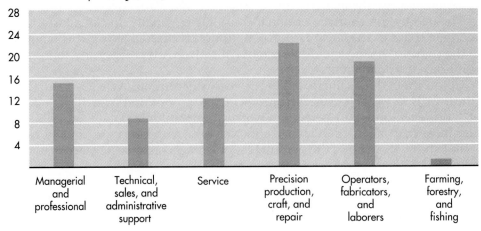

EXHIBIT 18-1 *Percentage of Employed Union-Represented Wage and Salary Workers, by Occupation, 1996*

Source: Adapted from ⟨http://stats.bls.gov/news.release/union2.t03.htm⟩.

STRUCTURE OF THE PRIMARY U.S. LABOR LEGISLATION AND THE MECHANISMS FOR ITS ENFORCEMENT

Three major pieces of legislation govern labor-management relations in the United States today: the Wagner Act of 1935, the Taft-Hartley Act of 1947, and the Landrum-Griffith Act of 1959 (the last is cited also as the Labor-Management Reporting and Disclosure Act, or LMRDA). The Taft-Hartley Act amended the Wagner Act, so they are jointly referred to as the National Labor Relations Act (NLRA). In this section, we briefly describe the primary features of each of these acts and discuss those situations in which the business manager is most likely to need an understanding of these laws.

TABLE 18-1 *The Two Faces of Unions*

COLLECTIVE FACE	MONOPOLY FACE
• Unions primarily provide a collective voice through which workers can express their job-related concerns.	• Unions are institutions that primarily serve to raise wages above competitive levels.
• Unions increase efficiency because unionized firms have lower employee turnover rates so the employer spends less money and time training new employees.	• Unions decrease efficiency by securing unmerited wage increases for their workers, thereby causing a misallocation of resources.
• Because unions usually negotiate contracts that base wage increases primarily on seniority, older workers are more likely to help newer ones and a more cooperative workplace will exist, thereby increasing efficiency.	• Unions decrease efficiency by causing strikes that result in lost production and obtaining special contract provisions that reduce productivity.
• Unions decrease inequality of wage distribution within the firm because they will try to raise the wages of the below-average workers up to those of the average; for solidarity purposes, they have to try to make the wages of those in the bargaining unit more equal.	• Unions increase the existing inequality of wage distribution by providing higher wages for unionized workers at the expense of non-unionized workers.
• Unions are democratic institutions, representing the interests of workers in general in the political process.	• Unions gain their power through coercion and the threat of physical violence and use that power to lobby for legislation to restrict competition in their respective industries.

Source: Adapted from R. B. Freeman and J. L. Medoff, What Do Unions Do (New York: Basic Books); 1994

THE WAGNER ACT OF 1935

The **Wagner Act** (cited also as the **NLRA**) was the first major piece of federal legislation adopted explicitly to encourage the formation of labor unions. Many supporters of this act recognized that a number of labor problems were caused by gross inequality of bargaining power between employers and employees. They hoped that the Wagner Act would bring about industrial peace and raise the standard of living of U.S. workers. The act was to accomplish those goals by facilitating the formation of labor unions as a powerful collective voice for employees and by providing for **collective bargaining** between employers and unions as a means of obtaining the peaceful settlement of labor disputes. The key section of the Wagner Act is Section 7. This section provides:

> *Employees shall have the right to self-organization, to join, form or assist labor organizations, to bargain collectively through representatives of their own choosing, and to engage in concerted activities for the purpose of collective bargaining or other mutual aid and protection.*

Employees' Section 7 rights are protected through Section 8(a) of the act, which prohibits specific "employer unfair labor practices." These practices are delineated in Table 18-2. Section 9 of the act sets forth the procedures, including the secret ballot election, by which the exclusive employee-bargaining-unit representative (union) is to be chosen.

The final important provision of the Wagner Act authorized an administrative agency, the **National Labor Relations Board (NLRB)**, to interpret and enforce the act. It also provided for judicial review in designated federal courts of appeal.

Wagner Act (NLRA) Guarantees the rights of workers to organize and bargain collectively and forbids employers from engaging in specified unfair labor practices. Also called National Labor Relations Act.

collective bargaining Negotiations between an employer and a union over, primarily, wages, hours, and terms and conditions of employment.

National Labor Relations Board (NLRB) The administrative agency set up to interpret and enforce the Wagner Act (NLRA).

THE TAFT-HARTLEY ACT OF 1947

The passage of the Wagner Act led to a growth in unionization and an increase in the workers' power. Given that they had almost no power before, any power workers obtained was bound to look like a dramatic increase. Thus the public's perception of union power may have been greater than the actual power of unions. At any rate, this perception led to the passage of the **Taft-Hartley Act**, which was designed to curtail the powers the unions had apparently acquired under the Wagner Act.

Section 8(b) of the Taft-Hartley Act, titled Union Unfair Labor Practices, (Table 18-3), bars unions from engaging in certain specified activities. The act also (1) amended Section 7 of the Wagner Act to include the right of employees to refrain from engaging in collective activity, (2) made collective bargaining agreements enforceable in federal district courts, and (3) provided a civil damages remedy for parties injured by certain prohibited union activities.

Taft-Hartley Act Bars unions from engaging in specified unfair labor practices, makes collective bargaining agreements enforceable in U.S. district courts, and provides a civil damages remedy for parties injured by certain prohibited union activities.

THE LANDRUM-GRIFFITH ACT OF 1959

The final major piece of labor legislation is the **Landrum-Griffith Act**, which primarily governs the internal operations of labor unions. This act's passage was prompted by congressional hearings that uncovered evidence of looting of union treasuries by some powerful union officials and of corrupt, undemocratic

Landrum-Griffith Act Governs the internal operation of labor unions.

TABLE 18-2   *Employer Unfair Labor Practices*

SECTION	PROHIBITED PRACTICE
8(a)1	Interference with employees' Section 7 rights.
8(a)2	Employer-dominated unions.
8(a)3	Discrimination by employers in hiring, firing, and other employment matters because of union activity.
8(a)4	Retaliation against an employee who testifies or makes charges before the National Labor Relations Board.
8(a)5	Failure to engage in good-faith collective bargaining with duly certified unions.

TABLE 18-3   *Union Unfair Labor Practices*

SECTION	PROHIBITED PRACTICE
8(b)1	Restraining or coercing employees' exercise of their Section 7 rights.
8(b)2	Forcing the employer to discriminate against employees on the basis of union or antiunion activity.
8(b)3	Failing to engage in good-faith collective bargaining with the employer.
8(b)4	Striking, picketing, and engaging in secondary boycotts for illegal purposes.
8(b)5	Charging excessive union dues or initiation fees in a union shop.
8(b)6	Featherbedding (charging employers for services not performed).
8(b)7	Picketing for recognition or to force collective bargaining under certain circumstances.

practices in some labor unions. The act requires certain financial disclosures by unions and establishes civil and criminal penalties for financial abuses by union officials. It also includes a section, known as "labor's bill of rights," that gives employees protection against their own unions. The rights established by the Landrum-Griffith Act are summarized in Table 18-4.

THE NATIONAL LABOR RELATIONS BOARD (NLRB)

STRUCTURE   The National Labor Relations Board (NLRB), as we stated earlier, is the administrative agency responsible for the interpretation and enforcement of the National Labor Relations Act. Its structure is diagrammed in Exhibit 18-2. The NLRB's three primary functions are:

1. Monitoring the conduct of the employer and the union during an election to determine whether workers want to be represented by a union.

2. Preventing and remedying unfair labor practices by employers or unions.

3. Establishing rules and regulations interpreting the act.

The NLRB is composed of five members, each appointed by the president with the advice and consent of the Senate. Members serve staggered five-year terms. The board meets in Washington, D.C. Three-member panels decide routine cases involving disputes between employees, union, and employer, but the entire board may hear significant cases.

TABLE 18-4   *Employee Rights under the Landrum-Griffith Act*

SECTION	RIGHT
101(a)1	*Equal Rights.* Every union member has an equal right to nominate candidates, to vote in elections, and to attend and fully participate in membership meetings, subject to the organization's reasonable constitution and bylaws.
101(a)2	*Freedom of Speech and Assembly.* Members have the right to meet freely with one another at any time and to express any views about the labor organization, candidates for office, or business affairs at organization meetings, subject to reasonable rules pertinent to conduct of meetings.
101(a)3	*Dues, Initiation Fees, and Assessments.* Increases in local union dues, initiation fees, or assessments must be voted on by a majority of the members through secret ballot.
101(a)4	*Protection of Right to Sue.* Labor organizations cannot prohibit members from bringing any legal actions, including those against the organization. Organizations may require that members first exhaust reasonable hearing procedures established by the organization.
101(a)5	*Safeguards against Improper Discipline.* No member may be fined or otherwise disciplined except for nonpayment of dues without being (1) served with written notice of specific charges, (2) given a reasonable time to prepare a defense, and (3) afforded a full and fair hearing.

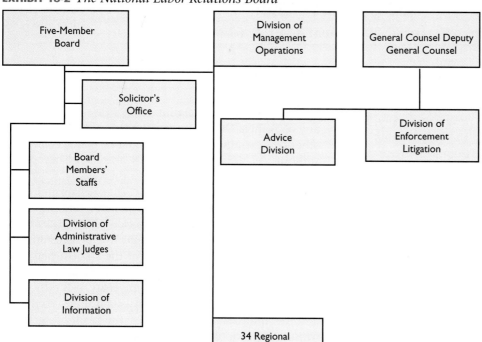

The *general counsel* of the NLRB, also appointed by the president with the advice and consent of the Senate, fulfills the role of a prosecutor in unfair labor practice cases by overseeing the investigation and prosecution of unfair practice charges before the board. If a board decision is subsequently challenged in court, it is the general counsel who represents the board before the appellate court.

Obviously, there are far too many cases for the board and general counsel to handle each one personally. Instead, most cases are handled by 34 *regional offices*, located in major cities across the country. These regional offices are headed by a *regional director*, appointed and overseen by the general counsel. The regional director and his or her staff are directly responsible for investigating charges of unfair labor practices, which they prosecute before *administrative law judges (ALJs)*. They are also responsible for conducting representation elections, in which employees of a firm decide whether they wish to be represented by a union.

JURISDICTION   Just as a civil court must have jurisdiction over the parties before it, the NLRB must have jurisdiction over the parties before it in both representation and unfair labor practice cases. The basis for NLRB jurisdiction is found in the NLRA, under which Congress granted jurisdiction to the NLRB over any business "affecting commerce," with certain specific exceptions. Any employer or employee not covered by the NLRA need not abide by its provisions. (Noncovered employees and employers, however, may be covered by state labor laws.) Employees specifically omitted from NLRA coverage are those who work in federal, state, and local government; employees in the transportation industry and those covered by the Railway Labor Act; independent contractors; agricultural workers; household domestics; and persons employed by a spouse or parent.

Also excluded from NLRB jurisdiction are supervisors and managerial employees and confidential employees. Much litigation has arisen over disputed definitions of "managerial employee." This debate has been particularly vigorous in institutions of higher education, where some faculty members have been seeking to organize labor unions. Their university employers claim that the National Labor Relations Act does not cover professors because they are managerial employees. The leading case in this area follows.

NLRB V. YESHIVA UNIVERSITY
UNITED STATES SUPREME COURT 444 U.S. 672 (1980)

Yeshiva University Faculty Association (union) filed a petition with the National Labor Relations Board seeking certification as the bargaining agent for full-time faculty members of certain schools of Yeshiva, a private university. The university opposed the petition on the grounds that the faculty were managerial or supervisory employees and hence not employees under the NLRA. The NLRB granted the union's petition and the union won the election. The university then refused to bargain, so the union filed an unfair labor practice charge. The board found an unfair labor practice, ordered the university to bargain with the union, and sought enforcement of its order from the court of appeals. The court of appeals denied the board's order, finding that the faculty members were not covered employees under the NLRA because of their extensive control over academic and personnel decisions and their crucial role in developing other university policies. The board appealed to the U.S. Supreme Court.

JUSTICE POWELL

Supervisors and managerial employees are excluded from the categories of employees entitled to the benefits of collective bargaining under the National Labor Relations Act. The question presented is whether the full-time faculty of Yeshiva University fall within those exclusions.

Managerial employees are defined as those who "formulate and effectuate management policies by expressing and making operative the decisions of their employer." Managerial employees must exercise discretion within, or even independently of, established employer policy and must be aligned with management. . . . [N]ormally an employee may be excluded as managerial only if he represents management interests by taking or recommending discretionary actions that effectively control or implement employer policy.

The Board . . . contends that the managerial exclusion cannot be applied in a straightforward fashion to professional employees because those employees often appear to be exercising managerial authority when they are merely performing routine job duties. The status of such employees, in the Board's view, must be determined by reference to the "alignment with management" criterion. The Board argues that the Yeshiva faculty are not aligned with management because they are expected to exercise "independent professional judgment" while participating in academic governance, and because they are neither "expected to conform to management policies [nor] judged according to their effectiveness in carrying out those policies." Because of this independence, the Board contends there is no danger of divided loyalty and no need for the managerial exclusion. . . .

The controlling consideration in this case is that the faculty of Yeshiva University exercise authority which in any other context unquestionably would be managerial. Their authority in academic matters is absolute. They decide what courses will be offered, when they will be scheduled, and to whom they will be taught. They debate and determine teaching methods, grading policies, and matriculation standards. They effectively decide which students will be admitted, retained, and graduated. On occasion their views have determined the size of the student body, the tuition to be charged, and the location of a school. When one considers the function of a university, it is difficult to imagine decisions more managerial than these. To the extent the industrial analogy applies, the faculty determines within each school the product to be produced, the terms upon which it will be offered, and the customers who will be served.

The Board nevertheless insists that these decisions are not managerial because they require the exercise of independent professional judgment.

. . . The Board's approach would undermine the goal it purports to serve: to ensure that employees who exercise discretionary authority on behalf of the employer will not divide their loyalty between employer and union. In arguing that a faculty member exercising independent judgment acts primarily in his own interest and therefore does not represent the interest of his employer, the Board assumes that the professional interests of the institution are distinct, separable entities with which a faculty member could not simultaneously be aligned. The Court of Appeals found no justification for this distinction, and we perceive none. In fact, the faculty's professional interests—as applied to governance at a university like Yeshiva—cannot be separated from those of the institution.

We certainly are not suggesting an application of the managerial exclusion that would sweep all professionals outside the Act in derogation of Congress' expressed intent to protect them. The Board has recognized that employees whose decisionmaking is limited to the routine discharge of professional duties in projects to which they have been assigned cannot be excluded from coverage even if union membership arguably may involve some divided loyalty. Only if an employee's activities fall outside the scope of the duties routinely performed by similarly situated professionals will he be found aligned with management.

Affirmed in favor of Defendant, Yeshiva.

Just because Congress has granted the NLRB the authority to act in a given case does not mean that the board *will* act. The board does not have unlimited funds. Consequently, the NLRB has established its own set of guidelines, which it uses to determine whether it will exercise jurisdiction over an employer. These guidelines are basically designed to determine whether a firm does a significant amount of business and thus has enough employees to justify the expenditure of NLRB resources; they are established industry by industry (e.g., a transit system must have a total annual business volume of at least $250,000). The employer must supply the figures the board needs to determine whether it should assert jurisdiction.

PROCEDURES IN REPRESENTATION CASES An important function of the NLRB and the general counsel is to ensure that employees will be uncoerced in their choice of a bargaining representative or in choosing *not* to be represented by a union. Under NLRB procedures, set out in Exhibit 18-3, a petition for a representation election is initially filed with the *regional director* (1) by the

EXHIBIT 18-3 *Steps in a Representation Proceeding*

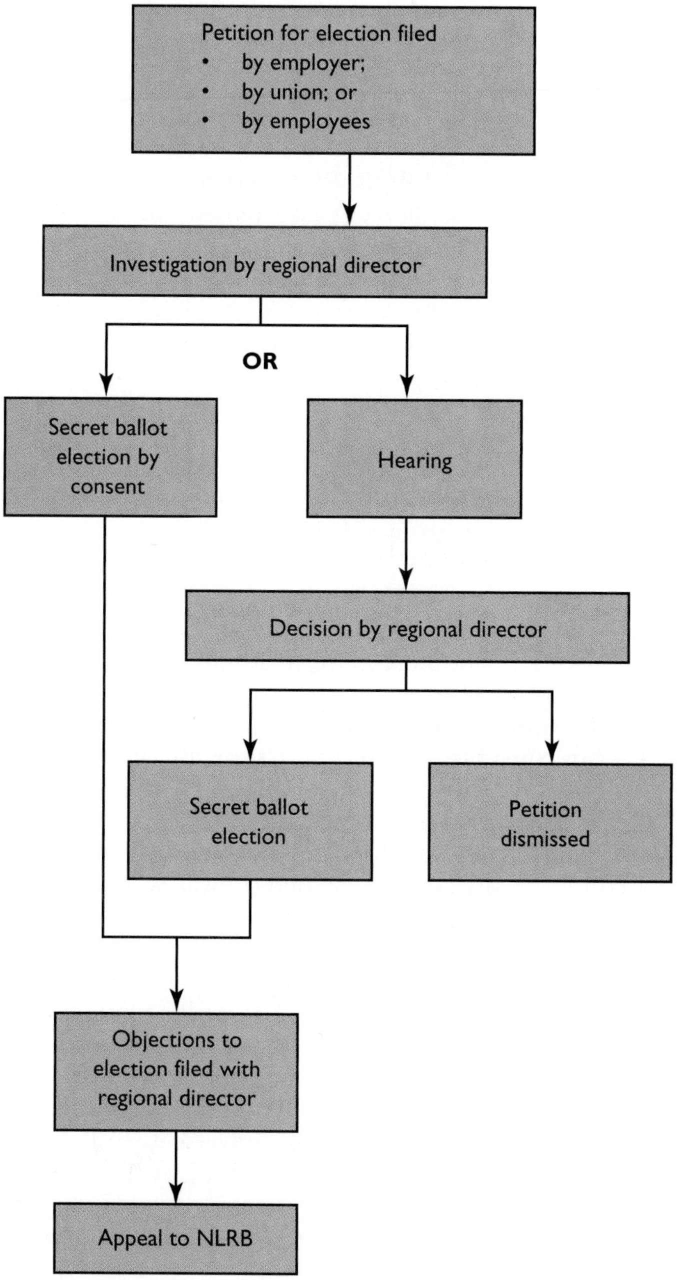

union, when it can demonstrate it has the support of over 30 percent of the employees it seeks to represent (known as "majority support"); (2) by the *employer*, when two or more unions are claiming to be the exclusive representative of the employees or when one union claims to have majority support; or (3) by the *employees* themselves. The union demonstrates its support by submitting authorization cards. Each card is signed by an employee and states that the employee gives the union the authority to act as the employee's exclusive bargaining representative.

Once the petition is filed, the regional director conducts an investigation to determine whether the employer is under the jurisdiction of the NLRB, whether the group of employees the union is seeking to represent is covered by the NLRA, whether the group of employees seeking representation is an appropriate bargaining unit (discussed in more detail later), and whether there is sufficient support (30 percent) for the union. If these findings are affirmative, the director will see whether all parties will consent to an election. If they will not, the regional office holds a hearing to receive evidence on whether an election should be held and, if so, which employees are entitled to vote. The transcript of the hearing is given to the regional director, who decides whether a question of representation exists and an election should be held. An affirmative decision results in an election by secret ballot, conducted by a representative of the regional office.

After the election, the losing party may file objections to the outcome of the election with the regional director, who either orders a new election or certifies the results. The decision may be appealed to the board.

PROCEDURES IN UNFAIR LABOR PRACTICE CASES A second important function of the NLRB is to prevent and remedy unfair labor practices by both employers and employees. An unfair labor practice charge is initiated when an aggrieved employee, union, or employer files an unfair labor practice *charge* with the appropriate regional office. (A sample charge is pictured in Exhibit 18-4.) After regional office employees, called *field examiners*, investigate the charge, the regional director decides whether to issue a complaint. If a complaint is issued, an attorney from the regional office tries to resolve the complaint informally.

If informal negotiations are unsuccessful, the regional office attorney prosecutes the case before an administrative law judge. The ALJ issues an order recommending a remedy or suggesting a dismissal, in either case stating the rationale and evidence for the decision. If no party objects to the decision within 20 days, it automatically becomes a final order of the NLRB. If an order is issued and any party fails to abide by it, the board must petition a U.S. court of appeals for an enforcement order. The procedure in unfair labor practice cases is diagrammed in Exhibit 18-5.

Given the cumbersome nature of this procedure, it is easy to see how an unfair labor practice can continue for a substantial period of time. During the mid-1980s, it took, on average, 48 days to complete an investigation, 94 days to hand down a decision after the close of an unfair labor practice hearing, and an additional 116 days before the board issued an order.

There are a couple of instances in which appeal to the board is available. First, if the regional director refuses to issue a complaint, the charging party may appeal to the general counsel in Washington, D.C. Such appeals are almost always denied. Second, a party dissatisfied with the administrative law judge's decision may file an appeal, called an *exception to the recommended order*, with the board in Washington. Briefs are then filed with the board, and, in extremely rare instances, oral arguments are heard. The board then issues its final order.

It should be noted that no one is actually required to honor an NLRB order because the board has no contempt-of-court powers. Instead, when its order is not followed, the NLRB brings an enforcement proceeding in a circuit court of appeals asking the court to order the parties to abide by its order. A party who is dissatisfied with the board's order may also appeal to a circuit court of appeals.

EXHIBIT 18-4 *Form for Filing an Unfair Labor Practice Charge*

UNITED STATES OF AMERICA
NATIONAL LABOR RELATIONS BOARD
CHARGE AGAINST EMPLOYER

DO NOT WRITE IN THIS SPACE	
Case	Date Filed

INSTRUCTIONS

File an original and 4 copies of this charge with NLRB Regional Director for the region in which the alleged unfair labor practice occurred or is occurring.

I EMPLOYER AGAINST WHOM CHARGE IS BROUGHT

a Name of Employer	b Number of workers employed

c Address, street, city, state, zip code	d Employer Representative	e Telephone No.

f Type of Establishment: factory, mine, wholesaler, etc.	g Identify principal product or service

h The above-named employer has engaged in and is engaging in unfair labor practices within the meaning of section 8 (a) subsections (1) and first subsections _____ of the National Labor Relations Act and these unfair labor practices are unfair practices affecting commerce within the meaning of the Act

2 Basis of the Charge (set forth a clear and concise statement of the facts constituting the alleged unfair labor practices)

By the above and other acts, the above-named employer has interfered with, restrained, and coerced employees in the exercise of the rights guaranteed in Section 7 of the Act

3 Full name of the party filing charge (labor organization give full name including local name and number)

4a Address (street and number, city, state and ZIP code)	4b Telephone No.

5 Full name of national or international labor organization which is an affiliate or constituent unit (to be filled in when charge is filed by a labor organization)

6 DECLARATION

I declare that I have read the above charge and that the statements are true to the best of my knowledge and belief.

B _____
Signature of representative making charge   (title if any)

Address _____
                    Telephone No.   (date)

WILLFUL FALSE STATEMENTS ON THIS CHARGE CAN BE PUNISHED BY FINE AND IMPRISONMENT (U.S. CODE, TITLE 18, SECTION 1001)

LABOR ORGANIZING

In a 1936 novel titled *In Dubious Battle*, John Steinbeck graphically described the extreme hardships faced by union organizers just after the passage of the Wagner Act. Derided as Communist sympathizers, they were often run out of town by company representatives and sometimes even by the workers they were trying to help.

This was an era in which many small-town law enforcement officers were indebted to business. The most protection they were willing to offer organizers was to advise them to get out of town. Many labor organizers lost their lives or were severely injured in these early unionization battles, and victories were often not clear-cut. Gradually, the violence directed against labor organizers subsided as companies realized that the National Labor Relations Act

EXHIBIT 18-5 *Procedures for an Unfair Labor Practice Case*

```
┌─────────────────────────────────────┐
│ Unfair labor practice charge filed   │
│ with the appropriate regional office │
│ by aggrieved employee, union, or     │
│ employer                             │
└─────────────────────────────────────┘
                  │
┌─────────────────────────────────────┐
│ Field examiner investigates charge.  │
│ Regional director decides whether to │
│ issue a complaint                    │
└─────────────────────────────────────┘
       │                    │
┌──────────────┐   OR   ┌──────────────────────┐
│ No complaint │        │ Complaint issued.     │
└──────────────┘        │ Informal resolution   │
                        │ attempted by regional │
                        │ office attorney       │
                        └──────────────────────┘
                                 │
              ┌─────────────┐  OR  ┌──────────────────────┐
              │ Case settled│      │ Regional office       │
              │ informally  │      │ attorney prosecutes   │
              └─────────────┘      │ case before           │
                                   │ administrative law    │
                                   │ judge                 │
                                   └──────────────────────┘
                                          │
                      ┌──────────────┐  OR  ┌──────────────────┐
                      │ Dismissal,   │      │ Remedy suggested, │
                      │ stating      │      │ stating rationale │
                      │ rationale and│      │ and evidence      │
                      │ evidence     │      └──────────────────┘
                      └──────────────┘              │
              ┌──────────────────────┐ OR ┌──────────────────────┐
              │ No objections in 20   │    │ Exceptions to order   │
              │ days, recommendation  │    │ filed with NLRB       │
              │ becomes final order of│    │ general counsel       │
              │ the NLRB              │    └──────────────────────┘
              └──────────────────────┘              │
              ┌──────────────────────┐    ┌──────────────────────┐
              │ Order issued but party│    │ Final order of        │
              │ fails to comply, board│    │ NLRB issued           │
              │ petitions United      │    └──────────────────────┘
              │ States Court of       │              │
              │ Appeals for           │    ┌──────────────────────┐
              │ enforcement order     │    │ Appeal to United      │
              └──────────────────────┘    │ States Court of       │
                                          │ Appeals               │
                                          └──────────────────────┘
```

would not be repealed and that the courts were going to enforce employees' right to organize.

Today, when employees are dissatisfied with their working conditions, they generally contact a national union representing other employees engaged in the same type of work. For example, employees of a shop that manufactures components for automobile engines would probably contact the United Auto Workers (UAW) Union. The union then sends a representative to meet with interested employees and explain what unionization would do for them. If the employees want to pursue a unionization effort, the organizer helps them engage in a campaign to convince a majority of the workers to accept the union as their exclusive representative.

During the course of this organizing campaign, certain activities of both employers and employees are prohibited by the NLRA and by "board rules"—that is, rules of conduct developed over the years by the NLRB in a number of cases. The constraints on employers' behavior under the NLRA are found primarily under section 8(a)1, which prohibits interference with employees' exercise of their Section 7 rights. It is important to distinguish conduct that constitutes an unfair labor practice from violations of board rules, because the remedies available for the two are different. A violation of board rules may result in the NLRB's setting aside the results of an election and ordering a new one. In contrast, the commission of an unfair labor practice by the employer may cause the board to ignore the election results altogether and order the employer to bargain with the union without a new election. The latter remedy occurs only in cases in which the employer's conduct was so egregious as to make it impossible to hold a fair election and the union had previously collected authorization cards signed by a majority of the employees.

BOARD RULES

Board rules are designed to guarantee a fair election. One very important rule, the **24-hour rule**, prohibits both union representatives and employers from making speeches to "captive audiences" of employees within 24 hours of a representation election. A captive audience exists when the employees have no choice but to listen to the speech.

24-hour rule Prohibits both union representatives and employers from making speeches to "captive audiences" of employees within 24 hours of a representative election.

Another important board rule requires employers to file with the regional director a list of the names and addresses of all employees eligible to vote within seven days after an election order is issued. This list, known as the *Excelsior list* (after the case that created it), is then made available to the union or union organizers by the regional director.

It is essential that employers be aware of these and other board rules because their violation may result in the setting aside of an election, even when the behavior does not constitute an unfair labor practice. All unfair labor practices, whether by employers or employees, are also considered violations of the board's election rules.

UNFAIR LABOR PRACTICES BY EMPLOYERS

INTERFERENCE WITH ORGANIZING   Section 8(a)1 of the National Labor Relations Act prohibits employer interference, restraint, or coercion of employees in the exercise of their Section 7 rights. It is sometimes difficult for a businessperson to know when her or his speech or conduct rises to the level of coercion, restraint, or interference. To make the issue even more complicated, Section 8(c) expressly provides that the expression of a view, argument, or opinion is *not* evidence of an unfair labor practice as long as it does not contain any threats of reprisals or promises of benefits.

As these sections have been interpreted since 1969, employers are allowed to communicate to employees their general views on unions or their specific views on a particular union, even to the point of predicting the impact that unionization would have on the company, so long as these statements do not amount to threats of reprisals or promises of benefits. To keep within these bounds, an employer must carefully phrase any predictions and be sure they are based on objective facts; in essence, the consequences that the employer predicts must be outside the control of the employer. Examples of threats of reprisals that constitute unfair labor practices are threats to close a plant if the employees organize, threats to discharge union sympathizers, and threats to discontinue present employee benefits, such as coffee breaks or employee discounts. An example of a promise of benefits that constitutes an unfair labor practice is the announcement of a new employee profit-sharing plan a few days before the election.

No-solicitation rules of employers may also constitute an employer unfair labor practice because they interfere with communications among employees.

In order for employees to exercise their Section 7 rights, they must be able to communicate with one another.

Businesspeople must understand what types of organizing behavior can lawfully be prohibited and what prohibitions would constitute unfair labor practices. Understandably, employers do not want employees to use work time or company property to organize, and, in general, they may prohibit union solicitation and the distribution of literature during work time. During nonwork time, such as lunch and coffee breaks, employers may prohibit organizing activity on company property *only* if there are legitimate safety or efficiency reasons for doing so and the restraint is not manifestly intended to thwart organizing efforts. The burden of proof is on the employer to demonstrate these safety or efficiency concerns. This prohibition against interference with employees' right to communicate extends beyond the organizing campaign, as the following case demonstrates.

EASTEX, INCORPORATED V. NLRB
UNITED STATES SUPREME COURT 437 U.S. 556 (1978)

Employees of petitioner Eastex, Inc., wanted to distribute a four-part newsletter to fellow employees in nonworking areas of petitioner's plant during nonworking hours. The first and fourth parts of the newsletter urged support of the union, the second urged employees to write letters opposing a right-to-work statute, and the third criticized the presidential veto of an increase in the federal minimum wage and urged employees to register to vote to defeat their enemies. Petitioners' representatives blocked the distribution of the newsletter, and the union filed an unfair labor practice charge. The NLRB found a violation of Section 8(a)1 and issued a cease-and-desist order requiring petitioners to cease refusing to allow distribution of the newsletter. Eastex appealed to the U.S. Supreme Court.

JUSTICE POWELL

The question presented is whether petitioner's refusal to allow the distribution violated § 8(a)1 of the National Labor Relations Act, . . . by interfering with, restraining, or coercing employees' exercise of their right under § 7 of the Act, to engage in "concerted activities for the purpose of . . . mutual aid or protection."

Two distinct questions are presented. The first is whether, apart from the location of the activity, distribution of the newsletter is the kind of concerted activity that is protected from employer interference by §§ 7 and 8(a)1 of the National Labor Relations Act. If it is, then the second question is whether the fact that the activity takes place on petitioner's property gives rise to a countervailing interest that outweighs the exercise of § 7 rights in that location. . . .

Petitioner contends that the activity here is not within the "mutual aid or protection" language because it does not relate to a "specific dispute" between employees and their own employer "over an issue which the employer has the right or power to affect." [I]n petitioner's view, under § 7 "the employee is only protected for activity within the scope of the employment relationship." Petitioner rejects

the idea that § 7 might protect any activity that could be characterized as "political," and suggests that the discharge of an employee who engages in any such activity would not violate the Act.

We believe that petitioner misconceives the reach of the "mutual aid or protection" clause. The "employees" who engage in concerted activities for "mutual aid or protection are defined by . . . the Act to include any employee, and shall not be limited to the employees of a particular employer, unless this subchapter explicitly states otherwise. . . ." This definition was intended to protect employees when they engage in otherwise proper concerted activities in support of employees of employers other than their own. In recognition of this intent, the board and the courts long have held that the "mutual aid or protection" clause encompasses such activity.

We also find no warrant for petitioner's view that employees lose their protection under the "mutual aid or protection" clause when they seek to improve terms and conditions of employment or otherwise improve their lot as employees through channels outside the immediate employee-employer relationship. Congress knew well enough that labor's cause often is advanced on fronts other than collective bargaining and grievance settlement within the immediate employment context. It recognized this fact by choosing . . . to protect concerted activities for the somewhat broader purpose of "mutual aid or protection" as well as for the narrower purposes of "self-organization" and "collective bargaining."

. . . Distribution of the second section, urging employees to write their legislators to oppose incorporation of the state "right-to-work" statute into a revised state constitution, was protected because union security is "central to the union concept of strength through solidarity" and "a mandatory subject of bargaining in other than right-to-work states." The newsletter warned that incorporation could affect employees adversely "by weakening unions and improving the edge business has at the bargaining table."

. . . [D]istribution of the third section . . . was protected despite the fact that petitioner's employees were paid more than the vetoed minimum wage. . . . [T]he "minimum wage inevitably influences wage levels derived from collective bargaining, even those far above the minimum," . . . Few topics are of such immediate concern to employees as the level of their wages. The Board was entitled to note the widely recognized impact that a rise in the minimum wage may have on the level of negotiated wages generally, a phenomenon that would not have been lost on petitioner's employees.

The question that remains is whether the Board erred in holding that petitioner's employees may distribute the newsletter in nonworking areas of petitioner's property during nonworking time. . . . An employer may not prohibit its employees from distributing union organization literature in nonworking areas of its industrial property during nonworking time, absent a showing by the employer that a ban is necessary to maintain plant discipline or production. This ruling obtained even though the employees had not shown that distribution off the em-

ployer's property would be ineffective. In the Court's view, the Board had reached an acceptable "adjustment between the undisputed right of self-organization assured to employees under the Wagner Act and the equally undisputed right of employers to maintain discipline in their establishments."

Petitioner contends that the board must distinguish among distributions of protected matter by employees on an employer's property on the basis of the content of each distribution. As already noted, petitioner made no attempt to show that its management interest would be prejudiced in any way by the exercise of § 7 rights proposed by its employees here. Even if the mere distribution by employees of material protected by § 7 can be said to intrude on petitioner's property rights in any meaningful sense, the degree of intrusion does not vary with the content of the material. Petitioner's only cognizable property right in this respect is in preventing employees from bringing literature onto its property and distributing it there—not in choosing which distributions protected by § 7 it wishes to suppress.

Affirmed in favor of Plaintiff, NLRB.

Critical Thinking about the Law

A PRINCIPLE GUIDING MOST PEOPLE'S LIVES is that the law should be followed. However, sometimes it is difficult to determine exactly what "the law" is.

The history of labor law litigation is riddled with cases consistent with the following scenario: Management and unions offer different interpretations of a particular statute's meaning. Each party interprets the statute in question as either (a) permitting themselves to take a certain action or (b) prohibiting the other party from taking a specific action. This conflict is resolved only when one interpretation is given the force of law by judges who support their decision with reasoning.

Eastex, Inc. v. NLRB is roughly consistent with this scenario, and the questions that follow are designed to make you think critically about how the scenario was played out in the context of this particular case.

1. The legal dispute in this case centered around the meaning of Section 7 of the National Labor Relations Act. As a future business manager, you need to recognize that ambiguity often plays a central role in labor-management conflict. What ambiguous phrase in Section 7 was an important factor in causing this particular dispute?

   CLUE You are being asked to find a phrase, so your answer will not be just an adjective. You want to find the phrase whose meaning as interpreted by the Court legally resolved the labor-management conflict.

2. The Court interpreted Section 7's ambiguous phrase in a manner favoring the union. What evidence would have been adequate to move the judgment in management's favor?

   CLUE To find this answer, go to the section of the decision where the Court discusses whether it was permissible for the employees to distribute the newsletter in nonworking areas of the business's property.

In a more recent case, _Guardian Industries Corp. v. National Labor Relations Board_,[1] a circuit court of appeals struck a slightly different balance between the employer's private property rights and the employees' rights to communicate with one another during an organizing campaign. Guardian had maintained a bulletin board upon which it would post, on its employees' behalf, "for sale" cards. When asked to post notices of upcoming union organizing meetings on this board, the employer refused. The union filed an unfair labor practice charge, arguing that once employees were given access to the bulletin board for one purpose, they should have access to it for all purposes, including organizing.

The court found that there was nothing unlawful about Guardian's behavior. The company had never allowed announcements of _any_ meetings to be posted, so it was not unlawfully discriminating against the organizing employees in this instance. It is only in instances in which an employer has opened up bulletin boards for all employee postings and then disallowed postings related to organizing that courts have found an employer violation of the National Labor Relations Act.

Thus far, we have been concerned with _employee_ solicitations and distributions. _Nonemployee_ organizers have fewer rights than employee organizers. As long as they have some way to communicate with employees (and they do in almost all cases now because they are entitled to the _Excelsior_ list of names and addresses of employees), nonemployee organizers may be prohibited from entering the employer's property, including private parking lots. The courts have held that in the case of nonemployee organizers, the employer's private property rights will be protected, as the following case illustrates.

LECHMERE, INCORPORATED V. NLRB
UNITED STATES SUPREME COURT 112 S. CT. 841 (1992)

Lechmere, Inc., owns and operates a retail store in a shopping plaza. The company also owns part of the plaza parking lot, which is separated from the highway by a 46-foot-wide strip of grass-covered public property. During a union organizing campaign, nonemployee organizers placed handbills on cars in the employee section of the parking lot. Lechmere then denied organizers access to the lot. The organizers responded by distributing handbills and picketing on the grassy strip. They also contacted about 20 percent of Lechmere's employees directly.

The organizers filed a charge with the NLRB, alleging that Lechmere's denial of access to the parking lot to the organizers constituted an unfair labor practice. An ALJ ruled in the organizers' favor, recommending that Lechmere be ordered to cease and desist from barring the organizers from the lot. The NLRB affirmed and issued the order. Lechmere appealed, and the U.S. Court of Appeals affirmed, enforcing the order. Lechmere appealed to the U.S. Supreme Court.

JUSTICE THOMAS

By its plain terms, the NLRA confers rights only on _employees_, not on unions or their nonemployee organizers. [H]owever, we recognized that insofar as the employees' "right of self-organization depends in some measure on [their] ability . . . to learn the advantages of self-organization from others," § 7 of the NLRA may, in certain limited circumstances, restrict an employer's right to exclude nonemployee union organizers from his property.

As a rule an employer cannot be compelled to allow distribution of union literature by nonemployee organizers on his property. As with many other rules, however, we recognized an exception. Where "the location of a plant and the living quarters of the employees place the employees beyond the reach of reasonable union efforts to communicate with them," employers' property rights may be "required to yield to the extent needed to permit communication of information on the right to organize."

"While an employer may not always bar nonemployee union organizers from his property, his right to do so remains the general rule. To gain access, _the union has the burden of showing that no other reasonable means of communicating its organizational message to the employees exists_ or that the employer's access rules discriminate against union solicitation. That the burden imposed on the union is a heavy one is evidenced by the fact that the balance struck by the Board and the courts under the _Babcock_ accommodation principle has rarely been in favor of trespassory organizational activity."

---

[1] 49 F.3d 317 (1995).

In *Babcock*, we held that the Act drew a distinction "of substance," between the union activities of employees and nonemployees. In cases involving *employee* activities, we noted with approval, the Board "balanced the conflicting interests of employees to receive information on self-organization on the company's property from fellow employees during nonworking time, with the employer's right to control the use of his property." In cases involving *nonemployee* activities, however, the Board was not permitted to engage in that same balancing. *Babcock*'s teaching is straightforward: § 7 simply does not protect nonemployee union organizers *except* in the rare case where "the inaccessibility of employees makes ineffective the reasonable attempts by nonemployees to communicate with them through the usual channels." Our reference to "reasonable" attempts was nothing more than a common sense recognition that unions need not engage in extraordinary feats to communicate with inaccessible employees—*not* an endorsement of the view that the Act protects "reasonable" trespasses. Where reasonable alternative means of access exist, § 7's guarantees do not authorize trespasses by nonemployee organizers, *even* "under . . . reasonable regulations" established by the Board.

The threshold inquiry in this case, then, is whether the facts here justify application of *Babcock*'s inaccessibility exception.

As we have explained, the exception to *Babcock*'s rule is a narrow one. It does not apply wherever nontrespassory access to employees may be cumbersome or less-than-ideally effective, but only where "the *location of a plant and the living quarters of the employees* place the employees *beyond the reach* of reasonable union efforts to communicate with them." Classic examples include logging camps, mining camps, and mountain resort hotels. *Babcock*'s exception was crafted precisely to protect the § 7 rights of those employees who, by virtue of their employment, are isolated from the ordinary flow of information that characterizes our society. The union's burden of establishing such isolation is, as we have explained, "a heavy one," and one not satisfied by mere conjecture or the expression of doubts concerning the effectiveness of nontrespassory means of communication.

The Board's conclusion in this case that the union had no reasonable means short of trespass to make Lechmere's employees aware of its organizational efforts is based on a misunderstanding of the limited scope of this exception. Because the employees do not reside on Lechmere's property, they are presumptively not "beyond the reach," of the union's message. Although the employees live in a large metropolitan area (Greater Hartford), that fact does not in itself render them "inaccessible" in the sense contemplated by *Babcock*. Their accessibility is suggested by the union's success in contacting a substantial percentage of them directly, via mailings, phone calls, and home visits. Such direct contact, of course, is not a necessary element of "reasonably effective" communication; signs or advertising also may suffice. In this case, the union tried advertising in local newspapers; the Board said that this was not reasonably effective because it was expensive and might not reach the employees. Whatever the merits of that conclusion, other alternative means of communication were readily available.

Thus, signs displayed, for example, from the public grassy strip adjoining Lechmere's parking lot would have informed the employees about the union's organizational efforts. (Indeed, union organizers picketed the shopping center's main entrance for months as employees came and went every day.) *Access* to employees, not *success* in winning them over, is the critical issue—although success, or lack thereof, may be relevant in determining whether reasonable access exists. Because the union in this case failed to establish the existence of any "unique obstacles," that frustrated access to Lechmere's employees, the Board erred in concluding that Lechmere committed an unfair labor practice by barring the nonemployee organizers from its property.

Reversed in favor of Plaintiff, Lechmere.

Critical Thinking about the Law

SUPPOSE THAT YOU ARE A MID-LEVEL manager in a firm who notices that one of the employees for whom you are responsible is not working very hard. After warning the employee several times, you finally go to your supervisor to report the situation. At this point, your supervisor must decide where she places the burden of proof with respect to your grievance. Basically, she can request either that you prove that the employee is slacking in his duties or that the employee prove that he is not slacking off. If she places the burden of proof on you, in essence she is saying: "I assume that the employee is working hard. That is the solid position from which you must move me to convince me of the validity of your grievance." In this case, the employee is innocent until proven guilty. On the other hand, if she places the burden of proof on the employee, a quite different situation arises. With that placement, she is conveying her assumption that the employee is less than diligent in his work and that he must prove otherwise. In this scenario, the employee is guilty until proven innocent.

As you can see, where the burden of proof is placed in a court of law is very important to the outcome of the case. In a very crude sense, by not placing the burden of proof on one party, those interpreting a law are saying that they tend to accept that party's argument. The other party has the burden of proof; it must disprove the first party's argument to the court's satisfaction.

Because the burden of proof is such a crucial factor in *any* dispute, it is important to be sensitive to who must bear that burden in particular conflicts.

1. Who had the burden of proof in *Lechmere*?

    CLUE The Court explicitly answered this question.

2. What ethical norm guided the placement and nature of the burden of proof in this case?

    CLUE Focus on the crucial role of private property rights in Justice Thomas's reasoning.

DOMINATION OR SUPPORT OF LABOR ORGANIZING   In addition to the NLRA's all-encompassing Section 8(a)1, there are other subsections of 8(a) that set forth specific behaviors that constitute unfair labor practices: a violation of any of these sections is simultaneously a violation of Section 8(a)1. For example, under Section 8(a)2, an employer cannot dominate, support, or interfere with a labor organization. Thus, in response to an organizing campaign by one union, the employer cannot aid some of its employees in contacting a different union to compete for the right to represent the workers at that plant. Nor can the employer play any role in establishing or operating any committee or other organization designed to represent or aid employees in their dealings with the employer over wages, rates of pay, or other terms and conditions of employment.

The employer must also be careful about voluntarily recognizing a union claiming to represent a majority of the employees. If the employer recognizes a union that does not represent the majority of employees, that is a violation of Section 8(a)2, even if the employer was acting in good faith.

A union *dominated* by an employer will be *disestablished;* that is, it may never again represent those employees. A union unlawfully *supported* by an employer will be *decertified;* that is, it will not be able to represent the employees until it has been certified as a result of a new representation election monitored by the NLRB.

One of the major concerns facing labor relations specialists at present is the impact of Section 8 on some of the more cooperative labor-management programs that employers are trying to put in place today. Many commentators from both business and academia have cited the traditional adversarial relationship between labor and management as being at least partially responsible for productivity problems in many industries.[2] Consequently, U.S. management has been experimenting with programs to increase cooperation between labor and management. There is strong evidence that these programs do boost productivity.[3] However, many of them have been found to constitute unfair labor practices.

We will discuss three of the most common of these new programs: quality circles, autonomous and semiautonomous work groups, and labor-management committees. All bring labor and management together in an attempt to solve mutual problems; yet, in instituting these programs, management may be violating the NLRA.

A **quality circle** is a small group of workers who meet regularly on a voluntary basis to analyze work problems and recommend solutions to manage-

quality circle A small group of workers who voluntarily meet on a regular basis, under the leadership of a supervisor, to discuss work problems and recommend solutions to management.

---

[2]C. Farrell and M. J. Mandell, *Industrial Policy*, Bus. Wk., April 6, 1992, at 70–75; and B. Childs, *Dew United Motor: An American Success Story*, 40 Lab. L.J. 453 (1989).
[3]Childs, *supra* note 2.

ment. Discussions are typically led by a supervisor from the area in which the employees work. Although the focus is typically on such production problems as reducing scrap, solutions may involve matters traditionally classified as "working conditions," such as plant layout and scheduling. Quality circles may also be used to educate workers in such areas as group dynamics, problem solving, and statistical quality control.

One of the best-known uses of quality circles is Ford's Employee Involvement program, a voluntary program developed in cooperation with the UAW. Workers meet voluntarily in small groups with their supervisors to provide suggestions for improving production. Participants also receive training in group problem-solving techniques. The recommendations and results of the groups are published. Since the implementation of this program, the number of grievances at Ford plants has fallen, and employee job satisfaction ratings have increased. So far, Ford's plan has not been challenged in the courts.

Autonomous work group programs organize workers into teams. Some teams are led by a supervisor appointed by management; others are led by a worker elected from among the team members. The group is given a task to perform, and it determines how it will accomplish the task. Depending on the industry, the "task" may be anything from building refrigerators to processing an insurance claim. The group's authority may range from deciding how and when subtasks are to be performed to disciplining group members, scheduling overtime, and interviewing job applicants for the team. Teams that have less authority are known as **semiautonomous work groups**.

The essence of the autonomous work team is that with increased responsibility will come increased motivation. A program using semiautonomous work groups has been successfully implemented at the General Motors-Toyota plant in Fremont, California, for example. This plant had a history of contentious labor-management relations, but after the semiautonomous work groups were set up, management noticed substantial improvements in the quality of the plant's products and a reduction in the number of grievances filed by workers.

Labor-management committees provide a forum where workers can communicate directly with upper management. Worker participants on these committees are either elected by their fellow workers or appointed by management. They usually serve for a limited time, such as six months, to ensure maximum participation.

Under a literal interpretation of the NLRA, most participatory committees would appear to constitute labor organizations. In fact, in the leading U.S. Supreme Court case on this issue, *NLRB v. Cabot Carbon Co.*,[4] the Court found that "employee committees" established by the employer to allow employees to discuss with managers such issues as safety, increased efficiency, and grievances at nonunion plants and departments are labor organizations. Numerous decisions since *Cabot* have followed this strict interpretation. The dilemma for management is that these committees are rather useless unless they are allowed to discuss issues that have an impact on working conditions, but having such discussions makes them illegal employer-dominated labor organizations under the NLRA.

Recently, the NLRB and a few appellate courts have created two narrow exceptions to the strict interpretation the Supreme Court set forth in *Cabot*. The first exception arises when all of the workers in a bargaining unit or plant participate in the program. In that situation, the committee does not "represent" the employees because it comprises all the employees; if it does not represent employees, it cannot be a labor organization, and hence cannot be construed as an employer-dominated union. In other words, *participation* in an employee group is legal, but *representation* of other employees is not.

The second exception involves a situation in which employees carry out a traditional management function. In such cases, the employee group no longer "deals with" management because it is performing the delegated function itself.

autonomous/semiautonomous work group A team of workers, led by either a supervisor appointed by management or a worker elected by the team, that determines for itself how it will accomplish the work task it is given to perform. Those groups with full authority over all subtasks, scheduling of overtime, and hiring of new team members are *autonomous*; those with less authority are *semiautonomous*.

labor-management committee A forum in which workers communicate directly with upper management. May be illegal under the NLRA if the committee has an impact on working conditions, unless all workers in a bargaining unit or a plant participate *or* the employees on the committee are carrying out a traditional management function.

---

[4]360 U.S. 203 (1959).

You can see from these examples that the National Labor Relations Board and some of the courts are trying very hard to find a way to allow cooperative labor-management programs to exist. Remember, even if a labor-management committee is found to constitute a labor organization, to be unlawful, the committee must be dominated or supported by the employer.

The traditional test[5] asks whether the committee is *structurally* independent of management. Most participatory committees have some minimal association with management that would render them unfair under this strict test. Again, however, some circuit courts are using two factors to minimize the impact of this holding on participatory programs. First, the court asks whether the employers had good motives in establishing the plan. Second, the court asks whether the employees are satisfied with it.

Applying this two-part analysis, the court may then distinguish illegal domination and support from legal cooperation.[6] In the case in which this two-part test was initially set forth, the court focused on the NLRA's goal, which is to protect employee free choice, and said that employees should be free to enter into cooperative arrangements with their employers as long as the employer does not try to use the plan to interfere with free choice.

So the courts are bending over backward to find these cooperative arrangements between labor and management legal. Yet, until there is a change in the NLRA to specifically allow such cooperative programs, or until the Supreme Court clearly upholds their validity, employers adopting such programs should be fully aware of the potential problems.

One final issue of concern with respect to employee-involvement plans is whether participation on some of the more powerful committees places workers in the category of managerial or supervisory employees, thereby putting them at risk of losing their right to bargain collectively under the NLRA. For example, after a union at the College of Osteopathy and Medicine won an increased managerial voice for its members, the employees lost their right to bargain collectively.[7]

DISCRIMINATION BASED ON UNION ACTIVITY   An employer who discriminates against employees because of their union activity is in violation of Section 8(a)3. An ambiguous situation arises when a marginal employee who is also an organizer for a union is fired. The NLRB will have to determine whether the firing was motivated by the employee's poor performance or by the employee's union activity. Discharge of even the most strident union activist is legal as long as the primary motivation for the firing was poor performance rather than union activity. In such cases, courts look at such factors as how others who engage in similar misconduct have been treated by the employer.

Firing is the ultimate form of discrimination, but other forms of discrimination, such as reducing break time and unfavorable treatment in job and overtime assignments, also constitute violations of Section 8(a)3.

UNFAIR LABOR PRACTICES BY EMPLOYEES

Unfair labor practices by employees are less common in organizing campaigns than unfair labor practices by employers, perhaps because when a union is trying to gain representational status, it generally does not have enough power to engage in such practices. The sections of the NLRA most applicable to unions during the organizing period are: 8(b)1, which prohibits restraint or coercion of employees in the exercise of their Section 7 rights; 8(b)2, which prohibits forcing the employer to discriminate to encourage or discourage union activity; and 8(b)7, which prohibits picketing for recognition when another union has been certified or when the picketing union has lost an election within the past year.

---

[5]This test was established in NLRB v. Newport News Shipbuilding and Drydock Co., 308 U.S. 241 (1939).
[6]Chicago Rawhide v. NLRB, 221 F.2d 165 (1955).
[7]265 N.L.R.B. 295 (1982).

The purpose of all organizing activity is for the union to gain the right to be the exclusive representative of employees in negotiations with the employer over wages, hours, and terms and conditions of employment. Because the potential power of the union clashes with the employer's desire to maintain control over the workplace, organizational campaigns can become very heated. In any organizing campaign, the first step for the union is to gain the support of a substantial number of the members (generally 30 percent) of an appropriate bargaining unit so that a board-run election may be ordered.

As mentioned previously, an important question in this initial stage is: What is the **appropriate bargaining unit?** The appropriate unit, as defined by the NLRA, is one that can "ensure the employees the fullest freedom in exercising the rights guaranteed by the Act." In making such a determination, the regional director of the NLRB examines a number of alternatives. An entire plant may be an appropriate unit; so may a single department of highly skilled employees; and so may all the employees of a single employer located at more than one facility (e.g., all employees of a group of retail stores located in a metropolitan area).

In determining whether a proposed bargaining unit is appropriate, the NLRB considers primarily whether there is a *mutuality of interest* among the proposed members of the unit. All proposed members should have similar skills, wages, hours, and working conditions, for only then is it possible for a union to look out for the interests of all members. Other factors considered include the desires of the employees, the extent of organization, and the history of collective bargaining of the employer and of the industry in which the employer operates.

The appropriateness of the proposed bargaining unit is the first issue that the staff of the regional office determines when it receives a petition for a representation election. Once that issue has been resolved, employer and union representatives try to reach an agreement on such matters as the time and place of the election, standards for eligibility to vote, rules of conduct during the election, and the means for handling challenges to the outcome of the election. If the parties cannot reach agreement, the NLRB regional director determines these matters and orders an election.

If the union obtains signed authorization cards from over 50 percent of the appropriate employee unit, it may ask the employer to recognize the union on the basis of this showing of majority support alone. Realizing it is futile to try to prevent the union from representing its employees, the employer may decide that it would ultimately be beneficial to recognize the union and begin the bargaining process on an amicable note. Such behavior is risky, however, because it may constitute a violation of Section 8(a)1, which prohibits employers from interfering with employees' Section 7 right of free choice. In other cases, the employer may wish to avoid the risk of violating Section 8(a)2, which prohibits employer-dominated unions, and may therefore request that the union file a petition for certification. Having a board-run election to ensure that there indeed is majority support protects the employer.

If a union receives a majority of the votes and the election results are not challenged, the board will certify the union as the exclusive bargaining representative of the employees of that unit. If two or more unions are seeking to represent employees, and neither one of the unions nor "no union" receives a majority of the votes, there will be a runoff election between the choices that got the first and second greatest number of votes. Once a valid representation election has been held and there has been either a certification of a representative union or a majority vote for no union, there cannot be another election for one year. Nor can there be an election during the term of a collective bargaining agreement, unless either the union is defunct or there is such a division in the ranks of the union that it is unable or unwilling to represent the employees.

appropriate bargaining unit May be an entire plant, a single department, or all employees of a single employer, as long as there is a mutuality of interest among the proposed members of the unit.

THE COLLECTIVE BARGAINING PROCESS

Shortly after a union has been certified, or recognized, the collective bargaining process begins. Both the employer and the bargaining unit representative are required by the NLRA to bargain collectively in good faith with respect to wages, hours, and other terms and conditions of employment. Note that the requirement is only to bargain in good faith, not to reach an agreement. The board has no power to order the parties to accept any contract provision; it can only order them to bargain.

good-faith bargaining
Following procedural standards laid out in Section 8 of the NLRA; failure to bargain in good faith, by either the employer or the union, is an unfair labor practice.

To a great extent, **good-faith bargaining** is defined procedurally. Under Section 8(d), the parties must: (1) meet at reasonable times and confer in good faith; (2) sign a written agreement if one is reached; (3) when intent on terminating or modifying an existing contract, give 60 days' notice to the other party with an offer to confer over proposals, and give 30 days' notice to the federal or state mediation services in the event of a pending dispute over the new agreement; and (4) neither strike nor engage in a lockout during the 60-day notice period.

Failure of the employer to bargain in good faith is an unfair labor practice under Section 8(a)5. Employers violate this section not only by disregarding proper procedural standards but also by assuming a take-it-or-leave-it attitude. So if the employer takes a position and says it will alter it only if new information shows its proposal to contain incorrect assumptions, this is not good-faith bargaining.

Employers who refuse to provide the union with relevant information that it requests and needs in order to responsibly represent the employees in the bargaining process are also engaging in an unfair labor practice. Relevant information includes job descriptions, time-study data, financial data supporting a company claim that it is unable to meet union demands, and competitive wage data to support a company claim that the union is demanding noncompetitive wage rates.

Taking unilateral action on a matter subject to bargaining is also an unfair employer labor practice under Section 8(a)5. One example is giving employees a raise or additional benefits during the term of a collective bargaining agreement without first consulting the union. This behavior would have the effect of undermining the union as a bargaining representative, and thus would be unlawful.

Because bargaining is meant to secure benefits for employees, there are fewer cases of union refusals to bargain, but failure of a union to bargain in good faith is a violation of Section 8(b)3. Thus unions may not violate any of the procedural requirements already delineated, nor may they refuse to sign a contract after an agreement has been reached or insist on bargaining for clauses that fall outside the scope of mandatory bargaining.

SUBJECTS OF BARGAINING

mandatory subjects of collective bargaining Subjects over which the parties must bargain, including rates of pay, wages, hours of employment, and other terms and conditions of employment.

permissive subjects of collective bargaining Subjects that are not primarily about conditions of employment and therefore need not be bargained over.

All subjects of bargaining are either mandatory or permissive. **Mandatory subjects of collective bargaining** are those over which the parties *must* bargain: rates of pay, wages, hours of employment, and other terms and conditions of employment. Failure to bargain over these subjects constitutes an unfair labor practice. All other bargaining subjects are **permissive** and need not be bargained over. Management decisions concerning the commitment of capital and the basic scope of the enterprise, for instance, are *not* primarily about conditions of employment, and thus are not mandatory. Inclusion of a permissive subject in the bargaining process in one year, even if that results in its inclusion in a collective bargaining agreement, does not make that subject an issue of mandatory bargaining in any future contract. The only subjects that *cannot* be included in the bargaining process are illegal terms, such as a contract clause that would require unlawful discrimination by the employer.

Unions have traditionally tried to expand the scope of mandatory items. Mandatory items concerning wages include piece rates, shift differentials incentives, severance pay, holiday pay, vacation pay, profit sharing, stock option plans, and hours (including overtime provisions). Mandatory items concerning conditions of employment include layoff and recall provision, seniority systems, promotion policies, no-strike and no-lockout clauses, grievance procedures, and work rules. In the following case, the U.S. Supreme Court examined the issue of whether changes in prices offered in a company cafeteria were subject to mandatory bargaining.

431

Chapter 18

Laws Governing Labor-Management
Relations

FORD MOTOR COMPANY V. NLRB
UNITED STATES SUPREME COURT 441 U.S. 488 (1979)

Ford Motor Co. provided its employees with in-plant cafeteria and vending services. Although Ford contracted out these services to an independent caterer, the company retained the right to review and approve the quality and price of the food. Ford notified the union of pending price increases, and the union sought to bargain over these increases. When Ford refused to bargain over the issue, the union filed an unfair labor practice charge with the NLRB, alleging a violation of § 8(a)5.

The NLRB decided in favor of the union, finding the prices of food available in the plant cafeteria to be within the scope of "other terms and conditions of employment," which the employer must bargain over. The U.S. Court of Appeals enforced the order to bargain. Ford then appealed to the U.S. Supreme Court.

JUSTICE WHITE

The Board has consistently held that in-plant food prices are among those terms and conditions of employment defined in § 8(d) and about which the employer and union must bargain under §§ 8(a) 5 and 8(b) 3. Because it is evident that Congress assigned to the Board the primary task of construing these provisions in the course of adjudicating charges of unfair refusals to bargain and because the "classification of bargaining subjects as 'terms or conditions of employment' is a matter concerning which the Board has special expertise," its judgment as to what is a mandatory bargaining subject is entitled to considerable deference.

Of course, the judgment of the Board is subject to judicial review; but if its construction of the statute is reasonably defensible, it should not be rejected merely because the courts might prefer another view of the statute. [W]e have refused enforcement of Board orders where they had "no reasonable basis in law," either because the proper legal standard was not applied or because the Board applied the correct standard but failed to give the plain language of the standard its ordinary meaning. We have also parted company with the Board's interpretation where it was "fundamentally inconsistent with the structure of the Act" and an attempt to usurp "major policy decisions properly made by Congress." [W]e could not accept the Board's application of the Act where we were convinced that the Board was moving "into a new area of regulation which Congress had not committed to it."

The Board is vulnerable on none of these grounds in this case. Construing and applying the duty to bargain and the language of § 8(d), "other terms and conditions of employment," are tasks lying at the heart of the Board's function. . . . [W]e conclude that the Board's consistent view that in-plant food prices and services are mandatory bargaining subjects is not an unreasonable or unprincipled construction of the statute and that it should be accepted and enforced.

The terms and conditions under which food is available on the job are plainly germane to the "working environment." Furthermore the company is not in the business of selling food to its employees, and the establishment of in-plant food prices is not among those "managerial decisions, which lie at the core of entrepreneurial control." The Board is in no sense attempting to permit the Union to usurp managerial decisionmaking; nor is it seeking to regulate an area from which Congress intended to exclude it.

Including within § 8(d) the prices of in-plant-supplied food and beverages would also serve the ends of the National Labor Relations Act. "The object of this Act was not to allow governmental regulation of the terms and conditions of employment, but rather to insure that employers and their employees could work together to establish mutually satisfactory conditions. As illustrated by the facts of this case, substantial disputes can arise over the pricing of in-plant-supplied food and beverages. National labor policy contemplates that areas of common dispute between employers and employees be funneled into collective bargaining. The assumption is that this is preferable to allowing recurring disputes to fester outside the negotiation process until strikes or other forms of economic warfare occur.

The trend of industrial practice supports this conclusion. In response to increasing employee concern over the issue, many contracts are now being negotiated that contain provisions concerning in-plant food services. In this case, as already noted, local agreements between Ford and the Union have contained detailed provisions about nonprice aspects of in-plant food services for several years. Although not conclusive, current industrial practice is highly relevant in construing the phrase "terms and conditions of employment."

Ford nevertheless argues against classifying food prices and services as mandatory bargaining subjects because they do not "vitally affect" the terms and conditions of employment and because they are trivial matters over which neither party should be required to bargain.

There is no merit to either of these arguments. Here, the matter of in-plant food prices and services is an aspect of the relationship between Ford and its own employees.

As for the argument that in-plant food prices and services are too trivial to qualify as mandatory subjects, the Board has a contrary view, and we have no basis for rejecting it. It is also clear that the bargaining-unit employees in this case considered the matter far from trivial since they pressed an unsuccessful boycott to secure a voice in setting food prices. They evidently felt, and common sense also tells us, that even minor increases in the cost of meals can amount to a substantial sum of money over time.

Ford also argues that the Board's position will result in unnecessary disruption because any small change in price or service will trigger the obligation to bargain. The problem, it is said, will be particularly acute in situations where several unions are involved, possibly requiring endless rounds of negotiations over issues as minor as the price of a cup of coffee or a soft drink.

These concerns have been thought exaggerated by the Board. Its position in this case, as in all past cases involving the same issue, is that it is sufficient compliance with the statutory mandate if management honors a specific union request for bargaining about changes that have been made or are to be made. The Board apparently assumes that, as a practical matter, requests to bargain will not be lightly made. Moreover, problems created by constantly shifting food prices can be anticipated and provided for in the collective bargaining agreement. Furthermore, if it is true that disputes over food prices are likely to be frequent and intense, it follows that more, not less, collective bargaining is the remedy. This is the assumption of national labor policy, and it is soundly supported by both reason and experience.

Finally, Ford asserts that to require it to engage in bargaining over in-plant food service prices would be futile because those prices are set by a third-party supplier, ARA. It is true that ARA sets vending machine and cafeteria prices, but under Ford's contract with ARA, Ford retains the right to review and control food services and prices. In any event, an employer can always affect prices by initiating or altering a subsidy to the third-party supplier such as that provided by Ford in this case, and will typically have the right to change suppliers at some point in the future. To this extent the employer holds future, if not present, leverage over in-plant food services and prices.

Affirmed in favor of Defendant, NLRB.

STRIKES, PICKETING, AND BOYCOTTS

The prudent businessperson needs to understand the National Labor Relations Act not only as it applies to labor organizing and collective bargaining but also as it applies to three other common occurrences in labor-management relations: strikes, picketing, and boycotts.

STRIKES

strike A temporary concerted withdrawal of labor.

A **strike**, simply defined, is a temporary, concerted withdrawal of labor. It is the ultimate weapon used by employees to secure recognition or to gain favorable terms in the collective bargaining process. However, not all strikes are legal, and employees engaging in certain types of legal strikes may still lose their jobs as a consequence of striking. The type of strike that one is engaged in is determined both by the purpose of the strike and by the methods used by the strikers.

economic strike A nonviolent work stoppage for the purpose of obtaining better terms and conditions of employment under a collective bargaining agreement.

LAWFUL STRIKES   A lawful **economic strike** is a nonviolent work stoppage for the purpose of obtaining better terms and conditions of employment under a collective bargaining agreement. Because this type of strike is a protected activity, strikers are entitled to return to their jobs once the strike is over. However, employers are allowed to fill economic strikers' jobs while the strike is taking place, and if permanent replacements are hired, strikers are not entitled to return to their jobs. This ability of the employer to replace economic strikers permanently tends to make the strike a less potent weapon than it at first appears.

Because of the ability of the employer to permanently replace workers engaged in an economic strike if they first hire permanent replacement workers, unions have fought to try to get Congress to pass legislation prohibiting the use of permanent replacement workers. Workers did achieve a minor victory in 1995, when President Clinton issued an executive order prohibiting federal contractors with government contracts worth over $100,000 from hiring permanent replacements for strikers. If any such firm does hire replacement workers, the labor secretary is to notify the head of any agencies who have contracts with such firms, and the contracts are to be terminated and no contracts are to be made with said firms in the future.

Even if replaced, however, economic strikers still are entitled to vote in representational elections at their former place of employment within one year of their replacement or until they find "regular and substantially similar employment" elsewhere, whichever comes first. Any permanently replaced economic striker is also entitled to be rehired when any job vacancies arise at the former place of employment.

Employees may also lawfully engage in a strike over employer unfair labor practices. An **unfair labor practice strike** is a nonviolent work stoppage in protest against an employer's committing an unfair labor practice. Employees engaged in such a strike are entitled to return to their jobs at the end of the strike. If the employer fires such strikers, they will be able to sue for reinstatement and back pay for the time during which they were unlawfully prohibited from working.

unfair labor practice strike A nonviolent work stoppage for the purpose of protesting an employer's commission of an unfair labor practice.

UNLAWFUL STRIKES   Strikes are unlawful when either their *means* or their *purpose* is unlawful. Strikes with unlawful means include: (1) *sit-down strikes*, wherein employees remain on the job but cease working; (2) *partial strikes*, wherein only some of the workers leave their jobs; and (3) *wildcat strikes*, which are strikes that are not authorized by the parent union and that are frequently in violation of the collective bargaining agreement. Strikes that include acts of violence or blockading of exits or entrances of a plant are also strikes with unlawful means.

Strikes with an unlawful purpose include *jurisdictional strikes*, which are work stoppages for the purpose of forcing an employer to resolve a dispute between two unions. Jurisdictional strikes are most common in the construction industry, where two unions often disagree over which trade (and thus which union's members) is entitled to do a particular type of work on a given project.

Also unlawful are a number of strikes that fall into the category of secondary strikes. A *secondary strike* occurs when the unionized workers of one employer go on strike to force their employer to bring pressure on another employer with whom the union has a dispute.

When employees engage in a strike with unlawful means or an unlawful purpose, they are not legally protected and therefore may be discharged by their employer.

BOYCOTTS

A **boycott** is a refusal to deal with, purchase goods from, or work for a business. Like a strike, it is a means used to prohibit a company from carrying on its business so that it will accede to union demands. *Primary boycotts* are legal; that is, a union may boycott an employer with whom the union is directly engaged in a labor dispute.

Secondary boycotts, like secondary strikes, are illegal. A secondary boycott occurs when unionized employees who have a labor dispute with their employer boycott another employer to force it to cease doing business with their employer.

One type of secondary boycott is legal under the NLRA in the construction and garment industries. That is the "hot cargo agreement," an agreement between the union and the employer that union members need not handle nonunion goods and that the employer will not deal with nonunion employers. This type of secondary boycott is considered an unfair labor practice under Section 8(b) in all other industries, however.

boycott A refusal to deal with, purchase goods from, or work for a business.

secondary boycott A boycott against one employer to force it to cease doing business with another employer with whom the union has a dispute.

PICKETING

Picketing is the stationing of individuals outside an employer's place of business for the purpose of informing passers-by of the facts of a labor dispute. Picketing usually accompanies a strike, but it may occur alone, especially when employees want to continue to work in order to draw a paycheck.

picketing The stationing of individuals outside an employer's place of business to inform passers-by of the fact of a labor dispute.

Just as there are numerous types of strikes and boycotts, there are multiple types of picketing with different degrees of protection. **Informational picketing**, picketing designed to truthfully inform the public of a labor dispute between an employer and employees, is protected. This protection may be lost, however, if the picketing has the effect of stopping deliveries and services to the employer. Picketing designed to secure a stoppage of service to the employer is called *signal picketing* and is not protected.

Jurisdictional picketing, like jurisdictional strikes, occurs when two unions are in dispute over which union's workers are entitled to do a particular job. If one union pickets because work was assigned to the other union's members, this action is unlawful; jurisdictional disputes are resolved by the NLRB under an expedited procedure, so there is no need to take coercive action against the employer. The other union or the employer may secure an injunction to preserve the status quo until the board resolves the dispute.

Organizational, or **recognitional, picketing**, which is designed to force the employer to recognize and bargain with an uncertified union, is illegal when: (1) another union has already been recognized as the exclusive representative of the employees, and the employer and employees are operating under a valid collective bargaining agreement negotiated by that union; (2) there has been a valid representation election within the past year; or (3) the union has been picketing for longer than 30 days without filing a petition for a representation election.

When (1) and (2) are not applicable, a union may picket for up to 30 days while attempting to secure signed authorization cards from over 30 percent of the employees. Once the appropriate signatures have been obtained, the union may then file its petition for recognition and continue picketing to inform the public of the company's refusal to recognize the union.

Picketing, like striking, may be illegal because of its means. *Violent picketing* is, of course, unlawful. So is *massed picketing*, though this type of unlawful activity is somewhat more difficult to define. It is said to exist when the pickets are so massed as to be coercive or to block entrances and exits. In cases interpreting this term, the courts have tended to find unlawful massed picketing when there have been so many picketers before a gateway to a plant that free entry or exit is made difficult or almost impossible.

INTERNATIONAL DIMENSIONS OF LABOR LAW

Many U.S. corporations have moved their operations overseas to obtain cheaper labor costs. Our laws permit this. But whereas a corporation's foreign operations are not subject to U.S. labor laws, most countries have labor laws of their own to which U.S. companies are subject. Likewise, foreign companies with plants in the United States must comply with our labor laws.

Many scholars argue that it would be desirable to have uniform labor laws across the world, or at least among all the industrialized nations. Their reasons differ. Some believe that there are certain inherent rights of workers that should be protected regardless of where they live and work. Others believe that uniformity would make it easier for multinationals that have a presence in many countries because then their labor practices could be uniform throughout all their operations.

The likelihood of a worldwide uniform labor law is almost nonexistent, if only because different countries' leaders have very different philosophies about the purpose of labor law. There are a few similarities, however, among most countries' labor laws. For example, in almost all countries a worker has the right to refuse to perform unsafe work.[8]

The International Labor Organization (ILO), to which 146 nations now send government, management, and labor delegates, has attempted to create some uniformity among the labor laws of member nations. The ILO formulates conventions and recommendations for labor legislation that can be adopted by

[8]M. Lennard, *The Right to Refuse Unsafe Work*, 4 Comp. Lab. L. J. 217 (1981).

all countries. These include minimum specifications and often provisions for national or traditional variations on those basics. Enforcement procedures are generally left to the individual nations.[9] The ILO has promulgated 156 conventions and 165 recommendations; there have been over 4,950 ratifications of these.[10] Although there are still more differences than similarities in labor laws from country to country, the ILO has generated some harmonizing of laws.

SUMMARY

The National Labor Relations Act is the primary legislation governing labor-management relations. Section 7 of the NLRA sets forth the rights of employees, and Section 8(a) identifies specific employer behaviors, called *unfair labor practices*, that are prohibited. Employee unfair labor practices are set out in Section 8(b). The Landrum-Griffith Act was passed to ensure proper internal governance of labor organizations.

The administrative agency responsible for oversight and enforcement of the NLRA is the National Labor Relations Board. The board is primarily responsible for ensuring that organizing campaigns are conducted fairly and that neither employers nor employees commit unfair labor practices.

Prospects for a worldwide uniform labor law are negligible, but the International Labor Organization is attempting to create some harmony among the labor laws of member nations.

REVIEW QUESTIONS

18-1. Explain why some people support unions whereas others oppose them.

18-2. Explain the relationship between Section 7 and Section 8 of the NLRA.

18-3. Explain why someone would argue that the existence of Section 8(a)1 really makes Sections 8(a)2–5 unnecessary.

18-4. Describe the roles of the National Labor Relations Board and its general counsel.

18-5. What is the difference between violating a board rule and committing an unfair labor practice?

18-6. What advice would you give to an employer who wants to adopt some form of employee participation program but is concerned about the legality of such programs?

REVIEW PROBLEMS

18-7. A national union wanted to organize the employees of Dexter Thread Mills. The company parking lot was adjacent to a public highway, separated from the highway by a ten-foot-wide grassy public easement. The union sought to distribute handbills in the parking lot; the company sought to exclude the union from the lot. Was the union allowed to distribute the handbills on the company lot?

18-8. Keystone, a producer of pretzels, employed about 40 people. Six months after the plant was sold, Local 6 obtained authorization cards from 17 employees out of a perceived potential bargaining unit of 29 employees. Keystone authorized one employee who had antiunion sentiments to conduct surveillance of union activities and report back to management. Keystone officials also interrogated two prounion employees and gave a raise to a union foe while denying one to a union adherent. They solicited and promised to resolve employee-grievances and to grant benefits. They conducted an employee meeting on a holiday: Employees who attended were paid and responded to an employee poll. Through its president, the company expressed satisfaction about the negative re-

---

[9]D. Ziskind, *Harmony and Counterpoint in Labor Law*, 4 Comp. Lab. L. J. 261, 267 (1981).
[10]*Id.*

sponse to unionization reflected by the poll. Could the union file a successful unfair-labor-practice charge?

18-9. Otis Elevator was acquired by United Technologies in 1975. A review of Otis's operations showed its technology to be outdated. The company's products were poorly engineered and were losing money. Its production and research facilities were scattered across the United States, with many duplications of work. Research, in particular, was done at two separate New Jersey facilities, one of which was extremely outdated. United Technologies (UT) did all of its research at a major research and development center in Connecticut; some research for Otis was also done there. UT decided to transfer Otis research from the two New Jersey locations to an expanded facility in Connecticut in order to strengthen the overall research effort and to allow Otis to redesign its product. The union representing Otis employees alleged that UT had engaged in an unfair labor practice by refusing to bargain with the union over its decision to relocate the work. Was UT's refusal to bargain over this decision a violation of Section 8(a)5?

18-10. The clerks at Raley's were represented by the Independent Drug Clerks Association (IDCA). When the Retail Clerks Union (Retail Clerks) began a campaign to oust IDCA, Raley's maintained a neutral posture. Retail Clerks picketed the store in July. Could Raley's obtain an injunction prohibiting the picketing?

18-11. The workers at the Big R Restaurant were trying unsuccessfully to negotiate a new contract. On Monday, all of the busboys called in sick. On Tuesday, all the cooks called in sick. On Wednesday, the waitresses all called in sick. Was there anything unlawful about the employees' behavior? If so, what recourse does the employer have?

18-12. Ajax manufacturing company was unionized in 1998 and had been operating under a contract negotiated at the beginning of that year. Several new workers were hired near the end of the year, and they thought a stronger union was needed. They began picketing the employer to get him to recognize a different union as the representative of the workers, or at minimum to have a decertification election. Is their picketing legal? Why or why not?

CASE PROBLEMS

18-13. Employees in the entertainment department of the Taj Mahal Casino were attempting to organize themselves into a union. The employees included state technicians, convention lounge technicians, and entertainment event technicians. The employer also maintained a list of 40 "on-call" employees who performed the same functions as the regular technicians on an intermittent basis, whenever more technicians were needed. Whenever the casino needed to hire new full-time employees, it hired the casuals with the greatest number of hours already worked at the casino. In 1990, casuals averaged 7 hours per week; in early 1991, 17 hours per week. The employees sought to have their bargaining unit include both full-time and casual employees. Apply the facts of this case to the criteria used in determining the appropriate bargaining unit and explain how the case should be decided. *Trump Taj Mahal Associates Ltd. v. Int'l Alliance of Theatrical Stage Employees*, 306 N.L.R.B. Cases No. 57 (1992)

18-14. Caremore licensed practical nurses (LPNs) spend most of their time providing direct patient care, but they also assign and direct nurses' aids. The LPNs call in off-duty aides to work and ask them to work overtime if necessary. They are also involved in the discipline and evaluation of aides. When the LPNs attempted to organize, their employer argued that they could not organize because they were supervisors. Why is the question of whether they are supervisors relevant? Do you think the court agreed with the employer? Why or why not? *Caremore v. NLRB*, No. 96-6116 (1997)

18-15. Local 2568 of the American Federation of State, County, and Municipal Employees began a campaign to organize Oakwood Hospital's 690 registered nurses. Gonzolez, a representative of the international union, was in charge of the internal organizing committee. The committee conducted mass mailings to the nurses and held organizational meetings at a local banquet hall. Gonzolez went to the hospital cafeteria every two weeks to try to get employees to support the union. He wore a button that said "Vote AFSCME," and ordered food and sat at a table talking to employees. The hospital did not interfere with him, despite the fact that a written policy adopted earlier prohibited nonemployees from soliciting employees on hospital premises without written permission.

In January 1988, the hospital issued booklets to visitors saying the cafeteria was closed to visitors from 11 A.M. to 1:00 P.M. and from 7:15 P.M. to 8:15 P.M., times when the cafeteria, which had been reduced in 1987 to a capacity of 110, was the most crowded.

On September 27, around midnight, Gonzolez was in the cafeteria and two supervisors asked him what he was doing. When he said organizing, he was asked to leave. He refused. When the head of hospital security asked him to leave, he again refused and stayed in the cafeteria until 4:30 A.M.

An unfair labor practice charge was filed against Gonzolez, along with a trespassing charge. Provide what you believe would be the rationale for a finding that Gonzolez did or did not commit an unfair labor practice. *Oakwood Hospital v. NLRB*, 983 F.2d 698 (1993)

18-16. Bernard Lamoureux, considered one of the firm's strongest union advocates, was fired by his employer for knowingly altering time reports and payroll records. Lamoureux admitted that he had not worked the precise hours stated on his time card, but he claimed that he had made up the time during other hours. He alleged that other workers had engaged in the same behavior as he had, but none had ever been terminated and that the firm was only firing him because of his union advocacy. Was his discharge lawful? *Wright Line, a Division of Wright Line, Inc.*, 251 N.L.R.B. No. 150 (1989)

18-17. Davis Supermarkets, a corporation, owned supermarkets in Greensburg and Hempfield township. The Greensburg store was represented by the United Steelworkers of America. The Hempfield Township store was not organized. In March, an organizing campaign began there. By mid-April, 13 workers had signed authorization cards. On that day, eight workers were summarily laid off, six of whom had signed cards. Two weeks later, two other workers who had signed cards were laid off, and a third worker met the same fate the following week. The employer could offer no legitimate reasons for laying off the workers. Explain why the court would or would not uphold their discharge. *Davis Supermarkets v. NLRB*, 2 F.3d 1162 (D.C. Cir. 1993)

18-18. Electromation, Inc., a manufacturer of electrical components, reduced wages, bonuses, and benefits for employees, while tightening attendance and leave policies. In response to employees' complaints, Electromation set up five "action committees," each made up of six employees and two management representatives. The purpose of the committees was to make suggestions to management about such policies as the treatment of absentee employees and employee remuneration. The Teamsters Union, which had been trying to organize Electromation's workers, filed an unfair labor practice charge against the company, arguing that the committees were comparable to a union dominated by management. The NLRB agreed. On appeal, did the Seventh Circuit Court of Appeals uphold the decision of the NLRB? Why or why not? *Electromation v. NLRB*, 35 F.3d 1148 (1994)

On the Internet

http://www.doc.gov/nlrb/homepg.html   This site is the home page of the
National Labor Relations Board.

http://www.aflcio.org/   Find out about the AFL-CIO at this site.

http://www.iisg.nl/~w3vl/   This site, Labor History and Business, is a virtual
library site that would be a good place to begin research on any labor topic.

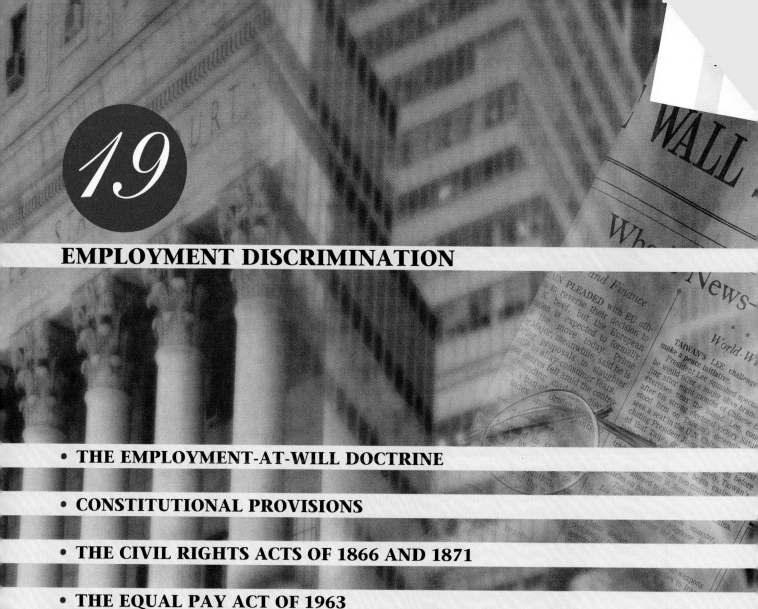

19

EMPLOYMENT DISCRIMINATION

- **THE EMPLOYMENT-AT-WILL DOCTRINE**

- **CONSTITUTIONAL PROVISIONS**

- **THE CIVIL RIGHTS ACTS OF 1866 AND 1871**

- **THE EQUAL PAY ACT OF 1963**

- **THE CIVIL RIGHTS ACT OF 1964, AS AMENDED (TITLE VII), AND THE CIVIL RIGHTS ACT OF 1991**

- **THE AGE DISCRIMINATION IN EMPLOYMENT ACT OF 1967**

- **THE REHABILITATION ACT OF 1973**

- **THE AMERICANS WITH DISABILITIES ACT OF 1991**

- **AFFIRMATIVE ACTION**

- **INTERNATIONAL DIMENSIONS OF EMPLOYMENT DISCRIMINATION LEGISLATION**

Being an employer was so much easier one hundred years ago. Managers could use almost any criteria for hiring, promoting, and firing employees. Today, employers' decision-making powers are restricted by both federal and state legislation. This chapter focuses on the laws that limit employers' abilities to use any criteria they wish in hiring, firing, and promoting employees.

Critical Thinking about the Law

YOU WILL SOON BE A BUSINESSPERSON, and you may be responsible for hiring, promoting, and firing people. When you do hold this position, you will need to be aware of federal and state laws that prohibit discrimination in employment. Why do you think the government has prohibited discrimination in employment? What ethical norm does the government emphasize by prohibiting discrimination in employment? The government seems to emphasize justice, in the sense that they want all human beings to be treated identically, regardless of class, race, gender, age, and so on. Reading the following case and answering the critical thinking questions will sharpen your thinking about laws prohibiting employment discrimination.

Tom, Jonathan, and Bob were hired to work as executive secretaries at a major corporation. The other secretaries for the corporation were surprised that three men were hired as secretaries when no man had ever been hired as a secretary at this corporation. All secretaries were required to type 20 five-page reports each day in addition to completing work for their respective departments. After the male secretaries had been working at the corporation for approximately one month, they received pay raises. None of the female secretaries received raises. When the women asked the manager why the male secretaries had received raises, the manager claimed that the men were performing extra duties and consequently received raises.

1. The manager claimed that the men received raises because they were performing extra duties. Can you identify any potential problems in the manager's response?

   CLUE What words or phrases are ambiguous in the manager's response?

2. The female secretaries have decided to bring a suit against the corporation. They claim that they did not receive raises because of their gender. Pretend that you are a lawyer, and the female secretaries have come to you with their complaint. After talking with the secretaries, you realize that you need to find out some additional information. What additional information might be helpful in this case?

   CLUE The female secretaries claim that the male secretaries received raises because they are male. Can you think of any alternative reasons why the men might have received raises?

3. You discover only one case regarding equal pay that was decided in your district. In this case, both men and women performed hard labor in a factory, but only men received offers to work during the third shift. Those workers who worked third shift received an additional $30 per hour. The women in this factory claimed that they were not asked to work the third shift because of their gender. The factory argued that the women who worked at the factory were not physically strong enough to endure the work of the third shift. The court ruled in favor of the women. Do you think that you should use this case as an analogy? Why or why not?

   CLUE How are the two cases similar? How are they different?

The right of the employer to terminate an employment relationship was originally governed almost exclusively by the employment-at-will doctrine, which is discussed in the first section of this chapter. The second section discusses the constitutional provisions that affect an employer's ability to hire and fire workers. The following six sections discuss each of the major pieces of federal legislation designed to prohibit discrimination in employment relations. These acts are discussed in the order in which they were enacted. The ninth section discusses the increasingly controversial subject of affirmative action. International dimensions of employment discrimination are discussed in the final section.

THE EMPLOYMENT-AT-WILL DOCTRINE

In all industrial democracies except the United States, workers are protected by law from unjust termination. The traditional "American rule" of employment has been that a contract of employment for an indeterminate term is terminable at will by either party. Thus, an employee who did not have a contract for a specific length of time could be terminated at any time, for any reason.

This **employment-at-will doctrine** has been justified by the right of the employer to control his or her property. It has also been justified on the grounds that it is fair because *both* employer and employee have the equal right to terminate the relationship. Some may question the latter justification because the employer can almost always replace a terminated employee, whereas it is not equally easy for the employee to find new employment. Thus, the employment-at-will doctrine places the employer in a position to treat employees arbitrarily.

Partially because of the abuse that can occur under this doctrine, it has been slowly restricted by state and federal legislation, as well as by changes in the common law. One of the first pieces of legislation to restrict the employer's right to freely terminate employees was the National Labor Relations Act (discussed in the previous chapter), which has reduced the number of employees covered by the employment-at-will doctrine. This reduction has occurred because the act gives employees the right to enter into collective bargaining agreements, which usually restrict the employer's ability to terminate employees except for "just cause." The employees covered by these agreements are thus no longer "at-will" employees.

The effect of the doctrine has also been restricted by a growing number of common law and state statutory exceptions. Such exceptions usually fall into three categories: implied contract, violations of public policy, and implied covenant of good faith and fair dealing. In some states, the courts find that an *implied contract* may arise from statements made by the employer in advertising the position or in an employment manual. For example, sometimes a company provides an employment manual delineating the grounds for termination but not containing any provision for termination "at-will." Under such circumstances, if the court finds that the employee reasonably relied on the manual, the court will not apply the employment-at-will doctrine and will allow termination only for reasons stated in the manual. Or, if certain procedures, such as notice and a hearing, are stated as being used to terminate an employee, such procedures must be followed or the termination is unlawful. Thirty-two states and the District of Columbia recognize this exception.

The **public policy exception** prohibits terminations that contravene established public policy. "Public policy" varies from state to state, but some of the more common terminations deemed unlawful include dismissals based on actions "in the public interest," such as participation in environmental or consumer protection activities and dismissals resulting from "whistleblowing." Many states have also cut away at the employment-at-will doctrine with laws that specifically prohibit the termination of employees in retaliation for such diverse activities as serving jury duty, doing military service, filing for or testifying at hearings for workers' compensation claims, whistleblowing, and refusing to take lie detector tests. A total of thirty-three states accept the public policy exception.

employment-at-will doctrine A contract of employment for an indeterminate term is terminable at will by either the employer or the employee; the traditional "American rule" governing employer-employee relations.

public policy exception An exception to the employment-at-will doctrine that makes it unlawful to dismiss an employee for taking certain actions in the public interest.

TABLE 19-1 *Exceptions to Employment-at-Will Doctrine*

PUBLIC POLICY EXCEPTION	IMPLIED CONTRACT EXCEPTION	GOOD FAITH AND FAIR DEALING EXCEPTION
Alaska, Arizona, California, Colorado, Connecticut, Florida, Georgia, Hawaii, Illinois, Indiana, Kansas, Kentucky, Louisiana, Maryland, Michigan, Minnesota, Missouri, Nevada, New Hampshire, New Jersey, New Mexico, New York, North Carolina, Ohio, Oklahoma, Oregon, South Carolina, Tennessee, Texas, Virginia, Washington, West Virginia, Wisconsin	Alabama, Arizona, California, Colorado, Connecticut, Georgia, Idaho, Illinois, Indiana, Kansas, Kentucky, Maine, Maryland, Michigan, Minnesota, Missouri, Nebraska, Nevada, New Jersey, New Mexico, New York, North Carolina, Ohio, Oregon, South Dakota, Tennessee, Texas, Vermont, Washington, West Virginia, Wisconsin, Wyoming, the District of Columbia	Alaska, Arizona, California, Connecticut, Massachusetts, Minnesota, Montana

Source: D.S. Hames, "The Current Status of the Doctrine of Employment-at-Will," *Labor Law Journal* 39 (January 19, 1988).

implied covenant of good faith and fair dealing An exception to the employment-at-will doctrine that is based on the theory that every employment contract, even an unwritten one, contains the implicit understanding that the parties will deal fairly with each other.

Seven states recognize the **implied covenant of good faith and fair dealing** exception. This theory holds that every employment contract, even an unwritten one, contains an implicit understanding that the parties will deal fairly with one another. Because there is no clear agreement on what constitutes "fair treatment" of an employee, this theory is not often used.

Many federal laws also restrict the employment-at-will doctrine. Employees cannot be fired for filing a complaint, testifying, or causing a hearing to be instituted regarding the payment of the minimum wage, equal pay, or overtime. Pursuit of a discrimination claim is likewise statutorily protected.

The doctrine of employment-at-will, however, still exists and is strongly adhered to in many states. So, although the doctrine is being cut back and therefore business managers of the future cannot rely on the continued availability of this doctrine, it may be a long time before the doctrine is no longer applicable. However, as its applicability varies from state to state, familiarity with the doctrine's parameters in one's own state is extremely important. Table 19-1 lists a breakdown of which states accept each of the three major exceptions.

CONSTITUTIONAL PROVISIONS

The beginnings of antidiscrimination law can be traced back to three of the constitutional provisions: the *Fifth Amendment*, which states that no person may be deprived of life, liberty, or property without due process of law; the *Thirteenth Amendment*, which abolished slavery; and the *Fourteenth Amendment*, which granted former slaves all of the rights and privileges of citizenship and guaranteed the equal protection of the law to all persons. These provisions alone, however, were not sufficient to prohibit the unequal treatment of citizens on the basis of their race, sex, age, religion, and national origin. Congress needed to enact major legislation to bring about a reduction of discrimination. These laws are referred to as *civil rights laws* and *antidiscrimination laws*. They are summarized in Table 19-2 and are discussed in detail in the following sections.

Civil Rights Act of 1866 Guarantees that all persons in the United States have the same right to make and enforce contracts and have the full and equal benefit of the law.

THE CIVIL RIGHTS ACTS OF 1866 AND 1871

The first major civil rights act was passed immediately after the Civil War: the **Civil Rights Act of 1866** (42 U.S.C.A. Section 1981). This act was designed to effectuate the Thirteenth Amendment and guarantees that all

LAW	PROHIBITED CONDUCT	REMEDIES
Civil Rights Acts of 1866 and 1871, codified as 42 U.S.C. Sections 1981 and 1982	Discrimination based on *race* and *ethnicity*.	Compensatory damages, including several years of back pay, punitive damages, attorneys' fees, court costs, and court orders.
Equal Pay Act of 1963	Wage discrimination based on *sex*.	Back pay, liquidated damages equivalent to back pay (if defendant was not acting in good faith), attorneys' fees, and court costs.
Civil Rights Act of 1964 (Title VII), 1991	Discrimination in terms and conditions of employment based on *race, color, religion, sex,* or *national origin*.	Back pay for up to two years, remedial seniority, compensatory damages, punitive damages (may be limited due to class), attorneys' fees, court costs, and court orders for whatever actions are appropriate including reinstatement and affirmative action.
Age Discrimination in Employment Act of 1969	Discrimination in terms and conditions of employment on the basis of *age* when the affected individual is age 40 or older.	Back pay, liquidated damages equal to back pay (if defendant acted willfully), attorneys' fees, court costs, and appropriate court orders including reinstatement.
Rehabilitation Act of 1973	Discrimination by government or governmental contractor based on a *handicap*.	Back pay, attorneys' fees, court costs, and court orders for appropriate affirmative action.
Americans with Disabilities Act of 1991	Discrimination in employment based on a *disability*.	Hiring, promotion, reinstatement, back pay, reasonable accommodation, compensatory damages, and punitive damages.

persons in the United States have the same right to make and enforce contracts and have full and equal benefit of the law. The **Civil Rights Act of 1871** (42 U.S.C.A. Section 1982) prohibited discrimination by state and local governments. Initially used only when there was state action, today these acts are also used against purely private discrimination, especially in employment.

Civil Rights Act of 1871
Prohibits discrimination by state and local governments.

APPLICABILITY OF THE ACTS

Initially, these acts were interpreted very narrowly to prohibit discrimination based only on race. For several years, circuit courts of appeals were split as to how race is defined. In June of 1986, the U.S. Supreme Court resolved that issue by holding that both an Arabic and a Jewish individual were protected by the Civil Rights Act of 1866. Justice White, writing the majority opinion in *Saint Francis College et al. v. Majid Ghaidan Al-Khazraji*,[1] said that it was clear from the legislative history that the act was intended to protect from discrimination "identifiable classes of persons who are subjected to intentional discrimination solely because of their ancestry or ethnic characteristics," even if those individuals would be considered part of the Caucasian race today. Thus, today these laws have a broader application.

---

[1]483 U.S. 1011 (1987). The accompanying case filed by a Jewish plaintiff was *Shaare Tefila Congregation et al.* v. *John William Cobb et al.*, 481 U.S. 615 (1987).

REMEDIES

The acts themselves do not have specific provisions for remedies. A wide variety of both legal remedies (money damages) and equitable remedies (court orders) have been awarded under these statutes. The courts are free under these acts to award compensatory damages, damages designed to make the plaintiff "whole" again, which may amount to several years of back pay. The courts may also award punitive damages, an amount intended to penalize the defendant for wrongful conduct. Finally, the courts may require the defendant to pay the plaintiff's attorney's fees.

PROCEDURAL LIMITATIONS

Unlike most antidiscrimination laws, the Civil Rights Acts of 1866 and 1871 do not require the plaintiff to first attempt to resolve the discrimination problem through any administrative procedures. The plaintiff simply files the action in federal district court within the time limit prescribed by the state statute of limitations, requesting a jury trial if one is desired. Often, a claim under the 1866 or 1871 Civil Rights Act will be added to a claim under another antidiscrimination statute.

THE EQUAL PAY ACT OF 1963

Equal Pay Act of 1963
Prohibits wage discrimination based on sex.

The next major piece of federal legislation to address the problem of discrimination was the **Equal Pay Act of 1963**, an amendment to the Fair Labor Standards Act. Enacted at a time when the average wages of women were less than 60 percent of those of men, the act was designed with a very narrow focus: to prevent *wage discrimination* based on *sex* within a business establishment. It was primarily designed to remedy the situations in which women, working alongside men or replacing men, were being paid lower wages for doing substantially the same job.

The act, as stated in 29 U.S.C.A. Section 206(d)1, prohibits any employer from discriminating within any "establishment"

> *between employees on the basis of sex by paying wages to employees in such establishment at a rate less than the rate at which he pays wages to employees of the opposite sex . . . for equal work on jobs the performance of which requires equal skill, effort, and responsibility, and which are performed under similar working conditions, except where payment is made pursuant to (i) a seniority system; (ii) a merit system; (iii) a system which measures earnings by quantity or quality of production; or (iv) differential based on any factor other than sex.*

In the typical Equal Pay Act case, the burden of proof is initially on the plaintiff to show that the defendant-employer pays unequal wages to men and women for doing equal work at the same establishment. Two questions result: What is equal work, and What is an establishment?

EQUAL WORK

The courts have interpreted *equal* to mean substantially the same in terms of all four factors listed in the act: *skill, effort, responsibility*, and *working conditions*. If the employer varies the actual job duties affecting *any* one of those factors, there is no violation on the act. For example, if jobs are equal in skill and working conditions, but one requires greater effort, whereas the other requires greater responsibility, the jobs are not equal. Obviously, a sophisticated employer could easily vary at least one duty and then pay men and women different wages or salaries.

Skill is defined as experience, education, training, and ability *required* to do the job. *Effort* refers to physical or mental exertion needed for performance of the job. *Responsibility* is measured by the economic and social consequences that would result from a failure of the employee to perform the job duties in question. *Similar working conditions* refers to the safety hazards, physical surroundings, and hours of employment. However, an employer is entitled to pay a shift premium to employees working different shifts, as long as he or she does not use sex as a basis for determining who is entitled to work the higher-paying shifts.

Extra Duties Sometimes employers try to justify pay inequities on the grounds that employees of one sex are given extra duties that justify their extra pay. The courts scrutinize these duties very closely. The duties are sufficient to preclude a finding of equal work only if:

1. The duties are *actually performed* by those receiving the extra pay.
2. The duties *regularly* constitute a *significant* portion of the employee's job.
3. The duties are *substantial*, as opposed to inconsequential.
4. Additional duties of a comparable nature are not imposed on workers of the opposite sex.
5. The extra duties are commensurate with the pay differential.
6. In some jurisdictions, the additional duties must be available on a nondiscriminatory basis.

ESTABLISHMENTS One business location is obviously an establishment, but if an employer has several locations, they may all be considered part of the same establishment on the basis of an analysis of the company's labor relations policy. The greater the degree of centralized authority for hiring, firing, wage setting, and other human resource matters, the more likely the courts are to find multiple locations to be a single establishment. The more freedom each facility has to determine its own human resource policies, the more likely a court will find it to be independent of other facilities.

Defenses

Once an employee establishes that an employer is paying different wages to employees of different sexes doing substantially equal work, there are certain defenses that the employer can raise. These are, in essence, legal justifications for paying unequal wages to men and women.

The first defense that an employer may use is that the pay differential is based on one of the four statutory exceptions found in the Bennet Amendment to the Equal Pay Act. If the wage differential is based on one of these four factors, the differential is justified and the employer is not in violation of the act. The four factors are:

1. A bona fide seniority system.
2. A bona fide merit system.
3. A pay system based on quality or quantity of output.
4. Factors other than sex.

The first three are fairly straightforward. Seniority, merit, and productivity-based wage systems must be enacted in good faith and must be applied to both men and women. As minimal evidence of good faith, any such system should be written down.

The fourth factor presents greater problems. Such factors as greater availability of females and their willingness to work for lower wages do *not* constitute factors other than sex. One factor that is frequently litigated is *training programs*. A training program that requires trainees to rotate through jobs that are normally paid lower wages will be upheld as long as it is a bona fide training program and not a sham for paying members of one sex higher wages for doing the same job. The court will look at each case individually, but factors that would lead to a training program's being found bona fide include: a written description of the training program that is available to employees; nondiscriminatory access to the program for members of both sexes; and demonstrated awareness of the availability of the program by employees of both sexes.

REMEDIES

An employer found to have violated the act cannot remedy the violation by reducing the higher-paid workers' wages or by transferring those of one sex to another job so that they are no longer doing equal work.

A person who has been subject to an Equal Pay Act violation may bring a private action under Section 16(b) of the act and recover back pay in the amount of the differential paid to members of the opposite sex. If the employer had not been acting in good faith in paying the discriminatory wage rates, the court will also award the plaintiff damages in an additional amount equal to the back pay. A successful plaintiff is also entitled to attorney's fees.

THE CIVIL RIGHTS ACT OF 1964, AS AMENDED (TITLE VII), AND THE CIVIL RIGHTS ACT OF 1991

Title VII The statute that prohibits discrimination in hiring, firing, or other terms and conditions of employment on the basis of race, color, religion, sex, or national origin.

The year after it passed the Equal Pay Act, Congress passed the Civil Rights Act of 1964. **Title VII** of this act is the most common basis for lawsuits premised on discrimination because it covers a broader area of potential claimants than do either of the previously discussed statutes. Title VII prohibits employers from (1) hiring, firing, or otherwise discriminating in terms and conditions of employment and (2) segregating employees in a manner that would affect their employment opportunities on the basis of their race, color, religion, sex, or national origin. These five categories are known as *protected classes.*

APPLICABILITY OF THE ACT

Employers covered by the act include only those who have 15 or more employees, this year or last, for 20 consecutive weeks, and are engaged in a business that affects interstate commerce. In 1994, the term *employer* was broadened to include the U.S. government, corporations owned by the government, and agencies of the District of Columbia. The act also covers Indian tribes, private clubs, unions, and employment agencies.

In addition to prohibiting discrimination by covered employers, unions, and employment agencies, the act also imposes recordkeeping and reporting requirements on these parties. Covered parties must maintain all records regarding employment opportunities for at least six months. Such records include job applications, notices for job openings, and records of layoffs. If an employment discrimination charge is filed against the employer, such records must be kept until the case is concluded. Annual reports (known as *EEO-1 forms*) that contain information concerning the number of minorities in various job classifications must be filed annually with the Equal Employment Opportunity Commission (EEOC) by employers of more than 100 workers. A copy of this form is provided in Exhibit 19-1. Finally, each covered employer must display a summary of the relevant portions of Title VII where the employees can see it. The notice must be printed in a language that the employees can read.

PROOF IN EMPLOYMENT DISCRIMINATION CASES

The burden of proof in a discrimination case is initially on the plaintiff. The plaintiff attempts to establish discrimination in one of three ways: (1) disparate treatment, (2) disparate impact, or (3) harassment.

disparate treatment cases Discrimination cases in which the employer treats one employee less favorably than another because of that employee's color, race, religion, sex, or national origin.

DISPARATE TREATMENT   **Disparate treatment** occurs when one individual is treated less favorably than another because of color, race, religion, sex, or national origin. The key in such cases is proving the employer's unlawful discriminatory motive. This process is referred to as *building a prima facie case.*

The plaintiff must establish the following set of facts: (1) The plaintiff is within one of the protected classes; (2) he or she applied for a job for which the employer was seeking applicants for hire or promotion; (3) the plaintiff possessed the minimum qualifications to perform that job; (4) the plaintiff was denied the job or promotion; and (5) the employer continued to look for someone to fill the position.

EXHIBIT 19-1 *EEO-1 Form*

EQUAL EMPLOYMENT OPPORTUNITY

EMPLOYER INFORMATION REPORT EEO—I
1994

Joint Reporting Committee
- Equal Employment Opportunity Commission
- Office of Federal Contract Compliance Programs (Labor)

I OF I

RETURN COMPLETED REPORT TO:
THE JOINT REPORTING COMMITTEE
P.O. BOX 779
NORFOLK, VA 23501

PHONE: (804) 461-1213

Section A—TYPE OF REPORT
Refer to instructions for number and types of reports to be filed.

1. Indicate by marking in the appropriate box the type of reporting unit for which this copy of the form is submitted (MARK ONLY ONE BOX).

(1) ☐ Single-establishment Employer Report

Multi-establishment Employer:
(2) ☐ Consolidated Report (Required)
(3) ☐ Headquarters Unit Report (Required)
(4) ☐ Individual Establishment Report (Submit one for each establishment with 50 or more employees)
(5) ☐ Special Report

2. Total number of reports being filed by this Company (Answers on Consolidated Report only) _____

Section B—COMPANY IDENTIFICATION (*To be answered by all employers*)

OFFICE USE ONLY

1. Parent Company

a. Name of parent company (owns or controls establishment in item 2) omit if same as label

a.

Address (Number and street)

b.

City or town	State	ZIP code

c.

2. Establishment for which this report is filed. (Omit if same as label)

a. Name of establishment

d.

Address (Number and street)	City or town	County	State	ZIP code

e.

b. Employer identification No. (IRS 9-DIGIT TAX NUMBER)

f.

c. Was an EEO-1 report filed for this establishment last year? Yes ☐ No ☐

Section C—EMPLOYERS WHO ARE REQUIRED TO FILE (*To be answered by all employers*)

☐ Yes ☐ No 1. Does the entire company have at least 100 employees in the payroll period for which you are reporting?

☐ Yes ☐ No 2. Is your company affiliated through common ownership and/or centralized management with other entities in an enterprise with a total employment of 100 or more?

☐ Yes ☐ No 3. Does the company or any of its establishments (a) have 50 or more employees AND (b) is not exempt as provided by 41 CFR 60-1.5. AND either (1) is a prime government contractor or first-tier subcontractor, and has a contract, subcontract, or purchase order amounting to $50,000 or more, or (2) serves as a depository of Government funds in any amount or is a financial institution which is an issuing and paying agent for U.S. Savings Bonds and Savings Notes?

If the response to question C-3 is yes, please enter your Dun and Bradstreet identification number (if you have one):

☐☐☐☐☐☐☐☐☐

NOTE: If the answer is yes to questions 1,2,or 3, complete the entire form, otherwise skip to Section G.

NSN 7540-00-180-6384

(continued)

Once the plaintiff has established those facts, the burden shifts to the defendant to articulate legitimate and nondiscriminatory business reasons for rejecting the plaintiff. Such reasons for a failure to promote, for instance, might include a poor work record or excessive absenteeism. If the employer meets this burden, the plaintiff must then demonstrate that the reasons the defendant offered were just a *pretext* for a real discriminatory motive. In other words, the alleged reason

EXHIBIT 19-1 *continued*

100 Page 2

Section D EMPLOYMENT DATA

Employment at this establishment Report all permanent full-time and part-time employees including apprentices and on-the-job trainees unless specifically excluded as set forth in the instructions. Enter the appropriate figures on all lines and in all columns. Blank spaces will be considered as zeros.

JOB CATEGORIES		NUMBER OF EMPLOYEES										
		OVERALL TOTALS (SUM OF COL. B THRU K)	MALE					FEMALE				
			WHITE (NOT OF HISPANIC ORIGIN)	BLACK (NOT OF HISPANIC ORIGIN)	HISPANIC	ASIAN OR PACIFIC ISLANDER	AMERICAN INDIAN OR ALASKAN NATIVE	WHITE (NOT OF HISPANIC ORIGIN)	BLACK (NOT OF HISPANIC ORIGIN)	HISPANIC	ASIAN OR PACIFIC ISLANDER	AMERICAN INDIAN OR ALASKAN NATIVE
		A	B	C	D	E	F	G	H	I	J	K
Officials and Managers	1											
Professionals	2											
Technicians	3											
Sales Workers	4											
Office and Clerical	5											
Craft Workers (Skilled)	6											
Operatives (Semi-Skilled)	7											
Laborers (Unskilled)	8											
Service Workers	9											
TOTAL	10											
Total employment reported in previous EEO 1 report	11											

NOTE: Omit questions 1 and 2 on the Consolidated Report.

1. Date(s) of payroll period used: 2. Does this establishment employ apprentices:
  1 ☐ Yes   2 ☐ No

Section E ESTABLISHMENT INFORMATION *(Omit on the Consolidated Report)*

1. What is the major activity of this establishment? (Be specific, i.e., manufacturing steel castings, retail grocer, wholesale plumbing supplies, title insurance, etc.) Include the specific type of product or type of service provided, as well as the principal business or industrial activity.

OFFICE USE ONLY

Section F REMARKS

Use this item to give any identification data appearing on last report which differs from that given above, explain major changes in composition or reporting units and other pertinent information.

Section G CERTIFICATION *(See instructions G)*

Check One   1 ☐ All reports are accurate and were prepared in accordance with the instructions (check on consolidated only).
   2 ☐ This report is accurate and was prepared in accordance with the instructions.

Name of Certifying Official	Title	Signature	Date
Name of person to contact regarding this report (Type or print)	Address (Number and Street)		
Title	City and State	ZIP Code	Telephone Number (Including Area Code.) / Extension

All reports and information obtained from individual reports will be kept confidential as required by Section 709(e) of Title VII.
WILLFULLY FALSE STATEMENTS ON THIS REPORT ARE PUNISHABLE BY LAW, U.S. CODE, TITLE 18, SECTION 1001.

was not the real reason; it was just put forth because it sounded good. One way in which the plaintiff can demonstrate pretext is by showing that the criteria used to reject the plaintiff were not applied to others in the same position. Introduction of past discriminatory policies would also be relevant, as would statistics indicating a general practice of discrimination by the defendant. At the pretext stage, the issue of proving an employer's intent to discriminate first appears and is usually the key to the plaintiff's winning or losing the case. Exhibit 19-2 shows how the burden of proof shifts in a disparate treatment case.

EXHIBIT 19-2 *The Shifting Burden of Proof in a Disparate Treatment Case*

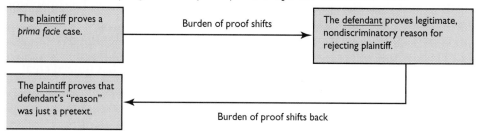

DISPARATE IMPACT   As complex as disparate treatment cases are, disparate impact cases are even more difficult to establish. **Disparate impact** cases arise when a plaintiff attempts to establish that an employer's facially neutral employment policy or practice has a discriminatory impact on a protected class. In other words, a requirement of the policy or practice applies to everyone equally, but, in application, it disproportionately limits employment opportunities for a particular protected class.

To establish a case of discrimination based on disparate impact, the plaintiff must first establish statistically that the rule disproportionately restricts employment opportunities for a protected class. Then, the burden of proof shifts to the defendant to demonstrate that the practice or policy is a business necessity. The plaintiff, at this point, can still recover by proving that the "necessity" was promulgated as a pretext for discrimination.

The first two steps for proving a *prima facie* case of disparate impact were laid out in *Griggs v. Duke Power Co.*[2] In that case, the employer-defendant required all applicants to have a high school diploma and a successful score on a professionally recognized intelligence test for all jobs except laborers. By establishing these criteria, he proposed to upgrade the quality of his workforce.

The plaintiff demonstrated the discriminatory impact by showing that 34 percent of the white males in the state had high school diplomas, whereas only 12 percent of the black males did, and by introducing evidence from an EEOC study showing that 58 percent of the whites, compared with 6 percent of the blacks, had passed tests similar to the one given by the defendant. The defendant could show no business-related justification for either employment policy, so the plaintiff was successful. Not all employees of Duke Power needed to be smart or possess high school diplomas. After all, when does a student in high school learn how to install power lines or repair company vehicles? Requiring a high IQ or high school or college diploma may be necessary for some jobs, but not for all jobs at Duke Power.

HARASSMENT   The third way to prove discrimination is to demonstrate harassment. Harassment is a relatively new basis for a discrimination claim; it first developed in the context of discrimination based on sex and then evolved to become applicable to other protected classes.

The definition of **sexual harassment** stated in the EEOC guidelines and accepted by the U.S. Supreme Court is "unwelcome sexual advances, requests for sexual favors, and other verbal or physical conduct of a sexual nature" that implicitly or explicitly makes submission a term or condition of employment; makes employment decisions related to the individual dependent on submission to or rejection of such conduct; or has the purpose or effect of creating an intimidating, hostile, or offensive environment.

The courts have recognized two distinct forms of sexual harassment. The first is often referred to as *quid pro quo*. This type of unlawful behavior occurs when a supervisor makes sexual demands on someone of the opposite sex and

disparate impact cases
Discrimination cases in which the employer's facially neutral policy or practice has a discriminatory effect on employees that belong to a protected class.

sexual harassment
Unwelcome sexual advances, requests for sexual favors, and other verbal or physical conduct of a sexual nature that explicitly or implicitly makes submission a term or condition of employment or that creates an intimidating, hostile, or offensive environment.

---

[2]401 U.S. 424 (1971).

this demand is reasonably perceived as a term or condition of employment. The basis for this rule is that similar demands would not be made by the supervisor on someone of the same sex.

The second form of sexual harassment involves the creation of a *hostile environment*. The following case demonstrates the standards used by the U.S. Supreme Court to determine whether an employer's conduct has indeed created a hostile environment.

TERESA HARRIS V. FORKLIFT SYSTEMS, INCORPORATED
UNITED STATES SUPREME COURT 510 U.S. 17 (1994)

Plaintiff Harris was a manager for defendant Forklift Systems, Inc. During her tenure at Forklift Systems, plaintiff Harris was repeatedly insulted by defendant's president because of her gender and was subjected to sexual innuendos. Numerous times, in front of other employees, the president told Harris, "You're just a woman, what do you know?" He sometimes asked Harris and other female employees to remove coins from his pockets and made suggestive comments about their clothes. He suggested to Harris in front of others that they negotiate her salary at the Holiday Inn. When Harris complained, he said he would stop. When he continued, plaintiff quit and filed an action against the defendant for creating an abusive work environment based on her gender.

The district court found in favor of the defendant, holding that some of the comments were offensive to the reasonable woman, but were not so serious as to severely affect Harris's psychological well-being or to interfere with her work performance. The court of appeals affirmed. Plaintiff Harris appealed to the U.S. Supreme Court.

JUSTICE O'CONNOR

In this case we consider the definition of a discriminatorily "abusive work environment" (also known as a "hostile work environment") under Title VII.

Title VII of the Civil Rights Act of 1964 makes it "an unlawful employment practice for an employer . . . to discriminate against any individual with respect to his compensation, terms, conditions, or privileges of employment, because of such individual's race, color, religion, sex, or national origin." As we made clear in *Meritor Savings Bank v. Vinson*, this language "is not limited to 'economic' or 'tangible' discrimination. The phrase 'terms, conditions, or privileges of employment' evinces a congressional intent 'to strike at the entire spectrum of disparate treatment of men and women' in employment," which includes requiring people to work in a discriminatorily hostile or abusive environment. When the workplace is permeated with "discriminatory intimidation, ridicule, and insult," that is "sufficiently severe or pervasive to alter the conditions of the victim's employment and create an abusive working environment."

This standard, which we reaffirm today, takes a middle path between making actionable any conduct that is merely offensive and requiring the conduct to cause a tangible psychological injury. As we pointed out in *Meritor*, "mere utterance of an . . . epithet which engenders offensive feelings in a employee," does not sufficiently affect conditions of employment to implicate Title VII. Conduct that is not severe or pervasive enough to create an objectively hostile or abusive work environment—an environment that a reasonable person would find hostile or abusive—is beyond Title VII's purview. Likewise, if the victim does not subjectively perceive the environment to be abusive, the conduct has not actually altered the conditions of the victim's employment, and there is no Title VII violation.

But Title VII comes into play before the harassing conduct leads to a nervous breakdown. A discriminatorily abusive work environment, even one that does not seriously affect employees' psychological well-being, can and often will detract from employees' job performance, discourage employees from remaining on the job, or keep them from advancing in their careers. Moreover, even without regard to these tangible effects, the very fact that the discriminatory conduct was so severe or pervasive that it created a work environment abusive to employees because of their race, gender, religion, or national origin offends Title VII's broad rule of workplace equality. The appalling conduct alleged in *Meritor*, and the reference in that case to environments "'so heavily polluted with discrimination as to destroy completely the emotional and psychological stability of minority group workers,'" merely present some especially egregious examples of harassment. They do not mark the boundary of what is actionable.

We therefore believe the District Court erred in relying on whether the conduct "seriously affected plaintiff's psychological well-being" or led her to "suffer injury." Such an inquiry may needlessly focus the fact-finder's attention on concrete psychological harm, an element Title VII does not require. Certainly Title VII bars conduct that would seriously affect a reasonable person's psychological well-being, but the statute is not limited to such conduct. So long as the environment would reasonably be perceived, and is perceived, as hostile or abusive, there is no need for it also to be psychologically injurious.

This is not, and by its nature cannot be, a mathematically precise test. But we can say that whether an environment is "hostile" or "abusive" can be determined only by looking at all the circumstances. These may include the frequency of the discriminatory conduct; its severity; whether it is physically threatening or humiliating, or a mere offensive utterance; and whether it unreasonably interferes with an employee's work performance. The effect on the employee's psychological well-being is, of course, relevant to determining whether the plaintiff actually found the environment abusive. But while psychological harm, like any other relevant factor, may be taken into account, no single factor is required.

Reversed and remanded in favor of Plaintiff, Harris.

Critical Thinking about the Law

AS HAS PREVIOUSLY BEEN TOUCHED UPON, the judiciary most often operates in relationship to shades of gray and not to the black and white between which those shades lie. The Court's decision in this case, in large part dependent on its determination of a definition, is illustrative of this point.

The Court's primary test was to decide what constitutes an "abusive work environment," the second type of sexual harassment actionable under Title VII. Deciding on such a definition is not as easy as going to a legal dictionary and looking up "abusive work environment." The Court had to interpret the meaning of such an environment, and important to this interpretation were legal precedent, ambiguity, and primary ethical norms.

Hence, the questions that follow will aid in thinking critically about these factors influential to the Court's interpretation.

1. What ambiguous language did the Court leave undefined?

   CLUE To find this answer, you want to look at the Court's definition of an "objectively hostile work environment." As always, remember that ambiguities most often are adjectives.

2. In her discussion of the *Meritor Savings Bank* precedent, Justice O'Connor made it clear that the district court misinterpreted the *Meritor* decision in rendering its decision. Contrary to the district court's decision, the existence of which key fact was *not* necessary for the Court to find the defendant guilty of sexual harassment?

   CLUE Revisit the paragraph discussing the district court's dismissal of Ms. Harris's claim. On what basis was this dismissal made? This is the key fact whose existence the Supreme Court found not to be necessary for judgment in favor of the plaintiff.

Since *Meritor*, conflicting lower court decisions have created confusion in the area of sexual harassment. It appeared that in a quid pro quo case, a company was liable regardless of its knowledge, but in a hostile environment case, a company could not be held liable without direct knowledge of the situation. Another question was whether there could be recovery when only empty threats were made.

For example, in *Jones v. Clinton*[3], the District Court Judge threw out Jones' sexual harassment case against the President because Jones had no clear and tangible job detriment necessary for a quid pro quo case, and she was not subject to a hostile environment when the totality of the circumstances were viewed. Even if the allegations were true, the contacts did not constitute "the kind of pervasive, intimidating, abusive conduct"[4] necessary for a hostile environment.

The U.S. Supreme Court attempted to clarify these issues in *Ellerth v. Burlington*.[5] Ellerth was subjected to a litany of dirty jokes and sexual innuendos from her boss. He propositioned her and threatened to make her life miserable if she refused him. She refused him without reprisals and was even promoted. She did

[3]No. LR-C-94-290 (E.D. Ark. 1998).
[4]*Id.*
[5]1998 WL 336326 (1998).

not complain about harassment, but quit after a year because she could not stand the threats and innuendos.

In a decision that offered something to both plaintiffs and defendants, the high court ruled that "an employer is subject to vicarious liability to a victimized employee for an actionable hostile environment created by a supervisor with immediate (or successively higher) authority over the employee. When no tangible employment action is taken, a defending employer may raise an affirmative defense to liability . . . [by showing that] (a) the employer exercised reasonable care to prevent and correct promptly any sexually harassing behavior, and (b) the plaintiff employee unreasonably failed to take advantage of any preventive or corrective opportunities provided by the employer or to avoid harm otherwise . . . No affirmative defense is available, however, when the supervisor's harassment culminates in a tangible employment action."[6] The court then remanded the case to the lower court for a new trial.

SAME-SEX HARASSMENT   Initially, same-sex harassment did not constitute sexual harassment. In the first appellate case on this issue, a Fifth Circuit Court of Appeals case decided in July 1994, a male employee sued his employer for sexual harassment, alleging that on several occasions his male supervisor had approached him from behind and grabbed his crotch.[7] The court of appeals affirmed the trial court's dismissal of the claim on the grounds that no prima facie case had been established. The court said that Title VII addresses gender discrimination, and harassment by a male supervisor of a male employee does not constitute sexual harassment, regardless of the sexual overtones of the harassment.

By 1997, however, the circuits were clearly split on whether one could be sexually harassed by a person of the same sex. The U.S. Supreme Court finally rendered a definitive answer to that issue in the following case.

JOSEPH ONCALE, V. SUNDOWNER OFFSHORE SERVICES
UNITED STATES SUPREME COURT 118 S.CT. 998 (1998)

Oncale was working for respondent Sundowner Offshore Services on a Chevron U.S.A., Inc., oil platform in the Gulf of Mexico. He was employed as a roustabout on an eight-man crew. Lyons, the crane operator, and Pippen, the driller, had supervisory authority. On several occasions, Oncale was forcibly subjected to sex-related, humiliating actions against him by Lyons, Pippen, and Johnson in the presence of the rest of the crew. Pippen and Lyons also physically assaulted Oncale in a sexual manner, and Lyons threatened him with rape. Oncale's complaints to supervisory personnel produced no remedial action; he eventually quit—asking that his pink slip reflect that he "voluntarily left due to sexual harassment and verbal abuse." Oncale stated, "I felt that if I didn't leave my job that I would be raped or forced to have sex."

Plaintiff Oncale brought a Title VII action against his former employer and against male supervisors and co-workers, alleging sexual harassment. The U.S. District Court granted summary judgment for defendants, and plaintiff appealed. The U.S. Court of Appeals affirmed. Plaintiff Oncale appealed to the U.S. Supreme Court.

JUSTICE SCALIA

[I]n the related context of racial discrimination in the workplace we have rejected any conclusive presumption that an employer will not discriminate against members of his own race. "Because of the many facets of human motivation, it would be unwise to presume as a matter of law that human beings of one definable group will not discriminate against other members of that group."

If our precedents leave any doubt on the question, we hold today that nothing in Title VII necessarily bars a claim of discrimination "because of . . . sex" merely because the plaintiff and the defendant are of the same sex. [W]hen the issue arises in the context of a "hostile environment" sexual harassment claim, the state and federal courts have taken a bewildering variety of stances. Some, like the Fifth Circuit in this case, have held that same-sex sexual harassment claims are never cognizable under Title VII. Other decisions say that such claims are actionable only if the plaintiff can prove that the harasser is homosexual (and thus presumably motivated by sexual desire).

---

[6]Id.
[7]Garcia v. Elf Atochem, 28 F.3d 466 (1994).

Still others suggest that workplace harassment that is sexual in content is always actionable, regardless of the harasser's sex, sexual orientation, or motivations.

We see no justification in the statutory language or our precedents for a categorical rule excluding same-sex harassment claims from the coverage of Title VII. [M]ale-on-male sexual harassment in the workplace was assuredly not the principal evil Congress was concerned with when it enacted Title VII. But statutory prohibitions often go beyond the principal evil to cover reasonably comparable evils, and it is ultimately the provisions of our laws rather than the principal concerns of our legislators by which we are governed. Title VII prohibits "discriminat[ion] . . . because of . . . sex" in the "terms" or "conditions" of employment. Our holding that this includes sexual harassment must extend to sexual harassment of any kind that meets the statutory requirements.

Respondents and their amici contend that recognizing liability for same-sex harassment will transform Title VII into a general civility code for the American workplace. But that risk is no greater for same-sex than for opposite-sex harassment, and is adequately met by careful attention to the requirements of the statute. Title VII does not prohibit all verbal or physical harassment in the workplace; it is directed only at "discriminat[ion] . . . because of . . . sex." We have never held that workplace harassment, even harassment between men and women, is automatically discrimination because of sex merely because the words used have sexual content or connotations. "The critical issue, Title VII's text indicates, is whether members of one sex are exposed to disadvantageous terms or conditions of employment to which members of the other sex are not exposed."

Courts and juries have found the inference of discrimination easy to draw in most male-female sexual harassment situations, because the challenged conduct typically involves explicit or implicit proposals of sexual activity; it is reasonable to assume those proposals would not have been made to someone of the same sex. The same chain of inference would be available to a plaintiff alleging same-sex harassment, if there were credible evidence that the harasser was homosexual. But harassing conduct need not be motivated by sexual desire to support an inference of discrimination on the basis of sex. A trier of fact might reasonably find such discrimination, for example, if a female victim is harassed in such sex-specific and derogatory terms by another woman as to make it clear that the harasser is motivated by general hostility to the presence of women in the workplace. A same-sex harassment plaintiff may also, of course, offer direct comparative evidence about how the alleged harasser treated members of both sexes in a mixed-sex workplace. Whatever evidentiary route the plaintiff chooses to follow, he or she must always prove that the conduct at issue was not merely tinged with offensive sexual connotations, but actually constituted "discrimina[tion] . . . because of . . . sex."

And there is another requirement that prevents Title VII from expanding into a general civility code: the statute does not reach genuine but innocuous differences in the ways men and women routinely interact with members of the same sex and of the opposite sex. The prohibition of harassment on the basis of sex requires neither asexuality nor androgyny in the workplace; it forbids only behavior so objectively offensive as to alter the "conditions" of the victim's employment. "Conduct that is not severe or pervasive enough to create an objectively hostile or abusive work environment—an environment that a reasonable person would find hostile or abusive—is beyond Title VII's purview." We have always regarded that requirement as crucial, and as sufficient to ensure that courts and juries do not mistake ordinary socializing in the workplace—such as male-on-male horseplay or intersexual flirtation—for discriminatory "conditions of employment."

[T]he objective severity of harassment should be judged from the perspective of a reasonable person in the plaintiff's position, considering "all the circumstances." In same-sex (as in all) harassment cases, that inquiry requires careful consideration of the social context in which particular behavior occurs and is experienced by its target. A professional football player's working environment is not severely or pervasively abusive, for example, if the coach smacks him on the buttocks as he heads onto the field—even if the same behavior would reasonably be experienced as abusive by the coach's secretary (male or female) back at the office. The real social impact of workplace behavior often depends on a constellation of surrounding circumstances, expectations, and relationships which are not fully captured by a simple recitation of the words used or the physical acts performed. Common sense, and an appropriate sensitivity to social context, will enable courts and juries to distinguish between simple teasing or rough housing among members of the same sex, and conduct which a reasonble person in the plaintiff's position would find severely hostile or abusive.

Judgment reversed in favor of Plaintiff, Oncale.

HOSTILE ENVIRONMENT EXTENDED   Hostile environment cases have also been used in cases of discrimination based on religion, race and even age.[8] For example, in a 1986 case[9], Hispanic and black corrections workers demonstrated that a hostile work environment existed by proving that they had been subjected to continuing verbal abuse and racial harassment by co-workers and that the county sheriff's department had done nothing to prevent the

[8]Crawford v. Medina General Hospital, 96 F.3d (1997).
[9]Snell v. Suffolk County, 782 F.2d 1094 (1994).

abuse. The white employees had continually used racial epithets and posted racially offensive materials on bulletin boards, such as a picture of a black man with a noose around his neck, cartoons favorably portraying the Ku Klux Klan, and a "black officers' study guide," consisting of children's puzzles. White officers once dressed a Hispanic inmate in a straw hat, sheet, and sign that said "spic." Such activities were found by the court to constitute a hostile work environment.

STATUTORY DEFENSES

The three most important defenses available to defendants in Title VII cases are the *bona fide occupational qualification (BFOQ)* defense, merit, and seniority. These defenses are raised by the defendant after the plaintiff has established a prima facie case of discrimination based on disparate treatment, disparate impact, or a pattern or practice of discrimination.

BONA FIDE OCCUPATIONAL QUALIFICATION   The BFOQ defense allows an employer to discriminate in hiring on the basis of sex, religion, or national origin when such a characteristic is necessary for the performance of the job. Note that race or color cannot be a BFOQ. Such necessity must be based on actual qualifications, not on stereotypes about one group's abilities. Being a male cannot be a BFOQ for a job because it is a dirty job or a "strenuous" job, although there may be a valid requirement that an applicant be able to lift a certain amount of weight if such lifting is a part of the job. Nor can a BFOQ arise because an employer's customers would prefer to be served by someone of a particular gender or national origin. Nor does inconvenience to the employer, such as having to provide two sets of restroom facilities, make a classification a BFOQ.

MERIT   Most claims of merit involve the use of tests to hire or promote. The use of a professionally developed ability test that is not designed, intended, or used to discriminate, is legal. Such tests may have an adverse impact on a class, but they do not violate the act as long as they are manifestly related to job performance. The "Uniform Guidelines on Employee Selection Procedures" (UGESP) have, since 1978, contained the policy of all governmental agencies charged with enforcing civil rights, and they provide guidance to employers and other interested persons about when ability tests are valid and job-related. Under these guidelines, tests must be validated in accordance with standards established by the American Psychological Association.

Three types of validation are acceptable: (1) *criterion-related validity*, which is the statistical relationship between test scores and objective criteria of job performance; (2) *content validity*, which isolates some skill used on the job and directly tests that skill; and (3) *construct validity*, wherein a psychological trait needed to perform the job is measured. A test that required a secretary to type and take shorthand would be content-valid. A test of patience for a teacher would be construct-valid.

SENIORITY SYSTEMS   A final statutory defense, available under Section 703(h), is a bona fide seniority system. A seniority system, in which employees are given preferential treatment based on their length of service, may perpetuate discrimination that occurred in the past. Nonetheless, such systems are considered bona fide and are thus not unlawful if (1) the system applies equally to all persons; (2) the seniority units follow industry practices; (3) the seniority system did not have its genesis in discrimination; and (4) the system is maintained free of any illegal discriminatory purpose.

PROTECTED CLASSES

As you know, five classes are protected under Title VII. Unique problems have arisen with regard to each of these protected classes, of which the astute business manager should be aware.

RACE AND COLOR   A primary goal of Title VII was to remedy the discrimination in employment to which blacks had been subjected since the founding of this nation. However, the act also contains a proviso stating that nothing in the act requires that preferential treatment based on an imbalance between their representation in the employer's workplace and their representation in the population at large be given to any protected class. This proviso thus paved the way for questions about "reverse discrimination," or discrimination against whites, as a result of employers' attempts to create a racially balanced workforce. This issue will be discussed in the section on affirmative action.

NATIONAL ORIGIN   The act prohibits discrimination based on national origin, *not* on alienage (citizenship of a country other than the United States). Thus, an employer can refuse to hire non-United States citizens. This prohibition applies even to owners of foreign corporations who have established firms in the United States. In the absence of a treaty between the United States and the foreign state authorizing such conduct, a corporation cannot discriminate in favor of those born in a foreign state.

SEX   Under Title VII, sex is interpreted as referring only to gender and not to preferences. Hence, homosexuals and transsexuals are not protected under the act. However, it would be sex discrimination to fire male homosexuals while retaining female homosexuals.

As noted earlier, sexual harassment is prohibited by Title VII's prohibition against discrimination based on sex. Although sexual harassment cases were not filed in large numbers immediately after Title VII's passage, there has been a tremendous increase in the number of such cases filed since law professor Anita Hill captivated the nation in late 1991 by testifying before Congress about the harassment to which she was subjected by U.S. Supreme Court nominee Clarence Thomas. According to the EEOC, there were 9,953 sexual harassment complaints filed in the year ending on October 1, 1992, an increase of 2,546 over the previous year. The number has continued to increase, and in 1996 alone 15,342 complaints were filed. Thus, it is increasingly important that businesspersons be able to recognize sexual harassment and to prevent its occurrence in the workplace. Exhibit 19-3 provides some suggestions for how managers can avoid liability for sexual harassment.

Shortly after Title VII's enactment, the U.S. Supreme Court ruled that discrimination on the basis of pregnancy was not discrimination on the basis of

---

EXHIBIT 19-3 *Tips for Avoiding Sexual Harassment Charges*

1. Senior management must make clear their position that sexual harassment in any form will not be tolerated.

2. Have an explicit written policy on sexual harassment that is widely disseminated in the workplace and given to every new employee.

3. Make sure employees know what is, and is not, sexual harassment.

4. Provide a gender-neutral training program on sexual harassment for all employees.

5. Establish an efficient system for investigating charges of sexual harassment and punishing violators.

6. Make sure that complaints are to be filed with a neutral party, not with the employee's supervisor.

7. Thoroughly investigate and resolve every complaint, punishing every violation appropriately. If no violation is found, explain to the complainant why there was no violation.

Source: Adapted from K. Swisher, "Corporations Are Seeing the Light on Harassment," *Washington Post National Weekly Edition*, February 14–20, 1994, p. 21.

sex under Title VII.[10] In response to that decision, Congress amended Title VII by passing the Pregnancy Discrimination Act (PDA), which specifies that discrimination based on pregnancy is sex discrimination; pregnancy must be treated the same as any other disability, except that abortions for any purpose other than saving the mother's life may be excluded from the company's medical benefits. In a 1986 case interpreting the PDA, the U.S. Supreme Court concluded that Congress intended the PDA to be "a floor beneath which pregnancy disability benefits may not drop—not a ceiling above which they may not rise."[11] Consequently, the High Court held that a California statute requiring unpaid maternity leave for pregnant women and reinstatement after the birth of the child was constitutional because the intent of the law was to make women in the workplace equal, not to give them favored treatment.

FETAL PROTECTION POLICIES While women's rights advocates worked to protect women from discrimination in the workplace and to get pregnancy treated like any other temporary disability, there was one way in which women were treated differently until 1991, and that is with respect to fetal protection policies. These policies, adopted by a broad range of companies, prohibited fertile women from working at jobs that could expose their unborn fetuses to hazardous substances that might harm the fetuses.

Employers understandably felt uncertain about whether to adopt such policies after passage of Title VII. On one hand, these policies do bar women from (often higher-paying) jobs on the bases of sex. On the other hand, allowing them to be exposed to these substances opened up the possibility of the women's bearing severely deformed infants and suing their employer.

Many employers decided to run the risk of a discrimination suit and adopted or retained fetal protection policies. One of the most extreme fetal protection policies was adopted by Johnson Controls, the nation's largest producer of batteries, in 1982. In the following lawsuit challenging Johnson Controls' policy, the U.S. Supreme Court addressed the legality of these policies under Title VII and the Pregnancy Discrimination Act.

UNITED AUTO WORKERS, INCORPORATED V. JOHNSON CONTROLS, INCORPORATED
UNITED STATES SUPREME COURT 499 U.S. 187 (1991)

Because scientific studies demonstrated that a pregnant woman's exposure to high levels of lead could harm her fetus, defendant Johnson Controls adopted a policy barring all women of childbearing age from working in its battery division. Plaintiff United Auto Workers (UAW) filed an action against defendant Johnson Controls, alleging that the policy discriminated in employment on the basis of sex in violation of Title VII.

The trial court ruled in favor of the defendant Johnson Controls, applying a business necessity defense. Because there was scientific evidence that high levels of lead had a considerably more dangerous effect on a fetus than on an adult, and because there was no other acceptable policy to protect the fetus, the policy was valid. The court of appeals affirmed. Plaintiff UAW appealed to the U.S. Supreme Court.

JUSTICE BLACKMUN

The bias in Johnson Controls' policy is obvious. Fertile men, but not fertile women, are given a choice as to whether they wish to risk their reproductive health for a particular job. Respondent's fetal-protection policy explicitly discriminates against women on the basis of their sex. The policy excludes women with childbearing capacity from lead-exposed jobs and so creates a facial classification based on gender.

Nevertheless, the Court of Appeals assumed that sex-specific fetal-protection policies do not involve facial discrimination. Consequently, the court looked to see if each employer in question had established that its policy was justified as a business necessity. The business necessity standard is more lenient for the employer than the statutory BFOQ defense.

---

[10]General Electric Co. v. Gilbert, 429 U.S. 125 (1976).
[11]California Federal Savings and Loan Association et al. v. Department of Fair Employment and Housing et al., 479 U.S. 272 (1987).

First, Johnson Controls' policy classifies on the basis of gender and childbearing capacity, rather than fertility alone. Respondent does not seek to protect the unconceived children of all its employees. Johnson Controls' policy is facially discriminatory because it requires only a female employee to produce proof that she is not capable of reproducing.

Our conclusion is bolstered by the Pregnancy Discrimination Act of 1978 (PDA), 92 Stat. 2076, 42 U.S.C. § 2000e(k), in which Congress explicitly provided that, for purposes of Title VII, discrimination "on the basis of sex" includes discrimination "because of or on the basis of pregnancy, childbirth, or related medical conditions." "The Pregnancy Discrimination Act has now made clear that, for all Title VII purposes, discrimination based on a woman's pregnancy is, on its face, discrimination because of her sex." Johnson Controls explicitly classifies on the basis of potential for pregnancy. Under the PDA, such a classification must be regarded, for Title VII purposes, in the same light as explicit sex discrimination. Respondent has chosen to treat all its female employees as potentially pregnant; that choice evinces discrimination on the basis of sex.

We concluded above that Johnson Controls' policy is not neutral because it does not apply to the reproductive capacity of the company's male employees in the same way as it applies to that of the females.

We hold that Johnson Controls' fetal-protection policy is sex discrimination forbidden under Title VII unless respondent can establish that sex is a "bona fide occupational qualification."

The BFOQ defense is written narrowly, and this Court has read it narrowly. The wording of the BFOQ defense contains several terms of restriction that indicate that the exception reaches only special situations. The statute thus limits the situations in which discrimination is permissible to "certain instances" where sex discrimination is "reasonably necessary" to the "normal operation" of the "particular" business.

Johnson Controls argues that its fetal-protection policy falls within the so-called safety exception to the BFOQ. Our cases have stressed that discrimination on the basis of sex because of safety concerns is allowed only in narrow circumstances.

In *Dothard v. Rawlinson* ... [we] found sex to be BFOQ inasmuch as the employment of a female guard would create real risks of safety to others if violence broke out because the guard was a woman. Sex discrimination was tolerated because sex was related to the guard's ability to do the job—maintaining prison security. We also required in *Dothard* a high correlation between sex and ability to perform job functions and refused to allow employers to use sex as a proxy for strength although it might be a fairly accurate one.

Similarly, some courts have approved airlines' layoffs of pregnant flight attendants at different points during the first five months of pregnancy on the ground that the employer's policy was necessary to ensure the safety of passengers.

The concurrence ignores the "essence of the business" test and so concludes that "the safety to fetuses in carrying out the duties of battery manufacturing is as much a legitimate concern as is safety to third parties in guarding prisons (*Dothard*). By limiting its discussion to cost and safety concerns and rejecting the "essence of the business" test that our case law has established, the concurrence seeks to expand what is now the narrow BFOQ defense. Third-party safety considerations properly entered into the BFOQ analysis in *Dothard* and *Criswell* because they went to the core of the employee's job performance. Moreover, that performance involved the central purpose of the enterprise. The concurrence attempts to transform this case into one of customer safety. The unconceived fetuses of Johnson Controls' female employees, however, are neither customers nor third parties whose safety is essential to the business of battery manufacturing. No one can disregard the possibility of injury to future children; the BFOQ, however, is not so broad that it transforms this deep social concern into an essential aspect of batterymaking.

Our case law, therefore, makes clear that the safety exception is limited to instances in which sex or pregnancy actually interferes with the employee's ability to perform the job. This approach is consistent with the language of the BFOQ provision itself, for it suggests that permissible distinctions based on sex must relate to ability to perform the duties of the job.

The PDA's amendment to Title VII contains a BFOQ standard of its own: unless pregnant employees differ from others "in their ability or inability to work," they must be "treated the same" as other employees "for all employment-related purposes." In other words, women as capable of doing their jobs as their male counterparts may not be forced to choose between having a child and having a job.

We conclude that the language of both the BFOQ provision and the PDA which amended it, as well as the legislative history and the case law, prohibit an employer from discriminating against a woman because of her capacity to become pregnant unless her reproductive potential prevents her from performing the duties of her job. An employer must direct its concerns about a woman's ability to perform her job safely and efficiently to those aspects of the woman's job-related activities that fall within the "essence" of the particular business.

We have no difficulty concluding that Johnson Controls cannot establish a BFOQ. Fertile women, as far as appears in the record, participate in the manufacture of batteries as efficiently as anyone else. Johnson Controls' professed moral and ethical concerns about the welfare of the next generation do not suffice to establish a BFOQ of female sterility. Decisions about the welfare of future children must be left to the parents who conceive, bear, support, and raise them rather than to the employers who hire those parents. Congress has mandated this choice through

Title VII, as amended by the Pregnancy Discrimination Act. Johnson Controls has attempted to exclude women because of their reproductive capacity. Title VII and the PDA simply do not allow a woman's dismissal because of her failure to submit to sterilization.

Nor can concerns about the welfare of the next generation be considered a part of the "essence" of Johnson Controls' business.

Johnson Controls argues that it must exclude all fertile women because it is impossible to tell which women will become pregnant while working with lead. This argument is somewhat academic in light of our conclusion that the company may not exclude fertile women at all; it perhaps is worth noting, however, that Johnson Controls has shown no "factual basis for believing that all or substantially all women would be unable to perform safely and efficiently the duties of the job involved."

A word about tort liability and the increased cost of fertile women in the workplace is perhaps necessary. One of the dissenting judges in this case expressed concern about an employer's tort liability and concluded that liability for a potential injury to a fetus is a social cost that Title VII does not require a company to ignore. It is correct to say that Title VII does not prevent the employer from having a conscience. The statute, however, does prevent sex-specific fetal-protection policies.

The tort-liability argument reduces to two equally unpersuasive propositions. First, Johnson Controls attempts to solve the problem of reproductive health hazards by resorting to an exclusionary policy. Title VII plainly forbids illegal sex discrimination as a method of diverting attention from an employer's obligation to police the workplace. Second, the specter of an award of damages reflects a fear that hiring fertile women will cost more. The extra cost of employing members of one sex, however, does not provide an affirmative Title VII defense for a discriminatory refusal to hire members of that gender.

Reversed in favor of Plaintiff, UAW.

Critical Thinking about the Law

THIS CASE PROMPTS US TO REVIEW the significance of a court's criteria selection to its legal reasoning and subsequent decision making. You will recall that different sets of criteria can yield different judgments.

In this case, the court identifies one important criterion to be mindful of in making its decision. In the questions that follow, you will be asked to identify that criterion as well as a key fact whose significance is almost wholly determined by this criterion.

1. What criterion did the Court use in determining whether a safety exception to Title VII's prohibition of sexual discrimination is legitimate?

   CLUE Go to the paragraph in which Justice Blackmun discusses case law.

2. What key fact is particularly significant in the Supreme Court's reversal of the lower courts' decisions?

   CLUE Consider that the Court ruled that the discrimination was not justifiable on the basis of its criterion. The key fact of the case will be the fact whose existence meant that the defendant did not meet this criterion in its discriminatory practices.

ENFORCEMENT PROCEDURES

Enforcement of Title VII is a very complicated procedure and is full of pitfalls. Failure to follow the proper procedures within the appropriate time framework may result in the plaintiff's losing her or his right to file a lawsuit under Title VII. An overview of these procedures is provided in Exhibit 19-4.

THE CHARGE The first step in initiation of an action under Title VII is the aggrieved party's filing of a charge with the state agency responsible for enforcing fair employment laws (a state EEOC) or, if no such agency exists, with the federal EEOC. A *charge* is a sworn statement that states the name of the charging party, the name(s) of the defendant(s), and the nature of the discriminatory act. In states that do not have state EEOCs, the aggrieved party must file the charge with the federal EEOC within 180 days of the alleged discriminatory act. In states that do have such agencies, the charge must be filed either with the

EXHIBIT 19-4 *Anatomy of a Title VII Case*

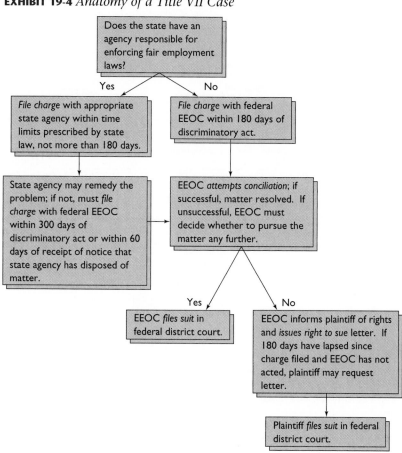

federal EEOC within 180 days of the discriminatory act or with the appropriate state agency within the time limits prescribed by local law, which cannot be more than 180 days. If initially filed with the local agency, the charge must be filed with the federal EEOC within 300 days of the discriminatory act or within 60 days of receipt of notice that the state agency has disposed of the matter, whichever comes first. Exhibit 19-5 is a typical charge.

CONCILIATION AND FILING SUIT Once the EEOC receives the charge, it must notify the alleged violator of the charge within ten days. After such notification, the EEOC investigates the matter in an attempt to ascertain whether there is "reasonable cause" to believe that a violation has occurred. If the EEOC does find such reasonable cause, it attempts to eliminate the discriminatory practice through conciliation. If unsuccessful, the EEOC may file suit against the alleged discriminator in federal district court.

If the EEOC decides not to sue, it notifies the plaintiff of his or her right to file an action and issues the plaintiff a *right-to-sue* letter. The plaintiff must have this letter in order to file a private action. The letter may be requested at any time after 180 days have elapsed since the filing of the charge. As long as the requisite time period has passed, the EEOC will issue the right-to-sue letter regardless of whether or not the EEOC members find a reasonable basis to believe that the defendant engaged in discriminatory behavior.

REMEDIES

The plaintiff bringing a Title VII action can seek both equitable and legal remedies. The courts have broad discretion to order "such affirmative action as may be appropriate."[12] Under this broad guideline, courts have ordered parties to en-

---

[12]Section 706(a).

EXHIBIT 19-5 *A Typical Charge of Discrimination Filed with the EEOC*

CHARGE OF DISCRIMINATION	AGENCY	CHARGE NUMBER
	☒ FEPA	
This form is affected by the Privacy Act of 1974; See Privacy Act Statement before completing this form.	☒ EEOC	

OHIO CIVIL RIGHTS COMMISSION ———— and EEOC
State or local Agency, if any

Name (Indicate Mr., Ms., Mrs.) Ms. Nellie Baldwin	Home Telephone (Include Area Code) (419) 863-4125

STREET ADDRESS 826 Potter Road	CITY, STATE AND ZIP CODE Toledo, Ohio 43602	DATE OF BIRTH 11/10/56

NAMED IS THE EMPLOYER, LABOR ORGANIZATION, EMPLOYMENT AGENCY APPRENTICESHIP COMMITTEE, STATE OR LOCAL GOVERNMENT AGENCY WHO DISCRIMINATED AGAINST ME *(If more than one list below.)*

Name Mancum Manufacturers	NUMBER OF EMPLOYEES, MEMBERS +15	TELEPHONE (Include Area Code) (419) 693-8296

STREET ADDRESS 896 Lewis Ave .	CITY, STATE AND ZIP CODE Toledo, Ohio 43605	COUNTY Lucas

Name	TELEPHONE NUMBER (Include Area Code)

STREET ADDRESS	CITY, STATE AND ZIP CODE	COUNTY

CAUSE OF DISCRIMINATION BASED ON *(Check appropriate basis)*

☐ RACE ☐ COLOR ☒ SEX Female ☐ RELIGION ☐ NATIONAL ORIGIN

☐ RETALIATION ☐ AGE ☐ DISABILITY ☐ OTHER *(Specify)*

DATE DISCRIMINATION TOOK PLACE

/ / 02/ 05/ 93

☐ CONTINUING ACTION

THE PARTICULARS ARE *(If additional space is needed, attach extra sheet(s)):*

1. I was employed by Canfield for 2 years as a machine operator general.
2. An opening for machine operator special, a higher position, was posted.
3. I applied for the position along with 4 other males and 2 females.
4. All applicants took a dexterity test.
5. I received the highest score on the test, but a male who scored second highest was promoted.
6. I was told that the posted job was "better suited for a male", but that with my test score I would be first in line when a more appropriate opening arose.

CXM/IFL:bd

☒ I also want this charge filed with the EEOC.	Notary - (When necessary for State and Local Requirements)
I will advise the agencies if I change my address or telephone number and I will cooperate fully with them in the processing of my charge in accordance with their procedures.	I swear or affirm that I have read the above charge and that it is true to the best of my knowledge, information and belief.
I declare under penalty of perjury that the foregoing is true and correct.	SIGNATURE OF COMPLAINANT *Ms. Nellie Baldwin*
	SUBSCRIBED AND SWORN TO BEFORE ME THIS DATE (Day, month, and year)
Date Charging Party *(Signature)* EEOC TEST FORM 5 (09/01/91)	

gage in diverse activities ranging from publicizing their commitment to minority hiring to establishing special training programs for minorities.

In general, a successful plaintiff is able to recover back pay for up to two years from the time of the discriminatory act. For example, if two years before the case came to trial the defendant refused a promotion to a plaintiff on the basis of her sex, and the job for which she was rejected paid $100 more per week than her current job, she would be entitled to recover back pay in the amount of $100 multiplied by 104. (If the salary rose at regular increments, these are also included.) The same basic calculations are used when plaintiffs were not hired because of discrimination. Such plaintiffs are entitled to the back wages that they would have received minus any actual earnings during that time. Defendants may also exclude wages for any period during which the plaintiff would have been unable to work.

If a plaintiff was not hired for a job because of a Title VII violation, the plaintiff may receive, in addition to back pay, remedial seniority dating back to the time when the plaintiff was discriminated against.

Perhaps the most significant change made by the 1991 Civil Rights Act was its impact on the availability of compensatory and punitive damages. Under the new act, not only plaintiffs discriminated against because of race, but also those discriminated against on the basis of sex, disability, religion, or national origin may recover both compensatory damages, including those for pain and suffering, and punitive damages. In cases based on discrimination other than race, however, punitive damages are capped at $300,000 for employers of more than 500 employees; $100,000 for firms with 101 to 200 employees; and $50,000 for firms with 100 or fewer employees.

Since the passage of the Civil Rights Act of 1991, there has been a definite increase in the damages awarded under Title VII, and in the amounts for which employers are willing to settle. In 1998, Astra USA agreed to the largest settlement in a sexual harassment case to date when they agreed to pay $10 million to end a lawsuit claiming widespread debauchery and sexual abuse by its management.[13]

Attorneys' fees are ordinarily awarded to a successful plaintiff in Title VII cases. They are denied only when special circumstances would render the award unjust. In those rare instances in which the courts determine that the plaintiff's action was frivolous, unreasonable, or without foundation, the courts may use their discretion to award attorneys' fees to the prevailing defendant.

THE AGE DISCRIMINATION IN EMPLOYMENT ACT OF 1967

Our society does not revere age. Many aspects of the culture reward and cater to youth. Older employees detract from a firm's "youthful" image. They are also expensive. They have accumulated raises over the years and thus earn more than younger employees. They have pension benefits, which the employer will have to pay if the employee retires from the firm. Thus, it is understandable that firms may attempt to discriminate against older employees. The **Age Discrimination in Employment Act of 1967 (ADEA)** was enacted to prohibit employers from refusing to hire, discharging, or discriminating in terms and conditions of employment on the basis of age. The language describing the prohibited conduct is virtually the same as that of Title VII, except that age is the prohibited basis for discrimination.

With all of the downsizing that has been taking place since the late 1980s and with the increasing number of employees over 40, some believe that age discrimination will become the main workplace issue of the twenty-first century. Older workers are increasingly being viewed as rigid, hard to retrain as

Age Discrimination in Employment Act of 1967 (ADEA) Prohibits employers from refusing to hire, discharging, or discriminating against people in terms of conditions of employment on the basis of age.

---

[13]M. Jackson, *Better Safe . . . Sexual Harassment Insurance is a Paton Company's Bottom Line*, Chicago Tribune, April 26, 1998, at 2.

technology changes, and expensive. During 1993 and 1994, the number of age discrimination suits increased by 14 percent, according to the EEOC.[14]

APPLICABILITY OF THE STATUTE

The ADEA applies to employers having 20 or more employees in an industry that affects interstate commerce. It also applies to state governments and their political subdivisions, to employment agencies, and to unions that have at least 25 members or operate a hiring hall.

The act does not protect *all* individuals from discrimination based on age; it protects only persons aged 40 or over. Thus, an employer can refuse to promote an employee under 40 because he or she is too old or too young.

PROVING AGE DISCRIMINATION

Discrimination under the ADEA may be proved in the same ways that discrimination is proved under Title VII: by the plaintiff's showing disparate treatment or disparate impact. Most of the ADEA cases today involve termination. In order to prove a prima facie case of age discrimination involving a termination, the plaintiff must establish facts sufficient to create a reasonable inference that age was a determining factor in the termination. The plaintiff raises this inference by showing that he or she: (1) belongs to the statutorily protected age group (40 or older); (2) was qualified for the position held; (3) was terminated; and (4) was replaced by a younger person. If the plaintiff does so, the burden of proof then shifts to the defendant to establish that there was a legitimate, nondiscriminatory reason for the discharge. If the employer meets this standard, the plaintiff may recover only if he or she can show by a preponderance of the evidence that the employer's alleged legitimate reason was really pretextual.

In an interesting case in 1994, the Third Circuit Court of Appeals attempted to clarify its position on the impact of age as a factor in the decision to terminate. The court said that the plaintiff need only show that "age played a role in the employer's decisionmaking process and that it was a determinative factor in the outcome of that process."[15] Rather than clarifying the standard, the decision may have in fact caused more uncertainty. In fact, shortly after the case was decided, the appellate court voted to rehear the case.[16]

STATUTORY DEFENSES

BONA FIDE OCCUPATIONAL QUALIFICATION As under Title VII, there are a number of statutory defenses available to an employer in an age discrimination case. The first is the bona fide occupational qualification. To succeed with this defense, the defendant must establish that he or she must hire employees of only a certain age to safely and efficiently operate the business in question. The courts generally scrutinize very carefully any attempt to demonstrate that age is a BFOQ. One example of an employer's successful use of this defense is provided by *Hodgson v. Greyhound Lines, Inc.*,[17] a case in which the employer refused to hire applicants aged 35 or older. Greyhound demonstrated that its safest drivers were those between the ages of 50 and 55, with 16 to 20 years of experience driving for Greyhound. Greyhound argued that this combination of age and experience could never be reached by those who were hired at age 35 or older. Therefore, in order to ensure the safest drivers, they should be allowed to hire only applicants younger than 35. In that case, the court accepted the employer's rationale.

---

[14]S. Shellenbarger and C. Humowitz, *As Population Ages, Older Workers Clash with Younger Bosses*, Wall St. J., June 13, 1994, at 1, col. 6.
[15]Miller v. Cigna Corp., 63 U.S.L.W. 2063 (3d Cir. 1994).
[16]Miller v. Cigna Corp., 65 Fair Emp. Practices Cases 1216 (1994).
[17]499 F.2d 859 (7th Cir. 1974).

Although safety considerations are important, to use them in establishing age as a BFOQ, the employer must prove that safety is indeed related to age. The following case demonstrates the level of scrutiny that the U.S. Supreme Court considers appropriate in determining whether age is a BFOQ.

WESTERN AIRLINES V. CRISWELL
UNITED STATES SUPREME COURT 53 U.S.L.W. 477 (1985)

Defendant Western Airlines required that its flight engineers (members of the cockpit crews who do not operate flight controls unless both the pilot and the copilot become incapacitated) retire at age 60. Federal Aviation Administration (FAA) regulations require pilots to retire at age 60. Flight engineers forced to retire at 60 and retired pilots who were not reassigned as flight engineers filed suit under the ADEA. The defendant argued that age was a BFOQ because "incapacitating medical events" and adverse psychological, emotional, and physical changes occur as a result of aging," and these changes could make a person over 60 incapable of safely operating a plane. The jury in the district court decided the case in favor of the plaintiffs. The court of appeals affirmed. The defendant appealed.

JUSTICE STEVENS

The question here is whether the jury was properly instructed on the elements of the BFOQ defense. The plaintiff's experts . . . testified that physiological deterioration is caused by disease, not aging, and that "it was feasible to determine on the basis of individual medical examinations whether flight deck crew members including those over age 60, were physically qualified to continue to fly." Moreover, several large commercial airlines have flight engineers over age 60 "flying the line" without any reduction in their safety record.

The jury was instructed that the "BFOQ defense is available only if it is reasonably necessary to the normal operation or essence of defendant's business." The jury was informed that "the essence of Western's business is the safe transportation of their passengers." The jury was also instructed:

One method by which defendant Western may establish a BFOQ in this case is to prove:

(1) That in 1978, when these plaintiffs were retired, it was highly impractical for Western to deal with each second officer over age 60 on an individualized basis to determine his particular ability to perform his job safely; and

(2) That some second officers over age 60 possess traits of a physiological, psychological or other nature which preclude safe and efficient job performance that cannot be ascertained by means other than knowing their age.

Throughout the legislative history of the ADEA, one empirical fact is repeatedly emphasized: the process of psychological and physiological degeneration caused by aging varies with each individual. As a result, many older American workers perform at levels equal or superior to their younger colleagues.

Congress offered only general guidance on when an age classification might be permissible by . . . providing that such a classification is lawful "where age is a bona fide occupational qualification reasonably necessary to the normal operation of the particular business."

First, the [Court of Appeals] recognized that some job qualifications may be so peripheral to the central mission of the employer's business that *no* age discrimination can be reasonably *necessary* to the normal operation of the particular business.

Second, the court recognized that the ADEA requires that age qualifications be something more than "convenient" or "reasonable"; they must be "reasonably necessary . . . to the particular business," and this is only so when the employer is compelled to rely on age as a proxy for the safety-related job qualifications validated in the first inquiry. This showing could be made in two ways. The employer would establish that it "'had reasonable cause to believe, that is, a factual basis for believing, that all or substantially all [persons over the age qualifications] would be unable to perform safely and efficiently the duties of the job involved.'"

Alternatively, the employer could establish that age was a legitimate proxy for the safety-related job qualifications by proving that it is "'impossible or highly impractical'" to deal with the older employees on an individualized basis. "One method by which the employer can carry this burden is to establish that some members of the discriminated-against class possess a trait precluding safe and efficient job performance that cannot be ascertained by means other than knowledge of the applicant's membership in the class."

. . . [W]e conclude that this two-part inquiry properly identifies the relevant considerations for resolving a BFOQ defense to an age-based qualification purportedly justified by considerations of safety.

Western argues that the jury should have been instructed to defer to "Western's selection of job qualifications for the position of [flight engineer] that are reasonable in light of the safety risks." This proposal is plainly at odds with Congress' decision, in adopting the ADEA, to subject such management decisions to a test of objective justification in a court of law. The BFOQ standard adopted in the statute is one of "reasonable necessity," not reasonableness.

The "rational basis" standard is also inconsistent with the preference for individual evaluation expressed in the language and legislative history of the ADEA. Unless an employer can establish a substantial basis for believing that all or nearly all employees above an age lack the qualifications required for the position, the age selected for mandatory retirement less than 70 must be an age at which it is highly impractical for the employer to insure by individual testing that its employees will have the necessary qualifications for the job.

When an employee covered by the Act is able to point to reputable businesses in the same industry that choose to eschew reliance on mandatory retirement earlier than age 70, when the employer itself relies on individualized testing in similar circumstances, and when the administrative agency with primary responsibility for maintaining airline safety has determined that individualized testing is not impractical for the relevant position, the employer's attempt to justify its decision on the basis of the contrary opinion of experts—solicited for the purpose of litigation—is hardly convincing on any objective standard short of complete deference. Even in cases involving public safety, the ADEA plainly does not permit the trier of fact to give complete deference to the employer's decision.

Affirmed in favor of Plaintiff, Criswell.

Critical Thinking about the Law

IN GENERAL, JUDGES IN THEIR LEGAL reasoning determine the primary ethical norm to which they will adhere to a great extent on the basis of the facts of the case. The case at hand illustrates this generalization.

In delivering the opinion of the Court, Justice Stevens implied that there are two primary ethical norms in contention for applicability to the case. Using legal reasoning, Justice Stevens rejected one and opted for the other.

In the questions that follow, you will be asked to identify those contending primary ethical norms and the set of facts particular to the case that were important in determining to which norm the Court would show allegiance.

1. What primary ethical norm was implicit in the Court's reasoning?

   CLUE Another way of thinking about this question is: In the absence of good arguments on the part of the defendant for its actions, which ethical norm did the Court feel should prevail?

2. In Western's defense, a primary ethical norm was implicit in Western's reasoning. Identify this ethical norm.

   CLUE Recall that Western Airlines argued that it should not have to individually test each flight engineer over the age of 60.

OTHER DEFENSES As under Title VII, decisions premised on the operation of a bona fide seniority system are not unlawfully discriminatory despite any discriminatory impact. Likewise, employment decisions may also be based on "reasonable factors other than age."

EXECUTIVE EXEMPTION Even if none of the foregoing defenses are available to the employer, termination of an older employee may be legal because of the **executive exemption.** Under this exemption, an individual may be mandatorily retired after age 65 if (1) he or she has been employed as a bona fide executive for at least two years immediately before retirement, and (2) on retirement, he or she is entitled to nonforfeitable annual retirement benefits of at least $44,000.

executive exemption
Exemption to the ADEA that allows mandatory retirement of executives at age 65.

AFTER-ACQUIRED EVIDENCE OF EMPLOYEE MISCONDUCT An important issue, not just for the ADEA but also for other employment discrimination claims, is whether an employer can use evidence of an employee's misconduct discovered *after* a charge has been found to defeat that charge. In the 1995 case of *McKennon v. Nashville Banner*,[18] a unanimous Supreme Court decided that issue in a manner that pleased lawyers that represented both businesses and plaintiffs.

In *Nashville Banner*, the plaintiff had feared being fired by the company because of age, so she copied confidential documents to use (if needed) in her subsequent lawsuit. She was, in fact, fired, and she filed a discrimination claim. The employer subsequently discovered that the plaintiff had copied the documents and argued that her ADEA action should be dismissed because she would have been fired anyway had the firm known that she had copied the documents. The circuit court held that she deserved to be fired because of her misconduct, and therefore she could not sue for discrimination.

The Supreme Court, however, overruled the appellate court and held that after-acquired knowledge of misconduct will not bar a discrimination action. However, the Supreme Court did *not* believe such conduct should be totally irrelevant. *If* the defendant can prove that the misconduct was actually substantial enough to have warranted termination of the employee, then reinstatement will not be required. The amount of back pay required will also be reduced. The employee's back pay will be calculated from the date of the unlawful discharge until the date that the evidence of misconduct was discovered. Thus, the after-acquired evidence may be used to reduce the plaintiff's relief but *not* to completely bar the action.

ENFORCEMENT PROCEDURES

Enforcement of ADEA is similar to the enforcement of Title VII. Under ADEA, the victim of age discrimination may file a charge with the appropriate state agency or with the EEOC within 180 days of the act. If a charge has been filed with the state agency, an EEOC charge must be filed within 300 days of the discrimination or within 30 days of receiving notice of the termination of state proceedings, whichever comes first. The charge must identify the defendant and specify the nature of the discriminatory act. On receipt of a charge, the EEOC must notify the accused and attempt to conciliate the matter. If conciliation fails, the EEOC may then bring a civil action against the violator.

Whereas a party who does not plan to file a private action may choose to file a charge with the EEOC only, if a party wishes to file a private civil action, complaints must be filed with both the appropriate state agency and the EEOC. If these complaints are filed within the appropriate time limits, a party then has three years from the date of the discriminatory act within which to file a private action under ADEA, assuming the alleged discriminatory act was willful. If the alleged discrimination is purportedly unwillful, the party has two years within which he or she must file the private action. The party, however, must wait 60 days from the date of the filing of the complaints with both the EEOC and the state agency before filing the lawsuit. If the EEOC or the state agency files an action on the matter during that time, the plaintiff is precluded from filing suit.

REMEDIES UNDER ADEA

First, the successful plaintiff is entitled to back pay, which is the difference between the pay that he or she received after the discriminatory act and the pay that he or she would have received had there been no discrimination. In addition, in a private action by a plaintiff, he or she may be able to recover liquidated damages in an amount equal to the back pay recovered if the plaintiff can prove that the employer acted willfully. *Willfully* means that the employer was substantially aware of the possibility that he or she was in violation of the ADEA but did not attempt to ascertain the legality of his or her actions. If no liquidated damages are granted, the plaintiff is generally entitled to interest on the back pay; interest is not awarded when liquidated damages have been granted. Compensatory damages for items such as mental distress from the dis-

---

[18]63 U.S.L.W. 4105 (1995).

Rehabilitation Act of 1973
Prohibits discrimination in employment against otherwise qualified persons who have a handicap. Applies only to the federal government, employers who have contracts with the federal government, and parties who administer programs receiving federal financial assistance.

crimination are occasionally, but *rarely*, awarded by a few courts. Likewise, punitive damages are rarely awarded.

THE REHABILITATION ACT OF 1973

In 1973, Congress broadened the class of individuals protected against discrimination to include the handicapped by passing the **Rehabilitation Act of 1973**. This act is designed to protect the handicapped from discrimination in employment and also to help them secure rehabilitation, training, access to public buildings, and all benefits of covered programs that might otherwise be denied them because of their handicap. It also requires that covered employers have a qualified affirmative action program for hiring and promoting the handicapped. A *handicapped individual*, for purposes of the act, is defined as one who has a "physical or mental impairment, which substantially limits one or more of such person's major life activities,"[19] or who has a record of such impairment. Even people who are falsely regarded as having such impairment are protected. The major provisions of this act are outlined in Table 19-3.

This act applies only to the federal government and employers who have contracts with the federal government, so its impact is relatively limited. In 1991, the *Americans With Disabilities Act (ADA)* was passed, which extends similar prohibitions against discrimination to private-sector employers who do not have federal contracts. Because of its broader impact, the ADA will be discussed in greater detail in the next section, but the principles discussed with respect to that act apply to the Rehabilitation Act as well.

The reader should notice that neither the Rehabilitation Act nor the Americans With Disabilities Act (ADA) requires any employer to hire an unqualified individual. The acts require only the hiring of a handicapped individual who, with reasonable accommodation for his or her handicap, can perform the job at the minimum level of productivity that would be expected of a nonhandicapped individual.

Nor does this act or the ADA prohibit an employer from terminating an employee whose disability does in fact prevent him or her from doing the job. For example, in a 1994 case, a disabled employee was terminated because her disability caused her to frequently miss work without calling in sick. She had an inner ear disorder that caused nausea and vomiting when she traveled, frequently making her so ill on the way to work that she could not continue or even call in. The plaintiff in that case had sued under the Rehabilitation Act, ar-

TABLE 19-3 *Summary of Major Provisions of Rehabilitation Act*

SECTION	POTENTIAL DEFENDANT	PROHIBITED CONDUCT	REQUIRED CONDUCT
501	Federal departments and agencies	Cannot discriminate against otherwise qualified workers because of a handicap.	Prepare and implement an affirmative action plan for hiring and promoting the handicapped.
502	Federal agencies entering into contracts with private employers for property or services and the private employers entering into these contracts	Private party with government contract cannot discriminate against otherwise qualified workers because of a handicap.	Contracts must contain clause requiring private employer to take affirmative action in hiring and promoting the handicapped and to not discriminate against them.
504	Parties who administer programs receiving federal assistance	Discrimination by those administering programs prohibited.	

---

[19]U.S.C. § 706(b).

guing that the Justice Department, her employer, should have reasonably accommodated her disability by allowing her to come in any time between 8 A.M. and noon and restructuring her job to allow others to do her time-sensitive tasks when she was absent. The Supreme Court disagreed, saying that such accommodation would place undue hardship on the department. The Court felt that an essential component of the job was being able to report to work and complete tasks within a reasonable period of time.[20]

THE AMERICANS WITH DISABILITIES ACT OF 1991

In July of 1991, the **Americans With Disabilities Act (ADA)** was passed. This law became fully operational on July 26, 1994, when its coverage expanded to include all employers of 15 or more workers. The purpose of the ADA is to prevent employers from discriminating against employees and applicants with disabilities by requiring employers to make reasonable accommodations to the known physical or mental disabilities of an otherwise qualified person with a disability unless the necessary accommodation would impose an undue burden on the employer's business.

The ADA now covers 660,000 businesses, so its impact has the potential to be significant. From July 26, 1992, when the law became effective, through December 31, 1996, the EPA received 77,388 charges, with 12,390 being resolved with outcomes favorable to the charging party.[21]

COVERED INDIVIDUALS

The definition of an *individual* with a disability, for purposes of the act, is essentially the same as the definition of a handicapped individual in the Rehabilitation Act. A disability is defined as "(1) a physical or mental impairment which substantially limits one or more of the major life activities of such individual, (2) a record of such impairment, or (3) being regarded as having such an impairment."[22] A wide variety of impairments are captured under such a definition. Individuals suffering from diseases such as cancer, epilepsy, and heart disease are included, as are those who are blind or deaf. In 1998, the U.S. Supreme Court held that those who are infected with the human immunodeficiency virus (HIV), but who are not yet symptomatic, are covered.[23] Those whose past records may harm them are also protected. For example, persons who suffer from alcoholism but are not currently drinking or who are former drug addicts are protected. However, an employee who is currently a substance abuser, whose abuse would affect job performance, is not protected.

Employers often find it difficult to know how the Americans With Disabilities Act applies to those who have mental disabilities. During the first year the law was in effect, claims by persons with mental disabilities constituted 11 percent of the total claims under the act, second only to back problems, which constituted 18 percent of the claims. And the number of such claims keeps skyrocketing. During the first nine months of 1996, almost 2,700 such claims were filed with the EEOC, more than were filed in all of 1995.[24]

Under the ADA, employers are not only forbidden from discriminating against persons with mental disabilities but also must make reasonable accommodations for them unless such accommodations could cause undue hardship. Typical accommodations include providing a private office, flexible work schedule, restructured job, or time off for treatment.

The major problems associated with responding to a mental disability are twofold. First, many employers are not sure how to accommodate a mentally disabled person. Second, many people are afraid of mentally disabled people be-

Americans With Disabilities Act of 1991 (ADA) Requires that employers make reasonable accommodations to the known disabilities of an otherwise qualified job applicant or employee with a disability, unless the necessary accommodation would impose an undue burden on the employer's business.

---

[20]Carr v. Reno, 23 F.3d 525 (D.C. Cir. 1994).

[21]P. S. Miller, *The Americans with Disabilities Act in Texas: The EEOC Continuing Efforts in Enforcement,* 34 Houston L. Rev. 777 (1997).

[22]42 U.S.C. 12102 (2).

[23]1998 WL 332958.

[24]S. Bocamazo, *ADA Mental Claims Skyrocket,* Lawyers Weekly USA 1, May 19, 1997.

cause some of them can be dangerous, especially people with mood disorders, who at times have violent tempers. And a firm that employs a worker who deals with the public could be liable in tort to a customer who is injured by a mentally disabled worker. How firms will respond to problems associated with mental disabilities remains to be seen.

Another major difficulty employers face under the ADA is ensuring that they do not violate the law during the interview process. The EEOC issued guidelines to help employers comply with the law. The guidelines emphasize that employers' questions must be designed to focus on whether a potential employee can do the job, not on the disability, but it is often difficult to know when a question violates the act. Exhibit 19-6 provides examples from the EEOC guidelines of acceptable and unacceptable questions.

It is well worth the prudent employer's time to study these guidelines because the liability for violating the "rules for job interviews" can be substantial. In 1995, a job applicant who was asked about his disability during an interview was awarded $15,000 in compensatory damages and $30,000 in punitive damages.[25] The plaintiff was partially disfigured, partially deaf, and partially blind as a result of two brain tumor operations. The plaintiff brought up the disability himself to explain a gap in his work record, but the interviewers told him they felt uncomfortable with his disability and asked him to make them feel more comfortable by describing the condition and its treatment. They also asked whether managers or customers had a problem with him because of his disability.

EXHIBIT 19-6

Interviewing Potential Employees Without Violating ADA

You May Ask
- Can you perform the functions of this job (essential and/or marginal), with or without reasonable accommodations?
- Can you meet the attendance requirements of this job?
- Do you illegally use drugs? Have you used illegal drugs in the past two years?
- Do you have a cold? How did you break your leg?
- How much do you weigh? Do you regularly eat three meals a day?

Do Not Ask
- Do you have a disability that would interfere with your ability to perform the job?
- How many days were you sick last year?
- What prescription drugs are you currently taking?
- Do you have AIDS? Do you have asthma?
- How much alcohol do you drink each week? Have you ever been treated for alcohol problems?

Source: Adapted from EEOC's "Enforcement Guidance on Pre-employment Disability—Related Inquiries and Medical Examinations Under the Americans with Disabilities Act.

[25] EEOC v. Community Coffee Co., No. H-94-1061 (S.D. Texas 1995).

The ADA is enforced by the EEOC in the same way that Title VII is enforced. To bring a successful claim under the ADA, the plaintiff must show that he or she (1) had a disability, (2) was otherwise qualified for the job, and (3) was excluded from the job solely because of that disability.

REMEDIES

Remedies are likewise similar to those available under Title VII. A successful plaintiff may recover reinstatement, back pay, and injunctive relief. In cases of intentional discrimination, limited compensatory and punitive damages are also available. An employer who has repeatedly violated the act may be subject to fines of up to $100,000.

AFFIRMATIVE ACTION

One of the most controversial workplace issues of the past decade has been the legitimacy of **affirmative action plans**. Ever since employers began to try to create balanced workforces by focusing on increasing their employment of minorities, there have been cries that such actions constitute **reverse discrimination**, which is a violation of the equal protection clause of the Fourteenth Amendment.

Many of the significant cases challenging affirmative action plans have arisen in contexts other than private employment. Other areas in which these programs have been challenged include school admissions policies and government policies to set aside contracts for minority businesses. Table 19-4 on page 472 summarizes the major affirmative action cases. A close reading of the cases reveals the increasing scrutiny that the courts have come to apply to affirmative action policies, and it now appears that any affirmative action plan that can withstand constitutional muster must (1) attempt to remedy past discrimination, (2) not use quotas or preferences, and (3) end or change once it has met its goal of remedying past discrimination. This standard was set forth by the Supreme Court in *Adarand Constructors, Inc. v. Pena*, a case challenging a federal affirmative action program (see Table 19-4).

Many interested observers were hopeful that in 1997 the U.S. Supreme Court would hand down a definitive decision regarding affirmative action cases in the employment setting, as the High Court had agreed to hear the case of *Taxman v. Board of Education*. However, the parties settled the case before it went to trial.

affirmative action plans
Programs adopted by employers to increase the representation of women and minorities in their workforces.

reverse discrimination
Discrimination in favor of members of groups that have been previously discriminated against; claim usually raised by white males.

TAXMAN V. BOARD OF EDUCATION OF THE TOWNSHIP OF PISCATAWAY
UNITED STATES COURT OF APPEALS 91 F.3D 1547 (3D CIR. 1996)

Defendant Board of Education of Piscataway Township needed to reduce its faculty by one. New Jersey law strictly circumscribed layoffs, leaving the school board no discretion except in cases in which faculty members had the same seniority. Plaintiff, a white female business teacher, had the same qualifications and was hired on the same day as a black female business teacher. In the past, when there was a tie for seniority, the board had used a random process to determine who would be laid off. In this case, the board decided to use an affirmative action policy as a basis for retaining the black teacher. The policy prohibited discrimination in all aspects of employment, requiring that the most qualified candidates be employed, but when

candidates had equal qualifications, minority candidates were to be recommended.

The district court found in favor of the plaintiff and enjoined the affirmative action plan. Defendant appealed.

CIRCUIT JUDGE MANSMANN

In this Title VII matter, we must determine whether the Board of Education of the Township of Piscataway violated that statute when it made race a factor in selecting which of two equally qualified employees to lay off. Specifically, we must decide whether Title VII permits an employer with a racially balanced work force to grant a non-remedial racial preference in order to promote "racial diversity." It is clear that the language of Title VII is violated when an employer makes an employment decision based upon an employee's race. The Supreme Court determined in *United Steelworkers v. Weber*, however, that Title VII's prohibition against racial discrimination is not violated by affirmative action plans which first, "have purposes that mirror those of the statute" and second, do not "unnecessarily trammel the interests of the [non-minority] employees."

The 1975 document states that the purpose of the Program is "to provide equal educational opportunity for students and equal employment opportunity for employees and prospective employees," and "to make a concentrated effort to attract . . . minority personnel for all positions so that their qualifications can be evaluated along with other candidates."

Asked to articulate the "educational objective" served by retaining Williams rather than Taxman, Kruse stated: "In my own personal perspective I believe by retaining Mrs. Williams it was sending a very clear message that we feel that our staff should be culturally diverse. [T]here is a distinct advantage to students to come into contact with people of different cultures, different backgrounds, so that they are more aware, more tolerant, more accepting, more understanding of [all] people."

[I]n the seminal case of *United Steelworkers v. Weber*, [the Court held] that Title VII's prohibition against racial discrimination does not condemn all voluntary race-conscious affirmative action plans. In *Weber*, the Court considered a plan implemented by Kaiser Aluminum & Chemical Corporation. [W]hile the local labor force was about 39% Black, Kaiser's labor force was less than 15% Black and its crafts workforce was less than 2% black.

The Court upheld the Kaiser plan because its purpose "mirror[ed] those of the statute" and it did not "unnecessarily trammel the interests of the [non-minority] employees": The purposes of the plan mirror those of the statute. Both were designed to break down old patterns of racial segregation and hierarchy. Both were structured to "open employment opportunities for Negroes in occupations which have been traditionally closed to them."

At the same time, the plan does not unnecessarily trammel the interests of the white employees. The plan does not require the discharge of white workers and their replacement with new black hires. Nor does the plan create an absolute bar to the advancement of white employees; half of those trained in the program will be white. Moreover, the plan is a temporary measure; it is not intended to maintain racial balance, but simply to eliminate a manifest racial imbalance.

In 1987, the Supreme Court decided *Johnson v. Transportation Agency*. There, the Santa Clara County Transit District Board of Supervisors implemented an affirmative action plan stating that "'mere prohibition of discriminatory practices [was] not enough to remedy the effects of past discriminatory practices and to permit attainment of an equitable representation of minorities, women and handicapped persons.'" The plan noted that women were represented in numbers far less than their proportion of the available work force in the Agency as a whole. The court of appeals further held that the plan had been adopted "to address a conspicuous imbalance in the Agency's work force, and neither unnecessarily trammeled the rights of other employees, nor created an absolute bar to their advancement." The Supreme Court affirmed.

We analyze Taxman's claim of employment discrimination under the approach set forth in *McDonnell Douglas v. Green*. Once a plaintiff establishes a prima facie case, the burden of production shifts to the employer to show a legitimate nondiscriminatory reason for the decision; an affirmative action plan may be one such reason. When the employer satisfies this requirement, the burden of production shifts back to the employee to show that the asserted nondiscriminatory reason is a pretext and that the affirmative action plan is invalid.

Title VII was enacted to further two primary goals: to end discrimination on the basis of race, color, religion, sex or national origin, thereby guaranteeing equal opportunity in the workplace, and to remedy the segregation and underrepresentation of minorities that discrimination has caused in our Nation's work force. This antidiscriminatory purpose is also reflected in the Act's legislative history.

In *Weber*, the Court carefully catalogued the comments made by the proponents of Title VII which demonstrate the Act's remedial concerns. The significance of this second corrective purpose cannot be overstated. It is only because Title VII was written to eradicate not only discrimination per se but the consequences of prior discrimination as well, that racial preferences in the form of affirmative action can co-exist with the Act's antidiscrimination mandate. Thus, based on our analysis of Title VII's two goals, we are convinced that unless an affirmative action plan has a remedial purpose, it cannot be said to mirror the purposes of the statute, and, therefore, cannot satisfy the first prong of the *Weber* test. The statute on its face provides that race cannot be a factor in employer decisions about hires, promotions, and layoffs.

The Board recognizes that there is no positive legislative history supporting its goal of promoting racial diversity "for education's sake," and concedes that there is no case law approving such a purpose to support an affirmative action plan under Title VII.

In *Johnson*, the Court held that the legality of the Santa Clara County Transportation Agency's plan under Title VII must be guided by the Court's determination in *Weber* that affirmative action is lawful if an employer can point to a "'manifest imbalance . . . in traditionally segregated job categories.'" [T]he Court determined that under the Constitution a public employer's remedial affirmative action initiatives are valid only if crafted to remedy its own past or present discrimination; that is, societal discrimination is an insufficient basis for "imposing discretionary legal remedies against innocent people."

In the plurality's words, affirmative action must be supported by "a factual determination that the employer had a strong basis in evidence for its conclusion that remedial action was necessary." . . . [R]acial classifications in the context of affirmative action must be justified by a compelling state purpose and the means chosen to effectuate that purpose must be narrowly tailored; that societal discrimination alone will not justify a racial classification; that evidence of prior discrimination by an employer must be presented before remedial racial classifications can be employed; and that the "role model" theory proposed by the employer as a basis for race-conscious state action was unacceptable because it would have allowed discriminatory hiring and layoff well beyond the point necessary for any remedial purpose and did not bear any relationship to the harm caused by prior discrimination.

Our analysis of the statute and the case law convinces us that a non-remedial affirmative action plan cannot form the basis for deviating from the antidiscrimination mandate of Title VII. The Board admits that it did not act to remedy the effects of past employment discrimination. The parties have stipulated that neither the Board's adoption of its affirmative action policy nor its subsequent decision to apply it in choosing between Taxman and Williams was intended to remedy the results of any prior discrimination or identified underrepresentation of Blacks within the Piscataway School District's teacher workforce as a whole. Nor does the Board contend that its action here was directed at remedying any de jure or de facto segregation. Even though the Board's race-conscious action was taken to avoid what could have been an all-White faculty within the Business Department, the Board concedes that Blacks are not underrepresented in its teaching workforce as a whole or even in the Piscataway High School. Rather, the Board's sole purpose in applying its affirmative action policy in this case was to obtain an educational benefit which it believed would result from a racially diverse faculty. While the benefits flowing from diversity in the educational context are significant indeed, we are constrained to hold, as did the district court, that inasmuch as "the Board does not even attempt to show that its affirmative action plan was adopted to remedy past discrimination or as the result of a manifest imbalance in the employment of minorities," the Board has failed to satisfy the first prong of the *Weber* test.

We turn next to the second prong of the *Weber* analysis. This second prong requires that we determine whether the Board's policy "unnecessarily trammel[s] . . . [nonminority] interests." Under this requirement, too, the Board's policy is deficient. We begin by noting the policy's utter lack of definition and structure. While it is not for us to decide how much diversity in a high school faculty is "enough," the Board cannot abdicate its responsibility to define "racial diversity" and to determine what degree of racial diversity in the Piscataway School is sufficient.

The affirmative action plans that have met with the Supreme Court's approval under Title VII had objectives, as well as benchmarks which served to evaluate progress, guide the employment decisions at issue and assure the grant of only those minority preferences necessary to further the plans' purpose. By contrast, the Board's policy, devoid of goals and standards, is governed entirely by the Board's whim, leaving the Board free, if it so chooses, to grant racial preferences that do not promote even the policy's claimed purpose. Indeed, under the terms of this policy, the Board, in pursuit of a "racially diverse" work force, could use affirmative action to discriminate against those whom Title VII was enacted to protect. Such a policy unnecessarily trammels the interests of nonminority employees.

Finally, we are convinced that the harm imposed upon a nonminority employee by the loss of his or her job is so substantial and the cost so severe that the Board's goal of racial diversity, even if legitimate under Title VII, may not be pursued in this particular fashion. This is especially true where, as here, the nonminority employee is tenured. In *Weber* and *Johnson*, when considering whether nonminorities were unduly encumbered by affirmative action, the Court found it significant that they retained their employment.

While we have rejected the argument that the Board's non-remedial application of the affirmative action policy is consistent with the language and intent of Title VII, we do not reject in principle the diversity goal articulated by the Board. Indeed, we recognize that the differences among us underlie the richness and strength of our Nation. Our disposition of this matter, however, rests squarely on the foundation of Title VII. Although we applaud the goal of racial diversity, we cannot agree that Title VII permits an employer to advance that goal through non-remedial discriminatory measures.

Affirmed in favor of Plaintiff, Taxman.

Because the parties settled this case when it was on appeal to the U.S. Supreme Court, this area of law is still unsettled.

The EEOC has issued guidelines in an attempt to help employers set up valid affirmative action plans. According to these guidelines, Title VII is *not* violated if (1) the employer determines that there is a reasonable basis for determining that an affirmative action plan is appropriate, and (2) the affirmative action plan is reasonable. Quotas are specifically outlawed by the 1991 Civil Rights Act amendments.

TABLE 19-4 *Major "Reverse Discrimination" Cases*

CASE	ALLEGED DISCRIMINATORY ACTION	OUTCOME
Bakke v. University of California, at Davis Medical School, 438 U.S. 265 (1978)	The school's special admissions policy reserved 16 out of the 100 available seats for minority applicants. Bakke was denied admission while minorities with lower test scores were admitted.	Although race could be one of a number of factors considered by a school in passing on applications, this special admission policy was illegal because a classification that benefits victims of a victimized group at the expense of innocent individuals is constitutional only where proof of past discrimination exists.
United Steelworkers v. Weber, 443 U.S. 193 (1979)	The employer and union enter into a voluntary agreement that half the openings in a skilled craft training program will go to blacks until the rough proportion of blacks in the program is equal to that of blacks in the labor force. A white male who would have been admitted to the training program absent the plan challenged the plan.	Court said it was clear that Congress did not intend to wholly prohibit private and voluntary affirmative action. To be valid, such plans must not unnecessarily trammel the rights of whites, should be temporary in nature, and should be customized to solve the past proven pattern of discrimination.
Johnson v. Santa Clara County Transportation Agency, 480 U.S. 616 (1987)	County affirmative action plan authorized agency to consider applicant's sex as a relevant factor when making promotion decisions for job classifications in which women have traditionally been underrepresented.	Court held that the plan represented a moderate, flexible case-by-case approach to gradually effecting an improvement of the representation of women and minorities in traditionally underrepresented positions. Court emphasized that the agency had identified a conspicuous imbalance in representation; that no slots were set aside for women or minorities; and no quotas were established. Race or sex could just be one of several factors considered.
Adarand Constructors, Inv. v. Pena, 515 U.S. 200 (1995)	Plaintiff submitted the lowest bid for a government contract, but the contract was awarded to a Hispanic firm submitting a higher bid. The job went to the Hispanic firm in accordance with a government program giving 5 percent of all highway construction projects to disadvantaged construction firms.	In a landmark decision, the U.S. Supreme Court held that any federal, state, or local affirmative action program that uses racial or ethnic classifications as a basis for making decisions is subject to strict scrutiny by the courts. This level of scrutiny can be met only when (1) the program attempts to remedy past discrimination, (2) does not use quotas or preferences, and (3) will be ended or changed once it has met its goal of remedying past discrimination.
Hopwood v. State of Texas, 84 U.S. 720 (3d Cir. 1996)	Two white law school applicants were denied admission to the University of Texas Law School because of the school's affirmative action program. That program allowed admissions officials to take racial and other factors into account when admitting students.	The Court of Appeals for the Fifth Circuit held that the program violated the equal protection clause because it discriminated in favor of minorities. The U.S. Supreme Court refused to hear the case.
Taxman v. Board of Education of the Township of Piscataway, 91 F.3d 1547 (3d Cir. 1996)	The Board of Education wanted to eliminate one teaching position at Piscataway High School. A black female and white female had the same seniority and qualifications. Because minority teachers were underrepresented in the school, the board chose to lay off the white teacher to promote racial diversity.	Taxman challenged the policy as violative of Title VII. The trial court granted summary judgment in her favor. The circuit court of appeals affirmed, awarding her complete back pay. The defendants appealed to the U.S. Supreme Court, but the case was settled prior to the hearing before the High Court.

CLAY BENNETT reprinted by permission of United Feature Syndicate, Inc.

INTERNATIONAL DIMENSIONS OF EMPLOYMENT DISCRIMINATION LEGISLATION

With many U.S. firms having operations overseas, the question of the extent to which the United States laws prohibiting discrimination apply to foreign countries naturally arises. The Civil Rights Act of 1991 extended the protections of Title VII and the ADA to U.S. citizens working abroad for U.S. employers. Amendments to the ADEA in 1984 had already extended that act's protection in a similar manner. The provisions of these acts also apply to foreign corporations controlled by a U.S. employer.

It is not always easy to determine whether a multinational corporation will be considered "American" enough to be covered by the acts. According to guidelines issued by the EEOC in October 1993, the EEOC will initially look at where the company is incorporated, but will often have to look to other factors. These other factors must also be considered when the employer is not incorporated, as for example, in the case of an accounting partnership. Some of these additional factors include: the company's principal place of business, the nationality of the controlling shareholders, and the nationality and location of management. No one factor is considered determinative, and the greater the number of factors linking the employer to the United States, the more likely the employer is to be considered "American" for purposes of being covered by Title VII and the ADEA.

In determining whether a foreign corporation is controlled by a U.S. employer, the EEOC will again look at a broad range of factors. Some such factors include the interrelation of operations, common management, centralized labor relations, and common ownership or financial control over the two entities.

However, a corporation that is clearly a foreign corporation and is not controlled by a U.S. entity is not subject to our equal employment laws. An employer may also violate ADA and Title VII if compliance with either law would constitute an illegal action in the foreign country in which the corporation is operating.

Thus, it is important for corporate managers to be familiar with Title VII and the ADA, even when they are going to be working outside the United States.

SUMMARY

During the early years of our nation's history, the employment-at-will doctrine governed the employment relationship. Under this doctrine, an employee without a contract for a set period of time could be fired at any time, for any reason. The doctrine has been gradually eroded, and most states today employ at least one of three exceptions to the employment-at-will doctrine: the public policy exception, the implied contract exception, and implied covenant of good faith and fair dealing exception.

Civil rights laws have also eroded the employer's ability to hire and fire at will. This chapter examined those laws in the order in which they were enacted. The Civil Rights Act of 1866 prohibits employers from discriminating against individuals because of their race.

The Equal Pay Act of 1963 prohibits employers from paying male and female employees doing the same job different wages because of their sex.

Title VII prohibits employers from discriminating in terms and conditions of employment on the basis of race, color, national origin, religion, and sex. This act was amended by the Pregnancy Discrimination Act, which essentially requires employers to not discriminate against pregnancy and to treat pregnancy like any other temporary disability. Title VII was also amended by the Civil Rights Act of 1991, which expanded the remedies available under Title VII.

The Age Discrimination in Employment Act prohibits discrimination based on age against persons aged 40 or over. The act is enforced similarly to the way in which Title VII is enforced.

The Rehabilitation Act requires federal agencies, those who have contracts with the federal government, and those receiving any type of federal funds to not discriminate against persons with handicaps. The Americans With Disabilities Act extended the basic protections of the Rehabilitation Act to private employers, requiring them to reasonably accommodate persons with disabilities.

Employers locating overseas must remember that they can no longer avoid Title VII and the ADEA simply by leaving the country. United States corporations operating in foreign nations, as well as foreign companies controlled by U.S. corporations must follow Title VII requirements.

REVIEW QUESTIONS

19-1. Explain the employment-at-will doctrine and why some people would prefer the abolition of this doctrine whereas others feel saddened by its gradual demise.

19-2. Explain why each of the following sets of jobs would or would not be considered equal under the Equal Pay Act:

a. Male stewards and female stewardesses on continental air flights.

b. Male checkers of narcotics and female checkers of nonnarcotic drugs at a pharmacy.

c. Male tailor and female seamstress.

19-3. Explain the following aspects of the Equal Pay Act:

a. Its purpose.

b. The remedies available under the act.

c. The defenses available to employers.

19-4. Explain the following aspects of Title VII:

a. Its purpose.

b. The remedies available under the act.

c. The defenses available to employers.

19-5. Explain two significant ways that the Civil Rights Act of 1991 has changed the application of Title VII.

19-6. What constitutes "reasonable accommodation" under the Rehabilitation Act and the Americans With Disabilities Act?

19-7. The City of Los Angeles provided equal monthly retirement benefits for men and women of the same age, seniority, and salary. The benefits were partially paid for by employee contributions and partially by employer contributions. Because women, on the average, live longer than men, the city required women to make contributions to the retirement fund that were 14.84 percent higher than those made by men. Was this a violation of the Civil Rights Act?

19-8. JoAnn, Ann, and Bryon were all laboratory analysts, performing standardized chemical tests on various materials. JoAnn was hired first, with no previous experience, and was trained on the job by the supervisor. She later trained Ann. When Bryon was hired, he was trained by the supervisor with the assistance of the two women. All initially worked the same shift and received the same pay. Then Bryon received a five cent per hour raise and was to work a swing shift every other two weeks. Was his higher wage a violation of the Equal Pay Act?

19-9. Administrators of an Ohio Christian school refused to renew a teacher's contract after she had become pregnant on the basis of their belief that "a mother's place is in the home." When she filed sex discrimination charges under the state civil rights statute, she was fired. Was the termination unlawful?

19-10. Ellen's immediate supervisor repeatedly required her to have "closed door" meetings with him, in violation of company policy. As a consequence, rumors began to spread that the two were having an office romance, although the meetings in fact involved her boss's trying to convince her to loan him money, again in violation of company policy. When Ellen asked her immediate supervisor to try to stop the rumors, he said he found them somewhat amusing and refused to do anything to stop them. As a consequence of the rumors, she began to be treated as an "outcast" by her co-workers and received low evaluations from other supervisors in the areas of "integrity" and "interpersonal relations." She was passed over for two promotions for which she had applied. She filed an action against her employer on the grounds that her supervisor had created a hostile environment by his refusal to stop the rumors. Do you believe she has a valid claim under Title VII? Why or why not? Are there any other causes of action she might raise?

19-11. A U.S. citizen was working at a multinational company's Zaire facility. The employer was incorporated in the state of Louisiana. When the employee was terminated, allegedly because of his age, he sought recovery under the federal ADEA and also under the Louisiana Age Discrimination in Employment Law. The employer argued that his overseas operations were not subject to the federal ADEA. Was the employer correct?

19-12. Davis, D'Elea, and Sims were former heroin or narcotics addicts. Davis and Sims were told by the city director that they could not be hired by the city because of their former habit. D'Elea was rejected from a city CETA program because of his former habit. The three sued the city, alleging that drug addiction was a handicap under the Rehabilitation Act of 1973 and that therefore, the city's refusal to hire them was unlawful under this act. Were they correct in their contention?

CASE PROBLEMS

19-13. In 1980, at fourteen years of age, Tyson was placed under the supervision of Cus D'Amato, a renowned boxing figure and manager. When Tyson's mother died in 1983, D'Amato also became his legal guardian. At the beginning of Tyson's boxing career, Rooney and D'Amato agreed that

Rooney would train Tyson without compensation until the fighter became a professional athlete, and when Tyson advanced to professional ranks, Rooney would be Tyson's trainer *"for as long as [Tyson] fought professionally."* Rooney trained Tyson for 28 months without compensation. In March 1985, Tyson turned professional and began enjoying meteoric success. D'Amato died that same year.

James Jacobs became Tyson's manager in 1986. When rumors started in some sports media that Rooney would be replaced as Tyson's trainer, Rooney queried Jacobs. To quell the speculation, Tyson allegedly authorized Jacobs to state publicly that "Kevin Rooney will be Mike Tyson's trainer as long as Mike Tyson is a professional fighter." Jacobs allegedly sent Rooney a copy of a press release to that effect. Thereafter, Rooney continued to train Tyson and was compensated for each of Tyson's professional fights until 1988. In 1988, apparently in connection with Rooney's alleged comments regarding Tyson's divorce and other business-related litigation, Rooney read a newspaper article stating that Tyson would no longer train with Rooney. Tyson formally terminated his boxer-trainer relationship with Rooney later that year.

A federal lawsuit claiming breach of the oral agreement was filed, and the jury returned its verdict in favor of Rooney. Tyson countered after the trial that the agreement was for an indefinite duration and was terminable at will under New York law and therefore unenforceable as a matter of law, regardless of the jury's verdict. The District Trial Court agreed with Tyson's legal position and granted him the post-trial victory. The trial judge concluded that "the alleged term of the employment contract, 'for as long as Tyson boxes professionally,' does not state a term of definite duration as a matter of law," and therefore "the nature of the proof offered at trial cannot sustain a finding that the employment relationship was anything other than one at-will." Rooney appealed.

Why do you believe the appellate court either reversed or affirmed the district court judge's ruling? *Rooney v. Tyson*, 1998 WL 286795 (NY)

19-14. Mardell brought an action against her former employer, alleging that she had been terminated in violation of Title VII and the ADA. In the course of preparing their defense, the employer discovered that Mardell had misrepresented her employment history on her résumé and on her application form when she was hired. They immediately filed a motion to dismiss, alleging that she would never have been hired in the first place had the firm known of these misrepresentations at the time of her employment interview. Was this motion successful? *Nancy Mardell v. Harrleysville Life Insurance Co.*, 31 F.3d 122 (1994)

19-15. The Plaintiff, a store manager of Petite Sophisticates, injured her hand at work, resulting in a 30 percent loss of function of her hand. When she sought to return to work, the store requested a release from her doctor stating that she was capable of returning to work. Her doctor provided a slip saying she could "return as tolerated." When contacted, the doctor said she could return to work, but must be allowed to leave work whenever her subjective level of pain toleration demanded. The employer refused to allow her to return, despite her claim that she could "work through any pain." She sued the employer, arguing that his refusal to rehire her constituted a violation of the ADA. Is she correct? *Carol J. Debris v. United States Shoe Corporation*, 30 A.D. Cases 1029 (1994)

19-16. A 375-pound college professor was fired. She did not regard herself as having difficulty doing her job, but when her contract was renewed, her employer mentioned her inability to get to her office when it snowed and her difficulty in walking during commencement. She was not disabled; on what grounds could she file her action? Do you think she had a legitimate claim under the act? *Nedder v. River College*, No. C-95-116 S.D. (1997)

19-17. An applicant with over 30 years experience was rejected for employment by an insurance company as a loss control representative because he was "overqualified." The insurance company then hired a 28-year-old applicant with no experience. In justifying their selection of the younger man, the company representative explained that they were afraid that with all his experience, he would have become "too involved in uncomplicated risks" and might "consume too much of the insureds' time." The company was concerned that he would simply "delve too deeply into acounts." The applicant, whose age placed him within the protected class of the ADEA, believed that he was unlawfully discriminated against because of his age. How should the circuit court have decided this case? *EEOC v. Insurance Co. of North America*, 49 F.3d 1418 (9th Cir. 1995)

19-18. Fernandez was employed by Wynn Oil Co. and had served in various positions. She was qualified and bid for a position as director of international marketing. She did not get it. She sued, alleging discrimination based on sex. The defendant argued that sex was a bona fide occupational qualification in this case because Latin American customers would be uncomfortable dealing with a woman in that position. Did the court find sex to be a bona fide occupational qualification in this case? *Fernandez v. Wynn Oil Co.*, 20 F.E.P. Cases 1162 (1979)

 On the Internet

http://www.law.cornell.edu/topics/employment_discrimination.html
Here is a page that will give you information about discrimination law, as well as allow you to search for statutes and cases related to employment discrimination.

http://aspe.os.dhhs.gov/96cfda/p30005.htm The objectives of this page are: to assist individuals who have filed a charge with the Equal Employment Opportunity Commission, or on whose behalf a charge has been filed, in contacting members of the private bar; and to provide technical assistance to aggrieved individuals and their attorneys.

http://www.legalshark.com/ This site was created by an attorney who practices discrimination law. She provides a lot of useful legal information.

20

ENVIRONMENTAL LAW

- **ALTERNATIVE APPROACHES TO ENVIRONMENTAL PROTECTION**

- **THE ENVIRONMENTAL PROTECTION AGENCY**

- **THE NATIONAL ENVIRONMENTAL POLICY ACT OF 1970 (NEPA)**

- **REGULATING WATER QUALITY**

- **REGULATING AIR QUALITY**

- **REGULATING HAZARDOUS WASTE AND TOXIC SUBSTANCES**

- **THE POLLUTION PREVENTION ACT OF 1990**

- **INTERNATIONAL DIMENSIONS OF ENVIRONMENTAL REGULATION**

As previous chapters have demonstrated, this country has often turned to the government to solve problems created by business enterprises. Early in the history of our nation, people recognized that certain problems, such as monopolization and labor strife, were national in scope and required a national solution.

Unfortunately, we did not exercise the same degree of foresight in thinking about protecting our physical environment. We looked at our smokestack industries with pride and saw them as symbols of our great productivity and technological advances. People did not fully appreciate that the billowing smoke was making the air less healthful to breathe and that the industrial sewage dumped into rivers was killing or contaminating many forms of aquatic life. The demands placed on nature to serve as a garbage disposal grew ever greater.

Some people eventually started to realize that pollution was a *negative externality*. It was a cost of the product not paid for by the manufacturers in their costs of production or by consumers in the purchase price. Rather, its costs were being imposed on the community as its members were forced to breathe dirty air and to fish in impure water. People who had the misfortune of living in industrialized areas were paying even higher costs than were people in rural areas through pollution-related diseases and discomfort. Not only were these costs being borne by those who did not use or manufacture the products whose production had led to the pollution, but, in many cases, these costs were higher than the cost of preventing the pollution would have been in the first place.

During the late 1960s, environmental problems became a major national concern. This concern resulted in the enactment of numerous pieces of legislation designed to protect the environment and to clean up previously created problems. Before introducing contemporary environmental legislation, this chapter briefly examines a few alternatives to the regulatory approach for solving pollution problems and examines the primary agency responsible for enforcing environmental laws, the Environmental Protection Agency. After discussing the primary direct regulations designed to protect the environment, this chapter examines the Pollution Prevention Act of 1990, an act that has the potential to shift the focus of environmental regulation. Finally, the chapter examines the international dimensions of environmental protection.

Critical Thinking about the Law

Why should you, as a future business manager, be concerned about environmental problems? First, you will need to be aware of environmental legislation that could affect your business. Second, as a citizen, you should be concerned about the quality of the environment for both you and future generations. Therefore, you should familiarize yourself with both environmental problems and legislation proposed as a solution to those problems. Asking the following questions about environmental law can help develop your critical thinking skills.

1. Companies are sometimes hesitant to support environmental regulation because the regulation may lead to higher costs for the business. Although a company might be required by law to comply with environmental regulation, devotion to which ethical norms might influence companies to voluntarily comply with environmental legislation?

   Clue Examine the list of ethical norms. Although compliance might add to a company's costs, what considerations may overrule monetary concerns?

2. You work for a major automobile maker, and you are responsible for monitoring the level of pollutants in the waste produced. If the level of pollutants rises above 75, you are required to contact the Environmental Protection Agency (EPA). One day, the pollutant level is 85; however, your supervisor advises you to correct the problem yourself and to not contact the EPA. You decide to notify the EPA. What ethical norms did you consider in making your decision? How did these norms conflict?

CLUE   Consider the list of ethical norms. What ethical norm seems most successful in convincing you to obey the EPA's regulation?

3. People hold beliefs, or assumptions, about the way the world is. For example, some people do not support environmental laws. They do not support those laws because they believe that it is wasteful to spend money and time on creating laws to protect the environment. Although they will not state so, they believe that there is no environmental problem. Therefore, they do not support environmental regulation. What is ambiguous in such analysis?

CLUE   Is it clear whether a particular event is wasteful or beneficial?

ALTERNATIVE APPROACHES TO ENVIRONMENTAL PROTECTION

TORT LAW

nuisance An unreasonable interference with someone else's use and enjoyment of his land.

Torts, as explained in chapter 11, are injuries to one's person or property. Pollution injures citizens and their property. Our first attempts to regulate pollution were through the use of tort law, in particular, through the use of the tort of **nuisance**. A nuisance is an unreasonable interference with someone else's use and enjoyment of his or her land. If a factory was emitting black particles that settled on a person's property every day, depositing a layer of dirt on everything in the vicinity, that person might bring an action based on nuisance. He or she would be asking the court to enjoin the emission of the particulates. Before the tort of nuisance began being used in attempts to stop pollution, an injunction was always granted when a nuisance was found. Nuisance, therefore would appear to be the perfect solution to the problem of pollution. The following case, however, demonstrates why the tort of nuisance is ineffective as a means of controlling pollution.

BOOMER, ET AL. V. ATLANTIC CEMENT COMPANY

NEW YORK STATE COURT OF APPEALS 257 N.E.2D 870 (1970)

Defendant Atlantic Cement Co. operated a large cement plant that emitted considerable amounts of dirt and smoke into the air. These emissions, combined with vibrations from the plant, caused damage to the plaintiffs, Boomer and other owners of property located close to the plant. The plaintiffs brought a nuisance action against the defendant, seeking an injunction. The trial court ruled in favor of the defendants; it found a nuisance but denied plaintiffs the injunction they sought. The plaintiffs appealed to the intermediate appellate court, and the judgment of the trial court was affirmed in favor of the defendant. Plaintiffs then appealed to the state's highest appellate court.

JUDGE BERGAN

[T]here is now before the court private litigation in which individual property owners have sought specific relief from a single plant operation. The threshold question raised on this appeal is whether the court should resolve the litigation between the parties now before it as equitably as seems possible, or whether, seeking promotion of the general public welfare, it should channel private litigation into broad public objectives.

A court performs its essential function when it decides the rights of parties before it. Its decision of private controversies may sometimes greatly affect public issues. Large questions of law are often resolved by the manner in which private litigation is decided. It is a rare exercise of judicial power to use a decision in private litigation as a purposeful mechanism to achieve direct public objectives greatly beyond the rights and interests before the court.

Effective control of air pollution is a problem presently far from solution even with the full public and financial powers of government. In large measure adequate technical procedures are yet to be developed and some that appear possible may be economically impracticable.

It seems apparent that the amelioration of air pollution will depend on technical research in great depth, on a carefully balanced consideration of the economic impact of close regulation, and on the actual effect on public health. It is likely to require massive public expenditure and to demand more than any local community can accomplish and to depend on regional and interstate controls.

A court should not try to do this on its own as a by-product of private litigation and it seems manifest that the judicial establishment is neither equipped in the limited nature of any judgment it can pronounce nor prepared to lay down and implement an effective policy for the elimination of air pollution. This is an area beyond the circumference of one private lawsuit. It is a direct responsibility for government and should not thus be undertaken as an incident to solving a dispute between property owners and a single cement plant—one of many—in the Hudson River Valley.

The cement making operations of defendant have been found by the Court at Special Term to have damaged the nearby properties of plaintiffs in these two actions. That court accordingly found defendant maintained a nuisance and this has been affirmed at the Appellate Division. The total damage to plaintiffs' properties is, however, relatively small in comparison with the value of defendant's operation and with the consequences of the injunction which plaintiffs seek.

The ground for the denial of injunction, notwithstanding the finding both that there is a nuisance and that plaintiffs have been damaged substantially, is the large disparity in economic consequences of the nuisance and of the injunction. . . .

[T]o grant the injunction unless defendant pays plaintiffs such permanent damages as may be fixed by the court seems to do justice between the contending parties. All of the attributions of economic loss to the properties on which plaintiffs' complaints are based will have been redressed.

The nuisance complained of by these plaintiffs may have other public or private consequences, but these particular parties are the only ones who have sought remedies and the judgment proposed will fully redress them. The limitation of relief granted is a limitation only within the four corners of these actions and does not foreclose public health or other public agencies from seeking proper relief in a proper court.

It seems reasonable to think that the risk of being required to pay permanent damages to injured property owners by cement plant owners would itself be a reasonably effective spur to research for improved techniques to minimize nuisance.

The damage base here suggested is consistent with the general rule in those nuisance cases where damages are allowed. "Where a nuisance is of such a permanent and unabatable character that a single recovery can be had, including the whole damage past and future resulting therefrom, there can be but one recovery." It has been said that permanent damages are allowed where the loss recoverable would obviously be small compared with the cost of removal of the nuisance.

Thus it seems fair to both sides to grant permanent damages to plaintiffs which will terminate this private litigation.

Reversed in favor of Plaintiff, Boomer.

Critical Thinking about the Law

I N THIS CASE, THE NEW YORK COURT OF APPEALS became the third court to find the Atlantic Cement Company guilty of committing a nuisance against the plaintiff Boomer. At the same time, the state's highest court also became the third court not to grant an injunction to halt the cement company's pollution.

At first glance, the finding of the court and its subsequent decision seem to contradict one another. However, a closer look at the case reveals that Judge Bergan, in delivering the decision, qualified when a nuisance warrants an injunction. The questions that follow will help you identify this qualification and determine the primary ethical norm to which such a qualification is tied.

1. To demonstrate your ability to follow legal reasoning, in your own words, run down the court's reasoning for its decision.

   CLUE Do not be too narrow here. You want to identify (1) why the court granted damages to the plaintiff and (2) why the court did not order an injunction.

2. The court argued that granting the plaintiff monetary damages should promote more environmentally friendly practices on the part of businesses, because they would develop technologies to prevent having to pay damages. What assumption was made by the court in this reasoning?

   CLUE Reread the court's reasoning. This assumption is related to the quantitative relationship between the damages imposed on businesses for polluting and the economic benefits of polluting for businesses.

standing The legal status necessary to file a lawsuit.

In *Boomer*, the plaintiffs technically "won" the case because they were granted a greater remedy than the lower courts had granted; they were granted an injunction in the event that the defendant failed to pay permanent damages within a set period of time. However, they did not achieve their objective, which was to eliminate the nuisance through receipt of an injunction, the traditional remedy in a nuisance action. Thus, in *Boomer v. Atlantic Cement Company*, the court decided that before it would apply the traditional nuisance remedy to stop the pollution, it would weigh the harms that would result from the injunction against the benefits. Because of a lack of scientific knowledge, judges at the time did not see the true costs that the polluting behavior was imposing on the community. Thus, a major problem with using nuisance laws to stop pollution is that the courts will not necessarily use their authority to issue an injunction to stop the polluting behavior even when they find that a nuisance exists.

Another problem with using the tort of nuisance as a remedy is **standing**: the legal status necessary to file an action. Under common law, there are two types of nuisances: public and private. A *public nuisance* is one that affects a substantial number of people. A *private nuisance* is one that affects only a limited number of persons, or one that generally affects a large group of persons but causes some special harm to one or a few.

The only person who has standing to bring an action for a public nuisance is a public official, such as the local prosecutor or the state attorney general. Such officials are often reluctant to sue polluting companies because a lawsuit might result in the closing down of that business and, consequently, a reduction in employment and tax revenues in the area.

In most states, only when the nuisance is a private nuisance does an individual plaintiff have standing to sue. Because most nuisances affect a large number of persons, there are many situations in which individuals cannot file an action and the prosecutor will not file one. In this situation, pollution continues unabated. A few states have resolved this problem by passing statutes giving private citizens standing to seek injunctive relief from public nuisances. In most states, however, this problem with tort solutions to environmental problems still exists.

The foregoing reasons amply demonstrate why nuisance actions alone are not sufficient to control pollution. Nuisance actions can be and are used, but they are primarily used as a way for plaintiffs injured by pollution to recover.

NEGLIGENCE, AN ALTERNATIVE TORT SOLUTION   The tort of negligence is also used sometimes in the fight against pollution. Plaintiffs must establish the elements of negligence as described in chapter 11: duty, breach of duty, causation, and damage. Negligence would most often be used in a case in which a defendant's polluting behavior harmed a plaintiff. For example, if a defendant buried hazardous waste in the ground and the waste seeped down into the water table, contaminating the plaintiff's well water and injuring the plaintiff, the plaintiff might bring a negligence action.

Negligence actions involving hazardous materials are often difficult to bring successfully, primarily because many of the pollutants do not cause immediate harm. By the time the harm occurs, it is often difficult to link the damage to the defendant's release of the material, making the element of causation extremely difficult to prove. The availability of defenses such as contributory or comparative negligence, as well as assumption of the risk, help weaken the effectiveness of this tort. It also shares with nuisance the attribute of being reactive rather than preventing pollution in the first place.

The primary method of controlling pollution today is through *direct regulation*, but before we discuss the regulatory approach, some additional alternatives to regulation should be considered. These approaches were proposed before much of the pollution control legislation was enacted, and they are being discussed again as the country attempts to find more efficient ways to protect the environment.

GOVERNMENT SUBSIDIES APPROACH

One such approach is the use of government subsidies. Under a subsidy system, the government pays polluters to reduce their emissions. Some subsidies that could be used are tax breaks, low-interest loans, and grants for the purchase and installation of pollution control devices. The primary problem with this approach is than when a subsidy is for less than 100 percent of the cost, the firm that limits its pollutants must still bear substantial expenses not borne by its competitors.

EMISSION CHARGES APPROACH

Another approach is simply to charge the polluter a flat fee on every unit of pollutant discharged. Each rational polluter would theoretically reduce pollution to the point at which the cost of reducing one more unit of pollutant is greater than the emission fee. The larger the fee for each unit, the greater the motivation of firms to reduce their emissions. Difficulties in monitoring every discharge of the pollutant and in calculating the amount that should be assessed for each unit of the various pollutants are major problems with this approach. A final problem with this approach is that it may amount to licensing a continuing wrong. Some firms might simply pay the charges and continue to emit pollutants that would be difficult to clean up even with the fees collected.

MARKETABLE DISCHARGE PERMITS APPROACH

Discharge permits provide a similar approach to pollution control. The government would sell permits for the discharge of various pollutants. These pollutants could be discharged only if the polluter had the appropriate permit. Polluters would be encouraged to reduce their emissions because this reduction would enable them to sell their permits. This approach is currently being attempted on a limited scale to reduce emissions of one air pollutant, sulfur dioxide (see the discussion of acid rain control later in this chapter).

From the perspective of people wishing to reduce the total amount of pollution emitted into the environment, the primary advantage that this system offers over a system of charges is that the government actually limits the total amount of pollution through the permits; no permits will be issued once a certain amount of emissions has been authorized. To reduce pollution, the government can simply reduce the number of permits that it issues. Again, however, there is the problem of monitoring the pollution sources.

DIRECT REGULATION APPROACH

Direct regulation is the primary device currently used for protecting the environment. During the late 1970s, a comprehensive set of regulations designed to protect the environment and specifically to improve air and water quality were adopted. These regulations set specific limits on the amount of pollutants that could be discharged. One issue that must be determined when direct regulations are going to be used is whether the standards set by the regulations are "technology-forcing" or "technology-driven." So-called **technology-forcing standards** are set primarily on the basis of health considerations, with the assumption that once standards have been established, the industries will be forced to develop the technology to meet the standards.

Technology-driven standards, on the other hand, try to achieve the greatest improvements possible with existing levels of technology. Most of the early environmental regulations in this country were technology-forcing. In some cases, this approach was highly successful, and impressive technological gains were made. In other cases, sufficient technology had not yet been developed, and we were unable to meet some rather lofty goals.

Environmental regulations are enforced primarily by administrative agencies. The judiciary is available as a last resort to ensure that these agencies will fulfill their obligations under the law. Because the administrative agencies are

technology-forcing standards Standards of pollution control set primarily on the basis of health considerations, with the assumption that once regulators have set the standards, industry will be forced to develop the technology to meet them.

technology-driven standards Standards that take account of existing levels of technology and require the best control system possible given the limits of that technology.

Environmental Protection Agency (EPA) The federal agency charged with responsibility for conducting an integrated, coordinated attack on all forms of pollution of the environment.

staffed by presidential appointment, the attitude of the chief executive has a substantial impact on an agency's behavior. Under different administrations, environmental regulations have been enforced with varying degrees of vigor.

The remainder of this chapter focuses primarily on direct regulation as a means of protecting the environment because, despite some minor changes in some of the environmental laws, direct regulation is still the primary means of protecting the environment. We will first examine the Environmental Protection Agency, which has primary responsibility for enforcing the direct regulations.

THE ENVIRONMENTAL PROTECTION AGENCY

Like other areas of administrative law, environmental law is primarily made up of regulations passed by a federal agency operating under the guidance of congressional mandates. The primary agency responsible for passage and enforcement of these regulations is the **Environmental Protection Agency (EPA)**.

The EPA is the largest federal agency, having over 17,000 employees in the year 1998. The agency was created by executive order in 1972 to mount an integrated, coordinated attack on pollution in the areas of air, water, solid waste, pesticides, radiation, and toxic substances—a rather substantial mandate for any agency! The reason for placing control of all types of environmental problems within one agency was to ensure that the attack on pollution would be integrated. In other words, Congress wanted to be certain that we would not have a regulation reducing air pollution that simply led to increased water pollution. Unfortunately, such integration did not occur. Within the agency, as Exhibit 20-1 reveals, separate offices were established for each of the areas of pollution, and there was very little interaction among them.

Recognizing the inefficiency of the EPA's organizational structure, in July 1993, EPA Administrator Carol Browner took one of the first major steps toward trying to make the agency one with a truly integrated focus. She announced her decision to move all enforcement actions from the various program offices into one main enforcement office. Environmentalists applauded this change because it would make multipronged enforcement routine, rather than extraordinary.

In October 1993, she carried out her plan by establishing an Office of Compliance, which has as its primary focus "providing industry with coherent information about compliance requirements." The office is divided into groups of regulators who will focus on separate sectors of the economy: energy and transportation, agriculture, and manufacturing. She also created a new Office of Regulatory Enforcement, which was established to take on the tough responsibility of deciding which polluters would be taken to court.[1]

One area of special concern to business managers, especially since 1990, has been the EPA's use of criminal sanctions, including incarceration, to enforce environmental laws. These cases are not actually tried by the EPA but are passed on by the EPA to the Justice Department with a recommendation for prosecution.

Criminal enforcement continues to be the fastest-growing component of the EPA's enforcement program. For example, in 1996, the EPA referred 262 criminal cases to the Department of Justice, as compared with the previous all-time high of 256 referred during 1995. During 1996, defendants were sentenced to a total of 1,160 months of jail time, as compared with 860 months the previous year. More than $76,660,670 in criminal fines and restitution were handed down in 1996, as compared with $23 million in 1995. The total of all criminal and civil fines during 1996 was $172.8 million, the highest in history.[2] Thus, compliance with environmental standards is clearly an area of importance to the business manager.

In 1994, the agency issued a policy statement to guide its special agents in their enforcement activities. Under this policy, the agents are to look for "sig-

---

[1]P. Wallach and D. Levin, *Using Government's Guidance to Structure Compliance Plan*, Nat'l L.J., August 30, 1993, at S.10.
[2]Office of Enforcement and Compliance Assurance, <http://es.epa.gov/oeca/>.

EXHIBIT 20-1 *U.S. Environmental Protection Agency*

U.S. Environmental Protection Agency

Office of the
Administrator/Deputy Administrator

Staff Offices

Executive Support
Executive Secretariat
Science Advisory Board
Cooperative Environmental Management
Office of Children's Health Protection

Administrative Law Judges
Civil Rights
Office of Reinvention
Small and Disadvantaged Business Utilization

Associate Administrators for

Regional Operations and State Local Relations
Congressional and Legislative Affairs
Communications and Public Affairs

Inspector General

Office of Audits
Office of Investigations
Office of Management and Technical Assessment

Assistant Administrator for International Activities

Office of International and Environmental Policy
Office of Management Operations
Office of Technology Cooperation and Assistance
Office of Western Hemisphere and Bilateral Affairs

Office of Chief Financial Officer

Office of Planning, Analysis and Accountability
Office of the Comptroller

Assistant Administrator for Enforcement and Compliance Assurance

Enforcement Capacity and Outreach Office
Office of Environmental Justice
Office of Planning and Policy Analysis
Federal Facilities Enforcement Office
Office of Compliance
Office of Criminal Enforcement, Forensics, and Training
Office of Federal Activities
Office of Regulatory Enforcement
Office of Site Remediation Enforcement

General Counsel

Air and Radiation Division
Grants, Contract, and General Law Division
Inspector General Division
International Activities Division
Pesticides and Toxic Substances Division
Solid Waste and Emergency Response Division
Water Division

Assistant Administrator for Policy, Planning and Evaluation

Office of Pollution Prevention
Office of Policy Analysis
Office of Regulatory Management and Evaluation

Assistant Administrator for Research and Development

Office of Research Program Management
Office of Technology Transfer and Regulatory Support
Office of Exploratory Research
Office of Health Research
Office of Environmental Process and Effects Research
Office of Environmental Engineering and Technology Demonstration
Office of Health and Environmental Assessment
Office of Modeling, Monitoring Systems and Quality Assurance

Assistant Administrator for Water

Policy and Resources Management Office
Office of Ground Water and Drinking Water
Office of Science and Technology
Office of Waste Water Enforcement and Compliance
Office of Wetlands, Oceans, and Watersheds

Assistant Administrator for Solid Waste and Emergency Response

Chemical Emergency Preparedness and Prevention Office
Technology Innovation Office
Office of Emergency and Remedial Response (Superfund)
Office of Solid Waste
Office of Underground Storage Tanks
Office of Waste Programs Enforcement

Assistant Administrator for Air and Radiation

Office of Program Management Operations
Office of Policy Analysis and Review
Office of Atmospheric and Indoor Air Programs
Office of Air Quality Planning and Standards (Research Triangle Park, NC)
Office of Mobile Sources
Office of Radiation Programs

Assistant Administrator for Prevention, Pesticides and Toxic Substances

Office of Program Management Operators
Office of Pesticide Programs
Office of Pollution Prevention and Toxics

Region 1
Boston

Region 2
New York

Region 3
Philadelphia

Region 4
Atlanta

Region 5
Chicago

Region 6
Dallas

Region 7
Kansas City

Region 8
Denver

Region 9
San Francisco

Region 10
Seattle

EXHIBIT 20-2 *Elements of a Successful Environmental Self-Auditing Program*

> Explicit senior management support for environmental auditing and the willingness to follow up on the findings.
>
> An environmental auditing function independent of audited activities.
>
> Adequate auditor training and staffing.
>
> Explicit audit program, objectives, scope, resources, and frequency.
>
> A process that collects, analyzes, interprets, and documents information sufficient to achieve audit objectives.
>
> A process that includes specific procedures to promptly prepare candid, clear, and appropriate written reports on audit findings, corrective actions, and schedules for implementation.
>
> A process that includes quality assurance procedures to verify the accuracy and thoroughness of such audits.

nificant environmental harm" and "culpable conduct." The first criterion is fairly straightforward, meaning that there has been actual environmental harm or a threat of significant harm. To satisfy the second criterion, the EPA will look for a "history of repeated violations," "concealment of misconduct," or "falsification of required records," "tampering with monitoring or control equipment," and "failing to obtain required licenses or permits."[3]

By issuing this policy, the EPA is trying to put firms on notice as to when their conduct is clearly unacceptable and may make them subject to criminal liability. The policy also reflects the intent of the EPA to target the worst violators and make examples of them, hoping that such prosecutions will have a deterrent effect.

A complementary policy issued in 1995, the Final Policy on Penalty Reductions,[4] encourages firms to engage in environmental self-auditing. If a firm can demonstrate that it discovered a violation and moved to correct it, the EPA will seek to reduce the penalty for the violation. Thus, the policy offers a significant benefit to firms that are trying to comply with the laws. Of course, the firm that engages in a self-audit, discovers a violation, and chooses to not change the harmful practice is setting itself up to be a candidate for a criminal prosecution. See Exhibit 20-2 for the elements of a successful environmental self-auditing program.

THE NATIONAL ENVIRONMENTAL POLICY ACT OF 1970 (NEPA)

One of the first major environmental laws passed in this nation set forth our country's policy for protecting the environment. This act, the *National Environmental Policy Act of 1970 (NEPA)*, has been regarded by many as the country's most influential piece of environmental legislation.

IMPLEMENTING THE NATIONAL ENVIRONMENTAL POLICY ACT

The National Environmental Policy Act is viewed as an extremely powerful piece of legislation because its primary purpose and effect has been to reform the process by which regulatory agencies make decisions. Title II of the act requires the preparation of an **Environmental Impact Statement (EIS)** for every major legislative proposal or agency action that would have a significant impact on the quality of the human environment. A substantial number of these statements are filed every year, over which a significant amount of litigation results.

Environmental Impact Statement (EIS) A statement that must be prepared for every major federal activity that would significantly affect the quality of the human environment.

---

[3]E. Devaney, *The Exercise of Investigative Discretion* (Washington D.C.: American Law Institute, 1995).
[4]60 Fed. Reg. No. 246 (December 22, 1995).

THRESHOLD CONSIDERATIONS   As the proceeding paragraph indicates, an EIS is required when three elements are present. First, the action in question must be *federal*, such as the grant of a license, the making of a loan, or the lease of property by a federal agency. Second, the proposed activity must be *major*, that is, requiring a substantial commitment of resources. Finally, the proposed activity must have a *significant impact* on the human environment.

CONTENT OF THE EIS   Once an agency has determined that an EIS is necessary, it must gather the information necessary to prepare the document. The NEPA requires that the EIS include a detailed statement of:

1. The environmental impact of the proposed action;
2. Any adverse environmental effects that cannot be avoided should the proposal be implemented;
3. Alternatives to the proposed action;
4. The relationship between local short-term uses of the human environment and the maintenance and enhancement of long-term productivity; and
5. Any irreversible and irretrievable commitments of resources that would be involved in the proposed activity should it be implemented.

A continuing problem under the act, however, is interpreting what is meant by environmental impacts. Clearly, they extend beyond the effects on the natural environment and in some cases have been held to include noise, increased traffic and congestion, the overburdening of public facilities such as sewage and mass transportation systems, increased crime, increased availability of illegal drugs, and in a small number of cases, damage to the psychological health of those affected by the agency action. Other cases, however, have not allowed all such damages. The loss of business profits resulting from a proposed agency action has not been considered an environmental impact.

One of the more controversial potential impacts is the impact of the proposed action on the psychological health of members of the community. The issue of whether such an impact must be included in an EIS was addressed in the following case.

METROPOLITAN EDISON COMPANY V. PEOPLE AGAINST NUCLEAR ENERGY
UNITED STATES SUPREME COURT 103 S.CT. 1556 (1983)

After the near disaster at Three Mile Island nuclear plant, the Metropolitan Edison Co. petitioned the Nuclear Regulatory Commission to resume operations of the TMI-1 nuclear reactor. Plaintiff People Against Nuclear Energy (PANE), an association of residents living near the nuclear plant, sought to enjoin the operation on the grounds that the EIS was insufficient because it failed to include a discussion of whether the risk of an another accident at TMI-1 might cause psychological harm to the residents. PANE believed that restarting TMI-1 would cause severe psychological risks to persons living in the area and severe damage to the stability, cohesiveness, and well-being of neighboring communities. The circuit court of appeals found in favor of PANE. Metropolitan appealed to the U.S. Supreme Court.

JUSTICE REHNQUIST

All the parties agree that effects on human health can be cognizable under NEPA, and that human health may include psychological health. The Court of Appeals thought these propositions were enough to complete a syllogism that disposes of the case: NEPA requires agencies to consider effects on health. An effect on psychological health is an effect on health. Therefore, NEPA requires agencies to consider the effects on psychological health asserted by PANE.

NEPA does not require the agency to assess every impact or effect of its proposed action, but only the impact or effect on the environment. If we were to seize the word "environmental" out of its context and give it the broadest possible definition, the words "adverse environmental effects" might embrace virtually any consequence of a governmental action that someone thought "adverse." But we think the context of the statute shows that Congress was talking about the physical environment—the world around us, so to speak. NEPA was designed to promote human welfare by alerting governmental actors to the effect of their proposed actions on the physical environment.

Some effects that are "caused by" a change in the physical environment in the sense of "but for" causation, will nonetheless not fall within 102 because the causal chain is too attenuated. For example, residents of the Harrisburg area have relatives in other parts of the country. Renewed operation of TMI-1 may well cause psychological health problems for these people. They may suffer "anxiety, tension and fear, a sense of helplessness," and accompanying physical disorders because of the risk that their relatives may be harmed in a nuclear accident. However, this harm is simply too remote from the physical environment to justify requiring the NRC to evaluate the psychological health damage to these people that may be caused by renewed operation of TMI-1.

Our understanding of the congressional concerns that led to the enactment of NEPA suggests that the terms "environmental effect" and "environmental impact" in 102 be read to include a requirement of a reasonably close causal relationship between a change in the physical environment and the effect at issue. This requirement is like the familiar doctrine of proximate cause from tort law.

PANE argues that the psychological health damage it alleges "will flow directly from the risk of [a nuclear] accident." But a risk of an accident is not an effect on the physical environment. A risk is, by definition, unrealized in the physical world. In a causal chain from renewed operation of TMI-1 to psychological health damage, the element of risk and its perception by PANE's members are necessary middle links. We believe that the element of risk lengthens the causal chain beyond the reach of NEPA.

It is difficult for us to see the differences between someone who dislikes a government decision so much that he suffers anxiety and stress, someone who fears the effects of that decision so much that he suffers similar anxiety and stress, and someone who suffers anxiety and stress that "flow directly" from the risks associated with the same decision. It would be extraordinarily difficult for agencies to differentiate between "genuine" claims of psychological health damage and claims that are grounded solely in disagreement with a democratically adopted policy. Until Congress provides a more explicit statutory instruction than NEPA now contains, we do not think agencies are obliged to undertake the inquiry.

Reversed in favor of Defendant, Metropolitan Edison.

Critical Thinking about the Law

WHEN JUDGES ENCOUNTER SIGNIFICANT AMBIGUITY IN statutory language, their subsequent interpretation is an important element of their reasoning. As we have discussed previously, such interpretation is influenced by primary ethical norms.

This case provides a good illustration of significant ambiguity whose interpretation has a significant, if not determinative, bearing on the Court's decision. Consequently, the questions that follow will focus on this part of the Court's reasoning with an emphasis on the impact of primary ethical norms.

1. What significant ambiguity did the Court confront in this case?

   CLUE Reread the section in which the Court discussed the statutory language relevant to the case.

2. How did the Court's interpretation of this ambiguity affect the plaintiff's claim?

   CLUE Reread the paragraph in which the Court directly addressed PANE's claim.

Another problem regarding the scope of the EIS pertains to the requirement of a detailed statement of alternatives to the proposed actions. What alternatives must be discussed, and how detailed must the discussion be? In general, any reasonable alternatives, including taking no action, must be discussed. The more likely the alternative is to be implemented, the more detailed the statement must be.

EFFECTIVENESS OF THE EIS PROCESS The EIS requirement has clearly changed the *process* of agency decision making, but many wonder whether the requirement has improved the quality of the decision making.

Now that the reader is familiar with this umbrella environmental act, we will examine some of the specific laws designed to protect various aspects of the environment. The focus will initially be on protecting the quality of the water.

REGULATING WATER QUALITY

Water pollution is controlled today primarily by two pieces of legislation: the *Federal Water Pollution Control Act* (FWPCA; also called the Clean Water Act) and the *Safe Drinking Water Act*. The first concentrates on the quality of water in our waterways; the second ensures that the water we drink is not harmful to our health. (Some people say that the former law protects the environment from humans, while the latter protects humans from the environment!)

Ohio's Cuyahoga River was so polluted that it actually caught on fire in 1969; the cleanup of that river is one of the many success stories of the Clean Water Act.

THE FEDERAL WATER POLLUTION CONTROL ACT

When Congress passed the 1972 amendments to the FWPCA, it established two goals: (1) "fishable" and "swimmable" waters by 1983 and (2) the total elimination of pollutant discharges into navigable waters by 1985. These goals were to be achieved through a system of permits and effluent discharge limitations. Obviously, these goals were not attained. Many argue that no one really expected their attainment. However, they set a high goal toward which we could aspire.

POINT-SOURCE EFFLUENT LIMITATIONS One of the primary tools for meeting the goals of the 1972 FWPCA amendments was the establishment and enforcement of point-source effluent limitations. **Point sources** are distinct places from which pollutants can be discharged into water. Factories, refineries, and sewage treatment facilities are a few examples of point sources. *Effluents* are the outflows from a specific source. **Effluent limitations**, therefore, are the maximum allowable amounts of pollutants that can be discharged from a source within a given time period. Different limitations were established for different pollutants.

Under the National Pollutant Discharge Elimination System (NPDES), every point source that discharges pollutants must obtain a discharge permit from the EPA or from the state if the state has an EPA-approved plan at least as strict as the federal standards. The permits specify the types and amounts of effluent discharges allowed. The discharger is required to continually monitor its discharges and report any excess discharges to either the state or federal EPA. Dis-

point sources Distinct places from which pollutants are discharged into water, such as papermills, electric utility plants, sewage treatment facilites, and factories.

effluent limitations Maximum allowable amounts of pollutants that can be discharged from a point source within a given time period.

charges without a permit or in amounts in excess of those allowed by the permit may result in the imposition of criminal penalties. Enforcement of the act is left primarily to the states where there is an approved program for regulation. However, the act provides for federal monitoring, inspection, and enforcement. Citizens may also bring suit to enforce the effluent limits.

Permissible discharge limits under the discharge system are based on technological standards. Most sources today must use the Best Available Control Technology, or BACT. All new sources must meet this standard, but some existing facilities are allowed to meet a slightly lower standard, Best Practicable Control Technology, BPCT. The EPA issues regulations explaining which equipment meets these standards.

THE SAFE DRINKING WATER ACT

The FWPCA ensures that the waterways are clean, but "clean" does not necessarily mean "fit to drink." The Safe Drinking Water Act (SDWA) therefore sets standards for drinking water supplied by a public water supply system. A public water supply system is defined by the SDWA as a water supply system that has at least 15 service connections or serves 25 or more persons.

The SDWA requires the EPA to establish two levels of drinking water standards for potential drinking water contaminants. *Primary standards* are to protect human health, and secondary standards are to protect the aesthetic quality of drinking water.

Primary standards are based on maximum contaminant level goals (MCLGs) and maximum contaminant levels (MCLs) for all contaminants that had the potential to have an adverse effect on human health. MCLGs are the levels at which there are no potential adverse health effects. These are unenforceable, health-based goals. They are the high standards to which we aspire. The MCLs are the enforceable standards. They are developed from the MCLGs but also take into account the feasibility and cost of meeting the standard. By 1991, the EPA was to have set MCLs for 108 of the hundreds of contaminants found in our drinking water, and MCLs for 25 more contaminants every three years thereafter. These goals were not met, and the 1996 amendments to the SDWA gave the EPA more flexibility in setting standards so that the agency could focus on first setting standards for the contaminants that posed the greatest potential health hazards. As the reader might guess, keeping up with the ever-increasing MCLs is a difficult task for public drinking water suppliers. Monitoring these systems is also a chore. Most states do monthly monitoring. Violations may be punished by administrative fines or orders. The 1996 amendments also imposed a "right to know" provision, requiring drinking water suppliers to provide every household with annual reports on water contaminants and the health problems they may cause.

REGULATING AIR QUALITY

A second major environmental concern is protecting the quality of the air. To that end, Congress enacted the Clean Air Act in 1970. Although air quality continues to improve, approximately 46 million Americans in 1996 lived in areas that did not meet the ambient air quality standards for at least one of six major conventional air pollutants: carbon monoxide, lead, nitrogen oxides, suspended particulates, ozone, and sulfur dioxide.[5]

Table 20-1 illustrates some of the most common health problems caused by these pollutants. In addition to these enumerated health problems, nitrogen oxides and sulfur dioxide contribute to the formation of acid rain, which defaces buildings and causes the pH levels of lakes to reach such low levels that most plants and animals can no longer survive in them. These pollutants, frequently referred to as *criteria pollutants*, have been regulated primarily through national air quality standards.

---

[5]42 USC § 7410 (1998).

TABLE 20-1 *Air Pollutants and Associated Health Problems*

POLLUTANT	ASSOCIATED PROBLEMS
Carbon monoxide	Angina, impaired vision, poor coordination, lack of alertness
Lead	Neurological system and kidney damage
Nitrogen oxides	Lung and respiratory tract damage
Ozone	Eye irritation, increased nasal congestion, reduction of lung function, reduced resistance to infection
Suspended particulates	Reduced resistance to infection; eye, ear, and throat irritation
Sulfur dioxide	Lung and respiratory tract damage

THE NATIONAL AMBIENT AIR QUALITY STANDARDS (NAAQSs)

The **national ambient air quality standards** (NAAQSs) provide the focal point for air pollution control. The administrator of the EPA establishes primary and secondary NAAQSs for criteria pollutants. *Primary standards* are those that the administrator determines are necessary to protect the public health, including an adequate margin of safety. *Secondary standards* are more stringent, as they are the standards that would protect the public welfare (crops, building, and animals) from any known or anticipated adverse affect associated with the air pollutant for which the standard is being established. Currently, the primary and secondary standards are the same for all criteria pollutants except sulfer dioxide. The administrator of the EPA retains the authority to establish new primary and secondary standards if scientific evidence indicates that the present standards are inadequate or that such standards must be set for currently unregulated pollutants.

Once each NAAQS is established, each state has nine months to establish a **state implementation plan (SIP)** that explains how the state is going to ensure that the pollutants in the air within a state's boundaries will be kept from exceeding the NAAQSs. Under the state SIPs, primary NAAQSs must be achieved within three years of their creation, and secondary standards are to be met within a reasonable time. The administrator of the EPA has to approve all SIPs. When a SIP is found inadequate, the administrator has the power to amend it or send it back to the state for revision.

In the 1990 Clean Air Act Amendments, Congress specifically addressed those areas of the country that had not yet met the NAAQSs, the so-called *nonattainment areas*. Such areas are classified in five categories ranging from "marginal" to "extreme," depending on how far out of compliance they are. New deadlines for meeting the primary standard for ozone were set ranging from 5 to 20 years. Nonattainment areas also must establish or upgrade vehicle inspection and maintenance programs.

In addition to establishing the NAAQSs, the EPA administration is also required to determine national, uniform emission standards for new motor vehicles, as well as for new and major expansions of existing stationary sources of pollutants. The standards for the new stationary sources are to reflect the best available control technology, taking into account the costs of compliance. The initial emission standards for automobiles and new stationary sources, like the NAAQSs, were not all met within the original timetables. Many of the deadlines were simply extended. In the 1990 amendments to the Clean Air Act, Congress imposed additional requirements on the automakers, mandating the use of tailpipe emissions-reduction equipment on newly manufactured vehicles, for example. In nonattainment areas, reformulated, cleaner gasolines were required beginning in 1995.

PREVENTION OF SIGNIFICANT DETERIORATION

One problem that arose under the Clean Air Act of 1970, and was subsequently addressed by the 1977 amendments, was how to establish standards for areas where the air was already cleaner than the 1970 act required. Congress commit-

national ambient air quality standards (NAAQSs) A two-tiered set of standards developed for the chief conventional air pollutants: primary standards, designed to protect public health; and secondary standards designed to protect public welfare.

state implementation plan (SIP) A plan, required of every state, that explains how the state will meet federal air pollution standards.

ted the country to the principle of the *prevention of significant deterioration (PSD)* in air quality. Under this principle, every area that had met the NAAQSs was originally designated Class I or II. A third classification, Class III, is now available on request of the governor.

The amount of deterioration of air quality allowable in the area now depends on an area's class designation. Class I areas include primarily national parks and wilderness areas. Very little deterioration is allowed in these areas. All other areas that had met the NAAQSs were originally designated Class II. Moderate increases in concentrations of pollutants are allowed in these areas. Degradation down to the secondary NAAQSs is *not* allowed in Class II areas.

Larger increases in pollutant concentration are allowed in Class III areas to provide for industrial development. However, even in Class III regions, the increased concentrations may not be so significant that the air quality no longer meets the NAAQSs. Before a new source of pollution can be constructed in any of these PSD areas, the firm must receive a permit, ensuring that the best available technology will be used in the new facility.

HAZARDOUS AIR POLLUTANTS

The conventional air pollutants discussed above can be emitted into the air in somewhat substantial quantities without posing a significant risk to human health or the environment. Other air pollutants, however, may pose a significant risk to human health when even very tiny amounts are emitted. These pollutants, which are likely to cause an increase in mortality or in serious, irreversible illness, are referred to as hazardous or toxic air pollutants.

Under the 1990 Amendments to the Clean Air Act, Congress identified 189 of these hazardous air pollutants, including asbestos, benzene, mercury, and vinyl chloride, and mandated that their emissions be reduced by 90 percent by the year 2000. This goal is to be met by requiring industries to use pollution control equipment that meets the maximum achievable control technology, or MACT, standard. The EPA publishes guidelines as to what equipment meets this standard.

INDOOR AIR POLLUTION

The Clear Air Act addressed primarily the outdoor air quality problems. In recent years, however, we have come to realize that the quality of the air inside the structures where people live and work has a significant impact on their health. Because Americans spend roughly 90 percent of their time indoors, indoor air quality is an important issue.

sick building syndrome
Indoor air pollution caused by the absence of fresh air in overly insulated new buildings and by the emission of harmful substances found in many building materials and office furnishings.

The major indoor air quality issue that has recently arisen is the **sick building syndrome**. During the 1970s, buildings were made as airtight as possible for purposes of saving energy; substantial insulation was used, and windows were sealed. Consequently, building occupants became completely dependent upon artificial heating and cooling systems for airflow and circulation. If filters are not properly cleaned and maintained, fungi, bacteria, and viruses can thrive, accumulate, and circulate in the building, having a detrimental impact on the health of the occupants.

A related problem is that many building materials, office furnishings, and carpets emit harmful substances, including pesticides, upon installation. In a well-sealed building, these substances may be concentrated for up to a year. The EPA estimates that 90 percent of people's exposure to pesticides may be through indoor exposure.[6]

Despite the costs to human health, the Clean Air Act does not address indoor air quality. The OSHA does have some air quality regulations for workplaces; however, no agency seriously addresses the residential threat, except that the EPA tries to publicize the potential problem (Exhibit 20-3).

---

[6]L. Wallace, *The Team Studies*, 19 E.P.A.J. 24 (Oct./Dec. 1993).

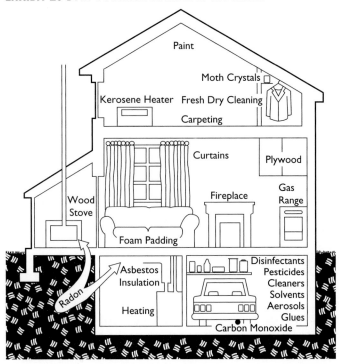

Source: U.S. Environmental Protection Agency, *Environmental Progress and Challenges: EPA's Update* (Washington, D.C.: U.S. Government Printing Office, 1988), p. 32.

THE ACID RAIN CONTROL PROGRAM

One of the major air quality problems facing the United States, as well as other countries, is **acid rain**. Roughly 75 percent of acid rain is caused by emissions of sulfur dioxide and nitrogen oxide from the burning of fossil fuels by electric utilities. The 1990 Clean Air Act Amendments included an innovative approach to controlling the sulfur dioxide emissions.

Under the 1990 Clean Air Act Amendments, Congress required the EPA to establish an emissions trading program that would cut the emissions of sulfur dioxide in half by the year 2000. Under the program, the EPA would auction a given number of sulfur dioxide allowances each year. A holder could emit one ton of sulfur dioxide for each allowance. Firms holding the allowances would be able to use the allowance to emit pollutants, "bank" their allowances for the next year, or sell their allowances to other firms. The purpose of the program is to reduce total emissions in the most efficient way possible. Those firms for whom emission reduction is the cheapest will reduce their emissions extensively, whereas those for whom emission reduction is extremely expensive will find it more efficient to buy allowances. Total emissions will fall because every succeeding year the number of allowances issued will be reduced, but the firms actually reducing their emissions will be the ones whose emissions can be reduced at the lowest cost.

On March 29, 1993, the first auction of EPA pollution allowances was held. More than 150,000 allowances were sold, with each allowance permitting the emission of one ton of sulfur dioxide. Prices for each allowance ranged from $122 to $450. Utilities were given a fixed amount of allowances and could bid for others at the auction. Some environmental groups also participated in the auction, buying allowances that they would retire unused to help clean the air.

By 1995, after three years of the program's operation, many observers were surprised that the price of the allowances had fallen to less than $140 per ton. Given the low price of allowances, it would have been cheaper for many firms to buy allowances, but many chose instead to install costly pollution control

acid rain Precipitation with a high acidic content (pH level of less than 5) caused by atmospheric pollutants.

equipment or to switch to less-polluting fuel. It is too early to tell whether this program will be successful in the long run, but many see it as being a model for achieving cost-effective pollution reduction.

REGULATING HAZARDOUS WASTE AND TOXIC SUBSTANCES

When people think about pollution, they often think of air and water pollution, yet the land can be polluted too, often with tragic results. Perhaps the most dramatic of such instances was the Love Canal incident.

In 1978, state officials ordered the emergency evacuation of 240 families from the Love Canal area of Niagara Falls, New York. This residential area had been built over the site of a Hooker Chemical Company dump that contained more than 300 million tons of industrial waste. The extremely high incidences of asthma, urinary tract disease, miscarriages, and birth defects among the residents were attributed to exposure to the waste.

Most of us want to enjoy the products that technology has developed. But what price are we willing to pay for these amenities? Most of us do not wish to pay the price paid by the former residents of Love Canal. Nor would any of us want to be the businessperson whose decisions were partially responsible for such a tragedy.

Until the mid-1970s, most people were content to take advantage of newly available products without giving much thought to the by-products resulting from their manufacture. Most businesspersons were primarily concerned about creating new products and using new technology to increase production and profits. Then came a growing awareness of the potential health and environmental risks posed by the waste created in the production process. In addition to the problems created by the waste, some of the new products themselves, and their newly created chemical components, were proving to be harmful.

The potential health risks from these chemicals and wastes include a plethora of cancers, respiratory ailments, skin diseases, and birth defects. Environmental risks include not only pollution of the air and water but also unexpected explosions and soil contamination. Species of plants and animals may be threatened with extinction.

During the mid-1970s, Congress began to take a closer look at regulating waste and toxic materials. One of the problems regulators face in this area, however, is a lack of scientific knowledge concerning the impact of many chemicals on human health. We know that exposure to many chemicals causes cancer in laboratory animals. We are unable, however, to ascertain the impact of each increment of exposure. For example, we know that saccharin in some quantity can cause cancer in humans, but we do not know what quantity or whether especially sensitive persons may be affected by substantially smaller amounts. Congress has responded to these and related problems in a variety of ways.

Four primary acts are designed to control hazardous waste and toxic substances: (1) the Resource Conservation and Recovery Act of 1976 (RCRA); (2) the Comprehensive Environmental Response, Compensation, and Liability Act of 1980 (CERCLA); (3) the Toxic Substances Control Act of 1979 (TSCA), and (4) the Federal Insecticide, Fungicide, and Rodenticide Act of 1972 (FIFRA).

THE RESOURCE CONSERVATION AND RECOVERY ACT OF 1976 (RCRA)

The Resource Conservation and Recovery Act regulates both hazardous and non-hazardous waste, with the primary emphasis on controlling hazardous waste. The focus of the act is on the treatment, storage, and disposal of **hazardous waste**. (Exhibit 20-4 defines *hazardous waste*.) The reason for this focus was the belief that it was not necessarily the creation of waste that was the problem but rather the improper disposal of such waste. Also, it was hoped that making firms pay the true costs of safe disposal would provide the financial incentive for them to generate less waste.

hazardous waste Any waste material that is ignitable, corrosive, reactive, or toxic when ingested or absorbed.

According to the Resource Conservation and Recovery Act of 1976 (RCRA) and the Hazardous and Solid Waste Amendments of 1984 (RCRA amendments), a hazardous waste may be "garbage, refuse, or sludge or any other waste material" that exhibits one or more of the following characteristics:

Ignitability

Corrosivity

Reactivity (unstable under normal conditions and capable of posing dangers)

Toxicity (harmful or fatal when ingested or absorbed)

Improperly handled, hazardous wastes can contaminate surface waters and groundwater, release toxic vapors into the air, or cause other dangerous situations, such as explosions.

Source: Council on Environmental Quality, *Environmental Quality*, January 1993, p. 126.

THE MANIFEST PROGRAM The best-known component of the RCRA is its **manifest program**, which is designed to provide "cradle to grave" regulation of hazardous waste. A waste may be considered hazardous, and thus fall under the manifest program, in one of three ways. First, it may be listed by the EPA as a hazardous waste. Second, the generator may choose to designate the waste as hazardous. Finally, according to the RCRA, a hazardous waste may be "garbage, refuse, or sludge or any other waste material that has any one of the four defining characteristics: ignitability, corrosivity, reactivity, or toxicity.

Once a waste is designated as hazardous, it falls under RCRA's manifest program. Under this program, generators of hazardous waste must maintain records called *manifests*. These manifests list the amount and type of waste produced, how it is to be transported, and how it will ultimately be disposed of. Some wastes cannot be disposed of in landfills at all. Others must receive chemical or biological treatment to reduce toxicity or to stabilize them before they can be landfilled. If the waste is transported to a landfill, both the transporter and the owner of the disposal site must certify their respective sections of the manifest and return it to the creator of the waste. The purpose of these manifests is to provide a record of the location and amount of all hazardous wastes and to ensure that such waste will be properly transported and disposed of. Exhibit 20-5 shows the hazardous waste manifest trail.

All firms involved in the transportation and disposal of hazardous waste must be certified by the EPA in accordance with standards established under RCRA. Because of the stringency of these standards, only one hazardous waste landfill has been licensed since 1980.

RCRA AMENDMENTS OF 1984 AND 1986 Congress amended RCRA in 1984 and 1986. The primary effect of the amendments was to make landfills, or hazardous waste dumps, a last resort for the disposal of many types of waste. Advanced treatment, recycling, incineration, and other forms of hazardous waste treatment are all assumed to be preferable to land disposal. Some wastes were banned from landfill disposal after 1988.

ENFORCEMENT OF RCRA RCRA is enforced by the EPA. However, states may set up their own programs as long as these programs are at least as stringent as the federal program. The EPA gives any state that has taken the responsibility for regulating its hazardous wastes the first opportunity to prosecute violators. This procedure is consistent with the EPA's enforcement of other environmental laws.

If the state fails to act within 30 days, the EPA takes action to enforce the state's requirements. The EPA may issue informal warnings; seek temporary or permanent injunctions, criminal penalties of up to $50,000 per day of violation, or civil penalties of up to $25,000 per violation, or both; or announce other penalties that the EPA administrator finds appropriate.

manifest program A program that attempts to see that hazardous wastes are properly transported to disposal facilities licensed by the EPA so that the agency will have an accurate record (manifest) of the location and amount of all hazardous wastes.

EXHIBIT 20-5

A one-page manifest must accompany every waste shipment. The resulting paper trail documents the waste's progress through treatment, storage, and disposal. A missing form alerts the generator to investigate, which may mean calling in the state agency or the EPA.

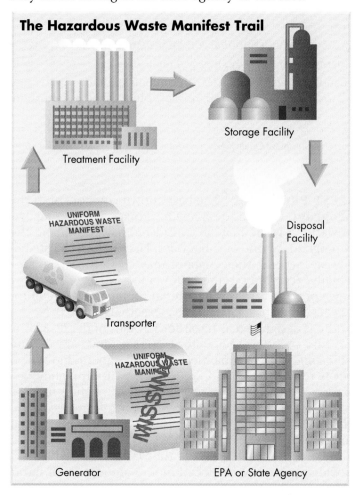

The Hazardous Waste Manifest Trail

Treatment Facility

Storage Facility

UNIFORM HAZARDOUS WASTE MANIFEST

Disposal Facility

Transporter

UNIFORM HAZARDOUS WASTE MANIFEST

MISSING

Generator

EPA or State Agency

Source: Environmental Programs and Challenges: EPA Updates (EPA, August 1988), p. 88.

THE COMPREHENSIVE ENVIRONMENTAL RESPONSE, COMPENSATION, AND LIABILITY ACT OF 1980 (CERCLA), AS AMENDED BY THE SUPERFUND AMENDMENT AND REAUTHORIZATION ACT OF 1986 (SARA)

If the manifest program is followed, waste will be disposed of properly and there will be no more incidents like Love Canal. But before RCRA was enacted there was extensive unregulated dumping. Something needed to be done to take care of cleaning up the sites created by improper disposal. Exhibit 20-6 shows some of the risks posed by these sites.

   To alleviate the problems created by improper waste disposal, CERCLA authorized the creation of the **Superfund**, primarily from taxes on corporations in industries that create significant amounts of hazardous waste. The money in Superfund is then used by the EPA or state and local governments to cover the cost of cleaning up leaks from hazardous waste disposal sites when their owners cannot be located or are unable or unwilling to pay for a cleanup. Superfund also provides money for emergency responses to hazardous waste spills other than oil spills. When an owner is found after a cleanup, or was initially unwilling to pay, the EPA may sue to recover the costs of the cleanup. Under CERCLA,

Superfund A fund authorized by the CERCLA to cover the costs of cleaning up hazardous waste disposal sites whose owners cannot be found or are unwilling or unable to pay for the cleanup.

EXHIBIT 20-6 *Environmental or Public Health Threats Requiring Superfund Emergency Actions*

Source: Office of Emergency and Remedial Response (Superfund), U.S. EPA, reprinted in *Environmental Programs and Challenges: EPA Updates,* (EPA, August 1988), p. 96.

liability for cleanup extends beyond the immediate owner. So-called *potentially responsible parties,* who may be held liable include (1) present owners or operators of a facility where hazardous materials are stored, (2) owners or operators at the time the waste was deposited there, (3) the hazardous waste generators, and (4) those who transported hazardous waste to the site.

Successful actions under the CERCLA to recover costs have been less frequent than originally hoped. The fund was originally intended to be self-replenishing but was not successful in that regard. The CERCLA was amended in late 1986 by the Superfund Amendment and Reauthorization Act of 1986 (SARA). These amendments provide more-stringent cleanup requirements and increased Superfund's funding to $8.5 billion, to be generated primarily by taxes on petroleum, chemical feedstocks, imported chemical derivatives, and a new "environmental tax" on corporations. Additional money will come from general revenues, recoveries, and interest.

Further reauthorization of the Superfund has been proposed every year since 1994 in an attempt to change some of the cleanup procedures to make the act more efficient. Congress, however, has been unable to agree on reauthorization legislation, so the debate arises anew every year.

THE TOXIC SUBSTANCES CONTROL ACT OF 1979 (TSCA)

Toxic substances are found not only as by-products in hazardous waste but also as integral parts of some products that we use every day. Neither RCRA nor CERCLA regulates these substances. The Toxic Substances Control Act (TSCA) attempts to fill this regulatory gap. It attempts to ensure that the least amount of damage will be done to human health and the environment while allowing the greatest possible use of these substances.

toxic substance Any chemical or mixture whose manufacture, processing, distribution, use, or disposal presents an unreasonable risk of harm to human health or the environment.

The term **toxic substances** has not been clearly defined by Congress. However, by reviewing the types of substances regulated under TSCA, one would probably conclude that a toxic substance is any chemical or mixture whose manufacture, processing, distribution, use, or disposal may present an unreasonable risk of harm to human health or the environment. That is a broad definition and encompasses a large number of substances. Thus, control of these substances is a major undertaking.

The primary impact of TSCA comes from its procedure for evaluating the environmental impact of all chemicals, except those regulated under other acts such as the Food, Drug, and Cosmetics Act. Under TSCA, every manufacturer of a new chemical must give the EPA a premanufacturing notice (PMN) at least 90 days before the first use of the substance in commerce. The PMN contains data and test results showing the risk posed by the chemical. The EPA then determines whether the substance presents an unreasonable risk to health or whether further testing is required to establish the substance's safety. The manufacture of the product is banned when the risk of harm is unacceptable. If more testing is required, a manufacturer of the product must wait until the tests have been satisfactorily completed. Otherwise, manufacturing may begin as scheduled.

THE FEDERAL INSECTICIDE, FUNGICIDE, AND RODENTICIDE ACT OF 1972 (FIFRA)

One category of toxic substances that has been singled out for special regulatory treatment is pesticides. **Pesticides** are defined as substances designed to prevent, destroy, repel, or mitigate any pest or to be used as a plant regulator or a defoliant. Insecticides, fungicides, and rodenticides are all forms of pesticides. Pesticides are obviously highly important to us. Their use results in increased crop yields. Some pesticides kill disease-carrying insects. Others eradicate pests, such as mosquitoes, that simply cause us discomfort. Yet many pesticides have harmful side effects. Pesticides may cause damage to all species of life. When a pesticide does not degrade quickly, it may be consumed along with the crops on which it was used, potentially resulting in damage to the consumer's health. The pesticide may get washed into a stream to contaminate aquatic life and animals who drink from that stream. Once the pesticide gets into the food chain, it may do inestimable harm.

pesticide Any substance designed to prevent, destroy, repel, or mitigate any pest or to be used as a plant regulator or defoliant.

In 1972, FIFRA created the registration system that is used to control pesticide use. In order for a pesticide to be sold in the United States, it must be registered and properly labeled. A pesticide will be registered when (1) its composition warrants the claims made for it; (2) its label complies with the act; and (3) the manufacturer provides data to demonstrate that the pesticide can perform its intended function, when in accordance with commonly accepted practice, without presenting unreasonable risks to human health or the environment.

A pesticide will receive *general use registration* if it can be sold without any restrictions. A *restricted use registration* will be granted if the pesticide will not cause an unreasonable risk only if its use is restricted in some manner. Typical restrictions would include allowing the pesticide to be used only by certified applicators or allowing it to be sold only during certain times of the year or only in certain regions of the country or only in certain quantities.

Registration is good for five years, at which time the manufacturer must apply for a new registration. If, at any time prior to the end of the registration period, the EPA obtains evidence that a pesticide poses a risk to human health or the environment, the agency may institute proceedings to cancel or suspend the registration.

The EPA believes that progress under FIFRA has been significant, although there are critics of the act. Since FIFRA's enactment, 34 pesticide registrations have been canceled and about 60 toxic chemicals have been eliminated from use as active ingredients in pesticides.[7] The following case illustrates the controversy that can arise when a pesticide's registration is canceled.

[7]N. Kubasek and G. Silverman, *Environmental Law* (Prentice Hall, 1990). p. 180.

ENVIRONMENTAL DEFENSE FUND, INC., AND NATIONAL AUDUBON SOCIETY, PETITIONERS, V. ENVIRONMENTAL PROTECTION AGENCY AND RUSSELL E. TRAIN, ADMINISTRATOR

UNITED STATES COURT OF APPEALS 510 F.2D 1292 (D.C. CIR. 1992)

The EPA administrator issued an order suspending the registration of pesticides aldrin and dieldrin on October 1, 1974. The EPA allowed the sale of existing stocks manufactured prior to August 2, 1974, the date Shell Chemical Co. was notified of the EPA intention to suspend the registration. Petitioners Environmental Defense Fund and National Audubon Society challenged the part of the order allowing the continued use and sale of the existing stock of pesticides. Shell Co., the manufacturer of the pesticides, challenged the suspension of the registration.

CIRCUIT JUDGE LEVENTHAL.

On August 2, 1974, the Administrator issued a notice of intent to suspend on the ground that evidence developed since December 1972 indicated that the continued use of aldrin/dieldrin presented an "imminent hazard" to the public. Shell and USDA requested a public hearing on the suspension question.

Turning first to the broad question of validity raised by cases like this, the court concludes: The EPA's order is a rational exercise of discretion, rather than arbitrary agency action. It is supported by the reasoning of the agency, and by substantial evidence in the record.

The primary challenge raised by Shell goes to the adequacy of the evidentiary basis of the EPA's finding that aldrin/dieldrin presents "an imminent hazard [to man] during the time required for cancellation."

We have cautioned that the term "imminent hazard" is not limited to a concept of crisis: "It is enough if there is substantial likelihood that serious harm will be experienced during the year or two required in any realistic projection of the administrative process." "FIFRA confers broad discretion" on the Administrator to find facts and "to set policy in the public interest." It does not require the Administrator to establish that the product is unsafe, but places "(t)he burden of establishing the safety of a product requisite for compliance with the labeling requirements at all times on the applicant and registrant."

The Administrator concluded that aldrin/dieldrin presented an "imminent hazard" to man on the basis of data indicating that it is carcinogenic in five strains of mice and, as corroboration, indications that "there is a strong probability that Aldrin-Dieldrin is a carcinogen in rats as well as mice."

Shell attacks the Administrator's reliance on mice data on the ground that the inadequacy of present knowledge regarding cancer and the difficulty of extrapolating from mice to men render his decision speculative.

The Administrator's failure to determine a threshold level of exposure to aldrin/dieldrin does not render his determination improper, for he has concluded that the concept of a threshold exposure level has no practical significance where carcinogens are concerned. This is due in part to the irreversibility and long latency period of carcinogens.

The administrator cited the data he interpreted as indicating a strong probability that aldrin/dieldrin is a carcinogen in rats. The rat data was derived from three tests, two by the FDA and one confirmatory test from Shell's Tunstall laboratories. At least six witnesses reviewing these studies found a carcinogenic effect or a strong probability of one.

The record supports the EPA's finding of "substantial likelihood" that serious harm will result from the uses defended by Shell.

EPA's conclusion that the prohibition of the predominant use would reduce the likelihood of increased exposure is not unreasonable. It is supported by the evidence of record as follows: Aldrin/dieldrin are highly mobile and persistent chemicals that are not lost by dilution in the inorganic components of the environment. The pesticides persist in the soil for several years, where they are absorbed by the roots and transported to the aerial parts of crops, such as soybeans, which are rotated with corn. Many of these products are important feed components for animals. The pesticide residues are thus incorporated, directly and indirectly, into the milk, meat, poultry, and soy products consumed by humans.

Shell, FCM and the USDA further challenge the Administrator's finding that the benefits derived from the suspended uses of aldrin/dieldrin do not outweigh the harms done.

The responsibility to demonstrate that the benefits outweigh the risks is upon the proponents of continued registration. The statute places a heavy burden on any administrative officer to explain the basis for his decision to permit the continued use of a chemical known to produce cancer in experimental animals.

EDF charges that the EPA's decision to exempt the sale and use of existing stocks of aldrin/dieldrin from the general suspension is arbitrary and capricious. EPA has responded that this decision was based on an assumption that no appreciable and realistically retrievable stocks existed at the time of the order. EPA counsel have informed us that EPA was presented in January 1975 with estimates that approximately 5 percent of the total 1974 amount of aldrin granules will be available for use in 1975, and that EPA intends to investigate the matter further, an ongoing re-evaluation that is entirely appropriate.

We affirm the agency's suspension order of October 1, 1974, except for the exemption of the sale and use of existing stocks.

Affirmed in favor of Respondents, EPA and Rusell E. Train, Administrator

PESTICIDE TOLERANCES IN FOOD   Under the Federal Food, Drug, and Cosmetic Act (FFDCA), the EPA establishes legally permissible maximum amounts of pesticide residues in processed food or on animal products such as meat or milk, as well as on food or crops such as apples or tomatoes. Before a pesticide can be registered, an applicant must obtain a tolerance for that pesticide. To obtain the tolerance, the applicant must provide evidence of the level of residue likely to result and data to establish safe residue levels. Under the 1996 Food Quality Protection Act, a safe residue level is one at which there is a "reasonable certainty of no harm" from exposure to the pesticide. The law also requires distribution of a brochure on the health effects of pesticides.

THE POLLUTION PREVENTION ACT OF 1990

By now the reader is familiar with the basic provisions of our primary laws designed to reduce the harmful effects of pollution. Tremendous gains have been made under these laws. However, after 20 years of implementing these controls, it has become more costly to get increasingly smaller reductions of pollutants. Whereas initially a $1 million expenditure on end-pipe controls might have reduced emissions by 80 percent, today that same investment is likely to result in only a 5 percent reduction.

Recognition of this decline in the effectiveness of direct regulation and the consequent need to look for alternative approaches to pollution problems led to passage of the Pollution Prevention Act of 1990, in which Congress set forth the following policy:

> *Pollution should be prevented or reduced at the source whenever feasible; pollution that cannot be prevented should be recycled in an environmentally safe manner, whenever feasible; pollution that cannot be prevented or recycled should be treated in an environmentally safe manner whenever feasible; and disposal or other release into the environment should be employed only as a last resort and should be conducted in an environmentally safe manner.*

The role of the government in encouraging this policy is one of providing a "carrot" as opposed to the "stick" of direct end-pipe regulations. The federal government is providing states matching funds under the act for programs to promote the use of source reduction techniques for business. A clearinghouse has been established to compile the data generated by the grants and to serve as a center for source reduction technology transfer.

Despite the voluntary nature of actions under this act, pollution prevention is becoming an important concept in business today. Chemical companies, for example, are beginning to see waste as avoidable and inefficient and are looking for ways to change their production processes to reduce the amount of waste they create.

Examples abound of firms that are joining the pollution prevention bandwagon. For example, at one DuPont plant that annually generated 110 million pounds of waste, engineers adjusted their production process to use less of one raw material and slashed their waste by two-thirds, with a resulting savings from the new process of $1 million a year.[8] The 3M Corporation claims to have saved over a half a billion dollars in the first 10 years of its voluntary "pollution prevention pays" or "PPP Program."[9]

Whatever the cause of this new emphasis on pollution prevention—whether it is the increasing cost of waste disposal, a fear of stricter direct regulations, public pressure for firms to be more "greener", or the federal government's new emphasis on pollution prevention—firms are changing their attitudes toward the environment. Whether this trend toward voluntary source reduction will continue remains to be seen. Certainly there is every indication that it will.

---

[8]S. McMurray, *Chemical Firms Find That It Pays to Reduce Pollution at the Source*, Wall St. J., June 11, 1991, at A1, col. 6.

[9]American Assembly of Collegiate Schools of Business, *Squeezing in Environmental Management*, 22 Newline, no. 2 (winter 1992), at 11–16.

INTERNATIONAL DIMENSIONS
OF ENVIRONMENTAL REGULATION

THE NEED FOR INTERNATIONAL COOPERATION

In most areas of regulation, the United States first enacted national legislation and only later, if at all, considered the worldwide implications of the problem that the law was enacted to resolve. This tendency was not the case with environmental regulation. In fact, the first major piece of environmental legislation, NEPA, addressed the global nature of environmental problems. The act instructed the federal government to

> *Recognize the worldwide and long-range character of environmental problems and, where consistent with the foreign policy of the United Sates, lend appropriate support to initiatives, resolutions, and programs designed to maximize international cooperation in anticipating and preventing a decline in the quality of mankind's world environment.*

THE TRANSNATIONAL NATURE OF POLLUTION

International cooperation on environmental matters is essential because environmental problems do not respect national borders. There are three primary means by which environmental problems originating in one area of the globe affect other areas: (1) movement of air in prevailing wind patterns; (2) movement of water through ocean currents; and (3) active and passive migration of numerous species of plants and animals.

Scientists have discovered that air tends to circulate within one of three regional areas, or belts, that circle the globe north and south of the equator. For example, between the latitudes 30° and 60° north (N) of the equator, the prevailing air currents are the westerly winds. Thus, the air between these latitudes circulates in a westerly direction all around the globe, remaining primarily within those latitudes.

The United States and China both have much of their land masses within these two latitudes. As a result, pollutants emitted into the air in the United States may be carried by these westerly winds to China, just as pollutants emitted into the air anywhere between 30°N and 60°N of the equator anywhere in the world may ultimately end up in the air above the United States. Consequently, the United States could have extremely strict air pollution laws, yet still have polluted air as a result of other countries' emissions. Likewise, our failure to enact adequate air pollution control laws can adversely affect air quality in other countries. Canada, for instance, attributes some of its pollution problems to the United States' failure to enact stricter control on sulfur dioxide emissions.

A similar situation exists with respect to the flow of water, except that the regions are not as clearly defined. All ocean currents ultimately connect with one another, so a pollutant discharged into any body of water that flows into an ocean may end up having a negative impact on water quality hundreds of miles away from the country in which it was dumped.

The migration of plants and animals also spread pollutants. Many animals, such as geese, whales, salmon, seals, and whooping cranes, travel across national borders seasonally. If an animal ingests a hazardous chemical in one country, travels to another country, and is eaten by an animal in that country, that pollutant has now been inserted into the food web in the second country.

THE GLOBAL COMMONS

Another closely related reason that international cooperation on environmental matters is necessary is that many of the planet's resources, such as the oceans, are within no country's borders and are therefore available for everyone's use. For this reason, these resources are often called the *global commons*. Because everyone has access to them, they are susceptible to exploitation and overuse. Cooperation to protect these global resources is the only way to preserve them.

PRIMARY RESPONSES OF THE UNITED STATES

The United States has played a role in establishing global environmental policies in four primary ways: (1) research, (2) conferences, (3) treaties, and (4) economic aid. It is important to recognize that these responses have not been extremely successful, nor has there been a major commitment of U.S. resources to the resolution of transnational environmental problems.

RESEARCH Research, the results of which are shared with other nations, is our typical response to international environmental issues. For example, in response to international concerns about changes in environmental conditions, the United States government sponsors research, in universities and in federal laboratories, by various governmental agencies. Some critics argue that we need to commit more money to research. Others claim that we use research as an excuse for not acting. Many environmentalists view a "commitment to research" as a stalling technique to prevent the imposition of needed controls. These environmentalists point out that conclusive scientific evidence on many matters is not likely to be available before irreparable harm has been done.

CONFERENCES Countries often have conferences to discuss specific transnational environmental problems. Many are arranged through the United Nations. The first such conference was the United Nations Conference on the Human Environment, held in Stockholm in 1972. The most recent was held June 1 through June 12, 1992, when delegates from over 120 nations met in Rio de Janeiro for the United Nations Conference on Environment and Development, commonly referred to as the Rio Summit. These conferences serve primarily to promote an understanding of the global implications of environmental problems. Often these conferences lead to the negotiation of treaties designed to help resolve environmental problems. For example, one of the agreements to come out of the Rio Summit was an agreement to reduce greenhouse gases. A subsequent summit was held in Kyto, Japan, in 1998 to try to work out a more precise treaty with specific time tables and an agreement that would be accepted by all nations that attended the meeting.

TREATIES Treaties are written agreements between two or more nations that specify how particular issues are to be resolved. The process of accepting a treaty varies from country to country. In the United States, a treaty must be negotiated and signed by a representative of the executive branch, generally the president. Then it must be approved by two-thirds of the U.S. Senate. A treaty's implementation then generally requires the passage of federal legislation that translates the objectives of the treaty into laws.

The United States has entered into numerous bilateral (signed by only two nations) and multilateral (signed by more than two nations) treaties, sometimes called conventions, in this area. One of the more successful multilateral treaties the United States has signed is the Montreal Protocol. Originally signed by 24 nations and the European Community on September 16, 1987, the Montreal Protocol on Substances That Deplete the Ozone layer ultimately led to an elimination of the production of ozone depleting chlorflourocarbons (CFCs) by January 1, 1996. A series of summits concerning the problem of ozone depletion have taken place since that initial meeting, and nations continue to amend the treaty to restrict production of more ozone destroying compounds as our understanding of these chemicals grows.

One of the problems with treaties, however, is that they are unenforceable when the signatories decide no longer to obey them. Many include clauses that allow a nation to withdraw from a contract or to cease abiding by particular terms after giving notice of its intent to the other parties to the treaty.

More recently, trade agreements have started to incorporate provisions regarding environmental protection. The North American Free Trade Agreement (NAFTA), for example, included a side agreement on the environment. Although it has been called the most environmentally sensitive trade agreement ever, there is concern that this agreement may ultimately result in a lessening of environmental protection.

In the preamble to NAFTA, the treaty does cite "sustainable development" as a goal. However, there are no specific provisions to ensure attainment of, or even progress toward, that goal. In the body of the agreement, parties have the right to establish a level of environmental protection each deems appropriate, as long as it is based on a "legitimate" objective. The ambiguity of the term *objective* causes concern for some environmentalists.

AID A final way in which the United States affects environmental policy transnationally is by the judicious use of foreign aid, either financing pollution control projects or giving economic aid for a particular project only when certain environmentally sound conditions have been met. Some aid is also given in the form of technical assistance and training. For example, the U.S. Soil Conservation Service (SCS) provides technical assistance in soil and water conservation to many Latin American and African countries. The SCS also teaches conservation techniques to students from these countries.

As the foregoing demonstrates, environmental problems are not simply a national affair. They are global in nature, and cooperation will be needed to alleviate them.

SUMMARY

There are many ways a nation can protect its environment. Some of these methods include tort law, subsidies, discharge permits, emission charges, and direct regulation. Beginning in 1970, with the passage of the National Environmental Policy Act (NEPA), our nation began a course of environmental protection based primarily on specific direct regulations.

The Federal Water Pollution Control Act established a discharge permit system designed to make the waterways fishable and swimmable. The Safe Drinking Water Act sets standards to make our drinking water safe. The Clean Air Act, as amended several times, establishes the National Ambient Air Quality Standards, standards designed to ensure that conventional air pollutants do not pose a risk to human health or the environment. This act also establishes standards for toxic air pollutants.

Hazardous wastes and toxic substances are primarily regulated by four pieces of legislation. The Resource Conversation and Recovery Act sets standards for waste disposal sites and established the manifest system for the tracking of hazardous wastes from creation to disposal. CERCLA, as amended by SARA, provides funding and a mechanism for cleaning up hazardous waste sites. The Toxic Substances Control Act provides a mechanism for testing new chemicals to ensure that they do not pose unreasonable risks before being used in commerce. Finally, FIFRA establishes a procedure for the regulation of pesticides through a registration system.

The newest trend in the environmental area is toward pollution prevention. This trend is encouraged by the Pollution Prevention Control Act of 1990.

Despite the comprehensive system of environmental laws that we have created, solving environmental problems requires cooperation among all nations. Four ways the United States tries to work to solve these problems on a global scare are through shared research, conferences, treaties, and aid.

REVIEW QUESTIONS

20-1. Explain the common law methods of resolving pollution problems, and evaluate their effectiveness.

20-2. Explain the circumstances under which an environmental impact statement must be filed, and describe the statement's required content.

20-3. Explain how emission charges and discharge permits could be used to help control pollution.

20-4. Present the arguments of those who would abolish the use of the EIS. How would you evaluate those criticisms?

20-5. Describe the structure of the amended Federal Water Pollution Control Act, and explain how each element of the act is designed to further the goals of the FWPCA.

20-6. Compare the structure of the FWPCA with that of the Clear Air Act.

REVIEW PROBLEMS

20-7. The defendant operated a mining company. Because of improper drainage techniques used by the defendant, drainage of pollutants from his mining operation contaminated the private water supplies of the plaintiff property owners located downstream from him. What legal theories would the plaintiffs use to sue the defendant? Would the plaintiffs be likely to win their lawsuit? Why or why not?

20-8. The lead industry challenged the EPA's establishment of a primary air quality standard for lead that incorporated an "adequate margin of safety." In setting the standard, the EPA had not considered the feasibility or the cost of meeting the standards. Must the EPA take such factors into consideration in setting primary air quality standards?

20-9. Ohio's SIP was submitted to the EPA. Approval of a portion of the plan was denied because it was not adequate to ensure the attainment and maintenance of the primary standard for photochemical oxidants in the Cincinnati area. The EPA supplemented the Ohio plan with a provision requiring a vehicle inspection and registration procedure for the Cincinnati area. Cincinnati set up the requisite inspection facilities but refused to withhold registration from those vehicles failing the inspection. The EPA sought an injunction ordering Ohio to implement "as written" the inspection and registration procedure described in the plan. Was the injunction granted?

20-10. The Idaho EPA, in developing its SIP, determined that the maximum sulfur dioxide emissions that could be captured from zinc smelters with the currently available technology was 72 percent. The state consequently adopted that standard for zinc smelters under the SIP. The federal EPA refused to accept that part of the SIP and promulgated an 82 percent standard. Did the federal EPA have authority to make such a change in the SIP?

20-11. Kantrell Corporation uses about 50 gallons a day of a highly corrosive acid as a cleaning agent in its production process. It collects the used acid and funnels it through a pipe out into a pond located entirely on company property that was dug to serve as a place in which to dispose of the acid and other wastes that could not be incinerated or recycled. Is Kantrell violating any federal environmental regulations?

20-12. The defendant operated a plant that had refined coal tar for 55 years. It had disposed of its wastes on the site. After the plant closed, the land was purchased by a municipal housing authority. The wastes buried on the site leaked into the groundwater, contaminating the drinking water of nearby cities. The state and the municipalities spent considerable sums of money cleaning up the site. The U.S. government joined the suit, seeking to hold the defendant liable under the CERCLA. Was the defendant responsible even though he no longer owned the dump site?

CASE PROBLEMS

20-13. Plaintiffs owned a piece of property on which they had a house and restaurant. Nearby was a Texaco Service Station. One evening, plaintiffs noticed the strong smell of gasoline in the basement of their restaurant. When fire officials investigated, they closed the restaurant because of the danger posed by the gasoline fumes. The fumes remained, and plaintiffs eventually sued the owner of the Texaco Station for trespass, negligence, and nuisance. Do you believe they were entitled to damages under any of those theories? *French v. Ralph Moore, Inc.*, 661 P.2d 844 (Mont. 1983)

20-14. Santa Fe Land Improvement Company sold some land to the city of Richmond. Richmond hired Ferry to excavate and grade a portion of the land for a proposed housing project. Ferry dug up soil containing hazardous chemicals and spread the contaminated soil over the property. Once the contamination was discovered, the city sought contribution from the excavator as a potentially responsible party under CERCLA. Was the excavator found to be a potentially responsible party? Why or why not? *Kaise Aluminum v. Catellus Dev.* 976 F.2d 1338 (1992)

20-15. A manufacturer sent waste containing only traces of hazardous metals to New York City landfills. When the city sought to enjoin him as a potentially responsible party, he argued that he should not be held responsible because he contributed such a minuscule amount of hazardous material to the site. Evaluate the quality of the manufacturer's argument. *New York City v. Exxon Corp.*, 744 F. Supp. 474 (S.D.N.Y. 1990)

20-16. Gratz was president of Lannett Company, which owned Astrochem, Inc. Gratz was notified by the town in which Astrochem was located and the landlord of the Astrochem property that chemicals left at Astrochem when it ceased operations were hazardous and needed to be removed immediately. He solicited bids for the removal of the waste but decided instead to move the barrels of chemicals to the property of Lannett Company and store them there. He eventually had Lannett employees flush them down a storm drain. Were any of Lannetts' actions violative of any federal environmental protection laws? *United States v. Gratz*, 39 E.R.C. 1469 (1994)

20-17. NEPCO manufactured a disinfectant at its Verona plant that produced hazardous by-products. Sometimes these wastes were stored on-site. While Lee was the vice president and superivisor of manufacturing, his plant manager arranged to have some of these waste-filled vats buried on Denny Farm. An anonymous tip led to the discovery of the improperly buried and leaking waste. The EPA undertook a cleanup under CERCLA. Explain why each of the defendants, NEPCO and Lee, either is or is not liable. *United States v. Northeastern Pharmaceuticals*, 810 F.2d 726 (1986)

20-18. DDT was the active ingredient in 31 pesticides registered for general use. Farmers sprayed these pesticides on cotton, soybeans, peanuts, and other crops to control insects. Subsequent to the registrations, the EPA received evidence that DDT is an uncontrollable chemical that persists in aquatic and terrestrial environments. Because it is insoluble, it collects in the food web and is passed up to the higher forms of life. It kills and injures birds, fish, and animals and affects their reproductive capacities. It is carcinogenic. The EPA, in light of this new evidence, brought an action to cancel the registrations. Was the EPA successful? Why or why not? *Consolidated DDT Hearings*, 37 Fed. Reg. 13,396 (1972)

On the Internet

http://www.epa.gov   The EPA home page is a source of valuable information about the main agency responsible for protecting the environment.

http://www.webcom/~staber/press-releases   This site contains the EPA press releases.

http://www.os.kcp.com/home/catalog/polprepro.html   Readers interested in learning about pollution prevention will find this page invaluable.

http://www.cais.com/tne/water.html   This site contains the National Environmental Information Services's most requested water documents.

http:www.house.gov/democrats/nt_environ.html   This address will lead you to state-by-state information about superfund sites.

21

RULES GOVERNING THE ISSUANCE AND TRADING OF SECURITIES

- **INTRODUCTION TO THE REGULATION OF SECURITIES**

- **THE SECURITIES ACT OF 1933**

- **THE SECURITIES EXCHANGE ACT OF 1934**

- **INTERNATIONAL DIMENSIONS OF RULES GOVERNING THE ISSUANCE**

  AND TRADING OF SECURITIES

In chapter 15, we said that the corporation was the dominant form of business organization in the United States—and also the most regulated. Two of the most strongly regulated aspects of corporate business are the issuance and trading of securities. Corporate securities—stocks and bonds—are, of course used to raise capital for the corporation. But they are also used by individuals and institutional investors to accumulate wealth. In the case of individuals, this wealth is often passed on to heirs, who use it to accumulate more wealth. Thus securities provide a means for one generation in a family to "do better" than the preceding generation. Securities also provide a means for financing pension funds and insurance plans through institutional investment.

Securities holders play a significant role in our society. They are powerful determinants of trends in business: If an individual company, industry, or segment of the economy is not growing and paying a good rate of return, investors will switch their funds to another company, industry, or segment in expectation of better returns. Securities holders (or their proxies) elect the board of directors of a corporation, who, in turn, select the officers who manage the daily operations of a corporation. Finally, securities holders' ability to bring lawsuits helps keep officers and directors honest in their use of investors' funds.

Both because of their importance to the operation of our free enterprise society and because of the ease with which they can be manipulated, securities have been regulated by the government for most of this century. This chapter examines the role of the federal government in regulating securities. We introduce the subject with a brief history of securities regulation that contains a summary of the most important federal legislation. Then we turn to the creation, function, and structure of the Securities and Exchange Commission, one of the most powerful regulatory bodies in the U.S. government. In the second section, we take up the provisions of the Securities Act of 1933 that govern the issuance of securities, paying special attention to the registration requirements for both securities and transactions and the allowable exemptions from those requirements. We then go through the provisions of the Securities Exchange Act of 1934 that govern trading in securities. We end with an examination of the international dimensions of the 1933 and 1934 securities acts.

Critical Thinking about the Law

BECAUSE SECURITIES CAN BE EASILY MANIPULATED by issuers, federal and state governments have strongly regulated the issuance and trading of securities. Studying the following case and answering some critical thinking questions about it will help you better appreciate the need for regulation of securities.

Jessica received a phone call from a man claiming to represent Buy-It-Here, a corporation that was relocating to Jessica's town. The man stated that the corporation was planning to issue new securities, and he was extending this offer to residents in Jessica's town. He claimed that Buy-It-Here would easily double its profits within six months. The man said that if Jessica would send $3,000, he would buy stock in Buy-It-Here for Jessica. Jessica sent the money; two weeks later she discovered that Buy-It-Here was in the process of filing for bankruptcy.

1. This case is an example of the need for government regulation. We want the government to protect citizens from cases like Jessica's buying stock in a bankrupt company. If we want governmental protection from potentially shady businesses, what ethical norm are we emphasizing?

   CLUE Put yourself in Jessica's place. Why would you want governmental protection? Now match your answer to an ethical norm listed in chapter 1. Think about which ethical norm businesses would emphasize.

2. Jessica wants to sue Buy-It-Here for misrepresentation. Before she brings her case, what additional information do you think Jessica should discover?

CLUE What additional information do you want to know about the case? Without having extensive knowledge about securities, you can identify areas where we might need more information about Jessica's case. For example, pay close attention to the role of the telephone caller.

3. Jessica did some research about securities cases in her state. She discovered a case in which a woman named Andrea Stevenson had purchased $100,000 in stock from a stockbroker. The company went bankrupt three months later. The stockbroker had known that the company had potential financial problems but had said nothing to Andrea. The jury in this case found in favor of Andrea. Jessica wants to use Andrea's case as an analogy in her lawsuit. Do you think that Andrea's case is an appropriate analogy?

CLUE What are the similarities between the cases? How are the cases different? Are these differences so significant that they overwhelm the similarities?

INTRODUCTION TO THE REGULATION OF SECURITIES

Securities have no value in and of themselves. They are not like most goods produced or consumed (e.g., television sets or toys), which are easily regulated in terms of their hazards or merchantability. Because they are paper, they can be produced in unlimited numbers and thus can easily be manipulated by their issuers.

The first attempt to regulate securities in the United States was made by the state of Kansas in 1912. When other states followed the Kansas legislature's example, corporations played off one state against another by limiting their securities sales to states that had less stringent regulations. Despite the corporations' ability to thwart state efforts at regulation rather easily, there was strong resistance to the idea of federal regulation in Congress. It was not until after the collapse of the stock market in 1929 and the free-fall of stock prices on the New York Stock Exchange—where the Dow Jones Industrial Average registered an 89 percent decline between 1929 and 1933—that Congress finally acted.

SUMMARY OF FEDERAL SECURITIES LEGISLATION

The following legislation, enacted by Congress since 1933, provides the framework for the federal regulation of securities.

- The *Securities Act of 1933* (also known as the *Securities Act* or the *1933 Act*) regulates the initial offering of securities by public corporations by prohibiting an offer or sale of securities not registered with the Securities and Exchange Commission. The 1933 Act sets forth certain exemptions from the registration process as well as penalties for violations of the act. This act is examined in detail in this chapter. Both the 1933 and 1934 Acts were amended by Congress and the SEC rulemaking process, much of which is summarized in the following pages.

- The *Securities Exchange Act of 1934* (also known as the *Exchange Act*) regulates the trading in securities once they are issued. It requires brokers and dealers who trade in securities to register with the Securities and Exchange Commission (SEC), the regulatory body created to enforce both the 1933 and 1934 acts. The Exchange Act is also examined in detail in this chapter.

- The *Public Utility Holding Company Act of 1935* requires public utility and holding companies to register with the SEC and to disclose their financial organization, structure, and operating process.

- The *Trust Indenture Act of 1939* regulates the public issuance of bonds and other debt securities in excess of $5 million. This act imposes standards for trustees to follow to ensure that bondholders are protected.

- The *Investment Company Act (ICA) of 1940*, as amended in 1970 and 1975, gives the SEC authority to regulate the structure and operation of public investment companies that invest in and trade in securities. A company is an "investment company" under this act if it invests or trades in securities and if more than 40 percent of its assets are "investment securities" (which are all corporate securities and securities invested in subsidiaries). Accompanying legislation, entitled the *Investment Advisers Act of 1940*, authorizes the SEC to regulate persons and firms that give investment advice to clients. This act requires the registration of all such individuals or firms and contains antifraud provisions that seek to protect broker-dealers' clients.

- The *Securities Investor Protection Act (SIPA)* of 1970 established the nonprofit Securities Investor Protection Corporation (SIPC) and gave it authority to supervise the liquidation of brokerage firms that are in financial trouble, as well as to protect investors from losses up to $500,000 due to the financial failure of a brokerage firm. The SIPC does not have the monitoring and "bailout" functions that the Federal Deposit Insurance Corporation (FDIC) has in banking; it only supervises the liquidation of an already financially troubled brokerage firm through an appointed trustee.

- Chapter 11 of the *Bankruptcy Reform Act of 1978* gives the SEC the authority to render advice when certain debtor corporations have filed for reorganization.

- The *Foreign Corrupt Practices Act (FCPA) of 1977*, as amended in 1988, prohibits the direct or indirect giving of "anything of value" to a foreign official for the purpose of influencing that official's actions. The FCPA sets out an *intent* or "knowing" standard of liability for corporate management. It requires all companies (whether doing business abroad or not) to set up a system of internal controls that will provide reasonable assurance that the company's records "accurately and fairly reflect" its transactions. The FCPA is discussed in the last section of this chapter.

- The *International Securities Enforcement Cooperation Act (ISECA) of 1990* clarifies the SEC's authority to provide securities regulators of other governments with documents and information and exempts from Freedom of Information Act disclosure requirements all documents given to the SEC by foreign regulators. The ISECA also authorizes the SEC to impose administrative sanctions on securities buyers and dealers who have engaged in illegal activities in foreign countries. Finally, it authorizes the SEC to investigate violations of the securities law set out in the act that occur in foreign countries. The ISECA is also discussed in the last section of the chapter.

- The *Market Reform Act of 1990* authorizes the SEC to regulate trading practices during periods of extreme volatility. For example, the SEC can take such emergency action as suspending trading when computer program–driven trading forces the Dow Jones Industrial Average to rise or fall sharply within a short time period.

- The *Securities Enforcement Remedies and Penney Reform Act of 1991* (the *1991 Remedies Act*) gives the SEC powerful new means for policing the securities industry: cease and desist powers and the power to impose substantial monetary penalties in administrative proceedings. The 1991 Remedies Act also gives the SEC and the federal courts the following powers over anyone who violates federal securities law:

  1. The imposition of monetary penalties by a federal court for a violation of the securities law on petition by the SEC.

  2. The power of the federal courts to bar anyone who has violated the fraud provisions of the federal securities laws from ever serving as an officer or director of a publicly held firm.

  3. The power of the SEC to issue permanent cease and desist orders against "any person who is violating, has violated, or is about to violate any" provision of a federal securities law.

     This act arms the SEC with some of the most sweeping enforcement powers ever given to a single administrative agency other than criminal enforcement agencies such as the Justice Department.

For your convenience, all this federal securities legislation is summarized in Table 21-1.

FEDERAL SECURITIES LEGISLATION	PURPOSE
Securities Act of 1933	SEC regulates the *initial public offering* of securities.
Securities Exchange Act of 1934	SEC regulates the *trading* in securities.
Public Utility Holding Company Act of 1935	SEC regulates public utility and holding companies through registering and disclosure processes.
Trust Indenture Act of 1939	SEC regulates the public issuance of bonds and other debt securities.
Investment Company Act of 1940	SEC regulates structure and operation of public investment companies.
Securities Investor Protection Act of 1970	Securities Investor Protection Corporation supervises the liquidation of financially troubled brokerage firms.
Bankruptcy Reform Act of 1978	SEC has authority to advise debtor corporations that have filed for reorganization.
Foreign Corrupt Practices Act of 1977	Prohibits the payment of anything of value to influence foreign officials' actions.
International Securities Enforcement Cooperation Act of 1990	SEC has authority to provide securities regulators of other governments with information on alleged violators of securities law in the United States and abroad.
Market Reform Act of 1990	SEC regulates trading practices during periods of extreme volatility.
Securities Enforcement Remedies and Penney Reform Act of 1991	SEC regulates securities industry through cease and desist powers and threat of substantial monetary penalties.

THE SECURITIES AND EXCHANGE COMMISSION (SEC)

CREATION AND FUNCTION The **Securities and Exchange Commission** was created under the Securities Exchange Act of 1934 for the purpose of ensuring investors "full and fair" disclosure of all material facts with regard to any public offering of securities. The SEC is not charged with evaluating the worth of a public offering of securities by a corporation (for example, determining whether the offering is speculative or not); it is concerned only with whether potential investors are provided with adequate information to make investment decisions. To this end, the commission was given the power to set up and enforce proper registration regulations for securities as well as to prevent fraud in the registration and trading of securities.

STRUCTURE Exhibit 21-1 lays out the structure of the SEC. It has five commissioners (inclusive of the Chairman) appointed by the president with the advice and consent of the Senate; each serves for a period of five years, and no more than three commissioners can be of the same political party. The Commission, based in Washington, D.C., has nine regional offices across the United States. There are five divisions: Corporation Finance, Market Regulation, Enforcement, Corporate Regulation, and Investment Management. (Note in Exhibit 21-1 that five major offices—i.e., Consumer Affairs, Public Affairs, etc.—also serve the commission, along with an executive director.)

Division of Corporation Finance This division is responsible for establishing and overseeing adherence to standards of financial reporting and disclosure for all companies that fall under SEC jurisdiction as well as for setting and administering the disclosure requirements prescribed by the 1933 and the 1934 securities acts, the Public Utility Holding Company Act, and the Investment Company Act. The Division of Corporation Finance reviews all registration statements, prospectuses, and quarterly and annual reports of corporations as

Securities and Exchange Commission (SEC) The federal administrative agency charged with overall responsibility for the regulation of securities, their registration and trading to see that investors receive "full and fair" disclosure of all material facts with regard to any public offering of securities. It has wide enforcement powers to protect investors against price manipulation, insider trading, and other dishonest dealings.

EXHIBIT 21-1 *The Securities and Exchange Commission*

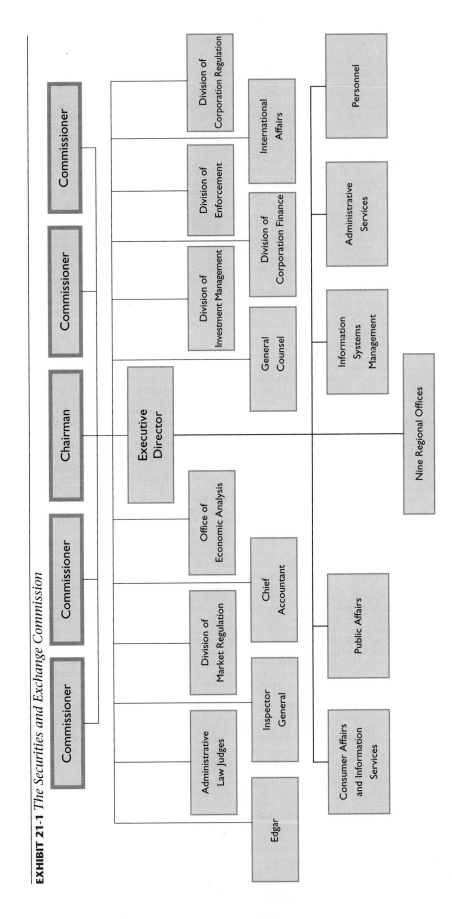

Source: The United States Government Manual, 1990/91 (Washington, D.C.: U.S. Government Printing Office, July 1, 1990), p. 698.

well as their proxy statements. Its importance in offering informal advisory opinions to issuers (corporations about to make a public offering of stock) cannot be overemphasized. Accountants, lawyers, financial officers, and underwriters all rely heavily on this division's advice.

Division of Market Regulation This is the SEC division that regulates the national security exchanges (such as the New York Stock Exchange) as well as broker-dealers registered under the Investment Advisers Act of 1940. Through ongoing surveillance of both the exchanges and broker-dealers, the Division of Market Regulation seeks to discourage manipulation or fraud in the issuance, sale, or purchase of securities. It can recommend to the full commission the suspension of an exchange for up to one year as well as the suspension or permanent prohibition of a broker or dealer because of certain types of conduct. In addition, the division provides valuable informal advice to investors, issuers, and others on securities statutes that come within the SEC's jurisdiction.

Division of Enforcement This division is responsible for the review and supervision of all enforcement activities recommended by the SEC's other divisions and regional offices. It also supervises investigations and the initiation of injunctive actions.

Division of Corporation Regulation This division administers the Public Utility Holding Company Act of 1935 and advises federal bankruptcy courts in proceedings brought under Chapter 11 of the Bankruptcy Reform Act of 1978.

Division of Investment Management This is the SEC division that administers the Investment Company Act of 1940 and the Investment Advisers Act of 1940. All investigations arising under these acts dealing with issuers and dealers are carried out by this division.

THE SECURITIES ACT OF 1933

In the depths of the Great Depression, Congress enacted this first piece of federal legislation regulating securities. Its major purpose, as we have said, was to ensure full disclosure on new issues of securities.

DEFINITION OF A SECURITY

When most people use the word *securities*, they mean stocks or bonds that are held personally or as part of a group in a pension fund or a mutual fund. However, Congress, the SEC, and the courts have gone far beyond this simple meaning in defining securities. Section 2(1) of the 1933 Act defines the term **security** as

> *any note, stock, treasury stock, bond, debenture, evidence of indebtedness, certificate of interest or participation in any profit sharing agreement, collateral trust certificate, preorganization certificate or subscription, transferable share, investment contract, voting trust certificate, certificate of deposit for a security, fractional undivided interest in oil, gas or other mineral rights, or, in general, any interest or instrument commonly known as a security . . .*

The words "or, in general, any interest or instrument commonly known as a security" have led to various interpretations by the SEC and the courts of what constitutes a security. In the landmark case *SEC v. Howey*,[1] the Supreme Court sought to discover the economic realities behind the facade or form of a transaction and to set out specific criteria that could be used by the courts in defining a security. The Court in that case held that the sale of rows of orange trees to the public with a service contract, under which the Howey Company cultivated, harvested, and marketed the oranges, constituted a security within the meaning of Section 2(1) of the 1933 Act. Its decision was based on three elements or characteristics: (1) There existed a contract or scheme whereby an individual invested money in a *common enterprise*; (2) the investors had *reasonable*

security A stock or bond or any other instrument of interest that represents an investment in a common enterprise with reasonable expectations of profits that are derived solely from the efforts of those other than the investor.

---

[1] 328 U.S. 293 (1946).

expectations of profits; and (3) the *profits* were *derived solely from the efforts of persons other than the investors*. These criteria are examined in detail here because they have been the basis of considerable litigation.

Howey test The three-part test used to determine whether an instrument or contract is a security for purposes of federal securities laws: (1) common enterprise and (2) expectation of profit that is (3) derived from efforts of others.

COMMON ENTERPRISE   The first element of the **Howey test** has been interpreted by most courts as requiring investors to share in a single pool of assets so that the fortunes of a single investor are dependent on those of the other investors. For example, commodities accounts involving commodities brokers' discretion have been held to be "securities" on the ground that "the fortunes of all investors are inextricably tied" to the success of the trading enterprise.

REASONABLE EXPECTATIONS OF PROFIT   The second element of the Howey test requires that the investor enter the transaction with a clear expectation of making a profit on the money invested. The U.S. Supreme Court has held that neither an interest in a noncontributory, compulsory pension plan nor stock purchases by residents in a low-rent cooperative constitute "securities" within the definition of Howey. In the case involving the pension plan,[2] the Court stated that the employee expected funds for his pension to come primarily from contributions made by the employer rather than from returns on the assets of the pension plan fund. Similarly, in the low-rent housing case,[3] the Court decided that shares purchased solely to acquire a low-cost place to live were not bought with a reasonable expectation of profit.

PROFITS DERIVED SOLELY FROM THE EFFORTS OF OTHERS   The third element of the Howey test requires that profits come "solely" from the efforts of people other than the investors. The word *solely* was interpreted to mean that the investors can exert "some efforts" in bringing other investors into a pyramid sales scheme but that the "undeniably significant ones" must be the efforts of management, not of the investors.

REGISTRATION OF SECURITIES UNDER THE 1933 ACT

PURPOSE AND GOALS   The 1933 Act requires the registration of nonexempt securities, as defined by Section 2(1), for the purpose of full disclosure so that potential investors can make informed decisions on whether to buy a proposed public offering of stock. As we noted earlier in the chapter, the 1933 Act does not authorize the SEC or any other agency to decide whether or not the offering is meritorious and should be sold to the public.

prospectus The first part of the registration statement the SEC requires from issuers of new securities. It contains material information about the business and its management, the offering itself, the use to made of the funds obtained, and certain financial statements.

REGISTRATION STATEMENT AND PROCESS   Section 5 of the 1933 Act requires that, to serve the goals of disclosure, a registration statement consist of two parts—the prospectus and a "Part II" information statement—to be filed with the SEC before any security can be sold to the public. The **prospectus** (Exhibit 21-2) provides: (1) material information about the business and property of the issuer; (2) the purpose of the offering; (3) the use to be made of the funds garnered by the offering and the risks involved for investors; (4) the managerial experience, history, and remuneration of the principals; and (5) financial statements certified by public accountants attesting to the firm's financial health. The prospectus must be given to every prospective buyer of the securities. Part II is a longer, more detailed statement than the prospectus. It is not given to prospective buyers but is open for public inspection at the SEC.

During the registration process, the SEC bans public statements by the issuers, other than those contained in the registration statement, until the effective date of registration. There are three important stages in this process: the prefiling, waiting, and posteffective periods. They are summarized in Table 21-2.

---

[2]International Brotherhood of Teamsters, Chauffeurs, Warehousers and Helpers of America v. Daniel, 439 U.S. 551 (1979).
[3]United Housing Foundation, Inc., v. SEC 423 U.S. 884 (1975).

EXHIBIT 21-2

515

PROSPECTUS

March 1, 1998

INVESTMENT OBJECTIVE:
LONG-TERM CAPITAL APPRECIATION

The Links Fund invests primarily in common stocks and securities convertible into common stocks, but may also invest in other securities that are suited to the Fund's investment objective.

INVESTMENT OBJECTIVE:
LONG-TERM CAPITAL APPRECIATION

The Links International Fund invests primarily in a diversified portfolio of international securities.

NO LOAD — NO SALES CHARGE

NO 12b-1 FEES

Minimum Investment	**Ticker Symbols**
Initial purchase—$1,000	The Links Fund—LNX
($500 for an IRA)	The Links International Fund-LNIX
Subsequent investments—$100	

The Funds may invest to a limited extent in high-yield, high-risk bonds. See "Risk Factors."

This prospectus contains information you should know before investing. Please retain it for future reference. A Statement of Additional Information regarding the Funds dated the date of this prospectus has been filed with the Securities and Exchange Commission and (together with any supplement to it) is incorporated by reference. The Statement of Additional Information may be obtained at no charge by writing or telephoning the Trust at its address or telephone number shown inside the back cover.

THESE SECURITIES HAVE NOT BEEN APPROVED OR DISAPPROVED BY THE SECURITIES AND EXCHANGE COMMISSION OR ANY STATE SECURITIES COMMISSION, NOR HAS THE SECURITIES AND EXCHANGE COMMISSION OR ANY STATE SECURITIES COMMISSION PASSED UPON THE ACCURACY OR ADEQUACY OF THIS PROSPECTUS. ANY REPRESENTATION TO THE CONTRARY IS A CRIMINAL OFFENSE.

TABLE 21-2 *Stages in the Securities Registration Process*

STAGE	PROHIBITIONS
1. Prefiling period	No offer to sell or buy securities may be made before a registration statement is filed.
2. Waiting period	SEC rules allow oral offers during this period, but no sales. A "red herring" prospectus that disavows any attempt either to offer or sell securities may be published.
3. Posteffective period	Registration generally becomes effective 20 days after the registration statement is filed, though effective registration may be accelerated or postponed by the SEC. Offer and sale of securities are now permitted.

Prefiling Period   Section 5(c) of the 1933 Act prohibits any offer to sell or buy securities before a registration statement is filed. The key question here is what constitutes an "offer." Section 2(3) of the act exempts from the definition any preliminary agreements or negotiations between the issuer and the underwriters or among the underwriters themselves. **Underwriters** are investment banking firms that purchase a securities issue from the issuing corporation with a view to eventually selling the securities to brokerage houses, which, in turn, sell them to the public. These underwriters—such as Goldman Sachs, Kidder Peabody, or First Boston—may arrange for distribution of the public offering of securities, but they can not make offerings or sales to dealers or the public at this time. During the prefiling period, the SEC regulations also forbid sales efforts in the form of speeches or advertising by the issuer that seek to "hype" the offering or the issuer's business. However, a press release setting forth the details of the proposed offering and the issuer's name, without mentioning the underwriters, is generally permitted.

Waiting Period   In the interim between the filing and the time when registration becomes effective, SEC rules allow oral offers, but not sales. The SEC examines the prospectus for completeness during this period. SEC rules permit the publication of a written preliminary, or **red herring**, prospectus that summarizes the registration but disavows in red print (hence its name) any attempt to offer or sell securities. Notices of underwriters containing certain information about the proposed issue are also allowed to appear in newspapers during this period, but such notices must be bordered in black and specify that they are not offers to sell or solicitations to buy securities.

Posteffective Period   The third stage in the process is called the posteffective period because the registration statement usually becomes effective 20 days after it is filed, although sometimes the commission accelerates or postpones registration for some reason. Underwriters and leaders can begin to offer and sell securities after the 20 days or upon commission approval, whichever comes first.

Under Section 8 of the 1933 Act, the SEC may issue a "refusal order" or "stop order," which prevents a registration statement from becoming effective or suspends its effectiveness, if the staff discovers a misstatement or omission of a material fact in the statement. Stop orders are reserved for the most serious cases. In general, the issuer is forewarned by the SEC in informal "letters of comment" or "deficiency" before a stop order is put out, so they have the opportunity to make the necessary revisions. The commission may shorten the usual 20-day period between registration and effectiveness if the issuer is willing to make modifications requested by the SEC staff. This procedure, in fact, is the present trend.

The 1933 Act requires that a prospectus be issued upon every sale of a security in interstate commerce except sales by anyone not an "issuer, underwriter or dealer." If a prospectus is delivered more than nine months after the effective date of registration, it must be updated so that the information is not more than 16 months old. The burden is on the dealer to update all material information about the issuer that is not in the prospectus. Dealers who fail to do so risk civil liability under Sections 12(1) and 12(2) of the 1933 Act.

In the following case, the U.S. Supreme Court defined the reach of Section 12(2). When reading the edited Court decision, you should note its reliance on legislative history in arriving at a conclusion.

ARTHUR GUSTAFSON ET AL. V. ALLOYD COMPANY, INCORPORATED, ET AL.
UNITED STATES SUPREME COURT 513 U.S. 561 (1995)

Alloyd Shareholders (plaintiff-respondent) sued Gustafson and others (defendant-petitioners) under Section 12(2) of the Securities Act of 1993 for rescission of a previous agreement with regard to its stock purchase of Alloyd Company made from Gustafson. Plaintiffs purchased substantially all of the stock of Alloyd from the defendants in a private contractual arrangement. Under the contract, if a year-end audit and financial statements revealed variances between estimated and actual increased value, the disappointed party would receive an adjustment as a result of the audit. The plaintiffs (shareholders of Alloyd) were entitled to recover an adjustment but instead sought a rescission (cancellation) of the whole contract under Section 12(2) of the 1993 Act. This section gives buyers the right of rescission against sellers who make material misstatements or omissions "by means of a prospectus." The district court granted the defendant Gustafson's motion for summary judgment, holding that Section 12(2) claims can arise only out of initial stock offerings and not from a private sale agreement. The court of appeals reversed in favor of the plaintiff, vacating the summary judgment. The court claimed that the definition of "prospectus" included "communication," which, therefore, includes all written communication included in the offering of a security for sale, and thus a 12(2) right of action for rescission applies to private sale agreements. The defendants, Gustafson et al., appealed.

JUSTICE KENNEDY

Under § 12(2) of the Securities Act of 1933, buyers have an express cause of action for rescission against sellers who make material misstatements or omissions "by means of a prospectus." The question presented is whether this right of rescission extends to a private, secondary transaction, on the theory that recitations in the purchase agreement are part of a "prospectus."

The rescission claim against Gustafson is based upon § 12(2) of the 1933 Act. In relevant part, the section provides that any person who

> offers or sells a security (whether or not exempted by the provisions of section 77c of this title, other than paragraph (2) of subsection (a) of said section), by the use of any means or instruments of transportation or communication in interstate commerce or of the mails, by means of a prospectus or oral communication, which includes an untrue statement of a material fact or omits to state a material fact necessary in order to make the statements, in the light of the circumstances under which they were made, not misleading (the purchaser not knowing of such untruth or omission), and who shall not sustain the burden of proof that he did not know, and in the exercise of reasonable care could not have known, of such untruth or omission, "shall be liable to the person purchasing such security from him, who may sue either at law or in equity in any court of competent jurisdiction, to recover the consideration paid for such security with interest thereon, less the amount of any income received thereon, upon the tender of such security, or for damages if he no longer owns the security.

As this case reaches us, we must assume that the stock purchase agreement contained material misstatements of fact made by the sellers and that Gustafson would not sustain its burden of proving due care. On these assumptions, Alloyd would have a right to obtain rescission if those mis-

statements were made "by means of a prospectus or oral communication." The parties (and the court of appeals) agree that the phrase "oral communication" is restricted to oral communications that relate to the prospectus. The determinative question, then, is whether the contract between Alloyd and Gustafson is a "prospectus" as the term is used in the 1933 Act.

It is understandable that Congress would provide buyers with a right to rescind, without proof of fraud or reliance, as to misstatements contained in a document prepared with care, following well established procedures relating to investigations with due diligence, and in the context of a public offering by an issuer or its controlling shareholders. It is not plausible to infer that Congress created this extensive liability for every casual communication between buyer and seller in the secondary market. It is often difficult, if not altogether impractical, for those engaged in casual communications not to omit some fact that would, if included, qualify the accuracy of a statement. Under Alloyd's view any casual communication between buyer and seller in the aftermarket could give rise to an action for rescission, with no evidence of fraud on the part of the seller or reliance on the part of the buyer. In many instances buyers in practical effect would have an option to rescind, impairing the stability of past transactions where neither fraud nor detrimental reliance on misstatements or omissions occurred. We find no basis for interpreting the statute to reach so far.

Nothing in the legislative history, moreover, suggests Congress intended to create two types of prospectuses: a formal and less formal one. The Act proceeds by definitions more stable and precise. The legislative history confirms what the text of the Act dictates: § 10's requirements govern all prospectuses defined by § 2(10). In discussing § 10, the House Report stated:

> Section 10 of the bill requires that any "prospectus" used in connection with the sale of any securities, if it is more than a mere announcement of the name and price of the issue offered and an offer of full details upon request, must include a substantial portion of the information required in the "registration statement."

> "Prospectus" is defined in section 2(1) [now § 2(10)] to include "any prospectus, notice, circular, advertisement, letter, or other communication offering any security for sale."

> The purpose of these sections is to secure for potential buyers the means of understanding the intricacies of the transaction into which they are invited.

In sum, the word "prospectus" is a term of art referring to a document that describes a public offering of securities by an issuer or controlling shareholder. Here the contract of sale, and its recitations, were not held out to the public and were not a prospectus as the term is used in the 1933 Act.

Reversed in favor of Defendant, Gustafson.

SHELF REGISTRATION Traditionally, the marketing of securities has taken place through underwriters who buy or offer to buy securities and then employ dealers across the United States to sell them to the general public. The SEC, with Rule 415, has established a procedure, called **shelf registration**, that allows a large corporation to file a registration statement for securities that it may wish to sell over a period of time rather than immediately. Once the securities are registered, the corporation can place them on the "shelf" for future sale and not have to register them again. It can then sell these securities when it needs capital and when the marketplace indicators are favorable. A company that files a shelf registration statement must file periodic amendments with the SEC if any fundamental changes occur in its activities that would be material to the average prudent investor's decision to invest in its stock.

SECURITIES AND TRANSACTIONS EXEMPT FROM REGISTRATION UNDER THE 1933 ACT

Section 5 of the 1933 Act requires registrations of any sale by any person of any security unless specifically exempted by the 1933 Act. The cost of the registration process, in terms of hiring lawyers, accountants, underwriters, and other financial experts, makes it appealing for a firm to put a transaction together in such a way as not to fall within the definition of a security. If that is impossible, firms often attempt to meet the requirements of one of the following four classes of exemptions to the registration process (summarized in Table 21-3).

PRIVATE PLACEMENT EXEMPTIONS Section 4(2) of the 1933 Act exempts from registration transactions by an issuer that do not involve any public offering. Behind this exemption is the theory that institutional investors have the sophisticated knowledge necessary to evaluate the information contained in a private placement, and thus, unlike the average investor, do not need to be protected by the registration process set out in the 1933 Act. The private placement exemption is often used in stock option plans, in which a corporation issues securities to its own employees for the purpose of increasing productivity or retaining top-level managers. Because various courts had different views on what factual situations constituted a private placement exemption, the SEC published Rule 146, which seeks to clarify the criteria used by the commission in allowing this exemption:

1. The number of purchasers of the company's (issuer's) securities should not exceed 35. If a single purchaser buys more than $150,000, that purchaser will not be counted among the 35.

TABLE 21-3 *Exemptions from the Registration Process under the 1933 Securities Act*

EXEMPTION	DEFINITION
Private placement	Transactions by an issuing company not involving any public offering. Usually the transaction involves sophisticated investors with knowledge enough to evaluate information given them (e.g., stock option plans for top-level management).
Intrastate offering	Any security or part of an offering offered or sold to persons resident within a single state or territory.
Small business	Section 3(b) of the 1933 Act allows the SEC to exempt offerings not exceeding $5 million. Regulations A and D promulgated by the SEC define the type of investors and the amount of securities that are exempt within a certain time period.
Other offering exemptions	By virtue of the 1933 Act, exemptions are allowed for transactions by any person other than an issuer, underwriter, or dealer. Also government securities are exempt (federal state or municipal bonds). Also exempt are securities issued by banks, charitable organizations, savings and loans institutions, and common carriers under the jurisdiction of the Interstate Commerce Commission.

2. Each purchaser must have access to the same kind of information that would be available if the issuer had registered the securities.

3. The issuer can sell only to purchasers who it has reason to believe are capable of evaluating the risks and benefits of investment and are able to bear those risks, or to purchasers who have the services of a representative with the knowledge and experience to evaluate the risks for them.

4. The issuer may not advertise the securities or solicit public customers.

5. The issuer must take precautions to prevent the resale of securities issued under a private placement exemption.

INTRASTATE OFFERING EXEMPTION Section 3 of the 1933 Act provides an exemption for any "security which is part of an issue offered or sold to persons resident within a single state or territory, where the issuer of such security is a resident and doing business within, or, if a corporation, incorporated by, or doing business within such a state." To qualify for this exemption, an issuer must meet the strictly interpreted "doing-business-within-a-state" requirement: The issuer must be a resident of the state and "do business" solely with (i.e., offer securities to) people who live within the state.

Courts have interpreted Section 3 very strictly. One federal court ruled that a company incorporated in the state of California and making an offering of common stock solely to residents of California did not qualify for the intrastate exemption because it advertised in the *Los Angeles Times*, a newspaper sold in the mails to residents of other states. Another factor in the court's decision in this case was that 20 percent of the proceeds from the securities sale were to be used to refurbish a hotel in Las Vegas, Nevada.[4]

After that decision, the SEC issued Rule 147, which sets standards for the intrastate exemption by defining important terms in Section 3 of the 1933 Act. For example, an issuer is "doing business within" the state if (1) it receives at least 80 percent of its gross revenue from within the state; (2) at least 80 percent of its assets are within the state; (3) it intends to use 80 percent of the net proceeds of the offering within the state; and (4) its principal office is located in the state. Rule 147 is also concerned with whether the offering has "come to rest" within a state or whether it is the beginning of an interstate distribution. An offering is considered "intrastate" only if no resales are made to nonresidents of the state for at least nine months after the initial distribution of securities is completed.

SMALL BUSINESS EXEMPTIONS Section 3(b) of the 1933 Act authorizes the SEC, by use of its rule-making power, to exempt offerings not exceeding $5 million when it finds registration not necessary. Under this authority, the Commission has promulgated Regulations A and D.

Regulation A exempts small public offerings made by the issuer—defined as offerings not exceeding $1.5 million over a 12-month period. The issuer must file an "offerings" and a "notification circular" with a SEC regional office ten days before each proposed offering. The circular contains information similar to that required for a 1933 Act registration prospectus, but in less detail, and the accompanying financial statements may be unaudited. It should be noted that for these small business offerings, the SEC staff follows the same "letter of comment" procedure associated with registration statements; thus a Regulation A filing may be delayed. Regulation A circulars do not give rise to civil liability under Section 11 of the 1933 Act (discussed later in this chapter), but they do make an issuer liable under Section 12(2) for misstatements or omissions (also discussed later in this chapter). The advantages of this regulation for small businesses are that the preparation of forms is simpler and less costly and the SEC staff can usually act more quickly.

Regulation D, which includes Rules 501–506, attempts to implement Section 3 of the 1933 Act. Rule 501 defines an accredited investor as a bank; an insurance or investment company; an employee benefit plan; a business develop-

---

[4]SEC v. Trustee Showboat, 157 F. Supp. 824 (S.D.Calif. 1957).

noninvestment company A company whose primary business is not in investing or trading in securities.

ment company; a charitable or educational institution (with assets of $5 million or more); any director, officer, or general partner of an issuer; any person with a net worth of $1 million or more; or any person with an annual income of more than $200,000. This definition is important because an accredited investor, as defined by Rule 501, is not likely to need the protection of the 1933 Act's registration process.

Rule 504 allows any **noninvestment company** to sell up to $1 billion worth of securities in a 12-month period to any number of purchasers, accredited or nonaccredited, without furnishing any information to the purchaser. However, this $1 billion maximum is reduced by the amount of securities sold under any other exemption.

Rule 505 allows any private noninvestment company to sell up to $5 million of securities in a 12-month period to any number of accredited investors (as previously defined) and to up to 35 nonaccredited purchasers. Sales to nonaccredited purchasers are subject to certain restrictions concerning the manner of offering—for example, no public advertising is allowed—and resale of the securities.

Rule 506 allows an issuer to sell an unlimited number of securities to any number of accredited investors and to up to 35 nonaccredited purchasers. However, the issuer must have reason to believe that each nonaccredited purchaser or representative has enough knowledge or experience in business to be able to evaluate the merits and risks of the prospective investment. Again, there are certain resale restrictions attached to offerings made under this rule as well as a prohibition against advertising. Rule 506 seeks to clarify Section 4(2) of the 1933 Act, dealing with private placement exemptions, already discussed.

OTHER OFFERING EXEMPTIONS Section 4(2) of the 1933 Act allows exemptions for "transactions by any person other than an issuer, underwriter or dealer." Since Sections 4(3) and 4(4) allow qualified exemptions for dealers and brokers, the issuer and the underwriters become the only ones not exempted. SEC Rule 144 defines the conditions under which a person is not an underwriter and is not involved in selling securities.

Government securities issued or regulated by agencies other than the SEC are exempt from the 1933 Act. For example, debt issued by or guaranteed by federal, state, or local governments as well as securities issued by banks, religious and charitable organizations, savings and loan associations, and common carriers under the Interstate Commerce Commission are exempt. These securities usually fall under the jurisdiction of other federal agencies, such as the Federal Reserve System or the Federal Home Loan Board, or of state or local agencies.

The collapse of the Penn Central Railroad in 1970 and the default of the cities of Cleveland and New York on municipal bonds led Congress and the SEC to reexamine certain exemptions with a view to eliminating them. In fact, the Railroad Revitalization Act of 1976 eliminated the 1933 Act exemption for securities issued by railroads (other than trust certificates for certain equipment), and 1975 amendments to the securities acts now require firms that deal solely in state and local government securities to register with the commission and to adhere to rules laid down by the Municipal Securities Rulemaking Board.

INTEGRATION

Often a company will seek to obtain a private placement or small business exemption by dividing a large issuance of securities into several small units. Under its integration and aggregation rules, the SEC prohibits this action by integrating (putting together) two exempt offerings that are similar and are made at nearly the same time by the same issuing company. The SEC integrates and aggregates two or more otherwise exempt offerings when:

1. The offerings are part of a unitary plan of financing by the issuing company.
2. The offerings concern the same class of securities.
3. The offerings are made for the same general purpose and at about the same level of pricing.

The SEC has also adopted a "safe harbor rule," which, in effect, states that any offering made six months before or six months after another offering will not be integrated with that offering.

Liability, Remedies, and Defenses under the 1933 Securities Act

PRIVATE REMEDIES   The 1933 Act provides remedies for individuals who have been victims of (1) misrepresentations in a registration statement, (2) an issuer's failure to file a registration statement with the SEC, or (3) misrepresentation or fraud in the sale of securities. Each is examined here along with some affirmative defenses.

Misrepresentations in a Registration Statement   These are untruths or omissions for which Section 11 of the 1933 Act imposes liability. Section 11 allows a right of action to "any person acquiring such a security" who can show (1) a material misstatement or omission in a registration statement and (2) monetary damages. The term *material* is defined by SEC Rule 405 as pertaining to matters "of which an average prudent investor ought reasonably to be informed before purchasing the security registered." In addition, the issuer's omission of such facts as might cause investors to change their minds about investing in a particular security are considered material omissions for the purposes of Section 11. These facts include an impending bankruptcy, new government regulations that may be costly to the company, and the impending conviction and sentencing of the company's top executives for numerous violations of the Foreign Corrupt Practices Act of 1977 (discussed later in this chapter).

Three affirmative defenses are available to defendants:

1. The purchaser (plaintiff) knew of the omission or untruth.
2. The decline in value of the security resulted from causes other than the misstatement or omission in the registration statement.
3. The statement was prepared with the due diligence expected of each defendant.

Whereas others associated with the company can raise the **due diligence defense**, the issuing company itself cannot. Section 11(a) is very specific about what other individuals may be held jointly or severally liable in addition to the issuing company:

1. Every person who signed the registration statement. (Section 6 of the 1933 Act requires signing by the issuer, the issuing company's chief executive officer, the company's financial and accounting officers, and a majority of the company's board of directors.)
2. All directors.
3. Accountants, appraisers, engineers, and other experts who consented to being named as having prepared all or part of the registration statement.
4. Every underwriter of the securities.

It should be noted that there are two exceptions to Section 11 liability:

1. An expert is liable only for the misstatements or omissions in the portion of the registration statement that the expert prepared or certified.
2. An underwriter is liable only for the aggregate public offering portion of the securities it underwrote.

Section 11 liability has made such a strong impact that today virtually all professionals and experts involved in the preparation of a registration statement make precise agreements concerning the assignment of responsibility for that statement. Failure to grasp the import of Section 11 and related sections of the 1933 and 1934 acts can lead to loss of reputation and employment by busi-

due diligence defense An affirmative defense raised in lawsuits charging misrepresentation in a registration statement. It is based on the defendant's claim to have had reasonable grounds to believe that all statements in the registration statement were true and no omission of material fact had been made. This defense is not available to the issuer of the security.

nesspersons and professionals. The first case brought under Section 11[5] sent tremors through Wall Street, the accounting profession, and outside directors. In that case, the court evaluated each defendant's plea of due diligence on the basis of each individual's relationship to the corporation and expected knowledge of registration requirements.

Failure to File a Registration Statement   Failure to file a registration statement with the SEC when selling a nonexempt security is the second basis for a private action by the purchaser for recission (cancellation of the sale). Section 12(1) of the 1933 Act provides that any person who sells a security in violation of Section 5 (which you recall from our discussion of the registration statement) is liable to the purchaser to refund the full purchase price. A purchaser whose investment has decreased in value may recover the full purchase price without showing a misstatement or fraud if the seller is unable to meet the conditions of one of the exemptions we discussed earlier. In short, a business that fails to file a registration statement because of a mistaken assumption that it has qualified for one of the exemptions could be making a very expensive mistake.

Misrepresentation or Fraud in the Sale of a Security   A third basis for a private action is *misrepresentation* in the sale of a security as defined by Section 12(2) of the 1933 Act, which holds liable any person who offers or sells securities by means of any written or oral statement that misstates a material fact or omits a material fact that is necessary to make the statement truthful. Unlike Section 11, Section 12(2) is applicable whether or not the security is subject to the registration provisions of the 1933 Act, provided there is use of the mails or other facilities in interstate commerce. The persons liable are only those from whom the purchaser bought the security. For example, under Section 12(2), a purchaser who bought the security from an underwriter, a dealer, or a broker cannot sue the issuer unless able to show that the issuer was "a substantial factor in causing the transaction to take place." A further requirement is that the purchaser must prove the sale was made "by means of" the misleading communications. The defense usually raised by sellers in such suits is that they did not know and, using reasonable care, could not have known of the untruth or omission at the time the statement was made. (See *Gustafson v. Alloyd*, set out earlier in this chapter.)

Fraud in the sale of a security is covered by Section 17(a) of the 1933 Act, which imposes criminal, and possibly civil, liability on anyone who aids and abets any fraud in connection with the offer or sale of a security. Although Section 17(a) is clearly a basis for criminal liability, an implied right of private action by a purchaser to recover against an individual is still in doubt because of the recent trend of Supreme Court decisions in this area. The Court has refused to infer a private right of action under the antifraud provisions of both the 1933 Act and the 1934 Exchange Act on the ground that it has not been shown that Congress intended such a right. Still, a few lower courts continue to recognize an implied private right of action under Section 17.

GOVERNMENTAL REMEDIES   When a staff investigation uncovers evidence of a violation of the securities laws, the SEC can (1) take administrative action, (2) take injunctive action, or (3) recommend a criminal prosecution to the Justice Department.

Administrative Action   Upon receiving information of a possible violation of the 1933 Act, the SEC staff undertakes an informal inquiry. This involves interviewing witnesses but generally does not involve issuing subpoenas. If the staff uncovers evidence of a possible violation of a securities act, it asks the full commission for a formal order of investigation. A formal investigation is usually conducted in private under SEC rules. A witness compelled to testify or to produce evidence can be represented by counsel, but no other witness or counsel may be present during the testimony. A witness can be denied a copy of the transcript of his or her own testimony for good cause, although the witness is allowed to inspect the transcript.

_____

[5]Escott v. Barchris Construction Corp., 283 F. Supp. 643 (S.D.N.Y. 1968).

Witnesses at a private SEC investigation do not enjoy the ordinary exercise of Fourth, Fifth, and Sixth Amendment rights. For example, Fourth Amendment rights are limited because the securities industry is subject to pervasive government regulation, and those going into it know so in advance. Fifth Amendment rights are limited because the production of records related to a business may be compelled despite a claim of self-incrimination. (See the sections on the Fourth and Fifth Amendments in chapter 4.) As for the Sixth Amendment, in a private investigation, the SEC is not required to notify the targets of the investigation, nor do such targets have a right to appear before the staff or the full commission to defend themselves against charges. The wide scope of SEC powers in these nonpublic investigations was reinforced when the U.S. Supreme Court upheld a lower court's decision to deny injunctive relief with regard to subpoenas directed at plaintiffs in an SEC private investigation.[6]

An *administrative proceeding* may be ordered by the full commission if the SEC staff uncovers evidence of a violation of the securities laws. This proceeding before an administrative law judge can be brought only against a person or firm that is registered with the commission (an investment company, a dealer, or a broker). The ALJ has the power to impose sanctions, including censure, revocation of registration, and limitations on the person's or the firm's activities or practice before the Commission.

In addition, after a hearing, the full commission may issue a *stop order* to suspend a registration statement found to contain a material misstatement or omission. If the statement is later amended, the stop order will be lifted. As we mentioned earlier in the chapter, stop orders are usually reserved for the most serious cases. **Letters of deficiency** are the more frequent method used by the SEC to obtain corrections in registration statements. The remedies available under the 1991 Remedies Act, discussed earlier in the chapter under "Summary of Federal Securities Legislation," apply here as well.

> **letter of deficiency** Informal letter issued by the SEC indicating what corrections need to be made in a registration statement for it to become effective.

Injunctive Action   The SEC may commence an injunctive action when there is a "reasonable likelihood of further violation in the future" or when a defendant is considered a "continuing menace" to the public. For example, under the 1933 Act, the SEC may go to court to seek an injunction to prevent a party from using the interstate mails to sell a nonexempt security. Violation of an injunctive order may give rise to a contempt citation. Also, parties under such an order are disqualified from receiving an exemption under Regulation A (the small business exemption). Again, the remedies available under the 1991 Remedies Act apply here.

Criminal Penalties   Willful violations of the securities acts and the rules and regulations made pursuant to those acts are subject to criminal penalties. Anyone convicted of willfully omitting a material fact or making an untrue statement in connection with the offering or sale of a security can be fined up to $10,000 for each offense or imprisoned for up to five years or both. The commission does not prosecute criminal cases itself but refers them to the Justice Department.

THE SECURITIES EXCHANGE ACT OF 1934

One year after passing the Securities Act of 1933, Congress crafted this second, extremely important piece of securities legislation to come out of the Great Depression. More comprehensive than the 1933 Act, it had two major purposes: to regulate trading in securities and to establish the Securities and Exchange Commission to oversee all securities regulations and bar the kind of large market manipulations that had characterized the 1920s and previous boom periods.

REGISTRATION OF SECURITIES ISSUERS, BROKERS, AND DEALERS

REGISTRATION OF SECURITIES ISSUERS   Section 12 of the Securities Exchange Act requires every *issuer* of debt and equity securities to register with both the SEC and the national exchange on which its securities are to be traded.

---

[6]SEC v. Jerry T. Obrien, Inc., et al., 467 U.S. 735 (1984).

Congress extended this requirement to all corporations that (1) have assets of more than $5 million, (2) have a class of equity securities with more than 500 shareholders, and (3) are involved in interstate commerce. Registration becomes effective within 60 days after filing, unless the SEC accelerates the process.

The commission has devised forms to ensure that potential investors will have updated information on all registrants whose securities are being traded on the national exchanges. Thus registrants are required to file annual reports (Form 10-K; Exhibit 21-3) and quarterly reports (Form 10-Q; Exhibit 21-4) as well as SEC-requested current reports (Form 8-K). This last form must be filed within 15 days of the request, which is usually brought about by a perceived material change in the corporation's position (e.g., a potential merger or bankruptcy) that the commission's staff believes a prudent investor should know about.

In a proposed Codification of the Federal Securities Law (CFSL), the American Law Institute has sought to streamline the registration process under the 1933 and 1934 acts by requiring single issuance registration under the 1933 Act and an annual company "offering statement" for securities traded on a national exchange under the 1934 act. At present, Section 22 of the Exchange Act makes a registering company liable for civil damages to securities purchasers who can show that they relied on a misleading statement contained in any of the SEC-required reports.

REGISTRATION OF BROKERS AND DEALERS Brokers and dealers are required to register with the SEC under the Exchange Act unless exempted. A **dealer**, as defined by the 1934 Act, is a "person engaged in the business of buying and selling securities for his own account," whereas a **broker** is a person engaged in the business of "effectuating transactions in securities for the account of others." We use the convenient term *broker-dealer* throughout to refer to all those who trade in securities, and the specific term *broker* or *dealer* where only one type of trader is meant.

> **dealer** A person engaged in the business of buying and selling securities for his or her own account.

> **broker** A person engaged in the business of buying and selling securities for others' accounts.

Broker-dealers must meet a financial responsibility standard that is based on a net capital formula; a minimum capital of $25,000 is required in most cases. Brokers are obliged to segregate customer funds and securities.

The *Securities Investor Protection Act (SIPA)* provides a basis for indemnifying the customers of a brokerage firm that becomes insolvent: All registered brokers must contribute to a SIPA fund managed by the *Securities Investor Protection Corporation (SIPC)*, a nonprofit corporation whose functions are to liquidate an insolvent brokerage firm and to protect customer investments up to a maximum of $500,000. Upon application to the SEC, SIPC can borrow up to $1 billion from the U.S. Treasury to supplement the fund when necessary.

Under Section 15(b) of the Exchange Act, which contains the antifraud provisions, the SEC may revoke or suspend a broker-dealer's registration or may censure a broker-dealer. (Municipal securities dealers and investment advisers are subject to similar penalties). In general, the commission takes such actions against broker-dealers either for putting enhancement of their personal worth ahead of their professional obligation to their customers—conflict of interest—or for trading in or recommending certain securities without having reliable information about the company. Broker-dealers are liable to both government and private action for failing to disclose conflicts of interest. When even the potential for such a conflict exists, a broker must supply a customer with written confirmation of each transaction, including full disclosure of whom the broker is representing in the transaction.

SECURITIES MARKETS

We defined a *security* earlier in this chapter as a stock or bond or any other instrument or interest that represents an investment in a common enterprise with reasonable expectations of profits derived solely from the efforts of people other than the investors. A security can also be considered a form of currency that,

SECURITIES AND EXCHANGE COMMISSION
Washington, D.C. 20549

FORM 10-K
ANNUAL REPORT

PURSUANT TO SECTION 13 OR 15(d)OF THE SECURITIES EXCHANGE ACT OF 1934

For the fiscal year ended   Commission File Number 1-9999

Kubasek and Brennan, Inc.

(Exact name of registrant as specified in its charter)

Delaware

(State or other jurisdiction of incorporation or organization)	13-4567784
15999 McCuthoonville Road	(I.R.S. Employer Identification Number)
Pemberville, Ohio	43450
(Address of principal executive officers)	(Zip Code)

(419) 654-4128
(Registrant's telephone number)
Securities registered pursuant to Section 12(b) of the Act:

Title of each class	Name of each exchange on which registered
Common Stock - Par Value $1 Per Share	New York Stock Exchange
	Pacific Coast Stock Exchange

Securities registered pursuant to Section 12(g) of the Act
4% Convertible Subordinated Debentures
(Title of class)
9 1/2% Sinking Fund Debentures orginally
(Title of class)

Indicate by check mark whether the registrant (1) has filed all reports required to be filed by Section 13 or 15(d) of the Securities Exchange Act of 1934 during the preceding 12 months and (2) has been subject to such filing requirements for the past 90 days.
        Yes X   No·

Indicate by check mark whether the registrant has filed all documents and reports required to be filed by Sections 12, 13 or 15(d) of the Securties Exchange Act of 1934 subsequent to the distribution of securities under a plan confirmed by a court.
        Yes X   No·

The aggregate market value of Common Stock, Par Value $1 Per Share, held by non-affiliates (based upon the closing sale price of the New York Stock Exchange) was approximately $38,998,000.
As of August 31, 1982, there were 7,799,584 shares of Common Stock Par Value $1 Per Share, outstanding.

DOCUMENTS INCORPORATED BY REFERENCE

Portions of the definitive Proxy Statement for the Annual meeting of Stockholders are incorporated by reference into Part III

Source: Securities and Exchange Commission, Washington, D.C. The names and company are purely fictitious. The form itself is correct.

EXHIBIT 21-4 *Quarterly Report Form 10-Q*

SECURITIES AND EXCHANGE COMMISSION
Washington, D.C. 20549
FORM 10-Q
QUARTERLY REPORT UNDER SECTION 13 OR 15(d)
OF THE SECURITIES EXCHANGE ACT OF 1934

For Quarter Ended   Commission File Number 1-2345

Kubasek-Brennan, Inc.
(Exact name of registrant as specified in its charter)

DELAWARE	13-4567784
(State or other jurisdiction of incorporation or organization)	(I.R.S. Employer Identification Number)

Kubasek-Brennan, Inc.
(address of principal executive officers and zip code)

Registrant s telephone number, including area code (419) 654-4128

Indicate by check mark whether the registrant (1) has filed all reports required to be filed by Section 13 or 15(d) of the Securities Exchange Act of 1934 during the preceding 12 months (or for such shorter period that the registrant was required to file such reports), and (2) has been subject to such filing requirements for the past 90 days.

Yes _X_   No ___

Indicate the number of shares outstanding of each of the issuer s classes of common stock, as of the latest practicable date.

Class	Outstanding
Common Stock, par value 66-2/3¢ per share	7,020,531

KUBASEK-BRENNAN, INC.
INDEX

Source: Securities and Exchange Commission, Washington, D.C. The names and company are purely fictitious. The form itself is correct.

once issued, can be traded for other securities on what is called a *securities market*. We are concerned here with the markets for stocks and how they are regulated under the Exchange Act.

There are generally two types of markets in stocks: exchange and over-the-counter (OTC) markets. The **exchange market** provides for the buying and selling of securities within a physical facility such as the New York Stock Exchange (NYSE) or regional exchanges such as the Boston, Detroit, Midwest (Chicago), Pacific Coast (Los Angeles and San Francisco), and Philadelphia exchanges. These exchanges traditionally prescribed not only the number and the qualifications of their broker-members but also the commissions they could charge. In 1975, commissions were deregulated by the SEC, and, since then, brokers have been free to set the commissions they charge their customers. Brokers do not trade directly on an exchange market but rather transmit a customer's order to a registered specialist in a stock, who buys and sells that security for his or her own account on the floor of the exchange.

The **OTC (over-the-counter) market** has no physical facility—computers and telephones link OTC members—and no qualifications for membership. Its commissions have always been determined by the law of supply and demand. OTC firms serve as dealers or market makers in stocks and deal directly with the public.

Today the National Association of Securities Dealers (NASD) and the exchanges help the SEC to regulate the securities market. In enacting the Securities Exchange Act in 1934, Congress recognized that the stock exchanges had been regulating their members for 140 years and did not seek to dismantle their self-regulatory mechanisms. Rather, it superimposed the SEC on already existing self-regulatory bodies by requiring every "national securities exchange" to register with the SEC. Under Section 6(b) of the Exchange Act, an exchange cannot be registered unless the SEC determines that its rules are designed "to prevent fraudulent and manipulative acts and practices" and to discipline its members for any violations of its rules or the securities laws. Both the New York Stock Exchange—the most important exchange market in the nation—and the NASD have promulgated rules relating to stock transactions and qualifications for those participating in such transactions. In general, these rules are enforced by the self-regulating bodies.

To clarify the SEC's supreme role, Congress amended the Exchange Act in 1975 to give the SEC explicit authority over all self-regulatory organizations (SROs). Any exchange or OTC rule change now requires advance approval from the SEC. The commission also has reviewing power over all disciplinary actions taken by the SROs. Moreover, as we mentioned earlier, the 1975 amendments eliminated the power of exchanges to fix minimum commission rates.

Two legal questions have arisen concerning Congress's delegation of power to the SROs to adopt rules that have the force of law: Can an exchange be held liable for damages resulting from its failure to enforce a rule it has adopted? Are SRO members who violate one of the organization's rules liable to a person injured by the violation? The courts have generally said yes to the first question and are split on the second.

PROXY SOLICITATIONS

PROCEDURAL AND SUBSTANTIVE RULES Section 14 of the Exchange Act and the accompanying SEC regulations set forth the ground rules governing proxy solicitations by inside management, dissident shareholders, and potential acquirers of a company. You will remember from our discussion in chapter 15 that proxies are documents by which the shareholders of a publicly registered company designate another individual or institution to vote their shares at a shareholders' meeting. They are often used by inside management to defeat proposals by dissident shareholders or to prevent a takeover by a "hostile," company. The real significance of the proxy solicitation process, however, is that it may result in materially changing the direction of the corporation with-

exchange market A securities market that provides a physical facility for the buying and selling of stocks and prescribes the number and qualifications of its broker-members. These brokers buy and sell stocks through the exchange's registered specialist, who are dealers on the floor of the exchange.

over-the-counter (OTC) market A securities market that has no physical facility and no membership qualifications and whose broker-dealers are market makers who buy and sell stocks directly from the public.

out its owners' (the shareholders') awareness. Because very few individual shareholders (under 1 percent) attend annual shareholders' meetings, proxy voting is management's major instrument for electing the directors and setting the policy it wants.

Against this background, Congress enacted Section 14 of the Exchange Act—the section known as the *Williams Act*—making it unlawful for a company to solicit proxies in "contravention of such rules and regulations as the Commission [SEC] may prescribe as necessary or appropriate in the public interest or for the protection of investors." With this broad statutory authority, the SEC has promulgated rules and regulations that require all companies registered under the Securities Act to file proxy statements with the commission ten days before mailing them to shareholders. During this ten-day period, the SEC staff comments on the statements and sometimes asks for changes, usually because it believes all material information has not been included. Under its Rule 22, the commission requires proxy statements to carry several items of information, ranging from a notice on the revocability of proxies to a notification of the interest that the soliciting individuals or institutions have in the subject matter to be voted on. The purpose of this procedure is to make sure that shareholders have full disclosure on a matter before they agree to any grant of their proxy. The SEC also requires companies to send shareholders a form on which they can mark their approval or disapproval of the subject matter to be voted on. If a proxy is solicited for electing new directors, the shareholders must receive an annual report of the corporation as well.

SHAREHOLDER PROPOSALS   If a shareholder of a registered issuing company wishes to place an item on the agenda, Rule 14(a)(8) requires that management be notified in a timely way before a regular shareholder meeting or a special meeting. Once notified, management must include the proposal (200 words or fewer) in the proxy statement it sends to all the shareholders. Management may also include its own view on the proposal. Shareholder proposals in recent years have included prohibitions against discrimination, pollution, dumping of wastes, "golden parachutes," "poison pills," and "greenmail" (the last three topics are discussed later in this section under the heading "Tender Offers and Takeover Bids"). In a sense, proxy solicitation became a form of "shareholder democracy"—one that corporate management felt was getting out of hand. After vigorous debate by all interested groups, the SEC amended Rule 14(a) in 1983 to allow management to exclude a shareholder proposal if:

1. Under the particular state law governing the corporation, the proposal would be unlawful if agreed to by the directors.
2. It involves a personal grievance.
3. It is related to ordinary operational business functions.
4. It is a matter not significantly related to the company's business. (The commission has defined this criterion as matters accounting for less than 5 percent of the assets, earnings, and sales of a company.)
5. The stockholder making the proposal has not owned more than $1,000 worth of stock or 1 percent of the shares outstanding for a period of one year or more. (Several shareholders may accumulate shares to meet this criterion.)
6. The shareholders proposal received less than 5 percent of the votes when submitted in a previous year. Further, shareholders are limited to one proposal per annual company meeting.

If management excludes a proposal, it must explain why, and the shareholder may then appeal to the SEC. The SEC staff decides whether the proposal should be placed on the agenda for the next annual meeting.

PROXY CONTESTS   Proxy contests normally come about when an insurgent group of shareholders seeks to elect its own slate of candidates to the board of directors to replace management's slate. Both insurgent shareholders and management may seek shareholder proxies in this contest.

The SEC has set out specific rules governing disclosure by insurgents and management and the rights of each. An information statement must be filed by the insurgents disclosing all participants in their group and the background of each, including past employment and any criminal history. When soliciting shareholder votes, insurgents must provide their own proxy statement, as must management. Insurgents have the right to obtain the company's shareholder list so they can mail their proxy statement directly to the shareholders. Alternatively, management must mail the insurgents' proxy request to the shareholders along with its own proxy statement, with the extra costs of the mailing borne by the insurgents.

Both criminal and civil liability attach to a company that sends a misleading proxy statement to its shareholders. The civil liability is based on a negligence standard (preponderance of evidence). The SEC may, through injunctive relief, prevent the solicitation of proxies or may declare an election of directors, based on misleading proxies, to be invalid. Under the Insider Trader Sanctions Act of 1984 (discussed later in this chapter), the commission may also institute criminal and administrative proceedings against a company. Furthermore, persons who rely on a misleading proxy statement to buy or sell securities have the right to institute a private action, as do insurgent shareholders in a proxy fight.

TENDER OFFERS AND TAKEOVER BIDS

A series of hostile takeovers in the 1980s, and creative defensive strategies used by management of some targeted companies, renewed concerned parties' interest in the regulation of tender offers and takeover bids.

In a takeover bid, the acquiring company or individual, using a public **tender offer**, seeks to purchase a controlling interest (51 percent) in another company—the *target company*—which would lead to a takeover of that company's board of directors and management. The acquiring company makes this public offer in such national papers as the *Wall Street Journal* or the *New York Times* to company shareholders, requesting that they tender their shares for cash or for the acquiring company's securities, or for both, usually at a price exceeding that quoted for the shares on a national exchange. Because of abuses in the 1960s, when shareholders frequently were given only a short time to make up their minds and thus could not properly evaluate tender offers, Congress enacted legislation to give shareholders more information and a longer period to make a decision. This legislation became Sections 13 and 14 of the Securities Exchange Act.

tender offer A public offer by an individual or corporation made directly to the shareholders of another corporation in an effort to acquire the targeted corporation at a specific price.

RULES GOVERNING TENDER OFFERS Sections 13 and 14 of the Exchange Act together constitute the regulatory framework for tender offers. *Section 13* requires any person (or group) that acquires more than 5 percent of any class of registered securities to file within ten days a statement with both the issuer (the target company) and the SEC. This statement must set forth (1) the background of the acquiring person or group, (2) the source of the funds used to acquire the 5 percent, (3) the purpose(s) of the acquisition of the stock, (4) the number of shares presently owned, (5) any relevant contracts with the target company, and (6) plans of the person or group for the targeted company.

Section 14 provides that no one may make a tender offer that results in ownership of more than 5 percent of a class of registered securities unless that person or group files with the SEC, and also with each offeree, a statement containing information similar to that required by Section 13. It also restricts the terms of the offer, particularly the right of withdrawal by the offerer and extensions or changes in the offer.

The SEC has issued detailed rules concerning Section 14. For example, even if the offer is a **hostile bid**—meaning the management of the target company opposes it—the target company must either mail the tender offer to all shareholders or promptly forward a list of the shareholders to the tender offerer. Management must also, within ten days of receiving a tender offer, state whether it opposes or favors it or lacks enough information to make a judgment. SEC rules also compel management to file a form called Schedule 14-9.

hostile bid A tender offer that is opposed by the management of the target company.

Schedule 14-9 requires top managers to (1) disclose whether they intend to hold their shares in the company or tender them to the offerer; (2) describe any agreements they may have made with the tender offerer; and (3) disclose, if the tender offer is hostile, whether they have engaged in any negotiations with a friendly or "white knight" company.

Section 14 of the 1934 act and SEC rules require that a tender offer be open for at least 20 days so shareholders will have a reasonable amount of time to consider it. The SEC has also set out certain withdrawal rights for shareholders who have tendered their shares.

REMEDIES AND DEFENSIVE STRATEGIES

REMEDIES Section 14(e) (known as the Williams Act) makes it a criminal offense to make an untrue or misleading statement or to engage in fraudulent acts or deceptive practices in connection with a tender offer. The emphasis here is on intent to deceive. Shareholders of a targeted company can bring civil actions under Section 14(e) for violations of Sections 13(d) and 14(b) if they can show they have been injured because they relied on fraudulent statements in the tender offer. In addition, under the Insider Trader Sanctions Act (discussed later in this section under "Securities Fraud"), the SEC may start administrative proceedings against violators, which is a much quicker remedy than going to court.

In the landmark case that follows, in which the U.S. Supreme Court interpreted the meaning of Section 14(e) of the Securities Act, note the Court's concern over the correct interpretation of the word *manipulative*, which is the basis for causes of actions brought under this section.

BARBARA SCHREIBER V. BURLINGTON NORTHERN, INCORPORATED
UNITED STATES SUPREME COURT 472 U.S. 1 (1985)

Petitioner Schreiber, on behalf of herself and other shareholders of El Paso Gas Company, sued respondent Burlington Northern, claiming that the company had violated Section 14(e) of the Securities Exchange Act of 1934. In December 1982, Burlington issued a hostile tender offer for El Paso Gas Company. Burlington did not accept the shares tendered by a majority of shareholders of El Paso but instead rescinded the December offer and substituted another offer for El Paso in January. The rescission of the first tender offer resulted in a smaller payment per share to El Paso shareholders who retendered after the January offer. The petitioners claimed that Burlington's withdrawal of the December tender offer and the substitution of the January offer were a "manipulative" distortion of the market for El Paso stock and a violation of Section 14(e). Respondent argued that "manipulative" acts under 14(e) require misrepresentation or nondisclosure and that no such acts had taken place in this case. Therefore respondent moved for dismissal of the case based on a failure to state a cause of action. The federal district court granted the motion for dismissal. The court of appeals affirmed. Schreiber appealed to the U.S. Supreme Court.

CHIEF JUSTICE BURGER

We are asked in this case to interpret § 14(e) of the Securities Exchange Act. The starting point is the language of the statute. Section 14(e) provides:

It shall be unlawful for any person to make any untrue statement of a material fact or omit to state any material fact necessary in order to make the statements made, in the light of the circumstances under which they are made, not misleading, or to engage in any fraudulent, deceptive or manipulative acts or practices, in connection with any tender offer or request or invitation for tenders, or any solicitation of security holders in opposition to or in favor of any such offer, request, or invitation. The Commission shall, for the purposes of this subsection, by rules and regulations define, and prescribe means reasonably designed to prevent, such acts and practices as are fraudulent, deceptive, or manipulative.

Our conclusion that "manipulative" acts under § 14(e) require misrepresentation or nondisclosure is buttressed by the purpose and legislative history of the provision. Section 14(e) was originally added to the Securities Exchange Act as part of the Williams Act.

It is clear that Congress relied primarily on disclosure to implement the purpose of the Williams Act. Senator Williams, the bill's Senate sponsor, stated in the debate:

Today, the public shareholder in deciding whether to accept or reject a tender offer possesses limited information. No matter what he does, he acts without adequate knowledge to enable him to decide rationally what is the best course of action. This is precisely the dilemma which our securities laws are designed to prevent.

The expressed legislative intent was to preserve a neutral setting in which the contenders could fully present their arguments. To implement this objective, the Williams Act added §§ 13(d), 13(e), 14(e), and 14(f) to the Securities Exchange Act. Some relate to disclosure; §§ 13(d), 14(d) and 14(f) all add specific registration and disclosure provisions. Others—§§ 13(e) and 14(d)—require or prohibit certain acts so that investors will possess additional time within which to take advantage of the disclosed information.

To adopt the reading of the term "manipulative" urged by petitioner would not only be unwarranted in light of the legislative purpose but would be at odds with it. Inviting judges to read the term "manipulative" with their own sense of what constitutes "unfair" or "artificial" conduct would inject uncertainty into the tender offer process. An essential piece of information—whether the court would deem the fully disclosed actions of one side or the other to be "manipulative"—would not be available until after the tender offer had closed. This uncertainty would directly contradict the expressed Congressional desire to give investors full information.

Congress' consistent emphasis on disclosure persuades us that it intended takeover contests to be addressed to shareholders. In pursuit of this goal, Congress, consistent with the core mechanism of the Securities Exchange Act created sweeping disclosure requirements and narrow substantive safeguards. The same Congress that placed such emphasis on shareholder choice would not at the same time have required judges to oversee tender offers for substantive fairness.

We hold that the term "manipulative" as used in § 14(e) requires misrepresentation or nondisclosure. It connotes "conduct designed to deceive or defraud investors by controlling or artificially affecting the price of securities." *Ernst Ernst v. Hochfelder*, 425 U.S., at 199. Without misrepresentation or nondisclosure, § 14(e) has not been violated.

Applying that definition to this case, we hold that the actions of respondents were not manipulative. The amended complaint fails to allege that the cancellation of the first tender offer was accompanied by any misrepresentation, nondisclosure or deception.

Affirmed in favor of Defendant, Burlington Northern.

Critical Thinking about the Law

SOMETIMES AMBIGUITY IS PRESENT IN THE court's own reasoning; a judge might argue that a "reasonable" person would not be offended by sexual advances made by a fellow employee. At other times, the court must interpret ambiguity in congressional legislation to make a legal judgment.

This case deals with the second of those judicial confrontations with ambiguity. It is important to be aware not only of the Court's interpretation of an ambiguity but also of the evidence it selects in supporting that interpretation. The very fact that an important term is ambiguous means that there might be other legitimate interpretations; thus, in judging whether you agree with the particular interpretation at hand, you must evaluate the evidence presented for it. It is also important to recognize the primary ethical norm that informed the Court's interpretation. The following questions address those considerations.

1. What legislative ambiguity was the Court dealing with in this case?

   CLUE   The meaning of this term is the central issue of the case.

2. Specifically, to what evidence did the Court refer to support its own interpretation of the ambiguity?

   CLUE   Reread the paragraph immediately following the quotation from Section 14(e).

3. In supporting its strict interpretation of legislative ambiguity, the Court stated that Congress intended to leave issues of fairness up to shareholders and not judges, making full disclosure the most important consideration. In this prioritization of the liberty (of shareholders) over potentially more just outcomes (allowing judges to decide fairness), one might argue that the primary ethical norm of liberty drove the Court's reasoning. What other primary ethical norm is implicit in this prioritization?

   CLUE   Consider the primary ethical norm that would be damaged if judges decided fairness (especially with the inevitable increase in court cases).

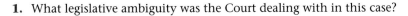

DEFENSIVE STRATEGIES   The *business judgment rule*, which we discussed in chapter 15, is based primarily on the 50 states' case law and the Revised Model Business Corporations Act. It has traditionally allowed wide latitude to managements of targeted companies, as long as they act in good faith in the best interests of the shareholders, do not waste the corporate assets, and do not enter into conflict-of-interest situations.

Here is a list of defensive strategies that managements of targeted companies have used to repel hostile takeovers in recent years.

- Awarding large compensation packages ("golden parachutes") to target-company management when a takeover is rumored.
- Issuing new classes of securities before or during a takeover battle that require a tender offerer to pay much more than the market price for the stock ("poison pill").
- Buying out a "hostile" shareholder at a price far above the current market price of the target company's stock in exchange for the hostile shareholder's agreement not to buy more shares for a period of time ("greenmail"). Congress has eliminated this defense by legislation.
- Writing super-majority requirements for merger approval into the bylaws and corporation articles ("porcupine provisions").
- Issuing treasury shares (stock that was repurchased by the issuing corporation) to friendly parties.
- Moving to states with strong antitakeover ("shark repellent") laws.
- Bankrupting the company ("scorched-earth" policy).
- Prevailing upon another company or individual (a "white knight") to buy out the hostile bidder to prevent the undesirable takeover.

SECURITIES FRAUD

The courts have had a difficult time defining securities fraud. An appellate court once stated: "Fraud is infinite, and were a Court of Equity once to lay down rules, how far they would go, and no further, in extending their relief against it, or to define strictly the species or evidence of it, the jurisdiction would be cramped, and perpetually eluded by new schemes which the fertility of man's invention would contrive." This is the philosophical position that has been adopted by the SEC: There cannot be a law against every type of fraud imaginable. Instead, the SEC staff has sought to use Section 10(b) of the Securities Act broadly, going beyond its exact language to develop a "fraud-on-the-market" theory that does not require the investor-plaintiff ever to have relied on false documents or specific acts but only on the integrity of the market and a fair stock price.

SECTION 10(b) OF THE SECURITIES EXCHANGE ACT   One of the purposes of the Securities Exchange Act of 1934 was to ensure the full disclosure of all material information to potential investors. Full disclosure enables the market mechanism to operate efficiently and ensures that consumers are provided with a fair price for securities. Section 10(b) prohibits the use of the mails or other facilities (e.g., truck or car and satellite or data transmission) in interstate commerce "in connection with the purchase or sale of any security, any manipulative or deceptive device or contrivance in contravention of such rules and regulations as the Commission may prescribe as necessary or appropriate in the public interest or for the protection of investors." This board statutory language signals a congressional intent to cover all possible forms of fraud. To that end,

it shall be unlawful for any person, directly or indirectly, by the use of any means or instrumentality of interstate commerce, or of the mails, or of any facility of any national securities exchange, (1) to employ any device, scheme, or artifice to defraud, (2) to make any untrue statement of a material fact necessary in order to make the statements made, in the light of circumstances under which they were made, not misleading or (3) to engage in any act, practice, or course of business which operates or would operate as a fraud or deceit upon any person, in connection with the purchase or sale of any security.

A private party's standing to sue under Section 10(b) and associated SEC Rule 10(b)-5 has been upheld in cases in which manipulative or deceptive acts were committed in connection with the purchase or sale of securities. The question of standing that the Supreme Court answers in the following case is whether civil liability under Rule 10(b)-5 extends also to those who aid and abet violators.

CENTRAL BANK OF DENVER, N.A. V. FIRST INTERSTATE BANK OF DENVER, N.A., AND JACK K. NABER
UNITED STATES SUPREME COURT 62 L.W. 4230 (1994)

After a default on certain bonds it had purchased, plaintiff First Interstate Bank of Denver (Interstate) sued Central Bank of Denver (Central Bank), the public building authority, the bonds' underwriter, and the land developer. Interstate alleged that defendant Central Bank was secondarily liable under Rule 10(b)-5 for its conduct in aiding and abetting the other defendants' fraud. Because the other defendants were primarily liable, Central Bank moved for a summary judgment, claiming that a private plaintiff does not have standing to bring an aiding and abetting suit under Rule l0(b)-5. The federal district court granted summary judgment for Central Bank. The tenth circuit court of appeals reversed in favor of the plaintiff, setting forth three elements that must be present in such a Section l0(b) suit: (1) a primary violation of Section l0(b); (2) recklessness by the aider and abettor as to the primary violation; and (3) substantial assistance given to the primary violator by the aider and abettor. The defendant appealed.

JUSTICE KENNEDY

As we have interpreted it, § l0(b) of the Securities Exchange Act of 1934 imposes private civil liability on those who commit a manipulative or deceptive act in connection with the purchase or sale of securities. In this case, we must answer a question reserved in two earlier decisions: whether private civil liability under § 10(b) extends as well to those who do not engage in the manipulative or deceptive practice but who aid and abet the violation.

We reach the uncontroversial conclusion, accepted even by those courts recognizing a § 10(b) aiding and abetting cause of action, that the text of the 1934 Act does not itself reach those who aid and abet a § 10(b) violation. Unlike those courts, however, we think that conclusion resolves the case. It is inconsistent with settled methodology in § 10(b) cases to extend liability beyond the scope of conduct prohibited by the statutory text. To be sure, aiding and abetting a wrongdoer ought to be actionable in certain instances. The issue, however, is not whether imposing private civil liability on aiders and abettors is good policy but whether aiding and abetting is covered by the statute.

As in earlier cases considering conduct prohibited by § 10(b), we again conclude that the statute prohibits only the making of a material misstatement (or omission) or the commission of a manipulative act. The proscription does not include giving aid to a person who commits a manipulative or deceptive act. We cannot amend the statute to create liability for acts that are not themselves manipulative or deceptive within the meaning of the statute.

From the fact that Congress did not attach private aiding and abetting liability to any of the express causes of action in the securities Acts, we can infer that Congress likely would not have attached aiding and abetting liability to § 10(b) had it provided a private § 10(b) cause of action. There is no reason to think that Congress would have attached aiding and abetting liability only to § 10(b) and not to any of the express private rights of action in the Act. In *Blue Chip Stamps*, we noted that it would be "anomalous to impute to Congress an intention to expand the plaintiff class for a judicially implied cause of action beyond the bounds it delineated for comparable express causes of action." Here, it would be just as anomalous to impute to Congress an intention in effect to expand the defendant class for 10b-5 actions beyond the bounds delineated for comparable express causes of action.

Our reasoning is confirmed by the fact that respondents' argument would impose 10(b)-5 aiding and abetting liability when at least one element critical for recovery under 10(b)-5 is absent: reliance. A plaintiff must show reliance on the defendant's misstatement or omission to recover under 10(b)-5. Were we to allow the aiding and abetting action proposed in this case, the defendant could be liable without any showing that the plaintiff relied upon the aider and abettor's statements or actions. Allowing plaintiffs to circumvent the reliance requirement would disregard the careful limits on 10(b)-5 recovery mandated by our earlier cases.

Because the text of § 10(b) does not prohibit aiding and abetting, we hold that a private plaintiff may not maintain an aiding and abetting suit under § 10(b). The absence of § 10(b) aiding and abetting liability does not mean that secondary actors in the securities markets are always free from liability under the securities Acts. Any person or entity, including a lawyer, accountant, or bank, who employs a manipulative device or makes a material misstatement (or omission) on which a purchaser or seller of securities relies may be liable as a primary violator under 10(b)-5, assuming all of the requirements for primary liability under Rule 10(b)-5 are met. In any complex securities fraud, moreover, there are likely to be multiple violators; in this case, for example, respondents named four defendants as primary violators.

Respondents concede that Central Bank did not commit a manipulative or deceptive act within the meaning of § 10(b). Instead, in the words of the complaint, Central Bank was "secondarily liable under § 10(b) for its conduct in aiding and abetting the fraud." Because of our conclusion that there is no private aiding and abetting liability under § 10(b), Central Bank may not be held liable as an aider and abettor.

Reversed in favor of Defendant, Central Bank.

Critical Thinking about the Law

THE SIGNIFICANCE OF HOW WE FORMULATE issues cannot be overstated. The answers that we find are to a large extent molded by the questions that we ask. Suppose that you are a business manager who is responsible for employee evaluations. Suppose further that in evaluating each employee, you can ask but one of two questions: Does the employee work quickly? or Does the employee do quality work? For each employee, you will probably get very divergent answers depending on which question you ask. One employee may work very quickly, but often has to redo assignments. Another employee may work more slowly, perhaps even to the point of missing deadlines, but still do superior work. Thus the issue you formulate—that is, the question you ask—will be the decisive factor in determining which of these two employees you evaluate more favorably. Of course, in a normal evaluation process, you would likely pose both questions; however, for the sake of highlighting the importance of issue formulation, this either-or example is illuminating.

What a court decides is the issue of a case is crucial to the legal outcome of that case. Consequently, we will explore this function of the Court in the questions that follow.

1. What issue did the Court seek to resolve here?

   CLUE Reread the first paragraph of the decision.

2. The lower court, in finding in favor of the plaintiff, based its judgment on a set of criteria. How did Justice Kennedy's formulation of the issue affect the significance of those criteria?

   CLUE You want to focus on the fact that the two courts handed down opposite opinions.

3. What key fact in the Securities Act's legislative history helped bolster the Supreme Court's decision that aiding and abetting liability did not properly come under the purview of the act?

   CLUE Reread the fourth paragraph, paying particular attention to private causes of action.

The use of Section 10(b) and Rule 10(b)-5 has been controversial in three major areas of securities fraud: insider trading, misstatements by corporate management, and mismanagement of a corporation (Table 21-4). After exploring each of these areas in turn, we will say something about a new concept that shareholder suits based on fraud have been invoking: "fraud-on-the market" theory.

insider trading The use of material, nonpublic information received from a corporate source by someone who has a fiduciary obligation to shareholders and potential investors and who benefits from trading on such information.

INSIDER TRADING AND SECTION 10(B) OF THE SECURITIES ACT   Insider Trading is the use of material, nonpublic information received from a corporate source by an individual who has a fiduciary obligation to shareholders and potential investors and who benefits from trading on such information. Insiders have been found by the courts to be (1) officers and directors of a corporation, (2) partners in investment banking and brokerage firms, (3) attorneys in a retained law firm, (4) underwriters and broker-dealers, (5) financial reporters, and (6) in a unique case, an employee of a financial printing firm that printed documents for a tender offer. (See Exhibit 21-5 for a look at Wall Street's army of insiders, from the general to the grunts.)

TABLE 21-4   *Securities Fraud under Section 10(b) of the Securities Exchange Act of 1934*

ACTIVITY	DEFINITION
Insider trading	The use of nonpublic information received from a corporate source by an individual(s) who has a fiduciary obligation to shareholders and potential investors and who benefits from trading on such information.
Misstatement of corporation	Any report, release, or financial statement, or any other statement, that is released by an officer, director, or employee of a corporation in connection with the purchase or sale of a security that shows an intent to mislead shareholders or potential investors.
Corporate mismanagement	Any transaction involving the purchase or sale of a security in which there is fraud based on an action of management. The plaintiff must be either a purchaser or a seller of securities in such transaction.

EXHIBIT 21-5 *Insider Traders*

THE INSIDERS
As part of their jobs, hundreds of people help to arrange mergers and buybacks that will push up stock prices once the deals become public. The process often begins in the executive suite, when chairpeople talk merger and bring in their top associates.

Vice Chairpeople   General Counsel   Boards of Directors

INVESTMENT BANKERS
Any company involved in a merger hires a Wall Street bank, with its numerous specialists.

Financial Experts   Research Analysts   Merger and Acquisition Teams

THE SUPPORTING CAST

Law Firms   Public Relations Advisers   Banks, Bond Dealers, Lenders

ON THE EDGE
Many others get insider information from the key players. These are the friends and relatives of the deal makers. Arbitragers, who speculate on mergers, can end up as well informed as the key players through constant sleuthing.

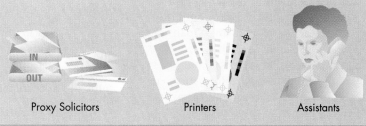

Proxy Solicitors   Printers   Assistants

Source: "Wall Street's Army of Insiders," reprinted from the *New York Times*, May 18, 1986, Sect. 3, p. F1. Copyright © 1986 by The New York Times Company. Reprinted by permission. Art reproduced by permission of John S. Dykes.

The expansion of targets in insider trading cases, from management and corporate directors to a *Wall Street Journal* reporter and a printer employee, has resulted from the SEC enforcement staff's determination that in order to provide full disclosure in the marketplace for potential investors, it had to extend its jurisdiction over tippers (insiders) and tippees (those who receive tips from insiders). The following case was the first in which the SEC staff was able to convince a U.S. Court of Appeals that a *misappropriation theory* could be the basis for liability for insider trading. This theory holds that if an individual misappropriates information and trades on it for personal gain, that individual should be held liable for securities fraud.

UNITED STATES V. CARPENTER
UNITED STATES COURT OF APPEALS 791 F.2D 1024 (2D CIR. 1986)

The prosecutor, the United States, charged defendants Winans and Felis with securities fraud for misappropriating material nonpublic information in connection with the purchase and sale of securities in violation of Section 10(b) of the Exchange Act of 1934 and SEC Rule 10(b)-5 and defendant Carpenter with aiding and abetting the fraud. Winans was a reporter for the *Wall Street Journal (Journal)* who wrote a column titled "Heard on the Street." Carpenter worked as a news clerk, and Felis and Brant were stockbrokers. Winans and Carpenter knew of the *Journal's* policy that all information gained by employees in the course of their employment was confidential. They nonetheless participated in a scheme whereby Winans gave Carpenter insider information that was about to be printed in the "Heard on the Street" column. Carpenter then turned the information over to Felis and Brant, who traded on it. Net profits for all amounted to $690,000.

All were convicted of fraud, with Carpenter convicted of aiding and abetting the fraud, by a federal district court. The defendants appealed.

JUDGE PEARCE

This case requires us to decide principally whether a newspaper reporter, a former newspaper clerk, and a stockbroker, acting in concert, criminally violated or conspired to violate or aided and abetted in the violation of federal securities laws by misappropriating material, nonpublic information in the form of the timing and the content of the *Wall Street Journal's* confidential schedule of columns.

Although the facts render the securities fraud issue herein one of first impression, we do not write on a clean slate in assessing whether this case falls within the purview of the "misappropriation" theory of section 10(b) and Rule 10(b)-5 thereunder. It is clear that defendant Winans, an employee of the *Wall Street Journal*, breached a duty of confidentiality to his employer by misappropriating from the *Journal* confidential prepublication information, regarding the timing and content of certain newspaper columns, about which he learned in the course of his employment. We are presented with the question of whether that unlawful conduct may serve as the predicate for the securities fraud charges hereon.

The core of appellants' argument is that the misappropriation theory may be applied only where the information is misappropriated by corporate insiders or so-called quasi-insiders . . . who owe to the corporation and its shareholders a fiduciary duty of abstention of disclosure. Thus, appellants would have us hold that it was not enough that Winans breached a duty of confidentiality to his employer, the *Wall Street Journal*, in misappropriating and trading on material non-public information; he would have to have breached a duty to the corporations or shareholders thereof whose stock they purchased or sold on the basis of that information.

The legislative intent of the 1934 Act is broad reaching. As this Court has noted in applying the misappropriation theory, "the antifraud provision was intended to be broad in scope, encompassing all 'manipulative and deceptive practices which have been demonstrated to fulfill no useful function.' " We perceive nothing "useful" about defendants' scheme. Nor, in our view, could any purported function of the scheme be considered protected given Congress' stated concern for the perception of fairness and integrity in the securities markets and the potential costs of forsaking such legislated concerns, including fewer market participants and greater reliance on fraud as a means of competing in the market.

Obviously, one may gain a competitive advantage in the marketplace through conduct constituting skill, foresight, industry and the like. Certainly this is as true in securities law as in antitrust, patent, trademark, copyright and other fields. But one may not gain such advantage by conduct constituting secreting, stealing, purloining or otherwise misappropriating material non-public information in breach of an employer-imposed fiduciary duty of confidentiality. Such conduct constitutes chicanery, not competition; foul play, not fair play. Indeed, underlying section 10(b) and the major securities laws generally is the fundamental promotion of " 'the highest ethical standards' . . . in every facet of the securities industry."

The information misappropriated here was the *Journal's* own confidential schedule of forthcoming publications. It was the advance knowledge of the timing and content of these publications, upon which appellants, acting secretively, reasonably expected to and did realize profits in securities transactions. Since section 10(b) has been found to prohibit fraudulent trading by insiders or outsiders, such conduct constituted fraud and deceit, as it would had Winans stolen material nonpublic information from traditional corporate insiders or quasi-insiders. Felis' liability as a tippee derives from Winans' liability given the district court's finding of the requisite scienter [intent] on Felis' part.

Nor is there any doubt that this "fraud and deceit" was perpetrated "upon a[ny] person" under section 10(b) and Rule 10(b)-5. It is sufficient that the fraud was committed upon Winans' employer. Appellants Winans, and Felis and Car-

penter by their complicity, perpetrated their fraud "upon" the *Wall Street Journal*, sullying its reputation and thereby defrauding it "as surely as if they took [its] money."

Thus, because of his duty of confidentiality to the *Journal*, defendant Winans—and Felis and Carpenter, who knowingly participated with him—had a corollary duty, which they breached under section 10(b) and Rule 10(b)-5, to abstain from trading in securities on the basis of the misappropriated information or to do so only upon making adequate disclosure to those with whom they traded.

Affirmed in favor of Plaintiff, United States.

COMMENT: The defendant filed a petition for review to the U.S. Supreme Court. The Court was divided 4–4 and the convictions were therefore upheld. More recently the Supreme Court of the United States has approved the misappropriation theory (See *U.S. V. O'Hagan*, supra at p. 539).

Insider Trader Sanctions Act and the Remedies Act   After the SEC was unable to persuade the Supreme Court to broaden its definition of insider trading in two cases, Congress enacted the *Insider Trader Sanctions Act (ITSA) of 1984*. This act continues the congressional policy of leaving the definition of insider trading up to the courts, but it provides that treble damages ("three times the profits gained or avoided") be levied against "any person who has violated any provision [of the 1934 Act] or rules or regulations while in possession of material nonpublic information." The treble-damage provision does not apply to aiders and abettors, but other provisions of the act do. The ITSA increases criminal penalties for insider trading and other violations of the Exchange Act from $10,000 to $100,000 for each violation. It also expressly allows the SEC to bring administrative proceedings against individuals within an organization that is responsible for such violations. Previously, the commission had to use an "aid and abet" theory against such persons, and the sole enforcement remedies available to it were an injunction against future violations and disgorgement of profits. Using the new administrative enforcement power granted to the commission by the ITSA, the SEC general counsel has proposed that members of boards of directors continually found guilty of insider trading be barred from serving as officers or members of the boards of any U.S.-registered corporation. Still, the ITSA leaves unresolved three important issues: (1) the legal definition of insider trading, (2) the availability of the treble-damage penalty to private plaintiffs who have been injured, and (3) the definition of "aiders and abettors" under the statute.

The *Remedies Act* discussed at the beginning of this chapter, under "Summary of Federal Securities Legislation," widens the scope of the Insider Trader Sanctions Act by giving the SEC additional new weapons such as cease and desist authority and the ability to impose substantial monetary penalties in administrative proceedings for those who violate, or are about to violate, the federal securities laws.

MISSTATEMENTS OF CORPORATIONS AND SECTION 10(b)

The second area of controversy to which Section 10(b) applies involves statements by corporate executives. Any report, release, or financial statement or any other statement that sets forth material information (information that would affect the judgment of the average prudent investor) falls within Section 10(b).

Whereas Sections 13 and 14 of the Exchange Act, which we discussed earlier, apply only to reports, proxy statements, and other documents filed by a company registered with the SEC and a national exchange, Rule 10(b)-5 applies to any statement made by any issuer, registered or not. To be considered a securities fraud, corporate misstatements must meet two requirements: (1) They must be issued "in connection with the purchase or sale of any security," and (2) there must be a showing of **scienter** (intent). As you read the landmark case set out here, you should try to determine how closely the defendants met those requirements.

scienter Knowledge that a representation is false.

The SEC (plaintiff) brought an action against the Texas Gulf Sulphur Company (TGS) and 13 of its directors, officers, and employees (defendants) for violation of Section 10(b) of the Exchange Act and SEC Rule 10(b)-5, seeking an injunction against further misleading press releases and requesting rescission of defendants' purchases and stock options. On June 6, 1963, TGS had acquired an option to buy 160 acres of land in Timmons, Ontario. On November 11, 1963, preliminary drilling indicated there would be major copper and zinc finds. TGS acquired the land and resumed drilling on March 31, 1964, and by April 8, it was evident that there were substantial copper and zinc deposits. On April 9, Toronto and New York newspapers reported that TGS had discovered "one of the largest copper deposits in America." On April 12, TGS's management said that the rumors of a major find were without factual basis. At 10 A.M. on April 14, the board of directors authorized the issuance of a statement confirming the copper, zinc—and silver—finds. On April 20, the New York Stock Exchange announced that it "was barring stop orders [orders to brokers to buy a stock if its price rises to a certain level to lock in profits in case of a sharp rally in that stock] in Texas Gulf Sulphur" because of the extreme volatility in the trading of the stock.

Approximately one month later, rumors circulated about insider trading. It was later found that when drilling began on November 12, 1963, TGS's directors, officers, and employees owned only 1,135 shares of stock in the company and had no calls (options to purchase shares at a fixed price). By March 31, 1964, when drilling resumed, insiders (tippers) and their tippees had acquired an additional 7,100 shares and 12,300 calls. On February 20, 1964, TGS had issued stock options to three officers and two other employees as part of a compensation package. From April 9, 1964, to April 16, 1964, when the confirmatory press release was issued, ten insiders and their tippees made estimated profits of $273,892 on the purchase of their shares or calls of TGS stock. The federal district court dismissed charges against all but two defendants. Those defendants, Clayton and Crawford, appealed, and the SEC appealed from that part of the district court decision that had dismissed the complaint against TGS and the nine other individual defendants.

JUDGE WATERMAN

Rule 10(b)-5 was promulgated pursuant to the grant of authority given the SEC by Congress in Section 10(b) of the Securities Exchange Act of 1934. By that Act Congress proposed to prevent inequitable and unfair practices and to insure fairness in securities transactions generally, whether conducted fact-to-face, over the counter, or on exchanges. The Act and the Rule apply to the transactions here, all of which were consummated on exchanges.

The essence of the Rule is that anyone who, trading for his own account in the securities of a corporation, has "access, directly or indirectly, to information intended to be available only for a corporate purpose and not for the personal benefit of anyone" may not take "advantage of such information knowing it is unavailable to those with whom he is dealing," i.e., the investing public. Insiders, as directors or management officers, are, of course, by this Rule, precluded from so unfairly dealing, but the Rule is also applicable to one possessing the information who may not be strictly termed an "insider" within the means of Sec. 10(b) of the Act. Thus, anyone in possession of material inside information must either disclose it to the investing public, or, if he is disabled from disclosing it in order to protect a corporate confidence, or he chooses not to do so, must abstain from trading in or recommending the securities concerned while such insider information remains undisclosed. So, it is here no justification for insider activity that disclosure was forbidden by the legitimate corporate objective of acquiring options to purchase the land surrounding the exploration site; if the information was, as the SEC contends, material, its possessors should have kept out of the market until disclosure was accomplished.

As we stated in *List v. Fashion Park, Inc.*, "The basic test of materiality is whether a reasonable man would attach importance in determining his choice of action in the transaction in question." This, of course, encompasses any fact "which in reasonable and objective contemplation might affect the value of the corporation's stock or securities." Such a fact is a material fact and must be effectively disclosed to the investing public prior to the commencement of insider trading in the corporation's securities. The speculators and chartists of Wall and Bay Streets are also "reasonable" investors entitled to the same legal protection afforded conservative traders. Thus, material facts include not only information disclosing the earnings and distributions of a company but also those facts which affect the probable future of the company and those which may affect the desire of investors to buy, sell or hold the company's securities.

The core of Rule 10(b)-5 is the implementation of the Congressional purpose that all investors should have equal access to the rewards of participation in securities transactions. It was the intent of Congress that all members of the investing public should be subject to identical market risks—which market risks include, of course, the risk that one's evaluative capacity or one's capital available to put at risk may exceed another's capacity or capital. The insiders here were not trading on an equal footing with the outside investors. They alone were in a position to evaluate the probability and magnitude of what seemed from the outset to be a major ore strike; they alone could invest safely, secure in the expectation that the price of

TGS stock would rise substantially in the event such a major strike should materialize, but would decline little, if at all, in the event of failure, for the public, ignorant at the outset of the favorable probabilities, would likewise be unaware of the unproductive exploration, and the additional exploration costs would not significantly affect TGS market prices. Such inequities based upon unequal access to knowledge should not be shrugged off as inevitable in our way of life, or, in view of the congressional concern in the area, remain uncorrected.

We hold, therefore, that all transactions in TGS stock or calls by individuals apprised of the drilling results of K-55-1 were made in violation of Rule 10(b)-5.

Reversed and remanded in favor of Plaintiff, SEC.

CORPORATE MISMANAGEMENT AND SECTION 10(b) The third controversial area of securities fraud under Section 10(b) is corporate mismanagement. Suits alleging corporate mismanagement and fraud brought by minority shareholders in class action or derivative suits must prove three elements: (1) that the transaction being attacked (e.g., the sale of a controlling stock interest in a corporation at a premium) involves the *purchase* or *sale of securities*, (2) that the alleged fraud is *in connection with* a purchase or sale, and (3) that the *plaintiff is either a purchaser or a seller* of securities in the transaction involved. The *Hochfelder* case, referred to in the *Schreiber* case, is an example of fraud perpetrated on shareholders by management. Other cases alleging fraud dealing with reorganizations and mergers have been brought, but since the mid-1970s, the Supreme Court has been reluctant to allow cases brought under Section 10(b) to preempt state laws, and thus has made plaintiffs meet all three elements in an exacting manner.

FRAUD-ON-THE-MARKET THEORY AND SECTION 10(b) The Supreme Court has attached stringent criteria to all private-party actions brought under Section 10(b)-5 and SEC Rule 10(b)-5. Defrauded investors generally need to show that their losses resulted from specific conduct of the company or its employees or agents and that they had relied on specific misstatements, omissions, or fraudulent actions in making investment decisions. Shareholders have more recently used an efficient-market concept as the basis for suits claiming fraud. That is, they have alleged that they relied on the integrity of an efficient market to assimilate all information about a company and to reflect this information in a fair price for securities. The plaintiff in such a suit argues that when a company makes fraudulent disclosures or omissions, it distorts the information flow to the market, and thus fixes the price of the company's securities too high, in violation of Section 10(b) and Rule 10(b)-5. This *fraud-on-the market theory* assumes that the market price reflects all known material information. In a landmark decision, the U.S. Supreme Court upheld this theory as outlined below.

UNITED STATES V. JAMES O'HAGAN
UNITED STATES SUPREME COURT 117 S. CT. 2199 (1997)

After Grand Metropolitan PLC (Grand Met) retained the law firm of Dorsey & Whitney to represent it regarding a potential tender offer for the Pillsbury Company's common stock, respondent O'Hagan, a Dorsey & Whitney partner who did no work on the representation, began purchasing call options for Pillsbury stock, as well as shares of the stock. After Dorsey & Whitney had withdrawn from the representation, Grand Met publicly announced its tender offer, the price of Pillsbury stock rose dramatically, and O'Hagan sold his call options and stock at a profit of more than $4.3 million. A Securities and Exchange Commission (SEC) investigation culminated in a 57-count indictment alleging, *inter alia*, that O'Hagan had defrauded his law firm and its client, Grand Met, by misappropriating for his own trading purposes material, nonpublic information regarding the tender offer. The indictment charged O'Hagan with securities fraud in violation of § 10(b) of the Securities Exchange Act of 1934 and SEC Rule 10(b)-5, with fraudulent trading in connection with a tender offer in violation of § 14(e) of the Exchange Act and SEC Rule 14(e)-3(a), and with violations of the federal mail fraud and money laundering statutes. A jury convicted O'Hagan on all counts, and he was sentenced to prison. The eighth circuit court reversed all of the convictions, holding that § 10(b) and Rule 10(b)-5 liability may not be grounded on the "misappropriation theory" of securities fraud on which the prosecution relied; that Rule 14(e)-3(a) exceeds the SEC's § 14(e) rulemaking authority because the rule contains no breach of fiduciary duty requirement; and that the mail fraud and money laundering convictions rested on violations of the securities laws, so could not stand once the securities fraud convictions were reversed.

JUSTICE GINSBERG

This case concerns the interpretation and enforcement of § 10(b) and § 14(e) of the Securities Exchange Act of 1934, and rules made by the Securities and Exchange Commission pursuant to these provisions, Rule 10(b)-5 and Rule 14(e)-3(a). Two prime questions are presented. The first relates to the misappropriation of material, nonpublic information for securities trading; the second concerns fraudulent practices in the tender offer setting. In particular, we address and resolve these issues: (1) Is a person who trades in securities for personal profit, using confidential information misappropriated in breach of a fiduciary duty to the source of the information, guilty of violating § 10(b) and Rule 10(b)-5? (2) Did the Commission exceed its rulemaking authority by adopting Rule 14(e)-3(a), which proscribes trading on undisclosed information in the tender offer setting, even in the absence of a duty to disclose? Our answer to the first question is yes, and to the second question, viewed in the context of this case, no.

A person who trades in securities for personal profit, using confidential information, misappropriated in breach of a fiduciary duty to the source of the information, may be held liable for violating § 10(b) and Rule 10(b)-5.

(a) Section 10(b) proscribes (1) using any "deceptive device" (2) "in connection with the purchase or sale of any security," in contravention of SEC rules. The Commission adopted Rule 10(b)-5 pursuant to its § 10(b) rulemaking authority; liability under Rule 10(b)-5 does not extend beyond conduct encompassed by § 10(b)'s prohibition. Under the "traditional" or "classical theory" of insider trading liability, a violation of § 10(b) and Rule 10(b)-5 occurs when a corporate insider trades in his corporation's securities on the basis of material, confidential information he has obtained by reason of his position. Such trading qualifies as a "deceptive device" because there is a relationship of trust and confidence between the corporation's shareholders and the insider that gives rise to a duty to disclose or abstain from trading. Under the complementary "misappropriation theory" urged by the Government here, a corporate "outsider" violates § 10(b) and Rule 10(b)-5 when he misappropriates confidential information

for securities trading purposes, in breach of a fiduciary duty owed to the source of the information, rather than to the persons with whom he trades.

Misappropriation, as just defined, is the proper subject of a § 10(b) charge because it meets the statutory requirement that there be "deceptive" conduct "in connection with" a securities transaction. First, misappropriators deal in deception: A fiduciary who pretends loyalty to the principal while secretly converting the principal's information for personal gain dupes or defrauds the principal. A company's confidential information qualifies as property to which the company has a right of exclusive use; the undisclosed misappropriation of such information constitutes fraud akin to embezzlement. Deception through nondisclosure is central to liability under the misappropriation theory. The theory is thus consistent with a decision underscoring that § 10(b) is not an all-purpose breach of fiduciary duty ban, but trains on conduct that is manipulative or deceptive. Conversely, full disclosure forecloses liability. Because the deception essential to the theory involves feigning fidelity to the information's source, if the fiduciary discloses to the source that he plans to trade on the information, there is no "deceptive device" and thus no § 10(b) violation. Second, § 10(b)'s requirement that the misappropriator's deceptive use of information be "in connection with the purchase or sale of (a) security" is satisfied by the misappropriation theory because the fiduciary's fraud is consummated, not when he obtains the confidential information, but when, without disclosure to his principal, he uses the information in purchasing or selling securities. The transaction and the breach of duty coincide, even though the person or entity defrauded is not the other party to the trade, but is, instead, the source of the nonpublic information. Because undisclosed trading on the basis of misappropriated, nonpublic information both deceives the source of the information and harms members of the investing public, the misappropriation theory is tuned to an animating purpose of the Exchange Act: to ensure honest markets, thereby promoting investor confidence. It would make scant sense to hold a lawyer-turned-trader like O'Hagan a § 10(b) violator if he works for a law firm representing the target of a tender offer, but not if he works for a firm representing the bidder.

The statute's text requires no such result. The Eighth Circuit erred in holding that the misappropriation theory is inconsistent with § 10(b). First, that court understood the theory to require neither misrepresentation nor nondisclosure; as this Court explains, however, deceptive nondisclosure is essential to § 10(b) liability under the theory. Concretely, it was O'Hagan's failure to disclosure his personal trading to Grand Met and Dorsey, in breach of his duty to do so, that made his conduct "deceptive" under § 10(b). Second, the Eighth Circuit misread this Court's precedents when it ruled that only a breach of a duty to parties to a securities transaction, or, at the most, to other market participants such as investors, is sufficient to give rise to § 10(b) liability.

Vital to this Court's decision that criminal liability may be sustained under the misappropriation theory is the Exchange Act's requirement that the Government prove that a person "willfully" violated Rule 10(b)-5 in order to establish a criminal violation, and the Act's provision that a defendant may not be imprisoned for such a violation if he proves that he had no knowledge of the Rule. The requirement of culpable intent weakens O'Hagan's charge that the misappropriation theory is too indefinite to permit the imposition of criminal liability. The Eighth Circuit may address on remand O'Hagan's other challenges to his § 10(b) and Rule 10(b)-5 convictions.

As relevant to this case, the SEC did not exceed its rulemaking authority under § 14(e) by adopting Rule 14(e)-3(a) without requiring a showing that the trading at issue entailed a breach of fiduciary duty. Section 14(e) prohibits "fraudulent ... acts ... in connection with any tender offer," and authorizes the SEC to "define, and prescribe means reasonably designed to prevent such acts." Adopted under that statutory authorization, Rule 14(e)-3(a) forbids any person to trade on the basis of material, nonpublic information that concerns a tender offer and that the person knows or should know has been acquired from an insider of the offeror or issuer, or someone working on their behalf, unless within a reasonable time before any purchase or sale such information and its source are publicly disclosed. Rule 14(e)-3(a) imposes a duty to disclose or abstain from trading whether or not the trader owes a fiduciary duty to respect the confidentiality of the information. In invalidating Rule 14(e)-3(a), the Eighth Circuit reasoned, *inter alia*, that § 14(e) empowers the SEC to identify and regulate "fraudulent" acts, but not to create its own definition of "fraud"; that, under *Schreiber v. Burlington Northern, Inc.*, 472 U.S. 1, 7–8, § 10(b) interpretations guide construction of § 14(e); and that, under *Chiarella,*

supra, at 228, a failure to disclose information can be "fraudulent" for § 10(b) purposes only when there is a duty to speak arising out of a fiduciary or similar relationship of trust and confidence. This Court need not resolve whether the SEC's § 14(e) fraud-defining authority is broader than its like authority under § 10(b), for Rule 14(e)-3(a), as applied to cases of this genre, qualifies under § 14(e) as a "means reasonably designed to prevent" fraudulent trading on material, nonpublic information in the tender offer contest. A prophylactic measure properly encompasses more than the core activity prohibited. Under § 14(e), the SEC may prohibit acts not themselves fraudulent under the common law or § 10(b), if the prohibition is reasonably designed to prevent acts and practices that are fraudulent. See *Schreiber, supra*, at 11 n. 11. In this case, the SEC's assessment is none of these. It is a fair assumption that trading on the basis of material, nonpublic information will often involve a breach of a duty of confidentiality to the bidder or target company or their representatives. The SEC, cognizant of proof problems that could enable sophisticated traders to escape responsibility for such trading, placed in Rule 14(e)-3(a) a "disclose or abstain from trading" command that does not require specific proof of a breach of fiduciary duty. Insofar as it serves to prevent the type of misappropriation charged against O'Hagan, the Rule is therefore a proper exercise of the SEC's prophylactic power under § 14(e). This Court declines to consider in the first instance O'Hagan's alternate arguments that Rule 14(e)-3(a)'s prohibition of preoffer trading conflicts with § 14(e) and violates due process. The Eighth Circuit may address on remand any such argument that O'Hagan has preserved.

Reversed in favor of Plaintiff, United States and *remanded*.

Short-Swing Profits

PURPOSE AND COVERAGE   Section 16(b) of the Exchange Act seeks to further the goal of complete disclosure of trading by insiders by requiring directors, officers, and owners of more than 10 percent of a class of stock of a registered company to file regular reports with the SEC and the exchanges the stock trades on. Directors and officers must file an initial statement of their holdings in the company when they take office, and the others must file when they come to own more than 10 percent. A follow-up statement is due monthly if they change their holdings in any manner. Any profits made by a director or officer or a 10 percent beneficial owner within a six-month period—known as **short-swing profits**—are presumed to be based on insider information. A plaintiff does not have to show that these insiders had access to, relied on, or took advantage of the insider information. In 1991, the SEC adopted new rules relating to Section 16 that (1) created a new form (Form 5) that must be filed by all insiders within 45 days of the end of the issuer's calendar year; (2) waive liability for insiders for transactions that occur within six months of becoming an insider; (3) make the acquisition of a derivative security (e.g., warrant) fall under Section 16; and (4) define an officer under Section 16 as people who have a policy function (e.g., chief executive officer, president, and vice president). Now those company officers who handle day-to-day operations do not fall under Section 16.

short-swing profits Profits made by directors, officers, or owners of 10 percent of the securities of a corporation as a result of buying and selling the securities within a six-month period.

LIABILITY   Suits based on short-swing profits seek to force the insiders to return the profits to the corporation. Only the issuers—meaning the directors and officers of the corporation—and the shareholders have standing to sue. Officers and directors generally do not sue other officers and directors, so virtually all suits are brought by other shareholders. However, the expense of such litigation makes use of this enforcement action infrequent.

INTERNATIONAL DIMENSIONS OF RULES GOVERNING THE ISSUANCE AND TRADING OF SECURITIES

The growing internationalization of money and securities markets has made it important to understand the transnational reach of U.S. securities regulations. Both the 1933 Act and the Exchange Act speak of the use of "facilities or instrumentation in interstate commerce." Interstate commerce is defined in the 1933 Act to include "commerce between any foreign country and the United States."

This section of the chapter is divided into two parts: (1) legislation prohibiting certain forms of bribery and money laundering overseas by United States–based corporations and (2) legislation governing foreign securities sold in the United States. You will notice throughout our discussion that provisions of the 1933 Act and the 1934 Exchange Act overlap.

LEGISLATION PROHIBITING BRIBERY AND MONEY LAUNDERING OVERSEAS

THE FOREIGN CORPORATE PRACTICES ACT (FCPA) OF 1977 AS AMENDED IN 1988   In the course of investigating illegal corporate payments made to President Nixon's 1972 reelection campaign, the SEC staff came across information showing that hundreds of corporations had also made questionable payments to foreign political parties, heads of state, and individuals to obtain business that they would not otherwise have gained. The companies argued that these payments were not illegal under U.S. law, and besides, they were necessary to compete with foreign state-owned and operated enterprises and with state-subsidized multinationals. The SEC, however, considered this information material under both the 1933 and 1934 securities acts because it affected the integrity of management and the records of the corporations involved. In 1974 and 1975, the SEC allowed approximately 435 companies to enter into consent orders whereby the companies did not admit to making illegal payments but agreed to report such payments in the future to the SEC. The SEC also urged Congress to enact legislation prohibiting bribery overseas by U.S. corporations.

The *Foreign Corrupt Practices Act of 1977 (FCPA)*, as amended in 1988, does just that. It applies both to companies registered under the securities acts of 1933 and 1934 and to all other domestic concerns, whether they do business abroad or not. Its antibribery provisions prohibit all domestic firms from offering or authorizing a "corrupt" payment to a foreign official, a foreign political party, or a foreign political candidate to induce the recipient to act, or to refrain from acting, so that a U.S. corporation can obtain business it would not ordinarily get without the payment. The standard of criminal conduct to which corporate officials and employees are held is "knowing." If such a payment is known to violate the FCPA, the corporation can be fined up to $2 million, and its officers, directors, stockholders, employees, and U.S. agents can be fined up to $100,000 and be imprisoned for up to five years. The FCPA prohibits not just the payment of a bribe, but the "offer" or "promise" of "anything of value," even if the offer or promise is never consummated. "Facilitating or expediting payments" to ensure routine governmental action is not prohibited. Also, under the 1988 amendments, liability can be avoided if the defendant proves that the payments were legal in the foreign country where they were made.

The FCPA's *accounting provisions*, enacted as amendments to Section 13(b) of the Exchange Act, apply only to registered nonexempt companies. They require that companies make and keep records and accounts in "reasonable detail" that "accurately and fairly" reflect transactions. Also, companies are required to maintain systems that provide "reasonable assurance" that transactions have been recorded in accordance with generally accepted accounting principles.

The FCPA is jointly enforced by the Justice Department and the SEC. The SEC can investigate and bring civil charges under the act's bribery provisions, but it refers criminal cases to the Justice Department for prosecution. The Justice Department can bring both civil and criminal charges against alleged violators of the FCPA. The SEC is charged with the enforcement of the accounting provisions and can bring both civil actions and administrative proceedings.

CONVENTION ON COMBATING BRIBERY OF FOREIGN OFFICIALS IN INTERNATIONAL BUSINESS TRANSACTIONS (CCBFOIBT)

In 1977, the U.S. Foreign Corrupt Practices Act was enacted. It was amended in 1988 to water down the original act. Twenty years later, the CCBFOIBT was signed in December 1997 by 34 countries after debate by the Organization for Economic Cooperation and Development (OECD). Signatories will be required to criminalize bribery of foreign officials, eliminate the tax-deductibility of bribes, and subject companies to wider disclosure. Russia (an observer) and China are not signatories; the 34 signatories include the United States, Canada, Japan, and Germany. The treaty creates one loophole: grease payments. It is acknowledged that these facilitating payments are the cost of doing business and can be paid to low-level officials.

The major change for the United States will be the need to amend the FCPA to cover foreign subsidiaries of U.S. companies whose activities have a nexus with interstate or foreign commerce. Under current U.S. law such subsidiaries are not subject to the FCPA.

THE INTERNATIONAL SECURITIES ENFORCEMENT COOPERATION ACT (ISECA) OF 1990

After it was found that many insider traders in the United States were holding secret accounts in Switzerland, the SEC in June 1982 entered into a memorandum of understanding with the Swiss government that established a procedure for processing SEC requests for information about Swiss bank clients suspected of insider trading. As reports of overseas "money laundering" of profits made from insider trading in the United States mounted throughout the late 1980s, the SEC encouraged Congress to clarify the Commission's authority to act, not only against those who were sheltering their profits from illegal insider trading in foreign countries but also against others who were violating U.S. securities laws abroad.

In 1990, Congress passed the *International Securities Enforcement Cooperation Act (ISECA)*. The most important provisions of this act are as follows:

1. It provides for giving foreign regulators U.S. government documents and information needed to trace laundered money and those suspected of doing the laundering.

2. It exempts from the Freedom of Information Act (FOIA) disclosure requirements documents given to the SEC by foreign regulators. Without this exemption, foreign regulators would be reluctant to provide U.S. regulators with information, and alleged violators could obtain information too easily.

3. It gives the SEC authority to impose administrative sanctions on buyers and dealers who engage in activities that are illegal under U.S. law while they are in foreign countries.

4. It authorizes the SEC to investigate violations of all U.S. securities laws that occur in foreign countries.

LEGISLATION GOVERNING FOREIGN SECURITIES SOLD IN THE UNITED STATES

Schedule B of the Securities Act of 1933 sets forth disclosure requirements for initial offerings by foreign issuers of stock on U.S. exchanges. Foreign issuers are entitled to some of the same exemptions in this area as domestic issuers, except that exemptions under Regulation A are granted only to U.S. and Canadian issuers. Also, the SEC has special registration forms for initial foreign offerings.

In Section 12(g)(3) of the Exchange Act, Congress gave the SEC power to exempt foreign issuers whose securities are traded on U.S. exchanges or the OTC markets from certain registration requirements if the Commission believed such action would be in the public interest. Under SEC Rule 12(g)(3)-2, the securities of a foreign issuer are exempt from annual and current reports if the issuer or its government furnishes the SEC with annual information material to investors that is made public in the issuer's own country. In 1983, the Commission published a list of exemptions for foreign-issued securities and adopted regulations that generally require foreign securities that are registered under the Exchange Act to be quoted also on the National Association of Securities Dealers Authorized Quotations (NASDAQ).

SUMMARY

The Securities and Exchange Commission (SEC) is the federal agency responsible for overseeing the securities markets and enforcing federal securities legislation.

Several pieces of legislation provide the framework for the federal regulation of securities issuance and trading, but the most important are the Securities Act of 1933 and the Securities Exchange Act of 1934.

The Securities Act of 1933 seeks to ensure that investors receive full and fair disclosure of all material information about a new stock issue. It prescribes a three-stage registration process for new securities: prefiling, filing, and postfiling. Several types of securities are exempt from registration, principally private placements, intrastate offerings, and small business offerings.

The Securities Exchange Act of 1934 governs six areas of securities trading: the registration of securities issuers and broker-dealers; securities markets; proxy solicitations; tender offers and takeover bids; securities fraud; and short-swing profits. Provisions of the act dealing with securities fraud include insider trading, misstatements by corporate management, and mismanagement of a corporation.

The increasing internationalization of securities markets has led Congress and the SEC to extend the reach of U.S. securities regulations through specific agreements with foreign governments and through provisions of the Foreign Corrupt Practices Act and the International Securities Enforcement Cooperation Act.

REVIEW QUESTIONS

21-1. Describe the differences between the national exchanges (e.g., the New York Stock Exchange) and the over-the-counter markets (OTC).

21-2. Explain what is meant by shelf registration of securities.

21-3. Under the proxy rules, when may the management of a registered issuing company exclude a shareholder proposal from the agenda of an annual meeting?

21-4. What criteria are used by the courts to determine whether an instrument or transaction will be called a security?

21-5. Which securities must be registered under the 1933 Act? Explain.

21-6. Which securities are exempt from registration under the 1933 Act. Explain.

REVIEW PROBLEMS

21-7. Livingston had worked for Merrill Lynch for 20 years as a securities sales representative ("account executive"). In January 1972, he and 47 other account executives were given the honorary title of "vice president" because of their outstanding sales records. None of their duties were changed, however, and they never attended a meeting of the board of directors. In November and December 1972, Livingston sold and repurchased the same number of shares of Merrill Lynch, making a profit of

$14,836.37. Merrill Lynch sued Livingston for recovery of the profits, claiming that he had violated Section 16(b) of the Securities and Exchange Act of 1934. Livingston denied such charges. Who won this case, and why?

21-8. Daniel had been a member of the Teamsters Union and an employee of the same trucking firm virtually for 23 years. The company had signed a collective bargaining agreement with the union that contained a pension plan. Under the plan, an employee had to work for 20 continuous years for the company. Daniel had not worked for 20 continuous years because he had had a single short break in his employment. He claimed that the pension plan constituted a "security" under the 1933 and 1934 securities acts, and he sued the union for fraud under Section 10(b) of the 1934 act and SEC Rule 10(b)-5. The union denied that the pension plan qualified as a security. Who won this case, and why?

21-9. Panzirer read an article in the *Wall Street Journal* stating that buying stock in a specific company would be a wise investment. She purchased stock in that company. The company later went bankrupt, and Panzirer lost her investment. She sued the company's officers, directors, and independent accountants under SEC Rule 10(b)-5, claiming that, although she had never read the company's annual report, she satisfied the reliance requirement for fraud because she had relied on the "integrity of the marketplace," and a "fraud on the market" had been committed by the company. Who won this case, and why?

21-10. Schlitz Brewing Company failed to disclose on its registration statement, as well as in its periodic reports to the SEC, certain kickback payments that it was making to retailers to encourage them to sell Schlitz products, as well as the fact that the company had been convicted of violating a Spanish tax law. The SEC claimed that the failure to include such information was a violation of the antifraud provisions of the 1933 and 1934 acts because it was material. Schlitz claimed that the information was not material because the kickbacks represented only $3 million, a tiny sum compared with the company's $1 billion in revenues. Was the information material, and was its omission thus a violation of Section 10(b) of the 1934 act and SEC Rule 10(b)-5? Explain.

21-11. International Mining Exchange and a person named Parker sold a "Gold Tax Shelter Investment Program. " Anyone who wished to invest had to write a check payable to an individual designated by International Mining and sign certain papers. Investors acquired a leasehold interest in a gold mine with proven reserves, and they agreed to allow International Mining to arrange for sale options to purchase the gold that would be mined. In effect, investors received the right to profits from the gold mined plus a tax deduction based on the cost of developing the mine. The SEC claimed that this transaction involved "securities" and thus was not exempt from registration under the 1933 Act. International Mining claimed that this transaction was not within the definition of a security. What was the result? Explain.

21-12. Continental, a manufacturer of cigarettes, sold to a group of 38 investors bonds with warrants attached to purchase common stock. The sales took place in a high-pressure atmosphere in a room with phones ringing and apparent new orders coming in. Each investor signed an agreement that she or he had received written information about the corporation, and each testified to having access to additional information if requested. The SEC brought an action claiming that Continental was in violation of the registration provisions of the 1933 Act for selling unregistered nonexempt securities. Continental argued that it qualified for a private placement exemption. What was the result? Explain.

21-13. Maresh, a geologist, owned oil and gas leases on land in Nebraska. He entered into an oral agreement with Garfield whereby the latter would provide investment funds for Maresh to drill for oil. Garfield promised to wire the money to Maresh, who began drilling immediately. Maresh found out that the land was dry before he received Garfield's money. Garfield refused to invest as he had promised, claiming that the offered lease investment was a "security" within the meaning of the Securities Act of 1933 and that it had not been registered. What was the result? *Garfield v. Strain*, 320 F.2d 116 (1963)

21-14. Truckee Showboat, incorporated in California, offered to sell its common stock to residents of California through the use of the U.S. mail. Its offer was made exclusively to residents of the State of California through an ad in the *Los Angeles Times*. Proceeds of the sale of the stock, minus commission, were to be used to acquire the El Cortez Hotel in Las Vegas, Nevada. Truckee Showboat, Inc. kept all its records in California. Its directors and officers were Californians. The SEC charged the company with issuing unregistered nonexempt securities under the 1933 Act. Truckee Showboat claimed an intrastate exemption. What was the result? *SEC v. Truckee Showboat, Inc.*, 157 F. Supp. 824 (1957)

21-15. Prior to the merger of Auto-Lite and Mergenthaler into the Mergenthaler Linotype Co., Mergenthaler owned 50 percent of Auto-Lite and dominated its board of directors. American Manufacturing Company in turn had control of Mergenthaler and through it controlled Auto-Lite. Auto-Lite's management at the time of the merger sent out a proxy statement to shareholders of Auto-Lite telling them that their board of directors recommended that they vote for approval of the merger. They failed to include in the proxy statement the fact that Mergenthaler dominated the board and that American Manufacturing through Mergenthaler controlled Auto-Lite. Mills and other minority shareholders filed a class action and derivative suit claiming that management had sent out a misleading proxy in violation of Section 14 of the Exchange Act of 1934 and that the merger should be set aside. Management and the board of directors of the merged company claimed that there was no material omission in the proxy statement. What was the result? Explain. *Mills v. Auto-Lite*, 396 U.S. 375 (1970)

21-16. Lakeside Plastics and Engraving Company (LPE) was a closed corporation incorporated in the State of Minnesota in 1946. It suffered losses until 1952, when it showed a yearly profit but still a large overall deficit. Fields and King in 1946 had each purchased 30 shares, which they held. Myzel, a relative of the Levine family, founders of the company, advised Fields and King in 1954 that the company stock was not worth anything and the company was going out of business. Both sold their shares to Myzel, who sold them to the Levine family at a substantial profit. Myzel failed to disclose before purchasing the shares that there were increased sales in 1953, a new Blatz contract, and profits of $30,000, along with the potential of 1954 sales. Fields, King, and others in separate actions sought damage for violation of 10(b) of the Exchange Act of 1934. What was the result? *Myzel v. Fields*, 386 F.2d 718 (1967)

21-17. In 1975 and 1976, Chiarella (defendant), a printer, worked as a "markup man" in the composing room of Pandick Press, a New York financial printer. Among documents that the defendant handled were five announcements of corporate takeover bids. When these documents were delivered to the printer, the identities of the acquiring and target corporations were concealed by blank spaces or false names. The true names were sent to the printer on the night of the final printing.

The defendant, however, was able to deduce the names of target companies before the final printing from other information contained in the documents. Without disclosing his knowledge, the defendant purchased stock in the target companies and sold the shares immediately after the takeover attempts were made public. By this method, the defendant realized a gain of slightly more than $30,000 in the course of 14 months. Subsequently, the SEC began an investigation of his trading activities. In May 1977, the defendant entered into a consent order with the commission in which he agreed to return his profits to the sellers of the shares.

In January 1978, the defendant was indicted on 17 counts of violating Section 10(b) of the Securities Exchange Act of 1934 (1934 Act) and SEC Rule 10(b)-5. After the defendant unsuccessfully moved to dismiss the indictment, he was brought to trial and convicted on all counts. Who won on appeal? Explain. *Vincent F. Chiarella v. United States*, 445 U.S. 622 (1980)

21-18. The federal Williams Act and implementing regulations govern hostile corporate stock tender offers by requiring offers to remain open for at least 20 business days. An Indiana act applies to certain business corporations chartered in Indiana that have specified levels of shares or shareholders within the state. The Indiana act provides that the acquisition of "control shares" in such a corporation—shares that, but for the act, would bring the acquiring entity's voting power to or above certain threshold levels—does not include voting rights unless a majority of all preexisting disinterested shareholders so agree at their next regularly scheduled meeting. However, the stock acquirer can require a special meeting within 50 days by following specified procedures. The appellee, Dynamics Corporation, announced a tender offer that would have raised its ownership interest in CTS Corporation above the Indiana act's threshold. Dynamics also filed in federal district court alleging federal securities violations by CTS. After CTS opted into the Indiana act, Dynamics amended its complaint to challenge the act's validity. The district court granted Dynamics' motion for declaratory relief, ruling that the act is preempted by the Williams Act and violates the Commerce Clause. The court of appeals affirmed, holding that the Williams Act preempts state statutes that upset the balance between target company management and a tender offeror. The court based its preemption finding on the view that the Indiana act, in effect, imposes at least a 50-day delay on the consummation of tender offers and that this time frame conflicts with the minimum 20-day hold-open period under the Williams Act. The court also held that the state act violates the Commerce Clause because it deprives nonresidents of the valued opportunity to accept tender offers from other nonresidents. On appeal to the U.S. Supreme Court, who won? Explain. *CTS Corp. v. Dynamics Corp. of America*, 481 U.S. 69 (1987)

 On the Internet

http://securities.stanford.edu/   The Securities Action Clearinghouse provides a wealth of information about federal securities litigation, including cases, statutes, reports, and settlements.

http://www.sec.gov/asec/secaddr.htm   Here is where you find the addresses of the regional and national offices of the Securities and Exchange Commission.

http://www.nasaa.org/   From this page, find out about the North American Securities Administrators Association, an organization devoted to investor protection.

http://www.moneypages.com/syndicate/stocks/sec/index.html   This site contains an archive of documents published or distributed by the SEC.

22

ANTITRUST LAWS

- **INTRODUCTION TO ANTITRUST LAW**

- **ENFORCEMENT OF AND EXEMPTIONS FROM THE ANTITRUST LAWS**

- **THE SHERMAN ACT OF 1890**

- **THE CLAYTON ACT OF 1914**

- **OTHER ANTITRUST STATUTES**

- **INTERNATIONAL DIMENSIONS OF ANTITRUST STATUTES**

There is disagreement in many areas of public law between those who believe that business conduct should be disciplined through government regulation and those who favor the marketplace and economic-efficiency criteria as the sole instruments of business discipline. Nowhere is this struggle sharper than in the area of antitrust law.

American attitudes toward government restraints in the area of contracts originated in the English common law, which traditionally upheld the freedom of the individual to contract. United States courts generally refused to interfere with commercial agreements: Price fixing and horizontal and vertical territorial divisions of markets were considered part of the business environment, and hence legal. This **laissez-faire** approach was accepted up to the second half of the nineteenth century, when the economic might of huge monopolies stirred Congress to enact the Interstate Commerce Act of 1887 and the Sherman Act of 1890.

The chapter begins with an introduction to the meaning of antitrust and a summary of the federal antitrust statutes. Then it discusses enforcement of the antitrust laws and exemptions made to those laws. Next it examines the types of business conduct that are forbidden by the Sherman Act as well as the Clayton Act, the Federal Trade Commission Act, and the Bank Merger Act of 1966. Because these acts have affected, directly and indirectly, almost every business and political institution in American society, and carry criminal and/or civil penalties, much of the chapter focuses on dissecting them. Finally, it examines the international dimensions of antitrust policy.

laissez-faire The concept that the owners of business and industry should be allowed to compete without government intervention or regulation.

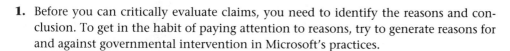

Critical Thinking about the Law

ANTITRUST LAW IS FULL OF CONTROVERSIAL cases. Should the government restrict businesses? To what extent? Should we prevent businesses from creating monopolies? These questions are addressed in a variety of laws regarding antitrust policy. A recent case of an antitrust action by the government involves Microsoft. Microsoft was charged with unfair monopolistic practices. The government claimed that Microsoft is unfairly restricting its competitors by forcing computer manufacturers to ship the Microsoft Internet Explorer along with Windows 95. Answering the following questions about Microsoft can help you think critically about antitrust law.

1. Before you can critically evaluate claims, you need to identify the reasons and conclusion. To get in the habit of paying attention to reasons, try to generate reasons for and against governmental intervention in Microsoft's practices.

   CLUE Reread the introduction. Why would Microsoft want to be free of governmental intervention? Why would the government want to regulate Microsoft?

2. Your roommate makes the following statement: "Businesses have to comply with far too many regulations. They should just be free to make their own rules. Businesses that aren't fair to the public will not be successful. The government shouldn't regulate Microsoft." How would you respond to your roommate?

   CLUE Even though you have not yet read this chapter, you can evaluate your roommate's statement. Do you see any problems with this statement?

3. Microsoft argues that the Internet Explorer is simply part of Windows. Furthermore, Microsoft claims that it is serving its customers by including the Internet Explorer. Customers don't have to worry about finding an additional World Wide Web browser. Thus, the government is essentially hurting the public by regulating Microsoft. Are you persuaded by Microsoft's argument?

   CLUE What information might be missing from Microsoft's argument? What more would you like to know about the World Wide Web industry?

INTRODUCTION TO ANTITRUST LAW

A DEFINITION OF ANTITRUST

trust A business arrangement in which owners of stocks in several companies place their securities with trustees, who jointly manage the companies and pay out a specific share of their earnings to the securities holders.

Trusts were originally business arrangements in which owners of stocks in several companies placed their securities in the hands of trustees, who controlled and managed the companies. The securities owners, in return, received certificates that gave each a specified share of the earnings of the jointly managed companies. The trust device itself was not—and is not today—illegal. However, in the late 1880s and 1890s, trusts were used by a few companies to buy up or drive out of business many small companies in a single industry. Standard Oil Company, for example, used this process to monopolize the oil industry. Unscrupulous methods of competition—such as bribery, setting up bogus companies, and harassing small companies with lawsuits—were used by large trusts to gain monopolistic profits. Magazine and newspaper exposures of scandalous transactions involving trusts shook the public's confidence in unregulated markets. Against this background, the Sherman Act was enacted in 1890. Because it was aimed at monopolies that called themselves *trusts*, it was called an *antitrust statute*.

LAW AND ECONOMICS: SETTING AND ENFORCING ANTITRUST POLICY

The formulation and enforcement of antitrust policy have been substantially affected by the disciplines of law and economics. And there is a strong difference of opinion about antitrust law between lawyers and economists who favor some government regulation of business and those who want to see deregulation or, more radically, no regulation at all. These two approaches to antitrust policy are known, respectively, as the Harvard School and the Chicago School after the universities where many of their proponents have taught and written.

Chicago School An approach to antitrust policy that is based solely on the goal of economic efficiency, or the maximization of consumer welfare.

The **Chicago School** argues that antitrust decisions should be based solely on the criterion of economic efficiency—that is, the maximization of consumer welfare, which may be defined as improving the allocation of scarce resources without in some way decreasing productive efficiencies. In our discussion of antitrust goals very shortly, you will find that one of those goals is the "promotion of the maximization of consumer welfare using market principles and efficiency criteria." But the Chicago School argues that unless efficiency is the sole criterion for antitrust policy making, consumers will not be able to obtain goods at the lowest price possible and United States–based multinationals will not be able to compete with foreign multinationals. Adherents of the Chicago School would like to see antitrust statutes enforced less strictly, especially in the areas of vertical price and territorial restraints, and would decriminalize many antitrust offenses. Finally, proponents of this approach believe that bigness in U.S. business is far from bad, considering that competitive foreign firms are big and are sometimes aided by their governments as well. You will see the Chicago approach at work when you come to read the *GTE Sylvania* case later in this chapter.

Harvard School An approach to antitrust policy that is based on the desirability of preserving competition to prevent the accumulation of economic and political power, the dislocation of labor, and market inefficiency.

The **Harvard School** favors the preservation of an economy characterized by many buyers and sellers, with little domination by any one. Adherents of this approach condemn the accumulation of economic power because they believe that it leads to substantial political power at the federal, state, and local levels as politicians are "bought" by the holders of economic power. The resulting concentration of economic and political power allows a small elite to dominate society and to dictate the closing of plants, downsizing, and the loss of jobs from a community. The Harvard School's position on the creation and enforcement of antitrust policy is embodied in all four of the antitrust goals we next discuss.

Try not to choose sides on this issue until you have read and critically analyzed this chapter. But it is important that you understand from the outset of your study of antitrust policy that the political, economic, and judicial systems of this country are profoundly affected by these two opposing schools of thought (Table 22-1).

TABLE 22-1 *Chicago and Harvard School Approaches to Antitrust Policy*

CHICAGO SCHOOL	HARVARD SCHOOL
1. Sole criterion for formulating antitrust policy is efficiency: the maximization of consumer welfare.	1. Several criteria, including: (a) preservation of many buyers and sellers in the economy; (b) prevention of concentration of political and economic power; (c) preservation of local control of business and prevention of dislocation of labor markets; and (d) efficiency of markets.
2. Decriminalize many offenses, including vertical restraints of trade and monopolies.	2. Enforce the antitrust statutes rigorously and increase the criminal penalties in most areas of antitrust.
3. Encourage joint ventures between U.S. and foreign multinationals without requiring government approval.	3. Allow joint ventures but retain strict oversight by the Justice Department and Federal Trade Commission to prevent worldwide concentration and division of global markets by multinationals.

THE GOALS OF THE ANTITRUST STATUTES

A century of debate by lawyers, economists, and others has not produced a real consensus on the goals of the antitrust statutes. Nonetheless, these four goals can be derived from the study of antitrust legislation and case law:

1. *The preservation of small businesses and an economy characterized by many sellers competing with one another.* Proponents of this goal would break up large corporations such as General Motors (GM) and International Business Machines (IBM).

2. *The prevention of concentration of political and economic power in the hands of a few sellers in each industry.* Proponents of this goal argue that there is a direct correlation between large corporations, economic power, and control of the political process. They point to 1980 and 1984 postpresidential election analyses indicating that well-financed political action committees (PACs) controlled by big businesses had a tremendous effect on the elections' outcomes.

3. *The preservation of local control of business and protection against the effects of labor dislocation.* The advocates of this antitrust goal argue that when large companies are allowed to merge, fix prices, and participate in joint ventures, jobs are lost and plants are shut down in some areas. The consequences are a dislocation of labor and a decline in local and state economies as their tax bases shrink because people are moving elsewhere in pursuit of jobs.

4. *The promotion of the maximization of consumer welfare using market principles and efficiency criteria.* Advocates of this goal define consumer welfare as an improvement in the allocation of resources without an impairment to productive efficiency. In effect, the proponents of this goal argue that, by encouraging the allocation of resources in an efficient manner, antitrust enforcement can make sure that consumers will be provided goods at the lowest possible prices.

Some of these goals are in conflict.[1] For example, the Harvard School proponents of goal 1 (preserving small businesses) are criticized by adherents of the Chicago School, who favor only goal 4 (consumer welfare maximization), because they believe that large firms are needed to manufacture goods at the lowest cost per unit. They point out that until Henry Ford introduced the assembly-line production of automobiles, few people could afford cars. Many small businesses are economically inefficient, they say, and attempts to preserve them through antitrust policy will be underwritten by consumers in the form of higher prices. The Chicago School also insists that if U.S. manufacturers are not

---

[1]For four conflicting opinions on the goals of antitrust, see T. Calvani, *Consumer Welfare Is Prime Objective of Antitrust,* Legal Times, December 24–31, 1984, at 14; B. Brennan, *A Legal-Economic Dichotomy: Contribution to Failure in Regulatory Policy,* 4 Am. Bus. L.J. 52 (1976); W. Cann Jr., *The New Merger Guidelines: Is the Justice Department Enforcing the Law?* 21 Am. Bus. L.J. 1, 2–13 (1983); R. Bork, *The Antitrust Paradox* (New York: Basic Books, 1978), pp. 6, 90–91, 104, 108.

TABLE 22-2 *Summary of Federal Antitrust Laws*

ACT	PROVISIONS
Sherman Act of 1890	
Section 1	Makes illegal every contract, combination, or conspiracy in restraint of trade; felony offense punishable by fine up to $10 million per corporation and up to $350,000 per individual; a person may be imprisoned up to three years, fined, or both.
Section 2	Forbids monopolizing, attempts to monopolize, or conspiracies to monopolize; penalties are the same as for Section 1.
Clayton Act of 1914	
Section 2	Forbids discrimination in price between different purchasers of goods of like grade and quality where the effect may be to lessen competition or to tend to create a monopoly in any line of commerce, or to injure, destroy, or prevent competition with the seller, the buyer, or either's customers.
Section 3	Forbids selling or leasing goods on the condition that the buyer or lessee shall not use or deal in goods sold or leased by the seller's or lessor's competitor, where the effect of such an agreement may be substantially to lessen competition or to tend to create a monopoly. In effect, this section outlaws exclusive dealing and tying arrangements.
Section 7	Forbids unlawful selling of corporate assets or stock mergers where the effect may be substantially to lessen competition or to tend to create a monopoly.
Federal Trade Commission Act of 1914	Forbids unfair methods of competition in commerce and unfair or deceptive acts in commerce.

allowed to merge and participate in joint ventures, they will be unable to compete with large foreign multinationals and foreign companies owned or subsidized by their governments. One of the reasons the Justice Department moved to dismiss an antitrust suit against the International Business Machines Corporation in 1982 was that the computer market had become international in character since the original government complaint against IBM in 1972. If IBM had been broken up, it would not have been able to compete with large foreign multinationals either in the United States or in other countries.

A summary of the Federal Antitrust statutes is provided in Table 22-2.

ENFORCEMENT OF AND EXEMPTIONS FROM THE ANTITRUST LAWS

ENFORCEMENT

Enforcement of the antitrust laws is carried out in both the public and the private sector. The Department of Justice and the Federal Trade Commission (FTC) (see Exhibit 16-4) are primarily responsible for enforcement in the public sector, whereas any individual or business entity in the private sector that establishes that it has been directly injured by illegal business conduct may bring an action under the federal statutes outlined here as well as under state antitrust statutes. Table 22-3 shows which parties have enforcement powers for the three major federal antitrust statutes.

PUBLIC ENFORCEMENT The Antitrust Division of the Justice Department exclusively enforces the Sherman Act and has concurrent jurisdiction with the Federal Trade Commission to enforce the Clayton Act. The FTC has exclusive jurisdiction to enforce the Federal Trade Commission Act (FTCA).

Usually, the Justice Department files civil suits in a federal district court. The remedy requested is ordinarily an injunction to prevent a particular action from occurring, along with a specific order requiring the business to change its conduct or operation. Most of the time, the defending parties, be-

	SHERMAN ACT	CLAYTON ACT	FEDERAL TRADE COMMISSION ACT
Justice Department	Civil and criminal enforcement powers	Civil enforcement power	No power to enforce
Federal Trade Commission	No power to enforce	Civil enforcement power	Civil enforcement power
Private parties	Power to enforce civil litigation	Power to enforce civil litigation	No power to enforce

cause of the cost of litigation and the attendant bad publicity, choose not to fight the case and instead agree to enter into a *consent decree* (consent order) with the Justice Department, which binds them to stop the activity complained of (e.g., attempting to manipulate a market). As you know from our discussion of administrative agencies in chapter 16, entering into a consent order does not involve admitting to any liability. The federal district court must approve the consent order.

For serious violations of the Sherman Act (e.g., price fixing among competitors), the Justice Department may bring a criminal action. A corporation convicted of criminal conduct under the act faces a fine of up to $10 million for each offense; individual officers and employees who are convicted face a maximum $350,000 fine for each offense, or up to three years in jail, or both. *Nolo contendere pleas* are often negotiated between the Justice Department and corporate or individual criminal defendants. This plea of no contest subjects the defendant to a lesser punishment than would result from conviction at a trial. Though technically not an admission of guilt, a nolo contendere plea is treated as such by a judge. Like a consent decree, it must be approved by the court.

Both *consent decrees* in a *civil action* and *nolo contendere pleas* in a *criminal action* are often entered into by defendants to avoid the cost of litigation and publicity. Another advantage of these decrees and pleas for defendants is that they cannot be used as a basis for shareholder-derivative or indemnity suits. For the Justice Department, such decrees and pleas save time and taxpayers' money.

In December of 1997 at the urging of the Justice Department a federal judge issued a temporary restraining order to prevent Microsoft from allegedly violating a 1995 court order by forcing computer makers to install its Internet browser software along with its Windows 95 operating system. Several days later the federal court issued a contempt order advising that the company was making a mockery of the court's order. Microsoft appealed in January of 1998. Violation of antitrust laws are at issue. On another front, 13 states have begun planning, as of April 1998, a separate antitrust action, which has wider implications than the mere tying of a browser system to Windows 95. In this case, the 13 state attorneys general will seek to show an effort by Microsoft to eliminate competition under the Clayton Act, Section 7 and to fix prices under Section 1 of the Sherman Act as well as several other anticompetitive practices to be studied in this chapter. This action by the states is a continuation of their joint efforts to pursue cases against the tobacco companies, telemarketing advertisers, and environmental violators, all under the name of consumer protection. For elected attorneys general, these are popular cases to be grouped.[2]

---

[2]See John Martott, "13 States Planning Broader Suits against Microsoft," *New York Times*, pp. A1 and C20, April 30, 1988. The federal district court entered a preliminary injunction forbidding Microsoft from licensing any of its personal computer software on the condition, express or implied, that the licensee (Microsoft) preinstall any of its Internet browser software (including Internet Explorer 3.0, 4.0, or any successor). U.S. v Microsoft, U.S. District Court, D.C. (no. 95cv 015 1998). On appeal, the U.S. Circuit Court of Appeals of the D.C. Cir. found that the district court erred procedurally in entering a preliminary injunction without notice to Microsoft and substantively in its implicit construction of the consent decree on which the preliminary injunction rested (see U.S. v Microsoft Corporation, U.S. D.C. Cir. Ct. of App. (1998) U.S. App. Lexis 13242).

The Federal Trade Commission can bring only civil actions, which are usually argued before an administrative law judge. The ALJ makes findings of fact and recommends action to the full five-member commission, which may issue a *cease-and-desist order*. The defendant has the option of appealing such an order to a U.S. Court of Appeals, and further to the Supreme Court. But usually such cease-and-desist orders are negotiated by the parties before a hearing by the ALJ and are approved by the commission. Failure to abide by a cease-and-desist order carries a penalty of $10,000 a day for each day the defendant is not in compliance.

PRIVATE ENFORCEMENT   Section 4 of the Clayton Act says that

> *any person who shall be injured in his person or in his business or property by reason of anything forbidden in the antitrust laws may sue [and] . . . shall recover threefold the damages by him sustained and the cost of suit including a reasonable attorney's fee.*

This section provides the incentive for private enforcement of our antitrust laws because it requires the court to triple the amount of damages awarded to a plaintiff by a jury or by a judge. It also awards reasonable attorney's fees to the plaintiff's attorney.

Private-action suits can be brought by individuals or businesses against perceived violators of the antitrust laws. In recent years, approximately 90 percent of all antitrust claims were brought by private party plaintiffs. Moreover, when a small company, such as Microwave Communication, Inc. (MCI), sues a large company, such as American Telephone and Telegraph (AT&T), for antitrust violations, victory has the double advantage of enhancing its cash flow and showing bond-rating agencies and investors that it is a viable entity able to take on a big company.

class-action suit A lawsuit brought by a member of a group of person on behalf of all members of the group.

parens patriae suit A lawsuit brought by a state attorney general on behalf of the citizenry of that state.

Individuals in a class-action suit and state attorneys general in *parens patriae* actions on behalf of their citizenry can also bring suits. In a **class-action suit**, one member of a group of plaintiffs injured by an antitrust violation (e.g., price fixing, which results in higher prices for direct purchasers) institutes an action on behalf of the group. This kind of suit is particularly useful when the amount of each individual claim is small. Similar to class actions are ***parens patriae suits***, which are usually brought by a state attorney general on behalf of purchasers and taxpayers in a state (previously discussed with action pending against Microsoft and actions against tobacco companies by attorneys general of several states).

EXEMPTIONS

Several activities and industries are fully or partially exempt from the antitrust statutes (Table 22-4). These exemptions are based on federally enacted statutes or case law of the courts. When exemptions are granted by statute, they are largely the result of successful lobbying of Congress by an industry. Soft-drink franchisors, for example, lobbied successfully in 1980 to obtain a limited exemption from the antitrust statutes, and shipping lines received a similar exemption in 1984.

THE SHERMAN ACT OF 1890

The Sherman Act of 1890 was intended to prevent control of markets by any one powerful entity. In other words, it is designed to thwart anticompetitive behavior. Sections 1 and 2 of the Act, covered here, profoundly affect decisions and behaviors of business managers. As we shall see the Sherman Act is also an important tool to protect consumers from a number of activities that will be discussed here.

ACTIVITY	BASIS FOR EXEMPTION AND EXAMPLES
Regulated industries	Transportation, electric, gas, and telephone.
Labor union activities	Collective bargaining.
Intrastate activities	Intrastate telephone calls are regulated by state public utility commissions.
Agricultural activities	Farmers may belong to cooperatives that legally set prices.
Baseball	The U.S. Supreme Court declared baseball a sport, not a trade. No other professional sport has been exempted by the Congress or courts.
Activities falling within the "State Action" doctrine	In *Parker v. Brown* [317 U.S. 341 (1943)] the U.S. Supreme Court held a state marketing program that was clearly anticompetitive to be exempt from the federal antitrust statutes because it obtained its authority from a "clearly articulated legislative command of the state." The Court looks at the degree of involvement before exempting any *activity* under this doctrine.
Cities', towns', and villages' activities	The *local Government Antitrust Act of 1984* prohibits monetary recovery under the federal antitrust laws from any of these local subdivisions or from local officials, agents, or employees.
Export activities	The *Webb-Pommerce Trade Act of 1918* and the *Export Trading Act of 1982* made the formation of selling cooperatives of U.S. exporters exempt. Also, the *Joint Venture Trading Act of 1983* exempted certain joint ventures of competing companies when seeking to compete with foreign companies that are private and/or state-controlled. Approval of the Justice Department is required. The *Shipping Act of 1984* allows shipping lines to enter into joint ventures and to participate in international shipping conferences that set worldwide rates and divide routes and shipments.

SECTION 1: COMBINATIONS AND RESTRAINTS OF TRADE

Section 1 of the Sherman Act reads:

> *Every contract, combination in the form of trust or otherwise, or conspiracy, in restraint of trade or commerce among the several States, or with foreign nations, is declared to be illegal. Every person who shall make any contract or engage in any combination or conspiracy hereby declared to be illegal shall be deemed guilty of a felony, and, on conviction thereof shall be punished by fine not exceeding one million dollars if a corporation, or, if any other person, one hundred thousand dollars or by imprisonment not exceeding three years, or by both.*

The **Sherman Act** requires three elements for a violation: (1) a *combination*, *contract*, or *conspiracy*; (2) *a restraint of trade* that is *unreasonable*; and (3) a *restraint* that is involved in *interstate*, as opposed to intrastate, commerce. We examined the third element in chapter 4, when we discussed the effects of the Commerce Clause on business. Here we will analyze the first two elements.

COMBINATION, CONTRACT, OR CONSPIRACY The Sherman Act requires a *contract, combination,* or *conspiracy,* so more than one person must be involved (one cannot make a contract, or conspire, or combine with oneself). Just as an offeror and an offeree are necessary parties to a contract, there must be co-conspirators in a conspiracy. In other words, there must be *concerted action* (action taken together) by two or more individuals or business entities. In antitrust language, there must be an "agreement," or **collusion**. Such an agreement can be *expressed* in writing or orally, or it can be *implied*, as established by circumstantial evidence such as trends toward uniformity in pricing in an industry and opportunities to conspire.

Sherman Act Makes illegal every combination, contract, or conspiracy that is an unreasonable restraint of trade when this concerted action involves interstate commerce.

collusion Concerted action by two or more individuals or business entities in violation of the Sherman Act.

It is in cases of implied agreements established by circumstantial evidence that the courts deal with two major problems: (1) whether there can be an *intra-enterprise conspiracy* that violates the Sherman Act and (2) what actions constitute conscious parallelism as opposed to price fixing. **Conscious parallelism** exists when identical actions (usually price increases) are taken independently and nearly simultaneously by two or more leading companies in an industry and thus have the apparent effect of having arisen from a conspiracy.

The courts' solution to the first problem has generally been that there can be no conspiracy between two divisions, departments, or subsidiaries of the same corporation. In answer to the second problem, the courts have generally held that if there is supportable evidence of conscious parallelism, as opposed to an expressed or implied agreement among competitors, no antitrust violation exists.

RESTRAINTS OF TRADE   The second element required to prove a violation of Section 1 of the Sherman Act is that there be a **restraint of trade** and that this restraint be "unreasonable" as defined by the courts. In enacting the Sherman Act, Congress gave no indication of whether it meant all restraints or just some.

Rule-of-Reason Standard   Taking its direction from the English courts, the U.S. Supreme Court adopted a **rule-of-reason standard**. Over time, the Court has followed certain indices, laid out by Justice Louis D. Brandeis in 1918, to determine whether a specific business activity is an unreasonable restraint of trade:

1. The nature and purpose of the restraint.
2. The scope of the restraint.
3. Its effect on the business and on competitors.
4. Its intent.

When using a rule-of-reason standard, the U.S. Supreme Court terms a restraint reasonable, and thus legal, if it has a procompetitive purpose and its effect does not go beyond that purpose. In the case of *NCAA v. University of Oklahoma and the University of Georgia* (excerpted later in this section), the Court found that National Collegiate Athletic Association regulations, which limited the two universities' right to negotiate football contracts individually with the major television networks, arguably had a good purpose (allowing exposure for all college teams and thereby encouraging amateur athletics by maintaining a competitive balance), but that their effects (setting prices and restricting output) violated the Sherman Act. A restraint is unreasonable and unlawful if it allows the parties to substitute themselves and their judgment for the laws of supply and demand. Restraints that are judged by a rule-of-reason standard, and therefore may be in violation of Section 1 of the Sherman Act, include some tying arrangements, activities of trade and athletic associations, some exclusive-dealing arrangements, nonprice vertical restraints, and some franchising arrangements. Most of these are discussed later.

Per Se Standard   Over time, the courts have judged certain business activities and arrangements facially so anticompetitive in nature that they have seen no need to listen to any procompetitive economic justifications. This **per se standard** favors the plaintiff because all that has to be proved is that the restraint (e.g., price fixing) took place; the only defense is that the activity did not occur. However, since the present Supreme Court began looking at the economic impact of previous per se rulings, the number of restraints of trade in this category has fallen. Restraints that are judged by the per se standard, and therefore are automatically in violation of Section 1 of the Sherman Act, include horizontal and vertical price fixing, some tying arrangements, some divisions of markets, and group boycotts. Table 22-5 compares the types of activities that come under each of those standards.

conscious parallelism
Identical actions (usually price increases) that are taken independently but nearly simultaneously by two or more leading companies in an industry.

restraint of trade Action that interferes with the economic law of supply and demand.

rule-of-reason standard A legal standard that holds that only unreasonable restraints of trade violate Section 1 of the Sherman Act. If the court determines an action's anticompetitive effects outweigh its procompetitive effects, the restraint is unreasonable.

per se standard A legal standard that is applicable to restraints of trade that are inherently anticompetitive. Because such restraints are automatically in violation of Section 1 of the Sherman Act, courts do not balance pro- and anticompetitve effects in such cases.

TABLE 22-5 *Sherman Act Section 1 Activities Judged by the per se Standard and Those Judged by the Rule-of-Reason Standard*

557

Chapter 22

Antitrust Laws

PER SE STANDARD	RULE-OF-REASON STANDARD
Price fixing—both horizontal and vertical	Restrictive convenant in a sales or employment agreement.
Group boycotts	Location and resale restraints by manufacturer on some tying arrangements.
Some tying arrangements.	Exchange of information.
Some divisions of markets.	Joint research and development ventures. Some horizontal price tampering based on unique nature of industry (see *NCAA* case in this chapter).

We discuss the various activities that are considered restraints of trade under two headings: *horizontal restraints* and *vertical restraints*.

HORIZONTAL RESTRAINTS **Horizontal restraints of trade** are those that take place between competitors at the same level of the marketing structure. Three types of activities are considered horizontal restraints: horizontal price-fixing, horizontal divisions of markets, and horizontal boycotts.

Horizontal Price-Fixing Suppose that competitors X, Y, and Z are the only manufacturers of a certain heat tape used in the construction of office buildings. They agree to take turns bidding on certain jobs, thus eliminating competition and holding up prices. From the viewpoint of these companies, this is a way to make high profits, stay in business, and keep their employees working. However, the Supreme Court views such **horizontal price fixing** as per se illegal restraints because they interfere with the price mechanism—that is, the law of supply and demand, which requires that competing sellers make decisions about prices on their own *without agreement* or *collusion*, either expressed or implied. Besides direct price-fixing agreements, the Court has struck down such indirect price-fixing arrangements as minimum fee schedules for lawyers and engineers, exchanges of price information among groups of competitors, and agreements between competitors about terms of credit when these become part of the overall price structure in an industry.

The case that follows illustrates an agreement among competitors that not only affected prices (price fixing) but also limited the output of the product and dictated to whom it would be marketed (division of markets and customer allocation). What's more, the defendant, the National Collegiate Athletic Association (NCAA), also threatened a boycott by its membership of those members (the universities of Oklahoma and Georgia and others who belonged to the College Football Association) who refused to follow its rules. Each of those activities had traditionally been considered per se illegal by the courts, but in this 1984 case the Supreme Court indicated that it would examine some of the activities on the bais of a rule-of-reason standard.

horizontal restraint of trade
Restraint of trade that occurs between competitors at the same level of the marketing structure.

horizontal price fixing
Collusion between two or more competitors to, directly or indirectly, set prices for a product or service.

NATIONAL COLLEGIATE ATHLETIC ASSOCIATION, PETITIONERS V. BOARD OF REGENTS OF THE UNIVERSITY OF OKLAHOMA AND UNIVERSITY OF GEORGIA ATHLETIC ASSOCIATION
UNITED STATES SUPREME COURT 468 U.S. 85 (1984)

In 1981, petitioner-defendant National Collegiate Athletic Association (NCAA) adopted a plan for the televising of college football games of its member institutions for the 1982–1985 football seasons. The plan's stated purpose was to reduce the adverse effects of live television on football game attendance. To that end, it limited the total number of intercollegiate football games that could be televised and the number of games played by any one college that could be televised. No member of the NCAA was permitted to enter into any sale of television rights except in accordance with the plan. The NCAA had separate agreements with the two networks that carried intercollegiate football games, ABC and CBS, granting each one the right to telecast the live "exposures" described in the plan. Each network agreed to pay a specified "minimum aggregate compensation" to the participating NCAA members and was authorized to negotiate directly with the members for the right to televise their games.

Respondent-plaintiff universities, in addition to being NCAA members, were members of the College Football Association (CFA). The CFA was originally organized to promote the interests of major football-playing colleges within the NCAA structure. Eventually, however, its members claimed that they should have a greater voice in the formulation of football television policy than they had in the NCAA. Thus the CFA negotiated a contract with NBC that would have allowed a more liberal number of television appearances for each member college and that would have increased the revenues realized by CFA members. In response, the NCAA announced that it would take disciplinary action against any CFA member that complied with the CFA-NBC contract. Respondents brought suit in a federal district court, which, after an extended trial, held that the controls exercised by the NCAA over televising college football games violated Section 1 of the Sherman Act and, accordingly, granted injunctive relief. The court of appeals affirmed. The NCAA appealed to the U.S. Supreme Court.

JUSTICE STEVENS

The plan adopted in 1981 for the 1982–85 seasons is at issue in this case. This plan recites that it is intended to reduce, insofar as possible, the adverse effects of live television upon football game attendance. It provides that "all forms of television of the football games of NCAA member institutions during the Plan control periods shall be in accordance with this Plan."

There can be no doubt that the challenged practices of the NCAA constitute a "restraint of trade" in the sense that they limit members' freedom to negotiate and enter into their own television contracts. In that sense, however, every contract is a restraint of trade, and as we have repeatedly recognized, the Sherman Act was intended to prohibit only unreasonable restraints of trade.

It is also undeniable that these practices share characteristics of restraints we have previously held unreasonable. The NCAA is an association of schools which compete against each other to attract television revenues, not to mention fans and athletes. As the District Court found, the policies of the NCAA with respect to television rights are ultimately controlled by the vote of member institutions. By participating in an association which prevents member institutions from competing against each other on the basis of price or kind of television rights that can be offered to broadcasters, the NCAA member institutions have created a horizontal restraint—an agreement among competitors on the way in which they will compete with one another. A restraint of this type has often

been held to be unreasonable as a matter of law (per se). Because it places a ceiling on the number of games member institutions may televise the horizontal agreement places an artificial limit on the quantity of televised football that is available to broadcasters and consumers. By restraining the quantity of television rights available for sale, the challenged practices create a limitation on output; our cases have held that such limitations are unreasonable restraints of trade. Moreover, the District Court found that the minimum aggregate price, in fact, operates to preclude any price negotiation between broadcasters and institutions, thereby constituting horizontal price-fixing, perhaps the paradigm of an unreasonable restraint of trade.

Horizontal price-fixing and output limitation are ordinarily condemned as a matter of law under an "illegal per se" approach because the probability that these practices are anticompetitive is so high; a per se rule is applied when "the practice facially appears to be one that would always or almost always tend to restrict competition and decrease output." In such circumstances a restraint is presumed unreasonable without inquiry into the particular market context in which it is found. Nevertheless, we have decided that it would be inappropriate to apply a per se rule to this case.

Our decision not to apply a per se rule rests in large part on our recognition that a certain degree of cooperation is necessary if the type of competition that petitioner and its member institutions seek to market is to be preserved. It is reasonable to assume that most of the regulatory controls of the NCAA are justifiable means of fostering competition among amateur athletic teams and therefore procompetitive because they enhance public interest in intercollegiate athletics. The specific restraints on football telecasts that are challenged in this case do not, however, fit into the same mold as do rules defining the conditions of the contest, the eligibility of participants, or the manner in which members of a joint enterprise shall share the responsibilities and the benefits of the total venture.

The interest in maintaining a competitive balance that is asserted by the NCAA as a justification for regulating all television of intercollegiate football is not related to any neutral standard or to any readily identifiable group of competitors. The television plan is not even arguably tailored to serve such an interest. There is no evidence that this restriction produces any greater measure of equality throughout the NCAA than would a restriction on alumni donations, tuition rates, or any other revenue producing activity.

Perhaps the most important reason for rejecting the argument that the interest in competitive balance is served by the television plan is the District Court's unambiguous and well-supported finding that many more games would be televised in a free market than under the NCAA plan. The hypothesis that legitimates the maintenance of competitive balance as a procompetitive justification under the Rule of Reason is that equal competition will maximize consumer demand for the product. The finding that consumption will materially increase if the controls are removed is a compelling demonstration that they do not in fact serve any such legitimate purpose.

Today we hold only that the record supports the District Court's conclusion that by curtailing output and blunt-

ing the ability of member institutions to respond to consumer preference, the NCAA has restricted rather than enhanced the place of intercollegiate athletics in the nation's life.

Affirmed in favor of Plaintiff, CFA.

COMMENT: In a dissenting opinion, Justice White—a former All-American college football player and a Rhodes scholar to boot—argued that the majority decision was wrong because it failed to see the noneconomic nature of the NCAA program of self-regulation. Such noneconomic values as the promotion of amateurism by spreading revenues among various schools and thus reducing financial incentives toward professionalism were sufficient in Justice White's view to "offset any minimal anticompetitive effects."

Critical Thinking about the Law

THE COURT'S USE OF A RULE of reason approach to particular restraints of trade is one requiring extensive use of critical thinking. It is one thing to say, "let's be reasonable about this particular restraint of trade." But the actual application of that standard requires a much deeper form of analysis than is required once a restraint has been labeled a per se violation.

By answering some critical thinking questions about the *NCAA* case, you can better appreciate the analysis involved in applying a rule of reason.

1. What reasons does the Court give for its decision?

   CLUE Ask yourself what the Court used to support its conclusion. The answer will be the Court's reasons.

2. Look at the reasons you found in answering the first question. Are there any key words in these reasons that need clarification for us to feel confident about the Court's conclusion?

   CLUE Check any descriptive adjectives or verbs that have multiple meanings.

3. Provide one piece of missing information that, had it existed in the fact pattern, might have led the Court to a different conclusion.

   CLUE Look at the social harm that is caused by *unreasonable* price-fixing restraints of trade.

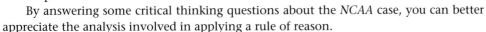

After the *NCAA* decision, a question was raised: How "per se" is the per se rule in the area of price fixing? For example, it is clear that certain forms of price fixing are per se legal by statute. Before deregulation of long-distance phone service in the early 1980s, prices for this service were set by the Federal Communications Commission and therefore were exempt from the Sherman Act. Similarly, before deregulation of the trucking industry, trucking rates were set by the Interstate Commerce Commission and therefore were exempt. In contrast, organizations of engineers, lawyers, and doctors have been found guilty of per se illegal price fixing when they set minimum or maximum schedules of rates or recommend certain minimum prices. The *NCAA* case is one of the few cases of price-fixing in which the Supreme Court was guided by a rule-of-reason standard. There is no "bright line" in this area of antitrust law showing which pricing activities will be judged per se illegal in the future.

horizontal division of markets Collusion between two or more competitors to divide markets, customers, or product lines among themselves.

Horizontal Division of Markets Territorial division, customer allocation, and product-line division of markets between competitors have traditionally been deemed illegal per se. The **horizontal division of markets** is considered particularly dangerous to a free-market economy because it eliminates all forms of competition, in contrast to price fixing, which eliminates only price competition. "Naked" horizontal agreements to divide markets, customers, or product lines have had no redeeming value in the eyes of the courts.

More recently, however, it has been argued that price fixing and division-of-market agreements that are part of cooperative productive activity (as opposed to "naked" restraints) are economically efficient and therefore desirable. Thus the advocates of these "more-than-naked horizontal agreements" contend that a rule-of-reason standard should guide the courts. They cite the *NCAA* case, in which the majority of the justices of the Supreme Court decided that horizontal agreements "placing an artificial limit on the quantity of televised football that will be available to broadcasters and consumers" by the NCAA had to be judged by the rule of reason because the industry (college sports) required horizontal restraints on competition if the product (college football) was to be available at all.

An example of price fixing and division of markets that has been long accepted is a law partnership. Lawyers who would ordinarily compete with each other eliminate competition by signing a partnership agreement that restricts work output to their specialization (market division) and that provides for an agreement on fees to be charged by partners and their associates (price fixing). In effect, an integrated economic unit fixes prices and divides markets (output) internally so that the partnership may operate more efficiently in competing externally with other law firms.

horizontal boycott A concerted refusal by a trade association to deal with members that do not follow the association's regulations.

Horizontal Boycotts Trade associations frequently promulgate rules among their memberships that amount to concerted refusals to deal with members that do not follow the association's regulations. This activity constitutes a **horizontal boycott** and is per se illegal because it takes away the freedom of other members to interact with the boycotted members and, in many instances, lessens the ability of a boycotted member to compete.

Many professional associations have rules that contain sanctions for violations, ranging from reprimands to suspension or expulsion from the association. These sanctions constitute a boycott and are per se illegal. In the *NCAA* case just excerpted, for instance, the NCAA's television regulations prohibited its members from independently negotiating with television networks concerning their individual games. Violation of the regulation to adhere to the NCAA-negotiated package of football games subjected a member college to sanctions, including expulsion from the organization and prohibitions against its team's appearing on television in a game against another member's team. The CFA schools that also belonged to the NCAA defied the regulation and negotiated on their own with a network. In response, the NCAA announced that it would take disciplinary action against any member of the CFA that went ahead and complied with the CFA-NBC contract. Disciplinary measures would not necessarily be limited to televised football programs, for the association warned all its members that did not also belong to the CFA about the seriousness of consorting with CFA members should the CFA go forward with its NBC television contract. This threat of a boycott and expulsion led two CFA members, the University of Georgia and the University of Oklahoma, to seek injunctive relief. Although the district court called the NCAA warning a horizontal boycott and per se illegal, the Supreme Court did not reach the boycott issue because it found against the NCAA on the price-fixing question.

In this era of deregulation, and thus indirect encouragement of industry self-regulation, certain antitrust cases have become extremely important. If an industry's own rules are arbitrary and capricious, or lacking in due process, the courts will generally not uphold them under the rule of reason. For example, when the New York Stock Exchange, without a hearing, ordered all exchange members to withdraw wire connection with a nonmember broker, the Supreme Court held that "concerted termination of trade relations which would ordinarily constitute an illegal boycott, might be exempt from the antitrust law as a result of the duty of self-regulation imposed on the Exchange [by Congress and the Securities and Exchange Commission], but only if fair procedures were followed, including notice and hearing."[3] In another case,[4] however, the Court found no unreasonable restraint of trade arising out of the program established by the National Sanitation Foundation (NSF) for testing production of and issuing a seal of approval for products that complied with the NSF's promulgated standards, which were strictly enforced among manufacturers. The Court has indicated that where an alleged boycott of an unapproved manufacturer takes place, the plaintiff must show either that it was discriminated against vis-à-vis its competitors or that it was subjected to anticompetitive conduct.

Clearly, self-regulatory associations will continue to be watched carefully by the courts for due process and reasonable conduct. In July 1985, the Supreme Court ruled that a wholesale purchasing cooperative's expulsion of a member without notice, a hearing, or an opportunity to challenge the decision could not be conclusively presumed to be a per se violation of Section 1 of the Sherman Act.[5] The Court remanded the case to the federal district court, directing that a rule-of-reason approach be used to determine whether the cooperative had the market power to exclude competitors and whether the expulsion of a member was likely to have an anticompetitive effect.

In the case of noncommercial refusals to deal, it is clear that the per se rule will not be applied by the courts. For example, when the National Organization of Women (NOW) organized a boycott of convention facilities in all states that had refused to endorse the proposed Equal Rights Amendment to the U.S. Constitution, Missouri sued NOW, claiming that the organization was in violation of Section 1 of the Sherman Act. The circuit court of appeals stated that the Sherman Act was nonapplicable in this case because the boycott had a noncommercial goal—to influence legislation in the political arena.[6] The court had used the rule-of-reason standard to determine whether the group's purpose was truly noncommercial in nature.

A conflict between constitutional principles—such as the right to free speech and to petition one's government under the First Amendment of the Constitution—and enforcement of the Sherman Act against boycotts or refusals to deal must often be resolved by the courts. Usually, as in the NOW case, constitutional principles have prevailed when noncommercial groups have been involved.

VERTICAL RESTRAINTS   Those restraints agreed to between individuals or corporations at different levels of the manufacturing and distribution process are called **vertical restraints of trade**. For example, manufacturers and retailers, as well as franchisors and franchisees, are often involved in the following types of vertical restraints: resale-price maintenance (*price fixing*), *territorial and customer restrictions*, *tying agreements*, and *exclusive-dealing contracts*. Although the latter two restraints involve violations of Section 3 of the Clayton Act, the courts have also condemned such actions under Section I of the Sherman Act.

vertical restraint of trade
Restraint that occurs between individuals or corporations at different levels of the marketing structure.

As we examine these vertical restraints, we would like you to focus on two policy implications for business managers:

1. What effect do court decisions have on intrabrand competition (retailers competing with one another in selling the same manufacturer's brand) and interbrand competition (competition between different manufacturers of a similar product when sold at the retail level)?

---

[3]*See* Silver v. New York Stock Exchange, 373 U.S. 341 (1965).
[4]Eliason Corp. v. National Sanitation Foundation, 614 F.2d 126 (1980).
[5]Northwest Wholesale Stationers, Inc. v. Pacific Stationery and Printing Co., U.S. 284 (1985).
[6]Missouri v. NOW, Inc., 620 F.2d 1301 (8th Cir. 1980), *cert. denied* 449 U.S. 8412 (1981).

2. Are the courts moving in the direction of judging such restraints by a per se or a rule-of-reason standard?

Vertical Price Fixing   When a manufacturer sells to a retailer, the company may attempt to specify what price it expects the retailer to charge for the product or, at least, a minimum price. **Vertical price-fixing** agreements of this type have been traditionally judged per se illegal by the courts if a "contract, combination, or conspiracy" exists under Section 1 of the Sherman Act. This has been true regardless of whether the manufacturer coerced the retailer into entering the agreement (by refusing to supply the product) or the retailer entered the agreement voluntarily.

The courts' major concern in this area has been whether the retailer made the pricing decision independently or by agreement with the manufacturer. For example, many manufacturers offer suggested prices to their retailers in the form of price lists. The question often before the court is what type of surveillance the manufacturer uses to coerce an initial agreement or to gain compliance. If the prices are truly suggested, how many times has the retailer deviated from such prices, and what has been the response of the manufacturer? The courts have scrutinized manufacturers' responses carefully, particularly when there is evidence of a manufacturer's refusal to deal. The courts have generally agreed that a manufacturer, on its own initiative, can announce in advance an intention not to deal with an individual retailer who does not sell the manufacturer's product at a specific price. No agreement is involved in these unilateral cases. However, the court will infer an agreement, and thus per se illegal price fixing, if the manufacturer refuses to deal with a retailer who fails to adhere to a resale then reinstates the retailer when it agrees to conform.

Vertical Territorial and Customer Restraints   The restraints used by a manufacturer to limit the territory in which a retailer may sell the company's product and to restrict the number of retailer-owned stores as well as the customers a retailer can serve in a location are classified as **nonprice vertical restraints**.

Lawyers, economists, and scholars in many disciplines have studied nonprice vertical restraints in great depth. Those urging that a rule-of-reason standard be applied to such territorial restraints argue that they encourage economic efficiencies and thus provide for spirited interbrand competition.

Vertical restraints allow a manufacturer to concentrate its advertising and distributional programs on one or two retailers in a location, making it better able to compete at the retail level with different brand manufacturers of the same product. Customer restrictions are also beneficial in this view because they enable a manufacturer to give better service and to cut out the costs of distributors' and retailers' services. For example, a manufacturer may reserve certain large commercial customers for itself, selling directly to them in large quantities and disallowing retailer involvement with them. Those arguing that a per se standard should be applied to vertical territorial restraints suggest that not only is intrabrand competition enhanced by this approach but also that customers are better able to compare the prices charged by different retailers selling the same brand. They argue that the elimination of intrabrand competition reduces the number of sellers of a leading brand in a market and increases overall market concentration in the product.

In the following landmark opinion, the U.S. Supreme Court changed the standard for judging vertical territorial and customer restrictions from per se to rule-of-reason. This was just ten years after it had gone in the opposite direction in another case.[7]

---

vertical price fixing
Stipulation by a manufacturer to a retailer to whom it sells products what price the retailer must charge for those products.

nonprice vertical restraint
Restraint used by a manufacturer to limit the territory in which a retailer may sell the manufacturer's products and the number of stores the retailer can operate, as well as the customers the retailer can serve, in a location.

---

[7]United States v. Schwinn and Co., 388 U.S. 365 (1967).

Before 1962, GTE Sylvania (plaintiff-respondent) found that it was losing market share to other television manufacturers, so it adopted a plan that placed both territorial and customer restrictions on its retailers and phased out its wholesale distributors. Sylvania limited the number of retailers selling its product in each area and designated the location within each area where the stores could be located. When Sylvania was unhappy with its sales in San Francisco, it established another retailer besides Continental (defendant-appellant) to carry the product. Continental protested, canceled a large order of Sylvania televisions, and ordered a competitor's product. Continental then requested permission to open another store in Sacramento. Sylvania opposed such an opening, claiming that it would be in violation of Continental's franchise agreement. When Continental advised Sylvania that nevertheless it was going to open in the new location, Sylvania cut Continental's credit line, and Continental, in turn, withheld all payments on inventory owed to the manufacturer's credit company. Sylvania terminated the franchise and sued for the money owed and the Sylvania merchandise in the hands of the defendant. Continental filed a cross-claim, alleging that Sylvania had violated Section 1 of the Sherman Act with its restriction on the location of the retailers that could sell its product. The district court found in favor of Continental on the cross-claim. The U.S. Court of Appeals reversed for Sylvania. Continental appealed to the U.S. Supreme Court.

JUSTICE POWELL

The Court [in *Schwinn* (1967)] proceeded to articulate the following "bright line" per se rule of illegality for vertical restrictions. "Under the Sherman Act, it is unreasonable for a manufacturer to seek to restrict and confine areas or persons with whom an article may be treated after the manufacturer has parted with dominion over it." But the Court expressly stated that the rule of reason governs when "the manufacturer retains title, dominion, and risk with respect to the product and the position and function of the dealer in question are, in fact, indistinguishable from those of an agent or salesman of the manufacturer."

In the present case, it is undisputed that title to the televisions passed from Sylvania to Continental. Thus, the *Schwinn* per se rule applies unless Sylvania's restriction on locations falls outside *Schwinn*'s prohibition against a manufacturer attempting to restrict a "retailer's freedom as to where and to whom it will resell the products."

Sylvania argues that if *Schwinn* cannot be distinguished, it should be reconsidered. Although *Schwinn* is supported by the principle of *stare decisis*, we are convinced

that the need for clarification in this area justified reconsideration. Since its announcement, *Schwinn* has been the subject of continuing controversy and confusion, both in the scholarly journals and in the federal courts. The great weight of scholarly opinion has been critical of the decision, and a number of the federal courts confronted with analogous vertical restrictions have sought to limit its reach. In our view, the experience of the past 10 years should be brought to bear on this subject of considerable commercial importance.

In essence, the issue before us is whether *Schwinn*'s per se rule can be justified under the demanding standards of *Northern Pac. R. Co.* (1958). The Court's refusal to endorse a per se standard in *White Motor Co.* (1963) was based on its uncertainty as to whether vertical restrictions satisfied those standards. Addressing this question for the first time, the Court stated:

> We need to know more than we do about the actual impact of these arrangements on competition to decide whether they have such a "pernicious effect on competition and lack . . . any redeeming virtue" and therefore should be classified as per se violations of the Sherman Act.

Only four years later the Court in Schwinn announced its sweeping per se rule without even a reference to Northern Pac. R. Co. and with no explanation of its sudden change in position.

The question remains whether the per se rule stated in Schwinn should be expanded to include nonsale transactions or abandoned in favor of a return to the rule of reason. We have found no persuasive support for expanding the rule. As noted above, the Schwinn Court recognized the undesirability of "prohibit[ing] all vertical restrictions of territory and all franchising. . . ." And even Continental does not urge us to hold that all such restrictions are per se illegal.

We revert to the standard articulated in *Northern Pac. R. Co.*, and reiterated in *White Motor*, for determining whether vertical restriction must be "conclusively presumed to be unreasonable and therefore illegal without elaborate inquiry as to the precise harm they have caused or the business excuse for their use." Such restrictions, in varying forms, are widely used in our free market economy. As indicated above, there is substantial scholarly and judicial authority supporting their economic utility. There is relatively little authority to the contrary. Certainly, there has been no showing in this case, either generally or with respect to Sylvania's agreements, that vertical restrictions have or are likely to have a "pernicious effect on competition" or that they "lack . . . any redeeming virtue." Accordingly, we conclude that the per se rule stated in Schwinn must be overruled. In so holding we do not foreclose the possibility that particular applications of vertical restrictions might justify per se prohibition under *Northern Pac. R. Co.* But we do make clear that departure from the rule of reason standard must be based upon demonstrable economic effect rather than—as in Schwinn—upon formalistic line drawing.

In sum, we conclude that the appropriate decision is to return to the rule of reason that governed vertical restrictions prior to Schwinn.

Affirmed in favor of Plaintiff, Sylvania.

TYING ARRANGEMENTS As discussed previously under the enforcement section of this chapter and the Microsoft case, a *tying arrangement* is one in which a single party agrees to sell a product or service (tying product, Windows 95) on condition that the other party agrees to buy a second (tied) product, Internet browser, or service. For example, if a company owns a patent on a tabulating machine (tying product), for example, it will attempt to get its customers to buy only tabulating cards produced by it (tied product); or if a franchisor owns a trademark symbol such as golden arches (tied product), it will seek to get its franchisees to use only products with the designated trademark symbol on them or products approved or manufactured by the franchisor (tying products). As noted in Table 22-2, tying arrangements are violations of Section 3 of the Clayton Act; however, that section of the act applies only to tying arrangements involving tangible commodities. Therefore, actions are frequently brought under Section 1 of the Sherman Act when either the tying or tied products have been *services* or *real property*.

Tying arrangements have generally been adjudged per se illegal if the manufacturer of the tying product has a monopoly on the tying product either by virtue of a patent or as a result of a natural monopoly situation. If the tying arrangement does not exist in a monopoly situation, it may still be an illegal vertical restraint of trade if the following three conditions are present:

1. The manufacturer or seller of the tying product has *sufficient economic power* to lessen competition in the market of the tied product. For example, if the owner (A) of a patent on salt-dispensing machines (tying product) leases the machines only to companies or individuals (B) who agree to buy salt (tied product) from A, such an agreement may be considered per se illegal because it limits the sellers of the tied product (salt) from competing vigorously in the salt market. However, if there are similar salt-dispensing-machine manufacturers and lessors that the lessees (B) can buy from, it is clear that A will not be able to lessen competition in the salt market.

2. A *substantial amount of interstate commerce* is affected. If the manufacturer and lessor of the salt machines, through a tying agreement, has little impact on the market of the tied product (salt), the courts will not consider this agreement to be per se illegal and, using a rule-of-reason approach, will dismiss the case.

3. *Two separate products or services* are involved. Some franchisors have argued successfully that their trademark (e.g., the golden arches) and their products and services (building, equipment, service contract) are one and the same package rather than separate products and thus that no tying arrangement exists.

EXCLUSIVE-DEALING CONTRACTS Agreements between manufacturers and retailers (dealers), or between franchisors and franchisees, requiring the second party to sell and promote only the brand of goods supplied by the first party are known as **exclusive-dealing contracts**. For example, the Standard Oil Company of California had exclusive-dealing contracts with independent stations in seven western states that required the stations to buy all their oil and other petroleum products from the company. Sales under that exclusive-dealing contract involved approximately 7 percent of all sales of such products in the seven states. Using a *comparative substantiability test* (one comparing the effect of such agreements on competing sellers of petroleum products in the geo-

exclusive-dealing contract
Agreement in which one party requires another party to sell and promote only the brand of goods supplied by the first party.

graph area), the U.S. Supreme Court found a violation of Section 3 of the Clayton Act.[8]

Since that case, the Court has generally followed a rule-of-reason approach in cases that involve exclusive-dealing agreements. Such agreements are found to be illegal when they foreclose a substantial portion of a relevant market. The Court has found that legitimate business reasons for exclusive-dealing contracts exist in certain industries. For example, it ruled that an exclusive dealing contract between an electrical utility and a coal supplier extending 20 years was lawful because it had procompetitive effects.[9] The contract assured the utility and its customers a regular supply of coal at a reasonably fixed rate and allowed the coal company to better plan its production and employment needs over a long period; in turn, it was allowed to offer the utility a lower price.

SECTION 2: MONOPOLIES

Section 2 of the Sherman Act reads:

> *Every person who shall monopolize, or attempt to monopolize, or combine or conspire with any other person or persons to monopolize any part of trade or commerce among the several states, or with foreign nations, shall be deemed guilty of a felony, and on conviction thereof shall be punished by a fine not exceeding one million dollars if a corporation or, if any other person, one hundred thousand dollars, or by imprisonment not exceeding three years, or by both.*

Section 2, therefore, prohibits monopolization, attempts to monopolize, and conspiracies to monopolize. Each of these prohibitions is examined in this section. In reading this material, keep the following four factors in mind:

1. One of the purposes of antitrust law, as we stated earlier in this chapter, is to promote a competitive model. Such a model traditionally assumes the existence of many buyers and sellers who have equal access to information about the marketplace and labor that is mobile.
2. In framing Section 2 of the Sherman Act, Congress was vague about what it meant by a **monopoly**. Therefore it has been up to the courts to define the concept case by case, sometimes with the aid of economic analysis.
3. Some claim that U.S. corporations need to be large in order to compete with state-owned and state-supported foreign multinationals.
4. Large companies that have attained their monopolistic position through innovation and research, leading to patents, may be forced in some cases to share the results of their efforts with competitors in order to avoid bringing down on themselves a Section 2 enforcement and possible penalties of fines or imprisonment or both.

monopoly An economic market situation in which a single business has the power to fix the price of goods or services.

MONOPOLIZATION The U.S. Supreme Court has developed three criteria, or steps, to determine whether a firm has attained a monopolistic position and is misusing its power in violation of Section 2 of the Sherman Act:

1. It determines the *relevant product and geographic markets* within which the alleged monopolist operates.
2. It determines whether the defendant has *overwhelming power* in the relevant markets.
3. It examines whether there is an *intent* on the part of the alleged monopolist to monopolize.

Relevant Product and Geographic Markets Markets are divided into product and geographic markets. How the courts determine the boundaries of those markets helps decide what market share a company has, and thus its market power.

---

[8]Standard Oil Co. of California v. United States, 337 U.S 293 (1949).
[9]Tampa Electric Co. v. Nashville Coal Co., 365 U.S. 320 (1961).

The courts have generally defined the relevant *product market* as that in which the company alleged to be a monopolist can raise or lower prices with relative independence of the forces of supply and demand. In a monopoly situation, the courts look to the concept of **cross-elasticity of demand** or **substitutability**.

Cross-elasticity of demand measures the impact that upward and downward changes in price have on the demand for the product. If cross-elasticity of demand is positive, an increase in price of the alleged monopolistic product will result in consumers' switching to a substitute product. For example, in a landmark case,[10] the government charged the Du Pont Company with monopolizing the cellophane industry because it produced 75 percent of all the cellophane sold in the United States. Du Pont argued that cellophane was not the correct product market because there were many substitutes for cellophane; rather, flexible packaging materials was the correct product market to consider in this case. If the court agreed, Du Pont would not be a monopolist because cellophane constituted only 25 percent of the flexible packaging materials market. The U.S. Supreme Court did rule in favor of Du Pont, on the basis of the availability of substitutes and the high elasticity of demand for cellophane. The Court noted that a slight increase in the price of cellophane caused many customers to switch to other flexible wrapping materials, which showed there was a positive cross-elasticity of demand and that Du Pont lacked monopoly status.

The courts generally have defined the *geographic market* as the area where the defendant's firm competes head-on with others in the previously determined relevant product market. Usually, geographic markets are stipulated (agreed to) by the plaintiff and the defendant as regional, national, or international. However, an exception occurred in a leading monopoly case decided by the Supreme Court.[11] In this case, the parties argued over whether the products that were sold were at a regional market level (Grinnell) or at a national level (United States). The products in which Grinnell had ownership interests included tires, sprinklers, plumbing supplies, and burglary systems, together called accredited central station protection services.

Overwhelming Power in The Market Once the relevant markets have been determined, the alleged monopolist's market power to control prices and to exclude fringe competition is significant. The courts are interested in whether the defendant has overwhelming market power, not absolute power, because there are usually small competitors who produce poor substitutes. The courts will ask: Do the pricing and output of the alleged monopolist control the conduct of the few competitors in the industry?

In order to answer that question, the courts have traditionally looked at five factors: market share, the size of other firms in the industry or market, the pricing structure of the market, entry barriers, and the unique nature of the industry. In the case of *Aspen Skiing Co. v. Aspen Highlands Skiing Corp.*,[12] the U.S. Supreme Court stated that in viewing market power, it would look not only at the *market share* that the alleged monopolist held but also at whether the power was acquired and maintained through *predatory conduct* that would be illegal or as a result of a superior product, business acumen, or historical accident. This approach is fair because a corporation attaining monopoly power through innovation and research could easily be punished instead of rewarded if market share were the sole measure of overwhelming market power. A company would then have little incentive to compete to gain a market share in excess of 50 percent because if it did gain that much (or perhaps even less), it would risk being charged a monopolist under Section 2 of the Sherman Act.

Intent to Monopolize After defining the relevant product and geographic markets and determining whether the company has overwhelming

---

[10]United States v. Du Pont Co., 351 U.S. 3717 (1956).
[11]United States v. Grinnell Co., 384 U.S. 563 (1966).
[12]472 U.S. 585 (1985).

market power, the courts must decide if the company has a general intent to monopolize the market. This step is significant because having overwhelming power by virtue of being "big" in the market is not enough to make a firm liable for a Section 2 violation. The courts will look at specific conduct that tends to show "intent," such as attempts to exclude competitors or to raise barriers to entry. They particularly look at the foreseeable consequences of an alleged monopolist's actions: Would these actions naturally lead to a monopoly position? For example, the Aluminum Company of America (ALCOA) anticipated every demand increase and expanded its output in the aluminum industry. It was thus able to exclude competitors from the aluminum ingot market by lowering prices. These generally would be good business practices if ALCOA had not been judged to have overwhelming market power in the relevant product market. The courts draw a fine line between a monopoly gained by innovation, patents, and business acumen and one attained by conduct whose foreseeable consequence is the reinforcement of a monopoly position. The first position is gained in a passive manner, the second in an active manner that shows intent to monopolize.

ATTEMPT TO MONOPOLIZE   Section 2 of the Sherman Act forbids not only monopolization but even *attempts to monopolize* because the drafters of the section were concerned about the damage that efforts to attain a monopoly could inflict on an industry even if such efforts failed. So great was their concern, in fact, that the penalties are the same for both monopolization and attempts to monopolize. Case law indicates that after determining the relevant geographic and product markets, the courts look for one or some combination of three factors when a firm is charged with an attempt to monopolize: specific intent, predatory conduct, a dangerous probability of success. We will discuss the first two; the third is self-explanatory.

Specific intent is shown by bringing forth evidence that a firm has engaged in predatory or anticompetitive conduct aimed at a stated or potential competitor.

Predatory conduct includes (1) stealing trade secrets, (2) interfering unlawfully in requirement contracts that third parties have with other competitors, and (3) attempting to destroy the reputation of a competitor through defamatory actions. Recently, the courts have added **predatory pricing**—pricing below average variable cost (or, in some cases, below average total cost)—to this list on the ground that when a company is pricing below average variable cost, it is not seeking to maximize profits but is intending to drive a competitor out of business.

predatory pricing Pricing below the average or marginal cost in order to drive out competition.

THE CLAYTON ACT OF 1914

The Clayton Act was enacted in 1914 after a major debate in the presidential campaign of 1912. The Supreme Court had ruled in 1911 that only restraints that were unreasonable by their nature or in their effect could be declared unlawful under the Sherman Act. This ruling left much room for interpretation by federal judges as well as by Justice Department prosecutors. Democratic candidate Woodrow Wilson argued during the presidential campaign that the Supreme Court was hostile to the antitrust laws and that businesspeople needed guidance as to what specific practices were illegal. He urged the creation of an agency to investigate trade practices and to advise businesspeople about which actions were lawful and which were not. Upon election, Wilson proposed a bill that, after great debate and compromise in Congress, was enacted into law as the **Clayton Act of 1914**. It declared the following acts to be illegal under certain circumstances:

Clayton Act Prohibits price discrimination, tying and exclusive-dealing arrangements, and corporate mergers that substantially lessen competition or tend to create a monopoly in interstate commerce.

1. Price discrimination (Section 2).
2. Tying arrangements and exclusive-dealing contracts (Section 3).
3. Corporate mergers and acquisitions that tend to lessen competition or to create a monopoly (Section 7).
4. Interlocking directorates (Section 8).

At the same time, Congress passed the Federal Trade Commission Act of 1914, setting up the Federal Trade Commission (FTC) and giving it authority to police these and other "unfair or deceptive acts or practices affecting interstate commerce."

SECTION 2: PRICE DISCRIMINATION

Section 2 of the Clayton Act (as amended in 1936 by the Robinson-Patman Act) prohibits each of the business activities set out in Table 22-6. As you read the table, pay attention to all the italicized words because they have been the source of litigation and acceptable defenses to that litigation.

Section 2(a) of the Clayton Act prohibits discrimination in *price* by seller between *two* purchasers of a *commodity of like grade* and *quality*, in *interstate commerce*, and resulting in *injury to competition*. Each of these elements must be proved by a plaintiff in any action brought under Section 2(a). Let us dissect these elements one by one.

price discrimination A price differential that is below the average variable cost for the seller; considered predatory, and therefore illegal, under the Clayton Act.

- *Price.* Section 2(a) forbids direct or indirect discrimination in price. **Price discrimination** is deemed by most courts and scholars to be a price differential that is below the average variable cost for the seller, and thus is "predatory" and illegal. An example of indirect price discrimination would be a seller's giving a *preferred buyer* a 60-day option to purchase a product at the present price, while giving another purchaser only a 30-day option. The courts have ruled that this situation constitutes price discrimination under Section 2(a).

- *Sales.* There must be *two actual sales* (not leases or consignments) by a single seller that are close in time. Say that seller A offers to sell to B a widget for $1.00 and then sells the widget to C for $.95. If B charges price discrimination, that claim will not be upheld because there was no sale between A and B but merely an offer to sell. A sale exists only when there is an enforceable contract.

- *Commodities.* Commodities are movable or tangible properties (e.g., milk or bicycle tires). Services and other intangibles are not covered by Section 2(a).

- *Like Grade and Quality.* The commodities must be of similar grade and quality; they need not be exactly the same. For example, price differences in milk cartons that are slightly different in size do fall under Section 2(a) jurisdiction. However, differences in price between car tires and bicycle tires are differences in prices of commodities of different grade and quality, so they do not fall under Section 2(a) jurisdiction.

- *Interstate Commerce.* The sales must occur in interstate commerce. If the two sales by a single seller to two purchasers take place in intrastate commerce, the Clayton Act, being a federal statute, does not apply.

TABLE 22-6   *Summary of Provisions of Clayton Act as Amended by Robinson-Patman Act*

SECTION	ACTION(S) PROHIBITED	DEFENSE
2(a)	Discrimination in price by seller between *two* purchasers of a *commodity of like grade* and *quality* where effect may be to *substantially lessen competition* or tend to create a monopoly.	Cost *justification* or a good faith attempt to *meet equally low prices of competitors*.
2(c)	Fictitious brokerage payments (or discounts where services not rendered).	None.
2(d)	Payments for promotions or allowances for promotional services by seller unless made available to all buyers on *proportionately equal terms*.	*Meeting competition*.
2(e)	Promotional services by seller unless provided to all buyers on *proportionately equal terms*.	*Meeting competition* for seller.
2(f)	*Inducing* to discriminate in price or knowingly receiving the benefits of such discrimination.	Cost *justification*.

- *Competitive Injury.* Finally, the plaintiff must show that the price discrimination caused competitive injury, which under the Clayton Act is price discrimination that either substantially lessens competition, tends to create a monopoly, or injures, destroys, or prevents competition with the person or firm that knowingly receives the benefits of discrimination.

Injury to competition includes:

1. **Primary-line injury** (at the seller level), which occurs when a seller cuts prices in one geographic area in order to drive out a local competitor.

2. **Secondary-line injury** (at the buyer level), which occurs when competitors of one of the buyers are injured because the seller sold to that one buyer at a lower price than he sold to the others. The buyer who received the lower wholesale price can then undersell the other buyers, which may substantially lessen competition.

3. **Tertiary-line injury** (at the retailer level), which occurs when a discriminatory price is passed along from a secondary-line buyer to a retailer. Retailers who get the benefit of a seller's lower price to a buyer will be able to undersell their competitors.

primary-line injury A form of price discrimination in which a seller attempts to put a local competitive firm out of business by lowering its prices only in the region where the local firm sells its products.

secondary-line injury A form of price discrimination in which a seller offers a discriminatory price to one buyer but not to another buyer.

tertiary-line injury A form of price discrimination in which a discriminatory price is passed along from a secondary-line party to a favored party at the next level of distribution.

THE MEETING-THE-COMPETITION DEFENSE Section 2(b) of the Clayton Act allows a seller to discriminate in price if able to show that the lower price "was made in good faith to meet an equally low price of a competitor." The seller can discriminate to meet the competition but not to "bury" or "beat" the competition. The breadth of the meeting-the-competition defense has long been debated.

SECTION 3: TYING ARRANGEMENTS AND EXCLUSIVE-DEALING CONTRACTS

Section 3 of the Clayton Act reads:

> *That it shall be unlawful for any person engaged in commerce, in the course of such commerce, to lease or make a sale or contract for sale of goods, wares, merchandise, machinery, supplies, or other commodities, whether patented or unpatented for use, consumption or resale within the United States or any territory thereof or the District of Columbia or any insular possession or other place under the jurisdiction of the United States, or fix a price charged therefore, or discount from or rebate upon, such price, on the condition, agreement or understanding that the lessee or purchaser thereof shall not use or deal in the goods, wares, merchandise, machinery, supplies, or other commodities of a competitor or competitors of the lessor or seller, where the effect of such lease, sale, or contact for sale or such condition, agreement or understanding may be to substantially lessen competition or tend to create a monopoly in any line of commerce.*

This is the section of the act that courts have generally relied on in cases concerning tying arrangements and exclusive-dealing contracts. Tying arrangements and exclusive-dealing contracts may not be per se illegal in a particular instance, despite past treatment of them as per se illegal in other instances by the courts.

SECTION 7: MERGERS AND ACQUISITIONS

Section 7 of the Clayton Act reads:

> *That no corporation engaged in commerce shall acquire, directly or indirectly, the whole or any part of the stock or other share capital and no corporation subject to the jurisdiction of the Federal Trade Commission shall acquire the whole or any part of the assets of another corporation engaged also in commerce, where in any line of commerce in any section of the country, the effect of such acquisition may be substantially to lessen competition, or to tend to create a monopoly.*

The purpose of Section 7 of the Clayton Act, as amended in 1950, is to prohibit anticompetitive mergers and acquisitions that tend to lessen competition at their incipiency—that is, in the words of Justice Brennan, "to arrest apprehended consequences of intercorporate relationships before those relationships [can] work their evil, which may be at or any time after the acquisition."[13]

The language of the statute has led to controversy and considerable litigation, especially since the business world went on a **merger** binge in the early 1980s. There were more than 2,000 mergers each year from 1983 through 1986, and some of this country's largest corporations were involved in the deal making. For example, in 1984, Chevron purchased Gulf Oil for $13.2 billion, and Texaco bought Getty for $10.1 billion. The emphasis in 1983 and 1984 was on large oil company acquisitions, but 1985 and 1986 saw acquisitions by companies in the manufacturing, technology, and service areas of the economy as well. Although the 1980s is the decade associated with big deal making, the merger frenzy continued into the 1990s (see Exhibit 22-1).

REASONS FOR THE INCREASE IN MERGERS IN THE 1980s Mergers are a method of external growth as opposed to internal corporate expansion. They may take place for one or any combination of the following reasons:

1. *Undervalued assets.* It is cheaper for a company such as General Motors (GM) to buy Electronic Data Systems (EDS) and Hughes Aircraft in order to obtain computer capabilities, a computer transmission network, and telecommunications capabilities than to borrow money and expand internally in those areas. In the opinion of GM and its investment banking advisers, both EDS and Hughes Aircraft were undervalued stocks in the marketplace and therefore a "good buy."

2. *Divestiture.* About 22 percent of all the companies acquired in mergers in 1981, 1982, and 1983 were subsidiaries of parent companies that had purchased them in the late 1950s and the 1960s and then decided to jettison them because they were no longer profitable or because they no longer fit in with the parent company's plans.

EXHIBIT 22-1 *Some of the Biggest U.S. Deals Since 1997**

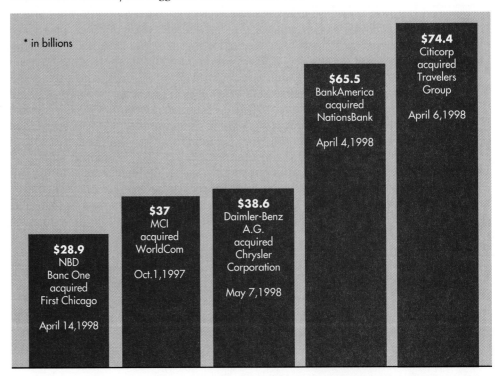

* in billions

$28.9
NBD
Banc One
acquired
First Chicago

April 14, 1998

$37
MCI
acquired
WorldCom

Oct. 1, 1997

$38.6
Daimler-Benz
A.G.
acquired
Chrysler
Corporation

May 7, 1998

$65.5
BankAmerica
acquired
NationsBank

April 4, 1998

$74.4
Citicorp
acquired
Travelers
Group

April 6, 1998

Source: Workload Report, Research in Statistics Bureau, Antitrust Division, U.S. Dept. of Justice (1997–1998).

[13]United States v. E.I. du Pont de Nemours & Co., 353 U.S. 586 (1957).

3. *Diversification.* During a recession (e.g., 1981–1983), when stocks are generally underpriced, companies may seek to diversify—that is, to reduce their risks in one industry's business cycle by investing in another industry. U.S. Steel's acquisition of Marathon Oil Company was an attempt at diversification by a steel company hit hard by recession and foreign imports.

4. *Tax credits for research and development.* Between the middle of 1981 and the end of 1985, the Internal Revenue Code allowed a 25 percent tax credit for increases in research capabilities acquired through mergers.

5. *Economies of scale.* A merger often brings about greater efficiency and lower unit costs, particularly in research and development and in manufacturing.

6. *The Reagan administration's philosophy* that "bigness" is not "bad." This flexible approach to mergers was embodied in the Justice Department's Merger Guidelines of 1982 and 1984, which are examined later in this chapter.

CRITERIA FOR DETERMINING THE LEGALITY OF MERGERS UNDER SECTION 7   The U.S. Supreme Court, the lower federal courts, the Justice Department, and the Federal Trade Commission use the following criteria, or steps, to decide on the legality of a merger:

1. They first determine the *relevant product and geographic markets.*
2. They then determine the *probable impact* of the merger on competition in the relevant product and geographic markets.

Relevant Product and Geographic Markets   We said in our discussion of monopolies that how courts determine the boundaries of the product and geographic markets helps them decide what market share a company has, and hence its market power. The same holds true when the courts are ruling on mergers: The market share of the new, combined company will have a strong bearing on the court's decision on the legality of the merger.

The primary criterion the courts use in determining the relevant *product market*, is, again, *substitutability*, or *cross-elasticity of demand* for a product. Other factors used are (1) public recognition of the product market, (2) distinct customer prices, (3) the product's sensitivity to price changes, (4) whether unique facilities are necessary for production, and (5) peculiar product characteristics. In the *Brown Shoe* case excerpted later in the chapter, you will note the courts' interest in these other factors.

When identifying the *geographic market*, what the courts are interested in is where the merging companies compete. The courts may decide that this geographic market includes all cities with a population of over 10,000, or they may judge this market to be regional, national, or international.

Probable Impact on Competition   The courts have traditionally gauged a merger's impact on competition by examining such factors as:

1. *Market foreclosure*, resulting from the merger of a customer and its supplier, so that competing customers may be foreclosed from the market if the supplier's goods are in demand and that demand exceeds supply.

2. *Potential elimination of competition* from a market if two competing firms merge.

3. *Entrenchment* of a smaller firm in a market if a large firm with "deep pockets" acquires it and supplies the capital the small firm needs to eliminate competitors.

4. *Trends in the market* revealing a high rate of concentration, as measured by percentage of the market that the leading four to six competitors in an industry have.

5. Postmerger evidence revealing *anticompetitive effects* on a market.

TYPES OF MERGERS   The courts have distinguished among horizontal, vertical, and conglomerate mergers because each type has a potentially different impact on competition. **Horizontal mergers** involve the acquisition of one firm by another that is at the same competitive level in the distribution system. This type of

horizontal merger A merger between two or more companies producing the same or a similar product and competing for sales in the same geographic market.

merger usually leads to the elimination of a competitor. For example, in 1984, Chevron's purchase of the Gulf Oil Corporation eliminated one oil company at the seller's level in the industry. **Vertical mergers** involve the acquisition of one firm by another that is at a different level in the distribution system. For example, if a shoe manufacturer acquires a company that has many retail shoe outlets, the merger is termed vertical because one company is at the manufacturing level and the other is at the retailing level of the distribution system. **Conglomerate mergers** involve the acquisition by one firm of another that produces products or services that are not directly related to those of the acquiring firm. For example, the acquisition by GM (an automobile company) of EDS (a technology company) merged two companies that did not produce directly related products and services.

Horizontal Mergers　In the 1960s and early 1970s, whenever a merger would result in what was labeled *undue concentration* in a particular market, there was a presumption of illegality. In a landmark case,[14] the Supreme Court termed a postacquisition market share of 30 percent or more prima facie illegal. In another, equally important case involving the merger of two retail grocery store chains,[15] the Court, perceiving a trend toward fewer competitors in the retail-store market, held a postacquisition share of 8.9 percent presumptively illegal. In both cases, the Court's initial determination of the relevant product and geographic markets and the percentage of market shares the merged company would have became determinative of the result.

It was in 1974 that a majority of Supreme Court justices first showed a willingness to examine economic factors such as the nature of the industry, barriers to entry, sources of supply, the financial condition of the acquired firm, and the economic impact of a merger on a particular industry. Each of those factors has been used ever since to rebut the presumption of illegality.

Vertical Mergers　Vertical mergers are termed *backward* when a retailer attempts to acquire a supplier and *forward* when a supplier attempts to acquire a retailer. In vertical merger cases, unlike in horizontal merger cases, the courts have tended not to put great emphasis on market share percentage. Instead, they have generally examined the potential for foreclosing competition in the relevant market. For example, if a retailer acquires a supplier of widgets, will other widget suppliers be foreclosed from selling to the retailer? What impact will that foreclosure have on the widget market? The courts also look at the trend in the supplier's market toward concentration, barriers to entry, and the financial health of the acquired firm.

Conglomerate Mergers　As with horizontal and vertical mergers, the courts, using a case-by-case approach, have developed criteria that they look at in conglomerate merger situations to determine whether Section 7 of the Clayton Act has been violated. Because conglomerate mergers result in the combining of firms in different fields that are not competing with each other, the courts have found for the plaintiffs when it can be shown that the acquiring firm was already planning to move into the field and did not move into it only because it had "acquired" its way in; in effect, the conglomerate merger had prevented a company that was a potential entrant from entering and increasing the number of competitors. The following case illustrates a potential entrant situation.

FEDERAL TRADE COMMISSION V. PROCTER & GAMBLE COMPANY
UNITED STATES SUPREME COURT 386 U.S. 568 (1967)

The Federal Trade Commission staff (plaintiff-appellant) sued Procter & Gamble (defendant-respondent), claiming that P&G's acquisition of the assets of the Clorox Chemical Company violated Section 7 of the Clayton Act. The full commission found the staff's complaint valid and ordered Procter & Gamble to divest itself of Clorox. The Sixth Circuit Court of Appeals reversed. The FTC appealed.

---

[14]United States v. Philadelphia National Bank, 374 U.S. 321 (1963).
[15]United States v. Vons Grocery, 384 U.S. 270 (1966).

vertical merger A merger that integrates two firms that have a supplier-customer relationship.

conglomerate merger A merger in which the businesses of the acquiring and the acquired firm are totally unrelated.

JUSTICE DOUGLAS

At the time of the merger, in 1957, Clorox was the leading manufacturer in the heavily concentrated household liquid bleach industry. It is agreed that household liquid bleach is the relevant line of commerce. The product is used in the home as a germicide and disinfectant, and, more importantly, as a whitening agent in washing clothes and fabrics. It is a distinctive product with no close substitutes. Liquid bleach is a low-price, high-turn-over consumer product sold mainly through grocery stores and supermarkets. The relevant geographical market is the nation and a series of regional markets. Because of high shipping costs and low sales price, it is not feasible to ship the product more than 300 miles from its point of manufacture. Most manufacturers are limited to competition within a single region since they have but one plant. Clorox is the only firm selling nationally; it has 13 plants distributed throughout the nation. Purex, Clorox's closest competitor in size, does not distribute its bleach in the Northeast or mid-Atlantic states; in 1957, Purex's bleach was available in less than 50% of the national market.

At the time of the acquisition, Clorox was the leading manufacturer of household liquid bleach, with 48.8% of the national sales—annual sales of slightly less than $40,000,000. Its market share had been steadily increasing for the five years prior to the merger. Its nearest rival was Purex, which manufactures a number of products other than household liquid bleaches, including abrasive cleaners, toilet soap, and detergents. Purex accounted for almost 6% of the nation's household liquid bleach sales, and together with four other firms for almost 80%. The remaining 20% was divided among over 200 small producers. Clorox had total assets of $12,000,000; only eight producers had assets in excess of $1,000,000 and very few had assets of more than $75,000,000.

In light of the territorial limitations on distribution, national figures do not give an accurate picture of Clorox's dominance in the various regions. Thus, Clorox's seven principal competitors did no business in New England, the mid-Atlantic states, or metropolitan New York. Clorox's share of the sales in those areas was 56%, 72%, and 64%, respectively. . . .

Since all liquid bleach is chemically identical, advertising and sales promotion are vital. In 1957 Clorox spent almost $3,700,000 on advertising, imprinting the value of its bleach in the mind of the consumer. In addition, it spent $1,700,000 for other promotional activities. The Commission found that these heavy expenditures went far to explain why Clorox maintained so high a market share despite the fact that its brand, though chemically indistinguishable from rival brands, retailed for a price equal to or, in many instances, higher than its competitors.

In 1957, Procter was the nation's largest advertiser, spending more than $80,000,000 on advertising and an additional $47,000,000 on sales promotion. Due to its tremendous volume, Procter receives substantial discounts from the media. As a multiproduct producer Procter enjoys substantial advantages in advertising and sales promotion. Thus, it can and does feature several products in its promotions, reducing the printing, mailing, and other costs for each product. It also purchases network programs on behalf of several products, enabling it to give each product network exposure at a fraction of the cost per product that a firm with only one product to advertise would incur.

Prior to the acquisition, Procter was in the course of diversifying into product lines related to its basic detergent-soap-cleanser business. Liquid bleach was a distinct possibility since packaged detergents—Procter's primary product line—and liquid bleach are used complementarily in washing clothes and fabrics, and in general household cleaning.

The decision to acquire Clorox was the result of a study conducted by Procter's promotion department designed to determine the advisability of entering the liquid bleach industry. The initial report noted the ascendancy of liquid bleach in the large and expanding household bleach market, and recommended that Procter purchase Clorox rather than enter independently. Since a large investment would be needed to obtain a satisfactory market share, acquisition of the industry's leading firm was attractive.

All mergers are within the reach of Section 7, and all must be tested by the same standard, whether they are classified as horizontal, vertical, conglomerate or other.

The anticompetitive effects with which this product extension merger is fraught can easily be seen: (1) the substitution of the powerful acquiring firm for the smaller, but already dominant, firm may substantially reduce the competitive structure of the industry by raising entry barriers and by dissuading the smaller firms from aggressively competing; (2) the acquisition eliminates the potential competition of the acquiring firm. . . .

Procter would be able to use its volume discounts to advantage in advertising Clorox. Thus, a new entrant would be much more reluctant to face the giant Procter than it would have been to face the smaller Clorox.

Possible economies cannot be used as a defense to illegality. Congress was aware that some mergers which lessen competition may also result in economies but it struck the balance in favor of protecting competition.

The Commission also found that the acquisition of Clorox by Procter eliminated Procter as a potential competitor. The Court of Appeals declared that this finding was not supported by evidence because there was no evidence that Procter's management had ever intended to enter the industry independently and that Procter had never attempted to enter. The evidence, however, clearly shows that Procter was the most likely entrant. Procter had recently launched a new abrasive cleaner in an industry similar to the liquid bleach industry, and had wrested leadership from a brand that had enjoyed even a larger market share than had Clorox. Procter was engaged in a vigorous program of diversifying into product lines closely related to its basic products. Liquid bleach was a natural avenue of diversification since it is complementary to Procter's products, is sold to the same customers through the same channels, and is advertised and merchandised in the same manner. Procter had substantial advantages in advertising and sales promotion, which, as we have seen, are vital to the success of liquid bleach. No manufacturer had a patent on the product or its manufacturing methods and processes. They were available, there was no shortage of raw material, and the machinery and equipment required for a plant of efficient capacity were available at reasonable cost. Procter's management was experienced in producing and marketing goods similar to liquid bleach. Procter had considered the possibility of independently entering but decided against it because the acquisition of Clorox would enable Procter to capture a more commanding share of the market.

It is clear that the existence of Procter at the edge of the industry exerted considerable influence on the market. First, the market behavior of the liquid bleach industry was influenced by each firm's predictions of the market behavior of its competitors, actual and potential. Second, the barriers to entry by a firm of Procter's size and with its advantages were not significant. There is no indication that the barriers were so high that the price Procter would have to charge would be above the price that would maximize the profits of the existing firms. Third, the number of potential entrants was not so large that the elimination of one would be insignificant. Few firms would have the temerity to challenge a firm as solidly entrenched as Clorox. Fourth, Procter was found by the Commission to be the most likely entrant. These findings of the Commission were amply supported by the evidence.

Reversed in favor of Plaintiff, FTC.

DEFENSES TO SECTION 7 COMPLAINTS   In cases brought under Section 7 of the Clayton Act, defendants have met complaints by private plaintiffs, as well as those filed by the Justice Department or the FTC, by asserting the following defenses.

1. *The merger does not have a substantial effect on interstate commerce.* In order for the Clayton Act to be applicable, the merger must be shown to have a substantial effect on interstate commerce, for the federal government may act—and a federal statute may be applied—only if interstate activity, as opposed to intrastate activity, is involved. As we noted in chapter 4, however, activities involving interstate commerce have been broadly interpreted under the Commerce Clause of the Constitution by the federal courts.

2. *The merger does not have the probability of substantially lessening competition or tending to create a monopoly.* Since the 1980s, firms have argued that mergers are procompetitive and beneficial to the economy and the nation because they improve economic efficiency and enable United States–based companies to compete with state-subsidized and state-owned foreign multinationals.

3. *One of the companies to the merger is failing.* This defense must meet three criteria: (a) The failing company had little hope of survival without the merger; (b) the acquiring company is the only one interested in purchasing the failing company or, if there are several interested purchasers, it is the least threat to competition in the relevant market; and (c) all possible methods of saving the failing company have been tried and have been unsuccessful.

4. *The merger is solely for investment purposes.* Section 7 does not apply to a corporation's purchase of stock in another company "solely for investment purposes," so long as the acquiring corporation does not use its stock purchase for "voting or otherwise to bring about, or attempting to bring about, the substantial lessening of competition." The courts look on this defense skeptically, especially when purchases of a company's stock by another company exceed 5 percent of the shares outstanding.

ENFORCEMENT   The Justice Department, the Federal Trade Commission, and private individuals and corporations can all enforce Section 7. The Justice Department divides authority with the FTC on the basis of areas of historical interest as well as according to the expertise of the staff of each agency.

When the Clayton Act was enacted, it provided no *criminal punishment* for violators but merely allowed the Justice Department to obtain injunctions to prevent further violations. Recall that Sections 1 and 2 of the Sherman Act do provide for criminal sanctions, and that Section 4 of the Clayton Act (see

"Goals of the Antitrust Statutes: Private Enforcement," at the beginning of this chapter) allows *individuals* to sue on their own behalf and to obtain triple damages, court costs, and attorneys' fees if they can show injury based on violations of either the Sherman Act or the Clayton Act. The Clayton Act also allows individuals to obtain injunctions. Further, if a business is found guilty of violating the Sherman Act in a suit brought by the Justice Department, this finding is prima facie evidence of a violation when a private party sues for treble damages under the Clayton Act. That is, the private party need not prove a violation of the antitrust statutes over again but merely introduces into evidence a copy of the court order that found the defendant guilty of a Sherman Act violation.

MERGER GUIDELINES The Justice Department has sought to put the business community on notice about what it views as violations of Section 7, and when it is most likely to bring an enforcement action, by issuing Merger Guidelines. These guidelines do not constitute law; they serve only an advisory function. They can be changed by each new administration to fit preordained political goals. The Federal Trade Commission generally follows the Justice Department's Merger Guidelines.

The first guidelines, issued in 1968, were based essentially on market share analysis. In 1982, the guidelines were substantially revised to reflect the courts' growing emphasis on economic analysis that goes beyond the traditional postacquisition market share criterion. The **Hertindahl-Hirschman Index (HHI)** is now used to determine whether the Justice Department will challenge a horizontal merger. This index is calculated by adding the squares of the market shares of a firm in the relevant product and geographic markets. For example, if two firms each control 50 percent of the relevant market, the HHI is equal to $50^2 + 50^2$, or 5,000. The smaller the HHI, the less concentrated the market, and the less likely the Justice Department is to challenge the merger. A postmerger HHI below 1,000 is unlikely to be challenged, and a postmerger HHI between 1,000 and 1,800 will probably be challenged only if the merger produces an increase in the HHI of more than 100 points. Whether a postmerger HHI of more than 1,800 will be challenged depends on whether a leading firm is involved, the ease of entry into the relevant market, the nature of the product, market performance, and certain other factors the department regards as relevant in a particular case.

In general, the Justice Department did not challenge vertical mergers in 1982–1992 unless they facilitated collusion or raised barriers to entry. Usually, the HHI has to exceed 1,800 in order to gain the department's attention. No mention is made of conglomerate mergers in the 1982 Merger Guidelines.

In 1984, the Merger Guidelines were revised again to set out changes and clarifications. One important difference was that the guidelines allowed the Justice Department to take into consideration foreign competition in determining whether to bring an enforcement action. This revision was prompted by the Commerce Department, which was concerned about the ability of large United States–based corporations to compete with foreign multinationals. Under the 1984 guidelines, if a foreign firm imports into a relevant U.S. product and geographic market in a particular merger case, its impact on that market will be considered by the FTC and the Justice Department when deciding whether to challenge the merger.

A new political administration in Washington in 1993 produced new guidelines with a five-step approach to challenging horizontal mergers:

Step 1. Before challenging a merger, the Antitrust Division of the Justice Department will determine whether the merger significantly increases market concentration. The definition of market participation was broadened to include all current producers and potential entrants. The 1982 HHI remains the measuring stick.

Step 2. Next the division will determine the potential adverse competitive effect of a merger. The focus here was changed from the potential for postmerger collusion to the potential for "coordinated interaction among participants."

Hertindahl-Hirschman Index (HHI) An index calculated by adding the squares of the shares of the relevant market held by each firm in a horizontal merger to determine the competitive effects of the merger. In using the HHI to decide whether to challenge a merger, the Justice Department considers both the level of the postmerger HHI and the increase in the HHI caused by the merger.

Step 3. The division will then look at whether entry into the market is so easy that prices will not profitably increase after the proposed merger.

Step 4. The 1993 Merger Guidelines omit the previous guidelines' requirement that the merging companies present clear and convincing evidence for these efficiencies of scale.

Step 5. Finally, the division will determine whether one of the merging companies is a "failing" firm or company division that would leave the market unless allowed to merge with the stronger company. Under the 1993 Merger Guidelines, the "failing" company defense will be limited to firms in liquidation; Chapter 11 reorganization under the bankruptcy laws will not be enough to meet the guidelines.

premerger notification requirement The legislatively mandated requirement that certain types of firms notify the FTC and the Justice Department 30 days before finalizing a merger so that these agencies can investigate and challenge any mergers they find anticompetitive.

PREMERGER NOTIFICATION   The *Hart-Scott Robinson Act of 1976*, which amended Section 7 of the Clayton Act, introduced a **premerger notification requirement** into the area of mergers. If the acquiring company has sales of $100 million or more, if the acquired firm has sales of $10 million or more, and if either affects interstate commerce, both firms must file notice of the pending merger with the Justice Department and the Federal Trade Commission 30 days before the merger is finalized. This notice enables the department and the FTC to assess the probable competitive impact of the merger *before it takes place.*

REMEDIES   When parties decide to go ahead with a merger despite being advised that an enforcement action will be brought, the Justice Department and the FTC have three basic civil remedies available: civil injunctions, cease-and-desist orders, and divestiture. However, the Antitrust Division of the Justice Department has tried to avoid using these remedies. Instead, it has sought compromise. Thus at times it has succeeded in getting the acquiring firm to agree to a divestiture of some subsidiaries of the postmerged firm. At other times it has prevailed on the acquiring firm to agree that the postmerged firm will refrain from some form of business conduct—for example, that it will not compete in certain geographic areas for a period of years.

Individuals and corporations may also bring private civil actions for triple damages against a firm that violates Section 7 of the Clayton Act. These private actions, which far outnumber government antitrust cases, are important for preserving a competitive business environment.

SECTION 8: INTERLOCKING DIRECTORATES

Section 8 prohibits an individual from becoming a director in two or more corporations if any of them has capital, surplus, and individual profits aggregating more than $51 million or is engaged in interstate commerce, or if any of them were or are competitors, or where agreements to eliminate competition between such corporations would be a violation of the antitrust law.

With the growing number of conglomerates and the rise of the "professional" director who sits on many companies' boards for a fee, this long dormant section of the Clayton Act has been the basis of some private civil litigation in recent years. The trend toward diversification by many large firms has resulted in overlapping areas of competition in many corporations, so there are potential violations of Section 8 for outside directors of these firms.

It should be noted that Section 8 excludes from its coverage banks, banking associations, trust companies, and common carriers subject to the Interstate Commerce Act of 1887. Directors of corporations in those industries, therefore, do not have to be concerned about a potential Section 8 violation.

OTHER ANTITRUST STATUTES

FEDERAL TRADE COMMISSION ACT (FTCA) OF 1914

The outburst of reform that produced the Clayton Act also produced the Federal Trade Commission Act (FTCA), which prohibits "unfair methods of competition." This broad, sweeping language, and the courts' interpretation of it, allow the Federal Trade Commission to bring antitrust enforcement actions against business conduct prohibited by the Sherman and Clayton acts. Where prosecution may be difficult because of the level of proof required under those acts, the FTC may bring a civil action under the FTCA. Also, business conduct that may not quite reach the level of prohibition under either the Sherman or the Clayton act may be actionable under the "unfair" competition language of the FTCA. The following case illustrates the reach of this statute.

FEDERAL TRADE COMMISSION V. BROWN SHOE CO.
UNITED STATES SUPREME COURT 384 U.S. 316 (1966)

The Federal Trade Commission brought an action against Brown Shoe Co., charging the defendant with a violation of Section 5 of the Federal Trade Commission Act by virtue of its use of a franchise agreement. The agreement required shoe retailers to purchase only Brown lines; it prohibited the purchase or stocking of competitors' shoes. Retailers who entered into this agreement and became Brown franchisees were given special treatment and valuable benefits that were not given to retailers who did not enter into the agreement. The trial examiner and the full commission ruled that this restrictive agreement was in violation of Section 5. The court of appeals reversed the commission and ruled in favor of Brown. The FTC appealed to the U.S. Supreme Court.

JUSTICE BLACK

The question we have for decision is whether the Federal Trade Commission can declare it to be an unfair practice for Brown, the second largest manufacturer of shoes in the nation, to pay a valuable consideration to hundreds of retail shoe purchasers in order to secure a contractual promise from them that they will deal primarily with Brown and will not purchase conflicting lines of shoes from Brown's competitors. We hold that the Commission has power to find, on the record here, such an anticompetitive practice unfair, subject of course to judicial review.

The Commission has broad powers to declare trade practices unfair. This broad power of the Commission is particularly well established with regard to trade practices which conflict with the basic policies of the Sherman and Clayton Acts even though such practices may not actually violate these laws. The record in this case shows beyond doubt that Brown, the country's second largest manufacturer of shoes, has a program which requires shoe retailers, unless faithless to their contractual obligations with Brown, to substantially limit their trade with Brown's competitors. This program obviously conflicts with the central policy of both Section 1 of the Sherman Act and Section 3 of the Clayton Act against contracts which take away freedom of purchasers to buy in an open market. Brown nevertheless contends that the Commission had no power to declare the franchise program unfair without proof that its effect "may be to substantially lessen competition or tend to create a monopoly" which of course would have to be proved if the government were proceeding against Brown under Section 3 of the Clayton Act rather than Section 5 of the Federal Trade Commission Act. We reject the argument that proof of this Section 3 element must be made, for our cases hold that the Commission has power under Section 5 to arrest trade restraints in their incipiency without proof that they amount to an outright violation of Section 3 of the Clayton Act or other provisions of the antitrust laws.

It is clear that the Federal Trade Commission Act was designed to supplement and bolster the Sherman Act and the Clayton Act . . . to stop in their incipiency acts and procedures which when full blown would violate these Acts as well as to condemn as "unfair" methods of competition existing in violation of them.

We hold that the Commission acted well within its authority in declaring the Brown franchise program unfair whether it was completely full blown or not.

Affirmed in favor of Plaintiff, FTC.

Critical Thinking about the Law

A S WE NOTED IN THE TEXT immediately preceding this case, the Federal Trade Commission Act makes it easier for the government to prosecute companies believed to be in violation of antitrust policies than either the Sherman or the Clayton act does. Although the burden of proof is the same as under the Sherman and Clayton acts, the degree of proof required under the FTCA is less.

This weakening of the standard for prosecuting antitrust violators has implicit ethical norms. The questions that follow will explore these ethical norms and certain facts that are related to this case.

1. What ethical norm is present in the Court's decision?

   Clue You can identify this norm by discovering what the judge thought the Court was protecting with its decision.

2. The Court implicitly held that the FTC's demonstration that the acts and procedures of Brown Shoe Co. would, when full blown, violate antitrust policies was sufficient to make the commission's claim actionable. If the FTC had been forced to prosecute under the Clayton Act, what evidence would it have needed to present in order to secure a favorable judgment?

   Clue Look toward the end of the second paragraph of the decision.

3. This opinion is littered with ambiguities. Find at least two.

   Clue Look for adjectives whose exact meaning is important in determining the outcome of the case.

BANK MERGER ACT OF 1966

The *Bank Merger Act of 1966* requires that all bank mergers be approved in advance by the banking agency having jurisdiction—that is, the Federal Reserve Board, the Federal Deposit Insurance Corporation (FDIC), or the Comptroller of the Currency. The agency with jurisdiction must obtain a report "on the competitive factors involved" from the U.S. attorney general, and from the other two agencies as well, before making a decision.

Even if the agency approves the merger, the Justice Department may bring a suit within 30 days. This action automatically stays the merger, and a federal district court must then review all issues concerning the merger de nova (newly, or from the beginning). If not challenged by the United States Attorney General within 30 days, a bank merger is still subject to liability under Section 2 of the Sherman Act if it is shown to have resulted in a monopoly. Acquisitions by bank holding companies are subject to the same antitrust standards that are applied to other industries.

The Bank Merger Act has become more significant in light of a 1985 decision of the U.S. Supreme Court approving regional banking and acquisitions by banks across state lines, where state legislatures have given prior approval.[16]

EXHIBIT 22-2 *The Biggest U.S. Banks**

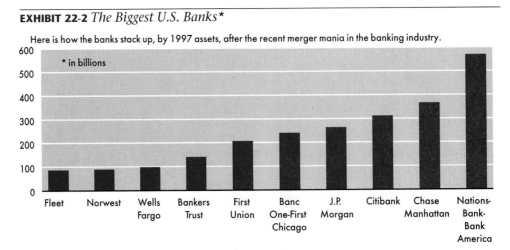

Here is how the banks stack up, by 1997 assets, after the recent merger mania in the banking industry.

Source: Workload Report, Research in Statistics Bureau, Antitrust Division, U.S. Dept. of Justice (1997–1998).

[16]Northeast Bancorp v. Board of Governors of Federal Reserve, 472 U.S. 86 (1985).

Further, major bank, insurance and brokerage companies (e.g. Travelers and Citicorp), and large banks are planning to merge (e.g. Bank One and National Bank of Chicago). See Exhibit 22-2.

INTERNATIONAL DIMENSIONS OF ANTITRUST STATUTES

TRANSNATIONAL REACH OF U.S. ANTITRUST LEGISLATION

Sections 1 and 2 of the Sherman Act explicitly apply to "trade or commerce . . . with *foreign nations*," so they obviously have transnational reach. In contrast, Sections 2 and 3 of the Clayton Act, because they apply to price discrimination, tying arrangements, and exclusive-dealing contracts for commodities sold for "use, consumption, or resale *within the United States*," have no transnational reach. However, Section 5 of the Federal Trade Commission Act is given express transnational reach by Section 4 of the *Export Trading Act (Webb-Pomerence Export Act)*, which extends the meaning of "unfair methods of competition" to practices in export trade against other competitors engaged in such trade even though acts constituting unfair methods of competition "are done without the territorial jurisdiction of the United States." The courts, using a case-by-case approach, have interpreted the language of these statutes so as to establish principles of law that guide companies and their management in determining whether certain activities are illegal because of their transnational impact.

In 1994, Congress passed the *Antitrust Enforcement Assistance Act of 1994* which gave the Department of Justice authority to negotiate "mutual assistance" agreements with foreign antitrust enforcers. Also in 1994, the Justice Department and the FTC issued guidelines, based on current statutory and case law, that tell foreign and U.S. companies when either of the agencies is likely to act against alleged anticompetitive action in international trade. The following kinds of behavior may be investigated under the guidelines:

1. A merger of foreign companies that have significant sales in the United States.
2. Conduct by foreign companies that has a direct, substantial, and reasonably foreseeable effect on commerce within the United States or on U.S. companies' export business.
3. Anticompetitive schemes by importers that have a significant impact on the United States.
4. Anticompetitive actions by foreign firms selling to the U.S. government.

INTERNATIONAL DIMENSIONS OF U.S. ANTITRUST LAWS

The general principle guiding the courts in the application of the Sherman Act (and other U.S. antitrust laws) has been that if U.S. or foreign private companies enter into an *agreement* forbidden by Section 1, and that agreement *affects* the foreign commerce of the United States, then the U.S. courts have jurisdiction. The question arises: *How much* commerce must be affected before U.S. courts will assume jurisdiction? The Department of Justice's guidelines on its foreign antitrust enforcement policy announced a jurisdictional standard that requires business practices to have a "substantial and foreseeable effect on the foreign commerce of the United States." An example would be an agreement by U.S. corporations selling roller bearings to divide up markets in Latin America. The department has stated that this country's antitrust laws will not be applied to certain business practices if they have no "direct or intended effect," and most commentators agree that trivial restraints affecting the foreign commerce of the United States are likely not to be prosecuted.

United States appellate courts have held that U.S. courts do have jurisdiction over business conduct by a foreign corporation that is based on a decision by the corporation's government to replace a competitive economic model with a state-regulated model. State-regulated models encourage price fixing and collaboration among competitors, especially when a government actually prohibits competition between firms. The courts of the United States do not evaluate the lawfulness of acts of foreign sovereigns performed *within their own territories*, even if the foreign commerce of the United States is affected by those acts, because the act-of-state doctrine forbids them to. Under this doctrine (discussed in chapter 3), when the illegal conduct is that of a foreign *government* (as opposed to that of foreign *individuals*), the courts are not permitted to examine and decide the merits of any claim alleged. This approach applies to any case in which a statute, a decree, an order, or a resolution of a foreign government or governments is alleged to be unlawful under U.S. law. For instance, when the International Association of Machinists brought a suit claiming that an agreement by member states of the Organization of Petroleum Exporting Countries (OPEC) to increase the price of crude oil through taxes and price setting was in violation of Sections 1 and 2 of the Sherman Act, the federal district court dismissed the case for lack of jurisdiction based on the act-of-state doctrine.

ENFORCEMENT

A court decision condemning certain business practices prohibited by U.S. antitrust laws—such as price fixing, allocation of markets, or boycotts—may give a plaintiff satisfaction, but no equitable relief. For example, if a U.S. corporation enters into a price-fixing agreement with a foreign corporation to determine the price of uranium worldwide, the foreign corporation may be made a defendant in a U.S. court and the plaintiff may win the case. But can the foreign defendant be forced to pay triple damages? Usually not, unless it has assets in the United States that can be seized, or there is a treaty of friendship and commerce between the United States and the foreign corporation's home country providing for the implementation of judicial decrees of U.S. courts in that country's courts. The second possibility is limited by the fact that there are very few treaties containing those terms. The first possibility is more promising, because many foreign corporations have assets, such as bank accounts, in the United States. The plaintiff can get a decree freezing those assets until the corporation pays the court-ordered damages because Section 6 of the Sherman Act provides *forfeiture of property* to enforce an antitrust decree.

In the OPEC case, referred to earlier, a group of *foreign* governments colluded to fix prices, but the crude oil was extracted, transported, and sold by *U.S.* oil corporations. Would it have been appropriate for the plaintiffs in that case to obtain a court decree ordering the seizure of the assets of the oil companies on the ground that they were co-conspirators in the price fixings? Would OPEC have cared about U.S. oil companies' assets? If it did care, would it have ceased selling oil to the United States? The answer to that question would probably depend on the supply and demand of oil on the world market.

SUMMARY

A history and summary of sections of the Sherman Act, Clayton Act, Federal Trade Commission Act, and Bank Merger Act are included in this chapter. We have sought to examine the policy implications of the acts for business managers and consumers (e.g. the Microsoft case). We have also examined the international dimensions of U.S. antitrust statutes in light of multinationals coming to the United States, as well as the impact of the U.S. antitrust statutes on those doing business in other countries. We have called this the transnational reach of antitrust legislation. The enforcement by the U.S. federal courts in both cases has become more frequent.

REVIEW QUESTIONS

22-1. Who is responsible for the enforcement of the antitrust statutes?

22-2. What industries and activities are exempt from the antitrust law?

22-3. Explain the difference between horizontal and vertical restraints under Section 1 of the Sherman Act.

22-4. List and define three types of mergers.

22-5. Describe the approach the Justice Department takes to horizontal mergers under its current Merger Guidelines.

REVIEW PROBLEMS

22-6. Ronwin was an unsuccessful candidate for admission to the Arizona State Bar. Under Arizona Supreme Court rules, a Committee on Examinations and Admissions appointed by the court was authorized to examine the applicants on specified subjects, to grade the exam on a formula submitted to the court before the exam, and then to submit its recommendation to the court. A rejected applicant could seek review of the state supreme court's decision. After he was rejected by both the committee and the state supreme court, Ronwin appealed to the U.S. Supreme Court, claiming that the committee had violated Section 1 of the Sherman Act by artificially reducing the number of attorneys in the state. He argued that the committee had set the grading scale with reference to the number of new attorneys it thought were desirable in Arizona, as opposed to a "suitable" level of competence. Defendants argued that they were immune from antitrust liability under the act-of-state doctrine. Who won this case, and why?

22-7. Topco is a cooperative association of 25 small and medium-sized regional supermarket chains that operate in 33 states. In order to compete with large supermarket chains, Topco buys and distributes for its members quality merchandise under private labels. Each member of the cooperative has to sign an agreement promising to sell Topco brand products only in a certain designated territory. The government sued Topco, claiming it was horizontally dividing markets in violation of Section 1 of the Sherman Act. The defendant argued that this territorial restriction was necessary to compete with large chains. Who won this case, and why?

22-8. Falstaff Brewing Company was the fourth-largest brewer in the United States, with 5.9 percent of the national market. Falstaff acquired a local New England brewery, Narragansett, in order to penetrate the New England market. Narragansett had 20 percent of that market. The Justice Department filed suit against Falstaff under Section 7 of the Clayton Act. What was the result? Explain.

22-9. Alcoa was the leading producer of aluminum conductors in the United States, with 27.8 I percent of the market. Alcoa acquired Rome Electric, which had 1.3 percent of the market. Rome ranked ninth among all companies in the aluminum conductor market. The Justice Department sued, claiming a violation of Section 7 of the Clayton Act and asking for a divestiture by Alcoa. What was the result? Explain.

22-10. Ford Motor acquired Autolite, an independent manufacturer of spark plugs that accounted for 15 percent of national sales of spark plugs. GM, through its AC brand, accounted for another 30 percent of national sales. After Ford's acquisition of Autolite, Champion was the only independent manufacturer of spark plugs remaining in the market. Its market share declined from 50 percent to 33 percent after the acquisition. The Justice Department sued Ford for being in violation of Section 7, and the federal district court ruled in favor of the United States. The court ordered Ford to do the following: (1) divest itself of Autolite; (2) stop manufacturing spark plugs for ten years; and (3) purchase 50 percent of its requirements from Autolite for five years. Ford appealed. Who won, and why?

CASE PROBLEMS

22-11. A group of lawyers in the District of Columbia regularly acted as court-appointed attorneys for indigent defendants in District of Columbia criminal cases. At a meeting of the Superior Court Trial Lawyers Association (SCTLA), the attorneys agreed to stop providing such representation until the district increased their compensation. Their subsequent boycott had a severe impact in the district's criminal justice system, and the District of Columbia gave in to the lawyers' demands for higher pay. After the lawyers had returned to work, the Federal Trade Commission filed a complaint against the SCTLA and four of its officers and, after an investigation, ruled that the SCTLA's activities constituted an illegal group boycott in violation of antitrust laws. *FTC v. Superior Court Lawyers Association*, 493 U.S. 411 (1990)

22-12. Febco, Inc., manufactured lawn and turf equipment. Colorado Pump and Supply Co. was a wholesale distributor of such equipment in Colorado. An important item that Colorado Pump distributed was a control device for sprinkling systems. Although Febco manufactured one of the better sprinkler controls, a number of other manufacturers in the field offered competitive and satisfactory substitutes for the Febco device. Under an agreement between Febco and Colorado Pump giving Colorado Pump the right to distribute Febco products, Colorado Pump was required to stock an entire line of Febco products. It could also stock other brands. Industry data proved that it was important for distributors to protect the goodwill of manufacturers by carrying a complete line of a manufacturer's goods or none at all. Is the agreement between Febco and Colorado Pump an illegal tying agreement? *Colorado Pump & Supply Co. v. Febco, Inc.*, 472 F.2d 637 (1973)

22-13. Excel Corporation, which is a wholly owned subsidiary of Cargill, Inc., is the second largest beef packer in the country. Excel operated five integrated beef-packing plants, that is, plants for both the slaughtering of cattle and the fabrication of beef. On June 17, 1983, Excel signed an agreement to acquire Spencer Beef, which operated two integrated beef-packing plants and was the third largest beef packer in the country. After the acquisition, Excel would still be the second largest packer but would command a market share almost equal to that of the largest packer, IBP, Inc. The beef-packing industry is highly competitive, and profit margins of the major beef packers are low. The current markets are a product of two decades of intense competition, during which time packers with integrated plants have gradually replaced packers with less modern plants. Monfort of Colorado, Inc., which operates three integrated plants and is the country's fifth largest beef packer, brought this action under Section 16 of the Clayton Act seeking to enjoin the merger between Excel and Spencer. The trial court held in favor of Monfort. The court of appeals affirmed. Cargill appealed. Was there an "injury" as required by Section 16 or Section 4 of the Clayton Act? Explain. *Cargill, Inc. v. Monfort of Colorado*, 479 U.S. 104 (1986)

22-14. The Lipton Tea Company was the second largest U.S. producer of herbal teas, controlling 32% of the national market. Lipton announced that it would acquire Celestial Seasonings, the largest U.S. producer of herbal teas, controlling 52% of the national market. R.C. Bigelow, Inc., the third largest producer of herbal teas, with 13% of the national market, brought suit, alleging that the merger would violate Section 7 of the Clayton Act and sought an injunction against the merger. What was the relevant market? *R.C. Bigelow, Inc. v. Unilever, N.V.*, 867 F.2d 102 (1989)

22-15. The G.R. Kinney Company, Inc., was the largest independent chain of family-owned shoe stores in the nation. Kinney announced that it would merge with the Brown Shoe Company, Inc., which was the fourth largest manufacturer of shoes in the country with assets of over $72 million and which sold over 25 million pairs of shoes annually. The United States brought this action, alleging a violation of Clayton Act Section 7 and seeking a preliminary injunction against the merger. Did the merger violate Section 7? *Brown Shoe Company, Inc. v. United States*, 370 U.S. 294 (1962)

On the Internet

http:www.vanderbilt.edu/Owen/froeb/antitrust/antitrust.htm. This site provides information about mergers, price fixing, and vertical restraints.

http://www.findlaw.com/01topics/01antitrust/mail_usenet.html This is a site where you can go to begin your search for legal resources related to antitrust law and policy.

http://www.stolaf.edu/people/becker/antitrust/antitrust.html The Antitrust Case Browser, located at this address, provides a collection of U.S. Supreme Court case summaries dealing with violations of antitrust statutes.

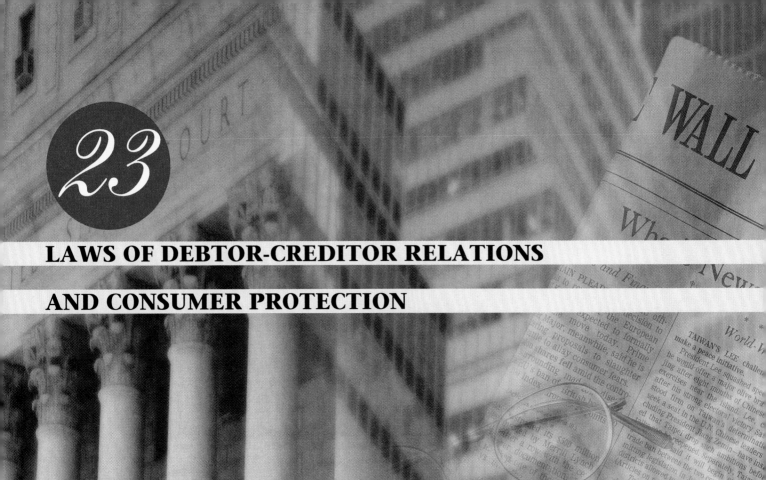

23

LAWS OF DEBTOR-CREDITOR RELATIONS

AND CONSUMER PROTECTION

- **DEBTOR-CREDITOR RELATIONS**

- **THE EVOLUTION OF CONSUMER LAW**

- **FEDERAL REGULATION OF BUSINESS TRADE PRACTICES**

  AND CONSUMER-BUSINESS RELATIONSHIPS

- **FEDERAL LAWS REGULATING CONSUMER CREDIT**

  AND BUSINESS DEBT-COLLECTION PRACTICES

- **STATE CONSUMER LEGISLATION**

- **INTERNATIONAL DIMENSIONS OF CONSUMER PROTECTION LAW**

In chapters 9 and 10 on contract law, we offered you a view of private law and how it governs the relationship between two individuals or corporations that buy and sell things. When you went to the bookstore to buy this textbook, you entered into a legally binding contract. The bookstore made an *offer*, and you, as buyer, accepted that offer. Your *acceptance* was signified by your picking out the book and paying for it at the cash register. Assuming there was consideration, mutual assent, competent parties, and a legal object (and we are convinced that this text is a legal object), you entered into an enforceable contract. Before taking this course, you probably never thought of the act of buying a textbook as a legally binding transaction. Most consumers do not. They generally see it as an exchange of money for something that they want or are required to buy.

Because consumers do not think of buying a product as a formal legal transaction, they are usually unaware of the legal implications of an exchange of money for a product or service until they have problems. The posttransaction business-consumer relationship then becomes the basis for angry exchanges, hurt feelings—and sometimes litigation. If both business managers and consumers had some knowledge of the requirements of contract law, as well as federal, state, and local statutes governing consumer transactions, there would be less friction between these two important parties in our economy (and fewer disputes over the types of product and service liabilities we discussed in chapter 12).

In this chapter, we describe debtor-creditor relationships and the evolution of consumer law through legislation and case law. Then we examine the major federal legislation governing such trade practices as advertising, labeling, and the issuance of warranties on products. Federal laws pertaining to the credit arrangements entered into by consumers and the debt-collection practices of businesses are explained. We also touch on state laws governing consumer transactions. The chapter ends with an examination of the international dimensions of consumer protection laws.

Critical Thinking about the Law

YOU HAVE ALREADY THOUGHT ABOUT THE law and contracts. But you probably never realized that you enter into a legally enforceable contract when you buy a product. If the principles of a contract apply to consumer behavior, why is it necessary to have federal and state agencies that regulate business and trade practices? In other words, why can't we rely on contract law to deal with consumer problems? Why create additional agencies to protect consumers?

These agencies often serve as watchdogs for consumers. Some agencies prevent unfair advertising, others monitor credit arrangements. You can use the following critical thinking questions to improve your thinking about consumer protection law.

1. You are the CEO of one of the largest corporations in the United States. You discover that one of your competitors is falsely representing the quality of one of your products. You decide to sue that competitor for deceptive advertising. You are thankful that you have a course of action through the legal system. What ethical norm seems to influence your thinking?

    CLUE While looking at the list of ethical norms, think about which norm promotes protection.

2. Your competitor receives the notification that her corporation is being sued for deceptive advertising. Your competitor is outraged, primarily because she believes that the government should not regulate advertising behavior. What ethical norm seems to dominate her thinking?

    CLUE Again, examine the list of ethical norms.

3. Advertisers typically have 30 seconds to convey a convincing message to consumers. Therefore, they must use quite persuasive language in a brief amount of time. Think about cases in which companies are sued for deceptive advertising. Why might ambiguity be a particularly important aspect of a case involving deceptive advertising?

   CLUE How might the ambiguity of a word serve as a defense for a business accused of deceptive advertising?

DEBTOR-CREDITOR RELATIONS

In this section we will briefly describe the rights and remedies for creditors and debtors. Both the case law of federal and state courts and federal and state statutory law play a significant role. The U.S. economy has more and more become a credit-based economy. One can use a Visa or MasterCard to purchase everything from a home and automobile to clothes and a computer. When these transactions take place a *creditor* and a *debtor* are created. We will define the **creditor** as the lender in the transaction (e.g., the bank that issues the credit card) and the **debtor** as the borrower (e.g., the business or individual who uses the credit card).

RIGHTS AND REMEDIES FOR CREDITORS

The following rights and remedies are most commonly used by creditors to enforce their rights. They include liens, garnishments, creditors composition agreements, mortgage foreclosures, and debtor's assignment of assets for the credits.

LIENS   A **lien** is a claim on debtor's property that must be satisfied before any creditor can make a claim. We have both statutory liens—mechanics's liens—and common law liens, which include an artisan and innkeepers lien.

A **mechanics lien** is placed on the real property of a debtor when the latter does not pay for the work done by the creditor. In effect a debtor-creditor relationship is created in which the real property becomes the security interest for the debt owed. For example when a contractor adds a room onto the house of the debtor, and payment is not paid, the contractor becomes a lienholder for the property after a period of time (usually 60–120 days), foreclosure may take place. Notice of foreclosure must be given to the debtor in advance.

An **artisan lien** is created by common law that enables a creditor to recover payment from a debtor on labor and services provided on the latter's personal property. For example, Andrew leaves a lawnmower at Jake's repair shop. Jake repairs the lawnmower, but Andrew never picks up his personal property. After a period of time, Jake can attach the lawnmower.

Once a debt is due and the creditor brings legal action, the debtor's property may be seized by virtue of a judicial lien. Types of judicial liens include attachment, writ of execution, and garnishment.

Attachment involves a court-ordered judgment allowing a local officer of the court (e.g., sheriff) to seize property of a debtor. On the motion of the creditor this order of seizure may take place after all procedures have been followed according to state law. This is usually a prejudgment remedy, but not always. If at trial, the creditor prevails, the court will order the seized property to be sold in order to satisfy the judgment rendered.

If the debtor refuses to pay the creditor or cannot pay, usually a clerk of the court will direct the sheriff, in a **writ of execution**, to seize any of the debtor's real or personal property (nonexempt) within the court's jurisdiction. An excess after the sale will be returned to the debtor.

A creditor may ask for a **garnishment** order of the court, usually directed at wages owed by an employer or a bank where the debtor has an account. This can be either a post- or a prejudgment remedy. The latter requires a hearing.

---

creditor The lender in the transaction.

debtor The borrower in the transaction.

lien A claim on a debtor's property that must be satisfied before any creditor can make a claim.

mechanics lien A lien placed on the real property of a debtor when the latter does not pay for the work done by the creditor.

artisan's lien A lien that enables a creditor to recover payment from a debtor on labor and services provided on the debtor's personal property; for example, fixing a lawnmower.

attachment A court-ordered judgment allowing a local officer of the court to seize property of a debtor.

writ of execution An order by a clerk of the court directing the sheriff to seize any of the nonexempt real or personal property of a debtor who refuses to or cannot pay a creditor.

garnishment An order of the court granted to a creditor to seize wages or bank accounts of a debtor.

Both the federal and state laws limit the amount of money that a debtor's take-home pay may be garnished for. Recently, the courts have been faced with the question of whether a debtor's pension can be attached by a creditor after it has been received by the debtor.

UNITED STATES V. SMITH

UNITED STATES COURT OF APPEALS 47 F.3D 681 (4TH CIR. 1995)

Smith (defendant-appellant) was indicted for criminal fraud. For nine years he promised to invest his friend's money in several businesses. Most of the money (some $350,000) was used by Smith for his personal expenses. Smith pleaded guilty to the crime. He was ordered by the federal district judge to turn over his entire pension to repay his former friends and acquaintances. Smith claimed that the court's order violated a provision of the Employee Retirement Income Security Act (ERISA), which prevented his pension fund from being transferred ("alienated") in any manner. The Department of Justice denied the applicability of ERISA to this case. Smith appealed.

JUDGE ERVIN

This court has long recognized a strong public policy against the alienability of ERISA [pension] benefits. The Supreme Court, as well, has found that it is not "appropriate to approve any exception." The government cannot require Smith to turn over his pension benefits. Understandably, there may be a natural distaste for the result we reach here. The statute, however, is clear. Congress has made a policy decision to protect the ERISA income of retirees, even if that decision prevents others from securing relief for the wrongs done them.

The Court of Appeals ruled in favor of Smith and ordered the lower court to determine the amount Smith had to pay on the basis of his other financial resources.

MORTGAGE FORECLOSURE Creditors called mortgage holders (mortgagees) have a right to foreclose on real property when a debtor (mortgagor) defaults. There are statutes in each of the 50 states calling for process of foreclosure. In general, a court-ordered sale of the property takes place when the debtor receives notice and cannot pay. After the cost of foreclosure and the mortgage debt has been satisfied, the mortgagor (debtor) may receive the surplus.

SURETYSHIP AND GUARANTY CONTRACTS A contract of **suretyship** allows a third person to pay the debt of another (debtor) which is owed to a creditor in the event the debtor does not pay. The suretyship creates an express contract with the creditor, and the surety is *primarily liable*. In chapter 9 on the law of contracts we discussed this matter under third-party beneficiary contracts.

A **guaranty** contract is similar to a suretyship arrangement except the third person is *secondarily liable* to the creditor. The guarantor is required to pay the debtor's obligation only after the debtor has defaulted and usually only after the creditor has made an attempt to collect. In chapter 9, we discussed primary and secondary liability under the Statute of Frauds, which requires that a guaranty contract to be in writing. The case of primary liability is the main exception to that requirement.

suretyship A contract between a third party and a creditor that allows the third party to pay the debt of the debtor; the surety is primarily liable.

guaranty Similar to a suretyship except that the third person is secondarily liable: i.e., is required to pay only after the debtor has defaulted.

RIGHTS AND REMEDIES FOR DEBTORS

Debtors are protected by the law as well creditors. For example, property is exempt from creditor's actions. Federal and state consumer protection statutes will be discussed at length in this chapter. Third, we will discuss bankruptcy laws as they apply to debtors and creditors.

freedom-to-contract doctrine Parties that are legally competent are allowed to enter into whatever contracts they wish.

EXEMPTIONS TO ATTACHMENTS   We have indicated that creditors can attach, or levy, real and personal property. In order to protect debtors, certain exemptions are made. The best-known exemption for debtors is the *homestead exemption*. Historically, people have been allowed to retain their home up to a specified dollar amount, or in the entirety. The purpose is to prevent a person from losing his home if forced into bankruptcy or faced with an unsecured creditor. For example, Texas and California offer by far the most generous homestead exemption in bankruptcy proceedings. Many people move to one of these states when faced with bankruptcy.

Some personal property is exempt depending on state statutory law. Some examples include household furniture, a vehicle to get to work with, equipment used in a trade, or animals used on a farm.

THE EVOLUTION OF CONSUMER LAW

As Adam Smith's *laissez-faire* philosophy with its revolt against government intervention in the economy gained popularity in the eighteenth and nineteenth centuries, the **freedom-to-contract doctrine** evolved through case law out of our state court systems. The courts said that, assuming parties were legally competent, they should be allowed to enter into whatever contracts they wished. Neither the courts nor any other public authority should intervene except in cases of fraud, undue influence, duress, or some other illegality. Governed by this doctrine, the U.S. courts throughout the nineteenth century generally refused to interfere in contractual relations merely because one party was more economically powerful or better able to drive a hard bargain. In effect, they upheld the principle of *caveat emptor* (let the buyer beware).

Since the 1930s, state courts (and some federal courts) have curtailed the traditional freedom to contract by establishing rules of public policy and doctrines of *unconscionability* and *fundamental breach* that allow the courts to interfere in contractual relationships, especially when the seller is in the stronger economic position and a consumer has no other source to buy from. The doctrine of freedom to contract has also been limited by the *implied warranty doctrine*, as well as by the courts' relaxation of strict *privity* relationships between manufacturers and consumers. (These aspects of contract and product and service liability law were discussed in chapters 9 and 12).

Then the consumer rights revolution that started in the 1960s inspired major pieces of consumer legislation at the local, state, and federal levels. Although this chapter deals largely with federal consumer legislation, you should keep three matters in mind as you read it:

1. Consumer law includes both statutory and case law. Case law at the state level began the consumer revolution by curtailing the freedom-to-contract doctrine.

2. Statutory law passed by Congress has served as a model for state and local consumer legislation. State and local enforcers of consumer legislation are very important, however, because they are closer geographically to the questionable transaction.

3. Privately funded foundations and legal aid societies do research and play a major role in enforcing consumer legislation at all levels of government.

FEDERAL REGULATION OF BUSINESS TRADE PRACTICES AND CONSUMER-BUSINESS RELATIONSHIPS

THE FEDERAL TRADE COMMISSION: FUNCTIONS, STRUCTURE, AND ENFORCEMENT POWERS

FUNCTIONS   The Federal Trade Commission (FTC) has been discussed throughout this book. It was created by the Federal Trade Commission Act (FTCA) expressly to enforce Section 5 of the act, which forbids "unfair methods of competition." Section 5 was originally intended to be used to regulate anticompetitive business practices not reached by the Sherman Act. In 1938, it was amended by the *Wheeler-Lea Act* to prohibit "unfair or deceptive acts or practices." From then on, even if a business practice did not violate the Sherman or Clayton antitrust statutes, the FTC could use the broad "unfair or deceptive" language of Section 5 to protect consumers against misleading advertising and labeling of goods as well as against other anticompetitive conduct by business. Thus the FTC became the leading federal consumer-protection agency.

Since 1938, Congress has passed several statutes delegating further administrative and enforcement authority to the FTC. Among them are the *Fair Packaging and Labeling Act,* the Lanham Act, the *Magnuson-Moss Warranty–Federal Trade Improvement Act*, the *Telemarketing and Consumer Fraud and Abuse Prevention Act*, important sections of the *Consumer Credit Protection Act*, the *Bankruptcy Reform Act*, Hobby Protection Act, the Wool Products Labeling Act, the Hart-Scott-Rodino Antitrust Improvement Act; and the Food, Drugs and Cosmetics Act. Those that are italicized are described in this chapter.

STRUCTURE AND ENFORCEMENT POWERS In chapter 16, we used the Federal Trade Commission in our example of the adjudicative process for federal administrative agencies, and we presented a diagram of the agency's structure in Exhibit 16-4. Before you read any further here, you may want to turn back to that exhibit to get a quick picture of how the agency is organized.

The Commission is composed of a chairman and four commissioners, who are nominated by the president and confirmed by the Senate. No more than three commissioners may come from the same political party.

The FTC's Bureau of Competition is responsible for the investigation of complaints of "unfair or deceptive practices" under Section 5 of the FTCA. If the bureau finds merit in the complaint and cannot get the offending party either to voluntarily stop the deceptive or unfair practice or to enter into a consent order, it issues a formal complaint, which leads to a hearing before an administrative law judge.

The FTC has other enforcement weapons at its disposal. It may assess fines, obtain injunctive orders, order corrective advertising (as it did in the *Warner Lambert* case excerpted in chapter 16), order rescissions of contracts and refunds to consumers, and obtain court orders forcing sellers to pay damages to consumers.

DECEPTIVE AND UNFAIR ADVERTISING

DECEPTIVE ADVERTISING In passing the 1938 Wheeler-Lea Act amending Section 5 of the FTCA, Congress made it clear that it wished to give the Commission the power "to cover every form of advertising deception over which it would be humanly practicable to exercise government control." Through their interpretation of the "unfair or deceptive" language of Section 5 over the years, the commission and the courts have evolved a three-part standard whereby the FTC staff must show:

1. There is a misrepresentation or omission in the advertising likely to mislead consumers.
2. Consumers are acting reasonably under the circumstances.
3. The misrepresentation or omission is material. Neither intent to deceive nor reliance on the advertising need be shown.

We look at three types of deceptive advertising in this section: (1) that involving prices, (2) that involving product quality and quantity, and (3) testimonials by well-known sports, entertainment, and business figures.

False price comparisons are one form of *deceptive price advertising*. Another is offers of a "free" item to a customer who buys one at a "regular" price, when, in fact, the "regular" price covers the cost of the "free" good. The classic deceptive price advertising, though, is the famous "bait and switch" tactic, or advertising one product at a low price to entice customers into the store, and then switching their attention to a higher-priced product. The *Tashoff* case that follows illustrates how this deceptive tactic works.

TASHOFF V. FTC
UNITED STATES CIRCUIT COURT OF APPEALS 437 F.2D 707 (D.C. CIR. 1980)

The FTC charged Leon Tashoff (defendant-appellant) with falsely advertising its discount eyeglasses and with several other unfair and deceptive practices. Tashoff owned the New York Jewelry Company (NYJC), which was located in a low-income neighborhood. The administrative law judge (formerly called a hearing examiner) dismissed the charges against Tashoff. The full commission disagreed with the administrative law judge, found the defendant guilty of unfair and deceptive practices under Section 5 of the Federal Trade Commission Act, and issued a cease-and-desist order. Tashoff appealed to the District of Columbia Circuit Court of Appeals.

JUDGE BAZELON

The Commission first found that NYJC employed a "bait and switch" maneuver with respect to sales of eyeglasses. The evidence showed that NYJC advertised eyeglasses "from $7.50 complete," including "lenses, frames and case." The newspaper advertisements, but not the radio advertisements, mentioned a "moderate examining fee." During this period NYJC offered free eye examinations by a sign posted in its store, and through cards it mailed out and distributed on the street. NYJC claimed that if offered $7.50 eyeglasses only to persons with their own prescriptions. But we have no doubt that the record amply supports the Commissions' finding that the advertising campaign taken as a whole offered complete eyeglass service for $7.50.

That much shows "bait." There was no direct evidence of "switch"—no direct evidence, that is, that NYJC dispar-

aged or discouraged the purchase of the $7.50 eyeglasses, or that the glasses were unavailable on demand, or unsuited for their purpose. The evidence on which the Commission rested its finding was a stipulation that out of 1,400 pairs of eyeglasses sold each year by NYJC, less than 10 were sold for $7.50 with or without a prescription. NYJC claims that this evidence does not support the finding. We disagree.

It seems plain to us that the Commission drew a permissible inference of "switch" from the evidence of bait advertising and minimal sales of the advertised product. At best only nine sales—64/100 of one percent of NYJC's eyeglass sales—were made at $7.50. The record leaves unexplained why NYJC's customers, presumably anxious to purchase eyeglasses at $7.50 found them unavailable. Further, NYJC continued to advertise the $7.50 glasses for a year and a half despite the scarcity of sales, a fact which tends to support a finding of a purpose to bring customers into the store for other reasons. This evidence, we think, was sufficient to shift the burden of coming forward to the respondent. NYJC offered no evidence to negate the inference of "switch." The relevant facts are in NYJC's possession and it was in the best position to show, if it could be shown at all, that $7.50 glasses were actually available in the store. Yet the most NYJC could produce was its sales manager's denial that the $7.50 glasses were disparaged.

Affirmed in favor of Plaintiff, FTC.

Critical Thinking about the Law

T HE FACTS OF A CASE ARE an essential ingredient in the court's reasoning. They are the building blocks of the story the court constructs to persuade us of its decision's appropriateness.

Facts are closely related to, but do not by themselves constitute, reasons. They become reasons only when the court interprets them as having meaning significant to the case. You want to recognize that different interpretations can have different consequences for the court's decision. For example, that a toothpaste company advertised that two out of three dentists prefer its brand will have different implications as a "fact" in a false advertising case, depending on the court's acceptance of this statistic's truthfulness.

In this case, the court finds that NYJC's practices were a "bait and switch" maneuver. The evidence for the "switch" is indirect and depends to a great extent on an interpretation of certain facts' meaning. Consequently, the questions that follow will focus on this part of the court's reasoning.

1. What key fact does the court cite in stating that the Commission "drew a permissible inference of 'switch' "?

   CLUE This fact is the same evidence on which the Commission based its ruling.

2. What missing information would be useful in evaluating the court's interpretation of this fact?

   CLUE Think of information that would help you to decide what kind of *impact* NYJC's advertising claim had on its sales. A low impact might suggest that NYJC was not using the "bait and switch" tactic.

Advertising about product quality and quantity is often found to be deceptive under Section 5 of the Federal Trade Commission Act. For example, when a car sales representative tells a customer, "This car is the best-running car that has ever been sold," is this mere puffery, or is it deception? This kind of hype is usually considered an acceptable form of **puffery**. However, had the sales representative said, "This car will run at least 50,000 miles without a change of oil," the claim would cross the line into the territory of deception.

The FTC staff does not have to show that a claim is expressly deceptive; it is sufficient to show that deception is implicit. Also, the FTC must present evidence that there is no basis for the claim made by the advertiser. When an advertiser claims a certain quality in a product on the basis of what "studies show," it must possess reasonable substantiation of its claim. The commission will consider the cost of substantiation, the consequences of a false claim, the nature of the product, and what experts believe constitutes reasonable substantiation before deciding whether the advertising was deceptive.

Years ago, American Home Products, manufacturers of Anacin, advertised that its drug had a unique pain-killing formula that was superior to the formulas of all other drugs containing analgesics. In 1982, the FTC staff charged that this claim was deceptive because there was insufficient substantiation to show that Anacin was either unique or superior to other nonprescription drugs containing the same ingredients (aspirin and caffeine).[1] The full Commission and the court of appeals agreed after examining the evidence presented by American Home Products. In a similar case in 1984, the FTC filed a complaint against General Nutrition (GN), charging it with deceptive advertising for claiming, purportedly on the basis of a National Academy of Science report, that consumption of its dietary supplement Healthy Greens was related to reduced rates of cancer in humans. General Nutrition entered into a consent order in which it agreed to cease such advertisng.[2] The case that follows turned on whether an implied claim in advertising was so subjective that it could not be considered consumer deception.

puffery An exaggerated recommendation made in a sales talk to promote the product.

KRAFT, INC. V. FTC
UNITED STATES COURT OF APPEALS 970 F.2D 311 (7TH CIR. 1992)

The FTC filed a complaint against Kraft, Inc., charging a material misrepresentation of the calcium content of its single-slice cheese and the benefits of this product relative to competitors' products. This complaint came after an investigation of Kraft's wrapped, or "single-slice," cheese, which Kraft claimed in advertisements was more expensive because it was made with 5 ounces of milk, and thus had more calcium than competitors' "imitation cheese." The administrative law judge ruled in favor of the FTC staff after finding that Kraft had failed to state that approximately 30 percent of that extra 5 ounces of milk was lost in processing. The ALJ also found that a majority of the "imitation cheese" sold contained about the same amount of calcium as Kraft's single-slice cheese. The commission affirmed the ALJ's recommended decision with modifications. Kraft appealed.

JUDGE FLAUM

Kraft makes numerous arguments on appeal, but its principal claim is that the FTC erred as a matter of law in not requiring extrinsic evidence of consumer deception. Courts,

[1]American Home Products v FTC, 695 Fed. 2nd 681 (3rd cir. 1982).
[2]General Nutrition Inc. Prohibited Trade Practices, 54 Fed. Reg. 9198, March 6, 1989.

including the Supreme Court, have uniformly rejected imposing such a requirement on the FTC, and we decline to do so as well. We hold that the Commission may rely on its own reasoned analysis to determine what claims, including implied ones, are conveyed in a challenged advertisement, so long as those claims are reasonably clear from the fact of the advertisement.

Kraft's [claim] has two flaws. First, it rests on the faulty premise that implied claims are inescapably subjective and unpredictable. The implied claims Kraft made are reasonably clear from the fact of the advertisements, and hence the Commission was not required to utilize consumer surveys in reaching its decision.

The Commissioners' personal experiences quite obviously affect their perceptions, but it does not follow that they are incapable of predicting [how] a particular claim is likely to be perceived by a reasonable number of consumers.

Affirmed in favor of Plaintiff, FTC.

---

testimonial A statement by a public figure professing the merits of some product or service.

The third form of deceptive advertising discussed here is **testimonials** by public figures (e.g., athletes and entertainers) endorsing a product. The FTC guidelines require that such figures actually use the product they are touting and prefer it to competitive products. The FTC's Bureau of Consumer Protection also monitors claims by public figures that they have superior knowledge of a product. For example, singer Pat Boone represented Acne Stain as a cure for acne when there was no scientific basis for the claim; he also failed to disclose a financial interest he had in Acne Stain. After the FTC filed a complaint against him, Boone agreed to enter into a consent order.[3]

UNFAIR ADVERTISING   Section 5 of the Federal Trade Commission Act also forbids "unfair" advertising. The FTC guidelines consider advertising to be unfair if consumers cannot reasonably avoid injury, the injury is harmful in its net effect, or it causes substantiated harm to a consumer. In 1975, the commission promulgated a rule for public comment that forbade all children's television advertising. This action came about after complaints by groups that advertising by cereal and toy companies on Saturday morning television programs was addressed to a select age group that could not weigh the advertising rationally; thus, the advertising was "unfair." In 1980, Congress terminated the FTC rule-making proceedings dealing with children's advertising for political reasons and, for good measure, forbade the FTC to initiate rule-making proceedings of any type based on the concept of "unfairness." The Commission may still challenge individual acts or practices as unfair under Section 5 of the FTCA in an adjudicatory context.

PRIVATE PARTY SUITS AND DECEPTIVE ADVERTISING   A company may sue a competitor under the *Lanham Act of 1947* (see the discussion in chapter 13 about trademarks), which forbids "false description or representation." Parties bringing actions based on violations of this act may request an injunction or corrective advertising. For example, McDonald's and Wendy's, in separate cases, accused Burger King of falsely portraying its hamburgers as superior to rivals' burgers on the basis of an alleged taste test. In their suits, McDonald's and Wendy's questioned the scientific basis of Burger King's survey and its analysis of the results. Both cases were settled out of court.[4]

THE FTC AND DECEPTIVE LABELING AND PACKAGING   Under the *Fair Packaging and Labeling Act (FPLA)*, the Department of Health and Human Services (DHHS) promulgates rules governing the labeling and packaging of products. The department has issued rules governing the packaging of foods, drugs, and cosmetics—all of which the FTC has enforcement jurisdiction over.

The FPLA and the enacted rules require that such product packaging contain the name and address of the manufacturer or distributor; the net quantity, which must be placed in a conspicuous location on the package front; and an

---

[3]In re Cooga Mooga, Inc. and Charles E. Boorea, 92 F.T.C. 310 (1978).
[4]McDonald's v Burger King, 82/2005 (S.D. Fla., 1982); Wendy's International Inc. v Burger King, C-2-82-1179 (S.D., Ohio, 1982).

accurate description of all contents. The purpose of the FPLA is to allow consumers to compare prices on the basis of some uniform measure of content.

CONSUMER LEGISLATION

FRANCHISING RELATIONSHIPS   Misrepresentation by franchisors of the potential profits to be made by franchisees is a violation of Section 5 of the Federal Trade Commission Act, which prohibits "unfair" methods of competition as well as "unfair and deceptive trade practices." To combat the blatant fraud taking place in the form of business associations (discussed in chapter 15), the FTC in 1979 promulgated rules governing franchise systems.

In its 1979 *Franchising Rule*, the commission defines a franchise as a commercial operation in which the franchisee pays a minimum fee of $500 to use the trademark of or to sell goods and services supplied by, a franchisor that exercises significant control over, or promises significant aid to, the franchisee's business operation. The fee must be paid within six months after the business is begun. For example, McDonald's franchisees receive the trademark (the "golden arches") in return for an initial fee and a percentage of revenues that go to the McDonald's Corporation (the franchisor). McDonald's, in its franchising agreement, specifies the products that must be bought from McDonald's, the quality of food to be served, the store hours, cleanliness standards, and grounds for termination of the franchising agreement.

The FTC rule governing franchising requires each franchisor meeting the definition to provide a disclosure document to prospective franchisees that tells such pertinent information as the names and addresses of the officers of the franchisor; any felony convictions; involvement in any bankruptcy proceedings; all restrictions on a franchisee's territories or the customers it may sell to; and any training or financing the franchisor makes available to franchisees. If a franchisor suggests a potential level of sales, income, or profits, all materials that form the basis of those predictions must be made available to prospective franchisees and the FTC.

Violations of the FTC Franchising Rule may lead to a fine of up to $10,000. The FTC can bring a civil action for damages on behalf of franchisees in federal district court as well as administrative enforcement actions before an administrative law judge.

CONSUMER WARRANTIES   The FTC is also in charge of enforcing the *Magnuson-Moss Warranty Act–Federal Trade Improvement Act of 1975*, which applies to manufacturers and sellers of consumer products that make an *express written* warranty. You recall from our discussion of product and service liability law in chapter 12 that an *express warranty* is a guarantee or promise by the seller or manufacturer that goods (products) meet certain standards of performance. Note that the act does not cover oral warranties, whether express or implied. "Consumer products," as defined by the act, are goods that are normally purchased for personal, family, or household use. The courts have interpreted this definition liberally.

The purpose of the Magnuson-Moss Warranty Act (its brief name) is to prevent sellers and manufacturers from passing on confusing and misleading information to consumers. To that end, the act requires that all conditions of a warranty be clearly and conspicuously disclosed for any product sold in interstate commerce that costs more than $5.00. Further, consumers must be told what to do if a product is defective.

Before this act was passed, a consumer purchasing a video recorder, for instance, could not be sure whether the "limited warranty" covered all labor and parts or only some labor and parts. Thus, after sending the video recorder back to the manufacturer or authorized dealer for repairs, the consumer might discover that the warranty covered a $50 part, but not $150 in labor costs—a rather nasty surprise.

Full or Limited Warranties   All written warranties of consumer products that cost more than $10.00 must be designated as "full" or "limited." A

full warranty Under the Magnuson-Moss Warranty Act, a written protection for buyers that guarantees free repair of a defective product. If the product can't be fixed, the consumer must be given a choice of a refund or a replacement free of charge.

limited warranty Under the Magnuson-Moss Warranty Act, any written warranty that does not meet the conditions of a full warranty.

full warranty means the manufacturer or dealer must fix the product or the warranty is breached and there are grounds for a breach-of-warranty suit. If efforts to fix the product fail, the consumer must be given a choice of refund or replacement free of charge. A manufacturer or supplier that gives only a **limited warranty** on its product can restrict the duration of implied warranties if the limit is designated conspicuously on the product. In effect, a limited warranty is any warranty that does not meet the conditions of a full warranty.

Second buyers and bailees as well as bystanders are covered by the act and pertinent FTC regulations. Also, manufacturers or sellers cannot limit the time period within which implied warranties of the product are effective. Finally, damages to the consumer cannot be limited unless the limits are expressly stated on the face of the product.

Remedies The Magnuson-Moss Warranty Act gives an individual consumer, or a class of consumers, the right to bring a private action for a breach of a written (remember, not an oral) warranty. Consumers who bring such actions can recover the costs of the suit, including attorneys' fees, if they win. However, before they file suit, they must give the manufacturer or seller a reasonable opportunity to "cure" the breach of warranty by replacing or fixing the product.

EXHIBIT 23-1 *Telemarketing Fraud*

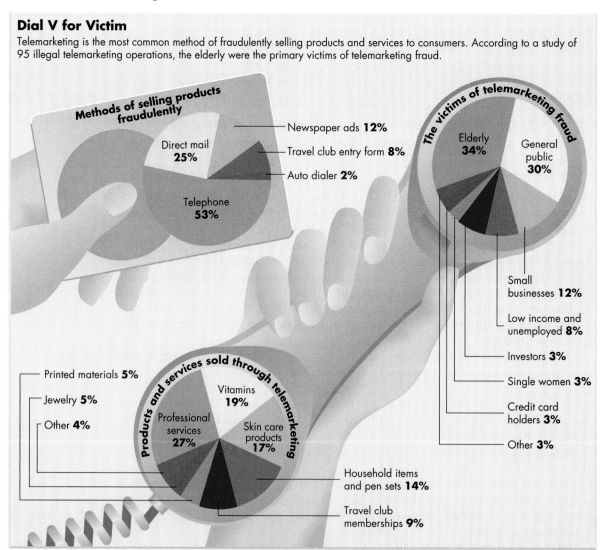

Dial V for Victim

Telemarketing is the most common method of fraudulently selling products and services to consumers. According to a study of 95 illegal telemarketing operations, the elderly were the primary victims of telemarketing fraud.

Methods of selling products fraudulently
- Direct mail **25%**
- Newspaper ads **12%**
- Travel club entry form **8%**
- Auto dialer **2%**
- Telephone **53%**

The victims of telemarketing fraud
- Elderly **34%**
- General public **30%**
- Small businesses **12%**
- Low income and unemployed **8%**
- Investors **3%**
- Single women **3%**
- Credit card holders **3%**
- Other **3%**

Products and services sold through telemarketing
- Printed materials **5%**
- Jewelry **5%**
- Other **4%**
- Professional services **27%**
- Vitamins **19%**
- Skin care products **17%**
- Household items and pen sets **14%**
- Travel club memberships **9%**

Source: New York Times, February 10, 1995, p. C10. Copyright 1995 by The New York Times Company. Reprinted by permission.

TELEMARKETING LEGISLATION FTC regulations that took effect on August 1, 1995, restrict the activities of telemarketers and ban certain interstate telephone sales practices altogether. Here are some of the prohibited practices:

- Calling a person's residence at any time other than between 8 A.M. and 8 P.M.
- Claiming an affiliation with a governmental agency at any level when such an affiliation does not exist.
- Claiming an ability to improve a consumer's credit records or to obtain loans for a person regardless of that person's credit history.
- Not telling the receiver of the calls that it is a sales call.
- Claiming an ability to recover goods or money lost by a consumer.

Each violation of these regulations is punishable by a fine of up to $10,000. Exempted are insurers, franchisers, on-line services, stocks and bonds salespeople regulated by the SEC, and not-for-profit organizations.

The FTC's regulations are an outgrowth of a federal statute, the *Telemarketing and Consumer Fraud and Abuse Prevention Act of 1994*. Congress passed this statute after holding hearings that revealed that some telemarketing firms ("budget shops") used imaginary sweepstakes and other schemes to bilk $40 billion a year from consumers (particularly the elderly) and small businesses (Exhibit 23-1).

The statute and the FTC regulations were made enforceable in the federal courts by the 50 state attorneys general as well as by the FTC. This broad scope was intended to put an end to the situation in which telemarketers who engaged in fraud moved quickly from one state to another without being caught because state attorneys general did not have the authority to pursue them under federal law. Moreover, state law often did not provide for suitable punishment when such telemarketers were caught.

FEDERAL LAWS REGULATING CONSUMER CREDIT AND BUSINESS DEBT–COLLECTION PRACTICES

Consumer credit means *buyer power*, which translates into *demand for products*, which, in turn, increases the *supply of products* produced by manufacturers. In short, this nation's economy runs on credit. With Americans owing over $1.5 trillion and businesses and banks mailing out thousands of credit card applications almost daily, it is imperative that both business managers and consumers understand the rules governing credit arrangements.

Until 1969, when Congress passed the *Consumer Credit Protection Act*, most consumer protection was left to the states. There were many abuses in the issuance and reporting of credit terms. Often, consumer-debtors were ignorant of the annual percentage rates they were being charged, which made it impossible for them to shop around and compare rates. The Consumer Credit Protection Act (CCPA) of 1969 was designed to give consumers a fair shake in all areas of credit. We examine here several important sections of this comprehensive act under their popular titles: the Truth-in-Lending Act; the Electronic Fund Transfer Act; the Fair Credit Reporting Act; the Equal Credit Opportunity Act; the Fair Credit Billing Act; the Fair Debt Collection Practices Act; and the Consumer Leasing Act (Exhibit 23-2). We also discuss certain provisions of the Bankruptcy Reform Act.

TRUTH-IN-LENDING ACT (TILA) OF 1969

GOALS The Truth-in-Lending Act of 1969 (TILA), as amended in 1982, seeks to make creditors disclose all terms of a credit arrangement before they enter into an agreement with a consumer-debtor. It also, by virtue of mandating uniform terms and standards, seeks to give consumers a basis for comparative shopping. The ability of consumers to shop around for the lowest interest rates or finance charges promotes competition in the consumer-credit market.

EXHIBIT 23-2 *Significant Sections of the Consumer Credit Protection Act*

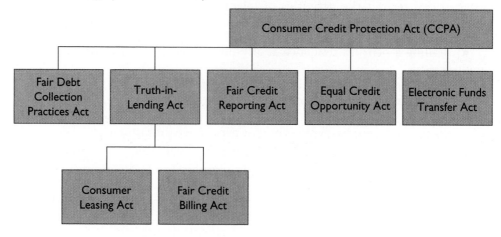

SCOPE The TILA applies to creditors that *regularly* extend credit for less than $25,000 to natural persons for personal and family purposes. Corporations and persons applying for more than $25,000 in credit (except for buying a home) are not covered by the act. To be covered by the act, creditors must regularly extend credit (e.g., banks, finance companies, retail stores, credit card issuers, or savings and loans), demand payment in more than four installments, or assess a finance charge.

PROVISIONS The TILA is a complex, detailed, and costly act for both management (creditors) and consumers (debtors). Six important provisions of the TILA deal with general disclosure, finance charges, the annual percentage rate, the right to cancel a contract, open- and closed-end credit transactions, and credit advertising.

General Disclosure The general disclosure provisions of the TILA require all qualified creditors to disclose all terms clearly and conspicuously in meaningful sequence and to furnish the consumer with a copy of the disclosure requirements. Additional information, as long as it is not confusing, may be incorporated into the disclosure statement. Exhibit 23-3 is an example of a Truth-in-Lending disclosure statement.

Finance Charges The finance charge provisions of the TILA—as well as the Federal Reserve Board's **Regulation Z**, which implements some provisions of the act—require a system of disclosing charges so that consumers can compare credit costs using *uniform* standards. A finance charge includes any dollar charges that make up the cost of credit to the consumer. These may be interest rates; service, carrying, or transaction charges; charges for mandatory credit life insurance on an installment loan in the event of the death of the debtor; loan fees; "points" when buying a home; and appraisal fees.

Annual percentage Rate The **annual percentage rate (APR)**—the *effective* annual rate of interest being charged by the creditor—must be disclosed in a meaningful and sequential way to all consumers of credit. Annual percentage rates differ according to the compounding period being used by the creditor, so this disclosure requirement makes it easy for consumers to see exactly what interest rate they are paying and to do some comparison shopping. The Federal Reserve Board publishes *Regulation Z Annual Percentage Tables*. If creditors use these tables and follow their instructions, there is a legal presumption of correctness.

Right to Cancel The right to cancel a contract applies only to home loans. A consumer has a right to cancel such a loan three days after entering the contract. The three days begin *after* the proper truth-in-lending disclosures have been made, usually at the closing by a bank employee. Because so many documents are being signed at this time, the disclosure statement is sometimes overlooked by both the bank employee and the borrower.

Regulation Z A group of rules, set forth by the Federal Reserve Board to implement some provisions of the Truth-in-Lending Act, that require lenders to disclose certain information to borrowers.

annual percentage rate (APR) The effective annual rate of interest being charged a consumer by a creditor, which depends on the compounding period the creditor is using.

Application#:
Loan#:

Borrowers

John Jones
15980 Main Street
Pemberville, OH

Property

15980 Main Street
Pemberville, OH

Itemization of Amount Financed

$ Total amount financed $

$ TAX SERVICE FEE
$ Interim interest
$ MI premium
$ MI renewal reserves
$ Total prepaid finance charges $

$ 1992 COUNTY TAXES
$ Appraisal fee
$ Credit report
$ Hazard insurance reserves
$ County tax reserves
$ Settlement or closing fee
$ Document preparation
$ Title insurance
$ Recording fees
$ State tax/stamps
$ SEPTIC INSPECTION
$ Proc/underwriting fee
$ Total amount paid to others

LOAN AMOUNT $

THE FIRST PAYMENT FOR YOUR ADVANCE 7/23

FOR: $200,000
AT: 7.65%

WHICH WILL PAY OFF IN 84 PAYMENTS

IS BROKEN DOWN AS FOLLOWS:

PRINCIPAL &/OR INTEREST $

Mortgage Insurance

Taxes

Insurance

Other

TOTAL OF PAYMENT $

ANNUAL PERCENTAGE RATE The cost of your credit as a yearly rate.	FINANCE CHARGE The dollar amount the credit will cost you. $	Amount Financed The amount of credit provided to you or on your behalf.	Total of Payments The amount you will have paid after you have made all payments as scheduled.

Your Payment Schedule Will Be:

THIS LOAN MUST EITHER BE PAID IN FULL AT MATURITY OF MODIFIED TO A MARKET LEVEL FIXED RATE OVER THE REMAINING 30 YEAR TERM. YOU MUST REPAY THE ENTIRE PRINCIPAL BALANCE OF THE LOAN AND UNPAID INTEREST THEN DUE IF YOU DO NOT QUALIFY FOR THE CONDITIONAL MODIFICATION AND EXTENSION FEATURE AS SPECIFIED IN THE NOTE ADDENDUM AND MORTGAGE RIDER. THE LENDER IS UNDER NO OBLIGATION TO REFINANCE THE LOAN IF QUALIFICATION CONDITIONS ARE NOT MET. YOU WILL, THEREFORE, BE REQUIRED TO MAKE PAYMENT OUT OF OTHER ASSETS YOU MAY OWN, OR YOU WILL HAVE TO FIND A LENDER, WHICH MAY BE THE LENDER YOU HAVE THIS LOAN WITH, WILLING TO LEND YOU THE MONEY. IF YOU REFINANCE THIS LOAN AT MATURITY YOU MAY HAVE TO PAY SOME OR ALL OF THE CLOSING COSTS NORMALLY ASSOCIATED WITH A NEW LENDER EVEN IF YOU OBTAIN REFINANCING FROM THE LENDER.

Security Interest: You are giving a security interest in the property located at

Late Charge: If payment is 15 days late, you will be charged 5.0000% of the payment.
Prepayment: If you pay off early, you will not have to pay a penalty.
               If you pay off early, you will not be entitled to a refund of part of the finance charge.
Assumption: Someone buying your home cannot assume the remainder of the mortgage on the original terms.
This Obligation: WILL have a demand feature.

Insurance: You may obtain property insurance from anyone you want that is acceptable to Lender. See your contract documents for any additional information about nonpayment, default, any required repayment in full before the scheduled date, prepayment refunds and penalties.

I (We) hereby acknowledge receiving a completed copy of this disclosure.   Date: ___/___/___

_____   _____

Nancy Kubasek

The following case concerns the right to rescission claimed by borrowers in a situation in which the creditor bank went into receivership and the Federal Deposit Insurance Corporation (FDIC) tried to foreclose on the property.

HUGHES ET AL. V. FIRST NATIONAL BANK OF LOUISVILLE
COURT OF APPEALS OF KENTUCKY 700 S.W. 2D 804 (1985)

The Federal Deposit Insurance Corporation (plaintiff) brought a foreclosure action on a mortgage taken out by Mr. and Mrs. Hughes (defendants). The Hugheses took out a loan from the Sixth Guaranty State Bank and in return gave the bank a security interest, or mortgage, on their home. The loan was to be used for remodeling the house. When the bank went into receivership, the Hugheses notified the FDIC that they had received disclosures from the bank of their right to rescind and cancel the loan on their home as required by the Truth-in-Lending Act (TILA).

JUDGE DOTY

The FDIC requests summary judgment on its claim for foreclosure on the Lombard loan. In response, the defendants request summary judgment dismissing FDIC's foreclosure action on the Lombard residence because Mr. Hughes effectively rescinded the Lombard Mortgage as allowed under the Truth-in-Lending Act and thereby voided FDIC's security interest in the residence.

The defendants request this Court to enforce their right to rescind a consumer loan. 15 U.S.C. § 1612(b) creates a statutory exemption for governmental agencies.

Because § 1612(b) clearly constitutes a statutory exemption, this Court cannot impose civil or criminal sanctions against the FDIC. The question then becomes whether rescission pursuant to § 1635 ... constitute(s) a civil penalty.

The Fifth Circuit held that the purpose of the TILA is to enable the individual consumer to credit shop and avoid the uninformed use of credit, that the recovery under § 1635 runs to the individual and that the purpose of the rescission remedy is to restore the parties, as much as possible, to the *status quo ante*.

Under this analysis, the right to rescission under § 1635 is not a civil penalty and, therefore, is a remedy outside of the scope of § 1612(b). This conclusion is consistent with the general policy of the Act "to assure a meaningful disclosure of credit terms." There is no public policy reason for disallowing a valid rescission merely because the creditor has become insolvent and has sold the underlying note and mortgage to a governmental agency.

Affirmed in favor of Defendants, Hugheses.

---

open-end credit Credit extended on an account for an indefinite time period so that the debtor can keep charging on the account, up to a certain amount, while paying the outstanding balance either in full or in installment payments.

closed-end credit A credit arrangement in which credit is extended for a specific period of time, and the exact number of payments and the total amount due have been agreed upon between the borrower and the creditor.

Open- and Closed-end Credit Transactions Regulation Z distinguishes between *open-end credit* and *closed-end credit*; each has separate disclosure requirements. An **open-end credit transaction** (e.g., MasterCard or a revolving charge account in a retail store such as Sears) is one that extends credit for an indefinite time period and gives the debtor the option to pay in full or in installments. The initial statement to the debtor with such an account must include such items as the elements of any finance charge and the conditions under which it will be imposed, the APR as estimated at the time of extending credit, if and when overcharges will be imposed, and the minimum payment for each periodic statement.

A closed-end credit transaction (e.g., a personal consumer loan, a student loan, or a car loan) is extended by the creditor for a limited time period. All conditions of the loan, including the total amount financed, the number of payments, and the due dates, have to be agreed on before the loan is extended. For this type of credit transaction, Regulation Z requires creditors to disclose the total finance charges, the APR, the total number of payments due, any security interest, and any prepayment penalties or rebates to the consumer if payment is made ahead of time.

Credit Advertising The TILA governs all advertising or "commercial messages" to the public that "aid, promote, or assist" in the extension of consumer credit. Thus many television and radio commercials, newspaper ads, direct mail, postings in a store, and all announcements of a "blue ribbon" extension of credit to customers in a store must meet certain disclosure requirements.

These include the amount of the down payment, the conditions of repayment, and the finance charges, expressed in annual percentage terms.

REMEDIES The Federal Trade Commission and seven other federal agencies are responsible for enforcement of the Truth-in-Lending Act. All these agencies have at their disposal uniform corrective actions that can be brought on behalf of a consumer-debtor.

First, a consumer can be reimbursed for a creditor's overcharging and for billing errors with regard to finance charges. Second, if the creditor has exhibited a pattern of negligence, misleading statements, or an intentional failure to disclose, the case may be referred to the Justice Department for criminal action. Conviction in such cases can bring a fine of up to $5,000, or imprisonment up to one year, or both.

Private parties, as in the *Walker Bank* case, excerpted later, are the major enforcers of the TILA. A private party who brings suit must show, first, that the transaction affected interstate commerce and, second, that the creditor failed to comply with the TILA or Regulation Z. Private parties (usually consumer-debtors) do not have to show that they were injured by the failure to disclose. Moreover, the creditor's noncompliance need only be slight. Damages recovered are usually actual damages plus a penalty of twice the finance charges imposed in connection with the transaction. "Reasonable attorney fees," as determined by the court, can also be collected.

Class actions brought on behalf of consumer-debtors are also permissible under the TILA. Usually, these are brought by legal aid societies or other non-profit groups against creditors with a history of blatantly unscrupulous dealings with consumers.

THE ELECTRONIC FUND TRANSFER ACT

GOALS In 1978 Congress amended the TILA and enacted the *Electronic Fund Transfer Act (EFTA)* to regulate financial institutions that offer electronic fund transfers involving an account held by a customer. The Federal Reserve Board was empowered to enforce the provisions of the act and adopted *Regulation E* to further interpret the act. Types of consumer electronic funds include automated teller machines (ATMs), point-of-sale terminals (e.g., debit cards), pay-by-phone systems, and direct deposit and withdrawals.

PROVISIONS Consumer rights established by the EFTA apply in the following areas:

1. *Unsolicited cards.* Banks can send unsolicited EFTA cards to a consumer only if the card is not valid for use when received.

2. *Errors in billing.* Customers have 60 days from the receipt of a bank statement to notify the bank of its error. The bank has 10 days to investigate. The bank can re-credit the customer account to gain 45 more days to investigate.

3. *Lost or stolen debit cards.* If the bank is notified within two days from the time a card is lost, the customer can be liable for only $50 for unauthorized use. Liability increases to $300 up to 60 days, and more than $500 after 60 days when no notice is given.

4. *Transactions.* A bank has to provide written evidence of a transaction made through a computer terminal.

5. *Statements.* Banks must provide a monthly statement to an EFTS customer at the end of a month in which a transaction is made. If no transactions are made, a quarterly statement must be provided.

The EFTA covers only transactions involving accounts held by natural persons for personal, family, or household purposes. Many fund transfers fall outside the EFTA. An attempt to create a uniform body of law in the 50 states took place in 1989 with the creation of Article 4A of the UCC. Article 4A and the EFTA are mutually exclusive. Article 4A does not apply to regulate any part of an electronic fund transfer that is subject to the EFTA.

REMEDIES   Under the EFTA, a financial institution is liable to any customer for all damages caused by its failure to make an electronic transfer in a timely manner and when instructed to do so by the customer. The institution is liable for damages caused by its failure to credit a deposit of funds and failure to stop a preauthorized transfer from a customer's account.

If an Act of God or other circumstance beyond its control or a technical malfunction take place, the financial institution is not liable.

The Walker Bank and Trust Company case, which follows, illustrates the stolen credit card situation covered by the Electronic Fund Transfer Act. Notice the court's emphasis on the "unauthorized use" of a credit card.

WALKER BANK AND TRUST COMPANY V. JONES AND HARLAN
SUPREME COURT OF UTAH 672 P.2D 73 (1983)

Two cases were consolidated for hearing by the Supreme Court of Utah. In both cases, the Walker Bank and Trust Company was the plaintiff-appellee.

In the first case, the bank sued Jones (the defendant) when she refused to pay a balance of $2,685.70 on her VISA and MasterCharge accounts. Initially, Jones and her husband had received credit cards jointly in both their names. Jones later notified the bank that she would not assume any liability for charges made by her husband to either account. The bank requested that the cards be returned and threatened to revoke the account. Neither Jones nor her husband returned the cards, and both continued to use them. Finally, a bank employee visited Jones's place of employment and got her to surrender her card. A portion of the balance due was charged by her husband after the time she had notified the bank not to honor his charges. Jones refused to pay any of the balance due.

In the second case, the bank also sued Harlan (the defendant) to recover a balance due. Harlan had requested that her husband be added to her VISA card account. When the couple separated shortly thereafter, she requested that either her account be closed or that her husband be denied further use of the card. After this request was made, several charges were made to her account by her husband.

In both cases, the bank argued that the husbands' use of the credit cards was not an "unauthorized use" within the meaning of the statute. The defendants argued that the Truth-in-Lending Act limited their liability to $50 for the unauthorized use of the cards by their husbands.

The trial court granted summary judgment in favor of the bank in both cases. The defendants appealed.

JUSTICE HALL

The term "unauthorized use" is defined (by statute) as:

Use of a credit card by a person other than the cardholder who does not have actual, implied, or apparent authority for such use and from which the cardholder receives no benefit.

A "cardholder" is described as:

Any person to whom a credit card is issued or any person who has agreed with the card issuer to pay obligations arising from the issuance of a credit card to another person.

Defendants contend that they alone occupied the status of "cardholder," by reason of their request to the bank that credit cards be issued to their husbands and their assumption of liability therefor. Accordingly, they maintain that their husbands were no more than authorized users of defendants' accounts.

Defendants further aver that the effect of their notification to the Bank stating that they would no longer be responsible for charges made against their accounts by their husbands was to render any subsequent use of the cards unauthorized. This notification, defendants maintain, was all that was necessary to revoke the authority they had once created in their husbands.

The bank's position is that unauthorized use is precisely what the statutory definition says it is, to wit: "Use . . . by a person . . . who does not have actual, implied, or apparent authority and that notification to the card issuer has no bearing whatsoever on whether the use is unauthorized, so as to entitle a cardholder to the statutory limitation of liability." We agree with this position.

The liability of the cardholder for unauthorized charges is limited to $50 regardless of any notification to the card issuer. Unless and until the unauthorized nature of the use has been established, the notification provision, as well as the statute itself, is irrelevant and ineffectual.

The language of the statute defining unauthorized use is clear and unambiguous. It excludes from the category of unauthorized users, any person who has "actual, implied, or apparent authority."

The Bank maintains that defendants' husbands clearly had "apparent" authority to use the cards, inasmuch as their signatures were the same as the signatures on the cards, and their names, the same as those imprinted upon the cards. Accordingly, it contends that no unauthorized use was made of the cards, and that defendants therefore cannot invoke the limitations on liability provided by the TILA.

Again, we find the Bank's position to be meritorious. Apparently authority exists:

> Where a person has created such an appearance of things that it causes a third party reasonably and prudently to believe that a second party has the power to act on behalf of the first person.

As previous pointed out, at defendants' request their husbands were issued cards bearing the husbands' own names and signatures. These cards were, therefore, a representation to the merchants to whom they were presented that defendant's husbands . . . were authorized to make charges upon the defendants' . . . accounts. This apparent authority conferred upon defendants' husbands by reason of the credit cards thus precluded the application of the TILA.

In view of our determination that the TILA has no application to the present case, we hold that liability for defendants' husbands' use of the cards is governed by their contracts with the Bank. The contractual agreements between defendants and the Bank provided clearly and unequivocally that *all* cards issued upon the accounts be returned to the Bank in order to terminate defendants' liability. Accordingly, defendants' refusal to relinquish either their cards or their husbands', at the time they notified the Bank that they no longer accepted liability for their husbands' charges, justified the Bank's disregard of that notification and refusal to terminate defendant's liability at that time.

Affirmed in favor of Plaintiff, Walker Bank.

THE FAIR CREDIT REPORTING ACT (FCRA) OF 1970

GOALS   The *Fair Credit Reporting Act (FCRA)* was enacted by Congress in 1970 as an amendment to the Consumer Credit Protection Act to ensure that credit information obtained by credit agencies would remain confidential. Individual privacy is a major concern in an era in which three major credit bureaus (TRW, TransUnion, and Equifax) hold files on a majority of U.S. citizens. At the same time, Congress wanted to force the agencies to adopt reasonable procedures to allow lenders, such as banks and finance corporations, to have access to information they needed to make decisions on whether to lend money.

The FCRA sought especially to correct three common abuses by credit agencies: the failure to set uniform standards for keeping information confidential; the retention of irrelevant and sometimes inaccurate information in their files; and the failure to respond to consumer requests for information.

PROVISIONS   These are the most important provisions of the FCRA:

1.   The creditor or lender must give *notice* to a consumer whenever that consumer has been unfavorably affected by an adverse credit report from a consumer reporting agency. A *consumer reporting agency* is defined as any entity that "regularly engages in the practice of assembling or evaluating consumer credit or other information on consumers for the purpose of furnishing consumer reports to third parties." If a company infrequently furnishes information to a third party or collects it for internal use only, it does not fall within the FCRA.

2.   The consumer may *go to the credit agency* that issued the adverse report and be "informed of the nature and substance" of the information on file. A written request for information by a consumer must also be honored.

3.   Credit reporting agencies are *required to keep files up to date* and to delete inaccuracies. If these inaccuracies have been passed on to lenders, the agencies are also required to notify them of their error. Agencies cannot retain stale information and must follow reasonable procedures to update information dealing with bankruptcies, tax liens, criminal records, and bad debts. If a credit transaction involves $50,000 or more, these agency actions are not necessary in issuing a credit report.

4.   If consumers *do not agree* with what is in their file, or with what has been reported by the credit agency to a lender, they can file a written report of one hundred words or fewer giving their side of the dispute.

5.   A consumer credit agency may issue *credit information reports* to (a) a court in response to a court order; (b) the consumer to whom the report relates (upon written request); (c) a person or entity who the agency has reason to

believe will use the information in connection with making a credit transaction, obtaining employment, licensing, or obtaining personal or family insurance; and (d) anyone having a legitimate business need for the information in order to carry on a business transaction with a consumer.

REMEDIES The FTC may bring actions in the federal courts to obtain cease-and-desist orders against credit agencies and users of information, or it may seek to obtain administrative enforcement orders from an administrative law judge. Violations of the FCRA are considered "unfair or deceptive practices" under Section 5 of the Federal Trade Commission Act. Seven other government entities can also enforce the FCRA: the Federal Reserve Board, the Comptroller of the Currency, the Federal Home Loan Bank Board, the National Credit Union, the Interstate Commerce Commission, and the Secretary of Agriculture.

Criminal liability is incurred by a person who "knowingly and willfully obtains information on a consumer from a consumer reporting agency under false pretenses." Anyone convicted of this charge is subject to a fine up to $5,000 and possible imprisonment for a maximum of one year.

Civil liability is incurred by a credit agency *for any user of credit agency information* (e.g., a bank) if a consumer, in a private action, can show that the agency *willfully* violated the FCRA through repetitive errors. For such violations, the court may assess punitive and actual damages, court costs, and attorneys' fees. A consumer who is able to show *negligence* on the part of the credit agency or user will obtain actual damages, court costs, and reasonable attorneys' fees.

Application of and remedies to the FCRA are illustrated in the case below.

STEVENSON V. TRW, INCORPORATED
UNITED STATES COURT OF APPEALS 987 F.2D 288 (4TH CIR. 1993)

Stevenson (plaintiff) filed suit against TRW, Inc. (defendant), claiming that TRW had violated the Fair Credit Reporting Act (FCRA) by failing to delete erroneous information promptly from his credit report. After Stevenson began receiving phone calls in 1989 from bill collectors concerning debts he did not owe, he discovered 16 accounts in his credit reports that he had never opened. He wrote TRW on October 8, 1989. TRW investigated and claimed that by February 9, 1990, all "negative" credit information had been removed from Stevenson's credit report. However, false information continued to appear on Stevenson's credit report. The federal district court ruled in favor of Stevenson, awarding him $30,000 in actual damages, $100,000 in punitive damages, and $20,700 in attorney's fees. TRW appealed.

JUDGE WILLIAMS

Allowing inaccurate information back onto a credit report after deleting it because it is inaccurate is [negligence]. Additionally, in spite of the complexity of Stevenson's dispute, TRW contacted the subscribers only through the CDV's. Although testimony at trial revealed that TRW sometimes calls subscribers to verify information, it made no calls in Stevenson's case. TRW relied solely on the CDV's despite the number of disputed accounts and the allegations of fraud. TRW also relied on the subscribers to tell TRW whether to delete information from Stevenson's report. In a reinvestigation of the accuracy of credit reports, a credit bureau must bear some responsibility for evaluating the accuracy of information obtained from subscribers.

TRW argues in its defense that the reinvestigation was complicated by the accounts fraudulently obtained in Stevenson's name and based upon accurate information. TRW urged at trial, however, that where fraud has occurred, the consumer must resolve the problem with the creditor. TRW's only obligation, it urges, is to publish a "victim of fraud" statement at the end of a credit report if fraud has been established by the parties. This response by TRW to Stevenson's complaint falls short of [the FCRA's] mandate that the "consumer reporting agency shall within a reasonable period of time reinvestigate" and "promptly delete" inaccurate or unverifiable information. The statute places the burden of investigation squarely on TRW. We conclude that there was no clear error in the district court's finding of negligence in failure to meet the prompt deletion requirement.

Affirmed for Stevenson but *reversed* as to punitive damages because TRW's noncompliance was found not to be willful.

Equal Credit Opportunity Act (ECOA) of 1974

GOALS When Congress enacted the Equal Credit Opportunity Act (ECOA) in 1974, it was trying to eliminate all forms of discrimination in granting credit, including those based on race, sex, color, religion, national origin, marital status, receipt of public assistance—and exercise of one's rights under the act. The Federal Reserve Board, which is charged with implementing ECOA's regulations, may exempt any "classes of transactions not primarily for household or family purposes." Thus most commercial transactions are exempt from the act.

PROVISIONS The ECOA—and *Regulation B*, promulgated by the Federal Reserve Board—provide that:

1. A creditor may not request information from a credit applicant about a spouse or a former spouse, the applicant's marital status, any alimony and child support received, gender, childbearing, race, color, religion, or national origin.

2. A creditor must notify the applicant of what action has been taken on the application within 30 days of receiving it. The notification must contain: (a) a statement of the action taken and, if the application is denied, either a statement of the reasons for the denial or a disclosure of the applicant's right to receive a statement of such reasons; (b) a statement of the basic provisions of the ECOA; and (c) the name and address of the relevant administrative agency that deals with compliance by creditors. There is a two-year statute of limitations to bring a suit under the EOCA. However, this sometimes does not apply when the act is used as a *defense*. For example, there is a conflict among state and federal court decisions in cases in which the wife is illegally required under EOCA to cosign a loan guarantee for her husband's business. When the bank later brings suit to collect on the promissory note that has been defaulted on by the husband, the wife raises the defense of a violation of the act even though the two-year statute of limitations has run out. Other ECOA violations besides requiring a spouse to cosign include: (a) asking for information about an applicant's spouse or former spouse when not relevant; (b) taking race, sex, or national origin into account when making a credit decision; (c) requiring certain types of life insurance before issuing a loan; (d) basing a credit decision on the area in which the applicant lives; (e) asking about an applicant's intent to have children.

REMEDIES The FTC and other agencies can bring administrative actions on behalf of consumers before an administrative law judge as well as civil injunctive actions in the federal district courts. In addition, if a creditor violates the ECOA, individuals who feel they have been injured under the act can bring an action in federal district court for actual and punitive damages. Punitive damages may not exceed $10,000 for an individual successful plaintiff, but they may go as high as $500,000 for successful class-action plaintiffs. Plaintiffs may also ask for injunctive relief to prohibit future discriminatory actions by the creditor.

The Fair Credit Billing Act (FCBA) of 1974

GOALS Congress enacted the Fair Credit Billing Act (FCBA) as an amendment to the TILA in 1974 in order to eliminate inaccurate and unfair billing practices, as well as to limit the liability of consumer creditors for the unauthorized use of their credit cards.

PROVISIONS The FCBA provisions cover (1) issuers of credit cards, (2) creditors who extend credit in more than four monthly installments, and (3) creditors who assess finance charges. The following provisions of the act establish a procedure for correcting billing errors:

1. All creditors must notify consumer-debtors of their rights and duties when an account is opened and every six months thereafter. They must notify debtors on the billing statement where they are to inquire when they notice a billing error.

2. Consumer-debtors who believe their billing statement contains an error must notify the creditor in writing within 60 days, identifying themselves, their account number, the item, and the amount in dispute. Within 30 days, the creditor must notify the debtor that it has received notice of the alleged billing error. Within 90 days, or two billing cycles, the creditor must notify the consumer-debtor of the outcome of its investigation. During this period, the creditor cannot take any action to collect the debt in dispute. It may continue to send billing statements listing the disputed item, but these statements must give notice to the consumer that the item in dispute does not have to be paid.

3. If after investigation the creditor finds that there was a billing error, it must correct the error and notify the consumer. If it finds no error, it must notify the consumer-debtor and substantiate its reason. A bad credit report cannot be filed until ten days after the substantiation has been sent out.

If a faulty product is purchased on credit, the consumer can withhold payment until the dispute is settled, provided he or she notifies the creditor immediately after finding the fault in the product. The creditor is then obligated to attempt to negotiate the dispute between the seller of the product and the consumer-debtor.

REMEDIES   Individual consumer-debtors, as well as government agencies, can bring actions against creditors who violate the FCBA. The only penalty set forth in the act is that creditors forfeit their right to collect up to $50 on each item in dispute on each periodic statement. This amount includes interest and finance charges on the amount in dispute.

THE FAIR DEBT COLLECTION PRACTICES ACT (FDCPA) OF 1977

GOALS   The purpose of the Fair Debt Collection Practices Act is to prevent harassment by creditors or debt collectors of consumer-debtors at their place of work or at home. The act defines *debt collectors* as those who are in the business of collecting debts from others. In 1986, attorneys who regularly perform debt activities were brought under the provisions of the FDCPA.

Approximately 5,000 debt collection agencies seek about $5 billion in debts from some 8 million consumers annually. Many use sophisticated WATTS telephone lines and computers. They are paid a 20 to 50 percent commission on what they collect, so they often are quite aggressive in their collection methods—as well as successful. So successful that in the 1980s the federal government turned over many outstanding federal loans (including student loans) to these private collection agencies.

States are exempt from FDCPA enforcement within their boundaries if they have laws meeting the FDCPA requirements. Actually, state laws are often more vigorously enforced than the federal law.

PROVISIONS   The FDCPA prohibits the following activities by debt collectors who are covered by the act:

1. They may not contact a third party (other than the debtor's family and lawyer) except to find out where the debtor is. The idea behind this provision is that the debtor's name should not be ruined among friends, acquaintances, or employers.

2. They may not contact a debtor during "inconvenient" hours. This provision seeks to prevent creditors from harassing a debtor in the middle of the night. "Inconvenient hours" are considered to be from 9:00 P.M. to 8:00 A.M. for a debtor whose workday is the normal 8:00 A.M. to 5:00 P.M. If the credit collection agency knows that the debtor is represented by a lawyer, it may not contact the debtor at all.

3. They cannot contact a debtor in an abusive, deceptive, or unfair way. For example, posing as a lawyer or police officer is forbidden.

In the abridged case below, the U.S. Supreme Court for the first time brought lawyers under the FDCPA. The reader should note what activities of lawyers the Court deemed are covered by the act.

GEORGE W. HEINTZ ET AL. V. DARLENE JENKINS
UNITED STATES SUPREME COURT 513 U.S. 1109 (1995)

Plaintiff, Darlene Jenkins brought suit under the FDCPA against Heintz, a lawyer, and his firm. Plaintiff borrowed money from the Gainer Bank in order to buy a car. She defaulted on her loan. The bank's law firm then sued Jenkins in state court to recover the balance due. As part of an effort to settle the suit, a lawyer with that law firm, George Heintz, wrote to Jenkins. His letter, in listing the amount she owed under the loan agreement, included $4,173 owed for insurance, bought by the bank because she had not kept the car insured as she had promised to do.

Jenkins then brought this Fair Debt Collection Practices Act suit against Heintz and his firm. She claimed that Heintz's letter violated the act's prohibitions against trying to collect an amount not "authorized by the agreement creating the debt" and against making a "false representation of . . . the . . . amount . . . of any debt." The loan agreement, she conceded, required her to keep the car insured "against loss or damage" and permitted the bank to buy such insurance to protect the car should she fail to do so. But she said, the $4,137 substitute policy was not the kind of policy the loan agreement had in mind, for it insured the bank not only against "loss or damage" but also against her failure to repay the bank's car loan. Hence, Heintz's "representation" about the "amount" of her "debt" was "false"; amounted to an effort to collect an "amount" not "authorized" by the loan agreement; and thus violated the act.

Pursuant to Rule 12(b)(6) of the Federal Rules of Civil Procedure, the district court dismissed Jenkins Fair Debt Collection lawsuit for failure to state a claim. The court held that the act does not apply to lawyers engaging in litigation. However, the court of appeals for the seventh circuit reversed the district court's judgment, interpreting the act to apply to litigating lawyers.

JUSTICE BRENNAN

The issue before us is whether the term "debt collector" in the Fair Debt Collection Practices Act applied to a lawyer who "regularly," *through litigation*, tries to collect consumer debts. The Court of Appeals for the Seventh Circuit held that it does. We agree with the Seventh Circuit and we affirm its judgment.

The Fair Debt Collection Practices Act prohibits "debt collector[s]" from making false or misleading representations and from engaging in various abusive and unfair practices. The Act says, for example, that a "debt collector" may not use violence, obscenity, or repeated annoying phone calls; may not falsely represent "the character, amount, or legal status of any debt"; and may not use various "unfair or unconscionable means to collect or attempt to collect" a consumer debt. Among other things, the Act sets out rules that a debt collector must follow for "acquiring location information" about the debtor; communicating about the debtor (and the debt) with third parties; and bringing "[l]egal actions." The Act imposes upon "debt collector[s]" who violate its provisions (specifically described) "[c]ivil liability" to those whom they, e.g., harass, mislead, or treat unfairly. The Act also authorizes the Federal Trade Commission to enforce its provisions. The Act's definition of the term "debt collector" includes a person "who regularly collects or attempts to collect, directly or indirectly, debts owed [to] . . . another." And, it limits "debt" to consumer debt, i.e., debts "arising out of . . . transaction[s]" that "are primarily for personal, family, or household purposes." Section 1692a(5).

There are two rather strong reasons for believing that the Act applies to the litigating activities of lawyers. *First*, the Act defines the "debt collector[s]" to whom it applies as including those who "regularly collec[t] or attemp[t] to collect, directly or indirectly, [consumer] debts owed or due or asserted to be owed or due another." Section 1692a(6). In ordinary English, a lawyer who regularly tried to obtain payment of consumer debts through legal proceedings is a lawyer who regularly "attempts" to "collect" those consumer debts. See, e.g., Black's Law Dictionary 263 (6th ed. 1990) ("To collect a debt or claim is to obtain payment or liquidation of it, either by personal solicitation or legal proceedings".)

Second, in 1977, Congress enacted an earlier version of this statute, which contained an express exemption for lawyers. That exemption said that the term "debt collector" did not include "any attorney-at-law collecting a debt as an attorney on behalf of and in the name of a client." In 1986, however, Congress repealed this exemption in its entirety without creating a narrower, litigation-related, exemption to fill the void. Without more, then, one would think that Congress intended that lawyers be subject to the Act whenever they meet the general "debt collector" definition.

Heintz argues that we should nonetheless read the statute as containing an implied exemption for those debt-collecting activities of lawyers that consist of litigating (including, he assumes, settlement efforts). He relies primarily on three arguments.

First, Heintz argues that many of the Act's requirements, if applied directly to litigating activities, will create harmfully anomalous results that Congress simply could not have intended. We address this argument in light of the fact that, when Congress first wrote the Act's substantive provisions, it had for the most part exempted litigating attorneys from the Act's coverage; that, when Congress later repealed the attorney exemption, it did not revisit the wording of these substantive provisions; and that, for these reasons, some awkwardness is understandable. Particularly when read in this light, we find Heintz's argument unconvincing.

Many of Heintz's "anomalies" are not particularly anomalous. For example, the Sixth Circuit pointed to Section 1692e(5), which forbids a "debt collector" to make any "threat to take action that cannot legally be taken." The court reasoned that, were the Act to apply to litigating activities, this provision automatically would make liable any litigating lawyer who brought, and then lost, a claim against a debtor. But, the Act says explicitly that a "debt collector" may not be held liable if he "shows by a preponderance of evidence that the violation was not intentional and resulted from a bona fide error notwithstanding the maintenance of procedures reasonably adapted to avoid any such error." Thus, even if we were to assume that the suggested reading of Section 1692e(5) is correct, we would not find the result so absurd as to warrant implying an exemption for litigating lawyers. In any event, the assumption would seem unnecessary, for we do not see how the fact that a lawsuit turns out ultimately to be unsuccessful could, by itself, make the bringing of it an "action that cannot legally be taken."

The remaining significant "anomalies" similarly depend for their persuasive force upon readings that courts seem unlikely to endorse. For example, Heintz's strongest "anomaly" argument focuses upon the Act's provisions governing "[c]ommunication in connection with debt collection." One of those provisions requires a "debt collector" not to "communicate further" with a consumer who "notifies" the "debt collector" that he or she "refuses to pay" or wishes the debt collector to "cease further communication." In light of this provision, asks Heintz, how can an attorney file a lawsuit against (and thereby communicate with) a nonconsenting consumer or file a motion for summary judgment against that consumer?

We agree with Heintz that it would be odd if the Act empowered a debt-owing consumer to stop the "communications" inherent in an ordinary lawsuit and thereby cause an ordinary debt-collecting lawsuit to grind to a halt. But, it is not necessary to read Section 1692c in that way—if only because that provision has exceptions that permit communications "to notify the consumer that the debt collector or creditor may invoke" or "intends to invoke" a "specified remedy" (of a kind "ordinarily invoked by [the] debt collector or creditor"). Courts can

read these exceptions, plausibly, to imply that they authorize the actual invocation of the remedy that the collector "intends to invoke." The language permits such a reading, for an ordinary court-related document does, in fact "notify" its recipient that the creditor may "invoke" a judicial remedy. Moreover, the interpretation is consistent with the statute's apparent objective of preserving creditors' judicial remedies. We need not authoritatively interpret the Act's conduct-regulating provisions now, however. Rather, we rest our conclusions upon the fact that it is easier to read Section 1692c as containing some such additional, implicit, exception than to believe that Congress intended, silently and implicitly, to create a far broader exception, for all litigating attorneys, from the Act itself.

Second, Heintz points to a statement of Congressman Frank Annunzio, one of the sponsors of the 1986 amendment that removed from the Act the language creating a blanket exemption for lawyers. Representative Annunzio stated that, despite the exemption's removal, the Act sill would not apply to lawyers' litigating activities. Representative Annunzio said that the Act.

> *regulates debt collection, not the practice of law. Congress repealed the attorney exemption of the act, not because of attorney[s'] conduct in the courtroom, but because of their conduct in the backroom. Only collection activities, not legal activities, are covered by the act. . . . The act applies to attorneys when they are collecting debts, not when they are performing tasks of a legal nature. . . . The act only regulates the conduct of debt collectors, through their attorneys, from pursuing any legal remedies available to them.*

This statement, however, does not persuade us.

For one thing, the plain language of the Act itself says nothing about retaining the exemption in respect to litigation. The line the statement seeks to draw between "legal" activities and "debt collection" activities was not necessarily apparent to those who debated the legislation, for litigating, at first blush seems simply one way of collecting a debt. For another thing, when Congress considered the Act, other Congressmen expressed fear that repeal would limit lawyers' "ability to contact third parties in order to facilitate settlements" and "could very easily interfere with a client's right to pursue judicial remedies." They proposed alternative language designed to keep litigation activities outside the Act's scope, but that language was not enacted. Further, Congressman Annunzio made his statement not during the legislative process, but *after* the statute became law. It therefore is not a statement upon which other legislators might have relied in voting for or against the Act, but it simply represents the view of one informed person on an issue about which others may (or may not) have thought differently.

Finally, Heintz points to a "Commentary" on the Act by the Federal Trade Commission's staff. It says:

"Attorneys or law firms that engage in traditional debt collection activities (sending dunning letters, making collection calls to consumers) are covered by the [Act], but *those whose practice is limited to legal activities are not covered.*"

We cannot give conclusive weight to this statement. The Commentary of which this statement is a part says that it "is not binding on the Commission or the public." More importantly, we find nothing either in the Act or elsewhere indicating that Congress intended to authorize the FTC to create this exception from the Act's coverage—an exception that, for the reasons we have set forth above, falls outside the range of reasonable interpretations of the Act's express language.

For these reasons, we agree with the Seventh Circuit that the Act applies to attorneys who "regularly" engage in consumer-debt-collection activity, even when that activity consists of litigation.

Affirmed in favor of Plaintiff, Jenkins.

REMEDIES A violation of the FDCPA is considered a violation of Section 5 of the FTCA. The FTC and individual debtors may both bring actions. The FTC may issue cease-and-desist orders and levy fines after an internal administrative agency proceeding.

Individual debtors may bring civil actions to recover actual damages, including those for embarrassment and mental distress. An additional $1,000 may be assessed for each violation for malicious damages. Attorneys' fees are recoverable by debtors who win their suits and also in the event that the creditor brings an action against the debtor and it is found to be "harassing." The case set out here illustrates a private debtor's use of a charge of harassment by a collection agency.

RUTYNA V. COLLECTION ACCOUNTS TERMINAL, INCORPORATED
UNITED STATES FEDERAL DISTRICT COURT 478 F. SUPP. 980 (N.D. ILL. 1979)

Plaintiff, a widow on Social Security, sued the defendant under the Fair Debt Collection Practices Act for harassment, abuse, and deception in attempting to collect a bill. Plaintiff owed a medical bill incurred for treatment of high blood pressure. She thought it had been paid, but it had not. Defendant, a collection agency, made several threatening telephone calls and wrote a letter promising to initiate an investigation of her in her neighborhood and to call on her employer if she did not pay. Defendant moved for a summary judgment.

JUDGE MCMILLEN

The first sentence of § 169 2d provides: "A debt collector may not engage in any conduct the natural consequence of which is to harass, oppress, or abuse any person in connection with the collection of a debt." This section then lists six specifically prohibited types of conduct, without limiting the general application of the foregoing sentence. The legislative history makes clear that this generality was intended. Plaintiff does not allege conduct which falls within one of the specific prohibitions contained in § 169 2d, but we find that defendant's letter to plaintiff does violate this general standard. Without doubt defendant's letter has the natural (and intended) consequence of harassing, oppressing and abusing the recipient. The tone of the letter is one of intimidation, and was intended as such in order to effect a collection. The threat of an investigation and resulting embarrassment to the alleged debtor is clear

and the actual effect on the recipient is irrelevant. The egregiousness of the violation is a factor to be considered in awarding statutory damages. Defendant's violation of § 169 2d is clear.

Section 169 2e bars a debt collector from using any "false, deceptive, or misleading representation or means in connection with the collection of any debt." Sixteen specific practices are listed in this provision, without limiting the application of this general standard. Section 169 2d(5) bars a threat "to take any action that cannot legally be taken or that is not intended to be taken." Defendant also violated this provision.

Defendant's letter threatened embarrassing contacts with plaintiff's employer and neighbors. This constitutes a false representation of the actions that defendant could legally take. Section 169 2c(b) prohibits communication by the debt collector with third parties.

Plaintiff's neighbors and employer could not legally be contacted by defendant in connection with this debt. The letter falsely represents, or deceives the recipient, to the contrary. This is a deceptive means employed by defendant in connection with its debt collection. Defendant violated § 169 2e(5) in its threat to take such illegal action.

The envelope received by plaintiff bore a return address, which began "COLLECTION ACCOUNTS TERMINAL, INC." Section 169 2f bars unfair or unconscionable means to collect or attempt to collect any debt. Section 169 2f specifically bars:

> Using any language or symbol, other than the debt collector's address, on any envelope when communicating with a consumer by use of the mails or by telegram, except that a debt collector may use his business name if such name does not indicate that he is in the debt collection business.

Defendant's return address violated this provision, because its business name does indicate that it is in the debt collection business. The purpose of this specific provision is apparently to prevent embarrassment resulting from a conspicuous name on the envelope, indicating that the contents pertain to debt collection.

On the subject of the return address on the envelope, defendant cites § 169 2k(c), which provides:

> A debt collector may not be held liable in any action brought under this subchapter if the debt collector shows by a pre-ponderance of the evidence that the violation was not intentional and resulted from a bonafide error notwithstanding the maintenance of procedures, reasonably adapted to avoid any such error.

Defendant states that it was "unaware that the return address could be considered a violation of any statute." No affidavit is offered. Section 169 2k(c) does not immunize mistakes of law, even if properly proven (as this one is not). Section 169 2k(c) is designed to protect the defendant who intended to prevent the conduct which constitutes a violation of this Act but who failed even though he maintained procedures reasonably adapted to avoid such an error. Defendant here obviously intended the conduct which violates the Act in respect to the return address, but it simply failed to acquaint itself with the pertinent law. . . .

Defendant's motion for summary judgment is *denied*.

Critical Thinking about the Law

A DUTY BASIC TO JUDGES IS reading and interpreting legislation. One cannot overstate the impact of the judge's performance of this duty on the court's reasoning. For example, if a judge decides that legislation cited by the plaintiff is not applicable to the case, then the grievance will likely be dismissed.

In this case, the court's reading of Sections 169 2d and 169 2k(c) determined in large part the decision rendered. Consequently, the questions that follow focus on the court's reasoning pertaining to those two sections.

1. The court held that § 169 2d, which covers illegal actions on the part of a debt collector, can be applied beyond the specific prohibitions listed in it. What reasons did the court provide for that holding?

   CLUE You are looking for the court's justification for its general application of the legislation.

2. The court rejected the defendant's claim to exemption from liability for printing its name on an envelope to the plaintiff. What reasons did the court provide for this rejection?

   CLUE Reread the court's discussion of § 169 2k(c).

THE CONSUMER LEASING ACT (CLA) OF 1976

GOALS Congress enacted the Consumer Leasing Act in 1976 as an amendment to the Truth-in-Lending Act for the express purpose of providing *meaningful disclosure* to consumers who lease goods. Before the CLA was passed, the lease terms for consumer goods were often so complex that the average consumer could not understand them.

PROVISIONS The CLA applies to leases of "consumer goods," which are defined as a "lease of personal property" for "person, family, or household" use. The lease period must be more than four months, and the dollar value of the lease obligation cannot exceed $25,000. The CLA defines a "lessor" as any natural person or legal entity (corporation, partnership, franchise, or individual proprietorship) that regularly engages in or arranges for leasing as a *normal part of business*. Apartment leases and leases between neighbors are not covered by the act.

When a lease falls under the CLA's definition, the creditor-lessor must provide the following information for the consumer-lessee in the lease agreement:

1. The date and name of the lessor and the lessee.
2. A description of the personal property being leased, plus an itemization of all financing charges, the date of lease payments, and any expressed warranties regarding the leased property.
3. The responsibility of consumer-lessee and the lessor-creditor for attorney's fees in the case of a suit by either party, insurance coverage, and the terms and conditions for terminating and transferring the lease.

REMEDIES   Violations of the Consumer Leasing Act are subject to the same penalties as violations of the Truth-in-Lending Act discussed previously.

The Bankruptcy Reform Act (BRA) of 1978

GOALS   The Bankruptcy Reform Act of 1978 (as amended in 1982 and 1984) is intended to protect consumer-debtors in need of assistance after "falling on hard times." Congress sought to give consumer-debtors, whether individuals or companies, a "fresh start" without being dragged down by past debts.

PROVISIONS   The Bankruptcy Reform Act (BRA) provides two forms of relief for consumer-debtors: (1) liquidation under Chapter 7, (2) a wage earner's plan set out in Chapter 13 of the act. Chapter 11 of the act is designed primarily for the reorganization of a financially unsound business, though it can also be used by individuals.

Consumer-debtors who file for bankruptcy either voluntarily or involuntarily under Chapter 7 (liquidation) generally see their assets sold and the proceeds distributed to creditors. All debts are discharged (excused) for a six-year period except taxes, child support and alimony, and credit obtained under *material* false pretenses. A debtor may elect to take *exemptions* under federal or state law. Federal exemptions tend to be more liberal than state exemptions. For example, federal law exempts the following debtor assets.

1. Trade tools up to $750 in value.
2. Household items and other property for personal use whose value is $200 or less.
3. State and federal payments such as Social Security, unemployment, and pensions necessary for "reasonable support."
4. Equity in a home not in excess of $7,500.
5. Equity in a motor vehicle up to $1,200.
6. Interest in life insurance policies.[5]

If a husband and wife petition for bankruptcy, each may claim separate exemptions under federal law.

Under Chapter 13 of the BRA (the wage earner's plan), a portion of the consumer-debtor's earnings is paid into the court for distribution to creditors over three years or, with court approval, five years. Both wage earners and individuals engaged in business whose unsecured debts are not in excess of $100,000 and who have secured debts not in excess of $350,000 may qualify under Chapter 13. Only voluntary petitions for bankruptcy may be filed under this chapter. Creditors cannot force petitioners into bankruptcy. Often, creditors agree to a *composition plan*, whereby each creditor receives a percentage of what the debtor owes in exchange for releasing the debtor from the debt.

Chapter 11 of the BRA is generally aimed at financially troubled businesses, but individuals (with the exception of stockbrokers) are also eligible. Its purpose

---

[5]12 C.F.R. 222 (1984).

is to allow a business to reorganize and to continue to function while it is arranging for the discharge of its debts. (Note the contrast to Chapter 7, which discharges the debts by selling off all assets; you can see why Chapter 11 is more advantageous for individuals who qualify.) Reorganization under Chapter 11 may be voluntary or involuntary. The court, after receiving the debtor's petition and ordering relief, appoints committees representing stockholders in the business as well as creditors. If these groups can agree to a fair and reasonable plan that satisfies their constituencies, the court will order its implementation. If some creditors or stockholders disagree on the plan, the court will still order it if the judge finds it fair and reasonable under the circumstances.

The 1984 amendments to the Bankruptcy Reform Act provide that (1) consumer-debtors who owe largely consumer-oriented debts and are petitioning for Chapter 7 bankruptcy must be advised of the availability of the more advantageous Chapter 13; (2) a Chapter 7 petition may be dismissed by a bankruptcy court if the petitioner has previously abused the bankruptcy process; and (3) consumer-debtors who purchase a large number of goods before filing in order to take advantage of exemptions will find it difficult to get those debts discharged.

STATE CONSUMER LEGISLATION

It has often been argued that state, city, county, and private agencies (e.g., the Better Business Bureau) are closer geographically to the problems that the average consumer encounters, and thus are more effective at resolving them than are federal agencies, particularly when relatively small amounts of money are involved. In this section, we examine some consumer-oriented legislation applied in the states. Though it is often overlooked in treatments of consumer protection law, it is important, because it touches the lives of many Americans daily.

UNIFORM CONSUMER CREDIT CODE

The *Uniform Consumer Credit Code (UCCC)* was drafted by the National Conference of Commissioners on State Laws in 1968 and was revised in 1974 and 1982. The commissioners' aim was to replace the patchwork of differing state consumer laws with a uniform state law in the area of consumer credit.

The UCCC takes a disclosure approach to consumer credit similar to that of the federal legislation discussed in this chapter. It regulates interest and finance rates, sets out creditors' remedies, and prohibits fine-print clauses. (It incorporates the TILA by reference.) Like the FTC regulations, the UCCC gives the consumer three days to cancel a sale when it is made as a result of home solicitations.

So far, only ten states have enacted the UCCC.

UNFAIR AND DECEPTIVE PRACTICES STATUTES

All states and the District of Columbia have statutes forbidding deceptive acts and practices in a way similar to Section 5 of the Federal Trade Commission Act. So closely are they modeled on the act, in fact, that these statutes are often called *baby FTC laws*.

State attorney general offices typically have consumer fraud divisions that investigate consumer fraud and false advertising and that seek injunctions, fines, or restitution in state courts. Often, notice of investigation by a state attorney general's office is sufficient to discourage the continuation of a practice such as false advertising. Furthermore, private consumer actions, as well as class actions, are permitted under most state statutes. Usually, consumers may obtain actual and punitive damages as well as court costs and attorney's fees.

Attempts to combat consumer fraud at the state level range from mandatory disclosure statutes requiring merchants to set out all terms and conditions in a financing agreement to laws requiring "cooling-off" periods that allow consumers a set number of days to cancel a purchase sold by a door-to-door salesperson. One class of state consumer laws, the "lemon laws," gives consumers warranty and refund rights on used cars when a material defect can be shown. Mandatory seat-belt-use laws and license-suspension statutes are also consumer-oriented in that they protect buyers and drivers of automobiles.

State attorneys general have recently been encouraging private groups, such as the Better Business Bureau, to play a role in exposing fraudulent sales tactics and in arbitrating disputes. One excellent example in this area is a formal agreement between General Motors (GM) and the Better Business Bureau that allows consumers to bring their complaints about car engines to the bureau. General Motors has agreed to be bound by the bureau's decisions, although consumers have the right to go to court if they disagree with a decision.

INTERNATIONAL DIMENSIONS OF CONSUMER PROTECTION LAW

As companies have become multinational there has become a need to look at varying national consumer protection laws and how they differ. For example in *advertising*, a company such as Coca-Cola seeks to standardize its advertising for purposes of reducing costs and improving quality and appeal to internationally mobile consumers. However, one of the factors that prevents complete standardization of advertising is legality. Differing national views on consumer protection, competitive protection, and standards of morality and nationalism prevent a multinational company from delivering the same advertising message in each nation where it sells goods.

In the area of *consumer protection*, countries differ on the amount of deception in advertising permitted. For example, the United Kingdom and the United States allow competing companies to advertise in a comparative way (for example, Burger King and McDonald's). In contrast, the Philippines prohibits this form of advertising. In the United States we are concerned with sexism in advertising, as well as tobacco. Most countries in Europe, Asia, and Latin America have few, if any, prohibitions in those areas.

In 1984, the European Union's Commission adopted what was termed a "Misleading Advertising Directive." Similar to Section 5 of the Federal Trade Commission Act, the Directive called upon member states of the European Union to prohibit misleading advertising by statute and to create means to enforce such laws. Similar to the U.S. laws, the directive requires that courts and agencies within member states be given the power to require companies to substantiate claims made in advertisements. Member nations have gradually enacted legislation that fits the cultural mores it is to be applied to.

In Mexico, the Federal Consumer Protection Act of 1975 (FCPA) was modeled in large part after several U.S. statutes. Some provisions dealing with advertising include the "principle of truthfulness" between customers and merchants. Labeling instructions must be clear as to content. There must be warnings on all advertised products, as well as truthfulness in advertising on radio and television. In addition to advertising, the FCPA covers areas such as warranties, consumer credit disclosure, and unconscionable clauses in contracts. Both private parties and the Federal Attorney General for Consumer Affairs may bring actions in courts of law. With the advent of NAFTA, the FCPA has become more important as the United States, Canada, and Mexico seek to bring some uniformity to their consumer protection laws.

SUMMARY

Consumer law began in the 1930s, in case law, and evolved fast during the consumer rights movement of the 1960s and 1970s. Federal regulation of business and trade practices is highly dependent on the Federal Trade Commission, which is the watchdog agency charged with enforcing Section 5 of the Federal Trade Commission Act, forbidding unfair or deceptive business practices and unfair methods of competition. Prohibited trade practices include deceptive and unfair advertising, misrepresentation by franchisors, deceptive or confusing warranties, and deceptive telemarketing practices.

Federal laws regulating consumer credit all come under the comprehensive Consumer Credit Protection Act. Important parts of this umbrella act are the

Truth-in-Lending Act, which forces creditors to disclose all terms of a credit arrangement to consumer-debtors before they sign the agreement; the Fair Credit Reporting Act, which seeks to ensure that credit agencies keep accurate, confidential records; the Equal Credit Opportunity Act; the Fair Credit Billing Act; the Fair Debt Collection Practices Act; the Consumer Leasing Act. The Bankruptcy Reform Act is intended to help debtors who have fallen on hard times.

State consumer legislation is important because state and local agencies are often closer to consumers' problems then federal agencies are, and therefore they are more effective.

As indicated in this chapter, as international business grows it is important to look at consumer protection laws around the world so that multinational companies are aware of their rights and duties.

REVIEW QUESTIONS

23-1. What is meant by the freedom-to-contract doctrine?

23-2. List the enforcement weapons the Federal Trade Commission has to use against a corporation or an individual who violates Section 5 of the Federal Trade Commission Act.

23-3. With which general types of deceptive advertising is the Federal Trade Commission most concerned?

23-4. What must franchisors disclose to prospective franchisees under the Federal Trade Commission rule governing franchising?

23-5. What must be disclosed by a consumer credit reporting agency under the Fair Credit Reporting Act?

23-6. What enforcement weapon does the FTC use against parties who violate the Equal Credit Opportunity Act? Explain.

REVIEW PROBLEMS

23-7. Robert Martin allowed a business associate, E. L. McBride, to use his American Express Card in a joint business venture that they were involved in. He orally authorized McBride to use the card and to charge anything up to $500. Martin received a statement from American Express three months later; the amount due on his account was $5,300. Martin refused to pay, claiming that he had not signed the invoices and therefore was liable, under the Truth-in-Lending Act, only up to $50 for "unauthorized use" of the card. American Express claimed that McBride was an "authorized" user and sued for the full balance of the account. Who won this case, and why?

23-8. Joe T. Morris received from the Credit Bureau of Cincinnati a bad credit rating based on a bankruptcy filing of his wife that had occurred before their marriage and two unpaid delinquent department-store accounts that were also his wife's. (The delinquent accounts had ended up in his file by accident.) He was denied credit in several instances. After he reported the error to the Credit Bureau, the bureau corrected his record, but by mistake it opened another account using the name "Joseph T. Morris" with the same inaccurate information. Once again, Morris was denied credit. He sued under the Fair Credit Reporting Act, requesting compensatory and punitive damages. Who won? Explain.

23-9. When Jerry Markham and Marcia Harris became engaged, they found a house that they wanted to buy and jointly applied for a mortgage to Colonial Mortgage Service Company, an agent of Illinois Federal Savings and Loan Association. Three days before the closing date for the purchase of the house, the loan committee of Illinois Federal rejected the couple's loan application, claiming that their separate incomes were not sufficient to meet the bank's criteria for "loan and job tenure." Markham and Harris sued, claiming a violation of the Equal Credit Opportunity

Act, which forbids discrimination based on marital status when the credit-worthiness of individuals is evaluated. Who won this case, and why?

23-10. Campbell Soup ran ads on television showing solid ingredients at the top of a bowl of soup in a "mock-up" display. The company placed marbles at the bottom of the bowl to force the solid ingredients to the top. The FTC claimed that this was a violation of Section 5 of the Federal Trade Commission Act in that it was deceptive advertising. Who won? Explain.

23-11. Tropicana Products, Inc., in a television advertisement had Bruce Jenner, U.S. Olympic decathlon champion, squeezing an orange. As the juice went into a Tropicana carton, he said, "It's pure, pasteurized juice as it comes from the orange." The voiceover then stated, "It's the only leading brand not made with concentrate and water." Coca-Cola, owner of Minute Maid, sued Tropicana for false advertising under the Lanham Act. It claimed that the juice was not freshly squeezed juice but was often heated and frozen before packaging. Who won this case, and why?

23-12. Millstone applied for a new automobile insurance policy after he moved from Washington, D.C. to St. Louis. He was told that a background investigation would be conducted in connection with the application. One week later he was notified that the policy would not be granted because of a report that the insurance company had received from Investigative Reports, a credit bureau. After repeated efforts to obtain his file, Millstone was informed by Investigative Reports that his former neighbors in Washington considered him a "hippie," a drug user, and a possible political dissident. Investigative Reports refused to discuss the matter further. Has Investigative Reports fulfilled its obligations to Millstone? Explain.

CASE PROBLEMS

23-13. *Reader's Digest* magazine tested seven leading cigarettes in order to find out which was lowest in tar and nicotine. It published the results, stating that the cigarette "whose smoke was lowest in nicotine" was Old Gold. The report went on to say that the differences between the brands was small and that no single brand was so superior to its competitors as to justify its selection as less harmful. Lorillard Company, manufacturer of Old Gold cigarettes, advertised: "Old Golds Found Lowest in Nicotine. Old Golds Found Lowest in Throat Irritating Tars and Resins. See Impartial Test by *Reader's Digest*, July issue." Was this deceptive advertising under Section 5 of the Federal Trade Commission Act? *P. Lorillard Co. v. FTC*, 186 F.2d 52 (1970)

23-14. The Colgate-Palmolive Company, manufacturer of a shaving cream, "Rapid Shave," sought to test the effectiveness of its cream on men's beards. In an advertisement broadcast on television, Colgate sought to show that its product could soften even sandpaper. However, when the advertisement was run, a sheet of Plexiglas with sand sprinkled on it was used in place of sandpaper. The FTC claimed that the commercial was deceptive and violated Section 5 of the FTC Act. Colgate claimed there was no deception because the viewer was simply being given a visual presentation of the test that had actually been made on sandpaper. Was there a violation of Section 5? *FTC v. Colgate Palmolive Co.*, 380 U.S. 374 (1965)

23-15. Kathleen Carroll, a single working woman, applied for an Exxon credit card in August 1976 and was advised by mail shortly thereafter that her application for credit was denied. No reason for the denial was given. Fourteen days after the denial she asked to be advised of the specific reasons. In a letter she was told by Exxon that a local reporting agency had not been able to supply sufficient information. The name of the credit bureau used by Exxon was not included in any of their communications. Upon filing the present lawsuit, Carroll was given the name and address of the credit bureau. Carroll did not have a major credit card, or a savings account and had been employed for one year. Did Carroll win the suit? What consumer protection statutes did she base it on? *Carroll v. Exxon*, 434 F. Supp. 557 (E.D. La. 1977)

23-16. For the price of $408 Linda Glaire obtained a seven-year membership in a health club owned and operated by LaLanne. The $408 was paid by Glaire over a two-year period at the rate of $17 monthly. The installment contract stated that there were no finance charges. The contract was sold to Universal Guidance Acceptance Corporation. LaLanne and Universal are in reality owned by the same shareholders, with Universal assisting LaLanne in financing. Glaire filed suit against LaLanne alleging violation of the Truth-in-Lending Act. Was there a violation of the Truth-in-Lending Act? *Glaire v. LaLanne-Paris Health Spa, Inc.*, 528 P.2d 357 (1974)

23-17. A key requirement of the Truth-in-Lending Act and Regulation Z is that each borrower receive two copies of the Notice of Right to Cancel. The lender gave Jacquelyn Elsner and her husband Max each one copy of the notice, along with other materials on the loan document they both signed. The Elsners later moved to tear up the loan agreement because they did not each receive two copies of the notice, which was a simple oversight by the lender. Is the loan good, or can they walk away? *Elsner v. Albrecht*, 1985 Mich. App. 72, 460 N.W.2d 232 (1990)

23-18. Seymour Roseman quit has job as an insurance agent after a company investigation found money missing from his account. The Retail Credit Company credit report on him had this statement in it: "We have handled [the investigation] at the home office in Boston and find that Roseman was employed as a debit agent [for the insurance company]. He resigned due to discovery of discrepancies in his accounts amounting to $314.84. This was all repaid by Roseman. His production in 1970, 1971, and 1972 was above average, and in 1973 and 1974, it was below average. This was the extent of the information available from [the insurance company] due to strict company policy." Roseman asked the credit company to check the accuracy of this information. The credit company did, confirmed its accuracy, and refused to remove the information from his credit history. He sued under the Fair Credit Reporting Act, claiming his rights had been violated. What was the result? *Roseman v. Retail Credit Co.*, 428 F. Supp 643 (E.D. Pa. 1977)

 On the Internet

http://www.state.nh.us/oag/cpb.html   Find out about the rights and protections of consumers in New Hampshire from this New Hampshire Consumer Protection and Antitrust Bureau site. This site provides an example of what one state does. Although not all states offer exactly the same protections, many similar protections are offered by all states.

http://www.lectlaw.com//tcos.html   Here is a 'lectric law library site that is a good place from which to begin your research about consumer protection issues.

http://www.agcm.it/inglese/b_links1.html   This site provides Australian and Canadian perspectives on consumer protection.

http://www.democrats.org.au/democrats/media/1997/subject/consumer. html   Find out about consumer protection in Australia from this site.

GLOSSARY

absolute privilege The right to make any statement, true or false, about someone and not be held liable for defamation.

acid rain Precipitation with a high acidic content (pH level of less than 5) caused by atmospheric pollutants.

act-of-state doctrine States that each sovereign nation is bound to respect the independence of every other sovereign nation and that the courts of one nation will not sit in judgment on the acts of the courts of another nation.

actual authority Includes expressed authority as well as implied authority, or that authority customarily given to an agent in an industry, trade, or profession.

administrative agency Any body that is created by the legislative branch to carry out specific duties.

administrative law Any rule (statute or regulation) that directly or indirectly affects an administrative agency.

administrative law judge (ALJ) A judge, selected on the basis of a merit exam, who is assigned to a specific administrative agency.

Administrative Procedure Act (APA) Establishes the standards and procedures federal administrative agencies must follow in their rule-making and adjudicative functions.

adversarial system System of litigation in which the judge hears evidence and arguments presented by both sides in a case and then makes an objective decision based on the facts and the law as presented by each side.

adverse possession Acquiring ownership of realty by openly treating it as one's own, with neither protest nor permission from the real owner, for a statutorily established period of time.

affirm Term used for an appellate court's decision to uphold the decision of a lower court in a case that has been appealed.

affirmative action plans Programs adopted by employers to increase the representation of women and minorities in their workforce.

Age Discrimination in Employment Act of 1967 (ADEA) Prohibits employers from refusing to hire, discharging, or discriminating against people in terms and conditions of employment on the basis of age.

agency A fiduciary relationship between two persons in which one (the agent) acts on behalf of, and is subject to the control of, the other (the principal).

agency by estoppel (apparent authority) An agency relationship in which the principal is estopped from denying that someone is the principal's agent after leading a third party to believe the person is an agent.

agency by implied authority Agency relationship in which customs and circumstances, rather than a detailed formal agreement, determine the agent's authority.

agency by ratification Agency relationship in which an unauthorized agent commits the principal to an agreement and the principal later accepts the unauthorized agreement, thus ratifying the agency relationship.

alternative dispute resolution (ADR) Resolving legal disputes through methods other than litigation, such as negotiation and settlement, arbitration, mediation, private trials, minitrials, and summary jury trial.

ambiguous Susceptible to two or more possible interpretations.

Americans With Disabilities Act of 1991 (ADA) Requires that employers make reasonable accomodations to the known disabilities of an otherwise qualified job applicant or employee with a disability, unless the necessary accommodation would impose an undue burden on the employer's business.

analogy A comparison based on the assumption that if two things are alike in some respect, they must be alike in other respects.

annual percentage rate (APR) The effective annual rate of interest being charged to a consumer by a creditor, which depends on the compounding period the creditor is using.

answer Defendant's response to the allegations in the plaintiff's complaint.

antidiscrimination/civil rights laws Laws designed to ensure that no one will be deprived of basic rights because of membership in a readily distinguishable minority.

appellate jurisdiction The power to review a previously made decision by the trial court.

appropriate bargaining unit May be an entire plant, a single department, or all employees of a single employee, as long as there is a mutuality of interest among the proposed members of the unit.

appropriation A privacy tort that consists of using a person's name or likeness for commercial gain without the person's permission.

arbitration A dispute-resolution method whereby the disputing parties submit their disagreement to a mutually agreed upon neutral decision maker or one provided for by statute.

arraignment Formal appearance of the defendant in court to answer the indictment by entering a plea of guilty or not guilty.

arrest To seize and hold under the authority of the law.

artisan's lien A lien that enables a creditor to recover payment from a debtor on labor and services provided on the debtor's personal property; for example, fixing a lawnmower.

assault Intentional placing of a person in fear or apprehension of an immediate, offensive bodily contact.

assignment The present transfer of an existing right.

assumption of the risk A defense to negligence based on showing that the plaintiff voluntarily and unreasonably encountered a known risk and that the harm that the plaintiff suffered was the harm that was risked.

attachment A court-ordered judgment allowing a local officer of the court to seize property of a debtor.

attorney-client privilege Provides that information furnished by a client to an attorney in confidence, in conjunction with a legal matter, may not be revealed by the attorney without the client's permission.

autonomous/semiautonomous work group A team of workers, led by either a supervisor appointed by management or a worker elected by the team, that determines for itself how it will accomplish the work task it is given to perform. Those groups with full authority over all subtasks, scheduling of overtime, and hiring of new team members are *autonomous*; those with less authority are *semiautonomous*.

award The arbitrator's decision.

bail An amount of money the defendant pays to the court upon release from custody as security that he or she will return for trial.

bailment A relationship in which one person (the bailor) transfers possession of personal property to another (the bailee) to be used in an agreed-upon manner for an agreed-upon period of time.

battery Intentional unwanted and offensive bodily contact.

bilateral contract The exchange of one promise for another promise.

bilateral investment treaty Treaty between two parties to outline conditions for investment in either country.

binding arbitration clause A provision in a contract mandating that all disputes arising under the contract be settled by arbitration.

blue sky laws State legislation providing for the regulation of securities.

bonds Long-term loans secured by a lien or mortgage on corporate assets.

boycott A refusal to deal with, purchase goods from, or work for a business.

bribery The offering, giving, soliciting, or receiving of money or any object of value for the purpose of influencing the judgment or conduct of a person in a position of trust, especially a government official.

broker A person engaged in the business of buying and selling securities for others' accounts.

business ethics The study of what makes up good and bad conduct as related to business activities and values.

business judgment rule A rule that says corporate officers and directors are not liable for honest mistakes of business judgment.

capital structure The percentage of each type of capital—debt, preferred stock, and common equity—used by the corporation.

case law Law resulting from judicial interpretations of constitutions and statutes.

Chicago School An approach to antitrust policy that is based solely on the goal of economic efficiency, or the maximization of consumer welfare.

civil law Law governing litigation between two private parties.

Civil Rights Act of 1871 Prohibits discrimination by state and local governments.

Civil Rights Act of 1866 Guarantees that all persons in the United States have the same right to make and enforce contracts and have the full and equal benefit of the law.

class-action suit A lawsuit brought by a member of a group of persons on behalf of all members of the group.

Clayton Act Prohibits price discrimination, tying and exclusive-dealing arrangements, and corporate mergers that substantially lessen competition or tend to create a monopoly in interstate commerce.

closed-end credit A credit arrangement in which credit is extended for a specific period of time, and the exact number of payments and the total amount due have been agreed upon between the borrower and the creditor.

closely held corporation One whose stock is not traded on the national securities exchanges but is privately held by a small group of people.

collective bargaining Negotiations between an employer and a union over, primarily, wages, hours, and terms and conditions of employment.

collusion Concerted action by two or more individuals or business entities in violation of the Sherman Act.

Commerce Clause Empowers Congress to regulate commerce with foreign nations, with Indian tribes, and among the states; found in Article I.

commercial impracticability Situation that makes performance of a contract unreasonably expensive, injurious, or costly to a party.

commercial speech Expression solely related to the economic interests of the speaker and the speaker's audience.

common stock A class of stock that entitles its owner to vote for the corporation's board of directors, to receive dividends, and to participate in the net assets upon liquidation of the corporation.

comparative negligence A defense that allocates recovery based on percentage of fault allocated to plaintiff and defendant; available in either pure or modified form.

compensatory damages Monetary damages awarded for a breach of contract that results in higher costs or lost profits for the injured party.

competency A party's ability to understand the nature of the transaction and the consequences of entering into it at the time the contract was entered into.

complaint The initial pleading in a case that states the names of the parties to the action, the basis for the court's subject matter jurisdiction, the facts on which the party's claim is based, and the relief that the party is seeking.

complete performance Completion of all the terms of the contract.

conclusion A position or stance on an issue; the goal toward which reasoning moves.

concurrent jurisdiction Applies to cases that may be heard in either the federal or the state court system.

condemnation The process whereby the government acquires the ownership of private property for a public use over the protest of the owner.

conditional estate The right to own and possess the land, subject to a condition whose happening (or nonhappening) will terminate the estate.

conditional privilege The right to make a false statement about someone and not be held liable for defamation provided the statement was made without malice.

condition precedent A particular event that must take place to give rise to a duty of performance of a contract.

condition subsequent A particular event that when following the execution of a contract terminates it.

conflict of interest A conflict that occurs when a corporate officer or director enters into a transaction with the corporation in which he or she has a personal interest.

conglomerate merger A merger in which the businesses of the acquiring and the acquired firm are totally unrelated.

conscious parallelism Identical actions (usually price increases) that are taken independently but nearly simultaneously by two or more leading companies in an industry.

consent order An agreement by a business to stop an activity an administrative agency alleges to be unlawful and to accept the remedy the agency imposes; no admission of guilt is necessary.

consideration A bargained-for exchange of promises in which a legal detriment is suffered by the promisee.

consumer expectations test A test used by courts to determine whether a product is so defective as to be unreasonably dangerous that asks whether the product performed as would be expected by a reasonable consumer.

contingency fee Agent's compensation that consists of a percentage of the amount the agent secured for the principal in a business transaction.

contract A legally enforceable exchange of promises or an exchange of a promise for an act.

Contract Clause Constitutional provision that prohibits the states from passing any laws that unreasonably impair contract obligations.

contributory negligence A defense to negligence that consists of proving the plaintiff did not exercise the ordinary degree of care to protect against an unreasonable risk of harm and that this failure contributed to causing the plaintiff's harm.

conversion Intentional permanent removal of property from the rightful owner's possession and control.

cooperative A not-for-profit organization formed by individuals to market products.

co-ownership Ownership of land by multiple persons or business organizations; all tenants have an equal right to occupy all of the property.

copyright The exclusive legal right to reproduce, publish, and sell the fixed form of expression of an original creative idea.

corporate opportunity doctrine A doctrine, established by case law, that says corporate officers, directors, and agents cannot take personal advantage of an opportunity that in all fairness should have belonged to the corporation.

corporation An entity formed and authorized by state law to act as a single person and to raise capital by issuing stock to investors, who are the owners of the corporation.

counterclaim Defendant's statement of facts showing cause for action against the plaintiff and a request for appropriate relief.

creditor The lender in the transaction.

creditor-beneficiary contract One in which the promisee obtains a promise from the promisor to fulfill a legal obligation of the promisee to a third party.

criminal fraud Intentional use of some sort of misrepresentation to gain an advantage over another party.

criminal law Composed of federal and state statutes prohibiting wrongful conduct ranging from murder to fraud.

critical thinking skills The ability to understand the structure of an argument and apply a set of evaluative criteria to assess its merits.

cross-elasticity of demand, or **substitutability** If an increase in the price of one product leads consumers to purchase another product, the two products are substitutable and there is said to be cross-elasticity of demand.

cross-licensing An illegal practice in which two patent holders license each other to use their patented objects only on condition that neither will license anyone else to use those patented objects without the other's consent.

culture The learned norms of a society that are based on values, beliefs, and attitudes.

dealer A person engaged in the business of buying and selling securities for his or her own account.

debentures Unsecured long-term corporate loans.

debtor The borrower in the transaction.

deed Instrument of conveyance of property.

defamation Intentional publication (communication to a third party) of a false statement that is harmful to the plaintiff's reputation.

defendant Party against whom an action is being brought.

deposition Pretrial testimony by witnesses who are examined under oath.

disclaimer Disavowal of liability for breach of warranty by the manufacturer or seller of a good in advance of the sale of the good.

disclosed principal One whose identity is known by the third party when the latter enters into an agreement negotiated by the agent.

discovery The pretrial gathering of information from each other by the parties.

disparagement Intentionally defaming a business product or service.

disparate impact cases Discrimination cases in which the employer's facially neutral policy or practice has a discriminatory effect on employees that belong to a protected class.

disparate treatment cases Discrimination cases in which the employer treats one employee less favorably than another because of that employee's color, race, religion, sex, or national origin.

donative intent Intent to transfer ownership to another at the time the donor makes actual or constructive delivery of the gift to the donee.

donee-beneficiary contract One in which the promisee obtains a promise from the promisor to make a gift to a third party.

due diligence defense An affirmative defense raised in lawsuits charging misrepresentation in a registration statement. It is based on the defendant's claim to have had reasonable grounds to believe that all statements in the registration statement were true and no omission of material fact had been made. This defense is not available to the issuer of the security.

Due Process Clause Provides that no one can be deprived of life, liberty, or property without "due process of law"; found in Fifth Amendment.

duress Any wrongful act or threat that prevents a party from exercising free will when executing a contract.

duress defense An affirmative defense claiming that the defendant was forced to commit the wrongful act by threat of immediate bodily harm or loss of life.

easement An irrevocable right to use some portion of another's land for a specific purpose.

economic strike A nonviolent work stoppage for the purpose of obtaining better terms and conditions of employment under a collective bargaining agreement.

effluent limitations Maximum allowable amounts of pollutants that can be discharged from a point source within a given time period.

embezzlement The wrongful conversion of the property of another by one who is lawfully in possession of that property.

eminent domain The constitutional right of the government to take privately owned real property for a public purpose in exchange for a just compensation to the owner.

employer-employee relationship One in which an agent (employee) who works for pay and is subject to the control of the principal (employer) may enter into contractual relationships on the latter's behalf.

employer-independent contractor relationship One in which the agent (independent contractor) is hired by the principal (employer) to do a specific job but is not controlled with respect to physical conduct or details of work performance.

employment-at-will doctrine A contract of employment for an indeterminate term is terminable at will by either the employer or the employee; the traditional "American rule" governing employer-employee relations.

enabling legislation Legislation that grants lawful power to an administrative agency to issue rules, investigate potential violations of rules or statutes, and adjudicate disputes.

enterprise liability (market share theory) A theory of recovery in liability cases according to which damages are apportioned among all the manufacturers of a product, based on their market share at the time the plaintiffs' cause of action arose.

entrapment An affirmative defense claiming that the idea for the crime did not originate with the defendant but was put into the defendant's mind by a police officer or other government official.

Environmental Impact Statement (EIS) A statement that must be prepared for every major federal activity that would significantly affect the quality of the human environment.

Environmental Protection Agency (EPA) The federal agency charged with responsibility for conducting an integrated, coordinated attack on all forms of pollution of the environment.

Equal Pay Act of 1963 Prohibits wage discrimination based on sex.

equitable remedies Nonmonetary damages awarded for breach of contract when monetary damages would be inadequate or impracticable.

estoppel A legal bar to either alleging or denying a fact because of one's own previous words or actions to the contrary.

ethical norms Standards of conduct that we consider good or virtuous.

ethics The study of what makes up good and bad conduct inclusive of related actions and values.

exchange market A securities market that provides a physical facility for the buying and selling of stocks and prescribes the number and qualifications of its broker-members. These brokers buy and sell stocks through the exchange's registered specialists, who are dealers on the floor of the exchange.

exclusive-dealing contract Agreement in which one party requires another party to sell and promote only the brand of goods supplied by the first party.

exclusive federal jurisdiction Applies to cases that may be heard only in the federal court system.

executed contract One for which all the terms have been performed.

executive administrative agency An agency located within a department of the executive branch of government; heads and appointed members serve at the pleasure of the president.

executive exemption Exemption to the ADEA that allows mandatory retirement of executives at age 65.

executive power The power delegated by Congress to an administrative agency to investigate whether the rules enacted by the agency have been properly followed by businesses and individuals.

executory contract One for which all the terms have not been performed.

express contract An exchange of oral or written promises between parties that is enforceable in a court of law.

expressed agency (agency by agreement) Agency relationship formed through oral or written agreement.

expressed authority Authority that arises from specific statements made by the principal (employer) to the agent (employee).

express warranty A warranty that is clearly stated by the seller or manufacturer.

expropriation The taking of private property by a host country government for political or economic reasons.

fair use doctrine A legal doctrine providing that a copyrighted work may be reproduced for purposes of "criticism, comment, news reporting, teaching (including multiple copies for classroom use), scholarship, and research."

false imprisonment The intentional restraint or confinement, by force or threat of force, of a person against that person's will and without justification.

false light A privacy tort that consists of intentionally taking actions that would lead observers to make false assumptions about the person.

Family and Medical Leave Act (FMLA) A law designed to guarantee that workers facing a medical catastrophe or certain specified family responsibilities will be able to take needed time off from work without pay, but without losing their medical benefits or job.

feasible alternatives test A test used by courts to determine whether a product is so defective as to be unreasonably dangerous; it focuses on whether, given available alternatives, the product's design was reasonable; the risk-utility test.

federalism A system of government in which power is divided between a central authority and constituent political units.

federal jurisdiction See exclusive federal jurisdiction.

federal preemption Doctrine stating that in an area in which federal regulation is pervasive, state legislation cannot stand.

federal supremacy Principle that states that any state or local law that directly conflicts with the federal Constitution, laws, or treaties is void.

Federal Trade Commission (FTC) An independent regulatory agency entrusted by Congress with promoting a competitive business environment.

fee simple absolute The right to own and possess the land against all others, without conditions.

felony A serious crime that is punishable by death or imprisonment in a penitentiary.

Fifth Amendment Protects individuals against self-incrimination and double jeopardy and guarantees them the right to trial by jury; protects both individuals and businesses through the Due Process Clause and the Takings Clause.

First Amendment Guarantees freedom of speech, press, and religion and the right to peacefully assemble and to petition the government for redress of grievances.

first appearance Appearance of the defendant before a magistrate, who determines whether there was probable cause for the arrest.

fixture An item that is initially a piece of personal property but is later attached permanently to the realty and is treated as part of the realty.

foreign subsidiary A company that is wholly or partially owned and controlled by a company based in another country.

Fourteenth Amendment Applies the entire Bill of Rights, excepting parts of the Fifth Amendment, to the states.

Fourth Amendment Protects the right of individuals to be secure in their persons, homes, and personal property by prohibiting the government from conducting unreasonable searches of individuals and seizing their property.

franchising A commercial agreement between a party that owns a trade name or trademark (the franchisor) and a party that sells or distributes goods or services using that trade name or trademark (the franchisee).

fraud Misrepresentation of a material fact made with intent to deceive the other party to a contract, who reasonably relied upon the misrepresentation and was injured as a result. *See also* criminal fraud.

freedom-to-contract doctrine Parties that are legally competent are allowed to enter into whatever contracts they wish.

full warranty Under the Magnuson-Moss Warranty Act, a written protection for buyers that guarantees free repair of a defective product. If the product can't be fixed, the consumer must be given a choice of a refund or a replacement free of charge.

future interest The present right to possess and own the land in the future.

garnishment An order of the court granted to a creditor to seize wages or bank accounts of a debtor.

general partnership A partnership in which management responsibilities and profits are divided (usually equally) among the partners, and all partners have unlimited personal liability for the partnership's debts.

general warranty deed A deed that promises that the grantor owns the land and has the right to convey it and that the land has no encumbrances other than those stated in the deed.

genuine assent Assent to a contract that is free of fraud, duress, undue influence, and mutual mistake.

good-faith bargaining Following procedural standards laid out in Section 8 of the NLRA; failure to bargain in good faith, by either the employer or the union, is an unfair labor practice.

grand jury A group of 12 to 23 citizens convened in private to decide whether enough evidence exists to try the defendant for a felony.

guaranty Similar to a suretyship except that the third person is secondarily liable: i.e., is required to pay only after the debtor has defaulted.

Harvard School An approach to antitrust policy that is based on the desirability of preserving competition to prevent the accumulation of economic and political power, the dislocation of labor, and market inefficiency.

hazardous waste Any waste material that is ignitable, corrosive, reactive, or toxic when ingested or absorbed.

hedging Exporting companies contract with a bank that guarantees the exporter a fixed number of U.S. dollars in exchange for payment of the goods it receives in a foreign currency. The exporting company pays a fee to the bank. The fee is based upon the risk the bank is taking that the foreign currency will fluctuate.

Hertindahl-Hirschman Index (HHI) An index calculated by adding the squares of the shares of the relevant market held by each firm in a horizontal merger to determine the competitive effects of the merger. In using the HHI to decide whether to challenge a merger, the Justice Department considers both the level of the postmerger HHI and the increase in the HHI caused by the merger.

horizontal boycott A concerted refusal by a trade association to deal with members that do not follow the association's regulations.

horizontal division of markets Collusion between two or more competitors to divide markets, customers, or product lines among themselves.

horizontal merger A merger between two or more companies producing the same or a similar product and competing for sales in the same geographic market.

horizontal price fixing Collusion between two or more competitors to, directly or indirectly, set prices for a product or service.

horizontal restraint of trade Restraint of trade that occurs between competitors at the same level of the marketing structure.

hostile bid A tender offer that is opposed by the management of the target company.

Howey test The three-part test used to determine whether an instrument or contract is a security for purposes of federal securities laws: (1) common enterprise and (2) expectation of profit that is (3) derived from efforts of others.

implied contract One that is established by the conduct of a party rather than by the party's written or spoken words.

implied covenant of good faith and fair dealing An exception to the employment-at-will doctrine that is based on the theory that every employment contract, even an unwritten one, contains the implicit understanding that the parties will deal fairly with each other.

implied warranty A warranty that automatically arises out of a transaction.

implied warranty of fitness for a particular purpose A warranty that arises when the seller tells the consumer a good is fit for a specific use.

implied warranty of merchantability A warranty that a good is reasonably fit for ordinary use.

impossibility of performance Situation in which the party cannot legally or physically perform the contract.

indemnity Obligation of the principal to reimburse the agent for any losses the agent incurs while acting on the principal's behalf.

independent administrative agency An agency whose appointed heads and members serve for fixed terms and cannot be removed by the president except for reasons defined by Congress.

indictment A formal written accusation in a felony case.

information A formal written accusation in a misdemeanor case.

informational picketing Picketing designed to truthfully inform the public of a labor dispute.

injunction Temporary or permanent court order preventing a party to a contract from doing something.

in personam jurisdiction (jurisdiction over the person) The power of a court to render a decision that affects the legal rights of a specific person.

in rem jurisdiction The power of a court to render a decision that affects property directly rather than the owner of the property.

insanity defense An affirmative defense claiming that the defendant's mental condition precluded understanding the wrongful nature of the act he or she committed or distinguishing wrong from right in general.

insider trading The use of material, nonpublic information received from a corporate source by someone who has a fiduciary obligation to shareholders and potential investors and who benefits from trading on such information.

intangible property Personal property that does not have a physical form and is usually evidenced in writings (e.g., an insurance policy).

intentional infliction of emotional distress Intentionally engaging in outrageous conduct that is likely to cause extreme emotional pain to the person toward whom the conduct is directed.

intentional interference with a contract Knowingly and successfully taking action for the purpose of enticing a third party to breach a valid contract with the plaintiff.

intentional tort A civil wrong that involves taking some purposeful action that the defendant knew, or should have known, would harm the person, property, or economic interests of the plaintiff.

international franchising A contractual agreement whereby a company (licensor) permits another company (licensee) to market its trader marked goods or services in a particular nation.

international licensing A contractual agreement by which a company (licensor) makes its intellectual property available to a foreign individual or company (licensee) for payment.

international trade The export of goods and services from a country and the import of goods and services into a country.

invasion of privacy A privacy tort that consists of encroaching upon the solitude, seclusion, or personal affairs of someone who has the right to expect privacy.

joint/several liability The legal principle that makes two or more people liable for a judgment, either as individuals or in any proportional combination. Under this principle, a person who is partially reponsible for a tort can end up being completely liable for damages.

joint stock company A partnership agreement in which members of the company own shares that are transferable, but all goods are held in the name of the members, who assume partnership liability.

joint tenancy Form of co-ownership of real property in which all owners have equal shares in the property, may sell their shares without the consent of the other owners, and may have their interest attached by creditors.

joint venture Relationship between two or more persons or corporations; or an association between a foreign multinational and an agency of the host government, or a host country national; set up for a specific business undertaking or a limited time period.

judicial activism A judicial philosophy that says the courts need to take an active role in encouraging political, economic, and social change.

judicial power The power delegated by Congress to an administrative agency to adjudicate cases through an administrative proceeding; includes the power to issue a complaint, hold a hearing by an adminstrative law judge, and issue either an initial decision or a recommended decision to the head(s) of an agency.

judicial restraint A judicial philosophy that says courts should refrain from determining the constitutionality of a legislative act unless absolutely necessary and that social, political, and economic change should come out of the political process.

jurisdiction The power of a court to hear a case and render a binding decision.

jurisdictional picketing Picketing by one union to protest an assignment of jobs to another union's members.

jurisprudence The science or philosphy of law; law in its most generalized form.

labor-management committee A forum in which workers communicate directly with upper management. May be illegal under the NLRA if the committee has an impact on working conditions, unless all workers in a bargaining unit or a plant participate *or* the employees on the committee are carrying out a traditional management function.

laissez-faire The concept that the owners of business and industry should be allowed to compete without government intervention or regulation.

Landrum-Griffith Act Governs the internal operation of labor unions.

larceny The secretive and wrongful taking and carrying away of the personal property of another with the intent to permanently deprive the rightful owner of its use or possession.

lease The contract that transfers possessory interest in a property from the owner (lessor) to the tenant (lessee).

leasehold The right to possess property for an agreed-upon period of time stated in a lease.

legal acceptance An acceptance that shows objective intent to enter into the contract, that is communicated by proper means to the offeror, and that mirrors the terms of the offer.

legal object Contract subject matter that is lawful under statutory and case law.

legal offer An offer that shows objective intent to enter into the contract, is definite, and is communicated to the offeree.

legislative power The power delegated by Congress to an administrative agency to make rules that must be adhered to by individuals and businesses regulated by the agency; these rules have the force of law.

letter of deficiency Informal letter issued by the SEC indicating what corrections need to be made in a registration statement for it to become effective.

libel Publication of a defamatory statement in permanent form.

lien A claim on a debtor's property that must be satisfied before any creditor can make a claim.

life estate The right to own and possess the land until one dies.

limited liability Liability limited to the amount of one's investment; the kind of liability that pertains to corporate shareholders.

limited liability corporation (LLC) A hybrid corporation-partnership like the Subchapter S corporation, but with far fewer restrictions.

limited partnership A partnership that has one general partner, who is responsible for managing the business, and one or more limited partners, who invest in the partnership but do not participate in its management and whose liability is limited to the amount of capital they contribute.

limited warranty Under the Magnuson-Moss Warranty Act, any written warranty that does not meet the conditions of a full warranty.

liquidated damages Monetary damages for nonperformance that are stipulated in a clause in the contract.

litigation A dispute-resolution process that involves going through the judicial system; a lawsuit.

long-arm statute A statute authorizing a court to obtain jurisdiction over an out-of-state defendant when that party has sufficient minimum contacts with a state.

malpractice suits Service liability suits brought against professionals, usually based on a theory of negligence, breach of contract, or fraud.

mandatory subjects of collective bargaining Subjects over which the parties must bargain, including rates of pay, wages, hours of employment, and other terms and conditions of employment.

manifest program A program that attempts to see that hazardous wastes are properly transported to disposal facilities licensed by the EPA so that the agency will have an accurate record (manifest) of the location and amount of all hazardous wastes.

market share theory *See* enterprise liability.

mechanic's lien A lien placed on the real property of a debtor when the latter does not pay for the work done by the creditor.

mediation An alternative dispute-resolution method in which the disputing parties select a neutral party to help them reconcile their differences by facilitating communication and suggesting ways to solve their problems.

merger One company's acquisition of another company's assets or stock in such a way that the second company is absorbed by the first.

mineral rights The legal ability to dig or mine the minerals from the earth below the surface of one's land.

minitrial An alternative dispute-resolution method in which lawyers for each side present the case for their side at a proceeding refereed by a neutral adviser, but settlement authority usually resides with senior executives of the disputing corporations.

Miranda rights Certain legal rights—such as the right to remain silent to avoid self-incrimination and the right to an attorney—that a suspect must be immediately informed of upon arrest.

misappropriation Use of an unsolicited idea for a product, service, or marketing method without compensating the originator of the idea.

misdemeanor A less serious crime than a felony that is punishable by fine or imprisonment in a local jail.

mistake Error as to material fact. A *bilateral mistake* is one made by both parties; a *unilateral mistake* is one made by only one party to the contract.

mistake-of-fact-defense An affirmative defense claiming that a mistake made by the defendant vitiates criminal intent.

mock jury Group of individuals, demographically matched to the actual jurors in a case, in front of whom lawyers practice their arguments before presenting their case to the actual jury.

modify Term used for an appellate court's decision that, although the lower court's decision was correct, it granted an inappropriate remedy that needs to be changed.

monetary damages Dollar sums awarded for a breach of contract; "legal" remedies.

monopoly An economic market situation in which a single business has the power to fix the price of goods or services.

motion to dismiss Defendant's application to the court to put the case out of judicial consideration because even if the plaintiff's factual allegations are true, the plaintiff is not entitled to relief.

multinational (transnational) corporation One whose production, distribution, ownership, and management span several nations.

national ambient air quality standards (NAAQSs) A two-tiered set of standards developed for the chief conventional air pollutants: primary standards, designed to protect public health; and secondary standards, designed to protect public welfare.

National Institute for Occupational Safety and Health (NIOSH) A research facility established by the OSH Act to identify occupational health and safety problems, develop controls to prevent occupational accidents and diseases, and disseminate its findings, particularly to OSHA.

National Labor Relations Board (NLRB) The administrative agency set up to interpret and enforce the Wagner Act (NLRA).

negligence Failure to live up to the standard of care that a reasonable person would meet to protect others from an unreasonable risk of harm.

negligence per se Legal doctrine that says when a statute has been enacted to prevent a certain type of harm and the defendant violates that statute, causing that type of harm to befall the plaintiff, the plaintiff may use proof of the violation as proof of negligence.

negligent tort A civil wrong that involves a failure to meet the standard of care a reasonable person would meet, and because of that failure, harm to another resulted.

negotiation and settlement An alternative dispute-resolution method in which the disputant parties come together informally to try to resolve their differences.

nolo contendere A plea of no contest that subjects the defendant to punishment but is not an admission of guilt.

nominal damages Monetary damages of a very small amount (e.g., $1) awarded to a party that is injured by a breach of contract but cannot show real damages.

noninvestment company A company whose primary business is not in investing or trading in securities.

nonprice vertical restraint Restraint used by a manufacturer to limit the territory in which a retailer may sell the manufacturer's products and the number of stores the retailer can operate, as well as the customers the retailer can serve, in a location.

norm A standard of conduct.

notes Short-term loans.

nuisance An unreasonable interference with someone else's use and enjoyment of his land.

Occupational Safety and Health Act (OSH Act) A regulatory act designed to provide a workplace free from recognized hazards that are likely to cause death or serious harm to employees.

Occupational Safety and Health Administration (OSHA) The agency responsible, under the OSH Act, for setting and enforcing standards for occupational health and safety.

Occupational Safety and Health Review Commission (OSHRC) An independent body that reviews OSHA citations, penalties, and abatement periods that are contested by an employer.

open-end credit Credit extended on an account for an indefinite time period so that the debtor can keep charging on the account, up to a certain amount, while paying the outstanding balance either in full or in installment payments.

original jurisdiction The power to initially hear and decide (try) a case.

organizational (recognitional) picketing Picketing designed to force the employer to recognize and bargain with an uncertified union.

over-the-counter (OTC) market A securities market that has no physical facility and no membership qualifications and whose broker-dealers are market makers who buy and sell stocks directly from the public.

parens patriae suit A lawsuit bright by a state attorney general on behalf of the citizenry of that state.

parol evidence rule When parties have executed a written agreement that is complete on its face, oral agreements made prior to, or at the same time as, the written agreement that vary, alter, or contradict it are invalid.

partially disclosed principal One whose identity is not known to the third party at the time of the agreement, though the third party does know the agent represents a principal.

partnership A voluntary association of two or more persons formed to carry on a business as co-owners for profit.

par value The nominal or face value of a stock or bond.

patent Grants the holder the exclusive right to produce, sell, and use a product, process, invention, machine, or asexually reproduced plant for 20 years.

permissive subjects of collective bargaining Subjects that are not primarily about conditions of employment and therefore need not be bargained over.

per se standard A legal standard that is applicable to restraints of trade that are inherently anticompetitive. Because such restraints are automatically in violation of Section 1 of the Sherman Act, courts do not balance pro- and anticompetitive effects in such cases.

personal property All property that is not real property; may be tangible or intangible.

pesticide Any substance designed to prevent, destroy, repel, or mitigate any pest or to be used as a plant regulator or defoliant.

petit jury A jury of 12 citizens impaneled to decide on the facts at issue in a criminal case and to pronounce the defendant guilty or not guilty.

petty crime A minor crime punishable, under federal statutes, by fine or incarceration of no more than six months.

picketing The stationing of individuals outside an employer's place of business to inform passers-by of the facts of a labor dispute.

piercing the corporate veil A legal doctrine whereby, when a corporation is used for improper purposes, the court can disregard the existence of the corporate entity and hold the shareholders liable for the corporation's debts and obligations.

plaintiff Party on whose behalf the complaint is filed.

plea bargaining The negotiation of an agreement between a defendant's attorney and the prosecutor whereby the defendant pleads guilty to a certain charge or charges in exchange for the dropping or reduction of the charges by the prosecution.

pleadings Papers filed by a party in court and then served on the opponent in a civil lawsuit.

point sources Distinct places from which pollutants are discharged into water, such as papermills, electric utility plants, sewage treatment facilities, and factories.

police power The states' retained authority to pass laws to protect the health, safety, and welfare of the community.

power of attorney An agency agreement used to give an agent authority to sign legal documents on behalf of the principal.

predatory pricing Pricing below the average or marginal cost in order to drive out competition.

preferred stock A class of stock that entitles its owner to special preferences relating to either dividends or the distribution of assets.

premerger notification requirement The legislatively mandated requirement that certain types of firms notify the FTC and the Justice Department 30 days before finalizing a merger so that these agencies can investigate and challenge any mergers they find anticompetitive.

preponderance of evidence A legal standard whereby a bare majority (51 percent) of the evidence is sufficient to justify a ruling.

price discrimination A price differential that is below the average variable cost for the seller; considered predatory, and therefore illegal, under the Clayton Act.

primary ethical norms The four norms that provide the major ethical direction for the laws governing business behavior: freedom, security, justice, and efficiency.

primary-line injury A form of price discrimination in which a seller attempts to put a local competitive firm out of business by lowering its prices only in the region where the local firm sells its products.

principal-agent relationship One in which the principal gives the agent expressed or actual authority to act on the former's behalf.

private international law Law that governs the relationships between private parties involved in international transactions. Includes international business law.

private law Law dealing with the enforcement of private duties.

private trial An alternative dispute-resolution method in which cases are tried, usually in private, by a referee who is selected by the disputants and empowered by statute to enter a binding judgment.

probable cause The reasonable inference from the available facts and circumstances that the suspect committed the crime.

procedural due process Procedural steps to which individuals are entitled before losing their life, liberty, or property.

procedural rule A rule that governs the internal processes of an administrative agency.

professional corporation One organized by doctors, dentists, lawyers, accountants, and other professionals specified in state statutes.

property A bundle of rights, in relation to others, to possess, use and dispose of a tangible or intangible object.

prospectus The first part of the registration statement the SEC requires from issuers of new securities. It contains material information about the business and its management, the offering itself, the use to be made of the funds obtained, and certain financial statements.

proxy A document by which a shareholder of a publicly held company can transfer his or her right to vote at a shareholders' meeting to a second party.

public disclosure of private facts A privacy tort that consists of unwarranted disclosure of a private fact about a person.

public international law Law that governs the relationships between nation-states.

public law Law dealing with the relationship of government to individual citizens.

publicly held corporation One whose stock is traded on at least one national securities exchange.

public policy exception An exception to the employment-at-will doctrine that makes it unlawful to dismiss an employee for taking certain actions in the public interest.

puffery An exaggerated recommendation made in a sales talk to promote the product.

punitive damages Monetary damages awarded in excess of compensatory damages for the sole purpose of deterring similar conduct in the future.

quality circle A small group of workers who voluntarily meet on a regular basis, under the leadership of a supervisor, to discuss work problems and to recommend solutions to management.

quasi-contract A court-imposed agreement to prevent the unjust enrichment of one party when the parties had not really agreed to an enforceable contract.

quitclaim deed A deed that simply transfers to the grantee the interest that the grantor owns in the property.

Racketeer Influenced Corrupt Organizations Act (RICO) Prohibits persons employed by or associated with an enterprise from engaging in a pattern of racketeering activity, which is broadly defined to include almost all white collar crimes as well as acts of violence.

real property Land and everything permanently attached to it.

reason An explanation or justification provided as support for a conclusion.

red herring A preliminary prospectus that contains most of the information that will appear in the final prospectus, except for the price of the securities. The "red herring" prospectus may be distributed to potential buyers during the waiting period, but no sales may be finalized during this period.

Regulation Z A group of rules, set forth by the Federal Reserve Board to implement some provisions of the Truth-in-Lending Act, that require lenders to disclose certain information to borrowers.

Rehabilitation Act of 1973 Prohibits discrimination in employment against otherwise qualified persons who have a handicap. Applies only to the federal government, employers who have contracts with the federal government, and parties who administer programs receiving federal financial assistance.

reformation Correction of terms in an agreement so that they reflect the true understanding of the parties.

remand Term used for an appellate court's decision that an error was committed that may have affected the outcome of the case and that therefore the case must be returned to the lower court.

rescission Cancellation of a contract.

res ipsa loquitur Legal doctrine that allows a judge or a jury to infer negligence on the basis of the fact that accidents of the type that happened to the plaintiff generally do not occur in the absence of negligence on the part of someone in the defendant's position.

respondeat superior Legal doctrine imposing liability on a principal for torts committed by an agent who is employed by the principal and subject to the principal's control.

restraint of trade Action that interferes with the economic law of supply and demand.

restrictive covenants Promises by the owner, generally included in the deed, to use or not to use the land in particular ways.

reverse Term used for an appellate court's decision that the lower court's decision was incorrect and cannot be allowed to stand.

reverse discrimination Discrimination in favor of members of groups that have been previously discriminated against; claim usually raised by white males.

rule-of-reason standard A legal standard that holds that only unreasonable restraints of trade violate Section 1 of the Sherman Act. If the court determines an action's anticompetitive effects outweigh its pro-competitive effects, the restraint is unreasonable.

rules of civil procedure The rules governing proceedings in a civil case; federal rules of procedure apply in all federal courts, and state rules apply in state courts.

scienter Knowledge that a representation is false.

secondary boycott A boycott against one employer to force it to cease doing business with another employer with whom the union has a dispute.

secondary-line injury A form of price discrimination in which a seller offers a discriminatory price to one buyer but not to another buyer.

Securities and Exchange Commission (SEC) The federal administrative agency charged with overall responsibility for the regulation of securities, their registration and trading to see that investors receive "full and fair" disclosure of all material facts with regard to any public offering of securities. It has wide enforcement powers to protect investors against price manipulation, insider trading, and other dishonest dealings.

security A stock or bond or any other instrument or interest that represents an investment in a common enterprise with reasonable expectations of profits that are derived solely from the efforts of those other than the investor.

separation of powers Constitutional doctrine whereby the legislative branch enacts laws and appropriates funds, the executive branch sees that the laws are faithfully executed, and the judicial branch interprets the laws.

service Providing the defendant with a summons and a copy of the complaint.

sexual harassment Unwelcome sexual advances, requests for sexual favors, and other verbal or physical conduct of a sexual nature that explicitly or implicitly makes submission a term or condition of employment or that creates an intimidating, hostile, or offensive environment.

shadow jury Group of individuals, demographically matched to the actual jurors in a case, that sits in the courtroom during a trial and then "deliberates" at the end of each day so that lawyers have continuous feedback of how their case is going.

shelf registration Procedure whereby large corporations can file a registration statement for securities it wishes to sell over a period of time rather than immediately.

Sherman Act Makes illegal every combination, contract, or conspiracy that is an unreasonable restraint of trade when this concerted action involves interstate commerce.

short-swing profits Profits made by directors, officers, or owners of 10 percent of the securities of a corporation as a result of buying and selling the securities within a six-month period.

sick building syndrome Indoor air pollution caused by the absence of fresh air in overly insulated new buildings and by the emission of harmful substances found in many building materials and office furnishings.

slander Spoken defamatory statement.

social responsibility Concern of business entities about profit and non-profit activities and their unintended impact upon others directly or indirectly involved.

sole proprietorship A business owned by one person, who has sole control over management and profits.

sovereign immunity doctrine States that a government expropriating foreign-owned private property is immune from the jurisdiction of courts in the owner's country.

specific performance A court order compelling a party to perform in such a way as to meet the terms of the contract.

standing The legal status necessary to file a lawsuit.

state-of-the-art defense A product liability defense based on adherence to existing technologically feasible standards at the time the product was manufactured.

state court jurisdiction Applies to cases that may be heard only in the state court system.

state implementation plan (SIP) A plan, required of every state, that explains how the state will meet federal air pollution standards.

statute of limitations A statute that bars actions arising more than a specified number of years after the cause of the action arises.

statute of repose A statute that bars actions arising more than a specified number of years after the product was purchased.

statutory law Law made by the legislative branch of government.

stock The capital that a corporation raises through the sale of shares that entitle their holders to certain rights of ownership.

stock option A stock warrant issued to employees; cannot be traded.

stock warrant A document authorizing its holder to purchase a stated number of shares of stock at a stated price, usually for a stated period of time; may be freely traded.

strict liability offense One for which no state of mind is required.

strict liability tort A civil wrong that involves taking action that is so inherently dangerous under the circumstances of its performance that no amount of due care can make it safe.

strike A temporary concerted withdrawal of labor.

Subchapter S corporation A business that is organized like a corporation but, under Internal Revenue Code Subchapter S, is treated like a partnership for tax purposes so long as it abides by certain restrictions pertaining to stock, shareholders, and affiliations.

subject matter jurisdiction The power of a court to render a decision in a particular type of case.

submission agreement Separate agreement providing that a specific dispute be resolved through arbitration.

substantial performance Completion of nearly all the terms of the contract plus an honest effort to complete the rest of the terms coupled with no willful departure from any of the terms.

substantive due process Requirement that laws depriving individuals of liberty or property be fair.

substantive rule A rule that creates, defines, or regulates the legal rights of administrative agencies and the parties they regulate.

summary jury trial An alternative dispute-resolution method that consists of an abbreviated trial, a nonbinding jury verdict, and a settlement conference.

summons Order by a court to appear before it at a certain time and place.

Superfund A fund authorized by the CERCLA to cover the costs of cleaning up hazardous-waste disposal sites whose owners cannot be found or are unwilling or unable to pay for the cleanup.

Supremacy Clause Provides that the U.S. Constitution and all laws and treaties of the United States constitute the supreme law of the land; found in Article V.

suretyship A contract between a third party and a creditor that allows the third party to pay the debt of the debtor; the surety is primarily liable.

syndicate An investment group that privately agrees to come together for the purpose of financing a large commercial project that none of the syndicate members could finance alone.

Taft-Hartley Act Bars unions from engaging in specified unfair labor practices, makes collective bargaining agreements enforceable in U.S. district courts, and provides a civil damages remedy for parties injured by certain prohibited union activities.

Takings Clause Provides that if the government takes private property for public use, it must pay the owner just compensation; found in Fifth Amendment.

tangible property Personal property that is material and movable (e.g., furniture).

technology-driven standards Standards that take account of existing levels of technology and require the best control system possible given the limits of that technology.

technology-forcing standards Standards of pollution control set primarily on the basis of health considerations, with the assumption that once regulators have set the standards, industry will be forced to develop the technology to meet them.

tenancy by the entirety Form of co-ownership of real property, allowed only to married couples, in which one owner cannot sell without the consent of the other and the creditors of only one owner cannot attach the property.

tenancy in common Form of co-ownership of real property in which owners may have equal or unequal shares of the property, may sell their shares without the consent of the other owners, and may have their interest attached by creditors.

tender offer A public offer by an individual or corporation made directly to the shareholders of another corporation in an effort to acquire the targeted corporation at a specific price.

tertiary-line injury A form of price discrimination in which a discrimatory price is passed along from a secondary-line party to a favored party at the next level of distribution.

testimonial A statement by a public figure professing the merits of some product or service.

title Ownership of property.

Title VII The statute that prohibits discrimination in hiring, firing, or other terms and conditions of employment on the basis of race, color, religion, sex, or national origin.

tort An injury to another's person or property; a civil wrong.

toxic substance Any chemical or mixture whose manufacture, processing, distribution, use, or disposal presents an unreasonable risk of harm to human health or the environment.

trademark A distinctive mark, word, design, picture, or arrangement used by the producer of a product that tends to cause consumers to identify the product with the producer.

trade secret A process, product, method of operation, or compilation of information used in a business that is not known to the public and that may bestow a competitive advantage on the business.

trespass to personalty Intentionally exercising dominion and control over another's personal property.

trespass to realty (trespass to real property) Intentionally entering the land of another or causing an object to be placed on the land of another without the landowner's permission.

trust A business arrangement in which owners of stocks in several companies place their securities with trustees, who jointly manage the companies and pay out a specific share of their earnings to the securities holders.

24-hour rule Prohibits both union representatives and employers from making speeches to "captive audiences" of employees within 24 hours of a representation election.

tying arrangement A restraint of trade wherein the seller permits a buyer to purchase one product or service only if the buyer agrees to purchase a second product or service. For example, a patent holder issues a license to use a patented object on condition that the licensee agree to also buy nonpatented products from the patent holder.

Ultramares Doctrine Rule making accountants liable only to those in a privity of contract relationship with the accountant.

underwriter Investment banking firm that agrees to purchase a securities issue from the issuer, usually on a fixed date at a fixed price, with a view to eventually selling the securities to brokers, who, in turn, sell them to the public.

undisclosed principal One whose identity and existence are both unknown to the third party.

undue influence Mental coercion exerted by one party over the other party to the contract.

unfair competition Entering into business for the sole purpose of causing a loss of business to another firm.

unfair labor practice strike A nonviolent work stoppage for the purpose of protesting an employer's commission of an unfair labor practice.

unilateral contract An exchange of a promise for an act.

unlimited personal liability Liability that allows creditors to recover claims against the business from the personal assets of a sole proprietor or a general partner.

valid contract One that meets all legal requirements for a fully enforceable contract.

variance Permission given to a landowner to use a piece of his or her land in a manner prohibited by the zoning laws; generally granted to prevent undue hardship.

venue County of the trial court; prescribed by state statute.

vertical merger A merger that integrates two firms that have a supplier-customer relationship.

vertical price fixing Stipulation by a manufacturer to a retailer to whom it sells products what price the retailer must charge for those products.

vertical restraint of trade Restraint that occurs between individuals or corporations at different levels of the marketing structure.

virus A computer program that destroys, damages, rearranges, or replaces computer data.

voidable contract One that gives one of the parties the option of withdrawing.

void contract One that at its formation has an illegal object or serious defects.

voir dire Process whereby the judge and/or the attorneys question potential jurors to determine whether they will be able to render an unbiased opinion in the case.

Wagner Act (NLRA) Guarantees the rights of workers to organize and bargain collectively and forbids employers from engaging in specified unfair labor practices. Also called National Labor Relations Act.

warranty A guarantee or binding promise that goods (products) meet certain standards of performance.

water rights The legal ability to use water flowing across or underneath one's property.

white collar crime A crime committed in a commercial context by a member of the professional-managerial class.

winding-up The process of completing all unfinished transactions, paying off outstanding debts, distributing assets, and dividing remaining profits after a partnership has been terminated, or dissolved.

workers compensation laws State laws that provide financial compensation to covered employees, or their dependents, when employees are injured on the job.

work-product doctrine Provides that formal and informal documents prepared by an attorney in conjunction with a client's case are privileged and may not be revealed by the attorney without the client's permission.

writ of execution An order by a clerk of the court directing the sheriff to seize any of the nonexempt real or personal property of a debtor who refuses to or cannot pay a creditor.

zoning Government restrictions on the use of private property in order to ensure the orderly growth and development of a community and to protect the health, safety, and welfare of citizens.

INDEX

642

The Legal Environment of Business, Second Edition • Kubasek, Brennan, and Browne
Prentice-Hall, Inc.

YOU SHOULD CAREFULLY READ THE TERMS AND CONDITIONS BEFORE USING THE CD-ROM PACKAGE. USING THIS CD-ROM PACKAGE INDICATES YOUR ACCEPTANCE OF THESE TERMS AND CONDITIONS.

Prentice-Hall, Inc. provides this program and licenses its use. You assume responsibility for the selection of the program to achieve your intended results, and for the installation, use, and results obtained from the program. This license extends only to use of the program in the United States or countries in which the program is marketed by authorized distributors.

LICENSE GRANT
You hereby accept a nonexclusive, nontransferable, permanent license to install and use the program ON A SINGLE COMPUTER at any given time. You may copy the program solely for backup or archival purposes in support of your use of the program on the single computer. You may not modify, translate, disassemble, decompile, or reverse engineer the program, in whole or in part.

TERM
The License is effective until terminated. Prentice-Hall, Inc. reserves the right to terminate this License automatically if any provision of the License is violated. You may terminate the License at any time. To terminate this License, you must return the program, including documentation, along with a written warranty stating that all copies in your possession have been returned or destroyed.

LIMITED WARRANTY
THE PROGRAM IS PROVIDED "AS IS" WITHOUT WARRANTY OF ANY KIND, EITHER EXPRESSED OR IMPLIED, INCLUDING, BUT NOT LIMITED TO, THE IMPLIED WARRANTIES OR MER-CHANTABILITY AND FITNESS FOR A PARTICULAR PURPOSE. THE ENTIRE RISK AS TO THE QUALITY AND PERFORMANCE OF THE PROGRAM IS WITH YOU. SHOULD THE PROGRAM PROVE DEFECTIVE, YOU (AND NOT PRENTICE-HALL, INC. OR ANY AUTHORIZED DEALER) ASSUME THE ENTIRE COST OF ALL NECESSARY SERVICING, REPAIR, OR CORRECTION. NO ORAL OR WRITTEN INFORMATION OR ADVICE GIVEN BY PRENTICE-HALL, INC., ITS DEALERS, DISTRIBUTORS, OR AGENTS SHALL CREATE A WARRANTY OR INCREASE THE SCOPE OF THIS WARRANTY.

SOME STATES DO NOT ALLOW THE EXCLUSION OF IMPLIED WARRANTIES, SO THE ABOVE EXCLUSION MAY NOT APPLY TO YOU. THIS WARRANTY GIVES YOU SPECIFIC LEGAL RIGHTS AND YOU MAY ALSO HAVE OTHER LEGAL RIGHTS THAT VARY FROM STATE TO STATE.

Prentice-Hall, Inc. does not warrant that the functions contained in the program will meet your requirements or that the operation of the program will be uninterrupted or error-free.

However, Prentice-Hall, Inc. warrants the diskette(s) on which the program is furnished to be free from defects in material and workmanship under normal use for a period of ninety (90) days from the date of delivery to you as evidenced by a copy of your receipt.

The program should not be relied on as the sole basis to solve a problem whose incorrect solution could result in injury to person or property. If the program is employed in such a manner, it is at the user's own risk and Prentice-Hall, Inc. explicitly disclaims all liability for such misuse.

LIMITATION OF REMEDIES
Prentice-Hall, Inc.'s entire liability and your exclusive remedy shall be:
1. the replacement of any diskette not meeting Prentice-Hall, Inc.'s "LIMITED WARRANTY" and that is returned to Prentice-Hall, or
2. if Prentice-Hall is unable to deliver a replacement diskette that is free of defects in materials or workmanship, you may terminate this agreement by returning the program.

IN NO EVENT WILL PRENTICE-HALL, INC. BE LIABLE TO YOU FOR ANY DAMAGES, INCLUDING ANY LOST PROFITS, LOST SAVINGS, OR OTHER INCIDENTAL OR CONSEQUENTIAL DAMAGES ARISING OUT OF THE USE OR INABILITY TO USE SUCH PROGRAM EVEN IF PRENTICE-HALL, INC. OR AN AUTHORIZED DISTRIBUTOR HAS BEEN ADVISED OF THE POSSIBILITY OF SUCH DAMAGES, OR FOR ANY CLAIM BY ANY OTHER PARTY.

SOME STATES DO NOT ALLOW FOR THE LIMITATION OR EXCLUSION OF LIABILITY FOR INCIDENTAL OR CONSEQUENTIAL DAMAGES, SO THE ABOVE LIMITATION OR EXCLUSION MAY NOT APPLY TO YOU.

GENERAL
You may not sublicense, assign, or transfer the license of the program. Any attempt to sublicense, assign or transfer any of the rights, duties, or obligations hereunder is void.

This Agreement will be governed by the laws of the State of New York.

Should you have any questions concerning this Agreement, you may contact Prentice-Hall, Inc. by writing to:
Director of New Media
Higher Education Division
Prentice-Hall, Inc.
1 Lake Street
Upper Saddle River, NJ 07458

Should you have any questions concerning technical support, you may write to:
New Media Production
Higher Education Division
Prentice-Hall, Inc.
1 Lake Street
Upper Saddle River, NJ 07458

YOU ACKNOWLEDGE THAT YOU HAVE READ THIS AGREE-MENT, UNDERSTAND IT, AND AGREE TO BE BOUND BY ITS TERMS AND CONDITIONS. YOU FURTHER AGREE THAT IT IS THE COMPLETE AND EXCLUSIVE STATEMENT OF THE AGREE-MENT BETWEEN US THAT SUPERSEDES ANY PROPOSAL OR PRIOR AGREEMENT, ORAL OR WRITTEN, AND ANY OTHER COMMUNICATIONS BETWEEN US RELATING TO THE SUBJECT MATTER OF THIS AGREEMENT.